S0-AQM-592

Why Do You Need This New Edition?

If you are wondering why you should buy this new edition of *Social Problems*, here are several good reasons:

- Social problems are ever changing. This edition includes many new topics, terms, data, and theory—including the latest on the following:
  RU486 (Chapter 1); feminist theory (Chapter 2); sex tourism (Chapter 3); pharm parties (Chapter 4); soldier rape (Chapter 5); the Ponzi scheme (Chapter 6); welfare queens (Chapter 7); genocide (Chapter 8); same-sex marriage versus civil unions (Chapter 9); medical malpractice (Chapter 10); the real divorce rate (Chapter 11); designer animals (chapter 12); the Green Party (Chapter 13); and narcoterrorism (Chapter 14).

- New features in this edition help you find related information on the Web and bring data to life by showing how things have changed over time:

  - **See For Yourself** lists Web sites that allow you to further explore topics in the chapter. (For example, in Chapter 6: visit www.equalitynow.org to see real laws influencing the lives of women in the Least Industrialized Nations).

  - **By the Numbers** highlights key data and statistics at the end of the chapter and shows trends over time. (For example, in Chapter 11: the number of cohabitating couples in the U.S. in 1980: 1.5 million; and in 2006: 5.1 million.)

- **MySocLab** for *Social Problems* is a state-of-the-art interactive site, built around a complete e-book version of the text, that provides practice tests for every chapter; a multimedia library containing video- and audio-based exercises; audio files of the chapters; and resources such as access to Research Navigator, interactive flashcards, Sociology in the News, and a blog. It is available at no additional cost to the student when the text is packaged with a MySocLab Website Student Access Code.

PEARSON

NINTH EDITION

Social Problems
A Down-to-Earth Approach

James M. Henslin
Southern Illinois University, Edwardsville

Lori Ann Fowler
Tarrant County Community College

Boston Columbus Indianapolis New York San Francisco Upper Saddle River
Amsterdam Cape Town Dubai London Madrid Milan Munich Paris Montreal Toronto
Delhi Mexico City Sao Paulo Sydney Hong Kong Seoul Singapore Taipei Tokyo

Publisher: Karen Hanson
Editorial Assistant: Courtney Shea
Development Editor: Jenn Albanese
Associate Editor: Mayda Bosco
Executive Marketing Manager: Kelly May
Editorial Production Service: Gary Kliewer, Nesbitt Graphics, Inc.
Manufacturing Buyer: Debbie Rossi
Electronic Composition: Nesbitt Graphics, Inc.
Interior Design: Gina Hagen, Nesbitt Graphics, Inc.
Photo Researcher: Katharine S. Cebik
Cover Administrator: Kristina Mose-Libon

Credits appear on pages 601–602, which constitutes an extension of the copyright page.

Copyright © 2010, 2008, 2006 by James M. Henslin
Copyright © 1983 by James M. Henslin and Donald W. Light

All rights reserved. Manufactured in the United States of America. This publication is protected by
Copyright, and permission should be obtained from the publisher prior to any prohibited reproduction,
storage in a retrieval system, or transmission in any form or by any means, electronic, mechanical, photo-
copying, recording, or likewise. To obtain permission(s) to use material from this work, please submit a
written request to Pearson Higher Education, Rights and Contracts Department, 501 Boylston Street,
Suite 900, Boston, MA 02116, or fax your request to 617-671-3447.

Many of the designations by manufacturers and sellers to distinguish their products are claimed as trade-
marks. Where those designations appear in this book, and the publisher was aware of a trademark claim,
the designations have been printed in initial caps or all caps.

If you purchased this book within the United States or Canada you should be aware that it has
been wrongfully imported without the approval of the Publisher or the Author.

Allyn & Bacon
is an imprint of

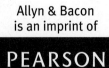

ISBN-10:   0-205-70504-9
ISBN-13: 978-0-205-70504-7

10 9 8 7 6 5 4 3 2 1   WEB   13 12 11 10 09

BRIEF CONTENTS

CONTENTS

CHAPTER 3   **Social Problems Related to Sexual Behavior**   **50**

CHAPTER 7 **Economic Problems: Wealth and Poverty**   202

CHAPTER 10 Medical Care: Physical and Mental Illness 318

BOXED FEATURES

A Global Glimpse

"What is happening now has simply never happened before in the history of the world," said Nicholas Eberstadt, a demographer (Specter, 1998). Never before has a country's birthrate plunged so low that its population shrank. But this is now happening in several European countries.

Is a birthrate too low to replenish a population really new in history? We have had instances in the past when a country's leaders thought that their nation had too few children. Usually this was because many young men had been killed in war, and they wanted new soldiers to replace them. Officials would then initiate *pronatalism*, policies that favor or promote births. They were successful. Men and women responded to the rewards and had more children.

Today's situation is different. Populations are shrinking not because of war but because women are bearing so few children that they aren't replacing the people who die. What is happening in Sweden, one of these countries, helps us understand some of the implications of the fourth stage of the demographic transition—and why pronatalism is failing.

If any country is pronatalist, it is Sweden. Health care for mothers and children is free. Maternity centers offer free health checks and free courses in preparation for childbirth. When a child is born, the parents are eligible for 15 months' leave of absence with pay. They can divide the leave between them any way they want, as long as the father gets at least one of the months. When a child is sick, either parent can stay home to care for it and receive full pay for missed work—up to 60 days a year per child (The Swedish Institute, 1992; Froman, 1994; Bernhardt & Goldscheider, 2001).

Births should be booming, families growing larger, the baby carriage industry prosperous. Instead, Sweden is becoming a lopsided society, one in which there are more old people than young, one in which there will not be enough workers to pay for the health care and pensions of the elderly.

The culprit? It is prosperity and freedom. Swedish women are staying in school longer, putting more emphasis on careers, marrying later—and having fewer children.

Like the Germans, Italians, Spanish, and other Europeans, the Swedes are developing different ideas about children and about what they want out of life. Here are some of their comments:

"People want their freedom. They see children as a burden, as an inconvenience."

"It's a sacrifice to have a child."

"Children cost more than they used to. Today you have to bring them to the pool, and you need to get a nanny, and they have to learn a foreign language. Children have more needs. Parents just didn't think of all these things before."

Ninni Lundblad, a biologist who works in Stockholm, said, "Did your parents sit down with a spreadsheet and figure out whether they could afford to have two or three children?"

No, they didn't. They just had them. But Ninni Lundblad, who said this so derisively, has no children (Specter, 1998).

So why don't Sweden's generous pronatalist policies work? Perhaps this statement by Jan Delanor of Stockholm best sums it up:

"I am supposed to have an extra child to help the system? Nonsense. I'll have a child if and when it makes sense to me, not because the government thinks it's a good idea."

Swedes are finding so much more that makes sense to them—education, travel, career, money, and spending time with friends. All these things come before having children.

A Global Glimpse — THE LOPSIDED SOCIETY: PRONATALISM IN SWEDEN

Reasons that Swedish couples, like this one, are choosing to have only one child or to remain childless are discussed in the text. Countries throughout Europe are experiencing similar low birth rates.

Issues in Social Problems

Issues in Social Problems — THE GRAY PANTHERS

WHO WE ARE

We are a group of people—old and young—drawn together by deeply felt common concerns for human liberation and social change. The old and young live outside the mainstream of society.

Ageism—discrimination against persons on the basis of chronological age—deprives both groups of power and influence. Besides being a movement of older and younger persons, as Gray Panthers we consider ourselves distinctive in the following ways:

We are against ageism that forces any group to live roles that are defined purely on the basis of age. We view aging as a total life process in which the individual develops from birth to death. Therefore, we are concerned about the needs of all age groups and ageism directed at any age group.

We have a strong sense of militancy. Our concern is not only for education and services, but also for effective nonviolent action with an awareness of timing and urgency.

We advocate a radical approach to social change by attacking those forces that corrupt our institutions, attitudes, and values, such as materialism, racism, sexism, paternalism, militarism, and extreme nationalism.

Over the years, the elderly have become more politically astute in their lobbying. They have influenced political decisions by both threatening bloc votes and by manipulating images of poverty and the elderly.

WHAT WE WANT

1. To develop a new and positive self-awareness in our culture that can regard the total life span as a continuing process in maturity and fulfillment.
2. To strive for new options for lifestyles for older and younger people that will challenge the present paternalism in our institutions and culture, and to help eliminate the poverty and powerlessness in which most older and younger people are forced to live, and to change society's destructive attitudes about aging.
3. To make responsible use of our freedom to bring about social change, to develop a list of priorities among social issues, and to struggle nonviolently for social change that will bring greater human freedom, justice, dignity, and peace.
4. To build a new power base in our society uniting presently disenfranchised and oppressed groups, realizing the common qualities and concerns of age and youth working in coalition with other movements with similar goals and principles.
5. To reinforce and support each other in our quest for liberation and to celebrate our shared humanity.

Reprinted by permission of The Gray Panthers.

Thinking Critically about Social Problems

Spotlight on Social Research

Technology and Social Problems

PREFACE

It is our pleasure to carry this text into its ninth edition, continuing our fine relationship with Pearson as its publisher. Jim Henslin is extremely pleased to welcome Lori Fowler as coauthor. Lori has worked on the supplements program that accompanies the Henslin Introductory Sociology textbooks for over a decade and is delighted that Jim agreed to sign her on as a coauthor. Lori's personal research focus is on race, class, and gender studies. She has spent a decade researching cosmetic surgery trends among adolescents. Lori teaches six courses at a community college, advises a Student Ambassadors program on campus, and develops distance learning courses as well. Teaching is her passion. Together, our aim is that the revisions made in this text will allow sociology students to easily grasp difficult sociological concepts.

Lori's revision was motivated by the desire to include the latest research as well as issues of pop culture and feminist theory, under the conflict theory umbrella, all the while maintaining Jim's encompassing view of social problems. As in earlier editions, we continue to highlight both theory and research throughout all chapters. Adopters have commented that they appreciate how consistently sociological theories are applied to social problems, and now feminist theory has been incorporated as well. In addition, we have expanded the emphasis on the *social* nature of social problems—explaining how objective concerns are essential in understanding all social problems. As we progress through the life span, specific social problems may change, but sociological frameworks will allow us all to better interpret changing conditions of society.

In this new edition, we've made several organizational changes. The discussion of homosexuality has been moved into a chapter that covers discrimination based on sexual orientation (Chapter 9). Previously in two separate chapters, the topics of population and urbanization have been combined into one, *Population and Urbanization Issues* (Chapter 12). Providing 14 chapters total allows for the entire text to be covered in a typical 16-week course (assuming most instructors have 14 teachable weeks). We trust that your students will react positively to this text, that it will be a source of provocative discussions surrounding major issues facing our society, and that the ideas presented here will provide a foundation for viewing social life and will become a part of their future perspectives.

Spotlight on Social Research

This edition maintains the popular feature called Spotlight on Social Research. Here, sociological researchers share their personal research experiences with students. The researchers explain how they became interested in a particular social problem and how they performed data collection. As they do so, they take students "into the field" with them, allowing readers to share in solving real-world social problems.

The authors of this boxed feature are

Phyllis Moen: Discovering that the elderly are "young people who got old," Chapter 2

Edward Laumann: Studying human sexuality—and the stigma that comes from this research, Chapter 3

James A. Inciardi: Learning about prescription drug abuse in the club culture of Miami, Chapter 4

Ruth Horowitz: Getting an insider's perspective on Chicano gangs, Chapter 5

William Chambliss: Discussing his personal journey into sociology, Chapter 6

Herbert Gans: Doing research on the exploitation of people in poverty, Chapter 7

Nazli Kibria: Studying the identity problems of Asian Americans, Chapter 8

Rafael Ezekiel: Studying neo-Nazis and Klans, Chapter 8

Kirsten Dellinger: Exploring the meanings of sexual harassment, Chapter 9

William Cockerham: Solving a medical mystery, Deaths in Russia, Chapter 10

Kathleen Ferraro: Gaining an insider's view of intimate violence, Chapter 11

Cynthia Shinabarger Reed and Robert E. Reed: Choosing not to have children, Chapter 11

Carl Haub: Doing research on population and food, Chapter 12

Robert Gottlieb: Discovering changing meanings of the environment, Chapter 13

Morten Ender: Studying the military as an "embedded" sociologist, Chapter 14

Scope and Coverage of the Ninth Edition

Social Problems is an enjoyable course to teach, and many students find it to be the most exciting course in sociology. Certainly the topics are fascinating, ranging from such controversial matters as prostitution and pornography to such deeply embedded problems as racism, poverty, and gender. Some of the issues are intensely personal, such as abortion, suicide, and victimization; others, such as war and unemployment, center on global stratification and capitalism. All are significant, but especially vital for our present and for our future are the changing relationships of power among the nation-states of the world.

For students, the benefits of this course are similarly wide-ranging. Not only do they gain a sociological understanding of social problems, but they are also able to explore—and evaluate—their own opinions about specific social problems. As the course progresses, they are also able to attain greater awareness of the social forces that shape their orientations to social problems and their perspectives on social life in general. The ideas in this book, then, can penetrate students' thinking and give shape to their sociological imagination.

The Sociological Task: The Goal of Objectivity

This process of insight and self-discovery—so essential to sociology and good teaching—is one of the most rewarding aspects of teaching Social Problems. But teaching this class presents a special challenge, for it requires objectivity in the midst of deep controversy. In this text, we attempt to present both sides of controversial topics objectively. We know, of course, that it is impossible to achieve total objectivity, no matter how ardently it may be desired or pursued, but we think that objectivity should be the hallmark of Social Problems, and we have tried to attain it. The most obvious example is found immediately in Chapter 1, where abortion is discussed as a substantive issue to illustrate basic sociological principles. Beginning the text with this topic jump-starts the course, placing us squarely in the midst of one of the most debated and heated issues in U.S. society. It also brings deep-seated attitudes to the surface. Used creatively, this approach allows us to illustrate the social origin of ideas, which is so essential to the objective understanding of social problems.

If we are successful in our efforts, both students and instructors who may be on extreme opposite ends of an issue should feel that their position is represented fairly. To verify whether or not objectivity was achieved in Chapter 1, for example, the first chapter was sent to national officers of both pro-choice and right to life organizations for review. *Both sides* responded that the text seemed "too fair" to the other side.

The goal of this text, then, is to present objectively the major research findings on social problems, to explain their theoretical interpretations, and to describe clearly the underlying assumptions and implications of competing points of view. In endeavoring to reach this goal,

we strive to present the best of the sociology of social problems and to introduce competing views fairly. Again using Chapter 1 as an illustration: the terms *proabortion* and *antiabortion* have been selected as more objective labels than *pro-choice* and *pro-life*. If we have been successful, readers should find themselves content when they encounter views with which they are in disagreement. This should hold true for readers of all persuasions, whether "radical," "liberal," or "conservative." This text should serve as a strong foundation for an exciting class.

Incorporating Theory into the Text

Students often find the word *theory* to be frightening: Indeed, they find theories vague, abstract, and difficult to understand. But theories can be easy to understand—even enjoyable—*if* they are presented in a creative way. Students and instructors alike have reacted favorably to the ways in which sociological theories are presented in this text. One of the main reasons for this favorable reaction is that we embed the theories in clarifying contexts. For example, when we introduce the *four* theories in Chapter 2—symbolic interaction theory, functional theory, conflict theory, and feminist theory—we make them concrete by applying each to problems that the elderly confront. This makes the theory more understandable.

In the following chapters, we consistently apply most of the theories to *each* social problem. This approach helps give students a cohesive understanding of what otherwise might appear to be a disparate collection of problematic events and issues. The effect is cumulative, for each new chapter allows students to broaden their understanding of these perspectives. As one reviewer said, most texts in social problems simply mention theory in an initial chapter and then dispense with it thereafter, whereas this text follows through with the "theoretical promise" of its introductory chapters.

Chapter Organization and Features

To foster student understanding, a consistent structure is used within each chapter. This gives students a "road map" to guide them through each social problem, letting them know what to expect in each chapter. In most chapters, we use the following framework to analyze each social problem:

Opening Vignette Intended to arouse student interest in the social problem and to stimulate the desire to read more, this brief opening story presents essential elements of the social problem.

The Problem in Sociological Perspective By presenting a broad sociological background, we set the stage for understanding the social problem.

The Scope of the Problem This section presents basic data on the extent or severity of the problem. It allows students to grasp the problem's wider ramifications.

Looking at the Problem Theoretically Here we present a theoretical analysis of the problem or some major aspect of it. We generally begin on the more personal level, with symbolic interaction theory, move from there to functional theory, and conclude with the perspective of conflict theory.

Research Findings Discussed here are both current and classic sociological studies—and, where relevant, studies from other academic disciplines as well. To allow students to become more familiar with primary research, we present many sociological studies in detail. In addition, the feature written by researchers themselves, *Spotlight on Research,* helps students understand how the researcher's personal background leads to interest in a social problem and how research on social problems is actually done.

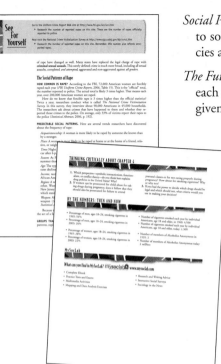

Social Policy This section focuses on actions that have been taken or could be taken to try to solve the social problem. We often spell out the assumptions on which these policies are based and the dilemmas that they create.

The Future of the Problem Because students want to know what lies ahead of them in life, each chapter concludes with an overview of the direction the problem is likely to take, given what we now know about the problem's dimensions and trends.

See For Yourself This new boxed feature provides information on Web sites that allow students to further explore topics in the chapter.

Summary and Review To reinforce what the students are learning, we provide a succinct point-by-point summary of the main ideas in the chapter. Students also find this summary helpful for review purposes, especially in preparing for tests. Some students also find it useful as a preview of the chapter, reading the summary *before* they read the chapter.

Key Terms When a term first appears in the text, it is set in bold type and is defined in context. Key terms are also listed at the end of each chapter.

Thinking Critically About the Chapter At the end of each chapter are several questions designed to help students evaluate what they have read. These questions also lend themselves to stimulating class discussions.

By the Numbers At the end of the chapter, this new feature highlights key data and statistics from the tables, figures, and text references in the chapter and shows changes over time.

New in This Edition

Writing about social problems is challenging because social problems are ever changing. This edition includes many new and updated topics, terms, data, and theory. Here are some of them:

CHAPTER 1

RU486 information ■ Public issues versus personal troubles ■ Sociology definition ■ Value definition ■ Paper–pencil questionnaires

CHAPTER 2

Feminist theory ■ Caretakers' role ■ Patriarchy ■ Radical feminism ■ Liberal feminism ■ Socialist feminism ■ Cultural feminism ■ Ecofeminism

CHAPTER 3

Single woman–married man Syndrome ■ Spitzer and prostitution ■ Paraphilia ■ Sex tourism

CHAPTER 4

Anna Nicole Smith and Heath Ledger overdose cases ■ Pharm parties ■ ADHD, updated information ■ Binge drinking on college campuses ■ Smoking, updated information ■ Trail mix ■ Pharming ■ Hillbilly heroin

CHAPTER 5

Virginia Tech massacre ■ Behavior modification ■ Criminal sexual assault ■ Soldier rape ■ Saturday Night special

CHAPTER 6

"Dumb" laws ■ Equality Now laws ■ New corporate crime cases ■ Power ■ Self-fulfilling prophecy ■ Sarbanes-Oxley Act ■ Juvenile delinquency ■ Status crime ■ Dysfunctional families ■ Criminal enterprise ■ Capital punishment ■ Ponzi scheme ■ Subprime mortgage crisis

CHAPTER 7

Cold War ■ Economic recession of 2008 ■ Poverty line ■ Ralf Dahrendorf ■ Feminization of poverty ■ Max Weber's definition of power ■ Social class ■ Welfare queen

CHAPTER 8

Achieved status ■ Ascribed status ■ Endogamy ■ Exogamy ■ Affinity groups ■ Ethnophaulisms ■ Ethnocentrism ■ Genocide ■ Perpetuity

CHAPTER 9

Female infanticide information ■ Patriarchal society ■ Glass ceiling ■ Kim Possible and My Life as a Teenage Robot ■ Same-sex marriage versus civil unions ■ Female infanticide ■ Gender accomplishment ■ Patriarchal society ■ Suffragists ■ Scholastic Assessment Tests (SATs) ■ Machismo ■ Testosterone ■ Misogyny ■ Sexual harassment ■ Domestic partnership ■ Defense of Marriage Act ■ Narrative data

CHAPTER 10

C-section risks ■ Health care for undocumented immigrants ■ Conversion therapy ■ Why women attempt suicide with pills ■ Medical malpractice lawsuits ■ Antiretroviral drugs ■ AIDS orphans ■ Occupational disease after 9–11 ■ Cesarean section ■ Infant mortality rate ■ Deinstitutionalization ■ Working poor ■ Pharmaceutical straitjacket ■ Domiciliary care ■ Depersonalization ■ Managed care

CHAPTER 11

Grandparents as child care providers ■ Real divorce rate ■ Women not remarrying after divorce ■ Impact of divorce on children ■ No-fault divorce ■ Feminist view of marriage ■ Child-free couples ■ Social institution ■ Modernity ■ Remarriage ■ Defective discipline ■ Pushouts ■ Pedophiles ■ Breadwinners ■ Incompatibility ■ Sexual revolution ■ Reproductive labor ■ Second shift ■ False consciousness ■ Intimate partner violence ■ Incest taboo ■ Pedophile Liberation Army

CHAPTER 12

Urban villagers ■ Urbanization ■ Alienation ■ Road rage ■ Torches ■ Supergangs ■ Diced in ■ Jumped in ■ Race riot ■ Sunbelt states ■ Snowbelt states ■ Death rate ■ Verstehen ■ Food politics ■ Carrying capacity ■ Deforestation ■ Agricompanies ■ Windrows ■ Indexing ■ Biotech society ■ Designer animals

CHAPTER 13

Carbon credits ■ Pollution ■ Air pollution ■ Fossil fuels ■ Resource recovery plants ■ Strip mining ■ *E. coli* ■ Bovine growth hormones (BGH) ■ Food chain ■ Optimistic environmentalists ■ Pessimistic environmentalists ■ Organization of Petroleum Exporting Countries (OPEC) ■ Scaled-back society ■ Community Right to Know Act of 1986 ■ Synfuels ■ Hydrocarbons ■ Geothermal energy ■ Nuclear fusion ■ Lo-Cal house ■ Solar envelope ■ Green Party ■ Extremophiles

CHAPTER 14

International Criminal Court (ICC) ■ Intercontinental Ballistic Missiles (ICBMs) ■ Long-distance surgery • Bourgeoisie ■ Proletariat ■ National Security or Homeland Security ■ Collateral damage ■ Combat fatigue and PTSD ■ Armaments ■ Pentagon capitalism ■ Disarmament ■ Agent Orange ■ Political theater ■ Sarin gas ■ Narcoterrorism ■ Targeted killings ■ Predator ■ Mutual assured destruction (MAD) ■ G8 ■ New World Order • North Atlantic Treaty Organization (NATO)

Suggestions for Using This Text

Authors of social problems texts, as well as those who teach this course, must decide whether they want to begin with a more "micro" or "macro" approach to social problems. Each approach is popular, and each has much to commend it. Our choice is to write first at the micro level. We begin by focusing on problems of personal concern to students—issues about which they are already curious and have questions they want answered. In our teaching experience, this approach provides a compelling context for helping students become familiar with the sociological perspective and sociological theory. From there, we move to an examination of broader social problems, those whose more apparent connections to global events often make them seem more remote to students.

This is nothing more than a preference, and it is as equally logical to begin with problems that involve large-scale social change and then to wrap up the course with a focus on more individualistic problems. Instructors who wish to begin with the more macro problems can simply move Part II of this text to the end of their course. Nothing else will be affected.

Because this book is written for students, we limit the amount of citations, the kind that read: "A fuller amplification of this position would include reference to the works of so-and-so," or "This theoretical position is really much more complex than can be described here, but because of lack of space. . . ." Such references are appropriate in a scientific journal. In a Social Problems course, we feel that too many citations hinder retention.

Invitation for You to Respond

This text flows from years of teaching social problems inside a traditional classroom setting. Especially formative have been the reactions of our students. This text also incorporates feedback that instructors have graciously shared. We have designed the book to help make your course more successful—so it would both challenge students' thinking and make the sociological perspective clear and readily understandable. What matters, then, is how this text actually works in your classroom. Consequently, we would greatly appreciate your feedback—whether positive or negative. Because your reactions are based on your own classroom experience, we will find them useful. Our e-mail addresses are as follows: *Henslin@aol.com* or *Lori.fowler@tccd.edu*

Acknowledgments

Lori Fowler would first like to thank Jim Henslin for welcoming her as a coauthor on this text—thank you for your unbelievable trust. Lori especially wants to thank Jeff Lasser for attending her course, providing her with endless opportunities, and carving an author out of a teacher; Lori wishes to thank Karen Hanson for answering every question ever surmised; Jenn Albanese for her continual research effort; Kate Cebik for the gorgeous new photos, the amazing ability to read my mind, and the fun Cypress tutorials; Judy Fiske, for her demeanor and optimistic outlook; Leah Strauss for catching every mistake and gently rearranging each word into an artistic presentation; and Gary Kliewer, who coordinated the production process.

We are grateful to the following instructors who have offered valuable comments during the development of *Social Problems*.

Reviewers of this edition:

Allison Camelot, *Saddleback College*

Shawna Cleary, *University of Central Oklahoma*

David Fasenfest, *Wayne State University*

Wayne Flake, *Eastern Arizona University*

Daniel Hall, *South Puget Sound Community College*

Sharon Jackson, *Fontbonne University*

Rosalind Kopfstein, *Western Connecticut State University*

Daniel Martorella, *Quinnipiac College*

Lesli Overstreet, *Bridgewater State College*

Bonni Raab, *Dominican College*

Adrian Rapp, *Lonestar College*

Annette Schwabe, *Florida State University*

Sheryl Skaggs, *University of Texas, Dallas*

Stephen Soreff, *Boston University*

Brian Ward, *University of Maryland*

Linda Whitman, *Johnson County Community College*

Gary Wyatt, *Emporia State University*

Reviewers of previous editions:

Gary Burbridge, *Grand Rapids Community College*

Carole A. Campbell, *California State University–Long Beach*

Cheryl Childers, *Washburn University*

Susan Claxton, *Floyd College*

Al Cook, *Trinity Valley Community College*

Sandra Emory, *Pensacola Junior College*

Michael W. Flota, *Daytona Beach Community College*

David D. Friedrichs, *University of Scranton*

Michele Gigliotti, *Broward Community College*

Rosalind Gottfried, *San Joaquin Delta College*

Charles Hall, *Purdue University*

Carl M. Hand, *Valdosta State University*

Rosa Haritos, *University of North Carolina at Chapel Hill*

Rachel Ivie, *South Plains College*

Cardell Jacobson, *Brigham Young University*

Joseph F. Jones, *Portland State University*

Victor M. Kogan, *Saint Martin's College*

Muketiwa Wilbrod Madzura, *Normandale Community College*

Paul Magee, *North Lake College*

Marguerite Marin, *Gonzaga University*

Mark Miller, *East Texas Baptist University*

John Mitrano, *Central Connecticut State University*

Sharon Erickson Nepstad, *University of Colorado–Boulder*

Kevin R. Ousley, *East Carolina University*

Dennis L. Peck, *The University of Alabama*

Richard P. Rettig, *University of Central Oklahoma*

Barbara L. Richardson, *Eastern Michigan University*

Daniel M. Roddick, *Rio Hondo College*

Edwin Rosenberg, *Appalachian State University*

Annette M. Schwabe, *Florida State University*

James P. Sikora, *Illinois Wesleyan University*

K. S. Thompson, *Northern Michigan University*

Richard T. Vick, *Idaho State University*

Lori also wants to thank her very supportive husband and four children—without you this wouldn't be possible. To mom, thanks for reading endless edits—who would have thought you would become so schooled in sociology! And to dad, thanks for assuring me that I had the stamina to grow.

Finally, we hope that this text provides understanding and insight into the major problems facing our country, many of which have global ramifications—and all of which have an impact on our own lives.

Lori Ann Fowler, Professor
Department of Sociology
Tarrant County College, Fort Worth

James M. Henslin, Professor Emeritus
Department of Sociology
Southern Illinois University, Edwardsville

A NOTE FROM THE PUBLISHER ON SUPPLEMENTS

Instructor's Supplements

Instructor's Manual and Test Bank (ISBN: 0-205-74727-2)

INSTRUCTOR'S MANUAL BY SHELLY BREITENSTEIN, WESTERN TECHNICAL COLLEGE
TEST BANK BY NAIMA PRINCE, SANTA FE COLLEGE

For each chapter in the text, the Instructor's Manual provides a list of key changes to the new edition, chapter summaries and outlines, learning objectives, a listing of key terms and people, classroom activities, discussion topics, recommended films, Web sites, and additional references.

The Test Bank contains approximately 1,500 questions, including multiple choice, true/false, short answer, essay, and open-book formats. All questions are labeled and scaled according to Bloom's Taxonomy.

Adopters can request a print copy of the Instructor's Manual and Test Bank or download the electronic file by logging in to our Instructor Resource Center at www.pearsonhighered.com/educator

MyTest (ISBN: 0-205-74744-2)

This software allows instructors to create their own personalized exams, to edit any or all of the existing test questions, and to add new questions. Other special features of this program include random generation of test questions, creation of alternate versions of the same test, scrambling question sequence, and test preview before printing. For easy access, this software is available within the instructor section of MySocLab for *Social Problems,* Ninth Edition, or at www.pearsonhighered.com/educator

PowerPoint™ Presentation (ISBN: 0-205-74728-0)

BY ROSE HUNTE-ROBERSON, METRO COMMUNITY COLLEGE

The online PowerPoint presentations for *Social Problems,* Ninth Edition, offer a new and robust suite of supplementary lecture materials. Professors have the option of choosing from any of the following types of slides: Lecture, Line Art, Integrated Lectures and Line Art, Clicker Response System, and Special Topics. Additionally, all of the PowerPoint presentations are uniquely designed to provide students with a clear visual of succinct content for each concept. They are available to adopters at our Instructor Resource Center at www.pearsonhighered.com/educator

MySocLab mysoclab

MySocLab for *Social Problems* is a state-of-the-art interactive and instructive solution for social problems, designed to be used as a supplement to a traditional lecture course, or to completely administer an online course. MySocLab provides access to a wealth of resources all geared to meet the individual teaching and learning needs of every instructor and every student. MySocLab is available at no additional cost to the student when a text is packaged with a MySocLab Access Code.

Student Supplements

Seeing the Social Context. Readings to Accompany *Social Problems* (ISBN: 0-205-56875-0)

EDITED BY JAMES M. HENSLIN

This brief reader contains one reading for each chapter of the text, chosen and introduced by James M. Henslin. The reader can be purchased separately at full price or packaged with this text for an additional $5 net to the bookstore.

Online Course Management

MySocLab mysoclab

MySocLab for *Social Problems* gives students the opportunity to explore important sociological concepts, by watching relevant television news stories, listening to interviews with prominent researchers and social scientists, reading current newspaper articles, analyzing the latest census data, and performing other hands-on activities.

Combining an e-book, streaming audio-files of the chapters, practice tests and exams, audio and video-based activities, interactive flashcards, research support, a guide for improving writing skills, and more, MySocLab is an ideal way to become more engaged with the subject matter and enhance performance in the classroom.

MySocLab is available at no additional cost to the student when a text is packaged with a MySocLab Access Code.

Social Problems

A Down-to-Earth Approach

CHAPTER 1

How Sociologists View Social Problems: The Abortion Dilemma

"But you don't understand! It's not a baby!" Lisa shouted once again. She felt desperate, at her wit's end. The argument with her grandmother seemed to have gone on forever.

With tears in her eyes, her grandmother said, "You don't know what you're doing, Lisa. You're taking the life of an innocent baby!"

"You're wrong! There's only one life involved here—mine!" replied Lisa. "It's my body and my life. I've worked too hard for that manager's job to let this pregnancy ruin everything."

"But Lisa, you have a new responsibility—to the baby."

"But you don't understand! It's not a baby!"

> ## "But you don't understand! It's not a baby!"

"Don't judge my life by your standards. You never wanted a career. All you ever wanted was to raise a family."

"That's not the point," her grandmother pressed. "You're carrying a baby, and now you want to kill it."

"How can you talk like that? This is just a medical procedure—like when you had your gallstones taken out."

"I can't believe my own granddaughter is saying that butchering a baby is like taking out gallstones!"

Lisa and her grandmother looked at each other, knowing they were worlds apart. They both began to cry inside.

The Sociological Imagination

Like Lisa and her grandmother, when we are confronted with problems, we usually view them in highly personal—and often emotional—terms. Our perspective is often limited to our immediate surroundings. Seldom do we connect our personal lives with the larger social context. Restricting our perspective in such a way often causes us to blame ourselves solely instead of blaming greater social forces. When we learn to connect broad social patterns to our own lives, it becomes easier to understand why certain social problems exist and to craft solutions.

What Is the Sociological Imagination?

Much of the responsibility for social problems lies in greater social forces, not individuals. Using the sociological imagination, we can discover how these greater forces create the problems that confront us. The term **sociological imagination** describes looking at people's behavior and attitudes in the context of the social forces that shape them. C. Wright Mills (1959b) described how individuals can understand their own experience by locating their place within a time period: "Neither the life of an individual nor the history of a society can be understood without understanding both."

The discipline of sociology attempts to understand and explain the connection between **personal troubles** and public issues. Broad changes in society influence our lives profoundly. For example, attitudes surrounding abortion have been influenced by the women's movement and the advance of medicine. New developments in technology

as well as new roles for women demanded changes in the law. With the legalization of abortion in 1973, attitudes changed as well. Abortion is now one of the most common medical procedures among women ages 15–44 in the United States (Guttmacher Institute, 2008). The sociological imagination, then, is an emphasis on how the larger events swirling around us influence how we think, feel, and act. Therefore, in using the sociological imagination, we can discover how forces greater than we are create the personal troubles that confront us.

APPLYING THE SOCIOLOGICAL IMAGINATION TO PERSONAL TROUBLES. Historical forces that are changing our society also have an impact on our individual lives. One major trend in global capitalism is the exportation of jobs to countries where workers earn just a dollar or two a day. This global exchange brings about beneficial and damaging effects. Beneficial effects may include reduced labor costs, for example, that lower what we pay for our clothing and cars. On the other hand, negative results include the loss of many American jobs and the transfer of workers to jobs that pay much less. Mills used the term *personal troubles* to refer to such phenomena, in which large-scale events of history bring trouble to people's lives. With all the publicity given to moving jobs overseas, "everyone" knows that this particular large-scale event causes a loss of jobs here. In most cases of personal troubles, however, people get so caught up in what is bothering them that they are unaware of how their problems are related to larger social forces.

To better understand this connection between personal troubles and larger social forces, let's apply the sociological imagination to the topic of abortion. Your values may reflect developments in society that were not part of your grandmother's consciousness when she grew up. Proabortion views have been shaped by the women's movement, which stresses that each woman has the right to make choices and to exercise judgment about her own body. From this perspective, a woman has the right to terminate her pregnancy. Abortion is simply one way that she controls her body. In the extreme, proponents of this view state that a woman's right in this area is absolute. For example, she can choose to have an abortion at any point in her pregnancy, even if she is 9 months along—without informing her husband if she is married or her parents if she is a minor.

The sociological imagination also illuminates the social forces that may have shaped your grandmother's point of view. When your grandmother was growing up, abortion was not only illegal but also considered so shameful that people did not even talk openly about it. Every woman was expected to become a mother, and almost all girls grew up with marriage and motherhood as their foremost goal in life. Careers and advanced education were secondary to a woman's becoming a wife and mother. Marriage and motherhood were a woman's destiny, her fulfillment in life. Without them, she was incomplete, not a full woman. During this time, almost everyone agreed that abortion was murder. Within this context, any woman who had an abortion had to keep her act a secret. Some women who had abortions were taken to their destination blindfolded in a taxi. They endured unsanitary surgery with a high risk of postoperative infection and death.

In the opening vignette, neither Lisa nor her grandmother sees this finely woven net that has been cast over them, turning their lives upside down. Instead, the impact of social change hits them on a personal level: This is where they feel it, in their intimate and everyday lives. It affects what they think and feel and what they do—and how they relate to one another.

In contrast, the sociological imagination (also called the **sociological perspective**) invites us to look at our lives from a new perspective. The sociological imagination asks us to understand how the social context shapes or influences our ideas, attitudes, behaviors, and even our emotions. The social context occurs on three levels: broad, narrow, and intimate. Broad social context may include historical events such as war and terrorism. Narrow social context may include gender, race–ethnicity, religion, and social class. Intimate social context would describe the relationships we share with family, friends, or coworkers. Together, these many levels combine to make up the social context that shapes the way we look at life.

See For Yourself

Go to the *Body Ritual among the Nacirema*, by Horace Miner, at https://www.msu.edu/~jdowell/miner.html

▶ Practice using your sociological imagination while researching the body rituals among the Nacirema on this site. This article highlights unique cultural practices within a well-known society.

THE SIGNIFICANCE OF SOCIAL LOCATION. The term **social location** describes the process of becoming aware of ourselves by evaluating our own identity in relation to other people. Peter Berger (1963) explained how social location controls what individuals may do and what they can expect in life.

> To be located in society means to be at the intersection point of specific social forces. Commonly one ignores these forces . . . no one knows how to locate oneself, one also knows that there is not an awful lot that one can do about this. (p. 40)

Table 1-1 below illustrates how significant social location is in influencing whether a woman has an abortion. From this table, you can see the difference that age, race–ethnicity,

TABLE 1-1 Who Has Abortions?

ABORTIONS	NUMBER OF ABORTIONS	PERCENTAGE OF ALL ABORTIONS	ABORTIONS PER 1,000 BIRTHS[1]	PERCENT OF PREGNANCIES THAT END IN ABORTION
Age				
Under 15	8,000	1%	519	52%
15–19	225,000	17	341	34
20–24	434,000	33	298	30
25–29	295,000	23	219	22
30–34	194,000	15	171	17
35–39	109,000	8	195	20
40 and over	38,000	3	276	28
Race–Ethnicity				
White	723,000	56	186	19
Black and other[2]	579,000	44	407	41
Marital Status				
Married	238,000	18	80	8
Unmarried	1,065,000	82	456	46
Weeks of Gestation				
Less than 9	772,000	59	NA[3]	NA
9–10	251,000	19	NA	NA
11–12	132,000	10	NA	NA
13 or more	147,000	11	NA	NA
Number of Prior Abortions				
None	700,000	54	NA	NA
1	349,000	27	NA	NA
2 or more	254,000	19	NA	NA

[1] The source calls this the abortion ratio, formulating it from the "number of abortions per 1,000 abortions and live births."
[2] This is the rather strange classification used in the source.
[3] Not Available or Not Applicable.

Source: By James M. Henslin. Based on *Statistical Abstract of the United States* (2006, Table 94).

marital status, and length of pregnancy make. Look at age: This table shows that half (519 of 1,000) of girls under the age of 15 who get pregnant have an abortion. Those who are the next most likely to have abortions are other teenagers and women in their early 20s. The rate of abortion keeps dropping with age until women reach their 40s, when it increases sharply. Now look at the influence of race–ethnicity. As you can see from this table, African American women are twice as likely to have abortions as are white women. The most striking difference, however—which cuts across age and race–ethnicity—is marital status: Unmarried women are 6 times more likely than married women to obtain an abortion.

Suppose, then, that you are a woman in her late 20s. Can you see how much more likely you would be to have an abortion if you were single than if you were married? Similarly, suppose that you are an unmarried white teenager, and you get pregnant. Can you see how much less likely you would be to have an abortion than if you were an African American teenager who got pregnant?

Social location does not determine your actions; rather, it means that people who experience certain locations in society are exposed to influences that are different from the influences on those who occupy other corners of life. If you are of a certain race–ethnicity and age, for example, it does not mean that you will necessarily perform a certain act, such as having or not having an abortion. These influences make a difference in people's attitudes and behaviors, but in any individual case, it is impossible to know in advance the consequences of those influences—such as whether any particular individual will have an abortion. But—and this is important—as Table 1-1 makes apparent, sociologists can make predictions along well-traveled social avenues.

IN SUM Sociologists stress the need to use the sociological imagination to understand social problems and personal troubles. The sociological perspective helps make us aware of how the social context—from our historical era to our smaller social locations—influences our ideas, behaviors, and personal troubles. This context also shapes our views of what is or is not a social problem and of what should be done about it. Let's look more closely at how this shaping occurs.

What Is a Social Problem?

Because the focus of this text is on social problems, it is important to understand clearly what social problems are. Social problems do not arise out of some natural state, but are socially constructed. Herbert Blumer (1971) explained how social problems become problems through a process of collective definition. This process of collective definition is dynamic, cyclical, and often competitive.

The Characteristics of Social Problems

TWO ESSENTIAL ELEMENTS. A **social problem** is some aspect of society that people are concerned about and would like changed. Social problems are often subjects of controversy and debate. They have two key components. The first is an **objective condition,** some aspect of society that can be measured or experienced. With abortion, this objective condition includes whether abortions are legal, who obtains them and under what circumstances. The second key component of a social problem is **subjective concern,** the concern that a significant number of people (or a number of significant people) have about the objective condition. Subjective concern about abortion includes the distress that occurs because some women give birth to an unwanted child whereas others terminate pregnancies. To see how subjective concerns about abortion differ in another part of the world, see the Global Glimpse box on the next page.

SOCIAL PROBLEMS ARE DYNAMIC. As society changes, so do these two essential elements: objective conditions and subjective concerns. In other words, social problems are dynamic.

A Global Glimpse
ONLY FEMALES ELIGIBLE: SEX-SELECTION ABORTION IN INDIA

"May you be the mother of a hundred sons" is the toast made to brides in India, where the birth of a son brings shouts of rejoicing, but the birth of a daughter brings tears of sadness.

Why? A son continues the family name, preserves wealth and property within the family, takes care of aged parents (the elderly have no social security), and performs the parents' funeral rites. Hinduism even teaches that a man without a son cannot achieve salvation.

A daughter, in contrast, is a liability. Men want to marry only virgins, and the parents of a daughter bear the burden of having to be constantly on guard to protect her virginity. For their daughter to marry, the parents must also pay a dowry to her husband. A common saying in India reflects the female's low status: "to bring up a daughter is like watering a neighbor's plant."

This cultural context set the stage for female infanticide, the killing of newborn girl babies, a practice that has been common in India for thousands of years. Using diagnostic techniques (amniocentesis and ultrasound) to reveal the sex of the fetus, many Indians have now replaced female infanticide with gender-selective abortion. If prenatal tests reveal that the fetus is female, they abort it. Some clinics even put up billboards that proclaim "Invest Rs.500 now, save Rs.50,000 later." This means that by paying Rs.500 (500 Indian rupees) to abort a female, a family can save a future dowry of 50,000 rupees.

Even though their husbands and other relatives urge them to have an abortion, some women who are pregnant with a female fetus resist. Since these abortions are profitable, medical personnel try to sell reluctant women on the idea. To overcome their resistance, one clinic has hit on an ingenious technique: Nurses reach under the counter where they keep the preserved fetuses of twin girls. When a woman sees these bottled fetuses, the horror of double vigilance and two dowries is often sufficient to convince her to have an abortion.

National newspapers headlined the events in one clinic: A male fetus had been unintentionally aborted. This news sparked protests, and the Indian legislature passed a law forbidding doctors to tell would-be parents the sex of their fetuses. Physicians who violate the law can be sent to prison and banned from their profession.

Going unenforced, however, this law has had little or no effect. An eminent physician has even stated publicly: "The need for a male child is an economic need in our society, and our feminists who are raising such hue and cry about female feticide should realize that it is better to get rid of an unwanted child than to make it suffer all its life."

What do you think? In answering this, try to put yourself in the position of Indians in poverty.

Based on Kusum (1993), Holman (1994), Raghunathan (2003).

As previously mentioned, abortion was illegal in the United States until 1973. In that year, the U.S. Supreme Court came to a landmark decision in a case known as *Roe v. Wade,* by which the Court legalized abortion. Before this decision, the social problem of abortion was quite unlike what it is today. The primary objective condition was the illegality of abortion. The subjective concerns centered on women who wanted abortions but could not get them, as well as on the conditions under which illegal abortions took place: With most abortions performed by untrained people, many women died from botched, underground surgeries. As growing numbers of people became concerned, they worked to change the law. Their success transformed the problem: Large numbers of people became upset that abortion had become legal. Convinced that abortion is murder, these people began their own campaigns to make their subjective concerns known and to change the law. Those who favor legal abortion oppose each step these people take. We'll look more closely at this process in a moment, but at this point we simply want you to see how social problem are dynamic, how they take shape as groups react to one another.

SOCIAL PROBLEMS ARE RELATIVE. As you can see from the example of abortion, what people consider to be a social problem depends on their values. A **value** may be defined as a shared belief about whether something is good or bad. A social problem for some is often a solution for others. While some were pleased with the *Roe v. Wade* decision of 1973, others found it disastrous. Obviously, mugging is not a social problem for muggers. Nor do Boeing and other corporations that profit from arming the world consider the billions of dollars spent on weapons to be a social problem. In the same way, nuclear power is not a social problem for the corporations that use it to generate electricity. From the Issues in Social Problems box on page 9 and from Table 1-2, you can see that the way people define abortion according to their values is the same process that leads to contrasting views of all social problems.

COMPETING VIEWS. Because we live in a pluralistic world of competing, contrasting, and conflictive groups, our society is filled with competing, contrasting, and conflictive views of life. This variety certainly makes life interesting, but in such a dynamic world, whose definition of a social problem wins? The answer centers on **power,** the ability to get one's way despite resistance. After abortion became legal, most observers assumed that because the opponents of abortion had lost, they would quietly fade away. As you know, this assumption was naive. Feelings were so strong that groups which had been hostile to one another for centuries, such as Roman Catholics and Baptists, began to work together in opposing abortion. Shocked at what they considered the killing of babies, they took to the streets and to the courts, fighting battles over this issue.

A NOTE ON TERMS. Before we go further in our analysis of abortion as a social problem, we need to pause and consider some terminology. Definitions and terms are always significant, but especially when we deal with highly sensitive issues such as abortion. The terms *pro-choice* and *pro-life,* chosen by advocates on each side of this social problem, represent attitudes and positions that sometimes provoke strong emotional responses. As you may have noticed in the box on the relativity of social problems, we use the terms *antiabortion* and *proabortion. Antiabortion* refers to those who oppose the legal right to abortion, and *proabortion* refers to those who favor this legal right. As discussed in the Preface, neither side involved in the abortion issue prefers these terms. (For detailed background, see pages xxiv–xxv). Even if readers do not like this choice of terms, both those who favor the legal right to abortion and those who oppose it will feel that there is a balanced presentation of each.

TABLE 1-2 How Definitions of Abortion Affect People's Views

WHO DOES THE DEFINING?	WHAT ABORTION IS	WHAT IS ABORTED	THE WOMAN	THE RESULTING VIEWS	
				The Act of Abortion	The One Who Performs the Abortion
People Who Favor Abortion	A woman's right	Fetus	Independent individual	A service to women	Skilled technician
People Who Oppose Abortion	Murder	Baby	Mother	Killing a baby	Murderer
People Who Do Abortions	Part of my work	Fetus	Client	A medical procedure	Professional

Source: Modified from Roe (1989).

Issues in Social Problems
A PROBLEM FOR SOME IS A SOLUTION FOR OTHERS: THE RELATIVITY OF SOCIAL PROBLEMS

To be socialized means to learn ways of looking at the world. As we participate in groups—from our family and friends to groups at school and work—their perspectives tend to become part of how we view life. Among the other perspectives that we learn is a way of viewing the objective conditions of social problems.

The meanings that objective conditions have for us are not written in stone. The views that we currently have arose from our experiences with particular groups and our exposure to certain ideas. Experiences with different groups, or encounters with different ideas and information, can similarly change our position on a social problem. We might think that the subjective concerns we have now are the only right and reasonable way of viewing some objective condition. But just as we arrived at our subjective concerns through our social locations, so our views can change if our journey takes us in a different direction. In short, our views, or subjective concerns, are relative to our experiences.

This relativity is illustrated in the social problem of abortion. The central issue is how people define the status of the unborn. Is the fetus a human being, as the antiabortionists believe, or only a potential human, as the proabortionists believe?

Let's look at the two main opposing views.

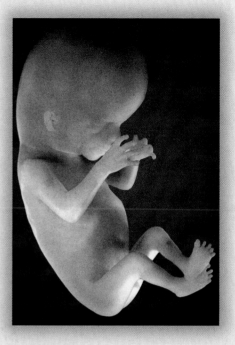

How people define the unborn relates to their position on abortion. Proabortionists may refer to this 11-week-old as a "fetus" or "product of gestation," while antiabortionists may call it a "baby" or "blessing."

THE FETUS IS NOT A HUMAN BEING

This is the position of most people who believe that abortion is a woman's right. "The fetus is a potential person that looks increasingly human as it develops" (NARAL Pro-Choice America). It follows, then, that abortion is not killing, but merely a medical procedure. It is the woman's right to have an abortion for whatever reason she expresses—from financial pressures to health problems—and for the purpose of attaining her goals, whether those be to limit family size, to finish school, to win a promotion at work, or to fulfill any other plans that she might have. The state, therefore, should permit abortion on demand.

WHAT DO YOU THINK?

THE FETUS IS A HUMAN BEING

This is the position of most people who oppose abortion. It follows, then, that abortion is murder, the killing of unborn babies. To simply want an abortion cannot justify murdering a baby. We need to protect and nourish these babies, not kill them. Women have no right to abortion, for it is not just their bodies that are involved but also the lives of other humans—their children. The exception is when another human life, the mother's, lies in the balance. The state has no business legalizing murder, and abortion should be illegal.

WHAT DO YOU THINK?

The Natural History of Social Problems: Four Stages

Sociologists claim that social problems evolve through four stages, called the natural history of social problems. Continuing with our abortion example, we will illustrate this process. First, it is important to explore the history of abortion in the United States. Before 1970, abortion was illegal in all 50 states. Although several states had liberalized their abortion laws, they still kept abortion illegal except for special circumstances, such as

when pregnancy endangered the mother's life. Then in 1970, in an unprecedented move, Hawaii legalized abortion. Hawaii's law defined abortion as a private, noncriminal act.

What made Hawaii receptive to such radical change? Three factors are significant (Steinhoff & Diamond, 1977). First, more than three-quarters of the population lived on the island of Oahu. Citizens there had a tradition of personally knowing their politicians and participating in public hearings. Second, two-income families had become common, and half of the women over age 16 worked. Finally, an epidemic of German measles hit Hawaii in 1964 and 1965. During this time, many obstetricians aborted fetuses to prevent them from being born with deformities. This was a turning point for Hawaiian physicians, and the rate of abortion never fell back to its pre-1964 level.

Now that we've set this brief background, we can trace the natural history of abortion. Let's look at how it developed in Hawaii, as well as in the United States as a whole. As we do so, you will see how social problems evolve through four stages.

The First Stage: Defining the Problem, the Emergence of Leaders, and Beginning to Organize

DEFINING THE PROBLEM. As you have just seen, for a social problem to come into being, people have to become upset about some objective condition. This concern involves a shift in outlook, a questioning of something that had been taken for granted. A change in perspective can come about in several ways. For example, if values change, an old, established pattern will no longer look the same. This is what happened with abortion. The 1960s brought extensive, wrenching social change to the United States. Young people—primarily teenagers and those in their 20s—challenged long-established values. Amidst political uproar, accompanied by widespread demonstrations, many new values were adopted. The women's movement challenged established ideas. As this movement gained followers, more and more women felt that they should not have to be viewed as criminals if they terminated a pregnancy. They convinced many that they had the right to legal abortions.

THE EMERGENCE OF LEADERS. As people discussed concerns about the legalization of abortion, leaders emerged who helped to crystallize the issues. In Hawaii, Vincent Yano, a Roman Catholic state senator and the father of 10, argued that if abortion were a sin, it would be better to have no abortion law than to have one that allowed it under certain circumstances (Steinhoff & Diamond, 1977). This reasoning allowed Yano to maintain his religious opposition to abortion while favoring the repeal of Hawaii's law against abortion.

ORGANIZING AROUND THE ISSUE. Another leader, Joan Hayes, a former Washington lobbyist, went even further. Hayes argued that the major issue at hand was the *right to choose* whether or not to have a baby. She invited leaders in medicine, business, labor, politics, religion, and the media to a citizens' seminar on abortion sponsored by the American Association of University Women.

The Second Stage: Crafting an Official Response

The stages of a social problem don't have neat boundaries. Their edges are blurry, and they overlap. In this case, between 1967 and 1968, legislators had introduced several bills to soften Hawaii's law against abortion. These bills, which would have broadened the circumstances under which abortion would be legal, were actually attempts to redefine abortion. Thus, the stages of defining the social problem and officially responding to it were intertwined.

The turning point came when Senator Yano announced that he would support the repeal of the abortion law. This stimulated other official responses from organizations such as the Chamber of Commerce and the Roman Catholic Church. Public forums and legislative hearings were held, generating huge amounts of publicity. This publicity served as a vital bridge between the public at large and the advocates of repeal. As Hawaiians became keenly aware of the abortion issue, polls showed that most sided with Yano, wanting to repeal the law against abortion. In 1970, Hawaii did just that.

The Third Stage: Reacting to the Official Response

As you can imagine, the response to a social problem often becomes defined as a social problem itself. This evolution of the problem occurred with abortion, especially after 1973, when the U.S. Supreme Court concurred with the Hawaiian legislation and struck down all state laws that prohibited abortion. Indignant about what they saw as murder, antiabortion groups picketed and used political pressure to try to sway public opinion.

Besides inspiring new opposition, responses to social problems also can change the definition of the social problem that is held by those who promoted the reform in the first place. In this case, proabortion groups noted that despite their Supreme Court victory, most counties did not offer abortions, and many women who wanted abortions could not obtain them. Consequently, they began to promote the development of abortion clinics to make abortion more readily accessible.

Figure 1-1 on page 12 shows the success of these efforts. In 1973, the first year of legal abortion, 745,000 abortions were performed. This number climbed quickly to one million, then to a million and a half, where it reached a plateau. From 1979 to 1994, the total number of abortions averaged 1.5 million each year. Beginning in 1995 the number began to drop. It now is about 1.3 million a year. Figure 1-2 on page 12 presents another overview of abortion. From this figure, you can see that the abortion ratio climbed sharply, plateaued for about 10 years, and then dropped. Today, for every 100 live births there are 32 abortions.

The Fourth Stage: Developing Alternative Strategies

The millions of legal abortions that took place after the Supreme Court's ruling led to a pitched battle that still rages. Let's look at some alternative strategies developed by the pro- and antiabortion groups to further their arguments.

ALTERNATIVE STRATEGIES OF THE ANTIABORTIONISTS. Antiabortion groups have tried to persuade states to restrict the Supreme Court's ruling. They have succeeded in eliminating federal funding of abortions for military personnel and their dependents, federal prisoners, and workers with the Peace Corps. They have also succeeded in eliminating health insurance coverage of abortions for federal employees. Their major victory on the federal level took place in 1976, when opponents of abortion persuaded Congress to pass the Hyde Amendment. This amendment prohibits Medicaid funding for abortions unless the woman's life is in imminent danger. When the Supreme Court upheld this amendment in 1980 (K. Lewis, 1988), the number of abortions paid for by federal funds plummeted from 300,000 a year to just 17. Despite repeated attempts to change the Hyde Amendment, the antiabortion forces have succeeded in retaining it.

Another highly effective strategy of antiabortion groups has been the establishment of "crisis pregnancy centers." Women who call "pregnancy hotlines" (sometimes called life lines or birth lines) are offered free pregnancy testing. When they accept it, they are directed to counselors who encourage them to give birth. The counselors inform women about fetal development and talk to them about financial aid and social support available to them during pregnancy. They also advise women about how to find adoptive parents or how to obtain financial support after the birth. Some activists also operate maternity homes and provide adoption services.

Strategies of Moderates ■ Antiabortionists are classified as moderates or radicals depending on techniques used to halt the practice of abortion. Moderates choose mild alternative strategies, less extreme than their radical counterparts. In an effort to oppose abortion, they call their friends, run newspaper ads, write their representatives, and picket abortion clinics. In the years after *Roe v. Wade,* some took their cue from the civil rights movement of the 1950s and practiced passive resistance. Lying immobile in front of abortion clinics, they allowed the police to carry them to jail. In the late 1980s, antiabortion groups practiced massive nonviolent civil disobedience, and thousands of demonstrators were arrested. This social movement grew so large and its members so

FIGURE 1-1 Number of Abortions and Live Births

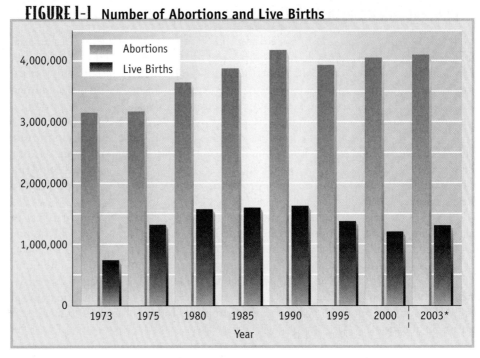

* This is the latest year listed in the 2007 source.

Source: By James M. Henslin. Based on *Statistical Abstract of the United States* (2007, Table 93).

FIGURE 1-2 Number of Abortions per 100 Live Births

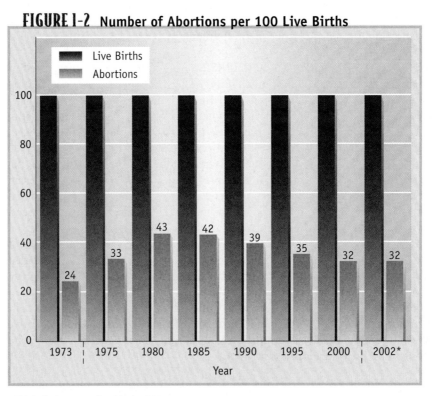

* This is the latest year listed in the 2007 source.

Source: By James M. Henslin. Based on *Statistical Abstract of the United States* (1988, Tables 81, 103; 2007, Table 93).

active that by 1990 more abortion protesters had been arrested than the number of people who were arrested in the entire civil rights movement (C. Allen, 1988; Lacayo, 1991; M. Kirkpatrick, 1992). Since then, with the U.S. Supreme Court upholding state laws that restrict demonstrations at clinics and the homes of clinic staff (Walsh & Goldstein, 2000), protesters have become less active, and arrests have dropped.

abortion is a major means of birth control, and the average Russian woman may have had six abortions in her lifetime (Yablonsky, 1981; Eberstadt, 1988). Although the rate of abortion has decreased, there are still more abortions than births in Russia (Deschner & Cohen, 2003; Greenall, 2003).

Nor is it true that women who have abortions don't know how to use contraceptives; some just choose not to use them. Sociologist Kristin Luker (1975), who studied an abortion clinic in California, found that many women avoided contraceptives because they interfered with intimacy, were expensive, were disapproved of by their boyfriends, or caused adverse side effects. Some even avoided contraceptives to protect their own image. If they used contraceptives, they might think of themselves as "available" or sexually promiscuous. Some women take chances—and when they get pregnant they have abortions.

Sociologist Leon Dash (1990) studied pregnancy among teens in Washington, D.C., and found that, contrary to what a middle-class perspective might suppose, many poor, young, unmarried teenagers get pregnant because they want to. Some want children so that, as they said, "I can have something to hold onto, that I can call my own." Some boyfriends also urge their girlfriends to get pregnant. This, they say, will make them "feel like a man." And, as Luker discovered, some women get pregnant to test their boyfriend's commitment. As many of these women found out, however, their relationships turned out to be short-term. After this discovery, the young women decided that they didn't want to bear a child after all, and they found abortion to be a way out of their situation.

PRINCIPLES UNDERLYING SOCIOLOGICAL RESEARCH. The research just discussed demonstrates that our commonsense ideas may not be correct. If common sense won't work, what guarantee do we have that sociological research will be any better? Three basic characteristics of sociological research help to ensure this:

1. Rather than basing conclusions on personal experience, hunches, assumptions, or opinions, sociologists use scientific methods to provide objective, systematic research findings.
2. Sociologists do not base their conclusions on emotions or personal values. To do so would obscure their perspective and prevent them from seeing things objectively. Even if sociologists discover things that contradict their own values, they are obligated ethically to report those findings.
3. Sociologists use the sociological imagination. To discover the underlying causes of social problems, sociologists interpret them within the framework of the larger picture. While common sense leads one to perceive matters on a personal level, the sociological imagination places them in the context of larger social patterns.

That sociologists can do objective research does not mean that sociology has all the answers. What?! Sociologists can suggest which consequences may result if some particular social policy is followed, but they have no expertise for determining which social policy should be followed. Social policy is based on values, on the outcomes that people want to see. *Because sociology cannot dictate that one set of values is superior to another, it provides no basis for making value decisions.* In short, sociologists can estimate likely outcomes of specific social policies, but they cannot determine which social policy should be chosen. We'll come back to this in a moment, but first let's look at how sociologists do their research.

Methods for Studying Social Problems

When sociologists investigate social problems, they can choose from several **methods** (ways of doing research). Which method they choose depends on the questions they want to investigate and issues of practicality. First, they must determine what they want to find out about a social problem, for different goals require different methods. Suppose, for example, that you want to find out how people form their ideas about abortion. To answer this question, a sociologist would use a different method of research than when comparing the abortion rates of high school dropouts and college-educated women. Second, not every method a researcher would like to use is practical. A sociologist

With each side of the controversy over abortion firmly committed to its cause, deeply entrenched in its views, and strongly convinced of its morality, this social issue seems to be eternally renewed.

might like to interview huge numbers of people or to conduct large-scale experiments, but limitations of money and time, or of ethics in the case of experiments, can make such methods impractical.

There are several methods sociologists use to study social problems. We shall first distinguish how sociologists design their studies, then describe how they gather their information.

FOUR BASIC RESEARCH DESIGNS. Most studies fall into one of four **research designs:** case studies, surveys, experiments, and field studies. Let's look at each.

Case Studies ▪ The **case study** is used to gather in-depth information on some specific situation. As the name implies, the researcher focuses on one case—an individual, an event, or even an organization such as an abortion clinic or a crisis pregnancy center. Let's suppose that you want in-depth information about how women experience abortion. You might want to know what emotions they undergo as they wrestle with the decision to give birth or to have an abortion, whom they talk to about it, even how they feel during the abortion and how they adjust afterward. A case study could provide this type of detail.

Surveys ▪ While the case study provides rich detail, it has issues with generalizability. If you focus on just one woman, how can you know whether her experiences are similar to those of other women who have abortions? The **survey** overcomes this limitation. In a survey, you focus on a **sample** of the group you want to study. (Sociologists use the term **population** to refer to your target group.) Samples are intended to represent the entire group that you are studying. Done correctly, surveys allow you to **generalize** what you find—that is, you are able to apply your findings to people who belong to the group but who are not in your sample.

The best sample is a **random sample.** This is a sample in which everyone in your population has an equal chance of being included in your study. When researchers do national surveys, whether on attitudes toward abortion or anything else, they need to get information from only about 2,000 people. Yet, random samples are so powerful that these surveys represent accurately the opinions of 300,000,000 Americans.

Experiments ▪ Another research method is the **experiment.** If you were to use this method, you would divide people who have certain characteristics (such as Latinas between the ages of 18 and 21 who have had an abortion) into two groups. You would expose half of them to some experience (an emotional film of a mother giving birth). These people are called the **experimental group.** You would do this to see how their reactions differ from those of the other half, who do not have this experience (the **control group,** which does not view the film). How the experimental group responds is thought to be generalizable to people who share their characteristics (all of those who have had an abortion).

Experiments are rare in the study of social problems, partly because ethics do not allow us to create problems for people (watching an emotional film after having an abortion may cause undue stress). However, you can use experiments in more limited ways. For example, you could measure attitudes toward abortion before and after listening to a lecture on abortion.

Field Studies ▪ In **field studies** (or **participant observation**), researchers go into a setting that they want to learn more about. (This is called "going into the field.") For example, Magda Denes (1976) wanted to know what an abortion clinic was like—for the women and the staff—so she obtained permission to be present and observe what took place. The result was a moving book, *In Necessity and Sorrow.* Denes, herself a proabortionist, found more than she expected while conducting field research in an abortion clinic. She describes picking up fetuses from the trash barrel, their little arms

broken, cut, and bleeding. Her book highlights conversations she has with doctors about how the fetus stops moving about half an hour after he injects the saline solution into the placenta. No other research method could obtain information like this.

Because each method (or research design) has its strengths and weaknesses, sociologists often use more than one. You might do field research in one abortion clinic and follow up with surveys of women from many abortion clinics.

FOUR METHODS FOR GATHERING INFORMATION. After choosing a research design, sociologists must decide how to gather their information. Four basic techniques are available: interviews, questionnaires, documents, and observations.

Interviews ▪ If you use an **interview,** you will ask people questions on the topics that you want to explore. You can choose from two types of interviews. If you use a **structured interview,** you will ask everyone the same questions (for example, "What is your relationship to the man who made you pregnant?"). If you use an **unstructured interview,** you will let people talk in depth about their experiences; you will, however, make certain that everyone covers specific areas (contraceptive history, family relations, the reasons for the abortion, and so on). Look at the Thinking Critically box on the next page. To learn how women interpret their abortion, Henslin used unstructured interviews. The women could talk about their experiences in any way they wanted, and he never knew where that would lead. Structured interviews may not have tapped into such in-depth feelings and perspectives.

Paper–Pencil Questionnaires ▪ If you were to use the second technique, **paper–pencil questionnaires,** you would ask people to answer written questions. Your questions could be either *open ended* (people answer in their own words) or *closed ended* (people choose from a list of prepared answers). An open-ended question might be "What is your relationship to the man who made you pregnant?" The woman would state the relationship in her own words. A closed-ended form of this question would ask the woman to check an item on a list, such as husband, boyfriend, casual acquaintance, other. It is easier to compare answers to closed-ended questions, but open-ended questions tap a richer world, eliciting comments and even topics that you might not anticipate.

Documents ▪ Written sources or records, called **documents,** can also provide valuable data about social problems. You might examine official records like census, crime data, or hospital records. Kristin Luker, for example, analyzed the records of 500 women who came to the abortion clinic that she studied. Or you might look at more informal records, such as journals, blogs, and letters. These documents can reveal people's behaviors and provide insight into how they cope with troubles.

Observation ▪ The fourth technique, **observation,** is just what the term implies: To use it, you observe what is occurring in some setting. You watch and listen to what is taking place and record or take field notes on people's actions or the statements they make. You might use a tape recorder, but if recording will interfere with what people are doing, you take notes instead, either while something occurs or afterward. If you use *overt observation,* you will identify yourself as a researcher, but if you use *covert observation,* the people in the setting will be unaware that you are studying them.

Sociologists often combine these methods. For example, in her study of the abortion clinic, Luker used three of these methods: observation, interviews, and documents. Not only did she observe women and abortion providers in the clinic, but she also interviewed women who were having abortions and then examined the clinic's records on its patients.

STRIVING FOR ACCURACY AND OBJECTIVITY. When doing research, it is essential to remain objective. You must be on guard against producing biased data. For example, it is obvious that if you were to ask a woman "What is your opinion about killing babies by abortion?" your study would be biased in an antiabortion direction. No one—whether proabortion or antiabortion—favors killing babies. This sort of question would not constitute

COPING WITH GUILT AFTER AN ABORTION

Having an abortion solves the immediate problem of an unwanted pregnancy, but it also creates new problems. One is how to define the abortion. For those who view the fetus as nonhuman, this can be relatively simple. For those who view the fetus as a human, however (as well as for those with mixed views, which appears to characterize most women), the situation is more complicated.

How do women cope? While abortions were still illegal (1971), Jim Henslin interviewed 22 college women who had abortions. These women used four major techniques to help them cope:

1. Some women think of abortion as the lesser of two evils. They view abortion as preferable to having a child and ruining their own life or the lives of people they love, as preferable to shifting the responsibility for rearing the child onto others, or as preferable to resenting the child for having been born. One woman said:

   We saved ourselves and a child and very numerous other people from a lot of hurt because of this. And besides that, it was the only thing I could do—the only thing that I wanted to do, let's put it that way.

2. Some women look at abortion as a positive good in and of itself:

   (My mom) thought it'd be the best thing. . . . After my mom told me, I started to talk to my girlfriend, and she decided it would probably be the best thing for me, too. . . . I told (my boyfriend). . . . He thought that would be the best thing. . . . I always told myself that, you know, I'd probably get one if I didn't get married, 'cause to me that would be the best thing for me.

3. Some women see themselves as having no responsibility because they had no choice:

   He (boyfriend) insisted that I do this. I was against it. . . . I knew that I didn't want to. . . . But when you have someone saying, "well, this is what I want you to do"—and he didn't want to get married, and he wouldn't let me just have the child like I wanted to do—so I really didn't have a whole lot of choices. You know what I mean?

4. Some women think in terms of a future pregnancy that will replace the "pregnancy-abortion":

   The mistake is past, if it was a mistake. At any rate, we can do nothing about it now. Now we have to look to the future. In another year John and I will hopefully have the start of our own family. Thoughts of being a mother have entered my mind frequently since the abortion. I really look forward to that day!

---

scientific research. Nor would this question, biasing answers in the other direction: "What is your opinion on forcing a woman to have a baby when she wants an abortion?"

You can see, then, that scientific studies require objectivity. Compare the biased questions just mentioned with these. Here is a neutral closed-ended question: "Do you favor or oppose abortion?" Here is a neutral open-ended question: "What is your opinion of abortion?" For either of these questions, you might specify the trimester being considered. Can you see that these questions are neutral, that they don't tilt answers in any direction? If you ask questions like these, your own opinions about abortion, whatever they might be, will not interfere with your research.

Like everyone else, those of us who are sociologists get our ideas and opinions from the groups with which we associate and the ideas to which we are exposed. No matter how we dislike it, this means that we have biases. Fortunately, we have a safeguard that helps to prevent our biases from contaminating our research on social problems. This safeguard is the publication of our findings. In our articles and books, we include details on the methods we use. Other sociologists examine these publications in detail, eager to point out any flaws they can find, including bias.

To help you better understand how sociologists do their research, we asked several researchers to share their experiences with us. The result is a feature in this text called Spotlight on Social Research. For an overview of this feature, see the box on the next page.

Spotlight on Social Research
AN OVERVIEW OF THIS FEATURE

Sociologists do a lot of research on social problems. In fact, this is one of their favorite areas of study. As we review the major social problems in this text, you will be introduced to both classic research and the most recent research findings.

To acquaint you with some of these researchers, 10 chapters have a boxed feature titled *Spotlight on Social Research*. Each box features a researcher who has studied a particular social problem. These boxes are unique, for the researchers themselves have written them.

The research that you will read about in Spotlight on Social Research is incredibly varied. With these researchers, you will visit a youth gang in Chicago, a bar in Chicago's inner city where gangsters hang out, and neo-Nazis in Detroit. You'll even be present at a Klan rally. In a study of workers at two magazines, you will learn how views of sexual harassment differ from one work setting to another. You will also learn how one

"That's the worst set of opinions I've heard in my entire life."

In an effort to remain objective and unbiased, sociologists do not reveal their own opinions.

(© The New Yorker Collection 1975. Robert Weber from cartoonbank.com. All rights reserved.)

sociologist became so interested in military matters that he went to Iraq. One researcher recounts how his picking beans in the fields of Washington led to a lifetime of doing research on crime. Another researcher shares how her own abuse at the hands of her husband while she was yet a student motivated her to do research on intimate violence.

As these researchers reflect on their studies, they pull back the curtains to let you look behind the scenes. This lets you see how research is actually conducted. To help provide a broader context for appreciating their research, we open each box by sharing a little about the researcher's background and how the researcher became interested in a particular social problem.

We think that you'll enjoy Spotlight on Social Research. The "inside" information that these researchers share gives a unique flavor to this text. From these reports, you will learn things about research that are not available anywhere else. We are grateful to these researchers for taking time out of their research and teaching to share their experiences with us. It was a pleasure corresponding with them and gaining insight into their work.

Should Sociologists Take Sides?

THE PROBLEM OF DETERMINING MORALITY. The four research methods described earlier allow us to gather objective information on social problems, but they do not reveal what attitude or social policy is "correct." This takes us back to the issue mentioned earlier, that sociology does not have the capacity to specify that one value is superior to another. Abortion, for example, is interwoven with thorny philosophical and religious issues concerning "great questions": life, death, morality, freedom, responsibility, and ultimate existence. Sociologists can study people's ideas about such topics, but sociology has no right to judge whether those ideas are right or wrong, much less determine the ultimate meaning that may underlie such issues.

To take a position on a social problem is to take sides—and because sociology is not equipped to make judgments about values and morality, sociology cannot tell us what side to take. Even so, the question of taking sides on social problems is debated hotly among sociologists, for, like other thoughtful people, sociologists have their own concerns and ideas about social problems.

Should sociologists, because they are scientists, forget their own subjective concerns and strive to remain dispassionate, detached, and value-free? If so, they would merely report the facts and not take sides on the social issues that affect our society. Or should they use their professional authority to promote the side of an issue that they see as right? For example, should they try to help the "oppressed," the "down and out," the poor, and others who are on the receiving end of social problems?

THE DEBATE AMONG SOCIOLOGISTS. Those who champion neutrality stress the position that sociologists enjoy no superior vantage point from which to make moral judgments. Sociologists do have knowledge and skills to offer, they say, but not morality. In their

study of social problems, sociologists can indicate the potential consequences of different social policies, but they should not promote any particular policy or solution. To do so would be to hide a moral or value position under the guise of sociology.

On the other side of this issue, some sociologists are convinced that they have a moral obligation to take a stand. "If sociology is not useful for helping to reform society," they ask, "of what value is it?" They stress that sociologists are in a strategic position to relate the surface manifestations of a social problem (such as poverty) to deeper social causes (such as the control of a country's resources by the wealthy and powerful). They say that sociologists should do their research objectively—and always side with those who are being hurt and exploited. Those on this extreme end of the debate also say that sociologists have a moral obligation to make the oppressed aware of their condition and to organize them to do battle against those who oppress them.

UNCOVERING VALUES. In order to fully participate in a debate, one must be aware of the position taken by each side, any hidden agendas, and future policy suggestions. What if a group of sociologists were to study unmarried pregnant teenagers and conclude that they all should have abortions? Arguments can be made for and against this position, of course, but should sociologists promote such a point of view? Or consider an even more extreme case. What if sociologists, after analyzing the soaring costs of Social Security and Medicare, became convinced that the solution to this severe problem would be to euthanize the physically and mentally handicapped? Or what if their conclusion was that all people, after celebrating their 80th birthday, should be "put to sleep" by means of painless drugs? Would professional activity on behalf of such proposed social policies be appropriate?

No sociologist is going to support such a position, but we think you get the point. Whenever someone takes a position on a social problem and advocates one solution or another, values of some sort underlie that person's views. Should sociologists, then, as sociologists, advocate or promote specific solutions to social problems?

TAKING SIDES: DIVISIONS AND AGREEMENT. This question of taking sides as professionals within sociology has created division within the discipline more than once—quite publicly during the Vietnam War and again with the Iraq War. The debate centers on whether the Society for the Study of Social Problems and other groups should make public antiwar pronouncements or not. Although wars come and go and issues change, this broad cleavage among sociologists remains. Some say that sociologists should work toward changing society in order to help the less powerful; others are just as convinced that sociology's proper role is only to investigate and report objectively. They say that if sociologists want to take sides on any issue, they should do so as private citizens, not as sociologists.

This debate keeps sociologists sensitive to the boundaries between objectivity and partisanship. Although there is little room for middle ground, most sociologists attempt to resolve this dilemma by separating research evidence from their own values and opinions. What they observe and measure, they attempt to report dispassionately and to analyze as accurately as possible.

Despite their disagreements about taking sides on social problems, sociologists agree that they are in a unique position to study social problems and that they should produce thorough and objective studies. Sociologists do possess the tools to do such research, and their studies can be valuable for both the public and policy makers.

A PERSONAL NOTE. As the authors of this book, we sincerely hope that the coming chapters help you to acquire a sociological imagination that will allow you to work toward creative solutions for the pressing social problems we face. Sociologists can provide facts on objective conditions, sensitize you to the broader context that nourishes social problems, and suggest the likely consequences of intervention. Your decisions about what should be done, however, will have to be made according to *your* values.

SUMMARY AND REVIEW

1. Sociologists use what is called the *sociological imagination* (or perspective) to view the social problems that affect people's lives. This means that they look at how social locations shape people's behavior and attitudes.

2. A *social problem* is some aspect of society that people are concerned about and would like changed. It consists of *objective conditions,* things that are measurable, and *subjective concerns,* the feelings and attitudes that people have about those conditions. Social problems are relative—one group's solution may be another group's problem.

3. Social problems go through a natural history of four stages that often overlap: defining the problem, crafting an official response, reacting to the official response, and pursuing alternative strategies.

4. Sociologists are able to make five contributions to the study of social problems: They can help determine the extent of a social problem, clarify people's attitudes toward social problems, apply the sociological imagination to social problems, identify potential social

policies for dealing with social problems, and evaluate likely consequences of those policies.

5. The sociological understanding of a social problem differs from a commonsense understanding because the sociological perspective is not based on emotions or personal values. Instead, sociologists examine how social problems affect people, view the causes of social problems as located in society rather than in individuals, and use scientific methods to gather information about social problems.

6. To study social problems, sociologists use four major research designs: *surveys, case studies, experiments,* and *field studies.* Sociologists gather information in four basic ways: *interviews, questionnaires, documents,* and *observations.* These methods are often used in combination.

7. Because social problems can be viewed from so many vantage points, sociologists disagree on whether they should choose sides as professionals. They do agree, however, that sociological studies must provide objective, accurate, and verifiable data.

KEY TERMS

Case study, 18
Common sense, 15
Control group, 18
Documents, 19
Experiment, 18
Experimental group, 18
Field study (or participant observation), 18
Generalize, 18
Interview, 19
Methods (research methods or methodology), 17

Objective condition, 6
Observation, 19
Paper–pencil questionnaire, 19
Participant observation (or field study), 18
Personal troubles, 3
Population, 18
Power, 8
Random sample, 18
Research design, 18
RU486 (Mifeprex), 14
Sample, 18

Social location, 5
Social problem, 6
Sociological imagination (or sociological perspective), 3
Sociological perspective, 4
Sociology, 15
Structured interview, 19
Subjective concern, 6
Survey, 18
Unstructured interview, 19
Value, 8

MySocLab

What can you find in MySocLab? mysoclab www.mysoclab.com

- Complete Ebook
- Practice Tests and Exams
- Multimedia Activities
- Mapping and Data Analysis Exercises

- Research and Writing Advice
- Interactive Social Surveys
- Sociology in the News

CHAPTER 2

Interpreting Social Problems: Aging

In 1928, Charles Hart, an anthropologist working on his PhD, practiced fieldwork among the Tiwi tribe, a preliterate people living on an island off the northern coast of Australia. The Tiwi were known to be uncomfortable around strangers. When Hart arrived, he was told that he must be assigned to a clan in order to belong. The tribe assigned Hart to the bird (Jabijabui) clan and gave him an adoptive mother. Hart was taken aback and described the woman as "toothless, almost blind, withered," adding that she was "physically quite revolting and mentally rather senile." He then described this remarkable event:

> How seriously they took my presence in their kinship system is something I never will be sure about. . . . However, toward the end of my time on the islands an incident occurred that surprised me because it suggested that some of them had been taking my presence in the kinship system much more seriously than I had thought. I was approached by a group of about eight or nine senior men. . . . They were the senior members of the Jabijabui clan and they had decided among themselves that the time had come to get rid of the decrepit old woman who had first called me son and whom I now called mother. . . . As I knew, they said, it was Tiwi custom, when an old woman became too feeble to look after herself, to "cover her up." This could only be done by her sons and her brothers and all of them had to

The Tiwi . . . sometimes got rid of their ancient and decrepit females.

agree beforehand, since once it was done they did not want any dissension among the brothers or clansmen, as that might lead to a feud. My "mother" was now completely blind, she was constantly falling over logs or into fires, and they, her senior clansmen, were in agreement that she would be better out of the way. Did I agree?

> I already knew about "covering up." The Tiwi, like many other hunting and gathering peoples, sometimes got rid of their ancient and decrepit females. The method was to dig a hole in the ground in some lonely place, put the old woman in the hole and fill it in with earth until only her head was showing. Everybody went away for a day or two and then went back to the hole to discover to their great surprise, that the old woman was dead, having been too feeble to raise her arms from the earth. Nobody had "killed" her; her death in Tiwi eyes was a natural one. She had been alive when her relatives last saw her. I had never seen it done, though I knew it was the custom, so I asked my brothers if it was necessary for me to attend the "covering up."

> They said no and they would do it, but only after they had my agreement. Of course I agreed, and a week or two later we heard in our camp that my "mother" was dead, and we all wailed and put on the trimmings of mourning.

—C. W. M. Hart in Hart and Pilling (1979, pp. 125–126)

Many find Hart's account rather shocking. He did not hesitate in agreeing that the old woman should be "covered up." His only concern was whether he would have to watch the woman die. In our society we devise our own ways of "covering up" when the elderly have outlived their social usefulness. "Why spend precious resources (all that money) on people who have only a few years—or just a few months—more to live?"

goes the reasoning. "Wouldn't we be better off ushering them off the stage of life—with dignity, of course?"

Such opinions elicit a wide range of reactions. Some agree that the frail elderly are a burden and that society is better off without them. This kind of thinking sends chills down the spine of others. If such programs of euthanasia were ever initiated, who would be put in charge of deciding which old people were "socially valuable" and which ones were not? Some fear that the frail elderly might simply be the first targets, to be followed by others whom some officials decide are "useless"—or at least of "less value" and, for the good of the general society, in need of being "covered up."

Although few human groups choose "covering up" as their solution, every society must deal with the problem of people who grow old and frail. You may have noted that the Tiwi "cover up" only old women. This is an extreme example of the discrimination against females that is common throughout the world. This topic is so significant that we shall spend all of Chapter 9 discussing issues of gender. In this present chapter, we will consider how theories help us to understand social life by exploring the social problem of the elderly.

Sociological Theories and Social Problems

As sociologists do research on social problems, they uncover a lot of "facts." If you have just a jumble of "facts," however, how can you understand what they mean? To make sense of those "facts," you have to put them in some order, so you can see how they are related to one another. To do this, sociologists use theories. A theory explains how two or more concepts (or "facts"), such as age and suicide, are related. A **theory,** then, gives us a framework for organizing facts, and in so doing it provides a way of interpreting social life. Theories often dictate the questions we ask when doing research.

In this chapter, we shall look at the three main theories that sociologists use—functionalism, conflict theory, and symbolic interactionism. Before we begin, you may want to look at an overview of these theories, which are summarized in Table 2-1. Because each theory focuses on some particular "slice" of a social problem, each provides a different perspective on the problem. As you study these theories, keep in mind that

TABLE 2-1 A Summary of Sociological Theories

	FUNCTIONALISM	CONFLICT THEORY	SYMBOLIC INTERACTIONISM
What is society?	A social system composed of parts that work together to benefit the whole	Groups competing with one another within the same social system	People's patterns of behavior; always changing
What are the key terms?	Structure Function System Equilibrium Goals	Competition Conflict Special interests Power Exploitation	Symbols Interaction Communication Meanings Definitions
What is a social problem?	The failure of some part to fulfill its function, which interferes with the smooth functioning of the system	The natural and inevitable outcome as interest groups compete for scarce or limited resources	Whatever a group decides is a social problem is a social problem for that group
How does something become a social problem?	Some part of the system fails, usually because of rapid social change	Authority and power are used by the powerful to exploit weaker groups	One set of definitions becomes accepted; competing views are rejected

Source: By James M. Henslin.

each theory is like a spotlight shining onto a dark area: It illuminates only a particular part of that area. Taken together, these theories throw much more light on problems that we want to understand.

Functionalism and Social Problems

Introducing Functionalism

The first major theory that sociologists use to interpret social problems is **functionalism** (or functional analysis). Functionalists compare society to a self-adjusting machine that is composed of many parts. Each part of a machine has a **function.** When a part is working properly, it fulfills that function, and the machine hums along. Functionalists also use the analogy of the human body. A human has many organs, and when an organ is working properly, it contributes to the well-being of the person. When one organ fails to work properly, another compensates. Like a machine or human, society is also composed of many parts. Each of society's parts also has a function. When a part is working properly, it contributes to the well-being (stability or equilibrium) of society. When a part is not working properly, it hurts the well-being of society.

To see how one part of society may compensate for other parts, consider health care and Social Security, two social services designed to help the elderly. Of the vast sums spent on health care for the elderly, some goes into medical research. The discoveries by medical researchers help not only the elderly but also children and adults of all ages. Similarly, not only do the 36 million retired and disabled workers who collect Social Security benefit from this program but so do the 64,000 people who work for this federal agency (*Statistical Abstract,* 2006, Tables 483, 537). Their families also benefit. The spending of these vast sums, in turn, helps businesses across the nation. In other words, functionalists stress how each part of society contributes to the well-being of other parts of society.

To see how the functionalist perspective applies to social problems, think of society as a single machine with many parts. When each part does its job, the machine runs smoothly. If some part fails, however, the whole machine can suffer. Functionalists call these failures **dysfunctions.** If a dysfunction creates instability or disequilibrium in society, it often becomes a social problem. *From the functionalist perspective, then, a social problem is the failure of some part of society, which then interferes with society's smooth functioning.* When analyzing the many social problems facing the aged from a functionalist point of view, one must consider "red tape." This term describes the strict guidelines and regulations set by the government that may prohibit an institution from performing the functions it sets out to perform. For example, strict regulations set by the government often create delays in receiving benefits. This extra layer of government bureaucracy makes it more difficult for health agencies to care for the elderly.

The Development of Functionalism

AUGUSTE COMTE: SOCIETY AS ORGANISM. Functionalism has its roots in the origins of sociology (Turner, 1978). Auguste Comte (1798–1857), who is called the founder of sociology because he coined the term, developed his ideas during the social unrest that followed the French Revolution. Comte regarded society as an animal: Just as an animal has tissues and organs that are interrelated and function together, so does society. For a society to function smoothly, its parts must be in balance.

HERBERT SPENCER: SOCIETY AS STRUCTURE. Herbert Spencer (1820–1903) built on Comte's ideas. He too emphasized that the parts of society work together in a structured fashion (a system, or whole). Just as each part of an animal, taken together, forms the animal's structure (or whole), so each part of society, taken together, forms its structure. Each part also makes some contribution to the structure, which Spencer called its function. Because the parts are interrelated, a change in one part affects other parts.

Emile Durkheim: "Members are united by ties which extend deeper and far beyond the moments during which the exchange is made. Each of the functions that they exercise is dependent on others, and with them forms a solidary system."

EMILE DURKHEIM: NORMAL AND ABNORMAL STATES. Later in the 19th century, Emile Durkheim (1858–1917) built on this idea that a society is composed of parts that perform functions. When society's parts perform their functions, he said, society is in a "normal" state. If society's parts do not fulfill their functions, society is in an "abnormal" or "pathological" state. According to Durkheim, in order to understand society, we need to look at both **structure**—how the parts of a society are related to one another—and function—how each part contributes to society: "Members are united by ties which extend deeper and far beyond the moments during which the exchange is made. Each of the functions that they exercise is dependent on others, and with them forms a solidary system" (Durkheim, 1893, p. 37).

ROBERT MERTON: FUNCTIONS AND DYSFUNCTIONS. A 20th-century sociologist, Robert Merton (1910–2003) defined functions as the beneficial consequences of people's actions. Functions help a social system to survive (to maintain stability or equilibrium). Functions can be either manifest or latent. A **manifest function** is an action that is intended to help some part of the system. For example, Social Security is intended to make life better for the elderly. Improving life for the aged, then, is a manifest function of Social Security. As Merton emphasized, our actions also have **latent functions.** These are consequences that arise from an action or institution but that were not part of the original purpose. For example, the salaries paid to the 64,000 employees of the Social Security Administration help to stabilize our economy. Because this beneficial consequence of Social Security is not intended, however, it is a latent function.

Merton (1968) stressed that human actions also have dysfunctions. These are consequences that disrupt a system's stability, making it more difficult to survive. If a part fails to meet its functions, it contributes to society's maladjustment and is part of a social problem.

Because the consequences of people's actions that disrupt a system's equilibrium usually are unintended, Merton called them **latent dysfunctions.** For example, the Social Security Administration has thousands of rules, written in incredible detail, designed to anticipate every potential situation. If the 64,000 employees of this agency were to follow each procedure exactly, the resulting red tape would interfere with their ability to serve the elderly. The rules are not intended to have this effect; therefore, they are latent dysfunctions.

IN SUM Although these theorists of functionalism have different emphases, they have this in common: They sensitize us to think in terms of systems, to see whatever we are studying as part of a larger unit. Functionalists emphasize that when we examine one part of a system, we must look at how it is related to other parts. As we do so, we analyze that part's functions or dysfunctions. Let's apply these terms of functionalism to the social problem of aging.

Applying Functionalism to Social Problems

From the functionalist perspective, *society* is a social system composed of interconnected parts that function together. When those parts work well, each contributes to the equilibrium of society. *Equilibrium* simply means that society's parts are balanced, that they have made an adjustment to one another. A *social problem,* then, is a condition in which the parts of society are not working well together. There is an imbalance of some sort.

SOCIAL PROBLEMS AS A RESULT OF CHANGE. A major source of social problems is the inevitable consequence of change. For institutional change in one area of society disrupts

the equilibrium of society's parts, forcing those parts to make new adjustments. From the functionalist perspective, a change in one part of society changes an interrelated part of society causing a new social problem to arise. Earlier we mentioned how red tape may cause difficulty for those institutions attempting to provide care to the elderly. The federal government is now asking hospices to repay millions of dollars in excess Medicare reimbursement because many hospice residents wound up living longer than expected. The federal government's demand for repayment is challenging those hospices who already spent the funds caring for other terminally ill residents. The result of this Medicare reimbursement demand will be the demise of many hospice organizations in the country.

FUNCTIONS. Now let's see how *functions* apply to another social problem among the elderly population—early retirement. Society needs to pass its positions of responsibility (jobs) from one group (the elderly) to another group (younger people). To entice the elderly to leave their positions, retirement bonuses and private pensions are dangled before them. In exchange for these benefits, the elderly transfer their jobs to younger people. In this view, called **disengagement theory,** the elderly get paid for not working and, in return, the younger people take over their jobs (Cumming & Henry, 1961; Cockerham, 1991). This trade-off is functional for society, for both old and young benefit from the exchange. From the functionalist perspective, this example demonstrates how society works as a self-regulating machine that compensates and makes the adjustments necessary to keep it humming along.

Nursing homes are also functional: They have helped society adjust to social change. Care of the elderly used to fall primarily upon women's shoulders. Because women worked at home and few people made it to old age, this was not a general problem. But then more women began to work outside the home, and life expectancy started to increase. The result was more frail elderly who needed care and fewer women available to care for them. Nursing homes were developed to replace these former caretakers, and today 4.5% of Americans over the age of 65 live in nursing homes (*Statistical Abstract,* 2006, Tables 11, 68). This is the total at any one time. Over the years, 37% of all people who reach age 65 will need such long-term care (Kemper, Komisar, & Alexcih, 2006). Most of these nursing home residents are not typical of older people: Most are ill, very old, or have no family. Again, society has compensated and adjusted to rapid social change.

As they analyze social problems, functionalists also look for latent functions. For many caretakers, providing care and shelter strained the relationship they shared with their parents. After they placed their parent in the nursing home, the love that had been obscured by duty gradually recovered. As one 57-year-old daughter reported, "My mother demanded rather than earned respect and love. We had a poor past relationship—a love/hate relationship. Now I can do for her because I want to. I can finally love her because I want to" (K. F. Smith and Bengtson 1979, p. 441). Although not intended, the restored love became a latent function.

Stereotypes of the elderly are inadequate. There are many types of elderly people. In general, people carry into their older years the habits and lifestyles developed during their younger years.

DYSFUNCTIONS. Functionalists also study dysfunctions. Few nursing homes are pleasant places. Some analysts refer to nursing homes as "houses of death" or "human junkyards." Many stink of urine, and it is depressing to see so many sad people clustered together. After being admitted to a nursing home, most elderly people decline physically and mentally. A chief reason is the dehumanized way they are treated: segregated from the outside world, denied privacy, and placed under rigid controls. Many nursing homes control their residents chemically, giving them psychotropic drugs such as Thorazine and Prozac (Gurvich & Cunningham, 2000). These "chemical straitjackets" keep elderly patients quiet, but they also can reduce them to an empty shell of their former selves. This particular dysfunction, elderly people being abandoned in abusive nursing homes, is concentrated among the poor who have few close family and friends.

Research on nursing homes has shown that abuse is common (Harris & Benson, 2006). Sociologists Karl Pillemer and David Moore (1989) surveyed nursing homes in New Hampshire. Thirty-one percent of the staff reported that during the past year they had seen physical abuse—patients being pushed, grabbed, shoved, pinched, kicked, or slapped. Eighty-one percent said they had seen psychological abuse—patients being cursed, insulted, yelled at, or threatened. When asked if they themselves had abused patients, 10% admitted that they had physically abused them, and 40% admitted to psychological abuse. The most abusive staff members were those who were thinking about quitting their jobs and those who thought of patients as being childlike.

Another dysfunction of nursing homes is neglect—ignoring patients or not giving medications on time. Some neglect comes from conscientious workers who are assigned so many responsibilities that they can't keep up with them all. Other neglect is purposeful, coming from workers who don't care about their patients or who even take pleasure in harming them. Here is an example of atrocious neglect:

> A nursing home patient was sent to the hospital for the treatment of a bedsore. The hospital staff treated the condition and gave the nursing home instructions on how to keep the wound clean and dressed. Several days later, family members noticed an odor and seepage from the wound and asked that the patient be returned to the hospital. The hospital staff looked at the bandage and saw that it had not been changed as they instructed. When the bandage was removed, insects crawled and flew out of the wound. (Harris & Benson, 2006, p. 87)

With the public painfully aware of abuse in nursing homes, the decision to place an elderly family member in a nursing home can be agonizing. Even though an aged parent may be too sick to be cared for at home, to place a parent in a nursing home is viewed by many as a callous denial of love and duty. Nursing homes don't have to be abusive places, however. To see how two major units of society, the government and the family, can work together to provide high-quality care for the elderly, see the Global Glimpse box on the next page.

Functionalism and Social Problems: A Summary

Table 2-3 on page 32 presents an overview of functionalism. As you look at this table, begin with the column marked *Action*. This column refers to actions that have taken place in the social system. The examples in this table refer to business, government, medicine, and the family, but we could include other social institutions. The column titled *Manifest Function* refers to the intended beneficial consequence of the action. The column titled *Latent Function* refers to a beneficial consequence of the action that was not intended. The last column, *Latent Dysfunction,* refers to an unintended harmful consequence of the action.

A Global Glimpse
THE COMING TIDAL WAVE: JAPAN'S ELDERLY

With one of the world's lowest birthrates, Japan's population is aging faster than that of any other nation. In 1950, only 66 Japanese turned 100. Now it is 1,700 a year. To see how rapidly Japan's population of elderly is growing, look at Table 2-2. In just a few years, one of every four Japanese will be age 65 or older.

Think about the implications of such a large percentage of elderly. What will happen to Japan's health care services? About half of the Japanese elderly will be age 75 and over. More than 1 million of them are expected to be bedridden. Another million are likely to be senile. By the year 2020, Japan's medical bill is likely to run 6 times higher than it is now. How will Japan be able to meet the health needs of this coming tidal wave of elderly?

This question must be placed within the context of Japanese culture, specifically, the obligations of one generation to another. The Japanese believe that because parents took care of their children, the children are obligated to care for their parents. Unlike in the United States, most aged Japanese live with their adult children. As the number of elderly mushrooms, will the Japanese family be able to carry on its traditional care-giving and protective roles?

Because Europe faces similar problems, Japanese leaders decided that they could learn from Europe's system. But when Japanese observers saw Europe's lower work ethic, higher taxes, and lower savings—all leading to a declining ability to compete in global markets—the Japanese decided to work out their own plan. One goal is to reduce inequality among the aged. With this goal in mind, the government has begun to unify the country's pension systems and has increased spending for social security. To care for the elderly who have no families and

"Robina," a robot made by Toyota Motor Corp., waves after being unveiled at a news conference in Tokyo, Japan. Toyota Motor Corp., the world's second-largest automaker, plans to start selling robots for use in housekeeping and elderly care to consumers next decade.

those who are the sickest, the government is building nursing homes. To improve the quality of life for the healthy elderly, the government is financing 10,000 day service centers.

These will be available to the poor and rich alike. The government will also provide transportation to physiotherapy centers and offer free testing for the early detection of cancer and heart disease. The government has also created a new position called "home helper." After passing a government examination, 100,000 specialists will help the elderly at home.

Japan's low birthrate amidst a surging older population has led to the search for alternative workers to care for the elderly. In an Orwellian twist, a Japanese company has come with an unusual answer—robots. These robots, called Hello Kitty Robo, are able to transmit both messages and images. To keep residents of nursing homes mentally active, the robots will ask riddles and quiz residents on math problems. They will also chat with residents and ask about their health.

These services and facilities are not intended to replace the family's care for the elderly but, rather, to supplement it. They are meant to strengthen, not crowd out the family. Gnawing at these ambitious plans, however, is a disturbing economic reality. For over a decade, Japan has been in the midst of a depression. Only now is the country coming out of it. With huge federal deficits, some of these plans will have to be shelved. Regardless of economic conditions or whether society is ready, the tidal wave of elderly is on its way. It will arrive on schedule.

Based on Freed (1994); Nishio (1994); Otten (1995); Mackellar & Horlacher (2000); "Hello Kitty Robot . . ." (2006).

TABLE 2-2	Japan's Population Age 65 and Older			
1950	1970	1990	2000	2020
4%	7%	12%	16%	24%

Remember that functionalists assume that society is like a well-oiled, self-adjusting machine. They examine how the parts of that machine (society, or the social system) are interrelated, adjusting to one another. As society undergoes change, a social problem arises when some part or parts of society do not adjust to the change and are not functioning properly.

TABLE 2-3 Old Age: A Functionalist Overview

RELATED PARTS OF THE SOCIAL SYSTEM[1]	ACTION	MANIFEST FUNCTION	LATENT FUNCTION	LATENT DYSFUNCTION
Economic (business)	Pension and retirement benefits	Provide income and leisure time for the aged	Jobs for younger workers	Displacement of the elderly; loss of self-esteem; loss of purpose
Political (government)	Social Security payments	Stable income for the aged; dignity in old age	Employment for 64,000 people by the Social Security Administration	Inadequate income; many recipients live on the edge of poverty
Medical	Technological developments; gerontological specialties	Longer lives for the population	A larger proportion of the elderly in the population	The Social Security system becomes much more expensive
	Medicare and Medicaid	Provide good health care for the elderly	Financing bonanza for the medical profession	"Rip-off" nursing homes
Family	Grown children live apart from their parents	Independence of both younger and older generations	Institutionalized care for the elderly; greater mobility of younger workers	Isolation of elderly parents; loneliness and despair

[1] As used here, "parts" of the social system are social institutions.
Source: By James M. Henslin.

Conflict Theory and Social Problems

Introducing Conflict Theory

"We couldn't disagree more," reply conflict theorists to the functionalist position. Parts of society do not work together harmoniously. If you look below the surface, you will see that society's parts are competing with one another for scarce resources. There are only so many resources to go around, and the competition for them is so severe that conflict is barely kept in check. Whether they recognize it or not, the elderly, for example, are competing with younger people for available resources. If the competition heats up, open conflict between the young and the elderly could erupt, throwing society into turmoil. In short, the guiding principle of social life is disequilibrium and conflict, not equilibrium and harmony, as functionalists say.

From the conflict perspective, social problems are the natural and inevitable outcome of social struggle. No matter what a social problem may look like on its surface, at its essence lies conflict over limited resources between the more and less powerful. As the more powerful exploit society's resources and oppress the less powerful, they create such social problems as poverty and discrimination. As those who are exploited react to their oppression, still other social problems emerge: street crime, escapist drug abuse, suicide, homicide, riots, revolution, and terrorism. To study social problems, we need to penetrate their surface manifestations and expose their basic, underlying conflict.

The Development of Conflict Theory

KARL MARX: CAPITALISM AND CONFLICT. Karl Marx (1818–1883), the founder of **conflict theory,** witnessed the Industrial Revolution that transformed Europe. Cities grew as farmers and laborers left rural areas to seek work in factories. The new factory

owners put rural farmers to work at near-starvation wages. As poverty and exploitation grew, political unrest followed, and upheaval swept across Europe.

Shocked by the suffering and inhumanity that he saw, Marx concluded that the hallmark of history is a struggle for power. In this struggle, some group always remains in the top position, and, inevitably, it oppresses those groups under it. Marx also concluded that a major turning point in this historical struggle occurred when **capitalism** became dominant in the Western world—that is, when a small group of people gained control over the means of production and made profit their goal. As machinery replaced workers' tools, the **capitalists** (owners of the capital, factories, and equipment) gained an exploitative advantage.

Because tens of thousands of people from farms and villages had crowded into the cities in a desperate search for work, the capitalists, who owned the means of production, were able to impose miserable working conditions. They paid workers little and fired them at will. The capitalists at this time also controlled politicians. When workers rebelled, they could count on the police to use violence to bring them under control. This misery led to a feeling of despair and desire to revolt: "The day of reckoning will finally come, and it will be bloody. The workers will overthrow their oppressors and will establish a classless society in which the goal will be not profits for the few but, rather, the good of the many."

In Marx's time, workers were at the mercy of their bosses. Workers lacked what many take for granted today—a minimum wage, eight-hour workdays, five-day workweeks, paid vacations, medical benefits, sick leave, unemployment compensation, pensions, social security, even the right to strike. Conflict theorists remind us that such benefits came about not because of the generous hearts of the rich but because workers fought for them—sometimes to the death.

Karl Marx: "The day of reckoning will finally come, and it will be bloody. The workers will overthrow their oppressors and will establish a classless society in which the goal will be not profits for the few but, rather, the good of the many."

GEORG SIMMEL: SUBORDINATES AND SUPERORDINATES. Conflict theory extends beyond Karl Marx's observations. Sociologist Georg Simmel (1858–1918), for example, compared the relationships of people who occupy higher positions (superordinates) with those who are in lower positions (subordinates). Simmel noted that a main concern of superordinates is to protect their positions of privilege. Because subordinates possess some power, however, the more powerful must take them into consideration as they make these decisions (Coser, 1977). Consequently, superordinate–subordinate relationships are marked not by one-way naked power but by exchange. If employers want to lower the benefits of a pension plan, for example, they must get unions to agree. In return, the workers will insist on a trade-off, such as increased job security.

Simmel argued that conflict does have its benefits. For example, when the members of a group confront an external threat, they tend to pull together. Similarly, if several groups face a common enemy, they tend to become more cohesive (Giddens, 1969; Turner, 1978). In times of war, for instance, antagonistic groups often shelve their differences in order to work together for the good of the nation. For example, the Army grants "moral waivers" to new recruits with criminal backgrounds in order to increase the number of available recruits. The bulk of moral waivers excuse soldiers with serious misdemeanors such as assault, burglary, robbery and vehicular homicide. The number of waivers granted increased 65 percent between 2003 and 2006 (Alvarez, 2007).

LEWIS COSER: CONFLICT IN SOCIAL NETWORKS. Sociologist Lewis Coser (1913–2003) analyzed why conflict is especially likely to develop among people who have close relationships. He pointed out that whether we refer to bosses and workers or to a husband and wife, each is part of a balance of power, responsibilities, and rewards. Through some

system of negotiation or imposition of power, the members have developed a relationship, one that is precariously balanced. Actions by either party, such as making new decisions—which are necessary to adjust to changing times—can upset the balances that people in the same network have worked out.

Applying Conflict Theory to Social Problems

SOCIAL CONFLICT UNDERLYING SOCIAL SECURITY. As we apply the conflict perspective to the elderly, let's see how Social Security came about. In this drama, the three major players are elderly workers, younger workers, and employers. A fourth, Congress, also appears. From this perspective, Congress represents the interests of the employers.

From the point of view of conflict theory, old people became a social problem when those in power found it advantageous to push them aside. When the Industrial Revolution spread across the United States, old people turned out to be a nuisance to the owners of big business. Not only did these older workers earn more than younger workers, but they were also not as docile. As the new machinery of the Industrial Revolution created types of work that required lesser or new skills, younger workers became as productive as the older workers, and the owners fired many of the elderly. This thrust most of the elderly into poverty, because in those days there was no unemployment compensation and Social Security. As a result, during the 1920s, two-thirds of all Americans over 65 could not support themselves (Holtzman, 1963; Hudson, 1978). In short, industrialization transformed the elderly from a productive and respected group to a deprived and disgraced group.

Then the Great Depression struck, bringing even more suffering to millions of elderly. In 1930, in the midst of national despair, Francis Everett Townsend, a physician, spearheaded a social movement to rally the elderly into a political force. He soon had one-third of all Americans over 65 enrolled in his Townsend Clubs. Recognizing their power, the elderly demanded benefits from the government (Holtzman, 1963). Townsend's ultimate goal was for the federal government to impose a national sales tax of 2% to provide $200 a month for every person over 65. This is the equivalent of about $2,200 a month today. Townsend argued that the

The U.S. elderly are a potent political force today. They were not considered so until Dr. Francis Everett Townsend (pictured here) organized them as a political force in the 1930s. Townsend proposed a radical $200 per month pension plan for the elderly in the midst of the Great Depression. His plan and campaign against Congress frightened politicians.

THE TOWNSEND PLAN
$200. PER MONTH FOR THOSE OVER 60 YRS OF AGE - THE SPENDING OF THIS MONEY WILL PUT THE CONTROL OF CREDIT IN THE HANDS OF THE PEOPLE - PREVENTING ECONOMIC CHAOS

sort of chain-letter arrangement by which the younger support the older. (2) The proportion of workers who collect Social Security benefits is growing, but the proportion of young people who are working—those who pay for these benefits out of their wages—is shrinking. This represents a major shift in the **dependency ratio,** the number of workers compared with the number of Social Security recipients. Presently, just fewer than five working-age Americans pay Social Security taxes to support each person collecting Social Security (5–1). In about a generation, this ratio will drop to about 3–1 (Melloan, 1994; *Statistical Abstract,* 2006, Tables 535, 537). (3) The U.S. government has collected $1 trillion more in Social Security taxes than it has paid to retirees. Supposedly, this huge excess has been placed into a trust fund, reserved for future generations. The "fund," however, exists in name only. Its billions of dollars disappear into thin air. Just as fast as they come in, the federal government "borrows" them and spends them on whatever it desires (Henslin, 2007b). The Social Security Trust Fund is supposed to prevent an intergenerational showdown. But there is no real fund, and one cannot rely on it. A day of reckoning between generations can't be far off.

To close this chapter, the Thinking Critically about Social Problems box applies the three sociological perspectives to the struggle between the generations. You'll see how different pictures emerge according to the theoretical perspective that examines the problem.

THINKING CRITICALLY about Social Problems

APPLYING THE THEORIES: UNDERSTANDING THE INTERGENERATIONAL BATTLE

Theories often appear vague and abstract. To help overcome this obstacle, as we introduced each theory in this chapter we applied it to the social problem of aging in the United States. Because these theories will be used throughout this text, it is important to understand them. Let's apply these three perspectives to the potential battle between the generations—the cutting edge of this social problem of aging and something that, in one way or another, you are likely to experience personally. Each theory yields a unique picture of a social problem, allowing us to compare their different interpretations.

Functionalism: Younger workers and the elderly are two major parts within the same social system. Because each part must work together if society is to function smoothly, these parts must also fit together well. If one of them absorbs too much of a society's resources, it creates an imbalance between these parts. Whenever an imbalance occurs, the parts must adjust in order for the larger unit (in this case, society) to attain equilibrium. Just as giving more resources to the elderly during the past two generations was an adjustment, so now, if those resources have become disproportionate, it will require another adjustment. Although the adjustment will be difficult, both the younger workers and the elderly are essential parts of society. The final result will be a harmonious balance between them.

Conflict Theory: Of course, there is a battle shaping up. Like other groups within society, the older and younger are marked by unequal power and privilege. Like other groups, each will struggle for its own interests. The AARP will push its own agenda, striving for greater advantage and as many resources as it can grab for itself. The concern of the elderly will be their own interests, regardless of how their gains may affect younger people. For their part, younger people will do the same, pursuing their own interests to the exclusion of other groups. Whenever one group gains a larger share of society's limited resources, others will resent those gains. The coming struggle between the generations is likely to be fierce, and the group with more power will win. Regardless of the outcome of this current competition for resources, conflict will continue in future generations.

Symbolic Interactionism: Symbols are the essence of social life, including social problems. We use symbols to interpret the events we experience in life. If we were to use different symbols, we would understand our experiences differently. Just as the meaning of old age shifted during industrialization, so this symbol is shifting again. Today's elderly have grown more affluent, and they are choosing new lifestyles: Their condos, motor homes, and vacations in exotic destinations make their new affluence highly visible. As a consequence, people's ideas of the elderly are changing. Out of the struggle that is shaping up between the generations will come a new set of symbols, one that will guide how we think about and act toward old people.

SUMMARY AND REVIEW

1. The frameworks that sociologists use to interpret their research findings are called *theories*. To interpret social problems, sociologists use three major theories: *functionalism, conflict theory*, and *symbolic interactionism*. Each theory provides a different interpretation of society and of social problems. No one theory is "right." Rather, taken together, these perspectives give us a more complete picture of the whole.

2. *Functionalists* see society as a self-correcting, orderly system, much like a well-oiled machine. Its parts work in harmony to bring the whole into equilibrium. Each part performs a function (hence, the term *functional analysis*) that contributes to the system's well-being. When a part is functioning imperfectly, however, it creates problems for the system. Those dysfunctions are called social problems.

3. *Conflict theorists* view social problems as a natural outcome of unequal power arrangements. Those in power try to preserve the social order and their own privileged position within it. They take the needs of other groups into consideration only when it is in their own interest to do so. As they exploit others, the powerful create social problems, such as poverty and discrimination. Other social problems, such as revolution, crime, suicide, and drug abuse, represent reactions of the oppressed to their exploitation. *Feminist theorists* also focus on the exploitation of the powerless by the powerful while claiming patriarchy is to blame.

4. *Symbolic interactionists* view social problems not as objective conditions but as views that are collectively held about some matter; that is, if people view something as a social problem, it is a social problem. As people's views (or definitions or symbols) change, so do their ideas about social problems.

KEY TERMS

THINKING CRITICALLY ABOUT CHAPTER 2

1. Of the three theories identified in this chapter, which one do you think does the best job of explaining social problems? Why?

2. Select a social problem other than aging:
   - How would functionalists explain the problem?
   - How would conflict theorists explain the problem?
   - How would symbolic interactionists explain this problem?

3. What do you think are the biggest problems that we are likely to face regarding the "graying of America" (the aging of the U.S. population)? Select a social problem other than aging:
   - Why do you feel your solutions might work?
   - What might prevent your solutions from working?

BY THE NUMBERS: THEN AND NOW

- Percentage of Japan's population, age 65 and older, in 1970: **7%**
- Percentage of Japan's population, age 65 and older, in 2000: **16%**

- Percentage of U.S. elderly living in poverty in 1970: **25%**
- Percentage of U.S. elderly living in poverty today: **9%**

- Percentage of U.S. children living in poverty in 1970: **15%**
- Percentage of U.S. children living in poverty today: **17%**

- Cost of Medicare to the U.S. government in 1975 (in billions): **$15**
- Cost of Medicare to the U.S. government today (in billions): **$440**

MySocLab

What can you find in MySocLab? mysoclab www.mysoclab.com

ALLYN & BACON
Where learning & the sociological imagination intersect.

- Complete Ebook
- Practice Tests and Exams
- Multimedia Activities
- Mapping and Data Analysis Exercises

- Research and Writing Advice
- Interactive Social Surveys
- Sociology in the News

CHAPTER 3

Social Problems Related to Sexual Behavior

Researcher Helen Rowland studies extramarital affairs. In her book, *Two Feminist Classics: Bachelor Girls,* she illuminates why some women date married men. One such woman states:

> I am 44 years old and separated from my husband a year ago. I am involved emotionally with a married man, even though I stopped the physical relationship six months ago. I am just shocked by the number of the successful, fabulous, divorced or never-married girlfriends in my age group who are involved with married men. It's an epidemic! What is the appeal?

> "Nothing so annoys a man as to hear a woman promising to love him "forever" when he merely wanted her to love him for a few weeks."
> —Helen Rowland, 2002

woman is currently enjoying dating another woman's husband. She continues, "I was married for over 30 years, raised my kids, and now I am free to be me and put me first. All I need is sexual release on a regular basis with a man who takes Cialis" (Amatenstein, 2007). She likes that his wife of 50 years "washes his clothes and makes his food." Amanda and her lover enjoy their current arrangement—seeing each other mainly on the weekends. Another woman, Ann, argues that her motivation for dating a married man is availability. As she put it, it is "slim pickings for girls over 40—married guys are often the only ones who can afford dates and have a decent conversation" (Amatenstein, 2007).

While few openly discuss this "phenomenon," sociologists have found that 1.5–3.6% of married couples engage in extramarital affairs (Leigh, Temple, & Trocki, 1993; Choi, Catania, & Dolcini, 1994; H. F. Smith, 1999).

Sherry Amatenstein of *More Magazine* exposes some motivating factors that may lead women to date married men. One woman in her exposé, Amanda, claims the appeal for dating a married man is "SEX, SEX and more sex without any strings attached." This 57-year-old divorced

Sociologist Judith Treas (2000) studied infidelity and found that people who generally are more interested in sex are more likely to have multiple partners. Sociologically speaking, adulterers tend to be (1) dissatisfied with the martial relationship itself; (2) permissive; (3) male, African American, and well educated (Treas, 2000).

Objective Conditions and Subjective Concerns

You will recall from our discussion in Chapter 1 that objective conditions alone are not adequate to make something a social problem. Also essential are subjective concerns: A lot of people must dislike the objective condition and want to see it changed. This principle applies to all the topics we discuss in this book, including deviant sexual behavior.

In this text, **sex** is defined as those activities associated with arousal, intercourse, and reproduction. *Deviance* often describes those behaviors not following the "norm." Psychology often uses an arbitrary rule of thumb that characteristics are deviant when

exhibited by less than 10% of a population. Therefore, engaging in sexually deviant behavior doesn't necessarily mean that a person is abnormal; instead, a sexual deviant uses nonmainstream sexual practices to become aroused. A person who practices sexual relations viewed as "not normal" may also be called a **paraphiliac.**

In American society, "normal" sexual behavior is defined as heterosexuality, monogamy, and fidelity. Sexual deviance, or paraphilia, is any behavior other than heterosexual monogamy. Major examples of deviant sexual behavior would then include homosexuality, sadism, masochism, sadomasochism, fetishism, rape, pedophilia, exhibitionism, transvestism, infidelity, sexual addiction, prostitution, and the like. *Normal* does *not* mean "good"—rather, *normal* means "mainstream."

Some people get upset when sociologists say that infidelity is a social problem. What many fail to realize is that sociologists are not passing judgment on those who have affairs with married people. Rather, as illustrated by the single woman–married man scenario at the beginning of the chapter, sociologists are simply pointing out that infidelity fits the definition of social problems perfectly—there is an objective condition ("cheating") that upsets large number of people (those being "cheated on"). As you read this chapter, keep in mind that saying infidelity is a social problem says nothing about whether having an affair with a married person is desirable or undesirable, only that large numbers of people are upset about it.

The same is true of prostitution and pornography. When sociologists say certain sexual problems qualify as social problems, they are not making value judgments. They are applying the essence of social problems—objective conditions (the existence of pornography and prostitution) and subjective concerns (people's negative reactions). When it comes to sexual deviance, the reaction to sociological objectivity often creates backlash: People sometimes get upset when they realize that sociologists are not taking a stand and stating that prostitution and pornography are bad.

Our job in this chapter is to examine human activities mired in controversy. As we do so, it is important to stress a sociological principle that is fundamental to this chapter: As much as we may prefer it to be otherwise, *sex is never only a personal matter.* All societies control or channel human sexual behavior, primarily through the institutions of marriage and family. Challenges to people's opinions of normal and deviant sexual behavior are difficult and not taken lightly.

Because many people view the topics of this chapter in moral terms, it is also important to stress another point made in the first chapter: *Sociology takes no stand in making moral judgments.* Sociology, in contrast, is well-equipped to report attitudes and social controversy—the concerns that make contemporary life so exciting. To help us understand the social problems related to sexual behavior, we will apply sociological theory to prostitution and pornography. As usual, we shall present both scientific evidence and public controversies that surround these behaviors. To learn more about studying sex in America, view the Spotlight on Social Research box on the following page.

Prostitution

Background: Getting the Larger Picture

Prostitution, the renting of one's body for sexual purposes, has been called "the world's oldest profession." Street prostitution occurs when a prostitute solicits customers while roaming "the track," or street. They usually dress in provocative clothing looking for customers, or "johns." Turning tricks, they service their customers in cars, alleys, or rented hotel rooms. Prostitutes are often driven by drug addiction, selling their bodies for their next high.

ATTITUDES TOWARD PROSTITUTION. Attitudes toward prostitution have varied immensely throughout history. Accounts of prostitution by both females and males reach back to the

Spotlight on Social Research
STUDYING SEX IN AMERICA

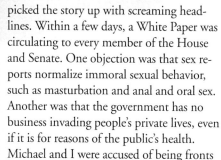

EDWARD LAUMANN, *dean of the Social Science Division at the University of Chicago, has done research on health, politics, power, status, and sex. Although he has pioneered theoretical work in how people form, maintain, and dissolve relationships, it is his research on sex that has received the most attention.*

In the 1980s, when we were in the midst of an AIDS epidemic so vicious that the number of people with this disease was doubling every 10 months, I organized a workshop on AIDS and Society. As I listened to the presentations, I became convinced that there would be no magic bullet to stop this epidemic through immunization. To contain the spread of AIDS, people would have to change their behavior. Robert Michael, an economic demographer, and I concluded that we needed a national sex survey to document the sex practices of Americans. With this information, we could design ways to persuade people to take defensive measures.

Research into human sexual behavior is often considered "illegitimate," even by many social scientists. Despite this disapproval, we wanted the University of Chicago to pool its strengths in survey and sample design to conduct this national survey. John Gagnon, a sexologist, joined our research team. When the National Institutes of Health announced a search for research proposals to combat AIDS, we submitted our design for a national sex survey. We won that competition.

When *Science* magazine reported that our proposal was under review at the White House's Office of Management and the Budget, the *Washington Times* picked the story up with screaming headlines. Within a few days, a White Paper was circulating to every member of the House and Senate. One objection was that sex reports normalize immoral sexual behavior, such as masturbation and anal and oral sex. Another was that the government has no business invading people's private lives, even if it is for reasons of the public's health. Michael and I were accused of being fronts for a cabal of homophiles who were attempting to legitimize gay sex.

Although the Senate Appropriations Committee recommended that our survey be funded, the House Appropriations Committee disagreed. For two years, we lobbied congressional staffers, senators, and representatives for their support in funding the research, but with few results. Then Senator Jesse Helms submitted an amendment to an appropriations bill that transferred the funding that had been intended for our sex survey to a "say no to sex" campaign. The Senate voted 66 to 34 in favor of the amendment, giving me the dubious distinction of having Congress trying to stop my research.

With government funding cut off, we turned to private foundations. The Robert Wood Johnson, Henry Kaiser, Rockefeller, and MacArthur foundations agreed to fund our research. To share the results of our survey with the scientific community, we wrote *The Social Organization of Sexuality.* This is a technical book, and as some have noted, it took the University of Chicago to take the fun out of sex.

We felt strongly that the public needed to know what we had discovered, and we wanted to have a hand in framing the public's understanding, not leave it to others. To do this, we arranged for Gina Kolata, a *New York Times* reporter who specializes in science and health news, to write a companion volume, *Sex in America.*

---

beginnings of recorded history. It exists in one form or another almost everywhere. Among early inhabitants of the Mediterranean area, Asia Minor, and West Africa, prostitution was an integral part of religious practice (Henriques, 1966). As a type of service to the gods, **temple prostitution** required every woman to perform an act of prostitution before she was allowed to marry. A woman was often dedicated to the gods as a sacred prostitute—either for a specific time or, more commonly, for life. In some villages in India, temple prostitution still exists.

In ancient Greece, high-class prostitutes, called *hetairae,* earned great respect. Their portraits and statues were placed "in the temples and other public buildings by the side of meritorious generals and statesmen" (Henriques, 1966, p. 64).

Today, in many Latin countries prostitution is seen as a necessary evil—something that keeps hot-blooded men away from pure, innocent girls and women. Although many Mexicans, Italians, and South Americans may consider prostitution disgusting,

Prostitution has existed in all cultures and is often referred to as the "oldest profession."

they are convinced it is necessary to protect the virtue of their own wives and daughters.

The attitudes of Americans toward the legalization of prostitution vary greatly. Those most likely to favor the legalization of prostitution are White male college graduates with high incomes living in the West. Those least likely to favor legal prostitution are Black female high school graduates with low incomes living in the Midwest. You may be surprised to learn that people between the ages of 50 and 64 are the most likely to favor the legalization of prostitution.

PROSTITUTION TODAY. In early 2008, Eliot Spitzer, then the governor of New York, was caught arranging to meet a high-priced prostitute at a Washington hotel. During an investigation, while Spitzer's phone was wiretapped, investigators overheard "Client Number 9" making plans to have a New York prostitute fly to Washington where he planned to meet her. (Mr. Spitzer was later identified as Client Number 9.)

With prostitution flourishing in the United States, researchers have tried to determine how many prostitutes there actually are. Given the secret nature of prostitutes' activities, this has proven to be a challenge. Using sampling techniques, researchers estimate that there are 23 prostitutes per 100,000 Americans. This comes to a total of 69,000 prostitutes in the United States (Brewer et al., 2000; Pottêrat et al., 1990). Generally 4% of these are thought to be under the age of 18.

The average length of a prostitute's career is 5 years, and a prostitute has sex with an average of 868 partners each year (Brewer et al., 2000). Some prostitutes, however, have over 5,000 customers a year (Brewer et al., 2000). If this seems high, note that prostitutes in Nairobi report even more clients: One reported 6 a day for 23 years, a total of about 50,000 clients (G. Cowley, 2006).

The only place in the United States where prostitution is legal is Nevada. Here, prostitutes are licensed to sell sex. Prostitution is not legal in several of Nevada's counties, including Reno, Las Vegas, and Lake Tahoe. Officials in these counties have banned prostitution for fear that it would drive out family vacationers. In Table 3-1 notice that the majority of Americans, whether male or female, think that prostitution should remain illegal in most areas. Those most likely to prefer that prostitution become legal in their state are white, middle-aged males living in the West.

Prostitutes have upgraded their industry, replacing the "whorehouses" of bygone days with massage parlors, escort services, corporate prostitution, and sex tourism. Under cover of legitimate service, "massage parlors" offer sex for sale. In an escort service, for a set fee a client arranges a date and privately negotiates the inclusion of sexual services.

Sometimes corporations hire prostitutes for their best-paying clients, as a perk. A New York telephone company, for example, held what its executives called a "pervert" convention, a weeklong, raucous session during which prostitutes provided sex for the company's best suppliers (Carnevale, 1990). In the Issues in Social Problems box on page 56, one of Jim Henslin's students explains how she became a corporate prostitute.

Similar to corporate prostitution, **sex tourism** occurs when an individual engages in prostitution while visiting a foreign country. Often prostitutes are chosen ahead of time through Internet-based advertisements. Some travel agencies now specialize in sex tourism, making all necessary arrangements for high-paying customers—from the booking of the flight to the purchasing of the hotel room. It is not accurate to think that sex tourism always involves sex with a child—often it involves two consenting adults.

TABLE 3-1 Attitudes Toward the Legalization of Prostitution by Percentage of Population Groups

Question: "In your opinion, should prostitution involving adults aged 18 years of age and older be legal or illegal in your state?"

	LEGAL	ILLEGAL	DON'T KNOW/REFUSED
National	26%	70%	4%
Sex			
Male	32	63	5
Female	21	77	2
Race/Ethnicity*			
White	27	70	3
Black	20	79	1
Age			
18 to 29 years	25	74	1
30 to 49 years	28	68	4
50 to 64 years	32	65	3
65 years and older	18	77	5
Education			
College graduate	28	69	3
High school	21	76	3
Income			
$50,000 and over	33	64	3
$30,000 to $49,999	26	70	4
$20,000 to $29,999	27	71	2
Under $20,000	18	80	2
Region			
East	28	68	4
Midwest	20	78	2
South	24	75	1
West	34	58	8

*Only these two groups are listed in the source.
Source: Sourcebook of Criminal Justice Statistics (1997, Table 2–99). Table dropped in later editions.

The branch of sex tourism that involves arranged sex with children of another country is becoming so common that there is now a movement to create an international court of some type that would punish offenders. The United States is actively partnering with other nations to combat this type of crime. In 2003 nearly $74 million in U.S. government funding was devoted to fighting this behavior. In his September 2003 speech to the United Nations General Assembly, President Bush described this international child prostitution ring as a type of "modern-day slavery—a special evil in the abuse and exploitation of the most innocent and vulnerable":

> The victims . . . see little of life before they see the worst of life—an underground of brutality and lonely fear. Those who create these victims and profit from their suffering must be severely punished. (Huhtala, 2004)

Some argue that prostitution serves social functions—from playing a role in religious rituals to giving some corporations a competitive edge. In the following section, we shall examine the social functions of prostitution in more detail.

Issues in Social Problems
ME, A PROSTITUTE?

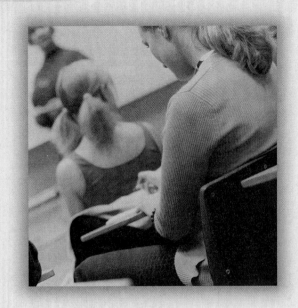

Some students among you may be secretly working as prostitutes or escorts.

Many women learn to be prostitutes gradually, going through a step-by-step process similar to the one recounted here. This account, written by one of Jim Henslin's students, has been reproduced as it was originally written (including typos and misspellings).

I am a average looking blond with blue eyes. I am a female of twenty years of age. My mother is a elementary school teacher with a doctorit degree. My father is the head of instramentation for a large oil company. He write books, makes movies and teaches around the world. I have one sibbling. She is 10 years old. My parents are very old fashioned. they are strickt with both my sister and I. We are Hard-Shell-Baptist, and attend church nomatter-what. They've instilled wonderful values in me. We live in the country on a farm (pleasure, we don't grow things). Our home is large and because both of my parents work we have a maid that comes three days a week to clean. I've always had to work around the house. Cooking meals, cleaning and doing farm chores such as, feeding the horses and cows, have always been a part of my dayly routine. Yet, there's never been anything I've ever done without. Anything that could be bought was automatically mine, just for the asking. Our entire family is close. We visit one another frequently and have get-togethers regularly.

I am from a family with an average annual income of over $100,000.00. My parents have never neglected me. No one has ever abused me. I've caused my share of trouble, but it was all jouvenile, never anything against the law of the state. I've never been a misfit. I was one of the "cool" kids. I was in with the "popular" crowd. I was in Student Government and Peer Leadership in High School. I was elected Snow Queen my junior year. I never had any problems with guys. There was always plenty around my house. I just could never get attached to guys my age, they came and they went . . . no big deal! I had a taste for older men even then.

When I was seventeen, I met a guy who was twenty-two. He was exciting and fun. He was my first love. He was also the first guy I'd ever had sex with. Kinky wouldn't even begin to explain him. We went out for about a year and a half. Through him I met Jesse. A gorgeous Spaniard, queer as a three dollar bill, but one of the nicest people you'll ever meet. Jesse is a "BIG" record promoter for a famous record corporation. We've been friends since the day we met. We call each other all the time and "dish" on guys.

I called Jesse up one day and asked if he'd get me tickets to go to a concert I wanted to see. He said sure as he had a million times before. Only this time he too had a request. He said, "I'm in a bit of a bind. I need someone to pick up a client and show him around town Friday!" "Cool!" I said. Jesse went on to explain,

Prostitution Viewed Theoretically: Applying Functionalism

THE SOCIAL FUNCTIONS OF PROSTITUTION. On the most obvious level, prostitution flourishes because it satisfies sexual needs that are not met elsewhere. This, of course, is precisely why prostitution will never be eliminated. In a classic research study, sociologist Kingsley Davis (1937, 1966) concluded that prostitutes provide a sexual outlet for men who

1. have difficulty establishing sexual relationships (such as disfigured or shy men or those with handicaps)

"You'll be given $200.00 to buy him dinner, go dancing, or whatever else he may want to do . . . what's left is yours to keep." "Wow, thats great," I exclaimed! I thought to myself, what could be better, a date in which we can do anything, the sky's the limit . . . you get payed for playing!!! What could possibly be better than that?

I made about $70. I had a wonderful time and so did the client. I told Jesse I loved being a escort and to fix me up as often as he liked. I was assigned many men after that. I'd say a good 75 percent wanted to finish off their evenings with sex. Some even would get quite insistent. I asked Jesse what to do. Jesse said do what you want to do, guys will offer you their own money (as a write off to their own company as entertainment). To sleep with me, I thought. He said, "Do what you want to do, if you want the money, go for it! If you don't keep standing firm!" I told Jesse I couldn't do it. So, he began to filter my dates more so and more so. He was always careful not to set me up with the weirdo's or the real wild party hardy guys. I mostly got the married with three kids and a dog type from then on.

I worked at the pace of picking up $20–$100 per date, for about three months; about 60 guys total. Then I met with a client from Europe for the second time. He was a very attractive man of 40. His black hair was salted with a whitened silver. He was a family man. Though, as was the story with many of the men I escorted, he was having alot of problems with his wife. While sitting at a bar he whispered in my ear, "Would you splease consider being with me tonight?" Knowing I'd turned him down the last time he was in town, he reached into his pocket for inspiration. $500.00 in crisp $100.00 bills he waved out like a fan and placed on the table. I looked at him and shook my head "No" I said. He put his hand on my arm and said, "How much do I have to offer you, $600, $700?" At this point I was getting pissed! In order to control my temper I flew off to the restroom in a rage. I remember standing at the sink, looking into the mirror, and thinking who in the hell does this man think he is!! I don't need his money! But still that much money, for sex?! . . . how could it be? I went back to the table with thousands of thoughts running through my mind. He looked at me and said, "I'm sorry if I upset you, but, I'm willing to give you all the money I have with me, $1000 dollars. Hows that sound?" My initial thought was to slap the crap out of him, however, the things I could do with $1000 cash. I agreed and it wasn't hard. No commitments, no future to worry about, and no love to get in the way of habitions. I went home that night with 10 crisp $100 dollar bills and two $20's left over from the date, in my coat pocket. There's nothing to it. I can spend $100 on myself and stick the rest in a savings account. It's no biggy!

I told Jesse about it. I told him I couldn't believe how easy or how much money I made. He laughed and asked me if I had plans of ever doing this again. I said sure, it's no problem. I made over $10,000 in the 4 months to follow. Enough to buy me a new car. I never have made $1000 in a evening again but, it became a game to me. How high can you raise the bid? How much will it take to make this man make an offer straight up? How much teasing can you get buy with, without having him drop his attention?

I've worked more than 2 yrs. I've totally mellowed out of the games. If it looks good to me, and if I find the man attractive I'll do it. I've become very secure financially. I have multiple CD's, bonds and ect. I have three savings accounts and alot of money tied up in the stock market. My only regrets are I have to keep it a complete secret from everyone. My parents, who mean more to me than the world, my family, and even my dearest friends. I miss out on the average everyday social life of a college student. I have to lie to practically everyone I meet. But, nowhere will I find a job in which I can save as much money for my future. Or for that matter when I get out of college and get a respectable job in advertising, make that kind of money. But, my life will be back to a "normal" one. One in which I can be proud of, one which I can share with my friends and family, one in which I can make a "honest" living.

2. cannot find long-term partners (such as travelers and sailors)
3. have a broken relationship (such as the separated or divorced)
4. want sexual gratification that they can't get from their wives or girlfriends

Other researchers (Freund, Lee, & Leonard, 1991; Gemme, 1993; Monto, 2004) have noted that prostitutes also provide a sexual outlet for men who

5. want quick sex without attachment
6. are sexually dissatisfied in marriage
7. want to have sex with someone who has a specific body type, age, or race–ethnicity

Although illegal, prostitution is practiced openly in some areas. In Las Vegas, vendors hand out cards like these advertising escort services.

Another motivation was discovered by sociologist Elizabeth Bernstein (2001), when she studied the customers of prostitutes and found that some men find emotional connections with prostitutes. They feel that they "connect" with the prostitute, are able to share personal feelings and thoughts that they cannot share elsewhere. Some are even convinced that the prostitute from whom they are buying sex has special feelings for them in return.

THE FUNCTIONALIST CONCLUSION: PROSTITUTION AS A WAY OF CONTROLLING SEXUAL BEHAVIOR. Although most of these findings may seem obvious, the conclusion that functionalists draw from them may not be. Functionalists argue that, by meeting needs, prostitution functions as *a form of social control* over sexual behavior. By this, they mean that prostitution channels sexual desires away from unwilling women to women who, for a price, are willing to satisfy those desires. For example, some people (whom prostitutes call "kinkies," "weirdos," and "freaks") achieve sexual gratification by inflicting pain on others (**sadists**) or by having others inflict pain on them (**masochists**). Some customers enjoy being sexually humiliated, being told by the prostitute that they are "no good" or being ordered to do humiliating things. Others combine the sex act with fantasy role playing; they may wear costumes or ask the prostitute to do so. Some even wear diapers, while others have sex in coffins (Hall, 1972; Millett, 1973; Prus & Irini, 1988). These extreme wishes that may not be acted out in traditional relationships are therefore redirected into an outlet that serves this purpose. The prostitute is paid, and the "john" is fulfilled.

These, however, are not the usual customers of prostitutes. Most johns are "regular" married, middle-aged men (Wells, 1970; Freund et al., 1991; Monto, 2004). So why do married men patronize prostitutes? Perhaps the two most common reasons are that they find their wives sexually unreceptive or they desire sexual variety that their wives are unwilling to provide—especially "frenching" (fellatio, or oral sex), apparently the act most requested of prostitutes (Melody, 1969; Heyl, 1979; Gemme, 1993).

Functionalists, then, see prostitution as a means of controlling or channeling sexual behavior. Prostitutes meet the needs of the sexually unattached and of those who want sexual acts that are not otherwise readily available to them. Prostitutes provide access to sexual variety in a nonemotional, unattached, random way. Furthermore, prostitutes do not threaten the male ego—it is unlikely that a john will ever be "turned down."

Functionalists stress that when people demand a service that is not supplied by legitimate sources, a hidden, or "subterranean," source will develop to meet the need. The underground channeling of illegitimate services to clients, called a **black market,** is built on **symbiosis** (a mutually beneficial relationship). Those who purchase a service, those who provide it, and those who suppress it all benefit from the illegal activity. The clients of prostitutes purchase the sex they want; prostitutes work with a minimum of legal hassles (even calling their occasional fines the price of "licensing"); pimps and criminal organizations earn untaxed income; and for a price, police who are "on the take" look the other way.

THE CONFLICT/FEMINIST PERSPECTIVE. The feminist perspective contrasts sharply with that of the functionalists. Taking this approach, feminists point out that prostitution is just one of the many ways that men exploit and degrade women. Some men use prostitutes as objects for their own pleasure. Other men (pimps, clients, and police "on the

take") exploit prostitutes for profit. The Global Glimpse box on page 60 explores the sexual exploitation of women in the Least Industrialized Nations.

Research on Prostitution

TYPES OF PROSTITUTES. Besides escorts and corporate prostitutes already mentioned, what kinds of prostitutes are there? Let's do a quick overview.

Call girls, the elite of the prostitutes, can be selective in choosing their customers. Building a steady, repeat business, they usually have their johns come to their own home (Lucas, 2005). To keep up with appointments, they use cell phones, pagers, fax machines, and e-mail. To meet clients' continuous demand for variety, some call girls fly from city to city, where new customers await them (Campo-Flores, 2002).

Convention prostitutes, as the name implies, are women who specialize in conventions. Posing as secretaries or sales agents, they roam hotel lobbies, display rooms, and cocktail parties. Some develop opinions about which professionals spend the most money, and they try to concentrate on them. Again, in the symbiotic manner referred to earlier, the organizers of conventions often make arrangements for prostitutes to be available.

Apartment prostitutes rent apartments outside of their own home and set up a "business" while their husbands are away at work. An apartment prostitute attempts to match her apartment hours to her husband's working hours. A husband who is ignorant of his wife's activities is likely to think that she has a regular job, whereas instead she is working as a prostitute during the day.

Stag party workers serve as topless waitresses or put on strip shows at stag parties— all-male parties. They arrange to meet customers after the party or in an adjoining room during the party.

Hotel prostitutes work out of a hotel and share their fees with the bell captain, desk clerk, or bellboys who steer johns to them (Reichert & Frey, 1985; Prus & Irini, 1988). Because this "added service" attracts male guests, some hotels provide their room free or at a discounted rate.

House prostitutes work in a "whorehouse." This form of prostitution has declined. During the 1800s and early 1900s, almost all large American cities and many small ones had brothels, which were located in an area known as the "red light district." A red bulb shining from a window or house informed outsiders of what went on behind those closed doors.

Barbara Heyl studied house prostitutes and reported on the selection process that occurs once a john enters the whorehouse. Typically the women gather in the living room while the john looks them over and makes his selection. While the prostitute makes her money in the bedroom, the manager of the house (the "madam") keeps 50%–60% as commission. House prostitutes try to persuade their johns to spend more than they intend. Heyl (1979, p. 120) found that this is especially difficult for the novice prostitute because she must vocalize graphic sexual acts.

Bar girls, also known as "B-girls," wait in bars for customers. Some pay or "tip" the bartender as commission for using the bar as their headquarters. Others hustle drinks (get johns to buy overpriced drinks), receiving a set fee for each drink they sell.

Streetwalkers have the lowest status among prostitutes and are the most frequently arrested. They are visible to the public, as they "work the street" in view of police and customers. In some American cities, streetwalkers are aggressive, hailing passing cars and opening the doors of cars that have stopped at traffic lights. Many are drug addicts involved in other criminal behaviors.

Parking lot lizards frequent truck stops, moving from one truck to another in search of clients.

Male prostitutes who service women are known as "gigolos." In 1980, sociologist Ed Sagarin concluded that this is "an infrequent behavior, for which there is little demand and probably more folklore than reality." Since then, sexual norms have changed, and now it is common for women to purchase male prostitutes (Sanchez Taylor, 2001). "Beach boys" in Bali even report that they prefer Japanese women as clients, saying that they are more generous than others (Beddoe, Hall, & Ryan, 2001).

A Global Glimpse
THE PATRIOTIC PROSTITUTE

A new wrinkle in the history of prostitution is the "patriotic prostitute." Patriotic prostitutes are young women who are encouraged by their government to prostitute themselves to help the country's economy. Patriotic prostitution is part of global stratification, the division of the world's countries into "have" and "have-not" nations. Some have-nots, or Least Industrialized Nations, view their women as a cash crop, encouraging prostitution as a way to accumulate capital for investment or to help pay interest on their national debt. A notorious example is Thailand, where in a country of 30 million females, between a half million and a million are prostitutes. About 20,000 are under the age of 15.

In some countries, government officials encourage prostitution by telling young women that they are performing a service to their country. In South Korea, officials issue identification cards to prostitutes, which serve as hotel passes. In orientation sessions, they tell these young women, "Your carnal conversations with foreign tourists do not prostitute either yourself or the nation, but express your heroic patriotism."

With such an official blessing, "sex tourism" has become a global growth industry. Travel agencies in Germany advertise "trips to Thailand with erotic pleasures included in the

In South Korea today officials have passed laws to reduce prostitution. In protest of such policies, these prostitutes wear funeral robes to signal the death of their industry.

price." Japan Air Lines hands out brochures that advertise the "charming attractions" of Kisaeng girls, advising men to fly JAL for "a night spent with a consummate Kisaeng girl dressed in a gorgeous Korean blouse and skirt."

The advertising, showing beautiful young women with "come hither" smiles, fails to mention the miserable slavery that underlies sex tourism. Many of the prostitutes were sold as children. Some are held in bondage while they pay off their families' debts. Some are even locked up to keep them from running away.

The enticing ads also leave out AIDS. In Nairobi, where about 10,000 prostitutes serve this thriving industry, perhaps half are infected with AIDS. Nor is the destruction of children mentioned. Although customers pay more for young girls and boys, especially for those who are advertised as virgins or "clean," the children are vulnerable to infection from lesions and injuries during intercourse. When they become too sick to service clients—or their disease becomes too noticeable—the children are thrown into the streets like so much rubbish.

Based on Gay (1985), Shaw (1987), Hornblower (1992), Beddoe et al. (2001), Leuchtag (2004).

Heidi Fleiss, famous for running a high-priced call girl operation that serviced wealthy men, decided to cater to a new clientele. She planned to open a brothel in Nevada servicing only women customers. Her plans included hiring 20 men to work as prostitutes. They would charge $250 an hour and split the fee with Fleiss. She has received more than 1,000 applications (Friess, 2005). As Fleiss said, "Women make more money these days, and let's face it, it's hard to meet someone." She added, "And then you've got the situation with the old husband leaving his wife for the younger girl, and the lady sitting at home crying. Well, now she has a place to go, and say, 'Right back at you, buddy, and on your credit card'" (Friess, 2005). Nevada authorities are challenging her licensing, since a convicted felon cannot apply for a brothel license. As of this writing, Heidi's Stud Farm, designed to be the world's first licensed brothel catering exclusively to female clients, remains unlicensed with a waiting list (Abowitz, 2008).

BECOMING A PROSTITUTE. Researchers typically focus on streetwalkers, who are most visible and accessible—which in essence means that most of the research on prostitution comes from poor women who have been arrested. Prostitutes who come from higher

social class backgrounds, such as the student featured in the Issues in Social Problems box on pages 56–57, engage in forms of prostitution that make them less accessible to the police—and to sociologists. Keep this biased sampling technique in mind as we examine how women become prostitutes.

The simplest answer to why someone becomes a prostitute is money—to make as much of it as easily as possible. This is an oversimplification, however, for running through the accounts that prostitutes give of their early home life are themes of emotional deprivation and sexual abuse (James & Meyerding, 1977; N. Davis, 1978; Williams & Kornblum, 1985; Hodgson, 1997). Sociologist Robert Gemme (1993) interviewed Montreal street prostitutes and found that before these women became prostitutes one-third had been raped and one-half had been sexually abused. Sociologist James Hodgson (1997) found that money or abuse was not the primary motivation for young prostitutes (ages 10 to 15). Instead, they fell "in love" with a pimp, who, after seducing them, insisted they "turn tricks" to help out.

Abused as children, most often by men, these women become locked into a way of life in which they continue to be victimized by men—by pimps who exploit their bodies for profit and by johns who exploit them for sexual pleasure.

Again, because of their accessibility, researchers have focused almost invariably on streetwalkers. The themes of abuse and emotional deprivation do seem to characterize these women, but these themes are less likely to appear among more privileged prostitutes. Call girls, for example, often become prostitutes much like anyone would choose any occupation (Lucas, 2005). The backgrounds of these women seem to reflect less abuse and deprivation, but to know this for sure we would need to compare the background of call girls with the background of all other prostitutes. We have no such data.

Prostitution has flourished in places, such as the "Old West," where men have outnumbered women. Pictured here is a prostitute from the late 1800s. It is not her clothing, but the cigarette, that indicates her status.

THREE STAGES IN BECOMING A PROSTITUTE. As you saw in the box "Me, a Prostitute?" on pages 56–57, becoming a prostitute is often a gradual process. Nanette Davis, a symbolic interactionist, documented how this occurs. She interviewed prostitutes in three correctional institutions in Minnesota, identifying three stages.

1. In the first stage, women *drift* from casual sex to the first act of prostitution. During this "drift," they face a series of forks in the road where choices they make channel them toward prostitution (James & Davis, 1982). Circumstances that lead to drifting include broken homes, dropping out of school, pregnancy, drug use, a juvenile record, and having sex at a young age. On average, these women first had sexual intercourse at age 13 (the youngest was age 7, the oldest 18). The girls engaged in casual sex for an average of 4 years before they drifted into prostitution. One of Davis's informants described it this way:

   > I was going to school and I wanted to go to this dance the night after. I needed new clothes. I went out at ten o'clock and home at twelve. I had three tricks the first time, and fifteen dollars (about $40 in today's money) for every trick. (Davis, 1978, p. 206)

2. Davis calls the second stage *transitional deviance.* During this stage, (which lasts an average of 6 months), girls experience **role ambivalence**—that is, conflicting emotions regarding their decision to become a prostitute. They feel both attracted to and repulsed by prostitution. To help overcome their ambivalence, many girls try to normalize their acts; that is, they try to convince themselves that what they are doing is normal. For example, although they sell sex, they may call it something else. As one girl said,

   > I'm a person who likes to walk. There's nothing wrong with picking somebody up while you're walking. I always like walking around at night, and girls will be tempted. Girls like the offer. They like to see what a guy is going to say. (Davis, 1978, pp. 203–209)

New York Gov. Eliot Spitzer announces his resignation amidst a prostitution scandal as wife Silda looks on Wednesday, March 12, 2008, in his offices in New York City.

3. Davis calls the third stage *professionalization*. During this stage, the girls no longer convince themselves that their behavior is normal; instead, they identify themselves as prostitutes. They begin to build their lives around this identity and defend their involvement in prostitution. Their argument rings true according to the functionalist approach—they claim they help wives by giving their husbands a sexual outlet that reduces marital tensions. Others say that prostitution helps prevent rape. Note how closely this statement spoken by a "madam" resembles the functionalist approach: "As to my claim about performing a useful social service, every lusty, tourist-jammed town like San Francisco needs safety valves and outlets for its males. Shut down a town and the rape rate soars higher than an astronaut" (Stanford, 1968, pp. 206–207).

AGE OF PROSTITUTES. Look at Table 3-2 to see how young and how old some prostitutes are. The involvement of children in the commercial sex trade is what angers most people. We shall return to this topic in the section on child pornography later in the chapter.

THE PIMP AND THE PROSTITUTE. Why would a woman rent her body, knowing she is likely to be hurt by sadists, risk death by AIDS, and then turn the money she makes over to a man? Let's use the sociological perspectives to see which best explains this.

Functionalists would state that pimps serve the following purposes: They locate customers, screen out sadistic johns, and bail arrested prostitutes out of jail. In actuality, however, pimps are not beneficial to their prostitutes. In reality, pimps are likely to make their girls find their own customers, be unconcerned if they are beaten up, and be unavailable when they are arrested (Hodgson, 1997). For this reason, we have to move beyond functionalism for an explanation.

Conflict–feminist theorists would claim simply that male pimps have the power. They, not the prostitutes, control the streets. To control women,

TABLE 3-2 Arrests for Prostitution and Commercialized Sex, by Age

AGE	PERCENT	NUMBER
Under 18	1.9%	1,204
Under 10	—	11
10–12	—	10
13–14	0.2	142
15–17	1.7	1,041
18–24	24.4	15,320
25–34	28.7	17,977
35–44	29.6	18,564
45–54	12.2	7,620
55–64	2.4	1,527
65 and older	0.7	456
Total arrested:		62,663

Note: The source does not list prostitution separately, but includes it in a category called prostitution and commercialized vice. Consequently, the totals include a large proportion (20 percent) of males (Table 39 of the *UCR*).

Source: By James M. Henslin. Based on *Uniform Crime Reports* (2006, Table 38).

See For Yourself

Go to the Stop Child Slavery Web site: http://stopchildslavery.com/2007/04/16/child-prostitution-three-stories/

▸ Research data on child prostitution and read victim stories posted online.

they use their greater physical strength, and they are ruthless. Consider what a former prostitute said:

> I saw a girl walk into a bar and hand the pimp a $100 bill. He took it and burned it in her face and turned around and knocked her down on the floor and kicked her and said, "I told you, bitch, $200. I want $200, not $100." Now she's gotta go out again and make not another hundred, but two hundred. (Millett, 1973, p. 134)

But there is more to the story than control through physical strength. Symbolic interactionists analyze what pimps represent to prostitutes. To better understand this relationship, we must take into account the background of a typical street prostitute, which we discussed earlier. As a victimized child, this girl often develops into an emotionally dependent woman. Pimps are known to play on the insecurities and fears of runaways and lost girls. Many offer a sense of belonging, affection, and tenderness. Some hold out the hope of marriage, children, even a home in the suburbs after they have saved enough money from the woman's earnings. Pimps, however, are exploiters, and a pimp may be making the same promises to several women. He may tell each that she is the special woman in his life, cautioning her not to tell the others so the two of them can use the earnings of the other women to fulfill their plans.

Pimps are unconcerned about the welfare of their women, except as it affects their earnings. To them, the women are mere money machines, objects to be used or abused at will. The pimp's real interest is in the prestige he gets from other street males. His status depends on the number of women he controls in his "stable"; on how aloof he can remain from these women while still making them bend to his will; and on his personal grooming, jewelry, cars, leisure, and free-spending ways (Milner & Milner, 1972; Williamson & Cluse-Tolar, 2002).

Symbolic interactionists stress that to understand deviants we need to grasp the definitions and meanings of the situation they are involved in. We need to understand how norms influence their and the dominant culture's behavior. When we take an insider's view into a deviant subculture, the world looks like a different place—and it is. This is precisely the point: to see from within in order to understand human behavior—especially when it contradicts the standards and experiences of mainstream society.

HOMOSEXUAL PROSTITUTION. Homosexual prostitution often takes place in areas known as "meat racks," public settings such as street corners, parks, and bars. A study in Rome found that some homosexual prostitutes have 1,500 sexual partners a year (Gattari et al., 1992). A study in Chicago by sociologist David Luckenbill (1986) found that male prostitutes have a hierarchy that parallels that of their female counterparts. At the top are escort prostitutes, those who work for modeling or dating agencies. In the middle are bar hustlers, and at the bottom are street hustlers. The charge per trick and respect received goes up with each level.

Sociologist David Pittman (1971) studied a house of male prostitution (exclusively for male clients) in St. Louis. To recruit male prostitutes, the "madam" (a man) advertises for male models. When young men apply, the madam explains why he really wants to

Prostitution by teenage boys has become more open since sociologists first studied it in the 1950s. In some urban areas known as "meat racks," boy prostitutes gather in search of customers.

hire them. He photographs those who take the job, placing photographs in a catalog of nude "models" that customers view. These male prostitutes face intense pressure because only those with the best bodies will remain employed. Many turn to stimulant drugs, steroids, and alcohol abuse. Their sexual performance declines, they lose customers, and ultimately they are fired.

In a classic study, sociologist Albert Reiss, Jr. (1961) found that teenagers who acted as prostitutes giving older men oral sex still maintained a heterosexual identity outside of work. As you can imagine, this required an intricate mental balancing act. The boys accomplished this by employing several techniques, including (1) no emotional attachment to the man, (2) seeing money as the only motivator, (3) tolerating nothing other than oral sex, (4) never seeing a homosexual outside of work, and (5) having a girlfriend in public.

Prostitution among young boys has become more prevalent since Reiss studied it (Cates & Markley, 1992; Beddoe et al., 2001). Many boy prostitutes are runaways from lower-class or welfare families. Some prostitute themselves to survive, others simply to have extra money. In some countries, such as Thailand, young boys are forced into prostitution. Many see the apparent increase in boy prostitution as a social problem in and of itself. A related problem is the growing epidemic of AIDS among homosexual prostitutes.

PROSTITUTION AS A SOCIAL PROBLEM. So why does prostitution arouse so much debate? Many subjective concerns surround this issue:

1. Sociologists would argue that morality is the primary reason (Brace, 1880, pp. 123–131). For most, morality is the primary issue because prostitution involves sexual relations among people who are not married to one another.
2. Still others view prostitution as immoral because the sex is sold for a price.
3. Prostitution exploits women's bodies, degrades their spirit, and subjugates them to men.
4. Prostitution ruins "good" neighborhoods, depressing property values by bringing in unsavory characters and illegal activities such as drug dealing.
5. Prostitution is a crime. Victimless or not, prostitution is illegal, and this makes it part of a larger social problem.
6. Profits from prostitution feed organized crime.
7. Profits are also used to corrupt police and judges, uniting these "enforcers of morality" with pimps, madams, and organized criminals.
8. Prostitutes spread disease. AIDS has given this concern special urgency.
9. There is also a concern about aesthetics—the disgust that people feel when they see used condoms and tissues left in public places, including schoolyards.

Let's now turn to another sexual behavior that has become widespread but that also arouses subjective concerns.

Pornography

Originally, *pornography* referred to writings by prostitutes or to descriptions of the life of prostitutes. (*Porna* is Greek for "prostitute.") For our purposes, we can define **pornography** as writings, pictures, or objects of a sexual nature that people object to as being filthy or immoral.

Materials intended to cause sexual excitement have existed since early history. Pornography abounded in the Roman Empire, as shown by excavations of the Mediterranean resort city of Pompeii, which was destroyed by an eruption of Mount Vesuvius in 79 CE. There archaeologists uncovered brothels decorated with mosaics of

Determining what is and what is not pornographic is difficult, for like beauty, pornography lies in the eye of the beholder. Adult film actress Jenna Jameson is photographed on the red carpet as she arrives for the 23rd AVN (Adult Video News) Awards Show in Las Vegas.

men and women engaging in a variety of sexual acts. The *Kama Sutra*, an Indian religious book dating from the 8th century, is explicit in sexual representation, including suggestions on how prostitutes can please their customers (Henriques, 1966).

Background: Getting the Larger Picture

Determining what is and what is not pornographic is difficult, for like beauty, pornography lies in the eye of the beholder. For example, are nude statues pornographic? Some think so, while others say they merely illustrate the beauty of the human body. Are movies that depict sexual intercourse pornographic? More would probably say they are. How about movies or photos that depict oral sex? A larger number would probably say yes. Or those that depict anal intercourse? The number would probably increase even more. How about movies that show sex between adults and children or between humans and animals? At this point, the rate of agreement that these are pornographic would increase sharply.

On one matter, almost everyone agrees—pornography, whatever it is, should be restricted. As shown in Table 3-3 on page 66, 56% of Americans think that the sale of pornography to teenagers should be banned, and another 38% would outlaw pornography altogether—representing a total of 94% in favor of legal restrictions. Those most likely to argue against pornography are White older women with only a high school education. Those least likely to want pornography to be illegal for everyone are African American young men who are college graduates.

THE PORNIFYING OF AMERICA. From its beginnings as an underground cottage industry, pornography has grown into an open and aggressive multibillion-dollar-a-year business. Behind today's pornography lies an extensive network of people who profit from it: writers, publishers, actors, and filmmakers; owners of bookstores, video stores, and theaters; corner newsstands and supermarket chains; and banks and financiers. HBO and Time Warner profit from selling pornographic movies, as do Holiday Inn, Marriott, Hyatt, Hilton, Sheraton, and other hotels that offer pay-per-view pornography to their guests.

TABLE 3-3 Attitudes About the Distribution of Pornography by Percentage of Population Groups

	SHOULD BE ILLEGAL FOR EVERYONE				SHOULD BE ILLEGAL ONLY FOR PEOPLE UNDER 18				SHOULD BE LEGAL FOR EVERYONE			
	1980	1990	2000	2002[1]	1980	1990	2000	2002	1980	1990	2000	2002
National	40%	41%	36%	38%	51%	52%	60%	56%	6%	6%	3%	5%
Sex												
Male	31	33	24	31	60	59	72	62	8	6	3	7
Female	47	47	45	43	45	47	51	52	5	5	3	4
Race/Ethnicity[2]												
White	41	42	36	39	52	51	60	56	6	5	3	5
African American	35	34	34	32	51	57	59	60	10	7	5	6
Education												
College	31	36	31	34	59	57	65	61	8	7	3	4
High School	42	44	41	40	52	51	55	52	5	5	3	8
Age												
18–20	12	17	18	29	79	65	77	59	9	13	4	12
21–29	23	29	17	17	69	67	78	75	7	3	4	8
30–49	32	36	29	32	60	60	68	64	7	4	2	4
50 and over	40	53	52	54	50	36	43	40	8	8	4	6
Religion												
Protestant	45	46	44	46	48	48	53	50	5	5	2	4
Catholic	40	39	31	34	52	56	66	61	6	4	2	4
Jew	25	25	20	19	10	59	53	79	75	20	5	2
None	8	22	16	21	74	66	76	68	15	9	7	11

[1] Latest year available.

[2] Only these two groups are given in the sources; African American is listed as Black/other.

Source: Sourcebook of Criminal Justice Statistics (1992, Table 2–98; 2003, Table 2–97).

To the extent that people subscribe to Internet service providers in order to gain access to pornography, even the cable and telephone companies get their share. Like politics, pornography makes strange bedfellows.

Pornography has become so common that we can say that the United States has become pornified. The basic reason is technology. The Internet allows people to pursue pornography privately, without risking their reputations by being seen in a porn shop in a seedy part of town. About one in four Internet users access adult sites, where they spend an average of 74 minutes a month (Paul, 2005). This does *not* count time spent visiting amateur sites. About 70% of 18–24-year-old men visit a pornographic site in a typical month.

Pornography Viewed Theoretically: Applying Symbolic Interactionism

ROTH V. UNITED STATES. The controversy about what is and is not pornography—and what should be done about it—has bedeviled the courts. In 1957, the U.S. Supreme Court tried to define pornography for the nation. In *Roth v. United States,* the Court ruled that materials are pornographic or obscene when

1. "taken as a whole," the "dominant theme" appeals to "prurient" sex
2. the material affronts "contemporary community standards"
3. the material is "utterly without redeeming social value"

Instead of settling anything, however, the *Roth* decision added fuel to the fire. *Prurient,* for example, means "lewd or impure." But the use of such a word solves nothing—it simply takes us back to the issue of what pornography is in the first place—for what is lewd or impure to one person is not to another. The guidelines, which were supposed to clear up matters, merely muddied the waters. If the terms were clear, they were clear only to the Court—and that is most unlikely.

As symbolic interactionists emphasize, until people attach meaning, words are merely sounds and human acts merely behavior. If two people look at the same photo or watch the same movie or stage play, one might see nudity or sexual intercourse as the expression of art and love, while the other perceives the filth of pornography. What, then, does the Court's phrase "redeeming social value" mean? Where does it leave us if I decide that the sexual content of a book or movie has "redeeming social value," but you do not?

And so the war of symbols marches on. Some claim that certain materials violate "contemporary community standards," whereas others say that those same materials reflect community standards. Still others say there are no community standards. The Internet, developed after the *Roth* decision, has complicated the matter even more. Do people who exchange sexually explicit photos on the Internet form a "community," and should it be their values by which we judge something as pornographic or not? Or does "community" refer to the place where the materials were produced? Or where they were downloaded?

CALIFORNIA V. MILLER. As you can see, the *Roth* decision didn't clarify a thing. Its ambiguities, however, made it difficult for prosecutors to obtain convictions for pornography. In 1973, in *California v. Miller,* the Court tried to remove these ambiguities. It kept the dominant "prurient" theme, said that "contemporary community standards" meant the local community, and, giving up on trying to figure out what it had meant by "redeeming social value," simply dropped the term (Lewis & Peoples, 1978, p. 1071).

Like the *Roth* decision, the *Miller* decision settled nothing. What is or is not pornographic still remained in the eye of the beholder. In some communities, the depiction of sexual acts symbolized filth and depravity to significant numbers of people (or to a number of influential people), and pornography was either banned or restricted to designated areas. In other communities, those same depictions were viewed differently, and not only images but also live presentations of those acts were allowed. With such inconsistencies, the matter was brought again before the Supreme Court. In 1976 (*Young v. American Mini Theaters*) and 1986 (*Renton v. Playtime Theatres*), the Court took a middle ground, ruling that it was constitutional to restrict the location of adult movie theaters (Sitomer, 1986).

A QUESTION OF "TASTE." Social class is significant in helping to determine people's perceptions of acts as pornographic or not. This became evident in a later Court ruling that some nudity, such as that in theater productions and art, is permissible because it is "tasteful." In contrast, other forms of nudity, such as striptease dancing, are not "tasteful." They are "low-art," if "art" at all, and not allowable (Heins, 1991). The question of "taste," of course, simply takes us back to the original question of what pornography is, for whose "taste" determines this? As conflict theorists would point out, it is not surprising that Supreme Court justices decide that their own class-based preferences for nudity are not pornographic, but those of the lower classes are.

CHILD PORNOGRAPHY. When it comes to depicting sex with children, hardly anyone finds "community standards" an adequate defense. Magazines that depicted children in sex acts with adults or with other children used to be easily accessible. Some of the children in these magazines were as young as 3 or 4, but most buyers of these magazines seemed to prefer prepubescents between the ages of 8 and 10. These publications bore such titles as *Lollitots* and *Moppets* (Dubar, 1980).

As states began to pass laws against child pornography and as judges grew willing to impose prison sentences for possessing these materials, such magazines and movies practically disappeared off of the back-wall racks. Child pornography, however, did not disappear. It just went underground, resurfacing on the Internet. There, people who are stimulated by sex with children "meet" in chat rooms, where they share stories of their exploits, real or imagined. They also buy, sell, and exchange files of children who have been bribed, tricked, or forced into sex acts. The photos, movies, and streaming videos are illegal, but the use of passwords and encryption make it difficult for law enforcement agents to track down those responsible for them (Ruethling, 2006). In the Technology and Social Problems box below, we explore the evolution of child pornography on the Internet.

In the coming years it may be even more difficult to restrict child porn. In 2002, in *Ashcroft v. Free Speech Coalition*, the U.S. Supreme Court ruled that it is legal to possess virtual child pornography—that is, computer-generated images of children in sex acts. Because no real child is involved, the Court concluded, there is no victim. This ruling handicaps law enforcement officials, because the improved quality of virtual images makes it difficult to tell the fake from the real thing. As a U.S. customs official said, "We're going to be forced to prove that every picture is of a real child" (Sager et al., 2002).

With perceptions and values varying so widely, it is impossible to pin down what pornography is. Cable operators, for example, try not to cross the line between "acceptable adult programming" and pornography. But where is this line, since showing vaginal penetration, anal sex, oral sex, and group sex is considered acceptable in some markets (Paul, 2005)?

Technology and Social Problems
"NOW TAKE OFF YOUR . . .": LIVE EXHIBITIONS BY CHILDREN ON WEBCAMS

When Justin was 13, he felt scrawny and didn't have many friends. He bought a Webcam and, projecting his image on his own Web site, waited for responses from other teenagers. Those responses never came. But responses from men did.

The men told Justin just what he needed to hear. He was handsome and intelligent. They asked Justin if he would take off his shirt so they could check him out a little more. They even offered him $50 and opened a PayPal account for him so he could collect the money instantly. "Why not?" thought Justin. "I sit at the pool without a shirt for nothing." When Justin took off his shirt, the men complimented him on his physique.

Justin began to look forward to these online chats. Eventually, the men asked him to pose in his shorts. After a while, they asked him to let them see him take them off.

So began Justin's secret life. Each request went only a little farther than the last one, so none of them seemed like a big deal. As the requests escalated, Justin ended up showing an erection for the men, then masturbating before the camera, and having sex.

Justin had become a cyberporn star or, as they are known in the vernacular of those who watch these teenagers, a camwhore. As Justin's popularity grew, he opened his own pay-for-view site, charging subscribers $45 a month. He also offered private shows, charging up to $300, depending on what the men wanted him to do on streaming video.

Justin's parents didn't catch on. They thought that their son, in his bedroom, was doing his homework.

Teenaged girls have also found the Webcam to be an easy way to supplement their allowances. They, too, operate pay-for-view Web sites, with their Webcams beaming their images around the world. The instant messages pour in: I would like to see you in jeans with a belt, in a miniskirt with your feet bare, in pantyhose, with bare legs, with a lacy bra, in red panties, wearing nothing . . .

FOR YOUR CONSIDERATION

Justin and others like him decide to show their bodies willingly, or to engage in sex acts, for a fee. If they are not forced into the act, why should this be considered part of a social problem?

Based on Eichenwald (2005); Brockman (2006).

Controversy and Research on Pornography

THE NATIONAL COMMISSION ON OBSCENITY AND PORNOGRAPHY. Like other social problems, pornography is not only a controversial issue but also an emotional one. A common fear is that pornography corrupts people, that it destroys their morals, perverts their sense of sexuality, and even encourages men to rape. In the 1960s, Americans were so concerned about pornography that President Johnson appointed a National Commission on Obscenity and Pornography. In 1970, the commission concluded that pornography affects some people more than others—that it stimulates the young more than the old, the college-educated more than the less educated, the religiously inactive more than the religiously active, and the sexually experienced more than the sexually inexperienced. Unlike Kinsey (1953), who reported that erotic material arouses males considerably more than females, the commission found that women and men are about equally aroused by watching pornography (Schmidt & Sigusch, 1970).

THE MEESE COMMISSION. The initial conclusions of the National Commission didn't argue that pornography was seriously harmful to society. As pornography proliferated, however, so did the commission's concerns. In the 1980s President Reagan asked the attorney general to appoint another commission to study the effects of pornography. This group, the Meese Commission (1986), concluded that pornography does indeed pose a serious threat *to women*: "The clinical and experimental evidence supports the conclusion that there is a causal relationship between exposure to sexually violent materials and an increase in aggressive behavior directed towards women" (p. 39).

An increase in pornography, said the commission, "will cause an increase in the level of sexual violence directed at women."

The commission's more specific findings (McManus, 1986) included the following:

1. Of 411 sex offenders examined, the average offender had 336 victims.
2. Rape increases where pornography laws are liberalized.
3. Rapists are much more likely than nonoffenders to have been exposed as children to hard-core pornography.
4. Pornography makes rape seem "legitimate."
5. States with higher sales of pornography have higher rates of rape.
6. Males exposed to sexual violence become desensitized and see rape victims as "less injured."

The Meese Commission (1986, p. 39) also concluded that "common-sense" makes it evident that violent pornography causes sex crimes. As illustrated in Chapter 1, not everything evident to our "common sense" is right. If all we need is common sense, we wouldn't need science, and science requires evidence. It is precisely this jump from the commission report (the frequency of pornography among sex offenders) to the conclusions drawn (pornography causes sex crimes) that caused critics to attack the report. Critics said that because the commission was predisposed to see pornography as evil and as the cause of crime, it misinterpreted the evidence and ignored studies that contradicted these notions (Baron, 1987; Brannigan, 1987; Linz, Donnerstein, & Penrod, 1987).

A QUESTION OF CAUSE AND EFFECT. Because neither the Meese Commission's report nor critics' rebuttals give us any final answers, we are still left with the question, Does pornography *cause* sex crimes? Or are sex criminals, such as rapists and child molesters, just more likely to use pornography? Or is it possible that violent pornography, even child pornography, satisfies deviant sexual urges and *decreases* attacks against women and children? Researchers have been able to document only **correlations** (two or more things occurring together). For example, although sex offenders tend to use more pornography than do nonoffenders, not all sex criminals do so. In addition, many non-criminals use pornography. Scientific proof (objective, consistent, verifiable) of a causal relationship, then, remains elusive, and these questions remain unanswered.

Some analysts point out that sex crimes against children in Denmark dropped after that country's lawmakers made hard-core pornography legal in 1965 (Kutchinsky, 1973). It is possible that some men who want to have sex with children find it more appealing to masturbate to pornographic images than to face the threat of prison if they indulge their fantasies with real children. Some child molesters may not even prefer children, taking them as substitutes because they are unable to relate sexually to adults. For these people, too, pornographic images may provide a substitute.

When Japan allowed hard-core pornography during the 1980s–1990s, there, too, the number of rapes dropped (Diamond & Uchiyama, 1999). It is the same in the United States. Although pornography—including that depicting violence against women—has become more common, rape has become less common. The rate of rape in the United States increased until the early 1990s, but since then has dropped 25% (*Statistical Abstract*, 2006, Table 293). It is difficult to determine cause and effect, but one thing seems clear: If pornography is proven to *increase* sexual attacks, there will be an outcry to get rid of it, but if it actually *reduces* sexual attacks, there is not likely to be an outcry to increase it.

The matter of cause and effect is seldom simple, but it is made all the more difficult because pornography has different effects on different people. Some researchers have found that pornography that shows violence against women tends to trigger sexual aggression against women among angry, aggressive men (Malamuth, Addison, & Koss, 2000), while it does not have these effects on more relaxed, "laid back" men. There certainly are problems with such categorizing of men, and even if these categories are valid, the findings are preliminary, and we need more research to determine whether the findings are valid.

SCIENCE VS. SOCIAL ACTION. This is science at work. When research is published, it enters what we might call the "court" of science, where it is judged by a jury of critical scientific peers. As researchers report their findings, other researchers meticulously examine their studies. They challenge the data and repeat the study or reanalyze the original data to publish their own conclusions. This critical process exposes researchers' biases and errors. The conclusions that emerge either replace or further establish the previous conclusions made by another researcher.

Some people find this rigorous and exacting process too slow. Convinced that severe consequences are at stake, they feel a pressing need to take a stand now. And based on their ideas about what is right and wrong and what they find offensive, they often do take a stand.

For example, many people are upset about how pornography portrays women. They are convinced that pornography teaches men to view women as "pieces of meat" and that it teaches women to devalue their own bodies. Whether pornography causes sex crimes is not the point, they insist. Even if it does not, the degrading portrayal of women is another way that women are debased and victimized in society. This is reason enough for pornography—at least the type that shows violence against females—to be banned. As discussed in the Thinking Critically about Social Problems box on the next page, resistance to pornography, though strongly rooted, has lost to the porn industry.

SAFETY VALVE OR TRIGGER? There is no doubt that pornography does influence people. To think otherwise would be absurd. A generation ago, sociologists Donal MacNamara and Edward Sagarin (1977, p. 205) made this point:

To say that pornography cannot influence a person is to contend that books and the printed word, graphics, art, and slogans cannot move people and cause changes in their thoughts and hence their actions.

The question, then, is not whether pornography influences people but, rather, *how*. Is the **safety valve theory** of pornography right? That is, do some types of pornography

THINKING CRITICALLY about Social Problems

THE PORNIFYING OF AMERICA: CRUSHING RESISTANCE AND CO-OPTING FEMINISTS

Pornography has become big business, but finding a market for the many magazines, millions of photographs, and thousands of pornographic movies produced first required a change in attitudes. To get Americans to change their attitudes, deep-seated resistance to pornography had to be overcome. How did porn overcome religion and feminists?

Religious conservatives have and probably always will view pornography as a moral issue. They view growing pornography industries as a sign of the growing depravity of U.S. culture. Conservatives continue to put up stiff resistance, but as pornography becomes more common, further resistance has come to be viewed as labor wasted on a lost cause. Occasionally, a religious leader will still bemoan pornography, but he or she is preaching to the choir.

Feminists didn't take the same moral route, as they didn't want to be seen as aligned with those they considered religious fanatics. But they, too, found something morally objectionable to pornography. Pornography exploits women, they say. Not only are women shown as a bunch of body parts to be used at the pleasure of men, but also many women who work in the porn industry suffer sexual and emotional abuse. Feminists who take this stance rally for better working conditions and health standards for those who have succumbed to the porn industry. Feminists who argue against pornography are in conflict with their counterparts who claim that women should have the right to choose to work in whatever industry they wish, even the sex industry. The porn industry has become delighted by this division among one of their greatest adversaries. Hence, feminist resistance, too, has quieted.

The victory of the porn industry has been so great that criticizing pornography has now become "uncool, unsexy, and reactionary" (Paul, 2005). Viewing pornography as part of women's freedom, not their oppression, makes it more difficult for conservatives to argue against it. Women's magazines discuss pornography from the perspective of equal opportunity for women—how women can introduce pornography into their sex lives and how it gives them the chance to get "in touch" with their sexuality (Paul, 2005). These articles, too, have become part of a greater acceptance of the porn industry as a whole, and of women's role in it.

Demonstrations against pornography seem to have lessened. For the most part, opponents seem to have resigned themselves to what they see as inevitable social change. Certain aspects of pornography, especially the depiction of children, however, still arouse protest.

protect women and children from rape and other sexual violence by providing the private release of sexual fantasies? If so, this type of pornography should be encouraged. Or is the **trigger theory** of pornography right? That is, do some types of pornography trigger sexual offenses by stimulating sexual appetites, often for deviance and violence? If so, these types of pornography should be banned.

Unfortunately, researchers have been unable to settle this question. Until they can—and if they can—social activists will continue to struggle for what they see as a better

social world. No matter which side of the issue they are on, however, they will be acting on their subjective concerns, not on irrefutable evidence.

Social Policy

Consensual acts behind closed doors are not always personal acts, but rather are public issues as well. For example, purchasing a prostitute's services or watching child pornography in one's own home may lead to criminal charges. Let's look at the issues of consent and legality in more detail.

The Question of Making Consensual Behavior Illegal

Sociologists use the term **victimless crime** to refer to illegal acts between consenting adults. The crime has no victim because the people agree to do something with or for one another. A man pays a woman for sex; someone sells or buys pictures of adults involved in sexual acts—both acts may be illegal, but they occur with the consent of the people involved.

In most crimes, someone does something against another person. There is a victim and a perpetrator. When a victim reports a crime, the police know where and when it happened and who the victim is. Without a victim, however, the police end up spending precious public resources attempting to determine that a crime occurred in the first place, and then prosecutors have difficulty in obtaining convictions because the people involved consented to what took place. Unless there is public outcry, both the public and the police prefer that law enforcement agents pursue criminals who have victims—thieves, muggers, rapists, and murderers.

Not all prostitution and pornography involve victimless crimes, however. There can be force, threats, or less than informed consent. If there is force, it is rape, a different matter entirely. If there is less than informed consent, there is also a victim. Child pornography, for example, is not a victimless crime. The children are not of age to give their consent, and child pornography often involves the abuse of adult authority. To deal adequately with social policy, we must separate such instances from those that involve full consent.

Alternatives to Making Consensual Behavior Illegal

LEGALIZING PROSTITUTION. Let's consider prostitution. Because prostitution is a commercial transaction—a business—some argue that it should be legal. We license and tax businesses, so why should we exempt prostitution? Proponents of legalization point out that prostitution will persist and suggest that it is time for the state to regulate it. For pro and con arguments on legalizing prostitution, see the Thinking Critically box on the next page.

THE MATTER OF PRIVACY. Central to deciding social policy is the issue of privacy. The argument is that if adults want to have sex in private, why should it concern the state? It may be a sin to some, but should it be a crime? There is yet another side to the privacy argument—the right of *privacy from* people who are involved in sexual acts. Those who find such activities morally repugnant should not have to see them. If the law were to permit these sexual acts, it should also prohibit street solicitation by prostitutes, sex in public places, and the display of sexual acts on the covers of magazines in supermarkets or on the Internet.

To allow people to pay for sex *and* ensure that others don't have to see it if they don't wish to, some suggest segregation—limiting these activities to specified areas. They also would insist on preventing blatant advertising even in those areas. For example, if prostitutes were segregated to a certain area of the city, they could advertise for customers

THINKING CRITICALLY about Social Problems

SHOULD WE LEGALIZE PROSTITUTION?

YES

1. Prostitutes perform a service for society. They provide sex for people who otherwise cannot find sexual partners. They even help marriages by reducing sexual demands on wives.

2. To keep prostitution illegal is dysfunctional. This stigmatizes and marginalizes women who want to work as prostitutes. It also corrupts many police officers, who accept bribes to allow prostitutes to work. Some prostitution is run by organized crime, with women held in bondage. Legalizing prostitution will eliminate these problems.

3. If prostitution is declared a legal occupation, the government can regulate it. The government can license prostitutes and tax them. It can also require prostitutes to have regular medical checkups and to display a dated and signed medical certificate stating that they are free of sexually transmitted diseases.

NO

1. Prostitution is immoral, and we should not legalize immoral activities. The foundation of society is the family, and we should take steps to strengthen the family, not tear it apart by approving sex as a commercial transaction outside the family.

2. The legalization of prostitution will not stop sexually transmitted diseases. For example, the HIV virus can be transmitted before the disease shows up in blood tests. Even though prostitutes are licensed, they will spread AIDS during this interval.

3. Prostitution degrades women. To legalize prostitution is to give the state's approval to their degradation. It also would affirm class oppression: Most prostitutes come from the working class and serve as objects to satisfy the sexual desires of men from more privileged classes.

Prostitute Shelly Duschel, 31, smokes a cigarette at one of Nevada's legal brothels, the Bunny Ranch, Mound House, Nevada, where top earners bring in thousands of dollars for a night's work.

through ads in newspapers or by a red light in an apartment window, but they could not walk the streets. Nor could pornographic sites show sexually explicit marquees or posters or pop-ups. This would allow the patrons of prostitutes and the consumers of pornography to be able to carry out their consensual activities in private, while respecting the rights of others to avoid seeing these activities.

THE MATTER OF CHILDREN. The use of children in prostitution and pornography is an entirely different matter. Almost everyone feels that children should be protected from sexual

Issues in Social Problems
APPLYING SOCIOLOGY:
TAKING BACK CHILDREN FROM THE NIGHT

Lois Lee isn't afraid to apply her sociological training to social problems. Lee did her master's thesis on the pimp–prostitute relationship and her doctoral dissertation on the social world of the prostitute. After receiving her PhD in sociology from United States International University in 1981, Lee began to work with adult prostitutes. They told her, "You know, it's too late for you to help us, Lois. You've got to do something about these kids. We made a choice to be out here . . . a conscious decision. But these kids don't stand a chance."

Lee began by taking those kids, the teenagers who were prostituting themselves, into her home. In three years, she brought 250 to her home, where she lived with her husband and baby son. Lee then founded "Children of the Night," which reaches the kids by means of "a 24-hour hotline, a street outreach program, a walk-in crisis center, crisis intervention for medical or life-threatening situations, family counseling, job placement, and foster home or group placement." By providing alternatives to prostitution and petty crime, Children of the Night has helped thousands of young runaways and prostitutes to get off the streets.

Lee's work has brought her national publicity and an award from the president. She credits her success to her sociological training, especially the sensitivities it gave her "to understand and move safely through intersecting deviant worlds, to relate positively to police and caretaking agencies while retaining a critical perspective, to know which game to play in which situation."

As Lee said during a CBS interview, "I know what the street rules are, I know what the pimp game is, I know what the con games are, and it's up to me to play that game correctly. . . . It's all sociology. That's why when people call me a social worker I always correct them."

Based on Buff (1987).

exploitation. The position: The purpose of the law is to protect the defenseless of our society. As the Issues in Social Problems box above shows, private citizens can help to protect children from sexual victimization.

The Future of the Problem

With the rapid social change that engulfs us, it is difficult to peer far into the future. Assuming that the United States does not devolve into a dictatorship, which could drive prostitution and pornography underground, we foresee the following.

Prostitution and the Future

Perhaps the easiest forecast in the entire book is this one: The demand for the services of prostitutes will continue. There will always be sexually deprived people who want to patronize prostitutes, as well as those who want to pay for the specialized sexual services that prostitutes offer.

Although prostitution will continue to flourish, it will remain illegal in almost all areas of the United States. The police will overlook all but the most blatant acts both because they feel that they have better things to do and because many of them are convinced that sexual acts between consenting adults should be legal. We are likely to see an increase in an aspect of prostitution that upsets both the public and the police, the prostitution of children. As the media give more publicity to prostituted children, subjective concerns among the public will grow. Spurred by the media, influential individuals will launch campaigns against the prostitution of children (and the exploitation of children in pornography), placing greater pressure on lawmakers. More laws will be passed. Most of them will have little effect.

Technology and Social Problems
PORNOGRAPHY ON THE INTERNET

Pornography vividly illustrates one of the sociological principles discussed in this chapter—that people adapt their sexual behaviors to social change. It was not long after photography was invented that pornographic photography appeared. Today a major issue is pornography on the Internet.

What is the problem? Why can't people electronically exchange nude photos with one another if they want to? If that were the issue, there would be no problem. The real issue, however, is something quite different. What disturbs many people are the photos that show bondage, torture, rape, and bestiality (humans having sex with animals). Judging from the number of such sites, apparently many people derive sexual excitement from such photos. To avoid legal prosecution, pornographers locate the sites that host such materials in countries with weak laws or enforcement.

The Internet abounds with "chat rooms" (people who "meet" online to discuss some topic). No one is bothered about the chat rooms that center on Roman architecture or rap music or turtle racing. But news groups that focus on how to torture women are another matter. So are those that focus on how to seduce children—or on the delights of having sex with preschoolers.

Any call for censorship raises the hackles of civil libertarians, who see all censorship as an attack on basic freedoms. Censorship, they say, is just the first step toward a totalitarian society. The extreme among them defend the right to display and exchange photos of children who are being sexually abused. But only the extremists. Most civil libertarians appear to draw the line at child pornography, but only reluctantly; and they don't want the line drawn any further.

Granted that such pornographic sites and related chat rooms will continue, the issue, then, is how to protect others from being exposed to them. For example, should school and public libraries be allowed to install Internet filters that screen out designated sites? One side insists that this violates the guarantee of the First Amendment's right of free speech, the other that it is only a reasonable precaution to protect children.

WHAT DO YOU THINK?

Based on Clausing (1998), Etzioni (1998), C. Kaplan (1998), Mendels (1998), O'Connell (1998), Locy & Biskupic (2003).

Pornography and the Future

Changes in pornography are likely to be driven by two forces: technology and profits. As each new communication technology appears, pornography will be adapted to fit it. With the increased ease of producing and viewing moving images, with Webcams and DVDs, for example, more people will produce pornography. Because pornography is so profitable, it is likely that the mainstream media will embrace it even more. Cable television, which offers subscribers XXX options, is likely to become even more explicit, perhaps even to broadcast live sex programs. As pornography becomes more mainstream, the line between pornography and art will become even more blurred. It will become increasingly difficult to distinguish between pornography and regular films. See the Technology and Social Problems box on electronic pornography on page 75.

Some continuing clash between the pro- and antipornography forces seems inevitable, for the values of these groups are contrary, and each desires to control the media. But pornography is now so entrenched in our society that it is likely that those who oppose it will limit themselves to an occasional statement decrying the fall of American values and then retreat into enclaves of people who agree with their views.

SUMMARY AND REVIEW

1. All societies attempt to channel sexual behavior in ways they consider acceptable. When the violation of sexual norms is felt to be a threat to society, especially to the family, it is considered a social problem.

2. The functionalist view holds that prostitution persists because it serves social functions. From a functionalist perspective, as prostitutes service customers who are sexually dissatisfied or whose sexual desires are deviant, they relieve pressures that otherwise might be placed on people who are unwilling to participate. The three stages in becoming a prostitute are drift (drifting from casual sex into selling sex), ambivalence, and professionalization. Some young men who sell sex to men manipulate symbols to maintain heterosexual identities.

3. Most Americans agree that the distribution of pornography should be restricted. Women favor greater restrictions than do men. Deciding what is and is not pornographic has confused many, including the U.S. Supreme Court, which, in the tradition of symbolic interactionism, has ruled that what a community decides is pornographic is pornographic—for them.

4. Social scientists have been unable to determine the social effects of pornography. Feminists are concerned that, by dehumanizing women, pornography encourages men to see women as sexual objects to be manipulated and exploited. Social activists take action on the basis of their convictions, not on the basis of proof about causation.

5. *Victimless crimes* are illegal acts to which the participants consent. Prostitution and pornography are classified as victimless crimes by sociologists when adults are involved, but not when children participate, since they cannot give full consent. The suggestion that the government legalize prostitution runs into huge opposition.

6. The interests of people who approve and disapprove of prostitution and pornography are likely to continue to clash, but those who disapprove of them are likely to be fighting rearguard actions.

KEY TERMS

THINKING CRITICALLY ABOUT CHAPTER 3

1. This chapter began by stating that all societies control human sexual behavior. Why do you think this is true? What is it about sex that makes us inclined to control the sexual behavior of others? Be sure to base your explanation on group aspects of society, not on personality or individuals.

2. How does one determine whether or not sexual behavior is "normal?" Who decides what qualifies someone as a paraphiliac?

3. What is your opinion of the following? Child pornography is illegal, and people are arrested and put in prison for possessing it. Pictures of tortured and sexually abused women are legal.

MySocLab

What can you find in MySocLab? mysoclab www.mysoclab.com

- Complete Ebook
- Practice Tests and Exams
- Multimedia Activities
- Mapping and Data Analysis Exercises

- Research and Writing Advice
- Interactive Social Surveys
- Sociology in the News

Alcohol and Other Drugs

"Debbie! What's this?"

Seeing the familiar plastic bag, Debbie felt her face redden. Why hadn't she put it away as she always did? She swallowed, then burst out defiantly:

"My purse! You've got no business snooping in my purse!"

"I was just looking for a match—but I found a lot more! I never expected a daughter of mine to be a drug addict."

"Drug addict, huh? That's funny! Just because someone smokes grass doesn't mean she's a drug addict."

"Everybody knows marijuana is just the first step to the hard stuff, like heroin."

"Mom, it's you who's hooked."

"Mom, it's you who's hooked. The first thing you do in the morning is light up a cigarette and have a cup of coffee. And after that you start popping Prozac."

"Don't you compare my medicine to your drugs. My doctor prescribes Prozac for my nerves."

"Okay, then what do you call your martinis? And I know why you dug in my purse for a match—it's because you're hooked on cigarettes."

"Don't you talk back to me, young lady. Ever since you started college you think you know it all. Just wait 'til your Dad gets home."

"Yeah, sure. Then you'll do the same thing you do every night—talk about it over a drink."

The Problem in Sociological Perspective

Just as Debbie's mother was shocked to discover that her daughter smoked marijuana, hundreds of thousands of other parents have had similar rude awakenings. The use and abuse of drugs for pleasure has become common in the West: on college campuses, in the suburbs, and in the executive suite. One president of the United States admitted to smoking marijuana—although, bringing laughter to millions, he said that he "didn't inhale." Additionally, in the most recent presidential race, Barack Obama openly discussed his use of marijuana as a young man.

Background of the Problem

DRUG USE IN ANCIENT SOCIETIES. Records of drug use stretch far back in history. Over 4,000 years ago, a Chinese emperor recommended marijuana for "female weakness, gout, rheumatism, malaria, beriberi, constipation and absent-mindedness" (Ray & Ksir, 2004). About 2,500 years ago, the famous physician Hippocrates recommended mandrake, taken with a little wine, to relieve depression and anxiety (Blum et al., 1969). And about 500 years ago, when the Spanish conquistadors landed in South America, they discovered that the natives chewed coca leaves for the stimulating effects of cocaine (DeRios & Smith, 1977; Goode, 1989).

DEFINING DRUG ABUSE. Just as drug use reaches far back into history, so does **drug abuse**—using drugs in such a way that they harm one's health, impair one's physical or

mental functioning, or interfere with one's social life. Noah, who is listed in the Bible as the ninth descendant of Adam, is reported to have abused alcohol. After the flood, he planted a vineyard, made wine from its first harvest, and drank himself into a stupor (Genesis 9). What qualifies as drug abuse, of course, depends on the social norms prevalent within a particular time period. In one group, smoking a joint of marijuana may be considered drug abuse, whereas in another group smoking marijuana might be considered just "normal."

THE SOCIAL HISTORY OF DRUGS. It is important to emphasize that *no drug is good or bad in and of itself* (Szasz, 1975). What is vitally important is how a group of people view the drug and react to it. And how perspectives change! You are familiar with today's dominant view of tobacco—and the health warnings on cigarette packages. But contrast today's perspective with that of the 1940s and 1950s. Back then, doctors actually recommended cigarettes as good for one's health. You will probably find the ad for Chesterfield on page 81, featuring a former U.S. president, rather different from today's tobacco ads.

Attempts to Deal with the Problem

THE FAILURE OF PUNISHMENT. When Christopher Columbus arrived on the shores of the New World, he found that Native Americans smoked tobacco regularly, something he hadn't seen before. He took some back with him to the Old World. Europeans tried it, and then smoking tobacco became common. King James I of England disliked this new habit, however, and in 1604 he wrote a pamphlet warning his subjects that tobacco was "harmful to the brain and dangerous to the lungs" (Ray & Ksir, 2004). Other rulers who viewed tobacco as evil went far beyond just issuing warnings. In 1634, the czar of Russia ordered the noses of tobacco smokers to be slit with a knife. The rulers of China had smokers' heads cut off. Turkish rulers also ordered smokers to be put to death (Goode, 1989). All of these harsh antitobacco campaigns failed.

Like many people today, King James was not one to let health concerns interfere with making money. When tobacco growing became profitable, he declared its trade a royal monopoly (Ray & Ksir, 2004). Today we have corporations that tout their concerns regarding health and social justice, but they can't resist the profitable dividends that tobacco stocks pay.

Although some people will risk their health for a good smoke, others will do the same for a popular beverage that may or may not be good to the last drop. After coffee was introduced to the Arab world during the 1500s, Islamic religious leaders became upset when people drank coffee to help them stay awake during long vigils. Stating that coffee was intoxicating and prohibited by the Koran, religious leaders ordered the coffee dealers to be beaten across the soles of their feet (Brecher et al., 1972). A century later, in 1674, a group of Englishwomen wrote a pamphlet titled "The Women's Petition Against Coffee." They complained that their men were leaving "good old ale" in order to drink "base, black, thick, nasty, bitter, stinking, nauseous" coffee. Their real complaint? The coffee, they said, was making their men less sexually active (Meyer, 1954).

CHANGING SOCIAL DEFINITIONS. In the United States attitudes toward drug use have undergone major change. Consider this: In the 1800s, you could buy opium and morphine

See For Yourself

Go to the U.S. Drug Enforcement Agency Website at: http://www.usdoj.gov/dea/statistics.html

▸ Research the number of DEA arrests and drug seizures on this site. Keep in mind these are only those cases that are officially investigated.

in drugstores, grocery stores, and general stores. If you found shopping inconvenient, you could order these drugs by mail. Opium was advertised as a cure for diarrhea, colds, fever, teething, pelvic disorders, even athlete's foot and baldness (Inciardi, 1986). Opium was so common that each year U.S. mothers fed their babies about 750,000 bottles of opium-laced syrup. To smoke cigarettes or drink alcohol was far more offensive than to use opium (Isbell, 1969; Duster, 1970; Brecher et al., 1972).

Society tends to project fear onto drugs and drug use. Drugs that may have initially been viewed as holy gifts are later defined as social problems. This drives home the point made in Chapter 1 about objective conditions and subjective concerns. It is not the *objective conditions* of drugs—such as whether or not they are harmful—that makes their use a social problem. Rather, it is the surrounding *subjective concerns that establish them as problems*. As in the case of tobacco and coffee, what once was considered normal drug use may be viewed as drug abuse at a later date—or vice versa. Just like topics already discussed—abortion and prostitution—drugs are a hub of social controversy. As with other social problems, people acquire different views of drugs and line up on opposing sides of the issue.

For generations, tobacco companies used well-respected icons to sell nicotine.

IN SUM Whether a drug is considered good or bad depends not on objective conditions but on subjective concerns. Subjective concerns are not fixed, but change over time. These concerns, and the views they generate, influence how people use and abuse drugs, whether a drug will become legal or illegal, and what social policies people ultimately adopt (see Table 4-1 on the next page). These subjective concerns are the central sociological principle of drug use and abuse, one that we shall stress over and over in this chapter.

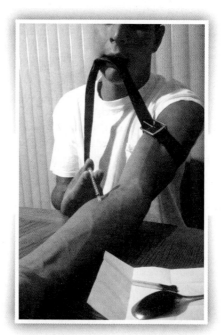

If a drug is in high demand, passing a law will not stop that demand. The law merely drives the use of the drug underground, to a black market that connects users and suppliers in an intricate, illegal relationship. Although coffee is broadly socially acceptable today, in some societies it was once an illegal drug, with severe penalties attached to its possession and consumption.

TABLE 4-1 Legal Status and Use of Drugs

| | USE OF DRUGS | |
	Legal Use	Illegal Use
Legal Drugs	a. Prescription b. Over the counter c. "Over the bar" and in vending machines	a. Forged prescriptions b. Black market sales of prescription drugs c. "After-hours" sales; "underage" sales
Illegal Drugs	a. Marijuana prescribed for medical problems b. Cocaine for surgery	a. Crack, heroin, etc.

Source: By James M. Henslin.

The Scope of the Problem

The Social Problem and the Pro-Drug Orientation of U.S. Society

Debbie, in our opening vignette, is like the other 15 million Americans who smoked marijuana during the past month (*Statistical Abstract*, 2006, Tables 11, 194). To Debbie, marijuana isn't a drug, it's just something that she likes to smoke with friends. It makes her feel good, and it is "no big deal." Debbie's mother is like most Americans—she drinks coffee, alcohol, and colas; smokes cigarettes; and ingests a variety of substances that *she* has a hard time thinking of as drugs.

Like marijuana, alcohol and nicotine are drugs. To qualify as a drug, a substance does not have to be sold in an alley or exchanged furtively for money in a van. A **drug** is a substance that people take to produce a change in their thinking, consciousness, emotions, or bodily functions or behavior. Obviously, people take many substances to cause such changes. The essential difference among these substances *is not which ones they use, but whether a substance is socially acceptable or disapproved of.* From this comes the clash in people's perspectives, such as those of Debbie and her mother.

Humans are often born with the aid of drugs, and drugs often ease our departure at the end of life. We use drugs for sickness and for pleasure; to relieve anxiety, queasy stomachs, and headaches; and for all sorts of other pains and discomforts. As with alcohol, we take drugs to help us become sociable. As with cigarettes, coffee, and colas, we take them routinely, unthinkingly, and habitually. (Yes, coffee, Coke, and Pepsi qualify as addictive, because they contain caffeine. Caffeine is addictive, and some people "just can't get going" in the morning without their "fixes" of it). *Far from being an antidrug society, we are actually pro-drug.*

Drug Abuse as a Personal or Social Problem

Most of us take this kind of drug use for granted. To us, it's like eating popcorn or munching on potato chips. When drug use interferes with someone's health or how that person gets along in life, though, we begin to question it. But we consider this a *personal* problem. If large numbers of people become upset about a drug, however, and want to see something done about it, then that drug becomes part of a *social* problem. Remember, a social problem is something about which people are concerned and that they want changed. This, of course, takes us back to the main point with which we began this text: objective conditions and subjective concerns. As we consider two common drugs, nicotine and alcohol, note how much more important subjective concerns are than objective conditions.

Let's suppose that you are on your way to the airport, leaving for a long-awaited vacation. You are listening to the radio and anticipating your arrival in sunny Hawaii. Suddenly, an announcer breaks into your reverie with a flash bulletin: Terrorists have hidden bombs aboard five jumbo jets scheduled for takeoff today. Each jet is going to crash. On each jet will be 200 passengers and crew, who will plummet from the skies, leaving a trail of agonizing screams as they meet their fiery destiny.

The announcer pauses, then adds: "The authorities have not been able to locate the bombs. Because no one knows which flights will crash, all flights will depart on schedule."

What would you do? My guess is that you would turn your car around and go home. Adios to Hawaii's beaches, and hello to your own backyard.

What does this have to do with nicotine? Nicotine is the addictive ingredient in tobacco. Cigarette smoking is the single most preventable cause of premature death in the United States. Each year, more than 400,000 Americans die from cigarette smoking. In fact, one in every five deaths in the United States is smoking related. Every year, smoking kills more than 276,000 men and 142,000 women (Surgeon General, 2007). This is the equivalent of five fully loaded jets, each carrying 200 passengers and 20 crew members, crashing each and every day. The crashes continue without letup, day after day, year after year. The passengers *know* that one of the jets will crash that day; yet they climb aboard anyway, thinking that it won't be *their* jet that crashes. Obviously no one would get on a plane if this were the case. And if planes crashed like this, the government would stop the flights and fix the problem. Who in their right mind would take the risk that *their* plane would not be among those that crashed? Yet smokers do. They know that nicotine is lethal. They also know that smoking-related deaths are lingering and painful, a burden to both the victims and their families. Although smoking cuts the average smoker's life span by 13 or 14 years, 20% of Americans continue to smoke (*Statistical Abstract*, 2006, Table 191). They put this deadly poison to their lips, thinking that it won't be their plane that goes down.

ALCOHOL AS A SOCIAL PROBLEM. Alcohol, too, is far more dangerous than its broad social acceptability would imply. Alcohol-related motor vehicle accidents kill 17,000 Americans each year. The death toll from alcohol-related accidents is about 47 a day (*Statistical Abstract*, 2006, Table 1092). To continue our analogy, this is the equivalent of two jumbo jets, each loaded with 165 passengers and crew, crashing each and every week of the year.

Alcoholics, their organs ravaged and decaying from long-term use, become a burden to themselves and to their families. Men are more likely to suffer the consequences of this drug, for most abusers of alcohol are men—about two or three men for every woman. In addition to the many health problems and deaths that come from alcohol abuse, like nicotine, this drug costs the nation billions of dollars a year in health care and in lost productivity.

Addiction and Dependence

A serious problem related to all drug use is **addiction,** or drug dependence. This occurs when people come to depend on the regular consumption of the drug to make it through the day. When people think of **drug addiction,** they are likely to think of addicts huddled in slum doorways, the dregs of society who gather at homeless shelters across the nation. Most people don't associate addiction with "good," middle-class neighborhoods and "solid citizens."

ADDICTION AND NICOTINE. Let's look at drug addiction a little more closely. Although most people may think of heroin or cocaine as prime examples of addictive drugs, we suggest nicotine as the better example. Even those who face horrible physical challenges from smoking maintain their habit to the end.

A guest speaker came into Lori Fowler's class once, to educate college students on the dangers of tobacco. He stood at the front of the class, looking very relaxed. The students were drawn to his inviting body language, and then he reached into his pocket and pulled out a vibrating voice machine. He lowered the large collar covering his tracheotomy and set the vibrating machine onto his throat. He spoke through the machine and told the students how even after losing his voice, he still smoked through his tracheotomy hole.

You'd think that developing emphysema, a more serious disease, would be enough to make a smoker quit, but chest specialists report that "even during the last months of their ordeal, when they must breathe oxygen intermittently instead of air, some smokers go right on alternating cigarette smoke and oxygen" (Brecher et al., 1972, p. 216). As emphysema progresses, breathing becomes increasingly difficult, resulting in death from respiratory failure.

Another example of risking all for nicotine occurs with Buerger's disease:

> In this disease the blood vessels become so constricted that circulation is impaired whenever nicotine enters the bloodstream. When gangrene sets in, at first a toe or two may have to be amputated. If the person continues to smoke, the foot may have to be amputated at the ankle, then the leg at the knee, and ultimately at the hip. Somewhere along this gruesome progression gangrene may also attack the other leg. Patients are told that if they will just stop smoking, this horrible march of gangrene in their legs will stop. Yet surgeons report that some patients vigorously puff away in their hospital beds following even a second or third amputation. (Brecher et al., 1972, p. 216)

AVOIDING WITHDRAWAL. Why don't drug addicts just quit? Even when they know that a drug is harming them, people continue to use it to avoid **withdrawal,** the intense distress—nausea, vomiting, aches and pains, nervousness, anxiety, and depression—they feel when they abstain from the drug. Withdrawal creates **cravings,** intense desires for the missed drug. Even after someone has kicked the habit, the craving may last for months or even years. Cravings are especially strong during times of emotional distress. Years after breaking the physical habit, people may still experience an occasional desire for the drug. This is referred to as **psychological dependence.**

Looking at the Problem Theoretically

Why is it legal to use drugs as lethal as alcohol and nicotine, and yet people are arrested and put in prison for using milder drugs? This answer lies in subjective concerns, objective conditions, and how the meanings we assign to drugs go far beyond their pharmaceutical characteristics. To understand the *social* significance of drugs, let's look at drugs through theoretical lenses.

Symbolic Interactionism

THE TEMPERANCE MOVEMENT AND THE MEANING OF DRUGS. The meaning of a drug depends on who is defining it. A physician might perceive a drug as a tool to help patients; a drug dealer might view the same drug as a high-profit product; the police might see it as an evil substance to be stamped out; users might perceive it as the pathway to an adventure, a "high," or even a religious experience. Some users might view the drug as simply a mild diversion that they can do without, whereas others view it as an absolute necessity for getting through the day. The meaning of a drug, then, does not depend on the drug itself, but on how people view the drug.

As the Issues in Social Problems box on the next page illustrates, alcohol has been a part of American culture from the beginning. If alcohol has always been so entrenched in our culture, why was it outlawed in 1919? Sociologist Joseph Gusfield (1963) analyzed how this perspective changed. Anglo-Saxon Protestants had settled in New England, and

Issues in Social Problems
THE PILGRIMS, BEER, AND THANKSGIVING

The *Mayflower* had completed its historic voyage. Now the Pilgrims faced the daunting task of settling the wilderness of the New World. They found the Indians friendly enough, but the bitter winter of 1620 was something else. Samoset, a tribesman, helped them survive that first harsh winter.

But beer also helped.

When winter hit, the colonists' buildings were still unfinished. To continue to work on them, the immigrants had to brave the icy February winds as they ferried back and forth from the *Mayflower*. Life was becoming unbearable, and the colonists were falling victim to pneumonia, scurvy, and exposure.

Adding to their misery was the first beer crisis in the New World. It wasn't as though the Pilgrims lacked foresight. They were careful planners, and they had brought with them a large supply of beer. Like other Europeans of the time, they distrusted water and thought of alcohol as essential for good health. A stiff drink kept off chills and fevers, aided digestion, made work easier to bear, and warmed the body on cold nights. The Pilgrims considered nondrinkers to be "crank-brained."

But the journey across the ocean had taken longer than expected, and so had their attempt to establish a beachhead in the wilderness. They had run out of beer, and now they were forced to drink water. Seeing their plight, the captain of the *Mayflower* shared beer from the crew's supplies. He could do this only so long, however, for he had to make sure that his crew had enough beer to drink on the long voyage back to England. When these supplies ran short, he had to stop sharing.

For the Pilgrims, the situation was desperate. William Bradford, who became the governor of Plymouth, pleaded for just one "can" of beer. The captain of the *Mayflower* refused him. As the deaths mounted, however, the captain took pity on the Pilgrims. To alleviate their suffering, from his personal supplies he gave beer "for them that hath need for it," particularly the sick.

With prayers, the help of Samoset, the *Mayflower*'s captain, and beer, the Pilgrims made it through that first bleak winter. And, unlike our grade school images, during their first Thanksgiving feast, the Pilgrims drank beer—and Samoset joined their merrymaking, for by this time he, too, had developed a taste for this frothy, heart-warming liquid.

Based on Lender & Martin (1982).

---

their customs and religion dominated the region. Then in the 1820s, millions of uneducated, poor immigrants poured in from Italy, Germany, and Ireland. The educated and well-to-do New England "aristocracy" found the customs of the new immigrants offensive—especially their religion (Roman Catholicism) and their practice of drinking wine, beer, and spirits. The established Protestant residents viewed the new immigrants as ignorant, Catholic drunkards.

To the dismay of the old New Englanders, the new immigrants continued to pour in. As the members of the old establishment gradually lost political power, they began a temperance (nondrinking) movement. They reasoned that if they couldn't control the politics of the region, they at least could control its morals. Their goal was to turn the new immigrants into clean, sober, and godly people whose customs would reflect the traditional Anglo-Saxon moral leadership of New England.

As a result, drinking and abstinence became two contrary symbols, identifying people as members of one of two major groups. Abstinence was associated with morality and respectability. It symbolized hard workers, people who were established and reputable. Drinking, in contrast, symbolized unreliable drifters, uneducated immigrants of questionable background. To abstain from alcohol became a requirement for anyone who strove for higher social standing.

As the United States grew more urban and secular, Protestants saw their power and values slipping even further. Intensifying their efforts to uphold temperance, they rejoiced

in 1919 when the Eighteenth Amendment to the Constitution was passed. Overnight, it became illegal for Americans to buy even a glass of beer. Prohibition, Gusfield says, marked the victory of middle-class, Protestant, rural values over working-class, Roman Catholic, urban values. Like earlier antidrug laws, however, Prohibition was a failure. It did not stop people from using alcohol. As the forces behind temperance weakened, 14 years later, in 1933, this grand experiment in drug control was repealed, and alcohol again was for sale.

CHANGING MEANINGS OF OTHER DRUGS. It may be difficult for us today to understand how any adult could have been arrested for possessing a bottle of beer or other alcohol. This illustrates another key point of subjective concerns, how our understanding of any drug use centers on the meanings that people attach to it. For example, many people view marijuana use as immoral, but for others it represents no threat. Throughout history, as long as marijuana had been confined to "bohemian" or marginal groups, the drug posed no cultural threat to mainstream society. But in the 1960s, rebellious middle-class youth formed a subculture that brought the use of marijuana into mainstream culture. To show their rejection of their parent's ethics, they promoted the use of marijuana and other psychedelic drugs. At that point, the meanings attached to marijuana use changed— and a social problem was born.

Functionalism

THE SOCIAL FUNCTIONS AND DYSFUNCTIONS OF DRUGS. When functionalists study a drug, whether it be legal or illegal, they examine its functions and dysfunctions. While *functions* are intended or recognized and have a positive effect on society, *dysfunctions* are unintended or unrecognized and have a negative effect on society. A function of recreational drug use is to "loosen" people up, or otherwise help remove tensions that interfere with sociability. These drugs are also functional for all those involved in growing, processing, distributing, and selling them. These same drugs are dysfunctional for the abuser or for the family members hurt by the addicted person.

Prescription drugs are functional both for the medical profession and for the patients they serve. These drugs, too, are dysfunctional for those who abuse them—or for those who have adverse reactions to them. A striking example of how prescription drugs can be functional is their increased use among mental health patients. In the 1950s, more than 500,000 Americans were locked inside psychiatric hospitals. Today, only 180,000 are institutionalized (*Statistical Abstract*, 2006, Table 173). This decline in institutionalization is due, in part, to the prescribing of mood-altering drugs (the psychopharmaceuticals). In just a few years the number of patients confined to psychiatric hospitals shrank by several hundred thousand. For these people, drugs have been functional.

Prescription drugs may also be dysfunctional. Some psychiatrists use them to put patients in "pharmacological straitjackets." Instead of trying to find out what is wrong with the patient or with the patient's social environment, the physician may take the easier route and prescribe mood-altering drugs. Such drug therapy exacts a price. "Doped-up" patients become befuddled and lethargic, some suffering permanent neurological damage.

In short, drug use is dysfunctional when it interferes with people's physical or social functioning. Nicotine, alcohol, heroin, barbiturates, and other addictive drugs create severe problems for abusers, addicts, and their families and friends.

The dysfunctions of drugs extend far beyond the individual. Although difficult to measure, these large-scale costs involve drug-related crimes, such as burglaries and muggings, that are committed in order to support addiction, unemployment, medical costs due to illness and disease, the spread of AIDS among addicts who share needles, the deaths and injuries suffered by people in automobile accidents, and the loss to society of a reservoir of human potential as people retreat into drugs.

LATENT FUNCTIONS OF DRUG CONTROL: THE EXAMPLE OF MARIJUANA. We can analyze the history of drug control in the United States to further understand function and

dysfunction. Making a drug illegal, for example, has the latent function (not its intended purpose) of strengthening the agencies that control that drug. Without these laws, some government agencies would go out of business. To protect their jobs, some bureaucrats eagerly try to define many drugs as dangerous to the public's welfare. The more drugs we have defined as illegal, the more secure government jobs remain.

Marijuana provides a beautiful illustration. In 1930, Harry Anslinger was appointed to head the Treasury Department's new Bureau of Narcotics. Congress cut his budget because the country was in the midst of the Great Depression. Although marijuana was legal at this time, Anslinger saw the drug as offering an opportunity to strengthen his faltering organization (Dickson, 1968). Embarking on a campaign to pass a federal law against marijuana, Anslinger became a **moral entrepreneur,** a crusading reformer who battles to enforce his or her idea of morality. Anslinger received support from an unexpected source, leaders of the liquor industry who feared that marijuana might compete with alcohol (Rockwell, 1972). With the help of these new allies, Anslinger was victorious, and Congress passed the Marijuana Tax Act in 1937. Anslinger's campaign to frighten people is recounted in the Issues in Social Problems box on page 88.

The Marijuana Tax Act has been functional for the Bureau of Narcotics, which is still going strong. This law, however, has been dysfunctional for the hundreds of thousands of Americans who have been caught in its enforcement web. When marijuana became popular with middle-class youth and it became impossible to enforce abstinence among millions of smokers, the drug enforcers did not stop searching out and arresting offenders. Drug use has kept them in business. This example illustrates a central tenet of functional analysis: What is dysfunctional for some is functional for others.

Conflict Theory

DRUG LAWS AS A WAY TO CONTROL SOCIETY. Common sense sometimes doesn't get us very far when it comes to the drug argument. As discussed in the Issues in Social Problems box on page 89, much more is involved in making a drug illegal than just illustrating the physical harm done by that drug. We must again consider power when analyzing this social problem. Some groups have the power to get laws passed to protect their interests; others don't. This situation brings us to the heart of drug use and the conflict perspective—drugs are often used as a political tool. If the use of a particular drug is common among some group (the poor), making the drug illegal allows authorities to unleash the police against them. In contrast, by keeping a drug legal (prescription drugs), the state can protect favored groups that make money from a drug (pharmaceutical companies).

U.S. history is littered with examples of how drug laws have been used as political tools. In the 1920s, the United States was in the midst of an economic boom, and workers from Mexico were viewed as a source of cheap labor. Then with the Great Depression of the 1930s, millions lost their jobs, and Mexicans came to be viewed as having stolen jobs from citizens (Galliher & Walker, 1977). Marijuana use was not popular among the mainstream in the United States, but it was common among Mexican immigrant workers. As we saw in the box "Marijuana: Assassin of Youth" on page 88, the head of the Bureau of Narcotics began a campaign to label the drug favored by this unpopular group as dangerous. In one of his articles, Anslinger even referred to "a hot tamale salesman pushing his cart about town . . . peddling marijuana cigarettes." The Marijuana Tax Act of 1937 became a political tool to drive competitive Mexican workers back across the border (Helmer, 1975).

Chinese immigrants have also been targeted by drug laws. In the 1800s, thousands of Chinese men came to the United States to help build the transcontinental railroad. They brought opium, a legal drug at the time, with them. When the railroad was completed, just a few years before the depression and financial panic of 1873, these workers were available to compete with mainstream Americans in the job market. But when the depression and financial panic hit, the Chinese—willing to work for less money than the White workers—posed a threat, and the White workers beat, tortured, and killed them. In 1875, San Francisco and other West Coast cities enacted laws to prohibit opium dens. These laws were not intended to target opium but, rather, the Chinese men

Issues in Social Problems
MARIJUANA: ASSASSIN OF YOUTH

In his campaign to make marijuana illegal, Harry Anslinger used dramatic accounts and exaggeration. To frighten people, he wrote articles for popular magazines (Reasons, 1974). In one of them, he tells this story:

> There was this young girl. . . . Her story is typical. Some time before, this girl, like others of her age who attend our high schools, had heard the whispering of a secret which has gone the rounds of American youth. It promised a new thrill, the smoking of a type of cigarette which contained a "real kick." According to the whispers, this cigarette could accomplish wonderful reactions and with no harmful aftereffects. So the adventurous girl and a group of her friends gathered in an apartment, thrilled with the idea of doing "something different" in which there was "no harm." Then a friend produced a few cigarettes of the loosely rolled "homemade" type. They were passed from one to another of the young people, each taking a few puffs.
>
> The results were weird. Some of the party went into paroxysms of laughter; every remark, no matter how silly, seemed excruciatingly funny. Others of mediocre musical ability became almost expert; the piano dinned constantly. Still others found themselves discussing weighty problems of youth with remarkable clarity. As one youngster expressed it, he "could see through stone walls." The girl danced without fatigue, and the night of unexplainable exhilaration seemed to stretch out as though it were a year long. Time, conscience, or consequences became too trivial for consideration.
>
> Other parties followed, in which inhibitions vanished, conventional barriers departed, all at the command of this strange cigarette with its ropy, resinous odor. Finally there came a gathering at a time when the girl was behind in her studies and greatly worried. With every puff of the smoke the feeling of despondency lessened. Everything was going to be all right—at last. The girl was "floating" now, a term given to marijuana intoxication. Suddenly, in the midst of laughter and dancing, she thought of her school problems. Instantly they were solved. Without hesitancy, she walked to a window and leaped to her death. Thus can marijuana "solve" one's difficulties.

Here's another story that Anslinger told.

> It was an unprovoked crime some years ago which brought the first realization that the age-old drug had gained a foothold in America. An entire family was murdered by a youthful addict in Florida. When officers arrived at the home they found the youth staggering about in a human slaughterhouse. With an ax he had killed his father, his mother, two brothers, and a sister. He seemed to be in a daze. . . . He had no recollection of having committed the multiple crime. The officers knew him ordinarily as a sane, rather quiet young man; now he was pitifully crazed. They sought the reason. The boy said he had been in the habit of smoking something which youthful friends called "muggles," a childish name for marijuana. . . .
>
> [People need to be] told that addicts may often develop a delirious rage during which they are temporarily and violently insane, that this insanity may take the form of a desire for self-destruction or a persecution complex to be satisfied only by the commission of some heinous crime. (Anslinger & Cooper, 1937)

If these stories didn't convince people, Anslinger had an ace up his sleeve. He said that this killer weed—his term—made men impotent (Galliher & Walker, 1977).

All things considered, it is little wonder that Anslinger's campaign resulted in Congress passing the Marijuana Tax Act in 1937.

Issues in Social Problems
SOCIOLOGY AND COMMON SENSE: LEGAL AND ILLEGAL DRUGS

COMMON SENSE

1. Common sense would suggest that illegal drugs are harmful, whereas legal drugs are not harmful.
2. Common sense would suggest that if a legal drug is discovered to be addictive, it will be made illegal.
3. Common sense would suggest that if a non-narcotic has been classified mistakenly as a narcotic, it should be reclassified differently.

Marijuana bars exist across the nation. Here, a man is sampling a style of marijuana before purchasing it.

SOCIOLOGY

1. Drugs do not become illegal (or remain legal) on the basis of the harm they cause. Drugs have a social history (page 80) that affects their legal classification. Classifying a drug as illegal involves a political process. If a drug is classified as illegal, some interest group has managed to get its argument translated into law.

2. Some addictive drugs that are backed by well-financed interest groups (alcohol, nicotine, Prozac, Valium, and OxyContin) remain legal.
3. Marijuana was classified incorrectly as a narcotic in the 1937 Marijuana Tax Act. Although knowledge of this error is acknowledged, no interest group has been powerful enough to get this classification corrected.

who threatened the jobs of Whites (Morgan, 1978). Even the U.S. Congress got involved. In 1887, it passed a law that prohibited the importation of opium *by the Chinese* but not by white Americans (Szasz, 1975).

Drug laws can be passed that either suppress or benefit a group's economy. Today, Japan's government is successfully manipulating laws regulating tobacco sales to increase revenue. Japan is currently debating a substantial cigarette tax increase that would triple the price of cigarettes to about $10.00 per pack. Japan Tobacco, Inc., is 50% owned by Japanese government officials. They are attempting to cut Japan's budget deficit and boost tax revenue by 8.5 trillion yen per year (Tabuchi, 2008).

Conflict theorists also stress that politicians use drug laws to control what are called "the dangerous classes," those whose members are likely to rebel. When oppressed people seek refuge in addictive drugs, their anger is diverted away from rebellion. Drugs, not social change, become their passion, the goal around which their life revolves. Contrary to the impression that news reports often create, drugs such as heroin and crack therefore stabilize society. They divert the attention and energy of the exploited away from their oppression, diluting their interest in social change. In addition, violence becomes directed toward members of their own community, not toward the ruling class. Conflict theorist Andrew Karmen (1980) said that heroin users become "too passive when nodding and too self-absorbed when they aren't high to fight for community control over the schools, to organize tenants for a rent strike, or to march on City Hall to demand decent jobs for all who want to work." Indeed, "since narcotics pacify those who suffer most from mental and physical degradation, it's likely that some astute members of the ruling circles have decided its benefits outweigh its costs" (p. 174).

Drugs can serve the interests of the powerful. A ploy sometimes used by groups in power to protect their position is to focus attention on some threat posed by a disfavored group. This tactic diverts attention from internal problems and makes people feel that they are all facing a common threat—and that they had better unite before the threat harms them all.

Our history provides numerous examples of how those in power have used drugs to consolidate sentiment against disfavored groups. During the 1800s, when China was deemed America's enemy, Chinese opium dens were pictured as outposts of corruption, places where evil Chinese men seduced innocent White women. By World War I the "enemy" label was now applied to Germans, and German pharmaceutical firms and anarchists were supposedly smuggling heroin into this country. With the outbreak of World War II, Japan as the new enemy was identified as the force behind the narcotics trade. Then during the Cold War of the 1950s with the USSR, the Soviet secret police were fingered as the sinister heroin supplier. During the Korean War, China became the culprit. During the Vietnam War, North Vietnam and the National Liberation Front were named as masterminds of the narcotics trade (Karmen, 1980). Today, with the Cold War over, the government is identifying a new enemy supplier. Top candidates, of course, are the "warlords" of Afghanistan (these are heads of clans who refuse to cooperate with the U.S. occupation).

IN SUM Each theory contributes to the understanding of drugs as a social problem. Symbolic interactionists stress how drugs become powerful symbols that affect social life, as was the case with alcohol and the great drug experiment known as Prohibition. Functionalists examine the functions and dysfunctions of drug use: For example, some psychiatric patients benefit from legal mood-altering drugs, but those same drugs impair the physical or social functioning of other patients. Conflict theorists examine drugs as part of a social order in which a privileged few are in control: Because drugs have been manipulated in the past for the purpose of enhancing power and control, some think that this same process may underlie the heroin and cocaine trade today.

Research Findings: The Use and Abuse of Drugs

Let's examine the medicalization of human problems, examine the drug-use patterns of students in the United States, and then try to explain why people have different experiences with the same drug.

Medicalizing Human Problems

The King, Elvis Presley, had a difficult time getting through the day—and the nights were no better. Middle age, unwelcome to almost everyone but especially dreaded by celebrities, had settled in, bringing a paunch and double chin that the Hollywood magazines ridiculed. To make matters worse, the breakup of his marriage had torn his only child from him. Throughout these ordeals, a longtime friend, Dr. George Nichopoulos, had been a great help. During the past 31 months he had prescribed 19,000 stimulants, depressants, and painkillers, some of which were highly addictive.

Now the King of Rock and Roll lay dead on his bathroom floor. The official report stated that Elvis had died from heart disease. Other medical examiners claimed that his death could have resulted from the interaction of the many drugs in his system. Presley's body contained toxic levels of the sedative methaqualone, 10 times more codeine than was needed for therapy, and low levels of 10 other drugs: morphine, Demerol, and phenyltoloxamine (painkillers); amobarbital, phenobarbital, and amitriptyline (sedatives); pentobarbital (a sedative and sleep-inducer); Valmid and Placidyl (sleep-inducers); and Valium (a muscle relaxant).

At his trial for overprescribing, Dr. Nichopoulos testified that his drug plan for Presley called for drugs to reduce his appetite, drugs to stimulate his bowels, drugs to help him urinate, drugs to relieve itching, drugs to help dizziness, drugs to relieve pain, and drugs to help him relax. Dr. Nichopoulos was found not guilty.

Anna Nicole Smith and Heath Ledger's autopsies revealed that the stars had both died from a prescription drug overdose.

Prescription drug use has caused the death of two other well-known celebrities: Anna Nicole Smith and Heath Ledger. Anna Nicole Smith, a former *Playboy* Playmate, was found unconscious in a hotel suite at the Seminole Hard Rock Cafe Hotel in Florida. Eight brown bags containing prescription drugs were taken from her room. Although pills were removed from her room, no pills were found in her stomach during the autopsy.

Heath Ledger, the actor known for his role in *Brokeback Mountain* and for playing the Joker in *The Dark Night,* was found dead at age 28 after an accidental prescription drug overdose. The coroner ruled the cause of death as an overdose from the combined effects of oxycodone, hydrocodone, diazepam, temazepam, alprazolam and doxylamine (Barron, 2008).

The abuse of a variety of prescription drugs does not affect only those in Hollywood. Abuse of prescription drugs to get high has become increasingly prevalent among teens and young adults. Past-year abuse of prescription pain killers now ranks second—only behind marijuana—as the nation's most prevalent illegal drug problem, according to the United States Council on Drug Abuse.

A new trend among our youth is the hosting of **pharm parties**—*pharm* is short for pharmaceuticals, such as the powerful painkillers Vicodin and OxyContin. At pharm parties, attendees bring mixed varieties of pills "**pharmed**" from their parents' medicine cabinets. This random collection of prescription medicine is often carried in baggies and then dumped into bowls of what is known as "**trail mix.**" Typically the teens share their trail mix with everyone else at the party, each grabbing a random handful of pills as they feel the desire (Jones, 2008).

Research on drug abuse among college students shows that Xanax and Valium—both antianxiety drugs—are the prescription drugs most often used for recreational purposes (Meadows, 2001). The drugs are easy to come by, work quickly, and often cause blackouts. Many college students drink while taking the pills, compounding the drugs' effects.

Along with Xanax and Valium, OxyContin has become a more popular choice as well. OxyContin is often prescribed for pain, but abusers take the drug while drinking alcohol to feel its narcotic effects. OxyContin has effects similar to those of heroin or opium, but is much cheaper—therefore, it is known among abusers as "**hillbilly heroin**" (Cahoun, Cox, & Chitale, 2008). OxyContin's popularity among addicts results from its long-lasting effects and easy ingestion. The drug provides a numbing sensation that can last up to 12 hours, and unlike heroin, OxyContin can be chewed in pill form, eliminating the need for painful injections.

Few parents realize that their own medicine cabinets house some of the most common drugs abused by teens today.

THE APPEAL OF MEDICALIZING HUMAN PROBLEMS. Though extreme, celebrity deaths pinpoint one of today's major drug problems: the abuse of legal prescription drugs. During the 1930s, the pharmaceutical industry began to manufacture psychoactive drugs, and production and use of these have increased significantly. Physicians now prescribe drugs for conditions that people used to assume were a normal part of life: anxiety and distress, feeling upset or uncertain, social unease, inability to concentrate, feeling "down," wrestling with perplexing problems, even sensing vague dissatisfactions or feelings of not "fitting in." All of these "normal emotions" have been redefined as "medical problems." This trend represents the medicalization of drug use. Before such drugs were available, the general attitude was that at some point we are all likely to confront problems like these, and we have to develop coping skills to deal with them. But with these drugs available, today's attitude is that ill feelings call for the use of prescription drugs. Sociologists call this **medicalizing human problems**—that is, offering a medical "solution" for the problems that people confront in everyday life.

Antidepressants and antianxiety drugs are a case in point. Effexor, Prozac, Valium, Xanax, and Zoloft promise help in getting through the problems of everyday life. Doctors prescribe these drugs for anxiety, depression, irritability, sleeplessness, restlessness, inability to concentrate, and even a pounding heart. Although the serenity offered by prescription drugs can be elusive, these drugs have side effects—as serious as suicidal tendencies.

The prescribing of legal drugs is highly profitable. Doctors make millions of dollars from scribbling the names of these drugs on little pieces of paper. Pharmacists make additional millions by counting the little pills and putting them in little bottles. The drug companies, of course, rake in billions of dollars from these drugs. Zoloft alone brings in $3 billion a year, while Effexor snags another $2.5 billion (Herper, 2006).

With so many people given the option of taking a pill to ease life's problems (and who wouldn't want all of their problems to disappear?), medicalizing everyday problems has given the power of diagnosing and treatment to the patient. In many cases, it is no longer the doctors who do the prescribing but, rather, the patients. Here's how it often works: Drug companies flood television and magazines with commercials for medications that you *cannot* buy over the counter. To get these drugs, you have to tell your doctor that you want that particular drug. This marketing strategy works. People see the commercials and imagine themselves living happy, carefree lives if they can just get their hands on Xanax, Prozac, or some other drug. Physicians don't want to lose business, so they write the prescriptions that their customers ask for. The doctors make money from writing—literally—millions of prescriptions. So do the pharmacists who eagerly fill them. And the drug companies laugh all the way to the bank.

The abuse of prescription drugs takes many forms, one of which includes the use of "club drugs." Use of club drugs is discussed in the Spotlight on Social Research box on page 93.

MEDICALIZING DEVIANT BEHAVIOR: PROBLEM KIDS AND REBELS. Imagine yourself sitting at your computer, crafting an e-mail message. Music playing in the background captures your attention—you drift off. The bell on your computer alerts you that a new e-mail message has arrived. This sudden alert jolts you back into focus; something interesting is happening. This daydreaming happens all the time, and you have quite a bit of trouble staying on task.

Scenes like this one, with endless variations, are played out across the United States every day in classrooms, in the workplace, and in homes. The American Psychiatric Association's (APA's) *Diagnostic and Statistical Manual of Mental Disorders,* Fourth Edition (DSM-IV), says that when a pattern of such behavior persists for 6 months or

Spotlight on Social Research
THE MIAMI CLUB CULTURE: PRESCRIPTION DRUG ABUSE AMONG ECSTASY USERS

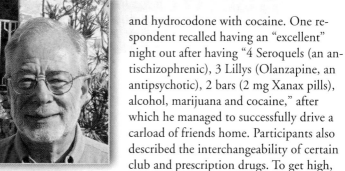

JAMES A. INCIARDI *is director of the Center for Drug and Alcohol Studies at the University of Delaware. He is also a member of the International Advisory Committee of the White House Office of National Drug Control Policy. His research focuses on substance abuse, criminal justice, and public policy.*

Miami, Florida, historically a major tourist destination—and since the 1970s a national center for cocaine importation, distribution, and use—is also a major player in the U.S. club drug scene. With the restoration of Miami's art deco districts and the popularity of the South Beach area, Miami has become an international destination for partying, sexual tourism, and club drug use. To a great extent, South Beach has also become an East Coast center for the club culture—setting trends that are replicated elsewhere in the United States, western Europe, and Latin America. The Drug Enforcement Administration has identified Miami as a destination for large amounts of prescription drugs that are channeled into the illegal marketplace. One of the more recent trends has been a significant incursion of prescription drugs into the club culture, accompanied by the health consequences associated with their abuse. To "get high," about 80% of ecstasy users in the Miami club culture appear to be using prescription narcotics (OxyContin, Vicodin, Percocet, and morphine), "downers" (Xanax and Valium), and stimulants (Ritalin and Adderall) (Kurtz et al., 2005).

To investigate this abuse of prescription drugs, we conducted focus groups with scores of young adults from a wide variety of racial–ethnic backgrounds. Although a few of the participants said that they had experimented with prescription drugs as early as their junior high years, most had recently begun to use prescription drugs to ease the "come down" from the "highs" produced by such party drugs as ecstasy, cocaine, ketamine, and methamphetamine. The demand for a "smooth landing" is so great that dealers often "package" ecstasy and methamphetamine with prescription depressants or narcotics. Antidepressants are also commonly used by ecstasy and methamphetamine users to ease withdrawal-related depression.

To achieve a "better high," prescription drugs are also used in *combination* with club drugs. Popular combinations include marijuana, Ritalin, and alcohol; prescription narcotics with methamphetamine and ecstasy; and hydrocodone with cocaine. One respondent recalled having an "excellent" night out after having "4 Seroquels (an antischizophrenic), 3 Lillys (Olanzapine, an antipsychotic), 2 bars (2 mg Xanax pills), alcohol, marijuana and cocaine," after which he managed to successfully drive a carload of friends home. Participants also described the interchangeability of certain club and prescription drugs. To get high, some would substitute phentermine (a diet drug) for methamphetamine; to feel drunk, they would substitute GHB for painkillers and combine this with alcohol. To ease withdrawal from stimulants, they used Xanax or marijuana.

Some participants described the practice of "colon rolling," also known as "booty bumping"—dissolving prescription and other drugs and then taking the solution rectally with an eye dropper or turkey baster. Some preferred this anal route of administration because it made the drugs' effects slower and more even. Of particular note in this regard was the "Royal Flush"—a dangerous combination of methamphetamine, ecstasy, and Viagra.

The focus group participants reported extremely diverse sources for obtaining the prescription drugs they abused. These included drug dealers, on the street and in nightclubs; HIV-positive patients, who have access to prescription medications through their physicians; parents and other relatives; pharmacy employees; online pharmacies; under-the-door apartment flyers advertising telephone numbers to call; Medicaid and Medicare fraud; doctor shopping; leftover supplies following an illness or injury; visits to Mexico, South America, and the Caribbean; prescriptions intended for treatment of drug dependence or mental illness; theft from pharmacies and hospitals; friends and acquaintances; and "stealing from grandma's medicine cabinet." All participants said they had no difficulty in obtaining prescription medications, although they were often happy to take what was available without seeking out a specific drug or brand name.

Those who relocated to Miami from other cities in the United States said that the illicit prescription drug market in Miami was much easier to navigate than the market in other places they had lived, including New York and Boston. They also said that street prices in Miami were much lower than those charged by online pharmacies.

Most participants described the "high" from prescription drugs as less exciting and less euphoric than that from illicit drugs, but they perceived prescription drugs to be purer, safer, more respectable, and more legal, as well as producing fewer withdrawal symptoms.

Note: This discussion was based, in part, on Kurtz et al. (2005).

longer and occurs in at least two different settings (e.g., in the classroom and at home), it may meet the criteria for a diagnosis of **attention-deficit/hyperactivity disorder (ADHD).** The combination of attention deficit and hyperactivity is common, but either can, and often does, occur without the other.

What, exactly, is ADHD? According to APA, this mental disorder is associated with distress and impairment of functioning resulting from some dysfunction within the individual. In the case of ADHD, the most quickly noticed behavioral and psychological patterns are hyperactivity and inattentiveness. Such children typically don't finish their homework, can't complete class assignments or exams in the time allowed, and are generally disorganized and forgetful. A diagnosis of ADHD requires that the symptoms have been present for at least 6 months, that they began before the child was 7 years old, and that they cause problems in both home and school (Iannelli, 2008). The adult version of the disorder shows the same patterns, rescaled to the tasks and settings of the grown-up world.

Existing data demonstrate that anywhere between 2% and 5% of the general population are living with ADHD symptoms (Barkley, 2006). The ADHD diagnosis has become highly controversial in recent years, with much of the controversy focused on the increasing use of the drug methylphenidate hydrochloride, an amphetamine, more popularly known by its trade name Ritalin, as the treatment of choice. Children in the United States now consume 90% of the 8.5 tons of methylphenidate produced worldwide each year. Ritalin is now being prescribed to 4 million schoolchildren in the United States (Livingston, 1997; Barkley, 2006).

Ritalin critics like child psychiatrist Carl L. Kline of the University of British Columbia state that Ritalin is "nothing more than a street drug being administered to cover the fact that we don't know what's going on with these children" (Livingston, 1997).

Pediatrician Julian Haber, author of *ADHD, The Great Misdiagnosis* (2000), claims that often children are misdiagnosed with ADD or ADHD because the diagnostic tests themselves are not valid. Symptoms of ADHD include a short attention span and hyperactivity. But having symptoms of ADHD does not necessarily mean that a child actually has the disease. Without valid measures, many children described as "hyper" or "out of control" by their teachers are wrongly classified as having ADHD. According to Haber, "the symptoms of ADHD may be present in more than thirty other disorders, [including] problems with the sensory systems, mental illness, or scholastic, psychosocial, and medical problems" (Haber, 2000). To be sure that a child actually has ADD or ADHD, children need to be thoroughly tested not only for this condition, but also for many others that Haber describes as "imitators." Imitators include things like hearing disorders and depression.

Those who view Ritalin favorably include many parents who give the drug to their children and appreciate the results. Ritalin administered at home is responsible for better behavior, improved performance at school, and less stress overall (Livingston, 1997). Treatment of ADHD with Ritalin also has been found to help children increase their sense of self-esteem (Konrad et al., 2004). Also, it has been reported that Ritalin treatment in childhood may prevent drug and alcohol abuse in adulthood (Biederman, 2003).

Whether ADHD is a true neurological condition is a medical issue; the social problem is that medicalizing human problems—thinking of them not as normal aspects of everyday life, but as a matter of "sickness"—has become so common that many people view it as part of the drug problem in the country. In their view, where we used to say that children who disrupted their classroom were *unruly* and in need of discipline by parents and school, we now label them *sick*—with an illness that medicine can cure.

FUNCTIONS AND DYSFUNCTIONS OF MEDICALIZING HUMAN BEHAVIOR. The functions of medicalizing disruptive behavior are obvious. "Drug therapy" helps authorities justify the confinement of the unruly. In the case of unruly children, most of the hundreds of thousands of American children who take Ritalin or other drugs for their "illness" sit still longer and appear to pay attention. The drugs work so well that doctors even prescribe

them for toddlers who are going through their "terrible twos" (Kalb, 2000). Treatment benefits not only the patient but teachers and parents as well.

There also are dysfunctions involved in the medicalizing of everyday life. Some schoolchildren get stuck with the label of hyperactive or mentally ill. For many, drug treatment brings with it horrible side effects: tics, lethargy, depression, even brain damage and cancer. There also are hallucinations, most commonly seeing or feeling snakes and worms (Harris, 2006, March 23). For younger toddlers who are medicalized to help *their parents* get through the "terrible twos," there is no recorded data. Their side effects are likely to be equally as unpleasant.

Because pills seem such a handy answer to problems that perplex us, medicalizing human problems has become a standard feature of contemporary life. If only we could find the perfect pill, our personal and social problems would disappear as we dip into the pharmacological treasury of medical miracles.

Illegal Drug Use by Students

HIGH SCHOOL. Let's look at some of the findings of sociologists who have studied the illegal drug use of high school students. We'll begin with Figure 4-1 below, which is based on a representative sample, allowing us to generalize these findings to all 8th-, 10th-, and 12th-graders in the United States. After reading the data, you will notice that during the past month about half of all U.S. high school seniors drank alcohol. In the last 30 days, about 3 in 10 got drunk.

You may think that high school seniors who have plans to attend college would abuse alcohol less than seniors with no future plans. You would be right! Look at Table 4-2 on page 96. From this table, you can see that high school seniors who plan on going to college use fewer drugs than those who don't. Although we know that college plans influence the decisions that high school seniors make, college attendance is also related to social class. The higher their parents' income, the more likely high school seniors are to head off to college (Carnevale & Rose, 2003). Drug use in high school, then, could be related more to social class than to future planning.

From Table 4-2, you may also notice that underage drinking is common—as though this would be a surprise. You may not have known, however, just how common marijuana smoking is among high school seniors. About 850,000 high school seniors

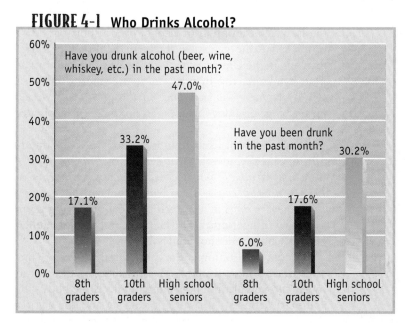

FIGURE 4-1 Who Drinks Alcohol?

Source: By James M. Henslin. Based on Johnston et al. (2006, Table 3).

TABLE 4-2 What Drugs Do High School Seniors Use? (in the last 30 days)

| | SEX | | COLLEGE PLANS | |
	M (%)	F (%)	None, or Less Than 4 Years (%)	4 years (%)
Alcohol	51.1%	45.1%	52.1%	47.0%
Been drunk	36.0	29.0	34.7	31.2
Alcohol daily	4.1	1.4	4.3	2.2
Cigarettes	25.3	24.1	36.8	21.6
Cigarettes daily	15.4	15.0	26.9	12.2
Marijuana	23.0	16.6	24.1	18.3
Marijuana daily	7.7	3.1	8.1	4.5
Amphetamines	4.6	4.5	6.5	4.0
Barbiturates (sedatives)	3.2	2.5	3.9	2.6
Powder cocaine	2.9	1.7	4.1	1.7
LSD	2.4	0.8	2.2	1.3
Steroids	2.1	1.0	2.5	1.3
Crack cocaine	1.2	0.7	1.9	0.7
Crystal meth (Ice)	1.1	0.6	1.8	0.5
Heroin	0.7	0.2	2.5	1.3

Source: By James M. Henslin. Based on Johnston et al. (2005, Tables 4-7, 4-8).

smoked marijuana during the past month. About 230,000 went to school stoned every day (Johnston et al., 2005, Tables 4-7, 4-8; *Statistical Abstract*, 2006, Table 211)!

COLLEGE. Now let's look at the drug use of college students. The representative sample on which Table 4-3 is based is generalizable enough to apply to *all* college students across the nation. Three main conclusions can be drawn from this data: (1) College students maintain the patterns of drug use they established in high school. (2) Alcohol is the most commonly used drug, followed by nicotine and marijuana. (3) Men use more illegal drugs than women.

College presidents agree that **binge drinking** is the *most serious problem* on campus. Binge drinking refers to the heavy consumption of alcohol over a short period of time. Today the generally accepted definition of binge drinking in the United States is the consumption of five or more drinks in a row by men—or four or more drinks in a row by women—at least once in the previous 2 weeks. Heavy binge drinking includes three or more such episodes in 2 weeks.

Students most likely to binge-drink are White fraternity or sorority members under the age of 23. *If they were binge drinkers in high school, they are three times more likely to binge in college.* Over half of binge drinkers binge *three or more times* in a 2-week period—qualifying them as heavy binge drinkers (Harvard School of Public Health College Alcohol Study, 2005).

Alcohol poisoning is the most life-threatening consequence of binge drinking. When someone drinks too much and gets alcohol poisoning, it affects the body's involuntary reflexes—including breathing and the gag reflex. If the gag reflex isn't working properly, a person can choke to death on his or her vomit.

TABLE 4-3 What Drugs Do Full-Time College Students Use? (in the last 30 days)

	TOTAL (%)	MEN (%)	WOMEN (%)
Alcohol	68.9%	70.2%	68.0%
Cigarettes	26.7	30.0	24.6
Marijuana	19.7	23.7	17.2
Amphetamines	3.0	3.2	2.8
Cocaine			
Powder	1.6	2.2	1.2
Crack	0.3	0.1	0.4
Ecstasy (MDMA)	0.7	0.9	0.7
LSD	0.2	0.4	0.1
Heroin[1]	0.0	0.0	0.0
Daily Use			
Cigarettes	15.9	16.6	15.4
Alcohol	5.0	7.0	3.7
Marijuana	4.1	5.7	3.0

[1] Certainly there are *some* college students who have used heroin in the past 30 days, but use of this drug is so rare that it does not register in this national survey of college students.

Source: By James M. Henslin. Based on Johnston et al. (2003, Tables 8-3, 8-4).

The Effects of Drugs

WHY DRUG EXPERIENCES DIFFER. Whether we are talking about college students or celebrities, the same drug can affect two people differently. Even when the same person takes a drug on different occasions, its effects can differ. What someone experiences from a drug depends on three main factors (Ray & Ksir, 2004). The first is the *drug*. Effects differ according to the amount of the drug, its quality, and how the drug is administered (ingested, smoked, shot into the bloodstream). The second is the *individual*. Effects can differ if users are anxious, depressed, or relaxed. They also differ according to individual body weight and metabolism, and for reasons yet unknown, drugs affect men and women differently (Acharyya & Zhang, 2003; Bell, 2006). The third factor is the *setting*, which can influence the individual's expectations and, in turn, can change a drug's effects.

We will use the example of LSD (lysergic acid diethylamide) to illustrate the effect a setting can have on a drug's outcome. When people first started using LSD, psychotic reactions and mass suicides made headlines across the nation. Sociologist Howard S. Becker (1967) studied the drug culture and found that people who took the LSD drug in its early days thought it would create panic—and they were expecting to experience panic. The subculture that was most often associated with LSD, hippies, educated new users on what to expect when taking LSD, so that when first-time users saw strange colors, walls breathing, or felt a unity with plants, their "trip guides" assured them that this was normal, that it was temporary, and that they should relax and enjoy the sensations. As a result, negative LSD experiences were replaced with positive ones. Trip guides educated the public and reduced mass panic surrounding the use of LSD and other mood-altering drugs.

Research Findings: The Recreational Mood Elevators

Alcohol

A little down? Want to feel better?
You feel fine, but you'd like to feel even finer?
A little uptight, and you want those problems to float away?
Going to a party, and you want to feel more at ease?
You want to get rid of tension?

When it comes to questions such as these, the answer seems to be an obvious yes. When Americans attempt to reduce anxiety, appear more sociable, or reduce tension, they most often reach for an alcoholic beverage. Each year, the average American drinks 25 gallons of alcoholic beverages—about 21.6 gallons of beer, 2.2 gallons of wine, and 1.3 gallons of hard liquor (*Statistical Abstract*, 2006, Table 201). The average alcoholic drinks *twice* this amount (*Statistical Abstract*, 2006, Table 194). Yes, you read that right: The average alcoholic consumes about 50 gallons of alcohol a year.

ALCOHOL CONSUMPTION AS A SOCIAL PROBLEM. About 10 million Americans are considered **alcoholics,** people who have severe alcohol-related problems. Relatively few of them wind up completely dysfunctional. Rather, almost all—whether working or middle class—continue with their routines but have impaired social relationships. Their work and loved ones suffer the most.

Alcohol abuse is so common that each year between 200,000 and 300,000 Americans are treated for alcoholism at substance abuse centers (*Statistical Abstract*, 2006, Table 193). The cost of such treatment runs several billion dollars a year, which everyone, including abstainers, must pay. If we consider reduced productivity and alcohol-related accidents, the total runs over $100 billion a year (Simon et al., 2005). Then, too, there are the costs of alcohol-related crime and social welfare. *These combined costs make*

alcohol the most expensive of all drug abuse problems. Alcohol abuse also brings with it those costs that cannot be measured in dollars—the abuse of spouse, family, children, and shattered marriages.

DRINKING AND MASCULINIZATION. As noted earlier, each year about 17,000 Americans die in alcohol-related car and truck wrecks. Most drunk drivers are young men. Why aren't just as many young women driving drunk? The basic reason centers on socialization in American culture. Men are taught that drinking is *macho,* a way by which young men prove their budding masculinity (Snow & Cunningham, 1985; Peele, 1987). Driving after drinking too much is often a symbol of male potency.

If American culture socialized women to believe that drunkenness represented femininity, we might have more young women drinking to excess. Based on data observations, this shift may be occurring. "Femininity" apparently is being redefined in more traditionally masculine terms. Getting drunk is now often part of a girl's rite of passage into womanhood. If this socialization pattern continues, we can also anticipate an increase in drunk driving accidents among women.

The liquor industry has also taken note of this increase in drinking by young women. Seizing the opportunity, the industry has targeted more of its advertising toward women—developing "feminine" beverages. "Alcopops," flavored premixed drinks that resemble alcohol-spiked soda, have become popular. Catering to this image of femininity, "Cocktails by Jenn" offers Lemon Drops and Blue Lagoon drinks for women. Never mind that "Jenn" is actually two men, Jason and Larry. These men have found that "Jenn" sells—especially when they make their drinks pastel-colored and put them in bottles with small metal charms—a high-heeled shoe, a purse, a diamond ring, and a heart (Ball & O'Connell, 2006).

HEALTH CONSEQUENCES OF DRINKING ALCOHOL. To adequately understand any social problem, we must examine sociological data—whether the results match preconceived notions or not. Research on alcohol, for example, shows both positive and negative consequences for one's health. Let's examine positive consequences first.

Light-to-moderate drinking—one to two drinks a day, 5 or 6 days a week—may have positive health consequences. Compared with people who don't drink alcohol, light-to-moderate drinkers have only one-third as many heart attacks (Rehm et al., 2003). Some researchers have found that 14 or more drinks a week are even better for people's health (Mukamal et al., 2006). Studies consistently show that red wine improves heart health. Whether someone drinks red wine, white wine, beer, whiskey, or vodka, alcohol stimulates production of HDL—"good" cholesterol.

Heavy binge drinking, on the other hand, increases the risk of sudden death from stroke and heart attacks (Rehm et al., 2003). Binge drinking is common, and within the next 30 days one-fifth of alcohol drinkers will binge-drink. Among drinkers between the ages 18 to 25, two of five will binge-drink during the next month (*Statistical Abstract,* 2006, Table 194).

Heavy drinkers are more likely to have heart attacks and problems with their endocrine, metabolic, immune, and reproductive systems. They are also more likely be diagnosed with diabetes, epilepsy, depression, cancer of the tongue, mouth, liver, lungs, esophagus, larynx, stomach, colon, and rectum. For women, heavy drinking increases the risk of breast cancer (*Seventh Special Report,* 1990; Rehm et al., 2003; Kruk & Aboul-Enein, 2006).

ALCOHOL, PREGNANCY, AND CHILDBIRTH. Embedded within this social problem is another problem, the use of alcohol by pregnant women. When a mother is pregnant and drinking, the alcohol enters the fetal circulatory system. Unlike the mother, however, a fetus cannot metabolize alcohol. When pregnant women drink, the alcohol becomes concentrated in the fetus's blood, raising its blood alcohol level to about *10 times* that of the mother.

The consequences of drinking while pregnant are anything but pleasant. Each year about 5,000 American babies are born with a cluster of problems called **fetal alcohol syndrome (FAS).** These children are born addicted to alcohol, and for a week

After Prohibition ended, Americans took advantage of their freedom to drink alcohol.

to 6 months they suffer painful withdrawal. They are irritable, their little hearts beat irregularly, and some go into convulsions. Brain damage reduces intelligence; corrupts learning, memory, speech, and coordination; and can cause lifelong disability (Howell et al., 2006). As you might expect, fetal alcohol syndrome occurs most often within groups that have higher rates of alcoholism. The most likely to suffer are Native Americans. The rate of FAS among Native Americans is 3 times the national average ("Congress," 1994; Carroll, 2000).

SIGNIFICANCE OF HOW PEOPLE LEARN TO DRINK. Social researchers have found that *how* one learns to drink is significant in setting the stage for having or not having alcohol-related problems. Studies of groups with low rates of alcoholism suggest five ways to ensure a low incidence of alcoholism (Hanson, 1995):

- Make drinking a regular part of life.
- View alcohol as neutral—neither poisonous or wonderful.
- Do not view drinking as a sign of adulthood or virility.
- Do not tolerate abusive drinking.
- Allow parents to provide an example of moderate (light, social, nonabusive) drinking.

These approaches are very important for teenagers newly exposed to alcohol. Handling alcohol in the ways described above can prevent alcoholism in the future. The following are most likely to lead to alcohol-related problems in the home:

- The family considers drinking alcohol as something special.
- Alcohol is viewed as either sinful or as a magical substance that makes the world more pleasant.
- Drinking is considered a sign of adulthood.
- The family looks at getting drunk as a favorable event.
- Family members learn to drink outside the home, in a sneaky manner.

BIOLOGY, SOCIOLOGY, AND ALCOHOL ADDICTION. Some research supports a biological basis for the development of alcoholism. Sons of alcoholic fathers run a higher risk than others of becoming alcoholics (Buck, 1998), and twins are more likely to have the same drinking patterns than nontwins (Prescott, 2004). As sociologists point out, however,

we cannot rule out *social* influences that may lead to alcoholism. Sons of alcoholic fathers, for example, may be following in the footsteps of alcoholic role models. As for twins, they grow up in environments so similar that they are likely to produce all sorts of similar behaviors. At this point, though, we can't rule out the possibility that biology makes a difference in how people's cells react to alcohol, predisposing some to alcohol abuse. The evidence that links alcoholism to genetics, however, is filled with contradictory findings.

Nicotine

Nicotine is the second most popular recreational drug in the United States. The surgeon general has identified smoking as "the chief, single, avoidable cause of death in our society, and the most important health issue of our time" (H. Smith, 1986). Tobacco is so harmful that "a nonsmoker has a better chance of reaching the age of 75 than a smoker has of reaching the age of 65" (Goode, 1989). Smoking costs the United States about $28 billion a year in health care and another $43 billion in lost wages.

The tobacco industry strives to recruit new smokers each year, spending $10 billion a year promoting cigarettes and chewing tobacco. Ad campaigns convince young people that smoking is sexy and adultlike (American Lung, 2003). Tobacco companies target youth, but perhaps none so brazenly as the company featured in the Global Glimpse box on the next page.

Teens think smoking is much more common, and thus acceptable, than it actually is. According to a survey, youth believe that about 62% of high school students are current smokers when, in fact, about 28% are. Similarly, the youth surveyed believe that about 64% of adults smoke, when national surveys show an adult smoking rate of 23%. Table 4-4 shows at the height of addiction, *most* men smoked, as did one of three women.

A new study confirms that fewer American kids are smoking and examines where those who do smoke get their cigarettes. According to a national survey of 8th–12th-graders, most kids get their cigarettes from friends or family members (Johnston, O'Malley, & Terry-McElrath, 2004). About 65% of children in each grade said they have friends or relatives buy them cigarettes.

TABLE 4-4 Cigarette Smoking by Sex and Age (percentage of population)

	1965	1975	1985	1995	2003
By Sex					
Male	52%	43%	33%	27%	24%
Female	34	32	28	23	19
By Sex and Age					
Males					
18–24 years	54	42	28	28	26
25–34 years	61	51	38	30	29
35–44 years	58	51	38	32	28
45–64 years	52	43	33	27	24
65 and over	29	25	20	15	10
Females					
18–24 years	38	34	30	22	22
25–34 years	44	39	32	26	21
35–44 years	44	40	32	27	24
45–64 years	32	33	30	24	20
65 and over	10	12	14	12	8

Source: By James M. Henslin. Based on *Statistical Abstract of the United States* (1994, Table 212; 1997, Table 221; 1998, Table 238; 2006, Table 190).

A Global Glimpse
FIRST DEATH, THEN SHAG: TARGETING COLLEGE STUDENTS

Every package of cigarettes sold in the United States contains a warning from the U.S. surgeon general. These are the four surgeon general's warnings that cigarette makers must rotate through on their packs:

- SURGEON GENERAL'S WARNING: Smoking Causes Lung Cancer, Heart Disease, Emphysema, and May Complicate Pregnancy.
- SURGEON GENERAL'S WARNING: Quitting Smoking Now Greatly Reduces Serious Risks to Your Health.
- SURGEON GENERAL'S WARNING: Smoking By Pregnant Women May Result in Fetal Injury, Premature Birth, and Low Birth Weight.
- SURGEON GENERAL'S WARNING: Cigarette Smoke Contains Carbon Monoxide.

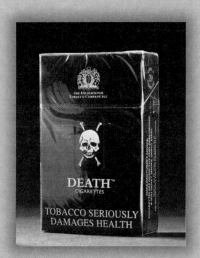

Americans assume these warnings couldn't possibly be true. After all, those thousands of happy, carefree young people who are smoking cigarettes in those countless ads wouldn't be happy and smiling if cigarettes really killed people. There are some companies who aim to get smokers to quit, and others who aim to make as much profit as possible. Death and Shag are two examples of polar opposite approaches in the world of cigarette ad campaigns.

In the 1990s, the Enlightened Tobacco Company of England began an advertising campaign called Death. They put cigarettes into black packages emblazoned with white skull and crossbones. The death logo was also stamped near the filter of each cigarette. Ads for Death were bordered in black, resembling funeral announcements. The company's position was that the tobacco industry has the right to sell cigarettes, people have the right to smoke, and smokers should know what they are doing to their bodies. To openly advertise death, they said, is morally superior to telling half-truths, being deceptive, or giving unbelievable health warnings.

In an effort to sell as many cigarettes as possible to college students, another tobacco company in Great Britain introduced a brand of cigarettes called Shag (British slang for sexual intercourse). The company's slogan: "Have you had one lately?" To promote Shag, the company handed out free samples to college students, along with a wink and a free Shag condom (Murray, 2004). Death and Shag—each a different approach in the world of advertising—represent the tobacco industry's influence in the market. But no matter how one tries to sell boxes of nicotine, smoking kills.

About half of all Americans who continue to smoke will die because of the habit, with 438,000 people dying each year from illnesses related to cigarette smoking. *Cigarettes kill more Americans than alcohol, car accidents, suicide, AIDS, homicide, and illegal drugs combined.* Death from smoking isn't merciful—nicotine deaths are agonizing and slow—often the result of emphysema.

Cigarette smoking accounts for at least 30% of all cancer deaths. It is a major cause of cancers of the lung, larynx (voice box), oral cavity, pharynx (throat), esophagus (swallowing tube connected to the stomach), and bladder, and it contributes to the development of cancers of the pancreas, cervix, kidney, and stomach, as well as to some types of leukemia. Smoking is responsible for about 87% of lung cancer deaths. Lung cancer is the leading cause of cancer death in both men and women, and is one of the most difficult cancers to treat. Only about half of the deaths related to smoking are from cancer. Smoking is also a major cause of heart disease, aneurysms, bronchitis, emphysema, and stroke, and it makes pneumonia and asthma worse.

Increasing knowledge about health problems related to smoking has aroused widespread subjective concern and legislation. These concerns have given birth to a strident, powerful antismoking campaign. Among the results are no-smoking sections in restaurants and a ban on smoking in offices, on flights, on buses, in government buildings—and, in some states, in virtually any public place, including bars. (Some of you will find this difficult to believe, but prior to this campaign, professors and students used to smoke in class.) The decline has been precipitous, to one of four men and one of five women.

FIGURE 4-2 Number of Cigarettes That Americans Age 18 and Older Smoke Each Year

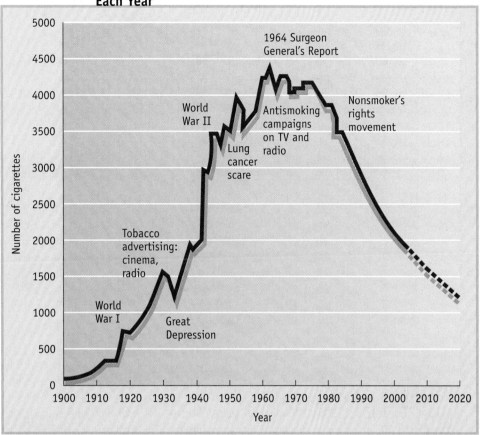

Source: By James M. Henslin. Based on Economic Research Service, U.S. Department of Agriculture, *Statistical Abstract of the United States* (2006, Table 989); projection by James M. Henslin.

The lowest rate of smoking—among those age 65 and over—does not represent results from the antismoking campaign. Rather, by this age so many smokers have died that there aren't many smokers left alive.

Figure 4-2 above depicts the sharp decline in smoking since tobacco awareness campaigns reached their peak. In a strange twist of logic, the tobacco industry itself claims credit for this decrease in smoking, stating that the decline is the result of its efforts "to deter youths from smoking" ("Frequent Tobacco Use" 1992)! For another perspective, read the Issues in Social Problems box on pages 104 and 105, which discusses the targeting of kids and minorities.

With Americans smoking less, tobacco companies face a shrinking market. Since they don't want to go out of business altogether, these companies are now turning to the Least Industrialized Nations to recruit new smokers. Many men in these countries already smoke, so the tobacco companies are recruiting women as new smokers (Preidt, 2003; Bansal et al., 2005). The global death toll from what is being called the *brown plague* is 5 million deaths a year, the result of tobacco sales. Most of these victims are men who live in the Least Industrialized Nations, but with women the new targets of heavy advertising, it is likely the death toll will increase.

Because the health care costs of tobacco victims fall largely on the government in the form of higher Medicaid bills, tobacco companies were sued by the individual states. In exchange for dropping their suits, each state was awarded $209 billion from cigarette manufacturers to be spent on health care. This huge settlement, to be paid over 25 years, insured that not a single cigarette company would be put out of business. To cover their settlement costs, cigarette manufacturers merely raised prices of cigarettes for their

addicted smokers. Since then the states have spent only about half of their award on health care, diverting the other funds to a variety of projects (GAO Delineates, 2003).

Marijuana

The third most popular recreational drug in the United States is marijuana, used almost as much as alcohol and nicotine. Marijuana once was used by only a few adventurous souls. Then came the norm-bending 1960s, and with it rebellious youth who embraced this drug. By 1979, one of three Americans ages 18 to 25 smoked marijuana at least once a month. Since then, the popularity of marijuana has dropped by half, and today 17% of Americans smoke marijuana this often (*Statistical Abstract*, 1998, Table 237; 2006, Table 194).

When marijuana surged in popularity during the 1960s, government officials panicked, thinking that the country was going to hell in a handbasket. The states didn't know what to do, so they each took their usual course of action and passed legislation banning marijuana use. While Nevada made the possession of even a single joint punishable by up to six years in prison, Alaska legalized the possession of marijuana for personal consumption (Goode, 1989, 30). Then both states decided they had made a mistake. Alaskans revoked their law, and Nevadans lightened up, making the possession of up to one ounce of marijuana punishable only by fines, with no jail time allowed.

Although marijuana has declined in overall popularity, it remains a common drug. As mentioned earlier, about 13 million Americans smoke marijuana. Figure 4-3 below summarizes marijuana use among high school and college students.

HEALTH CONSEQUENCES OF MARIJUANA USE. How does marijuana affect its users' health? Many assertions have been made—that marijuana harms the body's immune system, reduces male sex hormones, lowers fertility, damages chromosomes, and causes brain damage. Recent studies have not confirmed all of these previous findings.

We do know for sure that, as with cigarettes, smoking marijuana does damage the respiratory system. A study of 7,000 Americans showed that marijuana smokers suffer from more bronchitis, coughing, and wheezing than do nonsmokers (Moore et al., 2004). We are also certain that smoking marijuana impairs motor coordination and reduces awareness of external stimuli, such as red lights or stop signs (Carroll, 2000). As a consequence, people who drive after smoking marijuana are up to 7 times more likely to have an accident (Ramaekers et al., 2004).

FIGURE 4-3 Who Smokes Marijuana?

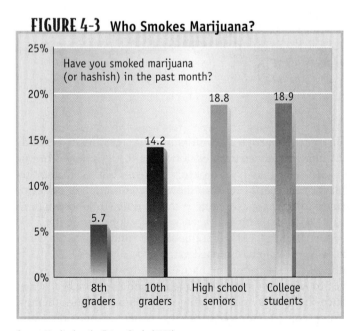

Source: Monitoring the Future Study (2007).

Issues in Social Problems
TARGETING KIDS AND MINORITIES

Let's listen to a conversation between Kent Reynolds, the CEO of a major tobacco company, and Chester Winston, director of sales.

"Chester, I want to show you something. My daughter brought this social problems text home from college. Look at this table on page 100."

"Yeah, that confirms our own studies. Our customer base is eroding. Too many people believe those lies the (expletive deleted) antismokers are telling—cancer and all that. We've got to get the kids started earlier."

"What've you got in mind?"

"Well, if we could get the kids hooked—I mean started . . . I was thinking about adding some flavor they like."

"Good idea. They've already added cherry to Skoal Long Cut. That's getting to a lot of kids. And they've been smart about it—keeping the nicotine down so the kids gradually get into it. Then they move on to Copenhagen after they're hooked—I mean, used to the taste. No one's done chocolate yet. Kids love chocolate."

"If you okay it, we can test-market Chocolate Smokeless Tobacco. And, of course, chocolate-flavored cigarettes. And we might try butterscotch and raspberry. We'll make 'em all low-nicotine and low-tar."

"What about the minorities?"

"We're already loading *Ebony* with ads. My research department reported that one of eight pages of *Ebony*'s color ads go to cigarettes."

"Great. How about sponsoring cultural events, like a jazz festival?"

"Kool's already got that covered."

"Come to think of it, Parliament's already got that World Beat Concert Series, too."

"Yeah, but we're underwriting the Harlem Week Festival in New York City."

"And don't forget all the money we're using to buy—I mean, contribute—to the National Black Caucus of State Legislatures."

"And the United Negro College Fund and the National Urban League are already in our budget."

The "Joe Camel" cigarette campaign may no longer be used after R. J. Reynolds Tobacco Company was charged with targeting youth.

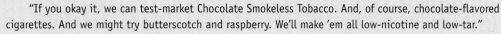

Although THC, the primary psychoactive agent in marijuana, remains in the body several days after smoking, its lingering effects are not noticeable to the smoker. In one study, pilots were tested 24 hours after they had smoked marijuana. Although they reported that they no longer felt the effects of THC, they showed deterioration in performing simulated landing maneuvers. Perhaps most telling is this finding: In a posthumous sample of 400 male drivers in California who had been killed in auto accidents, 37% had THC in their blood (Goode, 1989, p. 147). It seems safe to conclude that it is not prudent to ride or to fly with someone who has smoked marijuana.

Research findings are not all supportive of the harm created by THC. For example, marijuana has been proven to relieve symptoms of glaucoma and migraine headaches. Marijuana also helps to reduce the nausea and vomiting of patients in chemotherapy. Marijuana also relieves "asthma, epilepsy, muscle spasticity, anxiety, depression, pain, reduced appetite, and withdrawal from alcohol and narcotics" (Carroll, 2000).

"Sometimes I wonder if all this money is paying off."

"Don't worry about that! You never see any of that antismoking propaganda in *Ebony*—and that's no coincidence."

"I've never even seen a copy. But I depend on you to know these things, Chester."

"Well, the real payoff is that African American men are smoking more than the Whites."

"What about the women?"

"Sorry. Despite everything we've done, they've got the lowest rate of smoking."

"We've got to do better, Chester."

"We will."

"But we've got to be careful. They're starting to blame us for Blacks having higher rates of lung cancer and heart disease and stuff like that!"

"It's their soul food, Kent."

"What about Latinos?"

"Marlboro's got them pretty well covered. Remember those rodeos for Mexican Americans they sponsor in California?"

"That's right."

"And we're already buying off—I mean, contributing—all that money to the Hispanic Congressional Caucus and the National Association of Hispanic Journalists."

"How about the Native Americans, then? Maybe we're missing them."

"I think you've got something there. And the Chinese Americans, too. And then there's the Abyssinian Americans and the . . ."

"I'd like to bypass all that race and gender stuff and just target three-year-olds of every background."

"I'll get to work on that right away. I know it can be done. Ninety percent of 6-year-olds used to be able to match Joe Camel with Camel cigarettes. Too bad they can't use Joe any more." (laughs)

"Maybe we can make a kid's nicotine gum—just a little nicotine in the spearmint."

"Now you're talking."

"Yeah. And how about cute cutouts of our cigarette packs for the preschools—and maybe coloring books, too!"

"We can give the kids free colors in flip-top boxes that look like our cigarette packs."

"Great idea! We can call 'em Kiddie Packs. Maybe we can wrap the colors in white paper."

"Maybe we can include a play cigarette lighter, too."

That night both Kent and Chester enjoy their well-earned, peaceful sleep, dreaming of chocolate-flavored cigarettes, and butterscotch, and raspberry, and . . .

Based on Johnson (1992); Freedman (1994); Pollay (1997); *Statistical Abstract* (2006, Table 190).

To uncover marijuana's total effects, both positive and negative, we need further research. In today's political climate, however, such research is discouraged because of marijuana's social stigma.

ADDICTION AND MARIJUANA. When smoking marijuana reached the height of its popularity a generation ago, alarmed parents and officials warned youth that it was addictive. Those who smoked THC scoffed, saying that they could quit at any time. And they were right—or at least most of them were.

Recent research, however, shows that some marijuana smokers can't quit. Apparently some smokers do become dependent on cannabis, or THC, the active ingredient in marijuana. They become preoccupied with making certain that they are able to smoke every day, and they suffer symptoms of withdrawal when they try to stop smoking. Researchers estimate that 2% to 3% of marijuana smokers become addicted within

A man smokes a giant marijuana joint at a rave party during the annual Amsterdam Cannabis Cup, also known as the World Marijuana Championship.

2 years of smoking their first joint, that at some point up to 10% of smokers become cannabis-dependent (Roffman & Stephens, 2006). This means that more than 250,000 Americans are addicted to marijuana.

SOCIAL CONSEQUENCES OF MARIJUANA USE. When analyzing the long-term effects of marijuana use, researchers have discovered that marijuana smokers tend to receive poorer grades than those who don't smoke this drug, and they are more likely to drop out of high school (Kleinman et al., 1987; Fergusson et al., 2003). As we have learned throughout this text, when we analyze social problems, we must examine them from all perspectives.

For example, stating that those who smoke marijuana will do poorly in school is not representative of the complete picture. Compared with their classmates, heavy marijuana smokers are more likely to come from broken homes, to drink more alcohol, to commit more delinquent acts, and to be involved in a subculture that places less value on academic achievement. In other words, we can't be assured that pot smoking alone leads to poor performance. Marijuana smoking may be just "one element in a large and complex picture of interrelated problems and behaviors" (Kleinman et al., 1987; White, 1991).

Marijuana is associated with **amotivational syndrome**—heavy marijuana smokers become lethargic, lose their concentration, and drift away from long-range goals. The evidence for amotivational syndrome exists in narrative analysis and in monkey studies. One such narrative reads, "Before she smoked grass, Shirley had so many plans, but look at her now."

Several studies have examined the effects of marijuana addiction in monkeys. Researchers exposed the monkeys to THC and then measured their desire to go for bananas. Those monkeys that were given marijuana seemed less active than the monkeys that weren't exposed to marijuana. When researchers took the THC away from the exposed monkeys, their motivation returned to normal (Slikker, 1992). Although this study highlights monkey behavior, amotivation is a serious consequence of anyone engaged in heavy marijuana smoking.

SUBJECTIVE REACTIONS. Marijuana certainly is an excellent example of the subjective nature of social problems. Reactions are so subjective that they range from perceiving marijuana as a threat to society to viewing it as a treatment for medical problems. Until 1937, when the Marijuana Tax Act was passed, marijuana was an ingredient in about 30 medicines (Carroll, 2000). Physicians prescribed marijuana to treat a variety of conditions. If doctors did so today, they would be prosecuted. The possession of marijuana used to be legal for anyone in any state, but now marijuana possession is subject to punishment in all states.

Today, 13 million Americans pay illegal distributors to give them marijuana. At the same time, thousands of enforcement agents are arresting upwards of 87,000 distributors and 625,000 smokers and seizing 2.5 million pounds of marijuana each year (*Statistical Abstract*, 2006, Tables 318, 319).

Cocaine

THE SOCIAL HISTORY OF COCAINE. As with other drugs, cocaine has not always been viewed the way it is now. When the Spaniards invaded Peru in the 1500s, they conquered a people who chewed coca leaves. They witnessed many ill effects among the people and attributed them to the devil. The Spaniards at that time referred to cocaine as the "devil drug."

As more Europeans were exposed to the drug, cocaine gained social approval. By the late 1800s, physicians were praising cocaine, using it for medicinal purposes. Coca leaves

were a common ingredient in patent medicines. Famous people, such as Sigmund Freud, the founder of psychoanalysis, and Sir Arthur Conan Doyle, the creator of Sherlock Holmes, swore that cocaine got their creative juices going. When Angelo Mariana, a French chemist, introduced a wine that contained the coca leaf extract, the pope enjoyed the wine so much that he presented Mariana with a medal (Ray & Ksir, 2004). At this time, hundreds of thousands of Americans were sipping cocaine as a "pick-me-up," for cocaine had become an ingredient in Coca-Cola, a drink that is named after the coca leaf.

Yet by 1910, cocaine had been transformed from a medicine and a "pick-me-up" into a dangerous drug, much as Dr. Jekyll became Mr. Hyde—a story, by the way, that was written in three days by Robert Louis Stevenson while he was high on cocaine (Ashley, 1975). What led to the drug's downfall?

In the late 1800s, reporters began to link cocaine with poverty and criminal behavior. The media stated that gunmen used cocaine to get up their nerve to commit robberies (Ashley, 1975). These news stories led to public outcry, and in 1903 the Coca-Cola Company found it prudent to eliminate cocaine from its drink. Even today, however, Coca-Cola contains an extract from the coca leaf (Miller, 1994) In the early 1900s, it was still legal to use cocaine in products, but the products had to list it as an ingredient. Then in 1914, the Harrison Act classified cocaine as a narcotic (an error, because cocaine is a stimulant), making it illegal to sell or purchase the drug.

THE BLACK MARKET IN COCAINE. The Harrison Act paved the way for cocaine to be sold on the black market, a market that still exists today. The black market distributes cocaine effectively: About 15% of Americans age 12 and over—about 37 million people—have used cocaine, and about 2.5 million use this drug at least once a month (*Statistical Abstract*, 2006, Tables 12, 194). As we saw in Tables 4-2 and 4-3, in an average month 4% of all U.S. high school seniors and 2% of college students use cocaine. Though snorting is the preferred method of use, smoking cocaine base, called *freebasing*, is also popular.

USES OF COCAINE. Cocaine has a distinctive medical use. Surgeons apply cocaine as a local anesthetic and as a vasoconstrictor (a substance that reduces blood flow to the area to which it is applied). The drug is so effective that cocaine is the medical profession's anesthetic of choice for surgery involving the nose, throat, larynx, and lower respiratory passages. The most common use of cocaine, however, is to obtain a high—feelings of well-being, optimism, confidence, competence, and energy. Cocaine also has a reputation as an aphrodisiac; it is thought to create or heighten sexual desires, to increase sexual endurance, and to cure frigidity and impotence (Inciardi, 1986, pp. 78–79).

From the coca plant comes an abundance of legal products: soap, shampoo, toothpaste, flour, tea, calcium and iron supplements, hair growth supplements (Forero, 2006). Evo Morales, the president of Bolivia, the source of most cocaine, is a farmer of the coca plant. He argues that legal coca products should be accepted in the international commodities market. He wants to continue growing coca for legitimate purposes. U.S. government officials refuse to accept such a proposal because they want all coca plants eradicated.

DYSFUNCTIONS OF COCAINE. Cocaine's "high" is intense. Those who become addicted to cocaine report a craving so strong that "they will give up many of the things they value—money, possessions, relationships, jobs, and careers—in order to continue taking the drug" (Goode, 1989, pp. 198–199). In one form of cocaine—*crack*—the pleasure is so intense it is akin to orgasm. The high, which lasts from 5 to 12 minutes, is followed by a "crash" that leaves its users irritable, depressed, nervous, or paranoid. Crack is initially inexpensive, but users find that throughout life it is extremely costly—costly in the form of lost relationships. The desire for the intense pleasure is so great that some women rent their bodies for crack; and, as we saw in Chapter 3, a form of prostitute, the "crack whore," has emerged.

Singer Amy Winehouse is now suffering from the early stages of incurable lung disease due to her crack cocaine addiction.

Cocaine also creates health dysfunctions, including heart attacks, brain damage, and death (Kozel, 1996; Julien, 2001). Another dysfunction stimulating subjective concerns is the effect of a user's drug habit on her unborn child. "Crack babies" describe those fetuses born addicted to cocaine because of their mother's drug addiction while pregnant. To an unborn fetus the drug's concentration can equal or exceed that of the mother. The cocaine can interfere with the normal development of the heart, brain, and other organs. It can also cause the brain to bleed (Julien, 2001). In an attempt to prevent "crack babies," some authorities are following the controversial social policy discussed in the Thinking Critically about Social Problems box below.

CRACK COCAINE. Again, crack is inexpensive and can be produced easily in a home kitchen. With huge profits at stake, illegal drug entrepreneurs ("corner crack dealers") fight for territory ("turf") and customers. As a result, violence surrounds crack—coming from those who will do anything to get the drug and from those who will do anything to make money from selling the drug.

Crack cocaine's social history includes racial injustice. In 1986, the U.S. Congress made selling crack a federal offense. With the new law, judges began to give longer jail and prison sentences for cheap crack than for expensive powder cocaine. Because powder cocaine is more likely to be used by Whites and crack by African Americans (Lewis, 1996; Riley, 1998), Blacks charged the courts with racial discrimination. After 8 years of prison sentences that

THINKING CRITICALLY about Social Problems

ON PREGNANCY, DRUGS, AND JAIL

Consider the following court cases.

A pregnant woman in Washington, DC, was charged with check forgery. The usual sentence for first-time offenders is probation. When the woman tested positive for cocaine, the judge sentenced her to prison, saying, "I'm going to keep her locked up until the baby's born."

A California woman who had taken street drugs was charged with child abuse after she delivered a brain-damaged baby who died soon after birth.

An Illinois woman was charged with manslaughter when her 2-day-old infant died because she had snorted cocaine during pregnancy.

In Florida, a woman was convicted of two counts of delivering drugs to a minor. The prosecution alleged that the woman had passed cocaine to her newborn child through the umbilical cord after the baby was delivered but before the cord was cut.

In Texas, 18 pregnant women were charged with delivering drugs to their unborn children, using the umbilical cord as the delivery vehicle.

FOR YOUR CONSIDERATION

Should judges jail a pregnant woman because she uses drugs such as cocaine that can harm her fetus? If so, because alcohol and nicotine can harm a fetus, should judges jail pregnant women who smoke cigarettes or drink alcohol? If not, what's the difference?

In 2006, a Texas Appeals Court overturned convictions of two pregnant women for transferring drugs to their fetuses. What do you think about their conviction? About their conviction being overturned?

Based on Broff (1989); Humphries et al. (1992); Pagelow (1992); Chen (2006).

were handed down primarily to African American users, in *U.S. v. Ricky Davis* (1994) the U.S. District Court in Georgia declared that crack and powder cocaine are one and the same drug. Now sentences imposed for the use of crack can be no heavier than those imposed for the use of powder cocaine.

PRINCIPLES UNDERLYING A DRUG'S SOCIAL REPUTATION. From this brief social history of cocaine, we can see that several principles are involved in determining a drug's level of acceptability:

1. A drug's level of acceptance is not based on objective conditions. It does not, for instance, derive from experimental tests showing that one drug is more physically harmful than another. If such a scientific approach characterized a drug's social history, alcohol would be banned, and marijuana would be available in grocery stores (Ashley, 1975).
2. Like humans, drugs gain their reputation and acceptance through the types of people with which they are associated.
3. Drugs that are associated with respectable people are more likely to be defined as good and desirable, while drugs associated with poor people or deviants are likely to be defined as bad and undesirable.
4. The reputation or social acceptability of drugs changes over time.

Although illegal, drugs continue to be smuggled into and out of the country, satisfying the high demand.

Research Findings: The Hallucinogens

LSD

Perhaps the most famous of the hallucinogens is LSD (lysergic acid diethylamide). This drug was first synthesized in 1938 by Albert Hoffman, a Swiss chemist. Hoffman discovered that LSD was psychoactive when he accidentally inhaled a minute dose of the drug. Here is what he says happened to him:

> Last Friday, April 16, 1943, I was forced to stop my work in the laboratory in the middle of the afternoon and to go home, as I was seized by a peculiar restlessness associated with a sensation of mild dizziness. Having reached home, I lay down and sank in a kind of drunkenness which was not unpleasant and which was characterized by extreme activity of imagination. As I lay in a dazed condition with my eyes closed (I experienced daylight as disagreeably bright) there surged upon me an uninterrupted stream of fantastic images of extraordinary plasticity and vividness and accompanied by an intense, kaleidoscope-like play of colors. This condition gradually passed off after about two hours. (Hoffman, 1968, pp. 184–185)

Until 1960, LSD was thought to produce psychoses, and therefore people avoided it. Then Timothy Leary, a Harvard professor, began experimenting with LSD. After Leary was fired for violating experimental guidelines, he became a guru of the 1960s youth drug counterculture. Leary's message was that that everyone should take some LSD to experience changed consciousness and become nonconformist. Leary's slogan, "turn on, tune in, and drop out," struck a responsive chord with the youth of the time, and LSD use became widespread.

This tasteless, odorless substance, an ounce of which contains 300,000 doses, reached its height of media attention in the mid-1960s with the hippie culture (Goode, 1989, pp. 178–179). As we saw in Table 4-2 on page 96, about 3.2% of U.S. high school seniors took LSD within the past month. Although this is a small percentage, it totals about 60,000 high school seniors. The 0.2% of college students who used LSD in the past month equals about 30,000 students (*Statistical Abstract*, 2006, Table 204).

Peyote and Mescaline

The use of peyote is an old custom widely practiced among Native Americans. Native Americans were using this cactus product on the continent in the 1500s. In the United States today, peyote can be used legally—but only by members of the Native American Church for religious purposes (Schaefer, 2004). About 20 states forbid any use of peyote (Carroll, 2000). Mescaline, synthesized from peyote, produces similar effects. Both peyote and mescaline have had famous proponents: Havelock Ellis (1897, 1902) was enthusiastic about peyote, and Aldous Huxley (1954) sang the praises of mescaline. In the 1960s and 1970s, anthropologist Carlos Castaneda (1968, 1971, 1974) popularized the use of peyote among a cultlike following.

Psilocybin

The magic mushrooms of Mexico (*Psilocybe mexicana*) were also being used in the Americas in the 1500s. Because the mushrooms were associated with pagan rituals, rulers launched religious campaigns against them, causing a decline in their use. In the 1930s it was discovered that natives of southern Mexico were still using the mushrooms. Their active ingredient is psilocybin, which was isolated by Albert Hoffman in 1958 and later synthesized. As with peyote, reports about the effects of this drug often contain a spiritual or religious emphasis (Ray & Ksir, 2004).

A package of "magic" mushrooms bought legally from a store in Tokyo's trendy Shibuya district is displayed. Under Japanese drug laws, the compound that makes them hallucinogenic is illegal, but the mushrooms themselves are not.

PCP

PCP (phencyclidine hydrochloride), also called *angel dust,* was synthesized in 1957 by Parke-Davis and sold as a painkiller. As people soon discovered, this drug produces hallucinations. Because PCP requires little equipment to manufacture, it is often made in home laboratories. PCP affects the central nervous system, making it difficult to speak. It is known to produce altered body images and feelings of unreality. Some users report feeling euphoria and a sense of power, loneliness, or isolation. Others experience numbness and even feelings of dying (which is why users refer to PCP as "embalming fluid"). Higher dosages may result in loss of inhibition, disorientation, rage, convulsions, or coma (Crider, 1986; Ray & Ksir, 2004).

Ecstasy

Ecstasy (MDMA, methylenedioxyamphetamine) is a popular party drug. Ecstasy gives its user a euphoric rush like that of cocaine combined with some of the mind-altering effects of psychedelics. Users report that Ecstasy relaxes them, increases empathy and feelings of intimacy, and enhances sensual experiences, such as making touching more pleasurable. Side effects for some users are mental confusion and anxiety. The main concern about this drug, though, is that it may act as a toxic substance and cause permanent brain damage (Carroll, 2000).

Research Findings: The Amphetamines, Barbiturates, and Heroin

Amphetamines

Amphetamines—Benzedrine, Dexedrine, Methedrine, Desoxyn, Biphetamine, and Dexamyl—are often referred to as "uppers," "pep pills," "bennies," "dexies," "speed," "meth," "crystal," and "ice" (Carroll, 2000). Discovered in 1887, Benzedrine

became popular in the 1920s in over-the-counter inhalers intended to dilate the bronchial tubes. Later Benzedrine was available by prescription in tablet form for hyperkinesis and, in 1939, as an appetite suppressant. During World War II, the military gave amphetamines to soldiers to help them stay awake. At this time, people began to abuse the amphetamine from Benzedrine inhalers, and amphetamine abuse was born.

"Speed" (methamphetamine dissolved in liquid) is used by "speed freaks," who inject the drug, sometimes every 2 or 3 hours, for "runs" of 3 or 4 days. Each injection of this kind produces a "rush" or "flash," a sudden feeling of intense pleasure, followed by moderate feelings of euphoria. Some users hallucinate, while others develop feelings of paranoia, or become hostile and aggressive—symptoms that have been called the *amphetamine psychosis* (Ray & Ksir, 2004). Heavy amphetamine use is sometimes accompanied by behavioral fixations—a person repeating an activity over and over, such as counting the corn flakes in a box of cereal or cleaning the same room over and over again. Amphetamine withdrawal brings with it outbursts of aggression, feelings of terror, and thoughts of suicide or homicide (Carroll, 2000; Julien, 2001).

"Meth" addiction has become a growing epidemic across the country. Meth can be easily made at home using ordinary household items like Sudafed (pseudoephedrine, a common nonprescription cold or sinus medicine), matches, aluminum foil, and charcoal. Meth users experience such severe side effects—including high blood pressure and high fevers—that they have become a burden to the emergency services of hospitals (Zernike, 2006). Officials are so concerned about meth addiction and meth manufacturing that the White House Office of National Drug Control Policy runs television advertisements to discourage meth use, and a provision of the Patriot Act forces states to now restrict purchases of pseudoephedrine (Tierney, 2006).

Barbiturates

In 1862, Dr. A. Bayer of Munich, Germany (the Bayer of aspirin fame), combined urea with malonic acid and made a new compound, barbituric acid, from which over 2,500 drugs have since been derived. Of these, phenobarbital (Luminal), amobarbital (Amytal), pentobarbital (Nembutal), and secobarbital (Seconal) are best known. Medically, barbiturates are used as anesthetics or for treatment of anxiety, insomnia, and

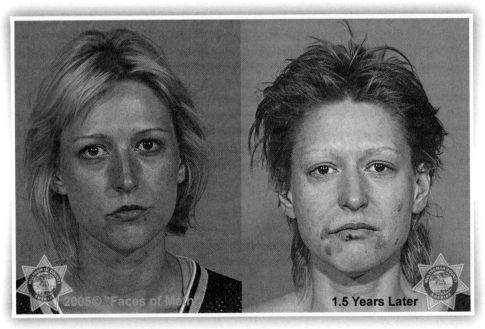

These photos are of the same person—before and after meth addiction. For some, it takes but a couple of years or less for this type of transition to occur.

epilepsy. Used for nonmedical purposes, the barbiturates provide an experience similar to that of alcohol. Regular barbiturate use leads to physical dependence. Withdrawal causes nausea, anxiety, sweating, dizziness, trembling, muscular twitching, and sometimes convulsions, coma, and death. Because the risk of death is higher for those who stop "cold turkey" (abruptly), physicians usually substitute a long-lasting barbiturate and then withdraw it slowly (Ray & Ksir, 2004).

Heroin

Flowers in our culture often come to be associated with emotion: Red roses symbolize love, and black lilies symbolize death. The social reputation of one flower became so negatively associated with drug use that in 1901 it was illegal to import it. By 1942, Americans couldn't even grow this flower without getting a license from the secretary of the Treasury. Government officials even made it possible to execute someone who sold derivatives of the flower to anyone under age 18 (Ray & Ksir, 2004).

What flower is this? It is the opium poppy. The derivative of the opium plant that is so feared and hated is heroin. The process by which opium yields heroin, illustrated by Figure 4-4, has been simplified by Afghans, who filter opium juice through a flour sack and dry it in the sun (Shishkin & Crawford, 2006).

As you probably know, Western nations decided years ago that to stop the heroin trade, they had to go to the source and destroy the poppy fields. If you've ever wondered why there is always plenty of heroin for those who want it, despite the money spent by Western governments to eradicate the poppy fields, read the Global Glimpse box on page 114.

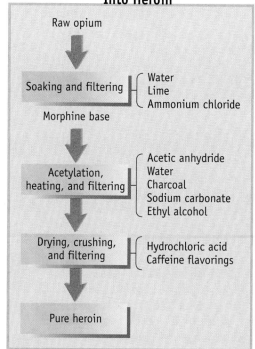

FIGURE 4-4 How Opium Is Converted Into Heroin

Source: By James M. Henslin, based on *Newsday* (1974) and Drug Enforcement Agency (2001).

ADDICTION TO HEROIN. The common view regarding heroin is that it is so addictive and the withdrawal pains so severe that addicts will do anything to avoid such withdrawal. Here is how novelist William Burroughs (1975, p. 135) described his own addiction:

> Junk (heroin) yields a basic formula of . . . total need. . . . Beyond a certain frequency need knows absolutely no limit or control. In the words of total need: "Wouldn't you?" Yes you would. You would lie, cheat, inform on your friends, steal, do anything to satisfy total need. Because you would be in a state of total sickness, total possession, and not in a position to act in any other way. . . . A rabid dog can't choose but bite.

This is and has been the conventional view of heroin. When a team of sociologists headed by Bruce Johnson (1985) explored heroin addiction, however, they found something different. These researchers rented a storefront in a Harlem neighborhood that had "the highest number of street-level heroin abusers in the country."

For two years, a research staff of former heroin users built rapport with 201 current users. From the day-to-day reports they collected from these addicts, the researchers found that many heroin users are *not* physically addicted. For a period of time, they use heroin once or twice a day, and then—without suffering withdrawal symptoms—they go for several days without the drug. Other researchers have noted that some people use heroin on an occasional basis, such as at weekend parties, without becoming addicted (Spunt, 2003).

Similar findings were found among heroin users in Vietnam. About 14% of U.S. soldiers in Vietnam used heroin, and it was far stronger than any available back home. After the soldiers left Vietnam, were reunited with family and friends, and went back to work, the vast majority ceased using heroin. They had few, if any, noticeable physical problems. As the assistant secretary of defense for health and environment said, "Everything that I learned in medical school—that anyone who ever tried heroin was

A Global Glimpse
"WHAT'S A POOR FARMER TO DO?"
HEROIN SUPPLIES FOREVER

Life is tough in Afghanistan, even outside the war-torn cities. Farmers barely eke out a living; their mud huts lack both electricity and running water.

Were it not for the poppies, they might not even have enough food for their children.

The lush poppy fields of the Afghan countryside bring the cash that allows farmers to survive, sometimes even enough to build a small house.

Why does Afghanistan produce three-fourths or more of the world's opium? First, growing poppies is a centuries-old custom. It's a part of the culture—the taken-for-granted, routine, normal part of life—of Afghan farmers. One of them, Ahmad Jan, said, "We will not abandon poppy cultivation until the end of this world." He thought about what he'd said for a moment, and then added, "If the government gives us something in return, we might stop" (Gall, 2006).

Second, the farmers face a dilemma. For survival a mechanic must have machines to fix, or a teacher must have students to teach. And farmers must have crops to grow. In some places in Afghanistan, the land is salty, because it was reclaimed from the desert. Little grows on it, except the hardy poppy plant. Because there is so little rainfall, the farmers have to pump water for irrigation from wells about 300 feet deep. No one would survive growing wheat or melons.

Third, even the farmers who are lucky enough to have more productive land must confront the political situation. The central government of Afghanistan remains weak, and its control over the countryside is fragile. Here, tribal chiefs and private armies are still in control (Scherer, 2003). If these local rulers tell farmers to grow poppies, how can they refuse?

In some areas, the Taliban is in control. The U.S. invasion after September 11 drove this political and religious group out of power in the cities, but it lives on in the more remote regions. For the Taliban, the poppy crop is a cash cow, and it even distributes leaflets ordering farmers to grow poppies. The Taliban takes opium production so seriously that its leaders provide armed protection for drug convoys and will battle government troops that dare to interfere with the drug smuggling (Gall, 2006).

Even so, at the urging—and with the healthy payments—of Western nations, the central and regional governments do send out soldiers and police to eradicate poppy fields. But the police and soldiers are poor, and it doesn't take much to bribe them into either skipping some farmer's land or leaving part of the crop.

When one group of farmers had their poppy fields destroyed, they figured that this was the cost of having a new government that was bringing them peace. When they learned that the farmers in a neighboring village had bribed the police to not destroy their crops, they felt indignant. "What kind of government is this?" they asked. When Alam, one of these farmers, was interviewed, he said, "Of course I will plant poppy! And if our neighbors give bribes to the police again, then we'll just give bribes that are three times as high. We understand the system now." (Aizenman, 2005)

Despite these obstacles, the West remains determined to get rid of the poppy fields. Western governments continue to pump hundreds of millions of dollars into Afghanistan. Not only do they try to eradicate the crop, but they also try to train farmers to grow fruit trees and plant vineyards instead of poppy fields. In a culture where the government is thought of as an illegitimate force, officials fight a losing battle. One farmer said that he does go along with the Western-financed program to grow alternative crops, but only to a certain extent. If he doesn't grow poppy on at least some of his land, the other villagers will accuse him of working for the government.

And how the West's plans can backfire! When the British government, which is leading the international efforts to combat Afghan drugs, offered farmers money to destroy their poppy crops, the word spread quickly. Many farmers rushed home to plant more poppies. Why not, since the British government was going to guarantee the price? When the British cash didn't arrive, the farmers harvested their poppies, giving the drug dealers a boom crop to turn into heroin (North, 2004).

FOR YOUR CONSIDERATION

Why is it unlikely that the poppy fields of Afghanistan will be eradicated? In addition to the scenario just outlined, keep yet another factor in mind: The situation is like a balloon. Squeeze one end, and the balloon expands on the other end. If eradication programs reduce crops in one area, crops increase in another region—or even in an adjacent country. Given what you have read here, what solutions would you suggest to stop heroin? Or would you support the legalization of heroin? Or something else entirely?

instantly, totally, and perpetually hooked—failed to prepare me for dealing with this situation" (Peele, 1987, p. 211).

These contradictory reports make it difficult to draw accurate conclusions. Certainly William Burroughs's description of his own addiction to heroin (and similar reports by other users) is accurate. He did not make it up. Nor did Johnson and his associates make up their findings either. How can we reconcile such mixed reports? The simplest explanation seems to be that heroin is addicting to some people, but not to others. Some users of heroin do become addicts and match the stereotypical profile. Others are able to use heroin on a recreational basis.

Both, then, may be right. With the evidence we have at this point, it would be inappropriate to side with either extreme. That is, it would not match research findings to conclude that anyone can use heroin without getting addicted or that anyone who uses heroin will automatically become addicted. We must await further research to find the key to heroin addiction.

FETAL NARCOTIC SYNDROME. As with alcohol and cocaine, pregnant women who use narcotics deliver babies who are addicted. Suffering from **fetal narcotic syndrome,** these newborns suffer greatly. They have tremors and can't sleep; they vomit, sneeze, and frantically suck their tiny fists (*Drug Dependence in Pregnancy*, 1979). They also are more likely to be born prematurely, to be underweight, and to be starting life with such a cluster of problems that they are less likely than other babies to survive (Choo et al., 2004).

Research Findings: Narcotics, Crime, and the Law

Heroin causes crime. It destroys people's incentive to work. It also devastates their users' health.

Everyone know that these things are true, so why even mention them? These statements bring us, again, face to face with sociology and commonsense assumptions about social life that should be challenged. In this section, we are going to report on some unusual research findings.

These common assumptions about crime, health, and work seem to be supported by sociological research. Sociologists James Inciardi and Anne Pottieger (1994), who studied Miami crack users, found that the average crack user had committed 6,000 crimes in just the preceding three months!

This astronomical number comes into somewhat better focus when we learn that 98% of their crimes were illegal drug sales. Similarly, sociologists Bruce Johnson, Kevin Anderson, and Eric Wish (1988), who interviewed 105 drug addicts, found that during just the preceding 24 hours these men had committed 46 robberies, 18 burglaries, and 41 thefts. Seventy-five percent of the $7,771 they netted went for drugs, and twenty-five percent for other things such as food. The average street addict commits 150 nondrug crimes a year, about one every 2 or 3 days (Johnson et al., 1985, p. 185).

Most Americans would argue that narcotics are the cause of crime, narcotics make people unproductive, and they destroy people's health. But here is a surprise: Some argue that narcotics are *not* the cause of these crimes. Narcotics do *not* make people unproductive nor do they destroy people's health. Researchers examined physicians who themselves had become addicted to narcotics. These doctors, high, did *not* hold up cabbies, mug pedestrians, burgle houses, or become prostitutes. Nor did they stop working. Nor did their health deteriorate (Winick, 1961).

Why not? The answer lies in the social position that physicians occupy. To obtain narcotics, physician addicts get them from legal sources, such as hospital supplies. They earn enough salary that they do not have to scramble for money to buy narcotics. With pure drugs cheap and readily obtainable, they have no need to prey on others. In addition, they continue to work at their medical practice. This research on doctors is supported by

the observations of middle-class weekend users of heroin. They, too, find no need to prey on others. They simply pay for their drug of choice from their earnings at work (Spunt, 2003). *Life circumstances make the difference, not narcotic addiction.*

In and of themselves, then, the narcotics do not drive people to crime, make people stop working, or destroy people's health. Although such conditions are common among street addicts, they are not the consequence of narcotics. Jerome Jaffe (1965, p. 292), a physician who studied physician addicts, concluded

> The addict who is able to obtain an adequate supply of the drug through legitimate channels and has adequate funds, usually dresses properly, maintains his nutrition, and is able to discharge his social and occupational obligations with reasonable efficiency. He usually remains in good health, suffers little inconvenience, and is, in general, difficult to distinguish from other persons.

This point must be underscored. Narcotics do *not* cause the things we commonly associate with them. Yet the observation that robbery, burglary, prostitution, unemployment, and poor health are associated with narcotic addicts is correct. The narcotics, however, are not the cause.

What then is the cause? It is *the laws* that make these drugs illegal. These laws create a black market, which provides a rich source of income for organized crime. Running a monopoly, the criminal underworld is able to command high prices, and *poor* addicts turn to crime to buy drugs. Spending their money on drugs, they don't eat right, and their health deteriorates. Physician addicts, in contrast, are not dependent on this black market. Middle-class users, who do use the black market in heroin, are able to afford the price. Both the physicians and the middle-class users are able to function in a comparatively normal fashion.

These laws force most addicts to use street narcotics, and with no state or federal drug agencies protecting the consumer, addicts never know what they are buying. For example, street heroin can be cut with substances that kill, or might not be cut enough and thereby be potent enough to kill. Users may develop allergies to the quinine commonly used to cut heroin, or even to the heroin itself, and die from acute congestion and edema of the lungs. Some users die so rapidly that the needle is still in their arm when they are found.

As we noted at the beginning of this chapter, making a drug illegal will not stop it from being available. Nor does attaching severe penalties to its use make drug use disappear. The law simply drives the transaction underground and makes a black market profitable. If tough laws are not the answer (recall the mutilation and the death penalty that once applied to tobacco use), then what is? Let's look at some alternatives.

Social Policy

The Dilemmas of Social Policy

Of all the social problems, developing adequate policies for drug use is most difficult. Like abortion, this problem is surrounded by irreconcilable differences of opinion, strong emotions, prejudices, and legislation. Complicating social policy even further are contrasting moralities, subcultural values, and vested financial and personal interests. For just one example of how difficult, perhaps impossible, it is to formulate "adequate" social policy, see the Issues in Social Problems box on the next page. For another, consider this: The health findings on alcohol suggest that we should encourage light to moderate drinking, but discourage heavy drinking. Which of our high schools and colleges—or our churches and state governments—would promote such a policy? ("Okay, class, this is why you should drink a beer or two almost every day.")

Issues in Social Problems
JUST WHAT *CAN* YOU DO?
THE LARRY MAHONEY CASE

This is the school bus that Larry Mahoney hit while driving drunk. Twenty-four children and three adults were killed.

"Larry Mahoney," said his friend, "wouldn't hurt anybody for the world." Another said that "since he was a little baby, he hasn't any meanness in him." Those are apt descriptions of this 34-year-old father from Kentucky. He is an all-around, pleasant, easygoing guy. How, then, could he have killed 24 teenagers and 3 adults?

It happened on a Saturday night in May. All Larry wanted was to have a good time, so he did what most of the "good old boys" of his town did: After a hard week of work at the chemical company, Larry headed for his favorite watering hole. There he met his friends, and he drank, and laughed, and drank some more. The time passed quickly, and Larry had to get home to his wife and children.

He climbed into his pickup truck and took off down the road. Things looked a little blurry, but they always did after his drinking sprees. This time, though, he didn't notice that he was going the wrong way on the interstate.

As if from nowhere, Larry saw a school bus headed toward him. Then he heard the sounds that he still can't shake—the loud crash of metal searing against metal, followed by piercing screams of agony as the bus and its passengers were engulfed in flames.

After he was charged with 27 counts of murder, Larry's friends rallied to his defense. Bobby Simmons, a gas station attendant, said, "It's a terrible mistake he made. But that boy ain't no murderer." Some families held bake sales and yard sales to raise money for his bail. Lillian O'Banion, a widow in her 80s, put up the deed to her farm.

Chris Rogers, a farm worker, pinpointed the attitude in Carrollton, Kentucky, where Larry grew up and lived all his life, when he said, "Let's tell the truth about it. That could be you or me sitting in that jail. What he done ain't no different than what a lot of people in this town or anywhere else have done. To hear people on TV talk, you'd think Larry don't even feel bad about this. Let me tell you, he feels himself like he ought to be killed."

Sickened at this outpouring of support for Larry, the national president of MADD (Mothers Against Drunk Driving) said, "This was no accident. People intentionally drink, and they intentionally drive. I'm sick and tired of people sugar-coating murder."

A few miles south, on Interstate 71, where Larry Mahoney killed the 24 children and 3 adults, someone erected a white wooden cross and planted roses in the grassy median. Forty of the passengers on that church outing escaped with their lives, but they wonder why their friends had to die just because Larry Mahoney wanted a good time.

FOR YOUR CONSIDERATION

Mahoney served 10 years in the Kentucky state prison at La Grange. Do you think this was just? Instead of going to prison, do you think that he should have been fined and had his driver's license revoked? Or should he have been given the death sentence, as some prosecutors demanded? What do you think would have been appropriate?

Based on Johnson (1988).

Even trying to analyze the health consequences of drugs poses a dilemma. As Oakley Ray (1998) put it,

> From a medical point of view no drug is safe. With some doses, modes of administration, and frequency of use, all drugs cause toxic effects and even death. It is equally true that at some doses, modes of administration, and frequency of use all drugs are safe. The concern here is whether a drug, used the way most people use it today, is physically harmful. From this position, alcohol and marijuana are relatively safe drugs the way most people use them. Nicotine, in contrast, is a very harmful drug, since the usual amount of cigarette smoking does increase the mortality rate.

THEORY AND SOCIAL POLICY. From a medical standpoint, then, no drug is safe and all drugs are safe. Rational social policy should be built around the dimension of *social harm*. Why prohibit drugs, for example, that don't cause social harm? But how do we determine harm? *Symbolic interactionists* would want to know from whose point of view we define social harm. For example, with their worlds so different, the middle class's definition of social harm would differ considerably from that of inner-city residents. And why should we force the perspective of one group on the other? For *functionalists,* the question would be, When do drugs interfere with people reaching their goals or when do they interfere with the welfare of society? And how do we determine this? *Conflict sociologists* might suggest something entirely different—that so-called social harm could be a prelude to wide-scale social change that actually leads to a more just society.

THE "GET TOUGH" APPROACH. U.S. officials have vacillated between extreme social policies in an effort to curb the drug problem. Currently, a *get-tough* approach appears to be the dominant sentiment in the United States—passing strict laws and putting teeth in them. What is wrong with a get-tough policy? Recall the discussion at the beginning of this chapter about other societies in history. Remember that in early societies some slit noses and cut off heads for smoking cigarettes or beat the soles of people's feet for drinking coffee. Even draconian measures don't work when people crave drugs.

In the 1980s, President George H. W. Bush declared a "war on drugs." He ordered the Coast Guard, the Customs Service, the Border Patrol, the Immigration and Naturalization Service, and the Drug Enforcement Agency to stop illegal drugs from coming into the United States. The Pentagon even attempted to build a "fence" of radar-equipped balloons at the Mexican border (Fialka, 1988). The result? After the war on drugs, an even larger supply of drugs flowed into the United States, enough that the price of heroin dropped, and its purity increased. So much for that war.

Some just shake their heads and say that if we can't stop the drugs from coming in, at least we can lock up the dealers and users. *This is impossible.* Consider that millions of Americans use illegal drugs, from cocaine and heroin to the hallucinogens, barbiturates, and inhalants. During just the past month, about 13 million Americans smoked marijuana. How could we possibly lock up all of these people? How many dealers does it take to supply just the marijuana smokers? If each dealer has twenty-five customers, there are a half million dealers. We simply don't have enough jails and prisons to lock all of these people up.

Some would say that we should just build new prisons. Perhaps, but consider this: To build one prison cell costs about $100,000. To keep one inmate locked up for one year costs a minimum of $25,000. If we skipped the users of illicit drugs and were going to lock up just the drug dealers, where would we get the money? Assume that there are a half million dealers (and there likely are more) and all were arrested. If we put two dealers in a cell, 250,000 new cells would run $25 billion. It would then cost another $12 billion a year to keep those dealers in prison.

Lurking in back of a "lock-'em-up" approach is the assumption that to jail a dealer is to eliminate that dealer's drug deals. The reality is quite different. An arrest of a dealer is a business opportunity for would-be dealers, who are waiting eagerly in line to take over vacated territory. Get rid of one dealer, and two more may fight to take his or her place.

Consider also what we reviewed earlier, that get-tough policies fuel black markets. They unintentionally produce fountains of profits for those who are willing to take the risk, for both independent entrepreneurs and for organized crime. This harsh reality surfaced when

the United States made drinking alcohol a criminal act under Prohibition. An underground network sprang up immediately to keep that drug supply going. It is no different with drugs such as marijuana, cocaine, and heroin. When a drug is criminalized, people will continue to buy it from an underground network. To get the money to buy addictive drugs, which are made expensive by the criminal laws, the poor who are addicted prey on others. These latent dysfunctions of criminalizing drugs—the bankrolling of organized crime and an increase in muggings, burglaries, thefts, prostitution, and premature deaths—become worse than the original problem that the laws address.

Or you might want to consider the situation in other countries and the controversial drug policy suggested in the Global Glimpse box below.

A Global Glimpse
DRUGS AND DRUG VIOLENCE: WHAT SHALL WE DO?

It was a typical night at El Sol y Sombra in Uruapan, a little town in Michoacán, Mexico. Some couples were dancing to Norteño, while others were flirting. As the drinks took effect, the problems of life receded.

The reverie was abruptly broken when several men burst into the nightclub, waving machine guns and shooting wildly into the air. The music stopped and the revelers, their alcohol-induced escape suddenly cut short, huddled against the walls. The men threw a garbage bag onto the middle of the emptied dance floor.

Five human heads rolled out, the eyes staring ghastly into space, the blood still dripping from the freshly severed necks.

"Now that's something you don't see every day," said a bartender at El Sol y Sombra when reporters talked to him later. "Very ugly."

That's an understatement, even here in Michoacán, where drug-related violence is an almost daily occurrence. The drug dealers have become so brazen that they kill even the police. They raided one police station with grenades and bazookas. In another town, after receiving death threats, 18 of the 32 policemen resigned.

The drug dealers have also killed judges and prosecutors.

No longer are the drug dealers content to threaten rival dealers, or even to kill them—or the police or reporters who are getting too close. Cutting off heads and putting them on display sends a more impressive message.

And since some people, for whatever reason, might not get the message, the dealers have begun leaving notes alongside the heads.

At El Sol y Sombra, the note said, "The family does not kill for money. It does not kill women. It does not kill innocents. It kills only those who deserve to die. Everyone should know, this is divine justice."

"The family" ("La familia") is the term this group has given itself.

At another location, this note accompanied more severed heads: "See. Hear. Shut Up. If you want to stay alive."

Not surprisingly, investigators are finding it difficult to locate anyone who has seen or heard anything.

If the drug dealers had their way, they would control Mexico. Some say they just about do so now. This, of course, is an exaggeration, but drug money and corruption go hand in hand. Throughout Mexico, corruption has overtaken both the police and politicians. According to some observers, drug corruption has reached into the presidential palace—at least in previous administrations.

In Colombia, drug dealers became so brazen in the 1990s that they assassinated three presidential candidates. Dealers are still powerful there, forging alliances with revolutionaries, paying for protection in the areas the rebels control so they can process cocaine without interruption. Despite massive antidrug efforts by the Colombian government, financed by the United States, Colombia accounts for about 80% of the world's cocaine—about 90% of the cocaine that flows into the United States.

FOR YOUR CONSIDERATION

What do you think can be done to solve this problem? The drug violence is fueled by a war over its tremendous profits. Some suggest that the most effective way to eliminate drug violence is to strike the problem at its root by making drugs legal. Removing the profits in illegal drugs would cause the problem to disappear overnight. At the same time, legalization would eliminate the thousands upon thousands of arrests for drug dealing and possession.

On the one hand, what reasons can you offer against the legalization of drugs, letting adults put whatever substances they want into their body? On the other hand, if the drugs that are now illegal were made legal, what social problems do you think this would produce?

Based on "Colombia" (2006); McKinley (2006a, 2006b); McKinley & Lacey (2006).

WHEN "REASONABLE" BACKFIRES. With illegal drugs so popular and attitudes so divergent, how can we ever develop a reasonable social policy? As functionalists stress, we must anticipate the unintended consequences of social policy. To discourage cigarette smoking, let's suppose that we raise taxes by, say, $3 more a pack. If we did so, as intended, cigarette smoking would decline. An unintended consequence, however, would be that crime would increase—that of smuggling cigarettes from Mexico and Canada. Even more serious, though, is that such a policy could have the *opposite* effect among teenagers. It might encourage more of them to smoke. An increase in smoking among teenagers is just what happened when lawmakers in Canada raised cigarette taxes (Izumi, 1997). The huge black market in cigarettes that sprang up made it easier for teenagers to obtain cigarettes.

Deciding Social Policy

BANNING ADVERTISING. One thought is that the United States could begin by banning *all* advertising for drugs known to be harmful. Nicotine is certainly a case in point. As it now stands, when young people open magazines and newspapers, they are greeted by smiling, happy, healthy young people beckoning them to join their carefree lifestyle of pleasurable smoking. If all advertising for cigarettes and tobacco products were eliminated, this source of enticement would be removed.

DRUG EDUCATION. Another attempt might include drug education based on scientific studies. Such a program would require that we determine *both* the beneficial and the harmful effects of drugs—and that we communicate those findings, even if they go against our biases. Our own values concerning "good" or "bad" drugs should be irrelevant. For example, if scientific evidence shows that marijuana is safer than tobacco, which appears to be the case, then, like it or not, we need to communicate that information. We cannot shy away from communicating either the good or the bad effects of marijuana just because we have a bias for or against this drug. This same principle applies to all drugs.

Drug education is a two-edged sword. On the one hand, students who are given information about drugs use drugs in greater moderation. On the other hand, giving students information piques their curiosity, and more of them use drugs (Blum et al., 1976; Levine, 1986). More drug use, but in greater moderation, then, is what we can expect from formal drug education programs. We stress formal, because an informal drug education program is already at work—the one that comes from the streets and is filled with misinformation. The alternative, no formal drug education, produces heavier drug use among a select few. In sum, although drug education stimulates interest in drugs, it also cuts down on abuse. If the purpose of drug education is to decrease drug *use,* it is missing the mark; if its purpose is to decrease drug *abuse,* it is on target.

DRUG ADDICTION. Adequate social policy dealing with drug addiction would be beneficial. Locking up addicted people does not address addiction, for upon release most of them go back to their drugs. A successful program cannot focus on addiction as though addicts live in a social vacuum. It must take into account the background factors of an addict's life. Addiction is often part of subcultural orientations and deprivations— often poverty, unemployment, dropping out of school, hopelessness, despair, and a bleak future. To reflect the life realities of drug abusers, drug programs must take multiple approaches.

People who become drug dependent are strongly motivated to continue their drug use. With cigarettes available legally, nicotine addicts have no difficulty obtaining their drug. Tobacco is available in any community, and tobacco crops are even subsidized by the Department of Agriculture. With the average cost of supporting a nicotine habit running $1,200–$2,000 or so a year, cigarette addicts do not mug, steal, or kill to obtain their drug. In contrast, heroin and cocaine are illegal, their cost is considerably higher, and many of their users are involved in crime. A successful drug addiction program,

A 39-year-old heroin addict with AIDS, named Pai, smokes heroin at home in rural China. Widespread heroin use has caused the transmission of AIDS among thousands of addicts and family members and has left many children as orphans.

then, might include free or very affordable drugs. For example, heroin addicts could be prescribed heroin by physicians who would treat them as patients. As Arnold Trebach (1987, p. 369) put it,

> The availability of prescribed heroin would mean that multitudes of addicts would be able to function as decent law-abiding citizens for the first time in years. Their health should be much improved because their drugs would be clean and measured in labeled dosages. The number of crimes they commit should drop dramatically. By implication, addicts to other narcotics, such as morphine and codeine, would also reap the same benefits. They would be eligible to receive maintenance doses of the drugs on which they are dependent. Hordes of potential crime victims would, accordingly, be denied the pleasure.

Such a policy would break the addicts' dependence on the black market, remove a major source of profit for organized crime, and eliminate the need for addicts to prey on others. If the program provided only such benefits, it would be a night-and-day improvement over the present situation, but still needed would be a three-pronged attack: counseling for personal problems, practical help in seeking and maintaining employment, and clinical services for those who want to end their addiction.

Methadone maintenance is a great example of how the labels *illegal* and *legal* play a key role in developing social policy. Methadone, a synthetic narcotic that is itself addicting, was developed by the Germans during World War II as a painkiller for wounded soldiers (Wren, 1998). Today, given orally in medically supervised clinics, methadone is used to help break addiction to heroin. This transfers addiction from an illegal drug, heroin, to a legal drug, methadone.

Why transfer someone's addiction from one narcotic to another? Freeing addicts from the black market in essence frees them from the need to commit crime. But if we are going to supply drugs to addicts, why not simply give them the narcotic to which they already are addicted? Obviously, the answer goes back to the labels of acceptable drugs. In this case, the narcotic heroin is evil; the narcotic methadone is good.

The original model of methadone maintenance programs was multipronged. A successful program would include counseling for patients and job training. For budgetary reasons, however, at most locations these elements are absent from the program. Only the

"bare bones" of the original plan are left—giving methadone to addicts. This failing alerts us to a danger of social policy: Politicians who fund a program may not see it in the same way as do the professionals who designed it. If politicians and bureaucrats cut costs, they dismantle the original program in all but name.

ALCOHOLICS ANONYMOUS. Alcoholics Anonymous (AA) has been a successful drug program whose principles have been applied to other addiction treatment programs, such as Cocaine Anonymous. The main principle of AA is that the program should be directed and staffed by people who have experienced the addiction themselves—and have overcome it. They know firsthand what the addicts are going through. Intimately familiar with the addicts' orientations, they can talk their language on a "gut level."

Alcoholics Anonymous was started in 1935 in Akron, Ohio, by two alcoholics. It is now a worldwide organization of 100,000 local groups numbering more than 2 million members in 150 countries ("AA Fact File," 2004). The essentials of Alcoholics Anonymous are summarized in what this group calls the Twelve Steps. To overcome addiction to alcohol, you must

1. Admit that you are powerless over alcohol and your life has become unmanageable.
2. Believe that a power greater than yourself can help restore you to wholeness.
3. Make a decision to turn your will and life over to God, as you understand God.
4. Make an honest moral inventory of yourself.
5. Admit to God, yourself, and another human being exactly what you have done wrong.
6. Be ready to work with God to remove your defects of character.
7. Ask God to remove your shortcomings.
8. Make a list of every person you have harmed and be willing to make amends to them.
9. Make amends whenever possible, except where it would harm them or others.
10. Continue to take personal inventory, and promptly admit your wrongs.
11. Through prayer and meditation, seek to improve your contact with God, as you understand God, praying for knowledge of God's will for yourself and the power to carry it out.
12. Have a spiritual awakening as a result of these steps; try to carry this message to other alcoholics; and practice these principles in all your dealings with others.

To put these steps into practice, members meet weekly with others who have overcome alcohol addiction or who are struggling to overcome. From their fellow members, they draw encouragement to continue their abstinence. They also carry the telephone number of a mentor, "someone who has been through it." They can call this person at any hour for personal support, learning to handle crises without turning to alcohol.

PRINCIPLES OF EFFECTIVE SOCIAL POLICY. To be effective, a social policy must match the subculture of its target group. A policy must be geared to the group members' age, race–ethnicity, gender, and social class, as well as to the members' values, lifestyle, and problems. This means that programs for different groups must have different emphases. For example, a program that is successful with middle-class youth will fail if it is transferred without modification to inner-city youth.

Successful social policies must also accept that individuals have the right to make their own choices. Applied to social policy, this value means the right of people to abuse their bodies with drugs they choose. Regardless of how we may feel about the abuse, it seems that people have the right to consume substances that you and I may choose not to.

Drug programs must also encourage active participation in our economic system. Encouragement by itself is not enough; to be effective, drug programs should offer job training and placement (Faupel & Klockars, 1987). This means that addicts need to be

integrated into a community of people where "clean" values are dominant, including social networks that value employment and nonexploitative relationships.

Finally, if drug education is to be successful, it is essential that it be related to *the realities of the users.* Nonusers' ideas about morality and the risks of using drugs are not the same as those of users. Attempting to impose some outside reality onto an experienced user is a recipe for failure.

A POSSIBLE NATIONAL GOAL. Owing to our backgrounds, all of us have biases. We all hold strong opinions about addicts and drugs, making it difficult to develop sound social policy. Legislators, for example, pass laws designed to punish the "evil" of drug use, "evil" as defined from their perspective. Because we see the world from different perspectives, no social policy can satisfy everyone, and all social policies are bound to displease many. You may have found some of the policies suggested in this chapter to be unreasonable, perhaps even ridiculous, while others see those same policies as reasonable and desirable. Despite these many differences, because ours is a drug-using society, it seems that a rational goal could be to teach people to *use* drugs sensibly, reducing the amount of drug *abuse.* This principle would apply to all drugs—not just to those that match *our* ideas of "acceptable" drugs.

The Future of the Problem

In light of the high numbers of drug users, we can expect drug use to remain high. Because drugs are subject to change, we can expect some drugs to decrease in popularity, while others will become more popular. As a young person partakes of the latest drug, we can expect alarm in the general public. Alarms then, will be sounded from time to time.

With advances in chemistry, a new generation of drugs will appear. Designed to work only on particular receptors of the brain, these drugs will be more precise in their effects. The market for these drugs will be high, because many people choose to take drugs to help them cope with their life. This high-tech market will stimulate the demand for new drugs, putting even greater pressure on "drug dispensers."

The social reputations and acceptability of drugs will continue to influence people's lives profoundly. Some drugs will remain in disrepute, their users disgraced and stigmatized. Other drugs will maintain their social approval. Advertised in glossy magazines and in other media, they will continue to be an accepted part of social life.

From the standpoint of functional theory, we can expect drug enforcement agents—in order to protect their jobs and enhance their positions—to try to keep many substances illegal. To do so, they will work with legislators and government agencies to influence drug legislation and policy. In 2006, the Federal Drug Administration did just this. Although a panel of scientists had examined the evidence regarding the medical uses of marijuana and made recommendations for this drug's limited medical use, the FDA rejected the panel's findings (Harris, 2006).

The refusal to accept the potential uses of medical marijuana, or refusal to fund research related to it, helps to keep the black market alive and profitable. This attitude by officials who determine social policy will continue to produce a familiar theme: The resulting crimes, especially the headline-producing violence, will continue to make the drug enforcement establishment seem vital for society. *Organized crime and drug enforcement agents,* then, sharing as they do a mutual interest in keeping drugs illegal, will remain partners, although reluctant symbiotic ones.

If we view ourselves as the "good, clean" people and them as "evil drug addicts," then drug use, treatment, and policy will continue to be what it has been in the past. The "good, clean" people can turn a blind eye to what happens to "evil drug addicts," ultimately denying them changes in policy. This perception impedes the development of new social policy, not only for drug abusers but also for the mentally ill and others who violate middle-class standards of behavior.

SUMMARY AND REVIEW

1. What constitutes *drug abuse* is a matter of social definition. What is considered drug use at one time or in one society may be considered drug abuse at another time or in another society. From the historical record, we know that drug use and abuse are ancient.

2. Americans have a strong pro-drug orientation, although they consider some drugs to be disreputable and those who use them to be part of a social problem. People generally consider the particular drugs that they use to not be part of a social problem.

3. A major problem in drug abuse is *addiction*—becoming dependent on a drug so that its absence creates the stress of withdrawal. One of the most highly addicting drugs is nicotine. Heroin appears to be less addicting than previously thought.

4. Symbolic interactionists emphasize the social meanings of drugs. Prohibition, for example, has been analyzed as a symbolic crusade: As the old order lost political control, it attempted to dominate society morally by wrapping itself in abstinence (morality) and associating drunkenness (immorality) with the newcomers.

5. In examining the functions and dysfunctions of drugs, functionalists stress not just that legal drugs are functional for the medical profession, their patients, and those who manufacture and sell these drugs, but also that illegal drugs are functional for their users, manufacturers (or growers), and distributors. The dysfunctions of drugs include problems with the law and abuse that harms people physically and socially. A major latent function of illegal drugs is to support agents of social control.

6. Conflict theorists stress how the criminalization of drugs is related to power. Opium, for example, was made illegal in an attempt to overcome the economic threat that Chinese immigrants posed to White workers. Similarly, marijuana legislation was directed against the Mexican working class in the United States. Some see the heroin trade as a means of defusing revolutionary potential.

7. Pharmaceutical companies, with the cooperation of the medical profession, play a central role in getting Americans to define drugs as *the way* to relieve the stresses of everyday life. Defining problems of living as medical matters, known as *the medicalization of human problems,* includes defining unruly children as in need of medication.

8. The same drug has different effects on different people and on the same person at different times. These differences are due to characteristics of the drug, the individual who is taking it, and the setting in which it is taken. Especially significant are the user's expectations.

9. Of all the drugs that Americans use, nicotine causes the most harm. Alcohol abuse, which destroys vital body organs, also causes *fetal alcohol syndrome.* The social setting in which people learn to drink influences their chances of becoming problem drinkers. We need more studies to determine the effects of marijuana and other drugs. Cocaine's social history illustrates how a drug's reputation depends on the people with whom it is associated.

10. Although addicting to many people, in and of themselves narcotics do not cause crime or destroy people's work incentive or health. Street addicts deal with a black market that demands high prices and motivates them to commit predatory crimes. Street addicts buy drugs whose purity is far from guaranteed—and suffer the consequences. In contrast, narcotic addicts who are physicians maintain normal lives because they need not deal with a black market and are able to obtain pure drugs.

11. Developing an adequate social policy is difficult because drugs arouse strong emotions and biases. At a minimum, an adequate social policy would involve drug education that presents scientific findings honestly, whether they are favorable or unfavorable to any particular drug. It would also break the addicts' dependence on a black market and provide help for their multiple problems. Alcoholics Anonymous appears to be a model recovery program.

12. We can anticipate that the future will bring new drugs from pharmaceutical companies, continuation of the symbiotic partnership between law enforcement agents and drug dealers based on their shared interests, and social policies that protect the users of favored drugs and penalize the users of those in disfavor.

KEY TERMS

THINKING CRITICALLY ABOUT CHAPTER 4

1. Which perspective—symbolic interactionism, functionalism, or conflict theory—do you think best explains drug policies in the United States? Why?
2. If women can be prosecuted for child abuse for taking drugs during pregnancy, does it follow that they should also be prosecuted for failure to attend prenatal classes or for not eating properly during pregnancy? How about for smoking cigarettes? Why or why not?
3. If you had the power to decide which drugs should be legal and which should not, what criteria would you use in making your decision?

BY THE NUMBERS: THEN AND NOW

- Percentage of men, ages 18–24, smoking cigarettes in 1965: **54%**
- Percentage of men, ages 18–24, smoking cigarettes in 2003: **26%**

- Percentage of women, ages 18–24, smoking cigarettes in 1965: **38%**
- Percentage of women, ages 18–24, smoking cigarettes in 2003: **22%**

- Number of cigarettes smoked each year by individual Americans, age 18 and older, in 1960: **4,500**
- Number of cigarettes smoked each year by individual Americans, age 18 and older, today: **1,500**

- Number of members of Alcoholics Anonymous in 1935: **2**
- Number of members of Alcoholics Anonymous today: **2 million**

MySocLab

What can you find in MySocLab? mysoclab www.mysoclab.com

- Complete Ebook
- Practice Tests and Exams
- Multimedia Activities
- Mapping and Data Analysis Exercises

- Research and Writing Advice
- Interactive Social Surveys
- Sociology in the News

CHAPTER 5

Violence in Society:
Rape and Murder

They killed their fellow students.

There wasn't much for teenagers to do in Littleton, Colorado. Not much happened in this quiet town of 35,000, a middle-class suburb southwest of Denver. To get attention, some of the high school kids wore black trench coats and black shirts with swastikas. They called themselves the "Trenchcoat Mafia" and threw around a few phrases in German.

The Trenchcoat Mafia had their own table in the cafeteria and their group picture in the yearbook. The caption: "Who says we're different? Insanity's healthy . . . Stay alive, stay different, stay crazy! Oh, and stay away from CREAM SODA!!"

Just another high school group: jocks, emos, cheerleaders, dorks, Goths, punks, and gamers. Every school has them.

The jocks despised the Trenchcoat Mafia. They threw them into lockers and called them scumbags, faggots, and inbreeds. They threw rocks and bottles at them from passing cars.

Two seniors, Eric Harris and Dylan Klebold, who were members of the Trenchcoat Mafia, talked about killing their classmates, especially the jocks. Eric even had his own Web page, where he named those he wanted to kill and the methods he would like to use to kill them. As a class project, Eric and Dylan made a video in which they pretended to kill the classmates they didn't like. Just talk. But when the pretend killings in *Doom*, the video game they loved, no longer satisfied them, the boys hatched a plan for real killing. It was risky. Maybe they would survive, maybe not. But if not, they would go out in a blaze of glory. April 20, Hitler's birthday, would be perfect.

The carnage left Columbine High School seared into national memory. TV viewers switched on their sets and found that a quiet Tuesday afternoon had been interrupted by stunning events. The drama heightened as SWAT teams moved in to assess the situation. Bodies lay strewn on sidewalks. No one knew how many were dead inside the school. The nation watched transfixed as events unfolded.

As bombs went off and shots rang out, students fled in terror. Some hid in closets; others crawled under tables. Harris and Klebold went from room to room in search of victims. In the library, they found several students hiding under a table. "Do you believe in God?" asked one of the shooters. "Yes," replied Cassie Bernall. "There is no God," the gunman retorted, as he placed a gun against her head and squeezed the trigger.

Before the boys turned their guns on themselves, they had killed 12 of their fellow students and one teacher. They wounded another 23 students (Bai, 1999; Gibbs, 1999).

The Virginia Tech massacre on April 16, 2007, in Blacksburg, Virginia, reminded all Americans that mass murder could again result when a student's unstable mental state was shaken by bullying classmates. Seung-Hui Cho used a .22 caliber and a semiautomatic handgun to kill 32 people in two separate buildings before committing suicide. Cho had moved to the United States as a young boy, at which time he was diagnosed with severe anxiety disorder and selective mutism. Cho had had his battles with the law, once being accused of stalking female students and on another occasion being declared mentally ill by a Virginia judge. This murder of 32 in Virginia—the deadliest school shooting in U.S. history—prompted Virginia to pass a new law: Those deemed mentally ill through the courts would never be able to buy handguns.

The Problem in Sociological Perspective

Violence grabs our attention, whether we see it on the street or on television. The media are filled with accounts of violence, and audiences are enraptured with the sordid details of the latest rape or murder. The more gruesome the violence, the greater

the attention. In this chapter, we will examine violence from many angles. Let's begin by using the sociological perspective to better understand violence.

The Sociological Perspective on Violence

Violence, the use of force to injure people or to destroy their property, involves not only individuals, but society as a whole. Some societies encourage "violent personalities" to develop, while others discourage it. As a result, some societies have high rates of violence, and others have low rates. Sociologists, then, don't focus on individual tendencies. Rather, sociology focuses on environmental influences. A key question would be, *What about society increases or decreases the likelihood of violence?* Throughout this chapter, we shall grapple with this central question.

TYPES OF VIOLENCE. Sociologists divide violence into two categories: individual violence and group violence. **Individual** (or **personal**) **violence** involves one person physically attacking others or destroying their property. **Group** (or **collective**) **violence** consists of two or more people doing these same things. Sociologists divide group violence into three types.

1. **Situational group violence** is unplanned and spontaneous. Something in the situation stimulates or triggers the violence. An example is a brawl among hockey players.
2. **Organized group violence** is planned, but unauthorized, like the school shooting in our opening vignette or acts committed by terrorists.
3. **Institutionalized group violence** is violence carried out by agents of the government, such as an army at war or the SWAT team responding to the shootings at Columbine High School.

Rape and murder, the focus of this chapter, can take any of these forms of violence. Let's see how these types apply to rape. Rape usually takes the form of individual violence, for most victims are raped by an individual. If a rape victim is attacked by two or more men, however, it is group violence. (The common term is "gang rape.") If two or more men happen to see a woman alone and think, "Why not? We can get away with it," it is situational group violence. In contrast, if two or more men plan a rape, it is organized group violence. Finally, if there is a mass rape by soldiers after they take over a territory, it is institutionalized group violence.

The Scope of the Problem

Let's see how extensive rape and murder are. In this brief overview, we will compare the rates of rape and murder in the United States with rates in other parts of the world. First, let's distinguish between violence on a personal level and violence as a social problem.

What Makes Violence a Social Problem?

If two people get into a fight and end up in the hospital, that is their *personal* problem. The same is true if a woman, enraged at discovering her husband with a lover, shoots them to death. And the same is true if a man rapes a woman. Although these examples involve severe, bitter violence, they portray only objective conditions. To qualify as a *social* problem, violence must also arouse widespread subjective concern. Many people must see the violence as negative enough that they want to do something about it.

THE SUBJECTIVE DIMENSION OF VIOLENCE. Violence has become a social problem in the United States, but it is important to note that it is not the amount of violence (an objective condition) that makes violence a social problem. Rather, *subjective concerns* about violence make it a social problem. Parents worry about their kids walking to school. Women feel vulnerable as they get on elevators or as they walk alone at night from their classrooms to their cars. They feel relief when they get inside their cars—after they've

Always be wary of crime statistics such as those depicted in Figure 5-3. The way these statistics are compiled makes them subject to so much error that, at best, these numbers merely *indicate* that one country has more or less violence than another. Comparing rape, for example, is notoriously difficult for several reasons. Not only do some countries keep poor records, but the definition of rape changes from one country to another as well. Even within the United States, not all states use the same reporting methods. In Islamic countries, rapes are so underreported that they cannot be shown on compilations like Figure 5-3. Consider Pakistan, which reports an impossible rate of 0.04 per 100,000 people. This is 4 per million. Why do so few Pakistani women report their rapes? If the accused is found not guilty, the woman is found guilty of fornication ("Cross National," 2004). A Pakistani woman guilty of adultery can be stoned to death. To say the least, this is a rather strong deterrent to reporting this crime.

Let's look at some of the theories social scientists have developed to explain violence.

Looking at the Problem Theoretically

Before we analyze violence from a sociological perspective, let's examine some theories developed in other academic disciplines.

Nonsociological Theories

BIOLOGICAL EXPLANATIONS. In the 1800s, Cesare Lombroso (1835–1909), an Italian physician, treated thousands of prisoners. It struck him that they looked different from his regular patients. Lombroso concluded that violent people (and other criminals) are *atavistic;* that is, they are biological throwbacks to an earlier period when humanity was violent and primitive. His evidence was their physical makeup. They had lower foreheads, larger ears, and receding chins. (Kurella, 1911).

Anthropologist Konrad Lorenz (1966) also claimed that evolution was the key to explaining violence. We humans, he said, are biologically ill equipped for killing: We don't have claws, slashing teeth, or great strength. Because we are not designed to murder, we also lack an inhibitory mechanism that stops violence. Dogs, wolves, and baboons, for example, all have such an inhibitory mechanism that stops violence when an enemy becomes submissive. Our powerful intellect, however, allows us to make weapons. The availability of weapons and lack of physical inhibition produce terrible violence. In our anger or desire to dominate, we use weapons to destroy one another. As Lionel Tiger and Robin Fox (1971, p. 210) remarked, if baboons carried hand grenades, few would be left.

Others have suggested a variety of biological factors as the cause of violence—from the shape of the skull (phrenology) to hormonal imbalance or faulty neurotransmitters (George et al., 2006). One theory taken seriously for a time was proposed by anthropologist Earnest Hooton (1939), who concluded that body type is the key to understanding violence: Tall, thin men, he said, tend to be killers, and short, heavy men tend to rape.

Psychologist John Dollard (Dollard et al., 1939/1961), who also stressed a biological explanation for deviance, proposed the **frustration–aggression theory of violence.** As you may have experienced, you feel frustrated when you can't have something you want. Dollard conducted a series of experiments on how people whose goals are blocked relieve their frustration by striking out at others. Often we strike out in mild ways, such as telling someone off, but sometimes people strike out more violently.

PSYCHOLOGICAL THEORIES. Some psychologists point to **behavior modification** as the cause of violence. Following the lead of B. F. Skinner (1948, 1953, 1971), they stress that if some behavior is rewarded ("reinforced"), that behavior will occur again. The "reward" (or "reinforcement") can be any gain—consumables such as candy or food or social symbols such as money, status, or even a smile. For a rapist, the reward may be sex and power. For a killer, the reward might be revenge, power, or satisfaction at exterminating an enemy.

Other psychologists emphasize that violence may be learned through **modeling,** copying another person's behavior. In a classic experiment, psychologists Albert Bandura and R. H. Walters (1963) found that children who witnessed others hitting a Bobo doll (blow-up clown) on film tended to do the same thing themselves. Children who had not seen this sort of behavior on film were less likely to perform it.

THE SOCIOLOGICAL APPROACH TO UNDERSTANDING VIOLENCE. Sociologists do not stress genetic or biological causes of violence; instead, they stress environmental causes. Rather than looking for violence-inducing characteristics *within* people, such as chromosomes and inhibitory mechanisms, sociologists focus on matters *outside* people. They examine how *social life* shapes and encourages—or discourages—violence. For example, in one society, violence may be channeled into approved forms, such as the social roles of warrior, boxer, or football player. Other societies, in contrast, may downplay violence and develop mechanisms to ensure that it rarely occurs.

Let's apply sociological perspectives to violence, attempting to understand why males are more likely than females to be violent and why violence is higher among members of the working or lower classes.

Symbolic Interactionism

What causes people to murder? Consider what a detective on the Dallas police force said back in the 1960s:

> Murders result from little ol' arguments over nothing at all. . . . Tempers flare. A fight starts, and somebody gets stabbed or shot. I've worked on cases where the principals had been arguing over a 10 cent record on a juke box, or over a dollar gambling debt from a dice game. (Mulvihill, Tumin, & Curtis, 1969, p. 230)

EDWIN SUTHERLAND: DIFFERENTIAL ASSOCIATION. Today, people still kill over "little" things. Symbolic interactionists have developed two theories that help us to understand why. In the first, Edwin Sutherland (1947) stresses that people learn criminal behavior by interacting with others. In its simplest form, Sutherland's theory goes like this: People who associate with lawbreakers are more likely to break the law than are people who associate with those who follow the law. Sutherland used the term **differential association** to describe this process. Lawbreakers and law-abiders associate with people or groups like them.

Sutherland's theory can be used to explain violence in five ways:

1. People learn violence by interacting with other violent individuals.
2. People learn techniques, attitudes, motives, drives, and rationalizations for violence from these individuals.
3. People use violence when the attitudes or definitions surrounding them support such acts. (Sutherland called this an *excess of definitions.*)
4. The most significant interactions in which people learn violence are those that take place earliest in life and those that are the most frequent, endure the longest, and are the most emotional or meaningful.
5. The mechanisms for learning violence are the same as those used to learn nonviolent compliant behavior.

MARVIN WOLFGANG: SUBCULTURES OF VIOLENCE. Another paradigm similar to differential association is **subcultural theory.** In a nutshell, this theory claims that people who grow up in a subculture that approves of violent behavior have a high chance of becoming violent. Sociologist Marvin Wolfgang wanted to discover why the homicide rate tended to be high among lower-class African American males. In a classic study (1958), Wolfgang examined convicted murderers in Philadelphia.

Wolfgang found that the men connected violence with honor and manliness. When confronted with a difficult situation, they felt violence was the appropriate response.

Triggers that others might perceive as trivial were *not* trivial to them. Anyone who backed down from a confrontation (even if it was about a "little" thing) was seen as less than a real man. If he were to back down, he risked being viewed as a "chicken" or a "woman"—and would be laughed at by others. The young men learned to carry weapons both for protection and as a symbol of masculinity. The carrying of weapons, in turn, attracted negative confrontations. As a result, cyclical violence among these men became common.

FITTING THE THEORIES TOGETHER. Differential association and subcultural theory complement one another well. Subcultural theory stresses that violence is woven into the life of some groups, and differential association explains how people learn that violence is a suitable response from other violent people.

Many groups associate violence with masculinity: inner-city young men, gang members, and the Mafia. Sociologist Elijah Anderson (1990, 2006) concluded that violence continues to be a feature of young African American men in the inner city. This explanation goes a long way toward explaining their high homicide rates.

In her participant observation of Chicano gangs, sociologist Ruth Horowitz (1983) found that these young men also equate manliness and honor with violence. In the Spotlight on Social Research box on page 136, Horowitz shares insights that she gained from her research.

Lastly, the situation is similar in the Mafia. Michael Franzese, a college-educated member of the Mafia, put it this way:

> If somebody were to dishonor my wife or my child, I would view it as something that I had to take into my own hands. I don't see why I have to go to the police. As a man, I would feel that it was an obligation that I had to take care of. And I would have to be prepared in my own mind to kill this guy. This is a basic principle. (Barnes & Shebar, 1987)

IN SUM Based on symbolic interactionist research, "manliness" (or "masculinity") is associated with violence. As a result, we find more violence among working-class males than females. The working class incorporates more violence into its definitions of appropriate male behavior than do the middle and upper classes. As a result, year after year, across racial–ethnic lines and in every region of the United States, violence is more prevalent among males than females and among working-class males than males from higher social classes. Until the association between masculinity and violence is broken, you can expect these patterns to continue.

Functionalism

EMILE DURKHEIM: ASKING THE SOCIOLOGICAL QUESTION. Violence has always been a key topic of study for sociologists. In the late 1800s, Emile Durkheim, the first university professor to be formally identified as a sociologist, examined murder rates in Paris and suicide rates in several European countries (1897/1951, 1904/1938). He was struck by how consistent these rates remained over time. Year after year, the countries that once had high rates of violence continued to have high rates, whereas those with low rates at one time continued to have low rates. Durkheim found that a country's rate of violence was so consistent that he could use it to predict future rates. He called this **normal violence**—the violence that a group normally (or usually) has.

Durkheim found this regularity intriguing. One would assume that because individual rates of murder change over time, that a population's overall rate would change as well. But Durkheim discovered that overall, regardless of individual numbers, a country's rate remained the same. Durkheim employed the *sociological perspective*. He concluded that a society regulates total murder rates.

To appreciate Durkheim's conclusion, consider what life used to be like in farming communities. Children followed in their parents' footsteps and either worked in the village in which they were reared or farmed nearby land. They spent their entire lives in a

When she was a graduate student at the University of Chicago, RUTH HOROWITZ (now professor of sociology at New York University) did a participant observation study of young people in a Chicano community in Chicago. Her purpose was not to understand violence, but to understand poverty. She wanted to see how the explanations of poverty that sociologists had developed matched what she observed in "real life."

Two major explanations of poverty are the culture of poverty and the social structure of poverty. According to the culture of poverty, poor people have different values than the middle class, and this is why they act as they do. According to the social structural perspective, the poor act as they do because, unlike middle-class people, they do not have the same opportunities to attend good schools or to obtain good jobs. Consequently, the poor turn to illegal opportunities, and crime becomes part of their life.

One afternoon, a month after I met the "Lions" gang and shook hands with all of them in the park, several 16-year-old young women introduced themselves. They asked me several questions about myself, and they were able to give me a definition of sociology. They told me about school and their trips around the city. Several of these women went on to college; others became pregnant and married. The life experience of siblings varied, too; some went to school and became white-collar workers, while others ran afoul of the legal system and went to prison.

When I first began my research, the "Lions" were 15 to 17 years old, had guns, and did a lot of fighting. Some had after-school jobs and dressed in tuxedos for *quinceañeras* and weddings. In the streets, these same young men had developed a reputation by being tougher than other gangs. They would even seek opportunities to challenge others. At home and during most parties, in contrast, they were polite and conformed to strict rules of etiquette.

For seven years, I did participant observation with these youths. When I returned after a three-year absence, many of the "Lions" were still hanging out together, but quite a few were working, had married, and had children. A few of the gang members attended college, and others remained in the street. One had been killed in a drug deal gone wrong. A major change was their relationship to violence. Instead of provoking incidents, now they responded only when someone challenged their reputations.

The two models of poverty did apply. Violence had been part of the culture they had learned, and a lack of opportunities did contribute to a sense of being left out. But there was more to it. Actual violence depended on how the "Lions" defined a particular situation. As sociologists phrase this: Violence was situational and constructed interactionally.

village where everyone knew one another. Their close bonds probably restrained whatever individual impulses they might have had to lash out violently. They needed the community to survive and therefore respected the rules. Their close relationships (or high social integration, in Durkheim's term) kept overall rates of violence low.

Now imagine that this same community underwent rapid social change. With industrialization, the villagers moved away from the farm into the city. Living in the midst of strangers, they faced being fired by bosses who cared about profits, not workers. There were evictions by landlords who cared more about collecting rent than about what happened to a family. Unlike the factors that promoted cohesion on the farm, these urban characteristics loosened social bonds. People felt fewer ties with one another, and the rules that used to apply no longer fit. Durkheim gave the name **anomie** to such feelings of normlessness and anxiety. When everything one used to expect suddenly changes, anomie occurs. In the new city, impulses to violence were not as restrained as they were in the village. As a result, the city became a more dangerous place to live.

ROBERT MERTON: STRAIN THEORY. Another functionalist, Robert Merton (1968), used Durkheim's anomie to explain crime in the United States. He developed what is called **strain theory.** Merton said that success—especially in the form of earning money or

material goods—becomes a **cultural goal;** the goal for Americans is to earn enough money to be "successful." Society offers approved (or legitimate) ways to reach this goal, such as education and career training. These are called **cultural means.** As a result of socialization to a cultural goal of success, almost all Americans learn to want money or material goods. The cultural (approved) means for reaching the goal, however, are limited. Those who find their way blocked in some way are more likely to turn to illegitimate means, such as robbery and theft. If one is taught the goal but does not have the means to achieve it, strain results. *Strain* (or frustration and anxiety) that comes from limited means may motivate some to commit crime. Therefore, strain theory explains why high crime rates exist among poor minorities—they experience fewer means to achieve success.

GOTTFREDSON AND HIRSCHI: CONTROL THEORY. Strain theory does not explain why some people become violent while others do not. We all face hurdles, but not all of us commit crime. To address this issue, sociologists Michael Gottfredson and Travis Hirschi (1990) developed a criminal theory—**control** (or **containment**) **theory**—that places the root cause of committing illegal acts on a lack of self-control. The primary element in Gottfredson and Hirschi's theory is low self-control. Criminal acts offer immediate gratification. People who lack self-control tend to be impulsive, insensitive, risk-takers, thrill-seekers, highly physical, shortsighted, and relatively nonverbal. These traits have a tendency to come together in the same people and to persist throughout life. They thus comprise a stable construct that is useful in explaining crime and other risk-taking behavior.

Individuals who possess such traits also tend to have difficulty finding and maintaining jobs, acquiring and retaining friends, and meeting the demands of long-term financial commitments as well as the demands of effective parenting. In many theories of crime the offender is automatically seen as the product of positive forces such as socialization, culture values, and reward-reinforced learning. In Gottfredson and Hirschi's theory, the causes of low self-control are negative and tend to show themselves in the absence of nurture, discipline, or training.

Gottfredson and Hirschi (p. 96) argue that social life is not enhanced by low self-control or its consequences. Crime cannot be a product of peer socialization, culture, or positive learning of any sort because the traits exhibited by criminals impede educational and occupational achievement, prevent interpersonal relationships, undermine physical health, and therefore are not helpful for enhancing social relationships of any kind.

Importantly, Gottfredson and Hirschi maintain that ineffective child-rearing practices are the major cause of low self-control. They identify the minimum requirements of effective child rearing as (1) adequate monitoring of the child's behavior, (2) recognition of deviant behavior when it occurs, and (3) fair and consistent punishment of such behavior when it occurs. Such child-rearing behavior makes the child more capable of delaying gratification, more sensitive to the concerns of others, more independent, more willing to constrain personal behavior, and less likely to use force or fraud in pursuit of self-interest.

Conflict Theory

VIOLENCE IS INHERENT IN SOCIETY. Conflict theory argues that we can expect violence because groups are competing with one another for highly desired but limited resources. Conflict is often hidden beneath surface cooperation and even goodwill. The true nature of human relationships is adversarial. When competition over resources emerges, violence often is the consequence.

One major division among people in society is social class. Conflict theorists argue that social classes find themselves competing over limited resources. The essential division is between those who own the means of production—the factories, the machines, and capital (investment money)—and those who work for the owners (Marx & Engels, 1848/1964, 1906). The workers, who must struggle to put food on the table, pay rent, and buy clothing, are at the mercy of the owners, who make their decisions on the basis of profit, not the workers' welfare. For example, owners of the factory in search of cheap labor export jobs out of the country. Those who used to work in the factory now struggle to make ends meet. With low pay and unemployment, workers are now likely to strike out violently at others.

United Auto Workers (UAW) union members picket outside the General Motors Detroit–Hamtramck Assembly plant.

This situation is particularly tense for working-class males. Traditionally, men of all social classes assume the role of breadwinner. This role has been threatened by capitalism's recurring boom and bust cycle, which makes working-class men expendable pawns in the capitalists' pursuit of profits. Today, men also compete with women who are qualified to hold the jobs that men have traditionally held. With their economic security fragile, working-class men commit more violent crimes than do either working-class women or men from higher social classes. And the most exploited—those who are confined to the inner city—have the highest rates of violence as they desperately strike out against others.

Conflict theorists also point out that one should look beneath the surface and realize that the capitalist class is actually *more* violent than the working class. Just as the wealthy own the means to produce wealth, so they control the police powers of the state, which they use to suppress the riots and strikes of the underclass. Thus, it is the *form* of violence that distinguishes workers from capitalists.

IN SUM Because violence is a universal characteristic of human societies, sociologists are interested in its causes. True to their calling, sociologists look for *social* causes. They want to know why some societies are more violent than others, as well as why some groups in the same society are more violent than others.

Symbolic interactionists stress that each group has its own ideas and norms about violence. Some groups prefer nonviolent ways of handling disagreements, whereas other groups consider violence an appropriate response to many situations. To solve problems, middle and upper social classes may turn to the legal system, which transcends personal confrontation. The lower classes, in contrast, are likely to take matters into their own hands—and this breeds violence. The groups with which one associates (differential association) may determine one's likelihood of becoming violent.

Functionalists emphasize that social conditions that strengthen social bonds reduce violence, and social conditions that produce *anomie* increase violence. Violence tends to be higher among groups whose access to culturally approved goals is blocked. Tendencies toward criminal behavior result in violence when control mechanisms are weak.

Conflict theorists stress that class exploitation underlies violence. Members of the working class have high rates of violence because they lack power. Seldom is their violence directed against their oppressors, however, for the capitalists control the powers of the state and use them to protect their privileged positions. Instead of targeting their oppressors, workers almost always misdirect their violence, aiming most of it against one another.

Research Findings

Let's now focus on two of the most serious forms of physical violence—rape and murder. Believe it or not, rape was labeled a social problem only after the persistent efforts of victims, advocates, and feminists during the last third of the 20th century. This chapter focuses on **forcible rape**—a form of assault where one individual forces another to have any type of sexual relations against that person's will. Consent is considered absent if the victim is threatened in any way or if the victim's judgment is impaired in any way. Judgment may be considered impaired if a person is disabled, intoxicated, or underage. **Statutory rape** describes sexual intercourse between an adult and a minor.

Rape

The Natural History of Rape as a Social Problem

FROM A PERSONAL TO A SOCIAL PROBLEM. Rape is not a new topic in the social sciences. On the contrary, documented accounts of rape go back thousands of years; examples can be found in the Old Testament and Greek mythology. What has changed is the perception of rape as a *social* rather than a personal problem.

As emphasized throughout this text, objective conditions are not sufficient for labeling something a social problem. A social problem also requires subjective concerns: A significant number of people (or a number of significant people) must be upset by the objective conditions. Subjective concerns about rape are common in our society, and many teach others to take proactive measures to prevent possible attacks. Children are taught not to talk to strangers. Women are taught not to walk alone at night. Teens are taught to stay in groups, to "stick together."

RECONCEPTUALIZING RAPE: FROM PASSION TO POWER. The natural history of defining rape as a social problem began during the 1960s when Western women began to question traditional roles revolving around husband, home, and children (Friedan, 1963; Millett, 1970). Many women began to think of themselves less as individuals who were facing unique circumstances and more as members of a social group facing similar situations. Feminists analyzed the conditions encouraging men to act as dominant oppressors of women. They stressed how women are taught to be supportive of men at the cost of their own education and careers.

Up to this time, a traditional view of rape dominated mainstream thinking: Rape was considered an act of passion. From this perspective, rape was a personal problem, a crime committed by one individual upon another. Feminists have since redefined rape, placing it in the light of sociological analysis.

Feminists argued that the traditional definition of rape places blame on the victim, not the perpetrator. Here's how: Men and women alike who buy into the notion that men are ruled by oversexed passions believe that a man can lose control of his own sex drive and take a woman by force. Therefore, from this patriarchal viewpoint, a woman had to be careful not to arouse a man. If a man raped a woman, it meant that she acted provocatively or somehow excited the man. If the woman hadn't given off some sexual cue stimulating the attack, it wouldn't have occurred. "What sexual cues?" asked Dorothy Hicks, a physician treating rape victims of all ages in Miami, Florida. "Is an 80-year-old victim or a 4-month-old baby responsible for triggering a man's sex drive as well?" (Luy, 1977).

The feminist revision to the traditional definition of rape removed any burden of guilt from the victim and placed it onto the perpetrator. The current perspective on rape views it as a *social* problem, not a personal problem. Rape is an outcome of **patriarchy**—control by men of a disproportionately large share of power. Through the fear of rape, women are socialized to be submissive. The root of the problem, then, is patriarchy and power, not sexual arousal. Ultimately, feminists argue, rape is a form of violence, not an act of passion.

This feminist view does not suggest that men deliberately use rape to frighten women into submissive positions. The practice of patriarchy is maintained by those in power. Men are taught "to associate power, dominance, strength, virility and superiority with masculinity, and submissiveness, passivity, weakness, and inferiority with femininity" (Scully, 1990; Scully & Marolla, 1985/2007). Teaching men that to be "masculine" one must be domineering pressures them to make aggression a normal part of their gender identity. Men are taught in the media that "real" men don't take "No" for an answer. The media lie continues—women say "No" when they don't really mean it, and, as some pornographic movies demonstrate, women actually like being forced into sexual acts they don't consent to (Reynolds, 1976; Finkelhor & Yllo, 1985, 1989).

The feminist view of rape as dominance contrasts sharply with the traditional view of rape as an outcome of passion. As these ideas have become more accepted, legal definitions

See For Yourself

Go to the Uniform Crime Report Web site at http://www.fbi.gov/ucr/ucr.htm
- ▶ Research the number of reported rapes on this site. These are the number of rapes officially reported to police.

Now visit the National Crime Victimization Survey at http://www.ojp.usdoj.gov/bjs/cvict.htm
- ▶ Research the number of reported rapes on this site. Remember, this number also reflects unreported rapes.

of rape have changed as well. Many states have replaced the legal charge of rape with **criminal sexual assault.** This newly defined crime is much more broad, including all sexual assaults, completed *and attempted,* aggravated and non-aggravated against *all genders.*

The Social Patterns of Rape

HOW COMMON IS RAPE? According to the FBI, 72,000 American women are forcibly raped each year (*FBI Uniform Crime Reports,* 2006, Table 15). This is the "official" total, the number reported to police. The actual total is likely 3 times higher. That means each year, over 200,000 American women are raped.

How do we know that forcible rape is 3 times higher than the official statistics? Twice a year, researchers conduct what is called *The National Crime Victimization Survey.* In this survey, they interview about 90,000 Americans in 45,000 households. The researchers ask about crimes that have happened to them and whether they reported those crimes to the police. On average, only 33% of victims report their rapes to the police (*Statistical Abstract,* 2006, p. 192).

PREDICTABLE SOCIAL PATTERNS. Here are several trends researchers have discovered about the frequency of rape:

Acquaintanceship: A woman is more likely to be raped by someone she knows than by a stranger.

Place: A woman is most likely to be raped at home or at the home of a friend, relative, or neighbor.

Time: Night hours are more dangerous than daytime hours: Two of three rapes occur after 6 p.m.

Season: As Figure 5-4 on the next page shows, rapes are more likely to occur in summer than in winter.

Age: The typical victim is between 12 and 24 years of age. After the age of 34, rape rates decline.

Income, race–ethnicity, and geography: Those most likely to become victims are poor African American women living in the South.

Region: A woman's chances of being raped vary tremendously from one state to another. Women in Alaska are 6 times more likely to be raped than are women in New Jersey or West Virginia. The Social Map on the next page (Figure 5-5) shows which states are the safest and which are the most dangerous.

Weapon: About four out of five rapists use their own physical strength as their only weapon (*Sourcebook of Criminal Justice Statistics,* 2004, Tables 3.4.2004, 3.11; *Statistical Abstract,* 2006, Tables 308, 311).

Because these patterns show up year after year, sociologists conclude that rape is not the act of a few sick men, but, rather, *is intimately linked to our patriarchal culture.*

GROUPS THAT ARE OVERREPRESENTED. As you can conclude from these sociological patterns, rapists are almost always men. Although women can rape, it is almost exclusively

FIGURE 5-4 Forcible Rape by Month

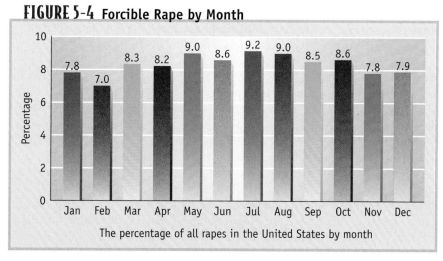

The percentage of all rapes in the United States by month

Source: By James M. Henslin. Based on *FBI Uniform Crime Reports* (2006, Table 2.1).

a crime committed by young males. Although only 7.5% of males in the United States are ages 17 to 21, they account for 23% of those arrested for rape (*Sourcebook,* 2005, Table 4.7.2004; *Statistical Abstract,* 2006, Table 11). Similar findings hold true for race–ethnicity: Only about 12% of the U.S. male population is African American, but African American males account for 32% of arrested rapists (*Sourcebook,* 2005, Table 4.10.2004; *Statistical Abstract,* 2006, Table 13).

Why are African American men overrepresented in rape statistics? For this answer, let's turn to two sociological theories. First, according to *conflict theory,* lower classes are oppressed—and, as we reviewed earlier, one reaction to oppression is violence. Compared with men from other social classes, lower-class men commit more forcible rapes (or are arrested most often). Because African Americans are overrepresented in the lower social classes, they are involved in rape cases disproportionately. Using strain theory as a second explanation, we see that African American men are often blocked from legitimate avenues

FIGURE 5-5 How Safe Is Your State? Rape in the United States

Source: By James M. Henslin. Based on *FBI Uniform Crime Reports* (2007, Table 5).

of attaining social status. These frustrations may lead them to turn against those less powerful than themselves. As some have suggested, rape may be a way of establishing power in the face of socially imposed powerlessness (McNeely & Pope, 1981).

INJURY, RAPE, AND RESISTANCE. Is a woman more likely to be raped if she resists or if she gives up without a struggle? In their interviews, sociologists Pauline Bart and Patricia O'Brien (1984, 1985) found that the women who had yelled, fled, or fought back were less likely to be raped. Other studies support this finding that women who resist are less likely to be raped (Kleck & Sayles, 1990; Zoucha-Jensen & Coyne, 1993; Ullman, 1998). Apparently the more strategies that a woman uses (scratching, biting, gouging, kicking, hitting, screaming, running), the greater her chances of avoiding rape (McIntyre et al., 1979; Block & Skogan, 1982).

Although a woman who resists her attacker is less likely to be raped, she is more likely to be injured. This is what sociologist Sarah Ullman (1998) found in her study of rape victims in Chicago. Other studies found the same to be true. Of 203,000 victims, about half reported that fighting back helped them, and only about one-seventh said that their resistance made their situation worse (*Sourcebook,* 1991, Table 3-20; *Sourcebook,* 2005, Table 3.20.2004). But not all rapists are the same. Fighting back may scare some rapists away, but it enrages other attackers, causing even more injuries. In addition, some rapists encourage their victims to struggle, for this excites them sexually. Unfortunately, *a woman who is being attacked does not know what kind of rapist she is facing, and she cannot know what the results of her resistance will be.*

At this point, let's look at types of rapists.

Profiling the Rapist

The following 10 profiles of rapists are based on the confessions of those who have been arrested and incarcerated (Cohen, Seghorn, & Calamas, 1969; Hotchkiss, 1978; Athens, 1980; Hills, 1980; Scully & Marolla, 1985/2007). Although these profiles illustrate many motivations for rape, it is impossible to know the proportion of rapists within each category.

At some point in his life, the *woman hater* was hurt by a woman who was significant to him. In many cases, this woman was his mother. This hurt inflicted an emotional wound and left him with a hatred of women. By sexually assaulting women, this man gains a sense of personal power. By degrading his victim and sometimes brutally assaulting her, he retaliates for his festering wound.

Although the *sadist* has no particular negative feelings toward women, he beats his victims because he has learned to receive pleasure by hurting others. By raping women, he combines the pleasure he receives from inflicting pain with the pleasure he receives from sex. Because he enjoys it when his victim begs, pleads, and shows fear, the sadist is likely to increase his sexual excitement by beating or torturing his victim before sexual penetration. He sometimes prolongs his pleasure by continuing to inflict pain on her during and after the rape.

For the *generally violence-prone* man, rape is just *another* act of violence. Unlike the previous two types of rapists, his pleasure in rape is rooted in sex, not violence. He uses only enough violence to make the woman submit. If she resists, he may hurt her because she is "holding out" on him.

The *revenge* rapist uses rape to get even. His victim may be the person he is angry at, or she may be just a substitute for his real target. For example, one such rapist went to collect money from another man who owed him a debt. When he discovered that the man was not home, he said, "I grabbed her and started beating the hell out of her. Then I committed the act. I knew what I was doing. I was mad. I could have stopped, but I didn't. I did it to get even with her and her husband" (Scully & Marolla, 1985/2007).

The *political* rapist also chooses his victim as a substitute for his enemy, but, in addition, he uses the rape to make a political statement. In *Soul on Ice* (1968), Eldridge Cleaver recounts how he raped White women to "strike out against the white establishment." **Soldier rape**—rape committed by a soldier on a country's inhabitants during

wartime—also qualifies as political rape. Soldiers are not motivated by a hatred of women, but by hatred of the enemy. Raping "the enemy's women" shows contempt for the enemy and declares superiority.

Generally passive and submissive, the *Walter Mitty* rapist has an unrealistic image of masculinity. He uses rape to bridge the gap between the way he perceives how men ought to be and the way he perceives himself. He fantasizes that his victims enjoy being raped—for he is an excellent sex partner. The Walter Mitty rapist is unlikely to beat his victim, but he will use as much force as necessary to make her submit.

Unlike the first six types of rapists, the *opportunist* does not set out to rape. Rather, he takes advantage of an unexpected opportunity, often during a robbery or burglary. For example, one man drove to a local supermarket looking for a robbery victim. The first person he found was a pregnant woman. As he threatened her with a knife, the woman, scared out of her wits, blurted out that she would do anything if he didn't hurt her. At that point, he forced her to a deserted area where he raped her. He explained, "I wasn't thinking about sex. But when she said she would do anything not to get hurt, probably because she was pregnant, I thought, '"why not"' (Scully and Marolla, 2007).

Date rapists, also called *acquaintance rapists,* feel that they deserve sex because they have invested time and money in a date or sexual seduction. They are simply collecting a sexual "payoff" for their investment. Date rapists generally prefer nonviolent encounters. It is uncommon for date rapists to be convicted, because their victims know them and feel as though they contributed to the situation—inviting them into their own home (Kanin, 2003). As the Issues in Social Problems box on page 144 shows, contrary to popular belief, date rape consists of much more than a man being more insistent than he should.

For the *recreational* rapist, rape involves not only him as perpetrator, but his friends as well. As sociologists Diana Scully and Joseph Marolla (1985/2007) discovered in their interviews of imprisoned rapists, one man may make a date with a victim and then drive her to a predetermined location, where he and his friends rape her. One participant said that this practice had become so much a part of his group's weekend routine that they rented a house just for the purpose of recreational rape.

Lastly, the *husband* rapist attacks his own wife. Contrary to common opinion, marital rape is real. It is not an innocuous event involving a husband who has simply become too insistent about having sex. After interviewing wives who had become victims of their husbands, sociologists David Finkelhor and Kersti Yllo (1985, 1989) concluded that marital rape can involve violence and sadism every bit as horrible as any we have discussed. Some wives are forced to flee their own homes in terror.

Reactions to Rape

Let's look at what happens to rape victims after their attack. We will focus first on personal reactions and then on the greater social problem—how the criminal justice system treats rape victims.

THE TRAUMA OF RAPE. Disbelief and shock are the first reactions reported by rape victims (McIntyre et al., 1979). The event is so frightening and alien that most victims report they could not believe it was actually happening.

The trauma of rape does not end with the physical attack (Littleton & Breitkopf, 2006). The woman typically finds her self-concept so wounded and her emotions in such tatters that her whole life is disrupted. Some rape victims deal with their trauma in an *expressive* style, venting their fear, anger, rage, and anxiety by crying and sobbing or by restlessness and tenseness. Others react in a *controlled* style, carefully masking their feelings behind a calm and composed exterior (Burgess & Holmstrom, 1974). Investigators often expect only an expressive style—talking with those demonstrating a controlled style is often confusing.

After a rape, life and relationships are no longer the same. Doubt, distrust, and self-blame plague rape victims. Some feel guilty for having been alone in that place at that time. Others feel it was their fault for letting themselves get in a compromising situation. If they didn't scream and fight back, perhaps they should have? They feel that there

Issues in Social Problems
DATE (OR ACQUAINTANCE) RAPE

The public has little understanding of date rape. Some seem to think that it involves a reluctant woman who needs a "push" to go along with what she really wants. Consider these two cases:

> Carol had just turned 18, and it looked as if her dreams had come true. It was only the beginning of her freshman year, and yet she had met Tom, the all-state quarterback. At Wiggins Watering Hole, the college bar, he had walked over to her table and made some crack about the English comp professor. She had laughed, and the two had spent most of the evening talking.
>
> When Tom asked to take her back to the dorm, Carol didn't hesitate. This was the man all the girls wanted to date! At the dorm, he said he would like to talk some more, so she signed him in. Once in the room, he began to kiss her. At first, the kisses felt good. But Tom was not about to stop with kissing. He forced her to the bed and, despite her protests, began to remove her clothing.
>
> With his 240 pounds, and her 117, there wasn't much of a contest. Carol always wondered why she didn't cry out; she was asked this at the trial, at which Tom was found not guilty. This brutal end to her virginity also marked the end of her college career. Unable to shake the depression that followed, Carol left college and moved back with her parents. After a hearing, the university suspended Tom for a few games. Tom then resumed his life as before. He still goes to Wiggins Watering Hole.
>
> For Letitia, age 27, the evening started out friendly enough. After a cozy dinner at her apartment, her boyfriend suggested that she lie down while he did the dishes. She grabbed this unexpected opportunity. As she lay in bed, though, he walked in with a butcher knife. Her formerly tender lover bound and raped her. When it was over, he fell asleep.

Convictions are difficult to get in date-rape cases. Some prosecutors discourage women from even bringing charges of date rape. A social worker at a rape treatment center summarized the problem well when she said, "Most people are sympathetic when a stranger breaks into your house with a gun and rapes you, but if you say you made a date with the rapist, they always wonder how far you went before you said no."

What can be done? Campus antirape groups—composed of both women and men—offer one remedy. Lectures and workshops introduce incoming freshmen to the reality and perils of date rape. Well-publicized prosecutions help reduce the risk, and antirape groups encourage women to press charges and insist that prosecutors file charges.

One rapidly growing nationwide college program, One in Four, has been shown to lead to reductions in rape and sexual assault. According to Matt Amalfitano, a college student and member of One in Four, "We're not like those antirape guys on campus. We want to be the pro-women guys."

"The name One in Four actually comes from the statistic that one in four women from the age of thirteen to the time they graduate college will have survived rape," Amalfitano said. "The scarier thing is that four out of five of these women will have known their rapists for a year on average." The presentation the group makes to students is titled "How to Help a Sexual Assault Victim: What Men Can Do."

This and similar student groups can pressure college administrations to react strongly to date rape. As one activist said, "If there were a pattern of assaults on quarterbacks, universities would respond very quickly."

Based on Engelmayer (1983); Seligmann (1984); Taslitz (2005); Seligmann (2008).

Events such as this appear often on college campuses across America.

See For Yourself

Go to the following Web sites that discuss false accusations: http://www.xyonline.net/Hines_False_accusations.shtml and http://www.anandaanswers.com/pages/naaFalse.html

▶ How many rapes among those reported are actually thought to be false reports?
▶ What are some of the possible reasons false reports are filed?

must have been something—*anything*—that they could have done—or not done—that might have changed the situation.

In addition to nightmares, many victims become afraid—of being alone, of the dark, of walking on the street, or of doing such ordinary things as shopping and driving. Anything that reminds them of the rape can send them into anxiety and depression—and they never know what will trigger the painful memories. The victim's personal relationships may also deteriorate, for, feeling hurt and less trusting, some women feel less intimate and withdraw emotionally. To complicate matters even further, some husbands and boyfriends wonder what "really" happened, and their suspicions feed this spiral of despair.

DEALING WITH THE LEGAL SYSTEM. As a result of the work done by many rape advocates and feminists, police departments have grown more sensitive to rape victims. They have trained women officers to do the interviewing and to collect the evidence needed to pursue a criminal case. Yet, the criminal justice system still places much of the blame on the victim (Madigan & Gamble, 1991; Jordan, 2001).

To conduct their investigation, police must collect evidence surrounding the attack. They ask intimate details—some officers get embarrassed, others are insensitive, and still others demonstrate disbelief. Some officers don't believe the attack qualifies as rape if the woman doesn't have bruises and cuts. Others suspect that the victim is using the police to "get even" with a boyfriend. Because some (very few) rape charges are bogus, this is a concern.

But just when the woman needs compassion the most, when her world has been turned upside down, she often finds herself the object of suspicion. One victim gave this account of her experience with the police:

> They rushed me down to the housing cops who asked me questions like, "Was he your boyfriend?" "Did you know him?" Here I am, hysterical. I'm 12 years old, and I don't know these things even happen to people. Anyway, they took me to the precinct after that, and there about four detectives got me in the room and asked me how long was his penis—like I was supposed to measure it. Actually, they said, "How long was the instrument?" I thought they were referring to the knife—how was I supposed to know? That I could have told them 'cause I was sure enough lookin' at the knife. (Brownmiller, 1975, p. 365)

Even if a woman is fortunate enough to be questioned by sensitive, compassionate police officers who have been trained in rape investigations, this is just the beginning of her experience in the criminal justice system. In only 42% of reported rapes is someone arrested (*Sourcebook,* 2005, Table 4.19.2004). The victim is now faced with a dilemma: If she fails to press charges, the rapist goes free—and he may well rape again. But if she prosecutes, she must relive her attack, perhaps repeatedly, as she goes over the details with the prosecuting attorney. Then she must describe everything in a courtroom in front of her rapist, his attorney, a judge, perhaps a jury, journalists, and even the general public. Here, the defense attorney may try to demean her character, for in some states her prior sex life can still be examined on the witness stand. Everything she says can and will be challenged. Any fuzziness in her account is an opportunity for the defense attorney

to attack her credibility. In the courtroom, the victim often becomes the accused. As one rape victim said of her experience,

> I had heard other women say that the trial is the rape. It's no exaggeration. My trial was one of the dirtiest transcripts you could read. Even though I had been warned about the defense attorney, you wouldn't believe the things he asked me to describe. It was very humiliating. I don't understand it. It was like I was the defendant and he was the plaintiff. I wasn't on trial. I don't see where I did anything wrong. I screamed, I struggled. (Brownmiller, 1975, p. 36)

This scenario describes a second victimization—some call it the "legal rape" of the victim. If someone is accused of a crime, the defense has the right to question the accuser (victim). The traditional/patriarchal view of rape influences some jurors. From this traditional perspective, men have a difficult time controlling their strong, almost overwhelming, sex drive. By their revealing clothing, some women provoke men sexually. Others are "asking for it," because they go into bars or go out alone at night. Then there are women who change their minds just before sex. When the aroused man continues with what they both had previously intended, these women cry rape. In the traditional view, women have no right to do any of these things.

HOMOSEXUAL RAPE. Although we have concentrated on male–female rape, other types of rape do occur. As we will discuss in Chapter 9, homosexual victimization can also occur. Male rape is not as frequent as female rape—but it is still all too common. Since homosexual rape became legally recognized in 1994, the number of rapes reported have escalated from 150 to 1,135 per year (Rumney, 2008). About 1 in 10,000 males over the age of 11 are raped each year by another man; 13 in 10,000 females are raped by men (Struckman-Johnson & Struckman-Johnson, 1992). Not all male rape is homosexual—a woman can also rape a man. The typical scenario of male rape by a female involves sodomy with a foreign object. Among the homosexual population, male rape is twice as common. It has been reported that in San Francisco, 24% of the male homosexual population has been raped (Cameron, 1999).

Murder

If people from another culture studied Americans, they might find our fascination with murder bizarre. The reenaction of murder has become a form of entertainment: Every night Americans watch beatings, bombings, shootings, slashings, stabbings, strangulations, and other mayhem on television. Beyond entertainment, however, real-life killings are occurring.

The Social Patterns of Murder

Let's examine statistics in order to uncover social patterns of murder.

THE "WHO" OF MURDER. Although most fears center on those murders committed by strangers, of all violent crimes, murder is the *least* likely to be committed by a stranger. As Figure 5-6 on the next page shows, of all violent crimes, murder is also the most likely to be solved. Table 5-2 on the next page shows the relationships between victims and their killers. As you can see, strangers account for only 23% of U.S. killings. Three out of four murder victims are killed by members of their family or by their lovers, friends, neighbors, or other acquaintances.

Perpetrators of murder share characteristics of social class, sex, age, and race–ethnicity with rapists. Poor young men are most likely to kill. Although males between the ages of 17 and 24 constitute only about 6% of the U.S. population, from this group come *one-third* of murderers (*FBI Uniform Crime Reports,* 2005, Table 2.5; *Statistical Abstract,* 2006, Table 11).

Figure 5-7 on page 148 illustrates how much more likely men are to kill than women. Men kill 90% of everyone who is murdered in the United States. Although women make up 51% of the U.S. population, they commit only 10% of the murders.

FIGURE 5-6 Crimes Cleared by Arrest

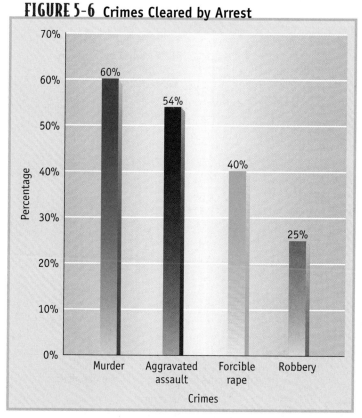

Source: Based on *FBI Uniform Crime Reports* (2006).

As you can see from Table 5-2, husbands are almost 4 times more likely to kill their wives than the reverse. You can also see how much more likely boyfriends are to kill their girlfriends than girlfriends are to kill their boyfriends.

Similar startling differences appear among the murders of African Americans and Whites. Although African Americans make up only about 12% of the U.S. population, in 49% of the cases where the race–ethnicity of the killer is known, the murderer is an African American (*FBI Uniform Crime Reports*, 2005, Table 2.7). From Table 5-3 on page 148, you can see that murder is overwhelmingly *intraracial;* 86% of White victims are killed by Whites, and 92% of Blacks are killed by Blacks.

TABLE 5-2 How Are Murder Victims Related to Their Killers?

THEIR KILLERS ARE (IN PERCENTAGES):

Family	**23.7%**	**Acquaintances**	**53.4%**
Wife	7.3	Girlfriend	5.6
Son	2.9	Friend	3.8
Daughter	2.7	Boyfriend	1.8
Husband	1.9	Neighbor	1.4
Father	1.4	Other Acquaintance	40.5
Mother	1.5		
Brother	1.1	**Strangers**	**22.9%**
Sister	0.1		
Other Family	3.5		

Note: These relationships refer to cases in which the relationship between the killer and victim is known. In 44% of killings this relationship is unknown, either because the crime was not solved or the police did not report the relationship.

Source: By James M. Henslin. Based on *FBI Uniform Crime Reports* (2006, Table 2.4).

FIGURE 5-7 Killers and Their Victims

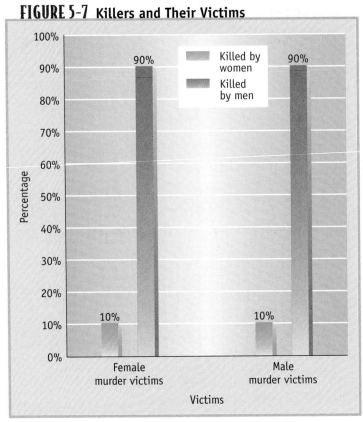

Source: By James M. Henslin. Based on *FBI Uniform Crime Reports* (2006, Table 2.7).

THE "WHAT" OF MURDER. Although people use a variety of weapons to commit murder, every year the number one murder weapon is the gun. As you can see from Figure 5-8 on the next page, all other weapons are far less popular. Guns may be the favorite choice for two obvious reasons: They are highly effective, and they are readily available in the United States. More subtle reasons may be that men as killers identify guns as masculine. Significant cultural stereotypes reinforce this image. For example, our culture romanticizes the display of guns among cowboys, hunters, and villains. To settle a quarrel, then, the U.S. male is much more likely to reach for a gun than, say, a kitchen knife or a bottle of poison.

THE "WHEN" OF MURDER. Murder is not evenly distributed across the seasons. July and August are consistently the highest months for murder, and February the lowest (*FBI Uniform Crime Reports,* 2005, Table 2.2). Statistics indicate that nighttime is more dangerous than daytime, and weekends more dangerous than weekdays. The most dangerous time of the week is Saturday night (McGinty, 2006). As sociologist Alex Thio (1978) observed long ago, this may explain why inexpensive handguns are often referred to as "**Saturday night specials.**" Saturday night specials are often sold on street corners to those criminals on a low budget.

TABLE 5-3 Race–Ethnicity of Killers and Their Victims

		KILLERS	
		White	**Black**
Victims	White	86%	14%
	Black	8%	92%

Note: Does not include victims or killers whose race-ethnicity is unknown.

Source: By James M. Henslin. Based on *FBI Uniform Crime Reports* (2006, Table 2.7).

THE "WHERE" OF MURDER. The good news is that U.S. murder rates have plunged 44%, dropping from 10 killings per 100,000 Americans to just 6 (*FBI Uniform Crime Reports,* 1992, 2005). Although the U.S. murder rate has declined sharply, when compared to other Western countries it remains high (see Figure 5-3 on page 132). As with rape, states vary tremendously in individual rates, and the region where you live affects your chances of becoming a murder victim. As you can see from Figure 5-9 on the next page, people

FIGURE 5-8 American's Choice of Murder Weapons

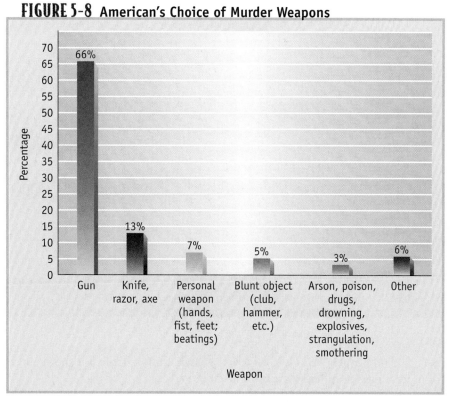

Source: By James M. Henslin. Based on *FBI Uniform Crime Reports* (2006, Table 2.9).

in Louisiana are thirteen more times likely to be murdered than are people in New Hampshire.

Most people think the chances of getting murdered are greater in the city than in the country—and they are right. In large cities (those with populations over 250,000), 6 of every 100,000 people are murdered each year. In rural areas, the murder rate drops

FIGURE 5-9 The "Where" of Murder: The Murder Rate per State

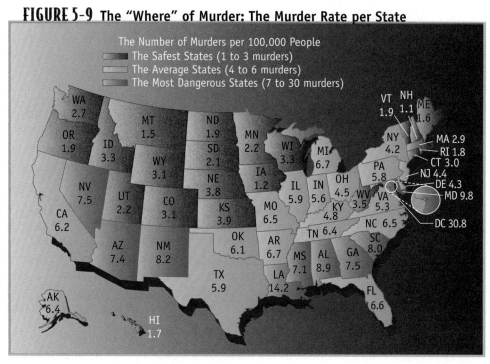

Source: Based on *FBI Uniform Crime Reports* (2007, Table 5).

TABLE 5-4 Murder: The Ten Safest and Most Dangerous U.S. Cities

	SAFEST			MOST DANGEROUS	
Rank	City	Murders per 100,000 People	Rank	City	Murders per 100,000 People
1	Honolulu, HI	1.7	1	New Orleans, LA	57.7
2	Mesa, AZ	3.2	2	Washington, DC	44.0
3	San Jose, CA	3.2	3	Baltimore, MD	41.9
4	El Paso, TX	3.6	4	Detroit, MI	39.4
5	Austin, TX	4.0	5	Atlanta, GA	34.3
6	Colorado Springs, CO	4.5	6	Oakland, CA	26.8
7	Wichita, KS	4.9	7	Philadelphia, PA	23.3
8	Portland, OR	5.0	8	Chicago, IL	20.6
9	San Diego, CA	5.1	9	Miami, FL	19.4
10	Virginia Beach, VA	5.5	10	Memphis, TN	19.3

Note: From data reported by police officials in cities over 250,000 people.
Source: By James M. Henslin. Based on *Statistical Abstract of the United States* (2006, Table 296).

to 4 per 100,000 people (*FBI Uniform Crime Reports,* 2005). Table 5-4 shows the variation of murder rates in different areas of the country.

THE "WHY" OF MURDER. Now that we have looked at the "who," "what," "when," and "where" of murder, let's examine the "why."

Explaining Social Patterns

Why do sociologists usually see the patterns just reviewed? They reflect societal trends.

ACQUAINTANCESHIP. Most murder victims are killed by someone they know; indeed, most murders are crimes of passion spurred by heated arguments. Many analysts have pointed out that we are much more likely to argue with people we know than with strangers. Those we know share our money, property, and love—which fuel the kinds of quarrels that sometimes lead to violent death.

POVERTY. Why are murderers so often represented among the poor? The sociological perspectives help us understand this pattern. *Conflict theorists,* who view the poor as oppressed people, see high murder rates as a direct result of poverty. As sociologist Elliott Currie (1985, p. 160) put it,

> Brutal conditions breed brutal behavior. To believe otherwise requires us to argue that the experience of being confined to the mean and precarious depths of the American economy has no serious consequences for personal character or social behavior.

Data reveal that most murder victims also live in poverty-stricken areas. Conflict theorists conclude that people in poverty may be striking out at one another instead of at their oppressors.

Functionalists adopt both strain theory and control theory in their explanations of deviance. Functionalists use strain theory to demonstrate how those who are blocked from achieving societal goals feel stressed. People who feel high stress are more likely to strike out at others. Functionalists who emphasize control theory point out that the poor have weaker internal and external controls inhibiting their desires to strike out at others. For example, the poor have "less to lose" if they go to jail. Compared with people from higher social classes, the poor are less likely to own their own homes, their jobs pay relatively little, and their reputations are not as fragile.

THE MEANING BEHIND MURDER. *Symbolic interactionists* help us understand that in some poor subcultures criminal behavior enhances a person's reputation. Young males become more "manly" if they are sent to "juvvie" (juvenile detention) or to jail. In some subcultures, the prison experience has become so common that young men expect to go there, just as young men in other social classes expect to go to college.

Symbolic interactionists stress that social classes also resolve disputes differently. Middle-class members are likely to seek legal recourse, whereas the poor not only can't afford lawyers, but they also don't have the same confidence in the legal system. As a result, poor people are more likely to settle disagreements outside the law. These direct confrontations more easily lead to heated words, physical assault, and death.

Symbolic interactionist theorists use subcultural theory and differential association to explain deviance. In a subculture of poverty, one settles scores directly with an antagonist. This is viewed as "macho." People who stand up to others are admired for doing so. Both men and women who grow up in this subculture are likely to learn to react violently to life's problems.

To trace the path by which people became involved in murder, Lonnie Athens, a symbolic interactionist, interviewed 58 prisoners. He found this general pattern: The killer was often retaliating against a victim when the murder took place. A spouse or lover might have refused sex or threatened to leave. Or someone may have spewed insults. The killer interpreted the act as one that called for retaliation, often because the act threatened the killer's self-image or social standing among friends. According to this interpretation of the situation, someone winds up dead for insulting the wrong person.

A woman prisoner whom Athens (1980, pp. 36–37) interviewed said that a stranger at a party had accused her of cheating him of $20. The man kept insulting her and laughing at her:

> Then I told myself, "This man has got to go one way or another; I've just had enough of this (man) messing with me; I'm going to cut his dirty . . . throat." I went into my bedroom, got a $20 bill and my razor. I said to myself . . . "now he's hung himself," and I walked out of the bedroom. I went up to him with a big smile on my face. I held the $20 bill in my hand out in front of me and hid the razor in the other hand. Then I sat on his lap and said, "O.K., you're a fast dude; here's your $20 back." He said, "I'm glad that you are finally admitting it." I looked at him with a smile and said, "Let me seal it with a kiss" . . . and then I bent over like I was going to kiss him and started slicing up his throat.

KILLING AS A MANLY ACT. This last example notwithstanding, why do men kill more often than women? As we have seen, men are more likely to associate violence with masculinity. Men in poverty believe that a "real man" should act violent. One's standing in the group may depend on being known as "the kind of guy who can't be pushed around." Not fighting back represents cowardice, the worst quality a young man can show in certain subcultures.

As we saw earlier, among some groups spilling blood brings honor. In the Mafia, killing an enemy is a demonstration of courage: Killing is the measure of one's *capacity as a man.* There, "the more awesome and potent the victim, the more worthy and meritorious the killer" (Arlacchi, 1980, p. 113).

Symbolic interactionists stress that women, on the other hand, are less likely to be socialized into violence. While men learn to associate masculinity with acting tough, showing bravery, and being violent, most women learn less violent ways of handling embarrassment. The result of this socialization is that *in every society around the world* men kill at a rate several times that of women (Daly & Wilson, 1988; Chernoff & Simon, 2000). Biological and evolutionary theorists point to this worldwide uniformity in the killing pattern as evidence for their theories of genetic inheritance. We will continue with a sociological focus on environmental theories.

RACIAL–ETHNIC DIFFERENCES. So why do African Americans kill at a higher rate than other races? African Americans are more likely to be poor, and the subculture to which lower-class African American males belong identifies masculinity with the willingness to

Visitors from other countries, such as this European woman visiting a "gun shop," are often shocked at how many Americans own guns and how easily guns can be purchased.

defend oneself aggressively. Functionalists would add that African Americans are socialized to strive for the cultural goal of material success, but discrimination blocks many of them from reaching that goal through legitimate means. This increases their strain, leading to a higher rate of violence, most of which is directed against people nearby. Because African Americans are forced into racially segregated housing, intraracial murder rates increase.

What about violence that crosses racial lines? To explain interracial patterns, functionalists stress a connection between race–ethnicity and money. If a burglary, robbery, or mugging results in a murder across racial lines, it is most likely to involve a poor African American robbing a White. Conflict theorists add that the oppression of African Americans by Whites produces racial hatred that has many negative consequences, including death. If African Americans possessed more wealth than Whites, we would expect this pattern to be reversed.

To better understand race–ethnicity and patterns of violence, in *The Declining Significance of Race,* William Julius Wilson (1978) analyzed how movement within social class affected murder rates. As African Americans were granted more access to education, they in turn occupied higher-paying jobs. Seizing the opportunity, they moved out of the ghetto and into more desirable areas of the city and suburbs. Left behind was an *underclass,* a group of people desperately poor and plagued with social problems: high unemployment, single-parent households, drug addiction, murder, robbery, and rape. As Wilson put it, this group "is increasingly isolated from mainstream culture." With successful African Americans moving out of the area, violence results among those blocked from success.

TEMPORAL PATTERNS. Murders are less frequent during weekdays when people are working and meeting personal and family responsibilities. Murders are higher on weekends when people are more likely to be socializing in public, drinking, and using drugs. The peak of violence occurs on Saturday night. Because people are more likely to get out of the house and socialize during warm weather, murder is higher during the summer months and lower during winter months.

GEOGRAPHIC PATTERNS. Last, geography plays a role in murder patterns as well. For more than a century, the South's murder rate has been higher than that of the rest of the country. This pattern is broadly evident in the Social Map you looked at earlier

(Figure 5-5 on page 149). That the South has a higher murder rate year after year has led some researchers to conclude that there is a *southern subculture of violence*. This subculture teaches southerners to resolve disagreements in confrontational ways. More violent themes run through southern music, literature, and jokes. Apparently, southerners are more likely to own guns, to know how to shoot them, and to use guns during quarrels. Sociologists find these explanations suggestive, but not totally satisfactory (Doerner, 1978; Huff-Corzine, Corzine, & Moore, 1986, 1991; Pridemore & Freilich, 2006). We need more research to establish adequate explanations.

Before concluding this section, let's look at two patterns of murder that have gripped the public's attention: mass murder and serial murder.

MASS MURDER. **Mass murder** is the killing of four or more people in a single episode (Fox & Levin, 2005). Examples are Richard Speck's murder of 8 nursing students in Chicago one July night in 1966 and Charles Whitman's killing of 16 people in a sniper attack from a tower at the University of Texas that same year. In 1981, Priscilla Ford killed 6 people in Reno, Nevada, by deliberately driving her car onto a crowded sidewalk during a Thanksgiving Day parade; James Huberty shot 21 people at a McDonald's in 1984; Julio Gonzalez torched the Happy Land Social Club in the Bronx in 1991, killing 87 people, because his girlfriend was breaking up with him. George Hennard shot 22 people at a Luby's Cafeteria in Killeen, Texas, in 1991; in 1993, Colin Ferguson went on a shooting spree on a New York commuter train. In Houston in 2001, Andrea Yates drowned her 5 small children in the family bathtub while her husband was at work. We have already discussed the school shootings, such as those described in our opening vignette, that have so alarmed the public.

When Timothy McVeigh blew up a federal building in Oklahoma City, Oklahoma, in 1995, 168 people died. This is the largest mass murder by a single individual in the history of the United States. (McVeigh may have been assisted by others, but, if so, only a small number of people were involved.) McVeigh's stunning number of victims was overshadowed by the events of September 11, 2001, of course, which claimed about 3,000 lives.

SERIAL MURDER. **Serial murder** is the killing of several people in three or more separate events. The murders may occur over several days, weeks, or even years. The elapsed time between murders distinguishes serial killers from mass murderers. Serial killers are generally less spontaneous than mass murderers and are generally more methodical in their planning.

Because many serial killers are motivated by lust and are aroused sexually by killing, the FBI sometimes uses the term "lust murder." A serial killer often keeps souvenirs or trophies—the victims' jewelry, underwear, even body parts—as reminders of the killing (Fox & Levin, 2005, p. 44). One of the most bizarre serial killers was Jeffrey Dahmer of Milwaukee. Not only did Dahmer kill young men, but he also had sex with their dead bodies and fried and ate parts of his victims. So he wouldn't go hungry, he kept body parts in his freezer. The serial killer with the most victims was Harold Shipman, a quiet, unassuming physician in Manchester, England. From 1977 to 2000, he killed 275 elderly women patients, giving them lethal injections while making house calls. The Spotlight on Social Research box on the next page focuses on one young man's development into a serial murderer.

Almost all serial killers are men, but occasionally women are perpetrators as well. In 1986, Blanche Taylor Moore poisoned her father, her first husband, and a boyfriend with arsenic. In 1988, Dorothea Montalvo Puente killed seven senior citizens. Her motive was cashing in their Social Security checks. In 1989, Faye Copeland and her husband killed five transient men. In 2002, Aileen Wuornos was executed after killing five middle-aged men she had sex with.

HAVE MASS AND SERIAL MURDERS BECOME MORE COMMON? Many assume that mass and serial murders are more common now than they used to be, but we cannot draw this conclusion. In the past, police departments had little communication with one another, and when killings occurred in different jurisdictions, it was difficult to link the killings. Today's more efficient investigative techniques make it easier for the police to conclude that a serial killer is operating in an area.

Spotlight on Social Research

DOING RESEARCH ON A SERIAL KILLER

BY JAMES M. HENSLIN

I researched one of the first serial killings to attract the attention of the U.S. public. In Houston, Texas, Dean Corll, with the aid of two teenaged accomplices, had tortured and killed 27 boys. The 33-year-old had befriended Elmer Wayne Henley, 14, and David Brooks,15, from broken homes. Corll became their father substitute, one who molded the boys into killers. Corll had a passion for teenaged boys, and from 1971 to 1973, Henley and Brooks picked up young hitchhikers and delivered them to Corll to rape, torture, and kill. Sometimes they even brought him their own neighbors and high school classmates.

The televised reports were shocking: Corpses, one after another, were being unearthed from a rented boat storage shed in Houston. As the police worked around the clock, the reports kept coming in. All the corpses seemed to be teenagers.

I decided to go to Houston. Summer classes ended in just a few days. As soon as I taught my last class, I took off for a straight-through drive from Illinois. My budget was low (nonexistent, actually), but these were "hippie" times, and it was easy to meet a stranger and find a place to stay for a few nights.

I went to the "morgue," the newspaper office that stores its back issues. There I read systematically about the case, from the first revelation of the killings to its current coverage. The accounts included the addresses of the victims. On a city map, I marked the home of each local victim, as well as the homes of the killers. As I drove around the neighborhoods, map in hand, I saw at one of the marked homes a man painting his porch. I stopped my car, went over and introduced myself. I asked him if he were the father of one of the boys who had been killed. Although

Elmer Wayne Henley being arrested in Houston, Texas, for the murder of Dean Corll. As detailed in this box, Henley was involved in the kidnapping, torture, and murder of dozens of boys.

reluctant to talk about his son's death, he did so. His son had left the house one Saturday to go for a haircut. He never made it home. He told me bitterly that the police had refused to investigate his son's disappearance. They insisted that his son was a runaway.

Elmer Wayne Henley, one of the accused killers, was a neighborhood kid who lived just down the street.

As I drove by Henley's home, I decided to stop and try to get an interview. As I drove up, Henley's mother and grandmother were entering the house, carrying bags of groceries. I told them who I was and what I wanted. Henley's mother said that she couldn't talk to me, that her attorney had ordered her not to talk to anyone. I explained that I had driven all the way from Illinois to talk to her, and I promised that I would keep whatever she said private until after her son's trial. She agreed to be interviewed, and I went inside her home. While I was talking to her and her mother, three of Henley's friends came over. I was also able to interview them.

My interviews revealed what since has become common knowledge about serial killers: They successfully lead double lives that catch their friends and family unaware. Henley's mother swore to me that her son was a good boy and that he couldn't possibly be guilty. His high school friends stressed that Elmer couldn't be involved in homosexual rape and murder because he was interested only in girls. (To prevent contamination—one person being interviewed influencing another—I interviewed each person separately.) I conducted my interviews in Henley's bedroom, and for proof of Elmer's innocence, his friends pointed to a pair of girls' panties that were hanging in the room.

There was no question about Henley's guilt or the guilt of Brooks or Corll. (The case had come to the attention of the police when Henley killed Corll, because Corll had tried to kill him.) Henley and Brooks had methodically delivered hitchhikers and acquaintances to Corll, and the three of them had raped, tortured, and killed the boys. Henley and Brooks were sentenced to life terms in Texas prisons, where they remain today.

Social Policy

While we could suggest many policies for dealing with offenders and their victims, the primary concern is the prevention of violence. Let's look at the potential.

Global Concerns: Preventing Violence

We suggest four social policies that may be used for the prevention of violence:

First, researchers have documented that rape is higher in societies in which women are devalued (Lalumiere et al., 2005). This finding has profound implications

for social policy. We can reduce rape by increasing the social value of women. To do this, we need programs in churches and schools, for families, and on television that teach equality.

Second, researchers have also documented that rape is higher when the perceived cost of raping is low (Lalumiere et al., 2005). This finding also has profound implications for social policy: To reduce rape, we need social policies that increase the likelihood that rapists will be punished. Of the many possibilities, here is just one. Some men are serial rapists, who commit a large number of rapes. Some rape several times a month until they are caught—which can take years. Long sentences for repeat offenders—with little chance of parole—may prevent some women from being raped.

Third, policy makers should support research to determine how our culture creates a climate of violence. Remember the sociological question that was posed at the beginning of this chapter: What in a society increases or decreases the likelihood of violence? As indicated above, we have proposed some answers to this question. But we need more research to determine what other aspects of our culture have led to high rates of violence. We suggest that researchers

1. Compare cultures having low levels of violence with cultures having high levels to determine the differences.
2. Focus on helping young men channel their aggression constructively.
3. Find ways to minimize antagonisms and increase respect among men and women.
4. Develop programs providing more opportunities for the disadvantaged, to address the violence that is based on economic inequality.
5. Resolve gun control policy issues.

The last suggestion highlights gun control. As we saw in Figure 5-8 on page 149, most murder victims die from gunshot wounds. Two opposing viewpoints argue over the value of owning personal weapons, and these extremes illustrate why it is difficult to establish social policy concerning the prevention of violence.

Proponents of gun control argue that because most murders are crimes of passion, emotional outbursts would be less lethal if guns were not easily accessible. They claim we could reduce the U.S. murder rate by registering all guns and licensing gun owners. They consider gun ownership as a custom that has "no redeeming social value."

Opponents argue that gun ownership is a constitutional right that should not be removed because a *few* abuse this right. Americans need and have the right to own as many guns as they desire. They argue that if all law-abiding citizens had guns, few rapists and killers would break into homes—and if they did, they wouldn't survive. Americans have access to more guns now than ever before—yet the rates of both murder and rape have dropped.

The Future of the Problem

Given our history, our rate of violence is destined to remain higher than that of most other nations. From time to time, our rape and murder rates will decline, offering hope that some fundamental change is taking place, but these events will be followed by increases in rape and murder. To attain a low and permanent rate of violence will require major structural changes in our society.

Viewing the future through the lens of our theoretical perspectives we can better understand the future of the problem. *Conflict theory* indicates that tensions will remain in our society. Short of revolution (which has proven no panacea for any society), the wealthy will retain control, and discrimination will continue. Thus, the poor, especially minorities—who suffer the two-edged sword of both poverty and discrimination—will continue to show up disproportionately in crime statistics. The *functionalist* perspective explains that violence is functional enough to be perpetuated and maintained: People do get revenge and other satisfactions from killing their enemies. The *symbolic interactionist* perspective focuses on violence as a cultural symbol used to resolve conflict. This potent

symbol links violence with masculinity. Violence, then, is likely to continue as men try to live up to valued cultural images.

The *sociological* perspective on violence is essential to understanding our present and future state. Social patterns of rape and murder represent a product of our history and current social structure. Without structural change removing social inequality, violence will remain a part of life. This understanding of the *social* basis of violence can be used to implement beneficial solutions.

SUMMARY AND REVIEW

1. Sociologists analyze how violence is rooted in society. How a society is organized—its social structure—increases or decreases its amount of violence.

2. Each society has a rate of violence that, without major social change, is fairly constant over time. Sociologists call this a society's *normal violence.*

3. Biologists, anthropologists, and psychologists have theories to account for violence. The sociological response is that whatever predispositions humans have toward violence are encouraged or inhibited by the society in which they live.

4. Symbolic interactionists use two theories to explain violence. The first, *differential association,* stresses that violence is learned in association with other people. The second, *subcultural theory,* emphasizes that some groups are more approving of violence than others. People who grow up or associate with groups that approve of violence are more likely to learn violence.

5. Functionalists stress that some people become dissociated from cultural norms. Durkheim used the term *anomie* to describe this uprooting and estrangement. Anomic individuals are more likely to rape and to kill. Merton's *strain theory* suggests that violence is an alternative path that some people choose when they find the *cultural means* (such as education and jobs) to reach *cultural goals* (such as financial success) blocked. *Control* (or *containment*) *theory* suggests that the inner and outer controls of rapists and murderers are

weaker than their pushes and pulls to commit these acts.

6. Conflict theorists emphasize that the various groups that form a society compete for scarce resources. The major division is between those who own the means of production and those who do not. Those at the mercy of the owners have few resources, and they lash out violently—misdirecting their violence onto one another.

7. Feminists challenged the traditional view of rape as a personal problem, a crime of passion. Researchers now consider rape a social problem, a crime of violence rooted in the structure of relationships between men and women.

8. Rape and murder are not random acts. Related to the larger social patterns of society, they reflect patterns of class, gender, age, race–ethnicity, timing, location, and acquaintanceship.

9. To prevent violence requires restructuring those aspects of society that foster violence. Without such restructuring, high rates of violence will continue. To determine a rational basis for social policy on these emotionally charged issues requires research on the social causes of violence.

10. Research indicates that we can reduce rape through social policies that increase the value of females and increase the perceived costs of raping. Rape may fade from the public's mind as a social problem. To find workable solutions, we must keep this issue alive.

KEY TERMS

Anomie, 136
Behavior modification, 133
Collective violence, 128
Containment theory, 137
Control theory, 137
Criminal sexual assault, 140
Cultural goal, 137
Cultural means, 137
Differential association, 134
Forcible rape, 138

Frustration–aggression theory of violence, 133
Group violence, 128
Individual violence, 128
Institutionalized group violence, 128
Mass murder, 153
Modeling, 134
Normal violence, 135
Organized group violence, 128

Patriarchy, 139
Personal violence, 128
Rate of violence, 130
Saturday night special, 148
Serial murder, 153
Situational group violence, 128
Soldier rape, 142
Statutory rape, 138
Strain theory, 136
Subcultural theory, 134
Violence, 128

THINKING CRITICALLY ABOUT CHAPTER 5

1. What is the sociological question of violence? What materials in this chapter indicate that this is the right question to ask?
2. Which five of the profiles of rapists that are discussed on pages 142–143 do you think are the most common? Explain your choices.

3. The authors suggest that, as a social policy to reduce rape, we should promote programs that increase the social value of females. Why is this policy suggested, and what specific programs do you think would work?

BY THE NUMBERS: CHANGES OVER TIME

- Percentage of U.S. women afraid to walk alone at night in 1980: **60%**
- Percentage of U.S. women afraid to walk alone at night in 2002: **47%**

- Number of violent crimes in the U.S., per 100,000 people, in 1991: **750**
- Number of violent crimes in the U.S., per 100,000 people: **400**

- Number of murders in the U.S., per 100,000 people, in 1991: **9.8**
- Number of murders in the U.S., per 100,000 people: **5.5**

MySocLab

What can you find in MySocLab? mysoclab www.mysoclab.com

- Complete Ebook
- Practice Tests and Exams
- Multimedia Activities
- Mapping and Data Analysis Exercises

- Research and Writing Advice
- Interactive Social Surveys
- Sociology in the News

CHAPTER 6

Crime and Criminal Justice

I was recently released from solitary confinement after being held therein for 37 months (months!). A silent system was imposed upon me and to even whisper to the man in the next cell resulted in being beaten by guards, sprayed with chemical mace, blackjacked, stomped and thrown into a strip-cell naked to sleep on a concrete floor without bedding, covering, wash basin or even toilet. The floor served as toilet and bed, and even there the silent system was enforced. . . . I have filed every writ possible against the administrative acts of brutality. The courts have all denied the petitions. Because of my refusal to let the thing die down . . . I am the most hated prisoner in (this) penitentiary, and called a "hard-core incorrigible."

> ## The floor served as toilet and bed.

Maybe I am an incorrigible. . . . I know that thieves must be punished and I don't justify stealing, even though I am a thief myself. But now I don't think I will be a thief when I am released. No, I'm not that rehabilitated. It's just that I no longer think of becoming wealthy by stealing. I now think of killing—killing those who have beaten me and treated me as if I were a dog. I hope and pray for the sake of my own soul and future life of freedom that I am able to overcome the bitterness and hatred which eats daily at my soul.

—A letter from a prisoner in a state prison, as quoted in Zimbardo (1972)

The Problem in Sociological Perspective

To better understand the social problem of crime, we will define exactly what crime is.

WHAT IS CRIME? Let's look at old "dumb laws" that remain in legal code today:

In Alabama: It is illegal to harm or scar oneself in order to escape duty.

In Arkansas: Schoolteachers who cut their hair short cannot get a raise.

In California: The mating of animals cannot take place within 1,500 feet of a church.

In Florida: The law allows pregnant pigs to roam free.

In New York: Women can go topless in public as long as they do not profit from the behavior.

In Texas: It is illegal to sell one's eye.

Your state more than likely has "dumb laws," and it probably has merchandising laws as well. Merchandising laws are often associated with the sale of alcohol and tobacco. In the case of alcohol sales, bars and taverns have "closing hours." To sell whiskey, wine, or beer one minute before closing is legal; to sell them two minutes later is a crime.

These examples illustrate the essential nature of crime. No activity is criminal in and of itself. **Crime** *is the violation of law.* If there is no law, there is no crime. Although we may agree that stealing, kidnapping, and rape are immoral or harmful, only the law can define them as criminal.

See For Yourself

Visit Equality Now at http://equalitynow.org/
▸ Discover real laws influencing the lives of women in the Least Industrialized Nations today.

THE CULTURAL RELATIVITY OF CRIME. Crime is influenced not only by temporal factors, but by region as well. *Crime is culturally relative;* that is, because laws differ from one society to another, so does crime. Travelers are sometimes shocked by this when they find that some behavior they take for granted at home is a crime abroad or that what is illegal at home is taken for granted elsewhere. For example, although consumption of pork and alcohol are illegal in some Muslim societies, a man there may take several wives as long as he can support them.

Within the same society, behavior that is criminal at one time can later be taken for granted or even encouraged as a virtue. In China, for example, selling goods to make a profit used to be illegal. This crime, called "profiteering," was so despised that it was punishable by death, and "profiteers" were hung in the public square as an example to others. As Chinese officials gradually adopted capitalism in the 1990s, however, they decided that letting people make profits would help the economy. The change has been so thorough that now Chinese capitalists can join the Communist party.

In the United States in the early 1900s, birth control was thought to injure the family and the state, and a federal law made it illegal to advertise its availability to women. Margaret Sanger broke the law when she advertised that birth control was available, and she was indicted for mailing "obscene, lewd, and lascivious" materials. Today, in contrast, most people consider the same act to be a service to an overpopulated world.

MAKING ACTS CRIMINAL IS A POLITICAL PROCESS. Before 1973, abortion was considered criminal, and those who performed it could be put in prison. After 1973, following the *Roe v. Wade* decision by the U.S. Supreme Court, abortion was made legal and no longer considered a crime. If antiabortion groups succeed in amending the Constitution or if the Supreme Court reverses its 1973 ruling, abortion will again become criminal. This example illustrates another point: Determining which behavior is criminal is a **political process.** The definition of some act as illegal is the outcome of a struggle among groups that have different interests and ideologies.

These two principles—that law defines crime and that crime is the outcome of a political process—illuminate the influence that power has on the legal process. **Power** may be defined as the capacity of some people to achieve goals in the face of opposition. What groups in a society have the power to get their views written into law? How do they get authorities to pass laws? Why do laws prohibit some behaviors but not others? Why do some societies punish behaviors while others ignore—or even encourage—it? Perhaps all these questions can be summarized into one: Whose interests do laws protect?

The Scope of the Problem

In considering crime as a social problem, we must also analyze the **criminal justice system**—those agencies that respond to crime: the police, courts, jails, and prisons. On the one hand, crime is a social problem when large numbers of people are upset about it, when they feel that crime threatens their safety, peace, or quality of life. On the other hand, the criminal justice system is a social problem if people are upset about how it fails to prevent crime, fails to rehabilitate offenders, or discriminates against some citizens. In this chapter, we will discuss crime and the criminal justice system.

Crime as a Social Problem

HOW EXTENSIVE IS CRIME? To see how extensive crime is in the United States, we must first look at the frequency of crime, the number of crimes occurring. Each year Americans are the victims of about 17,000 murders, 250,000 rapes, and 400,000 robberies. Another 10 million are assaulted or burglarized (*FBI Uniform Crime Reports*, 2007). We must also look at the **crime rate**—the number of crimes occurring per 100,000 people. Currently we are experiencing a drop in crime, signaling that the United States is safer today. Even with this decline, the U.S. crime rate remains one of the highest in the world! Crime in the United States is still so high that each year 4 of every 100 Americans fall victim to a crime. Figure 6-1 shows those countries with the highest total crime. Notice that the United States remains the highest.

THE UNIVERSAL NATURE OF CRIME. Although many societies have lower crime rates than ours, no society exists without crime. As Emile Durkheim, one of the earliest sociologists, pointed out in 1897, the very nature of crime makes it universal. Each society passes laws against behaviors that it considers a threat to its well-being. (Even tribal groups regulate behavior and impose severe penalties on violators.) Passing a law does not eliminate the behavior—it just identifies it as illegal. When there are laws (or rules), there always will be criminals (or rule breakers). As Durkheim stressed, no society or nation can ever be free of crime. For as behavior changes, definitions of crime change as well.

WHY IS CRIME CONSIDERED A SOCIAL PROBLEM? As stressed in earlier chapters, the mere existence of some objective condition is not enough to make it a social problem. Subjective concerns are also necessary. People have to be upset about a situation and want something done about it. Just a few years ago, Americans considered crime to be the number one social problem facing the nation. As the crime rate dropped, so did Americans' fears of becoming a victim of violent crime. As we saw in Chapter 5 (Table 5-1, page 129), however, Americans are still concerned about their personal safety, and each urban resident knows which areas of the city to avoid. Women, who have greater concerns about becoming a crime victim, are more cautious than men overall.

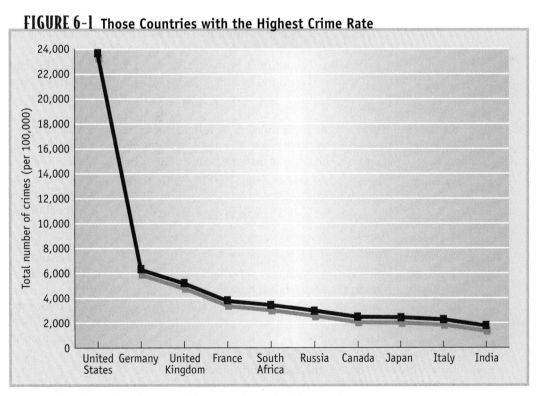

FIGURE 6-1 Those Countries with the Highest Crime Rate

Source: By Lori Fowler. Based on reports of total crime as contained in the *Nation Master Reports* (2008).

As we consider this grand social problem of crime, let's first look at the criminal justice system.

Looking at the Problem Theoretically

As we saw in Chapter 5, each of the theoretical perspectives provides different insight into the problem of criminal violence. We will now use these perspectives to look at property crime and the criminal justice system. Using symbolic interactionism, we will examine the social class bias of police enforcement and learn why we must view crime statistics with caution. Then, through a functionalist perspective, we will see how crime is an adaptation to a society's core values. Finally, using conflict theory, we will examine why the law comes down hardest on the poor who have stolen little, whereas it often is lenient toward the wealthy who have stolen much.

Symbolic Interactionism

THE SAINTS AND THE ROUGHNECKS: SOCIAL CLASS AND LABELING. For two years, sociologist William Chambliss (1973/2007) observed two groups of adolescent lawbreakers at "Hannibal High School." He labeled one group the "saints" and the other the "roughnecks."

These saints were "promising young men, children of good, stable, white, upper-middle-class families, active in school affairs, pre-college students." Despite their background, however, the saints were some of the most delinquent boys in the school, "constantly occupied with truancy, drinking, wild driving, petty theft, and vandalism." Yet their teachers and families considered the boys "saints headed for success." Not one saint was ever arrested.

The "roughnecks" were the same age and race–ethnicity as the saints, and from the same high school. These boys also were delinquent, although they committed somewhat fewer criminal acts than the saints. Their teachers saw them as "roughnecks headed for serious trouble," and the police often dealt with them.

Why did the community perceive these boys differently? Chambliss argued that this was due to *social class.* As symbolic interactionists emphasize, social class affects our perception and behavior. The saints came from respectable, middle-class families, the roughnecks from less respectable, working-class families. These backgrounds led teachers and authorities to expect good behavior from the saints but trouble from the roughnecks. And, like the rest of us, teachers and police saw what they expected to see.

The boys' social class also affected their *visibility.* The saints had automobiles, and they did their drinking and vandalism out of town. Because the roughnecks didn't own vehicles, they hung around their own street corners, where their boisterous behavior drew the attention of police.

Social class also affected the boy's *styles of interaction.* When police or teachers questioned the saints, they were apologetic. They showed respect for authority, important for winning authorities' favor. Their show of respect elicited a positive reaction from teachers and police, allowing the boys to escape school and legal problems. The roughnecks, reports Chambliss, were "almost the polar opposite." When questioned, they were hostile. Even when they put on a veneer of respect, teachers came down hard on the roughnecks, and the police were quick to interrogate and arrest them rather than to warn them.

The saints and the roughnecks illustrate differential association and subcultural theories introduced in Chapter 5. Unlike nondelinquent groups, both the saints and the roughnecks were immersed in vandalism and theft. Despite their similarities in delinquent behavior, however, the saints and the roughnecks were reared in subcultures that had different access to resources. The saints learned that college was their birthright; the roughnecks did not. The saints wanted good grades; the roughnecks didn't care. The saints learned middle-class politeness, which showed in their choice of words, tone of voice, and body language; the roughnecks did not. The reactions by authorities to these subcultural differences deeply affected the boys' lives.

Chambliss's research illustrates what sociologists call *labeling,* a practice that can set people on different paths in life. The labels "saint" and "roughneck," for example, carry

different expectations. They affect people's perceptions and channel behavior in different directions. All but one of the saints went to college. One became a doctor, one a lawyer, one earned a PhD, and the others went into management. Two of the roughnecks won athletic scholarships and went to college. They became coaches. One roughneck became a bookie. Two dropped out of high school, were convicted of separate killings, and ended up in prison. No one knows the whereabouts of the other. Although outcomes like these have many "causes," the boys lived up to the labels the community gave them—this is what we call a **self-fulfilling prophecy.** Robert Merton coined the term *self-fulfilling prophecy* to refer to something that becomes true because one said it might come true. In his book *Social Theory and Social Structure,* Merton gives as a feature of the self-fulfilling prophecy:

> The self-fulfilling prophecy is, in the beginning, a false definition of the situation, evoking a new behavior which makes the original false conception come "true." This specious validity of the self-fulfilling prophecy perpetuates a reign of terror. For the prophet will cite the actual course of events as proof that he was right from the very beginning. (Merton, 1957, p. 477)

POLICE DISCRETION. Sociologists Irving Piliavin and Scott Briar (1964) observed how levels of respect given to police officers can affect charges given by them:

> An 18-year-old white male was accused of statutory rape. The girl's father was prominent in local politics, and he insisted that the police take severe action. During questioning, the youth was polite and cooperative. He addressed the officers as "sir" and answered all questions. He also said that he wanted to marry the girl. The sergeant became sympathetic and decided to try to get the charges against the youth reduced or dropped. A 17-year-old white male was caught having sexual relations with a 15-year-old girl. When he was questioned, he answered with obvious disregard. The officers became irritated and angry. One officer accused the boy of being a "stud," interested only in sex, eating, and sleeping. He added that the young man "probably had knocked up half a dozen girls." The boy just gave back an impassive stare. The officers made out an arrest report and took him to juvenile hall.

Both young men had solid evidence against them. Police even had political pressure to prosecute the 18-year-old. His politeness and cooperation, however, changed the officer's perception. His deference—his respect and regard for police authority—sent a powerful message that put the police on his side. The 17-year-old's demeanor, in contrast, sent a negative message and elicited negative reactions from the police.

Symbolic interactionists emphasize that police operate within a system of labels as they administer the law. The more a suspect matches their idea of a "dangerous" criminal, the more likely they are to arrest that person. Using **police discretion,** deciding whether to arrest someone or to ignore a particular offense, is routine in police work.

CAUTION ABOUT CRIME STATISTICS. These examples illustrate why sociologists approach crime statistics with caution. As noted in Chapter 2, the "facts" of a social problem are not objective: Social "facts" are produced within a specific social context for a particular purpose. According to official statistics, working-class boys are much more delinquent than middle-class boys. Yet, as we have just seen, social class influences the reactions of authorities, affecting *who shows up in official statistics.* As we will see later in the chapter, in the cases of Buddy, Gary, and Clyde, many factors other than types of crime affect sentencing.

IN SUM Interpreting symbols is an essential part of social life. All of us make decisions based on what things mean to us. Police and judges use labeling and the interpretation of symbols in their work. As it is with everyone, social class, reputations, and demeanor are symbols that influence their evaluations and decisions. The impact of police and judicial discretion can have far-reaching effects on people's lives.

Functionalism

CRIME AND A SOCIETY'S CORE VALUES. Functionalists consider crime a natural part of healthy society. Crime is often a reaction to one core value stressed in society—that all should achieve material success. **Strain theory** states that illegitimate opportunity structures encourage some people to commit crime and provide that others will not have the need to.

Sociologists Richard Cloward and Lloyd Ohlin (1960) identified one crucial problem of industrial societies: locating and training the most talented persons of every generation—whether born wealthy or poor—to fill positions requiring ability and diligence. Because successful job skills are learned, society motivates *everyone* to learn skills in order to achieve success. Intense competition allows some of the talented to emerge as victors. "Regardless of race, sex, or social class, success can be yours" becomes the American value—one that drives intense competition. By making success a universal goal, society ensures its own survival.

Although almost all of us learn this goal of success, not all of us have the same access to resources allowing us to achieve this goal. There are only a limited number of high-paying positions, for example. It is easy to see how wanting success but being cut off from approved means to reach it may lead to strain.

A summary of sociologist Robert Merton's analysis of the ways that people react to strain is presented in Table 6-1.

Conformists don't experience strain; they have access to resources and strive for success without resistance. People who do not have equal access to such opportunities may adapt to resistance in four ways:

Innovators accept cultural goals but substitute other means of reaching them. An example is someone who decides to pursue wealth through fraud instead of hard work.

Ritualists give up on achieving success, but still work in culturally approved ways. An example is a worker who no longer hopes to get ahead, but does just enough to avoid getting fired.

Retreatists reject both the societal goal and the means to achieve it; some, such as street addicts, retreat into drugs, others into homelessness or convents.

Rebels are convinced that society is corrupt and reject both societal goals and the means to achieve them. They seek to replace the current social order with a new one.

Innovation is most often the cause of criminal behavior. Finding the legitimate means to success blocked, yet wanting to achieve the cultural goal of success, innovators turn to *illegitimate* means. Thus, a high proportion of crime is a response to wanting to achieve the cultural goal without the ability to do so, or, as Cohen (1955) said, "conformity to the American way."

SOCIAL CLASS AND ILLEGITIMATE OPPORTUNITIES. Using strain theory we can better understand why the poor commit the highest rates of burglary, theft, and robbery.

TABLE 6-1 How People Match Their Goals to Their Means

DO THEY FEEL THE STRAIN THAT LEADS TO ANOMIE?	MODE OF ADAPTATION	CULTURAL GOALS	INSTITUTIONALIZED MEANS
No	Conformity	Accept	Accept
	Deviant Paths:		
Yes	1. Innovation	Accept	Reject
	2. Ritualism	Reject	Accept
	3. Retreatism	Reject	Reject
	4. Rebellion	Reject/Replace	Reject/Replace

Functionalists stress how the poor are bombarded with messages that urge them to want material success. Television portrays vivid images of middle-class lives, suggesting that full-fledged Americans can afford the goods and services portrayed in commercials and programs. Education and job training are the main approved means of reaching success, but the middle-class school system does not always cater to the needs of the underclass. Their lack of education, poor grammar, relaxed view of punctuality and neatness, and lack of paper-and-pencil skills—all these differ from what wealthier children bring to the school experience. Poor children often attend schools which are inferior to those that educate the upper classes (Kozol, 1999). These barriers create higher dropout rates among working-class students, blocking them from many legitimate avenues of financial success.

Often, however, illegitimate opportunities are available to the underclass. Cloward and Ohlin (1960) define **illegitimate opportunity structures** as opportunities woven into the texture of life in urban slums: robbery, burglary, drug dealing, prostitution, pimping, gambling, and other income-producing crimes or "hustles." The "hustler" or "player" becomes a model for others—one of the few people in the neighborhood whose material success approximates the mainstream cultural stereotype. Such illegitimate opportunities beckon the poor in disproportionate numbers.

Martha Stewart spent time in jail for securities fraud and lying to federal investigators after she sold shares in the biotech company ImClone Systems just before the price fell.

The middle and upper classes are not free of crime, of course. Functionalists point out that *different* illegitimate opportunities attract them, ones that make *different forms* of crime functional. Instead of pimping, burglary, or mugging, members of the middle and upper classes commit white-collar crime—tax evasion, bribery of public officials, advertising fraud, price fixing, and securities violations. Martha Stewart is a remarkable example. She made over $1 billion the day her company, Martha Stewart Omnimedia, went public on the New York Stock Exchange. Yet, to gain a few thousand dollars, Stewart was enticed to engage in insider trading (trading stock on the basis of secret information). She was forced to resign her position as head of the company she founded, and she served a few months in a "country club" prison.

The case of Bernard Madoff is another remarkable example of white-collar crime. The largest-ever investment scandal was exposed in December 2008 when Madoff was charged by the Securities and Exchange Commission with operating a $50 billion Ponzi scheme. A **Ponzi scheme** occurs when high investment returns are paid to clients using other clients' money—not real investment profit. Madoff's clients were among the most wealthy individuals and established institutions.

WHY DO ONLY SOME PEOPLE COMMIT PROPERTY CRIMES? As you know, not everyone steals and robs. With the "Achieve Success" motto so prevalent, and with legitimate means to achieve success limited, why do so few engage in criminal behavior?

To answer this, sociologists use control theory to examine inner and outer controls that inhibit crime. *Inner* controls are what most of us mean by self-control. They include internalized morality, such as our ideas of right and wrong and our religious principles. They also include fears of punishment, feelings of integrity, moral beliefs, the desire to be a "good" person, and the ability to defer gratification (Hirschi, 1969; Brownfield & Sorenson, 1993; Schoepfer & Piquero, 2006). *Outer* controls include authorities such as the police, courts, and teachers; the potential damage to one's social standing and reputation; and the reactions of one's family.

IN SUM Functionalists view property crime as *inherent* in societies that socialize people of all social classes to desire material success while limiting the legitimate means to achieve that success. Since society cannot offer limitless opportunities, many people

This cartoon highlights the functionalist view of crime: it works for the good of the whole.

(By permission of Johnny Hart & Creators Syndicate, Inc.)

without resources find their options to achieve success limited. Some of them, then, turn to illegitimate means for achieving their own type of success. Through a combination of inner and outer controls, however, most people obey the law most of the time.

Conflict Theory

> Former WorldCom Chief, Bernard Ebbers, was sentenced to 25 years for covering up $11 billion in debt. Ebbers' attorney claims his client is innocent. (Lehrer, 2005)

INEQUITY IN THE LEGAL SYSTEM: POWER AND SOCIAL CLASS. Have you ever wondered about cases like that of Ebbers? In another corporate criminal case, John Rigas was sentenced to 15 years in prison for embezzling millions from a well known cable company—Adelphia. Rigas's son Timothy was sentenced to 20 years for hiding more than $2 billion in debt. By engaging in corporate corruption, top executives cost all of us.

Cases like these pressured Congress to react, and in 2002 it passed the **Sarbanes-Oxley Act.** For the first time company officers were held accountable for their company's actions. The first CEO charged with Sarbanes-Oxley violations was Richard Scrushy, HealthSouth founder. Scrushy was charged with more than 30 counts of fraud and money laundering.

Is the justice system fair? Although these men faced jail time, not all corporate criminals spend time in jail. Often, the *companies* pay for the fines out of their vast profits—and continue to chauffeur the executives who committed illegal acts between their exclusive offices and luxurious homes. Yet we read other news reports of young men or women from the working class who are sent to prison for stealing a $5,000 automobile.

How can we have such inequity in a legal system that is supposed to provide "law, liberty, and justice for all"? Conflict theorists, who ask such questions about crime and criminal justice, stress that every society is marked by power and inequality. The most fundamental division of a capitalist society exists between those who control the means of production and those who do not. The few people who control the means of production are able to exploit those who sell their labor. Those who own the means of production are called *the ruling class;* those who sell their labor are called *the working class.*

The working class is made up of three major groups: (1) Upper-level managers and professionals hold positions that are fairly secure and whose pay is good. (2) The stable working class is made up of white-collar and blue-collar workers who receive less pay. Their jobs, however, are adequate for survival. (3) The marginal working class receives the least of society's rewards. These people have little job security and their labor is in

low demand. This group includes most of the unemployed and people who are on welfare. From the marginal working class (also called the "reserve army" of the unemployed) come most burglars, muggers, armed robbers, and car thieves.

Conflict theorists emphasize that the law is not like the "innocent until proven guilty" ideology taught in grade school. Justice is not always fairly administered; rather, the law is controlled by the ruling class. The wealthy use the justice system to oppress the marginal working class and maintain their own privileges of power and wealth. Because of this, the criminal justice system does not harshly punish the owners of corporations (Coleman, 1989). Instead, the police and courts focus their attention on the marginal working class.

Violations by company owners—the ruling class—cannot be totally ignored. If their crimes were to become too flagrant, they could provoke an outcry among the working class and, ultimately, foment revolution. To prevent this, an occasional violation by the powerful is prosecuted—and given huge publicity—as was the case with Martha Stewart and the other executives discussed earlier. This demonstration that the criminal justice system applies to all helps to prevent revolt.

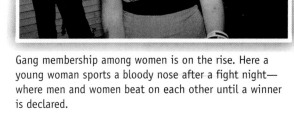

Gang membership among women is on the rise. Here a young woman sports a bloody nose after a fight night—where men and women beat on each other until a winner is declared.

Although the ruling class harshly punishes property crimes committed by the working class, it ordinarily ensures that lesser penalties are applied to its own versions of property crime.

Except for the rare prosecutions of the wealthy that are held out to the public as proof of the fairness of the judicial system, few criminals from the wealthy classes appear in court. Most go before a state or federal agency (such as the Federal Trade Commission) that has no power to imprison. The Federal Trade Commission (FTC), headed by people of privilege, levies small fines on those who are able to pay the most. Cases of the illegal sales of stocks and bonds, price fixing, restraint of trade, and so on are handled by "gentlemen overseeing gentlemen." In contrast, the property crimes of the working class are channeled into a court system that does have the ability to imprison. Burglary, armed robbery, and petty theft threaten not only the sanctity of private property but also, if allowed to continue, the positions of the powerful.

IN SUM　Conflict theorists stress that law enforcement is not a system of justice, but a device used by the powerful to carry out their policies and to keep themselves in power. They use the legal system to control workers, mask injustice, and prevent revolt. This point is highlighted in the Spotlight on Social Research box on page 168 written by William Chambliss, a conflict theorist who has done research on criminal justice systems in different parts of the world.

Types of Crime

To understand crime as a social problem, we'll analyze the following types of crime: juvenile delinquency, white-collar crime, professional and **organized crime,** and political crime. In each we will discuss typologies, rates, and trends.

Juvenile Delinquency

Our 21st-century views of child development make it difficult to realize how differently children used to be treated. Earlier generations did not make the same distinctions between children and adults that we do. Historically, children who committed crime were treated the same as adults. In the 1700s, girls as young as 13 were burned to death for their crimes, and 8- and 10-year-old boys were hanged for theirs (Blackstone, 1899).

Spotlight on Social Research
DOING RESEARCH ON CRIMINALS

WILLIAM CHAMBLISS, *professor of sociology at George Washington University in Washington, DC, became interested in criminology during his junior year in high school. That summer, he and a friend hitchhiked from Los Angeles to Walla Walla, Washington, where they worked with convicts picking peas. As Chambliss got to know the convicts, he was fascinated to discover what the bank robbers, drug dealers, burglars, and thieves were planning to do when they were released from prison—commit more crimes.*

After my experiences that summer, I knew that I wanted to be a criminologist. When I went to UCLA, I was exposed to sociology and criminology. There, I developed a passion for both that has never waned.

After college, I was drafted into the Army and sent to Korea where I spent 18 months as a special agent with the Counter Intelligence Corps. I was exposed to an immense amount of crime. But it was the crimes of the state and of the U.S. military that most interested me. They were the most egregious, not the crimes of the petty thieves and burglars or even what today we would call "terrorists." Between the pea fields of Walla Walla and the rice paddies of South Korea, I came to ponder what a short step it is from legitimacy to crime, from interrogation to torture, and from fighting soldiers to shooting and raping civilians.

Over the years, I have done research on organized crime, economic crime, juvenile gangs, and the creation of laws in the United States. I have also studied crime abroad: in England, Sweden, Norway, Nigeria, Zambia, and Thailand. Everywhere I have gone, from the slums and drizzling rain of Seattle to the steamy heat of Nigeria, I found the same story: Some of the worst offenders are the least likely to experience the sting of the criminal justice system, while the less powerful fill the courtrooms and the prisons. This bothers me. It just isn't justice.

In one of my books, *Power, Politics and Crime* (Westview, 2001), I suggest these social policies:

1. Mandatory minimum sentences be abolished (including three-strikes laws), and, in general, the trend toward more severe punishments be reversed.
2. Crime statistics be gathered by agencies that are independent of law enforcement agencies.
3. Law enforcement agencies be put under civilian control.
4. The prosecuting attorney's office be depoliticized (removed from political influence or control).
5. Drugs be decriminalized. The primary reason for this is that the enforcement of drug laws results in systemic bias against the poor and ethnic minorities.

My journey of discovery in criminology has exposed many shortcomings in the world we live in. It has also given me an opportunity to meet and work with wonderful people, some labeled criminals, others labeled heroes. Although I sometimes wish that "I didn't know now, what I didn't know then," more often I am eternally grateful for the opportunity to explore the world of crime and crime control and to do what I can to help make it more equitable—which is its supposed purpose.

Laws and changes in education created a perceptual shift in how children were viewed. As part of this cultural transformation, "teenagers" became a separate class of people. Previously, the teen years were just an age, much as ages 30 to 35 are now—there was nothing distinctive about them. As part of this perceptual shift, laws were passed that classified "juveniles" as a separate category in the criminal justice system (Platt, 1979). This change in the law produced a new category of crime—**juvenile delinquency**—the legal term for crime committed by children. In the United States, the maximum age limit to categorize a criminal as a juvenile varies, but is usually somewhere between 14 and 21 years.

Howard Snyder (1988) discovered that many juveniles had "delinquent careers." He studied the court records of 69,000 juvenile delinquents in Phoenix, Arizona and found the following:

1. After their first arrest, most youths (59%) never return to juvenile court.
2. The juveniles most likely to continue delinquent behavior are those arrested a second time before age 16.
3. Juveniles who are charged with a violent crime are likely to have already committed previous **status crimes**—those acts, like curfew violations, that pertain only to juveniles.

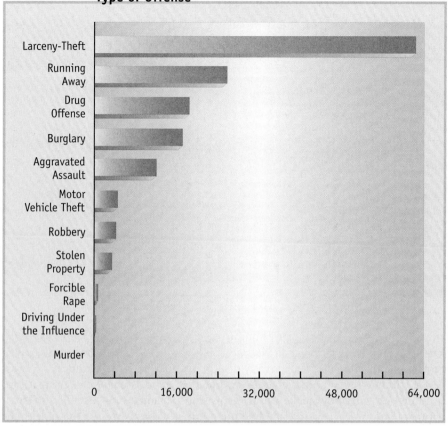

FIGURE 6-2 Number of Juveniles Under Age 15 Arrested by Type of Offense

Source: Crime in the United States (2006).

4. The younger a juvenile is when first charged with a violent crime, the greater the likelihood that he or she will be charged with subsequent violent crimes. (Those charged at age 13 are *twice* as likely to be arrested for a later violent offense).

5. The juveniles who are the *most* likely to be rearrested are those whose first charge was burglary, truancy, motor vehicle theft, or robbery (see Figure 6-2).

6. The juveniles who are the *least* likely to be rearrested are those whose first charge was underage drinking, running away, or shoplifting.

7. Girls are less likely to be rearrested than boys (29% versus 46%).

TYPOLOGY. Some delinquents grow up in **delinquent subcultures,** where criminal activities are seen as a normal part of everyday life. In these subcultures, they learn norms that support crime, as well as techniques for committing burglaries, robberies, and so on. In some of these subcultures, youths learn to rape, kill, and terrorize. For an example of such a subculture, see the Thinking Critically box on page 171. Not everyone who grows up in such environments becomes delinquent.

Some juvenile delinquents are found guilty of status crimes. Our definition of status crimes includes those acts that pertain only to juveniles. The court may charge teens with a status crime if they violate curfew, engage in drinking, or run away from home.

Often the public is less concerned with status crimes and more concerned with violent crime. Although adolescents age 13 to 17 make up only 3% of the population, they are responsible for 15% of **violent crimes**—murder, forcible rape, robbery, and aggravated assault. Juveniles are also responsible for another 25% of the nation's

TABLE 6-2 Arrests of People Under Age 18

	NUMBER OF ARRESTS				PERCENTAGE OF ARRESTS		
	1981	2000	2004	Percent Change	1981	2000	2004
Violent Crimes[1]							
Boys	47,415	48,169	53,154	+12%	89%	82%	81%
Girls	5,825	10,686	12,149	+109	11	18	19
Totals	53,240	58,885	65,303		100	100	100
Property Crimes[2]							
Boys	398,924	218,816	215,934	−46	81	70	66
Girls	95,010	94,888	110,378	+16	19	30	34
Totals	493,934	313,704	326,312		100	100	100

[1] Violent crimes are murder, forcible rape, robbery, and aggravated assault.
[2] Property crimes are burglary, larceny-theft, motor vehicle theft, and arson.

Source: By James M. Henslin. Based on *Sourcebook of Criminal Justice Statistics* (1993, Table 35); *FBI Uniform Crime Reports* (2000, Table 37); (2005, Tables 39, 40).

property crimes—burglary, larceny, motor vehicle theft, and arson (*FBI Uniform Crime Reports,* 2005, Table 39; *Statistical Abstract,* 2006, Table 11). In other words, juveniles are responsible for crime at a rate greatly disproportionate to their numbers.

Girls commit fewer crimes than boys, but this trend is changing. As you can see from Table 6-2, girls now make up an increasing percentage of juveniles arrested for both violent and property crimes. While the number of boys arrested for violent crimes has increased 12% since the early 1980s, the arrest rate for young girls has *doubled.* Historically, girls were charged with status crimes like underage sex and running away. Today, more than 12,000 girls are arrested each year for murder, robbery, and aggravated assault. Another 110,000 are arrested for larceny, theft, and arson.

TRENDS. Many argue that education prevents juvenile delinquency. "If we can keep them in school, we can keep them out of trouble. If they drop out, they're lost." Is this common statement based on reality? To find out, we need to compare arrests of delinquents who completed high school with arrests of delinquents who dropped out. This information is presented in Table 6-3. As you can see, by the time they are adults, delinquents who complete high school are only *half* as likely to be arrested as those who drop out of

TABLE 6-3 High School Graduation, Delinquency, and Adult Arrests

	ARRESTED AS ADULTS	
	African Americans	Whites
Delinquent in high school		
Dropped out	47%	33%
Completed high school	24	18
Not delinquent in high school		
Dropped out	30	22
Completed high school	16	6

Based on a longitudinal study of male Philadelphia high school students; no data for girls or other groups.
Source: By James M. Henslin. Based on L. Rosen et al. (1991), Tables 2, 5.

ISLANDS IN THE STREET: URBAN GANGS IN THE UNITED STATES

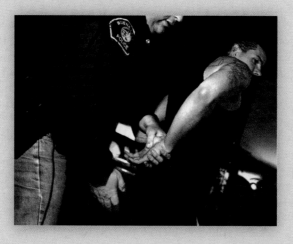

For more than 10 years, sociologist Martín Sánchez Jankowski (1991) used participant observation to understand 37 different gangs among African Americans, Chicanos, Dominicans, Irish, Jamaicans, and Puerto Ricans in Boston, Los Angeles, and New York City. The gangs earned money through gambling, arson, mugging, armed robbery, and selling moonshine, drugs, guns, stolen car parts, and protection. Jankowski ate, slept, and sometimes fought with the gangs, but by mutual agreement he did not participate in drug dealing or in other illegal activities. He was seriously injured twice during the study.

Contrary to stereotypes, Jankowski did not find that the motive for joining a gang was to escape a broken home (there were as many members from intact families as from broken homes) or to seek a substitute family (the same number of boys said they were close to their families as those that said they were not). Rather, the boys joined to gain access to money, to have recreation (including girls and drugs), to maintain anonymity in committing crimes, to get protection, and to help the community. This last reason may seem surprising, but in some neighborhoods, gangs protect residents from outsiders and spearhead political change (Martinez, 2003). The boys also saw the gang as an alternative to the dead-end—and deadening—jobs held by their parents.

Neighborhood residents are ambivalent about gangs. On the one hand, they fear the violence. On the other hand, many adults once belonged to gangs, the gangs often provide better protection than the police, and gang members are the children of people who live in the neighborhood.

Particular gangs will come and go, but gangs will likely always remain part of the city. As functionalists point out, gangs fulfill needs of poor youth who live on the margins of society.

FOR YOUR CONSIDERATION

What are the functions that gangs fulfill (the needs they meet)? Suppose that you have been hired as an urban planner by the City of Los Angeles. How could you arrange to meet the needs that gangs fulfill in ways that minimize violence and encourage youth to follow mainstream norms?

---

high school. The table also shows another remarkable finding: Children who are *not* delinquents who drop out of high school are *more* likely to be arrested as adults than delinquents who graduate from high school. This is one case where common sense and sociological research support each other.

White-Collar Crime

> After flashing photos of executives from Enron and Arthur Andersen on the television monitor, Jon Stewart, the anchor of *The Daily Show,* turned to the camera and shouted, "Why aren't all of you in jail? And not like white-guy jail—jail jail. With people by the weight room going, 'Mmmmm.'" (Leaf, 2004)

It is rare that corporate scandals hit the news, but when they do we learn about top executives who steal outrageous amounts of money. We have already discussed how a WorldCom executive and Martha Stewart were punished to demonstrate that the criminal justice system is in fact a fair system—that even corporate criminals get punished.

TYPOLOGY. Sociologist Edwin Sutherland (1949) coined the term **white-collar crime** to describe those crimes "committed by people of respectable and high social

status in the course of their occupation." The two major types of white-collar crime are those committed by employees *on behalf of* a corporation and those committed *against* a corporation. In crimes committed *on behalf of* a corporation, employees break the law in order to benefit a business organization. Examples include automobile manufacturers who knowingly sell dangerous vehicles, drug companies altering test data so they can keep their drugs on the market, and corporations engaging in price fixing and tax evasion.

Major corporations listed on the stock exchange create and support an environment conducive to crime. The corporate culture revolves around not only corporate profits but also personal achievement and recognition. Pressures to increase profits and to climb the corporate ladder, combined with the insulation of executives from the consequences of their decisions, can lead to "ethical numbness" (Hills, 1987).

Some of our most well known corporations participate in white-collar crimes, some of which result in death. In a factory producing Ball Park Franks, Sara Lee stopped testing for listeria, a deadly disease. The result was the death of 15 people who ate infected hot dogs. What was the punishment for Sara Lee? Sara Lee pled guilty to two misdemeanors and paid a fine (Mauer, 2004).

Corporate culture can so dominate its employees that executives of major companies even end up calculating the cold-blooded deaths of others for profit. This occurred in the famous "Pinto case." The Pinto was a car manufactured by Ford in the 1970s. After three young women in Indiana burned to death when their Pinto burst into flames following a rear-end crash, the Ford Motor Company was charged with reckless homicide (Strobel, 1980; Fisse & Braithwaite, 1987). No executives were charged, just Ford itself. It was alleged that Ford knew that in a rear-end collision the Pinto's gas tank could rupture, spew gas, and burn passengers to death (Dowie, 1977, 1979). (Never mind how a corporation can know anything. The commonsense view is that it is people in the corporation who know things, and they who make criminal decisions. Common sense and the legal system, however, often walk different paths.)

Disclosed at the trial was heart-wrenching evidence that revealed the cold-blooded malice of Ford executives. Installing a simple piece of plastic would have corrected the problem, at a cost of just $11 per car. The Ford executives faced a difficult decision—whether to pay the $11 or to sentence drivers and passengers to fiery deaths. Now, that is a difficult choice—at least it was for these executives. The memo on the next page, revealed during the trial, shows how the executives compared what it would cost the company to

Patty Ramge displays a sign on the rear of her Ford Pinto stating "Keep off my rear, I'm explosive." Mrs. Ramge put the sign on because of the fiery accidents involving Pintos whose gas tanks exploded after being hit from behind, killing or seriously injuring the occupants.

make the change ("Costs") or to pay for the deaths ("Benefits," meaning the amount of benefits that would have to be paid). As you can see, the cost of installing the plastic was high ($137 million) compared to the amount of money that would have to be paid if they simply allowed people to die ($49.5 million). To save $87 million for the company, the executives decided to let 180 people burn to death. Their estimates turned out to be too low: Several hundred people burned to death, and many others were disfigured.

With the right lawyers and connections, people can get away with murder. Ford was acquitted. The company recalled its 1971–1976 Pintos for fuel tank modification and launched a publicity campaign to maintain an image of a "good" company. Ford executives claimed that the internal memo was misunderstood. They said that it "related to a proposed federal safety standard and not to the overall design of the Pinto" (Fisse & Braithwaite, 1987, p. 253). Despite causing hundreds of deaths, not a single Ford executive was arrested or tried in court. They remained free, wealthy, and respected in their communities.

You might think that such a cold, homicidal act would never be repeated by a U.S. automobile company. Unfortunately, such an expectation would be wrong. In 1998, a 13-year-old boy was burned to death when the gas tank of an Oldsmobile Cutlass station wagon ruptured. When GM was sued, a memo was discovered in which GM calculated the cost to fix the problem at just $4.50 per vehicle. GM also calculated the cost of lawsuits and figured these would average just $2.40 per car. Able to save an estimated $2.10 per car, GM did not fix the problem (Boot, 1998).

Ford's Internal Memo on the Pinto. Benefits and Costs Relating to Fuel Leakage Associated with the Static Rollover Test Portion of FMVSS 208

BENEFITS.

Savings: 180 burn deaths, 180 serious burn injuries, 2,100 burned vehicles.
Unit cost: $200,000 per death, $67,000 per injury, $700 per vehicle.
Total benefit: $180 \times (\$200,000) + 180 \times (\$67,000) + 2,100 \times (\$700) = \$49.5$ million.

COSTS.

Sales: 11 million cars, 1.5 million light trucks.
Unit cost: $11 per car, $11 per truck.
Total cost: $11,000,000 \times (\$11) + 1,500,000 \times (\$11) = \$137$ million.

Sources: Dowie (1977); Strobel (1980, p. 286).

The Pinto and Cutlass cases confirm the perspective of conflict theorists: The powerful can and do manipulate our legal system. They can and do escape punishment for their crimes—including instances involving serial murder. Can you possibly imagine the same result if a "ma and pa" shop accidentally poisoned a couple of hundred people?

The main crime *against* the corporation is employee theft, ranging from snitching company supplies to embezzling company funds. This crime also includes sabotage by disgruntled employees. To avoid tarnishing their public images with the disgrace of internal crime, most corporations deal privately with such offenders.

Stealing company secrets, such as formulas, manufacturing processes, or even marketing plans, is a form of theft. If an employee sells one company's secrets to a competitor, the matter is easily recognized as a crime. A gray area emerges, however, when a key employee goes to work for a competitor. This employee steals nothing, but is hired specifically because he or she has vital knowledge about the former employer. The employee might even be given a higher salary and bonuses because of this knowledge. Because the knowledge is inside the individual's head, and no documents are stolen, this crime is difficult to prove.

Back in the 1950s, sociologist Donald Cressey (1953) did a classic study on embezzlement and found that employees embezzle because they have an "unshakable financial problem"—overdue taxes, children in college, sometimes gambling losses. He also found

that, like juvenile delinquents, embezzlers neutralize their crime. Many consider their embezzling to be a form of borrowing—the money stolen is simply an unauthorized loan to tide them over during a financial emergency. They intend to pay it back later. Some think of themselves as deserving the money because they are worth more than they are being paid or because their employer has cheated or somehow taken advantage of them. As with juvenile delinquents, the **techniques of neutralization** are usually effective. In this case, although violating the trust their company has placed in them, they still consider themselves to be respectable, law-abiding citizens.

Other researchers have found that not all embezzlers neutralize their crimes (Green, 1993). Some embezzle without trying to justify it at all (Benson, 1985). Embezzlers have many motives, not just financial problems. Some embezzle on an impulse; others embezzle because they are greedy (Nettler, 1974). Motives even change over the course of long-term embezzlement. Lori Fowler knew an embezzler who worked for her Uncle Vic. The secretary deposited a check into her personal account every week over the course of several years. By the time she was accidentally discovered by Lori's Aunt Sheri, she had stolen tens of thousands of dollars.

One of the most costly crimes against a corporation to date was the plundering of the U.S. savings and loan (S&L) industry in the 1980s. The crime was so widespread that corporate officers across the nation looted their banks of billions of dollars. The total cost ran $500 billion—$2,000 for every man, woman, and child in the country at that time (Kettl, 1991; Newdorf, 1991). Perhaps the most infamous culprit was Neil Bush, son of then president George H. W. Bush and brother of the second president Bush. As an officer of Silverado, a Colorado savings and loan, Bush helped bankrupt Silverado by approving $100 million in loans to a company in which he held secret interests (Tolchin, 1991a).

The subprime mortgage crisis that boiled over in the fall of 2008 pushed the nation into economic uncertainly. In an attempt to keep the U.S. economy afloat, Congress passed The Emergency Economic Stabilization Act in October 2008. The so-called "Wall Street bailout bill" allowed the Treasury to spend upwards of $700 billion on failing assets in an effort to boost the economy and represents the largest rescue bill ever passed (House Financial Services Committee, 2008).

Future generations will continue to pay for the S&L bank scandal of the 1980s and the credit crisis and financial bailout of 2008. The interest on the federal debt alone is exorbitant. At 5%, a year's interest on an increase of $700 billion in the national debt would run $35 billion, at 10%, $70 billion. Because the government does not pay its debt but merely borrows more to keep up with the compounding interest, the $700 billion owed now totals about $1.4 trillion. As the late senator Everett Dirksen once said, "A billion here and a billion there, and pretty soon you're talking about real money."

TRENDS. No one knows for sure how much white-collar crime costs the nation, but estimates place the bill at about $600 billion a year (McCain, 2004), more than the cost of all street crime combined. Most white-collar crime never gets reported, but that which does can be alarming. The most notorious example in recent years involved the fraud at Enron, which cost stockholders more than $50 billion. Eleven thousand employees also suffered huge pension losses. Bank robbers risk their lives for $10,000, but corporate executives manipulate documents earning millions of illegal dollars. White-collar criminals enjoy a privileged position within the criminal justice system. Because of their social position and ability to manipulate the law, few corporate criminals are punished. Some even get away with murder, as we saw with the automobile crime case. When arrested, which is seldom, white-collar criminals usually receive lenient sentences. Compared with street criminals, white-collar criminals (Carlson & Chaiken, 1987) are

1. More likely to have their cases dismissed by the prosecutor (40% versus 26%)
2. Less likely to have to put up bail (13% versus 37%)
3. More likely to get probation rather than jail (54% versus 40%)
4. More likely to get shorter sentences (29 months versus 50 months)

TABLE 6-4 Arrests for White-Collar Crimes, by Sex

	1981		2000		2004	
	Male	Female	Male	Female	Male	Female
Embezzlement	70%	30%	50%	50%	50%	50%
Fraud	58	42	55	45	55	45
Forgery and counterfeiting	68	32	61	39	60	40
Fencing stolen property	88	12	83	17	81	19
Average	71	29	62	38	61	39

Note: Not all these acts meet the definition of white-collar crime as developed by Sutherland. From the categories available in the source, however, these are as close as we can come.

Source: By James M. Henslin. Based on *FBI Uniform Crime Reports,* various editions, including *Crime in the United States* (2005, Table 42).

Social class not only operates within the criminal justice system, but also operates *among* white-collar criminals as well. Even within the same company, among all of those engaged in the same crime, executives who are higher up in the company are charged with lesser crimes and are given shorter sentences (Coleman, 1989).

It is rare for executives to be convicted for their crimes and, if convicted, unusual for them to serve even a single day in prison. In a study of the 582 largest U.S. corporations, sociologist Marshall Clinard (Clinard et al., 1979; Clinard, 1990) found that criminal charges had been filed against 1,553 executives. Only 56 were convicted, giving them a better than 96% chance of avoiding conviction if arrested. Of this small number, 40 served no time in prison. Their average stay was 37 days—about what a poor person would serve for disorderly conduct. Of 150,000 inmates in federal prisons, only 1,000 are white-collar criminals (Leaf, 2004). Similarly, Neil Bush, the president's son who was charged in the S&L scandal, had to pay only a $50,000 fine—after friends of the president paid his legal fees (Tolchin, 1991b; "Suit Settled," 1992). As sociologist Daniel Glaser (1978) stated, "criminal law has difficulty dealing with white-collar crime."

Back in 1975, sociologist Rita Simon predicted that as more women begin to work outside the home, more would become involved in white-collar crime. This is what happened. Like men, many women who join the corporate world are enticed by its opportunities for crime. Table 6-4 tracks this change. The largest increase has been in embezzlement, a crime that women are now as likely to commit as men. As you look at this table, you might notice how the increase in white-collar crime by women parallels the rise in crime by female juveniles that we noted earlier (Table 6-2 on page 170).

Professional and Organized Crime

Professional criminals are people who consider crime to be their occupation. Jewel thieves and counterfeiters—so highly romanticized in movies and books—are examples of professional criminals. So are fences—those who buy stolen goods for resale. Their activities, although illegal, are a form of work, and they pride themselves on their skills and successes. As some forms of professional crime, like safecracking and picking pockets, have declined, others, such as identity fraud, have increased. Thieves use computers today more than ever to commit fraud. As you can see from the Technology and Social Problems box on the next page, crime is keeping up with changing technology.

Another group of professional criminals include participants in organized crime or criminal enterprise. The FBI defines a **criminal enterprise** as crime committed within a highly organized gang. Among this gang of criminals there is significant organization and a hierarchical power structure. The group has strong networking skills and ties to legitimate power as well.

The idea that the **Mafia,** the most famous organized crime group, is made up only of Italians is a myth. The Mafia does exist, and it did originate in Sicily. As *The*

Technology and Social Problems
LEGOS AND MORE LEGOS: HIGH-TECH SHOPLIFTING

Shoplifting has been around as long as there have been shops. In the typical case, the shoplifter shoves some merchandise in a pocket or purse and walks away without paying for it. This is still the most common case.

But shoplifters are keeping up with the times by taking advantage of new technology. There is the bar code scam, for example. The shoplifter, if he or she can still be called that, replaces an item's bar code with the bar code of a lower-priced item. It is obviously awkward to remove an item's bar code in the store and then slap it on another item. Doing so could also draw some unwanted attention. Scammers get around this problem by buying the lower-priced item; then using scanners and computers, they reproduce the bar code. They go into the store with a supply of the fake bar codes, stick them on the more expensive item, and join the other shoppers in the checkout line.

Can this scam be profitable? Consider William Swanberg, who specialized in Legos, those perennially popular children's building toys. He printed $19 bar codes from the cheap sets of Legos and inserted them on the $100 sets. He would buy 10 sets at a time, all at his private 80% discount.

Swanberg liked Legos so much that he traveled around five Western states running his scam. He was meticulous, following an itinerary that specified his preferred "shopping" order: first Target, then Wal-Mart, followed by Toys-R-Us.

This image, taken from a surveillance videotape, shows a woman stuffing stolen items down her shirt.

What did Swanberg do with all the Legos? He didn't have a garage or basement filled with strange creations he was working on. Rather, technology again provided the answer. He became a vendor on Bricklink.com, which specializes in Legos. (Yes, there is even a Web site for Legos people.) There, not surprisingly, Mr. Swanberg became known as a vendor with a terrific inventory. Target officials figure that Swanberg stole $200,000 worth of Legos just from their stores.

Bar code swindlers are hard to catch, but don't get the idea that this might be a profitable side venture to honest work: Mr. Swanberg was sentenced to prison.

Based on Zimmerman (2006).

Godfather series depicts, the Sicilian government was overtaken by local strongmen who united to protect their families and communities from bandits. After establishing a private government, they also protected their communities from other strongmen—in return for regular tribute (Anderson, 1965; Blok, 1974; Catanzaro, 1992). As the formal government became more powerful, these men resisted, maintaining their control over areas of Sicily. After the 1860s, they became known as the Mafia. The idea that the Italians introduced organized crime to the United States in New York City is also a myth. New York City has had organized crime for more than 150 years. It has been dominated by successive waves of ethnic immigrants—first the Irish, then the Jews, and only after that the Italians (Bell, 1960). Today, no ethnic group dominates organized crime. It is shared among Sicilians and Italians, African Americans and Puerto Ricans, Japanese and Russians (Wagman, 1981).

In one classic study, Edwin Sutherland (1937) found that professional criminals organize their lives around their "work," just as people who work legitimate jobs do. They associate with like-minded people who share their approach to life, including

their values of loyalty, mutual aid, and scorn for the "straight world." They also teach one another technical skills for committing crimes and avoiding detection.

Although its forms change, professional and organized crime involves three main elements: (1) in-group loyalty, (2) scorn for the values of the straight world, and (3) pride in specialized skills. One researcher found these traits to be evident among the car thieves he studied. Based on the demand for parts, one owner of a "chop shop" ordered specific cars, paying set prices according to the make and model he wanted. He and his workers used acetylene torches and other tools to disassemble the cars. They sold the fenders, motors, transmissions, seats, doors, and so on to dealers in used auto parts. The small amount of metal that was left over was hauled away by an older man who sold it for scrap. Like small business owners across the country, the owner-manager of the "chop shop" carried a great deal of responsibility. He made the decisions, paid the rent on the shop, and had to meet the weekly payroll. Unlike "straight" employers, however, he paid wages in cash and did not pay taxes.

At this "chop shop," parts of a Jeep Cherokee are recovered by authorities.

Beyond the three main elements of organized crime listed above, the Mafia is also organized around the key principles of family and *omertá,* the vow of secrecy. These principles ensure a separation from outsiders. To maintain close connections, the Mafia encourages *village endogamy* (marriage between people from the same village) and *fictive kinship* (assigning obligations to people who are not related; a godfather, for example, unites two families).

In the Sicilian American Mafia, about 5,000 members belong to about 24 "families" of 200 to 700 members each. These families are linked to each other by understandings and "treaties." The leaders of the most powerful families form a "commission" or "combine" to take over weaker families (Cressey, 1969; Riesel, 1982a). Members call this structure the Mafia, or **Cosa Nostra** ("our thing").

Crime is Mafia business, and its members are successful at it. The Mafia continues to flourish—despite the U.S. government's perpetual "war" against it. Mafia groups—whether in Sicilian, Colombian, or Russian versions—are the major importers and wholesalers of narcotics. Mafia members also run loan-sharking operations (making private, illegal loans at high rates of interest). In some areas, they control the labor union and the construction trade (Penn, 1982; Riesel, 1982b; Trust, 1986). The Mafia also has infiltrated many legitimate businesses, such as the garment industry of New York City and the gambling industry of Las Vegas. Violence remains the mode of operation—despite claims to the contrary.

Why has the Mafia remained successful despite efforts of the U.S. government to shut it down? We cite the following reasons (*Organized Crime,* 1976):

1. Organized crime *is* organized. The Mafia has a **bureaucracy** with full-time specialists in many criminal pursuits.

2. Organized crime provides illegal *services in high demand* (prostitution, gambling, and loan sharking)—"victimless crimes" in which no one complains to the police.

3. Organized crime wields influence through *political corruption.*

4. Organized crime uses *violence and intimidation* against victims and its own members.

5. Conflict theorists highlight this reason—organized crime serves the goals of the U.S. ruling class.

According to sociologist David Simon (1981), the ruling class has used organized crime to keep U.S. labor from getting too organized or becoming too "radical." During the 1920s and the 1940s, periods of great labor unrest, corporations hired gangsters to

In *The Sopranos*, HBO depicts the stereotypical view of Italians as Mafia members. Organized crime follows waves of immigration; and Italian criminals have been joined by Irish, Russian, and now Asian Mafia members in this county.

break up strikes and infiltrate unions, especially among autoworkers and longshoremen. During World War II, U.S. Navy Intelligence asked Mafia boss Charles "Lucky" Luciano to protect the New York docks from sabotage. Luciano, who was directing Mafia operations from prison, cooperated. He also helped get the Sicilian Mafia to support the U.S. invasion of Sicily. As a reward, Luciano's prison sentence was commuted, and he was deported to Italy.

Some sociologists emphasize that organized crime threatens the well-being of the United States. The most serious problem is not gambling, prostitution, loan sharking, and so on, but the corruption of our social institutions. With its many millions of untaxed dollars, the Mafia bribes police, judges, and politicians, subverting the institutions and organizations that deal with crime. Thus violence, bribery, and other forms of corruption work their way into the social system (Cressey, 1969; Teresa, 1973; Gudkov, 1980; Schwidrowski, 1980).

It is certain that crime will continue, and along with it various versions of organized crime. The future of the Mafia, however, is uncertain. In recent years, *omertá* has weakened, and the FBI has infiltrated the organization. With the use of powerful surveillance devices, mobster confessions, and police indictments—even top Mafia bosses have been convicted. One of these bosses, John Gotti, captured the public's attention. Despite his crimes, which included murder, Gotti, who died in prison, was romanticized and became a darling of the media. The Mafia as a whole appears to be in decline, but it is too soon to sound its death knell. We will have to see how this group adapts to its changing situation.

Political Crime

I am innocent of the charges the U.S. Government is trying to pin on me. Just as many activists have experienced, I am being targeted by the U.S. Government and the FBI, not because I am guilty, but because I have chosen to challenge the status quo.

—Michael Scarpitti, aka Tre Arrow, radical environmental activist, accused ecoterrorist, political prisoner

Political crime is crime motivated by a particular ideology. Ideology refers to "the distinctive belief systems, ideas, and abstract ideals that are perceived as providing the true meaning of life" (Hagan, 1997, p. 1). In the United States, there is no official category of criminal behavior called political crime. This is because the First Amendment of the Bill of Rights in the U.S. Constitution restricts the government from taking action against individuals for expressing their views, peacefully assembling, and redressing the government. The First Amendment reads,

> Congress shall make no law respecting an establishment of religion, or prohibiting the free exercise thereof; or abridging the freedom of speech, or of the press; or the right of the people peaceably to assemble, and to petition the government for a redress of grievances.

In other words, those who disagree with governmental policies and practices can do so in a public forum without fearing arrest or punishment.

Political crime describes crimes designed either to change or to maintain the social order. Crimes to change the social order include treason (the betrayal of one's country), sedition (rebellion, an attempt to overthrow the government), and such activities as resistance to the draft. It is not the crime itself that defines the acts as political crimes, it instead is the motivation for the action.

Some people view the political actions of individuals as a major social problem, while at the same time viewing similar acts by the government as acceptable. Yet others view the politically motivated acts of the government as the real social problem. All political crime, whether committed by individuals or government officials, is a social problem because it is illegal. Within the context of political crime, there have been occurrences where both individuals and the government commit crimes simultaneously. For example, during the 1999 WTO riots in Seattle, both protesters and police were charged with committing offenses (Hagan, 1997). We're sure you can guess who was arrested though.

Crimes designed to *maintain the social order* include illegal surveillance of citizens by the FBI and illegal acts by the CIA such as assassinations and manipulation of foreign governments. Political crimes include the illegal activities of President Richard Nixon and his aides during Watergate and the activities of President Ronald Reagan and Lt. Col. Oliver North to support the contras of Nicaragua. Some allege that political crime also includes using drug money to finance President Bill Clinton's campaign (Reed & Cummings, 1994) and the unauthorized wiretapping and interceptions of e-mail by President George W. Bush. As you can imagine, political crime is especially difficult to prove.

Although there is no end to conspiracy theories—which flourish during political crises but vary from difficult to impossible to prove—we have ample evidence that U.S. politicians and bureaucrats do order illegal acts. In some cases, those acts become a routine part of the agency. Consider just one example: From the 1940s into the 1970s, the FBI committed thousands of burglaries and illegally opened and photographed tens of thousands of letters (Coleman, 1995). Data on political crime in research and course texts in criminology and criminal justice are sparse, and there is considerable confusion about what constitutes a political offense (Ross, 2003). A number of factors may contribute to this lack of consensus. First, all crimes can be viewed as political in that, by law, they have been deemed a threat to society. Some suggest that any attempt to categorize or classify "political crime" is itself a political act. Second, most ideologically motivated criminal behaviors fall under other categories of criminal behavior. Data are not collected through the Uniform Crime Reports, the U.S. Department of Justice, or elsewhere specifically for political crime, so it is a very difficult phenomenon to study empirically.

The National Counterterrorism Center (NCTC) is responsible for collecting data on global terrorist activity. In 2005, the Center reported that the number of terrorist attacks rose from 175 to 651 in one year alone (Glasser, 2005). In 2001, the U.S. Department of Justice published the 2000–2001 FBI terrorist report (U.S. Department of Justice, 2001). The report indicates that from 1980 to 2001, there were 345 acts of domestic terrorism, 136 acts of international terrorism, and 1 unclassified act (the 2001 anthrax mailings) of terrorism in the United States. Throughout the 21-year period, 14,047 individuals suffered minor injuries and 2,993 people were killed.

(The FBI estimates 12,000 as the number of 9/11 victims, both dead and injured; the actual number is unknown.) Of the 482 terrorist acts, 324 were bombings, 21 were assassinations, 19 were shootings, 19 were sabotage/malicious destruction, 15 were robberies, 10 were hostile takeovers, 6 were assaults, 6 were use of weapons of mass destruction, 3 were hijackings, 2 were kidnappings, 2 were rocket attacks, and 22 were other/ unspecified (Hagan, 1997).

The following are examples of a range of behaviors that could be defined as political crime:

- During World War II, the Nazis exterminated 6 million Jews and 5 million others.
- In September 1963, the Ku Klux Klan bombed a Baptist church in Birmingham, Alabama. When it was discovered that four girls were murdered, rioting broke out.
- During the civil rights movement in the 1960s, a number of political leaders were assassinated, including President John F. Kennedy, presidential candidate Robert F. Kennedy, Martin Luther King, Jr., and Malcolm X.
- In 1998, Matthew Shepard was killed by two men because he was openly homosexual (Hagan, 1997).

Political crime is motivated by a particular ideological perspective. Though it is not against the law in the United States to voice one's political opinion, people who do often face steep consequences. As we've seen, political crime has been woven throughout American history and remains prevalent on a global scale.

The Criminal Justice System

The Criminal Justice System as a Social Problem

We cannot fully understand crime as a social problem without examining the criminal justice system. For illustration purposes, we will follow the case of Buddy, Gary, and Clyde.

PLEA BARGAINING. On a Saturday night, Buddy Hudson, a 19-year-old African American, teamed up with two Whites, Gary Carson, 34, and Clyde Johnson, 21, to rob a liquor store. The robbery netted them $2,590. After a week's spending spree—their dreams of drugs and women realized—they tried their luck again. This time, though, their luck ran out. When an alarm went off, the three fled, but the police arrested them.

To ensure that the courts could not throw the case out for violating the suspects' rights, the arresting officers read the men the 1966 Miranda warning:

1. You have the right to remain silent.
2. If you do not remain silent, what you say can and will be used against you.
3. You have the right to be represented by a lawyer during questioning and thereafter.
4. If you cannot afford an attorney, the state will provide one at its expense.

The state did provide an attorney. Her advice was to say nothing—to let her talk to the prosecuting attorney, who would determine what crimes the suspects would be charged with. After meeting with the state's attorney, she told the men that the evidence against them was solid. They would be charged with armed robbery, resisting arrest, and assault with a deadly weapon. They could go to prison for up to 60 years. She added that she thought she could "cut

Social control is necessary for society's survival.

Issues in Social Problems
YOU DON'T HAVE TO BE POOR TO GO TO JAIL—BUT IT HELPS

It isn't a crime to be poor, but poverty sure doesn't help when you're in trouble with the law. If you can't pay a fine, you go to jail.

"It's the only practical alternative," declared Woodrow Wilson, a judge in Bastrop, Louisiana. "Otherwise, some people would never be punished."

In courtrooms across the nation, defendants with ready cash pay and leave. Those without money are ushered from the courtroom to the city jail to pay their debts with days rather than dollars—or at least to wait until someone bails them out.

In rural areas especially, authorities routinely jail defendants who are unable to pay fines for minor crimes such as public drunkenness, bad checks, and speeding. They jail the poor even though this appears to violate U.S. Supreme Court rulings. Legal aid lawyers charge—irrefutably, it seems—that it is unjust to give better treatment to defendants who have money. Still, indigent defendants keep winding up in jail.

Legal aid attorneys can't patrol all the courts, and most abuses occur in small, rural communities. The attorneys try to help people who are already in jail, but the process can be slow. Roger Baruch, a prisoners'-aid lawyer, recalls a man who spent 6 months in a Georgia jail because he couldn't pay traffic fines.

Many judges and prosecutors claim not to know that such defendants are poor. "If they raised the issue, they wouldn't be put in jail," asserts an Aurora, Colorado, city attorney, "but I don't see that it's the responsibility of the court or the prosecutor to check out their ability to pay fines."

It certainly must be difficult for these officials to know whether the people who are sitting in jail for petty offenses are poor or whether they have money but have chosen to be locked up so they can save a few bucks rather than being at work or home with their families.

Some officials have tried, or at least have given the appearance of trying. In Monroe, Louisiana, about 20 miles south of Bastrop, officials hired a priest to evaluate defendants' finances. They let him go, though, because he sided with the poor too often.

Few believe that this problem ever will be solved. The practice is too deeply ingrained in the legal system.

"The so-called administration of justice is arbitrary and somewhat capricious," says Jackie Yeldell, a Bastrop attorney. "One thing is certain, though. You can be sure there aren't any wealthy persons in jail."

Based on Schmitt (1982).

---

a deal" and get the charges of assault and resisting arrest dropped in return for a guilty plea to armed robbery. If so, she could reduce possible prison time from 60 years to 5 years.

Assuming that there would be some uncertainty on the part of the witnesses, the men figured that they could do better if they went to trial. Clyde's mother put up $20,000 to secure her son's release on bond. Unable to raise bond money, Buddy and Gary remained in jail during the 9 months it took for their case to come to trial. (Nine months? See the Issues in Social Problems box above.) Just before the trial, to everyone's surprise, Clyde pled guilty. The judge suspended Clyde's sentence and placed him on probation for 5 years. Buddy and Gary were found guilty of armed robbery. The judge gave Gary a 6-year sentence and Buddy a minimum of 15 years in prison.

A reporter asked about the differences in sentencing. The judge replied, "I have to show consideration for the defendant who cops a plea. It saves the court the expense of a trial" (Gaylin, 1974, pp. 188–189). He added that Clyde had a job and that to send him to prison would serve no purpose. Letting him keep his job, however, would increase his chances of staying out of trouble. When asked if the longer sentence for Buddy had anything to do with his race—he was African American—the judge stated that he had no racial bias. "That," he said, "is insulting. Race has nothing to do with this case. These are just facts: Gary Carson is older, but he has fewer 'priors' (previous arrests). He doesn't need as stiff a sentence to teach him a lesson. Buddy's 'priors' tell me he's more dangerous." The judge added, "For people like you, I wish Buddy were white and Gary black."

This case illustrates how the criminal justice system can be "more criminal than just" (Newman, 1966; Gaylin, 1974; Pattis, 2005):

1. Some of the poor spend months (even years) behind bars awaiting trial, while those with money use the bond system to buy their release.

2. Defense attorneys encourage **plea bargaining,** pleading guilty (whether or not one is guilty) in return for a lesser charge.

3. Prosecutors use threats of mandatory minimum sentences to get guilty pleas. ("Plead guilty to this lesser charge or I'll charge you with this more severe crime, which carries a longer sentence.")

4. Judges dislike "unnecessary trials" and impose harsher sentences on those who insist on them.

5. Age, employment, and the number of previous arrests affect sentencing. Even when offenses are the same, those who have better employment histories are given more lenient sentences.

6. The *number of arrests,* not the seriousness of those charges, influences a sentence. Judges discount the type of charge because they know that plea bargaining will affect the ultimate sentence handed down.

RECIDIVISM AND REHABILITATION. Recidivism rates—the percentage of former prisoners who are rearrested—show how inadequate attempts of rehabilitation in prison are (see Table 6-5). Most prisoners are simply warehoused—taken off the streets until they serve their time—and then they are taken back into their old neighborhoods, where they learned their criminal ways. They are not taught legitimate skills in prison, so when they are released without job training, they face a future of repeat offenses:

Over two million men and women are confined to jails and prisons in the U.S. Ninety percent of them eventually return home. After having served a median prison term of

TABLE 6-5 Recidivism of U.S. Prisoners

	REARRESTED	RECONVICTED	REINCARCERATED
All released prisoners	68%	47%	52%
Sex			
Men	68	48	53
Women	58	40	39
Race/Ethnicity			
White	63	43	50
African American	73	51	54
Latino	65	44	52
Other	55	34	50
Age at Release			
14–17	82	56	56
18–24	75	52	52
25–29	71	50	53
30–34	69	49	55
35–39	66	46	52
40–44	58	38	50
45 or older	45	30	41

Note: These percentages of former prisoners were rearrested, reconvicted, or reincarcerated within three years of being released from prison.
Source: Langan and Levin (2002, Table 8).

15 months, approximately 1600 inmates disgorge from state and federal prisons every single day of the week. In the greater Chicago metropolitan area alone roughly 1500 male ex-convicts return to their neighborhoods each month. They arrive home "wearing an X" on their backs, possessing meager skills of limited portability, and enjoying scanty resources on which to draw in their efforts to "make good," or live a life on the straight and narrow path of desistance. They almost always return to the same disaffected, marginalized neighborhoods in which they resided prior to incarceration but which now offer even fewer legitimate opportunities than before. The majority will stray from the path and wander into a gnarled grove of institutional failure, criminal opportunity, and the uniquely rewarding but ultimately self-defeating whorl of drug dealing and otherwise hustling street gangs. (G. Scott, 2004)

How effective is our U.S. criminal justice system? One study of 272,000 prison inmates reveals that within the *first year* after being released from prison, 46% of freed inmates are rearrested (see Figure 6-3). Within three years of freedom after arrest, 67% are rearrested.

You might be wondering about the crimes that these former prisoners committed after their release from prison. These statistics, too, are enlightening—and, some would say, frightening. As Table 6-6 on the next page shows, two-thirds of those who were rearrested during 3 years after release were charged with 750,000 new crimes, an average of 4 each. Over 100,000 of these charges were for violent crimes.

Keep in mind that these totals, as high as they are, are less than the actual number of crimes committed. How can we be certain of this? Simply put, few people are caught when they commit their first crime after being released from prison, and so, on average, offenders commit more crimes than they are charged with (Blumstein et al., 1988). In short, the crime rate of former prisoners is higher than their recidivism rate.

The likelihood of recidivism is influenced by gender, race–ethnicity, and age. Women, Whites, and older prisoners are less likely to get in trouble with the law again. Age at release is especially interesting. You can see how the rates of rearrest, reconviction, and reincarceration decrease with age. The two main possibilities are that the older these people get, the more they learn to stay away from crime—or the older they get, the more they are able to avoid getting caught when they commit a crime. They are either smarter older criminals or more-law-abiding former criminals.

FIGURE 6-3 Recidivism Trends

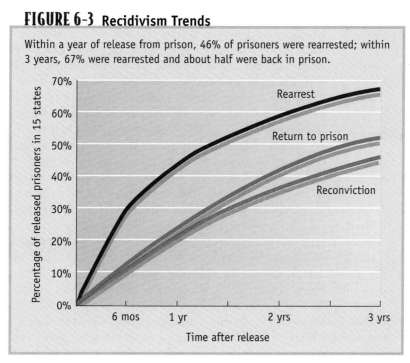

Within a year of release from prison, 46% of prisoners were rearrested; within 3 years, 67% were rearrested and about half were back in prison.

Source: *Confronting Confinement* (June 2006).

TABLE 6-6 Charges for 272,000 Offenders in the First Three Years After Their Release from Prison

Arrest Charge	Number of Arrest Charges in First 3 Years After Release
All offenses	744,480
Violent Offenses	100,531
Murder[1]	2,871
Kidnapping	2,362
Rape	2,444
Other sexual assault	3,151
Robbery	21,245
Assault	54,604
Other violent	13,854
Property offenses	208,451
Burglary	40,303
Larceny/theft	79,158
Motor vehicle theft	15,797
Arson	758
Fraud	21,360
Stolen property	21,993
Other property	29,082
Drug offenses	191,347
Possession	79,435
Trafficking	46,220
Other/unspecified	65,692
Public-order offenses	155,751
Weapons	25,647
Probation/parole violations	20,930
Traffic offenses	13,097
Driving under the influence	5,788
Other public-order	90,280
Other offenses	20,049
Unknown	68,351

[1] Murder includes non-negligent manslaughter and negligent manslaughter.

The more often someone has been put in prison, the greater that person's chances of going back to prison. How can this be? There are many reasons, of course, but for just one, recall our opening vignette: The treatment of that prisoner produced contempt and hatred, hardly the qualities we would recommend for bringing about law-abiding behavior.

To further demonstrate causes of recidivism, when inmates were asked "Do you think you could commit the same crime again without getting caught?" about 50% of inmates answer yes (Zawitz, 1998).

Not only do prisons fail to rehabilitate, but they also serve as socializing agents for future criminal behavior. People declared unfit to live in normal society are housed together for years in prison. One of their main topics of conversation is crime, and they boast to one another of those crimes they've gotten away with. Older, more experienced prisoners also teach younger ones how to commit crimes. It is an irony, of course, that the models for younger prisoners are criminals who have failed: *All* these mentors have been caught and put in prison. This irony may be part of the reason recidivism continues.

The Sting of Justice

Certain types of crime are easier to get away with than others. Least likely to be arrested are those who commit political crimes, for they are protected by the political system that they are supporting. Also at low risk of arrest are white-collar criminals who commit crimes in the name of a corporation or those involved in organized crime. Respectability, wealth, and power insulate many lawbreakers. Juvenile delinquents and other underclass members who commit street crimes run the highest risk of being apprehended.

ASSEMBLY-LINE JUSTICE. Keeping in mind, then, that the sting of the criminal justice system is more venomous for some than others, let's examine how this system operates. Buddy, Gary, and Clyde, whose defense attorney suggested that they plead guilty, represent in microcosm our criminal justice system. Prosecutors charge people with the most serious crimes possible and then offer to accept a guilty plea to lesser offenses. Despite their constitutional obligation to *defend* their clients, public defense attorneys often suggest to their clients that they plead guilty (Blumberg, 1967; Maynard, 1984). In *most* cases, what is supposed to be a trial is simply an arrangement of plea bargains worked out in the back room (Pattis, 2005).

Plea bargaining has become the standard in the U.S. criminal justice system. *In the vast majority of cases, people accused of a crime do* not *receive a trial.* On average, juries hear only 4% of criminal cases (*Sourcebook of Criminal Justice Statistics,* 2004, Table 5.43). Back in the 1960s, sociologist Abraham Blumberg explained that public defenders—despite their formal job description—develop "implicit understandings" about what their job *really* is: to be team players who produce "assembly-line justice" for the poor (Blumberg, 1967). Today, the situation remains unchanged. In urging his client to accept a jail sentence, one public defender said, "Even if you're innocent, it's a good deal" (Penn, 1985).

The criminal justice system is also slow and inefficient. Courtrooms are jammed with cases and available hours short. The slow pace is exasperating for police officers and other witnesses who must wait hours, even days, for cases to be called. Lawyers are expensive, and those assigned to the poor are overburdened. Rules for presenting evidence

are complex. For those who plead guilty, the average time between arrest and sentencing is 6 months. For those who choose a jury trial, it is twice as long, 12 months (*Sourcebook*, 2004, Table 5.43). During this time, some innocent people remain locked behind bars, while some guilty people are released to commit more crimes.

Plea bargaining and the inefficiencies of the court system subvert the Sixth Amendment to the Constitution, which declares that "the accused shall enjoy the right to a speedy and public trial, by an impartial jury of the State and district wherein the crime shall have been committed." The poor do not receive a speedy trial. Indeed, most do not even receive a trial.

Bias in the Criminal Justice System

Let's discuss racial–ethnic discrimination in the criminal justice system. As you will recall, Buddy, the only African American in the trio, received the most severe sentence. The judge claimed that this was only because of Buddy's "priors." What do you think?

"You look like this sketch of someone who's thinking about committing a crime."

A common perception is that bias in the criminal justice system works only against African Americans and Latinos. Sociological studies, however, indicate that this bias also favors these groups.

(© The New Yorker Collection 2000. David Sipress from cartoonbank.com. All Rights Reserved.)

The issue is complicated, and sociologists differ in their conclusions. At first glance, the judicial system certainly seems to discriminate along racial–ethnic lines, especially when it comes to African Americans. Although African Americans make up just 12% of the U.S. population, they make up 45% of prison inmates (*Sourcebook*, 2005, Tables 6.17, 6.34). From Table 6-7, you can see that the percentage of African Americans on death row is $3\frac{1}{2}$ times greater than you would expect from their percentage in the U.S. population. No other group makes up such a disproportionate share of prisoners or death row inmates. Perhaps no statement illustrates the impact of the criminal justice system on African Americans better than this one: On any given day, one of every eight Black males age 25 to 34 is locked up, and one-third of Black males born today can expect to spend time in prison (Mauer, 2004).

TABLE 6-7 Prisoners on Death Row, by Race–Ethnicity

Race–Ethnicity	Number on Death Row	Percentage of Death Row Inmates	Percentage of U.S. Population	More (+) or Less (−) Than What You Would Expect from the Group's Percentage of the U.S.Population[1]
White	1,531	45.4%	68.0%	−33%
African American	1,411	41.8	12.2	+243
Latino	353	10.5	13.7	−23
Native American	39	1.2	0.8	+50
Asian American	38	1.1	4.0	−72
Claim two or more races			1.3	
Totals	3,503	100	100	

[1] This total is computed by dividing the difference between the group's percentage of the U.S. population and its percentage of death row inmates by its percentage of the U.S. population.

Source: By James M. Henslin. Based on *Sourcebook of Criminal Justice Statistics* (2006, Table 6.80); Henslin (2007b, Figure 12.5).

Although these data do *not* let us draw conclusions about bias, they seem to hold true. Sociologists have analyzed victimization studies (which contain no police bias) comparing arrest rates for rape, robbery, and aggravated assault among African Americans and Caucasians. They find that the racial–ethnic makeup that victims report themselves closely matches arrest rates reported above by police (Hindelang, 1978; Shim & DeBerry, 1988; *Sourcebook,* 2005, Tables 42, 48).

Criminal conviction rates in the United States vary greatly among different racial groups. For example, among African Americans, 800/100,000 are likely to spend time behind bars. For Caucasians the rate is 166/100,000 (*Sourcebook,* 2005, Tables 42, 48).

The differences have been well documented throughout history, yet it still remains unclear why African Americans are most apt to be arrested and charged. Some contend that it is because African Americans commit more crime. Sociologists argue, on the other hand, that conviction rates among African Americans and other minorities are higher because the criminal justice system is biased (Sellin, 1928; Bridges & Stein, 1998; Mauer, 2004; Curry & Klumpp, 2007). Sociologists Douglas Smith and Christy Visher (1981) trained civilians to ride with the police in Missouri, New York, and Florida. After observing almost 6,000 encounters between police and citizens, they concluded that the police are more likely to arrest African American suspects. An examination of felony convictions in Florida showed that Whites were more likely to have their cases dropped or to receive probation, while African Americans were more likely to be convicted and to go to prison (Hale, 1980). Sociologist Gary LaFree (1980) examined the court records of a Midwestern city and found that African Americans who raped White women received more severe sentences than Whites who raped White women.

Other studies show that bias works in *both* directions: Sometimes Whites get more favorable treatment, but at other times minorities do. Consider these mixed findings: African Americans are given longer prison terms for rape and drugs, but Whites receive longer sentences for murder (Butterfield, 1999). Sociologist John Tinker (1981) found that Latinos in Fresno, California, were more likely than Whites to have their charges dismissed. If they were tried, however, they were more likely to go to prison. Sociologist Joan Petersilia (1983) found that minority suspects in California were more likely than Whites to be released after arrest. If convicted of a felony, however, they were more likely to be given longer sentences. Petersilia, along with sociologists Stephen Klein and Susan Turner (1990), found that race did not make a difference in sentences for assault, robbery, burglary, theft, and forgery. For drug offenses, however, Latinos were more likely to be sent to prison.

Sociologists Martha Myers and Susette Talarico (1986, p. 246) found that in Georgia, Whites were discriminated against: Once Blacks became a numerical majority, White offenders were at a distinct disadvantage. Put concretely, they were more likely than Blacks to be imprisoned.

We also find mixed results when we look at how juvenile delinquents are handled in the courts. While they wait for a judge to hear their case, Whites are more likely to be sent home, and Blacks are more likely to be kept in juvenile hall. When they do receive a hearing, however, African Americans are more likely to have their cases dismissed (*Sourcebook,* 1998, Table 5.77; 2004, Table 5.64).

At this point, then, we cannot conclude that the courts are biased for or against minorities or for or against Whites. The evidence is inconclusive.

The Death Penalty

Death penalty is administered differently based on factors such as race, gender, and region. A look at capital punishment tied to rape cases reveals much about discrimination in the justice system. **Capital punishment** may be defined as the decision by a jury in the sentencing phase of a capital (death penalty) case to put an inmate to death.

Donald Partington, a lawyer, examined all executions for rape and attempted rape in Virginia between 1908 and 1963. Convicted of these crimes were 2,798 men (56% White and 44% African Americans). Forty-one men were executed for rape and 13 for attempted rape. *All executed men were African Americans. Not one of the White men was executed.*

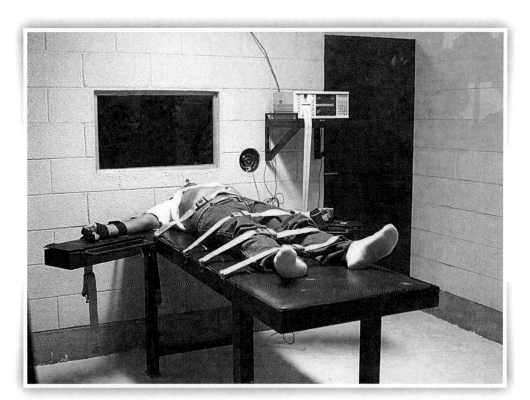

Throughout history many methods of execution have been used: death by hanging, a firing squad, the gas chamber, electrocution, and lethal injection.

When judges used to impose the death penalty for rape, what really made the difference was the race of the attacker *and* the race of the victim. In their study of rape and capital punishment in Georgia, sociologists Marvin Wolfgang and Marc Reidel (1975) found this: The best predictor of whether a man would be sentenced to death was knowing that the victim was White and the accused Black.

The death penalty was so biased that in 1972 the Supreme Court ruled in *Furman v. Georgia* that the death penalty was being applied unconstitutionally—in a discriminatory fashion. As Table 6-8 on the next page demonstrates, up to this point, 3,896 prisoners had been executed: 53% African American and 46% White. The states rewrote their laws, and since then 65% of those put to death have been White and 35% African American.

The death penalty apparently shows a strong gender bias: Of the 4,958 prisoners who have been executed between 1930 and 2007, only 43 have been women, a mere 0.9%. Since 1976, 1,088 men have been executed, and only 11 women (*Statistical Abstract*, 2009, Table 399). At present, only 1.5% of prisoners (51) on death row are women (Death Penalty Information Center, 2008). Do these totals indicate gender bias or real differences in criminal activity?

We do know that geography makes a huge difference in a person's chances of being executed. As the Social Map (Figure 6-4) on page 189 shows, 38 states use the death penalty while 12 states do not.

As you can see from Table 6-9 on page 190, some southern states are much more willing to order executions than are others. Texas holds the record for number of executions. One of every three executions (36%) since 1977 has taken place in Texas. Texas is a large state, though, with 23 million people living there. With a much smaller population of just 3.5 million, Oklahoma has had 75 executions since 1977. Therefore, a criminal is more likely to be executed in Oklahoma than in Texas.

The Prison Experience

Finally, let's look at the prison experience.

> I've been sentenced for a D.U.I. offense. My 3rd one. When I first came to prison, I had no idea what to expect. Certainly none of this. I'm a tall white male, who unfortunately has a small amount of feminine characteristics. And very shy. These characteristics have got me

TABLE 6-8 Prisoners Executed, by Race–Ethnicity

Year	WHITE		AFRICAN AMERICAN		NATIVE AMERICAN/ ASIAN AMERICAN		Total
	Number	Percentage	Number	Percentage	Number	Percentage	
Before the death penalty was abolished							
1930–34	371	48%	395	51%	10	1%	772
1935–39	456	51	421	47	14	2	891
1940–44	276	43	362	56	7	1	645
1945–49	214	33	419	66	6	1	639
1950–54	201	49	209	50	3	1	413
1955–59	135	44	167	55	2	1	304
1960–64	90	50	91	50	0	0	181
1965–69	8	80	2	20	0	0	10
Totals	**1,774**	**46**	**2,080**	**53**	**42**	**1**	**3,896**
Since the death penalty was reinstated							
1970–74	0	0%	0	0%	0	0%	0
1975–79	3	100	0	0	0	0	3
1980–84	19	66	10	34	0	0	29
1985–89	49	56	39	44	0	0	88
1990–94	85	62	50	36	2	2	137
1995–99	218	66	114	34	n/a	n/a	332
2000–04	233	68	109	32	n/a	n/a	220
Totals	**607**	**65**	**320**	**35**	**n/a**	**n/a**	**807**

n/a—not available

Note: Because this table does not include prisoners who were executed by the federal government, the total does not agree with that in Table 6-9.

Source: By James M. Henslin. Based on *Sourcebook of Criminal Justice Statistics* (1998, Table 6.88; 2004, Table 6.86); *Statistical Abstract of the United States* (2006, Table 342).

raped so many times I have no more feelings physically. I have been raped by up to 5 black men and two white men at a time. I've had knives at my head and throat. I had fought and been beat so hard that I didn't ever think I'd see straight again. One time when I refused to enter a cell, I was brutally attacked by staff and taken to segregation though I had only wanted to prevent the same and worse by not locking up with my cell mate. There is no supervision after lockdown. I was given a conduct report. I explained to the hearing officer what the issue was. He told me that off the record, he suggests I find a man I would/could willingly have sex with to prevent these things from happening. I've requested protective custody only to be denied. It is not available here. He also said there was no where to run to, and it would be best for me to accept things. . . . I probably have AIDS now. I have great difficulty raising food to my mouth from shaking after nightmares or thinking to hard on all this. . . . I've laid down without physical fight to be sodomized.

The preceding letter was written to the Human Rights Watch Organization in response to an article written by Stephen Donaldson of the organization Stop Prison Rape (Human Rights Watch, 1996).

THE ZIMBARDO EXPERIMENT. Philip Zimbardo, a social psychologist, conducted a fascinating experiment. Using paid volunteers, Zimbardo (1972/2007) matched 24 college students on the basis of their education, race, and parents' social class. He randomly assigned one group as guards and the other as prisoners. Without warning, one night real

FIGURE 6-4 Which States Have the Death Penalty?

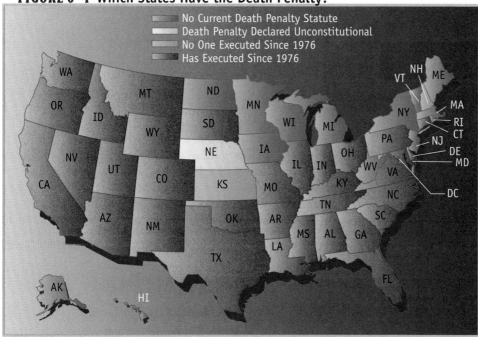

- No Current Death Penalty Statute
- Death Penalty Declared Unconstitutional
- No One Executed Since 1976
- Has Executed Since 1976

Source: Death Penalty Information Center, June 2008.

police cars arrived at the homes of those who had been designated prisoners. They were "arrested," fingerprinted, and taken to the basement of the psychology building at Stanford University, which had been turned into a prison. Both "guards" and "prisoners" were given appropriate uniforms.

Subject to the arbitrary control of their captors, the prisoners felt a loss of power and personal identity. The guards, in contrast, felt an increase in social power and status.

Some federal prisons are tougher on inmates than others. This photo depicts prisoners in Ohio performing manual labor.

TABLE 6-9 Number of Prisoners Executed, by Jurisdiction, 1930–2008

State	NUMBER EXECUTED	
	Since 1930	Since 1977
U.S. total	4,863	11,225
Texas	652	414
Georgia	405	43
New York	329	0
California	305	13
North Carolina	302	43
Florida	230	66
South Carolina	197	39
Ohio	191	26
Virginia	186	102
Alabama	169	38
Mississippi	161	10
Louisiana	160	27
Pennsylvania	155	3
Arkansas	145	27
Oklahoma	139	88
Missouri	128	66
Kentucky	105	2
Illinois	102	12
Tennessee	94	4
New Jersey	74	0
Maryland	73	5
Arizona	60	23
Indiana	57	19
Washington	51	4
Colorado	48	1
Nevada	41	12
District of Columbia	40	0
West Virginia	40	0
Federal system	36	3
Massachusetts	27	0
Delaware	26	14
Oregon	21	2
Connecticut	22	1
Utah	19	6
Iowa	18	0
Kansas	15	0
New Mexico	9	1
Montana	8	2
Wyoming	8	1
Nebraska	7	3
Idaho	4	1
Vermont	4	0
New Hampshire	1	0
South Dakota	1	1

Source: U.S. Bureau of Justice Statistics and Death Penalty Information Center: www.deathpenaltyinfo.org

They also developed strong in-group loyalty. After several days, rumors of a prison rebellion spread. The guards reacted brutally, with about a third treating the prisoners as though they were subhuman. Things started to get out of hand, and after 6 days Zimbardo stopped the experiment.

Zimbardo's experiment illustrates a fundamental sociological principle: The way society is structured and the groups to which we belong provide the basis for our orientations and how we act toward others. How a prison is organized is more important in determining how guards and prisoners act than are their individual personalities. As guards work in a prison, they come to see themselves as representatives of morality and the prisoners as enemies that need to be subdued, rather than as people who need to be helped. The guards' goal becomes upholding authority at all costs, even if this requires brutality, which in their view is justified. Eventually, the guards can come to see prisoners as "animals" who understand nothing but violence.

Zimbardo's experiment created a stir in the scientific community. Some fellow social scientists accused Zimbardo of being cruel and irresponsible. The federal government responded with strict guidelines for research on human subjects. Zimbardo's research, however, provides insight into what is wrong with our prisons, adding to our knowledge of why prisons fail to reduce crime. If prisons are not the answer, what is?

Social Policy

What is being done to solve these twin social problems of crime and the criminal justice system? We can never eliminate crime, but to the extent that we can encourage people to follow the law or prevent people from breaking it, we can reduce the problem. Because street crime bothers Americans the most, and street crime is linked to poverty, the *best policy* would be to reduce poverty. Education is an effective way to reduce poverty because, on average, the further that people can get in school, the more they will likely earn. In addition, researchers have found a direct link between adult crime and dropping out of high school, so any program that helps students graduate from high school should help prevent crime.

We will, of course, always have criminals, so we need effective policies for dealing with them. There are four basic approaches: retribution, deterrence, rehabilitation, and incapacitation. Let's consider each.

RETRIBUTION. *Punishing* criminals to uphold **values** (ideas of right and wrong) and to demonstrate that criminal behavior will not be tolerated is called **retribution.** Proponents of retribution view offenders as morally responsible for their violations. Violations create moral imbalance. To help restore moral order, punishment should fit the crime (Cohen, 1940). An interesting form of retribution is *shaming,* which is discussed in the Thinking Critically box on the next page.

Restitution requires offenders to compensate their victims for harm created. This is a form of retribution. Restitution is an attempt to mend the broken moral order, to help even things up. If people have stolen, for example, they need to pay the money back. Restitution is practical for property crimes, when the offender can repay the victim. It is

PUBLIC SHAMING AS SOCIAL POLICY

By James M. Henslin

"Shame on you!"

Do you remember those horrifying words from your childhood? If your childhood was like mine, you do. The words were accompanied by an index finger that pointed directly at me, while another index finger, rubbing on top of it, seemed to send shame in my direction.

With a harsh voice or one that showed disappointment, this gesture was effective. I always felt bad when this happened. I felt even worse when I saw the looks of disgust on the faces of my parents or grandparents in response to my childish offense, whatever it may have been.

These DUI offenders experience public shaming as part of their sentence.

If you have read Nathaniel Hawthorne's *The Scarlet Letter,* you know about shaming. Hester Prynne, who committed adultery, a serious offense at the time because it struck at the community's moral roots, had to wear a red A on her clothing. For life, wherever she went, she was marked as a shameful adulteress.

Some judges are bringing back this old-fashioned device. Not the scarlet A, but its equivalent.

A judge ordered thieves to wear sandwich boards that said, "I stole from this store." They had to parade back and forth outside the stores they stole from.

A Texas judge ordered a piano teacher who pled guilty to molesting his young students to give away his prized $12,000 piano and to not play the piano for 20 years. If you don't think this was harsh, consider the shaming that accompanied this punishment: He had to post a sign prominently on the door of his home declaring himself a child molester.

Judges have ordered drunk drivers to put bright orange bumper stickers on their cars that say, "I am a convicted drunk driver. Report any erratic driving to the police."

The Minneapolis police department has even organized "shaming details." Prostitutes and their johns must stand handcuffed in front of citizens who let loose with "verbal stones," shouting things like "You're the reason our children aren't safe in this neighborhood!"

Kansas City tried a different approach to prostitution. "John TV" shows the mug shots of men who have been arrested for trying to buy sex and of the women who have been arrested for selling it. Their names, birth dates, and hometowns are displayed prominently.

Rosters of convicted sex offenders are available at the click of a mouse. On your computer screen, you can see the individual's photo, name, date of birth, conviction, and, in some instances, even the offender's current address and a clickable neighborhood map. While this information is supposed to be intended to alert citizens to potential danger, it certainly is a shaming device.

Does shaming work? No one knows whether it reduces lawbreaking. But shaming certainly can be powerful. A woman convicted of welfare fraud was ordered to wear a sign in public that said, "I stole food from poor people." She chose to go to jail instead.

Even if shaming doesn't work, it does satisfy a strong urge to punish, to get even. In today's eager-to-punish climate, perhaps retribution is purpose enough. And perhaps it does help to restore a moral balance.

Examples are based on Gerlin (1994) and Belluck (1998)

---

less practical for offenders who don't have the means to pay back debt, although some judges require the unemployed to "work their debt off" in a variety of creative projects. Attempts to restore the "moral balance" are evident in the following attempts to "make the punishment fit the crime":

A Memphis judge invited victims to visit the thief's house and "steal" something back (A. Stevens, 1992).

A Florida judge sentenced a White man who was convicted of harassing an interracial couple to work weekends at an African American church.

These women volunteer for chain gang duty—picking up trash and burying bodies in order to get out of their jail cells.

A Texas judge ordered a deadbeat who had fathered 13 children to attend Planned Parenthood meetings (Gerlin, 1994).

For throwing beer bottles at a car and taunting a woman, a judge in Ohio sentenced two men to dress in women's clothing and to walk down Main Street (Leinwand, 2004).

Critics emphasize how difficult it is to decide that a crime merits a particular punishment and how inconsistent judges may be in making these decisions. For crimes of violence, retribution might require unusual measures, such as castration for rapists—acts that courts will likely declare unconstitutional. A California judge, for example, wanted to withhold AIDS treatment from a man who had raped two teenagers after he was released from prison for a previous rape (Farah, 1995). Proponents add that if retribution is the punishment, constitutional rights need to be addressed.

DETERRENCE. Deterrence aims to create fear by letting potential offenders know that they will be punished if they commit a crime. This approach views offenders as rational people who weigh the possible consequences of their actions. In this view, someone who is considering a crime will avoid it if punishment seems likely. Back in the 1970s, criminologist Ernest van den Haag (1975; van den Haag & Conrad, 1983) proposed that we treat juveniles who commit violent crimes the same way we treat adults ("adult crime, adult time"), abolish parole boards, and operate work programs for prisoners. With citizens demanding strong action, attempts at deterrence have become popular.

Researchers have discovered that the longer the interval between a crime and its punishment, the less the deterrence, or fear of the punishment. This underscores the need for speedy trials, already guaranteed by the Constitution, and for swift punishment of the guilty. Also, the more uncertain the penalty, the less deterrence works. To meet this principle, many propose **uniform sentencing,** the same sentence for everyone convicted of the same crime.

Critics of deterrence point out that offenders are not always rational about committing crime. Many act on impulse and do not weigh the consequences of their actions. For example, back in the 1700s, hanging was the known punishment for picking pockets in England. Hangings were public affairs, and one might think that such a severe punishment would stop this crime. Instead, when a pickpocket was being hung, other pickpockets worked the crowd. The hanging, with crowd's attention riveted on the gallows, provided them easier victims (Hibbert, 1963).

"Scared Straight" was once trumpeted by the mass media as a successful program of deterrence. To scare delinquents straight, they were taken on prison tours, where inmates gave them a close-up view of prison life. Leering and shouting obscenities, they said they could hardly wait for the youths to be sent to prison so they could rape them. Those who operated the program reported that it kept 80% to 90% of the youths from further trouble with the law. Follow-up studies by sociologists, however, showed that the program had backfired. Criminologist James Finckenauer (1982) matched delinquents on the basis of their sex, race–ethnicity, age, and criminal acts. He then compared those who had been exposed to the "Scared Straight" program (the experimental group) with delinquents who had not been exposed to it (the control group). Within 6 months, 41% of the experimental group were in trouble with the law while only 11% of the control group were in trouble.

How could such a program backfire? Finckenauer suggests that boys in particular were impressed by the macho performance of hypermasculine men. (Let your imagination go a little here: You've probably seen photos or TV programs that show the tattoos

James Settles helped start the faith-based halfway house called Aphesis in Nashville, Tennessee. He was inspired by his own experience in a halfway house after spending 8 years in prison for selling drugs.

and muscles and threatening posture that many male convicts display.) These boys were attracted to the images of the powerful men. Committing a crime after being through the program was one way to demonstrate that the talk hadn't frightened them, that they, too, were macho and couldn't be scared.

The failure of "scared straight" does not mean that programs of deterrence cannot work. It does, however, underline the need for sociological research to find out what actually works. We cannot *assume* that a program is successful just because it sounds good, because it appeals to our common sense, or because its operators say that it works. If we are to develop sound social policy, we need solid research so we can evaluate programs. This point is underscored in the Thinking Critically box on "prison boot camps" on page 194.

REHABILITATION. The focus of **rehabilitation** is resocializing offenders, to help them become conforming citizens. The following are major elements of current rehabilitation programs (Morash & Anderson, 1978):

1. *Probation:* keeping offenders in the community under the supervision of a probation officer
2. *Imprisonment:* confining prisoners with the goal of teaching them useful skills or educating them with high school courses
3. *Parole:* releasing prisoners before they serve their full sentence, both as a reward for good behavior and as a threat
4. *Furloughs:* giving prisoners freedom for a set time, such as a weekend, toward the end of the sentence, letting convicts adjust gradually to nonprison life
5. *Halfway houses:* allowing convicts to live away from a prison but requiring that they report back to parole officers about many aspects of their lives
6. *Honor farms:* allowing prisoners who have shown good behavior to live with less stringent supervision and training

The public is fed up with failed attempts at rehabilitation. Many perceive probation as an opportunity for felons to commit more crime—and this perception is accurate. Figure 6-5 on page 195 summarizes what happened to at-risk state and federal parolees over the last 8 years: More than 15% were rearrested and returned to incarceration (Bureau of Justice Statistics, 2007).

SQUEEZE YOU LIKE A GRAPE

As they step out of the police cars into the Georgia countryside, a guard shouts into their faces, "You're nothing! You're nobody! You're fools! You're maggots!"

The young people look dumbfounded. Another guard shouts, "I don't like ya. I got no use for ya, and I don't care who ya are on the streets. This is hell's half acre, and I don't give a damn if ya get tossed outta here into prison. I promise ya, ya won't last five minutes before you're somebody's wife. Do ya know what that means, tough guys?"

The offenders are ages 17 to 25. Convicted of nonviolent crimes, they were given a choice of either 1 to 5 years in prison or 90 days of prison boot camp, followed by probation.

Prison boot camps, like this one in Swan Lake, Montana, are intended to provide a structure of discipline which judges feel is lacking in the offenders' lives. We have no evidence that this punishment—or any other—is effective in changing offenders into law abiding citizens.

"You have to hit a mule between the eyes with a two-by-four to get his attention," explains a guard. "And that's what we do here." Within an hour of arriving, inmates are stripped of every sign of their previous life. Guards take their cigarettes and personal possessions. Their heads are shaved, and a white prison uniform with wide blue stripes replaces their jeans and T-shirts.

Inmates may not speak without permission. All responses must begin and end with "Sir." The lights go out at 10. Television watching is limited to one hour a day—only the news and PBS—all in black and white. No visitors are allowed for the first 45 days.

Inmates do hard physical labor. Up at 5 a.m., they cut grass with scythes and dig up tree trunks with shovels and pickaxes. If an inmate talks on the work crew without permission, he must do push-ups—or take the "chair position," unsupported, of course. Repeated violations mean being handcuffed and placed in a police car. Other inmates are made to watch as the violator is taken away to prison to serve the longer sentence.

Mississippi opened the first boot camp in 1985. Thirty-one states followed. Seven states opened camps for women.

The warden of this Georgia camp says, "They're not going to leave here any smarter, but we can provide some structure and discipline that they've never gotten. We can't fix the sociological problems that led to crime in the first place, but we can influence what they do next."

The sociologist, of course, replies, "Let's see the statistics. We need matched groups (offenders of the same background convicted of the same crimes) who go to prison and who go to boot camp. Or else we need randomized samples. When we compare the rearrest rate of each group, we'll know whether boot camps work."

It took some time, but we finally got random samples—and we now have measurements of the rearrest rates. Sociologists Jean Bottcher and Michael Ezell (2005) compared randomized samples of offenders who went through California's boot camp program with a control group of those who had not. The results are not encouraging. After 7 years, there were no differences between the groups in terms of how long it took to their first arrest or how often they were arrested. Other researchers who compared the recidivism of juveniles who went through prisoner boot camps with the recidivism of juveniles who were sent to prison have found nothing consistent. In some cases the recidivism rate of the juveniles who had gone to boot camp was lower, but in other cases it was higher. As a result, some states have shut down their boot camps and are sending their young offenders to traditional prisons.

Sources: Lamar (1986); Gest (1987); *Life* (July 1988, p. 82–83); Morash & Rucker (1990); MacKenzie & Souryal (1995); Bottcher & Ezell (2005); Lohn (2005); Willing (2005).

However, the concept of probation is not unsound, although our implementation of it is inconsistent. If probation were given to felons with the most promise, if they were provided with follow-up counseling, and if trained probation officers had small caseloads, it might work. As we have seen with the "Scared Straight" and boot camp programs, however, seemingly sound ideas can prove quite disappointing.

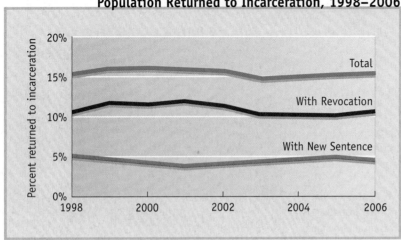

FIGURE 6-5 Percentage of At-Risk State and Federal Parole Population Returned to Incarceration, 1998–2006

Source: Probation and Parole in the United States, 2006.

Another approach to rehabilitation is **diversion,** diverting offenders *away from* courts and jails. The goal is to keep offenders out of the criminal justice system—to shift them to community organizations or to funnel them into administrative hearings rather than to criminal trials. Diversionary programs aim to avoid stigmatizing offenders and to keep them out of crime schools that socialize them into further deviance.

If rehabilitation programs were successful, almost everyone would favor them. The cost of rehabilitation would certainly be less than the price of crime—the cost to victims and the cost of prisons. The problem is that we do not have confident data demonstrating rehabilitation programs that work.

INCAPACITATION. Consequently, the public clamors for **incapacitation,** removing offenders from circulation. The view of those who propose imprisonment is direct and to the point: Everything else has failed. We cannot change people who don't want to change, so let's get them off the streets so they can't hurt people. Some offenders commit crime after crime ("career criminals"), so let's free ourselves of recidivists. For a new form of incapacitation, see the Technology and Social Problems box on page 196.

Incapacitation has aroused considerable debate in sociology. Criminologist James Wilson stated repeatedly that incapacitation is the *only* solution that makes sense. He advocated incapacitation in books, scholarly journals, and the popular media. Ernest van den Haag proposed "added incapacitation"—increasing an individual's sentence each time that person is convicted of a crime. Some estimated that if everyone convicted of a serious offense were imprisoned for 3 years, our rate of serious crime would drop by two-thirds (Shinnar & Shinnar, 1975). Others estimated that such sentencing would reduce crime by only 3%–4% (Greenberg, 1975; Cohen, 1978).

THE DEBATE OVER CAPITAL PUNISHMENT. One of the most provocative issues in social policy is the death penalty.

Its proponents argue that death is an appropriate punishment for heinous crimes because it deters and, of course, incapacitates absolutely. Its opponents argue that killing is never justified. If capital punishment did deter, then states with the death penalty would have a lower homicide rate than those without it—but they don't. In fact, the homicide rate of the states without the death penalty averages about *half* that of the states that have the death penalty (*Statistical Abstract,* 2006, Table 295). This fact doesn't faze those favoring the death penalty, who reply that it just goes to show that the states that have the death penalty really need it. Opponents also argue that the death penalty is capricious—jurors deliberate in secrecy and indulge their prejudices in recommending death—and that judges are irrational, merciful to some but not to others. Proponents

Technology and Social Problems
USING TECHNOLOGY TO STOP CRIME

The idea is simple. "It's expensive to keep people in prison, and not everyone who is convicted of a crime should go to prison. Yet we need to keep tabs on offenders. How can we use technology to do this?"

The ankle bracelet, simple and effective, is able to transmit an offender's location 24 hours a day. A transmitter is strapped around the offender's ankle, which transmits a signal to a central monitor. If the offender leaves home, it breaks the signal, setting off an alarm at the monitoring station.

The ankle monitor also lowers costs. To keep a juvenile in custody runs about $100 a day, but the cost for home monitoring is just $10 a day. To keep an adult in prison runs about $75 a day, but the cost to use the ankle device is just $12 a day. The costs include equipment and staff.

Some jurisdictions have even developed a pay-as-you go plan. Judges give adult clients a choice—go to jail or pay $12 a day for electronic monitoring. Not eligible are drug dealers, those who committed a violent crime, and those who used guns to commit their crime. In some Florida counties, even those accused of drunk driving have to wear this device and pay its daily cost (author's notes, 2005).

The ankle monitor is also suitable for probation and parole. Software can be programmed with an offender's work schedule and location. Probation officers can park outside a workplace to pick up a signal; better yet, failure to appear at work also sets off a signal. Probation officers check to make certain that it isn't a false call, then alert the police.

Hidden within this new technology is another benefit. Because electronic monitoring frees up prison cells, it allows courts to keep violent offenders in prison longer.

Victims of stalking get a special benefit. The software can be programmed to sound an alarm if an offender comes within a specified distance of a victim's home or workplace. Workers at the monitoring station warn the victim, who can leave the area.

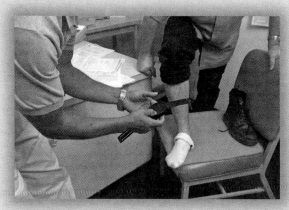

With the advent of technology, many parolees are now monitored with ankle bracelets. The Global Positioning System (GPS) signals police if the offender goes beyond his allotted boundaries.

Future technology will soon make this tool seem primitive. Signaling devices will be implanted in felons' bodies. The implant will be connected electronically to the Global Positioning System, satellites that can track the precise location of any object. Software will be programmed with the offender's schedule—times and location of work or rehabilitation classes, even routes to and from work and restricted places in the community. If the individual deviates from the schedule, a computer will notify the police to make an arrest.

Technology is moving rapidly. We already have the capacity to insert devices in an offender's brain that can send pain if an individual deviates from scheduled activities. Soon we may be able to implant devices that will direct the individual's movements. This capacity to monitor and control people, of course, leads to the question of potential abuse by authorities. Putting such devices on felons, some fear, is merely a step toward the goal of monitoring all citizens and residents. In light of the fear of terrorism, this is a chilling possibility. Implants and the marvels of the Global Positioning System—what more could Big Brother ask to control its citizens?

Based on D. Campbell (1995); McGarigle (1997); "GPS Creates Global Jail" (1998); Knights (1999).

reply that in their opinion judges and juries are doing a good job under difficult circumstances. Opponents stress that innocent people have been executed: They point to the men released from death row because of DNA testing. Opponents reply that they are happy that we have DNA testing, that now we can be even more certain of the guilt of the killers we execute.

Neither side convinces the other. Nevertheless, the public demands that "something be done," and as Figure 6-6 on the next page shows, about two-thirds of Americans favor

FIGURE 6-6 Americans' Changing Attitudes Toward Capital Punishment Question: "Are you in favor of the death penalty for persons convicted of murder?"

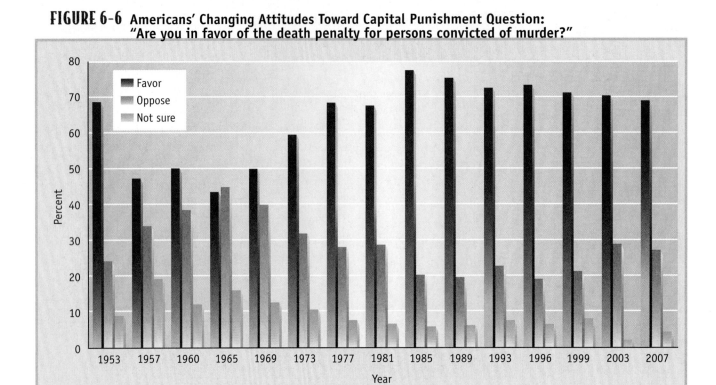

Source: By James M. Henslin. Based on various editions of *Sourcebook of Criminal Justice Statistics,* including 2008, Table 2.51.

the death penalty. Figures 6-7 and 6-8 on the next page show the increase in the number of prisoners sentenced to death and the numbers who have been executed.

GOALS AND PRINCIPLES. The United States has tried a variety of approaches to solve its crime problem. With little agreement on the basic purpose for the social response to crime (prevention, retribution, deterrence, rehabilitation, or incapacitation), our solutions are piecemeal and in disarray. To have rational social policy, we need to reform the criminal justice system. We suggest the following goals and guiding principles:

1. Clear laws based on the broadest possible consensus, rather than on the interests or moral concerns of small groups.

2. Swift justice based on legal evidence presented in adversarial proceedings. (This would require eliminating plea bargaining and lengthy delays based on legal technicalities; it would guarantee a speedy trial for all who plead not guilty and require more courts, more judges, and longer working hours for judges.)

3. More rehabilitation programs, including diversion for most first offenders who did not commit violent crimes, with the goal of integrating them into the community.

4. "Added incapacitation": Harsh penalties for violent offenders, with the penalty becoming harsher each time a person is convicted of a crime.

5. Task forces to investigate organized crime and white-collar crime (with the provision that, for a specified time, such as 5 years after they leave a task force, members cannot accept employment from the corporations they investigated).

6. Harsh penalties for people who are convicted of crime on behalf of a corporation, including jail for executives, the forced sale of any division found guilty of crime, and huge fines to reduce the motive of corporate profit (Liazos, 1981).

7. Prison reform, including making the position of prison warden a civil service job, training prison guards rigorously and paying them well, allowing prisoners to have

FIGURE 6-7 Persons Under Sentence of Death

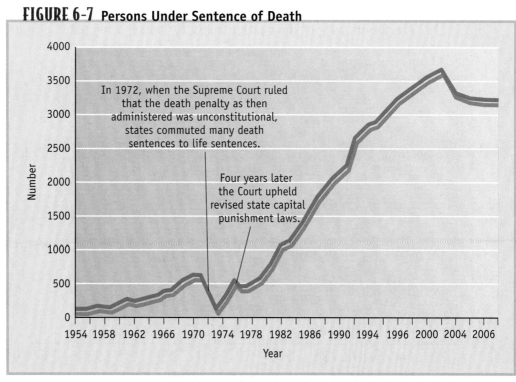

In 1972, when the Supreme Court ruled that the death penalty as then administered was unconstitutional, states commuted many death sentences to life sentences.

Four years later the Court upheld revised state capital punishment laws.

Source: By James M. Henslin. Based on Greenfield (1991); various editions of *Sourcebook of Criminal Justice Statistics; Statistical Abstract of the United States* (2006, Table 341 and Table 6.79); U.S. Department of Justice, Capital Punishment 2007.

conjugal visits, and giving *to the nonviolent* the right to visit friends and family on the outside.

8. Unbiased research to determine what works and what doesn't work. In the ideal case, we would compare experimental and control groups. We certainly have the capacity to make such determinations, but we need cooperative politicians and other government officials to approve and fund such research.

FIGURE 6-8 Executions 1930–2007

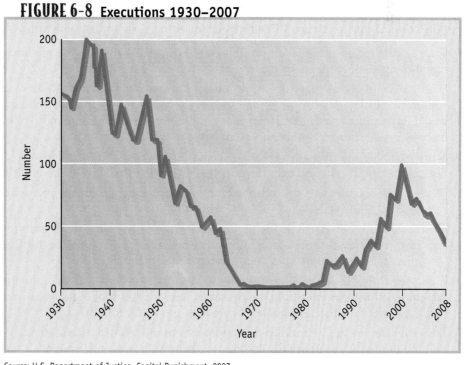

Source: U.S. Department of Justice, Capital Punishment, 2007.

The Future of the Problem

CHANGES IN CRIME. Will crime increase or decrease over time? The answer depends on the type of crime. Crime by women, for example, will probably increase as more women leave traditional roles at home to work in paid employment. Their opportunities for crime will increase, and, like men, they, too, will follow illegitimate opportunities.

We won't be able to tell whether white-collar crime increases or decreases. If more white-collar crime is handled by the judicial system, it will *appear* to increase. Because we lack a baseline of white-collar crime from which to draw accurate comparisons, however, official statistics could show a doubling or even more in any given year, and we would still not know whether this represented an increase or just a greater exposure.

Organized crime will continue, taking different forms as social conditions change. If enforcement efforts that are directed against one part of organized crime, such as the Sicilian American Mafia, succeed, that group will turn increasingly to legitimate businesses. The Mafia will more than likely remain criminal, however, as illegal activities are the heart of its existence.

The incidence of political crime will depend upon elections and political events. Economic distress and fears of election fraud could revive political protests like those of the 1960s and 1970s and lead to unrest. If we do have substantial illegal acts designed to change the political system, government officials may find the legal procedures too cumbersome to deal with and may, in turn, engage in illegal acts to protect a threatened political system.

THE CRIMINAL JUSTICE SYSTEM. The judicial system changes slowly. We anticipate that the criminal justice system will continue to focus on street crime and overlook the crimes of the powerful. We anticipate an increase in privately owned and operated prisons. Private firms now operate prisons with over 100,000 inmates (Harrison and Beck, 2006, Table 3). This change does not necessarily represent a change in the prison system, but a change in ownership.

NEED FOR FUNDAMENTAL CHANGE. If we ever get serious about preventing the poor from being recruited to street crime, we must open the doors to legitimate ways of achieving success. This means that we must provide access to quality education and training for careers. If the private sector doesn't create enough jobs for everyone who wants to work, then the government needs to create jobs—and, to be successful for this purpose, the jobs must pay a living wage. This is fundamental, as people who have a high investment in the social system commit fewer street crimes. To change the social system in ways that open the door to equal opportunity is a radical proposal; but, until we entertain radical change, crime will remain a serious social problem.

SUMMARY AND REVIEW

1. Whether an act is a *crime* depends on the law, which, in turn, depends on power relationships in society.
2. Crime is universal, because all societies make rules against acts they consider undesirable. Laws turn these acts into crimes. Because laws differ, crime differs from one society to another and in the same society over time.
3. The social problem of crime has two parts: the crimes committed and the criminal justice system. Crime is a problem because people are upset about the threat to their lives, property, and well-being; the criminal justice system is a problem because people are upset about its failures and want something done about it.
4. Chambliss's study of the "saints" and the "roughnecks" illustrates how social class affects the perception and reactions of authorities, as well as how crime statistics are distorted.
5. Functionalists note that property crimes represent conformity to the goal of success but rejection of the approved means of achieving success. Just as some

people have more access to legitimate opportunities, others have more access to *illegitimate opportunities.*

6. Conflict theorists regard the criminal justice system as a tool that the ruling class uses to mask injustice, control workers, and stabilize the social system. Law enforcement is a means that the elite use to maintain their dominance.

7. *Juvenile delinquents* use five major *neutralization techniques* to deflect society's norms: denial of responsibility, denial of injury, denial of a victim, condemning the condemners, and an appeal to higher loyalty.

8. *White-collar crime* is extensive but underreported. Corporations usually insulate white-collar criminals from the law, especially when the crimes benefit the corporation.

9. *Professional criminals* are people who make their living from crime. They have high in-group loyalty, scorn the "straight" world, and take pride in their specialized skills.

10. *Organized crime* is best represented by the Mafia, whose use of violence within a highly developed bureaucracy lies at the heart of its success.

11. *Political crime,* illegal activities intended to change the political system or to maintain it, ebbs and flows as political conditions change.

12. The criminal justice system fails to deliver justice because of overcrowded courts, *plea bargaining,* a team-player system that subverts public defense attorneys, possible racial–ethnic bias, and prisons that foster hostility and hatred.

13. Because our criminal justice system has no unifying philosophy with which to establish and evaluate social response to crime, our policies of social control are in disarray.

14. Social change—including the role of women, social policies toward crime, and economic and political events—will influence the direction of crime in the future.

15. To get at the root of this problem requires reform of the criminal justice system and a basic overhaul of our social institutions, especially changes that open more opportunities to the poor.

KEY TERMS

THINKING CRITICALLY ABOUT CHAPTER 6

1. Which of the three theoretical perspectives (symbolic interactionism, functionalism, or conflict theory) do you think does the best job of explaining the causes of crime? Why?

2. Which of the three perspectives (symbolic interactionism, functionalism, or conflict theory) do you think does the best job of explaining why white-collar criminals are treated differently from street criminals? Is your answer to this question different from your answer to Question 1? Explain.

3. Do you think that violent criminals should be treated differently from nonviolent criminals in terms of punishment? Why or why not? Consider the case of the criminally negligent manufacturer whose product kills people but who has no actual contact with victims versus the street criminal who kills someone during a robbery.

4. Which of the four basic approaches to treating criminals (retribution, deterrence, rehabilitation, and incapacitation) do you think is the most appropriate? Why?

BY THE NUMBERS: THEN AND NOW

- Number of girls, under age 18, arrested for violent crimes in 1981: **5,825**
- Number of girls, under age 18, arrested for violent crimes in 2004: **12,149**

- Percentage of all arrests for embezzlement made of men in 1981: **70%**
- Percentage of all arrests for embezzlement made of men in 2004: **50%**

- Percentage of all arrests for embezzlement made of women in 1981: **30%**
- Percentage of all arrests for embezzlement made of women in 2004: **50%**

- Number of U.S. prisoners executed before the death penalty was abolished: **3,896**
- Number of U.S. prisoners executed since the death penalty was reinstated: **1,136**

- Number of prisoners under sentence of death in 1978: **500**
- Number of prisoners under sentence of death in 2007: **3,220**

MySocLab

What can you find in MySocLab? mysoclab ALLYN & BACON www.mysoclab.com
Where learning & the sociological imagination intersect.

- Complete Ebook
- Practice Tests and Exams
- Multimedia Activities
- Mapping and Data Analysis Exercises

- Research and Writing Advice
- Interactive Social Surveys
- Sociology in the News

Economic Problems: Wealth and Poverty

At age 17, Julie Treadman faced more than her share of problems. Her boyfriend had deserted her when she told him that she was pregnant. Exhausted and depressed, Julie dropped out of high school. Now five months' pregnant, she wondered about her child's future.

When Julie had severe stomach pains, a neighbor called an ambulance, and she was rushed to Lutheran Hospital. When hospital administrators discovered that neither Julie nor her mother had insurance, money or

> ## Julie gave birth to a stillborn baby.

credit, they refused her admission. Before they could transfer her to a public hospital, however, Julie gave birth to a stillborn baby.

This situation perplexed hospital administrators who didn't want to serve those who wouldn't pay—but felt the need to provide care. They ordered the ambulance driver to take Julie—dead baby, umbilical cord, and all—to the public hospital.

—Based on an event in St. Louis, Missouri

The Problem in Sociological Perspective

In this chapter, we examine major economic problems facing our nation. Our primary focus will be on the unequal distribution of society's resources, especially as this inequality produces problems the poor face at the hands of the wealthy.

Economic Systems and Changes

COMPARING CAPITALISM AND SOCIALISM. The United States is made up of many **social classes.** The term *social class* refers to the way economic differences among groups or individuals in a society are measured. Picture social class like a ladder—where you are located on that ladder makes a vital difference in what your life is like. In this chapter, we shall look at sociological research and theory on the rich and the poor, the powerful and the powerless. Let's start by considering how the economy affects all our lives.

The **economy** represents the entire social institution that produces and distributes goods and services. How the economy functions affects the welfare of every individual, group, and community in the entire nation. At any given time, the U.S. economy is moving through a "boom–bust" cycle. During a "boom" everything seems to be affordable; during a "bust" nothing seems to be going right. These "boom–bust" cycles plague **capitalist economies,** which are based on the private ownership of property and the investment of capital for the purpose of making a profit. Some students who are taking this course will graduate during a "boom" and will have their choice of jobs. Others will graduate during a "bust," and even though they have worked just as hard as the others and earned the same degrees, they will end up struggling to find work.

In **socialist economies** the government owns property, and profit by individuals is illegal. Government committees decide what items—from cars to toilet paper—can be produced and distributed. The government also sets the price for items—taking into consideration neither the quality of the goods nor the demand for them. Everyone is guaranteed a job, and everyone works for the government, which owns everything.

Socialist and capitalist economies seem almost opposites of one another. Capitalists believe that socialism is immoral, that socialism denies people the freedom of choice—including the right to choose where they live and work. Socialists believe that capitalism is immoral, that capitalism puts profit ahead of the welfare of people, and that the poor are left to suffer. In what was known as the Cold War, proponents of each ideology viewed the other as the mortal enemy.

The **Cold War** (approximately 1945 to 1989) describes the political tension between the United States and the former Soviet Union or, more generally, to tensions between the "West" and "East." During this era, each side lived in constant fear of nuclear attack by the other.

THE TRIUMPH OF CAPITALISM. Under the socialist regimes of the Cold War era, workers were no longer rewarded for creativity or production. Committees governed all facets of production, and many workers lost the incentive to work hard. Capitalism's appreciation of individual effort proved much more efficient, and workers' standard of living in capitalist countries grew. Workers in socialist countries, in contrast, saw their living conditions—already at a low level—decline. As the Soviet economy deteriorated in the late 1980s, its leaders, under Mikhail Gorbachev, abandoned socialism and reluctantly turned to capitalism. The Soviet Union broke up into 15 independent states, and all of them, including Russia, pursued capitalism.

China still claims to uphold the principles of socialism, but is also on a journey to adopting capitalism. The Chinese are now encouraged to own property and to pursue profit. Since economic reforms began in 1978, international trade in China has dramatically risen. The domestic market in China is rapidly developing, showing indications that it will be as important as the United States in exports. China's economic system has successfully integrated the U.S. dollar into its reserve—allowing the country to import advanced technology and offer bargaining power (Satyananda, 2005).

At the beginning of the 21st century, then, capitalism seems to have triumphed. The new independent states adopting capitalism, however, have encountered economic problems. Russia was thrown into such economic and political disarray that its central authority was threatened. Organized crime figures, mentioned in the last chapter, in cooperation with corrupt politicians and military, took control of a large part of the Russian economy. They assassinated politicians and business leaders who stood in their way, as well as journalists who tried to expose them. This put the security of Russia's nuclear weapons in jeopardy. In 2008, the global economic crisis was especially threatening to new capitalist economies, many of them shutting down their fragile markets.

As capitalism has come to dominate the globe (with the primary holdouts being North Korea and Cuba), the leaders of major capitalist countries have divided the world's nations into three primary trading blocs: North and South America, dominated by the United States; Europe, dominated by Germany; and Asia, dominated by Japan, with China the newest contender. To control capitalism's troublesome cycle of "booms" and "busts," the most powerful eight nations, known as G-8 (the Group of 8) hold an annual summit, where they attempt to regulate global markets. This organization used to be called G-7, until Russia was invited to join. Soon it will be called G-9: China has been invited, another step toward China becoming a partner in world domination.

Capitalism's certainty of a "boom–bust" cycle is matched by the uncertainty of knowing when the economy will switch from "boom" to "bust" and back again. To try to control this cycle, G-8 uses the *International Monetary Fund,* a world bank that lends to nations that are in economic trouble. The "boom–bust" cycle continues, however, and entire regions may experience prosperity or poverty. In the 1990s, the region dominated by Japan went into the "bust" cycle, and formerly booming factories in Thailand, Indonesia, and South Korea closed their doors. As the value of these countries' currencies shrank, capitalist leaders feared a global "bust." Although G-8 members were able to pull this region out of the "bust," a danger facing global capitalism is that most of the world will be engulfed in these cycles.

Today, the evidence of a "bust," or recession, is compelling. In February 2008, not only did industries in the service sector lose more jobs than they created, but the index

Foreign investment in Asia made its economies boom. The wealthy search for ways to display their status, such as by driving this car in Brunei.

Poverty is a global issue, and every country has huge disparities between its wealthy and its poor. These young people in Siliguri, India, have no home. For them, every day is a fight for survival as they scrounge for scraps to eat, followed by fitful nights spent on the sidewalks.

of total weekly hours worked by production employees in the entire economy declined by one-tenth of 1% from January 2008 (Furchtgott-Roth, 2008). The real threat came not only from a slowing of economic growth but also from the possibility that weaknesses in the banking and housing sectors would affect the rest of the economy. Indeed, these two sectors did crash, leading to the economic crisis of late 2008, which has the potential for a long-term global "bust," a major recession or depression.

When socialist economies were functioning, their primary advantage was equality. They guaranteed jobs for everyone (although the jobs paid little) and provided medical care for everyone. If there was no wealth, neither was there hunger. With such equality, why did capitalism appeal to them at all? The simple answer is that capitalism is efficient at producing wealth. There certainly was greater equality in the socialist nations— almost everyone was poor. The capitalist countries are marked by tremendous wealth and **social inequality**—the unequal distribution of wealth, income, power, and poverty— but most people under capitalism have a high standard of living.

FOCUSING ON PROBLEMS. Capitalism offers both individual freedoms and the opportunity for economic success. These features are so appealing that millions of people immigrate to the United States, whether legally or illegally. For some people, however, such as Julie Treadman in our opening vignette, the social inequality of a capitalist system has dire consequences. Because Julie couldn't pay, she was denied medical treatment and human dignity. Because this book is about social problems, not social opportunities, our focus remains on the negative consequences of social inequality.

Economic Problems Facing the United States

Because the U.S. economy is essential to the well-being of its citizens, it is important to understand issues affecting its future. Let's look at four problems facing the U.S. economy.

STAGNANT INCOMES. The first problem is that people's **real income** (income adjusted for inflation) is stagnant. For 25 years, from the end of World War II until 1970, the real income of U.S. workers rose steadily. Even considering inflation, workers still had more money to spend. Since then, the paychecks of workers have continued to grow, but those paychecks contain dollars without calories. Although the paychecks show more and more dollars, making workers feel as though they are earning more than they used

FIGURE 7-1 Average Hourly Earnings, in Current and Constant Dollars

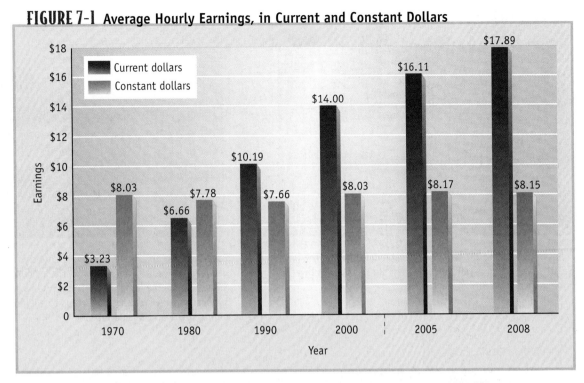

Note: *Current dollars* are the number of dollars a worker earns. *Constant dollars* means those dollars have been adjusted for inflation.

Source: *Bureau of Labor Statistics*, May 2008.

to, income in constant dollars of today's workers is little more than it was in 1970 (see Figure 7-1). In short, the raises that U.S. workers have been receiving have been eaten up by inflation. Look closely at Figure 7-1. You will see that it took 35 years for workers to get a real raise of 12 cents an hour.

What has softened the blow for the average family is that more family members are working. In 1940, only 16% of wives worked for wages. Today, about 60% of wives work for wages either full- or part-time (Davis & Robinson, 1988; *Statistical Abstract,* 2006, Tables 584, 585, 586, 587). How much do you think having this extra worker has added to family income? Do you think it doubled it? Maybe increased it by half? Despite two incomes, after adjusting for inflation, the average household today brings in just 16% ($6,000) more a year than it did in 1980 ($43,000 versus $37,000) (*Statistical Abstract,* 2006, Tables 585, 674). Despite 11 million more wives working for wages now than in 1980, the net gain to the average family's income is only 16%. This additional calculated income does not include the costs of child care, a second car, additional clothing, lunches, and so forth. After these costs are subtracted, one wonders whether there has been any gain at all.

TAXES. The second major problem involves income taxes. Someone coined the term *Tax Freedom Day* to refer to the day when the average worker has earned enough to pay his or her annual taxes. Politicians keep promising tax cuts, but they seldom deliver on that promise. Tax Freedom Day falls on April 26 (Tax Foundation, 2006). On average, each of us must work for the government 4 months before we have a cent for our own needs!

THE SAVINGS RATE. Figure 7-2 illustrates the third major problem. Americans are saving very little, even less than they saved in the midst of the Great Depression of the 1930s. Americans save less than the citizens of all other industrialized nations. The drop in savings shown in Figure 7-2 has significant consequences. It isn't just that the average family has less to draw on when they might need it. Reduced savings means that we have less

FIGURE 7-2 How Much Do Americans Save?

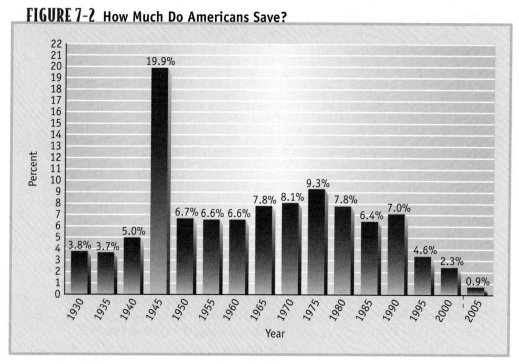

Source: By James M. Henslin. Based on American Savings Education Council (1999); *Statistical Abstract* (1990, Table 700; 1995, Table 710; 2007, Table 658).

money to invest in new plants and equipment, and this can undermine our ability to compete in today's global markets. This, in turn, undermines our standard of living.

A DEBTOR NATION. Fourth, we buy goods from other nations at such a frenzied pace that the United States has become the largest debtor nation in the world. When you calculate what we pay for the products we buy from other nations minus the products we sell to those nations, at the end of year we end up with an enormous shortfall. Year after year, we sell less than we buy. By the end of 2008, the national debt had surpassed $10 trillion. These mountains of debt have been piling up, and this cannot go on indefinitely. Just as individuals must repay what they borrow, so it is with nations. To finance the **national debt** (the total amount the U.S. government owes), we pay more than $180 billion a year in interest (*Statistical Abstract,* 2006, Table 460). The monies spent on interest alone are greater than the total amount spent on the Iraq war. These billions translate into funds that we cannot use to build schools and colleges, hire teachers, pay for medical services or job programs for the poor, operate Head Start, or pay for any other services to help improve our quality of life.

The Nature of Poverty

TYPES OF POVERTY. Let's turn now to the face of poverty. You might think that poverty would be easy to define, but its definition is neither simple nor obvious. There are three types of poverty. The first is **biological poverty,** which refers to starvation and malnutrition. It also refers to housing and clothing so inadequate that people suffer from exposure. Our homeless endure biological poverty.

More common is **relative poverty.** This term refers to people living below the standard of living for their society. Some relative poverty is serious, such as the poverty experienced by the Americans who try to get by on only half or even one-quarter of the average national income. Other relative poverty is not serious—those who report they feel impoverished because they don't belong to a country club or drive the nicest of cars. Relative poverty exists on a world scale: What is poverty in the United States may mean

See For Yourself

Visit the Poverty Calculator at www.livingwage.geog.psu.edu/
▶ Determine your living wage today.

comfortable living in India, where most families have little clothing and little food, and many people live in just one room or two.

Lastly, **official poverty** refers to the income level at which people are eligible for welfare benefits. People below this **poverty line** are defined as "poor"; those above it are not.

In the United States, these poverty guidelines were first created in 1962. Mollie Orshansky, an economist working in the Social Security Administration, developed a standard for measuring a family's poverty level. She considered the amount of money needed to buy food as the key factor in determining one's poverty level. Her research, reported in the 1965 *Social Security Bulletin,* allowed all others in government to better understand the social support that different family sizes would need to live a healthy lifestyle. In 1962, Orshansky used $3,000.00 as the standard cost of food for all families. Today, the Social Security Administration determines one's assistance by multiplying what they should spend on food by 3, on the assumption that most families spend one-third of their income on food (G. M. Fisher, 1988).

PROBLEMS WITH THE POVERTY LINE. Critics point out that the poverty line is stuck in a time warp. Sociologist William Julius Wilson (1992) and policy analyst Patricia Ruggles (1990, 1992) point out that food preferences and cooking patterns have changed since the 1960s, but not the government's definition of poverty. They say that because poor people actually spend only about 20% of their incomes on food, to determine a poverty line we ought to multiply their food budget by 5 instead of 3 (Uchitelle, 2001). Sociologist Michael Katz (1989) notes that the official poverty line assumes that everyone is a careful shopper who cooks all family meals at home and never eats out. Who lives like this, he asks? Others point out that except for Alaska and Hawaii, the poverty line is not adjusted for different costs of living. It costs a bit more to live in Albany, New York, than it does in Albany, Georgia, or in Philadelphia, Pennsylvania, than in Philadelphia, Mississippi. Finally, the poverty line does not even distinguish between urban and rural families. Despite decades of criticism, this magical line continues to be drawn across the income spectrum, supposedly separating the "poor" from the "non-poor." Because this is the standard of measurement, we will use it to look at "official poverty" in the United States.

The Scope of the Problem

Subjective Concerns and Objective Conditions

We need to stress again that objective conditions alone—whether defined officially or not—are not enough to make poverty a social problem. Subjective concerns are also essential and, actually, more important. How can subjective concerns be more important than objective conditions? Consider the extremes: On the one hand, according to our definition of social problems, if poverty is extensive but few people are concerned about it, poverty is *not* a social problem. On the other hand, if poverty is rare but its existence bothers many people and they want to address it, poverty *is* a social problem. Let's look at examples.

CHANGES IN CONCERNS AND CONDITIONS. During the early years of the United States, *most* people were poor. Yet at this time poverty was not considered a social problem. Life had always been a struggle for most of the population, so *people assumed that poverty was a natural part of life.* As industrialization progressed in the 19th century, it produced an abundance of jobs and wealth. As poverty declined, though, masses of poor people migrated to U.S. cities. Even though the standard of living had increased, this migration made poverty more visible, leading public leaders to declare that poverty was a social problem. As immigrants were absorbed into the expanding workforce, once again poverty receded from sight. Then the Great Depression of the 1930s thrust millions of people out of work.

As the ranks of the poor swelled and citizens protested, poverty was again visible. Declaring poverty to be the greatest problem facing the nation, government officials rushed through legislation that established emergency programs and created millions of jobs. Then came World War II, when factories began to operate at full capacity while millions of Americans were sent overseas to fight. Postwar prosperity followed, and poverty continued to recede from sight. Even though the objective condition—poverty—remained, subjective concerns lessened. Tucked in out-of-the-way rural areas and in urban slums, the poor once again dropped from popular view.

LAUNCHING THE WAR ON POVERTY. In 1960, President Kennedy made poverty a campaign issue, but subjective concerns were not really aroused until Michael Harrington wrote *The Other America* in 1962. Rarely has a single volume of social science transformed people's consciousness as this one did. Harrington passionately argued that in the midst of "the affluent society," one-quarter of the nation lived in squalor. Policy makers read this book, the media publicized it, and sociologists assigned it to their students.

Within two years of the book's publication, President Johnson declared a "war on poverty." The federal government began a raft of programs for the poor: child care, Head Start, legal services, medical services, job training, subsidized housing, and community health centers. The result was dramatic. As you can see from Figure 7-3, in just 10 years the number of Americans below the official poverty line dropped from 22% to 13%. This reduction made it clear that poverty could be addressed with social policy.

FIGURE 7-3 Americans Below the Poverty Line

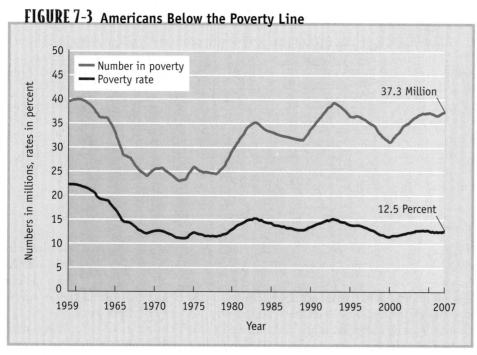

Source: U.S. Census Bureau, *Current Population Survey,* 1960–2008 Annual Social and Economic Supplements.

See For Yourself

Visit the U.S. Department of Labor at http://workforcesecurity.doleta.gov/unemploy/uifactsheet.asp

▶ What antipoverty programs are available in your neighborhood?
▶ Where might a person go to find out if they qualify for benefits?

The Situation Today

At the beginning of the 21st century, the war on terrorism and global economic threats caused subjective concerns about poverty to diminish. Although the media occasionally highlight the plight of workers in the steel, textile, or automobile industries, for the most part poverty has been relegated to tales of woe featured during Thanksgiving and Christmas. This changed somewhat when foreclosures and significant job losses across the economy began in 2008.

REACHING A PLATEAU. Since the initial reduction in poverty in the 1960s, progress has been limited. From Figure 7-3, you can see that during the past 30-plus years, the percentage of people below the poverty line has hovered between 12% and 14%. Currently, it is at 12.5%. With our larger population, today's 12.5% represents 37.3 million people, about the same number who were poor before the "war on poverty" began in the 1960s.

CONTROVERSY OVER NUMBERS. The poverty line, of course, is arbitrary in the first place, and the number of "poor" people can be reduced or increased at will by changing this official definition. Although some argue that the number of poor is higher than the official measure, others claim it is less. They point out that the government does not count as income many benefits that people receive from antipoverty programs. Medicare, Medicaid, food stamps, and HUD vouchers (the amount the government pays in rent for poor families) are not counted as income. If such items were counted, many people would no longer be officially poor.

THE SIGNIFICANCE OF POVERTY. Perhaps now you can better understand why it is difficult to address poverty as a social issue. Where should the cutoff for poverty be, and what should we count as income? How many poor people are there really? Despite this confusion, three facts stand out: First, no matter how we compute poverty, millions of Americans are poor. Second, how we define poverty has serious consequences for people's lives. The definition we use determines who will receive aid and who will not. Third, poverty lies at the root of many other social problems. In earlier chapters, we saw the connection between poverty and prostitution, rape, murder, and alcoholism and other forms of drug addiction. In coming chapters, we shall see how poverty is related to other social problems such as racism, physical and mental illness, and abuse in the family.

Social Inequality

The existence of poverty contradicts the ideal American vision of success. Americans often cope with this contradiction by denying it. For example, when researchers ask people what social class they belong to, most Americans—whether rich or poor—say that they are middle class. This tendency fascinates social researchers. Ann Getty (an heir to the Getty oil fortune) told a reporter, "I lead a very ordinary life" (*New York Times,* Sept. 7, 1980). Ordinary? Her "ordinary life" included not only living in a San Francisco mansion but also flying to Paris to shop for clothing by top designers—taking her personal chef with her.

Poverty is much more than having little money. Poverty means the reduction in life chances.

We know that all Americans are not equal, of course, and that the life chances of a waitress's daughter differ immensely from those of a son born to wealthy parents. We all know that the rich and politically connected pass these advantages on to their children and the poor and powerless pass disadvantages on to theirs. Because of this, we have social programs intended to help level the playing field. Affirmative action, as well as college scholarships and community colleges, are attempts to level the playing field.

Such programs run up against **structural inequality,** the inequality built into our economic and social institutions. For example, differences in wages are built into our capitalist structure. If a society has 100 million jobs, 20 million pay excellent wages, 50 million pay good wages, and 30 million pay low wages. Unemployment is another example of structural inequality. If a society has 107 million workers but only 100 million jobs, then 7 million workers will be unemployed, regardless of how hard they work. Job training programs cannot solve this structural problem. The solution requires changes in structure—that is, the creation of more jobs. No real social system has been devised that eliminates structural inequality.

Distribution of Income and Wealth

INEQUALITY OF INCOME. One major consequence of structural inequality is evidenced in the vast inequality in income among Americans. Look at Figure 7-4 on the next page. The poorest Americans are non-White or Hispanic, maintaining a median income $20,000 less than that of non-Hispanic Whites. Despite numerous antipoverty programs, *income inequality today is greater than it was in the 1940s.* The net worth of the average non-White is more than $100,000 less than the net worth of Whites.

INEQUALITY OF WEALTH. Another way to analyze financial inequality is to look at the distribution of **wealth:** how much property, savings, investments, and economic assets people own. Americans are worth about $50 trillion combined, mostly in the form of real estate, corporate stock, mutual funds, and bank accounts (*Statistical Abstract*, 2006, Table 703). This wealth is not evenly divided among Americans. To give you an idea of how concentrated assets are among the wealthy, look at Figure 7-5 on the next page. You can see that one-third of the nation's wealth is in the hands of just 1% of U.S. families. This 1% virtually controls corporate America.

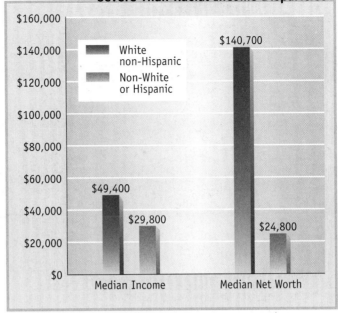

FIGURE 7-4 Racial Wealth Disparities Are More Severe Than Racial Income Disparities

Legend:
- White non-Hispanic
- Non-White or Hispanic

Median Income: $49,400 / $29,800
Median Net Worth: $140,700 / $24,800

Note: Median income and median net worth by race-ethnicity, 2004.

Source: Federal Reserve Board, Survey of Consumer Finances (2004).

With billions, the richest people in the United States are Bill Gates and Warren Buffet. Bill Gates dropped out of Harvard to cofound Microsoft Corp., the world's largest software company. (Gates's wealth fluctuates a few billion dollars up and a few billion dollars down as the price of Microsoft stock changes.) Gates and his employees developed MS-DOS and Windows, two popular computer operating systems. Microsoft gets a licensing fee each time a computer that uses these systems is sold. Having already given $30 billion to the Gates Foundation, Gates has often been labeled the most generous man in human history (Strom, 2006).

At 11 years old, Warren Buffet purchased his first stocks. In 2005, he purchased an energy company. His share-trading strategies have allowed him to amass more than $50 billion dollars. His "buy and hold" strategy involves purchasing downturned stock and then waiting patiently for them to regain their value in the market. In the recent economic crisis, Warren Buffet continues to buy, taking advantage of fears in the tumultuous market (Timmons & Romero, 2005; Cendrowski, 2008; O'Keefe, 2008). Like Gates, Buffet is a philanthropist; more than three-fourths of his fortune will go to the Gates Foundation.

How much is a billion dollars? The following illustration may help us grasp the enormity of a billion dollars— *one thousand million dollars:*

> Suppose you were born on the day Christ was born, that you are still alive today, and that you have been able to save money at the fantastic rate of one cent for every second that you lived—that is, 60 cents for every minute, $36 for every hour, or $864 for every day of your life during these past two thousand years. At that rate, it would take you another thousand years to save one billion dollars. (Shaffer, 1986)

WEALTH AND POWER. As research scientist James Smith said, "Wealth is a good thing, and everyone ought to have some" (Stafford et al., 1986–87, p. 3). Then why doesn't

FIGURE 7-5 Who Owns What? How the Wealth of the United States Is Distributed

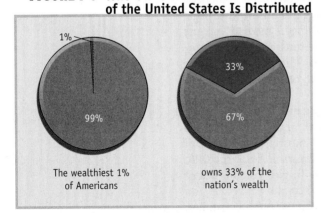

The wealthiest 1% of Americans — 1% / 99%

owns 33% of the nation's wealth — 33% / 67%

Source: Beeghley (2005).

everyone share? Part of the problem is that vast wealth brings vast power. Because owning 10% or 20% of a company's stock is enough to control it, the 1% of Americans who own over half of all corporate stock wield immense power over the economy (Beeghley, 2005). In their pursuit of even more wealth, these elite can move production to Mexico, India, or China, where labor is cheaper, closing down factories here. Thousands of people are thrust out of work. Most designer jeans, for example, which used to be made in the United States, are now made in Asian nations. The U.S. workers who lose their jobs in this global game of monopoly don't make these decisions, but they must live with the consequences.

Finally, because the rich can hire top financial advisors, attorneys, and lobbyists, they perpetuate their advantages. In their world of privilege, they are protected from unemployment, injustice in the courts, and an unresponsive political system. Let's turn our attention to those less advantaged who must cope with such conditions as part of everyday life.

The Impact of Poverty

Let's consider the impact of poverty. Living in poverty does not simply mean having less money and therefore going to fewer movies, buying fewer video games, and eating steak less often. Rather, people's economic circumstances envelop them, affecting profoundly every aspect of their lives. Let's look at some of these consequences.

"The poor are getting poorer, but with the rich getting richer it all averages out in the long run."

How we define reality depends to a large extent on where we are located in the social class structure. Poor Americans are not likely to have the view illustrated in this cartoon.

(© The New Yorker Collection 1988. Joseph Mirachi from cartoonbank.com. All Rights Reserved.)

HOUSING AND MORTGAGES. Most of the poor live in substandard housing. Many rent from landlords who neglect their buildings. The plumbing may not work. The heating system may break down in winter. Roaches and rats may run riot. And, unlike mortgage payments, the monthly rent does not build up equity in a home.

Even homeowners are at risk. During the first years of the 21st century, subprime mortgage rates and dishonest brokers allowed many people to buy homes they could not afford, especially when the value of their homes dropped below the amount of their mortgages—with home sales and home values dropping nationwide. Others were hit with rising payments because they had adjustable rate loans, and still other homeowners were facing unemployment as recession/depression loomed. By 2008, the banks that had made the loans or bought the loans were in crisis. As numerous homeowners started pleading with mortgage companies to lower payments, financial corporations continued with foreclosures. Many homeowners set appointments with "workout specialists" to restructure their home loans. Others declared bankruptcy when they could no longer pay their escalating mortgage rates.

One homeowner described his unsuccessful renegotiation as follows: "I told her that I probably spend $10.00 a day on groceries; and she said 'Maybe you can eat less'" (Morgenson, 2008).

Fannie Mae and Freddie Mac are government-sponsored enterprises that buy mortgages from lenders. They package those loans into securities to then sell to investors. Both companies reported a combined $11 billion loss in mid-2008 amid worry about whether they had enough capital to cover mortgage losses. Their plummet caused the Treasury Department to offer both companies a line of credit, and in September 2008, they were placed in government conservatorship; that is, the government basically took over their operations (Hagerty, Langley, & Pulliam, 2008; Labaton & Andrews, 2008).

The mortgage crisis is part of an overall financial downslide, compelling the government to intervene in the fate of the nation's largest insurance and investment banking firms. The months and years ahead will reveal the impact felt by American families.

EDUCATION. Although public schools are supposed to give all children an equal opportunity to succeed, the poor remain at a disadvantage. Because our schools are supported by property taxes, and property in poorer areas produces fewer taxes, the schools that the poor attend have smaller budgets. This translates into outdated textbooks, inexperienced teachers, and lower test scores (Kozol, 1999).

These lower test scores affect one's chances of going to college. Few, however, realize just how closely college and income are matched. If you rank families from the poorest to the richest, at each level of family income the likelihood that their children will go to college increases (Manski, 1992–1993; Reay et al., 2001). Similarly, the wealthier a family is, the more years of schooling their children complete (Conley, 2001).

And then there is the *type* of college that children attend. Most poor children who go to college attend community colleges where they are funneled into vocational programs. In contrast, most children of the middle class attend state universities, while the children of the wealthy go to elite private colleges. Before going to college, some children of the very wealthy first attend private boarding schools, where classes are small and teachers are well-paid (Persell et al., 1992). The college advisors at these schools have close ties with admissions officers at the most elite colleges. Some have networks so efficient that *half* of a private high school's graduating class will be admitted to Harvard, Yale, and Princeton (Cookson & Persell, 1985/2005).

JOBS. Unlike the career paths open to children of the middle class, the low-paying jobs of the working poor lead to fewer opportunities. Because workers are often laid off from dead-end jobs, their incomes, already low, are erratic. During unemployment, they have to cope with the complex bureaucracies of unemployment insurance, welfare, and other social programs. Such experiences add to the stress they are already experiencing.

CRIMINAL JUSTICE. The life experiences of the poor also make them more likely to commit crime. The most common crimes committed by those in poverty are robberies and assaults, crimes that are especially visible and for which offenders are punished severely. White-collar crime may be more pervasive and costly to society, but it is less visible and carries milder punishments. As mentioned in the previous chapter, when the poor are arrested, they lack the resources to hire good lawyers to defend themselves. Often, they cannot even post bail.

IN SHORT: QUALITY OF LIFE. Wealth and income represent privilege—received or denied. The net result is a quality of life that goes right to the core of one's being. Job insecurity brings stress to the poor. Their jobs offer no pension plans and no medical benefits. They then live one paycheck away from eviction. If they get sick, they can be laid off, and their job may not be there when they return to work. Among the stark repercussions: Those living in poverty don't eat as well, their children are more likely to die in infancy, they are more likely to have accidents at work and at home, and they die younger. And, like Julie Treadman in the opening vignette, they have less access to good medical care, which further jeopardizes their well-being.

Looking at the Problem Theoretically

As we learned in earlier chapters, each theoretical perspective gives a different view of a social problem. Let's look at poverty through these same lenses.

Symbolic Interactionism

THE RELATIVITY OF POVERTY

Andy, Sharon, and their two children live in a small house in a rural area. Andy farms 65 acres and works part-time at the local grocery store. Sharon works part-time as a cook at the Dew Drop Inn. She sews some of the children's clothing. Between their jobs and the farm, they make about $16,000 a year. They grow their own vegetables, buy milk from a neighbor, and fish in a nearby pond. Integrated into the community and with their basic needs satisfied, they don't think of themselves as poor. Neither do their friends and neighbors.

Leslie attends a private college. Her parents pay her tuition, fees, books, rent, utilities, insurance, medical bills, and transportation. They also pay about $800 a month for "extras." Unlike many of her friends, Leslie has no car, and she complains about how hard it is to get by. Her affluent friends feel sorry for her.

Between auditions, Keith, a struggling young actor works as a waiter. He earns about $900 a month, which has to cover his rent, food, and all other expenses. To make ends meet, he rooms with three other aspiring actors. "It's difficult to make it," he says, "but one day you'll see my name in lights." Keith sees himself as "struggling"—not poor. Nor do his actor friends think of him as poor.

Maria and her two children live in a housing project. Her rent is subsidized and cheap—$97 a month. Her welfare, Medicaid, and food stamps total $14,287 a year, all tax-free. Her two children attend school during the day, and she takes classes in English at a neighborhood church. Maria considers herself poor, and so do the government and her neighbors.

According to the government standards, all but Leslie are actually poor, yet Leslie *feels* poor. Why?

Symbolic interactionists stress that to fully understand poverty we must focus on what poverty *means* to people. All of us probably evaluate where we are in life. When doing so we *compare* ourselves with others. In some rural areas, simple marginal living is the norm, but in Leslie's cosmopolitan circle people often *feel* deprived if they cannot afford the latest upscale designer clothing from their favorite boutique. The meaning of poverty, then, is *relative:* What poverty is differs from group to group within the same society, as well as from culture to culture and from one era to the next.

It is not enough to understand how people view their own poverty. We must also focus on how the middle class views the poor. The dominant view is that the poor are good people who are down on their luck and need a helping hand. Another view is that the poor are "no-goods" who refuse to work—a drain on society's resources. Such differences in perception and meaning are significant, for they have an impact on social policy.

CHANGING MEANINGS OF POVERTY. The view of poverty in the early 1700s stands in marked contrast to today's perspective. At that time, Americans viewed poverty as God's will, and clergy preached that God put the poor on earth to provide an opportunity for the rest of us to show Christian charity (Rothman & Rothman, 1972). Poverty was viewed not as a social problem, but as a personal problem. Poverty was considered to be an ordinary part of life that required compassion on the part of others.

After Europeans settled in North America, the poor scattered among hundreds of villages along country roads. The American Revolution brought the poor out of seclusion into populated cities such as Boston, Philadelphia, and New York City. To address the visible poor, authorities set up welfare committees that distinguished between the deserving and undeserving poor. The deserving poor were the blind, the disabled, and deserted mothers. The undeserving poor were beggars, peddlers, idlers, drifters, and prostitutes. At this point, the meaning of poverty began to change. Increasingly, poverty was viewed not just as God's will, but also as the result of flawed character.

As the United States industrialized and more people moved to the cities, urban squalor bothered people of good intentions. Reformers launched campaigns to help the poor—and again the meaning of poverty changed. The reformers saw poverty as the product of corrupt cities. Urban temptations—alcohol, crime, and debauchery—held people in the bondage of poverty (Rothman & Rothman, 1972).

Although society no longer believes that poverty is God's will, the idea that poverty ought not to exist—and the suspicion that it is due to the character of the poor—remain part of our symbolic heritage. We have vacillated between viewing the poor as worthy people who deserve our help and as worthless people who deserve nothing. Symbolic interactionists help us understand that the meanings of poverty change as social conditions change.

Functionalism

HOW INCOME INEQUALITY HELPS SOCIETY. In their classic thesis, sociologists Kingsley Davis and Wilbert Moore (1945) developed the functionalist perspective on social inequality. Their argument was simple. Some tasks in society are more important than others. These positions require educated people who are willing to make a sacrifice to prepare for them. To attract such talented people, the positions must offer high income and prestige. Oil, for example, is vital to keeping the economy going, but to learn the advanced techniques to find oil or to manage oil fields takes years of training in geology. Consequently, petroleum geologists, especially geophysicists, must be offered both a substantial salary and the respect of others. Anyone can wash dishes, so unskilled workers earn poverty wages at jobs that require little training. Thus, disparities in income help society function.

HOW POVERTY IS FUNCTIONAL FOR SOCIETY. Functionalists go further in saying that poverty itself is functional for society. Sociologist Herbert Gans (1971/2007) points out that we need the poor because their poverty contributes to society's well-being. For a summary of this view, see the Thinking Critically box on the next page.

Functionalists also analyze the dysfunctions of poverty, including alienation and despair, drug abuse, street crime, suicide, and mental illness. In the Spotlight on Social Research box on page 218, Gans explains what he believes to be the true causes of poverty.

Conflict Theory

THE CAUSE OF SOCIAL INEQUALITY. Social inequality, argue conflict theorists, comes from a basic struggle over limited resources. At any point in history, some group has gained control of society's resources, and that group uses its power to secure its gains and to exploit those who are weaker. The result is a social class system in which the wealthy pass advantages to their children, whereas the poor pass disadvantages to theirs.

A GENERAL THEORY OF SOCIAL CLASS. Karl Marx (1818–1883) was the first sociologist to develop a general theory of social class and class relations. He argued that social class revolves around a single factor, the *means of production*—the tools, factories, land, and capital used to produce wealth (Marx, 1867/1967; Marx & Engels, 1848/1964). People are either capitalists (bourgeoisie), who own the means of production, or they are workers (*proletariat*), employed by the capitalists. The history of a society is best understood as a conflict between owners and workers, the wealthy and the poor. Because the capitalists are in power, they manipulate society's legal and political systems to promote the interests of owners to further control workers.

Marx wrote that the capitalists' control cannot continue forever. The day of reckoning will come when workers will revolt. Workers will lose their **false class consciousness,** the mistaken idea that they soon will start their own business and become wealthy. In its place will arise *class consciousness,* the realization that they are workers no matter what their

THINKING CRITICALLY about Social Problems

WHY WE NEED THE POOR: HOW POVERTY HELPS SOCIETY

Most of us think of poverty only in negative terms: Poverty is undesirable, and we should get rid of it. Functionalists, in contrast, identify the functions of poverty—that is, the positive consequences that poverty has for society. Consider these twelve functions:

1. The poor ensure that society's dirty work gets done at low cost. Many factories, restaurants, farms, and hospitals could not survive in their present state without this underpaid workforce. If there weren't poor people, who would do the dirty jobs at low wages?

2. The poor create jobs for others. Think of the social workers and welfare agencies that serve the poor and, not incidentally, shield the rest of us from them. Most police officers would be without jobs if it weren't for the poor. And what would social workers do for a living?

3. The poor serve as guinea pigs in medical experiments. The rest of us benefit from these advances in medicine. What would we do without those medicines and surgical techniques?

4. The poor make the economy more efficient. They spend their low wages and welfare money on leftover goods such as day-old bread and the many "seconds" that our factories produce. They also buy the furniture and cars that the rest of us discard. Where else would these undesirable items go if it weren't for the poor?

5. The poor make others wealthy. Many slum landlords, for example, would have to get jobs if it weren't for the poor. And what would the owners of the many liquor stores in the inner city do without the poor?

6. The poor help some people become upwardly mobile. Just above those who live in poverty are people who are striving to reach the fringes of the middle class. An example is the people who run the many small grocery stores in the inner cities. Without the poor, they would have to close their doors.

Generation after generation, there always are poor people. Why? The answer given by functionalists has stimulated controversy.

7. The poor provide the front-line soldiers for war. These youth are the ones who can be sacrificed during battle. (The Germans used to call them "cannon fodder.") Where else would we get the many people that we need to fill the "grunt" jobs in the armed services—or to test the roads for bombs in such places as Iraq and Afghanistan?

8. The poor stabilize our political system. Most poor people vote for Democrats, so to the degree that this party helps the U.S. political system, the poor contribute to that effort.

9. The poor provide entertainment. Their lives of despair become the story lines of novels, movies, and television programs. News programs gain followers—and advertising revenue—by documenting the murders and rapes committed by the poor. Some may disagree with this depiction, but to be shocked and frightened out of our ordinary lives by dramatic accounts of the lives of others is certainly one definition of entertainment.

10. The poor enrich our music. They have given us the blues, Negro spirituals, country music (from the Southern poor), rock (the Beatles came from the slums of Liverpool), and hip-hop/rap. Without the devastating experiences of the poor, the rest of us would have fewer tunes to hum.

11. The poor help motivate us. That there are "the projects," skid row, homeless shelters, and soup lines keeps the rest of us on our toes. We know that we had better get an education and work hard—doing whatever our teachers and bosses tell us—or else we could end up there. The poor have replaced the "bogeyman" of years past.

12. The poor also help our self-concept. They make us all feel superior. *We* are not like *them.*

By the time functionalists get through with their analysis, one wonders if society could even exist without the poor.

Based on Gans (1971/2007).

HERBERT GANS, *professor of sociology at Columbia University, is a past president of the American Sociological Association. He has written extensively on urban poverty and antipoverty policy.*

Ever since the 1950s, sociologists have led poverty researchers in studying America's victimized and demonized poor—although they have not done nearly enough research on their victimizers and demonizers.

Perhaps because I am a refugee from Nazi Germany and came to the United States dirt-poor, a significant part of my teaching and research has been about poverty and antipoverty policy. I have been concerned with the victimized and demonized, as well as the agencies and institutions that victimize and demonize the poor. In the early 1960s, I wrote *The Urban Villagers,* a book about a low-income neighborhood in Boston that was demonized as a slum and about its residents who were victimized when their neighborhood was torn down.

Later in the 1960s, I wrote a good deal about poverty and antipoverty policy—what is today called public sociology. Along with other sociologists, I analyzed and criticized the "culture of poverty" arguments, which suggested that the poor practice a culture that helps to keep them poor and prevents their escaping from poverty. We argued that blaming the victims for their victimization diverted attention away from what really keeps them poor: the shortage of secure and decent-paying jobs, the failures of the welfare program, and racism. Although their victimization resulted in depression and pathology, it was not a culture of poverty.

I returned to antipoverty research in the late 1980s, when a new version of, and a new term for, the culture of poverty argument appeared. This time, the poor were demonized as an "underclass," an alleged stratum that existed under respectable society. This underclass was accused of such moral shortcomings as not wanting to work, turning to welfare or street crime instead, being promiscuous, and avoiding marriage.

My interest in victimizers and demonizers made me wonder who invented and spread the new blaming term. In 1995, I wrote *The War Against the Poor,* which identified its inventors. The book also described how journalists, social scientists, and political conservatives combined to use and popularize the term.

Since the late 1990s, when welfare reform and a boom in low-wage jobs enabled more poor people to work, their demonization has declined—at least for the moment. However, if enough working poor lose their jobs to a weak economy, they will surely be demonized again—with the same old arguments, but perhaps with another new term. Then sociologists must show once more that blaming the victims only makes it harder for the poor to escape from poverty.

---

occupation, whether it be garbage collector or college professor. With their eyes finally opened and with the realization that they all are exploited workers, they will seize the means of production and use them for the good of all. Then poverty will be eliminated.

MODIFICATIONS OF CONFLICT THEORY. Most sociologists acknowledge that Marx provided valuable insight into relationships between the powerful and the poor, but they find his class division, consisting of just owners and workers, inadequate for today's society. Erik Wright (1979, 1985) made distinctions between office workers, factory workers, and managers. In fact, many top managers have more power than the stockholders they work for.

Unlike Marx, Ralf Dahrendorf (1959, 1973), a contemporary theorist, pointed to authority, not ownership, as the key dimension of social class, arguing that power and authority are the root causes of conflict within society (Ritzer, 2002). When two or more classes are living in the same society filled with constant change, this ultimately results in conflict.

Feminist theorists point out that women's labor in the home was not even included in Marx's capitalistic model. Such ignorance devalued women's contributions. Karl Marx considered the exploitation of workers in the paid sector, not women performing reproductive and household labor in the unpaid sector.

Functionalists argue that the highest salaries often go to the positions that perform the most important functions. Critics respond that if this were true, sanitation engineers would be among the highest paid.

Early conflict theory ignored key issues confronting the powerless—gender, race, and age. Feminist theory argues that these noncapitalist categories create venues for exploitation just as important as those that exist between the owners of production and workers.

IN SUM Conflict theory is like a long conversation. But no matter the speakers, conflict theorists always stress the relationship between those who have power and those who do not. The problems of the poor are due to their deprived position in a system of stratification, to their relative powerlessness, oppression, and patriarchy.

Summary of Theoretical Approaches

Each theoretical lens provides a unique understanding of wealth, poverty, and social inequality. Symbolic interactionists focus on the individual level, making us more sensitive to how social class works in our everyday lives. They explain, for example, why the amount of income that people have (the objective condition) is not the same as how they feel about that amount (subjective views that lead to relative poverty). Functionalists and conflict theorists look at a bigger picture. They examine social structure—in this case, the poor and the wealthy, the powerful and the powerless. Functionalists see inequality as originating from a broad social need to reward society's important positions. Conflict theorists stress that poverty originates and is maintained by those who own the means of production.

Research Findings

Who Are the Poor?

PERMANENCE AND POVERTY. It may surprise you that most people who fall below the poverty line do not stay there permanently. Most are poor only for short periods—for example, when they are injured, sick, or during layoffs or slow seasons. Although the total number of poor in the United States remains fairly constant from year to year, there is much change within this total. Each year millions of people rise above the poverty line, while millions of others fall below it. The likelihood that one will live in poverty is determined by region, race–ethnicity, age, and gender.

FIGURE 7-6 The Geography of U.S. Poverty

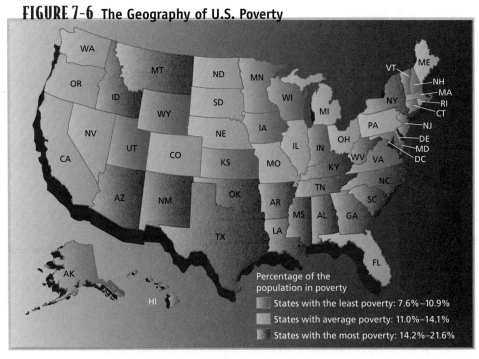

Percentage of the population in poverty

States with the least poverty: 7.6%–10.9%

States with average poverty: 11.0%–14.1%

States with the most poverty: 14.2%–21.6%

Note: Poverty varies tremendously from one state to another. In the extreme, poverty is about three times greater in Mississippi (21.6%) than in Connecticut and New Hampshire (7.6% each).

Source: By James M. Henslin. Based on *Statistical Abstract of the United States* 2007:Table 690.

REGION. A striking characteristic of poverty is that the poor are concentrated in the inner city and rural areas. The Social Map (Figure 7-6) shows how the rates of poverty differ among the states. As you can see, the regional differences are striking.

RACE–ETHNICITY. As you can see from Figure 7-7, poverty trends can also be predicted using race–ethnicity: African Americans and Native Americans, who have about the same rate of poverty, are about 3 times as likely as Whites to be poor. The poverty rate of African Americans has dropped considerably in recent years, and their rates are now

FIGURE 7-7 Minorities Are Much More Likely to Be Poor

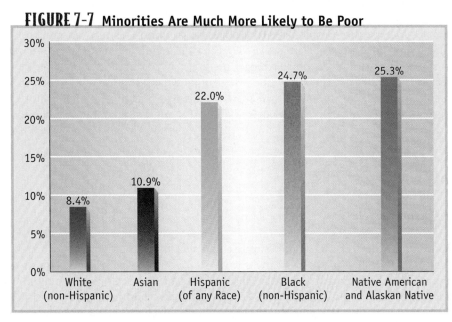

Note: Share in poverty by race–ethnicity.

Source: U.S. Census Bureau, *Current Populations Survey* (2006a).

FIGURE 7-8 Poverty Rates of Children and the Elderly

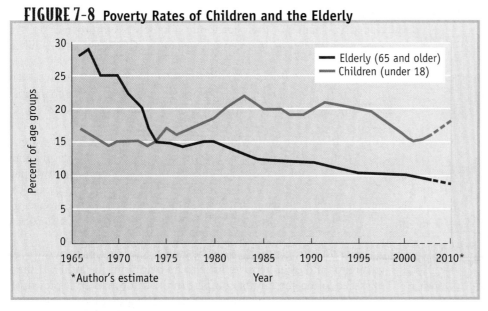

Source: Congressional Research Services; Statistical Abstract (1994, Tables 728, 731; 2009, Table 690).

close to where the national average was in 1960. The drop in poverty among African Americans is especially striking. It is now about half of what it used to be.

CHILDREN IN POVERTY. Poverty can also be predicted using age as a variable. The poverty rate of children is one-third *higher* than that of adults. Figure 7-8 illustrates the objective conditions concerning age and poverty. Note how poverty among the elderly has declined while poverty among children has fluctuated. Notice how 9% of U.S. elderly are poor while 17% of U.S. children live in poverty (*Statistical Abstract,* 2009, Table 690). Such extensive poverty in childhood will have severe implications for an entire generation of Latinos, Native Americans, and African Americans.

According to Figure 7-9, child poverty strikes some areas harder than others. Rural poverty is greatest in the South and lowest in the Northeast. Explanations for such discrepancies include jobs that pay low wages and high rates of immigration (Congressional Research Services; *Statistical Abstract,* 1994, Tables 728, 731; Koball & Douglas-Hall, 2006).

FIGURE 7-9 Rural Child Poverty Rates by Region

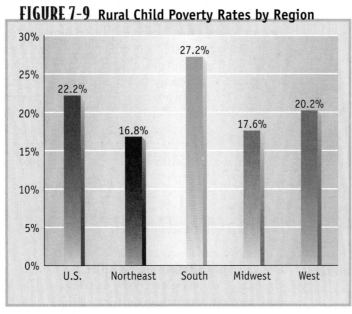

Source: Carsey Institute, U.S. Census (2007).

Poverty in the United States has become concentrated among women and children. Sociologists call this pattern *the feminization of poverty*. Poverty is especially high among teenage mothers.

THE ELDERLY. Poverty also used to plague the elderly, but, as mentioned in Chapter 2, their economic situation has improved. At 10%, the poverty rate of Americans over age 65 is now *lower* than that of the nation as a whole (*Statistical Abstract,* 2009, Table 691). Social Security and Medicare are the primary reasons for the reduction in poverty among the elderly. This development shows that changes in social policy can make a difference.

THE FEMINIZATION OF POVERTY. Children who live with both parents are seldom poor, while children who live in single-parent families are often poor. The reason for this is fairly simple: On average, two parents earn more. In addition, as you know, it is almost always the mother who heads single-parent families, and these women average *less than half* (43%) of what two-parent families earn (*Statistical Abstract,* 2006, Table 681).

Life for a single mother can be costly: She has a baby and herself to care for and often receives little to no help from the father. If she is unskilled, often she cannot compete in the labor market. If previously married, her income usually takes a nose-dive after divorce. A woman who has been out of the workforce usually finds it difficult to return after bearing and/or rearing children.

What about child support? As Figure 7-10 shows, only about half of single mothers receive what courts order fathers to pay. A fourth of these fathers skip out and pay nothing. Add all these factors together, and you can see why women and children are much more likely to be poor. (If you want to avoid poverty, see the Thinking Critically box on the next page.)

AN UNDERCLASS. People who earn minimum wage are likely to be poor. We are not referring to college students who take minimum wage jobs while they are preparing for careers that pay well. Rather, the United States has a large *underclass* made up of people who are locked into low-paying, minimum wage jobs. They do the "stoop labor" on farms and fill the sweatshops of our cities. Many work in the clothing industry's small factories or even at home, where they get paid a small amount for each piece of work they complete. Although there are no accurate counts, this underclass numbers several million.

SOCIAL STRUCTURE. The patterns we have reviewed indicate that poverty is not the result of people being lazy or stupid. Instead, poverty is *structural,* built into the social system. Poverty is influenced by the variables of region, age, gender, and race–ethnicity. Consequently, to understand poverty, sociologists examine features of the *social system:* discrimination, marriage and reproductive patterns, how welfare programs function, how the economy is changing, and how an underclass is created and maintained. In later chapters, we shall discuss some of these patterns, but for now let's consider an analysis of poverty that has generated considerable controversy in sociology.

Is There a Culture of Poverty?

We boast of vast achievement and of power,
Of human progress knowing no defeat,
Of strange new marvels every day and hour—
And here's the bread line in the wintry street!

Berton Braley, "The Bread Line"

FIGURE 7-10 Child Support Payments

From what the court ordered, the mother received	Percentage of mothers who received this	In one year, the mothers received
No payment	25%	$0
Partial payment	29%	$2,100
Full payment	46%	$5,700

Source: By James M. Henslin. Based on *Statistical Abstract of the United States* (2006, Table 558).

RULES FOR AVOIDING POVERTY

If you want to avoid poverty, follow these three rules:

1. Finish high school.
2. Get married before you have your first child.
3. Don't have a child until after you reach the age of 20.

This message is being delivered to the Black community by African American leaders (Herbert, 1998). Hugh Price, president of the National Urban League, and retired General Colin Powell say that 80% of African Americans who ignore these principles end up poor, but only 8% of those who follow them are poor. Although their statistics may not be exact, the rules are sound—and they apply to all racial–ethnic groups.

To not only avoid poverty but to also develop a financially secure life, we would add four more "rules":

1. Go to college.
2. Stay married.
3. Avoid the misuse of drugs, including alcohol.
4. Avoid credit card debt.

Poverty among people who follow these seven rules is practically nonexistent.

BLATANT POVERTY IN THE MIDST OF PLENTY. How things have changed! A generation ago, Americans associated bread lines and soup kitchens with the Great Depression, or perhaps with Charles Dickens's description of 19th-century London. Now the homeless are part of every large city across this rich land. Some are tucked out of sight, but the majority live on our cities' sidewalks. The homeless—ravaged by hunger and dressed in mismatched layers of out-of-date clothing—reveal the contrast between the American dream and its stark reality. Who are these homeless people, and how did they get that way? The Thinking Critically box on the next page summarizes some of what Jim Henslin discovered when he researched the homeless.

THE CULTURE OF POVERTY. Why do some people remain poor in the midst of plenty? After years of doing participant observation with poor people and gathering extensive life histories, anthropologist Oscar Lewis (1959, 1966) concluded that people who remain poor year after year have developed a way of life that traps them in poverty. He called this the **culture of poverty.** Perceiving a gulf between themselves and the mainstream, these people feel inferior and insecure. Concluding that they are never going to get out of poverty, they become fatalistic and passive. They develop low aspirations and think about the present, not the future. They also become self-destructive, as illustrated by their high rates of alcoholism, physical violence, and family abuse. Their lives become marked by broken marriages, desertion, single-parent households, and self-defeating despair. Their way of life, this culture of poverty, makes it almost impossible for them to break out of poverty.

TESTING THE CONCEPT. This is an interesting argument, but is it true? To find out, economist Patricia Ruggles examined national statistics of poverty and found that, contrary to popular belief, few people pass poverty on to the next generation: *Most children of the poor do not grow up to be poor.* Only 1 of 5 people who are poor as children are still poor as adults (Corcoran et al., 1985; Sawhill, 1988; Ruggles, 1989, 1990). In support of Lewis's culture of poverty, Ruggles found that 1% of the U.S. population remains poor year in and year out. They were poor 20 years ago, they are poor today, and they will be poor tomorrow. This group has three primary characteristics in common: Most are African American, most are unemployed, and many live in female-headed households.

In conclusion, some people do adopt a culture of poverty that perpetuates poor lifestyles. These people learn behaviors that keep them poor and pass them on to their

BEING HOMELESS IN THE LAND OF THE AMERICAN DREAM

By James M. Henslin

When I met Larry Rice, who runs a shelter for the homeless in St. Louis, Missouri, he said that as a sociologist I needed to know firsthand what was happening on our city streets. I resisted his "invitation," reluctant to leave my comfortable home and office to see who knew what. Then Larry hooked me: He offered to take me to Washington, DC, where he promised that I would see people sleeping on sidewalk grates within view of the White House. Intrigued at the sight of such a contrast, I agreed to go with him, not knowing that it would change my own life.

Like other people, the homeless consist of diverse people from many backgrounds. Some of the homeless have jobs and work regularly. Some are people with disabilities or elderly people trying to live on inadequate incomes. Similarly, there is no single route to homelessness. One route is environmental disaster.

When we arrived in Washington, it was bitter cold. It was December, and I saw what Rice had promised: sorrowful people huddled over the exhaust grates of federal buildings. Not all of the homeless survived that first night I was there. Freddy, who walked on crutches and had become a fixture in Georgetown, froze to death as he sought refuge from the cold in a telephone booth. I vividly recall looking at the telephone booth where Freddy's stiff body was found, still upright, futilely wrapped in a tattered piece of canvas. I went to Freddy's funeral and talked with his friends. To me, Freddy became a person, an individual, not just a faceless, nameless figure shrouded by city shadows.

This experience ignited my sociological curiosity. I was driven to find out more. I ended up visiting a dozen skid rows in the United States and Canada, sleeping in filthy shelters across North America. I interviewed the homeless in these shelters—and in back alleys and on street corners, in parks, and even in dumpsters. I became so troubled by what I experienced that for three months after I returned home, startled by disturbed dreams, I couldn't get through an entire night without waking up.

Among the many things that impressed me was that there are many routes to homelessness. Here are the types of homeless people whom I met:

1. *"Push-outs":* These people have been pushed out of their homes. Two common types of "push-outs" are teenagers who have been kicked out by their parents and adults who have been evicted by landlords.
2. *Victims of environmental catastrophe:* This type really surprised me, but they, too, live on our streets. The catastrophes I came across ranged from fires to dioxin contamination.

3. *The mentally ill:* These people have been discharged from mental hospitals. They are given little or no treatment for their problems, and they are unable to care for themselves.
4. *The new poor:* This group consists of unemployed workers whose work skills have become outmoded because of technological change.
5. *The technologically unqualified:* Unlike the new poor, these unemployed workers never possessed technological qualifications.
6. *The elderly:* These people have neither savings nor family support; they are old, unemployable, and discarded.
7. *Runaways:* After fleeing intolerable situations, these boys and girls wander our streets.
8. *The demoralized:* After suffering some personal tragedy, these people have given up and retreated into despair. The most common catalyst to their demoralization was divorce.
9. *Alcoholics:* The old-fashioned skid-row wino is still out there.
10. *Ease addicts:* These people actually choose to be homeless. For them, homelessness is a form of "early retirement." They have no responsibilities to others, and they can do mostly as they please. Some, in their 20s, spend their days playing chess in the parks of San Francisco.
11. *Travel addicts:* These people also choose to be homeless. Addicted to wanderlust, they travel continuously. They even have their own name for themselves: "road dogs."
12. *Excitement addicts:* These people, among the younger of the homeless, enjoy the thrill of danger. They like the excitement that comes from "living on the edge." Being on the streets offers many "edge" opportunities.

As you can see, the homeless are far from being one-dimensional. The homeless are not a single group, but rather are people who have arrived on our city streets by many "routes." Note how different the "routes" are for the last three types (those who choose homelessness, a minority of these people) than for the first nine types, those who do not want to be homeless. Because there are many "causes" of homelessness, it should be obvious that there can be no single solution to this social problem. We need multifaceted programs that are based on the various "routes" by which people travel to this dead-end destination.

Can a culture of poverty be transmitted across generations?

children. Because most people who are poor today will not be poor in just a few years, however, we can conclude that *most* poor people do not adopt such a culture of poverty.

Who Rules America?

WHO HAS THE POWER? Conflict theorists stress that to understand social life we must understand who controls scarce resources, especially power. Like wealth, power is a scarce resource, and some people have much of it, while others have little or none. Max Weber defined **power** as the ability to get one's way despite resistance (Weber, 1921). The possession of power is especially significant because it determines who gets the lion's share of resources in society. Let's ask, then, who rules in the United States?

THE POWER ELITE. Sociologist C. Wright Mills (1959a) argued that a **power elite** rules the United States. The power elite is made up of top military leaders, top political leaders, and owners of corporations. Mills argued that this small group makes decisions that direct the country—and the world. Figure 7-11 on the next page illustrates Mills's view of the power elite.

Mills stressed that the power elite is not a formal group. It meets neither in secret nor in public. In fact, some members may not think they belong to it. But, structurally, it exists. The power elite consists of people whose interests have merged. As people move within the highest levels of business, government, and military, the power elite gains cohesion. White House aides join powerful law firms. A law partner joins the president's cabinet or is appointed secretary of the treasury. The head of the treasury becomes the CEO of a leading bank or corporation. An air force colonel retires and then takes over the sales division of Boeing or General Dynamics.

Because these people share interests and experiences in business and politics, they think alike on major issues. In addition, they come from similar backgrounds, and they share similar values. Most are White Anglo-Saxon Protestants who attended exclusive prep schools and Ivy League colleges. Many belong to the same private clubs and vacation at the same exclusive resorts. These people, then, are united by shared backgrounds, contacts, ideologies, values, and interests (Domhoff, 1974, 1990, 2001).

Mills said that the three groups that make up the power elite—the top political, military, and corporate leaders—are not equal in power. Identifying who was dominant, Mills did not point to the president, however, or even to the generals and admirals, but,

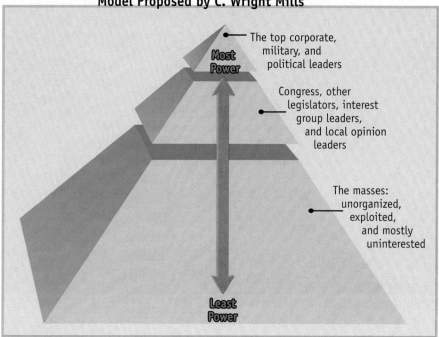

FIGURE 7-11 How Is Power Distributed in the United States? The Model Proposed by C. Wright Mills

Most Power

The top corporate, military, and political leaders

Congress, other legislators, interest group leaders, and local opinion leaders

The masses: unorganized, exploited, and mostly uninterested

Least Power

Source: Based on Mills (1959a).

rather, to the heads of corporations. Because all three segments of the power elite view capitalism as essential to the welfare of the country, national policy centers on business interests. Making decisions that promote capitalism works to the mutual benefit of all three groups.

Sociologist William Domhoff (1990, 1998, 2001) prefers to use the term "ruling class" instead of power elite. He studied the 1% of Americans who belong to the super-rich. These people are so wealthy that *they are worth more than 90% of the nation* (Beeghley, 2005). This 1% controls the nation's top corporations and foundations, even the boards that oversee our major universities. They also own the nation's major newspapers, magazines, and television stations. Members of this powerful group attempt, quite successfully, to shape the consciousness of the nation. It is no accident, says Domhoff, that from this group come most of the president's cabinet and top ambassadors.

Conflict theorists stress that we should not think of the power elite or ruling class as a group that meets and makes specific decisions. Rather, with their interlocking economic and political interests, their behavior stems not from a grand conspiracy to control the country but from a mutual interest in solving the problems that face large businesses (Useem, 1984). Able to ensure that the country adopts the social policies that it deems desirable—from fixing interest rates to sending troops abroad—this powerful group sets the economic and political agenda under which the rest of the country lives (Domhoff, 1990).

THE PLURALIST VIEW. Not all sociologists agree with this view. *Pluralists* argue that there is no power elite pulling the strings behind the scenes. Instead, many **interest groups** compete for social, economic, and political power. There are unions, industries, professional associations, and the like. *No one group is in control,* they stress. Sociologist David Riesman (1951) and his colleagues developed this *pluralist view of power.* He states that power is dispersed because the country's many groups are divided by essential differences. This makes a united policy or action impossible (Kornhauser, 1961; Marger, 1987; Beeghley, 2005). Mills would reply that members of the power elite settle important differences among themselves.

CONTINUING RESEARCH ON THE CONTROVERSY. The controversy between the pluralists and the sociologists who support the view of the power elite is long-standing and unresolved. In 1961, sociologist Robert Dahl published a study on power in New Haven, Connecticut, the home of Yale University. He demonstrated that the power elite did not exist in his own university town. Dahl's research became classic in support of the pluralistic view of power in the United States.

Conflict theorists remained unconvinced. William Domhoff (1978b), again in support of the power elite view, reanalyzed Dahl's data. Unlike Dahl, Domhoff found that Yale University, New Haven's businesses, and its other social institutions were interlocked extensively. Domhoff concluded that a power elite of corporate heads, bankers, social leaders, and politicians shaped New Haven's economy. He documented not only how the New Haven elites shape local decisions but also how they are connected to national elites. Domhoff argued that each major city in the United States has such a power center and that lines run from these cities to the national power structure.

Economists produced a study that has intriguing implications. They examined the relationships among 72 U.S. companies and found extensive connections among corporate directors. These companies are so bound together, the researchers concluded, that they form a power bloc (Hayden, Wood, & Kaya, 2002). It is possible, and perhaps likely, that each type of industry in the United States has its own similar interlocking power structure. To see how extensively the corporate elite is tied together on a national level, sociologist Michael Useem (1979) examined the nation's 797 largest corporations. These corporations had 8,623 directors. Of these, 1,570 were directors in two or more of the corporations. Most of those who did not hold multiple positions in these largest corporations held directorships in smaller firms. In another study, sociologist Gwen Moore (1979) examined the 545 top positions in key U.S. institutions. They were clustered into 32 issue-oriented cliques (see Table 7-1). One core circle of 272 people was linked to almost all smaller cliques. Moore (1979, 689) concluded,

> the evidence examined here indicates that considerable integration exists among elites in all major sections of American society. . . . The existence of a central elite circle facilitates communication and interaction both within that large, diverse group and between its members and those in more specialized elite circles and cliques.

TABLE 7-1 Members of the National Elite[1]

SECTOR	POSITION
Congress	Senators and members of the House of Representatives who are the chairpersons of major committees; all members of the Rules, Appropriations, and Ways and Means Committees
Federal administration— Political appointees	Secretaries and general counsel of cabinet departments; heads and deputy heads of independent agencies
Civil service	The two highest civil service grades from all cabinet departments and independent agencies
Industrial corporations	Fortune 500 largest industrial corporations
Nonindustrial corporations	Fortune 300 largest nonindustrial corporations
Wealthy individuals	Holders of fortunes worth at least $100 million
Labor unions	Presidents of unions with at least 50,000 members; top officials of the AFL-CIO
Political parties	The members of the Democratic and Republican National Committees; state and major city chairpersons of these parties
Voluntary organizations	The directors of certain public affairs organizations, including professional societies, farmers' organizations, women's groups, religious organizations, civil rights organizations, and business groups
Media	Editors of the largest-circulation newspapers and public affairs periodicals, including their major syndicated columnists and news executives; broadcasters and commentators of national networks

[1] This table lists the categories of people who, according to one study, make up the national elite of the United States.
Source: Based on Moore (1979).

Is there a *culture of wealth,* one that locks its members into wealth and privilege and is transmitted across generations? Sociologists have no difficulty in agreeing that such a culture (or, more accurately phrased, subculture) exists. We sociologists, like the rest of society, perceive through colored lenses, and a culture of wealth matches our bias in favor of the oppressed of society. As symbolic interactionists point out, it is impossible to perceive events except from some perspective. We use the research methods described in Chapter 1 to overcome our biases.

(© The New Yorker Collection 2001. Warren Miller from cartoonbank. com. All Rights Reserved.)

"Actually, it's one giant organism connected by blood, genes, and a common source of old wealth."

Useem and Moore concluded that there is indeed a national interlocking power elite. Yet, because they were unable to study how decisions are made (for example, policy on the Middle East), their studies do not demonstrate that U.S. elites form a cohesive ruling group.

THE CULTURE OF WEALTH. Although the question of a cohesive ruling group must remain open until we have more evidence, this brings us to another significant question: Does the culture of the elite—its set of institutions, customs, values, worldviews, family ties, and connections—allow the rich and powerful to perpetuate their privileges? In other words, is there a **culture of wealth** that keeps people from falling down the social class structure, just as some claim that a culture of poverty makes it difficult for poor people to pull themselves up? Of course there is. The elite of any city, region, or nation—indeed of any group—tend to develop common sentiments and share similar values and goals. The sociological problem is not to determine whether this occurs but to discover how it operates. That a culture of wealth exists, however, does not mean that the elite work together to rule the country. This is another matter entirely.

It is precisely here that many sociologists see danger—that the concentration of wealth and power violates the democratic processes on which our country is premised. Interlocking interests by wealthy people in powerful positions can result in a few non-elected individuals wielding immense control over the country.

Inequality and Global Poverty

GLOBAL STRATIFICATION. Just as the United States is stratified into different social classes, so the world's nations are stratified into rich and poor nations. The Most Industrialized Nations, which are wealthy, have **residual poverty,** or pockets of poverty. Most of the Least Industrialized Nations, in contrast, have **mass poverty:** many citizens living on less than $1,000 a year. Most are malnourished, chronically ill, and die young. The Global Glimpse box on the next page reports on the abysmal conditions of some children in nations that experience mass poverty.

One intriguing issue arises: Some nations remain poor year after year. Let's look at why this is so.

ECONOMIC COLONIALISM. The *first* proposed reason some countries remain impoverished is that rich nations exploit poor nations. Long ago, to obtain raw materials, the more powerful nations invaded and conquered weaker nations (*political colonialism*). Today, instead of invading weaker nations, wealthy nations exploit poor nations through

What is childhood like in the Least Industrialized Nations? As in the United States, the answer depends primarily on who your parents are.

If your parents are rich, childhood can be pleasant. If you are born into poverty but live where there is plenty to eat, life can still be good—although you will lack books, television, and education. But you probably won't miss them. If you live in a slum, however, life can be horrible, worse than in the slums of the Most Industrialized Nations. Let's look at the slums of Brazil.

You can take for granted alcoholism, drug abuse, child abuse, wife beating, a high crime rate, and not having enough food. Even in the inner cities of the Most Industrialized Nations, you would expect these things.

You might not expect the brutal conditions in which Brazilian slum (*favela*) children live. Poverty is so deep that children and adults swarm over garbage dumps to find enough decaying food to keep them alive. Sociologist Martha Huggins (1993) reports that the owners of these dumps hire armed guards to keep the poor out—so they can sell the garbage for pig food. The Brazilian police and death squads murder some of these children. Some associations of shop owners even put assassination teams on retainer and auction victims off to the lowest bidder! The going rate is half a month's salary—figured at the low Brazilian minimum wage.

Life is cheap in the Least Industrialized Nations—but death squads for children? To understand how this could possi-bly be, we need to note that Brazil has a fragile political structure and a long history of violence. With high poverty and a small middle class, mob violence and revolution always lurk just around the corner. The "dangerous classes," as they are known, threaten the status quo. Groups of homeless children, who have no jobs or prospects of getting work, roam the streets. To survive, these children clamber in and out of traffic to wash the windshields of cars that are stopped at red lights. They shine shoes, beg, steal, and sell their bodies.

These children annoy the "respectable" classes, who see them as trouble. Sometimes the children break into stores. They hurt business, for customers feel intimidated when they see poorly dressed adolescents clustered in front of a store. Some children even sell items in competition with the stores. Without social institutions to care for these children, one solution is to kill them. As Huggins notes, murder sends a clear message to the children, especially if it is accompanied by torture—gouging out the eyes, ripping open the chest, cutting off the genitals, raping the girls, and burning the victim's body.

FOR YOUR CONSIDERATION

Can the Most Industrialized Nations do anything about this situation? Or is it none of our business? Is it, though unfortunate, an internal affair for the Brazilians to handle?

economic colonialism. The Most Industrialized Nations import raw materials from the poor nations and export industrial products to them. With the Most Industrialized Nations dominating the global markets, the poor nations sell their food and natural resources—from bananas and coffee to tin and manganese—at prices so low that they are lucky if they can keep up with their expanding populations. Few actually do, and each year they find themselves deeper in debt to the Most Industrialized Nations. As a result, they do not have the capital to develop their own industries, and they remain poor.

Economic colonialism is often applied through political pressure. Oil-rich nations with high incomes remain economic colonies. What do you think would happen if one of these nations were to break out of this system? What if it were to gain control over its own resources? If that nation could control its flow of oil and set oil prices, it could lead the Most Industrialized Nations in wealth. Do you think that the Most Industrialized Nations would allow this? The answer should be obvious. When Iraq made an attempt to dominate its region, the result was the Gulf War of 1990–1991.

AN EXPLOITING NATIONAL POWER ELITE. A *second* answer as to why some nations remain poor is that their own ruling power elite exploits them. Although these nations are relatively poor, each has a wealthy elite that lives a sophisticated, upper-class lifestyle in the major city of its home country. This elite identifies with elites abroad and even sends its children to Oxford, the Sorbonne, or Harvard. Multinational corporations channel their investments through these elites, which profit from exploiting their own country's resources.

A CULTURE OF POVERTY. A *third* answer to why poverty continues in the Least Industrialized Nations is that they suffer from a culture of poverty (Landes, 1998). As ambassador to India, John Kenneth Galbraith (1979) observed what he described as a culture of fatalistic resignation, reinforced by religion. He pointed out that most of the world's poor make a living off the land. With barely enough to live on, they are reluctant to experiment with different ways of farming: If an experimental attempt fails, it could lead to hunger or death. Their religion also teaches them to accept their lot in life as God's will and to look for rewards in the afterlife. Galbraith emphasized that poor countries do not lack resources. Most have many natural resources—most much greater than resource-starved Japan. Their weakness in world markets, however, combined with their fatalistic culture, makes it unlikely that they will rise from poverty.

These three issues—economic colonialism, exploitation, and a culture of poverty—work together to form the plight of the least industrialized nations.

Social Policy

Historical Changes in Social Policy

SHIFTING VIEWS OF CAUSE AND POLICY. Our views of the causes of social problems influence the social policies that we favor. We reviewed how people's ideas about poverty have changed—how poverty was once considered God's will, then was thought to result from character flaws, and how it was even attributed to the evils of the city. As people's views changed, so did their ideas of which social policies were appropriate. In colonial times, when poverty was thought to be God's will, the proper response was the individual's religious duty to shelter, feed, and clothe the poor. The poor were cared for on a personal, individual basis.

During the American Revolution, when the poor were considered wayward and lazy, Boston opened a workhouse. There the poor had to work until they showed that they had acquired self-discipline and an appreciation of hard work. Philadelphia Quakers built almshouses that took in poor women and children. These social policies marked a departure from providing relief on an individual basis; instead, the government established institutionalized care of the poor (Nash, 1979).

In the 1830s, people believed that the squalor of cities caused poverty, so the logical solution was to take the poor away from the corrupting influence of the city. In the country, the basic sense of decency and order would be restored (Rothman, 1971). This attempt failed when institutions in the country filled up and budgets were cut. The institutions became human warehouses of the worst sort.

To appreciate the attitudes of the time, consider this statement from Henry Ward Beecher, the most prominent clergyman of his day:

> It is said that a dollar a day is not enough for a wife and five or six children. No, not if the man smokes and drinks beer. . . . But is not a dollar a day enough to buy bread with? Water costs nothing, and a man who cannot live on bread and water is not fit to live. A family may live on good bread and water in the morning, water and bread at midday, and good water and bread at night. (quoted in Thayer, 1997)

A dollar went a lot farther in those days, to be sure, and people did pump water freely from backyard wells. But to live on only bread and water?

Then came the 1930s, when the United States was thrown into the Great Depression. As businesses closed up all over the country and unemployment skyrocketed, so did poverty. Not having enough food to eat became common. So did bread lines. Finding economic security pulled out from beneath them, people who had once occupied the middle class lined up with the poor for a handout. At his 1937 inaugural address, President Franklin D. Roosevelt said, "Millions of families are trying to live on incomes so meager that the pall of family disaster hangs over them day by

day. . . . I see one-third of a nation ill-housed, ill-clad, and ill-nourished" (quoted in Fisher, 1988).

As masses of people became poor, the nation's perspective changed. No longer was poverty viewed as the result of God's will, flawed character, or the corruption of the city. Rather, poverty came to be seen as the result of institutional (economic) failure—the lack of jobs. To match this shift in view, the Roosevelt administration created basic welfare to help families survive until the husband-father could get a job, established massive work projects across the nation, and tried to revive the economy to create jobs. During World War II, the economy picked up and poverty declined sharply.

As work became available and men went back to work—and, during World War II, women also—less visible and more permanent kinds of poverty remained. As described earlier in this chapter, the rediscovery of poverty in the 1960s led to new social policies. Some programs provided education and training so the poor could get jobs. Other programs were based on the assumption that some of the poor, such as single mothers, children, and the elderly, needed to be subsidized.

THE BASIC DIFFERENCE—CAUSE AS INSIDE OR OUTSIDE OF PEOPLE. Views have shifted between attributing poverty to forces within the individual (laziness, stupidity, evil) and attributing poverty to forces outside the individual (God, evil cities, the economy). These differing assumptions bring with them contrasting ideas of appropriate social policy. Explanations of poverty that assume causes lie *within* people lead to such policies as teaching self-discipline and sterilization. Explanations that are based on causes *outside* the individual lead to programs of education, aid, social reform, job training, and stimulating the economy. Our cycles of social reform still reflect this duality of internal and external forces.

Although different generations define poverty differently, in each era these two core questions remain: What is the cause and what shall we do about it?

Progressive Taxation

One policy aimed at reducing inequality is **progressive taxation,** tax rates that progress (increase) with income. The federal and state governments tax wealthier people at higher rates and redistribute some of this money to the poor through welfare, Medicaid, housing subsidies, child care, and food stamps. Table 7-2 shows that as Americans earn more, they not only pay more dollars in taxes but also pay a larger percentage of their income in taxes.

TABLE 7-2 Income Taxes Paid by Americans

ADJUSTED GROSS INCOME	NUMBER OF RETURNS	TAX PAID AS A PERCENTAGE OF ADJUSTED GROSS INCOME	APPROXIMATE TAX PAID BY EACH INDIVIDUAL	TOTAL TAX PAID (Average paid per income group)
$1,000–$4,999	9,735	3.5	$103	$1,002,705
$5,000–$10,999	14,475	2.3	$194	$2,808,150
$11,000–$18,999	18,255,000	4	$627	$11,000,000,000
$19,000–$29,999	20,669,000	6	$1,444	$30,000,000,000
$30,000–$39,999	13,940,000	7	$2,457	$34,000,000,000
$40,000–$49,999	10,619,000	8	$3,526	$33,000,000,000
$50,000–$74,999	18,351,000	9	$5,307	$93,000,000,000
$75,000–$99,999	10,450,000	10	$8,324	$86,000,000,000
$100,000–$199,999	10,810,000	13	$18,000	$189,000,000,000
$200,000–$499,999	2,738,000	20	$58,000	$159,000,000,000
$500,000–$999,999	525,000	24	$162,000	$85,000,000,000
$1,000,000 or more	304,000	23	$777,000	$236,000,000,000

Source: Statistical Abstract of the United States (2009, Table 470).

Few wealthy people approve of the government taking their money in order to distribute it to the poor. A few wealthy individuals and corporations are so successful at finding loopholes in tax law that they manage to pay no taxes. These are exceptional cases, however.

Public Assistance Programs

SOCIAL INSURANCE. We can divide public assistance programs into four types. The first is designed to help people help themselves. This type includes social insurance programs such as unemployment compensation and Social Security. Money is deducted from paychecks, and workers draw on this pool when they need it. Few argue that workers who are laid off when an entire industry, such as steel or automobiles, is hit by recession don't deserve help.

TEACHING JOB SKILLS. The second type of program is intended to help the poor become self-supporting so that they no longer need social welfare. Most of these programs, such as the Job Corps, center on teaching job skills. Some teach personal grooming, punctuality, and politeness so that prospective workers can meet employer expectations.

WELFARE. A third type of program is *welfare*—money, food, housing, and medical care given to people who have a low enough income to qualify for them. Here the distinction between deserving and undeserving is replaced by a humanitarian notion that people in severe need should be helped regardless of who is responsible. Programs such as Temporary Assistance to Needy Families (TANF), food stamps, and public housing generate controversy because people think they encourage laziness and unwed motherhood. Many also think that people who receive this aid really can work and take care of themselves. One consequence is the topic of the Issues in Social Problems box on the next page.

WORKFARE. A fourth type of program is *workfare*. Critics claim that welfare reduces people's incentive to work. They say, "Why will people work if they can get aid free?" As U.S. welfare rolls swelled to 14 million people in the early 1990s, criticism grew louder. The media ran stories about "**welfare queens**" who collected welfare checks or excess amounts of government aid. This term first gained popularity in the 1970s, and it has been used since then to demean single mothers, especially Black women, needing assistance.

To help those suffering during the Great Depression of the 1930s, the federal government began the Works Progress Administration (WPA). Men often worked in construction while women likely canned food.

Issues in Social Problems
WELFARE: HOW TO RAVAGE THE SELF-CONCEPT

My husband left me shortly after I was diagnosed with multiple sclerosis. At the time, I had five children. My oldest child was 14, and my youngest was 7. My physician, believing I would be seriously disabled, helped get me on Social Security disability. The process took several months, and so it became necessary for me to go on public aid and food stamps.

By the time I needed to depend on my family in the face of a crisis, there weren't any resources left to draw on. My father had passed away, and my mother was retired, living on a modest income based on Social Security and my father's pension. Isn't it funny how there is no social stigma attached to Social Security benefits for the elderly? People look at this money as an entitlement—"We worked for it." But people who have to depend on public aid for existence are looked at like vermin and accused of being lazy.

I can tell you from my own experience that a great deal of the lethargy that comes from long periods on welfare is due primarily to the attitudes of the people you have to come into contact with in these programs. I've been through the gamut: from rude, surly caseworkers at Public Aid, to patronizing nurses at the WIC [Women, Infants, and Children] clinic ("You have *how* many children?"), to the accusing tone of the food pantry workers when you have to go begging for a handout before the 30-day time span has expired. After a while your dignity is gone, and you start to believe that you really are the disgusting human trash they all make you out to be.

Christine Hoffman, a student in Jim Henslin's introductory sociology class.

As criticism mounted, the federal government passed the 1996 *Personal Responsibility and Work Opportunity Reconciliation Act.* This law requires states to place a lifetime cap on welfare assistance and compels welfare recipients to look for work and take available jobs. Now the maximum length of time that someone can collect welfare is 5 years. In some states, it is less. Unmarried teen parents must attend school and live at home or in some other adult-supervised setting.

Workfare was met with severe criticism ("It's just a way of throwing the poor into the streets"), but national welfare rolls have plummeted. Overall, the number of Americans on welfare has been cut by 60% (Haskins, 2006). This huge reduction means that about a third of people who have been forced off welfare have no jobs (Hage, 2004). Perhaps there are a few who don't want to work, but most of these people can't work because of bad health, lack of transportation, or addiction to alcohol or other drugs. Many of those who do have jobs earn so little that they remain in poverty. On the bright side, however, about two of five who have left welfare for workfare are no longer in poverty.

The Feminization of Poverty

The **feminization of poverty** refers to the likelihood that those living in single-mother households are likely to live beneath the poverty line. Feminist theorists point out that rearing children in a mother-only home is difficult for obvious reasons, but especially because our patriarchal system hinders the success of single women in two key ways. First, women are not paid as well as men. Second, mothers often have to make child care arrangements that fathers do not. (For guidelines on avoiding poverty, see the Thinking Critically box on page 223.)

Poverty clustering around women and children is a special problem. To alleviate it, women should receive equal pay and necessary job training for career advancement. Our society also needs adequate child care facilities and policies that promote child care assistance.

It also seems reasonable that absent fathers, whether or not they were married to their children's mothers, should support the children they fathered, rather than letting these children become the government's responsibility. The courts can award child care support that better reflects the father's earnings, and as we saw in Figure 7-10 (page 222), they can also do a much better job of making sure that fathers pay child support. Unfortunately, some unemployed fathers pay little or nothing.

Private Agencies and Volunteer Organizations

When we think of aid for the poor, we generally think of the government. The United States also has thousands of private agencies and volunteer organizations that work to help the poor. Because these groups work mainly with the desperate poor, tucked in out-of-the-way urban centers and rural areas, few Americans see them in action. The Salvation Army, for example, runs soup kitchens and homeless shelters, as do other religious groups. The Salvation Army's efforts on behalf of the poor include alcohol counseling and job training.

Throughout our history, governments have not been allowed to lend aid to nonprofit religious charities. If they did so, they would violate the principle of separation of church and state. Under the George W. Bush administration, religious charities were allowed to compete for federal funds. For the first time "faith-based" organizations were awarded about $2 billion a year to help the poor (Loven, 2006).

Without weighing in on this issue of the government funding religious charities, we note that the efforts of religious groups are well intentioned, and without them the social problem of poverty would be much worse.

The Purpose of Helping the Poor

Why do some lend help to the poor? For faith-based organizations, the purpose is often connected with ideas of what God wants. For private groups, the purpose is simply humanitarian. Conflict sociologists suggest that when the government offers welfare, the underlying motive is quite different.

REGULATING THE POOR. Conflict sociologists Frances Piven and Richard Cloward (1971, 1982, 1989, 1997) argue that because capitalism expands and contracts, it needs a dependable supply of unemployed, low-skilled, temporary workers. These people can be put to work when the economy is booming and laid off when the economy slows. At a minimal cost, welfare maintains this pool of workers for capitalists. Welfare keeps the poor alive during business downturns so they can be used during the next business expansion. To support this assertion, Piven and Cloward point to the changing rules of welfare: In times of high unemployment, when political disorder looms, welfare rules soften. This makes the impoverished, who might band together in protest, quiet and submissive so they can receive their weekly check. In "boom" times, these workers are needed, so welfare rules are tightened. In short, conclude these theorists, the purpose of welfare is to control the unemployed, to maintain social order, and to provide capitalists a pool of cheap labor.

Following Piven and Cloward's analysis, it is no coincidence that the *Personal Responsibility and Work Opportunity Reconciliation Act* was passed during the longest "boom" in U.S. history. When more workers were needed, the federal government required states to force the unemployed into the labor market by tightening their rules for welfare eligibility. Some states even began to fingerprint applicants for welfare and send welfare investigators to their homes. During this time, as the states began to emphasize job training instead of welfare, New York City even changed the name of its locations from "welfare centers" to "job centers." Following this argument, then, it is reasonable to assume that states will loosen their rules for welfare eligibility during the next recession so that the expanding pool of unemployed, marginal workers can survive until capitalists need them again.

Providing Jobs

Perhaps the most direct way to deal with poverty would be to provide jobs. President Roosevelt lifted millions out of poverty during the Great Depression by providing construction jobs building bridges, roads, parks, and public buildings. Programs such as this stimulate the economy, for these workers spend the money that they earn. This, in turn, produces even more jobs. People who approve of job creation disagree violently, however, about how those jobs should be created. Some argue that it is the government's responsibility to create jobs, while others insist that this is the role of private business.

This debate may never be resolved. Rather than becoming embroiled in it, let's highlight two principles. First, what is important is that jobs become available. Second, to be really effective in fighting poverty, jobs should provide a wage that lifts people out of poverty. Dead-end jobs that keep people in poverty do not meet this goal. Additional factors affect whether job creation will help the poor. For example, good jobs are often in the suburbs, where they are inaccessible to inner-city poor. To overcome this limitation, we need to provide transportation for the poor. Finally, because much poverty clusters around women and children, quality child care facilities and mandated child-support orders need to be created.

Education Accounts

A promising proposal involves *education accounts*. The government would establish a credit of, say, $40,000 for *everyone* at age 18 who graduates from high school (Haveman & Scholz, 1994–95; Oliver & Shapiro, 1995). Based on their background, abilities, and preferences, students would choose from approved colleges and technical and vocational schools. This money (which would be adjusted annually for inflation) could be spent only for direct educational costs, such as tuition, books, and living expenses. Besides allowing individual choice, an attractive aspect of this proposal is that ultimately it would cost little or nothing: Not only would this program reduce welfare, but it would also increase people's earning power *for their entire lives*. The additional taxes from those larger earnings could be adequate to pay for the program.

Clients at the Hopelink Foodbank in Bellevue, Washington, receive food donations at a weekly distribution.

Giving the Poor More Money

One final social policy seems a bit radical. Why not eliminate poverty by giving poor people enough money so they are no longer poor?

This may seem an obvious solution, but what would happen if we did give people enough money to remove them from poverty?

THE INCOME MAINTENANCE EXPERIMENTS. As some social scientists were considering this obvious solution, they wondered what poor people would do in such a situation. To find out, they developed the *income maintenance experiments,* and they convinced the government to go along with their plan. In the 1970s, thousands of poor people were given weekly checks. Would they spend it on liquor? Would they work less? How would the free money affect relations between husbands and wives?

Random samples of poor people in Denver, Seattle, and New Jersey were given different amounts of money (West & Steiger, 1980; Moffitt, 2004). Both urban and rural people were selected. If they went to work, only part of the money they received was cut. This was to help avoid the **welfare wall**—the disincentive to work that comes when the amount that people earn from working is not much more than what they get on welfare. The families were guaranteed this money for either 3 or 5 years—no matter how they spent the money—so they could change their living habits without worrying that the program might suddenly end.

What were the results? Some people did work less. The reduction in work averaged 9% for husbands, 23% for wives, and 15% for female heads of households (West & Steiger, 1980). The people who quit their jobs enjoyed the extra money and were glad to get away from unpleasant jobs that paid poorly. Most people, however, continued to work as much as before.

Compared with control groups, the people in this program spent more on durable goods (cars, refrigerators, TVs) than they did on nondurable goods (food, entertainment) (Pozdena & Johnson, 1979). They also bought more housewares and clothing (Johnson, Pozdena, & Steiger, 1979). In households headed by women, most of the new spending went for better housing. With the security that came from a regular income over several years, they saved less and went into debt more—just like many families who are not poor.

ENDING POVERTY. Liberals and conservatives have engaged in endless verbal battles over welfare and every other program designed to help the poor. Liberals consistently favor giving more money or aid to the poor, while conservatives consistently favor programs that emphasize work and what they call personal responsibility. Now conservatives have come up with a radical plan, which we examine in the Thinking Critically box on the next page.

The Future of the Problem

Poverty begs a solution. The homeless, the rural poor, and those trapped in the inner cities can't be wished away. But no solution comes without a high price tag.

Some say, "Let's spend whatever it costs, because it's right. We can worry about the bill some other time. Besides," they add, "if we can afford all those weapons for the military, we can afford any program that will help the poor." Others, in contrast, argue that we should establish effective programs to help the poor, but that it is not right to saddle future generations with our spending. Their position is, "If we can't pay for programs now, we can't afford them."

THINKING CRITICALLY about Social Problems

THE UNIVERSAL GUARANTEED INCOME PLAN TO ELIMINATE POVERTY

Charles Murray (2006), a conservative who has been soundly criticized by liberals for various positions he has taken, has proposed the Universal Guaranteed Income Plan. The plan, designed to put an end to poverty, would work like this: First, we would end *all* services, subsidies, and programs for the poor, including housing, food stamps, and Medicaid. They wouldn't be needed because the plan is designed to eliminate poverty. Second, *all* U.S. adults would receive a cash grant large enough so no one would be poor. The grant would be large enough so everyone could live comfortably and afford health care and retirement. The grant would not be reduced for anyone's earnings, which would be unlimited.

That's the skeleton. The particulars go something like this: A health insurance policy would be purchased for everyone from private companies. With guaranteed payments for the entire life of each individual, companies would compete for this business, reducing the cost. At current rates, each policy would cost about $3,000 a year. For retirement, here's how everyone would have a comfortable income: Beginning at age 21, each person would get a retirement account, with $2,000 placed into it each year. This money would be invested in an index-based stock fund. This money would accumulate, with earnings, for 45 years until the individual retired at age 66. The worst that the stock market has ever done for *any* 45-year period, including the Great Depression, is 4.3% a year (1887–1932). If an individual were unlucky enough to get this worst historical return, he or she would have about $250,000. This would purchase an annuity, giving the individual $20,000 a year. On average, the return would be considerably better, giving each person closer to $30,000 or $40,000 a year at retirement.

But at its worst, an elderly couple would have an annual income of $40,000.

The Universal Guaranteed Income Plan certainly sounds like pie-in-the-sky. How could we ever afford it? According to Murray, we are a rich country going broke, and we have to do something about the situation. At current rates, by the year 2050 Social Security, Medicare, and Medicaid will consume 28% of the entire economic production of the nation (our gross domestic product), and this is what we can't afford. At first, says Murray, the Universal Basic Guaranteed Income Plan would be costly, but we could afford the additional taxes. Then in just 5 years, the cost of the plan would run about the same as what our current system is projected to cost at that time. In 10 years, this plan would run $500 billion a year *less* than the projected cost of our current system. In another 8 years, the savings would be twice this amount.

We don't know how accurate these projections are or how the assumptions on which they are based would hold over the years. No one does, as assumptions projected into the future are unknowns that often fail to follow projected paths. We do know, however, that if any plan holds the possibility of eliminating poverty—or even of reducing it to practically nothing—we should consider it. We also know that conservatives and liberals, who seem to have dog–cat natures when they try to communicate, will continue to quarrel. The one will continue to insist that individuals be responsible for their lives, while the other will stress the government's responsibility. If there is any possibility of actually eliminating poverty, perhaps both sides can put aside their biases and work together to develop a workable plan.

Most Americans seem to find themselves somewhere between these arguments—claiming it is not right to have homeless people huddled over heating grates or children's futures blocked or their lives cut short because of their parents' poverty, but not knowing what to do about the situation. With the politicians and the public not seeing any clear solutions, and with the poor remaining disorganized and having little political clout, we anticipate that we will continue with our present programs. From time to time, there will be the illusion of progress.

SUMMARY AND REVIEW

1. There are several types of *poverty. Biological poverty* refers to starvation and malnutrition. *Relative poverty* is the feeling of being poor in comparison with others, although one may be objectively well off. *Official poverty* refers to falling below arbitrary standards set by the government. Poverty follows lines of age, gender, geography, and race–ethnicity.

2. Symbolic interactionists examine how the meaning of income (for example, whether people see themselves as being rich or poor) differs from its objective measures. Functionalists emphasize that social inequality is a way of allocating talented people to society's more demanding tasks and less talented people to its less demanding tasks. They point out that although poverty may be dysfunctional for individuals, it is functional for society. Conflict theorists stress that those who win the struggle for society's limited resources oppress those who lose. They also stress that a *power elite* of top politicians and corporate and military leaders make society's big decisions. Pluralists disagree. They view society as made up of many groups that compete with one another in a marketplace of power and ideas.

3. Why do some people remain in poverty year after year? Some suggest that the reason is a *culture of poverty*, self-defeating behaviors that parents pass on to their children. Most sociologists, however, view what is called the culture of poverty not as the cause of poverty but, rather, as the result of poverty. Why do some countries remain in poverty year after year? Some suggest that this is due to a national culture of poverty. Others look to *economic colonialism* and exploitation by national elites.

4. Policies for dealing with poverty have been as diverse as the beliefs about its causes. In the 17th century, poverty was considered God's will, and it was a person's religious duty to help the poor. Personal moral failure has also been considered to be a cause of poverty. During the Great Depression, the poor were considered victims of economic conditions and were helped on a mass basis. Today, our welfare programs cause bitter debate. Rules have been tightened to make fewer people eligible for welfare and to "encourage" the poor to take jobs. Where conservatives think that individuals should take more personal responsibility, liberals view government action as more appropriate.

5. The future is not likely to bring an end to poverty but, rather, a continuation of our piecemeal welfare programs. It is likely that Americans will continue to be divided on the matter of the "deserving" and "undeserving" poor and to what extent they should be helped.

KEY TERMS

THINKING CRITICALLY ABOUT CHAPTER 7

1. What is your reaction to Herbert Gans's observations on how poverty helps society? Do you think Gans is serious? (See the Thinking Critically box on page 217.)
2. Review the different rates of poverty by age, geography, and race–ethnicity (see the text and Figures 7-6 to 7-9). Now explain them. To answer this question sociologically, you might want to begin by asking, "Why don't all groups have the same rate of poverty?"
3. A central debate in sociology has been whether the power elite or pluralist view is correct. Which do you think is right? Why?
4. What do you think can be done to solve the social problem of poverty?

BY THE NUMBERS: THEN AND NOW

- Average hourly earnings, in constant dollars, earned by American workers in 1970: **$8.03**
- Average hourly earnings, in constant dollars, earned by American workers now: **$8.15**

- Percentage of salary saved by Americans in 1975: **9.3%**
- Percentage of salary saved by Americans now: **0.9%**

- Percentage of Americans living below the poverty line in 1970: **13%**
- Percentage of Americans living below the poverty line now: **12.5%**

- Percentage of U.S. elderly, living in poverty in 1970: **25%**
- Percentage of U.S. elderly, living in poverty now: **9%**

- Percentage of U.S. children, living in poverty, in 1970: **14%**
- Percentage of U.S. children, living in poverty, now: **17%**

MySocLab

What can you find in MySocLab? mysoclab ALLYN & BACON www.mysoclab.com

- Complete Ebook
- Practice Tests and Exams
- Multimedia Activities
- Mapping and Data Analysis Exercises

- Research and Writing Advice
- Interactive Social Surveys
- Sociology in the News

8

Racial-Ethnic Relations

Damn right I'm teaching violence! It's about time somebody is telling you to get violent, whitey. You better start making dossiers, names, addresses, phone numbers, car license numbers on every damn Jew rabbi in this land.

—William Potter Gale, a former colonel who served under General Douglas MacArthur in the Philippines in World War II

Today we see the evil is coming out of government. To go out and shoot a Negro is foolish. It's not the Negro in the alley who's responsible for what's wrong with this country. It's the traitors in Washington.

—Thomas Robb, publisher of *The Torch,* a Klan newsletter

Hitler is the reincarnation of the prophet Elijah. *Mein Kampf* is part of the Bible. The "terrible day of destruction" is coming.

—Keith Gilbert, who started his own church, Restored Church of Jesus Christ, in Post Falls, Idaho

Damn right I'm teaching violence!

The Klan called the mother of a White teenage girl who had been seen with Black companions and warned her: "If you can't do anything about it, the Klan can, and will."

—According to Bill McGlocklin, the Grand Kaliff of the Invisible Empire, Knights of the Ku Klux Klan in Denham Springs, Louisiana

Outside Hayden Lake, Idaho, a neatly lettered sign—"Whites Only"—used to mark the entrance to the Church of Jesus Christ Christian. Members of the congregation carried rifles and wore Nazi swastikas. The group lost its property in a lawsuit. Richard Butler, the church's leader, argues that Jesus Christ was an Aryan, not a Jew, and Jews should be destroyed as the children of Satan. He keeps a photo of Adolf Hitler in his living room.

Based on King (1979); Starr (1985); Murphy (1999)

The Problem in Sociological Perspective

Prejudice, discrimination, and racial violence are an unfortunate facet of life in the United States. Hostilities and tensions among groups surface in street confrontations, disturbances in schools, and media-captivating quotes of individuals like those profiled in the opening vignette.

A WORLDWIDE PROBLEM. Prejudice and discrimination exist everywhere in the world. In Northern Ireland, Protestants and Roman Catholics discriminate against one another; in Israel, wealthier Jews, primarily of European descent, discriminate against poorer Jews of Asian and African backgrounds; in Japan, the Japanese discriminate against just about anyone who isn't Japanese, especially the Koreans and Ainu who live there (Spivak, 1980; Fields, 1986; "Law Enacted . . . ," 1997). And to move beyond any specific group, we note that in every society around the world, men discriminate against women.

Prejudice and discrimination are terms commonly misused in the media. **Prejudice** is an attitude—a prejudging of some sort. The prejudging is usually negative, but it can be positive. **Discrimination,** in contrast, is action, differential treatment. It refers to treating someone or some group unfairly. Unfair treatment is most often based on appearance— age, race–ethnicity, sex, height, weight, disability, clothing, and the like. People also

discriminate against others on the basis of their income, education, lifestyle, habits, and religious or political beliefs.

People who are discriminated against because they belong to a particular group are said to belong to a **minority group.** As sociologist Louis Wirth (1945) defined them, these are groups of people singled out for unequal treatment on the basis of their physical or cultural characteristics and who regard themselves as objects of collective discrimination. Discrimination denies a minority's full participation in society.

Minority in this sense does not necessarily mean *numerical* minority. In South Africa, the small number of Dutch settlers maintained political control of the country. They discriminated against the much larger population of Blacks in housing, jobs, education, and social relations. In colonial India, a handful of British discriminated against several hundred million Indians. Although there are more women than men, in every society men discriminate against women. Accordingly, we refer to those who discriminate as the **dominant group.** This group, which has more power, privileges, and higher social status can be either larger or smaller in numbers than the minority group.

THE ORIGIN OF MINORITY GROUPS. There are two ways minority groups come into being: political expansion or migration. Some groups are labeled minorities when a government expands its political boundaries. As anthropologists Charles Wagley and Marvin Harris (1958) pointed out, there are no minority groups in small tribal societies. This is because everyone in tribal society is "related"; they all speak the same language, practice the same customs, share similar values, and belong to the same physical stock. A second way that minority groups originate is through migration—when people migrate to a new country where a different dominant group already exists. This migration can be involuntary, as with Africans who were forcibly brought to the United States, or voluntary, as with Turks who chose to move to Germany for work.

Minorities come into existence, then, when people who have different customs, languages, values, or physical characteristics come under control of the same political system. There, some groups who share physical and cultural traits discriminate against those who have different traits. The losers in this power struggle are forced into minority-group status, while winners enjoy higher status and greater privileges that dominance brings.

CHARACTERISTICS OF MINORITY GROUPS. Wagley and Harris noted that minority groups share five characteristics:

1. Membership in a minority group is not voluntary (**achieved status**) but comes through birth (**ascribed status**).
2. The physical or cultural traits of the minority are held in low esteem by the dominant group (*prejudice*).
3. Members of the group are treated unequally by the dominant group (*discrimination*).
4. Minority members tend to marry within their group (**endogamy**).
5. They tend to feel group solidarity because of their physical or cultural traits—and the disadvantages that these traits bring.

Let's review this last characteristic. Because members of minority groups possess similar cultural or physical traits, tend to marry within their own group, and experience discrimination at the hands of a dominant group, a feeling of common identity often unites them. The term **affinity groups** describes this sort of voluntary segregation. Affinity groupings are natural and healthy. This identity (a sense of "we" versus "them") may be so strong that members of a minority group feel that they share a common destiny.

OBJECTIVES OF MINORITY GROUPS. Wirth (1945) identified the following objectives that minority groups have in regard to the dominant group:

1. **Pluralism:** The group wants to live peacefully with the dominant group, yet maintain its distinctive culture—the differences that set it apart and that are so important to its identity.

2. **Assimilation:** Focusing on the culture they share with the dominant group, members of the minority group become absorbed into larger society. They want to be treated as individuals, not as members of a separate group.
3. **Secession:** Wanting cultural and political independence, the minority seeks to separate itself and form a separate nation.
4. **Militancy:** Convinced of its own superiority, the minority wants a reversal in status and seeks to dominate the society.

POLICIES OF DOMINANT GROUPS. Dominant groups not only view minority groups differently, but they treat them differently as well. Figure 8-1 outlines six policies of dominant groups identified by sociologists George Simpson and J. Milton Yinger. As you can see from this figure, these practices can help or hinder minorities. Let's examine them now.

1. **Pluralism.** When a dominant group permits or even encourages cultural differences, *pluralism* exists. The "hands-off" policy toward immigrant associations and foreign-language newspapers in the United States is an example of pluralism. Switzerland provides an outstanding example of successful pluralism: Although the French, Italian, German, and Romish Swiss have retained their separate languages and other customs, they live peacefully together in a political and economic unit. None of them is considered a minority.
2. **Assimilation.** In contrast to pluralism, *assimilation* is an attempt to "eliminate" the minority by absorbing them into mainstream culture. In *forced assimilation,* the dominant group bans the minority's religion, language, and other distinctive customs. In the former Soviet Union, the Russians treated Armenians this way. *Permissible assimilation,* in contrast, permits the minority to adopt those dominant practices that it wishes. In the United States, we expect that cultural minorities will gradually and voluntarily give up their distinctive customs such as unique clothing and language and adopt the customs of the dominant group.
3. **Segregation.** Also known as *continued subjugation, segregation* is an attempt by the dominant group to keep a minority "in its place"—that is, subservient, exploitable, and "off by itself." During the period of Apartheid in South Africa between 1948 and 1990, a small number of Whites controlled the nation. Blacks were used for cheap labor. As Simpson and Yinger (1972) put it, who else would do the hard work? This small group established **apartheid** (ah-par´-tate), a system of elaborate rules that

FIGURE 8-1 Policies of Dominant Groups Toward Minority Groups

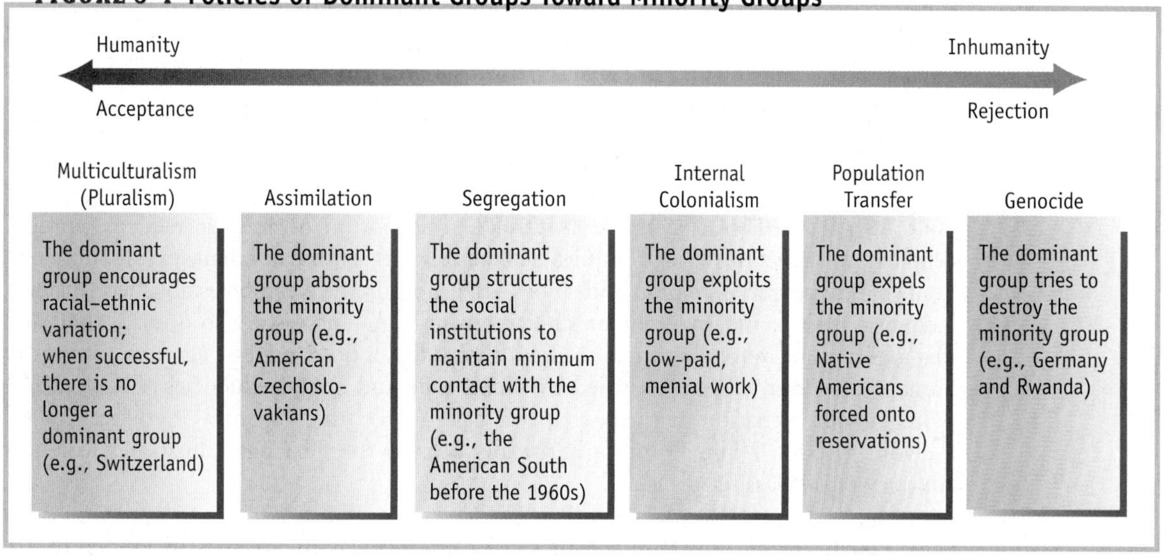

Humanity Acceptance					Inhumanity Rejection
Multiculturalism (Pluralism)	Assimilation	Segregation	Internal Colonialism	Population Transfer	Genocide
The dominant group encourages racial–ethnic variation; when successful, there is no longer a dominant group (e.g., Switzerland)	The dominant group absorbs the minority group (e.g., American Czechoslovakians)	The dominant group structures the social institutions to maintain minimum contact with the minority group (e.g., the American South before the 1960s)	The dominant group exploits the minority group (e.g., low-paid, menial work)	The dominant group expels the minority group (e.g., Native Americans forced onto reservations)	The dominant group tries to destroy the minority group (e.g., Germany and Rwanda)

Source: By James M. Henslin. Based on Simpson and Yinger (1972); Henslin (2007b).

maintained social distance between Blacks and Whites and forced the segregation of Blacks and Whites in almost all spheres of life. In the face of international sanctions that threatened the nation's economy, the Whites dismantled apartheid.

4. **Internal colonialism.** Whereas we usually think of colonialism as being external to a nation, *internal colonialism* refers to exploiting the minority group's labor. It accompanies segregation and precedes the next two policies, population transfer and genocide.

5. **Population transfer.** In *direct population transfer,* the dominant group forces the minority to leave. In the 1400s, for example, King Ferdinand and Queen Isabella (who financed Columbus's voyage to North America) drove the Jews and Moors out of Spain. In another example, during World War II the U.S. government placed Japanese Americans in internment camps. *Indirect population transfer* occurs when the dominant group makes life so miserable for a minority that its members "choose" to leave. Facing the bitter conditions of czarist Russia, for example, millions of Jews made this "choice."

6. **Genocide.** Hatred, fear, or greed can motivate the dominant group to use a policy of extermination, or *genocide.* The most infamous example was the Holocaust, when the Nazis ran death camps to systematically exterminate minorities. Between 1933 and 1945, the Nazis slaughtered about 6 million Jews, a quarter of a million Gypsies, hundreds of thousands of Slavs, and unknown numbers of homosexuals, communists, people with disabilities, and the mentally ill—all people whom Hitler did not consider "pure" enough to be part of his mythical Aryan race.

IDEAS OF RACIAL SUPERIORITY. Hitler was convinced that **race**—the inherited physical characteristics that identify a group of people—could be used to distinguish the deserving from the undeserving. He believed that the Aryans were responsible for the cultural achievements of Europe. These tall, fair-skinned, mostly blond-haired people—a biologically superior "super race" in his view—had as their destiny to establish a higher culture, a new world order. To fulfill their destiny, the Aryans had to avoid the "racial contamination" that breeding with "inferior races" would bring. Hitler believed that if he could isolate or destroy the "inferior races," they would not endanger Aryan biology or culture. Some "lower races" would remain to perform tasks too lowly for Aryans to perform.

Although most people today find Hitler's ideas bizarre, in the 1930s both the public and the scientific community took such ideas seriously. Many biologists and anthropologists, for example, believed that sharp lines divided the "races" and that some were inherently superior to others. It is not surprising that these scientists always concluded that Caucasians were the superior "race," for they themselves were Caucasian. *Eugenics*— attempts to improve the human "race" through selective breeding—was approved by scientists, health specialists, religious leaders, and prominent politicians of this period.

Ideas of racial superiority justifying one group's rule over another are certainly less popular today, but the idea of racial superiority remains a social reality. Almost everyone identifies with some "racial" group, classifies other people into "racial" groups, and treats them accordingly. Everyone has ideas, opinions, and attitudes that motivate people to treat some races better than others.

RACE AS AN ARBITRARY SOCIAL CATEGORY. The notion of a "pure race" is a myth. People have such a mixture of physical characteristics—skin color, hair texture, nose and head shapes, height, eye color, and so on—that no pure race can be established. Instead, biologists have found that human characteristics flow endlessly into one another, and this melding makes any attempt to draw sharp distinctions useless. Large groupings of humans, however, can be classified by blood type and gene frequencies. There can be more genetic variation within what we call a race than there is between "races" (Lewontin, 2006). The Thinking Critically box on the next page illustrates just how arbitrary racial classifications are.

CLARIFYING TERMS. Because the practice of racial classification is so embedded in our culture, "race" is an issue that sociologists confront. Preferring to avoid a term as

CAN A PLANE RIDE CHANGE YOUR RACE?

According to common sense, the title of this box is nonsense—our racial classifications represent biological differences. Sociologists, in contrast, stress that what we call races are *social* classifications, not biological categories.

Sociologists point out that *our "race" depends more on the society in which we live than on our biological characteristics.* For example, the racial categories that are common in the United States are merely one of *numerous* ways by which people around the world classify physical appearances. Although groups around the world use different categories, each group assumes that its categories are natural, merely a logical response to visible physical differences.

To better understand this essential sociological point—that race is more social than it is biological—consider this: In the United States, children who are born to the same parents are all of the same race. I am sure that you are thinking, "What could be more natural?" This is the common view of Americans. But in Brazil, children who are born to the same parents can be of different races—if their appearances differ. "What could be more natural?" assume Brazilians.

Consider how Americans usually classify a child who has a "Black" mother and a "White" father. Why do they usually say that the child is "Black"? Wouldn't it

What race is Tiger Woods? In his own words he states, "The media has portrayed me as African-American; sometimes, Asian. In fact, I am both. Yes, I am the product of two great cultures, one African-American and the other Asian. On my father's side, I am African-American. On my mother's side, I am Thai. Truthfully, I feel very fortunate, and equally proud, to be both African-American and Asian!

The critical and fundamental point is that ethnic background and/or composition should not make a difference. It does not make a difference to me. The bottom line is that I am an American . . . and proud of it! It is who I am and what I am. Now, with your cooperation, I hope I can just be a golfer and a human being."

Race is so social—and fluid—that even a plane ride can change a person's race. In the city of Salvador in Brazil, people classify one another by the color of their skin and eyes, the breadth of their nose and lips, and the color and curliness of their hair. They use at least seven terms for what we call White and Black. Consider again a U.S. child who has one "White" and one "Black" parent. Although she is "Black" in the United States, if she flies to Brazil, she will belong to one of their several "Whiter" categories (Fish, 1995).

On the flight just mentioned, did the girl's "race" actually change? Our common sense revolts at this, I know, but it actually did. We want to argue that because her biological characteristics remain unchanged, her race remains unchanged. This is because we think of race as biological, when *race is actually a label we use to describe perceived biological characteristics.* Simply put, the race we "are" depends on *where* we are—on who is doing the classifying.

"Racial" classifications are so fluid, not fixed, that you can see change occurring even now. In the United States, we recently began to

be equally logical to classify the child as "White"? Similarly, if a child's grandmother is "Black" but all her other ancestors are "White," the child is often considered "Black." Yet she has much more "White blood" than "Black blood." Why, then, is she considered "Black"? Certainly not because of biology. Rather, such thinking is a legacy of slavery. Before the Civil War, numerous children were born whose fathers were White slave masters and whose mothers were Black slaves. In an attempt to preserve the "purity" of their "race," Whites classified anyone with even a "drop of Black blood" as "not White."

use the term "multiracial." This new category indicates changing thought about race, a change picked up by the new classification on U.S. census forms, "two or more races."

FOR YOUR CONSIDERATION

How would you explain to "Joe Six-Pack" the sociological point that race is more a social classification than a biological one? Can you come up with any arguments to refute this view? How do you think our racial–ethnic categories will change in the future?

imprecise as *race,* many sociologists use the term *racial–ethnic group.* The term *ethnic* is derived from the Greek word *ethnos,* meaning "people" or "nation." A **racial–ethnic group** refers to people who identify with one another on the basis of their ancestry and cultural heritage. Their sense of belonging may center on unique physical characteristics, foods, dress, names, language, music, and religion. As we have reviewed, collective discrimination and intermarriage may also be significant factors in shaping that common identity.

The Scope of the Problem

Many racial–ethnic groups with different histories, customs, and identities populate the United States. The largest groups are listed in Figure 8-2.

THE MELTING POT. Throughout U.S. history, immigrants have confronted **Anglo-conformity;** that is, they are expected to maintain English institutions (as modified by the American Revolution), speak the English language, and adopt other Anglo-Saxon

FIGURE 8-2 U.S. Racial–Ethnic Groups

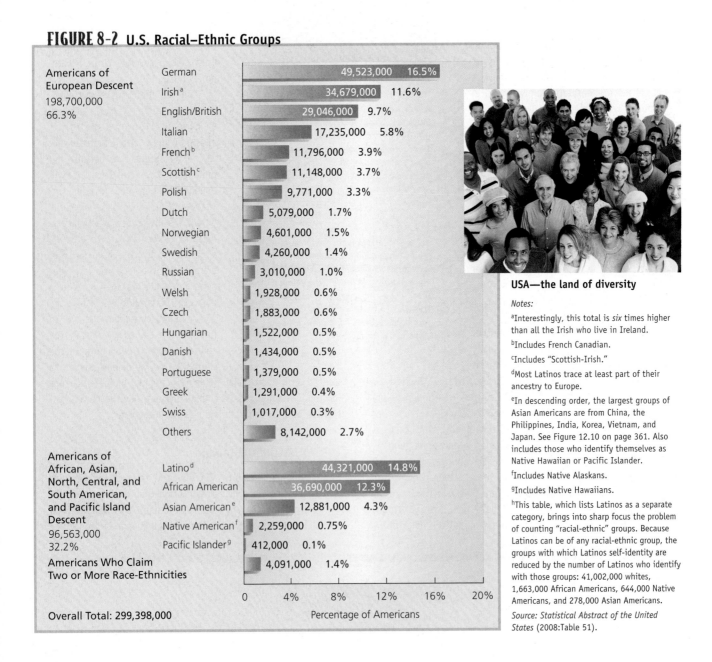

Americans of European Descent
198,700,000
66.3%

Group	Number	Percentage
German	49,523,000	16.5%
Irish[a]	34,679,000	11.6%
English/British	29,046,000	9.7%
Italian	17,235,000	5.8%
French[b]	11,796,000	3.9%
Scottish[c]	11,148,000	3.7%
Polish	9,771,000	3.3%
Dutch	5,079,000	1.7%
Norwegian	4,601,000	1.5%
Swedish	4,260,000	1.4%
Russian	3,010,000	1.0%
Welsh	1,928,000	0.6%
Czech	1,883,000	0.6%
Hungarian	1,522,000	0.5%
Danish	1,434,000	0.5%
Portuguese	1,379,000	0.5%
Greek	1,291,000	0.4%
Swiss	1,017,000	0.3%
Others	8,142,000	2.7%

Americans of African, Asian, North, Central, and South American, and Pacific Island Descent
96,563,000
32.2%

Group	Number	Percentage
Latino[d]	44,321,000	14.8%
African American	36,690,000	12.3%
Asian American[e]	12,881,000	4.3%
Native American[f]	2,259,000	0.75%
Pacific Islander[g]	412,000	0.1%

Americans Who Claim Two or More Race-Ethnicities
4,091,000 1.4%

Percentage of Americans (0% 4% 8% 12% 16% 20%)

Overall Total: 299,398,000

USA—the land of diversity

Notes:

[a]Interestingly, this total is *six* times higher than all the Irish who live in Ireland.

[b]Includes French Canadian.

[c]Includes "Scottish-Irish."

[d]Most Latinos trace at least part of their ancestry to Europe.

[e]In descending order, the largest groups of Asian Americans are from China, the Philippines, India, Korea, Vietnam, and Japan. See Figure 12.10 on page 361. Also includes those who identify themselves as Native Hawaiian or Pacific Islander.

[f]Includes Native Alaskans.

[g]Includes Native Hawaiians.

[h]This table, which lists Latinos as a separate category, brings into sharp focus the problem of counting "racial-ethnic" groups. Because Latinos can be of any racial-ethnic group, the groups with which Latinos self-identity are reduced by the number of Latinos who identify with those groups: 41,002,000 whites, 1,663,000 African Americans, 644,000 Native Americans, and 278,000 Asian Americans.

Source: Statistical Abstract of the United States (2008:Table 51).

ways of life. The United States was originally designed to become a modified version of England. Many thought that the evolving society would become a **melting pot,** that it would "melt" European immigrants together into a new cultural and biological blend. As sociologist Milton Gordon (1964) put it, "the stocks and folkways of Europe [would be], figuratively speaking, indiscriminately mixed in the political pot of the emerging nation and melted together by the fires of American influence and interaction into a distinctly new type."

For most European immigrants, the melting pot became a reality. Most lost their specific ethnic identities and merged into mainstream culture. Although individuals might identify themselves as "three-quarters German and one-quarter mixed Italian and Greek—with some English thrown in," they tend to think of themselves as "American." Some groups, however, have retained their unique cultures and ethnic identities. In recent years, large numbers of immigrants, especially those from Mexico, Cuba, Haiti, Vietnam, Laos, and India, have retained a strong immigrant identity.

Despite their desire to melt into U.S. culture, some non-European Americans find this melting elusive. Differences in appearance evoke stereotypes, as Nazli Kibria, who did research on Asian Americans, explains in the Spotlight on Research box on page 249.

Some immigrants are not welcome to join the melting pot. Americans of Western European background never intended for those of other ethnicities to become part of this "biological mix." On the contrary, in an effort to enforce "racial" purity they passed laws that made it illegal for Blacks and Whites to marry.

STEREOTYPES. As each new group of immigrants entered the United States, it confronted some level of prejudice. Prejudice is based on **stereotypes**—unrealistic generalizations of what people are like. For example, English immigrants despised Irish immigrants, viewing them as dirty, lazy, untrustworthy and drunkards. Members of minority groups also hold stereotypes of the dominant group; and, as you probably know from personal experience, various groups hold debasing stereotypes of one another (Leonard & Locke, 1993). The Thinking Critically about Social Problems box on page 251 explores the question of what to do about people who manipulate stereotypes to breed hatred.

What Is the Problem?

Prejudice, stereotypes, and discrimination are not necessarily social problems. Even people who are prejudiced against one another can coexist peacefully. A social problem arises when people get upset because prejudice and discrimination deprive minorities of the rights to which citizenship entitles them. When prejudice breeds hatred and conflict, group relations are troubled, and social problems develop.

As with other social problems, however, exactly what is problematic about racial–ethnic relations depends on one's vantage point. As the chapter's opening vignette indicates, for members of the Ku Klux Klan and its sympathizers, minorities are the source of the social problem.

Others are upset that prejudice and discrimination have thwarted their right to equality of "life, liberty, and the pursuit of happiness." This is how we shall look at the social problem of racial–ethnic relations—as discrimination that violates equality.

TRYING TO MEASURE DISCRIMINATION. The effects of discrimination reach beyond statistics about how many people

Exogamy—marrying outside one's race–ethnicity—is becoming increasingly popular. Here a White groom and his Black bride embrace and kiss after exchanging marriage vows at their church wedding ceremony in Atlanta, Georgia.

TABLE 8-1 Indicators of Relative Economic Well-Being

	FAMILY INCOME		FAMILIES IN POVERTY	
	Median Family Income	Percentage of White Income	Percentage Below Poverty	Percentage of White Poverty
White	$58,131		6.1%	
Asian American	$63,251	109%	9.2	151%
Native American	$34,641[1]	60	20.1	330
African American	$34,369	60	21.9	359
Latino	$35,600	61	20.4	334

[1] I doubt the accuracy of this total. It conflicts too greatly with the lower incomes for Native Americans that were reported in preceding years; it is suspiciously close to the incomes reported for African Americans and Latinos; and it does not account for the greater poverty of Native Americans. The explanation could be Indian casinos. If so, this total would mask huge disparities of income among tribes.

Source: By James M. Henslin. Based on *Statistical Abstract of the United States* (2006, Tables 37, 678).

are denied some particular benefit of society. Too often, we end up focusing on such numbers—missing how discrimination affects the lives of its victims. Because of discrimination, people often view themselves the way the dominant group does. They put down their own abilities, think of themselves as less capable, less worthy, and, ultimately, as less human. Discrimination, in short, can detract from people's sense of being and sense of self-worth.

Millions of Americans live with prejudice and discrimination. As Table 8-1 shows, family incomes of African Americans, Latinos, and Native Americans are generally 60% that of White families. Their poverty is more than triple that of Whites. Remember that underlying such statistics are people whose lives are affected adversely. At issue is whether they can afford health care, nourishing food, and education—not whether they can afford a boat, a new car, or a vacation out of state.

Such economic matters are so significant that they can translate into life and death situations. Look at Table 8-2. As you can see, an African American baby has *more than twice* the chance of dying that a White baby does, and the chances of a mother dying during childbirth are *four* times higher for African American women. You can also see that, on average, African American women die about 4 or 5 years younger than White women. In short, race–ethnicity and infant mortality is linked to income. African

TABLE 8-2 Health and Race–Ethnicity

	INFANT DEATHS[1]	MATERNAL DEATHS[1]	LIFE EXPECTANCY Male	LIFE EXPECTANCY Female
White	5.8	6.0	75.4	80.5
Black	14.4	24.9	69.2	76.1

[1] The death rates given here are the number per 1,000. Infant deaths refer to the number of infants under 1 year old who die in a year per 1,000 live births. The source does not provide data for other racial–ethnic groups.

Source: Statistical Abstract of the United States (2006, Tables 96, 104).

Spotlight on Social Research
BEING A "FOREIGN" AMERICAN

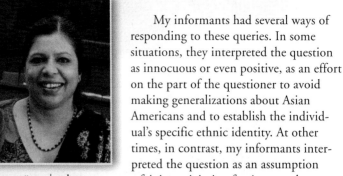

Nazli Kibria, *professor of sociology at Boston University, did research on second-generation Chinese and Korean Americans. She explored their experience of being identified by others as "Asian." In this essay, she reports on how "racial identities" serve as markers (or signals) in everyday social encounters. These "markers" are based on how people perceive the physical characteristics of others.*

I use the term "second-generation Chinese and Korean Americans" to refer to people of Chinese and Korean ancestry who were born and/or from a young age reared in the United States. Based on their encounters with people of non-Asian origin, I explored the ways in which they experience the identity marker of "Asian race" in their daily lives.

In their everyday social encounters, non-Asian Americans often assume that Chinese and Korean Americans are "foreigners." With the perception of "Asian" often comes an image of an unassimilable alien—a presence that is fundamentally and unalterably outside of, if not diametrically opposite to, what is "American." Many of my informants said that they frequently were asked, "Where are you from?" While this question may be intended as an inquiry about one's regional origin in the United States (e.g., "Are you from Southern California?"), when asked of Asian Americans it is often meant as a question about nationality and ethnic origins. In fact, informants told me that if they answered the question in local terms (such as, "I'm from Boston"), the person often followed up with something like, "Yes, but where are you really from?"

My informants had several ways of responding to these queries. In some situations, they interpreted the question as innocuous or even positive, as an effort on the part of the questioner to avoid making generalizations about Asian Americans and to establish the individual's specific ethnic identity. At other times, in contrast, my informants interpreted the question as an assumption that everyone of Asian origin is a foreigner and not American.

Among the strategies that my informants used to neutralize or at least to deflect the assumption of their foreignness were dis-identifiers. To remove an identity of "foreignness" and provide an identity of "American," they used symbols, such as language, dress, demeanor, and even the people with whom they were seen or associated. Language was one of their main dis-identifiers. During an encounter with strangers, they would deflect their presumed foreignness by speaking fluent and unaccented English. The need to use dis-identifiers produced an awareness among my informants that for Asian Americans, the achievement and acceptance of an American identity requires vigilance and work.

Ascribing "foreignness" to second-generation Chinese and Korean Americans not only casts doubt upon their identity as Americans, but also signals authentic ethnicity. That is, the dominant society assumes that second-generation Chinese and Korean Americans have ties to a community and culture that is either located or rooted outside the U.S. mainstream. These ties are assumed to be strong and genuine—authentic, rather than contrived or fake. My informants were especially aware of this assumption of ethnic authenticity when a non-Asian American would ask them to interpret Asian, Korean, or Chinese cultural practices or in some other way to display their ethnic cultural knowledge.

American men die 6 years younger than White men. Higher incomes afford better nutrition, housing, and medical care, and thus a longer life.

INSTITUTIONAL DISCRIMINATION IN THE PAST. To understand the effects of discrimination, we need to move beyond thinking in terms of **individual discrimination,** one person treating another badly on the basis of race–ethnicity. Although this certainly creates problems, as an individual conflict it does not qualify as a social problem. The law, however, may become involved if one person withholds something illegally—say, employment or housing—from someone on the basis of race–ethnicity.

Sociologists encourage us to move beyond individual situations and to think in broader terms. They point to **institutional discrimination** as the essence of social problems. This is discrimination built into the social system that oppresses whole groups. For example, for generations Whites denied African Americans the right to vote, join

Realty companies pose happy minority home buyers as part of their advertising campaigns. As indicated in the text, minority families are less likely to be approved for a loan even when their qualifications are identical to those of white applicants.

labor unions, work at high-paying prestigious jobs, attend good schools, or receive care at decent hospitals.

Throughout history, well-known institutions have practiced institutional discrimination. One group known to have practiced discrimination is the National Association of Real Estate Boards (NAR). This organization used to support racial discrimination as a *moral* act. Here is a statement from its 1924 code of ethics: "A Realtor should never be instrumental in introducing into a neighborhood . . . members of any race or nationality, or individuals whose presence will clearly be detrimental to property values in that neighborhood" (Newman et al., 1978, p. 149).

The federal government followed the same policy. If developers of subdivisions wanted to obtain a loan from the Federal Housing Authority (FHA), they had to exclude non-Whites (Valocchi, 1994; Oliver & Shapiro, 1995). Even after World War II, the FHA denied loans to anyone who would "unsettle a neighborhood." Again, the discrimination was considered a *moral* act, done to protect people. The FHA manual was explicit about this: "If a neighborhood is to retain stability, it is necessary that properties shall continue to be occupied by the same social and racial classes" (Duster, 1988, p. 288).

How times have changed. And with them, so have federal agencies and the NAR. In 1950, under pressure, the NAR deleted the reference to race or nationality. Fair housing was not fully practiced until 1972.

INSTITUTIONAL DISCRIMINATION TODAY. Do we still have institutional discrimination, or is it a distant memory from our past? Many aspects of institutional discrimination, as we have just seen with the NAR, certainly are a thing of the past, but institutional discrimination remains. Figure 8-3 on page 252, which summarizes a study of 9,000 U.S. financial institutions, shows that institutional discrimination is alive and well. This figure illustrates how discrimination has been woven into our social system and will remain for sometime.

When bankers were shown the findings reported in Figure 8-3, they cried foul, denying that they had discriminated. They claimed that they were fair to everyone and that they gave more loans to Whites because they had better credit histories. If this were true, it could account for the findings without pointing to racial–ethnic discrimination. To find out, researchers compared the history of late payments of the applicants, loan size, and incomes. The results? When two mortgage were identical in terms of debts, loan size relative to income, and even characteristics of the property they wanted to buy, African Americans and Latinos were 60% more likely to be rejected than Whites (Thomas, 1992; Passell, 1996).

UNINTENDED INSTITUTIONAL DISCRIMINATION. We don't know how many bankers intended to discriminate and how many did so without such intentions. We do know, however, that a fascinating aspect of institutional discrimination is that *it can occur even when those doing the discriminating are unaware of it*. Let's look at IQ testing as an example.

Imagine that you are in the fifth grade and your school is giving your class an IQ test. For "politically correct" reasons, the test is no longer called an IQ test. It has been renamed The Achievement Predictor (TAP). Your teacher tells you and your classmates to do your best because your results on TAP are going to affect your future. This is rather vague, but it makes you feel a little nervous. You intend to do your best anyway. You don't want anyone to think you're mentally challenged.

WHAT SHOULD WE DO ABOUT HATE SPEECH?

The Internet has proven a marvelous source of information. As sociologists, we are pleased that we have this tool. It enables us to live and travel in other countries and still have libraries, government agencies, and other sources at our fingertips—vast research that can be downloaded onto our computers.

The Internet is also a remarkable source of misinformation. Anyone can put up a Web site and fill it with distortions of truth or lies. People can nurse grudges, seek revenge for perceived wrongs, and fan hatred.

These negative communications are upsetting. Consider these statements:

Should hate speech be a protected right?

> Civil Rights come out of the barrel of a gun, and we mean to give the niggers and Jews all the civil rights they can handle. . . . Our security team will see that no live targets escape from the range. Any who refuse to run or can't for any reason will be fed to the dogs. The dogs appreciate a good feed as much as we do.
>
> —An invitation to a summer conference held by the Aryan Nations at Hayden Lake, Idaho. The group's founder, Richard Butler, is a former Lockheed executive (quoted in Murphy, 1999)

Who's pimping the world? The hairy hands of the Zionist. . . . The so-called Jew claims that there were six million in Nazi Germany. I am here today to tell you that there is absolutely no . . . evidence to substantiate, to prove that six million so-called Jews lost their lives in Nazi Germany. . . . Don't let no hooked-nose, bagel-eating, lox-eating, perpetrating-a-fraud so-called Jew who just crawled out of the ghettoes of Europe just a few days ago. . . .

—Statements of Khalid Abdul Muhammad (quoted in Herbert, 1988)

Hatred knows no racial–ethnic boundaries; the first statement was made by a White, the second by an African American.

Should we ban such statements from the Internet and other forms of the mass media? Should we punish their authors as lawbreakers? Should we allow such statements to be circulated as part of free speech, regardless of their inflammatory rhetoric, the twisting of fact, or the hatred they spew?

Canada has taken steps to ban hate speech. Ingrid Rimland of San Diego runs a Web site on which she sells anti-Semitic literature and publicizes the views of Ernst Zundel. An immigrant from Germany who lived in Canada for 40 years, Zundel denies the Holocaust took place and preaches anti-Semitism. Canadian authorities accused Zundel of controlling Rimland's Web site and charged him under laws that prohibit the use of telephone lines to spread hate messages based on race, religion, or ethnic origin ("Canada Tries to . . . ," 1998). Zundel was arrested in the United States on a charge of overstaying his visa and was deported to Canada. Canadian authorities then deported Zundel to Germany, where it is illegal to deny the Holocaust or to display Nazi symbols. Zundel was put in prison at Mannheim (Zundel, 2004).

FOR YOUR CONSIDERATION

Some say that in order to expose the ridiculousness of bad ideas, we should let them be viewed in the cold, hard light of logic. Others take the position that censorship even of hatred is wrong; as an attack on free speech, it threatens us all. That people can be put in prison for expressing ideas, as with Zundel in Germany, sends a chill up the spine of the advocates of free speech. They point out that it might be *your* ideas that are banned in the future. Still others say that hatred needs to be fought in any way possible, even by passing laws against certain kinds of speech and punishing those who express those ideas. What do you think?

FIGURE 8-3 Race–Ethnicity and Mortgages: An Example of Institutional Discrimination

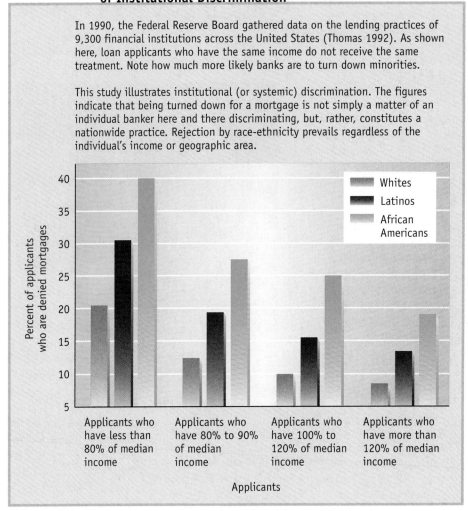

In 1990, the Federal Reserve Board gathered data on the lending practices of 9,300 financial institutions across the United States (Thomas 1992). As shown here, loan applicants who have the same income do not receive the same treatment. Note how much more likely banks are to turn down minorities.

This study illustrates institutional (or systemic) discrimination. The figures indicate that being turned down for a mortgage is not simply a matter of an individual banker here and there discriminating, but, rather, constitutes a nationwide practice. Rejection by race-ethnicity prevails regardless of the individual's income or geographic area.

The booklets are passed out face down. You fill out the blanks on the back, carefully printing the date, your name, class, school, and teacher. At your teacher's command, for this is a timed test, you turn the booklet over, open it, and eagerly read the first question. You can hardly believe your eyes when you read:

1. If you throw the dice and "7" is showing on the top, what is facing down?

___seven ___snake eyes ___box cars ___little Joe's ___eleven

This question confuses you. You haven't the slightest idea of what the correct answer might be. When you play Monopoly, you never look *under* the dice.

Since your teacher said that it is better to guess than to leave an answer blank, you put a check mark on something. Then you go to the second question, which only increases your confusion and frustration. Here is what you read:

2. Which word is out of place here?

___splib ___blood ___gray ___spook ___black

Again, you have no idea of what choice is correct, so you put a check on anything. The questions that follow are just like these first two. You continue to make marks, for the most part, meaninglessly. As this seemingly endless nonsense continues, somewhere in the process you realize that you've given up. No longer are you reading the questions thoroughly, for it doesn't seem to affect which blank you check.

It is obvious that you performed poorly on this test. It should also be obvious why— you were being tested on things that were not from your background of experiences.

"They just didn't ask the right questions." This is how it is on IQ (or "evaluation") tests. Some questions favor children from certain backgrounds. Consider this question from a standardized IQ test:

A symphony is to a composer as a book is to a(n) _____:
___paper ___sculptor ___musician ___author ___man

At first glance, this seems like an objective question, one that applies equally to everyone. Your experience with dice and splibs, though, should have made you more aware that children from some racial–ethnic backgrounds are more familiar with the concepts of symphonies, composers, sculptors, and musicians than are other children. This tilts the test in their favor.

It is important to note that those who write the questions for these evaluative tests are doing their best. They are trying to be objective. They do not intend to discriminate, and they are unaware that they are doing so. They are simply working out of their own backgrounds, from within their own taken-for-granted worlds.

The questions that "you" took were suggested by Adrian Dove (n.d.), a social worker in Watts (East Los Angeles). These questions are slanted toward a non-White, lower-class experience. With these *particular* cultural biases, is it not obvious that children from some social backgrounds will perform better than others?

Medical decisions illustrate another facet of unintended institutional discrimination. Researchers have found that physicians are more likely to recommend knee replacements for their White patients than for either their Latino or African American patients (Skinner et al., 2003). In yet another striking example, White patients are also more likely to receive coronary bypass surgery than Black patients. Those Blacks who do undergo bypass surgery are more likely to die within one year (Smedley et al., 2003). Why should this be? Actually, no one yet knows why or how race–ethnicity becomes a factor in making medical decisions. Even African American physicians are more likely to give preventive care to White patients (Stolberg, 2001). Discovering how unintended institutional discrimination is part of interracial dynamics in medical decisions and other aspects of social life would be a fascinating area of future research.

In short, institutional discrimination is built into our social system. It operates throughout society—with those involved often unaware of it.

Looking at the Problem Theoretically

Prejudice, discrimination, hostility, and tensions characterize many relations between racial–ethnic groups in the United States. To better understand them, social scientists use sociological theory. Although separately each perspective presents some illumination, taken together they bring more of the picture into focus.

Symbolic Interactionism

In human relations words are not meaningless labels. The labels we use color the way we see the world and influence what we experience. **Ethnophaulisms** describe those derogatory labels that are applied to racial–ethnic groups. The "N" word is an example of an ethnophaulism.

SOCIALIZATION INTO PREJUDICE. Symbolic interactionists examine how we are socialized into prejudice and discrimination. No one is born with prejudice or with a desire to discriminate. Indeed, we are born without standards, values, or beliefs. But all children are born into particular families and racial–ethnic groups. There they learn values, beliefs, and ways to perceive the world. If their family is prejudiced against another group, children are taught to dislike that group and to label its members negatively. Similarly, if discrimination is common, children learn to practice it routinely.

LABELS AND SELECTIVE PERCEPTION. Symbolic interactionists stress that labels (such as stereotypes or ethnophaulisms) affect prejudice by causing **selective perception.** Negative labeling leads us to see certain things while making us blind to others. As we view people through the lens of negativity, it shapes our perception, and we tend to look at the members of a group as though they all were alike. As Simpson and Yinger (1972) put it, we fit new experiences into old categories by selecting only those cues that harmonize with our prejudgment or stereotype.

THE SELF-FULFILLING PROPHECY. Labeling can be so powerful that it justifies prejudice and discrimination. The negative stereotypes that characterize a group can legitimize withholding of opportunities from members and justify placing them into positions considered appropriate for people "like them." This creates a **self-fulfilling prophecy.** For example, if a stereotype defines members of group X as lazy, then it legitimizes keeping them out of jobs that require dedication, industry, and energy. If "appropriate" jobs are not available, members of group X are liable to be seen standing around street corners while members of groups Y and Z are working. Seeing members of group X idle reinforces the original stereotype of laziness, whereas the basic discrimination that created the "laziness" passes unnoticed.

LABELS AND MORALITY. Racial–ethnic labels have special power over people. They are shorthand for emotionally laden stereotypes. The label "nigger," for example, has numerous connotations. By no means is it neutral. This term is so loaded with negative emotions that most won't say the word, using the phrase "the N word" instead. Nor are "cracker," "spic," "mick," "limey," "kraut," "dago," "wetback," or the many other words that people use to refer to members of racial–ethnic groups neutral. The emotional impact of such words blocks positive progress (Allport, 1954).

Dominant groups can be quite effective in using labels to demean others. For instance, in wartime the enemy is often given dehumanizing labels. In the 1960s, for example, U.S. soldiers sent to Vietnam soon began to refer to the Vietnamese as "the enemy," "slopes," and "gooks." The army bureaucracy adopted a similar strategy: Weekly it would release reports, not of *people* killed, but of "body counts" and "kill ratios." Such efforts helped soldiers **compartmentalize:** separate negative acts from other aspects of their lives.

Just as terms that dehumanized the Vietnamese helped U.S. soldiers commit acts that otherwise would have challenged their identities as moral people, so too in the 1700s White settlers labeled Native Americans "savages." Viewing Native Americans as something less than human, troops and settlers destroyed tribe after tribe (Garbarino, 1976). The Boers, Dutch settlers in South Africa, characterized the native Hottentots as jungle animals and wiped them out. Holding similar views, British settlers in Tasmania hunted the local population for sport and even for dog food. Today, much as in earlier U.S. history, miners, ranchers, and loggers in Brazil are wiping out Indian tribes as they seize their lands (Linden, 1991; "Guardian of Brazil Indians . . . ", 1997).

Ethnophaulisms, then, are dangerous. Not only do they create selective perception, but they can also lead to discrimination and mass murder. Groups that build an identity around hatred pose a special threat to society. In the Spotlight on Research box on the next page, Raphael Ezekiel discusses his research on such groups.

IN SUM Symbolic interactionists examine how labels (or symbols) affect our relationships: how we learn labels, how we

Master P and his son, Romeo, are taking the fight against what some people deem to be objectionable rap lyrics seriously: They co-founded Take a Stand Records, a label that will put out "hip-hop artists with street music without offensive lyrics."

Spotlight on Social Research
STUDYING NEO-NAZIS AND KLANS

RAFAEL EZEKIEL, *a senior researcher with the Harvard School of Public Health, says that his interest in racism was stimulated by the contradictions he experienced as a child growing up with liberal, northern, Jewish parents in a deeply racist East Texas town.*

Dear students,

Jim Henslin asked me to write about my fieldwork. I got stuck, so I decided to interview myself.

Interviewer: What did you do, Professor?

Rafe: I spent three years hanging out with a neo-Nazi group in Detroit. After that, I interviewed national leaders from neo-Nazi groups and from Klans. I also went to their national and regional meetings. My book, *The Racist Mind,* comes from that work.

Interviewer: Did they know you were a Jew?

Rafe: I made sure they knew I was a Jew and opposed to racism. Good interviewing is interplay between you and your respondent—kind of a dance. That requires trust; trust requires openness and honesty.

Interviewer: But, then, why did they talk with you?

Rafe: Because I told them the truth—that I believe every person creates a life that makes sense to him or her, and my professional work is to go onto the turf of people whose lives seem unusual to most folk and let these people tell me, in their own words, the sense their lives make to them. That made sense to them.

Interviewer: Did you find anything out?

Rafe: Yeah. The leaders and members are real different. The leaders are men—this is essentially a male movement—force, macho, blood, all that. The leaders are not motivated primarily by hate or by racism. They are motivated primarily by hunger for power: Power is the goal; racism is the tool. To move a crowd by what they say. To scare a community by saying that they're coming. To fill the media with scare stories. A whole lot of this is theater—they provide the stimulus; we provide the fantasies.

There are always suckers whom you can recruit by talking racism. If you line up 100 White Americans, ranked by how much they fear and dislike African Americans, the big leaders wouldn't be at the head of the line—they'd be about 30 places back.

Interviewer: And the ordinary members?

Rafe: That's a whole different story. This is not a movement built on hate. It's a movement built on fear. When you talk with a member, talk honestly about his life—his, again—the emotion you sense under the surface is fear. The kids in the Detroit group felt, deep down, that their own lives might be snuffed out at any moment, like a candle in the wind.

Interviewer: Do you have any hints on how to do good fieldwork?

Rafe: Yeah. First, check yourself out—why are you doing this? What does it mean to you? Second, be real—with them, with yourself. Third, field notes. When you finish your interview and start home, roll the interview around in your mind. Don't analyze, just let it play in your mind. Like remembering a dream. Don't talk to anyone—no phoning—don't listen to the radio—just keep the interview rolling around. Go straight home and start writing. Write first pure emotion—primary process stuff—associations, feelings. What's going on inside you after this interview? What does it remind you of? Then write your secondary process stuff—what went on and what you think it means. Then, in terms of your project, where does this take you? Do you need more questions? Respondents? Finally, ask yourself: "So what?" What difference does it make to the world what you think you are understanding? As you write that, you will be writing much of your book.

use labels to classify one another, how our classifications affect our perceptions and sort people out for different kinds of life experiences, how symbols of race–ethnicity change, and how symbols are used to justify discrimination and violence.

Functionalism

Why does racial–ethnic discrimination persist in the United States—and in other parts of the world? As you may recall, functionalists argue that the benefits of a social pattern (some characteristic of society) must be greater than its costs, or else that pattern will disappear.

The benefits (or functions) of discrimination, then, must outweigh its costs (or dysfunctions). How can this be?

FUNCTIONS AND DYSFUNCTIONS OF DISCRIMINATION. The discrimination woven into America's history benefited the dominant group for a time, but harmed others forever. Whites gained free land by killing Native Americans. Whites benefited from owning slaves. They acquired cheap labor and then sold the slaves' labor as masons, carpenters, or factory workers. Slave labor allowed many owners to live a "genteel" life of leisure or to pursue art, education, and other "refinements."

The legacy of slavery is forever dysfunctional. It bred tension, hostility, hatred, and fear among racial–ethnic groups. It would appear that the high costs of discrimination would lead to its elimination. But just as discrimination was functional for the dominant group in the past, today's dominant group benefits from it as well.

DISCRIMINATION AND DIRTY WORK. Racial–ethnic stratification, the unequal distribution of a society's resources based on race–ethnicity, serves major functions. It ensures that society's **dirty work** gets done. Sociologist Herbert Gans (2007) defines dirty work as society's "physically dirty or dangerous, temporary, dead-end and underpaid, undignified and menial jobs." Sociologist Emile Durkheim (1893/1964) stressed that society needs a **division of labor,** or people who perform specialized tasks. Dirty work, such as garbage collection, is a necessary but disagreeable task within this division of labor.

Society can fill its dirty-work jobs either by paying high wages to compensate for the work's unpleasantness and degradation or by forcing people to do them for low wages. To get society's dirty work done, then, it is functional for it to be assigned to minorities. This ensures that these jobs will get done and get done cheaply.

RACIAL–ETHNIC SUCCESSION IN DIRTY WORK. When a racial–ethnic group climbs the social class ladder, it leaves dirty work behind. Because the dirty work still has to be done, other groups are recruited to perform those tasks. For example, many African Americans have moved into the middle class, and unauthorized immigrants are doing much of the work they used to do. Mexicans and others who have entered the United States illegally have little control over their working conditions. They take jobs that practically no one else will accept, often working long hours in crowded, dirty, sometimes dangerous conditions. And they work cheaply, for many employers don't have to provide unemployment compensation, Social Security, hospitalization, overtime pay, disability compensation, or vacations.

Apart from what one could say about the injustice of this situation, it is functional. The dirty work gets done, and *most* Americans benefit: They eat the produce that the unauthorized immigrants pick and they wear the clothing they make. The immigrants also benefit: They earn far more than they would in their home country. Their families, left behind in desperate conditions, also benefit as their relatives in the United States send them part of their earnings. Even the government of Mexico benefits, for this vast migration siphons off millions of its more ambitious and dissatisfied citizens—those who otherwise might direct their energies toward overthrowing an oppressive Mexican elite.

ETHNOCENTRISM. Another function of racial–ethnic inequality is heightened **ethnocentrism,** a type of prejudice holding that "my group's ways are right and your group's ways are wrong." Ethnocentrism helps the dominant group justify its higher social position and greater share of society's resources. Members of the group don't have to question why they get more than others or feel guilty about it, for they claim superiority.

Racial–ethnic stratification also produces ethnocentrism among minority group members. Their visible differences and the discrimination they face because of their distinctiveness create cohesion, a sense of identity with one another. Seeing that other

groups have "made it" nourishes the hope that they, too, will succeed. This hope for the future strengthens the social system: It encourages minority groups to work hard, minimizes rebellion, and makes them willing to put up with demeaning circumstances—for the time being.

DYSFUNCTIONS. Discrimination is also dysfunctional; that is, it interferes with people's welfare and the functioning of society. If a group becomes too alienated, it might disrupt society and destroy human potential. Prejudice and discrimination can lower children's self-esteem, discourage high goals, and decrease the capacity to compete in school and work. Because they confront discrimination, many minority children drop out of school and waste their potential in low-level jobs or street crime. Society becomes the ultimate loser, denied the contributions that these youngsters could have made.

IN SUM Functionalists are often misunderstood: They identify social benefits that come from negative behaviors, such as discrimination. This can be seen as justifying or even promoting that behavior. Functionalists' main point, however, is that social characteristics persist only when they are functional. By analyzing the functions and dysfunctions of racial–ethnic stratification, functionalists uncover some of the hidden consequences of institutional arrangements.

Conflict Theory

What had seemed a personal hatred of me, an inexplicable refusal of southern Whites to confront their own emotions, and a stubborn willingness of Blacks to acquiesce, became the inevitable consequence of a ruthless system which kept itself alive and well by encouraging spite, competition, and the oppression of one group by another. Profit was the word: the cold and constant motive for the behavior, the contempt and despair I had seen. (Davis, 1974)

With these words, Angela Davis, an African American Marxist, recounted her understanding of U.S. racial–ethnic relations.

PITTING WORKERS AGAINST ONE ANOTHER. According to Marxist conflict theory, the dominant group pits racial–ethnic groups against one another in order to exploit workers and increase profit. Here is how the process works:

The United States has a **capitalist economy;** that is, our economic system is based on investing capital with the goal of making a profit. Profit results from selling items for more than what it cost to produce them. In conflict theory, this is called extracting the **surplus value of labor.** For example, if each item that a factory produces costs the owner of the factory $1 for materials; $1 for rent, utilities, and transportation; $1 for advertising, transportation, insurance, and the cost of borrowing money; and $1 for a worker to run a machine, the total cost of the item is $4. If the owner sells the item for $5, he or she makes $1 profit. Conflict theorists claim that the final profit represents a surplus value resulting from the labor used to produce the item. That is, the item increased in value *because* the worker added his or her labor to the item.

THE SPLIT-LABOR MARKET. Lower wages help investors and owners increase their profit. To keep wages low, capitalists use a **split-labor market;** that is, they weaken the bargaining power of workers by splitting them along racial–ethnic lines (Reich, 1972, 1981; Shafir & Peled, 1998). If employers can keep workers fearful and distrustful of one another, they can prevent them from uniting and demanding higher wages and more benefits.

The unemployed are especially valuable in maintaining a split-labor market. If everyone who wanted to work had a job, workers could threaten to quit unless they received higher pay and better working conditions. But when there are workers without jobs, owners have a pool of needy workers that they can dip into when they need them—to expand production or to break a strike. When the economy contracts or when

the strike is settled, these workers—called a **reserve labor force**—can be laid off to rejoin the unemployed, with no unsettling effects on society. Minority workers are ideal for the reserve labor force (Willhelm, 1980).

FALSE CLASS CONSCIOUSNESS. Besides the threat of unemployment, workers are also held in check by **false class consciousness.** Many workers buy into this false class consciousness, thinking that one day they will own a business and be rich too. Such false class consciousness prevents workers from realizing that their welfare is bound up with that of all workers, regardless of their race–ethnicity. If workers identify with capitalists instead of with their fellow working-class members, they cannot unite to bring about social change.

CONSEQUENCES OF A SPLIT-LABOR MARKET. The consequences of splitting labor along racial–ethnic lines are devastating, say conflict theorists. The system so distorts reality that it leads minorities and Whites to view one another as enemies, each able to gain some advantage over the other. Whites come to think of themselves as moral, hardworking taxpayers and view competing minority members as lazy people who swell welfare rolls, having to be supported by taxes that Whites pay. The minority, in turn, come to view Whites as ruthless, untrustworthy, hate-mongering hypocrites.

Dividing workers in these ways fosters disunity, keeping people from identifying with "the other." When this method is successful, Whites and minority group members fail to see that "the other" is an essential part of their own class interests. The reality, say conflict theorists, is that they both have a common enemy, the wealthy, who, to line their own pockets, use racial–ethnic divisions and hatred to oppress both.

Riots often result from similar situations. When the elite feel threatened, they often try to defuse the situation by offering concessions. They give a little here and there, whatever seems necessary to quiet the workers. They might increase welfare benefits, assign token representation on committees, or offer government aid to reconstruct inner cities. From the conflict perspective, these acts are not intended to change anything, but only to protect privileged positions of the powerful.

IN SUM Racial–ethnic antagonisms, encouraged by the powerful, divide the working class and strengthen the position of the powerful. A racist environment not only deflects working-class hostilities but also prevents working-class consensus. Such solidarity would allow workers to challenge control of the United States by the wealthy who own the means of production. Racial–ethnic discrimination will end only when White and minority workers see that they both are oppressed and that they have the same oppressor. If they become aware of their false class consciousness, workers of all groups will see the true source of their oppression. Then they can unite and create a new social order in which they will receive the full value of their labor. Workers can then create a new racial–ethnic harmony, a society that will no longer contain minority and dominant groups.

Summary of Theoretical Approaches

None of the theoretical perspectives has an exclusive claim to truth. Rather, each presents a particular truth. Each focuses on selected aspects of racial–ethnic relations, emphasizing those aspects above any other. Symbolic interactionists alert us to the powerful role of labels in defining human relations, how they are lenses through which we view ourselves and others. If those labels are demeaning, they help people discriminate with a clear conscience. Functionalists turn our attention not only to the dysfunctions of discrimination, but also to its benefits—its role in the division of labor and the consequences of the ethnocentrism it produces. Conflict theorists stress how the powerful of society use prejudice and discrimination to destroy worker solidarity so they can hold down wages and increase profits. Each theoretical lens, then, produces a unique understanding of racial–ethnic relations. Combined, these perspectives provide greater understanding of discrimination than does any one of them alone.

Research Findings

As demonstrated in Figure 8-2 on page 246, Whites make up 66% of the overall U.S. population, minorities 32% (African Americans 12%, Latinos 15%, Asian Americans 4%, and Native Americans 1%). About 1% of Americans claim two or more races. These groups are far from distributed evenly across the nation. As the Social Map (Figure 8-4) below shows, their distribution among the states seldom comes close to the national average. This is because minority groups tend to be clustered in regions. The extreme distributions are found in Maine and Vermont, which has only a 3% minority population, and Hawaii, where minorities outnumber European Americans 71% to 29%.

What major problems do minority groups in the United States face? How do the groups differ from one another? In what ways are relationships changing? What strategies are minority groups using to bring about social change? To answer these questions, we shall present an overview of the four largest minority groups in the United States: Native Americans, Latinos, African Americans, and Asian Americans.

Native Americans

NUMBERS. When Columbus arrived on the shores of the "New World," Native Americans numbered about 10 million (Schaefer, 2004). Four hundred years later, in 1900, Native Americans numbered 250,000. Today, there are 2 million Native Americans. These Americans represent more than 500 tribes (O'Hare, 1992).

CONFLICT. At first, relations between the European settlers and Native Americans were peaceful. Some American (and Canadian) authorities even encouraged marriage between Whites and Native Americans. In 1784, Patrick Henry introduced a bill in the Virginia House of Delegates offering tax relief, free education, and cash bonuses to Whites and Indians who intermarried. Such intermarriage is referred to as **exogamy** (Kaplan, 1990).

FIGURE 8-4 The Distribution of Dominant and Minority Groups in the United States

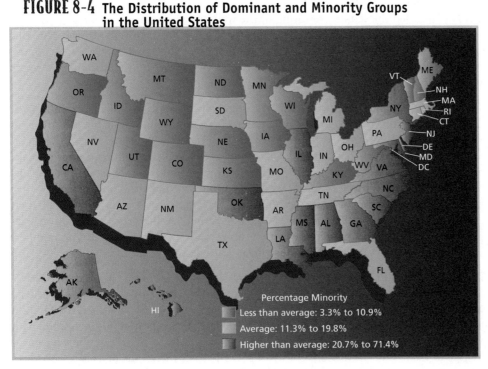

Percentage Minority
- Less than average: 3.3% to 10.9%
- Average: 11.3% to 19.8%
- Higher than average: 20.7% to 71.4%

This social map illustrates how unevenly distributed U.S. minority groups are. The extremes are Hawaii with 71 percent minority and Maine and Vermont with 3 percent minority.

Source: By James M. Henslin. Based on *Statistical Abstract of the United States* (2008, Table 18).

As more Europeans arrived, they began a relentless push westward. Native Americans stood in the way of expansion, so Europeans adopted a policy of *genocide*—the systematic extermination of racial minorities. As part of this policy (which they called "pacification"), the U.S. Cavalry slaughtered tens of thousands of Native Americans. When the cavalry butchered huge herds of buffalo on which the Great Plains Indians depended, many thousands more died from malnutrition and disease. Because Native Americans had no immunity to European diseases, more of them died from smallpox, measles, and the flu than from battle wounds (Kitano, 1974; Dobyns, 1983; Schaefer, 2004).

The barbarity of European Americans is evidenced in historical documents. One of the most grisly acts was the distribution of blankets contaminated with smallpox. The blankets were given as a peace offering. Another was the forced march to "reservations"—along the Trail of Tears—which took place after the government changed its policy from genocide to population transfer. The march along the Trail of Tears took place in midwinter from the Carolinas and Georgia to Oklahoma, a journey of 1,000 miles. Fifteen thousand Cherokees were forced to make this march in light clothing. Falling from exhaustion, 4,000 people, mostly elderly and children, were left to die.

TREATIES. Because each tribe was recognized as a separate nation, the U.S. government signed treaties with each tribe. These treaties, ratified by the U.S. Senate, granted the Native Americans specified lands forever. The treaties were broken when White settlers demanded more Indian land and natural resources. In 1874, for instance, when gold was discovered in South Dakota's Black Hills, Whites flooded the reservation lands. The cavalry supported the settlers, resulting in the well-known defeat of "General" Custer at Little Big Horn in 1876 (Churchill & Vander Wall, 1990). Afterwards, the symbolic end to Native American resistance may have been the 1890 massacre at Wounded Knee, South Dakota, where the cavalry killed 300 (out of 350) Native American men, women, and children (Kitano, 1974; Olson et al., 1997).

STEREOTYPES. As noted earlier, people use stereotypes and labels to justify inhumane acts. So it was with the U.S. Indian policy. The Europeans who populated the Americas viewed Native Americans as stupid, lying, thieving, murdering, pagan "savages" (Simpson & Yinger, 1972). Killing dangerous savages was viewed as an attempt to make the world a safer place for intelligent, civilized people. Those who have written our history books labeled Whites as "pioneers," not "invaders"; their military successes, they called "victories," those of the Native Americans "massacres"; they didn't call their seizure of Native American lands "invasion," but, rather, "settling the land"; and they labeled the Native Americans' defense of their homelands against overwhelming numbers not "courageous" but "treacherous" (Josephy, 1970; Henslin, 2007b).

EDUCATION AND CULTURE CONFLICT. After the federal government moved the Native Americans to reservations, the Bureau of Indian Affairs (BIA), an agency of the federal government assigned the responsibility of overseeing Native Americans, opened schools in an attempt to "civilize" the Indians—that is, to replace the Native American cultures with that of the European Americans. The BIA opened some schools on reservations, but in an attempt to make this effort more effective, the BIA took thousands of Native American children from their parents and forced them to attend school at off-reservation boarding schools. These efforts to replace Native American culture have had lingering effects, and even today many Native Americans mistrust the intentions of White authorities.

To "civilize" Native Americans, the U.S. government forcibly took children away from their parents and placed them in Eurocentric public schools so they could learn "White" ways.

Anthropologists Murray and Rosalie Wax (1964, 1965, 1967, 1971) found that a huge cultural gap existed between the home and school lives of Native American children. The parents taught their children to be independent, but at school they were rewarded for being dependent on their teachers. Native American parents taught their children not to embarrass their peers, but their teachers expected them to correct one another in public. Geared to European middle-class values, schools prepare Native American children for a life that few will lead. Because the school system, which is based on the values of the dominant group, denigrates Native American culture and teaches concepts that are largely irrelevant to reservation life, the parents are alienated from it and refuse to visit children's schools. The teachers, alienated by the rejection of their well-intended efforts, avoid the homes of their students.

Dead center in this conflict between schools and the reservation are the children. Torn between home and school, they generally choose the family and tribe. Lacking motivation to do well in school, they tend to drop out. As the Waxes expressed it, the deck is so stacked against Native American children that they are, in effect, pushed out of school. Their continuing low rate of college graduation indicates that such contrasting orientations continue.

ECONOMIC WELL-BEING. Table 8-1 on page 248 shows how Native Americans rank on indicators of economic well-being. As you can see from this table, their income is only 60% that of Whites, while their rate of poverty is 3 times higher than that of Whites. In addition, and not shown on this table, the life expectancy of Native Americans is less than that of the nation as a whole: 1 in 4 Native Americans dies before the age of 25, compared with the national average of 1 in 7. Their suicide rate is higher than that of any other racial–ethnic group, and their rate of alcoholism runs perhaps 5 times that of the nation (Snipp & Sorkin, 1986; O'Hare, 1992; Wallace et al., 1996). It seems fair to conclude that Native American life in dominant White society is far from satisfying.

CONTEMPORARY STRUGGLES. Native Americans are sometimes called the invisible minority. Because a third of Native Americans live on reservations, half in just four states—Oklahoma, California, Arizona, and New Mexico—most Americans are hardly aware of their presence (O'Hare, 1992). In addition, for the past 100 years or so, seldom have Native Americans made headlines by disrupting the dominant culture. Today's conflicts center on Native Americans trying to enforce the treaties they made with the United States. Minor legal skirmishes have centered on maintaining traditional fishing and hunting rights. Major legal battles are being fought over demands for the waters of the Arkansas, Colorado, San Juan, and Rio Grande rivers—which were

guaranteed by the treaty. What most upsets Whites, however, are the lawsuits that Native Americans have filed to reclaim millions of acres of land ranging from New England to the Southwest. Originally Congress guaranteed these lands to Native American tribes "in **perpetuity**"—for an unlimited time, generation after generation.

The federal government's primary legal strategy has been to obstruct the justice system through postponement. In some instances, legal cases are never heard. Those who originally filed the motion die; others lose interest as proceedings drag on for years, sometimes for generations. Some tribes, however, have won legal battles. Blue Lake, in New Mexico, a heavily forested area sacred to the Taos Pueblo tribe, has been returned to the tribe. Alaskan Native Americans, primarily the Inuits and Aleuts, were awarded a cash settlement of nearly $1 billion and legal title to 40 million acres.

Because real estate ownership is titled among families for generations, clouded titles interfere with the transfer of property. Whites in affected areas are upset—and understandably so. In the state of New York, clouded titles have made it difficult for owners to sell their land even though they have owned it for 200 years (Olson, 2002). Some Whites are currently trying to strip Native Americans of their legal status as separate nations. This would remove their immunity from lawsuits. So far, such attempts have failed (Anderson & Moller, 1998).

CASINOS. In 1988, the federal government passed a law allowing Native Americans to own and operate casinos. Now over 400 tribes do so, with their casinos bringing in about $18 billion a year. This is *twice as much as all of Nevada's casinos combined* (Butterfield, 2005). The Oneida tribe of New York has 1,000 members who used to live in low-cost trailers on 32 acres. Now their casino nets $232,000 a year for *each* man, woman, and child. This tribe employs 3,000 people in its casino, hotels, convention center, gasoline stations, bars, and restaurants. Not surprisingly, poorer White neighbors have grown resentful of the tribe's affluence (Dao, 1999; Peterson, 2003). Then there are the gambling profits of the Mashantucket Pequots of Connecticut. With 800 members, this tribe brings in about $2 million *a day* just from its slot machines, even when the economy is poor (Allen, 2008; Gannon, 2008). Native Americans who are wealthy are an exception, of course, as is evident from the data reviewed in Table 8-1 (page 248).

SELF-DETERMINATION. Native Americans had no overarching term for the many tribes that inhabited North and South America. The term *Indian* was given to them by Columbus, who mistakenly thought that he had landed in India. The name stuck, and many Native Americans still use it to refer to themselves (Shively, 1999). The term *Native American* was also made up by Whites. Thinking of the 500 culturally distinct tribes as "one people," then, is a European American way of labeling. The tribes see themselves as many nations, many peoples, and they insist on the right to self-determination—to remain unassimilated in the dominant culture and to run their own affairs as separate peoples.

These many separate identities have served the dominant Whites well, for they have not had to face a united Native American population. Perhaps, then, the most significant change in this aspect of group relations is the development of **pan-Indianism.** Moving beyond identification with only a particular tribe, some Native Americans emphasize common elements that run through all of their cultures. They are trying to build a united identity and work toward the welfare of all Native Americans. If effective, national Native American organizations will develop. These groups could help force courts to push through many Native American lawsuits and develop self-help measures centering on Native American values. Pan-Indianism, however, is a controversial topic among Native Americans. Some reject it in favor of ethnic diversity, preferring to stress the many Native American histories, languages, and even musical styles (Rolo, n.d.).

Latinos (Hispanics)

ARTIFICIAL TERMS. Today the largest ethnic group in the United States is Latinos (or Hispanics). Latinos trace their origins to the Spanish-speaking countries of Latin America and Spain. Like Native Americans, few Latinos consider themselves a single people. They

think of themselves as Americans of Mexican origin (*Mexicanos* or *Chicanos*), Americans of Cuban origin (*Cubanos*), Americans from Puerto Rico (*Puertoricanos*), and so on. Nor do most identify readily with the terms *Latino* or *Hispanic*. Most consider these words to be an artificial grouping of peoples. And so they are. *Latino* and *Hispanic* are umbrella terms that lump many people into a single category. It is also important to stress that *Latino* and *Hispanic* do not refer to race, but to ethnicities. Latinos may identify themselves as African American, White, or Native American. Some even refer to themselves as *Afro Latino*.

COUNTRY OF ORIGIN. The label "Latino" applies to 25 million people from Mexico, 3 million people from Puerto Rico, 1 million from Cuba, and 5 million from Central and South America (*Statistical Abstract,* 2005, Table 40). Although most Latinos of Mexican origin live in the Southwest, most Latinos from Puerto Rico live in New York City, and those from Cuba live primarily in Florida.

UNAUTHORIZED IMMIGRANTS. Officially tallied at 37 million, the number of Latinos in the United States is considerably higher than this. Although most Latinos are U.S. citizens, about 8 million have entered the country illegally (6 million from Mexico and 2 million from Central and South America) (Passel, 2005). Each year, over 1 million people are deported to their countries of origin (*Statistical Abstract,* 2009, Table 515). Some

Latinos are the largest ethnic group made up of many different cultures.

come to the United States for temporary work and then return home. Most do not. In 1986, the federal government passed the Immigration Reform and Control Act, which permitted unauthorized immigrants to apply for U.S. citizenship. Over 3 million people applied, the vast majority from Mexico (Espenshade, 1990). Similar proposals of amnesty and citizenship are being made today. To understand better what stimulates this vast subterranean migration, see the Issues in Social Problems box on the next page.

RESIDENCE. The United States has more Latinos than Canada has Canadians. As Figure 8-5 shows, two-thirds of Latinos are concentrated in just four states—California, Texas, Florida, and New York. The migration of Latinos into the United States is so vast that Latinos have become the largest minority group in the United States. With its prominent Latino presence, Miami has been called "the capital of South America."

SPANISH. The factor that clearly distinguishes Latinos from other U.S. minorities is the Spanish language. Although not all Latinos speak Spanish, most do. About 30 million Latinos speak Spanish at home (*Statistical Abstract,* 2009, Table 52). Many cannot speak English or can do so only with difficulty. Being fluent only in Spanish in a society where English is spoken almost exclusively remains an obstacle.

Despite the 1848 Treaty of Hidalgo, which guarantees Mexicans the right to maintain their culture, from 1855 until 1968 California banned teaching any Spanish in school. In a 1974 decision (*Lau v. Nichols*), the U.S. Supreme Court ruled that using only English to teach Spanish-speaking students violated their civil rights. This decision paved the way for bilingual instruction for Spanish-speaking children. (Vidal, 1977; Lopez, 1980).

The growing use of Spanish in the classroom has become a social issue. Senator S. I. Hayakawa of Hawaii initiated an "English-only" movement in 1981. Supporters of this movement have succeeded in getting 26 states to pass a law declaring English their official language (Schaefer, 2004).

ECONOMIC WELL-BEING. Latinos fare poorly on indicators of economic well-being (see Table 8-1 on page 248). Their family income averages only three-fifths that of Whites, and they are 3 times as likely as Whites to be poor.

FIGURE 8-5 Geographic Distribution of the U.S. Latino Population

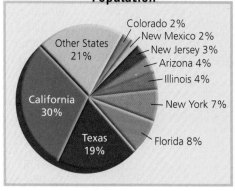

Source: By James M. Henslin. Based on *Statistical Abstract of the United States* (2008, Table 18).

Issues in Social Problems
THE ILLEGAL TRAVEL GUIDE

Manuel was a drinking buddy of Jose's, a man living in Colima, Mexico. At 45, Manuel was friendly, outgoing, and enterprising.

Manuel, who had lived in the United States for 7 years, spoke fluent English. Preferring to live in his home town in Colima, where he palled around with his childhood friends, Manuel always seemed to have money and free time.

Manuel made a decent living; he could afford a car, a luxury that none of his friends had. Manuel would sell used clothing that he had heaped in the back of his older-model Ford station wagon.

Manuel explained that he was not only selling clothing but was also lining up migrants to the United States. For $200 he would take a man to the border and introduce him to a "wolf," who, for another $200 would surreptitiously make a night crossing into the promised land.

Illegal immigration is destined to continue—unless the root causes are addressed.

Manuel stopped at one dirt-floored, thatched-roof hut. While chickens ran in and out, Manuel whispered to Juan, a slender man of about 23. Juan needed Manuel's help because the poverty in his homeland was overwhelming. Juan had a partial grade school education. He also had a wife, four hungry children under the age of 5, and two pigs—his main food supply. Although eager to work, Juan had no job, for there was simply no work available in this remote village.

Juan, borrowed every cent he could from every friend and relative he knew so he could pay Manuel $400. Although he risked losing everything if apprehended, Juan would make the trip, for wealth beckoned on the other side. He knew people who had been there and spoke glowingly of its opportunities. Manuel, of course, stoked the fires of hope.

Amidst the children playing on the dirt floor with chickens pecking about them was a man who loved his family. In order to make the desperate bid for a better life, he would suffer an enforced absence, as well as the uncertainties of a foreign land whose customs he did not know.

Juan opened his billfold, took something out, and slowly handed it to Manuel. Juan cried as he handled this piece of paper. It was his passport to the land of opportunity: a Social Security card made out in his name, sent by a friend who had already made the trip and who was waiting for Juan on the other side of the border.

Only the United States could fulfill his dream.

In addition, their unemployment rate is almost double that of Whites, and only 1 in 9 is a college graduate. At *every* level of education, whether it be a high school diploma or a doctorate, Whites earn more (*Statistical Abstract*, 2006, Table 217). In response to their position in U.S. society, some Latinos have begun a movement rejecting assimilation. Others insist on greater assimilation. Hundreds of thousands of unauthorized immigrants have taken to the streets to protest their illegal status, demanding citizenship.

POLITICS. Despite their numbers, Latinos hold only a fraction of elected positions. Because of their huge numbers, we might expect about 14 of the 100 U.S. senators to be Latino. How many are there? *Two.* Of the 435 voting representatives, 25 are Latino. Overall, of the 500,000 elected public officials in the United States, only 4,700 are Latino. Most serve at the county level or on school boards. Only 231 serve at the state level (*Statistical Abstract*, 2006, Tables 395, 404; "Some Facts . . . ," 2007). Yet, compared with the past, even these small totals represent substantial gains in political prowess.

It is likely that Latinos soon will play a larger role in U.S. politics, perhaps one day even beyond their overall numbers. This is because they are concentrated in four states that hold one-fourth of the 538 electoral votes: California (55), New York (31), Texas (34), and Florida (27). Latinos have received presidential appointments to major federal positions, such as Secretary of the Interior, Secretary of Transportation, and Secretary of Housing and Urban Development.

The potential power of Latinos has not been realized because of divisions based on national point of origin. These distinctions nourish disunity and create disagreements about social and economic policy. As mentioned, Latinos do not think of themselves as a single people, and national origin is highly significant. People from Puerto Rico, for example, feel little sense of unity with people from Mexico. It is similarly the case with those from Venezuela, Colombia, or El Salvador. Latinos from rural and urban areas also have different cultural traditions and, often, political views. It used to be the same with Europeans who immigrated from Germany and Sweden or from England and France. With time, however, the importance of identifying with the country of origin was lost and they came to think of themselves exclusively as Americans. Perhaps this will happen to Latinos as well.

Social class divisions also obstruct unity among Latinos. In some cases, even when they come from the same country, the differences in their backgrounds are severe. Most of the half million Cubans who fled their homeland after Fidel Castro came to power in 1959 were well-educated, financially comfortable professionals or businesspeople. The 100,000 "boat people" who arrived 20 years later, in contrast, were mainly lower-class refugees to whom the earlier arrivals would hardly have spoken in Cuba. The earlier arrivals have prospered in Florida and control many businesses and financial institutions: There continues to be a vast division between them and the more recent immigrants.

African Americans

It was 1955, in Montgomery, Alabama. As specified by law, Whites took the front seats of the bus, while Blacks went to the back. As the bus filled up, Blacks had to give up their seats to Whites.

When Rosa Parks, a 42-year-old African American woman and secretary of the Montgomery NAACP, was told she would have to stand so White folks could sit, she refused. She sat there stubbornly while the bus driver fumed, Whites felt insulted, and Blacks, observing from the back of the bus, also wondered what she was doing.

Mrs. Parks was arrested. Instead of passing as an incident of little importance, her arrest touched off mass demonstrations. Fifty thousand Blacks boycotted the city's buses for a year and thrust onto the stage of history Rev. Martin Luther King, Jr. He was an unknown preacher who had majored in sociology at Morehouse College in Atlanta, Georgia.

Dr. King, who was later murdered in Memphis, Tennessee, preached nonviolence. Incensed at King, segregationists bombed homes and churches.

CIVIL DISOBEDIENCE AND AMERICAN APARTHEID. In 1944, the U.S. Supreme Court decided that African Americans could vote in southern primaries. Just one year earlier the Court had ruled that African Americans had the legal right to attend public schools with Whites. Before this, they had to go to "colored" schools. During the 1950s, the South was practicing a form of apartheid. African Americans,

Rosa Parks is fingerprinted by police Lt. D. H. Lackey in Montgomery, Alabama, on February 22, 1956, two months after refusing to give up her seat on a bus for a white passenger. She was arrested with several others who violated segregation laws. Parks's refusal to give up her seat led to a yearlong boycott of buses by blacks, a tactic organized by the Rev. Dr. Martin Luther King, Jr., which ended after the U.S. Supreme Court deemed that all segregation was unlawful on December 20, 1956.

Dr. Martin Luther King, Jr. rallies the masses for equal rights while speaking outside the walls of an all-white college in 1965. The crowd gathered around the main gate of the school to hear the Nobel Peace Prize winner speak.

then called Negroes, were not allowed to stay at hotels or to eat in restaurants that Whites patronized. They had to use separate toilets, water fountains, and swimming pools. Virginia and South Carolina still had laws prohibiting marriage between Blacks and Whites (O'Hare, 1992). These were struck down in 1967.

In order to break institutional barriers supporting American apartheid, King led African Americans in **civil disobedience,** deliberately but peacefully disobeying laws considered unjust. Inspired by the writings of Henry David Thoreau and the acts of Mahatma Gandhi, King (1958) based his strategy on these principles:

1. actively resisting evil, but nonviolently
2. not seeking to defeat or humiliate opponents, but seeking instead to win their friendship and understanding
3. attacking the forces of evil rather than the people who are doing the evil
4. being willing to accept suffering without retaliating
5. refusing to hate the opponent
6. acting with the conviction that the universe is on the side of justice

King found no overnight success, but he and his followers persisted. Gradually the barriers did come down. In 1964 Congress passed the Civil Rights Act, making it illegal to discriminate in hotels, theaters, and other public places. Then, in 1965, the Voting Rights Act banned literacy tests that Whites had used to keep African Americans from voting.

Encouraged by these gains, African Americans experienced **rising expectations;** that is, they expected better conditions to follow right away. The lives of poor African Americans, however, changed little, if at all. Frustrations built, finally exploding in Watts in 1965, when residents of this central Los Angeles ghetto took to the streets in the first "urban revolt." The violence, which occurred despite the protests of Dr. King, precipitated a White backlash that threatened the interracial coalition that King had spearheaded. Congress refused to enact civil rights legislation in both 1967 and 1968. When King was assassinated on April 4, 1968, ghettos across the nation erupted in fiery violence. Under threat of the destruction of the nation's cities, Congress reluctantly passed the sweeping Civil Rights Act of 1968.

MILITANCY. After King's death, Black militants rushed in to fill the void in leadership. Like King, they emphasized Black unity and Black pride, but, unlike King, some of them proclaimed that violent confrontation was the way to gain equality. Flashed across the nation's television screens were images of the Black Panthers, brandishing rifles and parading in military-style uniforms. The statements and acts of Black militants stirred up fear and hostility among Whites. As a result, the authorities turned violently on the most outspoken leaders. Some were assassinated in nighttime raids, shot to death in their beds while sleeping.

With violence turned against them—and photos of the bloodied bodies circulating in the mass media—leadership became fragmented. Some argued for secession from the United States, others for total integration. Leaders also disagreed over whether violent confrontation, or peaceful protest, was the way to go. In the end, those who made the case for integration and political action won. As more moderate approaches replaced militancy, even the Black Panthers changed their tactics. Instead of challenging White authority and confronting police, they switched to productive techniques—providing breakfasts for schoolchildren and running for political office. Lacking a charismatic leader to replace King, the momentum that had propelled the struggle for equality faded.

POLITICS. Change has been gradual, but over time the change has been measurable. Today's race relations are vastly different from those that Rosa Parks experienced when she refused to

move to the back of the bus. The change, however, has come with positive and negative consequences. On a positive note, the governor of Massachusetts and the mayors of many major U.S. cities are now African American. Of the nation's 435 representatives, 42 are African American. And 9,000 African Americans hold lower-level political office, including over 600 at the state level (*Statistical Abstract,* 2006, Tables 395, 403; "Some Facts . . . ," 2007). Because African Americans make up about 12% of the U.S. population, though, we would expect about 12 African American senators. But since Reconstruction, there have been only 3 African American senators, never more than one serving at a time. In 2008, the third of these, Barack Obama, was elected president of the United States—the first African American to hold this powerful office. And in 2009, Eric Holder became the first African American U.S. attorney general. Although far from equitable, compared to the past, this change in political representation means African Americans have made substantial gains in the U.S. political system.

EDUCATION. In one of the ironies of race relations, the path-breaking 1954 Supreme Court decision to integrate U.S. schools led to schools becoming even more segregated. Following the 1954 decision, Whites fled the cities and relocated in all-White suburbs. Others remained in the city but opened all-White private schools. In Atlanta, Georgia, for example, "White flight" changed the school system from 55% White to 90% Black (Stevens, 1980). As White flight continued, most schools of the major U.S. cities became primarily African American. Facing this unanticipated result of the 1954 decision, in 1986 courts across the nation began to ease up on desegregation rulings. The result of these court actions has been the same as the 1954 ruling: even greater segregation (Frankenberg & Lee, 2002).

Barack Obama, the nation's first African American president, is pictured here with his family before delivering his victory speech to a crowd of some 200,000 supporters in Grant Park in Chicago at an election night rally.

African Americans, however, have made strong gains in education. The percentage of African Americans attending college increased from 43% in 1980 to 62% in 1998. Since then, however, the numbers have declined, and today 56% of African Americans who graduate from high school go to college (*Statistical Abstract,* 2009, Table 267). The reasons for this setback are uncertain, but it is ominous. To continue their hard-won economic gains, African Americans must reverse this decline: It is college graduates who enter the better-paying positions and join the middle class. Because African Americans are more likely than Whites to drop out of high school and now less likely to attend college than just a few years ago, a smaller proportion of African Americans will be prepared to compete in the job market.

RACE OR SOCIAL CLASS? A SOCIOLOGICAL DEBATE. The overall changes are stunning when one realizes that in the 1950s Whites in some areas kept African Americans from voting, forced them to sit at the back of the bus, refused to serve them in restaurants, and would not allow them to attend "their" schools. With progress made by African Americans in education, employment, politics, and legislation, the question is now whether race still underlies the relations between African Americans and Whites. Some sociologists have suggested that, rather than race, the significant factor is now social class.

This argument is evident in the following excerpt:

> In Westland, Michigan, the residents of Annapolis Park—a subdivision of expensive homes owned by African Americans—banded together to keep out White neighbors. The city council had voted to allow the construction of a trailer park near the Annapolis Park neighborhood. Residents of this neighborhood protested against the trailer park, in which Whites would live, because of the social class of the Whites, not their race–ethnicity. As one Annapolis Park homeowner said: "Let's face it. These are going to be lower-class Whites. You wouldn't want a $15,000 [trailer] home next to your place, would you?" (Associated Press, February 5, 1981).

Sociologist William Wilson (1978) put the matter this way: "Race relations in America have undergone fundamental changes in recent years, so much so that the life chances of individual Blacks have more to do with their economic class position than with their day-to-day encounters with whites." Wilson uses the term **social class** to refer to "any group of people who have more or less similar goods, services, or skills to offer for income in a given economic order and who therefore receive similar financial remuneration in the market-place." He says that the changes have been so great that social class, not race, is what most determines African Americans' **life chances**—their quality of life and experiences. Neither Wilson nor any other sociologist denies that race–ethnicity is significant in social life today, just that social class is more significant.

Wilson (1978, 1987) points out that social class now separates African Americans into two main groups—those with money and those without. Official statistics support this. Most African Americans are not poor. The African American middle class has expanded so greatly that it now holds 3 times the proportion of African Americans that it held in 1940. One of every three African American families makes more than $50,000 a year. Yet there is opposing evidence as well. One of every four African American families makes less than $15,000 a year (*Statistical Abstract,* 2009, Table 671). These figures indicate a division of African Americans into the "haves" and the "have-nots" and, with this, two contrasting worlds.

One world consists of middle-class incomes. People in this category work at jobs that offer advancement, earn good incomes and benefits, and live in middle-class suburbs or in exclusive areas of the city. They face little crime, and their children, who go to better schools, are motivated to go to college and prepare for careers. Not sociologically surprising, those who become successful believe in the "American dream."

The second category consists of those who are stuck in poverty in the inner city. Violent crime is a part of life, schools are terrible, jobs are dead-end, and they feel despair, apathy, or hostility. The aspirations and values of these two groups are very different.

Many sociologists take hearty exception to the idea that social class has replaced racial oppression. They say that this analysis misses one vital element, the discrimination that continues to underlie the relative deprivation of African Americans. They emphasize that at *all* levels of work—whether among factory workers, managers, or supervisors—an income gap separates African Americans and Whites. They point out that without exception Whites earn more. They also point out that at every level of educational attainment, whether it be a high school diploma or a doctorate, Whites earn more (*Statistical Abstract,* 2006, Table 217). Both Wilson and his critics agree that an African American child's chance of growing up poor is much greater than that of a White child. In Wilson's view, however, social class, not racial–ethnic discrimination, is mainly responsible for perpetuating this situation.

It seems fair to conclude that each position is valid. It is likely that both discrimination and a disadvantaged social class position contribute to fewer life chances. Those who are poor face far fewer opportunities and much greater discrimination; those who enjoy an advantaged class position face more opportunities and considerably less discrimination.

Asian Americans

It was a quiet Sunday morning, December 7, 1941, a day destined to live in infamy, as President Roosevelt was later to say.

At dawn, waves of Japanese bombers began an attack on Pearl Harbor, the United States' major naval station in the Pacific Ocean. At Oahu, Hawaii, the Japanese pilots found the U.S. Pacific Fleet anchored in shallow waters, unprepared for battle. The Americans were sitting ducks.

In response, the United States declared war on Japan, entering World War II and leaving no American untouched. Some left home to battle overseas; others left their farms to work in factories that supported the war effort. All lived with the rationing of food, gasoline, sugar, coffee, and other essentials.

In 1942, Japanese Americans were considered a threat to the security of the United States. They were taken from their homes and moved to internment camps.

DETENTION CAMPS. This event touched Americans of Japanese descent in a special way. Just as waves of planes flew over Pearl Harbor, so waves of suspicion and hostility surrounded the 110,000 Japanese Americans who called the United States "home." Overnight, Japanese Americans became the most detested racial–ethnic group in the country (Daniels, 1975). Many Americans feared that Japan would invade the United States and that Japanese Americans would sabotage military installations on the West Coast. Although not a single Japanese American had committed even one act of sabotage, on February 1, 1942, President Franklin Roosevelt signed Executive Order 9066, authorizing the removal of people considered threats to military areas. All people on the West Coast who were *one-eighth* Japanese or more were jailed in detention centers called "relocation camps." These people were charged with no crime; they were neither indicted nor given a trial. Having a Japanese great-grandmother on either your mother's or father's side of the family was sufficient reason to be put in prison.

DISCRIMINATION AGAINST CHINESE. This was not the first time that Asian Americans encountered discrimination. For years, differences in appearance and lifestyle had prompted Americans of European background to discriminate against Americans of Asian ancestry. Lured by gold strikes in the West and a huge need for unskilled labor, about 200,000 Chinese immigrated between 1850 and 1880. There was a rush to unite the West with the East, and the Chinese were put to work building the transcontinental railroad. Although 90% of the workers for the Central Pacific Railroad were Chinese, when the famous golden spike was driven at Promontory, Utah, in 1869 to mark the joining of the Union Pacific and the Central Pacific railroads, White workers prevented the Chinese from being present (Hsu, 1971). After the railroad was finished, many Chinese settled in the West. To intimidate their new competition, White workers formed mobs and vigilante groups to move them out.

As fears of "alien genes and germs" grew, legislators passed anti-Chinese laws (Schrieke, 1936). In 1850, the California legislature passed the Foreign Miner's Act, levying a special tax on Chinese (and Latinos) of $20 a month. At this time, the average Chinese person made a dollar a day. The Chief Justice of the California Supreme Court ruled that Chinese could not testify against Whites in court (Carlson & Colburn, 1972). In 1882 Congress passed the Chinese Exclusion Act, suspending all Chinese immigration for 10 years. Four years later, the Statue of Liberty was dedicated. The tired, the poor, and the huddled masses it was to welcome obviously did not include the Chinese.

Facing such severe discrimination, Chinese immigrants depended on one another, forming segregated communities known as "Chinatowns." Four stages were involved in their development (Yuan, 1963). The first was *involuntary segregation:* Discrimination forced the immigrants into separate living areas. The second was *defensive insulation:* The immigrants banded together for mutual help. The third was *voluntary segregation:* They chose to remain in the segregated community because that was where their friends and relatives lived. They avoided language barriers, and they could follow their customs and religion (Buddhism). The final stage, now in process, is *gradual assimilation:* As the Chinese become acculturated, individuals are now moving out of Chinatown and into mainstream culture.

DISCRIMINATION AGAINST JAPANESE. When the Japanese first began to immigrate, they met spillover bigotry that had been directed against the Chinese. They also confronted discriminatory laws. Even the U.S. Constitution became a tool that was used against them. Initially a document that allowed only Whites to be citizens, the Constitution was amended in the 1860s to include African Americans (Amott & Matthaei, 1991). Because Asians had not been named in the amendments, the Supreme Court ruled that this prohibited them from becoming citizens (Schaefer, 2004). This ruling provided an opportunity for California politicians. In 1913, they passed the Alien Land Act, prohibiting anyone who was ineligible for citizenship from owning land. (Most Native Americans were not granted citizenship in their own land until 1924; the Chinese gained citizenship in 1943; for those born in Japan, the exclusion remained until 1952.)

DIVERSITY. Contrary to media stereotypes that prevail in our society, the 12 million Asian Americans living in the U.S. are diverse. As you can see from Figure 8-6, they come from many different lands. As a result, Asian Americans are divided by many cultural heritages, including different languages and religions. Half of Asian Americans live in the western states, 1 of 3 in California (*Statistical Abstract*, 2006, Tables 23, 24). The two largest groups of Asian Americans, those of Chinese and Filipino descent, are concentrated in New York City, Los Angeles, San Diego, San Francisco, and Honolulu. The third largest group, those of Asian Indian descent, are the most geographically dispersed.

REASONS FOR SUCCESS. As you can see, like the terms *Latino* (*Hispanic*) and *Native American,* the category "Asian American" also lumps a lot of different groups together. As a result, any "average" that is computed for Asian Americans conceals a lot of differences. As you saw on Table 8-1 on page 248, the average family income of Asian Americans is higher than that of Whites, and their poverty is only 9%. Sociologists, however, stress that the income and poverty of Asian Americans differ according to country of origin: Poverty is the greatest among the Cambodians and the Hmong and least among those whose origin is China and Japan (Lee, 1998; Zhou & Xiong, 2005). Many of the Chinese who live in the urban settlements known as "Chinatowns" face the usual problems of ghetto poverty: poor health, high suicide rates, poor working conditions, and poor housing conditions.

One general conclusion that we can make, with the caution just indicated, is that most Asian Americans are remarkably successful. The general economic success of Asian Americans seems to be rooted in three factors: family life, education, and assimilation.

Of all racial–ethnic groups, including Whites, Asian American children are the most likely to grow up with two parents. The divorce rate of Asian Americans is low, less than half the rate of Whites (Reeves & Bennett, 2003). They also are the least likely to be born to single mothers (Lee, 1998; Zhou & Xiong, 2005). Most Asian American children grow up in close-knit families where they are socialized with values that stimulate cohesiveness and high motivation to succeed (Bell, 1991). Within a framework of strictness and constraints, they are taught self-discipline, thrift, and industry (Suzuki, 1985). This early socialization provides strong impetus for educational attainment and successful assimilation.

FIGURE 8-6 **The Country of Origin of Asian Americans**

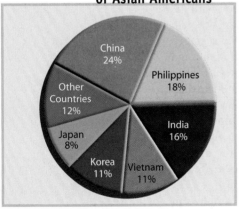

Source: By James M. Henslin. Based on *Statistical Abstract of the United States* (2006, Table 24).

Asian Americans are the most likely of any racial–ethnic group in the United States to complete college. Asian Americans have the highest intermarriage rate of any minority group: About 2 of 5 marry someone who is not an Asian American. Asian Americans are also the most likely to live in integrated neighborhoods (Lee, 1998). Japanese Americans are the most assimilated and financially successful (Bell, 1991). About 75% report that their best friend is of another race.

POLITICS. Although integrated, Asian Americans are underrepresented in U.S. politics. With their percentage in the population, we could expect 17 of the nation's 435 representatives and 4 senators to be Asian Americans. The actual numbers are well below that: 7 and 2 ("Some Facts . . . ," 2007). They are becoming more prominent in state politics, however. With 60% of its citizens being Asian American, Hawaii has elected Asian American governors and sent several Asian American senators to Washington (Lee, 1998; *Statistical Abstract*, 2006, Table 395). The first Asian American governor outside of Hawaii was Gary Locke, who in 1996 was elected governor of Washington. In 2008, Bobby Jindal became the second Asian American and the first Indian American governor when he was elected in Louisiana, a state in which Asian Americans make up less than 2% of the population.

Social Policy

Although the goal of a unified society is desired, we have more than adequate experience to know that it is futile to attempt to use our social institutions to force everyone into a White mold. Accordingly, it seems reasonable for social policy to center on the twin goals of encouraging cultural pluralism and preventing discrimination.

Encouraging Cultural Pluralism

APPRECIATING DIFFERENT BACKGROUNDS. The first goal of social policy encouraging cultural pluralism is "cultural integrity"—that is, an appreciation of different backgrounds. Here are steps to such progress:

1. establishing national, state, and local "cultural centers" that feature a group's heritage
2. holding "ethnic appreciation days" in public schools, where ethnic customs, dress, dances, history, and food are featured
3. teaching history (and all courses with an historical emphasis) in ways that recognize the contributions of the many groups that make up the United States
4. teaching foreign languages in our public schools, from grade school through high school—starting early enough that all students would learn two foreign languages

The first two suggestions are easy to implement and go a long way toward encouraging appreciation of cultural differences and pride in one's own heritage. Because of segregation in our urban schools, there should be cultural exchanges among public and private schools. There should be a changed emphasis in how we train teachers. For this proposal to be effective, the approach must be honest. Students will see through dishonest attempts to appear multicultural. Lastly, with the technical capacity for teaching foreign languages that we now have, students and teachers can be taught other languages. With the lowering of cultural boundaries and the development of a global society, the learning of other languages would benefit the nation as a whole.

PRIDE AND PARTICIPATION. Although one of the emphases of cultural pluralism is pride in one's own racial–ethnic heritage, this does not mean a retreat into one's racial–ethnic culture. Like members of the dominant group, members of minority groups need to be prepared to compete within dominant White institutions. Although children of minority groups should be encouraged to take pride in their rich heritage, like the children of the dominant group, they, too, need to become proficient at English and other basic skills that make them competitive in the marketplace. The school system is uniquely situated to equip them with these tools. Without the ability

to speak English, members of minority groups find themselves at a severe disadvantage in meeting their number one need—competing with Whites for jobs, especially positions that pay well and offer advancement.

Preventing Discrimination

USING THE LEGAL SYSTEM. Preventing discrimination involves using the legal system to ensure that minorities are not discriminated against in jobs, housing, education, or any other area of life. This requires that local, state, and federal governments participate. The Civil Rights Act of 1964, which forbids discrimination by race, color, creed, national origin, and sex, must be enforced. This law applies to unions, employment agencies, and, as amended in 1972, all businesses with 15 or more employees. This law also prohibits discrimination in voting, public accommodations, federally supported programs, and federally supported institutions such as colleges and hospitals. Preventing discrimination also requires funding the Equal Employment Opportunity Commission (EEOC)—the organization that is empowered to investigate complaints of discrimination and to recommend action to the Department of Justice.

EDUCATION VOUCHERS. As described earlier, "White flight" was a common reaction to forced integration in the public school system. U.S. parents have the right to send their children to any school they can afford, and this right needs to be protected. Although controversial, there is an effective solution to White flight. If education vouchers in the amount of the average cost per student in a district's schools were given to each student, their parents could choose any school they wanted their children to attend, private or public. Some voucher programs already exist, but none as generous as this suggestion. All schools, without exception, must be open to students of any racial–ethnic background.

The Dilemma of Affirmative Action

THE _BAKKE_ CASE. The Civil Rights Act of 1964 posed a dilemma: How do we make up for past discrimination without creating new discrimination? In the _Bakke_ case (1973), Allan Bakke argued that he was denied admission to the medical school of the University of California at Davis. Bakke sued when he learned that the school had admitted African Americans, Asian Americans, and Latinos who had scored lower than he had on the entrance exam and who had lower grade point averages than his. Bakke argued that had he been a member of a minority group he would have been admitted (Sindler, 1978). In other words, the university was racist—it had discriminated against him because he was White. The U.S. Supreme Court ruled that the Davis medical school had to admit Bakke because they had used illegal quotas.

CLOUDY GUIDANCE. Following the _Bakke_ case, the U.S. Supreme Court handed down a very inconsistent ruling: Colleges cannot use quotas to determine whom they admit, but they can use race as a factor to create a diverse student body (Walsh, 1996). In the 1989 precedent-setting _City of Richmond_ decision, the Court ruled that state and local governments "must almost always avoid racial quotas" in awarding construction contracts. "Almost always" left everyone confused about where and when and in what ways preferential treatment was or was not constitutional.

PROPOSITION 209. With the U.S. Supreme Court handing out cloudy guidance, national debate continued. Few were fond of affirmative action, but no one saw alternatives to erase the consequences of past discrimination. Then during the 1990s, the tide turned against affirmative action, with a series of rulings by circuit courts and the U.S. Supreme Court. Perhaps the most significant development was _Proposition 209,_ a 1996 amendment to the California state constitution that banned race and gender preferences in hiring and college admissions. Despite appeals by a coalition of civil rights groups, the U.S. Supreme Court upheld the California law.

THE UNIVERSITY OF MICHIGAN CASE. Another significant ruling was made in 2003. White applicants who had been denied admission to the University of Michigan claimed that they had been discriminated against because applicants from underrepresented minority groups had been given extra points just for being members of a minority. Again, the Court's ruling was ambiguous. The Court ruled that universities can give minorities an edge in admissions, but they cannot use an automatic system to do so. Race can be a "plus factor," but in the Court's words, there must be "a meaningful individualized review of applicants."

Such a confusing ruling left university officials—and, by extension, those in business and other public and private agencies—puzzled. Trying to increase racial–ethnic diversity is constitutional, but using quotas and mechanical systems is not. Michigan voters didn't like this ambiguity, and in 2006 they amended their constitution to make it illegal to use race–ethnicity (or gender) in college admissions (Walsh, 2004).

Absent constitutional amendments like those in Michigan and California, states that want to use race–ethnicity in college admissions must follow the Supreme Court's decision. Because the Court's ruling provides no specific guidelines and its University of Michigan ruling remains open to interpretation, we obviously have not yet heard the final word from the U.S. Supreme Court on this topic. And what we hear will likely depend not on the Constitution, which in this matter is open to contradictory interpretations, but, rather, on the political makeup of the Court.

Principles for Improving Relations

Social policies should follow sound sociological principles. The principles developed by social psychologist Gordon Allport (Pettigrew, 1976) provide a basic map for developing fair social policies:

1. People of different racial–ethnic backgrounds should have equal status (similar income and education for example). The occupants of interracial housing, for example, should have similar incomes.
2. People in interethnic contact should work together. Parents from different racial–ethnic backgrounds, for example, should work together to improve their children's school.
3. To achieve equality, groups must demonstrate cooperative dependence. For example, to improve an integrated school system, voters from different racial–ethnic groups must confer on how they vote.
4. Authority, law, and custom should support interaction among groups; when authorities stand behind school integration, for example, positive interaction among the groups is more likely.

The Future of the Problem

PROGRESS. Most Americans today reject the patterns of discrimination that were taken for granted in earlier times or that were assumed to be morally correct. Progress has been inconsistent and backwards at times, but the result has been expanding opportunities for minority groups. Even with our hesitant progress, huge gaps remain between our ideals of equality and the reality of racial–ethnic relations as we actually experience them. The United States has slowly moved toward greater equality, yet has much room for improvement.

World War II was especially significant for improving racial–ethnic relations in the United States. Prior to the war, the U.S. government was dominated by racist policies. During the war hundreds of thousands of African Americans migrated from the South to the North looking for work. Although they fought in all-Black units at this time, the several hundred thousand African American soldiers, dislodged from the segregation of home, were thrust into unexpected cultural experiences. Exposed to new ways of life in Europe, they returned home with visions of positive change. After the war, the federal

government, moving gradually from segregation to integration and social equality, broke many of the institutional barriers that had been directed against minorities. The future will not likely bring a return of the barriers that existed prior to World War II.

AN ONGOING STRUGGLE. Barriers to equality do remain, however, and racial–ethnic relations are haunted by them. Affirmative action was designed to overcome these barriers, but, as you know, it has come under heavy attack. By their very nature, court rulings are victories for one and defeat for the other. The disappointment is especially severe when the two sides hold incompatible philosophical positions. Inconsistent and vague court rulings, however, breed confusion. With effective mechanisms to remedy inequalities yet to be developed, the proper role of affirmative action in a multicultural society is likely to remain center stage for quite some time.

The major struggle in racial–ethnic relations will continue to revolve around equal employment. Access to careers determines much of people's quality of life. Removing structural barriers and increasing education will help ease conflict. Increasingly, workers must be prepared to compete in a world that demands more technical expertise. What occurs in education, then, is of vital importance for the future of racial–ethnic relations.

DISPARITIES IN EDUCATION. Education is the key to improving racial–ethnic relations. For most Americans, education holds the key to the future. Those who receive the better education get the better jobs and enjoy the more satisfying lifestyles. Any group that receives less schooling than the national average faces disadvantages in our technological society.

Granted this principle, then, look at Table 8-3. You can see that the rate of college graduation of Asian Americans far exceeds that of other groups: It is about 4 times higher than that of Latinos and Native Americans, and 3 times that of Native Americans, 3 times that of African Americans, and more than half as much as Whites. Note also that although the number of Asian Americans is less than a third that of Latinos, they earn almost twice the number of doctorates. This high achievement in education brightens the future for Asian Americans, opening doors to professions and managerial positions.

From the same table and for the same reasons, we conclude that the future looks good for Whites and African Americans and poor for Latinos and Native Americans. Nonetheless, the decline in the percentage of African Americans attending college must be addressed.

TABLE 8-3 Race–Ethnicity and Education

Racial–Ethnic Group	EDUCATION		COMPLETED		DOCTORATES		
	Less than High School	High School	Some College	College (BA or Higher)	Number Awarded	Percentage of all U.S. Doctorates	Percentage of U.S. Population
Whites	14.6%	30.0%	28.5%	27.0%	26,905	81.0%	68.0%
Latinos	47.6	22.1	19.9	10.5	1,432	4.3	13.7
Country or Area of Origin							
South America	23.8	24.0	27.0	25.2	NA	NA	
Cuba	37.0	20.0	21.7	21.2	NA	NA	
Puerto Rico	36.7	26.2	24.6	12.5	NA	NA	
Central America	54.0	19.1	17.4	9.5	NA	NA	
Mexico	54.2	20.9	17.5	7.5	NA	NA	
African Americans	20.0	35.2	27.4	17.3	2,397	7.2	12.2
Asian Americans	16.8	18.9	21.3	43.1	2,317	7.0	4.1
Native Americans	29.1	29.2	30.2	11.5	180	0.5	0.8

Source: By James M. Henslin. Based on *Statistical Abstract of the United States* (2005, Tables 34, 37, 38, 41, 283) and Figure 8-2 of this text.

Indicators of economic well-being shown in Table 8-1 on page 248 are related to education. Note from this table how closely each group's relative well-being in income and poverty matches its attainment in education. It isn't difficult to figure out why, since we all know that education opens doors of opportunity, and the lack of education closes them. Obviously, we need policies that produce greater educational achievement. To develop these policies, we suggest the funding of a "think tank" composed of top educators from various racial–ethnic groups, whose purpose will be to propose fair policies. There likely are already sufficient studies of multicultural education success stories. The "think tank" would suggest creative, testable policies.

AN UNDERCLASS. Some have severe reservations that, as a nation, we even want to change minority access to equal education. A disturbing possibility is that we have a permanent **underclass** (W. J. Wilson, 1978, 1987). That is, society may already have thrown up its collective hands and consigned to the ghetto an underclass that will endure. This alienated group, especially visible in our inner cities, has little education, lives primarily in single-parent families, and has high rates of violent crime, drug abuse, disease, births to single mothers, and death by murder. These self-defeating behaviors keep them from succeeding in mainstream society.

Unless social policy reaches this underclass, the tragic cycle will perpetuate. Many of the children born in those conditions will be fated to repeat their parents' behaviors. A primary structural factor that makes this sorry possibility likely is that most jobs are located in the suburbs. Those who live in the urban ghettos lack the means of transportation to reach those jobs and the financial ability to move closer to them.

These conditions carry severe implications for society as a whole. When large groups of people remain isolated from mainstream society, receive a meager education, can't get jobs, and are denied proper police protection, collective violence may result. With little being done about the problems of inner cities, it is likely that there will be turmoil. More riots, then, are likely, and at some point we may see a repeat of the 1992 riots in Los Angeles.

MILITANCY. Militants, whether from a minority group or the dominant group, are an unpredictable factor in future racial–ethnic relations. Although racial–ethnic pride is applaudable—as discussed in the social policy section, such pride should be encouraged—

After White LAPD police officers were cleared of charges that they had used excessive force when they beat Rodney King in the process of arresting him, riots broke out in Los Angeles. Demonstrators around the country protested what many viewed as racially motivated brutality upon the African American Rodney King by the White officers.

some people mistake pride as hatred of others. Any group, no matter its racial–ethnic background, that preaches hatred intends to create significant divisions by building on hostilities and negative stereotypes. The resurgence of the Ku Klux Klan indicates that racism is still alive and well in our country. Occasional outbursts by such hate groups, though dramatic, will pose no serious threat to those working toward a future of equality.

THE AMERICAN DILEMMA. In 1944, Gunnar Myrdal (1898–1987), a sociologist from Sweden, wrote that the United States was caught between two major forces. In his classic, *An American Dilemma,* Myrdal contrasted the "American creed," expressed in Christian ethics and the Declaration of Independence, with the un-Christian and undemocratic behavior he observed. Myrdal was confident that Americans could resolve racial tensions by adopting favorable values. Myrdal's prediction was right, and conditions are remarkably better today than they were in the 1940s.

Valleys of hatred and despair follow peaks of goodwill and high hopes. We have seen this in the past, and the future will bring more of the same. Although as individuals we have little power or influence, our actions, collectively, are significant. Ultimately, these actions give shape to racial–ethnic relations. None of us can overcome structural barriers alone, yet, together, we can dismantle them. C. Wright Mills realized we can help to create a more positive future through collective efforts.

SUMMARY AND REVIEW

1. *Discrimination* occurs worldwide, as *racial–ethnic groups* living in the same society struggle for dominance. *Dominant groups* develop *ideologies* and *stereotypes* to support their dominance.

2. *Minority groups* share five characteristics: unequal treatment, distinctive traits, solidarity, membership by birth, and marriage within their own group. Minority groups have four objectives: *pluralism, assimilation, secession,* and *militancy.* Five objectives of dominant groups are *assimilation, multiculturalism (pluralism), population transfer, continued subjugation,* and *genocide.*

3. Although the idea of *race* is significant in human behavior, biologically speaking, no human group represents a "pure race."

4. Discrimination is a life-and-death matter, affecting both the quality of life and mortality rates.

5. *Individual discrimination* consists of overt acts by individuals. *Institutional discrimination* is discrimination that is built into the social system.

6. Symbolic interactionists focus on how symbols of race–ethnicity divide people and influence their behavior, particularly how they affect perception, sort people into different life experiences, and justify discrimination and violence. Functionalists analyze functions of discrimination, such as fostering *ethnocentrism* and ensuring that society's *dirty work* gets done. They also analyze its dysfunctions, such as destroying human

potential. Marxist conflict theorists stress that racial–ethnic divisions among workers help capitalists control workers and increase their profits.

7. Discrimination in the United States is especially severe for Native Americans, Latinos, and African Americans. Members of these groups have less education, higher unemployment, lower incomes, and higher rates of poverty than Whites and Asian Americans. The pressures that these groups have placed on White-controlled social institutions have forced social change. Asian Americans have made the most social and economic gains—primarily through assimilation and family values that stress hard work, thrift, and education.

8. Major cleavages along social class lines divide U.S. racial–ethnic groups. Some sociologists argue that *social class* has become more significant than race–ethnicity in determining an individual's *life chances.*

9. Social policies should encourage cultural pluralism and prevent discrimination. Groups that attain the most education have the brightest future. The major struggle is over jobs. Dilemmas over affirmative action continue.

10. With the creation of an *underclass,* we can expect urban riots. In no foreseeable future will *prejudice* and discrimination be eliminated. A storm cloud on the horizon is the resurgence of groups that preach division and hatred.

KEY TERMS

THINKING CRITICALLY ABOUT CHAPTER 8

1. On page 242 is a list of five characteristics that minority groups share. Pick any minority group in the United States and give examples of how these five characteristics apply to that group.

2. On pages 242–243 is a list of four objectives of minority groups. Explain how each objective applies to African Americans, to Asian Americans, to Latinos, and to Native Americans. Do these groups emphasize these objectives in the same way? If not, why do you think there are differences?

3. Which of the six policies of dominant groups that Simpson and Yinger identify (pp. 243–244) do you

think that Whites are directing toward African Americans? Toward Native Americans? Toward Latinos? Toward Asian Americans?

4. What is your opinion about the laws against hate speech? Do you think that these laws should be eliminated or that they should be strengthened and enforced? Explain.

5. Which of the three sociological perspectives (symbolic interactionism, functionalism, or conflict theory) do you think best explains why prejudice and discrimination exist in the United States? Explain.

MySocLab

What can you find in MySocLab? mysoclab ALLYN & BACON Where learning & the sociological imagination intersect. www.mysoclab.com

- Complete Ebook
- Practice Tests and Exams
- Multimedia Activities
- Mapping and Data Analysis Exercises

- Research and Writing Advice
- Interactive Social Surveys
- Sociology in the News

CHAPTER 9

Inequalities of Gender and Sexual Orientation

Let's examine a birth scene in India—which would ordinarily be considered a happy event.

> Just outside the delivery room of a Delhi hospital, the expectant mother's family keeps vigil. The woman's husband is smoking and playing cards with the men. They tell a few jokes and laugh. None of the men mentions what everyone knows might happen. The women are knitting and recalling their own deliveries. They, too, don't bring up the taboo topic, although all are thinking about it.
>
> When the nurse brings the news, everyone falls silent. Faces drop—the newborn is a girl. Some relatives console the father; others curse the mother.

This scene is familiar in India. The birth of a son is seen as a gift from God; the birth of a daughter, at best, a disappointment.

> ## Strangling baby girls . . . might be a thing of the past.

An Indian girl stands little chance of earning money for her family. In Hindu society almost all women are expected to remain at home with their family. Jobs for women, especially uneducated women, are few—and most Indian women are uneducated.

The act of **female infanticide** represents the most awful consequence of gender discrimination in the world. Female infanticide persists, especially in India's tens of thousands of tradition-locked villages. As a result, many girls face early death.

Female infanticide is not uncommon, although authorities seldom document specific instances. "Strangling baby girls at birth might be a thing of the past," says Promilla Kapur, a sociologist who specializes in research on Indian women. "However, what used to be done in a fairly crude manner is still often achieved indirectly."

—Based on Chacko (1977); Page (2007)

The Problem in Sociological Perspective

You can see how important the sex of a child is in India. Parents living in poverty feel despair with the birth of a girl: They must feed and clothe her, but she can contribute little to the family's income. They rejoice at the birth of a boy, for it signals the arrival of a child who can help sustain them in their old age.

WOMEN AS A MINORITY GROUP. Although the Indian situation is extreme, *sex is the major sorting device in every society in the world.* In our own society, as we'll examine in this chapter, men are paid more for the same work; and, despite changes, they continue to dominate politics and public life. Even though females make up 50.7% of the U.S. population (*Statistical Abstract*, 2009, Table 7), sociologists consider women a minority group because of their position relative to men, the dominant group.

THE DEVELOPMENT OF SEXISM AS A SOCIAL PROBLEM. Sociologists have not always referred to women as a minority group. This labeling came about only gradually, as they began to note parallels between the social positions of women and men and those of African Americans and whites. In 1944 Gunnar Myrdal, a Swedish sociologist studied these parallels in *An American Dilemma*. He noted one main historical connection: The legal

status of African American slaves was derived from the legal status of women and children in the 17th century, whose lives were controlled by male heads of households. In 1951 an American sociologist, Helen Hacker, was the first to apply the term *minority* to women. Noting that discrimination against women "takes the form of being barred from certain activities or, if admitted, being treated unequally," Hacker said that women were marginal to a society dominated by men.

Just as the perception of sociologists was changing, so was that of women, who began to challenge the traditional relations between the sexes. Many came to see themselves not as *individuals* who had less status than men, but as a *group* of people who were discriminated against. During the 1960s and 1970s, women publicized their grievances at being second-class citizens dominated by men. Subjective concerns grew as large numbers of women in the United States and around the world agreed that something needed to be done. Recalling our definition of social problems, you can see that this new evaluation of the relative positions of women and men transformed what had been an objective condition of society into a social problem. Taking this issue seriously, sociologists began to investigate **sexism,** the belief that one sex is innately superior to the other and the discrimination that results from this belief.

Many social conditions have evolved since the 1960s and 1970s. Periods of unrest and agitation have been replaced with political and philosophical advancements. Let's see how extensive the problem of sexism is today.

The Scope of the Problem

IS MALE DOMINANCE UNIVERSAL? When did sexism begin? Some social scientists, such as anthropologist Marvin Harris (1977, p. 46), claim that men's domination of society "has been in continuous existence throughout virtually the entire globe from the earliest times to the present." After reviewing the evidence, historian and feminist Gerda Lerner (1986, p. 31) agreed, saying that "there is not a single society known where women-as-a-group have decision-making power over men (as a group)." She also concluded that the earliest societies had the least amount of gender discrimination. In those societies women contributed about 60% of the group's total food.

Conclusions of universal domination by men make some social analysts apprehensive: If people think that men have always dominated every society around the world, perhaps they will conclude that this behavior is innate. They might then use this conclusion to justify men's domination of women today. Not all sociologists accept the conclusion of the universality of male dominance (C. F. Epstein, 1989), a point to which we shall return shortly.

Don't women presidents, prime ministers, and monarchs disprove the universal domination of society by men? Sociologists point out that these are *individual* women in positions of power, not examples of women-as-a-group in control of a society. Even those societies led by a woman are dominated by men, for men hold almost all key positions in politics. Sweden comes closest to exhibiting political equality between the sexes: 45% of its cabinet ministers and 45% of its members of parliament are women ("Women in the Riksdag," 2003). Women hold many positions of power because Swedish laws limit the percentage of offices that men can control.

THE SEXUAL STRATIFICATION OF WORK. *Every* society stratifies its members by sex; that is, they single out males and females for different activities. Around the world, for example, most work is **sex-typed,** associated with one sex or the other. Because of this, early theorists argued that anatomy required men and women to be assigned particular work. In 1937, anthropologist George Murdock reviewed information on 324 societies. He found that what is considered "male" or "female" work differs from one society to another. For example, in some societies the care of cattle is women's work; in others, it is men's work. Three types of labor have almost always been defined as men's work—making weapons, pursuing sea mammals, and hunting. No specific work has been universally assigned to women. Making clothing, cooking, carrying water, and grinding grain have

When men do an activity that is usually assigned to women, the prestige of the activity increases.

commonly been defined as women's work, but not always. Biology, then, does not determine occupational destiny.

That one society assigns a certain kind of work to men while another assigns it to women—isn't this a type of equality? How is this relevant to a discussion of sexism? Social scientists have discovered a startling principle: *Universally, men's activities are always given greater prestige.* Whatever work is assigned to men is considered superior (Linton, 1936; Rosaldo, 1974). If taking care of cattle is men's work, then cattle care is thought to be important and carries high prestige. If taking care of cattle is women's work, however, it is considered less important and carries less prestige. To cite an example closer to home, when delivering babies was "women's work," the responsibility of midwives, this job was given low prestige. But when men took over delivering babies (despite opposition from women), its prestige shot up (Ehrenreich & English, 1973). *It is the sex that is associated with the work that provides its prestige, not the work itself.*

MAJOR AREAS OF DISCRIMINATION. Sexism pervades every society in the world, and it touches almost every aspect of our social life. In her classic 1951 article, Helen Hacker listed the following general types of discrimination against American women at that time:

1. *Political and legal.* Women were often barred from jury duty and public office.
2. *Education.* Professional schools, such as architecture and medicine, applied quotas for women.
3. *Economic.* Women were usually relegated to work that fell under the supervision of men, for which they received unequal pay, promotion, and responsibility.
4. *Social.* Women were permitted less freedom of movement, fewer deviations in dress, speech, and manners, and a narrower range of personality expression.

Hacker also described how women's three major roles—sister/daughter, wife, and mother—fit this pattern of discrimination. She said that a sister does more housework than her brother, a wife is expected to subordinate her interests to those of her husband, and a mother bears the stigma for an illegitimate child.

Sex discrimination in American society has changed drastically since Hacker's analysis. She seems to be describing another society—and in a sociological sense she is. Women are no longer barred from jury duty and public office, nor do they face quotas

in professional schools. You probably noticed that on a couple of significant levels, though, Hacker's analysis remains remarkably current. Women still struggle against unequal treatment in jobs, politics, and other areas of social life.

Looking at the Problem Theoretically

Why are societies sexist? Let's use our theoretical lenses to see what contrasting perspectives demonstrate.

Symbolic Interactionism

BASIC TERMS. We must distinguish between two terms. When we consider how males and females differ, we usually think first of **sex,** the different *biological* equipment of males and females. Then we might think about **gender,** how we express our "maleness" or "femaleness." Symbolic interactionists stress that sex is biological, and gender is learned, or social.

SOCIALIZATION INTO GENDER ROLES. Symbolic interactionists study how we are socialized into **gender roles.** Gender roles define the attitudes and behaviors expected of boys and girls. We accomplish our gender when our physical appearance matches the expectations of others. Each society has prescribed some activities as "male" and others as "female." To enforce these roles requires that a society's institutions work together. The result is so effective that people feel shame when **gender accomplishment** is not achieved. In the short space we have, we can indicate only a few of the elements involved in this orchestration of society's institutions.

The process of gender accomplishment begins *before* birth (Henslin, 2007a). While pregnant, expectant parents may imagine their future child's participation in sex-stereotyped activities. A father may see himself teaching his son how to play baseball; a mother may imagine dressing her daughter in lace while adoring her cute appearance.

J. Alexander is a runway expert and judge on *America's Next Top Model.*

When the child is born, the parents announce its sex to the world. Through cards, telephone calls, and e-mail, they proclaim "It's a girl!" or "It's a boy!" Even local newspapers report this momentous event. And momentous it is, for *in every society of the world this announcement launches people into their single most significant life-shaping circumstance.* Sex is a **master trait,** cutting across all other identities in life. Whatever else we may be, we always are male or female.

Cast onto the stage of life with a gender role to accomplish, we spend much of our childhood and young adult life learning how to manage this assignment. Throughout the world, parents—as "significant others"—teach children how to portray their gender role. In American society parents begin by dressing boys in blue and girls in pink. These colors have been imbued with gender-role significance. Parents continue coaching children through the stages of dating rituals and marriage preparations.

Difficulties of Interpretation ■ In a classic study, psychologists Susan Goldberg and Michael Lewis (1960) observed how parents teach gender roles subconsciously—that is, without being aware that they are doing so. Goldberg and Lewis recruited mothers of 6-month-olds to come into their laboratory so they could observe the socialization of their children. They observed how mothers interacted with their babies and found that they kept their girls closer to them than their sons. By the time the children reached 13 months of age, the girls were more reluctant than the boys to leave their mothers. During play, they remained closer to their mothers and returned to them sooner and more often than the boys did.

Goldberg and Lewis followed up their initial observations with an interesting experiment. They surrounded each mother with colorful toys and placed her child on the other side of a small barrier. The girls were more likely to cry and motion for help, while the boys were more likely to try to climb over or go around the barrier. The researchers concluded that without knowing it, the mothers had rewarded daughters for acting passive and dependent while rewarding their sons for acting aggressive and independent.

But are these conclusions unfounded? Were these differences brought about by the mother's behavior, as the researchers suggest? Or did the researchers observe biological differences that were beginning to appear at the age of 13 months? In short, were the mothers responding to differences inherent in their children (the boys wanting to get down and play more, and the girls wanting to be hugged more), or were the mothers creating those differences? In support of sociological environmental influences, we support the cultural argument.

In childhood, boys are generally allowed to be more active and to express more independence. Preschool boys, for example, are given more freedom to roam farther from home than their preschool sisters. They are also allowed to participate in more rough-and-tumble play—even to get dirtier and to be more defiant (Henslin, 2007a). Again, we face the same dilemma when trying to draw conclusions: Are the parents and teachers creating these differences in behavior? Or are the children responding to biological predispositions?

"Sex brought us together, but gender drove us apart."

The distinctions between sex and gender that sociologists have drawn are becoming part of public consciousness.

(© The New Yorker Collection 2001. Barbara Smaller from cartoonbank.com. All Rights Reserved.)

The Dominant Symbolic Interactionist Position ■ Most symbolic interactionists assume that gender differences are learned. They emphasize how stereotypes applied at birth tend to become reality through the self-fulfilling prophecy and continued socialization practices. If a male is labeled aggressive and dominant, he will tend to fulfill those expectations by acting aggressive and dominant. If a female is considered passive and submissive, she will tend to fulfill those expectations as well. Not everyone follows gender scripts, but so many do that often socialization gets confused with genetics.

IN SUM Symbolic interactionists highlight how society uses the labels of male and female to sort its members into separate groups. This process starts within the family and is then reinforced by other social institutions. As a result, males and females acquire different expectations of themselves and of one another. These labels then become an essential part of how we manage gender roles: physically identifying males and females, socializing them into appropriate categories, and then requiring males and females to pursue appropriate activities.

Functionalism

TWO THEORIES OF MALE DOMINANCE. If male dominance is universal, or even nearly universal, how did it come about? Although the origins of sexism are lost in history, functionalists have two theories to account for it.

Rewards for Warriors ■ The first theory was proposed by anthropologist Marvin Harris (1977). He said that male dominance is universal because it is based on two universal conditions. The first is social—the necessity to survive warfare. The second is biological—innate differences in the physical strength of men and women.

Harris's controversial explanation goes like this: In preliterate times, humans lived in small groups. Because each group was threatened by others, in an attempt to survive,

it had to recruit people who would fight in hand-to-hand combat. People feared injury and death, of course, so the recruiting wasn't easy. To coax people into bravery, groups developed rewards and punishments. Because an average woman is only 85% the size of an average man and has only two-thirds his strength, men were used in hand-to-hand combat. Men became warriors—and females became their reward, for sexual pleasure and as a labor resource. Some groups allowed only men who had previously faced an enemy to marry. Even today, in some tribal groups such as the Barabaig of Tanzania, women are rewards for men who show bravery (Aposporos, 2004).

Because some women are stronger than some men, to exclude all women from combat might seem irrational. But if women are socialized as rewards for men, they come to accept it as necessary. To make the system work, men have to be trained from birth for combat and women have to be trained from birth for submission.

In sum, the reward for male bravery often comes at the expense of females. In almost all band and village societies, men assign "drudge work" to women—weeding, seed grinding, fetching water and firewood, cooking, and carrying household possessions during moves. Because men prefer to avoid these onerous tasks—and could if they had one or more wives—women become an excellent resource.

Reproduction ■ The second theory used to explain gender stratification is based on human reproduction (Lerner, 1986; Hope & Stover, 1987; Friedl, 1990). It also stems from early human history. Life spans were much shorter in the past, so it was important to procreate as much as possible. Women attempted to have as many children as possible. Because women are responsible for giving birth and nursing infants, they have always struggled with work–life balance. To survive, an infant needs a nursing mother. Throughout history, with a child at her breast or in her womb and one on her hip or on her back, a woman has been encumbered physically—unable to participate fully in the labor market. Thus women everywhere took on tasks associated with home and child care, while men took over hunting large animals and other tasks that required longer absence from the base camp (Huber, 1990).

Through their separation from child-rearing responsibilities, men gained both power and prestige. They made and controlled the weapons used for hunting and warfare. They left the camp to hunt animals, returning triumphantly with prey. Leaving the camp, they also made contact with other tribes and accumulated possessions in trade. Men also gained prestige by bringing prisoners back from war. In contrast, little prestige was given to the routine activities of women, who didn't engage in warfare. The men's weapons, their items of trade, and the knowledge they gained from their contacts with other groups became future sources of power.

The ultimate result was a **patriarchal society**—one in which men ruled over women. As women became subject to the decisions of men, men justified their dominance. They developed ideas linking manhood with superiority. To avoid "contamination" by females, men shrouded some of their activities in secrecy and established rules and rituals excluding women.

IN SUM If either of these theories is true, the *origin* of male dominance is rooted in both biological and social factors. The *maintenance* of male dominance, however, is purely social—a perpetuation of millennia-old patterns. Although tribal societies developed into larger groups and hand-to-hand combat and hunting dangerous animals ceased to be routine, men, enjoying what they had, held on to their privileges and power. Reluctant to abandon this privileged position of dominance that is rooted in ancient custom, men continue to use cultural devices to control women. For an example, see the Global Glimpse box on the next page.

Conflict Theory

PRINCIPLES OF POWER. Conflict theorists provide a contrasting view of sexism. For background, consider these four principles.

CULTURE IS THE ANSWER

For sociologist Cynthia Fuchs Epstein (1986, 1988, 1989), the answer lies solely in social factors, especially socialization and social control. Here is her argument:

1. The anthropological record shows more equality between the sexes in the past than we had thought. In earlier societies, women, as well as men, hunted small game, devised tools for hunting, and gathered food. Studies of today's hunting and gathering societies show that "both women's and men's roles have been broader and less rigid than those created by stereotypes. For example, the Agta and Mbuti are clearly egalitarian. . . . " This proves that "societies exist in which women are not subordinate to men. Anthropologists who study them claim that there is a separate but equal status of women at this level of development."

2. Not biology but rigidly enforced social arrangements determine the types of work that women and men do in each society. Few people can escape these arrangements to perform work outside their allotted range. Informal customs and formal systems of laws enforce this gender inequality of work, which serves the interests of males. Once these socially constructed barriers are removed, women can and do exhibit the same work habits as males.

3. The human behaviors that biology "causes" are only those that involve reproduction or differences in body structure. These differences are relevant for only a few activities, "such as playing basketball or crawling through a small space."

4. Female crime rates, which are rising, indicate that the aggressiveness that often is considered a biologically dictated male behavior is related to social, not biological, factors. When social conditions permit, such as with women attorneys, females also exhibit "adversarial, assertive, and dominant behavior." Not incidentally, their "dominant behavior" also shows up in their challenging the biased views about human nature that male scholars have proposed.

In short, not "women's incompetence or inability to read a legal brief, to perform brain surgery, [or] to predict a bull market," but social factors—socialization, gender discrimination, and other forms of social control—are responsible for differences in the behavior of women and men. Arguments that assign "an evolutionary and genetic basis" to explain gender differences in social status "rest on a dubious structure of inappropriate, highly selective, and poor data, oversimplification in logic and inappropriate inferences by use of analogy."

Cynthia Fuchs Epstein, whose position in the ongoing "nature versus nurture" debate is summarized here.

This study of Vietnam veterans does *not* leave us with the ability to claim biology as the sole basis for aggression. Not all men who have high testosterone levels get into trouble with the law or mistreat their wives. A chief difference among those who do and do not is social class. High-testosterone men from higher social classes are less likely to be involved in antisocial behaviors than are high-testosterone men from lower social classes (Dabbs & Morris, 1990). Social factors (socialization, life goals, self-definitions), then, also play a role. Researchers are especially interested in uncovering particular social factors and discovering how they work in combination with biological factors.

RECONCILING THE FINDINGS. From the current evidence we can conclude that *if* biology provides males and females differences in temperament, personality, or some type of predisposition in behavior, culture often overrides those differences. Culture urges men and women to accomplish their gender in ways that promote functioning within society. Because people are often unaware of how environmental factors contribute to

differences among men and women, biology often presents overwhelming evidence of "natural" and "genetic" differences between the sexes.

In the years to come, unraveling the influences of socialization and biology should prove to be an exciting—and controversial—area of sociological research. Biological arguments will claim that differences in sex behaviors stem from genetics, while environmental arguments will claim that socialization is most important. This concerns us because, as sociologist Janet Chafetz (1990, p. 30) found, "different sexed" often results in "unequal treatment."

AVOIDING IDEOLOGY. At this point, we have no conclusive evidence as to whether nature or nurture singularly leads to aggression, nurturing, intelligence, and so on. Some researchers are convinced these qualities are innate, others that they are learned. Like other areas of science, we must examine data with an open mind. Unfortunately, research on differences between men and women has become emotionally charged, and arguing for or against biological influences indicates some adherence to that ideology. This, of course, is not scientific practice. Data, not ideology, may one day answer the nature versus nurture argument once and for all.

Let's now examine inequality between the sexes, with a focus on U.S. society.

Everyday Life

Leaning against the water cooler, two men—both minor executives—are holding coffee cups while discussing Sunday's *Cowboys* game.

A vice president hears them talking about sports. Does he send them back to their desks? Probably not. As a man he is likely to join the conversation—demonstrating that he is "one of the boys," feigning an interest in football that he may not share at all. These men in the office are his comrades-in-arms.

Now, assume that two women are standing by the water cooler discussing work, not sports. The same vice president sees them and complains that they are "gabbing" when they should be working. "Don't they know this is a workplace?" (Korda, 1973, pp. 20–21, paraphrased).

In everyday life, women encounter antagonistic attitudes from men. Their interests, attitudes, and contributions are often held in low regard. Masculinity and machismo represent strength while femininity is perceived as weakness.

Let's examine how males in the military and in sports are devalued when their masculinity is challenged. During World War II, a team of researchers headed by sociologist Samuel Stouffer studied the motivation of combat soldiers. Out of this research came a sociological classic, *The American Soldier*. This work (Stouffer et al., 1949, p. 132) explained how derogatory feminine terms are hurled at soldiers as insults to motivate them. Stouffer found that if a soldier did not measure up as a "manly" man, he heard comments like "Whatsa matter, bud—got lace on your drawers?" During the Vietnam War, military officers also used accusations of femininity to motivate soldiers. Drill sergeants would mock their troops by saying, "Can't hack it, little girls?" (Eisenhart, 1975). This practice continues today. In the Marines, male recruits suffer shame when their performance is compared to a woman's (Gilham, 1989). If a male soldier shows hesitation during maneuvers, others mock him, calling him a "girl" (Miller, 2007).

Social scientists have observed this same behavior in sports. Watching basketball, sociologists Jean Stockard and Miriam Johnson (1980) heard boys shout to others who missed the basket, "You play like a woman!" Anthropologist Douglas Foley studied high school football in Texas. He reported how alumni critiqued current football players—telling boys who had a bad game that they were "wearing skirts" (Foley, 1990/2006). Describing more of the same, sociologist Donna Eder (1995) reported that junior-high boys called one another "girl" if they didn't hit hard enough during a football game.

Women who congregate in the workplace are viewed differently than men.

Most people dismiss such remarks as insignificant: "That's just people talking." Stockard and Johnson point out, however, that such comments reveal a basic derogatory attitude toward women and things feminine, an attitude that women face as part of their everyday lives. They make this telling point: "There is no comparable phenomenon among women, for young girls do not insult each other by calling each other 'man.'"

Although we are seeing changes in male–female relationships, the devaluation of women continues to be a background feature of social life. As sociologist Carol Whitehurst (1977) stressed, this devaluation is important because it underlies all other forms of oppression.

Education

LOOKING AT THE PAST. To gain a better understanding of today's situation in education, let's take a glimpse into the past. About a century ago, leading educators claimed that women's wombs dominated their mental life. Dr. Edward Clarke, for example, a member of Harvard University's medical faculty, warned women that studying was dangerous for them:

> A girl upon whom Nature, for a limited period and for a definite purpose, imposes so great a physiological task, will not have as much power left for the tasks of school, as the boy of whom Nature requires less at the corresponding epoch. (quoted in Andersen, 1988, p. 35)

To preserve their fragile health, Clarke added that young women should study only one-third as much as men. And during menstruation, they shouldn't study at all.

Views like Clarke's certainly put women at an educational disadvantage. Women who followed his warning and studied less than men would obviously do worse overall. This, in turn, would confirm the stereotype that women's brains weren't as capable as men's—that their proper place was in the home.

TABLE 9-1	Of Students Enrolled in Secondary School, What Percentage Are Girls?

PERCENTAGE	COUNTRY
32%	Benin
36%	Equatorial Guinea
37%	Cambodia
38%	Djibouti
38%	Ethiopia
38%	Niger
39%	Burkina Faso
39%	Eritrea
39%	Mozambique
40%	Senegal
41%	Gambia
41%	Laos
41%	Nepal
41%	Papua New Guinea
42%	Burundi
42%	Congo
42%	Turkey
43%	Mauritania
44%	Angola
44%	Malawi
44%	Zambia

Note: These are the world's countries in which less than 45% of the students are females.

Source: By James M. Henslin. Based on U.S. Agency for International Development (2004).

LOOKING AT OTHER COUNTRIES. Women may not face discrimination as they did in the past, but in some countries women are still overtly discriminated against in education. Table 9-1 provides a glimpse of how education is disproportionately reserved for boys in some countries. This table lists 21 countries of the world in which girls make up less than 45% of secondary school students. You can see that 16 of those countries are located in Africa, 3 are in Asia, and 1 (Turkey) straddles Asia and Europe.

ACTIVE BOYS AND CHEERING GIRLS. There is great contrast between education in the United States and other countries. There are *2.7 million more* women than men in American colleges (*Statistical Abstract*, 2009, Table 268). With such great numbers of women attending college, how can sexism in education exist?

Some of it shows up in college sports: Boys often become football *players,* while girls join drill teams and pep squads—*cheering on* the players (Foley, 2006). As Carol Whitehurst (1977) put it, "The boys perform, the girls cheer."

GENDER TRACKING. Apart from this visible demonstration of men as active participants and women as voyeurs, another more hidden phenomenon exists as well. In college we find what sociologists call *gender tracking,* that is, women and men tend to cluster in different educational specialties. Women earn 92% of associate's degrees in home economics, for example, whereas men earn 95% of associate's degrees in building trades. Similarly, men dominate engineering, while women dominate library sciences

TABLE 9-2 Doctorates in Science, by Sex

Field	STUDENTS ENROLLED IN DOCTORAL PROGRAMS		DOCTORATES CONFERRED		COMPLETION RATIO (HIGHER OR LOWER THAN EXPECTED)	
	Women	Men	Women	Men	Women	Men
Computer sciences	27%	73%	20%	80%	−26	+10
Mathematics	36	64	27	73	−25	+14
Agriculture	45	55	34	66	−24	+20
Engineering	21	79	17	83	−19	+5
Biological sciences	55	45	46	54	−16	+20
Social sciences	53	47	45	55	−15	+17
Physical sciences	31	69	27	73	−13	+6
Psychology	74	26	67	33	−9	+27

Note: The formula for the completion ratio is *X* minus *Y* divided by *X*, where *X* represents the doctorates conferred and *Y* represents the proportion enrolled in a program.

Source: By James M. Henslin. Based on *Statistical Abstract of the United States* (2006, Tables 781, 783).

(*Statistical Abstract,* 2006, Table 288). It is socialization—rather than any presumed innate characteristics—that channels men and women into sex-linked educational paths.

A MAN'S WORLD. Another significant factor contributing to the devaluation of women is tradition. Most women are confronted with "a man's world" in college. Not only are most of their professors men, but they also study mostly male authors in their literature courses, discuss the thinking of men in their philosophy courses, and read almost exclusively about famous men in history courses. Even sociology concentrates on the contributions of men. Little is known about how this affects the orientations of female and male students, but it certainly has to be significant. Men who have taken courses in gender studies taught by women often get upset when they become immersed in "women's world of thought." Women's immersion in what we can call the "men's world of thought" is gradual and taken for granted, but the impact is just as severe.

COMPLETING THE DOCTORATE. Although women now outnumber men in college and earn 58% of all bachelor's degrees (*Statistical Abstract,* 2009, Table 288), something happens between the bachelor's and the doctorate. Look at Table 9-2, a snapshot of doctoral programs in the sciences. This table shows us how aspirations (enrollment) and accomplishments (doctorates conferred) are sex linked. In five of the eight doctoral programs, men outnumber women; in three, women outnumber men. Note that in *all* of them women are less likely to complete the doctorate.

No one is suggesting that graduate faculties purposely discriminate against women. Perhaps what we mentioned earlier about most faculty being men and most of the researchers, theorists, and writers being studied in the academic disciplines also being men has something to do with it. Apparently, though, the core reason is this: Women are more likely to get sidetracked with marriage and family responsibilities.

A DEVELOPING SOCIAL PROBLEM? We would like to conclude this section by referring back to an earlier point, the decrease in men's college enrollments. That we now have almost 3 million more women than men enrolled in college and earning 58% of all bachelor's degrees might indicate that we are on the verge of dramatic change in education. Following the basic model of social problems stressed throughout this text, at this point we have only an objective condition without subjective concern. If enough people become upset about the lack of men in college, a full-blown social problem may emerge—this time with men as objects of discrimination.

The Mass Media

The mass media help to shape gender roles by portraying certain behaviors as "right" for boys and other behaviors "right" for girls. The media send strong messages about "proper" sexual relationships and body image. To gain insight into how this occurs, we will look first at children's books, then television, music, and advertising.

CHILDREN'S BOOKS. Children's picture books have long been a focus for sociologists. Illustrated books for children are more than just entertainment. Little children learn about the world from the pictures they see and the stories read to them. The illustrations show girls and boys in stereotypical roles, doing what is considered "right" for the sexes.

When sociologists first examined children's picture books in the 1970s, they found it unusual to have a girl as the main character. Almost all the books featured boys, men, and even male animals. When they were pictured, girls were usually passive and doll-like, whereas boys were active and adventurous. While the boys did things requiring independence and self-confidence, girls were shown helping their brothers and fathers (Weitzman et al., 1972). Feminists protested these stereotypes and formed their own publishing companies. Now we have books depicting girls as leaders—active and independent. As a result of these efforts—as well as the changing role of women in society—today's children's books have about an equal number of boy and girl characters. Girls are now depicted in a variety of nontraditional activities.

One gender stereotype continues to linger in children's books, however: As researchers have pointed out, females are now portrayed as doing things that males do, but males are not portrayed as doing things that females do (Dickman & Murnen, 2004). Males, for example, are seldom depicted as caring for the children or doing grocery shopping, and they are rarely seen doing housework (Gooden & Gooden, 2001). As gender roles continue to change, we are sure that this, too, will change.

TELEVISION. More powerful perhaps than picture books are stereotypical gender roles shown on television. In the cartoons that so fascinate young children, males outnumber females, giving the message that boys are more important than girls.

A classic example of **misogyny**—hatred or strong prejudice against women—appeared in the children's cartoon *Teenage Mutant Ninja Turtles.* The original turtles were Michelangelo, Leonardo, Raphael, and Donatello—named after male artists whose accomplishments have been admired for centuries. A female turtle was added. Her name? Venus de Milo. The female turtle was named not for a person, but for a statue famous for curvaceous and ample breasts. One other significant point—she had no head or arms ("Getting the Message," 1997).

Adult television also creates and reinforces stereotypes of gender, age, and sexuality (Butler et al., 2006). On prime time, two-thirds of all characters are male, and men are more likely to be portrayed in high-status positions (Glascock, 2001; "Fall Colors," 2004). Women are depicted as losing their sexual attractiveness earlier than men; and starting at age 30, fewer and fewer women are shown. About 9 out of 10 women on prime time are below the age of 46, and older women practically disappear from television (Gerbner, 1998). Men are portrayed as aging more gracefully, with their sexual attractiveness increasing with age.

Body image is another key part of gender accomplishment, and television is effective in teaching us what we "should" look like. Sociologists have found that most female characters are below average in weight. They are often portrayed as dieting and slender. Viewers not only learn that thinness is desirable, but they also see, compared with what most women actually look like, a "distorted and unrealistic picture of women's bodies" (Fouts & Burggraf, 1999).

Lori Fowler studied the impact of media pressure on adolescents for over a decade and found (2008) that those teens who admire television icons are likely to adhere to televised beauty standards as well. She interviewed 10 mothers who gave breast implants to their daughters as high school graduation gifts. The key finding was that mothers paid for silicone breasts regardless of possible complications—stating it was worth any

Women are portrayed as more powerful in today's cartoons. Kim Possible is a fashionista, straight-A student, cheerleader, and superhero.

cost (including future surgeries and death) to allow their daughters to appear more attractive and confident.

Sociologists studying televised sports in Los Angeles found that it also maintains traditional stereotypes (Messner, Duncan, & Cooky, 2003). Women athletes rarely receive coverage. When they do, the stories often trivialize them by focusing on humorous events or by turning the women into sexual objects. Newscasters even emphasize breast size.

At the same time, though, some stereotypes are breaking. On new comedies women are appearing more verbally aggressive than men (Glascock, 2001). In children's television programming, gender role stereotyping is also changing. In *Kim Possible,* an animated beauty tackles the problems of the world with powerful fighting techniques. In yet another cartoon—*My Life as a Teenage Robot*—a towering robot named Jenny defends the planet against evildoers.

MUSIC. There are so many kinds (genres) of music that it is difficult to summarize sex roles in music accurately. In many songs for teens and preteens, boys learn to dominate male–female relationships. Lyrics instruct girls to be sexy, passive, and dependent—and to control boys by manipulating their sexual impulses. In music videos, females typically become background ornaments for dominant male singers. Studies show that those who watch music videos hold more traditional sex-role stereotypes (Ward, Hansbrough, & Walker, 2005). Some rap groups glorify male sexual aggression and revel in humiliating women. A common theme in country–western music is that men are aggressive and dominant, whereas women are passive and dependent.

ADVERTISING

Advertising is an insidious propaganda machine for a male supremacist society. It spews out images of women as sex mates, housekeepers, mothers, and menial workers—images that perhaps reflect the true status of most women in society, but which also make it increasingly difficult for women to break out of the sexist stereotypes that imprison them. (Komisar, 1971, p. 304)

How has the portrayal of men and women in advertising changed since Komisar's observation in the 1970s? Although fewer women are now depicted as "housekeepers, mothers, and menial workers," television advertising continues to reinforce stereotypical gender roles. Commercials aimed at children are more likely to show girls as cooperative and boys as aggressive. They are also more likely to show girls at home and boys outdoors (Larson, 2001). Men are more likely to occupy high-status positions (Coltrane & Messineo, 2000). Women make most purchases, are underrepresented as primary characters, and are still shown as supportive counterparts to men (Ganahl et al., 2003). Even when they are depicted as professionals, women are apt to be shown as less engaged in the situation or as a weaker employee needing a man's assistance (Lindner, 2004).

The use of the female body—especially exposed breasts—to sell products also continues. Feminists have persistently fought back. In one campaign, feminists re-created misogynist billboards into pro-woman messages (Rakow, 1992). One billboard that had a woman reclining on a car was repainted by feminists to say "When I'm not lying on cars, I'm a brain surgeon."

The average person views hundreds of ads each day (Draper, 1986). Therefore, a change in style of message can be very powerful. One major change in advertising has been the use of the male body. More than ever, sexy male ads are used for product association.

IN SUM The essential point is that the mass media—children's books, television, music, and advertising—influence us. They shape the expectations society holds regarding

Feminists have protested the degradation of women, including the exposure of the female body to sell products. The resulting change, however, has not been a decrease in the number of such ads. Instead, we now have ads that explicitly display the male body to sell products. This is a form of equality, although not the one that was intended.

the way people "ought" to be—how they should act and even feel—and we tend to view one another and ourselves through these images. Perhaps a cue to significant and influential change is the new portrayal of girls with masculine characteristics. Parents are changing the way they socialize their children—continuing to encourage traditional masculine characteristics in their sons while encouraging their daughters to display some of these same valued characteristics (Kane, 2006).

The images of the sexes that we learn as children and continue to assimilate as adults channel our behavior, becoming part of the process by which traditional sex roles are both maintained and changed. This includes politics, to which we now turn.

The World of Politics

THE CURRENT SITUATION. Despite the many changes that mark greater equality between the sexes, men remain dominant in politics. Analyzing politics can give us an excellent illustration of the relative position of men and women in the United States. Figure 9-2 on the next page illustrates how vastly underrepresented women are in political decision making. The higher the office, the less female representation. Twenty-nine women have held the office of governor, while none has ever held the office of president. Despite the gains women have made in recent elections, since 1789, nearly 1,900 men have served in the U.S. Senate, but only 37 women have served (Baumann, 2006; election results, 2008). Not until 1992 was the first African American woman (Carol Moseley-Braun) elected to the Senate. As of yet no Latina or Asian American woman has been elected to the Senate (National Women's Political Caucus, 1998; *Statistical Abstract,* 2009, Table 390). In 2007, Nancy Pelosi was the first woman to be elected Speaker of the United States House of Representatives. After the 2008 election, 74 of 435 House members were women. In the executive branch, three women have served as U.S. secretary of state, and others have also served at the cabinet level; two women have run for election as vice president on major party tickets; and in 2008, Hillary Clinton was the first woman to

One of the major changes occurring in the United States is the ascent of women into positions of power. Although we are not even close to a balance of men and women in power, the candidacy of Hillary Clinton for the presidency of the United States illustrates a fundamental change.

FIGURE 9-2 Who Controls U.S. Politics?

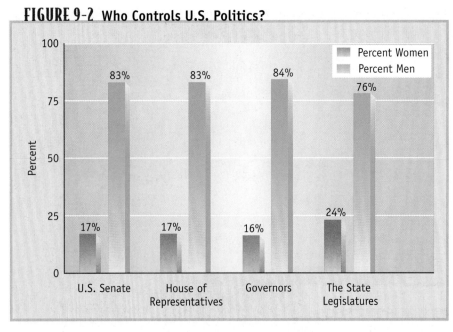

Source: James M. Henslin. Based on National Governors Association (www.nga.org); *Statistical Abstract of the United States* (2006, Table 395); 2008 election results; National Conference of State Legislatures.

win a presidential primary (in the end, she won 20 state contests but narrowly lost the nomination to Barack Obama). After the 2008 election, President Obama selected Senator Clinton to be U.S. secretary of state.

The Social Map below (Figure 9-3) shows the percentage of women who make up state legislatures in the United States. This is a rough indicator of how political power is distributed between men and women on the state level. It is difficult to decipher trends in this distribution of power among the states, but one does stand out—women hold the highest percentage of state offices in the West. There is also wide variation in the

FIGURE 9-3 Women in State Legislatures

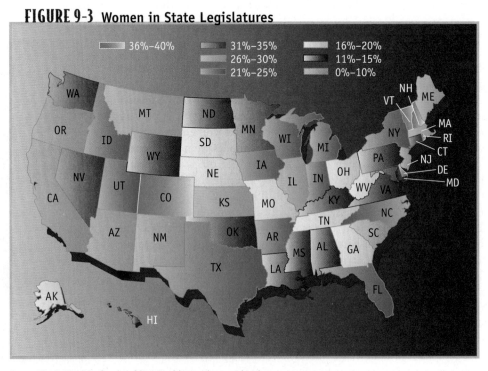

Source: The National Conference of State Legislatures (www.ncsl.org).

amount of political power distributed among women—from 10% in South Carolina to 40% in Colorado.

WHY DON'T WOMEN DOMINATE POLITICS? Consider these two facts. The first: About 8 *million* more women than men are of voting age. The second: Women who vote outnumber men who vote by 9 *million* (*Statistical Abstract*, 2006, Table 405). With their overwhelming numbers, why don't women take political control of the nation?

The Syllogism of Masculinity ■ A good answer appears to be socialization. As we have seen, social institutions continue to socialize men into positions of authority and women into subservience. This leads to the following illogical reasoning:

Dominance is masculine.
Politics is a form of dominance.
Therefore, politics is masculine.

This perception imposes severe restraints on women's recruitment, participation, and performance in politics.

The Power of Sex Roles ■ Other significant explanations for continued sexism center on the relative positions of men and women. First, women are underrepresented in law and business, the careers from which most politicians come. Most women also find the irregular hours that it takes to run for elective office incompatible with home life responsibilities. For men whose typical work schedules are more likely to take them away from home, this conflict is not as severe. Women are also less likely to have a supportive spouse who will play an unassuming background role while providing child care, encouragement, and voter appeal. Finally, men have been reluctant to bring women into decision-making roles or to regard them as viable candidates.

Changes ■ These restrictive patterns are changing, which indicates that we can expect more women to seek and win political office. More women are going into law and business, where they are doing more traveling and making statewide and national contacts. Child care is now the responsibility of both parents. A main focus for party candidates today is not their gender but their personal appeal. This generation, then, is likely to see a fundamental change in women's political participation—and perhaps a woman as president?

The World of Work

THE HISTORICAL PATTERN. To catch a glimpse of the overall participation of women in the workforce, look at Table 9-3. As you can see, for more than 100 years the number of American women employed outside the home has increased consistently. The one exception has been the period immediately following World War II. By 1945, 38% of women were in the labor force, working in factory and office jobs while the men fought in World War II. After the men came home from the war,

TABLE 9-3 Women in the Civilian Labor Force

YEAR	NUMBER	AS A PERCENTAGE OF ALL WORKERS	PERCENTAGE OF WOMEN IN THE LABOR FORCE
1890	4,000,000	17%	18%
1900	5,000,000	18	20
1920	8,000,000	20	23
1930	10,000,000	22	24
1940	14,000,000	25	29
1945	19,000,000	36	38
1950	18,000,000	30	34
1960	23,000,000	33	36
1970	32,000,000	37	41
1980	45,000,000	42	48
1990	57,000,000	45	54
2000	63,000,000	46	60
2010*	76,000,000	48	60

Note: Pre-1940 totals include women 14 and over; totals for 1940 and after are for women 16 and over.

*Estimate by the U.S. Dept. of Labor.

Sources: By James M. Henslin. Based on *1969 Handbook on Women Workers* (1969, p. 10); *Manpower Report to the President* (1971, p. 203, 205); Mills and Palumbo (1980, pp. 6, 45); U.S. Bureau of the Census, various years; *Statistical Abstract* (2003, Table 588; 2006, Table 577).

they reclaimed many of these jobs, and the percentage of women in the paid work-force dropped. As you can see, it took about 20 years for participation to get this high again.

The percentage of those ages 16 and older who are in the labor force at least part-time is referred to as the **labor force participation rate.** In 1985, for the first time in U.S. history, half of all American women were employed outside the home at least part-time. Today, close to half of all American workers are women. As the Social Map (Figure 9-4) below shows, the percentage of women working for wages differs by state. The rate ranges from 49% in West Virginia to nearly 70% in South Dakota.

Although it appears that work is becoming a level playing field for men and women, the world of work is no exception to the general pattern of discrimination against women. Women come up against "old boys' networks"—social contacts that keep jobs, promotions, and opportunities circulating among men. To overcome this exclusion, some women professionals have developed "new girls' networks." They pass opportuni-ties among one another, purposefully excluding men in order to help the careers of women.

THE GENDER PAY GAP. We need more than anecdotes to pinpoint discrimination at work—so sociologists analyze the *gender gap* in wages. *At all ages and at all levels of ed-ucation and no matter the type of work, the average man is paid more than the average woman.* If we consider all jobs, and if we look only at full-time, year-round workers, we find that women average only 77% of what men earn (*Statistical Abstract*, 2009, Table 627). Think about this—the average woman earns only a little over two-thirds of what the average man earns. Until the 1980s, women's earnings were 60% of men's, which means that today's 70% is an improvement! The European nations also have a gender gap in pay, but only Portugal has a gap as great as that of the United States (Clarke, 2001).

FIGURE 9-4 How Likely Are Women to Work for Wages?

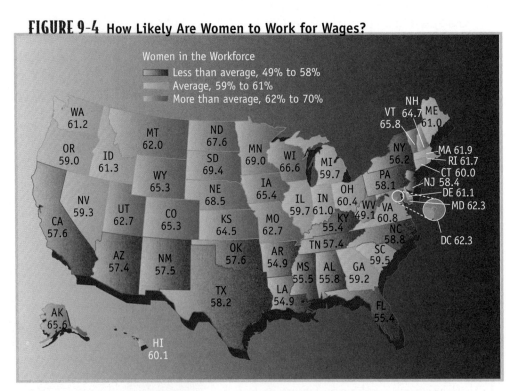

Note: Refers to women who are 16 years old and over who work for wages at least part-time in the civilian labor force; commonly called the *labor force participation rate.*

Source: By James M. Henslin. Based on *Statistical Abstract of the United States* (2007, Table 684).

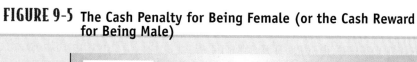

FIGURE 9-5 The Cash Penalty for Being Female (or the Cash Reward for Being Male)

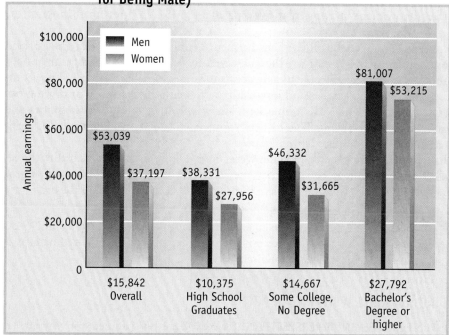

Note: These are the average (median) annual earnings of full-time workers.

Source: James M. Henslin. Based on *Statistical Abstract of the United States* (2007, Table 684).

We don't want to confuse things by comparing better educated men with poorer educated women, or some such thing, so look at Figure 9-5. Here we compare men and women who have the same level of education. Despite matching educations, the average man earns more than the average woman. This is true not only of all levels of education but also of all occupations. There isn't a single occupation in which the average woman outearns the average man. We can see now how powerful the connection is between gender and earnings!

From Figure 9-5 you can see the amount of money a woman may be discounted over her workforce lifetime. The gender gap in pay translates into an astounding total in favor of men: *Between the ages of 25 and 65, the average man who graduates from college earns about a million dollars ($1,100,000) more than the average woman who graduates from college.*

REASONS FOR THE GENDER PAY GAP. Why do we have a pay gap at all? Recall the tracking in education we mentioned earlier. Perhaps this leads to occupational tracking. Also, women are more likely to work at types of jobs that pay less. You know that most secretaries and food servers are women, for example, and that few people who do these jobs earn much. Another possibility is that the gender gap in pay exists because women professionals, such as physicians, work fewer hours than the men in the same profession (Steinhauer, 1999b).

Researchers who considered these possibilities did a study controlling these variables. They found that the factors mentioned above are indeed important. They account for about half the pay gap (Kemp, 1990). The other half may be attributed to pure gender discrimination.

THE FULLER-SCHOENBERGER STUDY. How does discrimination create this gap in income between men and women? The most insightful research was done in 1991 by economists Rex Fuller and Richard Schoenberger. While teaching in the business school at the University of Wisconsin, they noticed that women graduates seemed to be

starting off at lower salaries. To find out if their informal observation was true, they examined the starting salaries of 230 business majors, of whom 47% were women. They found that the women's starting salaries averaged 11% ($1,737) less than those of the men.

Were the women less qualified than the men? Perhaps they had lower grades? Had they done fewer internships? If so, they deserved lower salaries. As faculty members, Fuller and Schoenberger were able to gain access to students' college records. They compared men's and women's grades and internship participation. What they uncovered can be described as *deep* gender discrimination: The *women* had earned *higher* grades and done *more* internships. In other words, the women had to have higher qualifications than men in order to be offered lower salaries!

What happened after these graduates were hired? Did their employers realize the recruiters had made a mistake and later pay the women more? On the contrary. The gender gap grew. In 4 years, the women were earning 14% ($3,615) less than the men.

IN SUM Sociologically, it seems fair to conclude that men are so valued by employers that they pay more for them—a conclusion that applies to other industrialized nations as well (Rosenfeld & Kalleberg, 1990; Sorensen, 1990; Shellenbarger, 1995).

Why Is Our Workforce Segregated by Sex?

THE CONFLICT AND FEMINIST PERSPECTIVES. Two explanations compete for why our labor force is segregated by sex (Blau, 1975; MacKinnon, 1979). The first is based on conflict theory. As we saw in Chapter 7, Marxist conflict theory emphasizes how having a pool of low-paid labor helps the owners of businesses. They draw on those workers during periods of economic expansion, then lay them off when the economy slows down. The result is a **dual labor market**—better-paid workers who are employed regularly coupled with temporary, marginal, low-paid workers. Feminist theory argues further that women are singled out because they are women, African Americans and Latinos are singled out because of their race–ethnicity. All are placed into a pool of marginal labor because, as minorities, they are relatively powerless.

THE SYMBOLIC INTERACTIONIST PERSPECTIVE. The third explanation is based on symbolic interactionism (MacKinnon, 1979). Because men *perceive* women as less capable, less productive, and ultimately, less profitable, they pay them less. This stereotype is furthered by women's greater participation in child-rearing responsibilities. Employers view women as more dedicated than men to the family and less dedicated than men to corporations. With these perceptions, employers assign women more menial jobs and pay them less, while they assign men more responsible positions and pay them more.

IN SUM Each explanation contributes to the whole answer. Businesses do profit from marginal pools of labor, and women do confront structural barriers in the marketplace. Stereotypes of men and women do affect employers' expectations, influencing their reactions, including what they pay their workers. Whatever the factors that created the situation, sex discrimination tends to be self-perpetuating.

Sexual Harassment

Another form of sex discrimination that women face is **sexual harassment**—defined as unsolicited sexual advances made by a person in power. Such sexual advances are often tied to promotions or demotions in the workplace.

If power is unequal, the less powerful person is at a disadvantage in warding off such demands. The most vulnerable women are those who lack job alternatives.

A PERSONAL PROBLEM. The traditional view of sexual harassment makes it a *personal* problem, a matter of individual sexual attraction. A man gets interested in a woman and

See For Yourself

Visit the Equal Employment Opportunity Commission at http://www.eeoc.gov/stats/harass.html

▶ How many sexual harassment charges have been filed by men?

makes an advance; the woman accepts, rejects, or says "maybe." Perhaps her body language even "signals" that she *wants* to be approached sexually. There are always sexual attractions between men and women; some just happen to take place at work. These individual events do not qualify as *social* problems.

A SOCIAL PROBLEM. In 1979, Catharine MacKinnon, an attorney and professor, wrote a book on sexual harassment that changed our thinking. Rejecting the traditional view, MacKinnon argued that sexual harassment is a *structural* matter; that is, it is built into the marketplace. She noted that two conditions encourage sexual harassment. The first is that most women occupy an inferior status in boss–worker relations. The second is an emphasis on women as sex objects. Women are often hired because of their sexual attributes, a precondition that usually is hidden under the requirement that the newly hired be young, "attractive" women who can offer a "good appearance" to the public. In short, sexual harassment begins with hiring procedures that judge women on factors other than their job qualifications and that then places them in a position where they are responsible to men (Silverman, 1981).

Although MacKinnon's analysis is accepted widely now, at the time it was new and controversial. Until 1976, sexual harassment was literally unspeakable—because it had no name. The traditional view dominated, and women considered unwanted sexual advances as something that happened to them as individuals. They did not draw a connection between those advances and their lower position in the marketplace. As feminists raised awareness of the *group* nature of these objective conditions, women gradually concluded that the sexual advances by men in more powerful positions at work were part of a general problem. As more women came to the same conclusion—and became upset about it and demanded that something be done—sexual harassment as a *social* problem

Most charges of sexual harassment are settled quietly, but some make headlines. Shown on the left is Tim Nardiello, coach for the U.S. Olympic bobsled team, who was accused of sexual harassment by some of his female bobsledders. Denying the charges, he was suspended, reinstated, and then fired.

was born. To catch a glimpse of how this definitional process is occurring in Japan today, see the Global Glimpse box below.

DEFINING SEXUAL HARASSMENT. As MacKinnon pointed out, sometimes sexual harassment is just a single encounter at work, but sometimes harassment consists of a series of incidents. At times, sexual relations are made a condition for being hired, retained, or advanced. Sexual harassment can include "verbal sexual suggestions or jokes, constant leering or ogling, brushing against your body 'accidentally,' a friendly pat, squeeze, or pinch or arm against you, catching you alone for a quick kiss, the indecent proposition

A Global Glimpse
SEXUAL HARASSMENT IN JAPAN

The public relations department had come up with an eye-catcher: Each month the cover of the company magazine would show a woman taking off one more piece of clothing. The men were pleased. Never had they so looked forward to the company magazine.

Six months later, with the cover girl poised to take off her tank top, the objections of the female employees had grown too loud to ignore. "We told them it was a lousy idea," said Junko Takashima, assistant director of the company's woman's affairs division. The firm dropped the striptease act.

The Japanese men didn't get the point. "What's all the fuss about?" they asked. "Beauty is beauty. We're just admiring the ladies. It just adds a little spice to boring days at the office."

"It's degrading to us, and it must stop," responded women workers, who, encouraged by the feminist movement in the United States, broke their tradition of silence.

The Japanese (like Americans until the 1970s) have no word of their own to describe such situations. They have borrowed the English phrase "sexual harassment" and are struggling to apply it to their own culture. This is difficult, because a pat on the bottom has long been taken for granted as a boss's way of getting his secretary's attention.

The cultural expectation that all Japanese workers are part of a team that works together harmoniously also makes it difficult to complain. But some women have begun to speak out, using their new vocabulary—and the changed perception that comes with it. As a result, the Japanese government has designated a week in December as "Week for Prevention of Sexual Harassment of National Civil Servants."

Based on Graven (1990); "Implementation of Measures . . ." (2000).

What is considered sexual harassment can differ from one culture to another. Do you think that the striptease in the company magazine, discussed in this box, is sexual harassment? How about the photos at this magazine stand in Tokyo? What is the difference?

backed by the threat of losing your job, and forced sexual relations" (MacKinnon, 1979, p. 2). MacKinnon added,

> Sexual harassment takes both verbal and physical forms. . . . Verbal sexual harassment can include anything from passing but persistent comments on a woman's body or body parts to the experience of an eighteen-year-old file clerk whose boss regularly called her in to his office "to tell me the intimate details of his marriage and to ask what I thought about different sexual positions." Pornography is sometimes used. Physical forms range from repeated collisions that leave the impression of "accident" to outright rape. One woman reported unmistakable sexual molestation which fell between these extremes: "My boss . . . runs his hand up my leg or blouse. He hugs me to him and then tells me he is 'just naturally affectionate.' " (1979, p. 29)

The Equal Employment Opportunity Commission has broadened the definition of sexual harassment to include all unwelcome verbal or physical conduct of a sexual nature that explicitly or implicitly affects an individual's employment, unreasonably interferes with an individual's work performance, or creates an intimidating, hostile, or offensive work environment. The offender does not have to be a boss, nor does the victim have to be a female. The intimidating, hostile, or offensive behavior can be from fellow workers or agents of the employer ("Facts About . . . ," 2006). The definition has also been broadened to include unwanted sexual behavior from fellow students.

You can see that some of the key terms in this definition are broad and subject to interpretation. One person can find some behavior intimidating, hostile, or offensive, while another person can view that same act quite differently. The legal concept has become so fuzzy that a woman whose boss did *not* ask her for sexual favors—while he asked all the other women—was ruled a victim of sexual harassment (Hayes, 1991). In addition, as sociologist Kirsten Dellinger discusses in the Spotlight on Social Research box on page 306, what passes for acceptable behavior in one work setting can be taken as sexual harassment in another.

THE MITSUBISHI CASE. If a worker is sexually harassed by a boss, she or he has limited options. Objecting, submitting, or ignoring the act are all risky (MacKinnon, 1979, p. 52). Let's say that the victim is a woman. If she objects, she may be hounded into quitting or get fired outright. If she submits, the man may tire of her. If she ignores it, she can get drawn into a cat-and-mouse game with few exits: He may tire of the game and turn to someone else, or he may fire her so he can hire a more willing victim.

Or she can file a claim of sexual harassment. These claims are often settled privately, as they are usually difficult to prove. In addition, women who make legal claims run the risk of frustration, embarrassment, and retaliation at work. Victims who have taken these risks, however, have gradually transformed the workplace. The landmark decision came in 1998. Three hundred women who worked at the Illinois plant of Mitsubishi Motors claimed that the company tolerated a hostile work environment. Some claimed fellow workers had groped them; others said their bosses threatened to fire them if they didn't agree to have sex. The women were awarded $34 million, an average of $113,000 each. The size of the award caught employers' attention nationwide. They became aware that tolerating a hostile work environment could affect the corporate bottom line.

RACIAL–ETHNIC LINES. When sexual harassment crosses racial–ethnic lines, victims are put at a special disadvantage. If they protest, they can be accused of being insensitive to cultural differences—perhaps they misunderstood a "normal" sexual invitation from another racial–ethnic group. Or they can be perceived as prejudiced—offended by the sexual offer because it was made by someone of a different race–ethnicity—with the implication that they would have welcomed the suggestion had it been made by someone of their own race–ethnicity.

NOT JUST A WOMAN'S PROBLEM. Sexual harassment used to be perceived as an exclusively female problem. With more women in positions of power, men are now finding themselves victims (DeSouza & Fansler, 2003; Hill & Silva, 2005). One man claimed

Spotlight on Social Research

SEXUAL HARASSMENT AT TWO MAGAZINES

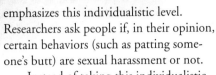

KIRSTEN DELLINGER, *associate professor of sociology at the University of Mississippi, says that her interest in gender and sexuality in organizations emerged from her own early work experiences. As she worked with autistic adults in one setting and children in another, she wondered why most workers were women and why they earned little and received little respect. From these initial observations, she turned her attention to how work is organized and the role of gender and sexuality in the work setting.*

I have been intrigued by the research that explores how organizations are "gendered" and "sexualized." One of the themes in this literature is how workplace policies create and maintain ideologies about masculinity and femininity. Another is how workers construct their gender identities through their everyday interactions. What is acceptable or not differs from one work setting to another. Take the example of sexual harassment.

Have you ever heard people say that sexual harassment is impossible to solve in the workplace because "it all depends on what an individual finds offensive"? Sally finds the joke about women's bodies funny, but Julie doesn't. Harry likes to tell stories about homosexuals, but Frank cringes when he hears them. Julie and Frank keep their mouths shut, because they hold lower positions at work. Much survey research on sexual harassment emphasizes this individualistic level. Researchers ask people if, in their opinion, certain behaviors (such as patting someone's butt) are sexual harassment or not.

Instead of taking this individualistic perspective, in my research I examine how the *social context* influences how people define sexual harassment. The research that I did with Christine Williams underlines the symbolic interactionist perspective that whether a behavior is sexual harassment or not depends on the definitions that people apply to it. And those definitions, as we found out, depend more on the social context than on individualistic perspectives.

We studied workers at two magazines who were doing the same jobs: editors, accountants, and administrative assistants. The magazines were quite different: a heterosexual men's pornographic magazine and a feminist magazine. Workers at the men's magazine, *Gentleman's Sophisticate,* worked in a "locker room" culture. Sexual joking was common, even about the magazine itself. At the same time, these workers had strict norms against discussing highly personal aspects of their own lives. Sexual harassment was defined as a violation of personal boundaries, not by how sexual a conversation was. In contrast, workers at the feminist magazine, *Womyn,* worked in something that was closer to what you find in an all-women's dorm: They expected one another to share personal aspects about their sexual lives. They wanted to analyze them through a feminist framework. These women defined sexual harassment as an abuse of power. Editors talked about being careful with the power that they had over interns, most of whom were college students. Workers at *Gentleman's Sophisticate* and at *Womyn* were using different workplace norms to define and to deal with sexual harassment.

that his chief financial officer—a woman—made sexual advances "almost daily." Another objected that his supervisor told him that she had dreamed about him naked. Some men who are victims receive little sympathy. Many men don't understand why a man would take offense at a woman's sexual advances, even from the boss (Carton, 1994). "Why not have some fun?" We anticipate that these norms will change to account for women's growing power in the workplace.

In 1998, the Supreme Court broadened sexual harassment laws to include people of the same sex. The Court ruled that sexual harassment is not limited to behavior between men and women, and it does not have to include sexual desire. This law now covers the harassment at work of homosexuals by heterosexuals (Felsenthal, 1998). By extension, the law includes the sexual harassment of heterosexuals by homosexuals.

We now turn to discussing homosexuality as a social problem.

Homosexuality

Let's begin by looking at what researchers have to say about the issues surrounding homosexuality. Despite strong social norms and early and continued efforts to socialize everyone as heterosexual, some become homosexual. How? How many people

claim to be homosexual? Do some who claim to be heterosexual secretly have sex with people of their own gender? With changing norms, how much opposition is there to homosexuality today?

Background: Getting the Larger Picture

HOMOSEXUAL BEHAVIOR VERSUS HOMOSEXUALITY. To better understand opinions surrounding homosexuality, we need to view the behavior in global perspective. Attitudes toward **homosexual behavior**—sexual *relations* between people of the same sex—vary widely around the world. To many Americans, the attitudes and behavior of the Sambia and the Keraki of New Guinea would be startling. The Sambia believe that boys do not grow into men if they do not swallow another man's semen. To ensure that they all successfully develop, Sambian boys have oral sex with other men of the tribe. The Keraki use anal intercourse as their puberty rite. At this time, older boys and the unmarried men have anal intercourse with younger boys. Until these boys marry (a woman), they, too, sodomize other younger boys (Ford & Beach, 1972). For both the Sambia and the Keraki, homosexual behaviors are considered a rite of passage toward "masculinization." Both Sambian and Keraki boys go on to live heterosexual lives; they marry women and become fathers (Gilmore, 1990).

No society in the world considers exclusive, or even predominant, **homosexuality**—the sexual orientation involving an attraction or preference for people of one's own sex—to be the norm. From a functionalist viewpoint, the primary reason for this is the family's role in human societies. To perpetuate the human group, adults are expected to become parents, and all societies build the family around some form of mother, father, and children. General homosexuality would upset this biologically based arrangement.

ATTITUDES IN THE UNITED STATES. In recent years Americans have grown more tolerant of those who identify as homosexual. This tolerance may be reflected in the changing attitudes of college freshmen. Look at Figure 9-6, which is based on national samples that

FIGURE 9-6 What Do College Freshmen Say About Homosexual Relationships Being Illegal?

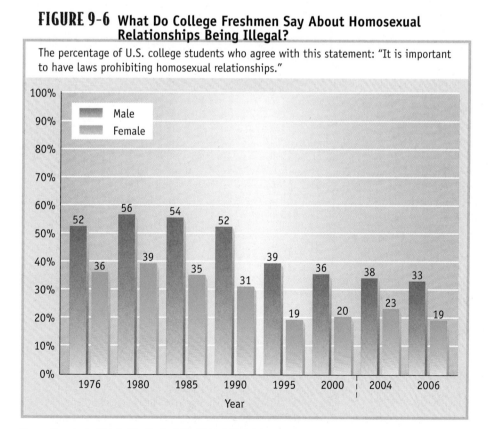

The percentage of U.S. college students who agree with this statement: "It is important to have laws prohibiting homosexual relationships."

Source: *Sourcebook of Criminal Justice Statistics* (2006, Table 2.99).

represent accurately the attitudes of all U.S. college freshmen. As you can see, attitudes were fairly consistent until 1990, after which a shift toward greater tolerance is notice-able. As you can also see, the attitudes of women are consistently more favorable than those of men.

In order to get a broader perspective on American attitudes, Table 9-4 illustrates the attitudes not only of college freshmen, but of Americans in general. The survey results shown in Table 9-4 are from a well-chosen national sample. From this table, you can see that 59% of Americans think that homosexual relations between consenting adults should be legal, and 37% want homosexual relations—even between consenting adults—to be illegal. The information from this table allows you to sketch a profile of

TABLE 9-4 Attitudes Toward the Legality of Homosexual Relations

QUESTION: "DO YOU THINK HOMOSEXUAL RELATIONS BETWEEN CONSENTING ADULTS SHOULD OR SHOULD NOT BE LEGAL?"

	LEGAL	NOT LEGAL	NO OPINION
National	59%	37%	4%
Sex			
Female	55	40	4
Male	62	35	4
Race–Ethnicity[1]			
White	60	37	3
Black	53	40	7
Age			
18–29 years	78	22	0
30–49 years	63	33	4
50–64 years	54	43	3
50 years and older	49	46	5
65 years and older	42	50	8
Education			
College postgraduate	75	21	4
College graduate	59	34	6
Some college	63	34	3
High school graduate or less	48	48	4
Income			
Under $20,000	58	36	5
$20,000–$29,999	56	43	1
$30,000–$49,999	52	44	4
$50,000–$74,999	60	37	3
$75,000 and over	67	29	3
Urban/Rural			
Urban area	66	29	5
Suburban area	57	39	3
Rural area	52	45	3
Region			
West	66	30	4
East	68	29	4
Midwest	56	40	5
South	49	47	4
Politics			
Independent	64	31	5
Democrat	71	27	2
Republican	38	58	4

[1] Only these two groups are listed in the source, other than an even more amorphous category, "Nonwhite."

Source: Sourcebook of Criminal Justice Statistics (2007, Table 2.99).

those who are most likely to support the legalization of homosexual relations: college-educated younger white women who live in a Western city or the suburbs, who make over $75,000 a year, and who are Democrats or Independents. Those most likely to want homosexual relations to be illegal are elderly black male high school graduates with low incomes who live in rural areas of the South and who vote Republican. Attitudes toward homosexual behavior, then, are related strongly to age, income, education, race–ethnicity, geography, and politics. The attitudes of men and women across the nation follow the same pattern as those of college freshmen: *Women are more likely to favor the legality of homosexual relations.*

HOMOSEXUALS AND THE LAW. The social institutions of U.S. society adopt the norm of **heterosexuality,** the sexual orientation involving an attraction or preference for people of the opposite sex. Until 1960, *in all states,* private, consensual sexual acts between adults of the same sex were illegal. In 2003, Texas and other states still had these laws on their books, but in that same year, the U.S. Supreme Court struck down the Texas law that made such sex illegal in *Lawrence et al. v. Texas* (Liptak, 2005). This decision currently applies to all states.

Over the years, homosexuals have been the victims of violent acts because of their sexual orientation. Until 1990 there was no way of tracking the extent of this victimization. When Congress passed the *Hate Crime Statistics Act,* the FBI began to collect data on "crimes that manifest evidence of prejudice based on race, religion, ethnicity, and sexual orientation." Later, disability and national origin were added to this list. **Hate crimes** are ordinary crimes such as assault motivated by dislike or hatred of the victim's personal characteristics. In the case of sexual hate crimes, the victim is chosen perhaps because he or she is a homosexual. Each year, about 1,500 homosexuals are the victims of such hate crimes (*Statistical Abstract,* 2009, Table 10). Remember that not all victims file reports and not all police agencies report these data to the FBI, so actual numbers are higher.

Homosexuals face less discrimination today because gay liberation groups, the American Civil Liberties Union, and tolerant Americans have changed mainstream attitudes. The Civil Service Commission used to deny federal employment to homosexuals, but no longer. Multinational corporations like AT&T, GM, Ford, and IBM no longer discriminate against homosexuals in hiring or promotion procedures.

The *Employment Equality (Sexual Orientation) Regulations* (2003) ban sexual discrimination in the workplace. Discrimination that draws on the assumption that a person is homosexual or bisexual, for example (regardless of whether the assumption is correct or not), is also against the law.

Despite such changes, discrimination against homosexuals persists and thrives, especially in hiring and promotion practices. Some groups continue to openly discriminate—the FBI and CIA will not hire known homosexuals. Although the Defense Department follows a "Don't Ask, Don't Tell" policy, soldiers who are discovered to be practicing homosexuals may be discharged from the military.

In order to understand homosexual–heterosexual relations from a sociological perspective, we will analyze them using the lens of conflict theory.

Homosexuality Viewed Theoretically: Applying Conflict Theory

In reaction to overt discrimination—differential treatment that is open and observable—homosexuals have found that politics is often the best way to forge social change. *Coming out of the closet*—publicly asserting their private homosexual identity—many have marched in public demonstrations campaigning for legal reform. Beginning with local campaigns in San Francisco and New York, homosexuals have made an impact on national politics, demanding equality and basic human rights. As a result, politicians now actively study homosexual voting patterns in an effort to win votes.

"Don't ask, don't tell" is the common term for the U.S. military policy that prohibits any homosexual or bisexual person from disclosing his or her sexual orientation or from speaking about any homosexual relationships, including marriages or other familial attributes, while serving in the United States armed forces.

As homosexuals have publicized their demands, homosexuality has become a more public political and social issue. The promotion of the acceptance of homosexuality as an alternative lifestyle has generated intense opposition. Conflict is inevitable when opposing groups such as this struggle for power and resources. One demands greater acceptance (homosexuals), and the other resists that demand (heterosexuals).

When conflict arises, a shift in power often results as a reevaluation of ideas, attitudes, and positions occurs. A common solution for maintaining the status quo is to allow competing groups to make compromises or trade-offs. In these instances, conflict eventually resurfaces. All it takes is for one side to try to shift the terms of this sensitive balance in favor of their position.

One example of this delicate compromise has been the legalization of same-sex marriages, civil unions, and domestic partnerships. **Same-sex marriage (SSM)** refers to the legally sanctioned marriage of two same-sex people. A legal same-sex marriage would grant both partners full legal rights in any state traveled to within the United States. A **domestic partnership** or **civil union,** on the other hand, is not a legal marriage. A domestic partnership refers to cohabitation among two same-sex people. Their union is recognized legally, but does not grant all 1,400 state and federal benefits available to heterosexual married couples. In a domestic partnership, the relationship is legally recognized only by the state that granted it. For example, if one is granted legal domestic partnership status in Maine and travels or moves to Iowa, the union would not be legally recognized in Iowa. This would be of great concern if one partner became gravely ill while traveling. The significant other would have no legal right to share in medical decision making.

The first country to recognize same-sex marriage was the Netherlands in 2001. By 2008, Belgium, Canada, Spain, Norway, and South Africa legally sanctioned same-sex marriage. Other Scandinavian countries, the United Kingdom, and several states in the United States allow homosexual couples to register their domestic partnerships—gaining some benefits. In addition to the **Defense of Marriage Act,** which Congress passed in 1996, a majority of states have enacted constitutional amendments or other laws that prohibit same-sex marriage or civil unions. A civil union, therefore, may be viewed sociologically as a "compromise" to the legality of same-sex marriage. By 2008, same-sex marriage was legal in California, Connecticut, and Massachusetts; in the 2008 election, however, California voters approved a proposition that made it once again illegal. The courts will have to decide the issue for California because the election results are being challenged on civil rights grounds.

Homosexuals and bisexuals are not the only ones in history who have fought for legal recognition of partnerships. Only after 1967 were mixed-race couples allowed to marry everywhere in the United States. Many are hopeful that same-sex marriage and full legal rights will be granted to all people of any sexual orientation in the future. Religious and social conservatives, on the other hand, view same-sex marriage as a threat to the institution of marriage. This conflict between those in power and the powerless will no doubt continue.

Research on Homosexuality

THE KINSEY RESEARCH. Let's turn now to sociological studies of homosexual behavior. Alfred Kinsey and his associates included homosexual behavior in their path-breaking study, *Sexual Behavior in the Human Male* (1948). To understand the Kinsey findings of more than a half century ago, keep in mind the distinction between homosexual behavior and homosexuality. Based on case histories of about 5,300 males, Kinsey found that 37% of men in the United States had at least one sexual experience with a same-sex partner that resulted in orgasm. Such experiences, however, do not translate into homosexuality. As Kinsey pointed out, most of these homosexual behaviors were a form of experimentation, and almost all of these

Although she never wanted to be a political figure or a spokesperson for the gay community, Ellen DeGeneres has walked through the fire and blazed a path for all gay and lesbian actors. She went through a period of intense depression, but has risen to be one of the most popular women on television.

males went on to live heterosexual lives. Kinsey concluded that only about 4% of American males are exclusively homosexual.

Kinsey's findings shocked the American public and unleashed a storm of criticism in the academic community. The primary problem was that Kinsey's sample was biased, and there was no scientific way to generalize from his findings. The reason social scientists argued that the sample was biased was because Kinsey recruited his subjects from prisons and reform schools. These men hardly represented the general population. He also interviewed only white lower-class males (Himmelhoch & Fava, 1955). Consequently, researchers no longer trust Kinsey's findings.

THE LAUMANN RESEARCH. In an effort to collect more accurate data, a team of researchers headed by sociologist Edward Laumann researched sexual behavior in the United States (1994). Laumann interviewed a representative sample of the U.S. population, allowing others to generalize his findings to the entire U.S. population. As you can see from Figure 9-7, Laumann found that during the preceding 5 years, 2.2% of women and 4.1% of men in the United States had had sex with a same-sex partner. When the time period is extended to include all the years of their lives, these totals increase to 3.8% for women and 7.1% for men. This is a far cry from Kinsey's 37% for men.

As Figure 9-7 also shows, 1.4% of American women and 2.8% of American men identify themselves as homosexuals. These percentages are almost identical to those who reported that they had sex with a same-sex partner during the preceding year (1.3% of women and 2.7% of men). Even these figures may be slightly high, as the Laumann researchers included bisexuals in the homosexual data.

In the Spotlight on Social Research box on page 53, Laumann explains why he did his research and the opposition he experienced while collecting such data.

Laumann's sampling technique allowed us to generalize to the broader U.S. population, but did not provide us with qualitative or narrative data. **Narrative data** is unstructured data that tells a story. It allows us to analyze people's thoughts and understand their perspectives. Qualitative data helps us understand how people construct their own world, as we discussed in Chapter 2 in exploring the social construction of reality.

FIGURE 9-7 Homosexual Identity and Sex with Someone of the Same Sex

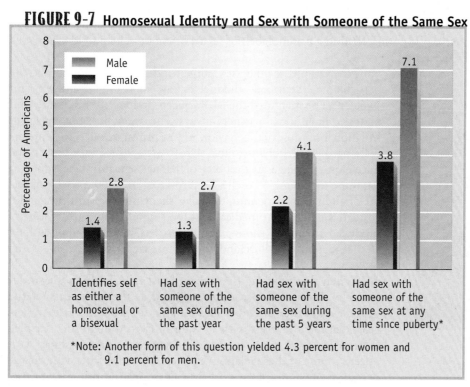

Source: Laumann et al. (1994, pp. 293–296).

THE HUMPHREYS RESEARCH. To collect unstructured data on homosexual behavior, sociologist Laud Humphreys devised an ingenious but widely criticized research method. Humphreys knew that some males engage in impersonal sex in public restrooms (these meeting places are called "tea-rooms," in homosexual vernacular); Humphreys (1970/ 1975) began hanging around these restrooms (literally). Taking the role of "watch queen," the one who gives warning to participants when strangers approach the restroom, he observed what went on in these tea-rooms. Humphreys recorded how these men used a system of gestures to initiate sex at the urinal and then moved to a toilet stall for fellatio (oral sex). Their random, anonymous sex often occurred without the exchange of a single word.

Humphreys wanted to know why these men engaged in random homosexual acts, so he decided to interview them. He wrote down their license plate numbers and then traced their home addresses. With the cooperation of his professors, who were conducting a health survey, he had these men unknowingly added to their study. Humphreys then interviewed the men in their homes, supposedly for the purpose of the medical study. Once there, he learned that 38% of the men he observed having tea-room sex were married. For this deception, Humphreys was criticized severely by other sociologists and the public.

He also learned that the men identified themselves as full-time heterosexuals, but when frustrated sexually with their wives, they sought pleasure in tea-rooms. They reported that having sex in a tea-room did not threaten their emotional commitment to their wives because it was anonymous. Humphreys also learned that these men sought out tea-room sex because it was convenient, a fast stop on their way home from work. In essence, the tea-rooms functioned as a free house of prostitution, a place where the men could obtain quick oral sex with no emotional entanglements. Sociologists Jay Corzine and Richard Kirby (1977) discovered similar homosexual acts at truck stops: Heterosexual truckers have sex with homosexuals who search out partners at highway rest areas.

SITUATIONAL HOMOSEXUAL BEHAVIOR: THE PRISON. Certain places, such as prisons and boarding schools, lend themselves to **situational homosexual behavior.** This term refers to homosexual acts committed by people who, if members of the opposite sex were available, would choose to be involved in heterosexual relations. To better understand situational homosexual behavior, let's look at a study of inmates in the state prison at Soledad, California. Within a prison, labels of sexual orientation help to identify one's preferences.

The queen does not engage in situational homosexual behavior, for, in prison or out, "she" prefers male partners.

For example, sociologist George Kirkham (1971) found that the participants identified themselves as "queens," "punks," and "wolves." The men used the label "queen" to identify an inmate who preferred male sexual partners always. The queen does not engage in situational homosexual behavior, for, in prison or out, "she" prefers male partners. Kirkham found that to attract fellow prisoners, the queen often exaggerates aspects of female sexuality. She adopts a feminine nickname ("Peaches," "Dee-Dee"), tears the back pockets off of tight prison denims to make them more form-fitting, uses cosmetics made from medical and food supplies, and wears jewelry produced in hobby shops. The queen lets her hair grow as long as the guards will allow and shows an exaggerated "swish" as she walks.

When first entering the prison, most men find the queen despicable. As months pass, however, and as the femininity of the queen evokes their memory and longing for women, staunch heterosexual men have sex with the queen. Even though they are heterosexual, some men enter into long-term relationships with queens. Some of these relationships resemble marriage, with the expectation of monogamous fidelity. These relationships are brittle,

though, for most queens are promiscuous, and some are forced into prostitution by prison pimps.

A situational homosexual within the prison system is called a "punk." A punk has the least social status among prisoners. There are two types: "canteen punks," who exchange sex for candy, cigarettes, or personal favors, and "pressure punks," who give sex to other men under threats of violence. Punks are despised by other prisoners because they sacrifice their manhood to obtain goods or services, or they show weakness in the face of violence.

Remember that sociology focuses on learned behavior, so how do prisoners become pressure punks? Some are beaten and gang-raped and then forced into this status for the rest of their prison term. Others are tricked into it. When a new inmate, unacquainted with prison ways, accepts cigarettes, money, or help of some sort from an experienced inmate, he is required to pay back this debt. Often he is told that he can give sex as payment. At this point, he only has two choices—to submit or fight. A new inmate who submits is marked as a punk from then on and must continue to provide sex for the rest of his prison term.

In some prisons in Texas, any identified homosexual who is incarcerated is "claimed" by a gang. This man is gang-raped by the gang members and forced into the role of sex slave for his entire prison term. He is rented out or sold, as the gang desires. Each gang typically owns only one sex slave, so when another homosexual is admitted to the prison, another gang claims that individual for its own use (Liptak, 2004).

Lastly, the "wolf" is a situational homosexual who has sex with punks, yet he does not lose his status as a "man." In order to remain a stereotypical "man" and still engage in sex with other men, he presents an image of machismo—excessive masculinity—or toughness. Because force and rape match the machismo image that prisoners live up to, the more violence that surrounds the wolf's sexual acts, the more he is seen as masculine. Some wolves "own" punks and prostitute them for cigarettes, drugs, or other favors. Situational homosexuality helps us understand how some are thrust into homosexual acts because of their environment.

IN SUM As stressed in Chapter 1, no social problem has only objective conditions. Like other social problems, homosexuality is a social problem because of subjective concerns. The major concern stressed by mainstream heterosexuals is that homosexuality is immoral, posing a threat to the family. Others argue that homosexuals should be protected under the law with their unions legally recognized.

Homosexuality and the Future

Two primary issues are generating controversy. The first is the political struggle by homosexuals to be allowed legal marriage. This issue is likely to reach the U.S. Supreme Court, where the decision will be decided not according to the U.S. Constitution, but by the justices who happen to make up the Court when the case comes before it. Obviously, then, the decision could go either way. The second issue also centers on a legal and social right: to serve as role models, to be openly homosexual, and to occupy positions, such as public school teachers and scout leaders, who mold the orientations of youth. The vast middle ground between those who espouse homosexuality and those who fear or despise it is likely to be occupied by those who believe that homosexuality should be discouraged but that homosexuals should not be oppressed.

Violence Against Women

RAPE AND MURDER. Fears of rape and murder surround women in this society. Women are warned that they can be abducted while out by themselves in public. We have already discussed rape and murder in Chapter 5, and there is no need to go beyond that chapter's materials. We need to stress one of the main points of that chapter, though: Women tend to be the victims, men the rapists and killers.

GENDERED VIOLENCE. In the United States women are disproportionately victims of spousal abuse and rape. In other countries women are victimized through female genital mutilation (FGM) and honor killings. FGM is the focus of the Global Glimpse box on page 285. Another form of violence alien to Western culture is "honor killings." These are killings of girls and women who have violated the family's honor by stepping outside the culture's sexual boundaries. In the typical case, the daughter or mother is accused of having sexual relations outside of marriage. It is the duty of a male family member, ordinarily the father, brother, or uncle, to restore the family's honor by killing the accused girl or woman. Honor killings are common in the Islamic world, especially in Pakistan.

APPLYING THE CONFLICT AND FEMINIST PERSPECTIVE. To explain why girls and women are the typical victims of violence, some sociologists use conflict theory and/or feminist theory. They argue that we can understand violence against women if we view it as an expression of power. Family violence, for example, stems from men expressing their greater power over women in the family. Men who are granted greater power in society exploit wives and children—the powerless.

APPLYING SYMBOLIC INTERACTIONISM. Sociologists also use symbolic interactionism to understand gendered violence. They stress that in American culture men learn machismo—to "associate power, dominance, strength, virility, and superiority with masculinity" (Scully, 1990). Strength and virility are goals American boys strive to achieve. Surrounding us are men in positions of power, men who dominate society.

But how does machismo turn into violence? Males are surrounded with models of violence. Of the many examples that we could select, let's highlight video games. In many of these games, the goal is to hunt down and kill enemies—from mythical creatures to iconic men. In some games, those who are to be hunted down and killed are barely clad young women (Pereira, 1993). Perhaps more than any other medium, video games send the message that women are not important. In many video games, male characters outnumber female characters 7 to 1 (Beasley & Standley, 2002). Video game themes are often sexist, violent, and sexually explicit. In one game, *Grand Theft Auto,* a male character can be made to rape a prostitute. We need to stress that most players of video games are boys and young men. Although the form may change, symbols of violence continue to be a feature of the male world.

Social Policy

Irreconcilable Ideologies

As we have seen with other social problems, improved social policy can be effective in reducing inequality. Let's turn now to an overview of social policy as it applies to inequalities of gender and sexual orientation.

As stressed earlier, those social policies that get approved depend on people's assumptions of justice, of what is right, or of how things in life should be. To view all possible proposals for reducing sex discrimination, let's look at *radical extremists* and *conservative extremists*. Each term combines several groups and organizations.

THE RADICAL EXTREMISTS. Radical extremists insist that society is so discriminatory that it must be restructured. As sociologist Jessie Bernard (1971) stressed, it is not enough to demand equal pay, break the glass ceiling, or reduce hate. Bernard claims we need strong social policies that eradicate the roots of sexism.

Because the roots of sexism reach back into childhood socialization, we need to remove distinctions between boys and girls. Girls and boys would have to be socialized in the same way. They would have to be treated equally throughout education, from preschool to graduate school. This would include athletics, sports, and sexual orientation.

Husbands and wives would have to share housework equally, and both parents would have to compete equally in the world of work. Ultimately, men and women would hold all positions in our social institutions equally (Bernard, 1971).

Such extreme social policies are not plausible in our society; therefore these goals are not likely to be achieved in our lifetime.

THE CONSERVATIVE EXTREMISTS. Opposing policies come from conservative extremists. They believe that heterosexual gender distinctions are natural and desirable and ought to be encouraged. They argue that a woman's proper role is as a homemaking wife and mother; a man's is as a breadwinning husband and father. This ideology would require parents to take full responsibility and care for their own preschool children. There would be no publicly supported child care. Girls would be encouraged to become full-time wives and mothers and boys to become the protectors and primary source of financial support of their wives and children. Children's picture books and school texts would present women and men in these traditional roles. Full-time homemakers would receive tax breaks, and job preference would be given to men who are supporting dependents.

Again, absent their enforcement, these social policies are likely to not be achieved anytime soon.

MIDDLE-OF-THE-ROAD POLICIES. Innumerable positions fall between these two extremes. It is likely that some of the more middle-of-the-road policies reflect your own views and the causes you support: well-run child care facilities for working parents, policies that foster closer relations of fathers with their children, the right for both mother and father to take extended leaves from work when a child is born or sick, same-sex marriage laws, enforcement of child support, the end of the gender pay gap, and, at home, a more equitable distribution of housework.

The Future of the Problem

Although sexism and discrimination are likely to remain facts of life, historical trends point toward greater equality between women and men of any sexual orientation. Today's and tomorrow's struggle centers on removing stereotypes, eliminating the gender gap in pay, and gaining greater access to leadership, especially in business and politics.

THE WORLD OF WORK. The most significant social trend that will affect gender discrimination is the future employment of women. As even larger numbers of women join and remain in the paid workforce, women will continue to reshape social relationships. Power relationships between husbands and wives will be altered, because wives who work outside the home have more control over family decisions than wives who do not. As more wives work outside the home, husbands will gradually take on greater responsibilities for housework and children. This will not result in equality in household responsibilities anytime soon, however, for studies show that men resist doing housework even in dual-earner families (Bianchi et al., 2000; Batalova & Cohen, 2002).

Women are likely to make greater use of the Equal Pay Act of 1963 (forbidding discrimination in salaries), Title VII of the Civil Rights Act of 1964 (forbidding discrimination on the basis of sex), and the Fourteenth Amendment (forbidding a state to "deny any person within its jurisdiction the equal protection of the laws"). Such legal pressures will not eliminate the problem, but they will continue to undermine the structure of sexism.

BREAKING GENDER STEREOTYPES. The increasing numbers of women in the workforce are already changing gender stereotypes, a change that will likely continue. More children are growing up with the model of a mother who more fully participates in family decisions. Children who see both mother and father bringing home paychecks take it for

granted that a man is not the exclusive breadwinner and that a woman is more than a mother and a wife. As stereotypes continue to fall, both men and women will be free to do activities compatible with their desires as *individuals*—not because the activity matches a stereotype. This will free men to play more supportive roles and "get more in touch with their feelings" and women to take leadership roles and become more assertive.

NEW ORIENTATIONS. As sociologist Janet Giele said in the 1970s, the ultimate possibility for the future is a new concept of the human personality (Giele, 1978). Stereotypes and gendered roles push us into activities dictated by our culture. As stereotypes are abandoned and as activities become gender-neutral, men and women will develop a new consciousness of who they are and of their potential. New paths will open, ones that allow feelings and expressions of needs that our current stereotypes deny. Women are likely to think of themselves as more active masters of their environment, men to feel and express more emotional sensitivity. Each will be free to explore these other dimensions of the self. As the future unfolds, it will reveal exactly what such "greater wholeness" of men and women looks like.

SUMMARY AND REVIEW

1. Although females make up 50.9% of the U.S. population, men discriminate against them. Consequently, sociologists refer to men as a dominant group and women as a minority group.
2. Every society *sex-types* occupations. That is, around the world, some work is thought suitable for men and other work appropriate for women. There is no inherent biological connection between work and its assignment to women or men, for "women's work" of one society may be "men's work" in another. In all societies, "men's work" is given greater prestige than "women's work."
3. Symbolic interactionists examine *gender* (masculinity and femininity), looking at how each society socializes the sexes into its ideas of what men and women ought to be like. Socialization includes learning *sexism,* the belief that one sex is innately superior to the other and the discriminatory practices that result from that belief.
4. Functionalists theorize that sexual discrimination is based on the need of early human groups to engage in hand-to-hand combat. Men had the physical advantage but needed to be motivated to become warriors. Women, offered as inducements for men to fight, were assigned the drudge work of society. A second functionalist explanation is that because women were encumbered physically through childbearing and nursing, men became dominant as they took control of warfare and trade.
5. Conflict theorists emphasize that the rights that American women enjoy came out of a power struggle with men. The confrontations and violence between the sexes in the late 1800s and early 1900s have been

replaced by legal pressure and economic and educational competition.
6. Given the inextricability of nature and nurture, we do not know the extent to which natural differences exist between the sexes. Both genetics and socialization can explain females' earlier proficiency in verbal skills and males' greater aggressiveness and abilities at mathematics.
7. Women confront discrimination in most areas of life, including a belittling attitude from men. The educational system and the mass media generally support existing gender roles. Although women outnumber men as voters, men dominate politics; women tend to see politics as incompatible with femininity and motherhood.
8. Women often work at jobs that pay less and that offer less advancement. They also confront *sexual harassment* at work. As more women have moved into power positions at work, men, too, experience sexual harassment.
9. In applying conflict theory to homosexuality, we see that fundamental tensions exist between homosexuals and heterosexuals and that their adjustment to one another is uneasy.
10. All social policies to deal with sex discrimination have ideological implications. Different groups of women propose antithetical social policies.
11. In the future, even larger numbers of women will be employed outside the home. This will continue to change power relationships at home and break down traditional stereotypes. The direction of the future is toward greater equality between the sexes.

KEY TERMS

THINKING CRITICALLY ABOUT CHAPTER 9

1. List 10 examples of sexism in the United States. In what ways do you think that your list would be different if you had written it 10 years ago? In what ways do you think it would be different if you were to write it 10 years from now?
2. Which of the three theoretical perspectives (symbolic interactionism, functionalism, or conflict theory) do you think best explains sexism in the United States? Why?
3. What are the main changes that you see occurring in gender roles? Why do you think we are experiencing these changes?
4. A developing social problem is mentioned on page 293: 2 million more women in college than men and women earning 58% of all bachelors' degrees. Do you think we should start affirmative action and special remedial and motivational courses for men? Why or why not?

MySocLab

What can you find in MySocLab? mysoclab ALLYN & BACON Where learning & the sociological imagination intersect. www.mysoclab.com

- Complete Ebook
- Practice Tests and Exams
- Multimedia Activities
- Mapping and Data Analysis Exercises

- Research and Writing Advice
- Interactive Social Surveys
- Sociology in the News

CHAPTER 10

Medical Care: Physical and Mental Illness

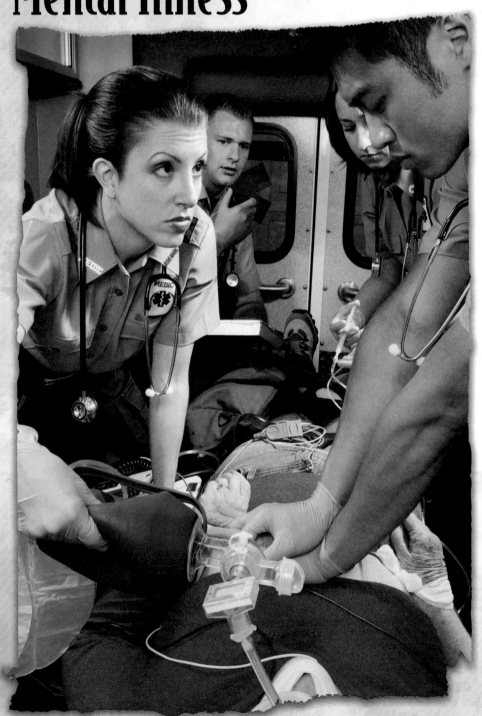

To prepare for the birth of their first child, Kathie Persall and her husband, Hank, read books and articles about childbirth and took childbirth classes together. At 5 o'clock one morning, as Kathie woke from a fitful sleep, the protective "bag of waters" that surrounds the fetus broke.

By 10 a.m., Kathie was on the maternity ward, hooked up to an electronic fetal monitor (EFM) and an intravenous feeding tube. She was informed of the hospital's rule that to prevent infection, delivery must take place within 24 hours after the waters break. At 11 a.m. the resident physician (not her own doctor) said that they would speed up Kathie's labor by using Pitocin, a powerful drug.

Kathie's sister, Carol, knew that inducing labor could lead to cesarean section. She urged Hank to get Kathie off Pitocin, but Kathie and Hank felt that they couldn't tell the doctor what to do. By evening, doctors decided that Kathie's cervix was not dilating rapidly enough. They increased the Pitocin. One nurse thought that the flow of Pitocin looked blocked. She wiggled the bottle, and a large dose sped through Kathie's veins. Kathie writhed in pain as a massive contraction took over her body. Five or ten minutes later, the fetal monitor indicated that the baby's heartbeat had dropped from 160

> ## Kathie was in pain and exhausted.

to 40 beats per minute. The doctor rushed in, cut off the Pitocin, and gave Kathie another drug to stop the contraction. He told them that a cesarean might be necessary. Hank, who had been trying to comfort Kathie, protested. The doctor told them that they could face an emergency, and they had to sign a consent form. On the form, Hank and Kathie read a long list of things that could go wrong. They did not want to sign the form, but how could they resist? Kathie was in pain and exhausted.

At midnight, the doctor told Kathie that a cesarean was necessary because she had dilated only 5 centimeters in 13 hours of labor and would need another 13 hours to dilate enough to have a vaginal birth. Kathie knew it was wrong to assume that just because the first 5 centimeters had taken 13 hours that the next would take as long. Nevertheless, she felt overpowered, and at 1:10 a.m. Kathie went into surgery.

When the baby was born, Kathie was vomiting too severely from the anesthetic to even look at her new son. It took Kathie 7 weeks to recover physically from the cesarean surgery. She was left with a disfiguring scar, but this was nothing compared with her anger at the doctors, the hospital, and the medical procedures that had created the need for surgery.

The Problem in Sociological Perspective

Earlier we focused on the twin problems of crime and the criminal justice system. As we consider medical care, we again need to focus on twin problems: illness and the medical care system. Our focus will be on how *social* factors affect health.

Subjective concerns about this medical problem run high. As Table 10-1 on the next page shows, the U.S. public views health care as the third most pressing social problem needing government attention. Health care outranks taxes, terrorism, and crime as problems the government needs to address.

TABLE 10-1 The Ten Most Important Problems Facing the Nation

RANK	PROBLEM	PERCENT WHO RANK IT NUMBER ONE OR TWO
1	The economy[1]	47%
2	War[2]	24
3	Health care[3]	18
4	Terrorism[4]	12
5	Education	11
6	Taxes	5
7	Budget deficit	5
8	Environment	4
9	Crime	3
10	Drugs	3

A random sample of Americans was asked "What do you think are the two most important issues for the government to address?" To compute these rankings, similar categories have been combined, namely:

[1] The economy (general) and unemployment
[2] War, Iraq, and defense (military)
[3] Health care and Medicare
[4] Terrorism and domestic security

Source: By James M. Henslin. Based on *Sourcebook of Criminal Justice Statistics* (2005, Table 2.2).

The Social Nature of Health and Illness

NOT JUST BIOLOGY. Most of us think of illness in biological terms, but there is a social component as well. What is considered healthy or sick is also culturally defined. This may seem strange—isn't a high fever always a sign of illness? Not always. Many dismiss low-grade fevers as "just a little temperature." Even when it is considered a sign of illness, interpretations of what that fever means differ among cultures and among medical authorities as well.

INDUSTRIALIZATION AND LIFESTYLE. The social nature of health and illness is also apparent when we consider industrialization and lifestyle. When the United States became an industrialized nation, heart disease became the number one killer. Industrialization brought with it greater affluence. People began to eat richer foods, exercise less, and suffer more stress. One consequence, then, was an increase in the number of heart attacks. Similarly, the pursuit of pleasure can often be a cause of disease. Consider those illnesses related to unprotected sex—HIV, gonorrhea, syphilis, and herpes. Then, too, there is the whole array of diseases that result from smoking, drinking, and doing drugs.

IATROGENESIS. Iatrogenesis refers to illness caused by medical care staff. An example of this occurred in our opening vignette, when the nurse jiggled Kathie's bottle of Pitocin and the baby's heartbeat plummeted. Iatrogenesis is not rare. Each year, about 90,000 Americans die at the hands of doctors. *If the number of Americans killed by medical errors became an official classification of death, it would rank as number 6 in the top 10 leading causes of death* (Health Grades, 2005). The discussion on medical incompetence in the Thinking Critically box on the next page focuses on another aspect of iatrogenesis.

CHANGING IDEAS ABOUT HEALTH AND ILLNESS. The way pregnancy is handled by physicians also highlights the *social* nature of health and illness. Physicians have defined a natural process (pregnancy and birth) as something requiring fetal monitors, powerful drugs, and medical supervision. Many doctors now define a woman as "ill" if she does not deliver within 24 hours after her water breaks. This arbitrary definition of "illness" is imposed on all women regardless of whether they deliver a baby in 1 hour or 48 hours.

The definitions of "diseases" are not fixed either. For example, coal miners used to think of lung cancer as an almost inevitable consequence of their job. Becoming short of breath and coughing up blood was something that "just happened" to longtime coal workers. They even wrote folk songs about "black lung." Eventually, however, coal workers were convinced that their symptoms were signs of true disease. In order to get adequate medical care and compensation, unions had to fight the medical profession. Doctors refused to acknowledge that coal mining caused these health problems. The coal miners' subjective concerns and their struggle to get their disease recognized brought about a new understanding of lung cancer and the environmental causes of illness (B. E. Smith, 1987).

ENVIRONMENT AND DISEASE ON A GLOBAL LEVEL. Medical researchers are investigating how the environment affects human disease. Specifically, they are looking at how human activities reshape the environment, which, in turn, has profound effects on the diseases that humans experience. This is the topic of the Global Glimpse box on page 322.

IN SUM We usually think of illness and disease as biological matters. Biology is certainly involved, but what is considered health and illness is also a *social* matter. At one

THINKING CRITICALLY about Social Problems

HOW INCOMPETENT ARE DOCTORS?

What are your thoughts surrounding these three statements?

1. Most physicians are competent, but all physicians make mistakes sometimes.
2. Some physicians are so incompetent that they should not practice medicine.
3. Some of the most incompetent physicians are so admired by their medical colleagues that they are promoted to leadership positions regardless of mistakes made.

You may agree with statements 1 and 2, but find statement 3 outrageous. During a postdoctoral fellowship, Jim Henslin studied suicide in Missouri. He discovered that a coroner missed "obvious" clues in cases of suicide and murder. This coroner had served as president of the Ohio State Medical Association 3 years before his exposure.

When these mistakes were brought to the attention of the public, the sheriff's department investigated the coroner. Among the coroner's mistakes were the following erroneous rulings of death:

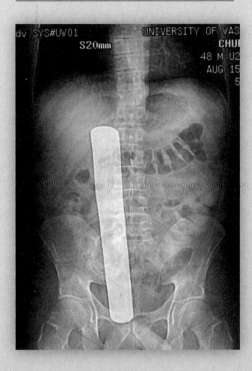

Supposedly, the surgeon at the University of Washington Medical Center who left this 13-inch steel retractor in a patient became "distracted" during the surgery. Some distraction!

- A man who had been run over with a bulldozer had his death reported as a suicide.
- A man's death was reported as carbon monoxide suicide from lawn mower fumes. The mower didn't work.

Other medical blunders include the following: (1) When a woman entered a New York City hospital because of a problem with her lungs, her surgeon did a hysterectomy. (2) A doctor removed the wrong kidney from a patient—leaving the cancerous one intact. (3) A woman awoke from surgery to find that the surgeon had removed the wrong breast. (4) In a Tampa hospital, a respiratory technician was supposed to disconnect a man from a ventilator. The technician disconnected the wrong patient. He died an hour later.

We trust that these medical professionals will not be promoted. But that coroner did become president of the state medical association. . . . What do you think?

Based on Associated Press (1995); Steinhauer (2001); Steinhauer and Fessenden (2001).

---

point in time, a physical condition such as pregnancy can be considered natural, and at another point in time it can be considered a medical matter. Similarly, what we claim are the causes of health problems are directly linked to society. The black lung problems once viewed as "weakness" on the part of coal miners were later redefined as a serious disease stemming from environmental conditions.

The Social Organization of Medicine as a Source of Problems

When we look at issues of health as social problems, we look not only at particular illnesses but also at the *system* of health care. Let's consider medical costs, cesarean births, and the quality of medical care.

AN EXPLOSION IN MEDICAL COSTS. As many of us realize, it can be very expensive to visit a doctor. View Figure 10-1 on page 323 to see how little it used to cost to deliver a baby in a hospital. The total bill of $113.85 in 1962 included a 3-day stay in the hospital for the mother, her anesthetic, lab fees, medicine, dressings, delivery room, nursery, and even

A Global Glimpse

A MEDICAL MYSTERY: ON BATS, FRUIT FLIES, AND ASTHMA

Why has the rate of asthma doubled among preschoolers in the United States? Why were people in Malaysia suddenly struck by the Nipah virus? Why has Lyme disease become a serious danger to wilderness campers?

Such changes in the prevalence of disease have alarmed the public and perplexed medical researchers. Medical mysteries like these often result from social change. Let's explore some conclusions being drawn by medical researchers studying the intricate relationship between the environment and disease.

One remarkable finding is that the destruction of the environment is directly related to an increase in human disease. For example, deforestation, the extensive cutting down of trees, can bring disease to humans. The early 1990s saw extensive deforestation in Malaysia and huge forest fires in Sumatra. These events destroyed much of the natural habitat of the fruit bats that carry the Nipah virus. In their search for food, the bats moved closer to where humans lived, settling in backyard fruit trees. From this contact, the Nipah virus moved from pigs to people.

The increase in malaria has been shown to stem from deforestation and human waste. Clearing forests of trees leaves holes that fill with water when it rains—these pools of standing water become breeding grounds for mosquitoes that carry malaria. The widespread use of inexpensive plastic bags has also produced an increase in malaria rates. When millions of these bags are discarded, they collect water, again increasing breeding sites for mosquitoes.

Globalization, too, is leaving its impact on disease. The world's increasing trade introduces plants and animals to new parts of the world, disrupting the balance of the ecosystem. Ships, for example, suck up water for ballast at one port and then disgorge the water at their destination in another region of the globe. The ballast contains plant and animal species, and the ships transfer them from one part of the world to another. In their new homes, some of these species don't have natural enemies to keep them in check, as they would in their home ecosystem. Algae from Asia, for example, have been transferred to Europe's North Sea. There they contaminate shellfish, which, when eaten, make humans sick.

Let's go back to the initial medical problem mentioned at the beginning of this box. Why has asthma more than doubled among U.S. preschool children? The answer to this huge increase has proved elusive to medical researchers, but they now think they are unraveling its cause. The major suspect turns out to be diesel emissions. Research shows that vehicle exhaust not only exaggerates asthma but also triggers it (National Resources Defense Council, 2002).

Diesel emissions, of course, are related to global warming, which in itself is having an impact on disease. Consider ticks. As the earth warms, ticks find more hospitable environments, and they multiply. The more ticks, the more humans get bit. The more that humans get bit, the more Lyme disease there is. Global warming is expected to continue, and researchers expect this to further increase rates of Lyme disease. With continued warming, the ticks that carry Lyme disease will move northward, from the United States into Canada. Soon not just American campers will be at risk, but so will their Canadian counterparts.

Understanding the root cause of disease has been of key concern for medical practitioners since the beginning of medical history. Back in the 1800s, London physicians were perplexed by the city's outbreak of deadly cholera. There was no cure, and healthy Londoners were struck dead almost overnight. Some areas were hit hard, while others had only a few cases. John Snow, a physician, painstakingly plotted the outbreak, noting on a map of London where each victim had lived. As he studied the map, it became apparent that the victims were clustered around certain wells. Snow speculated that some wells were contaminated and that if they were shut down, the epidemic could be halted. He removed the pump handle from one well in an area where 500 people had died in 10 days. The cholera was stopped in its tracks, defeated not by medicine but by medical investigation.

Today, medical researchers are trying to tease out more of these intricate connections between human activities and disease. One conclusion that we will be stressing in the coming chapter on the environment is that "everything is connected to everything else." The relationship between human activities, the environment, and disease is an example of this principle.

Based on Cooper (2002); Lloyd (2006).

---

the circumcision of her son. Due to the rising cost of health care, the dollar today buys what 19 cents would have bought in 1962.

Figure 10-2 on the next page provides another illustration of how medical costs have continued to soar. In 1960, the nation's cost of medical care was $27 billion. By 2006 it

had exploded to $2.1 trillion, *78 times higher*. During this time, the cost of other goods increased 6 times due to inflation. If medical costs increased at the same rate as average inflation, the nation's annual medical bill would be about $260 billion, one-eighth of what it is now.

Reasons for the Explosion in Costs ■ Why did the nation's medical bill explode? There are four reasons: (1) With an increase in the standard of living, people live longer. As a result of this new longevity, we now have more aged people in our population—and, overall, older people require more medical treatment than others. (2) The development of expensive technology continues as patients demand the latest treatment. (3) Most Americans seek out health care after illness arises, rather than investing time and energy in preventive care. (4) There is an accepted view that medical care is a commodity that should be sold for profit.

MEDICINE FOR PROFIT: A TWO-TIER SYSTEM OF MEDICAL CARE. Medicine for profit is also known as a *fee-for-service system*. Under this system, physicians collect a fee for each service they perform. Just like mechanics and plumbers, the more services that physicians sell, the more money they make. The fee-for-service system makes health care a commodity to be sold, not a right granted to citizens.

Through such social policy we have created a **two-tier system of medical care:** one for those who can afford insurance, and another for those who cannot. Because our society treats health care as a commodity to be sold to the

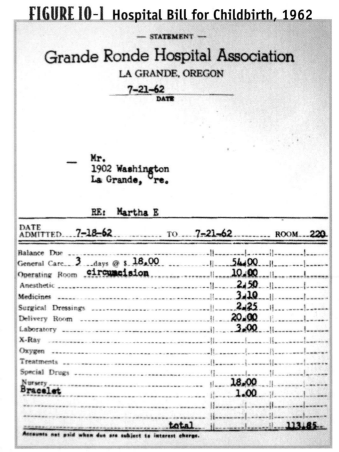

FIGURE 10-1 Hospital Bill for Childbirth, 1962

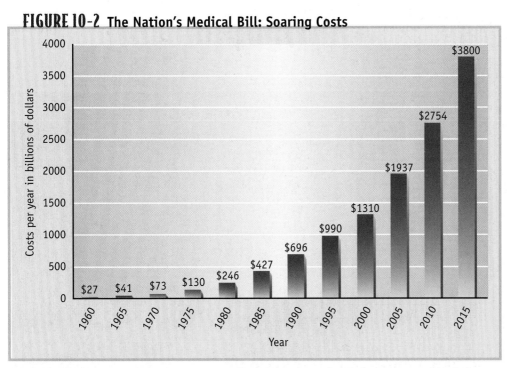

FIGURE 10-2 The Nation's Medical Bill: Soaring Costs

Note: Year 2010 is an estimate by the U.S. Centers for Medicare and Medicaid Services. The source also contains an estimate for 2015, to which a moderate increase has been added.

Source: By James M. Henslin. Based on *Statistical Abstract of the United States* (2006, Table 118).

highest bidder, our medical care ranges from the finest in the world at major universities to that provided by an underground network of unlicensed, foreign-trained physicians who can barely understand their patients.

WOMEN'S REPRODUCTIVE ORGANS. Sociologists who have done participant observation of doctors report a bias *against* women's reproductive organs. Sociologist Sue Fisher (1986), for example, was surprised to hear surgeons recommend total hysterectomy (the removal of both the uterus and the ovaries) even when no cancer was present. She found that male doctors regard the uterus and ovaries as a "potentially disease-producing" organ—useless and unnecessary after childbearing age. Some surgeons routinely recommend this profitable operation for every woman who has finished bearing children. *Most* of the 600,000 hysterectomies performed each year in the United States are unnecessary (Broder et al., 2000). It is no wonder that feminists refer to hysterectomies as a "war on the womb" (Fisher, 1986).

Many surgeons view hysterectomies as a money-making opportunity. To increase profits, they drum up business by "selling" the operation. Here is how one resident explained it to sociologist Diana Scully (1994):

> You have to look for your surgical procedures; you have to go after patients. Because no one is crazy enough to come and say, "Hey, here I am. I want you to operate on me." You have to sometimes convince the patient that she is really sick—if she is, of course [laughs], and that she is better off with a surgical procedure.

Some surgeons try to convince women to "buy" the operation they are offering for sale by scaring them. They tell a woman that her fibroids *might* turn into cancer. This statement is often sufficient, for the woman can picture herself lying in a casket, her tearful family inconsolable after the loss of their wife and mother. What the surgeon does *not* say is the rest of the truth—that fibroids are not likely to turn into cancer and that several nonsurgical treatments are available.

MEDICINE FOR PROFIT: CESAREAN DELIVERY. Consider our opening vignette: Do you think that Kathie's physician required cesarean surgery so that he could earn a larger fee? This is unlikely. But some physicians really are that driven by profit, performing

Today's rate of cesarean births is five times what it used to be.

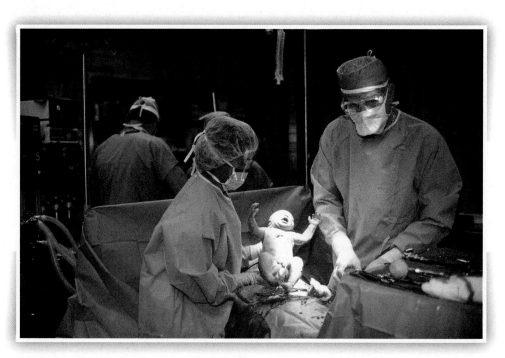

FIGURE 10-3 The Growth in Cesarean Births

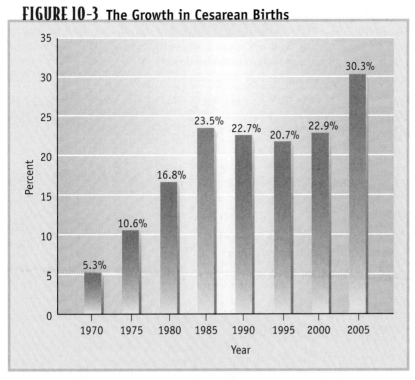

Source: By James M. Henslin. Based on *Statistical Abstract of the United States* (1990, Tables 88, 89; 2000, Table 90; 2007, Table 86).

unnecessary surgeries to increase their profits. As shown in Figure 10-3, in 1970 about 1 of 19 babies was delivered by cesarean section; now the total is 1 of every 3 or 4 (29%) (Finegold, 2006). During a **cesarean section** (C-section)—a baby is delivered through abdominal surgery.

Why have Cesarean Births Increased? ■ Have women in the United States become less healthy than they used to be and therefore less able to deliver babies naturally?

We know that women are living longer today than ever before, so there is no truth to the claim that today's women are less healthy. The answer, then, must have something to do with the medical profession's approach to childbirth. Some hospitals, for example, have a cesarean rate 5 times as high as that of other hospitals (Kilborn, 1998).

Please note that the number of C-sections has risen even though they carry greater health risks for the mother. These risks include bleeding, sterility, and death (Baldo, 2008). Compared with women who give birth vaginally, women who have cesarean births have to stay in the hospital longer and are more likely to be rehospitalized after childbirth ("Rates of . . . ," 2006). Finally, and most significantly, *most cesarean deliveries are medically unnecessary.*

Profit: Then why are so many U.S. births by C-section? The major factor seems to be the increase in income stream among obstetricians—doctors who specialize in childbirth. Being able to charge more for such births motivates doctors to encourage them. Obstetricians' income has increased so much that, with the exception of anesthesiologists and surgeons, it is higher than that of all the other medical specialties ("Physicians and Surgeons" 2006).

Convenience: Perhaps equally significant is that cesarean births *allow doctors to take control* of the delivery process. Instead of having to come into the labor and delivery room at 3 a.m.—no one likes this—the doctor can dictate when the baby will be born. *Both* convenience and higher profits motivate doctors to do more C-sections. Now that births are scheduled around the physician's preference, more births occur on Tuesday than on any other day of the week.

Technology: In addition to profit and convenience, the increased use of modern technology contributes to a higher rate of C-sections. Almost all American women who give birth do so in a hospital, and almost all of these women are attached to a fetal monitor prior to delivery. This monitor sets off an alarm when the fetus is in distress, which can call for a cesarean delivery. Almost all such distress signals are false (Beckett, 2005).

A Feminist Controversy ■ Cesarean birth has become not only a social issue, but also cause for controversy among feminists. The central issue is the relative power of women (Beckett, 2005). Some say that cesarean delivery takes power over childbirth away from women and places it in the hands of doctors. Some feminists, in contrast, take an opposing view. They say that cesarean delivery can empower women. They point out that it isn't always the physician who decides that a woman will have a cesarean delivery: Women also tell their doctors how they want to deliver their children. Because this argument is rooted in deep-seated ideology, it is likely to continue for some time.

The Scope of the Problem

To better understand the scope of medical problems, we will look at physical and mental illness.

Physical Illness as a Social Problem

LIFE EXPECTANCY AND INFANT MORTALITY. Social researchers analyze life expectancy when determining how healthy or ill a society is as a whole. In the United States, this rate has been rising for over a century, and those born today can expect to live 75–81 years (*Statistical Abstract,* 2009, Table 100). These are national averages, however, and do not always apply to individuals. As with so many other conditions in our society, life expectancy is related to income: Those who have higher incomes live longer. In addition, life expectancy is related to race–ethnicity: Asian Americans live the longest, while Native Americans die at young ages. Region also contributes to life expectancy: Those in Bergen County, New Jersey are likely to live 91 years, while those in South Dakota are likely to die before reaching their 59th birthday (Murray et al., 2006).

In conjunction with increased life expectancy, infant mortality is declining as well. The **infant mortality rate (IMR)** represents the number of babies who die before 1 year of age, per 1,000 live births. The IMR is one of the most accurate measures of a group's health conditions: It reflects the quality of nutrition, health of mothers and babies, and quality of health care. In 1960, the U.S. rate was 26 deaths per 1,000 births. Now it

In the United States, health care is a commodity to be sold. The result is a two-tier system of medical care—one for those who can pay, another for those who cannot. Shown here are two waiting rooms for medical patients, one way to illustrate the social class difference in medical care.

See For Yourself

Visit the Department of Health and Human Services at www.cdc.gov/nchs
► Read about collection procedures for the nation's health statistics.

has dropped to just 6.3 per 1,000 births (*Statistical Abstract* 1990, Table 110; 2009, Table 1295). As the Social Map (Figure 10-4) shows, infant deaths are not distributed evenly across the United States. As you can see from this map, the states with the highest IMR cluster in the Southeast, and those with the lowest IMR are in the Northwest. This, again, reflects *social* influences on health, illness, and even death.

Because life expectancy is increasing and infant mortality is dropping, we can conclude that the United States has no *health* crisis. (It does have a *health care* crisis, however, which we shall discuss later.) There are health problems, to be sure, and some are severe—cancer, AIDS, suicide, and others. Tremendous battles have been won against most infectious diseases, however, and many people survive even cancer and AIDS today. Overall, the nation's physical health has been improving.

All of the Least Industrialized Nations have higher infant mortality rates and a shorter life expectancy than the United States (*Statistical Abstract*, 2006, Table 131). Life expectancy in some of these nations is less than 50 years, and some infant mortality rates run 15 to 20 times higher than ours. That life expectancy and infant mortality improve with industrialization is another example of how *social* conditions affect the *biology* of health.

Although our infant mortality rate has improved greatly, many medical experts still find it a cause for concern. To see why, look at Figure 10-5 on page 328, which compares America's IMR with that of other nations. Our overall life expectancy (males and

FIGURE 10-4 The Geography of Death: Infant Mortality Rates

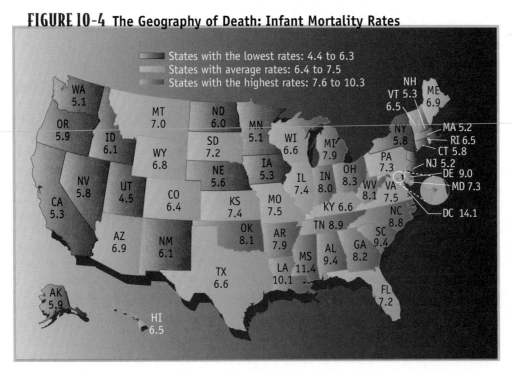

States with the lowest rates: 4.4 to 6.3
States with average rates: 6.4 to 7.5
States with the highest rates: 7.6 to 10.3

Source: By James M. Henslin. Based on *Statistical Abstract of the United States* (2008, Table 111: Infant Mortality Rates, 2005).

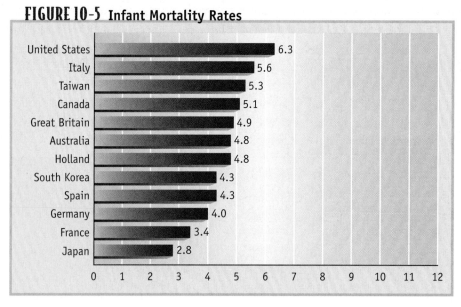

FIGURE 10-5 Infant Mortality Rates

Country	Rate
United States	6.3
Italy	5.6
Taiwan	5.3
Canada	5.1
Great Britain	4.9
Australia	4.8
Holland	4.8
South Korea	4.3
Spain	4.3
Germany	4.0
France	3.4
Japan	2.8

Note: These totals are infant deaths (babies who die before their first birthday) per 1,000 live births. For some reason, seven countries that had a lower rate of infant mortality than the United States have been dropped from the source. These countries are Belgium, Cuba, Czech Republic, Greece, Portugal, Sweden, and Switzerland.

Source: By James M. Henslin. Based on *Statistical Abstract of the United States* (2009, Table 1295).

females combined) of 78.1 years is also less than the life expectancy in most of the nations shown on Figure 10-5. Japan, with a life expectancy of 82.1 years, is highest on the list.

Why are life expectancy and the IMR better in other industrialized nations? Those countries with less poverty have better health. To put the matter in the simplest of terms: To live on the edge of survival is not good for people's health. Poor people are sick more often. They experience more stress, have more emotional problems, suffer more accidents and violence, and don't eat healthful foods. Poverty lies at the root of many health problems, and our advances in medical care are not reaching the poor to the same extent that they are reaching those who are wealthier.

LIFESTYLE. Although poverty is important, lifestyle may be even more significant. Sociologist Ruben Rumbaut and geographer John Weeks (1994) found that despite higher rates of poverty, Vietnamese and Cambodian refugees in California had lower IMRs than U.S.-born California women who were better off financially.

This backwards trend puzzled researchers who expected higher income to contribute to lower IMRs. They found the answer not in biology but in *social* conditions: The U.S.-born women had gained more weight during pregnancy, were more likely to have abused drugs, and had "surgically scarred uteruses" from previous abortions. Immigrant women lived a much more conservative lifestyle because they did not have the money to do otherwise.

It is difficult to overstate the importance of lifestyle in determining health and illness, for *lifestyle is the major cause of illness and death*. To mention the most obvious: Overeating and lack of exercise lead to heart attacks and strokes. Smoking causes cancer and the heavy consumption of alcohol harms essential body organs. These are all part of the *social* nature of physical illness.

Sexually transmitted diseases (STDs) also illustrate how lifestyle is related to health. To again state the obvious: Singles who practice abstinence run zero risk of STDs. Among couples who practice monogamy, the risk is also low. All others having intercourse with numerous sexual partners or who are having unprotected sex have a much

greater risk. Although the greater someone's promiscuity and unprotected sex, the greater that person's chances of acquiring an STD, it's possible to contract gonorrhea, syphilis, and even HIV after just one sexual encounter.

HEROIC MEDICINE. At the core of medical social problems lies this contradiction: We live in an age of *chronic* illness (lingering and ongoing medical problems), while our medical services are geared for *acute* illnesses (those that have a sudden onset, a sharp rise, and a short duration). Our approach to cancer, heart disease, and other chronic disorders is heroic, hospital-based, and expensive. Intervening at advanced stages of disease requires costly medical teams, highly trained specialists, technical equipment, and costly drugs. Patients who have serious illnesses want the best care, and the medical world has taught us that "the best" means complex, technical, and expensive. By promoting "cures," companies manufacturing medical equipment and drugs promote such heroism.

Prevention is not as exciting as a cure, but it is much more effective. We could limit untold suffering and save numerous lives through public health measures that reduce pollution, smoking, alcohol abuse, and poor eating habits. Such prevention efforts may seem costly during initial stages, but in the end are much less expensive than heroic measures.

EMERGENCY ROOMS AS DOCTORS' OFFICES. The United States creates a need for specialists in the pursuit of profit. This emphasis on specialists has led to a shortage of primary care doctors who treat routine problems. Consequently, for basic medical care many patients visit hospital emergency rooms. Because they stay open day and night and do not require appointments, they are seen as more convenient than visiting a doctor's office and perhaps receiving referrals for further care. These emergency services, however, are more costly in the long run. In an effort to halt such practices, insurance companies now refuse to pay for routine treatment given in emergency rooms. This has created a problematic situation: Insured patients have to prove that their visit to an emergency room is truly an emergency, while the poor without insurance coverage receive treatment. Among the uninsured are undocumented migrants, upon whom California, Texas, and Arizona are spending billions of dollars each year for medical treatment. *Health Affairs* estimates that the United States spends $1 billion on health care for illegal immigrants each year (Walters, 2006).

UNEVEN DISTRIBUTION OF MEDICAL SERVICES. Another problem with the medical delivery system in the United States is its uneven distribution of medical services. Some areas house an abundance of physicians, while other regions have very few doctors. Consider this extreme: Beverly Hills, California, has one doctor for every 275 residents, while just down the road in Bell Gardens there is one doctor for every 27,000 residents (Olivo, 1999). The Social Map (Figure 10-6) on the next page shows the national distribution of physicians.

Mental Illness as a Social Problem

MEASURING MENTAL ILLNESS. Some experts argue that the rates of mental illness have increased because people are experiencing more stress while their social support systems (family, friends, and community) are weaker. In reality, we do not know whether mental illness is more common today because we have no measurements of how much mental illness used to be. Attempts to measure rates of mental illness today are also inaccurate, resulting from pure speculation. Data are inadequate because experts rarely agree on definitions and classifications of mental illness. We can dispense, then, with the argument that mental illness is more common today, for there is no way of knowing one way or the other.

THE SOCIAL NATURE OF MENTAL ILLNESS. However we define mental illness—and this is another matter of dispute (Szasz, 1961; Caplan, 2006)—we do know that it has a strong social influence. That is, people who experience more stress are more likely to also

FIGURE 10-6 Where the Doctors Are

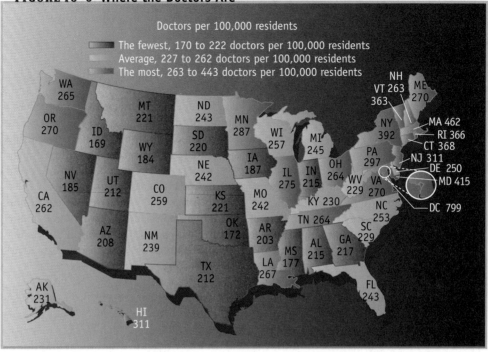

Source: By James M. Henslin. Based on *Statistical Abstract of the United States* (2008, Table 154).

experience what are known as mental problems. Mental problems, of course, would be part of the objective conditions of a social problem. Where are the subjective concerns that make mental illness a *social* problem? This is the focus of the Issues in Social Problems box on pages 332–333. From this box, you can see why even the intensely personal act of suicide is part of a *social* problem.

A TWO-TIER SYSTEM OF MENTAL HEALTH DELIVERY. Just as social problems surrounding physical illness are made up of two parts—the illness and the medical delivery system—so are social problems surrounding mental illness. Let's see how the medical delivery system fails in addressing mental health issues.

> An elderly nude man, looking confused, struggled to put on his clothing. The man had stolen from the homeless shelter. With the police in pursuit, he ran from one dark alley to the next. The officers were going to take the man to Malcolm Bliss—the state hospital. When asked how long the elderly man would be confined, the officer stated, "Probably for just a day or two. We picked him up last week when he was crawling under cars at a traffic light. They let him out after two days."

In the United States today, homeless people can be confined to a psychiatric institution only if they are a danger to others or to themselves.

During the 1970s, state psychiatric hospitals deinstitutionalized thousands of mentally ill patients. **Deinstitutionalization** is the release of hospitalized mental patients into the community. Ideally, these people could lead more normal lives in the community than they could in psychiatric hospitals. The plan was to support them with medication and community health services. In reality, few of the planned community centers were ever built. Most patients were simply abandoned on the streets to fend for themselves. A few were institutionalized again when no one could tolerate their presence, but most were left to wander the streets homeless.

It may be difficult to imagine medical and governmental authorities simply abandoning disoriented mentally ill patients on the streets, but they did precisely this. The cruel way that deinstitutionalization was carried out across the United States is further

illustrated by this one documented case in Texas: Patients from the state psychiatric hospital were loaded in a van and driven to Houston where they were dumped at the Greyhound bus station on skid row (Karlen & Burgower, 1985).

Looking at the Problem Theoretically

Lets look at how the sociological theoretical perspectives apply to health, illness, and the practice of medicine.

Symbolic Interactionism

DETERMINING THE MEANING OF SYMPTOMS AND BEHAVIOR. As you may recall, symbolic interactionists study how people use language and other symbols to define social reality. When we self-diagnose, for example, we are trying to label our symptoms. Should we go to bed, call a doctor, or just carry on with everyday life? To determine the meaning of some symbol (symptom), we use definitions our culture provides (illness).

Because different social classes and subcultures equip their members with distinct ways of thinking, people from different backgrounds interpret symptoms differently. People from the lower class, for example, are more likely to regard back pain as part of life. "This is what happens to me when I work too hard." People from the middle class, in contrast, are more likely to view back pain as a health problem that needs to be treated by a chiropractor. To many people cold or flu symptoms indicate a need to go to a doctor and "get a shot." To adherents of alternative medicine those same symptoms indicate a need to drink more water or to take vitamin C or other antioxidants. In short, we use cultural symbols to determine what our symptoms mean.

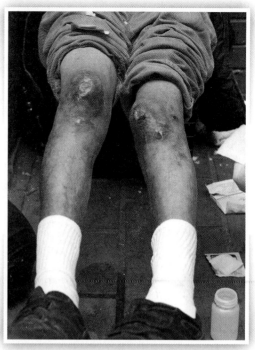

The homeless are the castoffs of postindustrial society. Unwanted and unneeded, they are left to wander the city streets and countryside. Only grudgingly are their needs attended to.

THE SIGNIFICANCE OF DEFINITIONS. Just as social classes and subcultural groups perceive health and illness differently, so groups compete to get their view of health accepted. This, in turn, changes the way we view health, illness, and medicine. For example, the American Psychiatric Association (APA) used to list homosexuality as a mental illness and had therapists attempt to treat it.

Using **conversion therapy** (sometimes called reorientation or reparative therapy), psychiatrists would attempt to change a person's sexual orientation. Often, conversion therapy was solicited by parents and other family members in an attempt to convert the "gay" loved one into a "straight" loved one.

Homosexuals object to this notion that sexual orientation is related to mental illness. Those against conversion therapy lobbied and put intense pressure on the APA to drop homosexuality as a mental illness. Their efforts were successful: Since 1973 the APA has not classified homosexuality as a mental illness, and most mainstream medical groups reject conversion therapy as useful or effective (American Psychiatric Association, 2000).

Just as medicine and psychiatry can declassify a behavior that had been considered an illness, so they can declare other behaviors as illnesses. Examples include the assertions that alcohol abuse is a disease and that children's inattentiveness is a symptom of attention-deficit disorder.

How we define health and illness has an impact on how we see the world and our behavior. If we define alcohol abuse as a disease, we perceive an alcohol abuser as sick; but if we define the abuser's behavior as drunkenness, we perceive the person as a drunkard. With such contrasting views, social policy also differs: If alcohol abuse is defined as a disease, sympathy and help might be viewed as appropriate responses; but if it is defined as drunkenness, condemnation might be viewed as appropriate. As with the classification

Issues in Social Problems
SUICIDE: THE MAKING AND UNMAKING OF A SOCIAL PROBLEM

Suicide—the act of deliberately causing one's death—chills the imagination. As sociologist Emile Durkheim (1897/1951) documented more than 100 years ago, suicide is more than an individual inclination or a sign of personal problems. Suicide, concluded Durkheim, is based on social conditions. Durkheim analyzed the suicide rates of different countries and noticed that year after year each country's rate remained about the same. Look at Figure 10-7. From one year to the next, these rates show little change. You can expect 30,000 to 32,000 Americans to kill themselves this year, and the next year, and the year after that (*Statistical Abstract*, 1994, Table 125; 2006, Table 109).

The funeral of a young man who committed suicide.

From Figure 10-7, you can also see that in each country men are much more likely to kill themselves than women. In the United States, many more women than men attempt suicide, but more men succeed at it. This is often misinterpreted as meaning that women's attempts are simply a "cry for help," whereas men's attempts are more serious. The reality is that women are more concerned about their children finding them—therefore, women are more likely to take pills in an attempt to prevent a gruesome death. Men typically use guns, allowing less time for someone to intervene.

FIGURE 10-7 International Suicide Rates

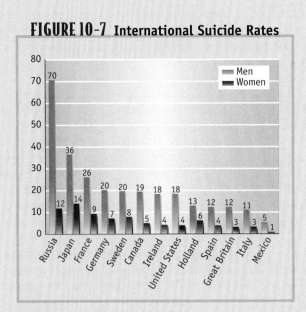

Note: The rate is per 100,000 people, as of 2003.

Source: By James M. Henslin. Based on "Suicide Rates" (2004).

Suicide illustrates the making and unmaking of a social problem. In the 1960s, mental health professionals began to publicize the idea that suicide was a national problem. There were no major changes in objective conditions at the time, but subjective concerns had grown. The National Institute of Mental Health (NIMH) took these subjective concerns and began to finance suicide prevention centers. The idea of swift intervention when people contemplate or attempt suicide was appealing, and across the nation suicide prevention centers were established to conquer what had become a social problem.

Overall, suicide prevention centers failed in reducing the suicide rate. For example, today suicide is the third most common cause of death among 15–24-year-olds in the United States, about the same as it was in the 1960s (*Statistical Abstract*, 2006, Table 108).

To prevent suicide, therapists must successfully manage patients known to be suicidal. This is difficult because psychiatrists receive inconsistent training. Some psychiatrists even contribute to their patient's suicide through a pattern of engagement and abandonment. The therapist initially responds to a suicidal patient with sympathy and concern, and the troubled individual begins to depend on the therapist as a helper. As treatment continues, the patient grows not only more dependent but also more demanding. Disliking this pressure, the therapist pulls back, calling the intense dependency "infantile regression." The therapist becomes less accessible just when the patient is most vulnerable. Feeling abandoned, the patient commits suicide (Light, 1973).

These treatment failures, along with lower funding, have resulted in prevention centers either closing their doors or broadening their focus to general crisis intervention.

IN SUM

Suicide illustrates how social problems are socially constructed. As Figure 10-7 shows, our suicide rate is not exceptional. Compared with other industrialized nations, our rate falls somewhere in the middle. Today's suicide rate is also about the same as it used to be. The overall rate, males and females combined, was 12.5 in 1960 and is 11.0 today (*Statistical Abstract*, 2006, Table 110). Suicide was labeled a social problem in the 1960s not because of an increase in suicide rates but because political activity increased subjective concerns. Mental health professionals and government officials used the mass media to arouse the public. Because of the resulting public outcry, suicide prevention centers were invented. Today we assume that suicide will occur and no longer consider suicide a pressing social problem.

of homosexuality by the American Psychiatric Association, political processes sometimes determine what definitions are adopted. In short, definitions are socially created, developing out of social interaction. We use symbols to determine whether we view something as a medical or social problem.

DIFFERENT REFERRAL NETWORKS. As they study how meaning is assigned in the practice of medicine, symbolic interactionists analyze symbolic interactions between doctors and patients. In classic research, Eliot Freidson (1961) examined how patients and doctors use different frames of reference. A patient's frame of reference lies within a **lay referral network**—friends, relatives, neighbors, and co-workers with whom the patient talks over medical problems. This network helps the patient decide which doctor to see—or even whether to see a doctor at all. In this lay referral network, a physician's knowledge and personality become important. Also important is the amount of confidence the doctor exhibits. Doctors who show uncertainty create fear, while those who appear confident instill confidence in their patients. People also want to be sure they get a shot or a prescription, not just empty advice.

The physician's frame of reference, in contrast, lies within a **professional referral network**—made up of other physicians and medical professionals. Here the meaning of "doctoring" is different, for medical schools put the emphasis on organs, symptoms, and

diseases apart from the person. Sympathy for the patient is less important than determining why some organ is malfunctioning and prescribing appropriate treatment (Haas & Shaffir, 1993; Conrad, 1995).

You can see, then, how patients' and physicians' referral networks produce definitions so contradictory that the expectations of patients and doctors can come into conflict with one another.

DEPERSONALIZATION. One consequence of the professional referral network is that some doctors treat patients not as people, but as objects—a process referred to as **depersonalization.** Patients detest being depersonalized, for it strips away their sense of humanity. To doctors who see patients as objects, psychological costs of procedures are of little importance. Because depersonalization may lead to a greater divide between patient and doctor, malpractice suits seem to be more common. But are they?

In 2002, the nation's insurance companies began to limit liability for doctors and hospitals. Most Americans believed this new limit came after a large number of lawsuits were filed against health care workers. In truth, the number of lawsuits did not increase, but the level of perceived threat did (Americans for Insurance Reform, 2007)

Since releasing its first study in 2002, the group Americans for Insurance Reform (AIR) has produced data demonstrating that the *threat* of lawsuits has created an environment in which health care workers now practice what is called **defensive medicine**—that is, a cautious practice incorporating the use of any and all available tests to ensure that an identifiable illness is not overlooked (Americans for Insurance Reform, 2007).

PROBLEMS IN COMMUNICATION. Different backgrounds and expectations often make it difficult for patients and physicians to communicate with one another. In the age of specialized medicine, doctors often neglect the personal or emotional needs of their patients:

> When Mrs. J., a 47-year-old schoolteacher, was told in a routine examination that she had a "uterine fibroid" and needed a hysterectomy (removal of her uterus), the only thing she could think of was "tumor." She asked the doctor if it was cancerous, and he frightened her more by saying, "Sometimes when we go in, we find them to be cancerous." Fearing cancer of the uterus, she consulted two other physicians and learned that the fibroid was small, common in middle-aged women, and soon likely to shrink on its own as she went into menopause (Larned, 1977, pp. 195–196).

> One man from Texas went in to see a specialist after he discovered a lump inside his testicle. He chose the urologist from a list of doctors provided by his insurance company; the urologist—Dr. Bamberger—was rated 4 stars. At the initial consult, the urologist warned the man that it was more than likely cancer, that he might have to consider prosthesis, and that chemotherapy was not out of the question. After literally passing out, the man scheduled emergency surgery for the very next morning. That same afternoon he had a sonogram done to view the exact size and location of the tumor. The technician warned the man that she could get in big trouble for telling him but said that he "did not have cancer." The man canceled the surgery, realizing that the doctor would have removed his testicle before even having the chance to see the sonogram results!

Functionalism

WHO BENEFITS? Because functionalists assume that customs or social institutions persist only if they fulfill social needs, this perspective raises interesting questions: Whose needs are met by a health care system that is hospital-based and oriented toward

In this age of specialized medicine, doctors spend limited time talking with their patients.

acute illnesses? Who benefits from allowing environmental diseases to flourish? What are the benefits of depersonalizing patients or of making childbirth a rigorous medical procedure?

FEE-FOR-SERVICE MEANS PROFITS. Let's start with the obvious: It is difficult for doctors to make money if people are not sick. Patients who get well quickly translate into less profit. An expensive, hospital-based system oriented toward acute illness creates profit for physicians, medical suppliers, hospitals, and drug companies. Each year, about 1 of every 8 Americans is admitted to a hospital and stays an average of 6 days (*Statistical Abstract,* 2006, Table 163). The average daily cost is shown in Figure 10-8. The shorter bars on this figure represent what a day's stay in the hospital would cost if medical costs had not outpaced inflation. This figure illustrates the skyrocketing costs of medical care in the United States today.

Not surprisingly, profits, not health care, are the engine that drives the U.S. health care system. Our fee-for-service system means that the more services doctors sell at the highest price, the more they earn. One result is unnecessary surgery, such as *most* cesarean sections and the testicular surgery described earlier. Another example involves hysterectomies, which we will review in the next section on conflict theory.

FIGURE 10-8 How Much Does It Cost to Stay in the Hospital? One Day's Cost Compared to Inflation

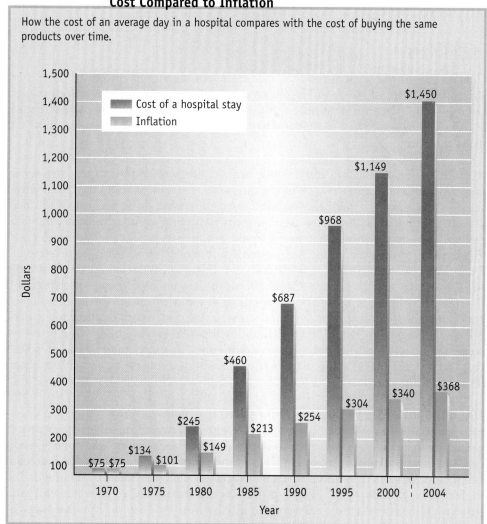

How the cost of an average day in a hospital compares with the cost of buying the same products over time.

Source: By James M. Henslin. Based on *Statistical Abstract of the United States* (1998, Table 137; 2007, Table 163).

Physicians, nurses, and investors in the U.S. health care industry, then, benefit from our fee-for-service system. Patients benefit, too, however, for this system lets them shop around. They can choose which doctor to see and what services to purchase. That this system is functional for patients is indicated by our rising life expectancy and decreasing infant mortality rates.

A SELF-CORRECTING SYSTEM. There are problems with a fee-for-service system, of course, and we have already mentioned some of them. Functionalists argue, however, that the system is self-correcting. For example, although the medical system is oriented to acute illnesses, after environmental health problems were recognized as serious, the government passed antipollution laws and formed the Environmental Protection Agency (EPA). Medical schools also responded, developing training programs in environmental medicine. Likewise, expensive insurance costs have led to the development of managed care (discussed later), outpatient surgery, and limitations on the number of days Medicare and Medicaid pay for hospitalization. In short, functionalists view fee-for-service health care as a system that responds to shifting needs of the nation.

THE GLOBAL LEVEL. Functionalists also analyze functions and dysfunctions of medicine on a global level. Exporting modern Western medicine to the Least Industrialized Nations provides an excellent example. The vaccines, immunizations, and medicines sent to these nations are functional for the United States because they reduce death rates on a global scale. But they are also dysfunctional because they encourage populations of these nations to surge. When populations grow so fast that they outpace the nations' food production, it can lead to mass starvation and political upheaval.

Conflict Theory

Conflict theorists argue that the U.S. medical system is not self-correcting. They view American patterns of illness and health care as the outcome of clashes between interest groups—which the most powerful control. They argue that the poor are more often sick because they lack sufficient income and high-quality education, food, housing, jobs, and medical services.

MEDICAID. What about Medicaid, which benefits the poor? Conflict theorists see this program, too, as the result of conflict. In the 1960s, resentment about the treatment of the poor had grown so vocal that politicians were forced to do something. With these pressures accompanied by a growing sentiment favoring socialized medicine, the U.S. medical establishment felt that its profitable fee-for-service system was threatened. Physicians used their union, the American Medical Association (AMA), to preserve the fee-for-service system. Viewing Medicaid as a first step to socialized medicine, the AMA fought against its passage. Caught between the public's demand for change and the intense lobbying of the AMA, Congress designed Medicaid to satisfy the public's criticism while still providing profit for doctors. In the eyes of conflict theorists, to consider, as functionalists would, that Medicaid was passed because health care providers wanted the poor to get free medical services is naive. It ignores the millions of dollars that the AMA spent lobbying to *prevent* the federal government from funding health insurance for the poor.

COLLIDING INTERESTS OF DOCTORS AND PATIENTS. Conflict theorists also have a different view of the doctor–patient relationship. Those adhering to the Marxist perspective emphasize that doctors and patients form two sorts of classes—those who control medicine and those who receive treatment. To maximize their incomes, physicians try to control the doctor–patient relationship. It is no accident that physicians commonly fail to explain their procedures and diagnoses but instead simply say a few words and send patients on their way. This is one way that physicians try to keep the oppressed class of patients ignorant and dependent (Waitzkin & Waterman, 1974). In a capitalist system of production for profit, the alienation of patient and physician is like that of owner and

worker, an inevitable result when the interests of the one (making a profit) oppose those of the other (getting well at the least expense).

IN SUM From a Marxist conflict perspective, the entire medical system is an industry whose goals are profit and power. To reach these goals, its practitioners exploit sick people (Reynolds, 1973). Marxists argue that their perspective best explains why medical care for the rich is so much better than that for the poor: Health care is *not* the goal of the U.S. medical system—the goal is profit for those who practice it. Physicians are businesspeople, patients are customers, and health care is the commodity they sell. The government pays an increasing proportion of the nation's health care bill because it perpetuates and underwrites the interests of capitalist industries—including medicine. Conflict theorists argue that health care should be a right of *all* citizens and that people's illnesses and diseases should never be exploited for profit.

Research Findings

After a brief overview of physical health problems in the United States, we will focus on social inequalities of health and health care. We will discuss the variables of age, race, and social class; examine our two-class system of medicine; and consider how health insurance creates its own inequalities. We will then discuss social inequalities in mental illness.

An Overview of Physical Health Problems

HISTORICAL CHANGES IN HEALTH PROBLEMS. Figure 10-9 compares today's 10 leading causes of death with those of 1900. This figure makes the *social* nature of death evident. As you can see, only 6 of the 10 leading causes of death have remained the same. A symbolic interactionist would point out that these labels are arbitrary—if we used

FIGURE 10-9 **The 10 Leading Causes of Death in the United States**

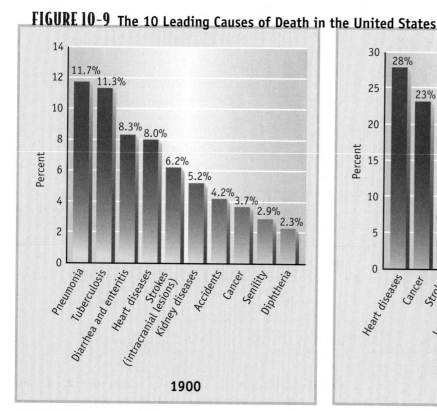

1900

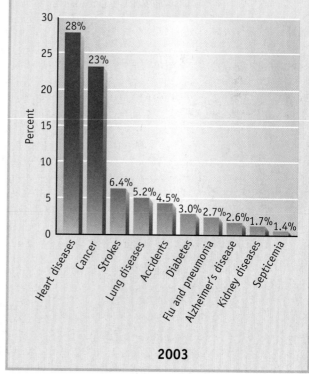

2003

Note: 2003 is the latest year available

Sources: By James M. Henslin. Year 2003 is based on Centers for Disease Control (2006b); year 1900 is based on Centers for Disease Control (2006c).

different classifications, we would end up with different causes of death. In fact, the CDC (Centers for Disease Control and Prevention) has revised these categories almost a dozen times since 1900. To see how arbitrary the categories can be, note the ninth leading cause of death in 1900. Today's definition of senility is obviously different from the one used in 1900. Today, senility (old age) isn't responsible for death, but it was considered a leading cause of death in 1900. When the aged didn't die from diarrhea or pneumonia, doctors categorized their deaths as "senility."

As arbitrary as these labels are, note that several of the top killers in both centuries are caused primarily by lifestyle and environmental pollution. In 1900 lifestyle factors like smoking cigarettes and the intake of high amounts of sugar weren't very common; therefore, lung diseases and diabetes did not make the top ten list. These changes in leading causes of death reinforce the point made earlier about how health and illness are related to lifestyle and the environment.

INFECTIOUS DISEASES. Figure 10-9 also reveals how significant infectious diseases have always been. As you can see, a hundred years or so ago pneumonia was the number one killer, with tuberculosis (TB) close behind. Every family feared polio, whooping cough, German measles, smallpox, and diphtheria. Then, during the first half of the 20th century, these diseases receded, death rates plummeted, and life expectancy rose from 47 years to over 70. What happened?

Two Reasons for the Decline in Infectious Diseases ■ First, prescription drugs and vaccinations have wiped out many diseases. Vaccinations have prevented deadly diseases from spreading, while prescription drugs, especially antibiotics, have played a significant role in treating disease. Second, clean running water accounts for much of the change.

Most infectious killers of the 19th century were already declining *before* antibiotics, immunizations, or specific drugs had been developed (McKeown, 1980). Although medical myth has it that new drugs and vaccinations conquered TB in the 1950s, as Figure 10-10 on the next page shows, TB had been declining since the 1800s. If modern medicine did not conquer the infectious diseases so feared by earlier generations of Americans, what did? *The answer is that cleaner public water supplies improved overall health.* Infectious killers declined as people became healthier and stronger from cleaner water, better food, and sustained water supplies.

Cleaner water has led to the decline in TB.

The Resurgence of Infectious Diseases ■ Infectious diseases, however, have a way of fighting back. They can go underground and develop new strains that are resistant to known drugs and vaccines. The Technology and Social Problems box on page 340 discusses worldwide implications of this problem. Even TB has resurfaced with deadly strains. More people around the world (about 1.7 million) die of TB now than when the vaccine for it was developed (Garrett, 1999). Some strains have become resistant to *all* known treatment (Rosenthal, 2006). Health officials in New York City and other states still fear the possibility of a TB outbreak and will arrest patients and lock them in guarded hospital rooms if they refuse treatment (Specter, 1992; Hench, 2006).

The most feared infectious disease today, however, is HIV/AIDS. Let's look at how this disease may be related to environmental factors.

How Disease Is Related to Behavior and Environment: The Case of HIV/AIDS

BACKGROUND. HIV/AIDS is an excellent example of the relationship between behavior, environment, and disease. When the disease was first brought to media attention, male homosexuals, intravenous drug users, and hemophiliacs were most likely victims.

FIGURE 10-10 The "Conquest" of Tuberculosis

Tuberculosis used to be one of the greatest killers. Many people believe that modern medicine "conquered" TB with the discovery of streptomycin in 1947 and a vaccine in 1954. As you can see, the death rate for TB had been declining steadily for almost 100 years before these discoveries. Many other infectious diseases "conquered" by modern medicine follow a similar pattern.

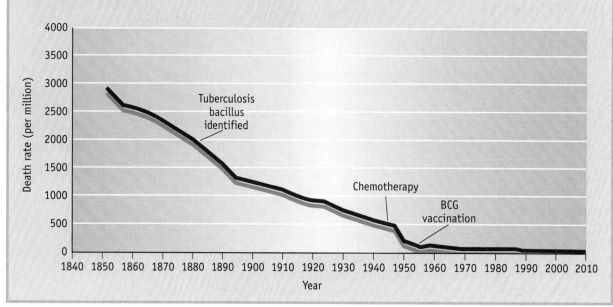

Source: McKeown (1980); *Statistical Abstract of the United States* (2006, Table 107).

Hemophiliacs and IV drug users were exposed to the disease through contaminated blood. Drug-addicted prostitutes also spread the disease to heterosexual men. The disease no longer discriminates—it affects all people from all walks of life. Today, women account for more than one quarter of all new HIV/AIDS diagnoses. Women of color are especially affected by HIV infection and AIDS.

A GLOBAL EPIDEMIC. HIV/AIDS is a global epidemic, perhaps the worst in the history of the world. About 25 million people have died from this disease, about 40 million people around the world are infected now, and about 5 million more people are being infected each year (Lamptey et al., 2006). Of all regions in the world, sub-Saharan Africa has been hit the worst. There, HIV/AIDS is the leading cause of death. HIV/AIDS is common in this region because there is a lack of sex education and protection, as well as a high prevalence of prostitution. In some African countries, HIV/AIDS is expected to kill half of the adolescent population. Hardest hit is Swaziland, where 2 of every 5 adults are infected with HIV/AIDS.

Worldwide, more than 15 million children have been orphaned as a result of AIDS (AVERT, 2008). Most of these orphans live in Africa, and some of them have also been infected with HIV. In 2005, HIV prevalence among orphans in Zimbabwe alone was estimated at 20% (Lopman et al., 2006).

HIV/AIDS IN THE UNITED STATES. Today, **antiretroviral drugs** (ARVs) halt the progression of AIDS. ARVs can prevent full-blown AIDS from appearing for up to 20 years after infection with the HIV virus. But ARVs are not equally available to all those who need them. For example, ARVs are expensive—costing an individual $10,000–$15,000 per year—and not all can afford them. Further, only some people in developing countries can access ARVs; they are not readily available in some least industrialized countries.

Although there are limited supplies at a high cost, when they are made available, those infected are more likely to admit they have the disease and seek treatment.

Technology and Social Problems
SUPERBUGS IN THE GLOBAL VILLAGE

imon Sparrow, a 17-month-old robust toddler, was just learning to feed himself. His family was startled out of their sleep one early morning when Simon let out a primal scream. They rushed Simon to the hospital, where he was diagnosed with a virus and asthma and sent home. Fifteen hours later, he was dead. (Chase, 2006)

What killed Simon? It was a new strain of staph infection. This germ can penetrate bones and lungs, leaving abscesses that require surgery. Simon died so quickly that he was spared this suffering.

This new form of staph (community-associated methicillin-resistant *Staphylococcus aureus,* which, fortunately has a shortened name—CA-MRSA) has also cropped up in Japan, France, England, and other countries. Health authorities are uncertain how to treat CA-MRSA and the other drug-resistant bacteria that are appearing at various spots around the world.

Their fear is that someone, somewhere, will come down with a germ that is resistant to every antibiotic—and that with global travel, in just a matter of days the new strain will spread throughout the global village.

Following the discovery of penicillin in the 1940s came a series of effective microbe killers. By the 1970s, more than 100 antibiotics sat on pharmacy shelves. The war against microbes had been won, or so the medical industry thought. Researchers relaxed and stopped developing new antibiotics. Promising new drugs, already in development, were even canceled as superfluous.

In the presence of antibiotics, the weaker germs die off, but the stronger ones can mutate, survive, and proliferate. This is especially likely to happen if people do not complete the full course of their medical treatment and stop taking a drug when they feel better. The more that antibiotics are used and misused, the more that drug-resistant bugs proliferate (Chase, 2006).

Are antibiotics misused? The Institute of Medicine reports that 20% to 50% of the 145 million prescriptions given to U.S. outpatients each year are unnecessary. The same goes for the 190 million doses of antibiotics given to hospital patients.

Bird flu is one of the diseases medical authorities fear can circle the globe and cause millions of deaths.

We all carry staph germs on our skin and in our nose. There they are harmless. When we get a scrape or cut or have a surgical incision, however, they can penetrate our body and attack our internal organs. This seldom leads to serious problems, as most of these staph germs are relatively mild. But when some of these are replaced by a mutant, virulent strain, simple cuts and scrapes can become mortal wounds. A patient who goes to the hospital for some strange pain, a sore throat, or routine surgery can be carried out in a coffin.

This threat has broken through the apathy of the medical industry. Pharmaceutical firms are searching for the next generation of antibiotics to fight the next generation of microbes. The race is close. Let's suppose that we win and are able to develop new antibiotics in time to prevent a global epidemic. Will we then repeat this process—overprescribing, not completing the course of treatments—with the microbes again mutating and developing resistance to the new drugs?

Granted the folly of much human behavior, we are certain that this will happen. In addition, certain social factors promote this self-defeating behavior—especially a medical establishment eager for profits and the tendency of patients to quit taking medicine when they feel better, but before invasive microbes are destroyed totally. A sage once said that those who do not learn from history are doomed to repeat it. We would add that although we study history, and even know its lessons, in some instances we set ourselves on a course destined to repeat it. This is one such case.

The combination of ARVs and education has caused AIDS deaths in the United States to decrease from 50,000 in 1995 to 14,000 in 2006 (*Statistical Abstract,* 1998, Table 144; 2006, Table 108). The availability of these drugs prevents people who are infected with the HIV virus from developing full-blown AIDS. They do *not* prevent people from infecting others with HIV.

Miley Cyrus performs at the "Idol Gives Back" show. The *American Idol* special charity event benefits relief programs for children and young people in extreme poverty.

No racial–ethnic group is more susceptible to HIV/AIDS because of biological factors. Some groups have higher rates of HIV/AIDS than others because of social factors: (1) they are sharing needles, (2) they are having sex with multiple partners, or (3) they are having unprotected sex.

One startling statistic is that although African Americans make up just 12% of the U.S. population, they account for almost *half* of HIV/AIDS infections. Why? The reasons are many: There is a distrust of doctors, a reluctance to talk about AIDS, a lack of education about its transmission, higher-than-average use of injected drugs, and a reluctance to use condoms. Another significant cause is that research funds for HIV prevention are not spread evenly among at-risk communities but rather are steered toward gay communities (Stolberg, 1998).

OMINOUS CHANGES. The HIV virus mutates rapidly, and medical researchers fear that drugs being used to fight HIV/AIDS might be only a temporary fix. Some individuals have contracted strains of HIV that are resistant to protease inhibitors, one kind of ARV (Bhattacharya, 2005). If drug-resistant strains become widespread, as is likely, the epidemic could surge again. Several new drugs, however, hold the promise of picking up where these drugs leave off.

Social Inequalities in Physical Illness

POVERTY AND HEALTH. Let's look more closely at social inequalities that create differences in U.S. health trends. From your reading of earlier chapters, you should not be surprised to learn that economic factors largely determine who will be healthy and who will be sick. Poor children, for example, are more likely to be undernourished or to lack a balanced diet. As a result, they are more vulnerable to disease. In general, the poorer people are, the sicker they are.

This takes us to the heart of the matter—social inequality—the essential factor that underlies our patterns of disease and death. Because the U.S. health care system focuses on acute health problems, it provides a temporary fix without curing the environment from which they came.

OCCUPATIONAL HEALTH HAZARDS. Health problems often stem from lower-class working environments. For example, workers in manufacturing plants are more likely to be

exposed to dangerous working conditions and toxic chemicals than are their managers. Some chemicals merely irritate the skin; others cause skin cancer or attack vital body organs. Carbon monoxide, mercury, and uranium destroy the kidneys; ethers, chlorines, and heavy metals invade the nervous system.

Occupational disease results from long-term exposure to specific substances or from continuous or repetitive physical acts. The noise level of some factories causes hearing loss for workers. Arc welding, lasers, and radar all damage the eyes.

After the collapse of the World Trade Center on September 11, 2001, many volunteers and transport workers were exposed to environmental contamination while working at Ground Zero; and many of them were never informed that contamination risks existed. During the initial recovery efforts, 74% of the volunteers and employees wore inadequate or no protection at all:

> For Jimmy Willis, a former subway conductor and Transport Workers Union (TWU) Local 100 representative, the collapse commenced a personal and physical struggle that has dogged him for over three years. On September 12, he rushed to the site to volunteer alongside thousands of fellow union members, who had been sent to the site by the city government. For about ten days, Willis and other transit workers helped clear out a towering six-story mass of rubble known as "the Pile," carving a path "five feet at a time" through a morass of concrete and bodies, with little or no respiratory protection. (Chen, 2007)

PAYING THE BILL. Looking at who pays medical bills helps to expose the social inequalities of health care. Before we had today's patchwork insurance coverage, there were private hospitals and clinics for those who could pay (considered "the worthy") and public facilities for those who could not (considered "the unworthy") (Rosenberg, 1987). Because medical students need patients to practice on and public hospitals provide them, public hospitals have become known as training centers. When these public facilities are associated with medical schools, medical care is often superior—but with lower salaries, worse working conditions, and outdated equipment, other public hospitals attract less-qualified doctors and nurses. Iatrogenesis, injury caused by medical professionals, often results.

Before World War II, professional health care was somewhat primitive. Health care often took place at home, and doctors made house calls to supplement and direct home health care. Hospitals, which were considered a last resort, were feared as "a place to go to die."

After World War II, medical technology improved, and the costs of treating illness increased. Many middle-class people who had serious health problems found that they could no longer afford hospital care. And as we've seen, physicians and hospital owners wanted to make more money. As a result, health insurance, which was first established in the 19th century, became a standard benefit for business and government employees (Thomasson, 2003). As a result, most working-class and middle-class people received medical care. The poor, unable to afford insurance, were left out of this health care revolution.

Those without insurance coverage suffered the most health problems. The poor and the elderly were most likely to suffer. In 1966, Congress tried to remedy this situation by offering Medicaid for the poor and Medicare for the elderly. Neither is comprehensive or generous, but overnight these plans provided medical coverage for millions who needed it the most. Because these programs did not control what health providers could charge, however, the cost of medical care rose rapidly. Soon, out-of-pocket expenses were as much as they had been before the government began these programs.

Unanticipated Consequences of Medicaid and Medicare ■ As functionalists stress, human actions have latent or unanticipated consequences. One of the latent consequences of Medicaid was its undermining of public hospitals. City and county officials figured that because the poor now had medical insurance, they no longer needed free facilities. Eager to save money, many cities and counties closed their public hospitals and clinics. Yet this left many of the poor without care: Because Medicaid's rates were low, many doctors and private hospitals refused to accept Medicaid patients. The **working poor**—those who are employed but receive low wages—have been hard hit. Their income

is so low that they cannot afford to buy insurance, but it is not low enough that they can qualify for Medicaid. Sixteen percent of the nation's population, or about 45 million people, have no health insurance (*Statistical Abstract,* 2006, Table 142).

MEDICAL INSURANCE. Lack of medical insurance highlights racial–ethnic inequalities undermining U.S. society. Because African Americans and Latinos are most likely to be members of the working poor, they are more likely to live without medical insurance. Whereas 15% of whites have no insurance coverage, 34% of Latinos and 21% of African Americans have no coverage (*Statistical Abstract,* 2009, Table 146).

Social Inequalities in Mental Illness

SOCIAL CLASS AND MENTAL ILLNESS. Do some social classes have more emotional problems than others? Yes. This intriguing question has been answered time and again. Since 1939, sociologists have found that people's emotional well-being declines with decreases in social class. Those in the lower social classes are more likely to be depressed, anxious, nervous, and phobic. Numerous studies have confirmed this finding (Faris & Dunham, 1939; Srole et al., 1978; Lundberg, 1991; Starfield, Robertson, & Riley, 2002).

As mentioned earlier, the definitions of *mental illness* are so vague that measurements are not reliable. To overcome this problem, sociologist Leo Srole and his colleagues at Columbia University did a classic study. The Midtown Manhattan Project interviewed a representative sample of New Yorkers in 1978. As shown in Figure 10-11, these researchers found that the poor have considerably more emotional problems.

FOUR EXPLANATIONS FOR THE GREATER EMOTIONAL PROBLEMS OF THE POOR. Why do the poor suffer more mental disorders than people in other classes? Four explanations have been suggested.

The Drift and Genetic Hypotheses ■ According to the *drift hypothesis,* people with emotional difficulties tend to be less successful in life, so they drift from higher-income families down into the lower classes (Fox, 1990). According to the *genetic hypothesis,* faulty genes cause schizophrenia, manic depression, and other severe disorders. So, do the poor have more of these faulty genes? The drift hypothesis would claim that many of

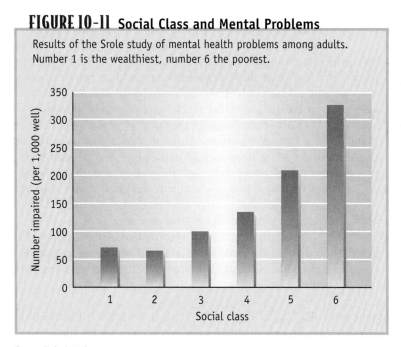

FIGURE 10-11 Social Class and Mental Problems

Results of the Srole study of mental health problems among adults. Number 1 is the wealthiest, number 6 the poorest.

Source: Srole (1978).

the people who have genetic predispositions for mental illness drift downward, leaving a disproportionate number of poor families with these traits.

The genetic explanation offered by psychologists and biologists for the most severe disorders, such as schizophrenia and manic depression, is widely accepted in the medical community. Sociologically, since the family that rears the child is usually the biological family, it is difficult to separate genetic influences from the effects of socialization. In an effort to prove genetic influences, biologists have studied twins from one set of biological parents. They have discovered that identical twins reared in different families have more mental problems than fraternal twins reared in the same family. They conclude that this research validates the genetic hypothesis. Critics of this explanation argue there are too many outside environmental influences to accept this conclusion. With the decoding of the human genome system, researchers are hopeful that they will be able to match specific genes with mental illnesses in the future (Pestka, 2006).

The Socialization Hypothesis ■ According to the *socialization hypothesis,* children who are reared by disturbed parents are more likely to learn pathological ways of coping with the world. They are less equipped to deal with the challenges of education and career. Without promises of further education and career opportunities, they are more likely to end up living in poverty.

The Environmental Hypothesis ■ Sociologists offer support for the *environmental hypothesis.* They focus on how different social class environments contribute to or restrict mental illness. Wealthier social classes tend to be happier, less depressed, less filled with anxiety, and less phobic. In short, they are "mentally healthier." People in the middle classes enjoy better job security, finances, physical health, medical care, and marriages. Not only do they have greater security at the present time, but they also have greater hopes for the future. They realistically plan and look forward to larger houses, better cars, exotic vacations, completing college, and a relaxing, enjoyable retirement. Therefore, their mental health is better.

Compare this with the stress-filled lives of those living in poverty: jobs without security, low wages, unpaid bills, high rates of divorce, alcoholism, violence, worse physical health, and less access to good medical care. Such conditions certainly deal severe blows to people's emotional well-being.

THE DELIVERY OF MENTAL HEALTH SERVICES. In order to understand how mental health services are related to social inequality, let's consider types of therapy and health care institutions. In **individual psychotherapy,** a therapist listens and tries to guide the patient toward a resolution of emotional problems. One type of psychotherapy is **psychoanalysis,** which Sigmund Freud pioneered as a way to uncover the subconscious motives, fantasies, and fears that shape people's behavior. The patient meets an analyst several times a week and talks about whatever comes to mind, while the analyst listens for hidden patterns, particularly those that reveal unresolved conflicts from early childhood. More common is **short-term directive therapy,** in which a counselor focuses on current situations to help clients understand their problems. In **group therapy,** several patients, with the guidance of a therapist, help each other to cope with their problems.

Another treatment option is **drug therapy,** the use of tranquilizers, antidepressants, and antipsychotic drugs to relieve people's problems and help them cope with life. As discussed in Chapter 4, some of these drugs have serious side effects. Drug therapy is often criticized as treating symptoms without offering a cure.

For some illnesses, especially depression, **electroconvulsive therapy (ECT)** (also known as electroshock therapy) is used. Wires are attached to either side of a patient's skull, and low-voltage electric shocks are sent repeatedly through the brain. Memory loss is a possible (and permanent) side effect.

Consequences of Ability to Pay ■ The type of therapy that a troubled person is likely to receive does not depend on the person's problems, but on the person's ability to pay. People who have money and good insurance are more likely to be guided through

Neither long-term counseling with psychiatrists nor quick takes with pop counselors have been proven to be effective.

their problems with **talk therapy**—psychotherapy, group therapy, and so on. "Talk" therapy is expensive, and it would be rare for a poor and uninsured person to receive it. The poor and uninsured are likely to receive no help at all, but when they do receive help, they are likely to be given drug therapy, which has been called a **pharmaceutical straitjacket**—drugs given in mental hospitals that make patients drowsy, lethargic, and easier to handle.

It is difficult, however, to say that these patterns of therapy and social class represent inequality: *We do not know which therapies work.* Costly psychoanalysis may be no more effective than drug therapy or even no therapy at all. Psychoanalysis may even be less effective. Consequently, we cannot say whether the poor are receiving worse—or better—treatment for their emotional problems. Rigorous studies demonstrating the effectiveness of therapy are yet to be done. An emerging type of therapy, described in the Technology and Social Problems box on the next page, is also likely to be claimed a success by its practitioners but remains unexamined and unproven.

Health care facilities for treating mental illness used to parallel the facilities for treating physical problems: public hospitals for the poor and private hospitals for the affluent. State and county hospitals had so many patients and so little money that thousands of patients languished in wards, a situation that could itself lead to mental illness. Few received proper treatment. With deinstitutionalization, described earlier in this chapter, the population of state and county psychiatric hospitals drastically declined. Although such places now offer short-term treatment and outpatient services, they still warehouse chronic patients who cannot cope in other environments.

As with physical illness, the type of payment that can be offered determines the type of care received. Medicare transferred the cost of treating the poor to the federal government. Because many of these patients were elderly, some nursing homes became what psychiatrists Fritz Redlich and Stephen Kellert (1978) called decentralized back wards. People who used to be placed in psychiatric hospitals are now placed in nursing homes. The primary force behind this change was Medicare legislation.

IN SUM Social inequality affects the treatment of both physical and mental problems. Because it is difficult to measure success related to psychotherapy, we cannot say that the poor are getting *less effective* treatment than the rich. However, we feel confident in stating that the poor receive less expensive treatment than the rich.

Technology and Social Problems
CYBERTHERAPY AND CYBERSHRINKS

The effectiveness of therapy is questionable. Talking to a friend or member of the clergy (or your mother-in-law, for that matter) may be as effective (or ineffective) as psychotherapy. Talking, in other words, may be helpful regardless of who the listener is—or it may not be helpful. We just don't know. It certainly is more pleasant to talk to a supportive, sympathetic, and understanding listener than to someone who challenges what you say—but we don't have evidence for which type of listener is more effective in helping with problems.

E-mail therapy has now made its appearance; patient and therapist send e-mail back and forth. Some therapists and patients use chat rooms. Others add video links so they can see each other. Some therapists offer a one-shot deal for a flat rate. Some sell their virtual couches by the minute, others by the month (E. Cohen, 1997).

Cybertherapy offers an advantage that the telephone does not: Time zones make no difference. Patients who are traveling around the world can zap off an e-mail whenever they like without waking the therapist in the middle of the night.

Because cybertherapy offers another profit center for therapists, it is being taken seriously by the American Psychological Association (APA). The APA has set up guidelines, and California requires that insurance companies pay for online therapy (Cohen, 1997). Therapists are also establishing ethical guidelines, which a skeptic might call rules for avoiding problems so the profits can flow without interruption (King & Poulos, 1999).

Cybertherapists are developing their own professional associations, such as the Interactive Media Institute. They hold national and international "telehealth" conferences, where they discuss such issues as how video games and robotics can "heal" patients.

There are also academic signs of acceptance: Some universities have set up programs in virtual counseling. The one at Duke University, called the Virtual Reality Program, recruits patients by saying that this type of therapy is more efficient, easier to schedule, and more confidential. (Efficient it may be—perhaps in bringing in profits—but in terms of results, totally unknown.) In the Duke program, the patients actually come to a university office, where they use computer simulations. The therapist, says an online ad for the program, can treat people who have a fear of flying by having the patient "repeatedly land the virtual airplane."

We have just entered the age of virtual therapy, barely able to envision its future. One form that is being developed is fascinating. In computer-enhanced therapy, the therapist and patient engage in discussions through computer-animated characters that represent themselves. From a supply of images, the patient chooses his or her character, as well as the character of the therapist and the online setting where their session takes place. The animated characters then talk to one another. Supposedly, this format reduces embarrassment for patients, encouraging them to talk about unflattering problems and feelings (Onion, 2004).

Does cybertherapy work? No one knows. But, then, no one knows whether other forms of therapy work either. So therapists might as well practice from the convenience of their homes.

Social Policy

We have reviewed several conditions contributing to the increasing cost of health care. (1) The fee-for-service system encourages physicians to sell specialized services to get patients to come back for visits. Doctors who are paid for every office visit, whether a visit is necessary or not, tend to encourage visits rather than discourage them or promote preventive medicine. (2) Focusing on acute problems creates depersonalization. (3) Malpractice insurance is expensive, and it further drives up the cost of medical care. (4) Concentrating on heroic intervention is more expensive and less effective than long-term prevention.

Being Paid to Stay Healthy

Some employers give their workers a rebate for staying healthy—or at least for staying away from doctors. In return for accepting a high annual insurance deductible, employees who spend less than the deductible are paid the difference between it and their insurance

claims. If the deductible is, say, $1,500, workers who claim only $100 for medical treatment collect $1,400, a very nice bonus. Where this program has been tried, employee health costs go down. As one employee said, "Now I feel I have an investment in my own health."

Prepaid Medical Care: The Example of Managed Care

Managed care plans are often purchased as a contractual package by employers in an effort to reduce the cost of providing health insurance to their employees. There are three main types of managed care: Health Maintenance Organizations (HMOs), Preferred Provider Organizations (PPOs), and Point of Service (POS) plans. In the best-known type of prepaid medical care, the **health maintenance organization (HMO),** a medical corporation (sometimes owned by physicians) covers the health needs of a company's employees. The business pays a monthly fee for each employee. If the health care of an employee runs more than this fee, the medical corporation loses money; if it costs less, it makes money. Because the medical corporation receives no more than this fee, its directors are motivated to reduce medical costs. Doctors are paid salaries, but they can receive bonuses if they reduce patient costs. The doctors try to strike a balance between reducing costs and providing good health care. They are also motivated to treat medical problems before they become serious and more expensive.

THE POSITIVE SIDE. Because doctors make more money when patients stay well, they encourage preventive care, such as immunizations, well-baby checkups, mammograms, and physicals (Ilminen, 2006). They urge patients to adopt a lifestyle that improves health, one based on better diet, exercise, rest, and avoiding the abuse of drugs, including alcohol. Unnecessary tests, surgery, and hospital admissions represent high costs to be avoided. For the same reason, they also keep the length of hospital stays to the bare minimum. The reduction in costs can be dramatic, as HMO patients have less surgery and fewer hospitalizations than fee-for-service patients (Ward, 1991; Cuffel, Goldman, & Schlesinger, 1999).

PROFITS AND A CONFLICT OF INTEREST. As you better understand HMOs, you may realize the built-in conflict of interest. The physicians face an ethical dilemma: profits or patient care? An unintended consequence of avoiding hospitalizing patients and conducting expensive tests or treatments is that HMO doctors withhold some *necessary* treatments, tests, and hospitalizations. For example, a woman was sent home from the hospital even though she was still bleeding from her surgery. If she had remained longer, she would have used up more than her "share" of allotted costs and eaten into the corporation's profits. This would not have happened to a fee-for-service patient who could afford to pay for the health care.

Physicians who argue against HMOs do so for two reasons: a loss of autonomy and reduced quality of care. Doctors have to gain permission to give certain treatments. This puts administrators of HMOs, even low-level ones, in the position of dictating to doctors what treatment they can offer (McGinley, 1999). ("You can do that if you want, but we won't pay for it.") Some HMOs even determine the number of patients the doctors must see each day. One HMO, for example, insisted that its physicians see eight patients an hour, limiting them to $7^1/_2$ minutes per visit. This did not leave the doctors enough time for completing paperwork, analyzing lab results, and of course, calling HMO officials to get approval for treatment (Greenhouse, 1999).

Limiting medical treatment in order to increase profits has led to severe problems. A mother tried to get her HMO doctor to refer her toddler to a specialist because of a persistent ear infection. She succeeded—*after a year* (Kilborn, 1998). A physician recalls how he fought with his HMO for 3 hours to get permission to do a procedure. The HMO officials kept refusing, even though the woman was coughing up life-threatening amounts of blood (Steinhauer, 1999a). Then there is the doctor who noticed a lump in one of her breasts. When she called the radiology department of the hospital where she worked to schedule a mammogram, she was told that she would have to wait 6 months.

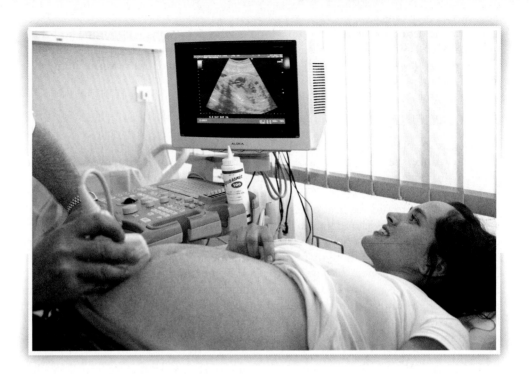

Patients demand—and doctors deliver—high-tech care.

The hospital's HMO allowed one mammogram every 2 years, and she had had a mammogram 18 months earlier. She had to appeal to the HMO's board of directors, who agreed to let her be an exception to the rule. She had breast cancer (Gibbs & Bower, 2006).

Physician Assistants

Another strategy for controlling costs is the greater use of *physician assistants*. Half to three-quarters of all the problems that are dealt with in a typical doctor's office are medically trivial. Physician assistants and nurses can provide much of this medical care and educate patients who have chronic disorders. To delegate routine and time-consuming responsibilities to assistants makes financial sense.

The use of physician assistants has led to an in-house rivalry, however, and the first volleys in a battle over turf have been fired. Physician assistants must work under the supervision of physicians, but they don't like doctors breathing down their necks. They want to be able to give more independent care, but their efforts at establishing greater autonomy have been met with hostility from doctors (Aston & Foubister, 1998). At this point, the attitude of the medical profession is, "If they want to do more, they can go to medical school."

Training Physicians

Medical schools graduate about 15,000 physicians a year, the same today as 20 years ago (*Statistical Abstract*, 2006, Table 291). As Figure 10-12 on the next page shows, a startling change has occurred in the gender makeup of those graduates: In 1960, only 6% of medical school graduates were women. Today, women make up almost half of the nation's medical school graduates, and we anticipate that women will soon outnumber men in the nation's medical schools.

We are unsure if this change in gender will have any significant effect on how medicine is practiced. The medical delivery system is in place, the characteristics reviewed are firm, and gender may be irrelevant to the practice of medicine. Female doctors are as likely as male doctors to be generous or greedy, patient or profit-oriented, in favor of heroic medicine or preventive medicine. They, too, will prefer fee-for-service medicine and will be just as likely to avoid the poor and to set up practices where they make more money. Such orientations are consequences of core values prevalent in general society and in medical school.

FIGURE 10-12 M.D. Degrees, by Sex

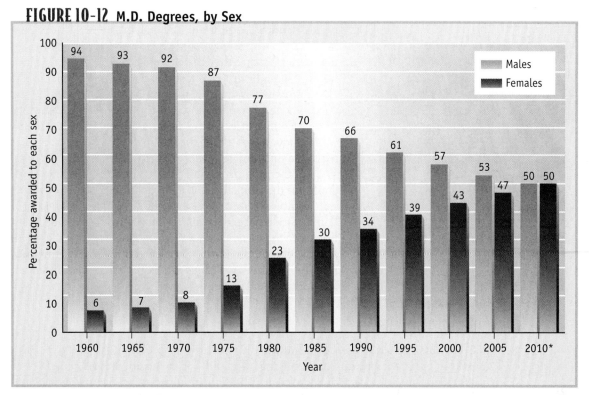

Note: Asterisk indicates estimate.

Source: Statistical Abstract of the United States (1994, Table 295; 2007, Table 293).

One social policy that might reduce costs and help provide care to the poor would be to train more physicians. The government could encourage the opening of new medical schools. It could either finance them or offer tax breaks to investors. This program could be similar to the National Health Service Corps, but more extensive. We suggest that students be allowed to go to college and medical school free of charge in return for spending a specified amount of time in areas where there is a doctor shortage. They would also be paid a monthly salary while they are in school. New physicians trained under this program would be required to give 4 years back for the 8 that they spend in training. These graduates would not be given their final certification until they completed those 4 years. During their years of service, the government would pay for their medical malpractice insurance and pay them a salary equal to the average U.S. wage.

Not only would such a program increase physician presence in poorer areas, but it would also increase competition among physicians. Currently, the American Medical Association stifles competition by limiting the number of medical graduates. If medical schools educated more people, patients would have a greater choice of physicians. As competition among doctors grew, they would likely reduce prices, and the rise in medical costs would slow. The waiting period in doctors' offices would also decrease as overcrowding and overscheduling decreased. Patients with choice would drive incompetent physicians out of business.

The outcry of physicians to such a proposal would be loud, for their income would drop as prices for their services fell. The physicians' labor union (or more accurately, their business organization), the American Medical Association, would mobilize to fight such a proposal. An abundant supply of medical practitioners would not be in the best interest of this powerful monopoly.

Domiciliary Care

Because hospitalization is expensive and many hospital stays are unnecessary, home health care is replacing hospitalization. **Home health care,** or **domiciliary care,** is treatment

Half of all deaths are preventable, and one of the main causes of preventable death is smoking.

given within a patient's home. This style of care is less expensive and often more humane than the care in nursing homes and hospitals. Many elderly people are put in nursing homes because they can no longer live independently at home. Home health care lets them remain at home, in the environment they are used to and that they prefer.

On a negative note, home health care may involve profiteering. For instance, a home health care company may pay its workers low wages to care for the homebound while charging Medicare much more than necessary for administrative costs.

Another approach would be to create domiciliary programs for the mentally ill. Care to deinstitutionalized patients can be provided long term in a group home or in their own home. Group homes and supervised apartments can be established for the mentally disturbed, the mentally handicapped, and the chronically ill who have difficulty living in the community on their own. Such programs are costly, of course, and many would object to providing care to the "unworthy."

Preventive Medicine

PREVENTABLE DEATHS. *Half* of all deaths in America are preventable. The two main causes of premature deaths are smoking (435,000 a year) and diet-related illnesses (400,000 deaths a year) (Mokdad et al., 2004). As subjective concerns and greater knowledge about preventive health have increased, the AMA has begun to emphasize preventive care.

THREE TYPES OF PREVENTIVE MEDICINE. Preventive medicine sounds ideal as a way to ensure good health and reduce medical costs, but how do you put it into practice? Health practitioners distinguish among three types of prevention. **Primary prevention,** such as improved nutrition and childhood vaccinations, keeps a disease from occurring in the first place. **Secondary prevention,** such as self-examination for breast cancer, involves detecting a disease before it comes to the attention of a physician. **Tertiary prevention** is not very different from medical care. It means to prevent further damage from an already existing disease. Examples are controlling pneumonia so that it does not lead to death and maintaining a diabetic on insulin.

FOOD AND HEALTH. Primary prevention is promising because with proper nutrition and exercise, and avoidance of tobacco, people can greatly reduce their susceptibility to many diseases. A diet rich in beta-carotene, raw fruits and vegetables, and vitamin E supplements reduces the risk of cancer. Wheat bran, canola oil, soy milk, cantaloupe, avocados, olive oil, and green vegetables such as cabbage also appear to reduce the risk. And leafy green vegetables—broccoli, brussels sprouts, and spinach—also seem to fight cancer (Biello, 2006).

Studies on the effects of milk on health are inconclusive. Some studies indicate that milk can reduce cancer (Cho et al., 2004; Larsson et al., 2004), whereas other research indicates that milk might increase the risk of cancer (Mayne et al., 1995). If milk does increase the risk of cancer, this could be due to pesticides, herbicides, and growth hormones that are fed to cows. Some researchers claim that bovine growth hormones pave the way for cancer by inhibiting the body's natural cancer fighters (Epstein, 1999). Some accuse Monsanto, a global corporate giant that produces bovine growth hormones, of caring more about profits than people's health.

IMMUNIZATIONS. Immunizing children is an effective prevention technique. Not only do immunizations save lives but also they save vast amounts of money that otherwise would be spent on medical treatment. Yet about 10 percent of American children have not been immunized against measles, mumps, diphtheria, pertussis, hepatitis, and polio (*Statistical Abstract,* 2006, Table 178). For many rural and poor areas, the figure is worse.

PREVENTING DRUG ABUSE AND HOMICIDE. Although not usually thought of as preventive medicine, no program would be complete unless it also focused on preventing drug abuse and homicide. From what we learned in Chapter 4, reducing drug abuse would prevent many serious health problems. Such programs could prevent the untimely deaths of many inner-city youths. In addition, drug abuse prevention programs that are directed against smoking and alcohol abuse could save hundreds of thousands of middle-class lives. Drug abuse programs, then, are another way to improve the nation's health.

EATING OURSELVES TO DEATH. Something disturbing is happening in the United States, and it does not bode well for our health or perception:

> In Cape Canaveral, Florida, a British couple in their 20s said that they had never seen so many overweight people in their lives! Another visitor from Spain wanted to know why there were so many overweight Americans.

Are these valid perceptions or ethnocentric observations made by foreigners?

In 1980, 1 of 4 Americans was overweight. By 1990, the percentage of overweight Americans had jumped to 1 of 3. Now, incredibly, it is 2 of every 3 (65%) (*Statistical Abstract,* 1998, Table 242; 2007, Table 198).

"So what?" Are the concerns being raised anything more than someone's arbitrary idea of how much we should weigh? It is a great deal more. Being overweight is more life-threatening to Americans than AIDS or even alcohol abuse. Health experts estimate that the extra weight kills 365,000 American adults each year. Some say that this total is exaggerated, that deaths from being overweight are actually 112,000 a year (Saguy, 2006).

Regardless of the exact number, people who are overweight are more likely to have strokes, to suffer heart attacks, and to come down with diabetes (Kumanyika, 2005). Compared with thinner people, when the obese come down with these health problems, they are more likely to die (Calle et al., 2003). The problem has become so extensive that some experts are predicting that the life expectancy of Americans will start to decline (Olshansky et al., 2005).

This increase in the weight of Americans, so apparent to people from other cultures, flies in the face of what we know about preventing health problems. For example, the average American drinks 46 gallons of soft drinks a year (*Statistical Abstract,* 2006, Table 201). Because this lifestyle is reinforced through advertising, it is more difficult to halt. Our culture encourages people to visit a doctor when health problems arise, rather than exercise and eat healthier.

THE PROBLEM WITH PREVENTIVE MEDICINE. Preventive medicine is quiet and unassuming. It often is obscured by the drama of heroic medicine—open-heart surgery, screaming ambulances, and doctors and nurses rushing about in emergency rooms. If you take care of your body and manage to stay well, no one thinks much about it. Become seriously ill, however, and people jump to attention. Preventing something from happening means that you may never see it happen. In fact, this is what most people want—not to get sick. Although society has the ability to reduce the risk of heart disease, unhealthy habits are appealing.

To see how severely lifestyle can affect people's health on a national basis, read the Spotlight on Social Research box on page 352.

Humanizing Health Care

Mary Duffy was lying in bed half-asleep on the morning after her breast surgery, when a group of white-coated strangers filed into her hospital room. Without a word, one of them, a man, leaned over her, pulled back her blanket, and stripped her nightgown from her

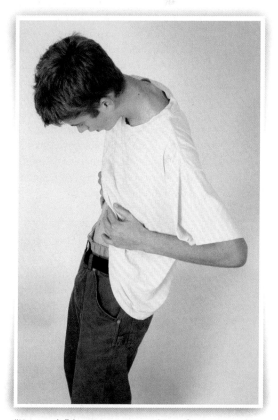

"Manorexia" is a term now used to refer to anorexia nervosa in males. This is not an officially recognized medical term but has been frequently used in media reports. Anorexia nervosa affects up to 1% of women at some point in their lives and is much less common in men. Males represent about 10% of people suffering from anorexia nervosa.

Spotlight on Social Research
SOLVING A HEALTH MYSTERY

WILLIAM COCKERHAM, *professor of sociology at the University of Alabama at Birmingham, studies international aspects of health. He has done research on health and lifestyles in Russia and Eastern Europe, and he is doing similar research in Japan.*

In the mid-1990s, I attended a medical sociology conference in Vienna. Sociologists from the former socialist countries in Eastern Europe reported that their countries were in the midst of a health crisis. They said that men were dying prematurely and that the life expectancy for women had either declined or stagnated. What was striking about their presentations and in the discussions that followed was that no one could explain why this was occurring. That in peacetime an entire group of industrialized societies was experiencing a prolonged deterioration in the health of the population was unexpected.

The lack of an explanation for this crisis presented an intriguing research question. The killer turned out to be an increase in heart disease that had begun in the mid-1960s. A review of the evidence showed that infectious diseases, environmental pollution, and poor medical care were not enough to cause this surge in mortality. A clue that social factors were important was the fact that the rise in death rates was not universal. Heart disease differed by gender, age, urban–rural locale, education, and region. Those most affected were middle-aged, urban men who did manual work.

We now knew the "what" and the "who," but not the "why." To discover the "why," I traveled to Russia and Eastern Europe. There, I collected data from clinics, hospitals, and ministries of health. I also interviewed public health experts, physicians, and sociologists. In addition, I observed how the people lived.

I uncovered three reasons for the increase in premature deaths. The first was policy failures: the failure to address the increase in heart disease and to adopt measures to lower smoking and drinking. The second seemed to be stress, which had increased with the collapse of communism: Workers had lost jobs and state benefits, such as housing and food subsidies. In addition, inflation had made their money worth less, driving down the value of their pensions and salaries. The third—and the primary reason—turned out to be unhealthy lifestyles. Heavy drinking and smoking and lack of exercise characterized the people who died prematurely from heart disease. To say "heavy" drinking is an understatement: adult Russian males, who comprise 25% of the population, drink 90% of the alcohol consumed in a country that averages 14 gallons per person annually.

I did not have enough data, however, to determine conclusively that stress—which has a well-established connection to heart disease—was especially important. A grant from the European Union provided funds to survey 18,000 people in eight countries of the former Soviet Union. This survey showed that women actually are more stressed than men. While stress undoubtedly makes the women's lives less pleasant and has consequences for their health, it is not killing enough of them prematurely to come close to the mortality rates of the men. As bad as the situation may be for the women, the key to explaining the health crisis ultimately lies in the men's behavior.

---

shoulders. He began to talk about carcinomas to the half-dozen medical students who had encircled her bed, staring at her naked body with detached curiosity. Abruptly, the doctor said to her, "Have you passed gas yet?" (Carey, 2005)

It's almost difficult to imagine such an event. No one likes *depersonalization*—being treated as an inanimate object, yet this happens routinely in medical settings. It is as though medical personnel think that when people check into a hospital, they have also checked their feelings and personal needs into their medical folder. Sociologists who have studied depersonalization in public clinics note how the poor have to wait for hours, aren't looked directly in the eyes when spoken to, and are addressed as numbers rather than humans, If they aren't able to see a doctor that day, it's just one of those things. After all, what do poor people have to do that's important, anyway?

If depersonalizing medical care is a problem, then the solution is to make it more humane. This process has to begin in medical school or even in pre-med training. The medical establishment recognizes depersonalization as a problem, and some medical schools have incorporated "bedside manner" training into their curriculum. So far, such

efforts have been feeble and ineffective. Even when medical students have a strong desire to treat patients as people, the pressures of their rigorous training, accompanied by their faculty's stress on organs, disease, and dysfunctions, changes the students' attitude and approach to patients. Listen to a medical student describe this change in her orientation:

> Somebody will say, "Listen to Mrs. Jones's heart. It's just a little thing flubbing on the table." And you forget about the rest of her . . . and it helps in learning in the sense that you can go in to a patient, put your stethoscope on the heart, listen to it, and walk out. . . . The advantage is that you can go in a short time and see a patient, get the important things out of the patient, and leave. (Haas & Shaffir, 1993, p. 437)

Ultimately, medical training needs to stress the *inherent worth* of patients—that each individual is valuable and deserves personal attention. Physicians and nurses also need to incorporate a *holistic approach,* a view that attempts to heal not only the body, but the spirit as well. Researchers suggest that hospital waiting rooms and hospital patient rooms be transformed into more comfortable settings (Howard & Strauss, 1975; Carey, 2005).

Making health care more personal is certainly an uphill battle. Depersonalization has become instinctive to medical personnel. Consider this event:

> Jeanne Kennedy, the chief patient representative at Stanford Hospital in Palo Alto, California, broke her knee cap rushing to a meeting. A member of her staff wheeled her to the employee health department, where a nurse practitioner she had worked with for years began to arrange for her care. But the nurse spoke to the woman pushing the wheelchair and ignored Mrs. Kennedy.
>
> "It was crazy," she said, "Here I was in my own hospital, hurt but perfectly capable, and she's being very professional, but she's talking over my head as if I were a child. And we worked together. She knew me!" (Carey, 2005)

The key to changing such deeply ingrained attitudes may require changing how fees are collected. Until physicians make more money by giving holistic treatment, this change is unlikely to come about. But it is a possibility, for there are indications that patients who feel their physicians have a personal interest in them and in the outcome of their treatment are less likely to sue for malpractice, even when doctors make mistakes. In addition, many people with medical problems are turning away from traditional medicine, which is eating at the profits of traditional medical practitioners. Let's look at one of these alternatives.

Self-Care Groups

One reaction to depersonalization and the high costs of health care is the emergence of self-care groups; in these groups, members discuss new developments in their diseases or problems, encourage one another to take preventive measures, and support one another emotionally. The goals of self-care groups are to maintain health, prevent disease, and provide diagnosis, medication, and treatment. Among the many who have formed groups to help each other are people with diabetes, heart attack victims, cancer patients, people who have had breast surgery, smokers, alcoholics, and people who suffer from rheumatism, arthritis, AIDS, disabilities, mental illnesses, and genetic problems.

IN SUM The social policies discussed in this chapter focus on three major problems of health and medical care: high costs, the general lack of preventive medicine, and depersonalization. The aim of these policies is to move health care away from the hospital into the home, with less emphasis on acute care and dysfunctional organs. These policies offer inexpensive alternatives to highly technological and costly medical care. To better understand the U.S. medical system and the policies discussed here, see the Global Glimpse box on the next page.

A Global Glimpse
HEALTH CARE IN SWEDEN, RUSSIA, AND CHINA

To better understand our own medical system, it helps to examine health care in other nations. Sweden, Russia, and China illustrate contrasting themes in health care around the world, helping us to place the U.S. medical system in cultural perspective.

HEALTH CARE IN THE MOST INDUSTRIALIZED NATIONS: SWEDEN

Sweden has the most comprehensive health care system in the world. National health insurance, which is financed by contributions from the state and employers, covers all Swedish citizens and alien residents. The government pays most physicians a salary to treat patients, but 5% work full-time in private practice (Swedish Institute, 1992). Except for a small consultation fee, medical and dental treatment by these government-paid doctors is free. The state also pays most of the charges of private physicians. The government reimburses travel expenses for patients and for the parents of a hospitalized child. Only minimal fees are charged for prescriptions and hospitalization.

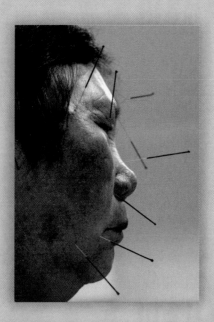

A patient receives traditional needle therapy to cure hemiplegia (a type of paralysis) at a hospital where Chinese medicine is practiced.

Medical treatment is just one component of Sweden's broad system of social welfare. For example, people who are sick or who must stay home with sick children receive 90% of their salaries. Swedes are given parental leave at the birth of a child and when a child is sick. They also are guaranteed a pension.

Sweden's socialized medicine, however, is inefficient. Swedes have not solved the twin problems of getting rid of waiting lines and motivating physicians to work hard. Because medical personnel know how much their pay will be, regardless of how many patients they see, they are not productive. When reporters visited Sweden's largest hospital on a weekday morning, when 80 of 120 surgeons were on duty, they found 19 of the hospital's 24 operating rooms idle. Their photos of empty operating rooms—at a time when there was a 1–2-year waiting period for hip replacements and cataract operations—provoked a public outcry (Bergström, 1992). The waiting list for cataract surgery has grown to 30,000 Swedes—in a population of 9 million ("Swedish Health Care . . . ," 2002). If the same percentage of Americans were waiting for surgery, the U.S. line would be 600,000 people long.

Swedish lawmakers have decided that to improve efficiency they need to abandon the socialized model, and they are gradu-

ally turning the health care system over to the private sector. The government has begun selling hospitals to private companies ("Social Darwinism . . . ," 2001). This privatization has created a two-tier system of health care. One tier is comprised of those who seek free universal health care, and the other is made of those who can afford private care. This has created a gap in patient service, and many private companies are now charging patients for treatments that would previously have been free (Templeton & St. Quinton, 2006).

HEALTH CARE IN THE INDUSTRIALIZING NATIONS: RUSSIA

Russia's medical system is in tatters. Under the Communist party, Russia had established a system that made free health care available to most people. Doctors would even visit patients at their homes (Gaufberg, 2004). Like the rest of the nation's production, the health care system was centralized. The state owned the medical schools and determined how many doctors would be trained in what specialties. The state paid medical salaries, which it set, and determined where doctors would practice. Physicians were poorly trained, had low prestige, and earned less than bus drivers.

Under Russia's fitful transition to capitalism, its health care system has deteriorated, and the health of the population has declined. An example is Moscow's ambulance system. It used to be efficient—dial 03, and an ambulance would arrive within minutes. When Russia turned to capitalism in 1991, ambulances sometimes took 8 hours to arrive because the drivers were using the ambulances as freelance cabs, and they kept emergency cases waiting (Field, 1998). Since then, ambulance service has improved, especially in Moscow (Gaufberg, 2004).

The only hospitals comparable to those of the United States are reserved for the elite (Light, 1992; Gaufberg, 2004). In the rest, conditions are deplorable. To be assured of care, some patients bring their own linens, medicines, and syringes with them to the hospital (Paddock, 1999). In some hospitals, surgeons resharpen scalpels until they break. Some even use razor blades for surgery (Donaldson, 1992). Outdated and broken equipment is not replaced. Some doctors face the choice of operating without anesthetic or not operating at all (Paddock, 1999). Physicians are paid so little that in order to

have food, they have to grow potatoes. They walk to work because they cannot afford the equivalent of a dime to take a bus (Goldberg & Kishkovsky, 2000).

The bright spot is that physicians continue to work despite their low status and miserable pay. Many are motivated by idealism and the desire to help, coupled with the hope that things will get better. A second bright spot is that some doctors are making the transition to private practice, which could be the beginning of a new medical system built on the rubble of the old (Goldberg & Kishkovsky, 2000).

In the meantime, Russia's medical system remains broken. Perhaps no event more pinpoints the disarray than this:

> Three patients lay unconscious in the intensive care unit, kept alive only by the Siberian hospital's life support system. Two were elderly; one was 39.
>
> On Wednesday, the hospital received a telegram from the local power company: "You haven't paid your bill for five years. You owe us $94,931. Pay up, or we'll shut off your electricity." The next morning, at 6 a.m., the company shut off the power. Forty minutes later, all three patients were dead. (Paddock, 1999)

The years of environmental degradation under the Communists have also taken their toll. Serious birth defects have jumped to 4 times the U.S. rate. A likely culprit is radiation pollution from decades of nuclear irresponsibility (Specter, 1995). Perhaps the single best indicator of the deterioration of health is the drop in life expectancy that began in the 1960s (Cockerham, 1997). As shown in Table 10-2, the health of Russians is more like that of the Chinese than that of citizens in the Most Industrialized Nations. Life expectancy is not only a medical issue, but also a barometer of a society's health.

HEALTH CARE IN THE LEAST INDUSTRIALIZED NATIONS: CHINA

Because this nation of 1.3 billion people has a vast shortage of trained physicians, hospitals, and medicine, most Chinese see "barefoot doctors," people who have only a rudimentary knowledge of medicine, are paid low wages, and travel from village to village. Until a few years ago, physicians were employees of the government, and the government owned all the country's medical facilities. With its emphases on medicinal herbs and acupuncture, Chinese medicine differs from that of the West. Although Westerners have scoffed at the Chinese approach, some have changed their minds, and on a limited basis, medicinal herbs and acupuncture are used in the United States.

Like Russia, China has begun the journey to capitalism. Physicians earn so little that, like American college students, some take "after work" part-time jobs. Deciding that profits should be part of the medical system, Chinese authorities withdrew government financing from the local health centers, which are now expected to sell their services (Beech, 2004). Most patients who cannot pay for their medical care go untreated. In one hospital, doctors insisted on being paid before they would give emergency care to a 3-year-old who had swallowed pesticides. The boy died, and the villagers rioted, ripping the hospital apart (Kahn, 2006).

At this point in its transition, China's medical system has deteriorated so greatly that the World Health Organization (WHO) ranked it 144 of 191 nations. WHO ranked the medical care system of Bangladesh higher (Beech, 2004).

FOR YOUR CONSIDERATION

In what ways would you say that the U.S. medical system is superior—and inferior—to each of these systems? Would you prefer to be treated within one of these three systems rather than in the American system? Why or why not? Short of socializing medicine, which goes against the values of Americans, how do you think the U.S. medical system can overcome the deficiencies reviewed in this chapter—and maintain its strengths?

TABLE 10-2 Indicators of Health

	SWEDEN	UNITED STATES	RUSSIA	CHINA
Life expectancy, years	79.2	77.3	66.8	71.6
Infant mortality[1]	3.9	6.6	16.0	26.4
Birthrate[2]	11.7	14.1	9.6	13.0
Death rate	10.8	8.3	14.7	6.9
Health costs as a percentage of Gross Domestic Product	9.2	15.0	2.3	4.8

[1] Per 1,000 live births.
[2] Per 1,000 population.

Sources: By James M. Henslin. Based on Field (1998); Liu (2004); Statistical Abstract of the United States (1998, Tables 1345, 1348; 2000, Tables 1355, 1358; 2006, Tables 98, 1318, 1323).

The Future of the Problem

To try to catch a glimpse of the future, let's look at trends in medical technology and in redirecting medicine.

Technology

MORE TECHNOLOGY. Just as the practice of medicine has been driven by the development of new technology, so it will be in the coming years. Patients will continue to demand cutting-edge technology when their lives are threatened—regardless of the cost. With this demand from patients—and from doctors and hospitals in competition with one another—the manufacturers of medical equipment will continue to develop and sell new products.

ETHICAL DILEMMAS. Out of these technological advances have arisen ethical problems that plague medical professionals and laypeople alike. If people can be kept alive artificially, must doctors keep them alive? Does "brain dead" really mean "dead"? If so, should physicians be allowed to "harvest body parts" from people who (only because of machines) are still breathing? Should medical researchers be allowed to test dangerous drugs on these people, because, after all, they are "really" dead? Another ethical controversy, **euthanasia,** is discussed in the Thinking Critically box on the next page.

THE INTERNET. The Internet has helped some patients regain control over their medical care. People who have rare diseases, for example, can participate in online discussion groups. Although people don't meet personally in this new type of self-care group, they share their experiences and knowledge with one another. Some doctors are surprised—and dismayed—when their patients know more than they do about a new treatment or some new research. Not only do physicians feel threatened because they no longer are the sole possessors of esoteric knowledge on rare diseases or even the treatment of common disorders, but they also fear that patients can be picking up misinformation on the Internet. Medical experiments can also be contaminated: By sharing information online, some patients are able to determine whether they are receiving an experimental drug or a *placebo,* a substance that is designed to look like a medicine but that has no medical value (Bulkeley, 1995).

Redirecting Medicine

THE CARLSON PREDICTIONS. In the 1970s, Rick Carlson (1975) said that in the year 2000 we would be living in a more complex and stressful society, we would have a large aging population with incurable degenerative diseases, and we would have more illnesses resulting from lifestyle and environmental deterioration. Carlson also argued that our medical system would still not use preventive medicine. He concluded that poverty would not be cured and that the poor would continue to have more illnesses than the affluent. He was right on all counts.

THE POTENTIAL. Carlson argued, however, that we can change our health care system, transforming it into a much better system for meeting health care issues. An effective system, he said, would *encourage people to demand better health rather than more medicine.* This requires an awareness of factors that influence health, from those under the individual's control to environmental factors under the community's control.

To take this essential element of an effective health care system seriously, we would need more research on self–health care and disease prevention. Some physicians would continue to provide acute and emergency care, but others would be retrained in preventive and environmental medicine. The elderly would be cared for in residential

SHOULD DOCTORS BE ALLOWED TO KILL PATIENTS?

Except for the name, this is a true story:

Bill Simpson, in his 70s, had battled leukemia for years. After his spleen was removed, he developed an abdominal abscess. It took another operation to drain it. A week later, the abscess filled, and required more surgery. Again the abscess returned. Simpson began to go in and out of consciousness. His brother-in-law suggested euthanasia. The surgeon injected a lethal dose of morphine into Simpson's intravenous feeding tubes.

Dr. Jack Kevorkian illustrating his suicide machine.

At a medical conference in which euthanasia was discussed, a cancer specialist who had treated thousands of patients announced that he had kept count of the patients who had asked him to help them die. "There were 127 men and women," he said. Then he added, "And I saw to it that 25 of them got their wish." Thousands of other physicians have done the same (Nuland, 1995).

When a doctor ends a patient's life, such as by injecting a lethal drug, it is called *active euthanasia*. To withhold life support (nutrients or liquids) is called *passive euthanasia*. To remove life support, such as disconnecting a patient from oxygen falls somewhere in between. The result, of course, is the same.

Two images seem to dominate the public's ideas of euthanasia: One is of an individual devastated by chronic pain. The doctor mercifully helps to end that pain by performing euthanasia. The second is of a brain-dead individual—a human vegetable—who lies in a hospital bed, kept alive only by machines. How accurate are these images?

We have the example of the Netherlands. There, along with Belgium, euthanasia is legal. Incredibly, in about 1,000 cases a year, physicians kill their patients without the patients' express consent. In one instance a doctor ended the life of a nun because he thought she would have wanted him to but was afraid to ask because it was against her religion. In another case, a physician killed a patient with breast cancer who said that she did *not* want euthanasia. In the doctor's words, "It could have taken another week before she died. I needed this bed" (Hendin, 1997, 2000).

Some Dutch, concerned that they could be euthanized if they have a medical emergency, carry "passports" that instruct medical personnel that they wish to live. Most Dutch, however, support euthanasia. Many carry a different "passport," one that instructs medical personnel to carry out euthanasia (Shapiro, 1997).

In Michigan, Dr. Jack Kevorkian, a pathologist (he didn't treat patients—he studied diseased tissues) decided that regardless of laws, he had the right to help people commit suicide. He did, 120 times. Here is how he described one of those times:

I started the intravenous dripper, which released a salt solution through a needle into her vein, and I kept her arm tied down so she wouldn't jerk it. This was difficult as her veins were fragile. And then once she decided she was ready to go, she just hit the switch and the device cut off the saline drip and through the needle released a solution of thiopental that put her to sleep in ten to fifteen seconds. A minute later, through the needle flowed a lethal solution of potassium chloride. (Denzin, 1992)

Kevorkian taunted authorities. He sometimes left bodies in vans and dropped them off at hospitals. Although he provided the poison, as well as a "death machine" that he developed to administer the poison, and he watched patients pull the lever that released the drugs, Kevorkian never touched that lever. Frustrated Michigan prosecutors tried Kevorkian for murder four times, but four times juries refused to convict him. Then Kevorkian made a fatal mistake. On national television, he played a videotape showing him giving a lethal injection to a man who was dying from Lou Gehrig's disease. Prosecutors put Kevorkian on trial again. This time, he was convicted of second-degree murder and was sentenced to 10 to 25 years in prison.

In 1997, Oregon became the first U.S. state to make medically assisted suicide legal; Washington joined it after the 2008 election. If Kevorkian had given that lethal injection today in either of those states, he would not have gone to prison.

FOR YOUR CONSIDERATION

Which state do you think is right? Why? In the future, do you think we will go the way of Oregon and Washington or Michigan?

As is evident in the Netherlands, physician-assisted deaths have a way of expanding. In addition to what is reported here, Dutch doctors also kill newborn babies who have serious birth defects (W. J. Smith, 1999). Their justification is that these children would not have "quality of life." Would you support this?

complexes that are humane and pleasant, such as those in Denmark and Sweden. Funds saved from spending less on acute and emergency medical care could go to programs that feature accident prevention, food safety, occupational safety, nutrition, and exercise. Efforts would be made to reduce the stresses of modern life by designing more relaxing work environments in offices and schools; building hiking and bike paths, tennis courts, and parks in our communities; and reducing noise pollution. Schools would teach nutrition and the benefits of a healthy lifestyle, while requiring students to get exercise through rigorous physical education.

The potential for improving the general health of our population is great. With the public's growing awareness of social factors underlying health and illness, the demand for preventive treatment will grow. The focus on preventive medicine, however, runs counter to our nation's current emphasis on heroic intervention in acute cases.

SUMMARY AND REVIEW

1. What people consider to be health and illness vary with culture and social class. Health problems are based on both biological and social factors.

2. Industrialization has brought better health, but with it has come an increase in some health problems—cancer, heart disease, drug addiction, and other chronic illnesses caused by lifestyle, aging, and environmental pollution. HIV/AIDS illustrates the relationship among behavior, environment, and disease. Physical and emotional problems are more common among the poor. To explain the relationship between social class and mental illness, sociologists prefer environmental explanations rather than genetic ones.

3. The U.S. medical system is centered on specialized, hospital-based, and heroic intervention. A fee-for-service system increases cost. In preventive medicine, the emphasis is on changing people's lifestyles and environment.

4. Social inequalities in medical and mental health services stem largely from the way we pay medical bills. In our fee-for-service system, health care is not a right but a commodity sold to the highest bidder. The United States has a *two-tier system of medical care*—public clinics

and poorer treatment for the poor and private clinics and better treatment for the more affluent.

5. Two policies designed to control medical costs are to pay patients to stay healthy and to pay doctors to reduce unnecessary medical care. HMOs are a form of managed care that provides a fixed amount of money to a medical corporation to attend to the health needs of a group of people. Medical services and tests come directly off the corporate bottom line, leading to a conflict of interest in treating patients. On the other hand, if HMO practitioners let their patients become too sick, it costs the medical corporation more than if they catch problems early.

6. The medical profession is experiencing a tension among its traditional focus on heroic intervention in acute problems, the need to treat chronic problems, and the emerging focus on medical problems caused by lifestyle and environmental pollution. Within this tension, there is likely to be increased emphasis on preventive medicine—better health habits, a cleaner environment, and education designed to teach people how to take care of themselves and to manage their illnesses.

KEY TERMS

Antiretroviral drugs, 339
Cesarean section, 325
Conversion therapy, 331
Defensive medicine, 334
Deinstitutionalization, 330
Depersonalization, 334
Domiciliary care, 349
Drug therapy, 344
Electroconvulsive therapy (ECT), 344
Euthanasia, 356

Group therapy, 344
Health maintenance organization (HMO), 347
Home health care, 349
Iatrogenesis, 320
Individual psychotherapy, 344
Infant mortality rate (IMR), 326
Lay referral network, 333
Managed care, 347
Occupational disease, 342
Pharmaceutical straitjacket, 345

Primary prevention, 350
Professional referral network, 333
Psychoanalysis, 344
Secondary prevention, 350
Short-term directive therapy, 344
Talk therapy, 345
Tertiary prevention, 350
Two-tier system of medical care, 323
(the) Working poor, 342

THINKING CRITICALLY ABOUT CHAPTER 10

1. What do you think the government's role should be in medical care? Why?
2. Why do you think the United States is the only industrialized country that doesn't have a national health care system?

3. Why do you think women live longer than men?
4. Which of the theoretical perspectives (symbolic interactionism, functionalism, or conflict theory) do you think best explains health care problems in the United States? Explain.

BY THE NUMBERS: THEN AND NOW

- Cost of U.S medical care, in billions of dollars, in 1990: **$696**
- Cost of U.S. medical care, in billions of dollars, now: **$2,754**

- Percentage of U.S. births by cesarean section in 1975: **10.6%**
- Percentage of U.S. births by cesarean section in 2005: **30.3%**

- Cost of one day's stay in the hospital in 1980: **$245**
- Cost of one day's stay in the hospital now: **$1,450**

- Percentage of U.S. deaths due to heart disease in 1900: **8%**
- Percentage of U.S. deaths due to heart disease in 2003: **28%**

- Percentage of M.D. degrees awarded to men in 1975: **87%**
- Percentage of M.D. degrees awarded to men in 2005: **53%**

- Percentage of M.D. degrees awarded to women in 1975: **13%**
- Percentage of M.D. degrees awarded to women in 2005: **47%**

MySocLab

What can you find in MySocLab? mysoclab www.mysoclab.com

- Complete Ebook
- Practice Tests and Exams
- Multimedia Activities
- Mapping and Data Analysis Exercises

- Research and Writing Advice
- Interactive Social Surveys
- Sociology in the News

The Changing Family

SHOULD DOCTORS BE ALLOWED TO KILL PATIENTS?

Except for the name, this is a true story:

Bill Simpson, in his 70s, had battled leukemia for years. After his spleen was removed, he developed an abdominal abscess. It took another operation to drain it. A week later, the abscess filled, and required more surgery. Again the abscess returned. Simpson began to go in and out of consciousness. His brother-in-law suggested euthanasia. The surgeon injected a lethal dose of morphine into Simpson's intravenous feeding tubes.

Dr. Jack Kevorkian illustrating his suicide machine.

At a medical conference in which euthanasia was discussed, a cancer specialist who had treated thousands of patients announced that he had kept count of the patients who had asked him to help them die. "There were 127 men and women," he said. Then he added, "And I saw to it that 25 of them got their wish." Thousands of other physicians have done the same (Nuland, 1995).

When a doctor ends a patient's life, such as by injecting a lethal drug, it is called *active euthanasia*. To withhold life support (nutrients or liquids) is called *passive euthanasia*. To remove life support, such as disconnecting a patient from oxygen falls somewhere in between. The result, of course, is the same.

Two images seem to dominate the public's ideas of euthanasia: One is of an individual devastated by chronic pain. The doctor mercifully helps to end that pain by performing euthanasia. The second is of a brain-dead individual—a human vegetable—who lies in a hospital bed, kept alive only by machines. How accurate are these images?

We have the example of the Netherlands. There, along with Belgium, euthanasia is legal. Incredibly, in about 1,000 cases a year, physicians kill their patients without the patients' express consent. In one instance a doctor ended the life of a nun because he thought she would have wanted him to but was afraid to ask because it was against her religion. In another case, a physician killed a patient with breast cancer who said that she did *not* want euthanasia. In the doctor's words, "It could have taken another week before she died. I needed this bed" (Hendin, 1997, 2000).

Some Dutch, concerned that they could be euthanized if they have a medical emergency, carry "passports" that instruct medical personnel that they wish to live. Most Dutch, however, support euthanasia. Many carry a different "passport," one that instructs medical personnel to carry out euthanasia (Shapiro, 1997).

In Michigan, Dr. Jack Kevorkian, a pathologist (he didn't treat patients—he studied diseased tissues) decided that regardless of laws, he had the right to help people commit suicide. He did, 120 times. Here is how he described one of those times:

I started the intravenous dripper, which released a salt solution through a needle into her vein, and I kept her arm tied down so she wouldn't jerk it. This was difficult as her veins were fragile. And then once she decided she was ready to go, she just hit the switch and the device cut off the saline drip and through the needle released a solution of thiopental that put her to sleep in ten to fifteen seconds. A minute later, through the needle flowed a lethal solution of potassium chloride. (Denzin, 1992)

Kevorkian taunted authorities. He sometimes left bodies in vans and dropped them off at hospitals. Although he provided the poison, as well as a "death machine" that he developed to administer the poison, and he watched patients pull the lever that released the drugs, Kevorkian never touched that lever. Frustrated Michigan prosecutors tried Kevorkian for murder four times, but four times juries refused to convict him. Then Kevorkian made a fatal mistake. On national television, he played a videotape showing him giving a lethal injection to a man who was dying from Lou Gehrig's disease. Prosecutors put Kevorkian on trial again. This time, he was convicted of second-degree murder and was sentenced to 10 to 25 years in prison.

In 1997, Oregon became the first U.S. state to make medically assisted suicide legal; Washington joined it after the 2008 election. If Kevorkian had given that lethal injection today in either of those states, he would not have gone to prison.

FOR YOUR CONSIDERATION

Which state do you think is right? Why? In the future, do you think we will go the way of Oregon and Washington or Michigan?

As is evident in the Netherlands, physician-assisted deaths have a way of expanding. In addition to what is reported here, Dutch doctors also kill newborn babies who have serious birth defects (W. J. Smith, 1999). Their justification is that these children would not have "quality of life." Would you support this?

complexes that are humane and pleasant, such as those in Denmark and Sweden. Funds saved from spending less on acute and emergency medical care could go to programs that feature accident prevention, food safety, occupational safety, nutrition, and exercise. Efforts would be made to reduce the stresses of modern life by designing more relaxing work environments in offices and schools; building hiking and bike paths, tennis courts, and parks in our communities; and reducing noise pollution. Schools would teach nutrition and the benefits of a healthy lifestyle, while requiring students to get exercise through rigorous physical education.

The potential for improving the general health of our population is great. With the public's growing awareness of social factors underlying health and illness, the demand for preventive treatment will grow. The focus on preventive medicine, however, runs counter to our nation's current emphasis on heroic intervention in acute cases.

SUMMARY AND REVIEW

1. What people consider to be health and illness vary with culture and social class. Health problems are based on both biological and social factors.
2. Industrialization has brought better health, but with it has come an increase in some health problems—cancer, heart disease, drug addiction, and other chronic illnesses caused by lifestyle, aging, and environmental pollution. HIV/AIDS illustrates the relationship among behavior, environment, and disease. Physical and emotional problems are more common among the poor. To explain the relationship between social class and mental illness, sociologists prefer environmental explanations rather than genetic ones.
3. The U.S. medical system is centered on specialized, hospital-based, and heroic intervention. A fee-for-service system increases cost. In preventive medicine, the emphasis is on changing people's lifestyles and environment.
4. Social inequalities in medical and mental health services stem largely from the way we pay medical bills. In our fee-for-service system, health care is not a right but a commodity sold to the highest bidder. The United States has a *two-tier system of medical care*—public clinics

and poorer treatment for the poor and private clinics and better treatment for the more affluent.
5. Two policies designed to control medical costs are to pay patients to stay healthy and to pay doctors to reduce unnecessary medical care. HMOs are a form of managed care that provides a fixed amount of money to a medical corporation to attend to the health needs of a group of people. Medical services and tests come directly off the corporate bottom line, leading to a conflict of interest in treating patients. On the other hand, if HMO practitioners let their patients become too sick, it costs the medical corporation more than if they catch problems early.
6. The medical profession is experiencing a tension among its traditional focus on heroic intervention in acute problems, the need to treat chronic problems, and the emerging focus on medical problems caused by lifestyle and environmental pollution. Within this tension, there is likely to be increased emphasis on preventive medicine—better health habits, a cleaner environment, and education designed to teach people how to take care of themselves and to manage their illnesses.

KEY TERMS

Antiretroviral drugs, 339
Cesarean section, 325
Conversion therapy, 331
Defensive medicine, 334
Deinstitutionalization, 330
Depersonalization, 334
Domiciliary care, 349
Drug therapy, 344
Electroconvulsive therapy (ECT), 344
Euthanasia, 356

Group therapy, 344
Health maintenance organization (HMO), 347
Home health care, 349
Iatrogenesis, 320
Individual psychotherapy, 344
Infant mortality rate (IMR), 326
Lay referral network, 333
Managed care, 347
Occupational disease, 342
Pharmaceutical straitjacket, 345

Primary prevention, 350
Professional referral network, 333
Psychoanalysis, 344
Secondary prevention, 350
Short-term directive therapy, 344
Talk therapy, 345
Tertiary prevention, 350
Two-tier system of medical care, 323
(the) Working poor, 342

THINKING CRITICALLY ABOUT CHAPTER 10

1. What do you think the government's role should be in medical care? Why?
2. Why do you think the United States is the only industrialized country that doesn't have a national health care system?

3. Why do you think women live longer than men?
4. Which of the theoretical perspectives (symbolic interactionism, functionalism, or conflict theory) do you think best explains health care problems in the United States? Explain.

BY THE NUMBERS: THEN AND NOW

- Cost of U.S medical care, in billions of dollars, in 1990: **$696**
- Cost of U.S. medical care, in billions of dollars, now: **$2,754**

- Percentage of U.S. births by cesarean section in 1975: **10.6%**
- Percentage of U.S. births by cesarean section in 2005: **30.3%**

- Cost of one day's stay in the hospital in 1980: **$245**
- Cost of one day's stay in the hospital now: **$1,450**

- Percentage of U.S. deaths due to heart disease in 1900: **8%**
- Percentage of U.S. deaths due to heart disease in 2003: **28%**

- Percentage of M.D. degrees awarded to men in 1975: **87%**
- Percentage of M.D. degrees awarded to men in 2005: **53%**

- Percentage of M.D. degrees awarded to women in 1975: **13%**
- Percentage of M.D. degrees awarded to women in 2005: **47%**

MySocLab

What can you find in MySocLab? mysoclab www.mysoclab.com

- Complete Ebook
- Practice Tests and Exams
- Multimedia Activities
- Mapping and Data Analysis Exercises

- Research and Writing Advice
- Interactive Social Surveys
- Sociology in the News

The Changing Family

Nancy and Antoine were pleased. Their 4-year-old daughter, Janelle, had been accepted at Rainbow Gardens Preschool in Manhattan Beach, California, a prosperous suburb of Los Angeles. The preschool came highly recommended by their close friends, whose son was attending the school. With Nancy's promotion and Antoine's new job, schedules had become more difficult, and Rainbow Gardens was able to handle their need for more flexible hours.

At first Janelle loved preschool. She would happily leave whichever parent drove her to school for the pleasures of her little friends and the gentle care of loving teachers. Then, gradually, almost imperceptibly, a change came over her. At first, Janelle became reluctant to leave her parents. Then she began to whimper in the mornings when they were getting her ready. And lately she had begun to have nightmares, waking up crying and screaming several times a week, something she had never done. The counselor they took Janelle to said it

> ## She had begun to have nightmares.

was nothing to worry about; all kids went through things like this from time to time. Janelle was going through a "developmental adjustment," and she would be just fine in a little while.

When allegations of sexual abuse of 3-, 4-, and 5-year-olds at Rainbow Gardens made headlines, it was devastating to parents around the nation. The unthinkable had become real. Had it happened at their preschool, too—with their child? But for Nancy and Antoine, it was more than a nagging question. Overnight, Janelle's nightmares, her crying, and her bed-wetting took on new meaning. Those gentle teachers, so affectionate with the children, child molesters? Janelle undressed, photographed, forced to commit sexual acts with adults, and threatened with the death of her puppy if she told?

Nancy and Antoine don't know. It is either this or simply a "developmental adjustment." Now it is Nancy's and Antoine's turn for nightmares.

The Problem in Sociological Perspective

"Nightmare at Rainbow Gardens" could be the title of a horror movie, a real-life one for some parents. Each year, an unknown number of children are sexually abused at day care centers. During the 1980s rumors spread that day care centers were filled with child molesters. Teachers were often tried and convicted, sometimes with weak evidence (Rabinowitz, 2004). A Massachusetts man served 18 years in prison before his pleas of innocence were finally acknowledged. Despite the publicity and convictions of the 1980s, many cases of child abuse in school go unreported. If the possibility of abuse does exist, why would 5 million U.S. children be entrusted to the care of strangers in a day care setting (*Statistical Abstract*, 2006, Table 568)?

According to the functionalist perspective, education and day care are considered necessary **social institutions**—enduring features of social life (Giddens, 1984, p. 24). Most institutions bring about both positive and negative outcomes—functions and dysfunctions.

Effects of the Industrial Revolution on the Family

The most significant event ever to affect the institution of the family was the Industrial Revolution. Before industrialization, economic survival was perilous. Both parents and children worked at home together. When industrialization moved production to factories, the effects on family life were so extensive that they continue today. We now explore some of those effects.

When men left the home to work in factories, they no longer shared home-life activities with their wives and children.

MEN LEFT HOME. Men left home to work in factories. This created a divide between husband as worker and husband as father. During workday hours the father left the farm to work in the factory while the rest of the family stayed home. Husband and wife no longer shared activities during working hours. Separated from the household, the husband's role as father changed.

CHILDREN BECAME AN ECONOMIC LIABILITY. Industrialization transformed children from an economic asset into an economic liability. When production was farm-based, children contributed to their family's survival—they fed chickens, milked cows, and worked in fields. When they no longer contributed to the bottom line but still consumed much of the family's limited resources, they became expensive.

FORMAL EDUCATION. To compete in the new industrialized world, one had to be educated. As children spent more years in school than ever before, they became dependent on their parents for a longer period. Their prolonged education and longer dependency made them even more expensive.

A LOWER BIRTHRATE. The discovery of vulcanized rubber during the 1840s made large-scale production of the condom possible. With further refinements in design and manufacture in the 1920s, the condom allowed working adults to limit the number of offspring (Douvan, 1980; Laslett, 1980). Because children had become nonproductive and expensive, the birthrate plunged. As Figure 11-1 on the next page shows, the U.S. birthrate is now the lowest in history, and it is expected to fall still further.

FROM RURAL TO URBAN. Industrialization changed how *and* where people lived. Until about 100 years ago, almost everyone in the world lived in the country. As production moved to city factories, workers moved with it. Because housing in the city was more expensive, couples reduced the number of their offspring even more.

LOSS OF FUNCTIONS. The early family was responsible for production, education, and medical care. As industrialization spread, other institutions began to replace the original functions of the family. Factories produced food and clothing, schools educated children, and health care systems took care of illness and well-being. As family functions were taken over by other social institutions, the institution of family weakened.

CHANGES IN WOMEN'S ROLES. Industrialization also changed women's roles within the family. The farm wife as mother was originally responsible for basic food production (milk, butter, eggs, vegetables), preparation (baking and cooking), and storage (canning). She also made, washed, ironed, and mended the family's clothing; cleaned the house; and took care of the children, the sick, and the elderly. With industrialization, her functions were reduced to that of "emotional provider"; that is, the wife became responsible for lavishing attention upon her breadwinner husband as well as her children.

FIGURE 11-1 U.S. Birthrate, 1890–2050

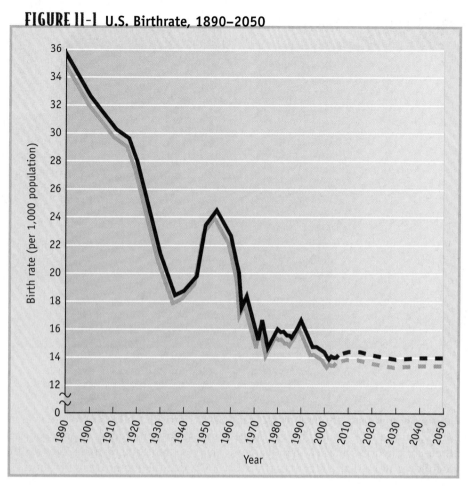

Note: Broken line indicates U.S. government projections.

Source: By James M. Henslin. Based on *Statistical Abstract of the United States* (various editions; 2001, Table 4; 2006, Table 76; 2009, Table 77).

One of the most fundamental changes involving women's roles—women leaving home to enter the paid workforce—began with the Industrial Revolution. About 150 years after the Industrial Revolution began, during World War II, millions of women took over jobs men had left vacant when they went off to war. In the 1980s, for the first time in history, more than half of married women worked for wages at least part-time outside the home. Today about 61% do (*Statistical Abstract*, 2006, Table 584). Because the movement of women from the home has been so tremendous—forcing change in all family relationships—it is sometimes called the *quiet revolution.*

GREATER EQUALITY. Industrialization also brought greater equality to the family. As women's roles changed, so did husbands', parents', and children's. This gradual change did not happen without struggle, as men were reluctant to give up their more privileged positions. Indeed, the struggle over equality (authority and decision-making power) is still a primary source of marital tension.

MORE DIVORCE. Industrialization and greater equality contributed to a higher divorce rate. Before industrialization, divorce was rare. But with the changes just outlined, especially the changes in roles, marriages became fragile.

LONGER LIVES AND MORE INTERGENERATIONAL TIES. Industrialization improved health care, and people lived longer than ever before. One consequence of this longevity has been the ability of more grandparents to participate in the lives of their grandchildren than at any other time in history (Bengtson, Rosenthal, & Burton, 1990). Numerous grandparents are now providing in-home day care while more mothers enter the paid workforce.

The family is always adjusting to changes that are taking place in society. As ideas of masculinity change, for example, behaviors that once were not acceptable for men come to be thought of as normal. After those changes become standard, a current generation may have difficulty understanding why such behaviors ever threatened men's sense of "masculinity."

No one knows exactly how many grandparents provide child care for their grandchildren. But the U.S. Census Bureau suggests that almost one-fourth of preschool-aged children are cared for by their grandparents. Many of these grandparents care for their grandchildren more than 20 hours each week; 7% watch them more than 30 hours each week (Benning, 2005).

Many grandparents babysit because they want to be involved in their grandchildren's lives. Also, many working parents today cannot afford the high cost of day care. Parents often would rather leave their children in the care of loving relatives at a much lower cost. Some working parents pay grandparents minimal amounts to compensate them for their time and effort.

IN SUM   The family has always been in transition. Just as the family adapted to large-scale social events during the Industrial Revolution, so it will adapt to current events today. The family is not an independent unit; rather, it coexists among other institutions in society.

The Scope of the Problem

It may seem to you that society is transforming the contemporary family into a weak institution. Some think that **modernity**—those social and cultural factors relating to recent times or the present—is so powerful that the family isn't going to be able to adjust. Some even feel that such social changes are causing the family to disintegrate. "The family used to be a viable social institution" goes this thinking, "but social change has been so far-reaching that the family no longer shelters us against societal pressures."

As always, we want to move beyond subjective concerns and examine objective conditions. What indications, if any, might suggest that the family is in trouble?

Divorce

One indication of declining family stability is the divorce rate. As Figure 11-2 shows, divorce has increased steadily since 1970. Another way to look at the trend in divorce is

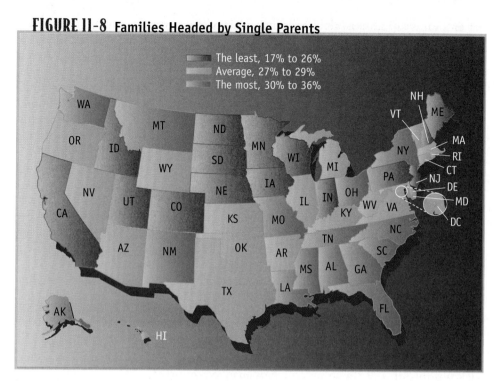

FIGURE 11-8 Families Headed by Single Parents

The least, 17% to 26%
Average, 27% to 29%
The most, 30% to 36%

Source: By James M. Henslin. Based on "Kids Count Data Sheet" (2004).

The Social Map (Figure 11-8) shows how the states compare in the percentage of families headed by single parents. The Southeast contains the greatest number of single-parent households, while the North contains the least.

Impact on Children ■ Being reared in a single-parent home has been proven to have significant impact on children. Researchers state several reasons why growing up in a single-parent household brings with it risk of experiencing mental, emotional, and economic difficulties. Most refer either to the economic and parental resources available to children or to the stressful events and circumstances to which these children must adapt.

Life for single mothers is usually filled with difficulties. In the typical case, these mothers are younger, have little education, and have an inadequate income. Although their resources are highly limited, their responsibilities are great.

For a variety of reasons, children living with single parents suffer economic disadvantages. Children living on single-parent incomes are less likely to benefit from resources that wealthier children have access to. For example, children living in poorer households are less likely to afford tutoring, computer access, and extracurricular activities. Many single-parent families live in poorer neighborhoods where schools are of lower quality and the crime rate is higher (McLanahan, 1996; Morrison & Cherlin, 1995; R. Simons, 1996).

Effective and involved parenting seems to be one of the greatest predictors of children's success and well-being. Single parents often find themselves less involved in the lives of their children because of work demands. Researchers have found that single parents without financial support are less involved, inconsistent with discipline, and more likely to argue with their children (McLanahan, 1996).

Most critiques of single parenthood focus on the mother's role. Fathers can also play a key role in their children's futures. Even when absent fathers do nothing more than pay child support, all benefit emotionally and economically (V. King, 1994; McLanahan, 1996). Furthermore, researchers have found that children excel when their nonresident fathers remain involved in their everyday lives (Hawkins, Amato, & King, 2007).

Hawkins et al. (2007) explained how nonresident fathers who are involved do a much better job at raising successful children than do those who are distant. However, involved fathers are not common. In fact, only 25% of nonresident fathers remain involved in their children's lives (Hawkins et al., 2007).

Absence of the Father ■ Absence of the father is proposed as one of the major explanations for some of the social problems analyzed in earlier chapters. The higher the number of single-mother families, for example, the higher the number of violent crimes. Such a statistic says nothing about the individual child, of course. Although children from mother-headed homes are more likely to drop out of school and get in trouble with the law, any particular child may grow up to become an artist, an astronaut, president of the United States, or a sociologist. But, *on average,* the absence of a father is more likely to lead to such problems.

Research studies prove how a mother by herself cannot do the same job of rearing children that a mother and father do together. Sociologist Travis Hirschi (Pope, 1988, pp. 117–118) says that, all else being equal, one parent is probably sufficient. The problem, he says, is that rarely is all else equal:

> The single parent (usually a woman) must devote a good deal to support and maintenance activities that are at least to some extent shared in the two-parent family. Further, she must do so in the absence of psychological or social support. As a result, she is less able to devote time to monitoring and punishment, and is more likely to be involved in negative, abusive contacts with her children.

Trying to Be Two Parents ■ One-parent families are not limited to fatherless families, of course. Our 3 million motherless households also present tremendous obstacles to fathers who rear children alone. How should a single father teach womanhood to his daughter? Whether man or woman, the single parent must try to be both mother and father, which, if not impossible, is certainly a formidable task.

Discipline ■ The essential problem appears to be **defective discipline**—excessive leniency or excessive control (Pope, 1988). To find the proper balance is difficult for any family, but more difficult for one parent to achieve than for two.

The Cross-Cultural Context ■ In an effort to determine cause and effect, sociologists examine cross-cultural data.

Equality is a goal with which most of us agree in principle. Because we all perceive reality from particular corners in life, however, putting "equality" into practice is problematic: What some see as gaining equality, others view as a demand for privileges. For one group to gain equality, then, some other group might undergo a reduction in privileges. Shown here is one example of this problem.

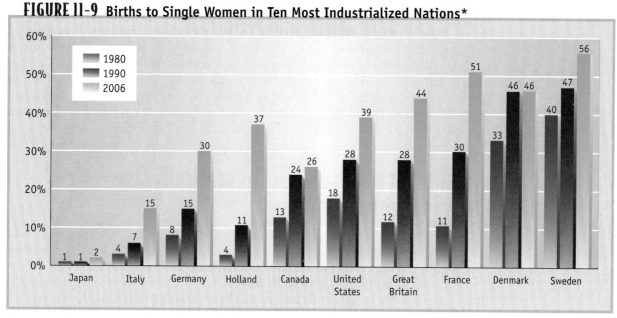

FIGURE 11-9 Births to Single Women in Ten Most Industrialized Nations*

Note: *As a percentage of all births. For some countries, the latest year available is 2003.

Source: By James M. Henslin. Based on *Statistical Abstract of the United States* (2009, Table 1291).

Figure 11-9 compares births to single women in 10 of the Most Industrialized Nations. Four of these nations have a rate higher than does the United States. Yet in none of them is the rate of juvenile delinquency or violent crimes as high as in the United States. Therefore, the culture and environment within which single-parent families live make a marked difference in rates of violence.

Other Problems

RUNAWAY CHILDREN. Although some might argue that divorce and single motherhood do not qualify as social problems, few would argue that the problem of runaway children is not a serious issue. Because no central agency keeps track of the number of runaways, we lack good data. The media sometimes advertise that 1 million children run away from home each year. This number is really unfounded, used to gain the public's attention. No one knows the real number, but whatever it is, each year the police arrest about 70,000 children on charges of running away from home (*Sourcebook of Criminal Justice Statistics,* 2005, Table 4.6). At a minimum, we can assume that runaways are not fleeing happy homes. They are often trying to escape intolerable situations—incest, beatings, and other debilitating family conditions.

The streets are tough, and survival is precarious. Some runaways or "**pushouts**"—children who have been shoved out by parents who no longer want them—fall into the hands of predators, making their already bruised lives even more desperate. **Pedophiles** (adults who are sexually attracted to children) and pimps search bus stations for victims, looking for children who appear lonely, confused, and vulnerable. As researchers studying runaways have observed, when children tire of sleeping in doorways, their alternative to starvation is to steal or to turn to the only thing they have—their bodies. Many runaways get involved in prostitution and pornography when they have no money and no place to go.

FAMILY VIOLENCE. Another indication of family problems is the presence of violence. Police and welfare workers report that about 75,000 people are arrested each year for "offenses against family and children" (*Sourcebook of Criminal Justice Statistics,* 2006, Table 4.6). Sociologists Steinmetz and Straus (1974/1992) stress that it would be hard to find a group or institution in the United States in which violence is more of an everyday occurrence than in the family. *Also note that data reflect only reported crimes, so these numbers are actually low.*

IN SUM Problems of violence, divorce, runaways, and so on indicate severe problems in the American family. They do *not* indicate, however, that the family is disintegrating. Although the contemporary family may seem in trouble, as a social institution it will endure. Despite family problems, humans have found no satisfactory substitute for the family, and millions of people report that marriage and family meet their needs for intimacy and sense of identity and belonging. In this book, however, our focus remains on the *problems* of marriage and family, not on the joys of marriage and family. At this point, we will turn to a theoretical analysis of the problem.

Looking at the Problem Theoretically: Why Is Divorce Common?

For most of us, the family is a major support system. Our family nourishes and protects us when we are young. It gives us security and love and shapes our personality. Sociologists call the family that rears us our **family of orientation** because it introduces us to the world and teaches us ways to cope with life. The family of orientation is the family in which we are raised. As a result, most people around the world try to establish stability, identity, and intimacy through marriage. When we marry, we form what is called a **family of procreation.** The family of procreation is the family formed when a couple has its first child.

With high value placed on marriage and family and the many benefits if offers, why is divorce common? Sociologists have used theoretical perspectives to better understand how divorce may be related to changes in society. As always, each perspective yields a unique interpretation; but, as you will see, taken as a whole, the perspectives work well with one another.

Symbolic Interactionism

AN OVERLOADED INSTITUTION. To explain why our divorce rate is so high, symbolic interactionists examine what people *expect* out of marriage. In 1933, sociologist William Ogburn noted that a mate's personality was becoming more important in the choice of husband or wife. A few years later, in 1945, sociologists Burgess and Locke observed that affection, understanding, and compatibility were becoming more central to marriage. These sociologists noted a major shift in mate selection: As society had become more complex and impersonal, people began to look to marriage to satisfy needs for intimacy.

These trends have continued. Society has grown even more impersonal, and today husbands and wives expect even greater emotional satisfaction from one another. Having come to view marriage as a solution to the tensions produced by our problem-ridden society (Lasch, 1977), we are likely to expect our spouse to meet most of our emotional needs. Because these expectations place a heavy burden on marriage, often more than it can manage, sociologists argue that marriage (and family) has become an *overloaded institution.* Let's look more closely at how marriage and family may have reached this state.

The Love Symbol: Engulfment Into Unrealistic Expectations ■ The once optional emotions—"affection, understanding, and compatibility"—that Burgess and Locke observed have now become mandatory emotions in a "healthy" marriage. They have all been symbolically bound into what we call "love." You may have heard phrases such as "Love conquers all," "Love is blind," and "Find your true love."

Ideas of love permeate our culture, often creating sentimental feelings when we see symbols of love. These feelings, in turn, motivate couples to marry and to take on the responsibilities of rearing children.

Society's demand that you find your one true love breeds disappointment. Americans expect marriage to deliver more than it possibly can, setting us up for inevitable disappointment. The media's portrayal of love is one of total and complete bliss: If we are "truly in love," we will be satisfied emotionally and, somehow, enjoy a continuous emotional high. For Americans, love has become *the* basis for marriage. The unrealistic expectations associated with love, however, often lead to marital breakup. When dissatisfactions arise in marriage, as they inevitably do, spouses tend to blame one another, each believing that the other has somehow failed the relationship. Their engulfment in the belief of love, or what love is supposed to represent, often blinds them to the reality of living day-to-day with another person. In effect, our culture promotes the idea that marriage should be based on a temporary emotional state.

In earlier generations children were seen as miniature adults.

Changing Ideas About Children ■ Expectations surrounding the treatment of children have undergone such great change that customs of earlier generations seem strange to us. These changes have also deeply affected the family. In medieval society, children were viewed as miniature adults (Aries, 1962). With no sharp separation between their worlds, adults and children mixed and mingled with one another. At the age of 7, boys began to work as apprentices in some occupations, while girls learned homemaking duties associated with marriage.

In modern society we consider age 7 a tender phase of early childhood, not a prime time for apprenticeship. In short, whereas people once viewed children as miniature adults, now we have culturally transformed them into impressionable, vulnerable, and innocent beings.

Changing Expectations of Parenting ■ Shifting ideas surrounding childhood often explain parenting expectations as well. Until 1940, American children "became adults" when they graduated from eighth grade and went to work. Parents at this time were expected to nurture young children to become members of a healthy workforce. Today, because we now view children as vulnerable, we expect them to be dependent much longer. We expect parents to give their children greater protection, to nurture them for longer periods of time, and to help their children "reach their potential." As the expected emotional ties between parents and children have become more intense, the family has been thrust into even greater "emotional overload" (Lasch, 1977).

Changing Marital Roles ■ You can expect that as parenting roles shift, marital roles shift as well. Traditional roles of wife and husband have been greatly altered. Society used to expect the husband to assume the role of **breadwinner,** the one whose earnings are the primary source of support for all dependents. It was his responsibility to provide for the family. If he did that well, he was considered a good husband and father. At the same time, society expected the wife to stay home, take care of the house and children, and attend to the personal needs of her husband. If she did those things well, she was considered a good wife and mother. Traditional roles—whatever their perceived faults—provided clear-cut guidelines for behavior. When a newlywed couple arrived home from the wedding ceremony, they knew exactly what to expect of one another.

Today, the roles of newlyweds are much less clearly defined. Although this gives them a great deal of freedom and flexibility, it also produces a major source of tension and conflict. A couple's expectations surrounding the balance of work and home life may not mesh. They may disagree over who should do what housework, to what extent the wife should be career oriented, how to make spending decisions, and how to divide child-rearing responsibilities. When guidelines are unclear, a role vacuum often creates discontent. How can one adequately fulfill a marital role if no one can agree on what that role is?

IN SUM Collectively, then, these fundamental changes in the meaning of marriage—our ideas about love, children, parenthood, and the roles of husband and wife—put tremendous pressure on spouses. Such pressure often leads to divorce. These historical changes have created "emotional overload" in today's marriages, becoming a burden to couples. We cannot expect marriage to provide unlimited emotional satisfaction.

PERCEPTION OF ALTERNATIVES. While these historical changes in the nature and expectations of marriage were occurring, more women began to work outside the home. This had a further fundamental effect on people's ideas about and expectations of marriage. As wives earned paychecks of their own, they began to find alternatives to living in unhappy marriages. Symbolic interactionists consider the *perception of alternatives* as an essential first step to making divorce possible.

CHANGING IDEAS ABOUT DIVORCE. In our society, divorce has never been taken lightly, but in our not-so-distant past, divorce used to represent failure, irresponsibility, and immorality. Divorced people were social outcasts. They were suspected of immoral behavior and were no longer welcome as dinner guests. As divorce became more common, its meaning changed: Divorce was transformed from a symbol of failure to one of self-fulfillment, of opportunity rather than shame. As divorce became a sign of personal fulfillment rather than shame, the stage was set for greater acceptance of divorce and, ultimately, higher rates.

Legal Changes ■ The law used to be much more strict about granting divorce—allowing it only if one spouse could prove severe abuse or adultery. In some states, such as New York, obtaining a divorce required that one spouse *prove* that the other had committed adultery, using witnesses and a trial. As the stigma attached to divorce lessened, laws against it relaxed. Today, in most states, "incompatibility" is adequate grounds for divorce. **Incompatibility** means that two people are no longer able to remain married because they are just "too different" and can no longer "get along." In no-fault divorce states, if one of the spouses wants to end the marriage, the judge can grant a divorce even if the other spouse wants to remain married.

In many states, couples can work out their own "no-fault" divorce, and judges simply sign the paperwork. In Florida, the couple can sign papers in a lawyer's office, and they don't even have to appear in court. Such legal changes have further reduced the stigma attached to divorce, which, in turn, has contributed to the high divorce rate.

Are These Changes Good or Bad? ■ Symbolic interactionists take the position that nothing is good or bad in and of itself. They view "goodness" and "badness" as value judgments that are imposed on people's behavior. Thus, different groups evaluate divorce differently. Depending on its assumptions, one group is alarmed at increases in divorce and changes in sex roles, ideas of how children are perceived, parenting, and so on. Another group looks at these same changes and feels pleased that the family is evolving. Symbolic interactionists do not take a stand that either is correct, for symbolic interactionism provides no framework for making value judgments.

IN SUM To explain why the divorce rate has increased, symbolic interactionists analyze how symbols—ideas and expectations—associated with the family have changed. They stress that symbols both reflect and create reality. That is, symbols not only represent people's ideas but also influence people's behaviors. Changing definitions of appropriate behaviors within the family influence future generations.

Functionalism

When functionalists analyze social change, they look at how change in one part of a social system affects its other parts. As an example, earlier we examined the impact of industrialization and urbanization on the family. We discussed how when child labor laws passed and children could no longer work, the birthrate fell because children became more costly. Change in one part of the system (work) influenced change in another (family).

HOW CHANGES IN THE TRADITIONAL FUNCTIONS OF THE FAMILY ARE RELATED TO DIVORCE.
Functionalists have identified seven key functions of every family. They point out that around the world the family provides

1. economic production
2. socialization of children
3. care of the sick and injured
4. care of the aged
5. recreation
6. sexual control of family members
7. reproduction

Let's see what effects the Industrial Revolution and urbanization have had on these seven traditional functions of the family—and how these changes are related to divorce.

Economic Production ■ Before industrialization, the family worked together in a tightly knit unit on the farm, gleaning food from their own property. For survival, the members of a family—like it or not—were forced to cooperate. *Industrialization moved production from home to factory, disrupting this operation.* This movement isolated the husband-father from the daily activities of the family, separated the wife-mother from the production of income, and made older children, who left the home to work for wages, less dependent on their family.

Socialization of Children ■ While economic production was changing, the state and federal governments were growing larger, more centralized, and more powerful. One consequence was that the government began to take over some of the family's functions, weakening family relationships. For example, lawmakers passed mandatory education laws, requiring parents to send their children to school. Parents faced fines and jail if they did not put their children in the government's care. In this momentous shift, the government took over much of the responsibility for socializing children.

Care of the Sick and Aged ■ Before industrialization, there were few trained physicians, and medicine had been a family matter. When someone was sick, the individual was cared for at home. As medical schools developed, along with hospitals and drugs, medicine came under government control. Gradually medical care shifted from the family to medical specialists. It was similarly the case with care of the aged. As the central government expanded and agencies multiplied, care of the aged, too, became a government obligation.

Recreation ■ As industrialization progressed, the country became more affluent. The family's disposable income increased, and businesses sprang up to compete for that income. Before the industrial age, entertainment and "fun" had consisted primarily of home-based activities—card games, parlor and barn dances, sleigh rides, and so on. As family-centered activities gave way to public-centered paid events, the family lost much of its recreational function.

Control of Sexuality ■ The family had also controlled the sexual behavior of its members, but even this has changed. Sexual relations in marriage used to be the only ones viewed as legitimate. Sexual relations outside of marriage—even between engaged couples—were considered immoral from the Victorian period onward. Although in reality this was only the ideal, for sexual relations have always taken place outside of marriage, the **sexual revolution** opened many alternatives to marital sex. During the sexual revolution there was a drastic relaxation in general standards of sexual behavior. Consequently, marital control over sexuality has become considerably weaker than it used to be.

Reproduction ■ Lastly, even something as personal as reproduction has been influenced by societal standards. In the United States, one-third of live births are to unwed

mothers outside the traditional family unit of husband and wife. Other significant changes have altered the face of reproduction today—now married women can get abortions without informing their husbands, and in some states teens can obtain birth control and abortions without parental consent. Influenced again by laws and government, then, complete control over reproduction has been removed from the family.

Can reproduction move even farther away from the sphere of the family? Some envision a future in which men or women, single or married, homosexual or heterosexual, can order DNA to match their specifications: sex, race–ethnicity, height, hair color, eye color, body type, even intelligence, personality traits, and ability in music, art, poetry, and sports (Bagne, 1992). Sociologist Judith Lorber (1980, p. 527) envisions a future of "professional breeding":

> A system of completely professional breeders and child rearers could be conducted with the best of modern technology—fertility drugs for multiple births, sperm banks, embryo transfers, and uterine implants to expand the gene pool and so on. Professional breeders could be paid top salaries, like today's athletes, for the 15–20 years of their prime childbearing time. Those who were impregnated could live in well-run dormitories, with excellent physical care, food, and entertainment.

IN SUM Many of the family's perceived traditional functions are undergoing rapid change. From a functionalist perspective, such changes have weakened the family unit. The fewer functions that family members have in common, the fewer the "ties that bind." As these bonds continue to weaken, functionalists argue, the family becomes more fragile. Divorce, then, is just the inevitable consequence of eroded functions.

Conflict and Feminist Theory

Conflict and feminist theorists point us in a different direction. They stress that marriage and family roles reflect basic social inequality that exists among men and women. In general, men control, dominate, and exploit women. Marriage is simply one of the means by which this is done.

MALE DOMINATION OF MARRIAGE AND FAMILY. Historically, men have dominated women in the family through traditional roles, mate selection, and abuse. In their traditional roles, women served men, as wife, sister, and mother. Women's role expectations included meeting men's emotional needs, preparing men for their work life, and supporting their career. A woman's labor therefore was defined as **reproductive labor**—that labor performed behind the scenes that allowed the breadwinner husband to flourish in public.

Fathers have traditionally controlled all the women in the family, usually deciding whom their daughters would marry. In ancient society, kings forged alliances with other kings by giving their daughters away in marriage. In modern society, fathers still manage to arrange marriages for their daughters. *Shaadi*, the word for marriage in many Indian languages, is still frequently arranged in modern Indian cultures. One father placed a matrimonial ad for his daughter online: "Match for Jain girl, Harvard-educated journalist, and 25, fair, slim." Such online advertisements are a natural extension of how things have been done in India for decades (Jain, 2008).

Our current wedding ceremony still reflects this traditional family power dynamic. While the mother sits passively on the side, the father walks down the aisle with his daughter and "gives"

Historically, fathers decided whom their daughters would marry. Our modern-day wedding ceremony reflects this age-old idea when fathers give away their daughters to be married.

her to her husband. This is but a pale reflection of the power men wield in other countries—able to choose their daughters' husbands—but it is a reflection nonetheless.

More dangerous is the power of physical discipline often granted to men. Both custom and the law have allowed men to discipline not only their children, but also their wives. Not too far in our distant past, a husband could spank his wife—if she "needed" it. Beating a wife was considered permissible if she became rebellious or had an affair. In some areas—such as Pakistan—a husband has been permitted to beat and even murder his wife (EqualityNow, 2007).

Marriage as an Arena for a Continuing Historical Struggle ■ Although men's control over the family has diminished somewhat, inequality between husband and wife remains. This, say conflict and feminist theorists, is the key to understanding today's family problems. In individual marriages, as husbands and wives argue, they typically don't view their personal problems as rooted in broad historical change. They experience personal trouble with their spouse, not historical underpinnings. At the root of personal marital strife, however, stress theorists, lies historical struggle between men and women over rights, obligations, and privileges.

In American history, as industrialization progressed, women's roles changed. As their experiences carried them beyond the home, women came to resent the strict arrangements that kept them isolated. Responsibility for housework became a primary source of resentment. Sociologist Arlie Hochschild (Hochschild & Machung, 2001) points out that even today, most wives, after returning home from an 8-hour shift of work for wages, put in a **second shift**—cooking, cleaning, and rearing children. In two-paycheck families, wives average 15 hours more work each week than their husbands. The cumulative total is incredible: Over a year, wives work an *extra month of 24-hour days—720 hours!*

Consciousness of Oppression ■ This analysis may not reflect everyone's reality: Many wives do not *feel* oppressed, and some husbands feel that *they* are oppressed. Many women do less housework than men, and many men are now more responsible for rearing children at home. Feminist theorists argue that a woman who does not feel oppressed is simply blind to her real situation and is suffering from a sense of **false consciousness**—a failure to recognize the state of one's exploitation because of having accepted the view of the dominant class (Rosen, 1996).

Power and the Marital Experience ■ This shift in the balance of power has greatly affected mate selection. In traditional arrangements, women expected to be wife and mother. Women sought out a mate who could provide financial and emotional security. The wife would emotionally invest in the man and offer a lifetime commitment (Firestone, 1970; Greer, 1972). For the sake of maintaining financial security and reputation, many women put up with unsatisfying relationships. Today's women, less dependent on mates for financial security, are not as willing to put up with relationships that they do not find fulfilling.

IN SUM Conflict theorists stress that marriage and family patterns simply reflect historical struggles between men and women. Historically, men have dominated women in every sphere of society. Increasing divorce rates are not a sign that the family is weakening but, rather, that women are making headway in gaining equality in marital relationships (Zinn & Eitzen, 1990).

The 1950s marked a watershed era in U.S. middle-class families. With the husband's income adequate to support a family comfortably, the wife was expected to focus on the home. This historical period is bathed in images that characterized only a minority of families, images that form a mythical lens through which we view that "ideal" period of family life.

Research Findings

We now examine the major trends defining marriage and family today: marrying at a later age, cohabitation, remaining single, living a child-free life, family violence, sexual abuse, and care of the elderly.

Cohabitation and Marrying at a Later Age

CHANGES IN AGE AT FIRST MARRIAGE. From 1890 to 1950, Americans married at younger and younger ages. By 1950, brides were younger than at any other time in U.S. history: The typical bride had just left her teens. In 1970, American grooms were the youngest since the U.S. government began keeping such records. After remaining steady for 20 years, there has been an abrupt reversal in the age of marriage, and *today's average first-time bride and groom are older than at any other time in U.S. history.*

COHABITATION. Why this reversal? Sociologists point to data like those shown in Figure 11-10 to explain. Look at the sharp increase in the number of unmarried couples cohabiting, living together in a sexual relationship outside of marriage. Some sociologists estimate that if **cohabitation** had not increased so drastically, the average age at first marriage might have changed very little.

It is not that most cohabitants are opposed to marriage. They are opposed, rather, to marriage at this particular time. For a variety of reasons, they do not feel that they are ready to handle the commitments and responsibilities of marriage. Although attracted to one another and wanting commitment, many couples fear that their relationship isn't strong enough to withstand the demands of marriage. They may feel that through cohabitation such commitment may develop, however, and they can marry when this happens.

Financial concerns also cause many to live together outside of marriage. Some couples do not want to commingle assets, and while cohabiting they can keep their own independent bank accounts and expenditure habits. Marriage is also considered a declaration of financial independence from parents; for many young people, especially college students, cohabitation keeps them eligible for support from their parents. For many widows and widowers, marrying after the death of a spouse would thrust them quickly into poverty, because they would lose the benefits (pensions and Social Security) earned by their deceased spouse. Thus, in old age it becomes common for elders to live together off of the benefits of one or more deceased spouses.

THE INCREASING NUMBER OF SINGLES. The number of women age 25 to 29 who are single today is almost 4 times higher than it was in 1970. The number of single men age 25 to 29 is 3 times higher (*Statistical Abstract,* 1993, Table 52; 1998, Table 62; 2006, Table 51).

REMAINING SINGLE. Few people view single life as a permanent alternative to marriage. Some do, however, and as sociologist Peter Stein (1992) found, those who plan on remaining single all their lives still feel a strong need for intimacy, sharing, and continuity. To attain these satisfactions, which marriage and family ordinarily provide, the permanent singles cultivate a network of people who feel as they do about marriage. Through these friendships, they satisfy needs for intimacy.

Child-Free Couples

PRESSURES TO HAVE CHILDREN. Although most married women give birth, about one of five (19%) do not (DeOilos and Kapinus, 2002). Child-free couples are now *twice* as common as they used to be 20 years ago. Child-free

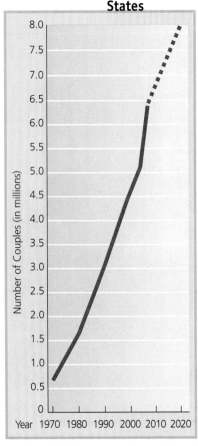

FIGURE 11-10 Cohabitation in the United States

Number of Couples (in millions)

Year 1970 1980 1990 2000 2010 2020

Note: The broken line is the author's estimate.

Source: By James M. Henslin. Based on U.S. Bureau of the Census 2007b and *Statistical Abstract of the United States* (1995, Table 60; 2008, Table 62).

Visit the National Center for Health Statistics at http://www.cdc.gov/nchs/PRESSROOM/02news/div_mar_cohab.htm

▶ What are cohabitation trends in the United States?

couples choose not to have children for a variety of reasons. The term "child-free" is preferred over "childless" as it infers freedom to choose, not stigma or loss. (See the Spotlight on Social Research box on page 380.)

THE PROCESS OF REMAINING CHILD-FREE. Sociologist Jean Veevers (1973, 1980) found that of 52 wives married at least 5 years who chose to remain child-free, about a third had made an agreement with their husbands before they married not to have children. In fact, they had sought husbands who would agree to remain, in their terms, child-free.

About two-thirds of the wives that Veevers studied, however, had planned to have children, but never did. Their permanent child-free life was the result of a four-stage process. First, these women had postponed the decision to get pregnant while they worked toward a specific goal, such as graduating from college or buying a house. Then they shifted their postponement to a vague future, a "sometime" (such as when they would feel financially independent) that never seemed to arrive. During the third stage, they decided that not having kids wasn't so bad, that they *might* want to remain child-free. When they reached the fourth stage, they viewed their child-free life as a permanent rather than a temporary state.

THE MYTHICAL CHILD. Many wives who decide to remain child-free feel somewhat stigmatized. Friends and relatives put pressure on them to bear children and make negative comments about not wanting to parent children. These pressures typically peak during the 3rd and 4th years of marriage, then decrease after 5 or 6 years. As a coping mechanism, Veevers says the couples often discussed a "mythical child" with relatives—one they claimed they might adopt "one day." Few couples, however, really made an effort to contact an adoption agency. None of those who attempted adoption followed up with their initial contact. The discussion of a "mythical child" helped the couples deal with inquisitive outsiders, for it made their childlessness appear temporary. Talking about adoption affirmed that they liked children. Even after many of the wives became too old to bear children, adoption remained a topic of discussion used to soften social stigma.

Family Violence

When she refused to give him money, the middle-aged man pushed the frail 70-year-old woman to the floor. She sprawled there, stunned and helpless, while he screamed insults. The woman became even more upset when the police arrived. She told them that she didn't want her attacker to be arrested.

This was not the first time—nor would it be the last—that this man would attack her. He was her son.

A NATIONAL STUDY. Murray Straus heads the Family Violence Research Program at the University of New Hampshire. He and fellow sociologists Susan Steinmetz and Richard Gelles have studied this cruel irony—that the social group we most often look to for intimacy and love (the family) is often the one most likely to be characterized by cruelty and violence. To determine the amount and types of violence in American homes, these

Spotlight on Social Research
CHOOSING NOT TO HAVE CHILDREN

Researchers Reed and Reed study child-free couple trends.

CYNTHIA SHINABARGER REED *is Professor of Psychology and Sociology at Tarrant County College.* **ROBERT E. REED** *is Adjunct Instructor of Sociology at Tarrant County College. Their research focuses on child-free individuals.*

People who choose not to have children have received little attention from social scientists. Textbooks on sociology of the family usually include no more than a paragraph or two on this topic.

We each became interested in researching individuals who have chosen not to have children while in graduate school. We are a child-free couple and when we learned that little research had been done on people like ourselves we were motivated to learn more about the child-free. One issue we encountered has to do with labeling: What should we call individuals who have chosen not to have children? Traditionally they have been referred to as "voluntarily childless" to differentiate them from people who would like to have children but have been unable to conceive ("involuntarily childless"). This term has been criticized for implying that people who choose not to have children are missing something important. Later, the term "child-free" was introduced, a term which many argued had a much more positive connotation. However, this term has also been criticized for implying that individuals who choose not to have children are free of something bad, as the terms "fat-free" and "cholesterol-free" imply. Another term that has recently been introduced is zero-child families. We perceive this term as having a negative connotation as well. This controversy led us to wonder what other people who have chosen not to have children would prefer to be called. In a recent study of men who have chosen not to have children, we found that the respondents preferred the label "child-free."

Although some couples, like us, make the decision not to have children prior to marriage, for the majority of child-free couples the decision is a gradual one that occurs after marriage. The process begins with a postponement of children for a definite period of time. The couple wants to wait until they have finished school or become established in their careers. This is followed by an indefinite postponement. The couple decides "it just isn't the right time." Later, when the couple realizes that their time for having children is running out, they begin to discuss the advantages and disadvantages of having children. This is followed by the acceptance of the choice to remain child-free.

People make the decision to be child-free for a variety of reasons. We have found most of these have to do with lifestyle issues. Many of the individuals we have interviewed stated they wanted more free time in order to focus on their marriage relationships and their careers. Many also mentioned the economic benefits of remaining child-free.

The United States is a pronatalist society and people who choose not to have children are often stereotyped negatively. They are often perceived as: materialistic, individualistic, career oriented, selfish, immature, child-haters, lazy, insensitive, lonely, and as unhappy. Our interviews with child-free individuals have revealed that some have encountered negative reactions from family, friends, and coworkers regarding their decision. Many were asked why they made this choice, implying that one must have a reason for making such an unpopular choice. Couples who have children are not typically questioned about their decision since it is consistent with society's norms. Some of the people we interviewed stated that others reacted to their decision by looking at them like they were crazy or by simply ignoring the decision and continuing to ask them when they were going to have children.

Our research with child-free individuals indicates that most of the stereotypes are not correct. While child-free women are typically very well educated and career-oriented, both child-free women and men usually indicate that they like children but do not want to be with children 24/7. While a few of the people we interviewed said at some point they had reconsidered their decision, all reported being happy with their choice and satisfied with their lifestyle.

researchers interviewed nationally representative samples of couples about intimate partner violence. **Intimate partner violence** refers to physical, emotional, and sexual abuse within a relationship. The research participants in this particular study were asked to report rates of slapping, pushing, kicking, biting, and use of weapons (Straus, Gelles, & Steinmetz, 1980; Straus & Gelles, 1988; Straus, 1992).

EXTENT OF VIOLENCE. The FBI reports violence rates per 100,000 people, but intimate partner violence is so common that sociologists report incidents occurring in rates per 100 people. They have discovered that each year, 16 of every 100 spouses physically attack their husband or wife. This is one spouse out of every six. No other violent crime even approaches this rate.

Because most couples (84%) were not violent during the past year and most violence is mild (such as slapping), some dismiss these figures with a "so what" attitude. To this, Straus and Gelles (1988) reply (paraphrased):

> Let's suppose we are talking about a university. Would anyone say that there wasn't much of a problem because, after all, 84% of the faculty didn't hit a student last year? Or would anyone argue that this isn't significant because, after all, most of the 16% of faculty members who were violent only slapped students, rather than punching or beating them?

Violence among spouses, whatever its form, is a common topic of research among sociologists. Sometimes sociologists become interested in a particular social problem because of their personal experience with it. This is how it was for sociologist Kathleen Ferraro, who shares her experiences in the Spotlight on Social Research box on the next page.

THE MOST VIOLENT. The most violent family members within a family are typically the children. During the year preceding the researcher's interviews, two-thirds of the children had attacked a brother or sister. Most had shoved or thrown things, but one-third had physically attacked a sibling. In rare instances, the attack involved a knife or gun. Straus suggests that these totals are severe underestimates because violence among siblings is often accepted.

EQUALITY BETWEEN THE SEXES? This may surprise you, but husbands and wives are about equally as likely to attack one another (Gelles, 1980; Straus, 1980, 1992). Even when a woman initiates violence, the effect is typically less than when a man does. As Straus points out, even though she may cast the first coffeepot, he usually casts the last and most damaging blow. Because most men are bigger and stronger than their wives, women are at a disadvantage in this literal battle of the sexes, and after episodes of spousal violence more women than men need medical attention. When a spouse murders another, 4 times out of 5 the wife is the victim (*FBI Uniform Crime Report,* 2006, Table 9). Like other crimes, marital violence has dropped in recent years, so much so that it is now *less than half* of what it was just 10 years ago (*Statistical Abstract,* 2006, Table 304).

SOCIAL CLASS AND VIOLENCE. Like other social problems, intimate partner violence is not distributed equally among the classes. Violence follows well-worn "social channels," which makes spouses in some social classes much more likely to be abusers—or victims—than others. The highest rates of violence (Gelles, 1980) are found among

families with low incomes

blue-collar workers

families in which the husband is unemployed

families with above-average numbers of children

people with less education

individuals who have no religious affiliation

people under 30

Poverty and Violence ■ Notice that poverty, age, and religion are variables related to intimate partner violence. Although family violence occurs in all social classes, blue-collar spouses, especially husbands, are considerably more violent than white-collar spouses. Researchers also suggest that blue-collar husbands experience more stress than their white-collar counterparts. Although it is likely that blue-collar husbands do experience much more stress, this does not explain why that stress gets translated into violence toward

Spotlight on Social Research
INTIMATE PARTNER VIOLENCE

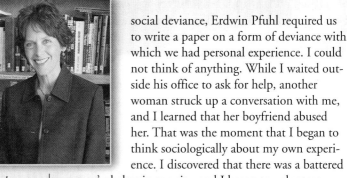

KATHLEEN FERRARO, *professor of sociology at Northern Arizona University, wanted to be a sociologist from the time she was 12. She never imagined, though, that her research would focus on "intimate partner violence," because she never knew that this existed.*

I found out about "intimate partner violence" at age 23 when I married my first husband. He went to high school with me and came from a well-respected family. He was a naturalist and a bird-watcher, did not drink or use drugs, and showed no violent tendencies. After we exchanged vows, however, he changed almost immediately, displaying the "power and control" tactics that have become so well known today. He monitored my movements, eating, clothing, friends, money, makeup, and language. If I challenged his commands, he slapped or kicked me or pushed me down.

I left him on these occasions, staying with other graduate students at Arizona State University, but I had no way to understand what was happening. My husband always convinced me to return. He stalked and threatened to kill me, even in front of police officers, but my faculty mentor, Albert J. Mayer, and my friends hid me until my father-in-law came to take my husband back to our hometown on the other side of the country. I obtained a single-party, no-fault divorce and never saw him again.

These events took place in 1974 and 1975, before the battered women's movement transformed public understanding of "domestic violence." In a graduate class on social deviance, Erdwin Pfuhl required us to write a paper on a form of deviance with which we had personal experience. I could not think of anything. While I waited outside his office to ask for help, another woman struck up a conversation with me, and I learned that her boyfriend abused her. That was the moment that I began to think sociologically about my own experience. I discovered that there was a battered women's shelter in my city, and I began to volunteer there and to interview staff members. This was the beginning of the battered women's movement and the beginning of a lifetime of research, teaching, and activism for me. I joined with a group of people to establish another shelter, and that is where I conducted the interviews and ethnographic work for my dissertation, *Battered Women and the Shelter Movement,* and for the *Social Problems* article, "How Women Experience Battering: The Process of Victimization."

The women taught me how difficult it is to make sense of the violence and emotional abuse that comes from a person they love and believe loves them. The rationalizations the women used to understand what was happening to them were similar to those used by people who commit crimes, the "techniques of neutralization" described by Gresham Sykes and David Matza [reviewed in Chapter 6 in this text]. For women at the shelter, these techniques included denial of victimization, denial of the victimizer, denial of injury, denial of options, appeal to higher loyalties, and the salvation ethic. Because of fear, lack of resources, and institutional failure to respond to battering, the women found escape from violent relationships to be difficult and precarious. Leaving an abuser does not necessarily end the violence—women are often at most risk during the time they are leaving the abuser.

---

their wives. To better understand this phenomenon, we need more research using sociological theory.

ALCOHOL AND VIOLENCE. Sociologists Glenda Kantor and Murray Straus (1987) also found that alcohol consumption was related to intimate partner violence. Based on a national probability sample, they found a direct relationship between alcohol consumption and wife battering. The more people drink, the more likely they are to beat their spouse. The lowest rates of violence occur in homes where couples do not drink; the highest rates of violence occur among alcoholics.

THE SOCIAL HEREDITY OF VIOLENCE. Straus, Gelles, and Steinmetz also discovered what they call the *social heredity of violence*—children learn from their parents that violence is a way to solve problems. After the children grow up and marry, they apply this lesson to their own family life. As Figure 11-11 shows, the more violence that children experience during their teen years, the more likely they are to be violent after they marry. Let's hear how the researchers (Straus et al., 1980, p. 113) explain Figure 11-11:

Those with scores of zero are the people whose parents did not hit them and did not hit each other. At the other extreme are people with scores of 9. They are the people whose parents frequently hit them when they were teenagers and whose parents were frequently violent with each other.

The researchers stress how powerful the social heredity of violence is:

When one member of a couple had experienced the double whammy of being hit as a child and observing his or her parents hitting each other, there was a one in three chance that at least one act of violence had occurred during the year of the study!

WHY DOESN'T SHE JUST LEAVE? Why does a woman remain with a husband who abuses her? This question has intrigued members of the public and sociologists alike. Researchers have studied many samples of women, and they have found remarkably consistent answers. Findings from one of these studies are featured in the Issues in Social Problems box on the next page.

SPOUSE ABUSE AS A DEFENSE FOR HOMICIDE. Some wives, of course, leave their husbands after the first attack and never return. Others remain in the relationship, only to murder their partners after enduring years of abuse. Wife beating has become a controversial defense for wives who have killed their husbands. Listen to Cindy Hudo, a 21-year-old mother of two in Charleston, South Carolina, who was charged with the murder of her husband, Buba. Here is what she said:

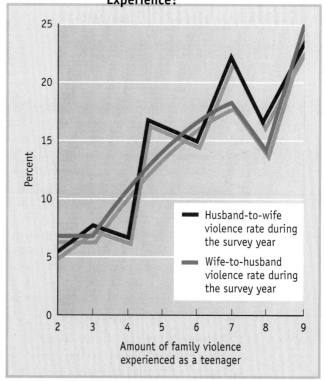

FIGURE 11-11 How Is Marital Violence Related to the Family Violence That Teenagers Experience?

Source: Straus, Gelles, & Steinmetz (1980, p. 112).

I start in the car and I get down the road and I see Buba walking, and he's real mad. I just look at him. So, I pull over, you know, and I'm trying, you know—"I didn't know to pick you up. You know, I'm sorry." And he didn't even say nothing to me. He just started hitting on me. And that's all I wanted to do, was just get home, because I was just self-conscious. I don't want nobody to see him hitting me, because I didn't want him to look bad. I had to go to work in a half-hour, because I was working a double-shift. And he told me I had forty minutes to get all my furniture out of the house and get my clothes and be out or he was going to throw them out.

And I was sitting there, because I could talk him down. You know, because I didn't want to leave him. I just talked to him. I said, "Buba, I don't want to leave." I said, "This is my house." And then he told me . . . (unclear) my kids. And I said, "No, you're not taking my kids from me. That's too much." And so I said, "Just let me leave. Just let me take the kids. And, you know I'll go, and you know, I won't keep the kids from you or nothing like that." And he said, "I'm going to take them and you're getting out."

[Buba then loaded a shotgun, pointed it at Cindy, and said] "The only way you're going to get out of this is if you kill me and I'll—I'll kill you." [Buba then gave the shotgun to Cindy and] just turned around and walked right down the hall, because he knew I wouldn't do nothing. And I just sat there a minute. And I don't know what happened. I just, you know, went to the bedroom and I seen him laying there and I just shot him. He moved. I shot him again because I thought he was going to get up again. . . .

I loved him too much. And I just wanted to help him. (*20/20*, October 18, 1979)

Although Cindy had shot and killed her husband, who at the time was unarmed and unresisting, a jury acquitted her on the basis that she was a battered wife.

Issues in Social Problems
"WHY DOESN'T SHE JUST LEAVE?"
THE DILEMMA OF ABUSED WOMEN

"Why would she ever put up with violence?" is a question on everyone's mind. From the outside, it looks so easy. Just pack up and leave. "I know I wouldn't put up with anything like that."

Yet this is not what typically happens. Women tend to stay with their men after they are abused. Some stay only a short while, to be sure, but others remain in abusive situations for years. Why?

Sociologist Ann Goetting (2001) asked this question, too. To get the answer, she interviewed women who had made the break. Goetting wanted to find out what it was that set these women apart. How were they able to leave, when so many can't seem to? She found that

Husbands or wives who are violent are likely to have been reared in homes in which their own parents were violent, a process sociologists call the "cultural transmission of violence."

1. These women had a positive self-concept.
   Simply put, they believed that they deserved better.
2. They broke with traditional values.
   They did not believe that a wife had to stay with her husband no matter what.
3. They found adequate finances.
   For some this was easy, but for others it was not. To accumulate enough money to move out, some of the women saved for years, putting away just a little each week.
4. They had supportive family and friends.
   A support network served as a source of encouragement to help them rescue themselves.

If you take the opposite of these four characteristics, you have the answer to why some women put up with abuse: They don't think they deserve anything better; they believe it is their duty to stay no matter what; they don't think they can make it financially; and they lack a supportive network. These four factors are not of equal importance. For some women, the lack of finances is the most significant, whereas for others it can be a low self-concept. For all women, the supportive network—or the lack of one—plays a significant role.

FOR YOUR CONSIDERATION

On the basis of these findings, what would you say to a woman whose husband or partner is abusing her? How do you think women's shelters fit into this explanation? What other parts of this puzzle can you think of—such as the role of love?

As with Cindy Hudo, in other cases wife battering as a defense has been upheld in court, and wives have been acquitted for killing their husbands. No matter how understandable the desire to kill may be under conditions of extreme duress and brutality, this defense raises questions about the justification of murder.

Sexual Abuse in the Family

MARITAL RAPE. How common is marital rape? This area of human behavior is shrouded in secrecy, making it difficult to gather valid data (Bennice & Resick, 2003). Sociologists

David Finkelhor and Kersti Yllo (1985, 1989) attempted to break through the shroud of secrecy, interviewing 330 women in Boston. Ten percent of the women reported that their husbands had used physical force to compel them to have sex. Another sociologist, Diana Russell (1980), estimated that 12% of married women had been raped by their husbands—this translates into 10 million women (*Statistical Abstract,* 2006, Table 50).

Types of Marital Rape ■ From interviews with 50 women whose husbands had raped them, Finkelhor and Yllo discovered there are three types of marital rape:

1. *Nonbattering rape.* In about 40% of the cases, the husband raped his wife without intending to do physical harm. The attack was usually preceded by a conflict over sex, such as the husband feeling insulted when his wife refused to have sex.
2. *Battering rape.* In about 48% of the cases, the husband intentionally inflicted physical pain during the rape. He was retaliating for some supposed wrongdoing on his wife's part.
3. *Perverted rape.* In these instances, about 6%, the husband seemed to be sexually aroused by the violence. These husbands forced their wives to submit to unusual sexual acts.

Effects of Marital Rape ■ Short-term effects of rape include anger, grief, despair, shame, and feelings of "dirtiness." The most common long-term effect was the woman's inability to trust intimate relationships or to function sexually.

The Timing of Marital Rape ■ Marital rape most often occurs while a couple is negotiating a separation or when a marriage is breaking up. In rare instances, however, husbands rape their wives throughout marriage. One woman, for example, had endured marital rape for 24 years—her marriage ended only when her husband divorced her!

Why Do Some Women Put Up with Marital Rape? ■ Although most women quickly leave a marriage after being raped by their husbands, some remain. Why? Just like women afraid to leave physically abusive situations, women who are raped inside their marriage are afraid to leave. They fear they do not have the skills to make it on their own, they don't have support networks, or they may have children. With low self-esteem and little support, they feel they cannot survive without their husbands.

INCEST. Another area long investigated by sociologists is **incest**—forbidden sexual relations between relatives, such as brothers and sisters or parents and children. The **incest taboo** states that sexual relations among siblings or with children are condemned universally. Revelations of incest are met with repugnance, and incest is one of the few issues on which most Americans strongly agree. Apart from rare exceptions, incest is viewed as abhorrent, sinful, or unnatural.

Rare circumstances include brother–sister marriages among the Egyptian pharaohs and the Incas of Peru. In East Africa, Thonga lion hunters may have sex with their daughters on the night before a big hunt (La Barre, 1954; Beals & Hoijer, 1965).

Extent of Incest ■ With such strong condemnation, one might think incest is rare, but is it? Sociologist Diana Russell (1986) interviewed 930 women in San Francisco. She found that before these women turned age 18, 16% had been victims of incest. Her definition included not only sexual relations with relatives but also unwanted kisses. In only 5 of 100 cases were the police informed. We can conclude that incest is much more common than the numbers that are officially reported.

Child advocates Bikers Against Child Abuse (B.A.C.A.) and survivor Angela Shelton stand against child abuse.

Who Are the Offenders? ■ Russell found that the most common offenders are uncles, cousins, fathers (biological, adoptive, step-, and foster), brothers, brothers-in-law, and step-grandfathers. In Russell's sample, incest between mother and son was rare, a finding confirmed by other researchers as well (Lester, 1972).

Effects on Victims ■ Incest creates enormous burdens for its victims (Bartoi & Kinder, 1998; Lewin, 1998). Susan Forward, a psychotherapist who was herself a victim of incest, reports:

> I understand incest not only as a psychotherapist but as a victim. When I was fifteen my father's playful seductiveness turned into highly sexualized fondling. This is a difficult admission for me to make, but even more painful is the fact that I enjoyed my father's attentions.
>
> I felt enormously guilty about my participation in the incest, as if I had been responsible. I know now I was not. It was my father's responsibility as an adult and as a parent to prevent sexual contact between us, but I didn't understand that at the time.
>
> I also felt guilty about competing with my mother—who was only thirty-three and very attractive.
>
> I was flattered by my father's attraction to me, and his caresses felt good, but after several months my guilt became too great. I somehow found the courage to tell him to stop, and he did. The psychological damage, however, had already been done.
>
> As my guilt feelings accumulated, my self-image deteriorated. I felt like a "bad girl." I began to punish myself unconsciously, most prominently by marrying an unloving man instead of pursuing the acting career I had dreamed of since I was five. Later, when my children were in school, I finally got a job on a television series. Good jobs followed and success was within my grasp. But my guilt still fought me on a [sub]conscious level, telling me that I didn't deserve success. So I allowed myself—[sub]consciously, of course, to become overweight and matronly at twenty-eight. My acting career stagnated. My marriage was a mess. I was desperately unhappy. Yet I had absolutely no idea that there was any connection between what my father had done to me and the problems in my life. (Forward & Buck, 1978, p. 1)

The Pro-Incest Lobby ■ There does exist a small group of people who claim that incest is not a problem. The problem, they say, is the *attitude* toward incest. The **Pedophile Liberation Army (PLA)** argues that if people changed their attitudes about sleeping with children, incest would no longer be an issue. This pro-incest lobby claims that there should be no law against incest because attraction toward children is healthy—just another sexual orientation. People who adopt this view also argue that prohibiting incest ruins relationships between children and adults (De Mott, 1980).

If the PLA ever were to succeed in removing what has been called the "last taboo," the change certainly would affect individuals everywhere—especially innocent children.

Old Age and Widowhood

PROBLEMS OF ADJUSTMENT. Most Americans today survive to old age. Old age brings many problems of adjustment, especially the need to adjust to deteriorating health, the death of loved ones, and the knowledge of one's own impending death. When the elderly retire, or disengage, their sense of social worth can be challenged. They may even face accusations of acting as parasites—of bankrupting the Social Security system, of taking energy from their children, and of draining the health care system.

THE FAMILY AS BUFFER. The family often acts as a buffer between the individual and outside social forces. Families that function well give their members a sense of belonging and personal worth. Most adults thrive on the love and acceptance that they find within their family. As it is for young children, it is for the elderly. The family is their chief source of identity. The warmth and acceptance they find in family life—if they do—counteracts negative stereotypes portrayed in society.

FROM EXTENDED TO NUCLEAR. Several generations ago, Americans lived in **extended families;** that is, other relatives, perhaps grandparents or aunts and uncles, lived with the parents and their children. During this agrarian period, the aged, who owned land, could maintain positions of authority, gradually relinquishing control while easing younger family members into responsible roles. Although we cannot be sure, the transition to old age may have been smoother and perhaps less painful than it is today. Even though they may have been living in a productive extended family, their adjustment to deteriorating health, the death of loved ones, and the knowledge that they, too, would soon die could not have been easy.

THE MYTH OF FAMILY ABANDONMENT. Today, the **nuclear family** (consisting of immediate parents and children) has become our dominant family form. This living arrangement has bred distance between adult children and their parents. The media often paint a grim picture of the elderly, abandoned and embittered, living out their last remorseful years stowed away in some isolated apartment, crammed full of newspapers and memorabilia from the past.

A team of sociologists who studied the residents of Muncie, Indiana, found that the elderly maintain close contact with their adult children (Caplow et al., 1982). As you will see in Figure 11-12, 64% of elder Americans are still living with their spouse. Only 1 of 4 lives alone. With increasing age the percentage of the very old that live alone increases, but even among the eldest it is only 2 of 5.

FIGURE 11-12 Living Arrangements of the Elderly

Living alone 23%
Living with other people 13%
Living with spouse 64%

People ages 65 to 74

Living with other people 16%
Living alone 38%
Living with spouse 45%

People ages 75 and over

Source: By James M. Henslin. Based on *Statistical Abstract of the United States* (2009, Table 57).

"Intimacy at a Distance" ■ Sociologist Elaine Brody (1978) says that in the United States both the elderly and the young *prefer* to live apart. The elderly prefer to live near, but not with, their children—a situation described as "intimacy at a distance." Sociologist Suzanne Steinmetz (1988) reports that parents and their adult children who live together tend to "get on one another's nerves." The elderly appear to be expressing their own independence and respecting the privacy of their own children when they want to live near, but not with, their children. Far from abandoning their aged parents, children remain key figures in their support system (Bengtson et al., 1990).

THE INSTITUTIONALIZED ELDERLY. Although 3% of the aged live in nursing homes, they are *not* typical of older people (*Statistical Abstract,* 2003, Tables 11, 68). In other words, 97% of the elderly do *not* live in nursing homes. Of those who do, most need help with bathing (95%), dressing (88%), and going to the toilet (58%). Most (63%) are in wheelchairs, and another 26% have to use walkers to get around. Seven out of ten report they can no longer manage money, take care of their personal possessions, or make telephone calls (*Statistical Abstract,* 2003, Table 185).

Nursing home residents who need constant care confirm common stereotypes about the elderly. They certainly are not a healthy group, but remember that nursing home residents do *not* represent elderly people in general. On the contrary, *most* elderly Americans enjoy good health and the company of their family and friends.

Although most of the elderly who end up in nursing homes do not have families available to care for them, some do. Contrary to common belief, elderly people living in nursing homes have not been "dumped" there by their ungrateful children. As Elaine Brody reported (1978, p. 20–21),

Nursing home residents do NOT represent the elderly population in general.

Prior to institutionalization, most families have endured severe personal, social, and economic stress in attempting to avoid admission [to a nursing home]; it is typically the last, not the first, resort; and the decision is made reluctantly. The "well" spouse usually is in advanced old age. The adult children are often approaching or engaged in the aging phase of life with attendant age-related stresses and often are subjected to competing demands from ill spouses or their own children.

ADJUSTING TO WIDOWHOOD. Even for people who enjoy good health and family relationships in their older years, death comes eventually. When death ends a marriage, the survivor is forced to face life without the partner who had become such an essential part of life. In the midst of disrupted family relationships and the loss of social roles, the widowed face three main problems: loneliness, anxiety, and financial strain (Hiltz, 1989).

Sociologist Robert Atchley (1975) studied retired schoolteachers and retired employees of a telephone company who were in their 70s. He found that the widowers generally did better than the widows. The men were more likely to be active in organizations, to have more contact with friends, and to be less anxious. The key to feelings of well-being in widowhood, Atchley found, was financial independence. The men were more secure financially, which made them less anxious about life. Atchley also found a surprising variable—the mobility that a car offered was *the* key factor in reducing social isolation, loneliness, and anxiety. Those who had cars, whether widows or widowers, got out of the house more, participated in more group activities, and visited their friends more often. Atchley's findings can be summarized as follows: In general, the more adequate people's income, the better they adjust to whatever challenges they face.

The Death of the Family?

MARRIAGE IN DECLINE. Is marriage doomed? Is the family destined for ruin? Let's review why some may think so. High divorce rates show that marriage is no longer a viable social institution. The many problems that we have reviewed in this chapter signal the end of the contemporary family. As we discussed earlier, 10 times more couples are cohabiting today than in the 1970s. If this trend continues, eventually most people will live together, not marry. Throughout U.S. history, most households have consisted of married couples with or without children. In 2006, these "traditional" households fell below 50%, and now *most* households consist of people in other living arrangements (alone, with other friends or relatives, cohabiting) (Roberts, 2006). As you can see in Table 11-1, the average household size has also been shrinking, and one-third of U.S. children are born to unmarried mothers. As more unmarried women bear children, marriage will become a quaint custom reserved for a few traditionalists.

MARRIAGE FLOURISHING. Although "traditional" households consisting of marrieds with children have dropped below 50% (to 49.7%), because the population has grown, more Americans are married than ever before. Young Americans are certainly taking longer to say "I do," but they are still taking those vows. Look at Figure 11-13, which shows that by the time women reach age 26, about one-half of them are married. By the end of their 30s, just 1 of 7 women and 1 of 5 men remain unmarried. Overall, about 96% of Americans marry—perhaps the *highest* percentage in our history.

The Middletown Studies ■ Other sociological research also indicates that the American family is not disintegrating. Muncie, Indiana, is one of the most thoroughly researched cities in the United States. In the 1920s and 1930s, sociologists Robert and Helen Lynd (1929, 1937) analyzed family life in this middle-American city, which they called "Middletown." In the 1980s, other sociologists went back to Muncie to find out whether the family had declined during those 50 years. To see whether it had, they checked rates of suicide, mental illness, and domestic violence.

TABLE 11-1 Average Size of U.S. Households (Persons per household)

1960	1970	1980	1990	2000	2005	2007
3.67	3.62	2.75	2.63	2.62	2.57	2.56

Source: By James M. Henslin. Based on *Statistical Abstract of the United States,* 1971, Table 44; 1989, Table 58; 1991, Table 61; 2007, Table 59; 2009, Table 58.

FIGURE 11-13 The Percentage of Americans Who Have Never Married

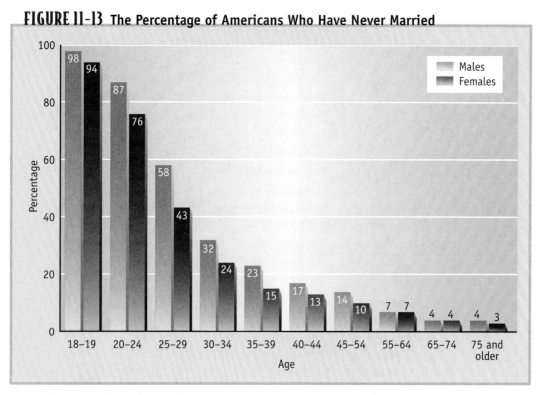

Source: By James M. Henslin. Based on *Statistical Abstract of the United States* (2008, Table 56).

To their surprise, Theodore Caplow and his fellow researchers (1982) found that these problems were *less* frequent in Middletown than they had been two generations earlier. They also found that people are not living in isolated nuclear families, as some stereotypes indicate. Rather, the nuclear families are embedded in larger kin networks, where people find economic support and satisfying personal relationships. Most parents and their grown children keep in close touch. Perhaps these researchers' most surprising finding was that marriage had become more vibrant. Marriage in the 1920s was shallower; husbands and wives didn't talk as much with one another. Now that male and female roles are less segregated, husbands and wives talk things over more—and they are *more satisfied* with marriage. Caplow concludes that "for most of their members most of the time, Middletown's composite families provide a safe and comfortable niche in a hazardous world." *The idea that the family has declined is a "sociological myth."*

VAST CHANGES, CHALLENGES, AND PROBLEMS. Despite such a positive Middletown assessment, in this chapter you've read about some of the problems that U.S. families are struggling against. Many of these challenges are severe. Figure 11-14 on the next page shows that less than a quarter of U.S. households consist of a married couple with children. Don't interpret the category—"Married couple, no children"—as meaning child-free couples. Married couples who have never had children are included in this category, to be sure, but most of these couples are "empty nesters": Their children have grown and left home.

"Money can't buy happiness" is an old saying. But it is not true. Money does buy happiness. Compared with poor people, wealthier people are more satisfied with life—and more optimistic about the future. Their health is better, they live longer, and even their marriages last longer.

FIGURE 11-14 What Are Americans' Living Arrangements?

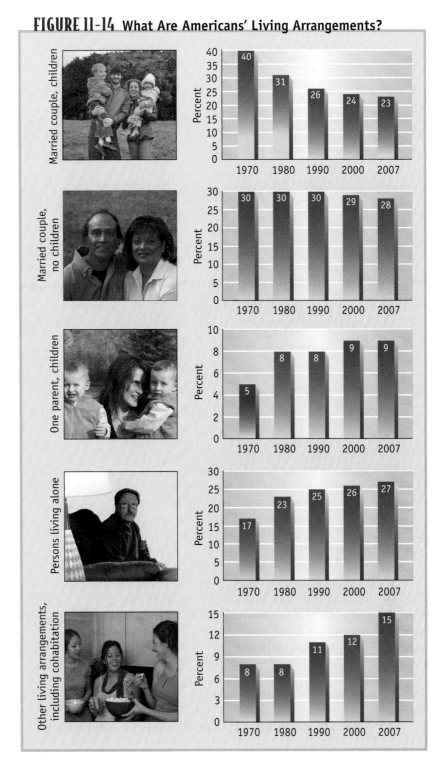

Source: By James M. Henslin. Based on *Statistical Abstract of the United States* (2000, Table 60; 2006, Table 53; 2008, Table 58).

Table 11-2 on the next page indicates the ways American families are changing: trends in cohabitation, living alone, and children living with only one parent.

IN SUM As symbolic interactionists stress, objective conditions are defined by society. Meanings are always determined by others, and it is no different in the case of the changes occurring in the family. We could become alarmed at changes facing the family and fear that the family is in serious trouble—but more than likely the family is undergoing vast change and doing what it always does—adjusting to social change.

TABLE 11-2 How U.S. Families Are Changing

	1970	1980	1990	2000	2004	Change Since 1970
Marriages	2,159,000	2,390,000	2,443,000	2,329,000	2,187,000	+1.3%
Divorces	708,000	1,189,000	1,182,000	1,179,000	1,108,000	+56
Married couples	47,500,000	52,300,000	56,300,000	56,497,000	57,719,000	+22
Unmarried couples	523,000	1,589,000	2,856,000	4,900,000	5,571,000	+1,065
People living alone	10,851,000	18,296,000	23,000,000	28,724,000	29,586,000	+273
Married couples with children at home	25,541,000	24,961,000	24,537,000	25,248,000	25,793,000	+1
Children living with both parents	58,787,000	48,648,000	46,499,000	49,760,000	49,632,000	−16
Children living with one parent	8,300,000	12,495,000	15,841,000	19,155,000	20,424,000	+246
Average size of household	3.14	2.76	2.63	2.62	2.57	−18
Married women who are employed	18,475,000	24,980,000	30,970,000	35,146,000	35,845,000	+194

Source: By James M. Henslin. Based on *Statistical Abstract of the United States* (1989, Table 58; 1992, Tables 49, 52, 56, 69, 73, 127, 619; 2001, Table 59; 2006, Tables 53, 57, 60, 72, 585).

Despite divorce, increased cohabitation, unwed births, family violence, and forces that pull people apart and even make them flee, Americans still have high hope for healthy marriage and family life. As Figure 11-13 demonstrates, Americans are marrying at a high rate. However, they are postponing the age at which they first marry, and fewer divorced people remarry. At the same time, sociological research demonstrates how some areas of family life have improved over the years, especially relationships between husbands and wives.

Social Policy

THE LASCH ACCUSATIONS: INTRUSIONS BY PROFESSIONALS. Social policy addressing family problems is mired in controversy. In *Haven in a Heartless World* (1977), social historian Christopher Lasch said that people are trying to find in the family a refuge of love and decency in a cruel and heartless world. The family, however, often cannot provide these comforts because it has been besieged by professionals—doctors, social workers, and "counselors" of various sorts. What Lasch meant was that these professionals have been trying to enlarge their own areas of specialty at the expense of the family. Under the guise of helping, they have stripped the family of some of its functions, eroding its capacity to provide protective intimacy.

Lasch came to this conclusion after researching sex counselors. He said these sex-perts write books and magazine articles about what sexual relations between husband and wife "ought" to be like. Hundreds of "Dr. Phils" appear as self-styled experts on radio and television, where they proclaim their expertise. As a result, husbands and wives feel less capable of working out their own sexual problems, for only "sexual experts" have the "real" answers.

Another example includes child development experts. They profess to know the best ways to rear children, sometimes even "the" correct way to do so. This makes parents worry that, as mere laypeople, they might be damaging their children through clumsy, improper parenting. They then turn to "professionals" who intrude into this traditionally private area of family life.

In short, we have become a "therapeutic society," one in which "experts" claim that all problems—including those in the family—are their domain. This "concern" by "experts" about the plight of the family, publicized on television and radio, in magazines and books, masks what is really happening—outside agents taking away the family's authority.

The situation is even worse than this, Lasch says, for there is no evidence that these so-called experts have benefited the family.

As you would expect, professionals have reacted bitterly to this attack on their profession. They deny that they have self-serving motives or that they intrude into family life, undermine its authority, and cause families to have less "self-sufficiency" (Joffe, 1978). On the contrary, their goal is to empower the family so that it can handle the problems of life successfully, making its members more competent and happy.

THE DILEMMA OF FAMILY POLICY: TAKING SIDES. Lasch's claims expose how any social policy addressing family needs often finds itself on one side or the other of issues that divide people who have the best interests of the family at heart. For example, consider what seems to be a neutral matter, making financial aid available to troubled families. One might argue that such a policy would aid the family; another side, however, may view it as an attack on family self-sufficiency, saying that it discourages families from looking out for themselves—making them further dependent on outside sources.

THE BATTLEGROUND OF DEFINITIONS: INTERVENTION OR INTERFERENCE? Consider a popular book that quickly stimulated national policy discussions—*It Takes a Village: And Other Lessons Children Teach Us* by Hillary Rodham Clinton. Clinton's declared purpose was to make the public aware of the need for community involvement in child care. Yet the book set off a storm of controversy: Some people argued it rallied for the state to eventually take child rearing away from parents.

Almost all policy falls on one side or the other of this explosive issue. Consider this case:

> Parents tell their 14-year-old girl that she cannot have sex because premarital sex is a sin. The daughter faces a dilemma. She is afraid that if she does not have sex with her boyfriend, he will date more cooperative girls. She also is "in love" and wants to please him. The girl goes to a family planning clinic and explains her plight. Counselors encourage her to assert herself against domineering and old-fashioned parents. They assure her that she can come to them for a free and confidential abortion if she becomes pregnant. They also offer her a Norplant.

Who is "right" in this example? As symbolic interactionists stress, our understanding of what "ought" to be depends on our values. Sociologist Carole Joffe (1978), who originated this example of the 14-year-old, put it this way: From one perspective, the decision of a teenager to seek out contraception is a step forward in gaining her independence. From another standpoint, to talk about giving contraceptives to a young teenager is to prejudge the issue. From this perspective, contraception does not represent a step toward independence but, rather, an intrusion into family privacy.

It is often difficult to face controversial social policy without being prejudiced. As symbolic interactionists stress, different family members experience family life differently. Arrangements that some family members find comfortable and satisfying, others find oppressive (Joffe, 1978). As the Thinking Critically box on children's rights on the next page highlights, what is government intervention to some is government interference to others. In the midst of this intense controversy and clash of values and opinions, there is one subject area about which most people agree—that young and defenseless children need to be protected from physical and psychological harm. But even here, trusting families to protect their own children from predators clashes with nonprofit organizations aimed at prosecuting offenders (Chilman, 1988).

THE ISSUE OF POVERTY. Apart from family problems such as marital rape and child abuse, many sociologists see poverty as the root of family troubles. Social policies to help families escape poverty are a central concern to many. A guaranteed family income,

THINKING CRITICALLY about Social Problems

CHILD RIGHTS I

In 1943, the U.S. Supreme Court determined that a cardinal principle of U.S. law is that "the custody, care, and nurture of the child reside in the parents." This decision is usually interpreted to mean that parents have a total right to decide matters concerning the welfare of their children, with the state able to intervene only to stop abuse or neglect.

Americans, however, are divided over the rights that parents should have over their children. The central question is, At what point does the authority of the state supersede the authority of parents? When does the privacy of the family take precedence over the concern of well-intentioned outsiders? Let's look at the major arguments.

TO PROTECT CHILDREN FROM DOMINEERING PARENTS, WE MUST STRENGTHEN CHILDREN'S RIGHTS

In the journal *Human Rights,* Patricia Wald (1974) wrote that a "very young child" has the right "to be consulted and informed about critical decisions in his life, and (the) right to be represented in those decisions." To protect the child from the "consequences of unilateral parental actions . . . the child's interests deserve representation by an independent advocate before a neutral decision maker."

Wald also suggested that communities provide homes for runaways under age 16 who do not want to return home. "Parents would have no right to forcibly take their children away from such homes," she proposed. A child ought to be able to seek legal advice to redress grievances against his or her family. Some also propose that children should be able to sue their parents for poor child rearing.

These proposals are designed to balance a system that currently favors the parents at the expense of children. For example, as things now stand, if parents want to take a job out of town, they do. The child has no choice in the matter and simply has to move with them. This, say critics, is a "crucial decision that affects the child's life." If the parents move, the child has to leave friends and attend a new school. The child should have the right to "an independent advocate to argue his or her case before a neutral decision maker." If the child does not want to go and the parents insist on moving, the independent advocate should be able to remove the child from the family.

TO PROTECT FAMILIES FROM DOMINEERING PROFESSIONALS WE MUST STRENGTHEN PARENTS' RIGHTS

To accomplish this, Phyllis Schlafly (1979) proposed the Family Protection Act. This act would guarantee that

1. Parents have the right to visit public school classrooms and school functions.
2. Parents can review textbooks before public schools adopt them.
3. No federal funding will be given for courses that encourage children to rethink the values that their parents have taught them, courses often called "values clarification" or "behavior modification."
4. Parents must give their consent for their children to enroll in courses about religion or "ethics," and they can keep their children out of such courses that they find offensive.
5. Parents must give consent for unmarried minors to get contraceptives or an abortion and must be informed if their child is treated for a venereal disease.
6. If a child's "right to self-expression" conflicts with the parents' "right to educate or discipline," in the absence of compelling evidence of parental unfitness, the courts must rule in favor of the parents.

a robust economy with full employment, and educational opportunities open to all would benefit many. Income, jobs, and education would not solve all family problems, but they would go a long way toward solving many of them.

The Future of the Problem

RAPID SOCIAL CHANGE AS NORMATIVE. Social change is the hallmark of American society. Seemingly overnight, familiar landmarks are torn down and replaced by a strip mall or by another of an endless series of fast-food outlets. Computers recognize your

speech, type your message, and check your grammar; devices connected to the Global Positioning System announce your location, even guide you through traffic in a strange city. On the Internet, type something in English and it can be translated instantly (if not 100% reliably) into German or Spanish or any other major language before being transmitted to someone in a distant part of the world. Soon you'll be able to have one telephone number that will stay with you for life and will be valid throughout the world. Change is so rapid and extensive that parents and children live in different worlds—so much so that grown children who are visiting their parents after an absence of months or even years often find that after the first hour or two they have little left to talk about.

FUTURE SHOCK. The speed, extent, and intensity of today's social change overpower us. Alvin Toffler (1971) coined the term *future shock* to refer to this dizzying barrage of change to which we have no leisure or opportunity to adjust. **Future shock** is the vertigo, the confusion, the disorientation that we experience when our familiar world is transformed.

The U.S. family is experiencing future shock. With industrialization and urbanization, the family has already had to adapt to social change so extensive that it has left little regarding human relationships untouched. Computers are changing the worlds of work, education, recreation, and entertainment. Parents and children text and e-mail one another from office, school, and home, giving brief updates on changing plans. Because the family is continuing to adapt to changing social conditions, its future is unclear. Let's examine changes we can expect.

CHANGES WE CAN EXPECT. The romantic notions of love and marriage are established firmly in our culture, and love will likely continue to be the "proper" basis for marriage. People will also continue to marry at a rate close to what we see today. The age at first marriage will continue upward a while longer, then stabilize. Cohabitation will continue to increase for about another decade and then level off. The proportion of married women who are employed outside the home will continue to increase, eventually reaching a plateau at about 75%. Marriage will become even more oriented around companionship. This orientation, coupled with more wives working outside the home—with their incomes increasing relative to those of men—will be a stimulus for husbands and wives to develop more equal relationships. Marriage will remain fragile, and the United States will continue to have one of the highest divorce rates in the world. With couples marrying at older ages after attaining greater levels of education, the divorce rate will likely decline. Day care and in-home child care will become more common for children of working parents (see the Issues in Social Problems box on the next page). Whether you interpret such changes as good, bad, or indifferent depends, of course, on your values.

THE IDEOLOGICAL STRUGGLE. The struggle among groups to influence family orientations and family policy will intensify. With their incompatible views of right, justice, and the good life, they will continue to battle one another. The future looks exciting, the outcome uncertain. This struggle is not theoretical or abstract: Much of it is bound to influence your own family life.

Issues in Social Problems
WHAT DOES DAY CARE COST A COMPANY?

Suppose that you are the president of Union Bank in Monterey, California. Some of your employees have asked you to provide a day care center. You would like to do so, but you can't spend stockholders' money on day care simply because you think it is a nice idea. You are accountable for the performance of your stock, and you have to know the bottom line.

"Find out what it would cost us to have a day care center," the manager told Sandra Burud, a social science researcher. At first, determining costs may sound fairly easy. You simply add the cost of the facilities and personnel, and you have the answer. But what you want to know is the *net* cost. After all, day care is supposed to benefit the company. Will the benefits be greater or less than the cost? How much in either direction?

Now the problem becomes difficult. How can you accurately estimate changes that the day care center will make in employee turnover? This, in turn, will change interview costs, hiring bonuses, and job advertisements. Then, too, you have to try to measure the productive time that will be lost while an employee is on maternity leave or is job hunting, while a job goes unfilled, or while a new employee is learning the ropes. Employee turnover is costly: Merck Pharmaceuticals has determined that during their first 14 months on the job new employees cost the company 5 months of work. Some costs are impossible to measure, such as poor morale and loss of reputation with the community, if a lot of employees quit. In fact, Burud decided that she couldn't put numbers on these variables and had to skip them.

In the midst of such uncertainties, Union Bank decided to go ahead and open a day care center. This cost the bank $105,000. Then Burud compared 87 employees who used the center with a control group of 105 employees who didn't use the center. She found that employee turnover among the center's users was 2%; among the control group, it was 10%. Employees who used the center were also absent an average of 2 days a year less than the control group. Their maternity leaves were also 1 week shorter.

The bottom line? After subtracting its costs of running the day care center, the bank saved $232,000.

Should you, the president, have your bank open a day care center? *Now,* that is an easy decision.

Such companies as Marriott Hotels have paid attention to the bottom-line results of corporate day care and have opened their own centers. Other companies, such as Levi Strauss and AT&T, subsidize their employees' child care.

Based on Solomon (1988); Shellenbarger (1994).

1. The family is always adjusting to social change. One of the most significant effects of the Industrial Revolution was the removal of economic production from the household.

2. Whether change within the family is perceived as a social problem or merely as a form of adaptation depends on people's values. Indicators that many see as evidence of a social problem are divorce, runaway children, births to single women, one-parent families, and violence and sexual abuse in the family.

3. In analyzing why the U.S. divorce rate is high, symbolic interactionists stress the changing ideas of sex roles and expectations of marriage; functionalists, the declining functions of the family; and conflict theorists, the unequal distribution of power in the family.

4. The average age at first marriage declined from 1890 to about 1950, then began to increase in about 1970. Today, the average age at first marriage is the highest in our history. The primary reason is *cohabitation*. As many people postpone marriage, a growing proportion of the young remain single.

5. Married couples remain child-free because of infertility, the decision not to have children, or the continuous postponement of children until childlessness becomes inevitable. Child-free couples face a stigma.

6. Physical violence between family members is common. Although wives initiate about as much violence as husbands, they are injured more often. People reared in violent homes are more likely to be violent to their own spouses and children. Incest and marital rape are more frequent than commonly supposed.

7. That the elderly are abandoned by their families is a myth: Most adult children and their parents keep in close touch. The elderly prefer to live near their children, but not with them, a preference called "intimacy at a distance." Widowhood appears to be easier for men than women: This is due not to gender, but rather to economics; those who are better off financially adjust better to the death of a spouse.

8. Despite its problems, the family is far from doomed and is much healthier than most imagine. More Americans are marrying today than ever before. The "Middletown" studies indicate that husbands and wives are more satisfied with married life than they were 50 years ago.

9. Social policy on the family is controversial because it pits individual rights against government intervention. Some even accuse "family professionals" of expanding their domain at the expense of the family.

10. These trends are likely to continue: increases in cohabitation, later age at first marriage, more wives working outside the home, more day care, and greater marital equality. Groups that are concerned about the family differ in their ideas about the way the family "should" be, and it remains to be seen which groups will be most influential in determining social policy.

KEY TERMS

Breadwinner, 373
Cohabitation, 378
Defective discipline, 370
Extended family, 387
False consciousness, 377
Family of orientation, 372
Family of procreation, 372
Future shock, 394

Incest, 385
Incest taboo, 385
Incompatibility, 374
Intimate partner violence, 380
Modernity, 364
Nuclear family, 387
Pedophile Liberation Army (PLA), 386

Pedophiles, 371
Pushouts, 371
Remarriage, 367
Reproductive labor, 376
Second shift, 377
Sexual revolution, 375
Social institution, 361

THINKING CRITICALLY ABOUT CHAPTER 11

1. What do you consider to be the five greatest benefits and the five greatest downsides of the changes in the composition of American families? Do you think that these changes are bringing more negatives or positives? Explain.
2. Which perspective (symbolic interactionism, functionalism, or conflict theory) do you think does the best job of explaining the changes that are taking place in American families? Explain.
3. Rank the seven traditional functions of the family according to how important you think they are in today's family. Explain your rankings.
4. With the huge increase in cohabitation, the high divorce rate, the number of runaways, and the extent of abuse in families, how can the authors not conclude that marriage is doomed? Explain.

BY THE NUMBERS: THEN AND NOW

- U.S. birthrate, per 1,000 people, in 1950: **24**
- U.S. birthrate, per 1,000 people, now: **14**

- Number of divorced Americans in 1975: **7,000,000**
- Number of divorced Americans in 2006: **23,000,000**

- Percentage of all African American births occurring to single African American women in 1970: **38%**
- Percentage of all African American births occurring to single African American women in 2005: **68%**

- Percentage of births to single U.S. women in 1980: **18%**
- Percentage of births to single U.S. women now: **34%**

- Number of cohabitating couples in the U.S. in 1980: **1,589,000**
- Number of cohabitating couples in the U.S. in 2006: **5,134,000**

- Number of U.S. children living with only one parent in 1970: **8,300,000**
- Number of U.S. children living with only one parent in 2004: **20,424,000**

- Percentage of households with one person, living alone, in 1970: **17%**
- Percentage of households with one person, living alone, in 2007: **27%**

MySocLab

What can you find in MySocLab? mysoclab www.mysoclab.com

- Complete Ebook
- Practice Tests and Exams
- Multimedia Activities
- Mapping and Data Analysis Exercises

- Research and Writing Advice
- Interactive Social Surveys
- Sociology in the News

Urbanization and Population Issues

Kellie Moiser was a 17-year-old high school student who worked part-time at the corner ice cream store. From childhood, she had dreamed of becoming a model. Kellie's mother encouraged her dream, hoping that it would be a way out of poverty.

But Kellie never got the chance.

Michael Hagan, 23, also lived in her area of south-central Los Angeles. He liked Olde English "800" Malt Liquor, especially when he smoked PCP.

He also liked guns.

And a little blood didn't bother him, either.

One Monday evening, Hagan was on a binge with other members of his gang, when they decided to go after a rival gang. They piled into an old Buick and sped toward enemy turf. There they spotted four teenagers, two boys and two girls.

The teenagers were not gang members. They were just kids who had gone out for ice cream. When they saw the gun, they ran. Kellie didn't run fast enough. Hagan methodically pumped 15 slugs into her, 6 into her back.

For the police, it was just one more crime in an endless stream of murders that occur in this part of the city. They didn't have much to go on, witnesses clammed up, and detectives had other priorities.

And a little blood didn't bother him.

Kellie's mother didn't have much to go on either, but she set out to solve her daughter's murder. Out of a fury born of grief, she stormed the streets in search of the killers. She even barged into local drug houses. The word got around, and a sympathetic inmate in the county jail sent her a letter telling her the name of the shooter.

Kellie's mother shook her head in disbelief when she found out who had killed her daughter. She said, "I knew these gang members when they were just babies. Now look at them. They've turned into killers."

Hagan, the shooter, says, "Jail ain't bad. To me, life ain't much better on the streets than in jail. I can live here; no problem."

"The gang is your family," Hagan explains. "If you're a Crip, I fight for you, no matter what the odds. If you're the enemy, it's do or die."

Hagan adds, "If I had a son, I'd give him a choice: Either he can go to school and be a goody-goody, or he can hit the streets."

Hagan smiles broadly as he adds, "I done did something, and I'm known. I consider myself Public Enemy Number 1."

—Based on Hull (1987)

Urbanization: The Problem in Sociological Perspective

Hagan represents an American nightmare—unsafe streets, drive-by shootings, senseless killings. Let's look at the history of cities and how they might influence violent behavior.

THE EVOLUTION OF CITIES. Somewhere between 6000 and 8000 BCE, people built cities with massive walls in Jericho (Homblin, 1973). By 3500 BCE, cities had been established

in several parts of the world. They appeared first in Mesopotamia, then in the Nile, Indus, and Yellow River valleys, around the Mediterranean, in West Africa, Central America, and the Andes (Fischer, 1976).

Agriculture was the key in the development of cities. Only when society produced a surplus of food were people able to stop farming and gather in cities to pursue other occupations. A **city,** in fact, can be defined as a large number of people who live in one place and do not produce their own food. As agricultural techniques became more efficient, they spurred urban development.

During the fourth millennium BCE, the plow was invented: As this invention spread, the resulting agricultural surplus stimulated the development of towns and cities around the world.

Early plows, although a great improvement beyond digging sticks, were primitive. For the next 5,000 years, the food surplus was only enough to allow a small minority of the world's population to live in urban areas. Then came the Industrial Revolution of the 1700s and 1800s, which sparked the urban revolution we still experience today. The Industrial Revolution stimulated not only the invention of mechanical means of farming, which brought food in abundance, but also mechanical means of transportation and communication. These inventions allowed people, resources, and products to be moved efficiently—factors upon which modern cities depend.

FROM RURAL TO URBAN. Two hundred years ago, almost everyone in the world lived in rural areas. Only 3% lived in towns of 5,000 or more (Hauser & Schnore, 1965). By 1900, the total number of city dwellers was up to 14%. Today, 50% of the entire world lives in cities (Massey, 2001). This process is called **urbanization**—the social process whereby cities grow.

In its early years, the United States was almost exclusively rural. In 1800, only about 6 of 100 Americans lived in towns of 2,500 or more. As Figure 12-1 on the next page shows, cities became increasingly popular places to live, and by around 1920 half of Americans lived in them. Today, four of every five Americans do. As you can see from the Social Map (Figure 12-2 on page 402), rates of urbanization differ considerably from state to state.

Cities are supposed to solve problems, to make life more convenient by transcending the limitations of farm and village. Cities offer the hope of a better life, of employment, education, and other advantages. With these benefits, cities have continued to grow around the world. Table 12-1 on page 402 lists the world's 10 largest cities in 1950 and the projected 10 largest cities in 2015. In 1950, three of the world's largest cities were in Europe, and two in North America. In 2015, seven of the world's largest cities will be located in Asia or the subcontinent. Thus, the major shift has been from the Most Industrialized Nations to the Least Industrialized Nations.

There are two primary reasons for this global change in the location of the largest cities. First, there is a lack of population growth in the Most Industrialized Nations and tremendous growth in the populations of the Least Industrialized Nations. Second, poverty is "pushing" people out of rural areas, and economic opportunities are "pulling" them into urban areas. In the Global Glimpse box on page 403 we explore why people in the Least Industrialized Nations are deserting their rural way of life and flocking to urban areas.

URBAN PROBLEMS. Cities have a difficult time addressing our desire for **community,** a feeling of belonging, the sense that others care what happens to us and that we can depend on the people around us. Some people do find community in the city, but others find **alienation**—a sense of estrangement—and they live in isolation and fear. Some people, like Hagan, even band together to create fear, making the city a miserable place to live.

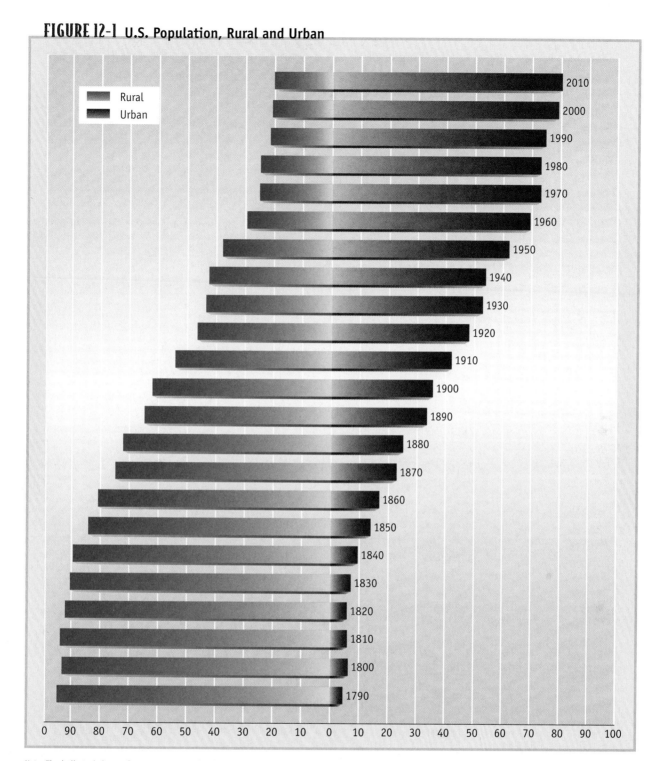

FIGURE 12-1 U.S. Population, Rural and Urban

Rural
Urban

2010
2000
1990
1980
1970
1960
1950
1940
1930
1920
1910
1900
1890
1880
1870
1860
1850
1840
1830
1820
1810
1800
1790

0 90 80 70 60 50 40 30 20 10 0 10 20 30 40 50 60 70 80 90 100

Note: The indicated change from 1990 to 2000 is misleading. In the year 2000 census, the U.S. Census Bureau began to use a more inclusive definition of "urban." Smaller areas that are dense ("urban clusters") are now counted as urban. If the old definition were used, the figure would show a 1% increase in urban population, not the 4% shown here.

Source: By James M. Henslin. Based on *Statistical Abstract of the United States* (2006, Table 27). The projections from 2000 to 2010 are by the author.

The Scope of the Problem

A DEEP AMBIVALENCE. Viewing the city as the source of problems is nothing new. In 1780, Thomas Jefferson said that cities contribute to the good government of a nation about as much as sores contribute to the strength of the body. He said that cities were

FIGURE 12-2 The Rural-Urban Makeup of the United States

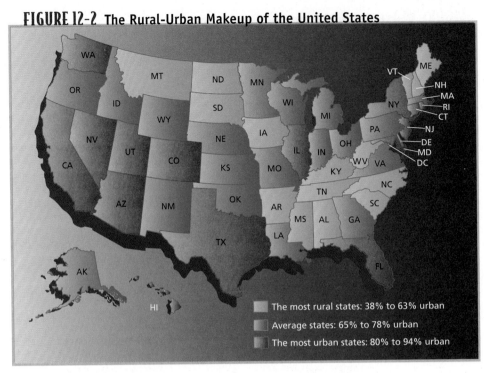

The most rural states: 38% to 63% urban

Average states: 65% to 78% urban

The most urban states: 80% to 94% urban

Note: The most rural state is Vermont (38% urban). The most urban states are California and New Jersey (94% urban).

Source: By James M. Henslin. Based on *Statistical Abstract of the United States* (2007, Table 33).

TABLE 12-1 The World's Ten Largest Cities, 1950 and 2015

		1950				2015	
Rank	City	Population (in millions)	Country	Rank	City	Population (in millions)	Country
1	New York	12.3	United States	1	Tokyo	36.4	Japan
2	Toyko	11.2	Japan	2	Mumbai (Bombay)	21.9	India
3	London	8.4	England	3	São Paulo	20.5	Brazil
4	Paris	6.5	France	4	Mexico City	20.2	Mexico
5	Shanghai	6.0	China	5	New York	20.0	United States
6	Moscow	5.4	Russia	6	Delhi	18.7	India
7	Buenos Aires	5.1	Argentina	7	Shanghai	17.2	China
8	Chicago	5.0	United States	8	Calcutta	17.0	India
9	Calcutta	4.5	India	9	Dhaka	17.0	India
10	Beijing	4.3	China	10	Karachi	14.9	Pakistan

Source: World Urbanization Prospects: The 2007 Revision, United Nations Department of Economic and Social Affairs/Population Division.

A Global Glimpse

WHY CITY SLUMS ARE BETTER THAN THE COUNTRY: THE RUSH TO THE CITIES OF THE LEAST INDUSTRIALIZED NATIONS

Thoughts of the Least Industrialized Nations often bring to mind images of people tending animals or harvesting crops, enjoying a peaceful life in the lush countryside or along babbling brooks. Such images no longer represent the reality that most people in the Least Industrialized Nations face—if ever they did. The rural poor of these countries are flocking to the cities at such a rate that, as shown in Table 12-1, the Least Industrialized Nations now contain most of the world's largest cities. In the Most Industrialized Nations, industrialization generally preceded urbanization, but in the Least Industrialized Nations *urbanization has preceded industrialization*. These cities cannot support their swelling populations.

The settlement patterns are also different in these cities. When rural migrants and immigrants move to U.S. cities, they usually settle in deteriorating housing near the city's center. The wealthy reside in suburbs and luxurious city enclaves. Migrants to cities of the Least Industrialized Nations, in contrast, establish illegal squatter settlements outside the city. There they build shacks from scrap boards, cardboard, and bits of corrugated metal. Even flattened tin cans are scavenged for building material. Squatters do not enjoy city facilities—roads, public transportation, water, sewers, or garbage pickup. After thousands of squatters settle an area, the city reluctantly acknowledges their right to live there and may add bus service and minimal water lines. Hundreds of people use a single spigot. About *5 million* of Mexico City's residents live in such squalid conditions, with hundreds of thousands more pouring in each year.

Why this rush to live in the city under such miserable conditions? At its core are "push" factors: (1) No longer is there enough land to divide up among children. (2) Without

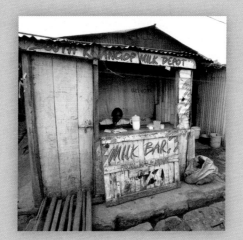

land, there is hunger. (3) People are deeply dissatisfied with the resulting character of rural life. Then, too, there are the "pull" factors that draw people to the cities—jobs, schools, housing, and a more stimulating life.

At the bottom of a ravine near Mexico City is a grand bunch of shacks. Some hold parents and 14 children.

"We used to live up there," Señora Gonzalez gestured toward the mountain, "in those caves. Our only hope was one day to have a place to live. And now we do." She smiled with pride at the hand-built shacks . . . each one had a collection of flowers planted in tin cans. "One day, we hope to extend the water pipes and drainage—perhaps even pave. . . ."

And what was the name of her community? Señora Gonzalez beamed. "Esperanza!" (McDowell 1984, p. 172)

Esperanza is the Spanish word for hope. Hope is often what lies behind the rush to cities—the hope of a better life. And this is why the rush has been so great. In 1930, only one Latin American city had over a million people—now 50 do! This change is so vast and so rapid that the world's cities are growing by one million people each week (Brockerhoff, 2000).

How will the Least Industrialized Nations ever be able to adjust to such extensive migration? They have no choice. Authorities in Brazil, Guatemala, Venezuela, and other countries have sent in the police and even the army to evict the settlers. It doesn't work. It does lead to violence, and sometimes the temporary removal of people, but the settlers keep streaming in. The adjustments that these nations must make will be painful. The infrastructure (roads, water, sewers, electricity, and so on) must be built, but these poor countries don't have the resources to build them. As the desperate rural poor flock to the cities, problems will worsen.

"pestilential to the morals, the health, and the liberties of man" (1784/1977). Other Americans viewed rural life as the source of virtue—an agrarian paradise where life is innocent, simple, and happy (Hadden & Barton, 1973). The cold brutality of urban life often makes people long for something better. The bottom line is a deep ambivalence toward the city: People dream of fleeing the city to find safety and security in a simpler area, yet they remain fascinated with the city, locating there for work, cultural attractions, and diversions.

This ambivalence toward the city—its threat and its allure—will be woven throughout this chapter as we examine major problems that face our cities.

WHAT IS URBAN ABOUT URBAN PROBLEMS? In one sense, almost all social problems are urban. Because most Americans live in cities, poverty, crime, unemployment, divorce, drug addiction, violence, and so forth are concentrated in cities. None of these problems is urban by nature, because these problems can—and do—occur everywhere.

What, then, is *urban* about social problems? First, city life *increases* rates of social problems. For example, the *rates* of burglary, robbery, suicide, alcoholism, and rape are *higher* in cities than in rural areas. Why do cities increase such behaviors? Or, conversely, why do rural areas inhibit them?

Second, the United States is facing an *urban crisis.* U.S. cities have areas that almost everyone fears and avoids. There, amidst burned-out and boarded-up buildings, addicts and the unemployed slouch on apartment steps. Drug dealers openly work "their" street corners, a lucrative turf that they defend by violence. Gang members prowl filthy streets, mugging and killing. Many who enter these areas are at peril. Lastly, there are other indications of further crisis. During economic downturns, some cities shorten the school year because they cannot meet payroll. Some slash budgets for the public library and garbage collection. Some even reduce police and fire protection. Across the nation the middle class has rushed to the suburbs, abandoning the inner city to the poor, a flight that has impoverished the city. **Urban sprawl** is the phenomenon that occurs as cities expand: They invade the countryside, devouring farmland, leaving in its place asphalt and buildings. The term **urban crisis** refers to this cluster of interrelated urban problems. We will use sociological theory to consider some solutions.

Looking at the Problem Theoretically

As usual, theoretical perspectives yield contrasting insights. We will apply symbolic interactionism to the inner city, looking at the social organization of the "slum." Functional theory will make visible the zones of activity that develop as a city expands. Finally, using the conflict perspective, we will see how class conflict creates urban problems.

Symbolic Interactionism

Americans often report they are fearful of the inner city. Middle-class citizens avoid the inner city—unable to understand why anyone would live "like that."

GAINING AN INSIDER'S VIEW. Symbolic interactionists try to see how life in the Least Industrialized Nations looks to the people who live in them. They try to discover the meanings that people attach to their own experiences, how they feel about their situation, and how they cope with their problems. As symbolic interactionists study the worlds of the urban poor, they try not to impose their own values or views on others. This approach to understanding urban life is called the **Chicago School of sociology,** because it represents the methods used by the sociology department of the University of Chicago in the 1920s. The scholars associated with the Chicago School produced classic studies of urban life. In 1923 Nels Anderson wrote *The Hobo,* followed in 1927 by Frederic Thrasher's *The Gang.* In 1929 Harvey Zorbaugh's *The Gold Coast and the Slum* contrasted the rich and the poor in Chicago. Then in 1932, Paul Cressey published *Taxi-Dance Hall,* about women who made their living dancing with men. Making the city their sociological laboratory, these sociologists, as others have done since, focused mostly on the lives of the poor.

DISTINCTIVE SOCIAL WORLDS. The contrasts of the city—its many groups with their distinctive ways of life—fascinated sociologists at Chicago. They were impressed with how people of different backgrounds developed unique subcultures and lived in separate

areas of the city. As Louis Wirth (1938) put it, the city is made up of "a mosaic of social worlds." Sociologists today are also fascinated by these contrasting social worlds, and they remain topics of sociological research. In these smaller social worlds, urban people live with unique codes and understandings of social life. Their differing interpretations of life and expectations of how to interact make it easy for people from different areas of the same city to misunderstand one another.

WHYTE'S CLASSIC STUDY. In this tradition, sociologist William Foote Whyte lived as a participant observer in an inner city for 3 years. In the classic book that he wrote to recount his experiences, *Street Corner Society* (1943, 1995), Whyte explains that what may look to outsiders to be disorganized is, in fact, a tightly knit way of life. By participating in residents' lives—hanging around the street corner with "the boys," going to dances, bowling, playing baseball—Whyte was able to identify the various types of people who lived in the inner city. The young men separated themselves into two main groups: "*the college boys,*" who were upward bound, and "*the corner boys,*" who remained in their old neighborhood. Each group had its own statuses, its own norms, and its own ways of controlling its members.

SUTTLES'S STUDY. Thirty years later, sociologist Gerald Suttles was a participant-observer in Chicago. He found social statuses and forms of communication equally as complex as those Whyte had uncovered among the Italians he studied. Suttles documented how African Americans, Puerto Ricans, Chicanos, and Italians, although sharing the same physical space, had their own forms of communication. One group's customary ways of expressing itself—its distinctive language, gestures, and clothing—may be offensive to members of another group. Here's what Suttles (1968, pp. 66–67) says:

> Whites say that Negroes will not look them in the eye. The Negroes counter by saying the Whites are impolite and try to "cow" people by staring at them. . . . The most subtle accounts are those which describe almost entirely nonverbal encounters: "When I went over to the Negro nurse, she didn't even look up," "I'd go again (to an Italian restaurant) but they really stare you down," "I can understand why those guys (older Italians) can't half speak English, but why they gotta eyeball everybody walk past?"

Within each area of the city, different groups stake out a unique existence. They develop their own ways to express themselves, live by their own codes, and evaluate their members accordingly. Although these background assumptions unite a group's members, they separate them from others and hinder communication with other groups. This can create hostility among diverse groups staking a claim in the city. These differences often lead to suspicion and misunderstanding, even death.

ANDERSON'S STUDIES. As a graduate student at the University of Chicago, Elijah Anderson conducted a participant observation study in another Chicago slum. He, too, emphasized how one cannot understand a group of people without taking on their perspective. For example, while studying a group of men who hung around at Jelly's, a bar and liquor store in an African American area, Anderson (1978) uncovered intricate boundaries that separated people from one another. He found three main groups at Jelly's:

Elijah Anderson used participant observation to study slum life.

The regulars. These men see and present themselves as hard-working. They subscribe to mainstream values, are proud of their involvement in families, and have aspirations of getting ahead. Their values can be summed up with the single word *decency*—working regularly and treating other people right.

The wineheads. These men neither value work, nor do they work regularly. Their main concern is getting enough money to buy wine. They beg from others and have low status.

The hoodlums. These men pride themselves on "being tough" and having access to easy money. Few work regularly. They are involved in petty theft, stickups, burglaries, and fencing stolen property. The other men at Jelly's do not trust them, nor do they trust one another.

When Anderson (1990, 2006) was hired as a sociologist at the University of Pennsylvania, he moved into a neighborhood in Philadelphia that was being "gentrified"; that is, more affluent people were moving into the area and rehabilitating its buildings. **Gentrification** creates tensions because it raises property values, taxes, and rents, forcing the poorer residents to move to lower-rent areas. Although the area begins to look prettier, the poor resent the invasion of the wealthy into their neighborhood.

The gentrified area bordered an African American ghetto, and tension between residents of the two areas was high. Just as Suttles had documented a couple of decades earlier, eye contact was a significant source of tension. Whites were afraid to look too long at African Americans whom they didn't know, fearing that their look might be interpreted as an invitation to interact. To avoid this problem, Whites either pretended not to see African Americans or else looked right through them without speaking. African Americans, in contrast, were used to more outgoing interaction, and they found failure of eye contact offensive. Only after people lived in the area for a while did they become adequately familiar with what Anderson called the *code of the street*—that is, its norms and etiquette—which reduced tension and allowed the two groups to coexist. Such coexistence, though, was never easy, and tensions remained.

IN SUM Groups living within each area of the city stake out territory, establish social boundaries between themselves and others, and work out a sense of identity and belonging. When you look beyond the run-down buildings, you will find intricate patterns of interaction. People there, like people everywhere, interact on the basis of background assumptions and within social networks. The assumptions, codes, and norms of inner-city residents, however, often differ sharply from those of the middle class.

Symbolic interactionists remind us that the poor do not experience urban problems in the abstract. They encounter specific problems. For example, the poor do not experience the *concept* of urban decay. Rather, they deal with cutbacks in city services; buses that run late or not at all; factories that move to Mexico or China and wipe out their jobs overnight—and killers who stalk their neighborhoods, hallways, and elevators. In short, symbolic interactionists focus on how people make sense of their experiences as they attempt to cope with urban life.

Functionalism

BURGESS'S MODEL OF CONCENTRIC ZONES. The University of Chicago also produced urban studies that reflect the functionalist perspective. Ernest Burgess analyzed how cities grow. Figure 12-3 is taken from one of his books. As you can see, Burgess identified five urban zones, each with distinct functions. Burgess visualized the city as expanding outward from its center, the central business district (Zone I). Zone II, which encircles the downtown area, contains the city's slums. To escape the slum, skilled and thrifty workers move to Zone III. Zone IV contains the better apartment buildings, residential hotels, single-family dwellings, and gated communities where the wealthy live. Still farther out, beyond the city limits, is Zone V, a commuter zone of suburbs and satellite cities.

Burgess used his **concentric zone theory** to explain the "tendencies of any town or city to expand radically from its central business district." He noted, however, that no "city fits perfectly this ideal scheme." Some cities face physical obstructions such as lakes or rivers that make their expansion depart from this model. As Burgess also noted, businesses deviate from this model when they locate in outlying zones.

MOBILITY AND THE CITY. This classic model of urban growth helps us understand urban problems. Burgess stressed that city dwellers are always on the move. In addition to commuting for work, school, shopping, and recreation, they move into better zones when they can afford to. This creates an **invasion–succession cycle** in which one group moves into an area already occupied by people who have different characteristics. The invasion creates antagonisms between the groups: The one resents displacement; the other feels unwelcome. Today, however, people move not only outward, away from a city's center, but also toward it.

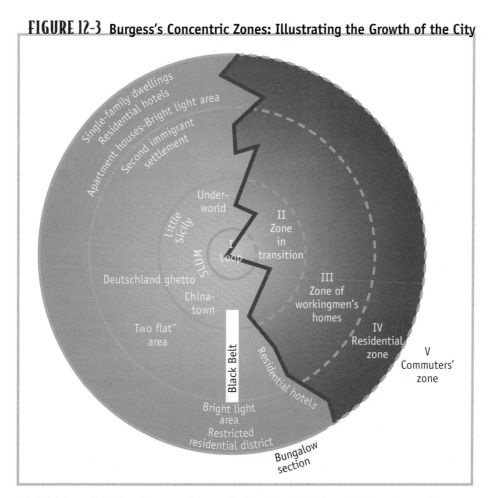

Note: This is Burgess's depiction of how concentric zones flow from the central business district as a city expands. The left side shows the city of Chicago in 1925. The jagged vertical line represents the shore of Lake Michigan.

Source: From Ernest W. Burgess, "The Growth of the City: An Introduction to a Research Project" in *The City,* Robert E. Park, Ernest W. Burgess, and Roderick D. McKenzie, eds. Chicago: University of Chicago Press, 1925. (Pages 47–62 in the 1967 edition). Reprinted with the permission of the University of Chicago Press.

THE ZONE IN TRANSITION. Burgess also noted that the most mobile areas have the most severe social problems: These areas lack a sense of community, they have fewer controls over people's behavior, and they suffer from *anomie,* or alienation. As Burgess put it, high mobility leads to promiscuity, juvenile delinquency, gangs, crime, poverty, and the breakup of families. Mobility and its accompanying problems are concentrated in Zone II, which Burgess called a *zone in transition.* He said that here we find the city's "poverty, degradation, and disease," the "underworlds of crime and vice." In Burgess's colorful phrase, this zone is "the purgatory of lost souls."

Within the zone in transition you can also find social workers, preachers, artists, and political radicals—all, says Burgess, "obsessed with the vision of a new and better world." To this, we can add that in recent years financiers have seen value in this area; and, in a process called *urban renewal,* they have constructed office buildings, financial centers, stadiums, and luxury hotels. This development moves people further *toward* the city center.

Because many cities diverge from Burgess's concentric zone model, his theory has many critics (Alihan, 1938; Harris & Ullman, 1945; La Gory, Ward, & Juravich, 1980). All cities, however, have *zones of functional specialties*—areas dominated by a type of business or activity—clusters of warehouses, auto dealerships, repair shops, boutiques, or fast-food restaurants. Cities also have zones that "specialize" in urban problems—skid rows, red-light districts, and regions of high crime and delinquency.

The functionalist approach claims that a city's problems are temporary. Over time, a city will absorb its dispossessed and poor and equip them for a better life. Movement in and away from the city is functional.

Conflict Theory

CLASS CONFLICT AND URBAN PROBLEMS. Conflict theorists argue that functionalists overlook basic class conflict that underlies urban problems. Manuel Castells (1977, 1983, 1989), for example, says that the problems that our cities face are the consequence of our capitalistic system. Mom-and-pop storefronts get bought out by more powerful businesses. Today, business leaders often run for office—dictating government policy.

As Castells points out, building interstate highways serviced the wealthy. In the early 1900s, capitalists built multistory buildings to house their factories. When assembly-line techniques were developed, these tall buildings became obsolete: It was inefficient to move raw materials and manufactured goods from one floor to another. Interstate highways (or expressways), built at taxpayer expense, enabled factory owners to relocate their production to the suburbs, where lower land prices and taxes allowed them to build single-story factories. These highways also allowed the corporate elite to maintain access to the city. There they could do business with the marketing and financial institutions while enjoying cultural benefits, such as professional sports, theaters, and concerts.

Moving factories and offices out of the city led to its ultimate decline. This flight by corporate management and skilled workers ravished the city's tax base, crippling the city's ability to maintain services and help the many poor who were left behind. Furthermore, corporate leaders voted against proposals designed to aid cities. In effect, corporate leaders abandoned areas they no longer needed and left the poor to fend for themselves.

The city remains the repository of the poor and powerless. Adjacent to resurrected areas live the huddled masses—the destitute in an affluent society. The poor are oppressed by leaders who pursue their own political and economic interests. The underclass can threaten the stability of society if they riot. This, in turn, threatens the position of the powerful and privileged. As a consequence, the police keep a sharp eye on the urban poor. Legions of social workers are dispatched into their midst, not from altruism, say conflict theorists, but to keep the poor quiet and preserve the status quo.

Research Findings

As we examine research findings, let's first consider alienation and community in the city and then look in depth at the decline of the inner city, urban violence, and the changes that are affecting cities in the United States.

Alienation in the City

GEMEINSCHAFT* AND *GESELLSCHAFT*.** From early on, sociologists were fascinated by the sharp contrast between the intimacy and community of village life and the anonymity and self-centeredness of urban life. In the 1880s, Ferdinand Tönnies noted that agricultural people share a sense of community because they share the same activities and values. Tönnies (1957) used the term ***Gemeinschaft to refer to the bonds of intimacy and shared traditions that unite people in rural areas. He used the term ***Gesellschaft*** to refer to the impersonality and self-interests associated with urban areas. (In German, *Gemeinschaft* means "community"; *Gesellschaft* means "society.")

IMPERSONALITY AND SELF-INTEREST. Impersonality and self-interest are ordinary characteristics of the bustling city. As you traverse city streets, you can expect people to avoid needless interaction with others, to be absorbed in their own affairs. These are normal

adjustments people have made to strangers with whom they temporarily share the same urban space. Sometimes, however, these characteristics of urban life are carried to extremes. The following event made national headlines when it occurred, upsetting the entire country:

> Twenty-eight-year-old Catherine Genovese, who was known as Kitty in her Queens neighborhood, was returning home from work. After parking her car, a man grabbed her. Kitty screamed, "Oh my God! He stabbed me! Please help me!"
>
> For more than half an hour, thirty-eight respectable, law-abiding citizens watched the killer stalk and stab Kitty in three separate attacks. Twice the sudden glow from their bedroom lights frightened him off. Each time he returned, sought her out, and stabbed her again. Not one person telephoned the police during the assault.
>
> When interviewed by the police, the witnesses said: "I didn't want to get involved," "We thought it was a lovers' quarrel," "I don't know," and "I was tired. I went back to bed." (*New York Times,* March 26, 1964)

It is possible that this incident was exaggerated, that due to darkness, distance, and obstructions people didn't understand that Kitty was being attacked ("Kitty Genovese," 2005). Regardless, anyone living in a large city understands that danger is a common element in city life. Even traffic accidents can breed serious **road rage:** violent behavior by a driver of an automobile.

> In crowded traffic on a bridge going into Detroit, Deletha Word bumped the car ahead of her. The damage was minor, but the driver, Martell Welch, jumped out. Cursing, he pulled Deletha from her car, pushed her onto the hood, and began beating her. Martell's friends got out to watch. One of them held Deletha down while Martell took a car jack and smashed Deletha's car. Scared for her life, Deletha broke away, fleeing to the bridge's railing. Martell and his friends taunted her, shouting, "Jump, bitch, jump!" Deletha plunged to her death. Whether she jumped or fell is unknown. (Stokes & Zeman, 1995)

HOW CITIES UNDERMINE COMMUNITY. How does the city cause alienation? In a classic essay, sociologist Louis Wirth (1938) said that urban dwellers live anonymous lives marked by segmented and superficial encounters. This undermines kinship and neighborhood, the traditional bases of social control and feelings of solidarity and identification with others. Urbanites then grow aloof and indifferent to other people's problems. In short, the personal freedom that the city offers comes at the cost of alienation.

Community in the City

The city is not inevitably alienating. Most drivers who witnessed the tragedy that befell Deletha Word did nothing. But after Deletha went over the railing, two motorists jumped in after her, risking injury and their own lives in a futile attempt to save her. Some urbanites, then, are more communal than alienating.

See For Yourself

Visit the World Bank at
http://youthink.worldbank.org/issues/urbanization/
▶ Investigate urbanization issues that affect people around the world who live in cities.

Urban life can be alienating. To feel anonymous in a crowd of strangers can make people grow aloof and indifferent to other people's problems.

THE GANS RESEARCH. Sociologist Herbert Gans, a symbolic interactionist, was so impressed with the sense of community in his research that he titled his book *The Urban Villagers* (1962):

> After a few weeks of living in the West End, my observations—and my perceptions of the area—changed drastically. The search for an apartment quickly indicated that the individual units were usually in much better condition than the outside or the hallways of the buildings. Subsequently, in wandering through the West End, and in using it as a resident, I developed a kind of selective perception, in which my eye focused only on those parts of the area that were actually being used by people. Vacant buildings and boarded-up stores were no longer so visible, and the totally deserted alleys or streets were outside the set of paths normally traversed, either by myself or by the West Enders. The dirt and spilled-over garbage remained, but, since they were concentrated in street gutters and empty lots, they were not really harmful to anyone and thus were not as noticeable as during my initial observations.
>
> Since much of the area's life took place on the street, faces became familiar very quickly. I met my neighbors on the stairs and in front of my building. And, once a shopping pattern developed, I saw the same storekeepers frequently, as well as the area's "characters" who wandered through the streets everyday on a fairly regular route and schedule. In short, the exotic quality of the stores and the residents also wore off as I became used to seeing them.

In short, Gans found community in Boston—there people identified with the area and with one another. Its residents enjoyed networks of friends and acquaintances. Despite the area's substandard buildings, most residents chose to live there. *To them, this was a low-rent district, not a slum.*

Most West Enders had low-paying, insecure jobs. Unlike the middle class, these people didn't care about their "address." The area's inconveniences were something they put up with in exchange for cheap housing. In general, they were content with their neighborhood.

DISINVESTMENT. Conflict theorists trace the decline of the city to capitalists, whose policies damaged cities and encouraged suburbanization. Banks and savings and loan associations tightened this noose by **redlining,** refusing to lend money for mortgages in areas they considered undesirable (Squires, 2003). (Loan officers used to draw a "red line" around neighborhoods they considered bad risks.) Redlined areas are usually located in the inner city.

As sociologist John Palen (2005) noted, redlining creates a *self-fulfilling prophecy*. When banks refuse to finance the sale of homes in the area, only people with cash or those who are eligible for government loans are able to buy homes. With few buyers, the inventory of homes for sale builds up, and prices drop. With home prices dropping and banks refusing to make loans for improvements, homeowners stop remodeling and making repairs to their homes. As the neighborhood declines, it justifies the decisions of the lending officials to avoid the area because it is a "bad risk." Bankers, of course, insist that **disinvestment,** their withdrawal of investments from an area, is the *result* of deteriorating housing, not its cause.

Redlining is now illegal, but it is still practiced behind the scenes:

> "It just doesn't pay," said Linda Kutz as she looked mournfully around her. "This used to be a good business. I could get good rents and keep my building up. I knew my tenants, and they respected me. But now—nothing but animals!" Linda muttered as she looked despairingly at the shambles of what had been a nice apartment just a few days before.

Like many other urban landlords, Linda Kutz is abandoning her apartment building. She is caught between the cross-pressures of high taxes, building codes, tenants who damage her property, and costly eviction processes.

ABANDONMENT. Each year, landlords abandon thousands of **housing units**—places of residence such as houses or apartments. With some of these buildings needing only minor repairs, why would they leave them? As Kutz indicates, vandalism, high taxes, a slow eviction process, and housing codes all play a role. Another landlord concurred:

> "Look at this building," he said, indicating the workers on the roof. "I don't know how long I can keep this up. I want to provide a nice place for my renters. Then comes the city inspector who says I have to add rain gutters. Every time someone moves in, an inspector examines my building. No one's ever said anything about gutters before. The building is over a hundred years old and has never had rain gutters. Why does it suddenly need them now?"

All these factors add up to higher risk and, sometimes, financial loss. Unable to find a buyer, some landlords stop paying their property taxes or making repairs. They collect as much rent as they can for as long as possible and then walk away from their deteriorating buildings. The abandoned buildings become a dangerous playground for children, a shelter for junkies, a target for looters, fun for vandals, and profit for arsonists.

ARSON. Some owners of buildings and businesses who face huge losses see fire as a solution. Those afraid to set the fire themselves hire "**torches**" (professional arsonists), who are seldom apprehended because arson often destroys the evidence of the crime. Many insurance companies prefer to pay off a blaze of "suspicious origin" and recover the cost in their general rates than to fight a case in court. Some cynically call arson the "modern way of refinancing."

Even when a company does fight a claim that is obviously arson, it can lose. As an insurance claims agent told Jim Henslin during an investigation:

> We won't have to pay on this one. The fire began in the basement on a pile of clothes. There was no source of fire [heating element or electricity] there. The insured was paid off on another fire just three years ago. The police have the case.

Henslin talked to the detective in charge of the case. The insured had lost his job, and the mortgage holder had begun foreclosure (the legal process of getting possession of the property), but the man stuck to his story. ("I don't know anything. I wasn't there.") The company paid.

Urban arson receives little publicity or concern. The public shows little interest, and often neither do the police. Functionalists can well see the core truth in the statement

Issues in Social Problems
A FAILED EXPERIMENT: CREATING ALIENATION

THE OLD EXPERIMENT: HIGH-RISE SEGREGATED HOUSING

Let's look at the problem of public housing in the 1980s and 1990s.

It is a summer afternoon in the Robert Taylor Homes in Chicago, no different from most other days in the nation's largest public housing complex, except for the intense heat.

Shots crackle from pistols near a play area. Laughter turns to screams as children dart for cover behind buildings and in stairwells crowded with craps shooters and winos.

The gunfire is soon over. The angry men bent on shooting each other have run off. The dice games and wine drinking resume. The basketball hoops again rattle above the scorching asphalt, and the children return to the dilapidated play equipment.

One of the few remaining buildings of Chicago's Cabrini-Green public housing project.

Fifteen blocks long and one block wide, Robert Taylor Homes was the world's largest public housing project. Taylor Homes consisted of 28 identical red and cream 16-story towers surrounded on all sides by other impoverished neighborhoods. Many residents viewed Taylor Homes as a separate city within Chicago, an island of poverty adrift in a city of plenty.

Mrs. Wallace had lived in Taylor Homes from the time they were built. "There are a lot of good people here," she said. "They go to work, come home, and close their doors. They take the attitude that if nobody bothers them, they won't bother anybody. They try to get their kids to do the right thing, which is hard when so many parents don't."

John Smith remembers better times at Robert Taylor Homes. He reared his children here. "And I sent all twelve to college," he said proudly with a deep, resonant voice. "I worked two jobs to do it, but I did it. I was firm with them and demanded that they do the right thing. They never gave me any trouble."

But by the 1990s, things were different. "Things are tense now. The young people have nothing to do. No jobs. No recreation programs. So they are rowdy. They don't go to school. They make trouble," said Mr. Smith, then 68 years old, from the chair in which he sat each day.

As he talked, a young man walked by several times wielding a metal pipe. Mr. Smith paused and gave the youth a stern look. The youth left.

"You have to watch them or they will hurt you," he said. "If they think you have something, they will slash you or knock you over the head and take it."

Asked why he didn't move, Mr. Smith said, "Son, things are bad all over. It's not just here."

One hundred fifty thousand people lived in Chicago's public housing. Single mothers occupied most of the units. Most of the residents were unemployed. Gangs controlled many of the buildings. The police gave up enforcing laws against drugs and burglaries. The head of Chicago's public housing put it this way:

As long as they don't go after and injure innocent people, it's fine. I can't stop them from using drugs. Everybody belongs to a gang. They are going to burglarize apartments to support their habits. You send a message. You don't say you can do these things, but over time they know that the only thing that's going to set me off is when they start hurting innocent people.

Robert Taylor Homes and Cabrini-Green public housing projects were badly mismanaged. Repairs weren't being made, rats infested apartments, and elevators broke down, leaving elderly and disabled people unable to get to upper-level apartments.

THE NEW EXPERIMENT: MIXED INCOME INTEGRATED HOUSING

After many attempts at reform, authorities finally gave up on public housing projects. They turned them over to the wrecking ball. The last of the Robert Taylor buildings was demolished in 2006. Its residents were dispersed into a series of low-rise buildings, none over four stories. Another key change in the city's public housing is not the height but the mixed-income format of the new dwellings. This new social experiment blends a variety of incomes.

Based on Sheppard (1980); J. Anderson (1995); "Granddaddy of All . . . " (2006).

Arson as a way of refinancing is discussed in the text. This fire at a landmark tavern in Beardstown, Illinois, was investigated as arson.

that "arson is the modern way of refinancing." Perhaps it is functional for society to let entrepreneurs refinance their losses by spreading the cost over tens of thousands of policyholders.

Urban Violence: Youth Gangs

In addition to physical decline, urban centers also house violence. We will examine violence by youth gangs and violence in the schools.

The topic of gangs intrigues both the public and sociologists. There is no such thing as *the* urban gang. There are many types of gangs, and not all of them are violent. In fact, not all of them are criminal. Some gangs protect their neighborhood, even help bring about social change that gives the poor a shot at the American dream—or at least try to make life better for people who are clinging precariously to the edge of society (DiChiara & Chabot, 2003; Martinez, 2003). Our focus, though, is on gang *violence*.

THE THRASHER STUDY: HOW GANGS FORM. Gangs have been a sociological topic for almost a century. In the 1920s, sociologist Frederic Thrasher studied 1,313 gangs in Chicago. He (1927) found that gangs start as ordinary play groups that begin competing for space in crowded and deteriorating areas of the city. The boys band together to gain a valued identity. The group then becomes the impetus for criminal activities.

Over and over sociologists have documented that it is primarily lower-class boys who are involved in gangs. They have also documented the *alternative identity* that gangs offer. Let's try to understand why gangs offer such an identity for lower-class boys.

THE COHEN STUDY: THE REJECTION OF MIDDLE-CLASS NORMS. In another classic study, sociologist Albert Cohen (1955) found that lower-class boys are measured by middle-class standards, but they lack the socially approved means to meet those standards. The schools these boys attend are immersed in middle-class values. They are run by middle-class teachers and administrators who use middle-class standards to judge the boys' speech, behavior, and performance on tests. The boys feel that they don't fit in, that their teachers look down on them. In their own defense, they form a gang of like-minded members. Their rejection of middle-class standards includes rejecting school standards and authority figures.

THE MILLER STUDY: SUBSTITUTE VALUES. Walter Miller (1958) examined the norms that make gangs so attractive to lower-class boys. He found that boys use gang membership to

build identities on the basis of six values: trouble, excitement, toughness, intelligence, autonomy, and fate. Making trouble not only provides excitement, but also allows the boys to show that they are tough, smart, and independent. The boys also view their lives as controlled by fate: If they get hurt or killed, this is simply because their number came up. The boys confer status on one another according to how they perform. In short, through gangs lower-class boys reject the world of middle-class values that seems to crush their spirits with constant rejection and failure, replacing it with a world of alternative values. Thriving in a gang offers the boys the opportunity to achieve a sense of self-worth through the positive recognition of peers.

SUPERGANGS. For the most part, all gangs in these classic studies were groups of adolescents who did nothing worse than get high, skip school, write graffiti, steal from parked cars, get into a fight now and then, and vandalize property. We say "nothing worse" because today we have **supergangs** such as the Crips and Bloods. These gangs, and many others like them, not only steal but also kill. The Crips and Bloods now have affiliated gangs in most major cities.

THE PRINCIPLES BENEATH THE FORMS. The El Rukins/Black P. Stone Nation, the Gangster Disciples, and the Vice Lords, as well as the more infamous Crips and Bloods, are all based on the rejection of middle-class norms. The names of gangs may change over time, but the basic principles on which they operate and by which they offer such attraction to lower-class boys remain the same.

GLOBAL ASPECTS OF GANGS. Gangs have been around for centuries, and there are local gangs in every large urban area around the globe. Today there are Muslim gangs in Norway, Latino gangs in Honduras, and Hells Angels in Germany. The MS-13 gang in Los Angeles has expanded to El Salvador, and gangs tied to Chinese Triads are found in Los Angeles; Russian gangs operate in Chicago; the Crips are in Holland; and Mexican gangs have moved into San Diego (Hagedorn, 2005).

Just as sociological studies have documented how gangs attract lower-class youth, so on the global level, gangs attract the disenfranchised, the neglected, those who are left out of the legitimate political process. Beyond establishing means of self-identity, which they do, on the global level gangs provide an alternative political structure. They give power to those who are bypassed by political systems. In some instances, the power of the gangs is so great that the established political powers must take them into account when they develop social policy (Hagedorn, 2005).

GIRL GANGS. Lower-class girls also find the middle-class values of school oppressive. For them, too, the contrarian values of gangs beckon. The girls reject the "soft feminism" of the middle class, replacing it with tough and aggressive behavior. Within their own gang, however, they are expected to be submissive to male gang members (Vigil, 2002). Girls are often **diced in:** When girls are initiated into the gang, the boys require them to have sex with several of the male gang members, corresponding to the number that appears on the roll of the dice. For the most part, girls play supportive roles in the boys' gangs; they hide weapons and drugs, providing alibis and sex. Almost all girl gangs, then, are counterparts of boy gangs (Vigil, 2002).

An occasional independent all-girl gang does appear on the urban scene, but this is unusual (Nurge, 2003). An example is *Las Locas* (the Crazies), an all-girl gang in Los Angeles. The members of this gang are unpredictably dangerous. Although such cases are rare, some girls will kill another just to get a pair of earrings (Faison, 1991).

NEIGHBORHOODS. It is difficult for some to understand what life is like in a lower-class neighborhood. Lower- and middle-class youths live in different worlds. To better understand the violence of youth gangs, we need to begin by analyzing the neighborhoods from which most gang members come.

Because gang members live in neighborhoods where violence is a normal part of life, they have learned an entirely different way of perceiving the world (Yonas et al., 2006).

Girl gangs have become more common, and not only in the United States. These girls in El Salvador, members of Gang 18, are making the symbol 18 with their hands.

They expect that people will be violent toward them and that they ought to be violent toward others first. Life is uncertain, violence routine, and killing normal. Violence is normative, the expected means by which members prove themselves and by which they receive valued recognition as worthy people (Scott, 1994). Initiation into a gang can require that an initiate do an anonymous drive-by shooting or be **jumped in**— beat up by fellow gang brothers (Vigil, 2002). Violence, then, is a means for expressing membership.

Urban Violence: Schools

That American schools would need guards and metal detectors to protect their students used to be unthinkable. The worst kids in school used to carry a switchblade, but today those kids take guns to class. Some bring guns to defend themselves from classmates who carry guns! As one 15-year-old in junior high school said, "You gotta be prepared— people shoot you for your coat, your rings, chains, anything." He then proudly displayed his "defensive" .25-caliber Beretta (Hackett, 1988).

And then, there are Columbine High School, Virginia Tech, and Northern Illinois University—schools where students have gone on killing sprees. In their wake, they have left dead students and teachers—and fear on the campus and in the community.

In some grade schools, teachers practice "duck-and-cover" drills to protect children from neighborhood shootings (Mydans, 1991). In some high schools and even middle schools, rapes and assaults go unreported. Guilt stops some teachers from reporting assaults; they feel that the assault would not have occurred if they had somehow done a better job in the classroom. Other teachers find it easier to ignore an attack, because assault cases usually require at least three appearances in court. Still others don't report attacks because they fear retribution. Often there are no witnesses, and it is the teacher's word against the student's.

Except for mass shooting incidents, school violence seldom comes to the attention of the police or public. School administrators want to run "a nice, quiet school." The last thing they want is to arouse the community with stories of violence or unsafe conditions at school. Administrators downplay incidents. This relieves pressure on them and protects their jobs, for one sign of their success—or failure—is the amount of violence in their schools.

Urban Violence: Riots

The year was 1747. The place was the bustling port of Boston. The Royal Navy had been impressing (kidnapping legally) local men for forced service. Fed up, seamen and others armed themselves and rioted. For three days, they dominated the city, forcing the governor to flee. The mobs freed the impressed men, gaining another victory for the urban rioters of the time.

RIOTS IN HISTORY. Urban riots reach far back in history. The book of Genesis in the Old Testament recounts a riot in the city of Gomorrah. Two thousand years ago, riots occurred in the city of Rome. In the United States, riots have been with us since the 1700s. According to historian Richard Brown (1969), rioting by the lower-class urban population bred the American Revolution.

In their early history, Baltimore, Philadelphia, New York, and Boston were the sites of numerous riots. During the 1830s–1850s, at least 35 major riots and numerous minor ones took place in these cities. There were labor riots, anti-Catholic riots, and riots by volunteer firemen (Wyatt-Brown, 2003).

COMMUNAL RIOTS. In a **race riot,** racial–ethnic groups direct violence against one another. Competition for jobs often underlies race riots, especially the riots of Whites against Blacks (Brown, 1969). Until the 1960s, the most common type of race riot was the **communal riot.** In this type, also called a *contested area riot,* one group would contest another's control of an area of the city. According to sociologist Morris Janowitz (1970b), the cities in which communal riots occurred contained large numbers of migrants—both African American and White—who were living in segregated areas. The police had little capacity to deal with outbreaks of mass violence and often conspired with White rioters against African Americans.

BACKGROUND FACTORS AND PRECIPITATING INCIDENTS. Sociologists note that riots are often preceded by tension between groups. Then comes a **precipitating incident,** something that triggers the riot. For example, between 1917 and 1919 Whites bombed more than 27 homes of Chicago Blacks. None of these incidents led to riots. What did, however, was the death of a 17-year-old Black youth who swam into an area of Lake Michigan used exclusively by Whites. When other Blacks challenged the Whites' use of this part of the beach, crowds of Blacks and Whites began throwing stones at one another. The Black youth, still in the water, drowned. Rumors abounded that he had been stoned to death, and Blacks rioted. Thirty-eight people were killed, 537 injured, and about 1,000 left homeless.

Until 1960, riots had been sporadic, but during the 1960s riots erupted across the nation—in Harlem, Brooklyn, the Watts neighborhood of Los Angeles, Newark, and Detroit, among other locations. Instead of challenging the control of some area of the city, as in communal riots, the rioters looted stores. Because of this, such riots are referred to as **commodity riots** (Janowitz, 1970a). Commodity riots peaked in 1967, with 41 major riots and 123 lesser ones.

So why does one incident set off a riot, whereas others do not? Social psychologists Kurt and Gladys Lang (1968) identified two necessary conditions for an incident to precipitate a riot: It must (1) be perceived as a threat to the group's well-being and (2) evoke moral outrage. For example, a precipitating incident has often been a confrontation between African Americans and White police officers. Rumors sweep the area, and the incident escalates. As one group concludes that "this time it has gone too far, and we won't take it any more," violence erupts.

THE LOS ANGELES RIOT OF 1992. The riot in Los Angeles in 1992 followed this scenario. Background conditions included the long-standing poverty of African Americans and Latinos and their oppression by the police. The precipitating incident was the acquittal of the policemen accused of assaulting Rodney King, an African American who was being arrested on traffic violations. A passerby had videotaped the police as they beat King. The videotape showed the officers as they pounded King with their nightsticks. Television stations repeatedly broadcast the videotape to stunned audiences across the nation. *Everyone* knew that the police officers were guilty.

Although riots are often thought of as a recent development in the United States, they are rooted in our history. Shown on the left is a riot in New York City in 1863. Rioters also looted stores—another behavior that is not new. The photo on the right is from a riot in Los Angeles 1992, discussed in the text.

Within minutes of the acquittal verdict, angry crowds gathered. That night, mobs set fire to businesses in south-central Los Angeles, and looting and arson began in earnest. The rioting spread to other cities—Atlanta, Tampa, and even Madison, Wisconsin, and Las Vegas, Nevada. The LA riot was spectacular—4,000 fires; dramatic footage of looting and beatings; the president federalizing the California National Guard and ordering the Seventh Infantry, SWAT teams, and the FBI to Los Angeles; and 60 dead, the most victims of a riot in the United States since the Civil War. Sociologically the LA riot was "routine," following patterns often identified.

THE RESULTS OF RIOTS. Beyond the obvious—the burning, looting, and killing—what are the usual results of riots? First, rioting can have positive consequences: Federal funds sometimes flow to the inner city. Most positive consequences, however, are short-lived. Second, as sociologists George Simpson and Milton Yinger noted (1972), riots increase segregation, for Whites flee the area. Although rioters may gain a sense of having struck a blow for freedom, they have only indicated their need for freedom: They have not shaken the basic institutions that support their oppression and enforce their poverty (Piven & Cloward, 1977). Not one riot in the history of the United States has eliminated the underlying discrimination and poverty that influence riots.

THE CONTINUING PROBLEM. Because background conditions remain—poverty, segregation, and the lack of opportunities—and precipitating events are bound to occur, riots have likely not come to an end in the United States. Periods of calm will inevitably be followed by more riots. When this occurs, there will be more commissions, more studies, and more recommendations—all about the same as those we've already had. The same background conditions will be newly "discovered," the same hand-wringing will occur, the same public denunciations of deplorable conditions will be uttered by politicians and other public officials; money will be funneled into emergency federal programs for the inner city, which will give the appearance of solving the problem. These will be but temporary measures. When the inner city is quiet, and some of it rebuilt, there will be no headlines about the debilitating poverty, the hopelessness and despair. The rest of the nation will go about its business as usual, with the inner city off the national radar, out of sight and out of mind. However, the same underlying background conditions will remain, festering in frustration and anger, destined to be ignited yet again by some other unexpected precipitating incident.

The City in Change

In addition to violence and general decline, American cities face extensive change. In this section we will examine changes in government, the emerging megalopolis, and the brightening of the sunbelt.

THE END OF THE CITY? "Are U.S. cities becoming obsolete?" John Teaford (1986), an urban historian, posed this question. He was referring to the problems we have reviewed here and in earlier chapters—gangs, rape, murder, drug addiction—that often make American cities threatening, alienating places to live. Some inner cities have become so frightening that most people avoid them. Locked in these pockets of poverty, many inner-city residents live short, brutal lives.

Although cities face severe challenges, they are located on valuable land, which draws resources for renewal when the price is right. Just as the World Trade Center will be replaced after its destruction, so U.S. cities will be renewed after they reach a certain point of decay. Consider the reversal of fortunes in Harlem, the topic of the Thinking Critically box on the next page.

GOVERNING THE CITY. The city must be governed. The **political machine**—an organization headed by a "boss" that operates behind the scenes to circumvent the city's official procedures—often manages inner city issues. In return for loyalty, the political machine distributes jobs and favors. In a practice called *patronage,* the machine puts its members on the city payroll.

Merton's Study: "Machine Politics"

In a functionalist study, sociologist Robert Merton (1968) examined big-city "machine politics." He wanted to know why, despite repeated attempts at reform, the political machine was able to continue year after year. Merton understood that (1) something does not exist in a society unless it contributes to that society, and (2) no part of society exists in isolation; each part is related to the other parts of the social system.

Merton found that the political machine helped three groups: the disadvantaged, businesspeople, and individuals. The machine helped the disadvantaged obtain food, welfare, jobs, scholarships, and legal assistance when children ran afoul of the law or when bill collectors became too threatening. Those who received such favors knew without question whom to vote for in the next election.

Businesspeople also needed favors. They wanted to bypass building codes and bureaucratic regulations that impeded their efforts to expand their businesses. In return for under-the-table payoffs, the political boss would pull strings at the appropriate government agency. The boss served as a mediator between the demands of urban bureaucrats and the needs of businesspeople.

The machine also helped the third group, people who wanted to move up the social-class ladder. Ambitious people always confront obstacles in their pursuit of success, and the ambitious poor are no exception. They don't have the money to start their own businesses, and many don't have the grades to attend professional schools. In return for their loyalty, the machine helped some get jobs at local businesses. Others went to work for the machine.

In short, Merton found that the political machine existed because the official channels of society failed to provide needed services; the machine stepped in to fill the void left by the more culturally approved structures of society.

The Decline of the Political Machine

The machine, which had dominated politics during the first half of the 20th century, gradually declined. Here is why:

1. Immigration slowed in the middle part of the 20th century. This removed a major function of the machine (serving unmet needs in return for loyalty) and undermined one of its major bases of power.
2. Education increased. As many people moved into the mainstream of society, they became less dependent on favors from the machine.
3. Suburbanization occurred. As Whites and jobs left the city, the machine lost the broad revenue base on which its power depended.
4. Civil service laws were passed. As city workers came under the protection of these laws, it became difficult for the machine to demand their loyalty.
5. New standards of city management came into vogue. The public wanted the heads of city agencies to be professionals rather than political operatives being rewarded for their service.

RECLAIMING THE CITY: THE NEW HARLEM

The story is well known. The inner city is filled with crack, crime, and corruption. It stinks from foul, festering garbage strewn on the streets and piled up around burned-out buildings. Only those who have no choice live in this desolate, despairing environment where danger lurks around every corner.

What is not so well known is that affluent African Americans are reclaiming some of these areas.

Howard Sanders was living the American Dream. After earning a degree from Harvard Business School, he took a position with a Manhattan investment firm. He lived in an exclusive apartment on Central Park West, but he missed Harlem, where he had grown up. He moved back to Harlem, along with his wife and daughter.

African American lawyers, doctors, professors, and bankers are doing the same.

What's the attraction? The first is nostalgia, a cultural identification with the Harlem of legend and folklore. It was here that Black writers and artists lived in the 1920s, here that the blues and jazz attracted young and accomplished musicians.

The second reason is a more practical one. Harlem offers housing value. Five-bedroom homes with 6,000 square feet are available. Some feature Honduran mahogany. Some brownstones are only shells and have to be renovated; others are in good condition. Prices, though, have soared.

What is happening is the rebuilding of a community. Some people who "made it" want to be role models. They want children in the community to see them going to and returning from work.

When the middle class moved out of Harlem, so did its amenities. Now that young professionals are moving back in,

"Brownstones" in a gentrified Harlem neighborhood. This photo was taken on West 132nd Street.

the amenities are returning, too. There were no coffee shops, restaurants, jazz clubs, florists, copy centers, dentist and optometrist offices, or art galleries—the types of things urbanites take for granted. Now there are.

The police have also returned, changing the character of Harlem. Their more visible presence and enforcement of laws have shut down the open-air drug markets. With residents running a high risk of arrest if they carry guns, the shootouts that used to plague this area have become a thing of the past. With the enforcement even of laws against public urination, the area has become much safer, further attracting the middle class.

The same thing is happening on Chicago's West Side and in other American cities.

The drive to find community—to connect with others and with one's roots—is strong. As an investment banker who migrated to Harlem said, "It feeds my soul."

"But at what cost?" ask others. This change might be fine for investment bankers and professionals who want to move back and try to rediscover their roots, but what about the people who are displaced? Gentrification always has a cost: residents of an area being pushed out as the area becomes middle class and more expensive. Tenant associations have sprung up to protest the increase in rents and the displacement of residents.

The "invasion–succession cycle," as sociologists call it, is continuing, this time with a twist—a flight back in.

Sources: Based on Cose (1999); McCormick (1999); Scott (2001); Taylor (2002); Leland (2003); Hampson (2005).

The political machine may be less powerful, but it isn't dead. City bosses, sometimes called "power brokers," continue to operate behind the scenes of city politics. New Jersey is famous for continuing this tradition (Kocieniewski & Sullivan, 2006). In Boston, rumors abound about political connections so corrupt that during the construction of a highway tunnel (the "big dig") millions of dollars were siphoned off for payoffs. The machine might even be due for a resurgence. Our cities are again flooded with immigrants, legal ones as well as millions of undocumented workers from Mexico and central and South America. Their unmet needs may be best met by the renewal of the political machine.

The New City Management ▪ In most cases, the political machine has been replaced with professional city management. Mayors or city managers head a complex bureaucracy of urban departments. Each department is assigned a particular task and works fairly independently of the others. Communication often breaks down, and the result can be disastrous (Lowi, 1977). Here's an example from Granada, Spain. The rundown buildings on one of its main streets were an eyesore. To present a better image to tourists, the city spent huge amounts painting and repairing the concrete, iron, and stonework on these buildings. The results were impressive. The only problem was that another unit of the government had slated these same buildings for demolition (Arías, 1993).

The Transition to Minority Leadership ▪ Another major change in city governance is the transition of power from Whites to African Americans and Latinos. Data show that in 1964, there were only 70 elected African American officials at all levels of government in the United States. Today there are 9,000. From 70 to 9,000 in 40 years! Latinos have also increased their total, to more than 4,000 (Eisinger, 1980; *Statistical Abstract*, 2006, Table 404).

Sociologist Peter Eisinger (1980) studied this transition to minority power. If a city is to be well-governed, all major groups must cooperate. If Whites were to withdraw their cooperation from an elected minority mayor, winning control of the formal apparatus of government would be a hollow victory. To see what happened after African Americans were elected as mayors of Detroit and Atlanta, Eisinger interviewed the business, political, and social leaders of these cities. Instead of engaging in confrontational politics, the White elite had chosen to cooperate and build coalitions.

The Megalopolis

MERGING CITIES. Another major change is the development of the **megalopolis**—urban areas spilling into one another. Small towns and cities have become interconnected. The first U.S. megalopolis runs from Boston to Washington, D.C., and includes New York City, Philadelphia, and Baltimore. It covers 10 states, the District of Columbia, and hundreds of local governments. Areas between Chicago and Cleveland and between San Francisco and San Diego are now becoming megalopolises.

These metropolitan areas are so intertwined that some people use air shuttles to taxi back and forth between the part of the megalopolis they work in and the part they live in. Air shuttles tie Washington, D.C., New York City, and Boston together. From dawn to dusk, commuters can catch a flight every few minutes between these cities. As sociologist John Palen (2005) has observed, in some instances these air shuttles make it faster to travel from city to city than to travel between parts of a single large city.

EDGE CITIES. Another way that cities are expanding beyond their traditional political boundaries is through *edge cities*. This term refers to a clustering of buildings and services near the intersection of major highways (Garreau, 1991; Lang, 2003). Shopping malls, hotels, office parks, and residential areas overlap boundaries and can include parts of several cities or towns. Edge cities are not cities in the traditional sense; that is, they are not political units with their own mayor or city manager. Well-known edge cities are Tysons Corner, Virginia (near Washington, D.C.) and Richardson–Plano (near Dallas, Texas).

Regional Restratification ▪ Another major change having a deep impact on U.S. cities is **regional restratification,** a shift in a region's population, wealth, and power. Tables 12-2 and 12-3 depict how the population has shifted. As you can see from Table 12-2, all 10 of our fastest-growing cities are in the West and South. This area is called the **sunbelt**—the southern and southwestern United States known for warm climate. Of the cities that are the slowest growing, except for New Orleans, which is an exceptional case because of Hurricane Katrina in 2005, most are in the Northeast. Table 12-3 illustrates this restratification on a *regional* basis. You can see how greatly the South and the West have grown and how little increase there has been in the Northeast and the Midwest. About half of the country's total population growth occurred in just the western states.

TABLE 12-2 The 10 Fastest-Growing and Shrinking U.S. Cities

THE 10 FASTEST-GROWING CITIES	THE 10 SHRINKING OR SLOWEST-GROWING CITIES
1. +24.3% Las Vegas, NV	1. −1.9% Buffalo-Niagara Falls, NY
2. +23.6% Cape Corl-Ft. Myers, FL	2. −1.9% Pittsburgh, PA
3. +22.2% Naples, FL	3. −1.8% Scranton, PA
4. +20.2% Provo, UT	4. −1.6% Youngstown, OH
5. +20.1% Riverside, CA	5. −1.0% Cleveland, OH
6. +19.3% Port St. Lucie, FL	6. −1.0% Charleston, WV
7. +19.2% Raleigh, NC	7. −0.9% Huntington, WV
8. +19.1% McAllen, TX	8. −0.7% Utica-Rome, NY
9. +18.9% Phoenix, AZ	9. −0.5% Dayton, OH
10. +17.8% Stockton, CA	10. −0.4% Toledo, OH

Note: Population change from 2000 to 2005.
Source: By James M. Henslin. Based on *Statistical Abstract of the United States* (2007, Table 25).

TABLE 12-3 Population Change of U.S. Regions

	MILLIONS OF PEOPLE				Increase in Millions 1970–2000	Increase in % 1970–2000
	1970	1980	1990	2000		
West	35	43	53	63	28	80%
South	63	75	85	100	37	59
Midwest	57	59	60	64	7	12
Northeast	49	49	51	54	5	10

Source: By James M. Henslin. Based on *Statistical Abstract of the United States* (various years and 2006, Table 24).

The political implications of this regional shift are enormous. Only during one other period of U.S. history—the Civil War—has the balance of power among the states undergone such rapid and deep transformation. With population growth comes wealth and political power. Regarding wealth: The tax base is growing dramatically faster in the West and the South than in other regions. Regarding power: The West and South are gaining representatives in Congress whereas the Northeast and Midwest are losing representatives. Even so, in the 2008 election, the South lost some of its new political power, because it voted primarily for Republicans, whereas the Democrats took control of the executive branch and both houses of Congress—by wide margins. How this political shift will play out, especially in a time of economic crisis, is yet to be determined.

This population shift also brings problems, the same ones that other urban centers face: traffic congestion, air pollution, urban sprawl, and pressures on educational systems. Many problems in this newly expanding sunbelt mostly affect the poor. Leaders in these expanding areas are not unlike their counterparts in the older industrial centers: Few are willing to devote many resources to help the poor.

Let's look at the potential for improving the quality of life in U.S. cities.

Social Policy

Many despair that the crises facing our cities cannot be solved. Some say that the government has simply shuffled money from one fashionable urban program to another, with little, if anything, to show for it. Some even insist that government programs

have made the problems worse. Shortly before she died, Jane Jacobs, an influential urban expert, warned that things were becoming so bad in our civilization that a dark age threatened to engulf us and our cities. She indicated, however, that there was still hope (Jacobs, 2004). A few have given up on cities altogether, saying that their problems are too complex and deep-rooted to be solved: We should abandon our cities and disperse the urban population throughout the countryside, to new, planned-from-scratch small cities with designated maximum populations (Webber, 1973).

THE ESSENTIAL CONDITION: ESTABLISHING COMMUNITY. Let's stop short of such an extreme approach and take the view that urban problems are human problems that can be solved. Although outcomes of social policy are always uncertain, there are reasonable solutions. Sociologists stress that urban policy must create a sense of community (Karp, Stone, & Yoels, 1991). If social policy does not do this, it is doomed to fail, for community is the essence of quality of life, of social control over destructive tendencies, of the social support that provides the social nurturance on which we depend. We must preserve and develop neighborhoods that people enjoy living in. We must avoid "urban renewal" programs that destroy neighborhoods and social relationships.

Granted the need and goal of preserving and developing community, then, what programs seem reasonable?

Specific Programs

Programs that can halt decline and revitalize urban areas include condominium in-filling, urban homesteading, tax reduction, enterprise zones, job deconcentration, and regional planning. Let's look at each of them.

CONDOMINIUM IN-FILLING. Many young adults of the middle class are moving away from the **snowbelt** states. The snowbelt refers to the northern region surrounding the Great Lakes. To reverse this migration, policy analyst Jan Newitt proposes **condominium in-filling,** building small energy-efficient condominiums for older urban homeowners. Because many older people stay in the homes in which they reared their children, they often have more room than they need and more maintenance than they can handle. Building condominiums in the neighborhoods in which people reared their children—where many older people want to remain—would give these older people a place to live. Helping them to remain in the area would also help stabilize the neighborhood. The larger, older housing the elderly vacate would be available to younger families with children, who have the energy, enthusiasm, and incomes needed to maintain and improve these homes. Such quality housing would encourage younger adults to remain in the city, often in the same neighborhoods where they spent their childhood. Of all programs, this has the most exciting potential because it meets the sociological requirement to foster a sense of community.

URBAN HOMESTEADING

> Paul Gasparotti bought two abandoned adjacent houses from the city for a dollar each. After tearing everything out but the exterior bricks, roof rafters, and floor joists, he connected the two houses and dug out the basement. (Kirkpatrick, 1981)

Urban homesteading is sometimes called "sweat equity," because people provide hard work rather than money for their down payment. In this program, a city sells (usually for $1) derelict housing that it has acquired by tax foreclosure. The buyer agrees to stay for some specified time, ordinarily at least 3 years, and to bring the house up to code within 2 years. As the mayor of Wilmington, Delaware, said, "We are not trying to provide housing for people. We are trying to find people for [abandoned] housing."

This program aims to stabilize neighborhoods by inspiring confidence. The idea is that salvaging buildings will encourage neighbors to stay and to improve their own properties. Deterioration will stop, neighborhoods will be rebuilt, and people will be

lured back from the suburbs. Despite its promise, however, urban homesteading has not been popular among remodeling experts. In total, 75,000 homes have been reclaimed through urban homesteading, but owners abandon approximately 150,000 homes and apartments in the inner city *each year* (Palen, 2005).

Urban homesteading is a mixed blessing, because only people with good incomes and credit can undertake the cost of rehabilitating buildings. Even if times are prosperous and the unskilled poor get jobs, what happens when they lose them? Urban homesteading threatens to displace the poor, for as a neighborhood is upgraded, rent and property values increase.

REDUCING TAXES. Another promising program is the reduction of taxes. No one wants to abandon buildings. The current tax system discourages homeowners from making improvements. Because taxes are based on a percentage of a property's assessed value, when someone improves a property, the assessed value goes up and so do the taxes. To encourage owners to improve their properties, legislation can allow city and county officials to *reduce* taxes when specified improvements are made to buildings—say, a new roof or an upgrade to the heating or electrical systems. Some may object that this policy would help landlords, and it would, but it also would make them a vehicle for improving and maintaining neighborhoods. Everyone wins. Social policies that penalize homeowners and landlords sow seeds of neighborhood degradation.

ENTERPRISE ZONES. The third program, **enterprise zones** (also known as *empowerment zones*), has been tried by most states. Here are the general principles of enterprise zones:

1. Businesses that locate in a designated zone—an economically depressed area with high unemployment—receive tax breaks and wage credits for each full-time, qualified employee they hire.
2. Businesses in the enterprise zone that improve their facilities receive credits on their property tax.
3. Businesses that locate in the enterprise zone, or that remain there, are eligible for low-interest loans.

Enterprise zones are designed to stimulate economic growth and generate employment. A danger is that enticing businesses to move into the zone may create blight in the areas they leave behind. It is also difficult to attract businesses, because the costs of additional security in the zone can outweigh the benefits offered for locating there. Another problem is that the jobs usually available in the enterprise zones are marginal, not paying enough for employees who are hired from the zone to move out.

Evaluating the results of enterprise zones has been difficult. The basic problem facing researchers is this: If you measure employment, earnings, or poverty in an enterprise zone, how do you know what they would have been if the enterprise zone had not been there? If the goal is to improve the lives of the residents in the enterprise zone, the results have been disappointing: Researchers have concluded that enterprise zones have had little impact on those who live in the zone (Ferguson, 2001).

JOB DECONCENTRATION. Another promising policy is **job deconcentration,** the rational planned location of jobs through a master plan. This policy, which helps control urban and **suburban sprawl,** presupposes a regional master plan and a regional authority to enforce it. Job deconcentration also lets planning bodies develop public transportation that serves workers outside the central city. Toronto has such a plan. Factories, offices, shopping centers, and housing subdivisions can be built only in specified areas adjacent to the city. If there is no regional authority, however, this policy is impossible, and the fierce rivalries for power and resources between our urban and suburban areas make such a policy difficult.

REGIONAL PLANNING. As you can see with job deconcentration, there is an overarching need for *regional planning* (Savitch & Vogel, 2004). Metropolitan areas are fragmented into numerous small, competing political divisions. Each jealously guards its own turf

against other jurisdictions. Governments responsible for regional development can be created without abolishing the individual, smaller governments. States, from which cities receive their charter to operate, can force cities to give some of their authority to regional bodies (such as decision making about water and sewer systems, police and fire protection, and building codes). These agencies would then implement policies for the region as a whole.

Educating the Poor

To be successful, urban programs must educate the poor. As sociologist Herbert Gans said back in the 1960s,

> The public-school system has never learned how to teach poor children, mainly because it has not needed to do so. In the past, those who could not or would not learn what the schools taught dropped out quietly and went to work. Today, such children drop out less quietly, and they cannot find work. Consequently, the schools have to learn how to hold them, not only when they drop out physically, but long before, in the early elementary grades, when they begin to drop out in spirit. (Gans, 1968, p. 292)

It is despairing to read Gans's policy suggestion made in the last century and note that there has been little or no change. As noted earlier, the educational system is still middle class, and it still bypasses the poor. Only now, with unskilled work seldom available, the educational dropouts live in greater despair—and with a greater propensity for violence.

PRINCIPLES FOR SUCCESS. When it comes to improving education, it is not that we don't have concerned teachers. We have good-hearted teachers in abundance, people with sincere intentions to make a difference in the lives of the children entrusted to their care (Gerstl-Pepin, 2006). It is that educators seldom examine the results of their teaching or probe the consequences of their educational programs with the goal of improving their teaching effectiveness with the poor. Rather, what they usually propose is the improvement of buildings or educational facilities.

Good schools for the poor require more than new buildings. Teachers must nourish their students' motivation to learn. Few poor children lack the desire to learn when they begin school. As they stay in school, however, they often come to view education as irrelevant to their lives and future. To do a better job of educating the poor, Gans (1968) pointed out that we need

1. motivated teachers
2. new teaching methods
3. smaller classes
4. innovative curricula that build on the aspirations of inner-city youth
5. a more decentralized and less bureaucratized school system
6. work-study programs
7. scholarships to encourage adult dropouts to return to school

We may wish to add cooperative learning, child care facilities, and positive reinforcement. More controversial, but quite defensible, is renewed emphasis on memorization in grade school (such as multiplication tables), a de-emphasis on "feelings of self-worth" as an educational goal and its replacement with the learning of academic subjects, and a strong trades program that leads to apprenticeships. (Why assume that every high school student should go to college?) Certainly, we can all agree that to produce an effective learning environment, violence and gang activity must be reduced—or, better, eliminated.

ABC. One successful program is ABC (A Better Chance). Financed by corporations, foundations, and individuals, ABC identifies and recruits gifted inner-city students, starting in junior high school, and matches them with top prep schools. Given scholarships, these high-performing youngsters attend schools such as Phillips Academy in

Andover, Massachusetts, and Cate Preparatory School in Carpinteria, California. The program is so successful that most graduates go on to college.

THE POTENTIAL VERSUS SHORT-TERM SOLUTIONS. ABC enrolls 1,000—2,000 students, but we need to touch the lives of more poor children. As the Thinking Critically box on the next page shows, we *can* design and implement successful programs. Although these programs appear expensive, they would pay back their cost many times over: Getting young people in school and out of criminal pursuits reduces the cost of crime and punishment. When they become working adults, these students also pay taxes.

IN SUM If we have learned anything from the recent past, it is that *replacing buildings does not cure urban ills*. Real problems remain: Poverty, crime, unemployment, dysfunctional families, gang violence, riots, arson, drug addiction, and juvenile delinquency are all conditions that are not solved by fixing or replacing old buildings. As sociologist William Julius Wilson (1987) said, the key to solving urban problems is a revitalized economic system that offers work. Perhaps the simplest summary is this: Greater access to jobs, housing, education, and justice will reduce urban problems, but those problems will persist to the same degree that these inequalities persist.

The Future of the Problem

Based on the current trends, we foresee the following trends as likely to continue.

INCREASING COSTS AND REDUCED INCOME. Many cities are confronting rising costs and demands for services in the face of reduced income. Our cities depend on federal money to finance many programs, from urban transit to gentrification. Caught in a financial squeeze, some cities have cut back on education, street cleaning, recreation programs, and activities for children and the elderly. Because reducing services, except in the poor areas of the city, upsets voters, urban governments have deferred the maintenance of their infrastructure—their sewers, bridges, water systems, and city buildings. Although this cutback is less visible, making it less subject to voter outcry, deferred maintenance borrows from the future.

THE URBAN VILLAGERS. Herbert Gans's report on urban renewal in Boston is the most well documented story of a neighborhood destroyed by urban renewal. Sixty-three percent of the families displaced were Italians, African Americans, and Hispanics. The little piece of Italy that Gans described was bulldozed in 1959—replaced by high-rise, expensive apartment buildings.

THE HOMELESS. The homeless will continue to live on our city streets, but they will be persecuted by city officials. To foster tourism and profits, politicians will disperse the homeless. This will create an outcry—there will be calls to remove the homeless from sight, to put them in "asylums" somewhere, as though hiding them might solve the problem.

HOUSING COSTS. Two major forces will increase the demand for affordable housing. First, each year about 4 million Americans turn 30, the typical first-time home-buying age (*Statistical Abstract*, 2006, Table 12). Second, the American dream of owning a home is nourished by developers and financial institutions. Middle-class Americans, although they have few children, want larger homes with more amenities (large master baths with his-and-her sinks, whirlpools, hot tubs, and so on). Although there will be fluctuations in cost, these two factors will feed urban sprawl and inflate the cost of housing.

POTENTIAL IN-MIGRATION. Higher housing costs could spearhead a change in our cities. The higher the cost of commuting to the city for work, the more attractive the lower-priced

THINKING CRITICALLY about Social Problems

EDUCATING FOR SUCCESS: REESTABLISHING COMMUNITY IN THE LEARNING PROCESS

Education is in crisis. Children are being promoted from one grade to another whether they learn or not. Some students graduate from high school illiterate, unable to even read help wanted ads. Many don't know how to do simple math, are unable to prepare a résumé, and have no idea how to prepare for a job interview. Budgets are cut, programs trimmed, teachers burned out, and students unmotivated.

"Sow the wind and reap the whirlwind," said Hosea, an Old Testament prophet. And sowing a future of illiterate children having babies and of unemployment, welfare dependency, crime, and despair will bring a whirlwind of shattered community. We can sever the nation into two, those who have and those who don't. Make this extensive enough, and it can destroy a society.

Can education make a difference in this sorry picture? How about for the most impoverished of society, the children of the inner city? To find out, a team from Yale worked with the staff and parents in two grade schools in New Haven, Connecticut. The schools were in low-income neighborhoods that were 99% Black and plagued by the usual inner-city problems. Student achievement, which had been the lowest in the city, soared to the third and fourth highest. As measured on standardized tests, the students' achievement levels jumped to 9 months *above* their grade level in one school, and 12 months ahead in the other. Attendance and behavior also improved dramatically.

How was this accomplished? First, the team made a radical assumption—that the problem was not "poor students," but, rather, the educational system. This is radical because it goes against the unspoken educational philosophy that permeates

Regardless of their backgrounds, when students are challenged educationally, they can do well. Students in this highly disciplined and demanding inner-city school in The Bronx, New York, have 9 1/2-hour school days and 2 hours of homework a night. Is it any wonder that their test scores are the highest in The Bronx?

U.S. education. It puts the responsibility on the shoulders of the staff. It made the staff responsible for meeting the needs that the children's background created. Second, the staff fostered a feeling of common cause. Leadership was transferred from a central office to the grass roots—to those who worked on the daily educational problems and rubbed shoulders with the students—and this group discussed problems and made decisions together. Third, parents, staff, and students interacted frequently. This allowed students to identify with adults who valued and encouraged learning, reflecting a solid educational principle that learning is based on modeling and imitation. Fourth, a sense of community was engendered as trust, mutual respect, and a sense of common cause developed among teachers, administrators, parents, and students.

Using this same assumption—that inadequate teaching, not inadequate students, is the reason poor children do not do well in school—Jaime Escalante motivated his students in an East Los Angeles inner-city school to perform so well on national calculus tests that officials thought that they had cheated. It is obvious that students in poverty can do well—if schools teach well.

FOR YOUR CONSIDERATION

How would you apply these principles to change a troubled school in your area? What other principles from this text would you use?

Based on Comer (1986); Escalante and Dirmann (1990); Hilliard (1991); J. Levine (2004).

houses in deteriorated areas of the city. Gentrification holds the potential of reversing the exodus from the city. It may also signal another major racial–ethnic change, for it may increase the proportion of Whites in central areas. Gentrification, of course, will fuel another controversy, for it will mean accommodating the middle class at the expense of the poor, who then are displaced.

REGIONAL RESTRATIFICATION. Because our cities are undergoing restratification, their future will be region-oriented. Sunbelt cities hold the brightest future. With their influx of capital, jobs, workers, and an expanding tax base, they appear best-equipped to weather problems.

PRINCIPLES FOR SHAPING THE FUTURE. The future of our cities depends on trends yet to appear and on the social policies we adopt. The following three principles provide a solid foundation for shaping that future:

1. As a cultural center of work and play, the city offers vast potential for human happiness.
2. The city is a social creation, and so are its negative features. As such, they can be overcome.
3. To design a future that overcomes urban problems, our policies must incorporate basic human needs—social, psychological, physical, and spiritual. As stressed in this chapter, the shorthand word for this is *community*.

These three principles can help us forge a future that enhances the quality of life, maximizes human potential, and creates urban areas that satisfy the human need for community.

Population: The Problem in Sociological Perspective

Earlier in the chapter, we discussed the growth in population in the world's cities. Now let's examine current population trends and their global implications. Is population growth a social problem?

The definition of **demography**—the study of the size, composition, growth, and distribution of human populations—makes it sound like a pretty dry subject. Yet this area of sociology is anything but dry, for demographers study some of the most far-reaching changes taking place in today's world.

A STARTLING CHANGE. Changes in population are especially important. For most of history, the world's population increased in very small intervals. When Jesus Christ was born, the population of the entire world was the same as that of the United States today. In 1750, all of Europe had 140 million inhabitants. Then there was an abrupt change: Within 50 years, Europe's population jumped by 48 million. Fifty years later, in 1850, it had increased by another 68 million, reaching a total of 256 million. What caused this unprecedented change?

PUBLIC HEALTH OR THE POTATO? In 1926, G. T. Griffith argued that this increase was due to improved public health. Better medical knowledge, hospitals, housing, water, and sanitation, he said, lowered the **death rate,** the number of deaths per 1,000 people. More people lived longer, and the population increased.

Griffith's explanation is widely accepted, but some demographers suggest a different explanation. Thomas McKeown (1977), for example, claimed that the population of Europe remained low until 1750 because Europeans practiced **infanticide,** killing infants shortly after birth. This practice declined when the food supply was able to support more people.

Europeans practiced infanticide when their food supply could not support large numbers of people. Infanticide ensured that the family would not suffer starvation. When the Europeans discovered an untapped food supply, the potato, they stopped practicing infanticide, and their population increased.

Did the potato have such an impact on history? It seems so. When the Spaniards conquered South America in the 1500s, they discovered the potato, cultivated in the Andean highlands. When they brought the potato back home with them, Europeans first viewed this strange food with suspicion. As the years passed, Europeans gradually began to think of the potato as a good food. By 1800 the potato had become the main food of

the poor in northern and central Europe. This "miracle" plant expanded Europe's food supply, allowing the population to almost double in 100 years.

Demography, then, emphasizes such a relationship between population and environment. When a population increases dramatically, demographers look for changes in customs. These changes range from the adoption of new medical and sanitation practices to simple changes in diet.

THOMAS MALTHUS, THE GLOOMY PROPHET. Thomas Malthus, an English economist, viewed Europe's surge in population growth as a sign of doom. In 1798, he wrote an influential book, *An Essay on the Principle of Population.* Malthus argued that although population grows geometrically, that is, from 2 to 4 to 8 to 16 and so forth, the food supply increases only arithmetically, that is, from 1 to 2 to 3 to 4 and so on. This means that if births go unchecked, the population of the world will outstrip the food supply.

THE PESSIMISTS: THE NEW MALTHUSIANS. Malthus's conclusions are still debated today. One group, whom we call the *New Malthusians,* argue that Malthus was right. Today's situation is as grim, if not grimmer, than he ever imagined. The world's population is growing out of control. It is following an **exponential growth curve.** This means that growth doubles during equal intervals of time.

To illustrate the implications of exponential growth, sociologist William Faunce (1981, p. 84) told a parable about a man who saved a rich man's life. The rich man, of course, was very grateful, and he offered a reward:

> The man replied that he would like his reward to be spread out over a four-week period, with each day's amount being twice what he received on the preceding day. He also said he would be happy to receive only one penny on the first day. The rich man immediately handed over the penny and congratulated himself on how cheaply he had gotten by.
>
> At the end of the first week, the rich man checked to see how much he owed and was pleased to find that the total was only $1.27. By the end of the second week, he owed only $163.83. On the twenty-first day, however, the rich man was surprised to find that the total had grown to $20,971.51. When the twenty-eighth day arrived, the rich man was shocked to discover that he owed $1,342,177.28 for that day alone and that the total reward had jumped to $2,684,354.56!

This acceleration is precisely what alarms New Malthusians. They claim that we have just entered the "fourth week" of an exponential growth curve. Figure 12-4 illustrates why they think the day of reckoning is just around the corner. It took from the

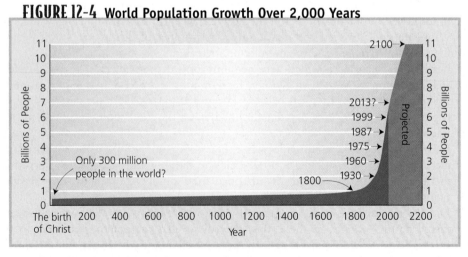

FIGURE 12-4 World Population Growth Over 2,000 Years

Sources: Modified from Piotrow 1973; McFalls 2007.

FIGURE 12-5 How Fast Is the World's Population Growing?

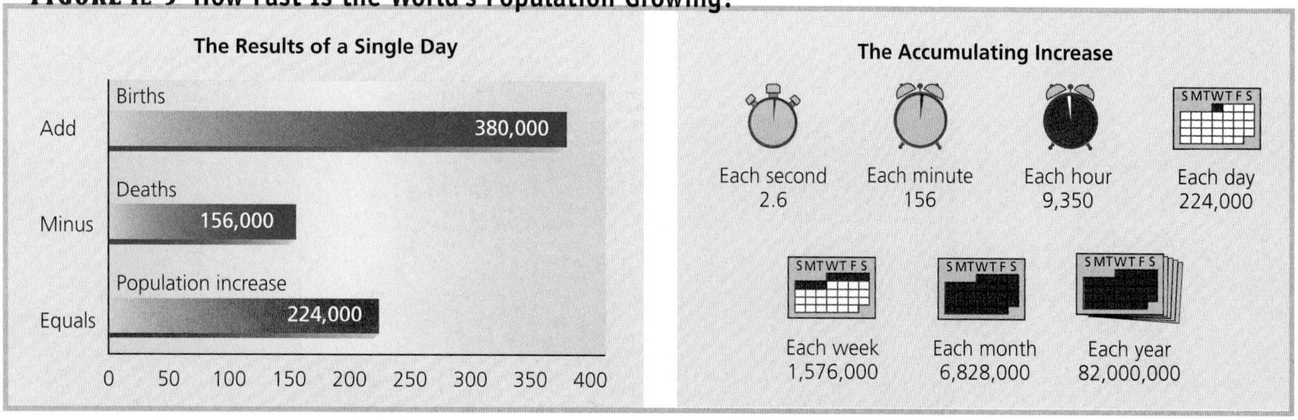

The Results of a Single Day

	Births	380,000
Add		

	Deaths	156,000
Minus		

	Population increase	224,000
Equals		

0 50 100 150 200 250 300 350 400

The Accumulating Increase

Each second	Each minute	Each hour	Each day
2.6	156	9,350	224,000

Each week	Each month	Each year
1,576,000	6,828,000	82,000,000

Source: By James M. Henslin. Based on Haub (2006) and Kent (2008).

beginning of time to 1800 for the world's population to reach its first billion. It then took only 130 years (1930) to add a second billion. Just 30 years later (1960), the world population hit 3 billion. The time it took to reach the fourth billion was only 15 years (1975). Then just 12 years later (in 1987), the total reached 5 billion, and in another 12 years it reached 6 billion (in 1999).

On average, every minute of every day, 156 babies are born. As Figure 12-5 shows, at sunset the world has 224,000 more people than it did the day before. In one year, this amounts to an increase of 82 million people. In just 4 years, the world increases by an amount greater than the entire U.S. population (Haub, 2006; *Statistical Abstract*, 2006, Table 1314). *In just the next 12 years the world's population will increase as much as it did during the first 1,800 years after the birth of Christ.*

These totals terrify New Malthusians. They are convinced we are headed toward a supply and demand crisis. In the year 2025, the population of just India, Pakistan, and Bangladesh is expected to be more than the entire world's population was 100 years ago (Haub, 2005). It is obvious that we will run out of food if we don't curtail population growth.

THE OPTIMISTS: THE ANTI-MALTHUSIANS. "You're wrong!" reply the Anti-Malthusians.

> Assume there are two germs in the bottom of a bucket, and they double in number every hour. . . . If it takes one hundred hours for the bucket to be full of germs, at what point is the bucket one-half full of germs? A moment's thought will show that after ninety-nine hours the bucket is only half full. The title of this volume [*The 99th Hour*] is not intended to imply that the United States is half full of people but to emphasize that it is possible to have "plenty of space left" and still be precariously near the upper limit. (Price, 1967, p. 4)

Anti-Malthusians say that fitting the world's current population growth onto an exponential growth curve and then projecting it into the future indefinitely is totally incorrect. This approach ignores people's intelligence and rational planning when it comes to having children. To understand what people actually do, we need to study historical records. After analyzing historical evidence we learn that people generally limit reproduction to available food. This principle applies today, as shown in the Global Glimpse box on page 431. The current "explosion" in world population, then, means that the world is producing *more food* than ever before.

To better understand future projections, consider Europe's **demographic transition.** As diagrammed in Figure 12-6 on the next page, Stage I consists of a fairly stable population—high death rates offset by high birthrates. Throughout most of its history, Europe was in Stage I. Then in about 1750 Europe entered Stage II, ushering in the "population explosion" that so frightened Malthus. Europe's population surged because death rates

FIGURE 12-6 The Demographic Transition

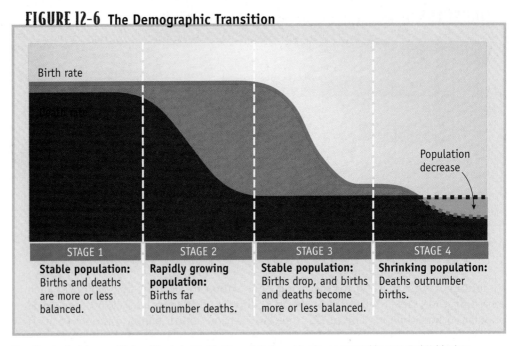

STAGE 1	STAGE 2	STAGE 3	STAGE 4
Stable population: Births and deaths are more or less balanced.	**Rapidly growing population:** Births far outnumber deaths.	**Stable population:** Births drop, and births and deaths become more or less balanced.	**Shrinking population:** Deaths outnumber births.

Note: The standard demographic transition is depicted by Stages 1–3. Stage 4 has been suggested by some Anti-Malthusians.

declined rapidly while birthrates remained high. When Europe moved to Stage III, its population stabilized as people brought birthrates in line with lower death rates.

Demographic transition was so successful that European countries now worry about *not having enough babies.* Having moved into Stage 4, Western European leaders fear **population shrinkage,** a failure to produce enough children to replace people who die. Italy was the first country in the world to have more people over age 65 than children under age 15. Of the 42 countries of Europe, 40 no longer produce enough children to maintain their populations (McDonald, 2001). They are now filling more coffins than cradles.

Anti-Malthusians predict that this demographic transition will also occur in the poorer nations of the world. The rapid growth of these nations today is not a cause for concern, for it merely indicates that they have reached the second stage of demographic transition. Already their growth rate has slowed. Look again at Figure 12-4. It took the world's population 12 years to grow from 4 to 5 billion, and then another 12 years to grow from 5 to 6 billion. If population continued accelerating as it had been, another billion babies would have been born in less than 12 years. Instead, population growth has tapered off, the precise slowing that Anti-Malthusians would expect. These nations have just penetrated the third stage of demographic transition.

In the Spotlight on Social Research box on page 432, Haub touches on many of the issues we have just reviewed.

The Scope of the Problem

SITTING ON THE SHOULDERS OF THE NEW MALTHUSIANS. Let's suppose that the world's population doubles during the next 50 years, as it will if present growth rates continue. Can the world support twice its present population? To answer this question, we will look at how the world is providing for its current population. Famine and malnutrition stalk the earth. Six hundred million people are malnourished and go to bed hungry each night. Eleven million children die each year before they reach the age of 5. One-half of these deaths are caused by hunger and malnourishment. One hundred twenty million children receive no education ("State of Food . . . ," 2005). In some of the world's poorest nations, such as Bangladesh, *half* the population never eats enough protein. Every

A Global Glimpse
"I'D LIKE TO HAVE TWENTY CHILDREN"

In 1976, an anthropologist making a documentary in an African village in Kenya asked a 26-year-old mother of two how many children she wanted. The woman looked at her bulging stomach, giggled, and said, "I'd like to have 20 children."

The documentary then went into a freeze frame, with a subtitle stating that the woman had given birth to twins.

This image haunted John Tierney, a *New York Times* reporter. "What is wrong with her?" he wondered. "What would become of her family?" Ten years later, Tierney went to Kenya to follow up the story. He found the woman, Fanisi Kalusa, living in the same hut, the twins healthy. She was now 36, with seven children, aged 4 to 16.

When Tierney asked about her wanting 20 children, Fanisi laughed, and said, "I've rejected that idea because there is not enough food to meet the demand."

Most African men dislike birth control, but her husband had agreed to limit their family size. He had his mother put a curse on his wife to make her barren—a standard practice in the area.

This photo of eleven children of a Himba family in Namibia, posing in front of their home, says more about the population explosion in the Least Industrialized Nations than I could ever say.

Fanisi went along with the curse—but without telling her husband, she visited a clinic for a free IUD.

Initially, she wanted 20 children who would be available when she needed help on the farm and support in old age. But now, children have become expensive in Kenya. For each child, parents must pay $10 a year in tuition, a burden many poor cannot afford. In addition, many children are moving to the city, breaking close family bonds and threatening the custom of adult children providing support for their aged parents.

Fanisi told her 16-year-old daughter to have only six children. Fanisi's daughter told Tierney that she thought four would be about right.

FOR YOUR CONSIDERATION

What do you think? Will Africa successfully move to the next stage in the demographic transition? Anti-Malthusians point to Fanisi Kalusa as evidence that they will. But the New Malthusians worry that Kenya is growing at 2.3% each year—4 times as fast as the United States.

Based on Tierney (1986); Haub (2005).

---

year thousands of people in Africa, Asia, and Latin America are born deaf-mutes because of iodine deficiency (Pollack, 2004). Several hundred million people survive on *less* than $1,000 a year. In Ethiopia, which is growing so fast that by the year 2050 it will be the 10th largest country in the world, the *average* income is less than $100 for an entire year (*Statistical Abstract*, 2006, Table 1327).

As bad as it may appear now, the future looks even worse. Urban sprawl is devouring productive farmland. In the United States alone, each year developers turn 3 million acres of farmland into subdivisions and businesses. This is enough land to form a corridor a mile and a half wide stretching from San Francisco to New York. The land taken through urban sprawl represents less food production, further sealing the fate of the world's malnourished.

SITTING ON THE SHOULDERS OF THE ANTI-MALTHUSIANS. "It isn't like that at all," reply Anti-Malthusians. The idea that the United States is being "paved over" is absurd, argued economist Julian Simon (1981). The United States has about 2 billion acres. All the land taken up by cities, highways, roads, railroads, and airports amounts to only 75 million acres—less than 4% of our total land. We are in no danger of running out of farmland.

Spotlight on Social Research
EXPERIENCING THE DEMOGRAPHIC TRANSITION

CART HAUB, *senior demographer at the Population Reference Bureau, became interested in population growth in the 1970s when he learned that the populations of some of the world's poorest nations would double in 23 years. He has conducted research in Belarus, Honduras, India, Jamaica, Trinidad and Tobago, and Vietnam.*

The populations of the world's poorest nations began to grow rapidly when their death rates declined because of factors like immunization campaigns, but their birthrates remained high. As a result, their growth rates shot up. In Europe, on the contrary, birth and death rates tended to decline together.

Most of the Least Industrialized Nations have adopted policies to slow their rates of growth. Without this, it would be impossible for them to improve health conditions and have any hope of feeding their people. A key point for demographers is the length of time it takes for a country's birthrate to decline to what we call the *replacement level.* This is achieved when couples average about two children each. When this happens, a country's population reaches zero growth, neither growing nor declining, since the average couple simply "replaces" itself.

Since most Least Industrialized Nations do not have thorough registration systems of their births and deaths, how do we know what a country's growth rate is? We glean trends in its population growth from its national census data. In addition, we take demographic surveys to fill the gaps in our knowledge.

Birthrates have declined remarkably in some countries, such as Brazil, South Korea, Thailand, and Tunisia. In others, especially the countries of sub-Saharan Africa, progress has been slow. In some sub-Saharan countries, progress has even stopped. In Asia and Latin America, the story is mixed. India, with one billion people, has seen some success, especially in its more educated areas. But in Uttar Pradesh, India's largest state with 170 million people, women still give birth to nearly five children each. In Costa Rica, the birthrate has declined to the replacement level, but in Guatemala it remains high.

The green revolution was truly a revolution; it improved food supplies in the Least Industrialized Nations. But the story does not end there. Poverty remains widespread in these nations, and malnutrition is still common. Without declines in population growth, alleviating poverty will be difficult. Consider these two countries: In Yemen, a country of high poverty, women still average about seven children. In Thailand, where much of the population is still rural, women average less than two.

Two recent developments are of major concern to demographers: HIV/AIDS and population shrinkage. HIV/AIDS has taken a toll, particularly in Africa, where, in some countries, over 30% (or more) of the population is infected. This has drastically changed the population outlook for these countries. The population of Africa, however, is still growing rapidly. In contrast, population shrinkage, not growth, is the situation in many of the Most Industrialized Nations. In all of Europe and in Japan, low birthrates are causing concern. In Germany and Italy, for example, women now average only 1.3 children. These low birthrates will lead to social problems.

Today's demographic trends will have significant impacts on society. The future will bring new developments, which will add to the developing demographic story.

Urban sprawl is not taking food out of the mouths of starving children, as New Malthusians would have us believe. In fact, urban sprawl has not even slowed food production. The problem of starvation has nothing to do with the earth having too large a population, nor with the earth failing to produce enough food. The amount of food available for every person on earth has actually been *increasing,* not decreasing. Every country records how much food it produces. As Figure 12-7 on the next page shows, *despite the billions of people who have been added to the earth's population, more food is available per person now than in the past.* The United States produces so much food that the problem is where to store it all. The U.S. government even pays its farmers *not* to farm land. Americans have so much to eat that obesity has become a major health problem.

What about those alarming images we see of starving children—those scrawny bony arms, protruding stomachs, and flies crawling over their faces? How can anyone deny

FIGURE 12-7 How Much Food Does the World Produce Per Person?

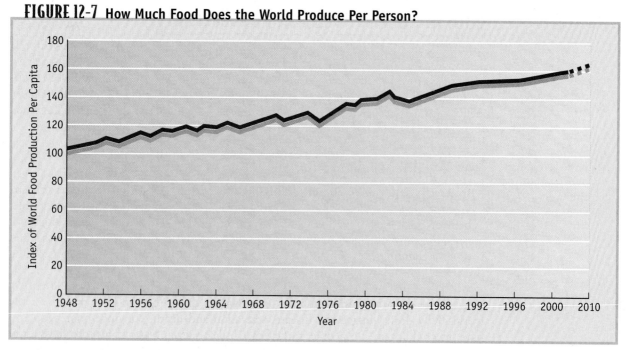

Note: Projections from 2004 are by James M. Henslin.

Sources: J. L. Simon (1981, p. 58); *Statistical Abstract of the United States* (1988, Table 1411; 1998, Tables 1380, 1381, 1382, 1383; 2006, Tables 817, 1346, 1350); recomputed to 1948–52 base.

that there is a food shortage? Of course, the starving people in those photos aren't getting enough food, reply the Anti-Malthusians. The reason for this, though, is not that the earth is failing to produce enough food for them. The problem is that the abundance of food is not distributed equally. If we were to redistribute a mere 5% of the grain grown in the Most Industrialized Nations, we could prevent *all* the malnutrition and starvation in the entire world (Conti, 1980).

How about the perception that Africa is overcrowded, that it has such a large population that it is outstripping its resources? The starvation in Africa that upsets the world does *not* occur because there are too many people, but because of drought and civil war. Africa is rich in resources, and—contrary to common belief promoted by the media—*Africa has fewer people per square mile than either Europe or the United States* (Haub, 2005). Civil wars in Africa disrupt food production and block humanitarian aid from reaching its suffering people.

To argue that starvation comes about either because the earth has too many people or the earth does not produce enough food is erroneous. The problem is a combination of agricultural inefficiency, inadequate incentives, political corruption, maldistribution of the earth's abundance, poor governments, and war—not too little food.

IN SUM New Malthusians and Anti-Malthusians arrive at different conclusions gleaned from the same evidence. The New Malthusians argue that population growth is so great that we are about to run out of land and food. Anti-Malthusians conclude that our era enjoys the greatest abundance that the world has ever known and that the abundance is continuing to grow. The scope of the population problem depends on one's theoretical approach.

According to symbolic interaction theory, we must place a phenomenon within a framework that gives it meaning. As we consider issues of population and food in the coming pages, we will return to this basic principle from time to time. For now, let's apply the frameworks provided by sociological theories.

Looking at the Problem Theoretically

As usual, our theoretical lenses provide contrasting perspectives. We will use symbolic interactionism to better understand why the population of the Least Industrialized Nations is growing so fast. Functionalism will illuminate the relationship between modern medicine and the twin problems of population and food. Finally, conflict theory yields a controversial analysis of food, profits, and international relations. Together, these perspectives help us understand the whole phenomenon of population growth.

Symbolic Interactionism

WHY DO THE POOR HAVE SO MANY CHILDREN? Let's start with something that doesn't seem to make sense. Look at Figure 12-8, which shows population change over time. When you track the population increase of the Least Industrialized Nations, it looks as if you're going up a steep hill. In contrast, the population of the Most Industrialized Nations is standing still. Why is *almost all* the increase in the world's population coming from the Least Industrialized Nations?

It may seem obvious that if you are poor, you would want to have few children. Yet you can see that the world's population growth is driven by the poor nations of the world. Why don't hunger and disease, starvation and death, convince poor people to have fewer children? Do people in the Least Industrialized Nations *want* to have fewer children, but not know how to prevent pregnancy? The truth is, cheap and effective birth control techniques are available, but many of the poor won't use them. They continue to have many children because they *want* large families (Burns, 1994).

TAKING THE ROLE OF THE OTHER. The focus of symbolic interactionism—understanding meaning attached to symbols—helps explain why the poor desire large families. What to Americans seems to be irrational behavior makes sense in the Least Industrialized Nations. Only by **taking the role of the other**—that is, seeing things from another person's perspective—can we make sense of people's experiences.

To understand the desires of billions of poor people we must move beyond our own American culture. First, in the Least Industrialized Nations, people's identities center on their children. Motherhood is the most exalted status a woman can achieve. It is what

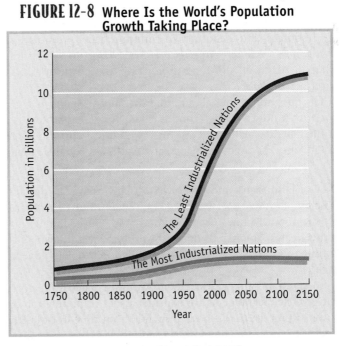

FIGURE 12-8 Where Is the World's Population Growth Taking Place?

Sources: "The World of the Child 6 Billion" (2000); Haub (2005).

With political conflicts common, the world is awash in refugees, who need to be fed, clothed, and sheltered. Their care is usually a temporary matter, as in this scene from Afghanistan, but in some instances the turmoil continues or the refugees' government refuses to allow them back into the country. In such situations the "temporary" arrangement can continue for decades.

she was born for. Through childbearing, she fulfills her destiny and finds personal worth. The more children she bears, the more she fulfills this purpose. Similarly, the more children that a man fathers, the more he proves his manhood. It is especially sons that he desires, for through them, his name lives on.

Second, most of these people live in small communities where they share values and identify with one another. It is in this *Gemeinschaft* community of like-minded people that they are given or denied status—their rank in the family and among friends and neighbors. Bearing many children is viewed as a sign of God's blessing on their lives. As people produce more children, then, the community grants them higher status. The barren woman, not the woman with a dozen children, is to be pitied.

Last, for the poor in the Least Industrialized Nations, children are *economic assets*. This may be difficult for Americans to grasp. We live in an urbanized, postindustrialized world where children are economic liabilities. When we left the agrarian world where children helped on the family farm, children became optional luxuries. They are expensive to bear and to rear for 18+ years. In the Most Industrialized Nations, couples consider having children in much the same way they consider buying a new car: "Can we afford it?" or "Should we put it off until later?"

How, then, can poor people afford to have many children, and why do they view children as economic assets? It is important to understand the world they live in. They have no social security, no medical insurance, and no unemployment benefits. The lack of benefits motivates people to have *more* children, not fewer, for when parents become too old to work, they rely on their adult children to take care of them. Their children are their social security, and the more children they have, the firmer their security is. In addition, children start to contribute financially to the family long before the parents are old. Figure 12-9 on the next page should help you take the role of the other, which is essential if we are to understand why the surge in the world's population is coming from the Least Industrialized Nations.

Consider this incident reported by a government worker in India:

A water carrier . . . Thaman Singh . . . welcomed me inside his home, gave me a cup of tea (with milk and "market" sugar, as he proudly pointed out later), and said: "You were trying to convince me . . . that I shouldn't have any more sons. Now, you see, I have six

FIGURE 12-9 Why the Poor Need Children

Children are an economic asset in the Least Industrialized Nations. Based on a survey in Indonesia, this figure shows that boys and girls can be net income earners for their families by the age of 9 or 10.

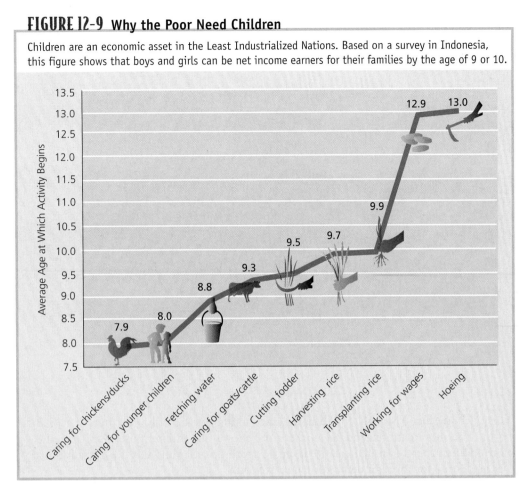

Source: U.N. Fund for Population Activities.

sons and two daughters and I sit at home in leisure. They are grown up, and they bring me money. One even works outside the village as a laborer. You told me I was a poor man and couldn't support a large family. Now, you see, because of my large family I am a rich man." (Mamdani, 1973, p. 109)

IN SUM Our ideas of the "right" number of children reflect our own life experiences. To superimpose American ideas onto people in other cultures is dangerous and not sociological practice. To understand the behavior of any group, we must understand it from their vantage point—a practice Max Weber referred to as **Verstehen.**

Functionalism

CATASTROPHES ARE FUNCTIONAL. When using the functionalist perspective, keep in mind that functionalists aim to determine *objectively* what the functions or dysfunctions of behaviors are, without judging those behaviors to be good or bad. As seen in instances of poverty, rape, murder, drug addiction, and racial–ethnic discrimination, functionalists find that even deviant, illegal, or abhorrent events serve functions. With regard to the social problem of population and food supply, functionalists stress that even war, natural disasters, disease, and famine are functional. Historically, these mass killers held the world's population in check, ensuring that humans did not outstrip their food supply.

MODERN MEDICINE AND PUBLIC HEALTH: LATENT DYSFUNCTIONS. Modern medicine, however, upset this precarious balance between population and food. The birthrates and death rates of the Least Industrialized Nations, both being high, had more or less

canceled one another out, leading to a stable population. Then came better nutrition and sanitation, coupled with Western pharmaceutical drugs that brought under control those nations' major killers—smallpox, diphtheria, typhoid, measles, and other communicable diseases. As a result, the death rates in these nations plunged. These advances didn't reduce their birthrates, though, which still remain high. Not only did millions of people who otherwise would have died survive, but they also reproduced. This has forced the Least Industrialized Nations into the second stage of demographic transition (see Figure 12-6 on page 430).

POPULATION PYRAMIDS. When a country is in the second stage of demographic transition, it has a lot of young people; if it is in the third or fourth stage, it has a lot of older people. Obviously, countries with more young people have higher birthrates, and those with older people have lower birthrates. Demographers use the term *age structure* to refer to countries having larger or smaller proportions of younger and older people. To illustrate age structures, demographers produce **population pyramids,** like Figure 12-10, which contrasts Mexico, in Stage 2 of demographic transition, with the United States, in advanced Stage 3. As you can see, different age structures produce different "shapes" of populations.

Let's consider one of the implications of Figure 12-10. If Mexico and the United States had the same number of people, Mexico would still grow faster than the United States. The reason? A larger proportion of Mexico's population is young, in childbearing years. This is the case with all Least Industrialized Nations, causing them to have *population momentum.* What accounts for the growth that you saw in Figure 12-8 on page 434, then, isn't only that the families are larger in the Least Industrialized Nations. This is important, but underlying this surge in growth is also the population momentum of the Least Industrialized Nations.

FIGURE 12-10 Population Pyramids of Mexico and the United States

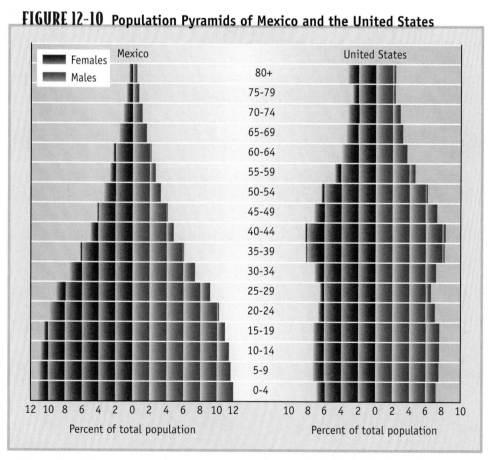

Source: By James M. Henslin. Computed from the U.S. Bureau of the Census (2006c, Table 94).

As stressed in the text, events in life do not come with built-in meanings. All of us use frameworks of thought to interpret life's events. How do New Malthusians and Anti-Malthusians interpret this scene in India? Why do they see things so differently?

DOUBLING TIMES. The combined force of large families and population momentum has a tremendous impact on population growth. The Most Industrialized Nations average only 0.1% population growth per year. At this rate, it will take 583 years for their population to double. The Least Industrialized Nations, in contrast, are growing 15 times faster, and they will double in just 40 years (Haub & Cornelius, 1999). Table 12-4 below shows extremes: Chad will double its population in just 21 years, while it will take Austria 2,310 years to do so. The doubling time of the world's nations is shown on the Social Map (Figure 12-11 on the next page).

TABLE 12-4 How Long Will It Take a Country to Double Its Population?

SOME MOST INDUSTRIALIZED NATIONS	POPULATION (IN MILLIONS)	BIRTHS (PER 1,000 WOMEN)	DEATHS (PER 1,000 POPULATION)	ANNUAL NATURAL INCREASE	YEARS IT TAKES TO DOUBLE
United States	290	15	9	0.6	116
Canada	31	11	7	0.4	162
Japan	127	10	7	0.2	318
Great Britain	59	12	10	0.2	423
Denmark	5	12	11	0.1	472
Belgium	10	11	10	0.1	693
Austria	8	10	10	Slightly over 0	2,310
SOME LEAST INDUSTRIALIZED NATIONS					
Chad	8	50	17	3.3	21
Nicaragua	5	38	6	3.2	22
Ethiopia	60	46	21	2.5	28
Algeria	31	30	6	2.4	29
Mexico	100	27	5	2.2	32
India	1,000	28	9	1.9	37
China	1,254	16	7	1.0	73

Source: By James M. Henslin. Based on Haub 2005.

FIGURE 12-11 How Long Will It Take for Population to Double?

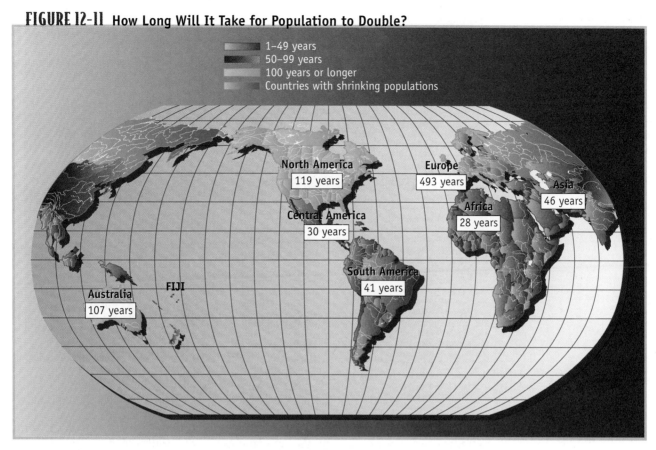

1–49 years
50–99 years
100 years or longer
Countries with shrinking populations

North America
119 years

Europe
493 years

Asia
46 years

Central America
30 years

Africa
28 years

South America
41 years

Australia
107 years

FIJI

Source: Population Growth Rates and Doubling Time. By Matt Rosenberg, About.com

The implications of doubled population are mind-boggling. *Just to stay even* a country must double its food production and factories; its medical and educational capacities; its transportation, communication, water, gas, sewer, and electrical systems; its housing, churches, civic buildings, stadiums, theaters, stores, and parks; its automobiles, electronics, and household appliances; as well as jobs and all else that constitutes "decent living standards."

The Least Industrialized Nations, then, appear destined to fall still further behind the industrialized nations, for they start with less, and their swelling numbers drain their limited economic resources. In contrast, the Most Industrialized Nations (such as the United States) *can spend much more on fewer people.* With an annual growth rate of 1.0%, the United States is at the low end of the world's growth rate. Much of the increase in our population size is due to immigration. The U.S. rate of natural increase (growth without immigration) is 0.6% (Haub, 2005; *Statistical Abstract,* 2006, Table 4).

IN SUM Functionalists analyze how exporting Western medicine and public sanitation into the Least Industrialized Nations caused a surge in their population. Their rapid population growth outstripped their food supply, resulting in malnutrition, mass starvation, and political unrest. Because these negative consequences were not anticipated or intended, sociologists call them **latent dysfunctions.**

The debate continues, though, as to whether these consequences are functions or dysfunctions. Anti-Malthusians believe that in the long run the increase in the world's population is functional. The Least Industrialized Nations are fighting through the difficult second stage in demographic transition, but they will enter the third stage and begin to limit their populations. In the meantime, growing populations will stimulate industrialization and food production. Consequently, they will increase their food supply and

The United States is experiencing one of its largest waves of immigration (approximately a million immigrants a year). Like earlier arrivals, today's immigrants form ethnic neighborhoods in which they maintain customs from their homeland while they adjust to the norms of their new land. Today's immigrants, like those before them, also have special educational needs.

match their growing populations. Functionalists argue that warnings to reduce world population are unwarranted, and the population surge that some now find upsetting will turn out functional for humanity.

Conflict Theory

POWER AND PROFITS. Conflict theorists focus on the global distribution of power and resources. They stress that social and economic arrangements, not nature, produce poverty, hunger, and starvation. The Least Industrialized Nations have problems feeding their populations not because of Malthusian inevitabilities but because they have too little income. As sociologist Michael Harrington (1977) stressed, their income is restricted because global political and economic arrangements favor rich nations. If they had access to more income, they could buy all the food they need but don't produce.

Conflict theorists point out that the Most Industrialized Nations exploit the Least Industrialized Nations today just as the European powers used to exploit their colonies. They extract the mineral and agricultural wealth of the Least Industrialized Nations at the lowest possible cost, turning those raw materials into products that they sell throughout the world. As the Most Industrialized Nations buy tin from Bolivia, copper from Peru, sugar from Cuba, coffee from Brazil, and so forth, the Least Industrialized Nations are left out of this cycle of profits.

Poor nations also contribute to the diet of rich nations. For example, each year the United States imports $42 billion in food, much of it from the Least Industrialized Nations (*Statistical Abstract*, 2003, Table 825). Although the ultimate consumers of these products pay for them, poor countries themselves receive little for the food they sell. Long ago, social critic Michael Harrington (1977) pointed out that global arrangements put real profits in the pockets of the middlemen in the Most Industrialized Nations.

FOOD POLITICS. The United States exports $60 billion in food (*Statistical Abstract*, 2006, Table 821). Food is a money-making enterprise, not a means of dealing with world hunger. The United States (accounting for 60% of the world's corn exports and

50% of its soybean exports) sells its grain surpluses first to those who pay the highest prices, not to the most needy (Conti, 1980; *Statistical Abstract,* 2006, Table 817).

Why does the U.S. government pay farmers billions of dollars *not* to grow crops, even though people in some nations are starving? Conflict theorists argue the answer is **food politics,** controlling food production to control food prices. Paying farmers to leave their land fallow creates an artificial shortage that drives up grain prices. This reduces the charges for storing grain—as there is less grain to store—and caters to the farm vote by keeping grain prices high. Food politics, stress conflict theorists, is done for profit, with no concern for moral implications

IN SUM Conflict theorists conclude that food production is just another tool used by the wealthy to exploit the poor. The food crisis that affects the undernourished is the result of food politics, not Malthusian inevitabilities.

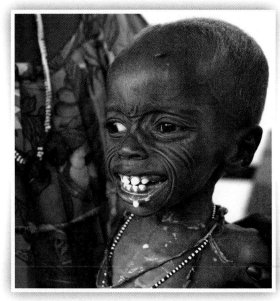

We have starvation not because the earth produces too little food, but because the earth's food is not equally distributed.

Research Findings

Let's first examine the position of the New Malthusians: the harm to fisheries, forests, and grasslands; the threat of plant disease and the intensification of natural disasters; and the momentum in world population growth. Then, after considering the views of the Anti-Malthusians, we'll examine why it is difficult to predict population growth accurately. We'll lastly consider whether the United States has a population problem.

The New Malthusians

THREE NATURAL SYSTEMS. As you have seen, New Malthusians are convinced that the world is outstripping its food supply. They argue that the world's huge population has put unsustainable pressure on the earth's three natural systems—its fishing grounds, forests, and grasslands—on which we all depend for food. Each has a **carrying capacity,** limits fixed by nature, and we are straining those limits.

Fishing Grounds ■ One natural system seems to offer an endless supply of food. When you go to a fish market or order fish at a restaurant, there is bountiful choice. There is no shortage. From flounder and catfish to lobster and shrimp, animals from the ocean are plentiful. Could there possibly be any concern? Indeed, according to some scientists, it is folly to view the ocean as a source of food that can supply our needs infinitely as long as we continue to develop better harvesting techniques (Arnason et al., 2005). In the 1970s, scientists pointed out that 90% of the ocean is a biological desert (Ehrlich & Ehrlich, 1972). The upper layer of open sea, which gets enough sunlight for photosynthesis, lacks nutrients for high productivity. Almost all fish come from areas close to shore, and these are the most polluted waters. Others warn that we are devastating the world's fragile fishing populations with our far-ranging fishing fleets equipped with sonar and mile-long drift nets.

In 2006, the loudest alarm was sounded. This report came from scientists at Dalhousie University in Nova Scotia, who had collected all the fishing data available from around the world from 1950 to 2003 (Worm et al., 2006). These data are so complete that they cover all 64 of the marine ecosystems worldwide, which produce 83% of the world's fish and invertebrate catches. The researchers' conclusions: If we continue to harvest fish at the rate we are doing now, more and more species will vanish, the marine ecosystems will unravel, and there will be a global collapse of all the species we currently fish. Unless we make changes, this collapse will occur in the year 2048.

Forests ■ The world's forests also seem eternally renewable. For every tree cut down, a tree can be planted. Each year, however, the world's forests shrink by an area the size of Cuba. In many places **deforestation**—the cutting down of trees—is not balanced by planting. In Peru and Chile, for example, vast areas have been cut for farming. With the soil unprotected against wind and rain, some hills have become as barren as the moon. Pressure on the world's forests continues to increase, as the demand for newsprint and packaging soars worldwide.

Grasslands ■ The grasslands are also under mounting pressure. Over the past four decades, individual family farms have been purchased by **agricompanies,** which operate farms of thousands of acres. To make these farms efficient, corporate owners have joined field to field, bulldozing **windrows,** the row of trees between the fields that farmers had planted to break the wind. By reducing the force of the wind, windrows keep topsoil from blowing away. Now that many have been removed, some fear the Midwest will see a repeat of the dust bowl of the 1930s.

Much of the agricultural production in the Midwest and West is dependent upon the Ogallala aquifer, an extensive underground water system. Extensive irrigation has depleted this reservoir. Soon we may have to curtail extensive irrigation, which supplies many of the farms in the western United States.

Around the world, the pressing need for food is pushing into production land that is basically unsuitable for cultivation (Little & Horowitz, 1987). The steep hillsides of Indonesia are being eroded; slash-and-burn agriculture is destroying tropical forests in many countries, including Brazil and the Philippines. Attempts to apply farming techniques that work in the temperate zone to the tropical soils of Brazil and Sudan have caused **laterization,** the transformation of soils into laterite—a rocklike material. This occurs when cultivation exposes certain soils to the air.

A DANGER: DISEASE OF SPECIALIZED STRAINS. In addition to pressure on the world's three natural systems, expanding populations face other dangers. First, the world's agricultural system now depends on only a few specialized strains of crops. In the quest for higher yields, a few specifically bred, high-yield strains have replaced the world's wide range of traditional varieties of wheat and rice. Although these high-yield varieties allow farmers to produce more food, they also increase the potential of widespread crop failure from insects and disease.

Back in the 1970s, biologists John Holdren and Paul Ehrlich (1974) warned that what happened in Ireland could happen to the United States on a much larger scale:

> The Irish potato famine of the 1800s is perhaps the best-known example of the collapse of a single agricultural ecosystem. The heavy reliance of the Irish population on a single, high productive crop led to 1.5 million deaths when the potato monoculture fell victim to a fungus.

In other words, if a treacherous pest or plant disease infects our crops, we could have a worldwide calamity. Our extensive cultivation of single high-yield grains is "an accident waiting to happen." The benefits it now yields may come at the future cost of epidemic starvation, malnutrition, and disease. This could occur suddenly and in surprising ways. For example, the storms of the 2004 hurricane season (one of the worst that the United States ever experienced) brought with them a fungus from South America that attacks soybeans.

ANOTHER DANGER: INTENSIFICATION OF NATURAL DISASTERS. Another danger is the intensification of natural disasters. As human populations grow, they expand into areas less likely to protect them from the elements. The Ehrlichs (1972, p. 243) provided this account of how overpopulation intensifies natural disasters:

> In November of 1970, a huge tidal wave driven by a cyclone swept over the Ganges Delta of East Pakistan. There a large, mostly destitute population lived exposed on flat lowland, in spite of the ever-present danger of climatic disaster for which the region is famous.

A mother cries as she holds a photo of her daughter who was killed in an earthquake in China on May 29, 2008, while in school. China's central government has promised to punish harshly anyone found responsible for poor construction.

They live in constant jeopardy because in grossly overpopulated East Pakistan the choice of places for them is greatly restricted. In November, 1970, 300,000 people died who need not have died if their nation had not been over-populated. This cataclysm has been described as the greatest documented national disaster in history.

INCREDIBLY RAPID POPULATION GROWTH. In poor, overcrowded Bangladesh (as East Pakistan is now known), evacuation was impossible. Despite the death toll of 300,000 from the tidal wave, the population in Bangladesh grew so fast that in only 6 weeks new births made Bangladesh's population as large as it had been before the catastrophe (Waddington, 1978). In 2004, a large tsunami struck Indonesia, where 233,000 people died. With Indonesia's growth rate of over 3 million a year, it took Indonesia just under 4 weeks (26 days) to replace *all* the people it lost in the tsunami (Henslin, 2007b).

ZERO POPULATION GROWTH? Suppose it was possible to achieve **zero population growth**—that is, adults having only enough children to replace themselves. It seems obvious that the world's population problem would disappear, right? Wrong. *The population momentum that we discussed earlier would keep the world's population growing for 50 to 70 years before it leveled off.*

Consider Africa as an example. Forty-two percent of Africans are not yet age 15 (Haub, 2005). This means that more Africans will enter the reproductive ages each year than will leave them. If Africa attained zero population growth, with each woman bearing an average of 2.1 children, the growth *rate* of Africa would fall for 50 or 70 years, but Africa's population would continue to increase during this time before it finally leveled off.

And, the New Malthusians add, Africa isn't even close to zero population growth. The average African woman gives birth to five children, not two (Haub, 2005). Despite the many deaths from HIV/AIDS and mass starvation, Africa has the fastest-growing population of any continent.

A BLEAK FUTURE FOR THE WORLD. The future looks desperate. Famine, malnutrition, and starvation are striking the earth. We are also suffering from pollution and environmental destruction as too many people try to carve a living from the earth's surface. The world's swelling population even threatens world peace. When the governments of the Least Industrialized Nations cannot feed their people, riots will likely break out.

The Anti-Malthusians

LARGER POPULATIONS ARE GOOD. Anti-Malthusians scoff at worrisome conclusions. Anti-Malthusians claim that more people are *good* for a country; larger populations lead to *higher* standards of living (J. L. Simon, 1977, 1982, 1991).

To support their position, Anti-Malthusians make four points. First, a growing population means that more geniuses will be born, who will contribute to everyone's welfare. Second, population growth forces countries to use their land more efficiently, which increases productivity. Third, larger populations create larger markets. This promotes more efficient manufacturing, lowering the production cost per unit. This makes more goods available. Fourth, a larger population makes many social investments profitable, especially railroads, highways, irrigation systems, and ports. Investments on this scale don't pay off in sparse populations. These investments, in turn, spur productivity and increase a country's capacity to deliver productivity to its people.

FOOD PRODUCTION IS OUTPACING POPULATION GROWTH. Anti-Malthusians stress that we should not lose sight of how the world's food production has *outpaced* the world's population growth. (Recall Figure 12-7 on page 433.) Today there is *more* food for each person in the entire world than there was 25, 50, or even 100 or 200 years ago. Moreover, this increase in per capita food occurred while the world's population "exploded." During this same time, the United States, the "breadbasket of the world," decreased the number of acres that it farmed. As Figure 12-12 shows, the United States now has *less* land under the plow than in 1920, yet the food production of the United States continues to increase. If the world's population increase is dramatic—and it is—then the world's food increase is more dramatic still.

When it comes to fishing grounds, Anti-Malthusians argue that the world's fish harvest has not fallen. According to U.S. government records, the world's fish harvest is now 36% *higher* than it was in 1990 (*Statistical Abstract*, 2006, Table 1347).

NOT EVEN A LAND SHORTAGE. And running out of land? Not in any realistic future, say Anti-Malthusians. According to the U.N. Food and Agricultural Organization, more than 2 billion acres of rain-fed land go unfarmed (Livernash & Rodenburg, 1998).

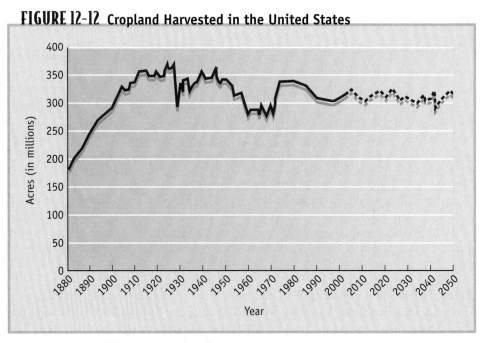

FIGURE 12-12 Cropland Harvested in the United States

Sources: By James M. Henslin. Based on *Statistical Abstract of the United States* (1991, Table 1154; 1998, Table 1126; 2006, Table 797). Broken line is the author's estimate.

Contrary to common belief, then, the world contains enough land to feed even more people. If we should ever farm all this unused land, and need more, then we could reclaim wasteland and make it productive.

Has the Population Explosion Peaked?

THE ANTI-MALTHUSIANS. Anti-Malthusians point out that the world's rate of population growth is slowing. The world's population grew an average of 2% each year between 1965 and 1975. Then it dropped to 1.7% during the 1980s. Now it has dropped to 1.2% (*Statistical Abstract,* 1991, Table 1434; Haub, 2005). This means that the world's population growth has dropped 40%.

Population growth has slowed not only in industrialized nations but also in poorer nations on all continents. Population growth is slowing—just as we would expect, according to the demographic transition model. Perhaps the most startling statistic is this: Today's birthrate in the Least Industrialized Nations is less than *half* what it was in the 1950s. Back then, the average woman in the Least Industrialized Nations gave birth to 6.2 children. The birthrate has dropped so drastically that today the average woman in these nations has just 3.0 children (Livernash & Rodenburg, 1998; Haub, 2005).

The "Luther Burger"—a bacon cheeseburger on a Krispy Kreme Donut—is an example of the excessively caloric fast food Americans so often eat.

THE NEW MALTHUSIANS. Advocates of zero population growth agree that these figures are correct, but they don't mean what Anti-Malthusians think they do. These figures do indicate that the *rate* of population growth has slowed, but they don't mean that the world's population has leveled off or that it is getting smaller. On the contrary, the world's population is still exploding.

Problems in Forecasting Population Growth

DEMOGRAPHERS' PREDICTIONS: Forecasting population growth is often difficult (Conner, 1990). Consider this:

> During the depression of the late 1920s and early 1930s, birthrates plunged as unemployment reached unprecedented heights. Demographers issued warnings about the dangers of depopulation almost as alarmist as some of today's forecasts of overpopulation (Waddington, 1978). Because each year fewer and fewer females would enter the childbearing years, they felt that the population of countries such as Great Britain would shrink.

Instead, at the end of the Great Depression and the outbreak of World War II, the birthrate rose. After the war, both the United States and Britain had a "baby boom." The inaccuracy of the population forecasters of the 1930s made many skeptical of demographic forecasts.

To get around this, today's demographers make several predictions, each based on different assumptions. Look at Figure 12-13 on the next page, which shows three projections of U.S. populations. The population of the United States grew to 300 million in 2006, so these estimates are low.

CHANGES IN THE U.S. BIRTHRATE. Two remarkable changes shown in Figure 12-14 on the next page further illustrate how difficult it is to make accurate demographic projections. As you can see from this figure, through the years the African American birthrate has been consistently higher than the White birthrate. Although the difference in the birthrates between these two groups fluctuated slightly, African American women always averaged more children than did White women. But look at how these birthrates have

FIGURE 12-13 Three Projections of the U.S. Population

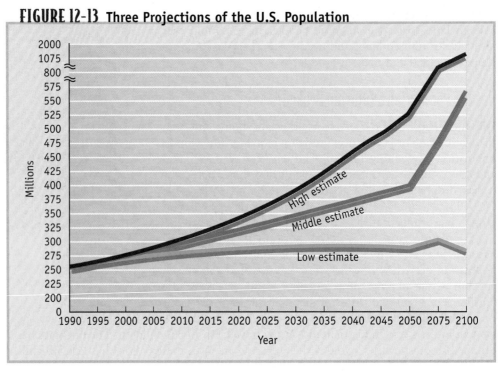

Source: Statistical Abstract of the United States (2006, Table 3).

converged. From 2002 to 2004, for the first time in U.S. history, African American women had lower birthrates than Whites. Projections of the U.S. population made in the past may be proved inaccurate because of failure to anticipate this development.

The totals on Figure 12-14 are rounded, and in 2005, the latest year available, the more precise totals were 2,071 children per 1,000 African American women and 2,056 children per 1,000 White women.

FIGURE 12-14 The Birthrates of African American and White Women

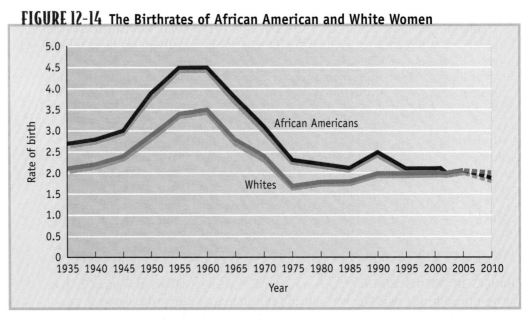

Note: These are the only groups listed in the source. For 1935 to 1960, the totals for African Americans are listed as Negro and Other. These are *fertility rates,* the number of births per woman. The source lists the number as per 1,000 women.

Source: By James M. Henslin. Based on U.S. Bureau of the Census (1975, Series B 36-41); *Statistical Abstract of the United States* (1989, Table 87; 2007, Table 81; 2008, Table 82).

FIGURE 12-15 U.S. Population by Race–Ethnicity

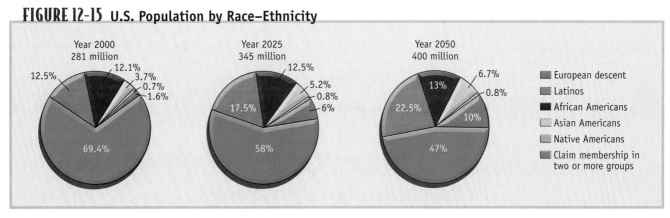

Year 2000
281 million

12.5%
12.1%
3.7%
0.7%
1.6%
69.4%

Year 2025
345 million

12.5%
5.2%
0.8%
6%
17.5%
58%

Year 2050
400 million

6.7%
0.8%
13%
10%
22.5%
47%

■ European descent
■ Latinos
■ African Americans
■ Asian Americans
■ Native Americans
■ Claim membership in two or more groups

Source: Henslin 2007b.

Figure 12-14 also shows that we have achieved Zero Population Growth. Because some children die, the average woman must give birth to 2.1 children to maintain growth. (Or, as demographers say, every 1,000 women must give birth to an average of 2,100 children.) As you can see from Figure 12-14, the U.S. birthrate has been on the decline. Today our birthrate is below the replacement level for a population.

IMMIGRANTS OFFSET LOW BIRTHRATES. If American women give birth to fewer children than it takes to replace the population, then the U.S. population should be shrinking. And it would be, except for immigration. Each year, about 1 million immigrants enter the United States legally (*Statistical Abstract,* 2006, Table 6), and several hundred thousand more arrive illegally. This vast immigration is having dramatic effects on the United States. Figure 12-15 shows how immigration is expected to change the racial–ethnic makeup of the United States.

DO IMMIGRANTS PAY THEIR WAY? People worry that immigrants depress wages and take jobs away from citizens. Because immigrants are viewed as a drain on taxpayers, the federal government made immigrants ineligible for welfare benefits (Martin & Midgley,

Among the reasons that it is difficult to project population growth accurately is the uncertainty of immigration. Shown here are U.S. immigrants from Korea who are performing a traditional dance as they celebrate at a dance festival in Los Angeles, California.

1999). Some economists argue that when you subtract what immigrants collect in welfare and then add back what they produce, they make a positive contribution to the economy (J. L. Simon, 1986). Others argue there is an "immigrant deficit," concluding that immigrants are a drain on taxpayers (Huddle, 1993).

The situation is complicated, but the data show that immigrants with low education collect more in benefits than they pay in taxes, whereas those with high education pay more in taxes than they collect in benefits (Smith & Edmonston, 1997). On average, each adult immigrant who has less than a high school education costs taxpayers $89,000 over his or her lifetime. Immigrants who have more than 12 years of schooling contribute $105,000 to the economy (Martin & Midgley, 1999).

Does the United States Have a Population Problem?

THE ANTI-MALTHUSIANS. As Table 12-5 shows, the United States has considerably fewer people per square mile than the world average. Anti-Malthusians stress that even if we continue to have high immigration, the country will have enough space, industry, and food to meet our needs. A larger population would prove an economic boom to the

TABLE 12-5 Density of Selected Countries

COUNTRY	NUMBER OF PEOPLE PER SQUARE MILE, 2008	COUNTRY	NUMBER OF PEOPLE PER SQUARE MILE, 2008
Macau	50,475	Egypt	213
Monaco	42,471	Greece	212
Singapore	17,500	Spain	210
Hong Kong	17,446	Morocco	199
Gibraltar	12,088	Ethiopia	191
Malta	3,307	Iraq	169
Bangladesh	2,970	Ireland	156
Bahrain	2,798	Mexico	148
South Korea	1,276	Afghanistan	133
Netherlands	1,272	Colombia	112
Puerto Rico	1,156	Iran	104
India	1,000	South Africa	104
Japan	880	United States	86
Israel	906	Venezuela	78
Haiti	839	Zimbabwe	76
Philippines	834	Brazil	60
Vietnam	686	Peru	59
Germany	611	Sweden	57
Pakistan	575	New Zealand	40
Italy	512	Norway	39
North Korea	505	Argentina	38
Nigeria	416	Saudi Arabia	34
China	369	Russia	21
Indonesia	337	Guyana	10
Denmark	335	Canada	9
Poland	328	Botswana	8
Portugal	301	Australia	7
Cuba	267	Mongolia	5
France	259	**WORLD**	**133**
Turkey	242		

Source: By James M. Henslin. Based on *Statistical Abstract of the United States* (2003, Table 1322; 2006, Table 1314; 2009, Table 1288).

United States, because industries would have to supply what they needed. In short, Anti-Malthusians say that the United States does *not* have *enough* people, and we ought to encourage immigration, especially of the educated (J. L. Simon, 1991).

THE NEW MALTHUSIANS. The New Malthusians claim that the United States does have a population problem. The average American uses 5 times more energy than others in the world, 26 times more energy than a citizen of India (*Statistical Abstract,* 2003, Table 1365). If each American costs the earth as much as 26 Indians, then in terms of energy our 300 million inhabitants use the same amount as 8 billion Indians. Put somewhat differently, if the population of India multiplied until it was larger than the earth's total population is now, only then would India put as much pressure on the earth's resources as we Americans already do.

THE ANTI-MALTHUSIANS. Americans do contribute to the earth. Our science, technology, financing, and industry give the world the capacity to increase production and enhance the standard of living for even the poorest nations. If we had more people, we would have even more creativity. We could then develop more potential, increase production, and help poorer nations even more (J. L. Simon, 1981).

OBJECTIVE CONDITIONS VERSUS VIEWPOINTS. How should we view population growth? The clashing views of the Malthusians highlight the relevance of symbolic interactionism, for conclusions on either side depend on how people interpret objective conditions. How we interpret population growth ultimately influences social policy.

Social Policy

Although the New and Anti-Malthusians disagree on almost everything, they do agree that we should increase food production. Let's consider the possibility of increasing food production by exporting Western agricultural techniques.

Exporting Western Agriculture

THE APPEAL OF EXPORTING WESTERN AGRICULTURE. American farming techniques are so efficient that, as discussed, our problem is what to do with excess production. Because we have such advanced technology, why not help the world's nations increase food production by exporting our agricultural techniques to the Least Industrialized Nations? "Give people a fish and you feed them for a day. Teach them to fish, and you feed them for a lifetime." If these nations were to adopt our farming techniques, couldn't they produce food in abundance?

The **green revolution**—the rapid expansion in food production that occurred in the 1950s—originated during a period of cheap energy and seemingly unlimited amounts of fresh water. The development of high-yield wheat and rice, coupled with effective fertilizers, raised hopes that impoverished nations could abolish famine.

THE LACK OF WATER AND FERTILIZER. It didn't happen. Water and fertilizer, essential to these high-yield plants, are in short supply in poor nations. To maximize yields, fields must be covered with 150 pounds of nitrogen fertilizer per acre, and they also require massive amounts of water to keep the fertilizer from burning the crops.

Nitrogen fertilizer is expensive. Even some American farmers find its cost prohibitive, and few farmers in poor nations can afford it at all. What rural poverty is like in the Least Industrialized Nations is difficult for Americans to imagine. Many farmers cannot afford even gasoline or electricity to irrigate their fields: "Oh, yes, we know about the green revolution," said Patal Mukherjee, a primary-school teacher in India who farms a few acres of rice and wheat. "But it does not change anything here. We are too poor."

Mukherjee's primitive farming methods are typical of India's 700 million village dwellers. He knows that different fertilizers will increase crop yields. And he knows how

to apply them. But he rarely has the money to buy them. He is locked into an endless cycle of defeat. When he most needs fertilizers—to make up for a bad harvest—he cannot afford to buy them (Wallace, 1980).

THE LACK OF AN AGRICULTURAL INFRASTRUCTURE. Food production is only one aspect of successful food production. Agricultural products must be distributed quickly to consumers or they rot. Our *agricultural infrastructure*—our network of railways and trucking, with many units refrigerated—allows us to move agricultural products from field to storage or directly to consumer. Our superhighways are subsidized by the federal government, which, in turn, depend on a vast system of tax collection. We also have regional and national systems of supermarkets to deliver products to consumers. We cannot export only one or two pieces of this interconnected, elaborate, and expensive support system of production, processing, and distribution to poorer nations and expect them to duplicate our success (Harrington, 1977).

Policy Implications of the Anti-Malthusians

ENCOURAGING POPULATION GROWTH AND TECHNOLOGICAL DEVELOPMENT. If larger populations are good for the world, then it follows that social policy ought to encourage larger families, that we need to avoid polices that would discourage women from having children. To implement Anti-Malthusian positions, we could take the following steps:

1. Reduce the age of consent to have sex to match the age at which girls are biologically able to reproduce. This would get more young women pregnant.
2. Encourage teenagers to experiment sexually.
3. Offer incentives for women to become mothers. These might include reduced taxes, paid maternity leave, subsidized housing, free nannies and child care, and free education and medical care. Cash bonuses could be paid, with larger bonuses for each successive child.
4. Discourage the education of women, because the more education women attain, the fewer children they bear.
5. Make abortion and birth control illegal.
6. Export Western medicine and public health techniques to the Least Industrialized Nations, in order to reduce maternal deaths and infant deaths and prolong the lives of the elderly.
7. Offer incentives to encourage science, technology, industry, and agriculture. Developments in these areas can help improve the standard of living of huge populations.

Policy Implications of the New Malthusians

MALTHUS'S MACHIAVELLIAN PROPOSAL. Malthus's main suggestion for limiting population was sexual abstinence. In *An Essay on the Principle of Population* (1798/1926), he proposed a solution that most may find outrageous:

> We should . . . encourage . . . destruction. . . . Instead of recommending cleanliness to the poor, we should encourage contrary habits. In our towns we should make the streets narrower, crowd more people into the houses, and court the return of the plague. In the country, we should build villages near stagnant pools, and particularly encourage settlements in all marshy and unwholesome situations. . . . But above all, we should reprobate [abandon, reject] specific remedies for ravaging diseases.

EFFECTIVE BUT GENERALLY UNACCEPTABLE POLICIES. If we were to implement Malthus's recommendations, some rather severe social policies would be called for. Among them would be mandates to

1. Withdraw modern medicine from the Least Industrialized Nations, especially vaccines and antibiotics.
2. Refuse to train students from the Least Industrialized Nations.
3. Refuse to send food to areas of famine and starvation.
4. Encourage infanticide.
5. Raise the age of sexual consent and the age at which people are allowed to marry—or, alternatively, lower the age of sexual consent and encourage promiscuous unprotected sex, while withholding medicines for HIV/AIDS.
6. Require a license to have children.
7. Require abortions for women who become pregnant without a license.
8. Encourage homosexual unions, since they don't produce children.
9. Sterilize enough baby girls to assure zero population growth.
10. Sterilize each woman who gives birth to a second child.
11. Establish a national system of free abortions on demand to any woman of any age for any reason.

Some New Malthusians take even more extreme positions. Pentti Linkola suggests that we annihilate most of the human race (Milbank, 1994). He compares humanity to a sinking ship with 100 passengers and a lifeboat that can hold only 10. He says, "We need to end aid to the Third World, stop giving asylum to refugees—and a war would be good, too." To prove that he is serious, he adds, "If there were a button I could press that meant millions of people would die, I would gladly sacrifice myself."

ZERO POPULATION GROWTH. New Malthusians usually support zero population growth. Most people decide to have fewer children not because of a world population problem but because of the attitudes, beliefs, and values produced by their location in an industrial or postindustrial society.

Perspectives Depend on Social Conditions ■ For zero population growth to occur in the Least Industrialized Nations, small families must meet people's needs. Adults must be confident that they do not need their grown children to take care of them when they are sick or old.

Proposals to Achieve Zero Population Growth ■ If we want to achieve zero population growth, here are some social policies that can help to achieve it.

1. Encourage women to go to college and graduate school. Again, the more education that women attain, the fewer children they bear.
2. Encourage women to want careers. Careers reduce commitment to motherhood: Women find satisfactions in their careers, and their families become dependent on their income for a higher standard of living.
3. Distribute free or low-cost birth control devices to everyone, including teenagers.
4. Teach zero population growth to schoolchildren.
5. Pay women to be sterilized. The payment can be small, for $20 or $30 in the Least Industrialized Nations goes a long way when annual incomes are less than $1,000.
6. Make international aid, including the exporting of Western medicines, dependent on a country lowering its birthrates.
7. Tie food aid to agricultural reform.

In what might seem a very cold, brutal policy, the United States used food to force agricultural reform in India: Each month's shipment depended on progress in meeting monthly agricultural goals. Today India can feed itself (L. R. Brown, 1985).

The other Least Industrialized Nations also have the potential to produce enough food to feed them. Asia used to have famines that killed millions. Now Asia *exports* excess food. China broke up its communal farms and, using capitalist (profit-oriented) incentives, produces more food than it needs for its 1.3 billion people (Critchfield, 1986).

NOT A REMEDY. Population control is not a remedy. First, as we reviewed earlier, if we were to achieve zero population growth, population momentum would keep the world population growing for another 50 years or so. Second, even if the world's population were to stabilize exactly where it is now, all the other social problems that we discuss in this text would remain. A population not growing could not solve poverty, sexism, racism, ageism, urban blight, drug addiction, violence, discrimination, and environmental decay.

Restructuring Global Markets

Some agree that the root of the population problem is poverty and that to eradicate poverty we need to restructure global markets. To do this, however, would mean that rich nations would have to redistribute their wealth. Why would they do this? Their people do not want to lower their standard of living.

DEBTS, TRADE, AND STABLE PRICES. Other than redistributing the world's wealth, then, what can we do? Back in the 1970s, Michael Harrington suggested a moderate policy. He said that the imbalance in global trade loads crushing debt onto the shoulders of the Least Industrialized Nations. This debt prevents them from developing their own standard of living. Harrington (1977) called for canceling their debt and increasing trade with them. He also pointed out that nations with specialized economies (such as coffee, bananas, or oil) suffer from fluctuations in the price they receive for their commodities. To stabilize prices, he suggested that we create a world organization to buy commodities when the price dips below a specified level and to sell them when they rise to a certain point. He also suggested **indexing**—tracking the amount poor nations pay for products. Indexing could lower the price that poor nations pay for manufactured goods.

SELF-INTEREST, GLOBAL MARKETS, AND GEOPOLITICS. Such proposals require altruism on the part of the Most Industrialized Nations, not self-interest. It may well be in the interest of the wealthy nations to restructure global markets to give greater benefits to the Least Industrialized Nations. If they don't, they may face a more hostile world. The Iraqi invasion of Kuwait in 1990 may have been an attempt by a Least Industrialized Nation to restructure global markets. The counterattack by the Western nations under the leadership of the United States (the Gulf War) may also have been an attempt by the Most Industrialized Nations to maintain the structure of global markets. As more Least Industrialized Nations gain access to nuclear, biological, and chemical weapons, it is going to be more difficult for the Most Industrialized Nations to maintain their control of global markets.

Illegal Immigration

To close this section, let's look at illegal immigration in the United States. We should note that such immigration is also taking place around the globe: Russians enter Latvia illegally, Poles rush into Great Britain, and North Koreans settle in China. Let's look more closely at this problem in the United States—focusing on the experience of the illegal immigrant. The Thinking Critically about Social Problems box on the next page offers you one perspective.

The Future of the Problem

As we saw earlier, demographers cannot even agree what the future population of a given country will be, much less the future population of the world.

The New Malthusian Viewpoint

THE PESSIMISTIC VIEW: EXHAUSTING THE WORLD'S RESOURCES IS INEVITABLE

High Food Prices ■ If population outstrips food production, as the New Malthusians say it will, supply and demand will raise the price of food. Some Americans already find

THINKING CRITICALLY about Social Problems

GOING NORTH: THE DREAM AND THE REALITY

Our news media are filled with accounts of the "invasion" of millions of Mexicans who thumb their nose at immigration laws, who fill jobs few others want, who work for so little they drive down the price of labor, who commit crimes here, and who demand citizenship despite their illegal status. But what is *their* experience? What is life like for them?

To Americans, it looks as though Mexicans, after crossing the border, disperse throughout the country. On the contrary, when Mexicans enter the United States, most have a specific destination in mind, not just "someplace where I can find work." Some *migrant paths,* the routes between sending and receiving areas, are so established that they connect specific towns in Mexico with specific towns in the United States.

Nathan Thornburgh (2006), a reporter, studied the connection that has developed between Tuxpan, Mexico, and the Hamptons on New York's Long Island. It all started 30 years ago when a tourist from the Hamptons asked directions from a skinny Mexican kid, Mario Coria. The two struck up a conversation, and the tourist offered Mario a job as his gardener. He arranged for Mario to receive plane tickets and a visa.

Mario was a hard worker, and he prospered. He sent money back home and built a nice house. On his return visits, other men from Tuxpan asked for his help in getting to the United States. Their destination, of course, would be where Mario had experience, the Hamptons. A few friends found ways to cross the border and travel to Mario, who helped them find jobs. Over the years, the one grew into a dozen, and the dozen into the hundreds of Tuxpeños who now work in the Hamptons as gardeners, house cleaners, roofers, and day laborers.

You have to work hard to make it in the Hamptons. You have to line up on the street early in the morning and scramble to the cars that stop, ready to take any job anyone offers you—unless you're one of the lucky ones who had a relative come earlier and arrange a regular job for you.

It is crowded where you live. An entrepreneur has purchased a suburban house and placed a padlock on each of its four bedroom doors. You share one bedroom with two other men. The neighbors are angry that so many single men are living in one house, and they shout at you. Since they shout in English, you don't know what they are saying, but you do know that they are hostile.

You miss home. You knew everyone in Tuxpan, and life was so laid back. Some mornings you are so depressed that you can hardly force yourself out of bed.

But your dream keeps you going—to send enough money to your wife in Tuxpan so you can go back home and open your own little business. Maybe, even, if you work hard enough, you'll have enough money to build a pretty house, one with flowers and bright colors.

Right now, though, you've got to live with these other men and keep sending your wife enough money so she and the kids can keep eating.

You've heard the stories. Some of the wives back home have taken lovers while their husbands are up North. There's even a name for the guy, Sancho. And the running joke. "I've got to send more money to my wife. Sancho needs a new pair of shoes."

Your wife knows better. Your mother keeps you informed. But then there is that gnawing thought—would she really tell you, since she loves you and she knows how disturbed you would be? Then, too, she needs your remittances to survive, and if you came home the money would dry up.

And you know of the husbands here in the Hamptons who have found other women. After all, to achieve the dream, you have to be here for years, and with the increased surveillance at the border and that 700-mile-long wall being built, it has become more difficult to make the trip back home.

To make matters worse, you learn about some Tuxpeños who have achieved the dream. They've gone home and opened their businesses—and found there weren't enough customers to make a living.

To top it off, those who go home are seen as too American to be real Tuxpeños. Some neighbors even call them gringo.

You are caught in the middle. Too Mexican to be a gringo, and too gringo to be a Mexican. The dream of earning enough money to have a good life back home, though, keeps you going. It helps you get up in the morning, even though the dream recedes a bit each day.

FOR YOUR CONSIDERATION

The proposals to solve the problem of having millions of illegal immigrants in the United States range from hunting them all down and deporting them to granting amnesty to them all. What do you think we should do?

food expensive, but the burden on the Least Industrialized Nations will be greater. Already poor, and burdened by debt to the Most Industrialized Nations, they cannot afford to import food.

More Famines ▪ If the New Malthusians are right, millions of people will starve each year, and the world will face a flood of economic refugees. Neither the Least Industrialized Nations nor the Most Industrialized Nations will be willing to accept the stream of hundreds of thousands of poor, uneducated, culturally foreign people. To do so would heighten social tension. Consequently, huge numbers of dislocated people may live in "temporary" refugee camps.

Riots, Revolutions, and Repression ▪ If there is not enough food to feed the masses flocking to the cities in search of work and a better life, the Least Industrialized Nations will face riots and revolution. In response, governments will become more repressive. Because political and civil disorder can upset the global balance of power that the Most Industrialized Nations try to control, these more powerful and wealthy nations may encourage such repression.

The Anti-Malthusian Viewpoint

THE OPTIMISTIC VIEW: THE FUTURE IS WHAT WE MAKE IT. The Anti-Malthusians, of course, foresee a different future. The idea that famines are inevitable is a myth. Such images are a scare tactic designed to encourage people to have fewer children (J. L. Simon, 1981). The earth can support several times more people than it does now.

TECHNOLOGY AND ABUNDANCE. Poorly managed, the earth's natural systems (fishing grounds, forests, and grasslands) can collapse, causing a loss of productivity and bringing terrible suffering to humanity. These are renewable resources, however, and, carefully managed, they can produce all that the world, even a growing one, will ever need.

In a future **biotech society,** bioengineering will produce pest-resistant plants that produce their own fertilizers. From gene splicing will come cereals that replace nitrogen in the soil, allowing farmers to bypass expensive petroleum-based fertilizers. We will produce low-fat cows and chickens that lay several eggs a day. Not only can the so-called inevitable cataclysm so widely touted by the New Malthusians be prevented, but the world will also be able to enjoy a future of abundance.

If any of this sounds unrealistic, note that biotech agriculture already exists. We have not just cloned animals, but we also have produced **designer animals,** gene-spliced farm animals that produce more meat and milk. We have corn that makes its own insecticide (Kilman, 2006). Our goats produce spider silk, and other animals produce medicine (Kristoff, 2002; Osborne, 2002).

THE FOURTH STAGE OF THE DEMOGRAPHIC TRANSITION: THE COMING POPULATION SHRINKAGE. If you want to peer into the future, look at the nations that have entered the fourth stage of demographic transition. (This stage is illustrated on Figure 12-6 on page 430.) The populations of these nations have begun to shrink. The world's other nations will also enter this fourth stage; and, despite their current rapid population growth, they, too, will fill more coffins than cradles. As this process continues, the population of the world will reverse itself, and it will become smaller. When this occurs, we don't know at what point the world's population will stabilize.

UNBALANCED STAGES AND GLOBAL UPHEAVAL. Before this occurs, however, we face a global realignment of nations that will likely bring global disorder. Consider one

dilemma facing nations entering the fourth stage of demographic transition. Because their birthrates are so low, they don't produce enough workers for their factories. Yet to maintain their standard of living, they need to keep those factories operating. Wanting those jobs—and waiting not so patiently—are masses of unemployed young people in the Least Industrialized Nations.

The Example of France ■ Those who emigrate from the Least Industrialized Nations to the nations that have entered the fourth stage of demographic transition bring with them customs that differ from those of their host nations. Germany and France have millions of workers from Turkey and other Muslim countries. The French are vocal in their opposition to "non-French" customs that immigrants bring with them. French officials and politicians have spoken openly against Muslim women wearing veils in public, and they prohibit Muslim girls from wearing scarves in school. One political party, whose slogan is "France for the French," has even made anti-immigration its cornerstone. Within this context of hostility, Muslim youth throughout France have rioted.

PRONATALIST POLICIES. Fearful of a shrinking population and the arrival of more immigrants that don't share French culture, the French government has initiated **pronatalist policies,** policies that encourage women to bear children. If French women bear more children, there will be more French to operate the offices and factories. But if the French government offers women benefits for giving birth, these benefits must also go to the "new" French. This will increase births among a group that already has a high birthrate, a group that is feared by the traditional French immigrants.

THE LONG-TERM FUTILITY OF PRONATALIST POLICIES. With the factors that lower the birthrate firmly in place around the globe, it is unlikely that social policies can have anything more than a short-term effect on a country's fertility. Facing a shrinking workforce amidst the increasing needs of a growing elderly population, accompanied by a possible wave of culturally distinct immigrants, countries in the fourth stage of demographic transition are trying to increase birthrates. To better understand this dilemma, read the Global Glimpse box on the next page.

THE ROLE OF IMMIGRANTS. In addition to uncertain birthrates, a nation's policy toward immigrants can change. A nation may turn inward and exile immigrants, or it may welcome them. If the United States did not welcome immigrants, its population would be shrinking. Only its millions of immigrants keep it growing. The United States, however, is one of the world's largest land masses, and as we have seen, it is relatively unpopulated.

Which Will It Be?

Will the earth be filled with so many people that there is not enough food for them all, with famine and suffering stalking the earth, as the New Malthusians anticipate? Or are the Anti-Malthusians right, and without curtailing population growth, the world's nations will be able to manage their resources, feed and clothe themselves, and provide a high standard of living for everyone?

It certainly appears that the world has the potential to meet its nutritional needs, but this would require that the Most Industrialized Nations cooperate to meet the challenge. Perhaps they will rise to the occasion.

"What is happening now has simply never happened before in the history of the world," said Nicholas Eberstadt, a demographer (Specter, 1998). Never before has a country's birthrate plunged so low that its population shrank. But this is now happening in several European countries.

Is a birthrate too low to replenish a population really new in history? We have had instances in the past when a country's leaders thought that their nation had too few children. Usually this was because many young men had been killed in war, and they wanted new soldiers to replace them. Officials would then initiate *pronatalism*, policies that favor or promote births. They were successful. Men and women responded to the rewards and had more children.

Today's situation is different. Populations are shrinking not because of war but because women are bearing so few children that they aren't replacing the people who die. What is happening in Sweden, one of these countries, helps us understand some of the implications of the fourth stage of the demographic transition—and why pronatalism is failing.

Reasons that Swedish couples, like this one, are choosing to have only one child or to remain childless are discussed in the text. Countries throughout Europe are experiencing similar low birth rates.

than young, one in which there will not be enough workers to pay for the health care and pensions of the elderly.

The culprit? It is prosperity and freedom. Swedish women are staying in school longer, putting more emphasis on careers, marrying later—and having fewer children.

Like the Germans, Italians, Spanish, and other Europeans, the Swedes are developing different ideas about children and about what they want out of life. Here are some of their comments:

"People want their freedom. They see children as a burden, as an inconvenience."

"It's a sacrifice to have a child."

"Children cost more than they used to. Today you have to bring them to the pool, and you need to get a nanny, and they have to learn a foreign language. Children have more needs. Parents just didn't think of all these things before."

Ninni Lundblad, a biologist who works in Stockholm, said, "Did your parents sit down with a spreadsheet and figure out whether they could afford to have two or three children?"

If any country is pronatalist, it is Sweden. Health care for mothers and children is free. Maternity centers offer free health checks and free courses in preparation for childbirth. When a child is born, the parents are eligible for 15 months' leave of absence with pay. They can divide the leave between them any way they want, as long as the father gets at least one of the months. When a child is sick, either parent can stay home to care for it and receive full pay for missed work—up to 60 days a year per child (The Swedish Institute, 1992; Froman, 1994; Bernhardt & Goldscheider, 2001).

Births should be booming, families growing larger, the baby carriage industry prosperous. Instead, Sweden is becoming a lopsided society, one in which there are more old people

No, they didn't. They just had them. But Ninni Lundblad, who said this so derisively, has no children (Specter, 1998).

So why don't Sweden's generous pronatalist policies work? Perhaps this statement by Jan Delanor of Stockholm best sums it up:

"I am supposed to have an extra child to help the system? Nonsense. I'll have a child if and when it makes sense to me, not because the government thinks it's a good idea."

Swedes are finding so much more that makes sense to them—education, travel, career, money, and spending time with friends. All these things come before having children.

1. The world is seeing an urban explosion. In 1900, about 13% of the world's population lived in *cities*. Today about 50% do. The U.S. figure is almost 80%.

2. Symbolic interactionists emphasize that those areas of the city that appear undesirable, disorganized, and threatening to outsiders may be viable communities to their inhabitants. Slums are worlds in miniature, with their own hierarchies of status, standards, and controls over behavior. It takes an insider's frame of reference to understand such worlds.

3. According to functionalists, specialized zones develop naturally as a city grows. Each zone meets certain needs of a city's residents, and people with distinctive characteristics live there. Antagonisms result from the *invasion–succession cycle,* as one group displaces another. Urban problems are generally concentrated in the area adjacent to the central business district.

4. According to the conflict perspective, business leaders caused the decline of the inner city. They influenced politicians to subsidize the relocation of their businesses to the suburbs and to build a transportation system to move their products. Suburban development came at the city's expense; it reduced its tax base and spurred the flight of the middle class.

5. Violence is such a problem that youth gangs even control some areas of our cities. Violence is also common in our urban schools. Poverty and discrimination remain background factors, but riots require a *precipitating incident.*

6. Ethnic minorities have gained political clout in our urban areas, and the transition of power has gone quite smoothly. *Megalopolises,* interconnected metropolitan centers that once were a series of smaller towns and cities, have emerged. The move to the sunbelt is forcing *regional restratification* in terms of capital, human resources, and political power.

7. *Demographers* study the size, composition, growth, and distribution of human populations. They disagree as to why Europe's population surged after 1750. Some cite improved public health, others a change in diet.

8. In 1798, Thomas Malthus predicted that the world's population would outstrip its food supply. His prediction is still controversial. The New Malthusians fear that the population of the world is entering the latter stages of an *exponential growth curve,* and most of this growth is in the nations least able to afford it. They favor an immediate cutback in population. The Anti-Malthusians claim that the world is producing more than enough food; the problem is the poor distribution of food due to political arrangements.

9. By applying symbolic interactionism, we can see why the birthrate is higher in the Least Industrialized Nations. There children are viewed as a blessing from God: They give the parents status in the present, and they provide security for the future.

10. By applying functionalism, we can see that exporting medicine and public health techniques from the Most Industrialized Nations was a *latent dysfunction* for the Least Industrialized Nations. It created problems by upsetting the balance between their birthrates and death rates.

11. Conflict theorists stress that the hunger that some nations experience is due to *food politics,* political and economic arrangements that favor the Most Industrialized Nations. Food politics creates and intensifies problems in the Least Industrialized Nations.

12. Demographers who take a New Malthusian position stress the pressures being placed on the earth's three natural systems: fishing grounds, forests, and grasslands. Two dangers are the threat of famine as the result of our dependence on specialized strains of grains and the intensification of natural disasters. Even if we attain zero population growth, because of *population momentum* it would still take 50 to 70 years for the world's population to stabilize.

13. Demographers who take an Anti-Malthusian position argue that the earth can support many more people. Food production is outpacing population growth, fewer people are dying from famines, and much land remains uncultivated. A growing population can spur us to greater productivity.

14. The New Malthusians recommend social policies to curb population growth. The Anti-Malthusians advocate policies that encourage (or do not discourage) population growth. Both sides agree that we should stimulate agricultural development. Exporting Western agricultural techniques to the Least Industrialized Nations is not viable, because it requires a vast support system that these nations cannot afford.

15. The New and Anti-Malthusians envision different futures. The New Malthusians anticipate widespread hunger in the Least Industrialized Nations, which may lead to more repression. The Anti-Malthusians stress that the world's nations hold the potential for meeting human needs, that one day the world will face the problem of population shrinkage.

KEY TERMS

THINKING CRITICALLY ABOUT CHAPTER 12

1. Do you think that symbolic interactionism, functionalism, or conflict theory does the best job of explaining urban problems? Why?
2. If a bank finds that a certain area within a city contains many "risky" investments and makes a business decision to "redline" the area (refusing to give loans to people who live or work in the area), do you think it is proper for government to interfere with the bank's business and to ban such a practice? Explain.
3. Do you think the New Malthusians or the Anti-Malthusians are right? Explain.
4. Which perspective (symbolic interactionism, functionalism, or conflict theory) do you think best explains the world's problems of population and food? Explain.

BY THE NUMBERS: THEN AND NOW

- Population of U.S. southern region in 1970: **63,000,000**
- Population of U.S. southern region in 2000: **100,000,000**

- Population of U.S. northeastern region in 1970: **49,000,000**
- Population of U.S. northeastern region in 2000: **54,000,000**

- Index of world food production per capita in 1952: **100**
- Index of world food production per capita in 2006: **160**

- Population, in billions, of the Least Industrialized Nations in 1950: **3**
- Population, in billions, of the Least Industrialized Nations now: **9**

- Population, in billions, of the Most Industrialized Nations in 1950: **1**
- Population, in billions, of the Most Industrialized Nations now: **1.75**

- Birthrate of White American women in 1960: **3.5**
- Birthrate of White American women now: **2.1**

- Birthrate of African American women in 1960: **4.5**
- Birthrate of African American women now: **2.1**

MySocLab

What can you find in MySocLab? mysoclab™ ALLYN & BACON www.mysoclab.com

- Complete Ebook
- Practice Tests and Exams
- Multimedia Activities
- Mapping and Data Analysis Exercises

- Research and Writing Advice
- Interactive Social Surveys
- Sociology in the News

CHAPTER 13

The Environmental Crisis

Jim Henslin hadn't been teaching very long at Southern Illinois University when he decided that he wanted to move to a farm. This is how he recounts his experience:

Them's red-tagged, boys.

I advertised for a farm in the county papers. The third one I visited was exactly what I was looking for. It was remote ("in the boonies," as the phrase goes), 165 acres of trees and pastures, with its own pond for swimming and fishing. (The pond was also my water source.) At $150 an acre, I knew I couldn't go wrong. My fellow professors were paying as much for a house as I would for the entire farm.

Being a town boy, I had a lot to learn about farm life. Eventually, I owned a dog, a horse, a sheep, and 25 head of cattle. My inexperience led to several humorous events (I can laugh at them now): the sharpie farmer sticking me with the runt of his herd, the horse I bought refusing to let me ride her, the cattle breaking through the fence and running away.

One of my most insightful lessons in farm life came one Saturday morning when I went to a cattle auction. Area farmers bring their excess cattle to these auctions, and fellow farmers—and meat companies, as it turned out—bid on them.

Standing amidst men wearing hats emblazoned with "Allis-Chalmers," "John Deere," and "Nutra-Feeds," I realized that I was entering a new culture. I was enjoying the moment, lost in reverie as I observed the auctioneer and the bidding. When one group of animals was brought into the ring, the auctioneer said, "Them's red-tagged, boys. Them's red-tagged."

I asked a man standing next to me what that meant. He said, "You can't buy 'em. They've got some disease. You can't take 'em back to your farm."

I nodded, then asked, "What happens to 'em, then?"

He replied, "Only guys from the meat packing plant can bid on 'em."

I let this sink in, relieved that I didn't eat much sandwich meat.

Then I recalled something my grandfather had told me when I was a child. He farmed on Minnesota's brutally cold Canadian border, and to earn money to buy his farm he had worked at a meat packing plant in St. Paul. I noticed that he always refused sandwich meat and had asked him about it. He said that it was because of what he had seen at the meat packing plant. He mentioned guys spitting into the meat.

I suppose I was too young for my grandfather to explain his revulsion, but I think I felt something similar on that Saturday morning. Animals too diseased to live on farms were judged by our government perfectly acceptable to be turned into lunch meat.

The Problem in Sociological Perspective

To better understand today's environmental problem, let's look into the distant past.

Environmental Destruction in the Past: The Myth of the Noble Savage

THE MYTH. Throughout history, Native American Indians have been known to live in harmony with their environment. They considered themselves one with the water, earth, sky, animals, and plants. Unlike people today, who destroy their environment for short-sighted

Many of our historical impressions are shrouded in myth. One example is the notion that Native Americans lived in perfect harmony with the environment.

gains, people used to use earth's resources wisely. Their presence did not disrupt the earth's natural systems. One old woman of the Wintu tribe explained:

The White people never cared for land or deer or bear. When we Indians kill meat, we eat it all up. When we dig roots, we make little holes. . . . We shake down acorns and pine nuts. We don't chop down trees. We only use dead wood. But the White people plow up the ground, pull up the trees, kill everything. . . . How can the spirit of the earth like the White man? . . . Everywhere the White man has touched it, it is sore. (Lee, 1959, p. 163)

This view evokes an image of a primitive past where humans were in harmony with the natural world and its resources. But as we will discuss below, this image does not reflect the entire truth of how humans have treated their environment historically.

EARLY HUMANS AND THE EXTINCTION OF ANIMALS. Humans have been destroying the environment for as long as they have existed. Carnivorous kangaroos, giant lizards, and horned turtles became extinct when humans set fire to trees and shrubs to keep warm or clear the land (Hotz, 1999). In North America, early inhabitants burned forests to help them hunt and control mosquitoes. As a result, prehistoric hunters wiped out three-fourths of the animals weighing more than 100 pounds (Lutz, 1959; Martin, 1967; Hotz, 1999). In translation: Early settlers extinguished more species of large animals than humans have in all the years since they started to record such events.

THE DESTRUCTION OF ENTIRE CIVILIZATIONS. Some early destruction of the environment may have been so extensive that it brought down entire civilizations.

The Mesopotamians ■ In the lush river basin of the Tigris and Euphrates, in what is now Iraq, the Mesopotamians developed a highly advanced civilization (Ozturk et al., 2004). Their extensive irrigation system provided abundant food, allowing their civilization to flourish. Their irrigation system, however, did not have drainage. As water evaporated, it left the remaining water salty. Over the centuries, as the water seeped into the earth, the underground water table rose, making the land too salty for crops. Eventually, agriculture collapsed and, with it, so did the Mesopotamian civilization.

The Mayans ■ In what is today Guatemala and Yucatán, another civilization met a similar fate. The Mayans developed their civilization over 17 centuries, reaching their peak in agriculture, architecture, and science in 900 CE. Then, within decades, 90% of the Mayans disappeared, their population dropping from 5 million to fewer than half a million. The cause may have been environmental destruction. Samples from lake beds indicate heavy soil erosion. As the population increased, Mayans cleared the land of trees. The topsoil washed from the denuded land, and with it went the agricultural productivity on which their civilization depended (Fernandez et al., 2005).

The Anasazi ■ In what is now Arizona and New Mexico (Budiansky, 1987), the Anasazi built roads, an irrigation system, and pueblos of stone and masonry. Some pueblos were four or five stories high and had up to 800 rooms. As they became more civilized, the Anasazi cut down so many trees in the canyons that they had to travel 50 miles or more to gather wood for fuel. Having stripped the forest beyond its ability to replenish itself, the civilization collapsed.

The Tragedy of the Commons

Far from being thoughtful conservationists or caretakers of their environment, earlier humans destroyed limited resources thoughtlessly. Because today's civilizations are larger, however, our capacity for destruction is greater.

Self-interest often works against the logic of environmental preservation. Biologist Garrett Hardin (1968) shares the following parable known as *the tragedy of the commons.*

Let us picture a pasture open to everyone. The number of cattle exactly matches the amount of available grass. Each herdsman, however, will seek to maximize his own gain. He thinks to himself: "If I add a cow to my herd, I will receive all the proceeds from the sale of this additional animal. The little overgrazing that this extra animal causes will be shared by all the other herdsmen."

This herdsman adds another animal to his herd. This works, so he eventually adds another . . . and another. And, for the same reason, the other herdsmen who share the commons do the same. Each is part of a system that rewards individuals for increasing the size of their herds. And therein lays the tragedy of the commons. The pasture is limited, and additional stress eventually causes it—and the civilization that depends on it—to fail. As each pursues his or her own interest, all rush to their collective ruin.

IN SUM   One irony of civilization is that our efforts to improve life often destroy the very environment on which life depends. Our civilization's contribution to environmental destruction is woven throughout history. With new technology, incessant demands for an ever-rising standard of living, and more people on earth than ever before, we have magnified our destructive capacity.

The Scope of the Problem

To understand the scope of environmental problems, we must perceive the environment in interconnected, global terms.

"Everything Is Connected to Everything Else"

PERCEIVING INTERCONNECTIONS.   Even local events are part of a global problem. Consider this example:

Long ago, farmers such as Jim Henslin's grandfather in Northern Minnesota sprayed their fields with DDT, the practice at the time. The excess DDT, a virulent pesticide, often ran from fields into creeks. These creeks ran into local rivers. From there, the chemicals flowed into larger waterways, ultimately creating higher than average rates of cancer. These cancer-causing chemicals moved from rivers through oceans, ultimately affecting many nations.

The connections between us and others are not always apparent, but we all are part of an interrelated system that encompasses humanity, technology, and the environment. Sociologists must view social problems in global perspective.

THREATENING THE PLANET.   Human actions are upsetting our planet's precarious balance. The population explosion we discussed in the last chapter, the industrialization emphasized throughout this text, and the drive for higher living standards are prime examples. If we deplete natural resources, as some civilizations of the past have done, our civilization, too, may collapse. This is a common fear among *ecologists,* scientists who study **ecology**—the relationship between living things and their environment.

For many, the primary threat to our environment and humanity's future is pollution. **Pollution** is the accumulation in the air, water, and land of substances harmful to living things. This is a good definition, but for our purposes we want to look at pollution in *social* terms. Consequently, we can define *pollution* as the presence of substances that interfere with socially desired uses of the air, water, land, or food (Davies & Davies, 1975).

Pollution by humans first occurred when fires were lit for warmth, cooking, or visual delight. Since then it has intensified beyond anything the world has ever seen. Today pollution comes from the world's industrial giants as well as nations that are industrializing rapidly. Two significant examples are China and India, the world's largest countries. Their headlong rush to industrialize is placing considerable additional strain on the earth's fragile environment.

LEAVING A LEGACY OF DEATH. The depletion of resources and pollution is due to short-sighted self-interest. In the former Soviet Union, pollution was dealt with in secret (Feshbach, 1992). Scientists and journalists could not even mention pollution in public. Those who demonstrated against pollution faced possible imprisonment. With little public attention and stifled social policy, pollution greatly increased.

Citizens of Russia and the other former Soviet states have been left to deal with harmful pollutants—from abandoned factories that used to manufacture chemical and germ weapons to billions of pounds of nuclear waste that were simply dumped into rivers or holes in the ground (Garelik, 1996; J. Miller, 1999; Gessen, 2001). Birth defects in Russia have increased while life expectancy has declined. The effects are so devastating that the average Russian man dies at age 58, compared to 75 in the rest of Europe. Russian women live to be 72, while most European women live to be 82 ("WHO/Europe" 2006).

How do we avoid such a legacy in the United States? We must implement those tools necessary to avoid such lethal consequences of our actions. The materials in this chapter can contribute to this effort.

Looking at the Problem Theoretically

Each theoretical perspective helps us understand the environmental crisis. Using symbolic interactionism, we will examine how the environment became a social problem. Through functionalism, we will focus on the interdependence of people and their environment. Lastly, we will use conflict theory to examine the clashing interests of environmentalists and those who pollute.

Humans have been treating their environment as though it were a garbage bag. The bill for the wanton destruction is coming due.

Symbolic Interactionism

How did environmental issues become a social problem? To many it seems obvious that the environment is endangered. On an everyday level, for example, in 2007 San Francisco became the first U.S. city to outlaw plastic grocery bags at checkout stands. The bags that were once considered environmentally friendly have been found to kill marine life (Goodyear, 2007).

On a broader level, people who have never seen a tropical rain forest are upset that they are being cut down to harvest lumber and to clear land for cattle and crops. Around the world, people are bothered by the harm that is done to whales, seals, dolphins, and owls and by the loss of plants and animals. A worldwide protest movement has begun.

But it was not always this way. Little more than two generations ago, people rarely thought of the environment as a problem. Let's find out how the environment became a social problem.

OBJECTIVE CONDITIONS BUT LITTLE SUBJECTIVE CONCERN. Even when objective conditions are widespread and harmful, they are not automatically considered social problems. Objective conditions must be translated into subjective concerns. For the environment, this transformation took many years. In the 1800s, hundreds of steel plants in the United States polluted the air, and no one considered poor air quality a social problem. Ever since the automobile was invented, people have been discarding worn-out tires in gullies and creeks, but only recently have these actions been regarded as part of a social problem. The same is true of the disappearance of animal species, which began millennia ago: Many European Americans welcomed the near extinction of the bison, seeing it as a way to defeat the Indians. The passenger pigeon, during its mass annual migration, used to darken the skies for days. Its extinction in 1914 was seen as unfortunate—an interesting bit of history, perhaps—but not tragic.

THE GROWTH OF SUBJECTIVE CONCERNS. So how did environmental decay and animal extinction become part of a pressing, worldwide social problem? That is, how did subjective concerns grow? The environment became a hot topic in the 1960s. This period was characterized by high social activism among college students, who adopted the environment as one of their concerns. Students began to participate in environmental protests, and "Earth Days" began on college campuses. How did this high subjective concern—marked by activism and demonstrations—come about? This is just what sociologists Clay Schoenfeld, Robert Meier, and Robert Griffin (1979) set out to discover.

Humans have destroyed many animal species, extinguishing some without remorse. Few elephants are left in the wild. Poachers hunt them for their tusks, selling the ivory on the black market. Soon, the only elephants left will be those in zoos, circuses, and in state preserves (such as this one in the Kruger National Park, South Africa).

Shown in this 1910 photo is Teddy Roosevelt, president of the United States from 1901 to 1909. Roosevelt, who headed a conservation movement, loved to kill "big game." The text explains how the concern for "conserving" wilderness areas to prevent hunters from running out of moving targets evolved into today's environmental concerns.

The Conservation Movement ■ As these researchers looked through historical records, they found that the 1960s were not the first time that Americans had become concerned about the environment. The issue had emerged earlier—in 1900. At that time, Theodore Roosevelt, who was the president of the United States from 1901 to 1909, spearheaded a conservation movement. Roosevelt was an avid hunter, and he had grown concerned that the wildlife he liked to hunt was disappearing from our wilderness areas (Morrison, Hornback, & Warner, 1972; Gale, 1972). In one of the ironies of history, Roosevelt, who liked killing animals so much that he also roamed Africa in search of elephants, tigers, and lions, supported bills that established our national park system, setting aside millions of acres for public use.

From Conservation to Environment ■ There is vast difference between conserving wilderness areas and concern over the quality of our food, air, and water. How, then, did "conservation" transform into "environmental concern"? Schoenfeld, Meier, and Griffin found that environmental transformation moved through five stages:

1. *Professionals* were the first to become troubled by problems in the environment. Knowing that we depend on natural resources, some professionals concluded that the situation was crucial. In 1959, geographers began to write journal articles about environmental problems and to present papers at their conventions.
2. *Interest groups* then began to form around specific issues.
3. *Government agencies,* aroused by the activities of the interest groups, began to issue environmental reports.
4. The *news media* publicized the issue. At first, reporters had difficulty understanding environmental issues. It was especially difficult for them to communicate the idea that people, resources, and technology are all part of a single, larger system. They tended to view environmental issues on an individual basis—such as an oil spill or a train wreck that spewed contaminants. As reporters began to understand the basic environmental principle that "everything is connected to everything else," they began to broaden their global perspective.
5. The *public* became alarmed as media gave more coverage to environmental issues, three in particular: (1) The first was the publication of Rachel Carson's *The Silent Spring* in 1962. Focusing on the dangers of pesticides, this blockbuster alerted Americans to environmental hazards. The book, however, focused on a single issue and didn't lead the public or the news media to explore the interconnections among environmental events. (2) In 1969 an oil well erupted off the coast of Santa Barbara, California. Each day for weeks 20,000 gallons of oil poured into the water. Americans were riveted by this environmental disaster as national headlines reported the oil's slow drift to the coast. When the oil finally hit Santa Barbara and blackened 20 miles of beautiful beaches, people were outraged (Davies & Davies, 1975). (3) Later that same year came the single most effective environmental message of the century—the view from the moon of earth. The Apollo 11 moon landing helped make the public aware that we live on a fragile, finite planet. With that first glimpse of us from the "outside," the public became much more aware that we all are partners on a small planet.

IN SUM Symbolic interactionists focus on the symbols that people use to communicate with one another, how those symbols develop, and how they are used to create and maintain our ideas of reality. The social problem of the environment did not appear in a social vacuum. Rather, the problem is a "social creation." Over the course of the five

stages summarized here, people's perceptions of the environment changed fundamentally. Professionals, reporters, and the general public began to see individual events as interconnected parts of a global problem. This changed perception transformed opinions of ourselves, our relationship with other living things, and even what we consider to be our place in the universe.

This change in how we symbolize ourselves and our world is ongoing: We still have a difficult time connecting what we do now with our distant future.

Functionalism

THE ESSENCE OF FUNCTIONALISM: INTERCONNECTIONS. The idea that community is connected to global policy is becoming more prevalent. We all know that though we are individuals, we are part of a larger group. We also know that the small groups to which we each belong are parts of a larger society and that our nation is part of a global network. Slowly, we are coming to grasp that we all are part of a global social system, that what each of us does—whether individual, group, or nation—affects others.

According to functionalists, each unit is part of a larger structure, with the activities of one part having functional or dysfunctional consequences for the other parts. In our **ecosystem** all life on the planet is interconnected in a finely balanced cycle rotating on the dynamic layer of the earth's surface.

THE ECOSYSTEM. Both biologists and sociologists who analyze environmental problems emphasize the interconnections between people and the earth's resources. No matter where we live on this globe, we need air, water, and soil to survive. Our survival depends on this ecosystem. Green plants produce oxygen for human and animal life. Plants, animals, and microorganisms purify the water in lakes and streams. Biological processes in the soil provide food and fuel. Anything that disrupts the earth's ecosystem threatens these finely balanced cycles. The major offender in disrupting the ecosystem has been industrialization.

FUNCTIONS AND DYSFUNCTIONS OF INDUSTRIALIZATION. Humans are intelligent and highly adaptable. We have settled into every habitable region of the globe. Technology has allowed humans to adapt to mountains and plains, to deserts and oceans, even to steamy jungles and ice-bound regions. Our intelligence has allowed us to dominate the earth. We have domesticated plants and animals. To improve our lives, we have harnessed the energy of animals and rivers, the sun and the wind.

It was the steam engine, though, that allowed us to harness energy on a scale unknown in history. The Industrial Revolution that followed its invention created countless new jobs and great wealth. Because of this revolution, the average person today enjoys a standard of living that previously was attained only by the wealthy.

Industrialization, however, also brought severe dysfunctional consequences for the earth's ecosystem. Production of material wealth damaged the air, water, and soil on which our existence depends. Our frenetic drive for a higher material standard of living has produced highly toxic industrial wastes, which we have strewn into almost every corner of the earth. In another irony of life, the expansion of our industrial systems to create a better life has damaged the environment that allows us life in the first place.

IN SUM Functionalists focus on how the parts of a social system are interconnected. As with earlier civilizations such as the Mesopotamians, the Mayans, and the Anasazi, our economic and political systems depend on a fragile ecosystem. Although we still have problems conceptualizing it, we have begun to think in terms of our being part of a complex, living machine called the environment. If our ecosystem fails, our society will collapse.

Conflict Theory

Opposing sides are lining up on environmental issues. Some view us as being on the verge of catastrophe, and they act politically to protect the environment. Others resist

what they consider arbitrary and irrational controls over their right to pollute. No one ever defends dirty water or filthy air, of course, for clean air and water have become commodities. Nevertheless, some groups fight efforts to reduce pollution. Let's look at this conflict.

ON ONE SIDE: ENVIRONMENTAL GROUPS. On one side are the groups organized to fight what they view as environmental threats. These environmental action groups consist of such organizations as Greenpeace, the National Wildlife Federation, the Izaak Walton League, the Sierra Club, Americans for Safe Food, and Earth First! Here is a statement from the Izaak Walton League that expresses this position:

> There is no justification for water pollution. The people of the United States are entitled to wholesome surface and groundwater, usable for all human needs. At a minimum, surface water should be of suitable quality for both recreational contact and for the protection and propagation of fish and wildlife. . . . The public goal should be maximal removal of pollutants from all waters. (Izaak Walton . . . , 2000, p. 11)

Environmental action groups have become a powerful political force. With chapters across the nation, these groups maintain lobbyists in Washington and state capitals, they promote legislation aggressively, and they hire lawyers to fight environmental cases in the courts. Many politicians support their efforts.

ON THE OTHER SIDE: POLLUTERS. Other groups oppose pollution control. At their core are the industrial polluters. Their dilemma is obvious. Pollution control is expensive and adds nothing to the value of their products. Manufacturers in the Most Industrialized Nations must compete with businesses that are located in the Least Industrialized Nations. Manufacturers in these nations enjoy not only the advantage of low-cost labor, but also the additional edge of not having to pay for pollution controls in the manufacturing process.

Manufacturers in the Most Industrialized Nations can't take a public stand in favor of pollution, of course. But they, too, lobby in Washington and the state capitals. As the Technology and Social Problems box on the next page illustrates, in some instances the polluters even have enough political clout to get laws passed that allow them to profit from their own pollution.

The polluters also hire lawyers who specialize in finding loopholes in pollution controls. Consider the automobile industry:

> In 1951, when it was discovered that automobiles were the major cause of smog in Los Angeles, the suggestion was made to develop electric cars. The auto industry formed a committee to study this proposal. The White House stacked the committee with representatives from the auto and oil industries. Their "surprising" conclusion: a recommendation against research on electric vehicles. (Davies & Davies, 1975)

The automobile industry's fight against pollution controls and alternative transportation—which continues today—illustrates a basic principle of conflict theory: that society is composed of competing groups whose interests often collide. It isn't just the interests of business and the public that collide, however. The interests of one business group can also conflict with those of another. Here is an obvious example:

> While the car manufacturers were opposing the control of automobile emissions, another group of manufacturers tried to pass laws that would require pollution control devices. This group was made up of the businesses that manufacture the pollution control equipment. For them, the more regulation the better—more stringent laws mean more profit.

A SPECIAL CONSEQUENCE: ENVIRONMENTAL INJUSTICE. Conflict and unequal power have led to a situation that sociologists call **environmental injustice**—the fact that pollution is more likely to hurt minorities and the poor (Ramo, 2003; Stolz & Wald, 2006).

Technology and Social Problems

HOW TO GET PAID TO POLLUTE: CORPORATE WELFARE AND BIG WELFARE BUCKS

Welfare is one of the most controversial topics in the United States. It arouses criticisms among the wealthy and middle class, who view welfare recipients as parasites. But have you heard about *corporate welfare?*

Corporate welfare describes handouts given to corporations. A state will reduce a company's taxes if it will remain within the state. A state may even provide the factory building at a bargain price if the business will provide future employment.

Corporate welfare even goes to companies that are known polluters. Borden Chemicals in Louisiana has buried hazardous wastes without a permit and released clouds of hazardous chemicals so thick that to protect drivers, the police have sometimes had to shut down the highway that runs near the plant. Borden even contaminated the groundwater beneath its plant, threatening the aquifer that provides drinking water for residents of Louisiana and Texas.

Borden's pollution has cost the company dearly: $3.6 million in fines, $3 million to clean up the groundwater and $400,000 for local emergency response units. That's a hefty $7 million. But when we take into account corporate welfare, the company didn't make out so badly. Its $15 million in reduced and canceled property taxes have brought Borden a net gain of $8 million (Bartlett & Steele, 1998). And that's not counting the savings the company racked up by not having to properly dispose of its toxic wastes in the first place.

Louisiana offers an incentive to help start-up companies. The problem is how they define "start-up." Although Exxon Corporation (now Exxon Mobil, the largest corporation in the United States, which has regularly posted record-setting U.S. quarterly profits) opened for business about 125 years ago, it had $213 million in property taxes canceled under this start-up program. Another company that Louisiana considered a "start-up" was Shell Oil Company, which had $140 million slashed from its taxes (Bartlett & Steele, 1998). Then there were a few other well-known companies redefined as "start-up": International Paper, Dow Chemical, Union Carbide, Boise Cascade, Georgia Pacific, and Procter & Gamble.

Near Baton Rouge, Louisiana.

Consider this:

Let's suppose that poor people were burning their old tires, fouling the air all around them, and the state said, "We know that we can't stop you from burning tires, so we'll give you a certificate for each tire that you don't burn. Other people want to burn tires, so you can make money by selling these certificates to them, giving them the right to burn a tire for each one that you don't burn."

This would be nonsense.

When a treaty was negotiated in Japan to reduce emissions of greenhouse gases, U.S. industries hit on a novel way to reap billions of dollars. They proposed a new corporate welfare law. This new law would issue credits to companies that reduce their emissions early—and even give them credits for reductions that took place years before the treaty. The average carbon-credit produced by a Least Industrialized Nation grants permission to a corporation in a Most Industrialized Nation to emit 1 ton of carbon dioxide (Ball, 2008). The company could then sell the credits for billions of dollars to companies that didn't reduce their emissions, allowing them to continue to pollute (Cushman, 1999). Now that's a great way to clean up—without cleaning up. The United Nations regulates the impact of pollution caused by the Least Industrialized Nations. In recent months (2008), the United Nations has objected to hydroelectric power, wind farms, and conservation efforts emerging in poorer countries because they suspect that their carbon-credits are being purchased by polluters in the Most Industrialized Nations.

This is because polluting industries locate where land is cheaper, places where the wealthy do not live. As a result, low-income communities, often inhabited by minorities, are more likely to be exposed to pollution. Sociologists have studied, formed, and joined environmental justice groups that fight to stop polluting industries.

IN SUM As conflict theorists examine environmental problems, they look at groups whose interests are being served. The efforts of environmentalists to eliminate what they see as dangers to public welfare conflict with what other groups see as their inherent right to make profits regardless of pollution. Those who campaign to develop a more healthy society run head on into the interests of powerful groups who see the cure as worse than the illness. This basic conflict runs throughout the environmental crisis.

Research Findings

How badly has our environment deteriorated? To answer this question, we will first examine the pollution of our air, land, water, and food supply. Then we will look at energy and resources. Finally, we will consider whether the whole environmental crisis has been exaggerated.

Air Pollution

A mixture of fog and smoke settled over Donora, Pennsylvania, during the last five days of October 1948. By Sunday, October 31, wind and rain finally cleared the smog.

Of the 12,300 people who lived in this steel mill town, about half (5,910) became sick. Another 1,440 were "severely affected." Seventeen died.

Front-page news stories compared Donora to the Meuse Valley in Belgium, where 60 people died in 1930. Both were heavily industrialized, and both had **thermal inversions,** a layer of cold air sealing in a lower layer of warm air. Thermal inversions trap smoke, exhaust, and particles causing more harm.

By Tuesday, November 2, most of Donora's dead were buried. The residents' reactions sound hauntingly familiar. The local doctor described the deaths as murder. An air pollution expert from a nearby university said the lungs of the people in the valley had suffered chronic damage. The superintendent of the steel factory, however, said, "I can't conceive how our plant has anything to do with the condition. There has been no change in the process since 1915." The workers, who saw dense smoke and fog as part of their way of life, said, "That smoke coming out of those stacks is putting bread and butter on our tables." And most of the public shrugged their shoulders and went about their business. (Bowen, 1972)

A few years later, in 1952, a "killer smog" settled on London. In just 5 days, 4,000 people were dead (Thorsheim, 2004). People became fearful as facts about air pollution emerged. **Air pollution** is a poison that accumulates in the human body. Besides causing eye, nose, and throat irritations, it can cause bronchitis, emphysema, and lung cancer, which lead to a slow, agonizing death.

CAUSES OF AIR POLLUTION. With air pollution a problem many of us will face, let's examine its main causes.

Fossil Fuels ■ The main cause of air pollution is the burning of **fossil fuels**—substances such as wood, coal, petroleum, and natural gas that are derived from living things. To produce electricity and manufacture the goods we consume, power plants and factories pour pollutants into the air. The worst polluter, however, is the internal combustion engine. The exhausts of cars, trucks, and buses emit poisons—sulfur dioxide, nitrogen oxide, hydrocarbons, and carbon monoxide. Vehicles also leave behind **carcinogens** (cancer-causing substances) from the asbestos particles in their brake linings.

Pollution is almost always unintended. On occasion, however, pollution is the result of deliberate, spiteful acts. The most dramatic example occurred in 1991 after U.S.-led forces defeated the Iraqi army in Kuwait. During their retreat, the Iraqi military ignited 600 oil wells, storage tanks, and refineries. The soot from the fires circled the globe (Naj, 1992).

Waste Incineration ■ A second major source of air pollution is waste incineration. The burning of plastics is especially damaging to our health because it creates PCBs (polychlorinated biphenyls), a potent toxin. Plastics are not **biodegradable;** that is, they do not disintegrate after being exposed to normal bacteria. Even steel rusts, but plastics endure almost indefinitely. Consequently, we burn them.

Fluorocarbon Gases ■ A third source of air pollution is fluorocarbon gases. These gases are suspected of damaging the **ozone shield,** the layer in the earth's upper stratosphere that screens out much of the sun's ultraviolet rays. High-intensity ultraviolet rays harm most life forms. In humans, they cause skin cancer and cataracts; in plants, they reduce growth and cause genetic mutations. When the danger of fluorocarbon gases was realized, their use in aerosol cans, refrigerators, and air conditioners was reduced or eliminated. The damage to the ozone layer is expected to be repaired, but it will take another 60 years (U.S. Department of State, 1997; U.S. Environmental Protection Agency, 2008).

GLOBAL WARMING. Besides damage to the ozone shield, another major consequence of air pollution is global warming. The pollutants in the air lead to what is known as the **greenhouse effect.** Carbon dioxide and water vapor form an invisible blanket around the globe that allows the sun's light to enter, but traps the heat. Without this blanket, temperatures would plummet, and the earth would be unable to support life. If the blanket is too thick, however, it traps too much heat and has devastating consequences for our environment.

The blanket seems to be growing thicker. Because of the Industrial Revolution, we burn more fossil fuels than humans did in the past, releasing more carbon dioxide into the air. In effect, the carbon dioxide blocks the atmospheric window through which our earth's daily heat escapes to outer space. This increased temperature of the earth is known as **global warming.**

Peru's 7.5-mile-long mountain glacier, the Quelcayya, is the world's largest tropical glacier. Sitting at 18,600 feet above sea level, it often gets snow but never rain. The Quelcayya is shrinking by about 100 feet a year. As the ice receded, researchers discovered a moss-like plant that had been frozen in the glacier. Carbon dating showed the plant to be over 5,000 years old.

To get an idea of how extensive today's global warming is, consider this: The last time this plant wasn't covered with snow and ice, the Egyptians were busy inventing hieroglyphics. (Regaldo, 2004)

Likely Consequences of Global Warming ■ If global warming continues, some scientists say that it will disrupt the earth's climate and biological system (D. A. Brown, 2001; Parmesan & Yohe, 2003; Kluger, 2006). If so, they say that we can expect these consequences:

1. Climate boundaries will move about 400 miles north, resulting in a longer growing season in the United States, Canada, and Russia.
2. The oceans will rise several feet as the polar ice caps melt.
3. The world's shorelines will erode. (Most of the beaches on the East Coast of the United States will be gone in a generation.)
4. Some small island nations will be destroyed, and the United States will lose an area of land the size of Massachusetts. Large portions of Florida will be under water.
5. Coastal fisheries will be damaged.
6. Summers will be hotter, increasing the demand for electricity.
7. There will be more forest fires, droughts, floods, and outbreaks of pests.
8. There will be more hurricanes.
9. There will be outbreaks of diseases—malaria, dengue fever, cholera.
10. Many species of plants and animals will become extinct.
11. Problems in the Least Industrialized Nations will be worse, as they have fewer resources to meet the crisis.

In the Maldives, an island nation of 270,000 people, the highest point is about 5 feet above sea level. With the threat of polar ice caps melting and oceans rising, the ministry of tourism created this national slogan: "Come see us while we're still here" (Dickey & Rogers, 2002).

DIFFERENCES OF OPINION. Global warming is a fact, but what is causing it? Throughout history, the earth has gone through periods of warming and cooling, and there is no exact correlation between carbon dioxide and these periods. During the ice age the atmosphere had an even higher concentration of carbon dioxide than we do today. With such inconsistent evidence, scientists disagree on whether global warming is due to natural or human causes. Some suggest that the cause might be changes in sun cycles or sea currents or in the cosmic rays that hit the earth (Broad, 2006a).

If a natural cycle is the cause of global warming, we can't do anything about it. If the cause is human activity, however, we can possibly take action to reduce or even reverse global warming. In 1997, the Kyoto Protocol united 37 countries in their efforts to decrease greenhouse gas emissions by 5% below 1990 levels by 2012. In 2005 the Protocol began monitoring emissions and offering compliance guidelines for those countries that did not meet such regulations. Of the current 183 countries involved in the Protocol, some are progressing better than others. France has moved to nuclear power, and Britain has shut down its coal mines. But Russia's emissions are rising due to its oil and gas boom. Japan hasn't developed its nuclear industry as predicted. The United States and Canada have abandoned their Kyoto targets altogether because of high oil prices (Stutchbury, 2008).

CHANGES IN U.S. AIR POLLUTION. With today's pollution control devices and the actions of environmentalists, is our air getting cleaner? Figure 13-1 shows some striking improvements. As you can see, emissions of nitrogen dioxide and volatile organic compounds have been nearly cut in half. The most stunning change is the amount of lead in our air; it is now only 1% of what it was in 1970. The primary reason for this change is lead-free gasoline. (Gasoline used to contain lead as an anti-knock additive.) With all of these improvements, we still have a long way to go. Carbon dioxide emissions continue to increase, and our air still contains 188 chemicals that have been linked to cancer, birth defects, and other health problems (Getter, 1999; "U.S. Greenhouse Gas Inventory," 2006).

FIGURE 13-1 U.S. Air Quality: The Emission of Pollutants

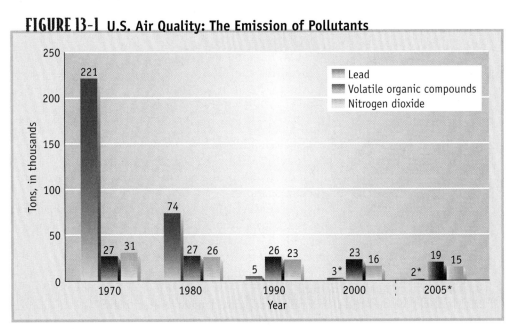

* The last time the source lists a measurement for lead is 1996. Latest year available.

Source: By James M. Henslin. Based on *Statistical Abstract of the United States* (2008, Table 360).

Land Pollution

It was such a beautiful day that Tamara and Bill decided to skip their social problems class and have a picnic on the beach. As they walked hand in hand, they found that they had to step around sewage that had washed ashore the night before. Their stomachs turned when they saw blood samples and contaminated needles that must have come from a hospital. All that came to mind was possible AIDS contamination.

GARBAGE. Cities and towns across the nation have to dispose of their waste. From Figure 13-2, you can see how much garbage one American produces each day. At 4.4 pounds of solid waste per American per day, we produce *240 billion pounds* of garbage each year (*Statistical Abstract*, 2006, Table 363). About a pound and a half of this waste is recovered (paper, glass, metals, plastics, rubber, wood), but each day every American still sends about 3 pounds of solid waste to landfills.

Humans have always dumped their wastes around them. We can identify many Stone Age villages by the mounds of oyster and mussel shells their inhabitants left behind. Today we produce so much trash that it is getting difficult to safely dispose of it. Many towns bury their wastes in gullies and swampy areas, but areas convenient to urban centers are filling up—and groundwater contamination has become a problem. Available landfills are incapable of absorbing the huge amounts of garbage that we produce.

Cities used to throw waste into a pit and light it. But with today's awareness of how burning waste pollutes the air and adds to global warming, this is no longer allowed. Cities must now use garbage incinerators approved by the Environmental Protection Agency (EPA). These incinerators are fancifully called **resource recovery plants.** With federal regulations requiring utilities to buy power generated by these garbage-burning plants, they partially pay for themselves. When studies showed that these incinerators also spewed toxic gases into the air, the EPA required the installation of multimillion-dollar pollution controls. Many communities were unable to afford this bill, so they abandoned their incinerators (Schneider, 1994).

Unable to burn their garbage, some states tried to ship their wastes to other states. When these states refused to accept the shipments, the case went to the Supreme Court. The Court ruled that the states to which the garbage was sent could not refuse the shipments. This decision opened landfills across the Midwest to the hard-pressed, more populated eastern states (Bailey, 1992). As a consequence, some Midwestern states have become the "garbage cans" of other states.

STRIP MINING. Another problem of land pollution is **strip mining,** which occurs where coal lies so close to the surface that it can be retrieved by stripping away the soil. Strip mining has scarred more than 5 million acres of U.S. land. Strip mining not only makes the land ugly but also poisons it because salt leeches from the coal when the land is stripped bare of its forest and plant life. In West Virginia a vast tract of land has been deemed unfit for farming. Although current federal regulations require mining companies to return land to its original condition, many believe that doing so is impossible. Today the western areas of the United States and huge areas in Canada are vulnerable, for vast amounts of shale and coal lie just beneath the surface.

FIGURE 13-2 Ounces of Solid Waste Each American Generates Each Day

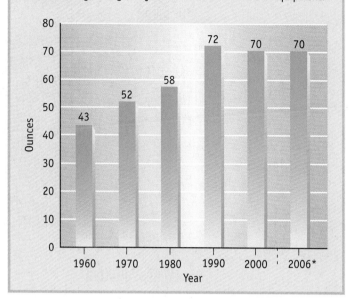

These totals are based on the solid wastes from residential and commercial trash collections. The totals do not include mining, agricultural, and industrial processing, demolition and construction wastes, sewage sludge, or junked autos and obsolete equipment.

* Latest year available.

Source: By James M. Henslin. Based on *Statistical Abstract of the United States* (1994, Table 370; 2007, Table 362; 2008, Table 361).

Pollution is a global problem, taking many forms around the world. One of the most common is the dumping of human excrement around dwellings. This photo was taken in Manila, Philippines.

Water Pollution

A silent spring has fallen over parts of the western Adirondacks. Brook trout have vanished from Big Moose Lake—along with crayfish and frogs, loons, kingfishers, and most of the swallows.

Pollutants from Midwest factories, borne by rain, wind, and snow, have left more than 300 lakes devoid of fish. The acid rain is also killing the trees. (Blumenthal, 1981; Ehrlich & Ehrlich, 1981; W. K. Stevens, 1996)

ACID RAIN. How do factory emissions in the Midwest destroy lakes in Canada and the northeastern states? This begins when power plants in the Midwest burn coal and oil to generate electricity. Burning fossil fuels releases sulfur dioxide and nitrogen oxide into the atmosphere. Moisture in the air turns these emissions into sulfuric and nitric acid. After traveling hundreds of miles, these acids fall to the earth's surface as **acid rain.**

Acid rain is not new. Ice samples from glaciers show heavy concentrations of acids 350 years ago, probably from volcanic activity and organic decomposition (LaBastille, 1979; Lynch, 1980). Our intensified use of fossil fuels, however, has transformed acid rain into a global social problem. To burn coal, utility companies in the Midwest built more than 175 smokestacks 500 feet tall or higher. These "megastacks" send pollutants high into the air, where they remain aloft for days, even weeks, before becoming part of a "chemical soup" that falls as rain on areas hundreds of miles away.

Canadians are upset by the "airborne sewer" that spills across their border from the United States. Acid rain has destroyed fish and normal plant life in hundreds of lakes in the province of Ontario. Acid rain also damages crops and forests around the world, as well as such world-famous landmarks as the Colosseum in Rome, the Taj Mahal in India, the Parthenon in Athens, and the Lincoln Memorial in Washington. Acid rain also threatens human health. Apparently, acid rain produces chemical reactions that release toxic metals into the water table. From there, these metals enter the public water supply.

As you saw in Figure 13-1, the amount of nitrogen dioxide emissions has been cut in half. Although this has reduced acid rain, the problem continues. Some lakes are regaining the chemical balance that will support plants and animals, but for reasons that scientists are trying to figure out, some of the affected lakes are not recovering ("Acid Rain Called Peril . . . ," 2006).

MERCURY RAIN. Half of the nation's electricity comes from burning coal. As coal burns, it releases traces of mercury, which become part of the smoke released by the coal-fired power plants. The mercury can stay airborne for up to two years, spreading around the globe. Some of the mercury reacts with chlorine and falls with rain. This rainwater washes into lakes, rivers, and oceans, where microorganisms ingest it. From there, it goes up the **food chain** into fish and from there into humans. As a result, some species of fish, especially swordfish and shark, are off limits to young children and to pregnant and nursing women (S. Levine, 2004).

GROUNDWATER. As you know, pollution also contaminates groundwater, the source of drinking water for millions (J. Lewis, 1990; Raloff, 1990; Bartlett & Steele, 1998). In addition to mercury, some of our drinking water also contains arsenic, asbestos, benzene, carbon tetrachloride, chloroform, PCBs, and other chemical wastes. Some wells on which large populations depend have had to be closed. For example, a well in the San Gabriel Valley of California that supplied drinking water to 400,000 people was closed after it became contaminated with the solvent TCE. Large portions of water supplies in southern Michigan are so polluted that state officials have suggested that it might be "cheaper to simply write off the groundwater supplies" than to try to clean them.

LAKES AND STREAMS. Our groundwater will rid itself of most pollutants eventually. This self-cleansing process takes significant time, though, since groundwater recycles so slowly that it remains in aquifers for an average of 1,400 years (Bogo, 2001). It is easier to solve the problem of the pollution of our lakes and streams, as these can be cleaned up.

The Infinity Tower in Dubai will have a total of 80 stories, rising to a height of 330 meters (1,083 feet). It was designed by Skidmore Owings & Merrill (SOM), and the building has been called the highest twisting tower in the world. Along with other architectural masterpieces, the Infinity Tower is threatened by acid rain.

The Mississippi River ■ The Mississippi River is a special case in point. Although thousands of industries discharge their wastes into this river, hundreds of cities still retrieve their drinking water from it. To "purify" the water, companies add more chemicals. Water from the Mississippi and other rivers treated in this way meets the standards set by the EPA. One of ten Americans, however, does not have access to drinking water that meets even these minimal health standards (Duskin, 2003).

The Great Lakes ■ The pollution of the Great Lakes is of special concern, for this giant network of waterways—Erie, Superior, Michigan, Huron, and Ontario—contains *1 of every 5 gallons of the entire world's surface freshwater.* Yet hundreds of toxic chemicals are pouring into the Great Lakes (Ashworth, 1987; Downing, 2006). The pollution of these formerly pristine waters by industry is so bad that people are warned not to eat bottom-feeding fish (which are exposed to heavier concentrations of poisons in the lakes' sediment). Disturbed by this pollution, environmentalists pressured Congress, which mandated that the EPA clean up these lakes (Environmental Protection Agency, 1994, 1998). Although the concentration of heavy metals has been reduced, the problem remains (McCool, 2006).

While the problem of toxic chemicals was being addressed, an additional problem surfaced, that of foreign species introduced into the lakes through the ballast of boats. Some of these species, which have hitchhiked across the world, no longer face the forces that keep them in check in their natural habitat. In the Great Lakes they multiply, threatening the native species ("To Restore . . ." 2005). Environmentalists are putting pressure on government bodies to work on this problem, too.

OIL SPILLS. Our industrial culture demands a continuous supply of oil. Transporting those vast quantities of oil is risky. Although industry and government assured environmentalists that they could handle oil spills, those promises proved hollow in 1989 when the *Exxon Valdez,* a 1,000-foot-long supertanker, ran aground and ruptured. Eleven million gallons of crude oil spewed into the pristine waters of Alaska's Prince William Sound, soiling 1,300 miles of coastline (K. Wells & McCoy, 1989; Y. Rosen, 1999). Left dead were 250,000 sea birds, 2,800 sea otters, 300 harbor seals, 250 bald eagles, 22 killer whales, and vast numbers of fish (Y. Rosen, 1999). Exxon spent over $2 billion to clean up the mess (K. Wells, 1990). Prince William Sound has largely recovered from the spill, but some species have not fully recovered (NOAA, 2006).

Oil spills are a global problem. As huge and tragic as the Exxon oil spill was, oil spills in Russia have been worse (Rosett, 1994; Garelik, 1996). When a cross-country oil pipeline burst in Siberia in 1994, it dumped 300 million gallons onto the tundra and into rivers. This is 27 times more oil than was dumped in the Exxon spill. Russia's rusting oil pipes continue to spew oil.

Chemical Pollution

The incidents of pollution discussed so far all involve toxic chemicals. These chemicals are so poisonous to land, air, and water that it is difficult to overstate the extent to which they threaten our well-being. To grasp the potential destruction, we'll look at a couple of examples.

LOVE CANAL. Perhaps the most infamous case of chemical pollution in the United States occurred in Love Canal, New York, where

> Hundreds of families unwittingly purchased homes adjacent to a waste dump that had been covered over with clay. Over the years, deadly poisons seeped into their homes. Neurological damage was common. So were urinary tract infections, kidney damage, swollen joints, sleepiness, clumsiness, headaches, fragile bones, irritability, and loss of appetite. One-third of Love Canal residents suffered chromosome damage (J. W. Brown, n.d.). One child was born with two rows of teeth, another with one kidney, and a third with three ears (Shribman, 1989).

Eventually, the federal government ordered all pregnant women and children under age 2 to move out of Love Canal (J. E. Brody, 1976; J. W. Brown, n.d.). In 1978, 239 families abandoned their homes, and in 1980 the federal government and the state of New York relocated 710 families before bulldozing another 128 homes (Shribman, 1989).

How did a nice little community called Love Canal get so polluted?

Beginning in the early 1940s, Hooker Chemical Company buried and covered with clay 44 million pounds of chemical waste in a canal it owned (Mokhiber & Shen, 1981). When Niagara Falls officials unwittingly chose the covered-over canal as the site for an elementary school, Hooker said that the city had chosen a "desirable site" for the school and deeded the land to the city for a token $1. The company warned no one about the chemicals, but the deed stated that Hooker was not liable for any injuries or deaths that might occur at this site (M. H. Brown, 1979).

"That account," replied Hooker, "is only part fact, combined with a lot of lies." The truth, claimed Hooker, is that "We warned the board about the risk. We even told them on what part of the property to locate the school so they would not disturb the buried chemicals." Moreover, when the board considered selling part of the property, Hooker sent an attorney to the board meeting to warn them that the buried chemicals could have a "serious deleterious effect on foundations, water lines, and sewer lines" and that it was "quite possible that personal injuries could result from contact therewith." The attorney also stated that "only the surface of the land" should be used because "the subsoil conditions make it very undesirable and possibly hazardous if excavations are to be made therein" (Wilcox, 1957).

Despite these warnings, the Niagara Falls Board of Education approved the removal of dirt from the canal for top grading, the city constructed a storm sewer through the landfill, and the Department of Transportation built an expressway across part of the site. These construction projects disturbed industrial waste that had been buried properly, causing the resulting damage, said Hooker.

Researchers are studying the long-term effects of chemical exposure on those who lived in Love Canal at the time of the contamination, but surprisingly, they have discovered little ("Serum Results . . . ," 2006). No matter who is to blame, we can draw several conclusions about Love Canal. It seems reasonable to conclude that it is not good to bury chemical waste and that we need to safeguard people from harm. How can we do this without implementing and monitoring effective controls over the disposal of chemicals?

DISPOSING OF CHEMICAL WASTES. U.S. industries produce over a trillion pounds of hazardous chemical wastes each year (*Statistical Abstract,* 2006, Table 380). Companies used to simply discharge wastes into the air or pour them into rivers and oceans. Today, we attempt to bury waste in landfills. The containers buried in our dumps—that is, our landfills—disintegrate slowly, allowing lethal chemical wastes to rise to the surface or to leach into rivers and groundwater.

Not all chemicals can be buried, however, and some must go through expensive processes to render them harmless. As officials have cracked down on making companies dispose of toxic wastes properly, it has created new opportunities for greed—including opportunities for members of organized crime operations (J. W. Brown, n.d.). Legal disposal of a tank full of chemical waste might cost $40,000, but criminals will dispose of it for half that amount. Their disposal methods don't match those approved by the EPA, though: They drive an 8,000-gallon tank truck full of waste to a wooded area and dump it in 8 minutes flat. The industrial company that produced the waste (a legitimate business) feigns ignorance. On 21 acres of marshland on Staten Island, men "well known to law enforcement agents" deposited 700,000 gallons of waste oil in barrels. In North Carolina, one "midnight dumper" simply opened the spigots on a tankload of PCBs and then drove until the tank was empty.

HAZARDOUS WASTE SITES: THE NATIONAL PRIORITY LIST. With inadequate disposal and thousands of toxic dump sites, chemical waste is a ticking time bomb. You can check to see how your state ranks on the Social Map (Figure 13-7 on page 493), which shows the *worst* of the many hazardous waste sites in the United States. These are the sites placed on the national priority list. Designated by authorities as posing such a risk to people's health that they need *immediate* attention, these sites will be cleaned up *when* and *if* Congress appropriates money to do so.

Nuclear Pollution

THE WORLD'S FIRST NUCLEAR WASTE DISASTER: KYSHTYM. Russia's Ural River Valley is a remote place, and it was here that the Soviet government decided to develop its first atomic bomb. In Kyshtym, the Soviets built a nuclear reactor to obtain plutonium. Accounts vary as to how they disposed of the millions of gallons of nuclear waste produced by this reactor. Some say they bored holes into the ground and poured the liquid wastes into them (Solomon & Rather, 1980). Others report that they piled the waste onto a dry lake bed (Clines, 1998). Perhaps they did both. In the winter of 1957 a chemical reaction occurred, and the waste exploded, sending radioactive dust high into the sky.

The fallout from this explosion devastated the area. Maps before the explosion show 30 villages and towns around Kyshtym, but on maps printed after 1958, those communities are nowhere to be seen. Thousands of people had to be evacuated permanently from a 1,000-square-kilometer area.

THE PUNY NUCLEAR REACTOR ACCIDENT: THREE MILE ISLAND. In comparison, the worst nuclear accident in the United States was much smaller. It occurred in 1979 at Three

Mile Island, Pennsylvania, when a reactor leaked. Panic ensued, and 100,000 residents fled (Rabinovitz, 1998). The contamination was minimal, however, and people quickly moved back to their homes. Some say that this accident may cause up to 50 future diagnoses of cancer (Milvy, 1979), but others claim that the accident was simply a minor loss of coolant that exposed people to less radiation than they get at the dentist's office (R. C. Williams, 1980).

THE WORLD'S WORST NUCLEAR REACTOR DISASTER: CHERNOBYL. Then there was Chernobyl, in the Ukraine:

> *Meltdown.* The word froze in the mouth of the operating engineer. No one wanted to even think it could happen. Yet the evidence was undeniable. An explosion had blown a 1,000-ton steel cover off a nuclear reactor. The containment structure was obliterated.
>
> It was too late to flee: No one could outrun the deadly radiation. For 10 days, the world watched the drama, the fire raging and radioactive materials spewing into the air.
>
> Chernobyl's cloud of radioactive gases traveled slowly around the world. In 2 weeks, its airborne waste was detected in the United States and Tokyo (Flavin, 1987). Canadians were advised not to drink rainwater, and farmers in Great Britain were ordered not to grow certain crops because of the radioactive fallout (Dufay, n.d.).

Over 300,000 people were evacuated. International medical teams rushed to the scene, and despite emergency transplants of bone marrow and fetal liver cells, 31 people died during the first months. About 12,000 square miles of farm- and forestlands were contaminated so badly that they may have been rendered useless for at least two generations. Unfortunately, some people aware of the risk have moved back into the contaminated areas around Chernobyl (Dufay, n.d.). Some farmers are again growing crops and raising livestock in areas contaminated by the Chernobyl disaster, which is presenting a concern for consumers. The residents of Eastern Europe are wary, and some avoid products that come from the Ukraine and Byelorussia. Since these products are sold at a cheaper price, others buy them (Henslin's notes, 2007).

Experts anticipate that perhaps tens of thousands of people will die from radiation-caused cancers. United Nations researchers did a 20-year follow-up study of Chernobyl and found that the health effects were much milder than expected. The levels of leukemia—one of the main fears—turned out to be within the normal range. About 4,000 cases of thyroid cancer were found, primarily among adults who had been children at the time; they had consumed milk from cows that had eaten radiation-contaminated grass. This disease, though, is treatable and has resulted in only a few deaths ("Stakeholders and Radiological . . . ," 2006).

Food Pollution

We may not be buying food from the Ukraine, but we face **food pollution** daily. There are three types of food pollution: (1) disease-causing germs in our food, (2) chemicals added to food, and (3) genetically modified food. Let's look at all three.

DISEASE-CAUSING GERMS IN OUR FOOD. *Escherichia coli (E. coli)* is a bacterium that lives in our digestive systems, where it has a beneficial role; but it becomes dangerous when our food or water is contaminated with feces. Many cases come from restaurant workers who don't wash their hands after defecating. But *E. coli* is only one of the many disease-causing substances in our food.

Chickens ■ If you have the stomach for it, consider how chickens are processed (Ingersoll, 1990). Slaughter lines run so fast that inspectors have two seconds to scrutinize each carcass, inside and out, for signs of disease and feces. "After a while, it gets to be a blur," inspectors say.

Our food processing is supposed to reduce food contamination, but the way we process chickens can increase it. In one plant, 57% of chickens arrived already contaminated with

disease-causing bacteria such as salmonella. This is horrible to contemplate, but listen to this: 76% left the plant infected. During processing, contaminants are passed from carcass to carcass. The two primary culprits of this bird-to-bird contamination are automatic disemboweling knives and vats of chilled water in which the chickens are dipped before going into the freezer. Says a microbiologist, "Even if you chlorinate the chilled water, it's still like soaking birds in a toilet." To this, industry officials reply reassuringly, "It may spread bacteria from bird to bird, but it also dilutes the overall effect."

Why doesn't the U.S. poultry industry switch from chilled water to blasting the chickens with cold air, as they do in Europe? The reason is cost. Federal regulations allow each chicken carcass to soak up to 8% of its weight in water. This allows the chicken industry to sell hundreds of thousands of gallons of disease-ridden water at poultry prices.

Contaminated chicken is so common that over one million Americans get sick each year from diseased birds. Scientists at *Consumer Reports* bought chickens at supermarkets in 25 cities nationwide ("Of Birds and Bacteria," 2003). These included major brands, supermarket brands, and chicken sold at health food stores. Tests showed that *half* of the chickens were contaminated with *Salmonella* or *Campylobacter,* bacteria that can make people sick. To prevent disease from filthy chickens sold in our stores, researchers suggest that we buy chickens located low in the supermarket freezer (where it is colder), separate raw chicken from other foods, not let any foods touch the area where we prepare the chicken, and cook the chicken thoroughly. They also warn us to wash our hands thoroughly to remove chicken juices—the blood and the filthy water (recall that "chill water") that the U.S. Department of Agriculture allows the chickens to absorb.

Our focus on contaminated chicken helps us to understand why European nations sometimes refuse to import food from the United States. This may come as a shock to you, for we are used to thinking of American food as safe. European resistance to U.S. food is the topic of the Technology and Social Problems box on the next page.

The Danger is Real ■ Contaminants aren't just in chickens, of course. Some of our food is so contaminated that it kills. Such a statement must sound like an exaggeration, but here are some cases: Twenty people died after they ate hot dogs produced by a subsidiary of Sara Lee—they were contaminated with *Listeria monocytogenes*. Forty people died after eating Jalisco brand soft cheese—this, too, was contaminated with listeria (Burros, 1999). After eating Schwan's ice cream, 224,000 Americans became sick. The ice cream mix had picked up salmonella when it was transported in tanks that had been used to carry raw eggs (Neergaard, 1998). Odwalla produced apple juice that was infected with an especially lethal strain of *E. coli*—14 children developed a life-threatening disease that ravages kidneys, and a 16-month-old girl died (Belluck, 1998a). In early 2009, a nation-wide outbreak of salmonella occurred, traced to peanuts from the Peanut Corp. of America. Products made with peanuts from the Georgia company at the heart of the salmonella outbreak sickened 600 people, were linked to nine deaths, and led to one of the largest product recalls in history, with more than 1,800 food products pulled off the market. *Each year, about 75 million Americans get sick from contaminated food, 300,000 are hospitalized, and 5,000 die* (Widdowson et al., 2005).

CHEMICAL ADDITIVES. Let's turn to the second type of food pollution, chemicals added to our food to process it, lengthen its shelf life, enhance its appearance, or alter its taste.

Food Flavorings and Colorings ■ Food companies sprinkle our food with artificial additives. Just to flavor our foods, they use 2,000 different chemical compounds. The "cherry" flavor in soft drinks, pies, and shakes, for example, is made of 13 different chemicals.

The information we have about the safety of food additives is not reassuring. The U.S. agency that is responsible for overseeing the safety of food is the Food and Drug Administration (FDA). Red Dye No. 2 used to be the most common food coloring in the United States. Because it enhances colors, the food industry added more than a million pounds to our food each year. In 1970, researchers discovered that rats and mice who ate Red Dye No. 2 developed cancer. It took 5 years for the FDA to ban this dye—and only after the agency was flooded with petitions from public interest groups.

Technology and Social Problems

"DO YOU EAT PLASTIC FOOD?" WHY EUROPEANS DON'T LIKE U.S. FOOD

A Spanish man asked an American, "Do you eat plastic food?"

In Spain egg yolks are brighter, almost orange. Fruits and vegetables are picked ripe. People buy them daily and eat them fresh. The meat is more tender and tasty. It doesn't come prepackaged or frozen. Each grocery store has its own butcher; in small stores, the butcher is also the owner. The butcher will cut the meat you order in the fashion you prefer. Bread is freshly baked and also purchased daily. The Spanish use a lot of fresh herbs—especially garlic and parsley. They also cook with olive oil—always. But why should this contrast in food customs lead someone to ask, in sincerity, if Americans eat plastic food? A rumor had traveled throughout Europe that U.S. food companies do strange things to food, so much so that our food had become synthetic. The term *plastic* was a poor translation of the word *synthetic*. Perhaps this term is not too far off the mark.

Officials of the European Union (EU) are also suspicious about American food. EU scientists claim that **bovine growth hormones (BGH)**—the hormones fed to cattle to make them grow faster—can cause cancer. The EU banned beef with BGH. Since this ban was aimed primarily at U.S. beef, the United States retaliated by slapping millions of dollars in tariffs on EU food products ("Dispute Between EU . . . ," 2004).

This dispute between proponents of "natural" versus "synthetic" foods, and the related positions that one is healthy and the other unhealthy, seems destined to continue for some time. The European Union and the United States continue to quarrel before the World Trade Organization.

FOR YOUR CONSIDERATION

How "synthetic" do you think American food is? Do you have any concerns about the safety of the food you buy? Do you avoid foods with chemical preservatives?

Many find little comfort in knowing that Red Dye Nos. 3, 8, 9, 19, 37, and 40 replaced No. 2 to color food. Some of these dyes also damage DNA and cause cancer in animals—yet the FDA allows them to be used (Brooks, 1985, 1987; Tsuda, 2001). Red dye No. 40, for example, has been banned in Austria, Belgium, France, Germany, Norway, Sweden, and Switzerland—yet it continues to be added to American foods (Hanssen, 1997).

Food Preservatives ■ The food industry uses sulfites to keep food from discoloring. The sulfites are spread over raw fruits and vegetables, especially at salad bars, to keep them "looking fresh." Sulfites are also added to beer, wine, and bakery goods, sprinkled over shrimp and fish, mixed with dairy and grain products, and added to fruit juices and frozen potatoes.

The problem is that the sulfites also make some people sick. A few even die from allergic reactions. Sulfites have been linked to deaths involving pizza, wine, and beer, and they pose a special danger to asthmatics. After years of complaints—and no regulation—the FDA decided to limit the amount of sulfites in our food and require a warning label (Dingell, 1985; Ingersoll, 1988; Food and Drug Administration, 1994; Magee et al., 2005).

SYNERGISM AND CUMULATIVE EFFECTS. Because they are **synergistic**—that is, because they interact with one another—chemical food additives are a complicated hazard. For example, the nitrites that give hot dogs, ham, and bacon their inviting red color appear to be safe in and of themselves. In the presence of amines, however, nitrites become nitrosamines—potent carcinogens. Every organ in every species of animal ever exposed to nitrosamines developed cancer. Amines are commonly added to beer, wine, cereals, tea, fish, cigarettes, streptomycin, Librium, and Contac cold medicine. Thus, hot dogs and beer are an unhealthy combination, as are a ham sandwich and a cup of tea.

Some Chinese imports have come under scrutiny lately for their high melamine content. Melamine is a powder found in plastic that boosts the test results for a food's protein content. Contamination experts have found milk, baby formula, ice cream, and yogurt to all be contaminated with melamine powder. More than 6,000 babies so far have developed kidney stones as a result of drinking the poisoned powder. Four of them have died (Callick, 2008). Companies that use Chinese milk in their own products are now suspending the purchase of Chinese milk. Starbucks, for instance, with about 150 stores in China, said that it would stop using milk from its former chief supplier, Mengniu, one of China's biggest dairy companies (Callick, 2008).

See Figure 13-3 for another illustration of polluted food.

Many chemical additives are harmless until they build up in our bodies. When they reach a certain level, then they begin to destroy tissues and organs. That level of destruction varies from person to person.

PROFITS AHEAD OF HEALTH. The food industry adulterates our food with harmful chemicals not because it is necessary but because it is profitable. The chemicals retard spoilage and increase sales by making food that appeals to the public's conditioned taste

FIGURE 13-3 Bon Appétit?

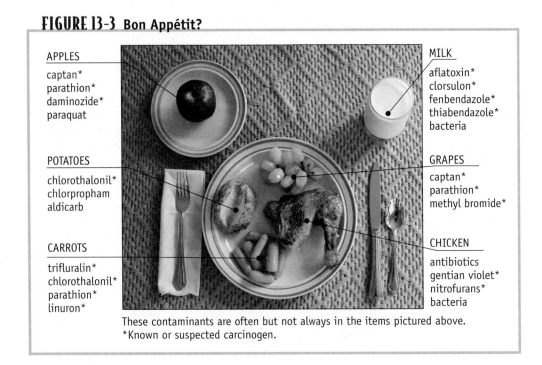

APPLES
captan*
parathion*
daminozide*
paraquat

POTATOES
chlorothalonil*
chlorpropham
aldicarb

CARROTS
trifluralin*
chlorothalonil*
parathion*
linuron*

MILK
aflatoxin*
clorsulon*
fenbendazole*
thiabendazole*
bacteria

GRAPES
captan*
parathion*
methyl bromide*

CHICKEN
antibiotics
gentian violet*
nitrofurans*
bacteria

These contaminants are often but not always in the items pictured above.
*Known or suspected carcinogen.

and sight. Because the food industry can use alternative ways to preserve food, from a conflict perspective we can say that those who control the food industry put profits ahead of health. Certainly the food chain is long—that is, getting food from grower to consumer is a lengthy process—and we must have effective ways to preserve food. Older preservation techniques like pickling, smoking, salting, canning, freezing, and drying, work as well as modern freeze-drying and vacuum packing.

Some of our food is polluted before it is processed and marketed. To keep cows, chickens, and other animals from getting sick and to cause them to grow faster so they can be marketed sooner, they are fed antibiotics and growth hormones. Some of these substances end up in our own bodies when we eat these animals or their products, such as milk and cheese. This use of antibiotics is also contributing to the rise of drug-resistant organisms (Iovine & Blaser, 2004). Similarly, farmers spray pesticides on fruits and vegetables to prevent insect damage. Because the fruits and vegetables absorb some of these chemicals, they enter our bodies when we eat them.

Food production is the largest industry in the United States. Sales in our 120,000 grocery stores amount to about $475 billion a year (*Statistical Abstract,* 2006, Table 1029). Adulterating our food is so profitable that our food industry adds more than 1 billion pounds of chemicals to our food each year—about 5 pounds of chemicals for every man, woman, and child in the United States. Researchers associate these chemicals with our high rates of cancer.

GENETICALLY MODIFIED FOODS. It does not take an expert to figure out that pollution can be harmful to health. At the very minimum, almost everyone agrees that we should avoid diseases in our foods and that at least some chemicals added to foods can be harmful to our health. However, when it comes to **genetically modified foods**—foods derived from plants or animals in which genetic materials have been transferred from one species to another or in which genes have been manipulated in a way that does not occur in nature—we land in the midst of controversy. Not only are governments and businesses, with their competitive power and economic interests, quarreling with one another, but so are scientists. They simply cannot agree whether genetically modified foods are harmful or not.

Even placing the topic of genetically modified foods in this section of the book is controversial. It might imply that modifying foods genetically is a form of food pollution. But locating this topic here is not intended to communicate such a message, only to stress that some scientists take this position.

The issue is simply this. Genetically modifying foods is new practice. This technology has the potential to greatly increase the world's food supply, but its consequences are unknown. U.S. companies have spearheaded the development of genetically modified foods, and they stand to reap huge profits if the new strains are accepted around the world. European agricultural interests, which fear competition, spearhead opposition. They are joined by environmentalists who fear both unknown health consequences of these foods and the harm they might bring to the environment if they replace natural varieties.

The continuing controversy has become an economic and political issue (Umberger, 2005). Depending on the outcome of scientific studies, American and European agricultural interests stand to gain or lose hundreds of millions of dollars a year. The United States and European Union don't order scientists to produce studies proving their position, but scientists on both sides of the Atlantic know that the European Union wants to prove that genetically modified foods are harmful, whereas the United States and Canada want to show that they are not harmful. Although research is being conducted within this highly charged political context, science—not economics or politics—will win. No matter who produces a study, the other side will examine it rigorously. Subjected to impartial, objective techniques of replication (repetition) and measurement, these studies will ultimately demonstrate that one or the other economic-political side is correct. Our prediction is that each side is partially correct—that is, that some genetically modified foods are harmful, while others are not. We will have to await the data to know for sure.

Pollution in the Industrializing Nations

Although pollution most often occurs in the industrialized nations, those that are industrializing also contribute to this problem. A third of the children in China have levels of lead in their blood that exceed the World Health Organization's limit (Oster & Spencer, 2006). After the United Nations declared that Mexico City had the worst air in the world, Mexican authorities banned leaded gasoline, shut down some factories, and embarked on a tree-planting program (Mandel-Campbell, 2001). Mexico City's air improved, and there now are fewer patients admitted to hospitals.

For a snapshot of how harmful conditions can get in industrializing nations, see the Global Glimpse box on the next page.

REASONS FOR THIS POLLUTION. Four main reasons underlie the extensive pollution of industrializing nations. Let's look at them.

Use of Banned Chemicals ■ First, many of the chemicals outlawed in the industrialized nations remain legal in the industrializing countries. Although these chemicals cannot be used in the United States, chemical companies still manufacture them here. They ship these chemicals to the industrializing nations, where they are used by workers who cannot read the warnings on the label. The chemicals poison the workers, the land, and the water. In a strange way, they also often poison the food that we eat, for they return to us in our coffee, fruit, nuts, and so on:

> The EPA banned domestic use of the pesticide ethylene dioromide (EDB) because it causes cancer. The State Department, fearing bad relations with Mexico and Haiti, and, not incidentally, damages to U.S.-financed mango growers in Belize and Guatemala, pressured the EPA to allow foreign mango growers to continue using the pesticide. (Meier, 1987)

Production of Banned Chemicals ■ Second, industrializing nations manufacture chemicals that the United States bans—often in factories that U.S. corporations own. Those factories represent jobs, and if an industrializing nation were to insist on stringent safeguards in manufacturing or in pollution controls, it would risk its economic security. Other nations would welcome the polluting company—without safeguards.

The cost of such practices, however, can be high. Consider Bhopal, the world's most infamous chemical accident:

> It was an unseasonably cold night in Central India. In the shantytowns of Bhopal, thousands of poor families were asleep. At a nearby railway station, a scattering of people waited for early-morning trains. At the local Union Carbide plant, a maintenance worker noticed that a storage tank holding methyl isocyanate (MIC), a chemical used in making pesticides, was showing a high pressure reading. The worker heard rumbling in the tank, then the sound of cracking concrete. The plant superintendent was notified, and he sounded an alarm. But it was too late. A noxious white gas had started seeping from the tank and had begun to spread through the region on the northwesterly winds.
>
> At the Vijoy Hotel near the railroad, sociologist Swapan Saha, 33, woke up with a terrible pain in his chest. "It was both a burning and a suffocating sensation," he said. "It was like breathing fire." Wrapping a damp towel around his nose and mouth, Saha went outside to investigate. Scores of victims lay dead on the platform at the train station. "I thought at first there must have been a gigantic railway accident," he recalled. Then he noticed a pall of white smoke on the ground, and an acrid smell in the air. People were running helter-skelter, retching, vomiting, and defecating uncontrollably. Many collapsed and died. Dogs, cows, and water buffaloes also lay on the ground, twitching in death agonies. Saha made his way to the railway office, only to find the stationmaster slumped over his desk. For a moment, he thought that an atom bomb had hit Bhopal. Staggering back to the hotel, half blind himself by now, he sat down to write a farewell letter to his wife.
>
> Saha survived. More than 2,500 others did not. (Whitaker, 1984; Spaeth, 1989)

A Global Glimpse
WHERE NEW LIFE BRINGS DEATH

"The factories, they give us life, but they kill us at the same time," sighs Maria Alves, who awakens at night to the sounds of her six children gagging in the polluted air. "It isn't fair, but what can we do? We need to work."

This is Cubatão, Brazil, a village nestled in the Serra do Mar mountains. It used to be pretty, but now people call it "the valley of death."

As nations rush to industrialize, they often skip health and safety standards. Their problems with hazardous chemicals don't grab the world's attention, but they still kill.

Cubatão is one of the most polluted cities on earth. With its factory pollutants and the worst acid rain ever recorded, half of its more than 100,000 people have respiratory ailments. Pollution is causing people to die from heart attacks and strokes.

This photo was taken in Cubatão, Brazil.

A benzene gas leak caused hundreds of workers to develop leucopenia, an abnormality of the blood cells. Three developed leukemia and died. The company was fined $4,000.

The phosphates spewing from the fertilizer factories make it look like winter—little white chemical flakes fluttering down, burning the skin.

Adimar dos Santos Lima, who works in a steel plant for $70 a month and is happy to have a job, says, "I make a living. But I live in a sewer."

A slum neighborhood blew up after gasoline leaked from an underground pipe owned by Petrobras, Brazil's national oil company. The recovery team found 90 bodies. Another 500 had been incinerated.

Based on Schuster (1985); Pereira et. al. (2004).

Not all the deaths occurred immediately. The leak contaminated the area's groundwater, claiming more lives over the following years. The Indian government estimates that this accident caused 22,000 deaths (Hertsgaard, 2004).

Although this accident took place in India, it could happen anywhere that chemicals are manufactured. As an expert on workplace safety put it, "It's like a giant roulette wheel. This time the marble came to a stop in a little place in India. But the next time it could be the United States" (Whitaker, 1984).

The Rush to Industrialize ▪ The third factor is the intensity with which these nations are trying to industrialize. Their pressing concern at the moment is to increase their standard of living and their position in the global power structure, not to manage pollution. China and India, the two most populous nations in the world, are industrializing at such a furious pace that they may well become the world's two largest polluters.

Dumping Grounds ▪ Fourth, industrialized nations have found that some of these nations are a convenient dump for their toxic waste. Corporate leaders negotiate deals with weak governments allowing the United States to ship them chemical waste that under our regulations would not be allowed (Polgreen & Simons, 2006).

In Alang, India, 35,000 men work for $1.50 a day breaking up ships whose parts are laden with asbestos, PCBs, lead, and toxic sludge (Englund & Cohn, 1997). The men work unprotected, and each year 2 out of 1,000 die from accidents, making ship-breaking the most dangerous occupation in India (S. Jain, 2006). Without witnessing such conditions firsthand, it is difficult to grasp the desperate misery that the poor of India face on a daily basis. One man who works in this setting, earning $1.50 for a full day's toil with the smell of death hovering over him, said, "It is better to work and die than starve and die."

Getting the Other Side

THE OPTIMISTIC ENVIRONMENTALISTS. Almost everything about the environment reviewed thus far has reflected negative findings and opinions. There is another side, one that is seldom heard. Some experts—**optimistic environmentalists**—say that groups of alarmist doomsayers have captured the attention of the media with their stress on negative findings, dire predictions, and exaggerations. Isolated incidents such as Bhopal, although tragic, have been blown out of proportion. If we take a more realistic, dispassionate view, they say, we will see that things are not so bad.

The Technological Fix ■ Optimistic environmentalists claim that improved technology will solve whatever threat pollution may pose to the environment. We have had predictions of disaster in the past, they argue, and our technology has always seen us through. The present is no exception. They point to the pollution problem of 1900. At that time, horses were common, and so was their manure. Huge amounts of this substance were piling up on city streets. When motorized vehicles replaced horses, that problem disappeared. The present is no different, and we will develop technology to counter threats to our environment.

Environmentalism Can Cause Disease ■ The optimistic environmentalists also point out that solutions can backfire, that they can do more harm than good. Edward Teller (1980), the man most responsible for the hydrogen bomb, said that strict environmental regulations are not only expensive but also create poverty and disease in poor nations. He made this point: When environmentalists objected to the use of DDT as environmentally harmful, it was banned. Look what happened just in Sri Lanka. The banning of DDT let mosquitoes multiply, and 2 million people came down with malaria. To combat this disease, DDT had to be brought back. Teller said, "I challenge anybody to show me a case where lack of environmental protection has made two million people as seriously sick as the disease caused by the environmentalists."

Things Are Getting Better ■ The optimistic environmentalists further claim: We can use a number of measures to evaluate the condition of the environment, but the best single one is life expectancy. When the environment deteriorates, life expectancy drops, as it did in Russia. When an environment improves, life expectancy increases. The best measure of the state of the environment, then, is life-expectancy—as shown in Figure 13-4 on the next page. Why are Americans living longer? Because our environment has improved, not deteriorated (J. Simon, 1981). Optimists claim we need to stop worrying about what *might* go wrong, much less twist reality in order to match some woeful view of life. Life is getting better, so let's enjoy it.

Of Special Concern: The Tropical Rain Forests

We don't have to be alarmists to see that, at a minimum, we must deal with toxic waste, provide wholesome food, and learn how to preserve, create, or—at least—not destroy a healthy environment. And we don't have to be alarmists to be concerned that plant and animal species are being extinguished. Especially ominous for humanity's future is the destruction of the tropical rain forests.

The tropical rain forests have been called the "lungs of the earth." They help to regulate the earth's exchange of oxygen and carbon dioxide, and they absorb carbon gases that create global warming. The rain forests also help keep the earth's climate in balance by giving off water vapor that keeps the ground from drying out. The "lungs of the earth" are gasping; and as the environmental pessimists say, if action is not taken soon, they will collapse.

Although rain forests cover just 7% of the earth's total land area, they are home to *one-third* of all plant and animal species. Many species of plants, still unstudied, possess medicinal or nutritional value (Cheng, 1995; Simons, 2005). Some of the discoveries from the rain forests have been astounding: A flower from Madagascar is used in the

FIGURE 13-4 Life Expectancy in the United States, by Year of Birth

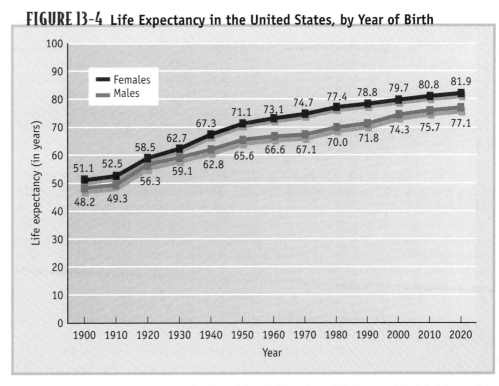

Females
Males

Females: 51.1, 52.5, 58.5, 62.7, 67.3, 71.1, 73.1, 74.7, 77.4, 78.8, 79.7, 80.8, 81.9

Males: 48.2, 49.3, 56.3, 59.1, 62.8, 65.6, 66.6, 67.1, 70.0, 71.8, 74.3, 75.7, 77.1

Life expectancy (in years)

Year: 1900 1910 1920 1930 1940 1950 1960 1970 1980 1990 2000 2010 2020

Sources: By James M. Henslin. Based on *Historical Statistics of the United States* (1976, Table B 116, 117); *Statistical Abstract of the United States* (1989, Table 106; 2009, Table 100).

treatment of leukemia, and a frog in Peru produces a painkiller more powerful, but less addictive, than morphine (Wolfensohn & Fuller, 1998). A chemical from a rain forest plant in Panama is thought to be effective in treating malaria (Roach, 2003).

Even knowing that the rain forests are essential for humanity's welfare, we keep clearing them. In the process, we extinguish thousands of plant and animal species (Durning, 1990; Wolfensohn & Fuller, 1998; "The Price of Success," 2004). As biologists remind us, a species lost is gone forever. We are exchanging our future for some lumber, farms, and pastures.

Ecotourism has developed to educate people about the environment and to generate profits to help sustain the environment. This ecotourist in Costa Rica's Rincon de la Vieja National Park is *zip-lining* over a rain forest canopy. Strapped in a harness, she uses the cable to propel herself to the next platform.

Energy and Resources

THE WAY IT WAS. Americans used to think that gasoline was limitless. We even had "gas wars." To attract people to buy their gas, service stations kept undercutting one another's price. Gas stations even used to give away glasses and dishes with a gasoline purchase. This ended abruptly in 1973 when OPEC (Organization of Petroleum Exporting Countries) surprised the West with an oil embargo. Overnight, long lines appeared at gas stations, and for a moment Americans became acutely aware of how fragile their energy supply was. But only for a moment. Although a few changes were permanent, such as more fuel-efficient cars and better-insulated homes, when the embargoes were removed, we went back to our old habits.

How concerned should we be about energy and resources? Let's examine opposing views.

THE PESSIMISTIC ENVIRONMENTALISTS. One group of experts argues that we are facing energy and resource shortages so vast that they will shatter the foundations of the industrialized world. These **pessimistic environmentalists** can't understand why most of us are so short-sighted that we become concerned only when the price of gasoline surges. Even then, our concern focuses not on the coming shortage of oil but on what it costs to fill our gas tank or heat our homes. We miss this bigger picture—that for its existence, our civilization depends on substances whose supply is limited.

The Water Shortage ■ The shortage of oil is all too familiar, but most of us are less aware that we are already running short of freshwater. We used to think that freshwater was endless, but gradually we are learning a bitter lesson. Of all the water on earth, 97% is salt water. A little over 2% is frozen in glacial ice. This leaves about 1% for all agricultural, industrial, and personal uses. Across the world, industrial societies are making huge and increasing demands on this limited supply of freshwater. In the United States, communities have even begun to quarrel about who has a right to the water in the Great Lakes (Barringer, 2005).

To illustrate the coming crisis in freshwater, consider the Ogallala aquifer. As shown in Figure 13-5, this aquifer runs from South Dakota to Texas. It waters nearly 12% of the nation's corn, cotton, grain sorghum, and wheat (Frazier & Schlender, 1980; L. R. Brown, 1987). In this area, ranchers raise nearly half the nation's cattle. Yet we are depleting this underground formation (Stroud, 2006). Some say that the natural condition of much of this area, now in pasture and farmlands, is Sahara-like desert, that eventually its outstanding characteristic will be its giant sand dunes (W. K. Stevens, 1996). Frank Popper, the head of the Department of Urban Studies at Rutgers University, says that one day hardly anyone will live in this region. He suggests that the federal government buy huge chunks of the land, replant the native prairie grasses, reintroduce the buffalo, and turn off the lights (Farney, 1989).

Minerals, Too ■ Pessimistic environmentalists foresee a bleak outlook for essential minerals. Economies around the world are expanding. India and China are joining the United States and the other industrialized nations in the competitive demand for the earth's limited, irreplaceable, essential resources. Soon we will run out of metals—copper, zinc, aluminum, nickel, and so on. Although substitute materials may buy us time, we are

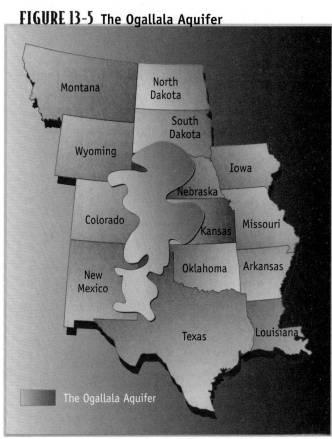

FIGURE 13-5 The Ogallala Aquifer

The Ogallala Aquifer

reaching limits that will stop the expansion of the world's economies and bring our civilizations to a screeching halt.

IN SUM That our resources are finite and we are depleting them is so obvious that it confronts us often: There is only so much oil, natural gas, and freshwater, and our mineral deposits are limited.

THE OPTIMISTIC ENVIRONMENTALISTS. Such a view misreads and distorts evidence, reply the optimistic environmentalists. Why would they take this position?

Resources Are Not Getting Scarcer ▪ Seeming to fly in the face of logic and reality, economist Julian Simon insisted that raw materials are *not* getting scarcer. He said that when something that people want grows scarce, its price increases. To see whether raw materials are becoming scarcer, all we have to do is to look at their price. The long-term trend is lower prices, which means *less scarcity.* Here is how Simon put it (1980, p. 11):

> The cost trends of almost every natural resource—whether measured in labor time required to produce the resource, or even in the price relative to other consumer goods—have been downward over the course of recorded history. These trends imply that the raw materials have been getting increasingly available and less scarce.

This view so infuriated the pessimistic environmentalists that it led to one of history's famous bets. This fascinating bet is recounted in the Thinking Critically box on the next page.

To illustrate how the prices of raw materials have been falling relative to wages, Simon used copper as an example. As Figure 13-6 illustrates, it takes less and less time to earn enough to buy a pound of copper.

Energy ▪ And energy? Here too, Simon stressed, the answer lies in long-term price trends. The historical prices of electricity and coal, for example, are downward, indicating a stable and even increasing supply of energy. Beware of short-term trends, which can yield a distorted picture. The escalation of oil prices in the 1970s, for example, did not indicate scarcity, but the futile attempt of OPEC to control prices.

FIGURE 13-6 The Price of Copper Relative to Wages

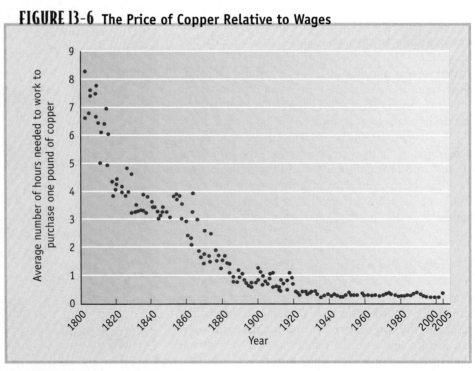

Sources: Historical Statistics of the United States 1976; Statistical Abstract of the United States 2007: Tables 630, 865.

PUT YOUR MONEY WHERE YOUR MOUTH IS: THE SIMON–EHRLICH BET

To say that Professors Julian Simon and Paul Ehrlich didn't like each other would be an understatement. *Detest* would be a more appropriate term. Simon was an economist who taught at the University of Maryland. Ehrlich, a demographer and ornithologist, taught at Stanford.

Ordinarily, their paths would not have crossed. They lived a continent apart, and they worked in different fields.

But then life changed for both of them.

Ehrlich came out swinging. In 1968, he wrote a book that scared mil-

Anne and Paul Ehrlich, authors of Betrayal of Science and Reason

Julian L. Simon, author of Hoodwinking the Nation

lions of people and fueled the environmental movement. He said that the world's population was growing so fast that food would soon be scarce. Prices were going to soar, and life expectancy would drop. His book, with the pop title, *The Population Bomb,* sold 3 million copies. The book scared the American public, aroused an environmentalist movement, and made Ehrlich rich. He was sought after as a guest on talk shows.

Fame and fortune. A prestigious job at Stanford. Unless he started to sexually harass his students or come to class drunk, how could that be spoiled?

Then along came Simon. Simon started grumbling in public, muttering that Ehrlich's book was a piece of, well, you know what—rotten catfish. Simon even claimed that the truth was the opposite of what Ehrlich had said. Larger populations, asserted Simon, would mean more abundance, not less. Prices would drop, not increase. Life expectancy would increase, not drop.

Simon and Ehrlich began to call each other names. They wrote nasty comments about one another in academic journals.

Ehrlich still had the public on his side. He kept repeating his predictions of doomsday. He was a founder of Earth Day, and he spoke to a crowd of 200,000 at the first gathering in 1970.

Simon was there, too, telling his side of the story. He had an audience of 16.

Simon didn't like this, but there wasn't much he could do about the public latching on to Ehrlich's ideas, not his.

Then Simon made an intriguing proposal. Without mentioning Ehrlich by name, he challenged any pessimistic environmentalist to a bet (Toth, 1998). The opponent could select *any* commodity, and Simon would bet that its price would

drop. "After all," he said, "contrary to common sense, resources are growing more plentiful, and they will drop in price."

"Put your money where your mouth is," Simon boasted, none too gently.

This was too much for Ehrlich—who knew that he was the target of the challenge. In October 1980, he accepted the bet. Then he did a little boasting of his own. He said, "I'll accept Simon's astonishing offer before other greedy people jump in" (Tierney, 1990).

The bet was on. If the prices of chrome, copper, nickel, tin, and tungsten were higher in 10 years, Ehrlich would win; if they were lower, Simon would win. To be sure there could be no misunderstandings, the two wrote their bet down, signed a contract, and publicized it widely.

During the ensuing years, the two kept goading one another—and the world's population kept growing. During the next ten years, it soared by more than 800 million people, the greatest increase in history.

Ten years later to the day, the two checked prices.

Ehrlich was chagrined. The price of all five metals had dropped. He quietly sent Simon a check. He enclosed no letter.

Simon gloated publicly. "Now you know who's right," he said. "And if you think this was just a fluke, let's do it again. And this time, let's put up some real money. How about $20,000?"

Ehrlich refused, saying that the matter was of minor importance.

Simon laughed and continued to poke fun at Ehrlich. Then students started to do the same, calling Ehrlich the nuttiest professor at Stanford.

Julian Simon died at age 65 in 1990. Paul Ehrlich stayed on at Stanford, where he still teaches. The two never reconciled.

The higher oil prices we face today may prove to be similar—increases because of war, political instability, higher demand, and the manipulation of output by oil companies. For example, whereas the year 2008 saw record high prices for oil when prices reached a record high of nearly $150 per barrel in July 2008, it also saw those prices drop by half toward the end of the year—a result of multiple factors, including a drop in demand because of the world economic crisis. By the end of January 2009, the price for oil had dipped below $40 per barrel.

Technology ■ The optimistic environmentalists also argue that if we should ever exhaust a particular resource, our technology will produce a substitute. New technology will also replace older technology. In fact, technology is rushing so headlong into the future that it produces new materials before old ones are threatened. Fiber-optic cable, for example, is replacing copper wire for the transmission of sound and images. Just a few years ago, the optimists point out, the pessimists were saying that we would run out of copper. Take another look at Figure 13-6.

IN SUM The price of commodities bounces around a little each year, and any given season will give you a distorted picture. It is necessary to focus on the larger picture—the historical price of resources relative to wages. The long-term picture indicates less scarcity and a growing standard of living.

Reconciling the Positions

In Chapter 12, where we discussed population and food, we saw that the experts fell into opposing camps. So it is with energy and resources. These topics, too, lead into controversy and debate. How do we reconcile contrary positions among the "experts"?

FRAMEWORKS OF INTERPRETATION. As stressed in Chapter 2, objective conditions—or the things that we call social facts—do not come with built-in meanings. We have to attach meaning to them. All of us, as the symbolic interactionists stress, fit "facts" into some framework. The framework that we choose influences our conclusions. This basic principle applies to "experts" and "nonexperts" alike.

Consider how this principle works when it comes to the environment—whether pollution, energy, or resources: If we assume that the environment is deteriorating and our vital resources are disappearing, we interpret data one way. If we assume, in contrast, that resources are infinitely abundant and will not shrink, other interpretations follow. The framework within which we interpret objective conditions makes all the difference in how we interpret "facts."

Science at Work ■ Does this mean that we are left only with opinions, and opposing ones at that? Not at all. As pointed out earlier, science is being used and objective studies will win out. Barring political interference, as opposing sides present their evidence, air their views, and try to disprove the other, the best data will become apparent. This isn't always the case, mind you, but it usually is. As scientists produce more data on the environmental crisis, the exaggerations of each side should become apparent, and better data on pollution, energy, and resources should become evident.

IMPLICATIONS OF THE FRAMEWORKS. Meanwhile, we must draw our own conclusions—which affect how we perceive the problem and the solutions we favor. On an individual level, our conclusions influence our choices about energy use and lifestyles. On the political level, the conclusions have infinitely greater implications: The well-being of billions of people depend on them—including future generations. Everyone will benefit if this debate and its related research are allowed to continue, unencumbered by politics, so that social policies can be based on sound data and logic.

Social Policy

Before we examine specific social policies, let's first consider how these contrasting frameworks of interpretation lead to vastly different social policies.

Oppositional Viewpoints and Overarching Solutions

Three approaches to social policy flow from these contrasting frameworks.

THE STEADY-STATE SOCIETY. As we have seen, pessimistic environmentalists argue that it is folly to expect the world's economies and standards of living to increase endlessly. Based on their position that pollution is endangering the world and resources are diminishing, they have come up with an overarching solution called the **steady-state society.** When using this term, pessimistic environmentalists state that we must stabilize industrial output at the level it is now. If we do this, we will slow the rate at which we pollute the environment and use up resources. This will give us time to solve problems of pollution and to develop alternative resources before a crisis of shortages develops. To reach a steady-state society will require painful adjustments; it will require us to curb our growing appetite for material goods that support our current lifestyles.

THE SCALED-BACK SOCIETY. An even more pessimistic group of environmentalists argues it is not enough to develop a steady-state society. Our current rate of pollution and use of resources are so far beyond anything that the earth can sustain that we must develop a **scaled-back society.** That is, we must immediately reduce our industrial output and our standard of living. Only after we cut back to some optimal level—one that experts will determine—can we move to a steady-state society. This will require not "adjustments" but, rather, considerable sacrifice; yet it is necessary for the survival of earth. All of us, except the poorest, must learn to get by with less. To lower our material standards so that we can reduce our dependence on depleting fossil fuels, we must scale back our expectations. Some who take this position add that once we have reduced our expectations and have learned to live simpler, less-materialistic lifestyles, we will find life more satisfying.

THE EXPANDING SOCIETY. Optimistic environmentalists scoff at the arguments of the pessimists. Their position is that not only can we solve the current environmental crisis but at the same time we can also enjoy high and even increasing standards of living. We can bring pollution under control through international agreements and develop alternative resources for any that are running short. As we do so, we can increase our industrial output and create a world of even greater material abundance. It is foolish to even consider a steady-state or scaled-back society. Such a society would deny billions of people a better life.

Regardless of whether we agree—partially, reluctantly, or wholeheartedly—with pessimistic or optimistic environmentalists, it seems reasonable to take the position that we need social policies addressing pollution and energy. Let's consider them.

To save the environment, some insist that we must drastically reduce the world's population and our standard of living. Few of us, however, want to go back to this way of life. There must be a balance that we can strike between population, standard of living, and the environment.

Pollution

PREVENTING THE MISUSE OF TOXIC CHEMICALS. A pressing problem is the misuse of toxic chemicals. Let's see what can be done.

International Controls ■ As the Global Glimpse box below highlights, it is not enough to ban the use of some toxic chemical in the United States. That chemical will return to us by way of a food chain that stretches to us from the Least Industrialized Nations. To protect the people in these nations, hazardous chemicals need to be labeled in the language of the country to which they are shipped, their proper use and dangers clearly stated in plain words. To protect people everywhere, no company or its subsidiaries should be allowed to manufacture chemicals whose use is banned in the company's home country. The United States can call a summit to enact international controls.

Holding Industry Accountable ■ To prevent misuse, industry must be held accountable. Congress has already passed the **Community Right to Know Act of 1986.** It requires companies to annually submit to a state agency and to local fire departments a list of the hazardous chemicals they use or manufacture. Some states have passed their own right-to-know laws, requiring businesses to inform their employees of the hazardous chemicals they will be exposed to at work.

Some environmentalists say that this is not enough, They want a comprehensive policy for toxic chemicals. In this "cradle-to-grave" approach, all toxic chemicals would be approved for sale and use, registered as they enter the marketplace, and monitored throughout their lifetime. The public would have access to information on chemical releases, and the worst polluters would be publicized (Friends of the Earth, 2004).

PREVENTING FOOD POLLUTION. A second pressing problem is food pollution. Recall the chapter's opening vignette on the sorry state of our meat industry. No compelling reason

A Global Glimpse
THE CIRCLE OF POISON

In U.S. ports from Gulfport, Mississippi, to Oakland, California, you can watch forklifts loading 55-gallon drums onto the decks of vessels bound for Central and South America.

What's in the drums? Heptachlor, chlordane, BHC, and other chemicals on their way to the plantations of Latin America. These pesticides, linked to cancer and sterility, are banned or severely restricted in the United States. U.S. companies, however, manufacture them here and in other nations and market them in the industrializing countries. There, most workers who handle these chemicals cannot read. They have no idea what the warnings on the labels say. Yet these chemicals will contaminate them, their family, and their food.

The pesticides that this girl in Pisco, Peru, is selling include DDT, which, although banned in the United States, is still manufactured for export.

Pesticides that are banned here don't disappear—they come back to haunt us. The fruit grown in these countries appears on our kitchen tables— along with the poisons used to protect them from insects. BHC comes back in your coffee. DDT, applied to cotton in El Salvador, shows up in beef carcasses imported through Miami. Nearly half of the green coffee beans we import are contaminated with pesticides, potential carcinogens. And the situation worsens, for the free trade zones that stimulate the globalization of capitalism increase the importation of these products.

Based on a newsletter from Frances Moore Lappe, founder of Food First; Ingersoll (1990); Allen (1991); "U.S. Pesticide Exports" (1994).

exists that should allow diseases to be transmitted in food. With our alternative forms of food processing and preservation, there also is no compelling reason to add dangerous chemicals to make our food look or taste better, to make it easier to transport, or to lengthen its shelf life. At a minimum, no chemical should be added to our food until it is proven safe for human consumption.

State-of-the-art testing procedures can be used to detect banned chemicals in our food, whether imported or domestic. We can shut down U.S. companies that violate chemical restrictions and ban food imports from countries where this occurs. To be effective, the legal penalties need to be directed against the *managers and directors* of companies that violate such laws.

PREVENTING POLLUTION THROUGH INDUSTRIAL WASTES. A third area of concern is proper disposal of the unwanted by-products of industrialization.

Detoxifying Wastes ■ We already know how to detoxify most industrial wastes. We probably could learn to detoxify the rest. Recycling waste products is especially promising because it turns noxious wastes into safe and usable products. To develop better technology to recycle and detoxify wastes, we could establish a superfund to finance cooperative research by scientists.

Hazardous Waste Sites ■ Scattered across the nation are thousands of sites where we have discarded oil, battery acid, PCBs, pesticides, paint, and radioactive wastes. As you see on Figure 13-7 below, the EPA has drawn up a National Priority List of the most dangerous of these hazardous waste sites. Table 13-1 on page 494 ranks the states on the basis of the number of priority waste sites they contain. Congress established a superfund to clean up these sites and has spent $20 billion to begin the cleanup. Some estimate that the bill for cleaning up these sites will run $50 billion; others say that it will total $500 billion. No one knows, of course, but if the lower total is correct, that's $160 for every person in the United States. If the higher figure is right, the cleanup will cost each of us $1,600.

FIGURE 13-7 Hazardous Waste Sites on the National Priority List

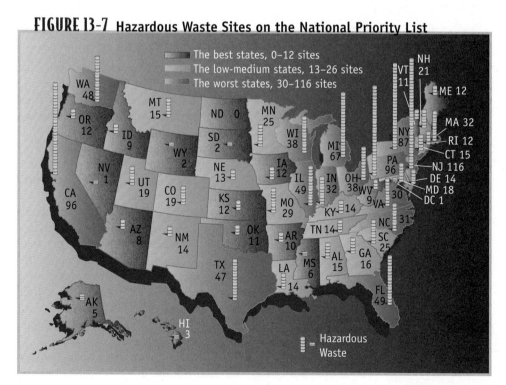

Note: New Jersey is in a class by itself. This small state has 20 more hazardous waste sites than its nearest competitor, Pennsylvania, with 96.

Source: By James M. Henslin Based on *Statistical Abstract of the United States* 2009, Table 367.

TABLE 13-1 How the States Rank in Number of Hazardous Waste Sites on the National Priority List

State	Number of Sites
1. New Jersey	116
2. Pennsylvania	96
3. California	96
4. New York	87
5. Michigan	67
6. Florida	49
7. Illinois	49
8. Washington	48
9. Texas	47
10. Wisconsin	38
11. Ohio	38
12. Massachusetts	32
13. Indiana	32
14. North Carolina	31
15. Virginia	30
16. Missouri	29
17. South Carolina	25
18. Minnesota	25
19. New Hampshire	21
20. Colorado	19
21. Utah	19
22. Maryland	18
23. Georgia	16
24. Connecticut	15
25. Alabama	15
26. Montana	15
27. Louisiana	14
28. Delaware	14
29. Kentucky	14
30. Tennessee	14
31. New Mexico	14
32. Nebraska	13
33. Iowa	12
34. Kansas	12
35. Maine	12
36. Oregon	12
37. Rhode Island	12
38. Oklahoma	11
39. Vermont	11
40. Arkansas	10
41. Idaho	9
42. West Virginia	9
43. Arizona	8
44. Mississippi	6
45. Alaska	5
46. Hawaii	3
47. South Dakota	2
48. Wyoming	2
49. Nevada	1
50. North Dakota	0
Total	**1,294**

Source: By James M. Henslin. Based on *Statistical Abstract of the United States*, 2009, Table 367.

Nuclear Waste ■ Because they stay lethal for thousands of years, leftover plutonium and other nuclear wastes have perplexed experts. For decades, while scientists debated how to store something that was beyond human experience, *millions* of pounds of radioactive waste have been stored in temporary containers (Campbell, 1987; Schneider, 1992). The waste's new home is supposed to be in Yucca Mountain near Las Vegas, Nevada. Storage chambers have been carved from an ancient salt bed, nearly half a mile below ground. Geologists assure us that this salt deposit has been stable for 250 million years (Brooke, 1999). Critics point out that this may be so, but the waste will be stored in stainless steel containers lined with lead. No one knows if those containers will last a thousand years, much less ten thousand years. Others say that we have so much waste waiting to be buried that even this depository won't hold it all (Ashley, 2002). Nevada officials don't want this waste, and they are suing to stop it from coming into their state (Tetreault, 2006). To make the issue even more controversial, Las Vegas officials have said that they won't allow the waste to pass through their city on the way to the mountain. If necessary, they say, they will use armed force to stop the trucks and railroad cars carrying the waste.

THE GREENHOUSE EFFECT. What can we do to solve the greenhouse effect? An immediate step would be to plant vast numbers of trees around the world, for they thrive on carbon dioxide. To the extent that carbon dioxide is a danger to the world, nations must reduce the amounts that they produce. The 1997 Kyoto Protocol was a giant step in this direction. As mentioned, this agreement may prove difficult to implement. Fearful that compliance could cost millions, Canada and the United States withdrew from it. Other nations seem ready to do so, too (Struck, 2006). We will have to see what the future holds in this regard, especially with a new U.S. administration.

THE RAIN FORESTS. We must also develop social policies that stop the destruction of the world's rain forests. We propose two policies: (1) Make it illegal to import timber that comes from rain forests. This will require an international agreement; the ban won't work if only a nation here and there passes such laws. (2) Industrialized nations need to *purchase the rights to not develop the rain forests.* Because most of the rain forests are in nations that have not industrialized, those funds could pay off their huge debts, thus helping to solve another problem. This policy would preserve millions of acres and thousands of plant and animal species for future generations. The rights would extend indefinitely and be overseen by an international watchdog agency.

No social policy is simple, of course, and policies concerning the rain forests bring their own complications. Brazil, for example, which has extensive rain forests, knows that the United States prospered by cutting down most of its forests for farmland. Brazilian officials find it ironic that the United States wants them to preserve Brazil's forests for the benefit of Americans. Some Brazilian officials even fear that the concern the United States has expressed is a prelude to an invasion, and they have trained jungle forces to repel it (Goering, 1998; Zibechi, 2005).

AN OVERARCHING SOLUTION. To address environmental problems once and for all, we need to produce less of what harms the environment. We can change our production techniques and equipment, redesign our products, and do more in-process recycling (Doran, 2006). We have the capacity to take these steps, but to take them we must be convinced that our fragile environment is being harmed and that it is worth the effort and cost to change our ways. Whether or not we have this perspective, of course, depends on the framework of interpretation we are using.

Energy

Aside from discovering new deposits of gas and petroleum, only two types of solutions for energy exist: alternative forms of energy and energy conservation.

ALTERNATIVE FORMS OF ENERGY. What forms of energy can be alternatives to our heavy dependence on gas and petroleum?

Coal ▪ We have enough coal in the United States to satisfy our energy needs for centuries. We can transform coal into liquids and gases. South Africa already operates a coal liquefaction plant that produces a fuel that is competitive in cost with petroleum, and China is in the process of developing such plants (Wu, 2006). We would have to ensure that such processes do not contribute to pollution.

Synthetic Fuels ▪ **Synfuels** can be developed from garbage, sawdust, and other waste. The decay of organic substances such as sewage and straw produces methane and methanol, gases that motors can burn efficiently. Synfuels offer the potential to solve two problems at once: (1) the disposal of our organic garbage and (2) the production of alternative fuels. We may see fields of common milkweed turn into flourishing "petroleum farms" as factories extract **hydrocarbons**—the backbone of motor fuels, lubricants, turpentine, and rubber—from those plants.

To encourage the development and production of synfuels, Congress offered huge tax breaks to those who undertook these efforts. This incentive drew the attention of scam artists who would spray pine tar or latex on coal, meeting the IRS requirement that the new product be chemically different from the original. Although there was no real new product, no real synfuel, the spraying met the letter of the law and qualified these con artists for the tax break. Companies that conduct such scams have to sell their coated coal at a loss—otherwise, the utility companies they sell to would simply buy coal that doesn't have the coating. Although these supposed synfuels companies lose money on their fake product, they reap real profits from the tax credits that they sell to wealthy investors (Biddle, 2001; Hogan, 2001). The losers in this setup are the taxpayers who have to make up the taxes that the IRS doesn't collect from those who profit from this legal scam.

Other Alternative Fuels ▪ Hydrogen, too, holds great potential. As a basic component of air and water, hydrogen is available in limitless amounts. Other alternative sources of energy include the wind, ocean tides, **geothermal energy** (heat from beneath the earth's crust), and **nuclear fusion** (combining atoms, as opposed to nuclear fission, which splits atoms). Especially promising is harnessing the sun. Solar power is infinite, and technologies such as the photovoltaic cell, which changes sunlight into electricity, can trap it.

Supporting alternative fuel initiatives may take a long time to adopt, but when gasoline reaches $5 a gallon and remains there, it is likely that Americans will get serious about alternative forms of energy.

ENERGY CONSERVATION. The simpler solution would be to conserve energy. Conservation involves everything from insulating homes, businesses, and factories to working four 10-hour shifts instead of five 8-hour shifts a week. Such a change in working patterns would cut commuting expenses by 20% and allow factories to fire up their boilers less often.

Increasingly popular as alternative sources of energy are wind turbines. Those depicted in this photo are located in Palm Springs, California. Wind turbine generators are much less harmful to the environment than burning fossil fuels, but they do require average wind speeds of at least 21 km/h (13 mph). The largest of these windmills stands 150 feet tall with blades half the length of a football field.

The potential savings from conservation are dramatic, but it does involve changing patterns of behavior that are rooted firmly in culture, hardly an easy matter.

Our Homes ■ As the price of energy has gone up, we have made our homes more energy efficient (*Statistical Abstract,* 2006, Table 896). But we still have a long way to go. The **Lo-Cal house,** developed at the University of Illinois, can cut fuel bills by about two-thirds. These savings are made simply through the design of the house, without help from solar equipment. About 85% of the total window area in the house faces south, the house is heavily insulated, and its roof overhangs by 30 inches, letting sunshine in during the winter but excluding it during the summer. Another home design is the **solar envelope.** This house is built within a second set of walls that provide a "skin" to trap and distribute the sun's heat. Even in northern climates, a furnace is needed on only the cloudiest days of winter. Its ingenious design also cools the house in the summer by drawing in cool air from a chamber under the house.

Our Cars ■ We have also increased the energy efficiency of our cars, and we get much better mileage than we used to. Although the automobile industry dragged its feet, after California increased its standards for cars sold in that state, car companies began researching alternatives in earnest. Their main innovation has been the hybrid. Using both electricity and gasoline to propel them, hybrid cars burn about 25% less gasoline than regular cars. They even convert the car's motion to electricity when the brakes are applied ("Hybrid Car . . . ," 2004). Other hybrids burn hydrogen. Toyota has developed a car that can travel 300 miles on a single tank of compressed hydrogen (T. Murphy, 2003). Propelling cars by burning hydrogen can also reduce global warming, because water, instead of carbon dioxide, flows out of the exhaust.

Cogeneration ■ Another form of conservation is **cogeneration,** producing electricity as part of normal operations, such as generating electricity from the heat and steam that industrial boilers produce. This is not a new idea. In 1900, cogenerators produced more than half of the nation's electricity. Now they produce only about 3%. To encourage cogeneration, federal law requires that utility companies purchase a firm's excess production at the utility's standard costs (Paul, 1987). The advantage for utility companies is that they can add to their capacity to provide electricity without having to invest in building new power plants (Devine, 2004).

IN SUM We seem to be at a watershed in social policy. If pessimistic environmentalists are correct, we soon will see the end of some of the resources on which our civilization depends. If we haven't implemented good social policy before this happens, these shortages will force us to do so. If optimists are right, we won't have to make difficult choices. Market forces will point us in the right direction. If we run short of something, the pursuit of profits will lead people to develop alternative sources. Those optimists convinced of this view tell us, "Just don't interfere with those market forces, and the balance will occur naturally."

Moral Issues in a Global Age

In addition to the fundamentally differing perspectives presented by the pessimists and optimists, determining social policy touches on basic philosophical and moral issues.

THE DILEMMA OF GLOBAL SOLUTIONS. Because the environmental crisis is global, its solution requires global social policy. Some organization—whether the United Nations or

the World Trade Organization or another international body—will need to take the lead in solving environmental problems by proposing international laws to benefit all nations. Because such laws will conflict with the individual sovereignty of nations, some nations are likely to reject this type of legislation as violating their national interest. This brings us face-to-face with philosophical, moral issues.

Consider these questions. Do nations have a fundamental right to use resources—whether from their own land or those they import—in any way they wish? Do they even have a fundamental right to pollute, if they choose to do so? If not, then do nations possess some fundamental right to impose their view of pollution and resources on others? If so, what is the basis of that right? Is it some "greater good" for the world's benefit? If so, who decides what that "greater good" is and how it should be enforced? Assumptions of a "greater good," as conflict theorists remind us, can be excuses for the Most Industrialized Nations to bully the Least Industrialized Nations. If there is such a right, it certainly isn't likely that the weaker nations would be able to impose their ideas of pollution and resource depletion on the more powerful nations.

The Future of the Problem

As we glimpse into the future, let's first examine energy conservation and pollution. After this, we'll again look through the eyes of the pessimists and optimists.

Energy

As our expectations of attaining higher standards of living continue to grow, we increase our demands for energy. Since 1970, the average U.S. family has diminished from 3.6 people to 3.1, but the average size of a new home has risen by over 50%—from 1,500 square feet to over 2,350. We also furnish our homes with more energy-eating appliances. In 1970, 34% of new homes had central air conditioning; now 90% do (*Statistical Abstract,* 1989, Tables 58, 1231; 2006, Table 932). We might complain about the price of gasoline, but the higher cost hasn't affected our driving. We drive our cars more than we used to, averaging 40% more miles per car today than in 1980 (*Statistical Abstract,* 2006, Table 1084).

Our efforts at energy conservation have been quite effective. Although the size of an average new house has increased over 50% since 1970, it uses only 17% more energy (*Statistical Abstract,* 2006, Table 896). Similarly, although we have increased our driving by 40% since 1980, our cars are so much more efficient that we burn only 6% more gasoline per car (*Statistical Abstract,* 2006, Table 1985). You can see, however, that although we have made great strides in conservation, we have *not* reduced our energy usage. Instead, we have increased it.

It is likely that we and the rest of the industrialized world will continue our wasteful ways. It is also likely that as shortages occur and prices go up, we will turn to alternative sources of energy, especially our vast reserves of coal. We likely will continue to develop technology to harness alternative forms of energy, making these sources of energy widely available at low prices. Doubtless, international oil companies will turn alternative forms of energy into profitable enterprises.

Pollution

The picture of pollution is less positive. We have no overarching plan for chemical and nuclear pollution that ensures the long-range health of our population.

If bringing pollution under control required only technology, we could assume a future with cleaner air, water, and land. But political thrust is required—particularly a national determination to make our environment as free of pollution as possible. Although this depends on public awareness, any administration can strengthen or weaken standards.

THE GREENS. Environmentalists in Europe have formed their own political parties. The **Green Party,** as the one in Germany is called, holds seats in the parliament; and in several of Germany's states it has become a key player in coalition governments. The United

States, too, has a Green Party, but it has a difficult time mustering enough support to get on the ballot, much less to win a major election. Even support for Ralph Nader, the closest we have had to a national Green candidate, decreased in 2004. That the Green Party in the United States has not been able to muster strong political support does not mean that this will continue indefinitely. Some unexpected event could etch the environment into national consciousness, making it a top political issue. In the meantime, as Robert Gottlieb discusses in the Spotlight on Social Research box on the next page, environmentalists have begun to apply their perspective to urban life.

A LACK OF UNITY. As conflict theorists would stress, the future of pollution depends on a fragile balance of power among groups whose interests coalesce. At this point, there is little to indicate that people will drop their other political interests to join under a green banner. However, some startling event yet to come could act as the stimulus uniting fragmented groups around the world, forging them into a global political alliance. Certainly people are concerned about the world they will leave for their children, but environmentalists, often local in orientation or fragmented by multiple visions and political strategies, lack a unifying voice. Even so, opposing groups can overcome differences in order to make the environment a top priority, as illustrated by the Christians and Jews joining forces under the banner "Creation Care." Their message: "We are called to be stewards, not exploiters, of the earth" (Watanabe, 1998). Though the potential is present, the voice remains weak.

THE ENVIRONMENTAL PESSIMISTS AND OPTIMISTS. Finally, let's look at the future through the eyes of the two groups who see practically nothing alike.

The Picture Painted by the Pessimists ■ Pessimists paint a gloomy future, of course. Pollution will continue with only superficial improvements here and there, and the depletion of resources will accelerate. The countdown has already begun, and "RDP Day" (Resource-Depletion and Pollution Day) is on its way. This is the day when we will have depleted our vital resources and pollution will have gone so far that we won't be able to fix it. With its industrial base undermined, modern society will disintegrate, bringing tragedy to all. Desperate, people will flee. But to where? Even the countryside will be too polluted to support anything but a minimum of life.

Can such a gloomy future be averted? Yes, reply the pessimists, but only if we develop a steady-state or scaled-back society. To level off our energy consumption or reduce it severely we need to eliminate our desire for material wealth. Because we have built a society on the assumption of inexhaustible resources, withdrawal symptoms will bring enormous pain. But once we recover from the shock of being forced into a drasti-

The future? The Hummer has the worst gas mileage of any civilian vehicle—it hovers somewhere around 9 mpg. The Smart Car, on the other hand, gets 33–41 mpg.

Spotlight on Social Research

THE MARRIAGE OF COMMUNITY AND ENVIRONMENT

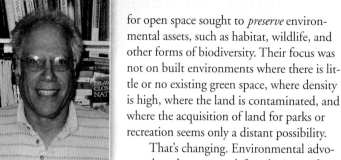

ROBERT GOTTLIEB, *professor of urban environmental policy at Occidental College, has found that something new is happening in the environmental movement. He calls it a marriage of community and environment. Living in Los Angeles and writing and teaching about the urban environment make this "marriage" particularly compelling for him.*

When I first arrived in Los Angeles in 1969, the city, with its sprawling landscapes of subdivisions and freeways, had a reputation as the "anti-environment." I never focused on the fact that Los Angeles had a river until the 1980s, when one of my students brought to my attention the growing advocacy around the revitalization of the asphalt-and-concrete-encased Los Angeles River. Since then, I've been able to document the creation in Los Angeles of a new kind of community-based environmentalism: where urban rivers and streams and other green spaces and community places in the city are re-envisioned.

This marriage of community and environment has made an impact on environmental groups. Open space has long referred to places outside urban areas or at the urban edge where there is little or no development. Earlier battles for open space sought to *preserve* environmental assets, such as habitat, wildlife, and other forms of biodiversity. Their focus was not on built environments where there is little or no existing green space, where density is high, where the land is contaminated, and where the acquisition of land for parks or recreation seems only a distant possibility.

That's changing. Environmental advocates have begun to redefine the issue of open space as the need to re-envision *community spaces* and to reclaim rather than simply preserve such places. Many environmentalists now embrace community gardens, farmers markets in low-income communities, re-landscaping projects, and recreational opportunities in densely populated areas. I had the opportunity to direct an educational program on the Los Angeles River—the very symbol of both the anti-environment and efforts to re-envision the river as a community and environmental asset.

If you define the marriage of community and environment as an effort to re-envision—or reconstruct or reclaim—these kinds of community and environmental assets, then a different kind of environmental agenda begins to emerge. This agenda would focus on a neighborhood's transportation needs, on access to and quality of food, on health concerns like asthma, and on schools as re-landscaped, livable places rather than fortress-like, asphalt jungles. In this marriage, the greening agenda becomes a justice agenda. It leads us to understand that nature belongs in the city as well as outside it.

---

cally different lifestyle, we may find that a simpler way of life is rewarding: We may be less rushed, enjoy social relationships more, and feel less compulsion to own things.

The Picture Painted by the Optimists. And what does the future look like to optimists? Our present path is fine, they say. We already have more resources than we need for the foreseeable future, but as scientists continue to make breakthroughs, they will put even more energy at our disposal. The development of hydrogen fuel cell technology holds the potential for giving us energy in unlimited quantities. From this source alone, we might meet all the world's needs now and in the future (Bishop & Wells, 1989; C. Stevens, 1989; Low, 2008).

For the optimists, neither is pollution a fearsome problem. Scientists have discovered a bacterium that has adapted to 15 times the dose of radiation it takes to kill humans. This bacterium, and others yet to be discovered, **extremophiles,** will eat our nuclear wastes, breaking them down into relatively harmless components (Fialka, 2004). The principle is this: Pollution will be solved to the extent that people demand a cleaner environment and are willing to pay for prevention and cleanup. Because people are demanding it, the environment is already getting cleaner—and it will continue to improve. Consequently, the future promises a healthier environment, an even higher standard of living, and a continued lengthening of our life expectancy.

WHO IS RIGHT? What *is* the future of the environmental crisis? Is humanity at a crossroads, as the pessimists insist, with our current course dooming us to destruction? Or are the optimists right, with our current course taking us to a delightful future? Could the

future turn out to be even gloomier than imagined, with nuclear war, the worst pollution of all, destroying our ecosystem—and humanity?

We who are the audience—and either beneficiaries or victims of—this unfolding drama will have to await its outcome.

SUMMARY AND REVIEW

1. The destruction of the environment began millennia ago and may even have destroyed ancient civilizations. Industrialization has intensified this process.

2. The nations of the world share a common *ecosystem*. The environmental crisis is a global matter: Even individual acts of *pollution* can have international consequences. Pollution comes primarily from industrialization and is common in both capitalist and socialist nations.

3. Symbolic interactionists have studied how the environment became a social problem, how objective conditions were translated into subjective concerns. Concerns about the environment began with professionals, were picked up by interest groups and government agencies, and then by the press, which aroused the public.

4. Functionalists stress that all life on earth is interdependent. ("Everything is connected to everything else.") We all are part of a huge, complex living machine called the environment. Industrialization has dysfunctional consequences for the ecosystem.

5. Conflict theorists stress the conflict between environmentalists, who battle to reduce environmental threat, and industrial leaders, who fight for the right to pollute while earning a profit.

6. Some measures of air and water pollution show improvement, but the results are mixed, and pollution continues. The *greenhouse effect* could cause climatic change that would have far-ranging consequences for humanity.

7. Strip mining and the disposal of solid wastes despoil the land. Industrial wastes threaten our drinking water and many of our lakes and rivers. *Acid* and *mercury rain* imperil animal and plant life.

8. Chemical pollutants pervade our environment. Leaching from landfills is extensive. Nuclear pollution is ominous, as illustrated by the Kyshtym and Chernobyl disasters. Food additives are a form of pollution. Genetic modification might be another form.

9. Alarmed at the environmental crisis, pessimists advocate a *steady-state society*—one based on no economic growth—or a *scaled-back society*, based on deliberately shrinking the economy. Optimists, convinced that we can continue industrial growth and use technology to solve environmental problems, advocate an expanded economy. Regardless of who is right, pollution is a global problem that requires international social policies.

10. The environmental pessimists and optimists paint contrasting pictures of the future. We don't yet know who is right, but with our coal reserves and other alternative forms of energy, accompanied by developing technology, our energy future looks positive. The outlook for pollution, however, is less positive. The currently fragmented environmental movement has the potential to become a powerful global force.

KEY TERMS

Acid rain, 474
Air pollution, 470
Biodegradable, 471
Bovine growth hormones (BGH), 480
Carcinogen, 470
Cogeneration, 496
Community Right to Know Act of 1986, 492
Corporate welfare, 469
Ecology, 463
Ecosystem, 467
Environmental injustice, 468
Escherichia coli (E. coli), 478

Extremophiles, 499
Food chain, 475
Food pollution (food contamination), 478
Fossil fuels, 470
Genetically modified foods (GMF), 482
Geothermal energy, 495
Global warming, 471
Green party, 497
Greenhouse effect, 471
Hydrocarbons, 495
Lo-Cal house, 496
Nuclear fusion, 495

Optimistic environmentalists, 485
Ozone shield, 471
Pessimistic environmentalists, 487
Pollution, 463
Resource recovery plants, 473
Scaled-back society, 491
Solar envelope, 496
Steady-state society, 491
Strip mining, 473
Synergistic, 481
Synfuels, 495
Thermal inversion, 470

THINKING CRITICALLY ABOUT CHAPTER 13

1. Which of the perspectives (symbolic interactionism, functionalism, or conflict theory) do you think does the best job of explaining the environmental crisis? Why?
2. How far do you think the government should go to reduce pollution? Should the executives who run polluting corporations be jailed? Should the government shut down polluters? What else could or should the government do?
3. The scientists represented by, among others, the conservative think tank the Heritage Foundation, argue that problems of pollution and the scarcity of resources are best solved by free enterprise. They believe that the market is better equipped than governments to solve these problems. What do you think of their position? Explain.
4. Do you think that U.S. corporations should be allowed to manufacture and export to other countries chemicals that are banned in the United States? Explain.
5. Do you think that the U.S. government has the power or authority to demand a steady-state society? Do you think it is advisable? Why or why not?

BY THE NUMBERS: THEN AND NOW

- Emission of lead into the air, in tons, in the U.S. in 1970: **221,000**
- Emission of lead into the air, in tons, in the U.S. in 2002: **3,000**

- Ounces of solid waste generated by each American each day in 1970: **52**
- Ounces of solid waste generated by each American each day in 2003: **70**

- Female life expectancy in the U.S. in 1920: **58.5**
- Female life expectancy in the U.S. in 2005: **80.4**

- Male life expectancy in the U.S. in 1920: **56.3**
- Male life expectancy in the U.S. in 2005: **75.2**

MySocLab

What can you find in MySocLab? mysoclab www.mysoclab.com

- Complete Ebook
- Practice Tests and Exams
- Multimedia Activities
- Mapping and Data Analysis Exercises

- Research and Writing Advice
- Interactive Social Surveys
- Sociology in the News

War, Terrorism, and the Balance of Power

Most of us can remember vividly where we were on September 11, 2001, a day that has become embedded in our own memories—seared into national consciousness. This day, which began like so many before it—a bright dawn, shining sun, and people going about their everyday lives—was destined to change the United States. No longer would our assumptions about life be the same.

When the commercial jets that had been transformed into lethal missiles struck the Twin Towers and the Pentagon, the United States was shaken to its roots. At dawn, these two global symbols, one of capitalism and the other of military power, had stood tall and proud. Just a few hours later, one had been destroyed, the other crippled.

Americans shook their heads in dismay and confusion. Why had they been attacked? And who could have done this? As confusion turned to anger, and the face

It's a strange war

of the enemy was beamed throughout the media to the United States and the world, the nation's response was swift and violent. U.S. Special Forces, accompanied by missiles directed from remote locations, attacked al-Qaeda in Afghanistan.

The United States declared war on terrorism—as it steeled itself against further attacks by an enemy that remained hidden. Where would this unseen enemy strike next? The White House? A nuclear plant? Some NFL football game? Even the local mall?

This event brought back memories of the surprise attack at Pearl Harbor in 1941. This led to the United States declaring war on Japan. Just as in 1941, Americans feared that sleeper cells in the United States could attack at any time, from almost anywhere.

How will we know when this new war has ended? After all, will there ever be an end to terrorist threats against the United States?

The Problem in Sociological Perspective

After the attack at Pearl Harbor, the United States entered World War II. The Soviet Union (a union of communist countries) and the United States (a capitalist country), although avowed enemies, became uneasy allies, fighting on the same side. From the end of that war in 1945 until the end of the 1980s, the Soviet Union and the West were caught up in an **arms race.** Each furiously developed and produced new weapons, threatening one another and trying to outmatch the other's war capabilities. During these decades, called the **Cold War,** the West and the Soviet Union built arsenals of nuclear weapons that had (and still have) the capacity to destroy the world many times over.

When the Soviet Union accepted capitalism in the 1980s, the Cold War came to an end, but the nuclear weapons that these nations developed did not. They remain, still so powerful that they threaten human existence. In an instant, these weapons could reduce major cities to rubble and transform world powers into barren deserts. If we could put all the catastrophes that the world has ever experienced throughout its history into a single event, it would pale in comparison with nuclear war.

Why Is War Common?

Although the magnitude of the terrorist threat we face today is new, war itself is not. Human groups have always fought each other. Why do they do so?

AN INSTINCT TO FIGHT? Because war has been common throughout history, some analysts suggest that humans have an instinct for aggression. Anthropologist Konrad Lorenz said (1966) that our instinct for aggression used to be functional, ensuring that the fittest survived. It also forced humans to colonize the whole world as they fled from one another's innate aggression. In modern society, however, as Lorenz put it, this instinct has become a "hereditary evil" left from our primitive past.

THE SOCIOLOGICAL ANSWER: SOCIETIES CHANNEL AGGRESSION. To find the answer to why warfare exists, sociologists (and most anthropologists) do not look *within* people. Whether humans have an instinct for aggression is not the point. People will always disagree about something, so conflicts always arise among people living nearby. *What is significant are the norms that groups establish to deal with those conflicts.*

To illustrate this principle, let's look at two extremes. The first is a society that nourishes aggression. As you read about the Yanomamö in the Global Glimpse box on the next page, you will see why they represent this extreme. The other extreme is represented by the Eskimos of East Greenland. Instead of fighting, their norms require that hostile individuals *sing* to one another! Actually, they sing about their grievances, and the contest goes like this:

> The singing style is highly conventionalized. The successful singer uses the traditional patterns of composition which he attempts to deliver with such finesse as to delight the audience to enthusiastic applause. He who is most heartily applauded is "winner." . . . One of the advantages of the song duel carried on at length is that it gives the public time to come to a consensus about who is correct or who should admit guilt in the dispute. . . . Gradually more people are laughing a little harder at one of the duelist's verses than at the other's, until it becomes apparent where the sympathy of the community lies, and then opinion quickly becomes unanimous and the loser retires. (Fromm, 1973)

Other groups channel aggression into rituals involving violence. It is common for the Tiwi of northern Australia to settle differences through spear-throwing duels.

> When a dispute is between an accuser and a defendant, which is commonly the case, the accuser ritually hurls the spears from a prescribed distance, while the defendant dodges them. The public can applaud the speed, force, and accuracy of the accuser as he hurls his spears, or they can applaud the adroitness with which the defendant dodges them. After a time, unanimity is achieved as the approval for one or the other's skill gradually becomes overwhelming. When the defendant realizes that the community is finally considering him guilty, he is supposed to fail to dodge a spear and allow himself to be wounded in some fleshy part of his body. Conversely, the accuser simply stops throwing the spears when he becomes aware that public opinion is going against him. (Fromm, 1973)

WAR IS NOT UNIVERSAL. Although hostilities, aggression, and even murder characterize all human groups, war does not. War is just one option that some groups use for settling disagreements, but not all societies offer this option. The Mission Indians of North America, the Arunta of Australia, the Andaman Islanders of the South Pacific, and the Eskimos of the Arctic, for example, have established ways to handle quarrels, but they do not have organized battles that pit one tribe against another. These groups don't even have a word in their vocabulary for war (Lesser, 1968).

The Yanomamö men of the Amazon rain forest often attack neighboring villages, killing the men and kidnapping the women. Villagers also fight with one another. Fights often begin over sex: infidelity, seductions, or failure to give a promised girl in marriage. Sometimes the men challenge one another to a duel. One man stands, muscles tensed, feet firmly planted, while the other hits him as hard as he can once in the chest. Then the other man gets his turn. This continues until one man can no longer return the blow. Sometimes men take turns pounding one another over the head with a long wooden club. At other times, they even use axes and machetes—and neglect to await their turn. When relatives are drawn in, fights turn into brawls. These games can trigger feuds between villages. When someone is killed, relatives seek revenge. A feud is self-feeding, for each killing requires retaliation.

Why do the men fight like this? Anthropologist Napoleon Chagnon, who lived with the Yanomamö and analyzed their relationships, concluded that the basic reason is *social status*. Because violence is considered to be the mark of a true man, a reputation for violence gives a Yanomamö man high status. Almost everyone everywhere wants more status, to be looked up to by others, and the Yanomamö have developed a system that integrates acts of violence and status.

There is also another factor, one that is less apparent: Success at violence brings men more access to women.

The origins of warfare go back to the origins of history. Because war is so common, some theorists suggest that aggression is a part of human nature. If so, it is socially channeled into cultural forms. Shown here are men of a Yanomamö tribe.

Chagnon found that the men in this northern Venezuelan jungle who have killed at least one other person have more wives and children than those who have never killed. An especially successful warrior may have six wives. The higher status that comes with killing makes a man an attractive candidate for marriages—which are arranged by the men.

"How primitive they are!" we might say, smugly acknowledging our higher technology and education. But the Yanomamö are not that different from us, as Chagnon points out. Although we don't reward our war heroes with additional wives, we do award them medals, seats in the U.S. Senate, and even the presidency. As Chagnon points out and as presidential campaigns illustrate, the military record of candidates is important in U.S. politics.

Are we any different, then, from the Yanomamö—aside from being more indirect in the ways we reward "war behaviors"?

FOR YOUR CONSIDERATION

In what ways do we encourage (reward) and discourage human aggression? In what ways do we channel human aggression into socially acceptable forms? What prevents us from breaking down into little groups that are at war with one another?

Based on Allman (1988); Chagnon (1988).

Why Do Some Groups Choose War?

War—an organized form of aggression that involves armed conflict between politically distinct groups—is often part of national policy. Why do some groups use war to handle disputes when less drastic solutions are available?

THREE ESSENTIAL CONDITIONS OF WAR. Sociologist Nicholas Timasheff became interested in this question. After studying armed conflicts, he (1965) identified three essential conditions of war. The *first* is a cultural tradition for war. Because war has become part of a people's thinking, they view war as a way to resolve conflict with another nation. The *second* is an antagonistic situation in which states confront incompatible objectives. Each, for example, might want the same land or resources. A cultural tradition for war and an antagonistic situation are essential, but they are not enough.

They provide the fuel, but there also has to be a spark to ignite it. This *third* condition moves the nations from thinking about war to actually engaging in it.

SEVEN "SPARKS" THAT SET OFF WAR. To identify the sparks that ignite a war, Timasheff studied wars throughout history. He found that seven sparks ignite antagonistic situations, causing them to flame into war. They include the opportunity to

1. get revenge (settle "old scores" from previous conflicts)
2. dictate one's will to a weaker nation
3. protect or enhance prestige (to preserve the nation's "honor")
4. unite rival groups within one's country
5. protect or exalt the nation's leaders
6. satisfy the national aspirations of ethnic groups (to bring "our people" who are living in another country into our borders)
7. convert others to different religious and ideological beliefs

IN SUM To understand war, sociologists do not look for factors *within* humans, such as an instinct for war. Instead, they look for *social* causes—conditions in society that encourage or discourage aggression and that shape aggression into organized combat between nations.

The Scope of the Problem

When you turn on the evening news, you almost always hear a report of a war being fought somewhere. The United States always seems to be sending troops somewhere, to assist in our own battles and those of other countries. Have countries always fought this much?

War in the History of the West

To find out how common war has been throughout history, sociologist Pitirim Sorokin (1937) examined the wars in Europe from 500 BCE to 1925 CE. He identified 967 wars, an average of one war every 2 to 3 years. Counting years in which a country was at war, Germany spent the least amount of time in war (28%) and Spain the most (67%). Sorokin found that Russia had experienced only one peaceful quarter century during the previous 1,000 years. Since William the Conqueror took power in 1066, England had been at war for 56 of each 100 years.

And the United States? It turns out that we are one of the most aggressive nations in the world. From 1850 to 1980, we sent troops to other parts of the world more than 150 times (Kohn, 1988). That's more than once a year. We continue this today, and at our current rate, it won't be long before the total reaches 200. Although we have been "at war" with no nation, in recent years we have "intervened" in numerous military efforts: El Salvador, Honduras, Libya, Grenada, Panama, Afghanistan, Iraq, Somalia, Haiti, Bosnia, Sudan, Kosovo—and then back again to Afghanistan and Iraq, where we still have troops. The media now report the need for "military interventions" in Korea and Iran. Only the targets of our "military interventions" differ throughout time, not our readiness to attack.

Measuring War in Terms of Deaths

War may be hell, as William T. Sherman said, but some wars are more grueling than others. Consider the following. Since 1829, there have been approximately:

- 80 wars in which 3,000–30,000 people died
- 42 wars in which 30,000–300,000 people died
- 12 wars in which 300,000–3,000,000 people died
- 2 wars (World Wars I and II) in which 3,000,000–31,000,000 people died (Richardson, 1960; updated to 2007)

OUR GROWING CAPACITY TO KILL. To understand war we need to recognize how industrialization has increased our capacity to kill. Consider bombs. During World War I, fewer than 3 of every 100,000 people in England and Germany died from bombs. During the next 20 years, scientists "advanced" this new technique of human destruction as well as the aircraft able to deliver them, and during World War II bombs killed about 300 of every 100,000 English and Germans (Hart, 1957). Scientists have continued to "advance" our technology in war, and if nations were to unleash nuclear weapons against one another today, the deaths of past wars would seem minute. Some of our more "advanced" weapons have the capacity to destroy every living thing on earth.

THE SLAUGHTER CONTINUES. Many have hoped that war would become the relic of a primitive past. With the world's higher levels of education, many have thought that we humans would finally achieve a more advanced method of resolving political conflict.

Two generations ago, the United States fought in Vietnam for 7 years—with a loss of 58,000 American lives and several hundred thousand Vietnamese. The death toll of the Soviet Union's 9-year war in Afghanistan ran about 1 million Afghans and perhaps 20,000 Soviet soldiers (Armitage, 1989). Iran and Iraq fought an 8-year war at a cost of 400,000 lives. We don't yet know the total number of troops lost from our "interventions" in Afghanistan and Iraq, but they will be higher than they are now. At the time of this writing, about 4,000 U.S. and other coalition soldiers have died, while estimates of Iraqi deaths are running over a half million (Tavernise & McNeil, 2006).

IN SUM   War, then, as Sorokin sadly concluded in the 1930s, is a common element in history. Sorokin added that his era was one of the bloodiest, most turbulent periods in the history of Western civilization—and perhaps in the history of humanity. Our era certainly has been violent as well. In recent years, we have seen Serbs kill Bosnians, and Bosnians kill Serbs—each claiming rightful revenge for the atrocities of the past. After generations and even hundreds of years, these groups claim the right to continue passing this bitter heritage on to their children. Israelis and Palestinians do the same. As they kill one another, each group is convinced that its views are just and that God is on its side. Among other nations, India and Pakistan also claim the right to perpetuate ancient warfare, threatening nuclear destruction. The soldiers of the United States, NATO, Russia, and the European Union stand armed and ready to battle. Recent train bombings in Madrid and bus bombings in London only fueled the fight against terror. Individual suicide bombers have caused the launching of armies around the globe.

Looking at the Problem Theoretically

Let's use sociological theory to better understand the social problem of war. Using symbolic interactionism, we will examine the basis of the nuclear arms race. Applying functionalism, we will consider why a nation at war can be functional for society. Through conflict theory, we will explore how conflicting interests and the desire for more territory lead to war.

Symbolic Interactionism

Symbolic interactionists emphasize how significant *perceptions* are in human behavior. They stress that we choose courses of action based on how we perceive events. When we apply this principle to war, we see that, at times, the fate of the world can actually hinge on the perceptions of the powerful. Let's see how this occurred during the Cold War.

PERCEPTIONS AND THE ARMS RACE. During the Cold War, the United States and the Soviet Union were spending enormous amounts of money developing weaponry. To underestimate the enemy could prove fatal, so each magnified the evil intentions and destructive capacity of the other. Without valid data, each had to guess what the other intended, and they then used their imaginations to choose what seemed to be the most practical response.

This guessing game led to an arms race. When one superpower thought that the other might build a certain weapon, it began to build that weapon itself. Sometimes, however, the other nation had no intention of building the weapon, and the so-called countermeasure turned out to be an aggressive step that stimulated the other nation to build the weapon. Robert McNamara, who was the U.S. Secretary of Defense, explained how such mistakes in perception led to a buildup of nuclear warheads (Kurth, 1974):

> In 1961 when I became Secretary of Defense, the Soviet Union possessed a very small operational arsenal of intercontinental missiles. However, they did possess the technological and industrial capacity to enlarge that arsenal very substantially over the succeeding several years. We had no evidence that the Soviets did plan, in fact, fully to use that capability. But, as I have pointed out, a strategic planner must be conservative in his calculations; that is, he must prepare for the worst plausible case and not be content to hope and prepare merely for the most probable.
>
> Since we could not be certain of Soviet intentions, since we could not be sure that they would not undertake a massive buildup, we had to insure against such an eventuality by undertaking ourselves a major buildup of the Minuteman and Polaris forces. . . . But the blunt fact remains that if we had more accurate information about planned Soviet strategic forces, we simply would not have needed to build as large a nuclear arsenal as we have today.

This buildup of **intercontinental ballistic missiles (ICBMs)** illustrates a primary principle of symbolic interactionism—that meanings applied to symbols are central to human behavior. Because U.S. officials perceived Soviet plans a certain way, they assumed they were preparing for war. When we built weapons to retaliate, this signaled to the Soviets that they needed to build ICBMs. The entire nuclear arms race was based on symbolic interpretations of what each nation thought the other would do.

This example illustrates how *symbols are so powerful that they can take on a life of their own.* Once put into play, symbols wield power over human affairs. Although McNamara's initial perception of Soviet intentions might have been wrong, our buildup of missiles became proof to the Soviets that they needed to build more missiles. This, in turn, became proof to us that our interpretation was right in the first place—and that we needed to build even more powerful weapons. *Perceptions, not facts, often guide human behavior.*

PERCEPTIONS AND THE "FIRST STRIKE." This principle occurs in other areas of human life. We might like to think that we always act on facts alone, but we really act on our perceptions of "facts," on how we "think" things "are." This underlying uncertainty of perceptions takes on special significance when two rival nations are considering war. As long as these nations perceive war as a no-win situation, they are likely to avoid it. If there is long-standing hatred and fear between them, however, and one nation thinks that striking first may destroy the other's capacity to strike back, that nation may strike first.

During the Cold War, generals of the U.S. Air Force advocated a "first-strike" policy if it meant that we could win the war (Kurth, 1974). Apparently, Soviet generals did the same. You can see how tense and dangerous the situation was at that time. Each nation felt that it had to signal to the other that it would be victorious, that a strike against it would be foolish. As a result, both the Soviet Union and the United States would let information slip about new weapons and defense systems. It is scary to think that our lives—and those of the world—depended upon the correct interpretation of one another's signals!

Functionalism

THE FUNCTIONS OF WAR. In 1939, the world was in turmoil. Hitler's tanks and *Luftwaffe* (air force) were tracking through Europe. Japan had invaded China and was threatening the South Pacific. During this time, Robert Park (1941) decided to analyze the social functions of war. Here are the functions that he and others have identified.

Extension of Territory ■ Park surveyed the literature on war and found that the world's countries had been born in war. The nations that existed in 1939—like those of today—had come into being as one group extended its political boundaries by conquering other groups. What is today's United States, for example, would not exist if it hadn't been for the Indian wars and the wars with France, Great Britain, Spain, and Mexico. A major function of war, said Park, is the *extension of territory,* an enlargement of a group's political power.

Social Integration ■ Another function of war is *social integration.* If groups within a country are in conflict, war labels another nation as "a mutual enemy." The groups put aside their differences, close ranks, and cooperate to repel their common threat (Coser, 1956; Timasheff, 1965; Hoffman, 2006). After the war, divisions may return among the temporary allies. Afghanistan, for example, was fragmented into groups separated by rigid lines and bitter divisions: religious, class, tribal, and clan loyalties that reached back for centuries. When the Soviets invaded Afghanistan in 1979, these groups put aside their differences to work together to repel their common enemy. As soon as they defeated the Soviets, which took 10 years, they renewed their divisions and turned on one another. Today, the United States' presence is the threat that certain groups in Afghanistan and Iraq are joining together to repel.

Social Change ■ Sociologist Georg Simmel (1904) identified *social change* as a third function of war. One form of social change stimulated by warfare is the development of science and technology. Five centuries ago, for example, Leonardo da Vinci designed war machines for his patron. Since then, war has prompted aerodynamic designs, the harnessing of nuclear energy, and satellites. We even owe our interstate highways and the Internet to war. General Eisenhower was impressed by the *autobahns* he saw in Germany when he arrived after its defeat in World War II. When he became president of the United States, he decided that we needed highways like these so we could move soldiers, weapons, and supplies rapidly across the country in case the Soviets attacked. Military personnel developed the Internet as an alternative form of communication.

War also stimulates developments in surgical techniques: Officers want soldiers patched up as quickly as possible so they can return to battle faster. Currently under development is **long-distance surgery:** The surgeon in the United States (with the aid of computers) can operate on a wounded soldier in some remote region of the world.

Economic Gain ■ A fourth function of war is *economic gain:* access to treasure, trade routes, markets, raw materials such as oil, and outlets for investment (Pruitt & Snyder, 1969). Industrialization has increased production, profits, and employment. For example, World War II put millions of unemployed people to work and helped lift the United States out of the Great Depression. Even the threat of war can bring economic gain. As sociologist C. Wright Mills (1958) noted back in the 1950s, "war readiness" requires increased spending that benefits big corporations.

Other Functions ■ Another function of war is *ideological*—advancing one nation's political or religious system over an opposing one. Between the 11th and 14th centuries European Crusaders traveled to the Holy Land to fight Islam. Today, al-Qaeda and its supporters have a similar agenda. *Vengeance* or *punishment* is another function of war, occurring when a country teaches another nation "a lesson" or avenges an attack (Pruitt & Snyder, 1969). Much of the warfare in Bosnia and Kosovo, including rapes and other atrocities, has been conducted on the basis of vengeance. *Military security* also serves as a function of war. That is, a nation does not desire an asset in and of itself, but attacks to prevent an enemy from using that asset against it. This is why Israel bombed Iraq's nuclear plants in 1981 and why Iran and North Korea may be targets. Lastly, another function of war serves to *increase the credibility* of a nation's threats or guarantees. By going to war, other nations will see that a nation means what it says.

Multiple Functions ■ No war serves a single function. A single war can involve territory, revenge, ideology, and military security. When a conflict gets drawn out, the functions

After Roman military campaigns, soldiers would bring captive slaves to Caesar.

themselves can even change. The Crusades began in 1095 when Pope Urban II urged Christians to go to war and reclaim the Holy Land. Ideological purposes may have dominated at first, but the Crusades also functioned to provide treasure and territory. Nine Crusades and 200 years later, all the functions of war had been incorporated in this single prolonged war. If the "war against terrorism" goes on for decades, as seems likely, it, too, will have served all functions of war.

Functions for the Victors ■ War is usually highly functional for the victors. Rome, for example, conquered most of the known world, subjugating one region after another to Roman power, exploiting their resources. To the acclaim of citizens and Caesar alike, generals would return in triumph to Rome, marching in formation down the main avenue and into the main square, laden with treasure and slaves. Such treasure enriched the government and its elite, as the captives acted as slaves. Some of the slaves brought to Rome after the fall of Greece were educated Greeks, who served as tutors for the elite's children. In the latter part of the empire, slaves provided entertaining drama, their deaths in the Colosseum yielding pleasure for Rome's jaded and bloodthirsty citizens.

Functions for the Losers ■ Although war is highly dysfunctional for losers, especially in terms of deaths, property destroyed, territories lost, and humiliation, losers can also benefit from war. One of the most remarkable examples occurred in Japan. After their defeat in World War II, the Japanese embraced Western technology. This change not only increased their standard of living and life expectancy, but also placed them in a world leadership position that they had failed to win through war. No social change is without its dysfunctions, however, and Japan's, too, has come at a price: the disruption of its traditional ways of life.

Functions for Individuals ■ War also has functions for soldiers and leaders. Soldiers often report that battle presents them with the challenge to "see what I'm made of." Some even report that when they enter a battle they feel an excitement that verges on sexual arousal. More significant, however, are the satisfactions that war brings its leaders. Officers who organize battles derive intense satisfaction from outmaneuvering the enemy, gaining advantage through surprise attacks, and being acclaimed as the victor. War also serves as an avenue of social mobility. Generals George Washington, Andrew Jackson, Ulysses S. Grant, and Dwight D. Eisenhower, for example, moved from being generals in the army to presidents of the United States. Colin Powell went from general to national security advisor. From there, he became secretary of state, one of the most powerful positions in the world.

DYSFUNCTIONS OF WAR. Standing in stark contrast are the dysfunctions of war. Defeat is war's most well-known dysfunction, as are the destruction of cities and the deaths of troops and citizens. There also remain fatherless or motherless children, a decline in education, and bitterness that can span generations. Even military victory can bring dysfunctions. The victor can grow dependent on the exploitation of subjugated peoples; when that control ends, as inevitably it does, economic pain is severe. Spain experienced this when it lost its colonies in the 1820s. For decades, Great Britain suffered withdrawal pains after it lost many of its colonies as a result of the fervor for independence ushered in by World War II. With the breakup of the Soviet empire, forged by war, Russia is undergoing this same dysfunction today.

Conflict Theory

THREE REASONS THAT NATIONS GO TO WAR. Conflict theorists have developed three major explanations for why nations go to war.

Resources ■ It has been a common practice in history to go to war to get another group's resources—its pastures, flocks, or wealth. Back in the 1300s, Ibn Khaldun of Tunis stressed that as human groups struggle to survive, they compete over scarce resources. Inevitably, they come into conflict with one another. War is simply one form of human conflict.

Conflict theorists claim that the central force in human history is the struggle for control over society's resources. In each society, some group maintains control. This group, which conflict theorists call the **bourgeoisie,** uses resources to keep itself in power and to exploit the less powerful. As the bourgeoisie expands its power beyond its borders, it comes into conflict with the bourgeoisie of another country. Their quarrel over resources often leads to war. The elite don't fight themselves, of course. They hold power, so to do battle for them they send young men and women from the groups they control (the poor, workers, the **proletariat**). The German generals used the term "cannon fodder" to describe the young men among the poor who died in such outrageous numbers in their wars.

Expansion of Markets ■ The second explanation focuses on the expansion of markets. In 1902, John Hobson, an economist, noted that as capitalism grows, surplus capital develops. Business leaders want to invest this capital, so they look for ways to expand their markets. They then persuade the government to go to war and take over other lands. The result is **imperialism,** the pursuit of profits and markets by war and threat of war.

A Military Machine ■ Another economist, Joseph Schumpeter, proposed a third explanation in 1919. He said (1919/1955) that the military and political elite build a strong military machine because it brings them power and prestige. Because the military machine was built for war, its very existence encourages war. Its use brings prestige to the elite.

The Military Machine Today

Conflict theorists stress how today's military machine has increased the threat of war. They note that after World War I the United States dismantled its military, and U.S. war industries returned to their peacetime pursuits (Barber, 1972). Then came World War II, which was a turning point in U.S. history. When this war was over, the United States did not dismantle its war machine, as it had previously done (Eisenhower, 1961/1972). Today, the United States maintains *a couple of million* soldiers and pumps vast amounts of money into upgrading weapons and equipment. After World War II, the Soviet Union, Great Britain, France, and others also kept their military machines. With its archenemy turning away from communism and transforming itself into a capitalist ally, the West did not suggest that it and Russia disarm and join together in a new world of peace. Instead, the West continued to arm millions of its people and to develop new weapons, even those that are designed to turn space into a new venue of warfare. As Russians reestablish their economy through oil sales and regain some of their lost political might, they are eager to rebuild their military machine and reclaim a more prestigious position in the world.

THE MILITARY MACHINE, THE POWER ELITE, AND THE GLOBALIZATION OF CAPITALISM. To understand why the military has become a permanent institution, conflict theorists stress that we need to analyze the structure of power. Of great importance is the *power elite*—the top leaders of the military, business, and politics. As sociologist C. Wright Mills stressed, we should look closely at the power elite to see how the interests of these powerful groups benefit from a strong military. Generals support a more powerful military, of course: This is their reason for being, and greater power bolsters their position. Generals typically support expanding the military.

In the world of global capitalism, to protect worldwide investments, today's business leaders also support a powerful military. At any moment, they might need armed intervention at home—or on the other side of the globe. Politicians are sensitive to what the business elite wants because, as conflict theorists stress, they owe their positions to support

among the business elite. If businesses were to withdraw their support, politicians would have little chance of being reelected. Consequently, politicians find it in their best interest to support a strong military: In the name of national security, politicians levy taxes to finance the military machine so desired by generals and business leaders. The term **national security** or **homeland security** refers to the protection of the nation, in terms of threats from outside. One of the major goals of homeland security is to ensure the safety of the nation.

Today, stress conflict theorists, the U.S. military machine is used to advance capitalism around the globe. U.S. armed forces join with Great Britain, France, Canada, and Australia to be sure that the world is being made safe for capitalism. The result, says Mills (1958, p. 2), is that "war is no longer an interruption of peace; in our time, peace itself has become an uneasy interlude between wars. . . . "

Research Findings

With war so prevalent—and today's weapons so powerful that they jeopardize even the existence of humanity—it is important to identify those factors that reduce the likelihood of war. After identifying root causes, we will examine the costs of war, both economic and human. Finally, we'll consider the significance of the military–industrial complex, the possibility of accidental nuclear war, biological and chemical warfare, and terrorism. To get an idea of how sociologists further examine war, see the Spotlight on Social Research box on the next page.

What Reduces War?

MAJOR FINDINGS ABOUT WAR AND PEACE. To understand those factors that reduce war, Quincy Wright (1942), a professor of international law, studied war throughout history. His findings, combined with those of physicist-mathematician Lewis Richardson (1960), are not encouraging. They are summarized in the following (Nettler, 1976):

1. Type of religion does *not* reduce warfare. A nation in which Christianity is dominant does not go to war less than a nation in which Islam is dominant.
2. Type of government does *not* reduce warfare. Democracies and republics are neither more nor less peaceful than dictatorships and monarchies.
3. Prosperity does *not* reduce warfare. Prosperous nations are neither more nor less peaceful than poor nations. Nor do periods of prosperity reduce fighting.
4. A shared religion does *not* reduce warfare between nations.
5. A common language does *not* reduce warfare.
6. Education does *not* reduce warfare. Education does not create an "enlightened" preference for peace; countries with high education are as likely to go to war as those with low education.
7. Being "neighbors" does *not* reduce warfare. The opposite is true: Shared boundaries stimulate fights over territory, and the more boundaries that countries share, the more wars they fight with one another.

It seems only rational that democracy, prosperity, increased education, and a shared religion would reduce war. Despite efforts to reduce war, the world's nations are *not* becoming more peaceful. Today's wars have become more lethal, killing more people than ever before in history. As sociologist Gwynn Nettler (1976) ruefully observed, the Nobel Peace Prize is typically awarded to a citizen living in a war-torn nation.

The Costs of War

War takes a huge toll on humanity. Certainly, its costs must be measured not only in dollars, but in the loss of life as well.

Spotlight on Social Research
ADVENTURES IN MILITARY SOCIOLOGY

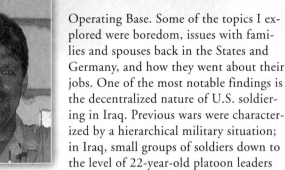

MORTEN ENDER, *professor at the United States Military Academy at West Point, does research on war, peace, and the military. In this essay, he discusses how he became interested in doing research on the military and his research experiences in Iraq.*

Although an American, I spent many years living in West Germany during the Cold War. I often reflected on the impact that World War II had on the German people as well as on the Americans living there. Both world wars had a profound impact on my own family. After WWI, my maternal great-grandparents were forced to move to the hinterland of Germany and a more meager lifestyle. U.S. bombers destroyed my paternal great-grandfather's printing plant during WWII, and a generation later, my mother married an American soldier stationed in Germany. I came to the United States for the first time on a U.S. troop ship. My family's many moves during my formative years and the stories I heard of war sparked my interest in social change, especially radical and intense change, at the individual level.

When I began studying the military I tried to develop knowledge in areas that had received little sociological attention, such as death and dying in a military context and military children. We learned that when a member of the military dies, the response is highly bureaucratic and task-focused, yet the notification and casualty officers keep the best interests of the survivors in mind. We also discovered that military children, who often live outside the country of their passport because of their parents' careers, have much in common with children of foreign service workers, missionaries, and those in international business.

I also had the opportunity to travel to Iraq and apply my sociological research skills to studying the Iraqi people. In a dangerous and compelling research environment, my research team helped assess the attitudes and opinions of Iraqis about their major social institutions—economics, politics, criminal justice, the family, education, the military, and medical care. We also studied Iraqi adolescents—their self-esteem and how they perceived their personal safety.

Because I was "embedded" with U.S. soldiers in Iraq, I was able to interview them, as well as observe their day-to-day activities on and off the Forward Operating Base. Some of the topics I explored were boredom, issues with families and spouses back in the States and Germany, and how they went about their jobs. One of the most notable findings is the decentralized nature of U.S. soldiering in Iraq. Previous wars were characterized by a hierarchical military situation; in Iraq, small groups of soldiers down to the level of 22-year-old platoon leaders make profound leadership decisions. For example, one might be responsible for training an entire police force for a neighborhood, or another might interact with the local leadership in a community, working with local mayors. This decentralized soldiering offers the opportunity to be creative and exercise autonomy. I asked soldiers an open-ended question on a survey about whether they use any creativity. A typical response was

Everyday! This place was not what we expected and therefore we have had to adapt on many occasions. One example is up armoring of vehicles. Soldiers are very adaptive and creative and come up with very good ideas that other units are now using. Scheduling is another example. We are short many soldiers and have had to develop shift work that fits the number of people we have.

I also studied the soldiers' morale, cohesion, preparation, leadership, and attitudes toward the mission. In many of these areas I found evidence contrary to common expectations. For example, morale is high among soldiers in Iraq—in some cases higher than when they are at home. Further, many soldiers told me they enjoyed the mission in Iraq. They liked being a part of something larger than themselves. I found the soldiers to be very focused and committed to their jobs—the small-scale, daily missions. One day, at one of the larger post-exchanges (PX)—which is affectionately called Wal-Mart because it has everything—I struck up a conversation with a 23-year-old Army reserve specialist from Woodstock, New York. He owned a small business back home, and his brother and wife were managing it for him. He was headed home for his once-a-year two-week R&R (rest and relaxation), but with great misgivings. His job in Iraq involved responsibility for training two 44- and 47-year-old Iraqi police officers. He appeared genuinely worried that although his "guys" had received the proper socialization into the policing role, without his structure and discipline, although for only a short while, they would fall back into bad habits, possibly putting themselves and others at risk. I asked why he didn't stay, and he said his sergeant was making him take some time off.

TABLE 14-1 What Has the United States Spent on Its Wars?

War	Cost
War of 1812	$600,000,000
Mexican War	$1,100,000,000
American Revolution	$2,000,000,000
Spanish–American War	$6,000,000,000
Civil War	$46,000,000,000
Gulf War	$145,000,000,000
Korean War	$260,000,00 0,000
World War I	$370,000,000,000
Vietnam War	$553,000,000,000
Iraq War	$648,000,000,000
World War II	$3,000,000,000,000
Total	$4,590,000,000,000

Note: The costs listed in *Statistical Abstract* are in 1967 dollars. To account for inflation, these amounts were increased by 350% and the costs of service-connected benefits were added. Where a range was listed, the mean was used. The costs do *not* include interest payments on war loans, nor are they reduced by the financial benefits to the United States, such as the acquisition of territory such as California and Texas in the Mexican War.

Keep in mind that these are rough estimates, not actual costs. The costs of the many "military interventions" such as in Grenada, Panama, Somalia, and Haiti are not listed in the source.

Sources: By James M. Henslin. Based on *Statistical Abstract of the United States* (1993, Table 553); this table was dropped after 1993. The cost for the Gulf War is from Conahan (1991), adjusted for inflation; for the Iraq War, the number is not final, but in 2008, various news sources, such as the *Washington Post* and NBC News, were estimating costs would be $1 trillion to $3 trillion in current dollars.

MATERIAL COSTS: MONEY. It would be an understatement to say that war is expensive. Table 14-1 summarizes what the United States has spent on major wars. This amount does not include other interventions in places such as Bosnia, Kosovo, and Afghanistan. If you look at Figure 14-1, you will see how much the United States has spent on its military operations and national defense since 1990. Today's higher spending reflects the wars in Afghanistan and Iraq.

A more realistic picture of total expenditures on war would include the costs of running the Central Intelligence Agency, the National Aeronautics and Space Administration, the Agency for International Development, and the Department of Homeland Security. Some argue it should also include what we spend on the Overseas Private Investment Corporation, the International Monetary Fund, and the World Bank (Greenberger, 1994).

On average, since 1960 the United States has spent $334 billion a year on what is euphemistically called national defense. To fully comprehend how much we are spending, consider this:

> Each dollar bill is about 6 inches long. If you laid a million of them end to end, you would just about cover the distance from Los Angeles to San Diego. A billion dollar bills would take you around the equator 4 times. If you laid the dollar bills of today's defense budget end to end, they would circle the earth more than 1,800 times! (Cf. Shaffer, 1986)

Lost Alternative Purchases ▪ Picturing a billion dollars may be difficult. We might also want to compare what we spend on war to other items that could be purchased with the same billions:

1. For the price of one aircraft carrier, we could build 12,000 high schools.
2. For the price of one naval weapons plant, we could build twenty-six 160-bed hospitals.
3. For the price of one jet bomber, we could provide school lunches for 1 million children a year.
4. For the price of one new prototype bomber, we could pay the annual salaries of 250,000 teachers (de Silva, 1980).

Money stretches further in the Least Industrialized Nations. There, the price of one tank would buy 1,000 classrooms. Many people dream of a more peaceful world in

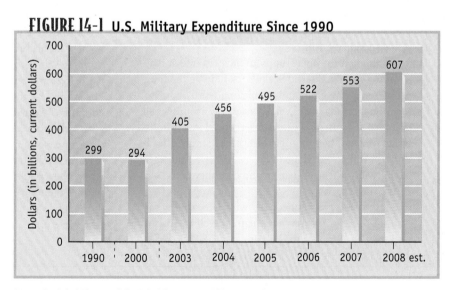

FIGURE 14-1 U.S. Military Expenditure Since 1990

Source: Statistical Abstract of the United States 2009: Tables 453 and 455.

which military dollars get redirected toward education, medicine, and the enlightenment of nations. We do not live in such a world—and from all indications, we may never live in one.

Our armed forces employ 1.4 million military personnel and 650,000 civilians. Add the 1.1 million men and women in the reserves and National Guard, and the total comes to almost 3 million people (*Statistical Abstract,* 2009, Tables 496, 499, and 500). For the cost of employing these 3 million men and women to fight in or be ready for war, we could pay 3 million people to work for the public good. We are already sending tens of thousands of soldiers abroad each year; for the same amount we could send tens of thousands of people to poorer countries to build schools, hospitals, and reduce suffering. You probably can think of other uses for the large amounts of money spent on the military institution.

But What Choice Is There? ■ Like other nations, the United States finds itself facing a dilemma. Although the military is costly in terms of money spent and benefits forgone, not spending this money would leave us vulnerable to attack. In light of the world's history, an assumption of danger appears well founded. Only if all nations were to become pacifists and all dangers of attack cease, would military preparedness become unnecessary.

MONEY SPENT BY OTHER NATIONS. The nations of the world spend about $1,100 billion a year arming themselves (Stalenheim et al., 2006). This is about $165 a year for every man, woman, and child on the entire planet. The dollars spent by the world's nations on war would stretch around the earth more than 4,000 times. Or if you laid them end to end, you could make over 200 round trips to the moon!

Any way you look at it, the cost of military preparedness is extremely high.

Table 14-2 shows which countries spend the most and least on their military. On a per capita basis, three of these countries outspend the United States; on the basis of gross national product, six do. Sweden, hardly a wartime nation, is one of the world's top spenders. As you can see, the nations that spend the least are also the least industrialized. Keep in mind that these are poor nations. Most of their citizens live in poverty, and they use every dollar for everyday survival. It is also true that some of these countries are so split by factions that only the power of their military holds them together.

HUMAN COSTS: DEATHS. War's greatest cost, of course, is the number of lives lost. During the 1700s, wars were fought according to aristocratic ideals. Small professional armies waged short, limited campaigns. In battle, the soldiers marched in formation, accompanied by flying flags and teenaged boys playing drums, flutes, and other musical instruments. War was similar to a chess game back then, with generals from an aristocratic background matching wits with opponents who also came from the upper class. Opposing generals often came from the same military school. Military officers, who considered war a test of bravery, looked forward to fighting on the "field of honor."

TABLE 14-2 What Do Countries Spend on Their Military?

COUNTRIES THAT SPEND THE MOST

RANK	COUNTRY	$ PER CAPITA	PERCENTAGE OF GROSS NATIONAL PRODUCT
1	Israel	$1,510	8.8%
2	Kuwait	1,410	7.7
3	Singapore	1,100	4.8
4	United States	1,030	3.0
5	Saudi Arabia	996	14.9
6	Taiwan	690	5.2
7	France	658	2.7
8	Great Britain	615	2.5
9	Sweden	601	2.3
10	Greece	573	4.7

COUNTRIES THAT SPEND THE LEAST

RANK	COUNTRY	$ PER CAPITA	PERCENTAGE OF GROSS NATIONAL PRODUCT
1	Tanzania	$4	1.4%
2	Bangladesh	5	1.3
3	Indonesia	7	1.1
4	Kenya	7	1.9
5	India	11	2.5
6	Nigeria	13	1.6
7	Philippines	14	1.4
8	Pakistan	25	5.9
9	Mexico	27	0.6
10	Egypt	36	2.7

Source: By James M. Henslin. Based on *Statistical Abstract of the United States,* 2003: Table 1383. This table was dropped in later editions of the source.

See For Yourself

View the Iraq Body Count at http://www.iraqbodycount.org/

▶ How many civilians have been killed since the start of the U.S. invasion in 2003?

Townspeople often viewed military encounters as a form of entertainment—riding in carriages to the site, eating picnic lunches while watching the "entertainment."

Napoleon instituted **total war,** or "no-holds-barred" warfare. Battles became wars and onlookers ran for shelter (Finsterbusch & Greisman, 1975). The American Civil War may be described as a "total war." During 4 brutal years, 620,000 Americans died, more than in all our other wars combined, from the Revolution to the present. With today's mass armies, the capacity to deliver wholesale death, industries creating advanced weapons, and civilians equal targets, the old image of war as pageantry no longer applies.

Most fearful of all, today's weapons are so destructive that they threaten human existence itself. Killing in the past was comparably inefficient. Even though more than 100 million people have died in all wars since 1700 (Gartner, 1988), if there were another world war, deaths could number in the hundreds of millions.

HUMAN COSTS: DEHUMANIZATION. Although we often calculate the cost of war in terms of money and deaths, war involves more than these measures. Among war's other costs is a loss in overall "quality of life." At the very minimum, war increases insecurity, fear, and worry. It may become difficult to plan for the future. Soldiers may postpone getting married and starting a family because they don't know what lies ahead.

Morality is often affected by war as well. Conflict tends to break down norms that regulate human behavior. Soldiers exposed to brutality and killing learn to **dehumanize** their opponents. That is, they come to see them as objects, not people. Dehumanization removes the obligation to treat others as human beings.

Over the centuries, the form and weapons of war have changed. Here is a Stealth bomber on display at El Toro Air Force base, Irvine CA.

Characteristics of Dehumanization ■ Social scientists have identified four key characteristics of dehumanization (Bernard, Ottenberg, & Redl, 1971):

1. *Increased emotional distance from others.* The individual stops identifying with others, seeing them as lacking basic human qualities. They become not people, but an object called "the enemy."
2. *An emphasis on following procedures.* Regulations become all-important. Those who do the "dirty work" do not question their orders, even if they involve atrocities. A person will say, "I don't like it, but it's necessary" or "We all have to die some day."
3. *Inability to resist pressures.* Fears of losing one's job or the respect of one's group or of having one's integrity and loyalty questioned become more important than morality.
4. *Diminished personal responsibility.* People see themselves as a small cog in a large machine. They are not responsible, because they have no choice. They are simply obeying orders. The superiors know best, for they have the information to judge what is right and wrong. The individual reasons "Who am I to question this?"

When dehumanization occurs, consciences become so numbed that people can dissociate killing—even torture—from their "normal self." Torture and killing become "dirty work" that has to be done. Those who complete this "dirty work" are duty-bound to obey orders, not to question them. The "higher-ups" who make the decisions are responsible, not the simple soldier who remains powerless.

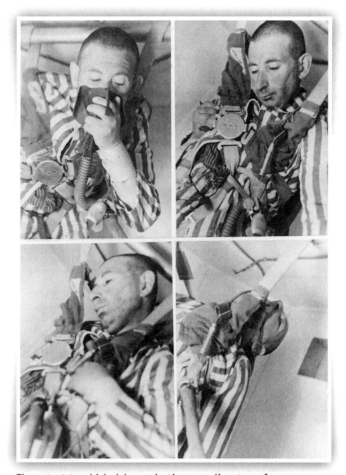

The extent to which dehumanization can alienate us from ordinary human feelings is incredible. To measure the effects of compression and decompression, German doctors placed this inmate of a concentration camp in a pressure chamber. As the doctors manipulated the air pressure, they observed and photographed the man's death.

Dehumanization in Prolonged Conflicts ■ Sociologist Tamotsu Shibutani (1970) pointed out that dehumanization is especially prevalent in prolonged conflicts. Long wars come to be viewed as a struggle between good and evil. People who don't want to torture or kill, for example, conclude that because the survival of good (democracy, freedom, the nation, and our way of life) hangs in the balance, they must suspend moral standards. War, then, exalts treachery, brutality, and killing. Soldiers are granted medals of honor that glorify murder we would otherwise condemn.

Dehumanization by the Nazis and Japanese ■ Sometimes soldiers must learn to distance themselves from their own moral values. During World War II, ordinary Germans—not Nazi soldiers—staffed concentration camps. They viewed the Jewish inmates as a blight on society. For example, German surgeons educated at top universities, whose profession called for them to be highly sensitive to people's needs, viewed the inmates as less than themselves. Methodically and dispassionately, they would mutilate Jewish inmates in experiments just to test for results. Some doctors immersed Jews in vats of ice water, considering their deaths insignificant because the results of the experiments would later save the lives of German pilots shot down over the North Atlantic (Gellhorn, 1959). The photos on this page are part of a documentary that these intelligent medical personnel produced.

One might think that the horrors of the Nazis were so severe that no one could match them. Yet the Japanese did. During World War II, they beheaded U.S. prisoners of war and buried others alive (Chang, 1997). They also tortured prisoners and performed

medical experiments on them (Daws, 1994). In one experiment, Japanese doctors pumped U.S. prisoners full of horse blood. In others, they injected them with typhus, typhoid, smallpox, and other diseases. In one test, they lined up 10 prisoners "behind a protective screen with their naked buttocks exposed to see what damage would result when a bomb was detonated" (Leighty, 1981). In China, the Japanese experimented with germ warfare, killing perhaps hundreds of thousands of Chinese using anthrax, typhoid, and plague (S. H. Harris, 1994).

DEHUMANIZATION BY THE U.S. MILITARY. The Germans and Japanese carried dehumanization to horrifying limits, but they were not unique. U.S. soldiers in Vietnam also dehumanized their victims. To U.S. soldiers the Vietnamese became less than human. They were transformed into "gooks," "dinks," and "slants." Some soldiers, effective at dehumanization, shot mothers fleeing with their babies. For others, dehumanization was more difficult, but it was better not to question the morality of the act, better to think of the act as part of the larger scheme of things, such as saving a people from communism—or as rightful retaliation for fellow soldiers who had been killed: "I don't like doing this, but this is war."

Something similar is happening today. When U.S. (and coalition) forces bomb military targets, civilians are often killed unintentionally. The military does not refer to them as "murdered children, mothers, and fathers" or even as "dead people" or "dead civilians." Instead, the military uses the term **collateral damage,** which refers to the unintentional murder of civilians during combat operations.

WHEN DEHUMANIZATION FAILS. Techniques of neutralization occur to protect the self. If a soldier were unable to disassociate his military behavior from his personal identity, he would live a guilt-ridden existence. Tim, for example, was a Marine interrogator during Vietnam. Beating prisoners to gain vital information was part of his job. When beating did not work, he used electric shock by attaching "two wires of a field telephone to the earlobe, the cheek, the temple, or sometimes the balls or the crotch" (P. Smith, 1980, p. 27). Tim did not enjoy his work, and one day while he was interrogating a 16-year-old girl, he began to wonder:

> Why are we killing all these people? These aren't soldiers. I'm beating on this girl—and it all hit me. I'm beating up this girl, what for? Who am I? . . . It was as if for the first time I was looking at myself. Here's this guy, slapping, beating on this girl—for what?
>
> No longer dehumanizing his prisoner, Tim added, "For the first time I was looking at this person, a detainee, as a real human being, not as a source of information." This change in perspective directly affected Tim's job performance. As he said, "I wasn't a very good interrogator from that time on. I lost all motivation."

Soldiers are surrounded by other soldiers who are also taught that the enemy is less than human. Upon returning home, however, former soldiers find themselves associating with people who do not practice dehumanization—and the definitions that worked for them during the war tend to break down. As this occurs, many former soldiers become greatly disturbed by harm they have caused others during the war. Before a Vietnam veteran committed suicide, he wrote:

> I can't sleep anymore. When I was in Vietnam, we came across a North Vietnamese soldier with a man, a woman, and a 3- or 4-year-old girl. We had to shoot them all. I can't get the little girl's face out of my mind. I hope that God will forgive me. I hope the people in this country who made millions of dollars off the men, women, and children that died in that war can sleep at night (I can't, and I didn't make a cent). (Smith, 1980, p. 15)

The norms of dehumanization also failed some of the Japanese soldiers who had participated in the atrocities of World War II. Although they had kept quiet for 50 years, some of them publicly confessed their mass rapes and killings. These confessions, which made international news, were denied by fellow soldiers.

HUMAN COSTS: COMBAT FATIGUE AND PTSD: Combat stress reaction, or **shell shock,** is a term used to describe the emotional and physical reaction a soldier faces immediately after combat. It should not be confused with **post-traumatic stress disorder (PTSD).** PTSD describes the long-term emotional distress a soldier experiences after combat. Shell shock can last for months, PTSD for years (Satcher, 1999). Most soldiers who suffer from immediate combat stress reaction do not develop PTSD symptoms. If a soldier does suffer with PTSD, he or she is likely to experience the following: clinical depression, night terrors, memory loss, and anxiety. A soldier diagnosed with PTSD can receive beneficial treatment from military or civilian therapists. If the symptoms are severe and persistent, the soldier will ultimately be discharged from the military.

Let's turn from what has been a symbolic interactionist analysis of war to the conflict perspective and examine how organizations profit from modern warfare.

The Military–Industrial Complex

THE MILITARY AS AN ECONOMIC FORCE. As an industry, the military requires vast industrial support. Those that specialize in **armaments**—guidance systems, bombs, missiles, tanks, planes, guns, ships, submarines, and other weapons—have become a powerful force in the U.S. economy. Military weapons are like personal computers; they quickly become obsolete and need to be replaced with more sophisticated models. This is so costly that *one of every four tax dollars* collected by the federal government goes to the Department of Defense and the Department of Veterans Affairs (*Statistical Abstract,* 2006, Tables 464, 490).

The Military–Industrial Complex ■ Like other businesses, corporations that manufacture armaments aim to increase profits. Unlike other businesses, however, their main customer is the Department of Defense. This relationship benefits the military and corporate employees. The defense industry hires top-ranking military officers when they retire, people who know the complex military system inside and out.

Their mutual interests are so intertwined that military and defense industries have become a threat to Congress. The **military–industrial complex,** as it is known, pressures Congress to increase military spending. Members of Congress tolerate this pressure because the Defense Department benefits them in return by channeling contracts into their districts, increasing their chance of being reelected. Some use the term **Pentagon capitalism** to describe interlocking relationship between Pentagon armaments and U.S. businesses (Melman, 1970).

Table 14-3 on the next page shows the 10 states that receive the most income from military contracts. As you can see, they each receive several billion dollars. The several hundred thousand military employees in these states support the local economy. Consider the impact of military spending on the state of Virginia. This state of 8 million people has a payroll of over $16 billion in military contracts. The state's 209,857 military workers bring in several more billions a year. With such income streams, closing a military base becomes a hefty economic dilemma. Unions and businesses often send lobbyists to Washington to fight in support of maintaining military bases. In this case, a popular slogan—NIMBY (Not In My Back Yard) has changed to KIMBY (Keep It In My Back Yard).

THE GROWING CAPACITY TO INFLICT DEATH. With all the profit and employment opportunity they bring, it is easy to forget that military industries represent the loss of human life. During the arms race, the West and the Soviet Union put some of their top scientists to work in an effort to increase the destructive power of weapons. At that time, our capacity for inflicting death grew so sharply that in 1970 a critic noted that *if a bomb the size of the one dropped on Hiroshima had exploded every single day from the birth of Christ until that year, the total force of those bombs would be less than the destructive capacity of the United States in 1970* (Melman, 1970). Of course, our capacity to inflict death has increased since then.

The preceding description applies only to the United States. If we include the nuclear weapons of Russia, France, Great Britain, and other countries shown on the Social

TABLE 14-3 Where Defense Dollars Go: The Top 10 States

RANK	STATE	PAYROLL FOR MILITARY CONTRACTS	MILITARY EMPLOYEES	CIVILIAN EMPLOYEES
1	Virginia	$16,693,000,000	128,515	81,342
2	California	15,270,000,000	149,481	55,709
3	Texas	11,908,000,000	119,176	41,462
4	Florida	8,864,000,000	58,100	26,072
5	Georgia	7,409,000,000	68,928	32,862
6	North Carolina	7,132,000,000	102,845	17,447
7	Washington	5,652,000,000	49,887	24,501
8	Maryland	5,334,000,000	29,626	30,749
9	Hawaii	4,064,000,000	45,366	17,079
10	South Carolina	3,431,000,000	38,090	9,640

Note: Military employees refers to active-duty military personnel who are living in a particular state. *Civilian employees* refers to civilians employed by the military; the totals do not include workers in the defense industries who fulfill the military contracts listed in column 3.

Source: By James M. Henslin. Based on *Statistical Abstract of the United States* (2009, Tables 490 and 492).

Map on pages 522–523 (Figure 14-2), it becomes impossible to calculate the destructive capacity that these nations now possess. Consider this: The explosive energy of nuclear weapons is measured in megatons. If you had 1 million tons of TNT, you would have one **megaton.** The United States has over 3,000 megatons of explosive power. Think of a freight train filled with gunpowder stretching from the earth to the moon. Now *triple* that—make the gunpowder train 925,000 miles long—and you would have the equivalent of 3000 megatons (see *Nucleus,* 1981).

Such an image alarms many. But then consider this thought: Russia's nuclear capacity is just as great. France and Great Britain also have nuclear capacity, although theirs is less. Israel, India, Pakistan, China, and a few other nations have nuclear weapons as well, although theirs are much less. North Korea and Iran are feverishly working to achieve their own nuclear capacity.

A GLIMMER OF HOPE. In the midst of this nuclear futility lies a glimmer of hope. Russia and the United States have been negotiating agreements that would eliminate ICBMs with multiple warheads and reduce nuclear stockpiles. No longer do Russia and the United States target each other's major cities. (Since ICBMs have to be directed somewhere, one wonders just where those nuclear missiles are targeted.) Although Russia and the United States have destroyed some weapons, this small amount does not qualify as **disarmament.** Disarmament is the act of reducing arms/weapons. Russia and the United States have destroyed outdated weapons and *reduced excess capacity:* Each nation can still destroy the other many times over—and take with them the rest of the world.

A GROWING DANGER. Of special concern is the availability of nuclear weapons in the hands of a single individual or a small group. Part of that concern involves dictators or groups of terrorists wishing to retaliate against the United States. If a rogue dictator possesses nuclear weapons, what would stop that individual from launching those missiles? This, of course, is why the West is fearful of nuclear weapons being developed in North Korea. A cynic might add that if the leader of a Western nation decided to launch nuclear-tipped missiles, could she or he really be stopped?

Nuclear proliferation increases the likelihood that nuclear weapons will be used. Not only do more countries possess these weapons, but in addition a few individuals (or governments) are willing to sell their knowledge of how to design, engineer, and build them. Pakistan, for example, is thought to be the source of advanced technology behind

This is Hamburg, Germany, after the defeat of the Nazis in 1945.

North Korea's nuclear weapons program. Accompanying this dismaying situation is the growing demand among potential customers—the smaller nations of the former Soviet Union and al-Qaeda.

Is it any wonder, then, that some anticipate that our civilization will end in one gigantic mushroom cloud? Look again at Figure 14-2, the Social Map, which pinpoints the major sources of this danger.

The Possibility of Accidental War

COMPUTER FAILURE. As things now stand, the threat of nuclear attack comes not only from dictators and terrorists, but also from the possibility that missiles will be unleashed accidentally. We have come close to such unintended launchings in the past. Here is a depiction of an actual event:

> Back in 1980, a military computer reported that Russia had fired missiles at the United States. The United States immediately went to red alert. U.S. bombers plotted courses toward pre-selected targets in the Soviet Union, and we prepared our missiles for launching. The countdown toward nuclear devastation had begun. (*U.S. News & World Report,* June 24, 1980)

Russia had *not* launched any missiles. A computer had malfunctioned, and the error was recorded. It's a chilling thought—the end of the world could result from a computer malfunction.

HUMAN ERROR. The obliteration of humanity could also come from simple human error. Here's another real-life event:

> On October 28, 1962, the North American Defense Command was informed that Cuba had launched a nuclear missile. It was about to hit Tampa, Florida. The U.S. began a countdown for its retaliatory strike. Then someone noticed that there had been no explosion in Tampa. (Sagan, 1994)

FIGURE 14-2 The Nuclear Club

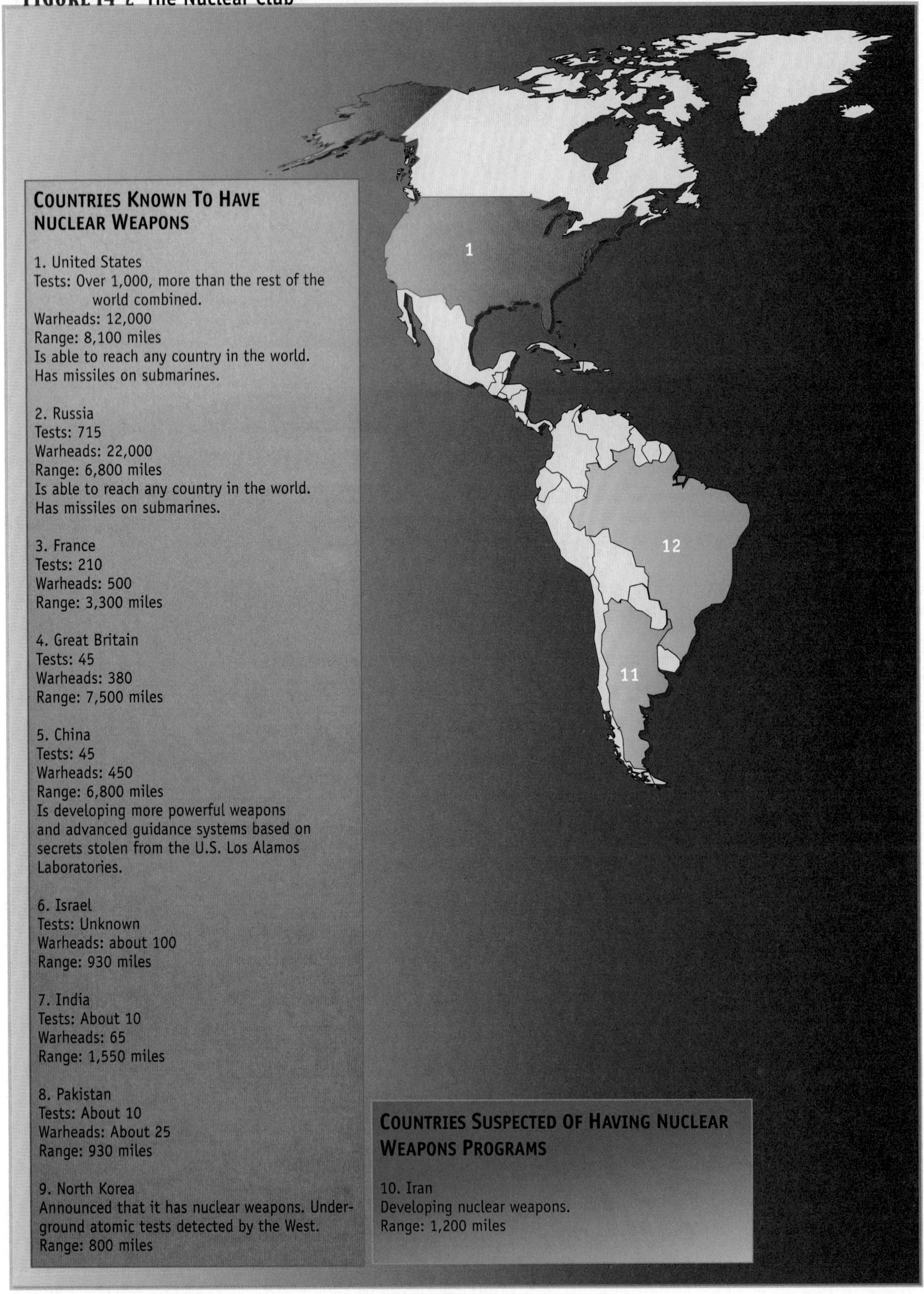

COUNTRIES KNOWN TO HAVE NUCLEAR WEAPONS

1. United States
Tests: Over 1,000, more than the rest of the world combined.
Warheads: 12,000
Range: 8,100 miles
Is able to reach any country in the world.
Has missiles on submarines.

2. Russia
Tests: 715
Warheads: 22,000
Range: 6,800 miles
Is able to reach any country in the world.
Has missiles on submarines.

3. France
Tests: 210
Warheads: 500
Range: 3,300 miles

4. Great Britain
Tests: 45
Warheads: 380
Range: 7,500 miles

5. China
Tests: 45
Warheads: 450
Range: 6,800 miles
Is developing more powerful weapons and advanced guidance systems based on secrets stolen from the U.S. Los Alamos Laboratories.

6. Israel
Tests: Unknown
Warheads: about 100
Range: 930 miles

7. India
Tests: About 10
Warheads: 65
Range: 1,550 miles

8. Pakistan
Tests: About 10
Warheads: About 25
Range: 930 miles

9. North Korea
Announced that it has nuclear weapons. Underground atomic tests detected by the West.
Range: 800 miles

COUNTRIES SUSPECTED OF HAVING NUCLEAR WEAPONS PROGRAMS

10. Iran
Developing nuclear weapons.
Range: 1,200 miles

Sources: Various, including "Iran Test Fires . . . ," 2006.

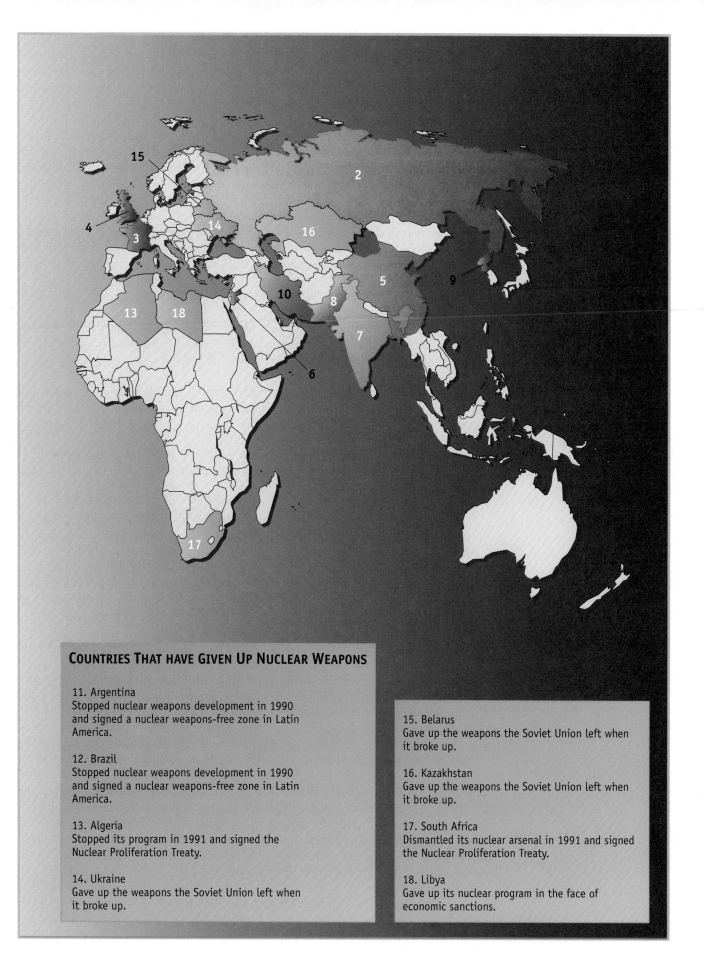

COUNTRIES THAT HAVE GIVEN UP NUCLEAR WEAPONS

11. Argentina
Stopped nuclear weapons development in 1990 and signed a nuclear weapons-free zone in Latin America.

12. Brazil
Stopped nuclear weapons development in 1990 and signed a nuclear weapons-free zone in Latin America.

13. Algeria
Stopped its program in 1991 and signed the Nuclear Proliferation Treaty.

14. Ukraine
Gave up the weapons the Soviet Union left when it broke up.

15. Belarus
Gave up the weapons the Soviet Union left when it broke up.

16. Kazakhstan
Gave up the weapons the Soviet Union left when it broke up.

17. South Africa
Dismantled its nuclear arsenal in 1991 and signed the Nuclear Proliferation Treaty.

18. Libya
Gave up its nuclear program in the face of economic sanctions.

It turned out that a radar operator had accidentally inserted into the system a test tape that simulated an attack from Cuba. If the United States had launched immediately, instead of waiting a few moments, Cuba would have been destroyed. The Soviet Union, Cuba's ally at the time, might have responded with an attack of its own—and you probably would not be here to read this book.

NUCLEAR ACCIDENTS. It can make your hair stand on end—since the unintended detonation of a nuclear weapon could signal the end of human civilization—but here are some real-life nuclear accidents. These are reported by Rear Admiral Gene LaRocque, U.S. Navy (retired):

The *George Washington,* a missile submarine, ran into a Japanese ship and sank it.
The *Scorpion* and the *Thresher,* two other nuclear attack submarines, sank in the ocean.
When a mechanic dropped a wrench in a missile silo in Arkansas, a missile was launched.
Several nuclear weapons have fallen out of planes, through open bomb bays. (Keyes n.d.)

As a symbolic interactionist, though, this is my favorite:

A nuclear weapon fell from a plane into a swamp in the Carolinas. The Air Force was unable to find it. The Defense Department bought the land, put a fence around it and, in Orwellian fashion, called it a "nuclear safety area." (Keyes n.d.)

Fortunately for us, in none of these incidents did a nuclear weapon detonate. We have no assurance that similar accidents will not happen again or that, if they occur, the weapons will not detonate.

NUCLEAR SABOTAGE. The U.S. government has repeatedly assured us—and the world—that a missile cannot be launched without proper authorization. Any talk to the contrary, they say, is alarmist.

The year was 1962. Kennedy had backed down in the Bay of Pigs invasion of Cuba, and the Soviet military thought that Kennedy would back down from them as well. Khrushchev, the premier of the Soviet Union, decided to ship missiles to Cuba. The CIA reported that the missiles would be capable of destroying the Pentagon, New York City, and other U.S. cities. Kennedy warned Khrushchev to order the ships back and set up a blockade to intercept them. The world waited tensely, television reporting the location of the ships as they neared the blockade.

Many Americans were not aware of the following:

At the height of the Cuban crisis, officers at Malmstrom Air Force Base in Montana, who also doubted the resolve of President Kennedy to give the order to bomb the Soviets, did what was supposedly impossible: They manipulated their Minutemen missiles so they could launch them on their own.
　　After the crisis, the Air Force investigated the manipulation and then kept secret the fact that officers at Malmstrom had given themselves the ability to launch missiles. (Sagan, 1994)

THE SIGNIFICANCE OF SYMBOLIC INTERACTION. This frightening event demonstrates the significance of symbolic interaction. To gain an understanding of an event's meaning, all symbols must be interpreted. If a missile were launched, or a city destroyed, as could happen with a computer malfunction or an unauthorized launch, military and political leaders would have to answer this question: Is this an accident, an unauthorized attack by a madman, or the effort of an orchestrated attack?
　　Fortunately, the United States and Russia have agreed to notify the other if either spots a missile—and to help each other track and destroy it (Greenberger, 1992). Although their intention is to protect one another against missile attacks by a third nation, their cooperation also helps to prevent accidental nuclear war.

Biological and Chemical Warfare

An interesting irony of warfare is that killing with bullets or bombs is considered normal, while killing with gas is deemed abnormal. During World War I, the French and Germans shocked the world by using poison gas. After that war, in 1925, the major powers met in Geneva, where they signed an agreement banning the use of poison gases in warfare. In 1972, they agreed not to use biological weapons either (Seib, 1981). In 1989, 145 nations met to try to put an end to chemical weapons once and for all (Revzin, 1989). But they failed.

USE OF BIOLOGICAL AND CHEMICAL AGENTS. Only a few nations have used biological and chemical agents throughout history. In World War I, France and Germany used mustard gas on each other. In World War II, as we have already mentioned, Japan used biological weapons against the Chinese.

In the 1960s and 1970s, the United States rained **Agent Orange**—a chemical defoliant—on the jungles of Vietnam. It and other chemicals, however, were not intended as weapons, but as a way of destroying crops and clearing terrain. Spraying stopped only when Vietnamese women gave birth to deformed babies, such as the children shown in the photo below. After the war, thousands of Vietnam veterans claimed that Agent Orange had damaged their health. The Veterans Administration (VA) replied that Agent Orange caused only a "severe skin rash" and could not be the cause of "cancer, birth defects, miscarriages, impotency, respiratory problems, and liver, skin, nerve, and emotional disorders" (Feinsilber, 1981). When the Department of Health and Human Services investigated the matter, it found that the United States had dropped 12 million gallons of Agent Orange on Vietnam. In some emergency situations, the gas had been dumped near military bases. In 1989, each soldier who had sued the government was awarded about $12,000.

There are other instances of chemical warfare. Iran and Iraq used mustard gas against one another in the 1980s. The Soviets have also been accused of using chemicals in Afghanistan and Laos, not against plants but against people (Douglass, 1998). They deny all allegations. For using poison gas to quell an uprising by the Kurds, Saddam Hussein was sentenced to death. His tortured victims were one motivation for the United States to initiate the Iraq War.

The human costs of war far outnumber the soldiers who are killed and maimed. Shown here are two victims of Agent Orange, a defoliant used by U.S. troops in Vietnam to clear the forests and disrupt the movement of troops and supplies from the north. Birth defects, especially the absence of vital organs (brains, eyes, kidneys, and so on) were a major factor in terminating the massive use of chemical defoliants during this war.

THE PRODUCTION OF THESE AGENTS. The justification for producing biological and chemical agents is the same used for producing nuclear weapons. During the Cold War, the Pentagon warned Congress that the Soviet Union's weapons gave it an advantage over the United States. Congress then funded the development of nuclear weapons and chemical warfare agents. At one point, the Pentagon reported that the United States needed to develop **binary chemical weapons.** These are shells or bombs in which two benign chemicals are kept in separate chambers. When the weapon is detonated, the chemicals mix, releasing a lethal agent.

THE TREATY WITH A HUGE FLAW. Because the Pentagon does not have a budget of its own, it has to have all weapons development approved by Congress. The Pentagon once attempted to convince Congress that chemical weapons could help bring about peace. With U.S. development of more powerful chemical weapons, other nations (Soviets) would agree to "a complete and verifiable ban on the development, production, and stockpiling of chemical weapons" because the United States would be "dangling the threat of retaliation over the heads of the Soviets" (*Wall Street Journal,* February 9, 1982).

The United States, Russia, and other nations have signed a Chemical Weapons Convention. They have agreed not to produce, stockpile, or use chemical weapons. By 2012, all nations are supposed to have destroyed their total supply of chemical weapons. The flaw? Biological weapons are not covered by this treaty.

CONTINUED RESEARCH AND PRODUCTION. When the Cold War ended, the United States and Russia continued to develop lethal biological weapons. Russia announced that it has genetically engineered an anthrax microbe that attacks blood cells, making vaccines useless (Broad & Miller, 1998). Supposedly, Russia has armed its ICBM warheads with plague, anthrax, and smallpox (Douglass, 1998). If so, we may assume that the United States has done the same. If Russia and the United States continue their peaceful alliance, it is likely that the race toward increasing biological destruction will come to an end; but many factors cause tensions between the two nations, and a permanent peaceful alliance is not guaranteed.

Although major nations have begun to scale back on the development of biological weapons, the possibility that terrorists will get their hands on some of these weapons still remains. Let's consider this possibility.

Terrorism

How times change. Merely 20 years ago, terrorism was only a theoretical topic. There had been no terrorist attacks on the United States, although they were taking place elsewhere.

Now, in contrast, terrorism has become a part of daily life. With 9/11, the world changed, and U.S. officials—and those throughout the West—became extremely concerned that terrorists would strike again. Our nuclear plants have become vulnerable targets. Boarding a plane used to be a delight, but no longer. Armed security agents scrutinize our baggage and body, while screening devices do the same. Billions of dollars have been spent to fortify our embassies around the world, and yet they too remain vulnerable.

POLITICAL TERRORISM. Although it is not outright war between nations, **political terrorism** involves the use of threats of war—intimidation, coercion, and violence—to achieve political objectives (Boston, O'Brien, & Palumbo, 1977). Political terrorists use random acts of violence to instill fear in the general public. They do not recognize civilians as "noncombatants." On the contrary, they often target civilians because they are easier to reach, and the apparent randomness of the attack sows fear. There are four types of political terrorism: revolutionary, repressive, state-sponsored, and criminal. Let's look at each.

REVOLUTIONARY TERRORISM. In the first type, **revolutionary terrorism,** enemies of the state use terrorism in an attempt to overthrow the government. Walter Laqueur (1977), a political scientist, identified these causes of revolutionary terrorism:

1. Existence of a segregated, ethnic, cultural, or religious minority
2. Perceptions of being deprived or oppressed
3. Higher-than-average unemployment or inflation
4. External encouragement (often from an ethnic, cultural, or religious counterpart living elsewhere)
5. A historical "them" (a group they blame for their oppressed condition)
6. Frustrated elites who provide leadership and justify ideological violence

Goals of Revolutionary Terrorism ■ Revolutionary terrorism doesn't appear overnight out of nowhere, as though it spontaneously sprang into existence in some social vacuum. The group initiating revolutionary terrorism has already gone through official channels in an attempt to change its situation:

> The Boston Tea Party, which helped lead to American independence, John Brown's raid on the federal arsenal at Harper's Ferry, which helped lead to the abolition of American slavery, and the bombing of the King David Hotel, which helped drive the British out of Palestine and thereby made possible the establishment of the State of Israel, were all terrorist acts under current U.S. law. (Seto, 2002)

Finding authorities unresponsive to their grievances, terrorist group members attempt to

1. publicize the group and its grievances
2. demonstrate the government's vulnerability
3. force political and social change

In Uganda, revolutionary soldiers kidnapped children from their villages. They trained the boys to use guns and forced them to kill. They used the girls as sex slaves and cooks. How do you compute the costs of war, in terms of quality of life—in this case lost childhoods, brutalized consciences, nightmares?

Terrorists often want to make public their "cause," and terrorism is sometimes called **political theater.** As political scientist Brian Jenkins (1987) put it, "Terrorists want a lot of people watching, not a lot of people dead." Consequently, terrorists choose targets that will attract media attention. In light of 9/11 and the Madrid train bombings in 2004, however, political terrorists today seem to want a lot of people dead as well. Suleiman Abu Ghaith, a spokesman for al-Qaeda, said that al-Qaeda's goal is to kill 4 million Americans (S. Simon, 2004).

Some terrorists have another motive for violence—this is discussed in the Global Glimpse box on pages 528–529. During the Russian Revolution of 1917, communist terrorists argued that "false consciousness" deluded the masses, blinding them to their own oppression. Terrorist acts were designed to illuminate harsh and brutal oppression of the people. If the terrorists revealed how horrible the political system was, the masses would become aroused (Rubenstein, 1987). Al-Qaeda, too, attempts to convince others they should fight against those who attack Islam—specifically, the repressive West. Not all Arabs are in agreement with al-Qaeda's mission; in fact, many of Osama bin Laden's greatest enemies are other Arabs (Wright, 2007).

The Global Glimpse box explores this issue in more detail.

The Oklahoma City Bombing ■ Although the truck filled with fertilizer and fuel oil that exploded in Oklahoma City in 1995 was not the first act of terrorism on U.S. soil, it was the most destructive to that time. The resulting destruction of a federal building and the deaths of almost 200 people, including 19 children in a day care center, opened the eyes of Americans to a new form of warfare. Up to that time, they assumed that terrorism only happened "someplace over there."

A Global Glimpse

AL-QAEDA AND THE WEST: POWER, RESOURCES, AND LOST GLORY

How can we make sense of 9/11, as well as the bombings in Madrid and London? Certainly, we need to look beyond those particular events to understand what causes them. To do this, let's sketch a broad historical context:

1. In earlier centuries, the Arabs were a powerful political force. They led an advanced civilization and were world leaders in agriculture, architecture, astronomy, mathematics, medicine, and metallurgy. They ruled an empire that extended into Europe. The terraced fields developed by the Arabs are still a distinctive feature of southern Spain.

2. In the late 1400s, Queen Isabella and King Ferdinand married, uniting two major provinces of what is now Spain. They turned their united armies against their neighbors, including the Arabs, who ruled vast parts of this region.

3. In addition to motives of gaining territory and treasure, this was a religious war. The goal was to drive out all non-Catholics from the Iberian peninsula (Spain). The pope blessed the armies, wanting the infidels out of Europe. The Jews, who were not a political force, were given three choices: to convert to Christianity, to leave the area, or to die by the sword.

4. After a series of battles, with heavy losses on both sides, the Christian armies defeated Islamic armies. The Arabs retreated back to Africa, although they continued to control other parts of Europe for another hundred years. Their political and economic power declined, as well as their leadership in academics and arts.

5. As Europeans developed strong economies and political power, they conquered peoples around the globe. The sands of Arab lands, many of them under the control of the Ottoman Empire, were of little interest to them, but the British (and the French) conquered Arabs to extend their global empire.

6. When vast pools of oil were discovered beneath those sands, that interest changed. The global dominance of the British depended on uninterrupted supplies of oil, which were not present in the British Isles. They needed oil for their economic machinery—for factories, homes, and maritime warships.

7. In the 1920s, after the defeat of the Ottoman Empire in World War I, the British, to help maintain their rule over the Arabs and to help settle squabbles among them, divided the land into countries. To do so, they drew lines on maps, declaring that those lines marked one country from another. They also set up Arab rulers in those territories. Until this time, the Arabs were loose confederations of tribes and kin.

8. Americans possessed vast sources of oil in their own country. As the nation grew more powerful and populous, its need for oil increased. Americans looked beyond their borders for additional sources of this essential commodity. As England's power weakened, the British began to lose control over Arab lands. The United States quickly stepped in.

9. The American public did not like troops fighting in foreign lands, so U.S. politicians were careful to use them only for limited excursions. To control access to oil, they supported cooperative Arab leaders, keeping them submissive by giving them military aid in return for oil. At times the Americans even set up puppets to head a country, as with the Shah of Iran, who was deposed by revolutionaries in 1979.

10. Many in Arab nations longed for their past—times of grandeur and wealth, of power and prestige. Those memories stood in sharp contrast to the shame of the present—domination by the West and, despite vast oil wealth, populations living mostly in poverty.

September 11 ■ As recounted in this chapter's opening vignette, an even more lethal act of terrorism followed, the destruction of the World Trade Center in New York City on September 11, 2001. This attack, accompanied by the attack on the Pentagon in Washington and the crash of another plane headed for Washington on that same day, caused several thousand deaths. These two targets were not random choices. The leaders of al-Qaeda chose the World Trade Center because it symbolized U.S. dominance of global capitalism. They targeted the Pentagon because it symbolized the U.S. military. To strike at the heart of two of the country's major symbols exposed the vulnerability of the United States. Al-Qaeda was right, and the attack struck widespread fear in Americans when they realized that nothing was safe.

September 11 became a sort of theater, in precisely the way that analysts had predicted. The timing—a busy Tuesday workday morning—meant that a huge audience could gather immediately. The act was larger than even the terrorists could imagine, of course, for they did not anticipate the dramatic collapse of the Twin Towers. Yet they did

Having sketched this brief historical outline, let's move to the present. Using symbolic interactionism, we will try to understand how al-Qaeda and similar groups perceive the West as an evil infidel.

11. A revolutionary movement needs an inspirational ideology to spur people into action, especially if it involves personal sacrifice. It must be built around a cause greater than the individual. Islam serves this purpose. Images of the Great Infidel (the West) polluting a holy land strike that responsive chord. So do images of the Evil One (the West) plundering resources and holding people captive through their puppet leaders. It also helps that this Great Satan (the West) supports Israel, the Arab archenemy.

12. Killing the Great Infidel, then, becomes an act of service to Allah. Losing one's life in that service becomes a sacrifice to God. The loss of individual life is nothing in comparison with this noble cause.

13. The Great Infidel possesses vast military power—soldiers, planes, ships, missiles, and bombs. The United States also equips Israel with military weapons. With such strong political power, America's military cannot be defeated in traditional warfare.

14. The solution for terrorists is to attack where the United States has the fewest defenses—on its own soil. This requires long-range planning, coordination, patience, and people so dedicated that they will give their lives to the holy cause. Suicide attacks by insurgents have been effective because it is difficult for Americans to pinpoint when they are coming.

15. The entire culture of the United States is seen as evil—dominating and exploiting Arab lands.

16. The goal of suicide attacks is not to destroy the Infidel but, rather, to strike fear and create outrage, especially to provoke large-scale violent retaliation. When Americans kill Arabs, the faithful do not move through legitimate channels to retaliate. Instead, they recruit others to join the movement for independence. If the Great Infidel is provoked and sends an invading army into sacred lands, so much the better.

17. The ultimate goal is pan-Arab unity, which surpasses any artificial boundaries drawn by Western powers. It will not be Iraqis, Syrians, Saudi Arabians, or any such group, but united Arabs, who will defeat the West.

18. Because the West will not easily give up its control over Arab oil, the struggle will likely last for decades.

FOR YOUR CONSIDERATION

Placed within this context, the activities of al-Qaeda—and the many groups destined to join this independence movement—take on different meaning. Suicide attacks are viewed as current manifestations of long-term historical events.

---

collapse and, in even more dramatic fashion, took with them over 300 firefighters. The message could not have been clearer, nor a worldwide audience as quickly summoned.

A Sense of Morality ■ To themselves, the Islamic terrorists' acts of bloodshed seem righteous acts. Using neutralization techniques discussed earlier, terrorists appeal to a higher morality in justifying their actions. It does not matter to them that almost everyone else in the world views their actions as evil—these terrorists are convinced of their moral superiority. As they see it, their "cause" justifies mass, indiscriminate murder of civilians, for these deaths can usher in their apocalyptic vision of Islamic rule.

It is this conviction (no matter how heinous) that makes revolutionary terrorists such formidable opponents of the established order. Some revolutionaries become as dedicated to "the cause" as any other dedicated religious follower would. Listen to Karari Mjama, a Mau Mau insurgent (the Mau Mau were a militant group whose goal was to liberate Kenya from British rule):

No one can serve two masters. In order to become a strong faithful warrior who would persevere to the last minute, one had to renounce all worldly wealth, including his family. . . . In fact, I had said to my wife . . . not to expect any sort of help from me for at least ten years' time. I had instructed her to take care of herself and our beloved daughter. I had trained myself to think of the fight, and the African Government; and nothing of the country's progress before independence. I had learned to forget all pleasures and imagination of the past. I confined my thoughts (to) the fight only—the end of which would open my thoughts to the normal world. (Schreiber, 1978, p. 32)

Japanese Subways ▪ Japan had prided itself on being a "community nation" insulated from the "profane" social problems of the West. This soothing, assuring myth was shattered when a religious leader launched a poison gas attack on Tokyo subways in 1995. Twelve people died, and 5,000 were injured (Miller & Broad, 1999). The chemical weapon—**sarin**—can be manufactured from chemicals used in pesticides bought at a local hardware store. Other frightening recipes for chemical weapons are now found on the Internet—a sort of Betty Crocker cookbook on how to devastate the world (Greenberger & Bishop, 1995).

REPRESSIVE TERRORISM. A second type of terrorism is **repressive terrorism,** that waged by a government against its own citizens. For example:

> Diana, a dedicated Christian, worked among the poor in Buenos Aires. One midnight, soldiers broke down her door, rushed in, and knocked her to the floor. They blindfolded her and beat her across the head. They then threw her into a car and drove to a building with an underground chamber. Here she was threatened, tortured, and interrogated for six straight hours about church leaders, the Vatican Council, and the Jews.
>
> Beaten beyond all tears, she suddenly blurted, "Good God, aren't you Christians?"
>
> Abrupt silence followed. One of the soldiers grabbed her hand and pressed her fingers to a metal cross on his chest. Afterward, they seemed to give up on her. "I'm convinced that small incident saved my life," she says. "The man apparently wanted to be recognized as a person rather than a torturer. He couldn't have that recognition without making me a person, too, rather than an object to be disposed of."
>
> Diana was later taken back to her apartment and held there for two more days by four officers who took turns raping her. The police then released her. (Cornell, 1981)

Such massive brutality and killing is typical of repressive terrorism: In this case, the generals who headed the military dictatorship of Argentina felt vulnerable. Fearful of their government's collapse, they became afraid. They arrested tens of thousands of people like Diana between 1976 and 1983. Thousands were tortured and executed, others were dumped in public places, and some captives were dropped alive from airplanes into the ocean.

The Khmer Rouge ▪ Pol Pot, the dictator of Cambodia, directed perhaps the most horrific repressive terrorism that any government has ever inflicted on its people. The extent of his regime's devastation is mind-boggling. For almost 4 years, from April 1975 to January 1979, Cambodia was Pol Pot's private slaughterhouse. On an average day, the Khmer Rouge killed 1,500 Cambodians. In just 45 months, the government killed about 2 million people (Wain, 1981). Many were beaten to death with rubber hoses and bamboo sticks. Some were tortured for weeks before their death. Others were killed instantly.

The Khmer Rouge targeted *all* intellectuals, for they represented an elite, and the Pol Pot government was attempting to develop a classless society (Miles, 1980). Being able to speak a foreign language was enough to merit execution. In one area of Cambodia, members of the Khmer Rouge could count only to 10. Anyone who could count higher was an "intellectual." To ferret them out, the Khmer Rouge would have someone count other people—they executed those who counted to 20, instead of counting two groups of 10. Only 50 of Cambodia's 800 doctors survived.

> Pol Pot's slaughterhouses remain on the outskirts of Phnom Penh, the capital of Cambodia. The buildings of torture have become memorials—reminding others of a gruesome past. There are metal cots on which the prisoners had been chained, torture devices used to break the men, women, and children before they were executed. There is a cabinet of skulls—larger ones of adults and smaller ones of children—each cracked where someone struck them to death. There is also a huge vat that once had a wooden bar above it. The vat was filled with water, and the victims, hung upside down, were lowered slowly head first into the water. They could be immersed as many times as the torturers wanted, until they finally were forced to drink their death.

At Tuol Sleng Prison outside of Phnom Penh, Cambodia, the Khmer Rouge tortured and killed thousands of people during its bloody reign from 1975 to 1979. The prison is now a museum and tourist attraction.

Russia ■ To dictators, who hold power unchecked, repressive terrorism is a way to silence criticism and suppress ideas they don't like. Soviet officials were sensitive to criticism of any sort, and they even persecuted poets and artists who dared to express "incorrect" political thought. They also felt threatened by religion, with party leaders referring to the Church as "the enemy within" (Ra'anan et al., 1986). Authorities felt so threatened by alternative views that they arrested Christians who witnessed to Christ, beating them to death (Wurmbrand, 1970). Andrei Sakharov (1977), a dissenter, told about the persecution of Baptists, the Orthodox church, Pentecostals, and uniates:

> It is a common practice of the Russian government to take children away from parents who are evangelical; that is, they believe that Jesus of Nazareth is God incarnate or the Savior who should be placed ahead of the State. Pastors of underground churches are regularly arrested, beaten, tortured, and killed.

STATE-SPONSORED TERRORISM. In the third type, **state-sponsored terrorism,** a government finances, trains, and arms terrorists. Colonel Moammar Gadhafi of Libya viewed terrorism as a legitimate extension of the state. He bankrolled terrorists and provided training camps for them. After the U.S. Air Force tried to kill him by bombing his palace, Gadhafi became more clandestine in his support of terrorism. Later, after years of economic sanctions that worsened conditions in his country, Gadhafi renounced his support of terrorism and invited international inspectors to verify that he had dismantled his nuclear weapons.

CRIMINAL TERRORISM. Beyond political terrorism, but often affiliated with it, is **criminal terrorism** in which criminals use terrorism to attain their objectives. The most well-known example involves the Russian Mafia. To maintain their sources of wealth, these gangsters intimidate and kill anyone who opposes them. They terrorize both the public and government into submission. As the executions of reporters, prosecutors, judges, and other government officials attest, death awaits anyone who dares to investigate or prosecute the Russian Mafia.

Narcoterrorism is a form of criminal terrorism that revolves around drugs. Some narcoterrorists use drug dealing to finance their ambitions. Mehemet Ali Agca, for example, sold drugs to finance his attempted assassination of Pope John Paul II (Oakley, 1985;

Ehrenfeld, 1990). For other narcoterrorists, money is the primary objective; terrorism is simply a way to protect their drug operations. In Colombia, international drug dealers hired thugs to assassinate the justices of the Colombian supreme court. They also terrorized the Colombian government until it abandoned its extradition treaty with the United States.

NUCLEAR AND BIOLOGICAL TERRORISM. Nuclear and biological weapons could be used by any type of terrorist, but because the effects are so devastating, we will focus special attention on this possibility.

Nuclear Terrorism ▪ Because plutonium is often used in the manufacture of nuclear weapons, you would think it would be guarded carefully—right? Wrong! About 5,000 pounds—2 1/2; tons—of plutonium are currently missing from U.S. nuclear facilities. A former security agent reported that protective measures at the Rocky Flats weapons factory near Denver were so lax that it was "like having a window in a bank vault" (Hosenball, 1999). When the missing plutonium was broadcast to the general public, officials took a cavalier attitude. "What's to worry?" they asked. The plutonium "probably got stuck in pipes and manufacturing tools." The solution? Simple. They suspended the individual who discovered that the plutonium was missing.

Even after 9/11, safeguards remain inadequate. Some nuclear materials in Russia are said to be secured only by a chain-link fence and a night watchman (Bunn & Weir, 2005). The situation in Russia is of special concern. The breakup of the Soviet empire brought with it a void of legitimate power that was soon taken over by the Russian Mafia. These gangsters stole plutonium and uranium and offered them for sale to Iraq and other dictatorships ("The Wild Wild East," 1995). Part of the difficulty in securing Russia's nuclear weapons is that the Soviet Union produced 1,300 tons of enriched uranium and 220 tons of plutonium and stored them in 40 to 50 different places (Gordon, 1996). With the cooperation of and financing by the West, about half of this nuclear material has been destroyed (Bunn & Weir, 2005). Some enriched uranium has been smuggled out of nuclear plants, however. One worker simply hid nuclear material in his protective gloves when he walked out the gate (Zaitseva & Hand, 2003).

As mentioned, the West's nightmare scenario has a dictator developing nuclear-tipped missiles and, unrestrained by the checks and balances built into democracies, terrorizing an entire region—and, with advanced delivery systems, perhaps the world. These concerns are not unrealistic. The "father of the Pakistani bomb," Abdul Qadeer Khan, who headed Pakistan's nuclear program, sold blueprints and parts for making nuclear bombs to Iran and North Korea (Rubin, 2004).

Because damage from nuclear attack would be unimaginably destructive, at some point nuclear terrorists could hold major governments, including the United States, captive. They could simply smuggle "dirty bombs" or other nuclear weapons into the country. Few of the tens of thousands of containers arriving each day at U.S. ports are searched. What would American officials do if terrorists threatened to detonate a nuclear weapon in the heart of New York City or Los Angeles? The thought of nuclear weapons in the hands of a ruthless, hell-bent-for-destruction dictator or terrorist sends chills down the spine of the industrialized nations.

Biological Terrorism ▪ Perhaps an even greater threat is biological terrorism. The components for weapons such as anthrax, smallpox, and the plague are cheaper to obtain than nuclear weapons, and they can be transported in tiny containers. Terrorists could infiltrate the United States or any other country and simultaneously release anthrax or other killer germs in several cities. If this were to occur in the United States, deaths could number in the millions. In 2001, lone suspect Bruce Ivins sent anthrax through the U.S. mail system. He mailed the letters from New Jersey, more than 160 miles from where he worked in a medical research institute. The U.S. government claims Ivins had a history of mental illness, the only possible motive for killing five others with anthrax. Ivins committed suicide before he could be formally charged (Bohn, 2008).

Other aspects of biological terrorism are highlighted in the Technology and Social Problems box on the next page.

Technology and Social Problems
OUR FUTURE: BIOLOGICAL TERRORISM IN THE TWENTY-FIRST CENTURY

Consider this scenario:

Over a period of years, agents of a nation whose leader despises the United States quietly infiltrate the United States. Most gain admission as university students across the country. All have been trained by their country's secret police. On a predetermined day, at a specified hour, they release anthrax and smallpox into the air of 20 major cities. Within days, a third of Americans are dead.

Scenarios like this haunt U.S. officials. Few safeguards exist to protect against such an attack. There will be no warning, no attempt to hold the United States hostage in order to extort billions of dollars. The motive will be revenge for humiliations suffered at the hands of the United States. The goal will be not profit or fear, but the annihilation of the United States itself.

How seriously officials are taking threats by terrorists is indicated by the federal budget: in 2008, for example, over forty-seven billion dollars were spent by the Department of Homeland Security (*Statistical Abstract*, 2009, Table 509). Officials have stockpiled vaccines around the country, and emergency medical teams have been trained in major cities. All military personnel, active and reserve, are being vaccinated against anthrax, as well as all civilian employees of the Department of Defense who are designated essential workers ("Anthrax Vaccination . . . ," 2004).

If a biological attack occurs, U.S. officials have a plan. It is not to evacuate populations, but to try to prevent the disease from spreading. Their plans to halt the spread of biological contamination include police blockades and military encampments (Miller & Broad, 1999). For at least a while after a biological attack, the Pentagon would have direct control over the United States.

An ancient Chinese proverb states "May you live in exciting times." We live in exciting times. Let's hope that the curse with which we live—weapons of mass destruction, hatreds engendered by foreign domination, and retaliatory action by terrorists—does not result in our destruction.

Social Policy

Let's examine existing social policies that attempt to address two major problems we have reviewed in this chapter, political terrorism and nuclear war.

Political Terrorism

THE OVERARCHING PRINCIPLE IN SOCIAL POLICY. The key principle in dealing with terrorists is "Don't give in to their demands, for this encourages further terrorism." This stance poses a dilemma—not meeting demands can bring high immediate costs: property damage, injuries, and deaths. Giving in to terrorists encourages further terrorism—because their tactics work. In short, giving in to terrorists' demands only escalates terrorism.

TEN BASIC POLICIES. Legal and government experts suggest the following as effective social policies (Bremer, 1988; Ehrenfeld, 1990; FBI, 1998; "National Strategy . . . ," 2006):

1. Promise anything during negotiations. Promises made under threat are not valid.
2. Make no distinction between terrorists and their state sponsors. Even though they hide behind the scenes, states that sponsor terrorists are not neutral and should not be treated as neutrals. This principle allows both retaliatory and preemptive acts.

3. Use economic and political sanctions to break the connection between terrorists and the states that provide them weapons, financing, safe houses, training areas, and identity documents in return for terrorism done on their behalf.

4. Treat terrorists as war criminals. Track them, arrest them, and punish them. Bomb them, if that is what it takes.

5. Discourage media coverage because publicity is a prime goal of terrorists. Make it illegal for the media to pay terrorists for interviews.

6. Establish international extradition and prosecution agreements: Terrorists need to know that if they are caught anywhere, they will be extradited or tried.

7. Develop an international organization to combat terrorism. This organization would coordinate worldwide intelligence and advise nations. It would also direct international teams to respond to specific events—such as freeing hostages or locating evidence to identify sponsors of terrorists.

8. Offer large rewards for information leading to the disabling of known terrorists. Just as in the old west, rewards can be paid on a "dead-or-alive" basis. With rewards of $50,000, or $1 million, or $5 million, terrorists will never know whether associates can be trusted. Informants should also be guaranteed safe passage and offered new identities.

9. Cut the funding of terrorist organizations. For travel, weapons, training, and other activities, they need money, so disrupt their remittance systems.

10. Infiltrate terrorist organizations.

APPLICATION OF SOCIAL POLICIES. Some of these policies are currently being put into use. Consistently viewing others as potential terrorists is controversial. The Iraq War, for example, represents the policy of preemptive strikes. Because Saddam Hussein supposedly possessed weapons of mass destruction and was intending to use them against the West, the United States (with troops from a few other nations) made a preemptive strike.

Targeted Killings ▪ **Targeted killings** are also disturbing. When the CIA determines that a certain individual is responsible for a terrorist attack or is planning such an act, she or he is put on a "hit list" and marked for assassination (Risen & Johnston, 2002).

The attacks of September 11, 2001, have had far-reaching effects on the United States. Whether the country ever returns to its more easygoing ways based on feelings of internal security remains to be seen. The anti-terrorism laws passed after 9/11 give the police more authority than they have had since the Civil War.

Launching a Predator—an unmanned plane—the CIA tracked suspected terrorists traveling by car in Djibouti. CIA agents in Yemen then fired a Hellfire missile, which struck the automobile, killing all six (Hersh, 2002).

How often this occurs is anyone's guess; but since targeted killings are effective, we suspect that this policy is implemented regularly by the CIA. This practice of target killings is also used by the KGB (now FSB) of Russia and the Mossad of Israel.

Nuclear Warfare and the Elusive Path to Peace

MUTUAL DETERRENCE. The primary policy that the United States and the former Soviet Union pursued after World War II was **mutual deterrence**—using threats and the fear of mutual destruction to prevent the other from striking first. Each was afraid to use its nuclear arsenal, because even out of the ashes missiles would be launched that would destroy the other. Because neither country would survive, there was no benefit in attacking the other. The resulting balance of power became **mutual assured destruction (MAD).**

A Strange Path to Peace ■ The path to peace, then, has been a MAD one. Each superpower stockpiled weapons of mass destruction—nuclear, chemical, and biological—and signaled to its counterpart that it was willing to unleash those weapons. Thus the superpowers struck a balance of power—or terror—that kept them from attacking each other. Sociologist Nicholas Timasheff (1965, p. 291) explained how it worked:

> Each party may consider that it has a fair chance to win, but each party also knows that the cost of victory would be prohibitive; physical destruction of 90–95% of the total population, almost complete destruction of industrial equipment, transformation of almost the total territory into an uninhabitable area because of radiation, contamination of air, water, plants and animals and other natural resources. Under these circumstances, victory can be worse than the most crucial defeat before this atomic age. Each of the parties to the possible conflict has full reason to refrain from attack.

THE BALANCE OF POWER. G-8, the association of the world's eight most powerful nations, is working out a new balance of power—sometimes called the **New World Order.** Those countries that form the G-8 are Canada, France, Germany, Italy, Japan, Russia, the United Kingdom, and the United States. The balance, however, is precarious. Of its many sources of disequilibrium, perhaps the most disturbing is the proliferation of nuclear weapons. Poor nations may not be able to make it to G-8's bargaining table, but if they join the nuclear club, G-8 will listen to them. The proliferation of nuclear weapons to desperately poor nations like Pakistan and North Korea makes this balance of power even more precarious. India has developed a missile system that can be fired from mobile launchers. Not only can India's missiles hit targets in Pakistan, its neighbor and historical enemy, but they can also reach Beijing and Shanghai (Norris & Kristensen, 2005). Look again at the Social Map (Figure 14-2) on pages 522–523.

Even local conflicts, ordinarily of little interest to G-8, can upset the balance of power. Local conflicts can heat up, bringing in other nations as allies. Such fear led to the quick action taken against Serbia by **NATO (North Atlantic Treaty Organization).** Bombs speak louder than words, as the president of Serbia, Slobodan Milošević, discovered when a minor, hostile nation comes close to possessing nuclear weapons or, as in the case of Hussein's Iraq, is suspected of doing so. Serving to restrain the United States and G-8, though, are fears of Iran unleashing terrorists; the million soldiers that North Korea can unleash on South Korea; and, uncertainty regarding China's reaction to North Korea's nuclear capacity.

Few of us realize how fragile our current balance of power is. Consider this event from the 1970s:

> For nearly four years, the public library of the Los Alamos Scientific Laboratory in New Mexico had on its shelves a report that provided precise details of the devices that trigger hydrogen bombs (Mintz, 1979). Only a few pages of the report were supposed to have

been declassified, but through a "clerical error" the entire report was made available to the public, both Americans and foreigners, for inspection and copying. A nuclear expert, Dimitri Rotow, who copied this report, was quoted as saying: "It was easier than getting something out of the Library of Congress. At the Library of Congress, they at least check your briefcase." (*Associated Press*, May 25, 1979)

Apparently, this event did not alarm U.S. officials. In March 2005, federal officials posted on the Web what critics called "a guide" on how to make atomic bombs. When someone suggested that these instructions might be inappropriate, they quickly yanked the information off the Web (Broad, 2006b).

THREE POTENTIAL POLICIES. Assuming we continue to keep manuals on "how to make your own bomb" off Web sites, social policies that can help ensure peace include disarmament, interlocking networks of mutual interests, and international law. Let's look at each.

Disarmament ▪ Disarmament can occur on two levels: bilateral and unilateral. Some propose **bilateral disarmament;** that is, both nations in conflict agree to disarm simultaneously. Others favor **unilateral disarmament;** that is, one nation announces its intention to disarm and dismantles its weapons system. When its antagonist sees that it has made itself vulnerable, it, too, disarms. Just as each step of armament has led to the escalation and proliferation of weapons systems, so each step of disarmament would reduce and ultimately eliminate that stockpile.

Others claim that disarmament of any kind is useless. Only a strong military and the will to use it makes a nation secure. Although full military preparedness may indeed prevent war, extremists feel that when all nations possess nuclear weapons, we will achieve peace. The West, then, should help other industrializing nations build nuclear weapons (Sagan, 1994).

Russia and the United States have signed treaties to reduce their stockpiles of nuclear weapons, and the nations in the G-8 that possess nuclear weapons have stopped testing them, even China. This is not disarmament, however, as none of these nations intends to rid itself of nuclear weapons. This testing of nuclear weapons is frightening to many because such practices could stimulate the United States and other countries to develop a new generation of nuclear weapons (Wirtz, 2006).

Developing Interlocking Networks of Mutual Interest ▪ Others claim that the key to peace is the development of interlocking networks of mutual interest. They argue that the more a nation depends on another for its own well-being, the less likely it is to destroy that nation. The route leading to such dependence could be global capitalism. The expansion of capitalism has produced a **global economy,** one that links the world's nations to one another. As a nation's trade becomes more interwoven with other nations, its affairs become more dependent on the other. To develop further interlocking interests, then, we should encourage trade among the world's nations. To stimulate peace, we encourage communication, travel, and scientific exchanges.

International Law. ▪ International law is essential for world peace. If each nation is a law unto itself and feels free to wage war when its goals are frustrated, we may never achieve peace. The major obstacle to implementing international law is the unwillingness of nations to yield sovereignty to an international organization. The United Nations was dealt a severe blow when NATO bombed Kosovo. Despite the "good" reason for the bombing—the prevention of further ethnic slaughter—NATO placed itself above international law by attacking without the approval of the United Nations. Another rebellion occurred when the United States refused to submit to the **International Criminal Court** (Sewall & Kaysen, 2000). This court, established in 2002, is used to investigate war crimes.

SURVIVAL AS A MUTUAL BENEFIT. In the end, perhaps it will be the desire for self-preservation that will prevent the nuclear annihilation of humanity. Leaders don't want themselves, their families, or their own country destroyed. Unfortunately, there may be exceptions to this rule—madmen who want to dominate and destroy the world. As Albert Speer (1970), one of Hitler's close associates, noted, when Hitler realized that the war was lost, he wanted to destroy his own country.

IN SUM The best social policies would remove weapons of mass destruction from humanity. We foresee no such policy eliminating these weapons, whether nuclear, biological, or chemical. The knowledge of how to produce weapons of mass destruction has proliferated. The best we can hope for are social policies that limit and prevent the use of these weapons.

The Future of the Problem

ARMS SALES AND WAR. There certainly is no indication that war will disappear. On the contrary, it appears that wars will continue indefinitely. Some of these wars will likely be fueled by the merchants of death, listed in Table 14-4. As you can see, the United States currently sells twice as many weapons as its nearest competitor.

Recall that U.S. factories produce more weapons than the military can possibly use. The recipient nations listed in the second part of Table 14-4 provide an excellent outlet for this excess capacity. It is unlikely that this profitable merchandising in death will diminish—regardless of the destruction of human life that ensues.

Look again at the nations that spend the most for weapons of war. As you can see, some poor nations pay huge amounts for arms. Some of the buyers, Egypt, India, Malaysia, and Pakistan, are using money they desperately need to feed, house, and educate their people. The potential of aggression by neighboring countries requires such spending.

POLITICAL TERRORISM. It is likely that political terrorism will not only continue but also increase. The unshackling of the central dictatorship in the former Soviet Union unleashed ethnic antagonisms that have been nourished by centuries of animosity. This uncorking has increased prejudice and hatred among Serbs, Croats, Muslims, Albanians, Kurds, and Turks. Groups in India, Pakistan, and Africa fight one another for precious territory.

Revolutionary Terrorism ■ Some revolutionary terrorists are motivated by hatred every bit as bitter as the antagonisms just mentioned. Others simply want political change. It seems almost inevitable that as time goes on, revolutionary terrorists, such as those who bombed the World Trade Center in New York in 2001, will acquire more sophisticated weapons. Supposedly available on the black market are shoulder-fired, precision-guided surface-to-air missiles that can bring down jumbo jets. That we will one day face weapons of mass destruction—nuclear, chemical, and biological—is also likely. With advances in genetic engineering, the potential of using biological weapons haunts officials.

Repressive Terrorism ■ Despite the growing acceptance of democracy, repressive terrorism will continue, particularly in China, Central and South America, Africa, and the Middle East. Demands for more democratic government will likely be met with heavy-handed repression. Political repression, in turn, may stimulate resistance—and war will continue.

TABLE 14-4 The Global Arms Trade: Buying and Selling the Weapons of Death

THE TOP 10 SELLERS

RANK	SUPPLIER	1998–2005
1	United States	97,100
2	Russia	41,600
3	France	30,000
4	Germany	17,000
5	United Kingdom	14,900
6	China	9,100
7	Israel	7,900
8	Sweden	6,800
9	Spain	5,700
10	Italy	5,600

THE TOP 10 BUYERS

RANK	RECIPIENT	1998–2005
1	Saudi Arabia	50,100
2	China	14,300
3	Taiwan	13,900
4	United Arab Emirates	11,400
5	Egypt	10,300
6	India	9,500
7	Israel	9,200
8	South Korea	7,600
9	Pakistan	4,400
10	Malaysia	3,400

Source: By James M. Henslin. Based on Grimmett (2006, Tables 8C, 2I).

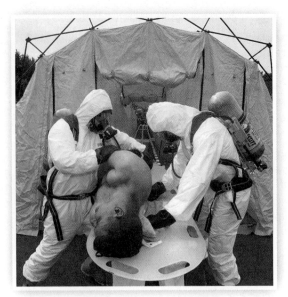

Authorities around the world are holding their collective breath, awaiting the next terrorist attack in some unexpected way at some unanticipated location. To test how prepared we are for such an attack, this man is being prepared for decontamination.

State-Sponsored Terrorism ■ It is likely that state-sponsored terrorism will decrease. We won't see a decrease in the number of rulers in weaker countries who would like to sponsor terrorists and send them against their enemies. Rather, investigative techniques have become more powerful, enabling state-sponsored sources to be more easily tracked and destroyed.

Russia ■ After seven decades of persecution in Russia, people gained freedom of speech, press, politics, education, religion, and the arts. Increased trade and cultural exchanges with the West reduced suspicions and hostilities on both sides. Russia's membership in NATO symbolizes hope for the entire world. Nothing about Russia is certain, however. The nation's arduous experiment with democracy may prove too threatening—bringing, as it has, inflation, poverty, the Russian Mafia, and criticism. With an arsenal of nuclear weapons hanging in the balance, dictatorship or anarchy could again threaten world peace.

SUMMARY AND REVIEW

1. The three essential conditions of war are a cultural tradition for *war,* an antagonistic situation, and a "spark" that sets off the war. Wars have occurred throughout history, but today's wars are much more destructive.

2. Symbolic interactionists analyze how symbols (perceptions) underlie war. The West and the Soviets saw each other as mortal enemies arming for deadly combat. Each felt obliged to arm itself, setting off a nuclear arms race. In this view, nuclear weapons are not intended to be used, but to symbolize a country's capacity to destroy an enemy.

3. Functionalists identify these functions of war: the extension of political boundaries, social integration, economic gain, social change, ideology, vengeance, military security, and credibility. The dysfunctions of war are defeat, dependence, and destruction. Apply these functions to the U.S. war on terrorism. How about the dysfunctions?

4. Conflict theorists identify four causes of war: competition for resources, a conflict of interests, a surplus of capital, and the dominance of a military machine.

5. Humans are no more peaceful today than in earlier times. The following do *not* diminish the chances of warfare: the type of government, the group's religion, prosperity, a common language or religion, shared political boundaries, or level of education.

6. Modern weapons are expensive and come at the cost of alternative expenditures. A major cost of war is *dehumanization.*

7. Both the military and business gain from producing, selling, and using weapons. The *military–industrial complex* is a powerful force in promoting war.

8. One of the more serious threats facing humanity is weapons of mass destruction: biological, chemical, and nuclear. Unless effective international controls are put into place, these weapons will proliferate, one day leading to vast destruction.

9. Today's nations are vulnerable to various forms of terrorism. *Political terrorism*—that is, the use of war to achieve political objectives—is of three types: *revolutionary terrorism,* waged by groups (or in rare cases, individuals) against the state; *repressive terrorism,* waged by the state against its own people; and *state-sponsored terrorism,* waged by one state against another. *Criminal terrorism* cuts across these types.

10. Disarmament, international law, and growing interlocking interests among the nations of the world could increase the chances for peace.

11. The future likely holds more terrorism and war. All-out nuclear war is unlikely because it means mutual destruction. Revolutionary terrorism will continue. This, in turn, will stimulate repressive terrorism. The ethnic antagonisms unleashed in the former Soviet Union will lead to more terrorism. Al-Qaeda and its supporters are likely to remain agents of terrorism. The Russian Mafia is likely to be brought under control, but political instabilities may bring hard-liners back into power.

KEY TERMS

Agent Orange, 525
Armaments, 519
Arms race, 503
Bilateral disarmament, 536
Binary chemical weapons, 526
Bourgeoisie, 511
Cold War, 503
Collateral damage, 518
Combat stress reaction
  (shell shock), 519
Criminal terrorism, 531
Dehumanization, 516
Disarmament, 520
G-8, 535
Global economy, 536
Imperialism, 511

Intercontinental Ballistic Missiles
  (ICBMs), 508
International Criminal Court
  (ICC), 536
Long-distance surgery, 509
Megaton, 520
Military–industrial
  complex, 519
Mutual assured destruction
  (MAD), 535
Mutual deterrence, 535
Narcoterrorism, 531
National security or homeland
  security, 512
NATO (North Atlantic Treaty
  Organization), 535

New World Order, 535
Pentagon capitalism, 519
Political terrorism, 526
Political theater, 527
Post-traumatic stress disorder
  (PTSD), 519
Proletariat, 511
Repressive terrorism, 530
Revolutionary terrorism, 526
Sarin gas, 530
State-sponsored terrorism, 531
Targeted killings, 534
Total war, 516
Unilateral disarmament, 536
War, 505

THINKING CRITICALLY ABOUT CHAPTER 14

1. Sociologist Nicholas Timasheff identified three essential conditions of war and seven "sparks" that can ignite these conditions into war (pages 505–506). Analyze a war that the United States has participated in. In this war, what were the essential conditions and the sparks?

2. Which of the three perspectives (symbolic interactionism, functionalism, or conflict theory) do you think best explains why countries go to war? Explain.

3. The functions of war are summarized on pages 508–510. Apply these functions to the U.S. war on terrorism. How about the dysfunctions?

4. Do you think that the United States would ever be able to trust the other nuclear countries of the world

if a worldwide treaty to destroy all nuclear weapons were signed? How would we be able to protect ourselves if just one country decided to secretly retain its weapons?

5. Do you think that the United States has the right to intervene in another country to protect our economic or political interests? Under what conditions is intervention justified? Explain.

6. Do you think that other countries have the right to intervene in the United States to protect their economic or political interests? Under what conditions is intervention justified? Explain.

7. Do you think that nuclear war is more or less likely now than it was during the Cold War? Explain.

MySocLab

What can you find in MySocLab? mysoclab ALLYN & BACON Where learning & the sociological imagination intersect. www.mysoclab.com

- Complete Ebook
- Practice Tests and Exams
- Multimedia Activities
- Mapping and Data Analysis Exercises

- Research and Writing Advice
- Interactive Social Surveys
- Sociology in the News

A

achieved status Positions or statuses that are acquired—through effort and accomplishment.

acid rain Rain with heavy concentrations of sulfuric and nitric acids.

addiction Dependence on a substance to make it through the day.

affinity group A form of voluntary segregation in which people of the same racial–ethnic group choose to associate with one another. Affinity groupings are natural and healthy.

ageism Discrimination against people on the basis of their age; this concept is not limited to older people.

Agent Orange A chemical defoliant used in Vietnam that caused birth defects and had other serious side effects.

agricompanies Large agricultural firms that operate farms of thousands of acres.

air pollution Environmental consequence of burning fossil fuels and other human activities—as well as of some natural events, like volcanic eruptions. Effects include eye, nose, and throat irritations; bronchitis, emphysema, and lung cancer.

alcoholic A person with severe alcohol-related problems.

alienation A sense of estrangement; often a consequence of urban life.

amotivational syndrome The tendency for people who smoke marijuana extensively to become apathetic, lose their concentration, and become unable to carry out long-range plans.

Anglo-conformity Requiring or expecting everyone in the United States to adopt the dominant culture, the customs inherited from English settlers.

anomie The feeling of being estranged, uprooted, unanchored, normless—not knowing what rules to apply to the situations one faces.

anti-retroviral drugs (ARVs) Medication that can slow down and even reverse the progression of HIV infection, delaying the onset of AIDS by 20 years or more.

apartheid The enforced segregation of people on the basis of their perceived race or ethnicity.

armaments Guidance systems, bombs, missiles, tanks, planes, guns, ships, submarines, and other weapons.

arms race The attempt by nations to match one another's war capabilities, usually referring to the buildup of weapons during Cold War standoff between the Soviet Union and the West.

ascribed status A position or role held as a result of one's birth.

assimilation The absorption of a minority group into the mainstream culture.

attention-deficit hyperactivity disorder A condition, as defined by the medical community, that causes children not to pay attention and to disrupt classroom activities. Also known as hyperactivity, attention-deficit disorder, and hyperkinesis. The social problems associated with it include possible overmedication of children and medicalization of everyday problems.

B

behavior modification Principle holding that if some behavior is rewarded ("reinforced"), it will occur again.

bilateral disarmament Situation in which two or more nations disarm simultaneously.

binary chemical weapons Shells or bombs in which two benign chemicals are kept in separate chambers in the weapon. Upon detonation, they mix, forming a lethal agent.

biodegradable Capable of disintegrating in outdoor weather, when exposed to microorganisms, as in a landfill.

biological poverty Material deprivation so severe that it affects one's health (biological functioning).

biotech society A future society in which bioengineering will take advantage of genetic knowledge to produce food and other materials.

black market The underground channeling of illegitimate goods or services.

bourgeoisie Marx's term for the group that uses resources to keep themselves in power and to exploit the less powerful; the capitalists.

bovine growth hormones (BGH) The hormones fed to cattle to make them grow faster; European Union scientists believe that they can cause cancer, although the U.S. Food and Drug Administration has deemed them to be safe.

breadwinner One whose earnings are the primary source of support for all dependents.

bureaucracy A highly structured hierarchy with specialized personnel.

C

capital punishment The decision by a jury in the second phase of a capital case that a convicted defendant should be put to death.

capitalism An economic system that is based on the private ownership of property and investing capital (wealth) to make a profit.

capitalist economy An economy based on the private ownership of the means of production, the pursuit of profit, and market competition. See *socialist economy.*

capitalists Owners of the means of production (land, factories, tools) who control the labor of workers.

carcinogen A cancer-causing substance.

carrying capacity Limits fixed by nature on how many people the land can support.

case study A type of research design that focuses on a single case. The case or subject of the study can be an individual, an event, or an organization, such as a church, hospital, or abortion clinic.

cesarean section (C-section) A form of surgery in which a baby is delivered through an incision made in the mother's abdomen and uterus.

Chicago school of sociology An approach to research that originated with the Department of Sociology at the University of Chicago in the 1920s. It emphasized participant observation, symbolic interactionism, and seeing things from an insider's point of view.

city Place of residence for a large number of people who live there permanently; city residents do not produce their own food.

civil disobedience Deliberate but peaceful refusal to obey laws that are considered unjust.

civil union (domestic partnership) A legal or personal relationship between two individuals who live together and share a common domestic life but are not joined in a traditional marriage.

cogeneration Production of electricity as a by-product of a business's ordinary operations.

cohabitation Situation in which a couple live together in a sexual relationship outside marriage.

Cold War A period of hostilities after World War II between the former Soviet Union and nations of the West.

collateral damage Inadvertent casualties and destruction inflicted on civilians in the course of military operations.

collective violence Another term for *group violence*.

combat stress reaction (shell shock) The emotional and physical reaction a soldier faces immediately after combat.

commodity riot Collective violence that involves extensive looting.

common sense The ideas common to a society or to some group within a society that people use to make sense out of their experiences.

communal riot Collective violence between the residents of two areas for control of a contested area.

community Identification people make with an area and with one another, sensing that they belong and that others care about what happens to them.

Community Right to Know Act of 1986 Legislation requiring that companies annually submit to a state agency and to local fire departments a list of the hazardous chemicals they use or manufacture.

compartmentalize To keep separate in one's mind feelings, attitudes, and behaviors that are incompatible with one another or that threaten the self-concept.

concentric zone theory A theory developed by Ernest Burgess suggesting that cities develop outward from their center, resulting in areas, or zones, that have specialized functions. The area closest to the central business district—the zone in transition—has the most severe urban problems.

condominium in-filling An urban policy in which condominiums for older people are built in vacant areas of their neighborhood, and the larger homes they vacate are taken over by younger families.

conflict theory A sociological theory that views society as a system in competition and conflict. Each group in society attempts to further its own interests, even at the expense of others. Those who gain power exploit people and resources for their own benefit. Social problems stem from exploitation and resistance to exploitation.

containment theory A functionalist theory that focuses on the pushes and pulls thought to cause people to commit criminal acts. Whether one commits a violent act depends on the relative strength of inner containment (controls within the individual) and on outer containment (controls outside the individual).

control group The group in an experiment that is not exposed to an experience (or independent variable).

control theory Another term for *containment theory*.

conversion therapy A form of psychotherapy aimed at changing gay, lesbian, and bisexual people's sexual orientations to heterosexual, or at eliminating or diminishing same-sex desires and behaviors.

corporate crime Crime committed either against a business, agency, or corporation (such as embezzlement and fraud) or on behalf of the corporation (such as price fixing, fraudulent advertising, antitrust violations, and corporate tax evasion).

corporate welfare Handouts given to corporations, usually in the form of tax breaks; may also be reductions in rent or bargain-priced real estate.

correlation Situation in which two or more things occur together; one does not necessarily cause the other.

Cosa Nostra The term by which East Coast mobsters refer to the Mafia. See *Mafia*.

craving An intense desire for a drug.

crime Any act prohibited by law. What constitutes crime varies from one social group to another.

crime rates The number of crimes per some unit of population, most commonly the number of crimes per 100,000 people.

criminal enterprise A group of individuals with an identified hierarchy engaged in significant criminal activity. These organizations often engage in multiple criminal activities and have extensive supporting networks.

criminal justice system The agencies that respond to crime, including the police, courts, jails, and prisons.

criminal sexual assault Category of crime that replaces the category *rape* in crime statistics; includes all sexual assaults, completed *and attempted*, aggravated and non-aggravated against all genders.

criminal terrorism People in organized crime using terrorism to achieve their objectives.

cultural feminism Branch of feminism which argues that there are biological differences between men and women and that women should celebrate these differences. Cultural feminists claim that women are inherently more kind and gentle.

cultural goal A goal held out as legitimate for the members of a society.

cultural means The approved ways of reaching cultural goals.

culture of poverty Characteristics of the poor—such as family violence, alcoholism, and low self-esteem—that help the poor stay poor.

culture of wealth Characteristics of the wealthy—such as social connections—that help keep them from falling down the social-class ladder.

D

death rate The number of deaths per 1,000 people.

defective discipline Excessive leniency or excessive control in raising children; often a problem in single-parent households.

Defense of Marriage Act Legislation that forbids federal government from treating same-sex marriages as legal; also allows states to refuse to recognize same-sex marriages that are legal in other states.

defensive medicine Medical procedures performed by physicians to protect themselves in case they are sued for malpractice.

deforestation Logging practices that are not counteracted by new plantings.

dehumanization Process of viewing and treating a person as an object not deserving the treatment ordinarily accorded humans.

deinstitutionalization The release of institutionalized people, especially psychiatric patients, from an institution for placement and care in the community.

delinquent subculture A subgroup in a culture whose members are oriented toward illegal acts.

demographic transition A four-stage process of population growth. The first is high birthrates and high death rates. The second is high birthrates and low death rates. The third is low birthrates and low death rates. The fourth stage is birthrates so low that a population shrinks.

demography The study of the size, composition, growth, and distribution of human populations.

dependency ratio In terms of Social Security, the number of workers compared with the number of recipients.

depersonalization Situation where a patient is treated as an inanimate object in medical settings.

designer animals Gene-spliced farm animals that produce more meat and milk.

deterrence The attempt to prevent crime by producing fear.

(to be) diced in During a girl's initiation into a gang, to be forced by the male gang members to have sex with one or several of them, according to whatever number appears on the roll of the dice.

differential association A symbolic interactionist theory that stresses how criminal behavior is learned. Applied to violence, it assumes that people learn to be violent in the same way that people learn to be cooperative.

dirty work The tasks in society that few people want.

disarmament A nation's reduction of its arms and weaponry.

discrimination The act of singling people out for unfair treatment.

disengagement theory The view that society prevents disruption by having the elderly disengage from (or give up) their positions of responsibility so that the younger generation can step into their shoes.

disinvestment A policy of withholding investments from an area.

diversion A response to crime that diverts offenders away from courts and jails to keep them out of the criminal justice system.

division of labor Situation in which people perform different sets of specialized tasks.

documents Written sources or records used as a source of information.

domestic partnership A legal or personal relationship between two individuals who live together and share a common domestic life but are not joined in a traditional marriage.

domiciliary care (home health care) Health care provided in the patient's home by health care professionals.

dominant group The group that has more power, privilege, and social status and that discriminates against minority groups.

drug A substance taken to change bodily functions, behavior, emotions, thinking, or consciousness.

drug abuse Use of drugs in such a way that they harm one's health, impair one's physical or mental functioning, or interfere with one's social life.

drug addiction Dependence on the regular consumption of a drug in order to make it through the day. Also known as drug dependence.

drug therapy The use of drugs such as tranquilizers and antidepressants to treat emotional problems.

dual labor market A pool of workers divided into two main segments: (1) regularly employed and better-paid workers and (2) low-paid temporary workers.

dysfunction Interference with the functioning of one part of a system or disruption of the stability (or equilibrium) of the entire system by one part of a social system.

E

ecofeminism Branch of feminism which states that patriarchy is bad for women and the environment and that women must play a role in preserving the environment.

ecology The study of the relationship between living things and their environment.

economic colonialism Situation in which one nation exploits another nation's resources.

economy A society's system of producing and distributing goods and services.

ecosystem The interconnection of life on the planet's outer surface; the web made up of organisms and their environment.

electroconvulsive therapy (ECT) A treatment for emotional problems in which a low-voltage electric current is passed through the brain. Also known as electroshock therapy.

endogamy The practice of marrying within one's ethnic–racial or other group.

enterprise zones An area where private enterprise (investment) is encouraged through reduction of taxes and government regulations.

environmental injustice Situation in which polluting industries (and other forms of pollution, such as dumping) are located in places inhabited primarily by the poor and minorities.

Escherichia coli (E. coli) A dangerous bacterium that comes from food or water contaminated by feces.

ethnocentrism A type of prejudice stating that my group's ways are right and your group's ways are wrong.

ethnophaulisms Derogatory labels that are applied to racial–ethnic groups.

euthanasia The hastening of another's death, through human action (often of a medication professional), usually out of a sense of mercy or compassion.

exogamy The practice of marrying outside of one's racial–ethnic or other group.

experiment A research design that divides a group into an *experimental group* (those who are exposed to some experience) and a *control group* (those who are not exposed to the experience). Measurements are taken before and after to determine the effects of the experience.

experimental group The group in an experiment that is exposed to an experience (or independent variable).

exponential growth curve Pattern in which, as growth doubles during approximately equal intervals, it accelerates in the latter stages.

extended family A family in which other relatives, such as the "older generation" or unmarried aunts and uncles, live with the parents and their children.

extremophiles Bacteria that eat our nuclear wastes, breaking them down into relatively harmless components.

F

false consciousness A failure to recognize the state of one's exploitation, having accepted the view of the dominant class.

family of orientation The family into which people are born and from which they receive their basic orientations to life.

family of procreation The family that is formed by marriage and that generally results in procreation, or the birth of children.

female infanticide Murder of female babies, usually because only sons are desired.

feminist theory A sociological theory that aims to transform society as well as study it; argues that women need to be made aware of their oppression in order to change it.

feminization of poverty Poverty clustered among women and children.

fetal alcohol syndrome A cluster of congenital problems caused by the alcohol consumption of the newborn's mother.

fetal narcotic syndrome A cluster of congenital problems caused by the narcotic use of the newborn's mother.

field study (or *participant observation*) A method of gathering information through direct observation of some setting.

food chain The arrangement of organisms according to food sources; each organism on the chain is a food source for the organism above it.

food politics The control of food production to control food prices: Paying farmers to leave their land fallow creates an artificial shortage that drives up grain prices.

food pollution (also called food contamination) The transmission of disease during food processing or the addition of chemicals to food to help process it, lengthen its shelf life, or enhance its appearance or taste.

forcible rape Nonconsensual or forced sexual relations.

fossil fuels Substances such as wood, coal, petroleum, and natural gas used as fuels that are derived from living things.

frustration–aggression A psychological theory that stresses that aggression is likely when a goal is blocked.

function The contribution of a part to its system; or people's actions that contribute to the equilibrium of a social system.

functionalism (also called functional analysis, functional theory, and the functional perspective) A sociological theory that views society as a system of interconnected parts, each part contributing in some way to the equilibrium or stability of the system. The contribution of each part is called its function. Functionalists view social problems as the failure of some part of the system to function correctly.

future shock The confusion or disorientation that accompanies rapid social change.

G

G-8 The association of the world's eight most powerful nations, whose goal is to work out a new balance of power.

Gemeinschaft A group of people characterized by bonds of intimacy combined with a sense of tradition and belonging. See also *Gesellschaft*.

gender How we express our "maleness" or "femaleness." Refers to socialization or culture. Commonly called femininity or masculinity. See also *sex*.

gender accomplishment Situation in which one's physical appearance and activities match the expectations of others, as determined by one's sex.

gender roles The behaviors and attitudes expected of males and females.

generalize To apply universally the findings that were learned from one setting, group, or sample.

generalized other Basically, the community or groups in general that people take into account as they consider a course of action.

genetically modified foods (GMF) Foods, either plant or animal, that contain genetic materials from another species or whose genes have been modified in a way that does not occur in nature.

genocide The systematic extermination of other people, usually racial–ethnic minorities.

gentrification A process in which the relatively affluent displace the poor and renovate their homes.

geothermal energy Heat from beneath the earth's crust.

Gesellschaft A group of people characterized by impersonality and the pursuit of self-interest. See also *Gemeinschaft*.

glass ceiling Invisible barrier that keeps women from rising to levels of authority within an organization.

global economy The economic interdependence of the nations of the world.

global warming An increase in the earth's temperature because of the *greenhouse effect*.

Green Party Political party formed by environmentalists.

green revolution The world's rapidly expanded food production during the 1950s and 1960s as the result of new fertilizers and high-yield strains of wheat and rice.

greenhouse effect The concentration of gases in the atmosphere that serve as a blanket around the earth, allowing sunlight to enter but inhibiting the release of heat.

group therapy A treatment for emotional problems in which members of the group talk about how they interact with others and help one another to cope with their problems.

group violence A number of people attacking others or destroying their property.

H

health maintenance organization (HMO) A comprehensive prepaid health care organization designed to reduce costs by minimizing unnecessary medical services.

heterosexuality The sexual preference for people of the opposite sex.

hillbilly heroin Slang term for oxydocone.

home health care Organized health services for people who are living at home with chronic or disabling diseases.

homosexual behavior Sexual relations between people of the same sex, regardless of their sexual preference.

homosexuality The sexual preference for people of one's own sex.

housing unit A place of residence normally occupied by a family, individual, or group of people. Examples are a detached house, a mobile home, an apartment, and a condominium.

hydrocarbons Materials whose essential elements are hydrogen and carbon; the backbone of motor fuels, lubricants, turpentine, and rubber.

I

iatrogenesis Accidental causation of illnesses or other health problems as a result of medical care; illnesses acquired in a hospital are iatrogenic.

illegitimate opportunity structure The opportunity, built into one's environment, to learn and participate in illegal activities.

imperialism The pursuit of unlimited geographic expansion.

incapacitation A response to crime that focuses on removing offenders from circulation.

incest Sexual relations between relatives, such as brothers and sisters or parents and their children.

incest taboo Prohibition of sexual relations among siblings or with children.

incompatibility In terms of marriage and family issues, inability to live together as husband and wife due to irreconcilable differences.

individual discrimination Discrimination by one person against another.

individual psychotherapy One-on-one treatment for emotional problems; a therapist listens and tries to guide the client toward a resolution of his or her problems.

individual violence One person attacking another.

infant mortality rate (IMR) The number of babies who die before one year of age, per 1,000 live births.

infanticide Killing infants shortly after birth, usually as a form of population control.

institutional discrimination Discrimination that is built into the social system.

institutionalized group violence Group violence that is carried out under the direction of legally constituted officials.

intercontinental ballistic missiles (ICBMs) Long-range nuclear weapon, part of the Cold War arsenal of the United States and Soviet Union.

interest groups Groups organized around different interests (from the dairy industry to animal rights).

internal colonialism A nation's exploitation of a minority group's labor within its own borders.

International Criminal Court (ICC) Court established in 2002 as a tribunal used to investigate and prosecute genocide, crimes against humanity, and war crimes.

interview A method of gathering information whereby the researcher asks questions. In a *structured* interview, specific questions are asked, whereas in an *unstructured* interview, people are simply encouraged to talk about their experiences, with the researcher making certain that specific areas are covered.

intimate partner violence A pattern of assaultive and coercive behaviors, including physical, sexual, and psychological abuse.

invasion–succession cycle One group moving into an area that is inhabited by a group that has different characteristics. Moving in represents the invasion; dominating the area, the succession.

J

job deconcentration An urban policy that moves jobs to specified areas adjacent to a city.

(to be) jumped in To be beat up by fellow gang members.

juvenile delinquency The legal term for behavior of children and adolescents that among adults would be considered criminal. In the United States, the maximum age limit varies, but is usually somewhere between 14 and 21 years.

L

labeling Stereotyping, or putting a tag on someone, and treating him or her accordingly.

labor force participation rate The proportion of the population 16 years and older that is in the labor force.

latent dysfunctions The unintended consequences of people's actions that disrupt the equilibrium or stability of a system or the adjustment of its parts.

latent functions The unintended consequences of people's actions that contribute to the equilibrium or stability of a social system or the functioning of its parts.

laterization The tendency of certain tropical soils to become laterite, a rocklike material, when they are exposed to the air.

lay referral network Friends, relatives, and acquaintances from whom sick people get suggestions about what to do about their illnesses. See also *professional referral network*.

lesbian A female homosexual.

liberal feminism Branch of feminism which claims that all people are created equal and deserve equal rights and which believes that oppression exists because of the way men and women are socialized.

life chances What one may expect to get out of life (because of the conditions of the group into which one is born).

Lo-Cal House Design for a house, developed at the University of Illinois, that can cut fuel bills by about two-thirds.

long-distance surgery Process by which a surgeon in the United States (with the aid of computers) can operate on a wounded soldier in some remote region of the world.

looking-glass self Cooley's idea that our self-images are dependent on what we think others think of us. We see ourselves, in other words, as a reflection in the eyes of others; hence the term *looking-glass self*.

M

machismo A strong or exaggerated sense of masculinity stressing attributes such as physical courage, virility, domination of women, and aggressiveness.

Mafia An organized crime group. The Sicilian-American version is bureaucratized with specialized personnel and departmentalization.

manifest function The consequences of people's actions that are *intended* to contribute to the adaptation, adjustment, or equilibrium of a system or its parts.

masochists People who receive sexual gratification by having pain inflicted on themselves.

mass murder The killing of four or more people at one time in one location.

mass poverty Poverty so widespread that most people are poor.

master trait A trait considered so important that it overrides an individual's other characteristics. One's sex is an example.

matriarchy A society in which women-as-a-group dominate men as a group.

medicalization of human problems Process by which the problems of daily life have come to be seen as a matter of sickness to be properly handled by the medical profession.

megalopolis Urban areas spilling onto one another, making them an interconnected region.

megaton The explosive power of 1 million tons of TNT.

melting pot The expectation that the European immigrants to the United States would "melt" or blend together—that is, interact, intermarry, and form a cultural and biological blend.

methadone maintenance A program for heroin addicts in which the narcotic methadone is substituted for the narcotic heroin.

methods (research methods or methodology) Ways of doing research.

militancy Seeking to dominate society (in Wirth's terminology).

military–industrial complex The merged interests of the military and business to pressure politicians to produce armaments.

minority group A group of people who, on the basis of physical or cultural characteristics, are singled out for unequal treatment and who regard themselves as objects of discrimination.

misogyny Hatred or strong prejudice against women.

modeling Copying another's behavior.

modernity Those things relating to recent times or the present.

moral entrepreneur A crusading reformer who wages battle to enforce his or her ideas of morality.

mutual assured destruction (MAD) Balance of power between two nations that comes to exist because neither country would survive a war; therefore, there is no benefit in attacking the other.

mutual deterrence Preventing a first strike by making the enemy fear that a massive retaliation would follow, which would also destroy them.

N

narcoterrorism A form of criminal terrorism that revolves around drugs. Some narcoterrorists use drug dealing to finance their ambitions.

narrative data Unstructured data that tell a story, which allows us to analyze people's thoughts and understand their perspectives.

national debt The total amount that a nation owes; computed by adding its annual deficits and subtracting its annual surpluses.

national security (or homeland security) The condition of the nation, in terms of threats from outside. One of the major goals of homeland security is to ensure the security of the nation.

New World Order Term applied to the new balance of power being attempted by the G-8 nations.

normal violence The amount of violence that a group usually has.

normalization (of deviance) Thinking of one's norm violations as normal; a second meaning is *mainstreaming*, when acts previously defined as deviant or criminal become accepted.

nuclear family A family that consists of a husband, wife, and their children.

nuclear fusion Process of combining atoms, as opposed to nuclear fission, which is the splitting of atoms.

O

objective condition A condition of society that can be measured or experienced. See also *subjective concern*.

observation A means of gathering information whereby the researcher directly observes what is occurring in a setting. In the *overt* form, people know they are being studied; in the *covert* form, they do not.

occupational disease Illness or injury resulting from long-term exposure to specific substances or from continuous or repetitive physical acts.

official poverty The level of income that a government recognizes as constituting poverty.

optimistic environmentalists Those environmentalists holding the viewpoint that groups of alarmist doomsayers have captured the attention of the media with their stress on negative findings, dire predictions, and exaggerations.

organized crime Organizations devoted to criminal activities.

organized group violence Violence that a group plans and carries out, although the group is not authorized to do so.

outrageous killing A killing that the public does not define as "usual" or "normal"—because of the method, the victim, or some other factor.

ozone shield A layer of the earth's upper stratosphere that screens out much of the sun's ultraviolet rays.

P

Pan-Indianism A movement that goes beyond tribal identification to work for the welfare of all Native Americans.

paper–pencil questionnaire The use of written questions to gather information. *Closed-ended* questions provide specific choices, while *open-ended* questions allow people to answer in their own words.

participant observation (or *field study*) A method of gathering information through direct observation of some setting.

patriarchal society A social system in which the father is the head of the family and men have authority over women and children.

patriarchy Rule by men, understood by feminists to be the root of gender inequality.

Pedophile Liberation Army (PLA) Group which argues that if people changed their attitudes about sleeping with children, incest would no longer be an issue.

pedophiles Adults who are sexually attracted to children.

Pentagon capitalism Interlocking relationship between Pentagon armaments and U.S. businesses.

perpetuity An unlimited time, generation after generation.

personal trouble An individual's own experience of a social problem.

personal violence Another term for *individual violence.*

pessimistic environmentalists Group of environmentalists who argue that we are facing energy and resource shortages so vast that they will shatter the foundations of the industrialized world.

pharm parties Parties that include illegal drugs or prescription drugs taken for recreational purposes.

pharmaceutical straitjacket Term that refers to drugs given in mental hospitals that make patients drowsy, lethargic, and easier to handle.

pharming From *pharm,* short for pharmaceuticals: collecting pills from the family medicine chest.

phenomenological sociology The study of the connection between human consciousness and social life, between social life and how people think and talk about it.

plea bargaining Pleading guilty to a lesser crime in exchange for a reduced sentence.

pluralism Situation where different racial–ethnic groups live peacefully with one another, while maintaining their distinctiveness and tolerating differences in others.

police discretion The decisions that the police make about whether to overlook or to enforce a law.

political crime Illegal acts that are intended to alter or to maintain a political system.

political machine A political organization that distributes municipal government jobs or favors. Essential to its operation is an informal, behind-the-scenes working arrangement that circumvents the official ways of handling a city's business.

political process A power struggle between interest groups and ideologies.

political terrorism Using the means of war to try to achieve political objectives. The four types are revolutionary terrorism, repressive terrorism, state-sponsored terrorism, and criminal terrorism.

political theater A name sometimes given to terrorism because terrorists seek to dramatically make public their "cause."

pollution The presence of substances that interfere with socially desired uses of air, water, land, or food.

Ponzi scheme a fraudulent investment operation that pays returns to investors out of the money paid by subsequent investors rather than from profit.

population In research, term for the group that one wishes to study.

population pyramid A graphic representation of a population, showing its age levels by sex.

population shrinkage The shrinking of a country's population because its birthrate and immigration are too low to replace the people who die or emigrate.

population transfer A minority relocating within a society or leaving the society altogether. In direct transfer, the minority is moved forcibly; in indirect transfer, the dominant group makes life so miserable for the members of a minority group that they "choose" to leave.

pornography Writings, pictures, or objects of a sexual nature that are considered filthy.

post-traumatic stress disorder (PTSD) The long-term emotional distress a soldier experiences after combat; also refers to other forms of long-term emotional distress after other kinds of trauma—such as rape, terrorist attacks, etc.

poverty line The official measure of poverty; originally calculated in the 1930s as 3 times a low-cost food budget and since then adjusted for inflation.

power The capacity of some persons to achieve goals in the face of opposition.

power elite A small group of wealthy, powerful people who are said to make the major economic and political decisions in the United States.

precipitating incident An incident that triggers something else, such as a riot.

prejudice An attitude whereby one prejudges others, usually negatively.

primary prevention Measures that keep a disease from occurring, such as vaccinations. See also *secondary prevention, tertiary prevention.*

professional criminals People who earn their living from crime.

professional referral network In the health care system, the physician's frame of reference—the network of other health care professionals who emphasize the science of medicine rather than connection with the patient.

progressive tax Tax rates that increase with income.

proletariat Marx's term for the workers, those whose labor is exploited.

pronatalist policies Social policies that encourage women to bear children.

property crime Obtaining or destroying property illegally; includes burglary, theft, robbery, vandalism, arson, and fencing.

prostitution The renting of one's body for sexual purposes.

psychoanalysis A treatment for emotional problems created by Sigmund Freud; the goal is to uncover subconscious motives, fantasies, and fears by having patients speak about whatever comes to mind.

psychological dependence The craving for a drug even though there no longer is a physical dependence on that drug.

pushouts Children who have been shoved out of the family home by parents who no longer want them.

R

race Identification of a group people by the inherited physical characteristics that distinguish it; a problematic term because it has traditionally been used in a way that has no scientific basis; race is a social construct.

race riot Racial–ethnic groups directing extreme violence against one another in incidents precipitated by some event, usually involving prejudice or a hate crime.

racial–ethnic group A group of people who identify with one another on the basis of their ancestry and cultural heritage. Also called an ethnic group.

racial–ethnic stratification Society divided along racial–ethnic lines; the unequal distribution of resources on the basis of race–ethnicity.

radical feminism Branch of feminism which believes that society must be changed at its core in order to dissolve patriarchy; radical feminists want to free men and women of rigid gender roles by raging war against patriarchy.

random sample A sample that gives everyone in the group being studied an equal chance of being included in the research.

rate of violence The number of violent acts per some unit of measurement of population, usually per 100,000 people.

real income Income in constant dollars; that is, adjusted for inflation.

recidivism rate The percentage of people released from prison who are rearrested.

redlining The refusal to service a designated area, such as a bank's not offering mortgages or an insurance company not writing insurance in a neighborhood that is primarily Black or Hispanic.

regional restratification A shift in the population and relative wealth and power of the regions that make up a country. The current shift in the United States is toward the sunbelt.

rehabilitation A response to crime that is designed to resocialize or reform offenders, so that they can become law-abiding citizens.

relative poverty Deprivation as measured by the standards of one's society and culture. On a personal level, people think of themselves as poor or not poor on the basis of their reference groups.

remarriage The act of marrying again.

repressive terrorism Terrorism directed by a government against its own citizens.

reproductive labor That labor performed behind the scenes allowing the breadwinner husband to flourish in public.

research design The methods that sociologists use to study social life. For social problems, these are *case studies, experiments, field studies,* and *surveys*.

reserve labor force The unemployed, who can be put to work during periods of labor strife or economic expansion and laid off when these conditions change. Also called reserve labor army.

residual poverty Pockets of poverty in an otherwise affluent society.

resource recovery plants Garbage-burning plants that generate power; utilities are required by the federal government to buy the power, which means that the plants partially pay for themselves.

restitution A form of retribution by which offenders compensate their victims.

retribution A response to crime based on upholding moral values and restoring the moral balance upset by a criminal act. Making thieves repay what they stole is an example.

revolutionary terrorism Terrorism used in the attempt to bring about change in the political structure.

riot Violent crowd behavior aimed against people and property.

rising expectations The belief that better conditions will come soon. Rising expectations develop when institutional barriers begin to fall; if conditions do not change immediately, frustration builds, sometimes resulting in group violence.

road rage Violent behavior by a driver of an automobile.

role ambivalence Feeling indecisive, or both positive and negative, about one's role.

RU486 (Mifeprex) An oral drug, used both as "a morning-after pill"/emergency contraceptive to prevent attachment of a fertilized ovum to the uterine wall and as an abortion agent to terminate pregnancy in women up to the 7th week of pregnancy.

S

sadists People who receive sexual gratification by inflicting pain on others.

safety valve theory (of pornography) The view that pornography protects people by providing a private release of sexual fantasies.

same-sex marriage (SSM) A term for a governmentally, socially, or religiously recognized marriage in which two people of the same sex live together as a family.

sample A relatively small number of people who are intended to represent the larger group from which it is selected.

Sarbanes-Oxley Act Federal legislation that holds executives responsible for the financial goings-on at their companies.

sarin gas A chemical weapon that can be manufactured from chemicals used in pesticides bought at a local hardware store.

Saturday night special Slang used in the United States and Canada for any inexpensive handgun.

scaled-back society Reduction of industrial output and standard of living. Prerequisite to a *steady-state society*.

Scholastic Assessment Tests (SATs) Standardized tests first administered in 1926; women as a group never score higher than men as a group on the mathematical portion of the test, bringing up issues of gender bias versus innate abilities.

secession A minority withdrawing from a society to establish its own nation.

second shift Term applied to the fact that most wives, after returning home from an 8-hour shift of work-for-wages, put in more hours of work, cooking, cleaning, and rearing children.

secondary prevention Early detection and precautions that keep a disease from getting worse.

segregation Confining an activity to specified geographical areas.

selective perception Seeing only certain things, while being blind to others.

self-fulfilling prophecy A prediction that directly or indirectly causes itself to become true.

serial murder Killing several victims in three or more separate events.

sex The physical identity of a person as male or female. Refers to biology. See also *gender*.

sex tourism Travel to another country to engage in sexual intercourse with a prostitute.

sex-typing Associating something with one sex or the other. "Men's work" and "women's work" are examples of sex-typing of occupations.

sexism The belief that one sex is innately superior to the other and the discrimination that supports such a belief.

Sexual harassment Unwelcome sexual advances, requests for sexual favors and other verbal or physical conduct of a sexual nature when part of an employment situation.

sexual revolution Drastic relaxation in general standards of sexual behavior, starting in the 1960s.

short-term directive therapy A treatment for emotional problems in which a therapist actively tries to solve the client's problems.

situational group violence Spontaneous group violence, such as a brawl among hockey players.

situational homosexual behavior Homosexual behavior by someone who has a heterosexual identity; often occurs in same-sex settings such as prisons or boarding schools.

snowbelt The northern region of the United States surrounding the Great Lakes.

social class The hierarchical distinctions between individuals or groups in society.

social construction of reality The attempt to make sense of life by giving meaning to one's experiences.

social inequality The unequal distribution of wealth, income, power, and other opportunities.

social institution Enduring features of social life, such as education, the family, the justice system.

social location An individual's position within the greater social system.

social problem Some aspect of society that large numbers of people are concerned about and would like changed.

socialist economy An economy based on the public ownership of the means of production, central planning, and the distribution of goods without a profit motive. See *capitalist economy.*

socialist feminism Branch of feminism that believes there is a direct link between class structure and the oppression of women.

sociological imagination (or sociological perspective) A framework of thought that looks at the broad social context that shapes people's experiences. This perspective helps people transcend personal values and emotions in order to see the larger picture that affects their situation.

sociological perspective Another term for *sociological imagination.*

sociology The systematic and objective study of human society.

solar envelope A second set of walls around a house that provide a "skin" to trap and distribute the sun's heat.

soldier rape Rape committed by a soldier on a country's inhabitants during wartime—also qualifies as political rape.

split-labor market Workers who are split along lines of race–ethnicity or gender; those in charge try to take advantage of this split to keep wages low by sowing distrust.

state-sponsored terrorism A country supporting terrorism against another nation.

status crimes Crimes that are so defined because of someone's status: for a juvenile, a status crime means conduct "illegal only for children," such as truancy or breaking curfew.

statutory rape Consensual sexual relations in which one person is under the legal age of consent.

steady-state society A society in which the economy does not grow or shrink.

stereotype A belief that consists of unfounded generalizations of what people are like.

strain theory A functionalist theory that stresses how people adapt when their access to the cultural means to reach cultural goals is blocked.

strip mining Form of mining that takes place where coal lies so close to the surface that it can be retrieved by stripping away the soil.

structural inequality Inequality that is built into social institutions.

structure The interrelations between the parts or subunits of society or some other social system.

structured interview Interviews that use closed-ended questions.

subcultural theory A symbolic interactionist theory that stresses a group's orientations: its distinctive norms, attitudes, values, beliefs, and behaviors.

subjective concern The concern or distress that people feel about some aspect of society.

suburban sprawl The disappearance of open areas as a suburb expands into the countryside.

suffragists Advocates in the 19th and early 20th centuries of the extension of political voting rights to women.

sunbelt The southern and southwestern regions of the United States, known for their warm climate.

supergangs Especially violent gangs whose members not only steal but also kill.

surplus value of labor Profit (extra amount, or surplus value) that results when an item sells for more than it costs to produce; the surplus value exists because of the value of the labor that went into producing the item.

survey Research that focuses on a sample of respondents from a target population. The sample is intended to represent the larger group from which it is selected.

symbiosis A mutually beneficial relationship.

symbolic interactionism A sociological theory that views society as consisting of the patterns common to a group of people. Social problems are not considered objective conditions but, rather, the issues that people have decided to call social problems.

symbols Items of social life to which we give meaning and that we then use to communicate with one another. Symbols include signs, gestures, words, and even our posture and appearance.

synergistic (literally, "working together") Applied to chemicals, it refers to their interactions.

synfuels Alternative fuels developed from garbage, sawdust, and other waste.

T

taking the role of the other Putting oneself in someone else's shoes to try to see things as that person sees them.

talk therapy Treatments of emotional problems that are based on "talking" (psychotherapy, group therapy, etc.).

targeted killings Assassinations undertaken by the CIA when it determines that a certain individual is responsible for a terrorist attack or is planning such an act.

techniques of neutralization Ways that people justify their norm-breaking activities, making their behaviors more acceptable to themselves and others.

temple prostitution Prostitution that takes place in a temple, as a type of worship.

tertiary prevention Medical care of an existing disease aimed at preventing further damage.

testosterone A male hormone produced by the testes that encourages the development of male sexual characteristics.

theory An explanation of how two or more concepts, such as age and suicide, are related to one another.

thermal inversion A layer of cold air sealing in a lower layer of warm air.

torches Professional arsonists who are seldom apprehended because arson often destroys the evidence of the crime.

total war No-holds-barred warfare.

trail mix Part of the drug culture: bowls and baggies of random pills.

trigger theory (of pornography) The view that pornography triggers sexual offenses by stimulating people's sexual appetite.

two-tier system of medical care A medical delivery system in which the poor receive one type of medical care and the affluent another.

U

underclass Alienated people who live primarily in the inner cities; they have little education and high rates of unemployment, female-headed families, welfare dependency, violent crimes, drug abuse, disease, births to single women, and murder.

uniform sentencing Imposing the same sentence on everyone who is convicted of the same crime.

unilateral disarmament One nation disarming itself. When used to refer to a social policy, it generally refers to one nation's taking some dramatic step in disarmament in order to encourage a similar step by the enemy.

unstructured interview Interviews that use open-ended questions.

urban crisis The interrelated problems of governing and financing cities, including their poverty, violence, crime, and deterioration of services.

urban homesteading An urban policy whereby a city sells at a token price tax-foreclosed property to an individual who agrees to bring it into compliance with city codes and to live in it for a designated period of time.

urban sprawl The expansion of a city onto adjacent farmland.

urbanization The social process whereby cities grow.

V

value A shared (or individual) belief about whether something is good or bad.

Verstehen Seeing things as others see them, including—and perhaps especially—behavior that appears irrational to us; Max Weber's term.

victimless crime An illegal act to which the participants consent.

violence The use of physical force to injure people or to destroy their property.

violent crimes A classification used by the FBI and other police to refer to murder, forcible rape, robbery, and aggravated assault.

W

war Violent armed conflict between countries.

wealth Savings, property, investments, income, and other economic assets.

welfare queen A woman who collects welfare checks or excess amounts of government aid; a derogatory label placed on poor mothers, often carrying racial connotations.

welfare wall The disincentive to work when the income from working is not much more than the income from welfare.

windrows Rows of trees between the fields that farmers had planted to break the wind and keep topsoil from blowing away.

withdrawal The distress that people feel when they don't take a drug to which they are addicted.

working poor Those who maintain regular employment but remain in relative poverty due to low levels of pay.

Z

zero population growth Lack of population growth because women bear only enough children to replace those who die.

All new references are printed in blue.

AA Fact File. (2004). *Alcoholics Anonymous.* Retrieved from http://www.aa.org/pdf/products/m-24_aafactfile.pdf

Abowitz, R. (2008, July 21). Trying to find Heidi Fleiss. *Los Angeles Times.* Retrieved from http://www.latimes. com

Acharyya, S., & Zhang, H. (2003). Assessing sex differences on treatment effectiveness from the Drug Abuse Treatment Outcome Study. *American Journal of Drug and Alcohol Abuse, 29*(2), 415–444.

Achenbaum, W. A. (1978). *Old age in the new land: The American experience since 1970.* Baltimore: Johns Hopkins University Press.

Acid rain called peril to Ontario lakes. (2006, November 10). *New York Times.* Retrieved from http://www.nytimes.com

Aizenman, N. C. (2005, July 15). Opium trade not easily uprooted, Afghanistan finds. *Washington Post.* Retrieved from http://www.washingtonpost.com

Alihan, M. A. (1938). *Social ecology.* New York: Columbia University Press.

Allen, C. L. (1988, December 8). Anti-abortion movement's anti-establishment face. *Wall Street Journal,* p. A14.

Allen, F. E. (1991, May 28). Environment. *Wall Street Journal.*

Allen, H. (2008, October 31). In shadow of troubled year, Mashuntuckets to choose two tribal councilors. *New London Day.* Retrieved from http://www.theday.com

Allman, W. F. (1988, April 11). A laboratory of human conflict. *U.S. News & World Report,* 57–58.

Allport, G. (1954). *The nature of prejudice.* Reading, MA: Addison-Wesley.

Alvarez, L. (2007, February 14). Army giving more waivers in recruiting. *New York Times.* Retrieved from http://www.nytimes.com

Amatenstein, S. (2007). *Reinventing Romance: Single Women, Married Men.* Retrieved April 30, 2008. http://www.more.com/ sex-dating/dating/reinventing-romance/ single-women-married-men

American Lung Association. (2003, November). *Search Lung USA.*

American Psychiatric Association. (2000). Therapies focused on attempts to change *sexual orientation (reparative or conversion therapies): Position statement.* Retrieved from http://www.psych .org/Departments/EDU/Library/APAOfficialDocumentsandRela ted/PositionStatements/200001.aspx

American Savings Education Council. (1999). *Personal savings rate, 1929–1998.* Online.

Americans for Insurance Reform. (2007). *New data confirms that doctors were price-gouged by the insurance industry during this decade.* Retrieved from http://www.insurance-reform.org/pr/070328.html

Amott, T., & Matthaei, J. (1991). *Race, gender, and work: A multicultural economic history of women in the United States.* Boston: South End.

Andersen, M. L. (1988). *Thinking about women: Sociological perspectives on sex and gender.* New York: Macmillan.

Anderson, E. (1978). *A place on the corner.* Chicago: University of Chicago Press.

Anderson, E. (1990). *Streetwise: Race, class, and change in an urban community.* Chicago: University of Chicago Press.

Anderson, E. (2006). Streetwise. In J. M. Henslin (Ed.), *Society: Readings to accompany sociology: A down-to-earth approach, core concepts* (pp. 54–63). Boston: Allyn & Bacon.

Anderson, J. (1995, March 24). Chicago's public housing official tries to thwart gangs. *Alton Telegraph,* A6.

Anderson, J., & Moller, J. (1998, January). Gorton under Republican fire for Indian Wars. *Washington Merry-Go-Round* syndicated column.

Anderson, R. T. (1965, November). From Mafia to Cosa Nostra. *American Journal of Sociology, 71,* 302–310.

Anslinger, H. J., & Cooper, C. R. (1937, July). Marijuana: Assassin of youth. *American Magazine.*

Anthrax vaccination immunization program. (2004, November 14). Online.

Aposporos, D. (2004, July). Hunting for glory with the Barabaig of Tanzania. *National Geographic.*

Arías, J. (1993, January 2). La Junta rehabilita en Grenada casas que deberá tirar por ruina. *El Pais,*(1).

Aries, P. (1962). *Centuries of childhood: A social history of family life* (Robert Baldick, Trans.). New York: Vintage.

Arlacchi, P. (1980). *Mafia, peasants and great estates: Society in traditional Calabria.* Cambridge: Cambridge University Press.

Armitage, R. L. (1989, February 7). Red army retreat doesn't signal end of U.S. obligation. *Wall Street Journal,* p. A20.

Arnason, V., Bartley, D., Garcia, S., Haraldsson, R. H., Sveinbjornsson, D., & Watanabe, H. (2005). *Ethical issues in fisheries.* Rome: Food and Agriculture Organization of the United Nations.

Ashley, R. (1975). *Cocaine: Its history, uses, and effects.* New York: St. Martin's.

Ashley, S. (2002). Divide and vitrify. *Scientific American, 286*(6), 17–19.

Ashworth, W. (1987, November–December). The great and fragile lakes. *Sierra,* 42–50.

Associated Press. (1995, February 12). *Father's persistence pays off.*

Aston, G., & Foubister, V. (1998). MD and physician extender turf war. *American Medical News, 41*(27), 9–10.

Atchley, R. C. (1975, April). Dimensions of widowhood in later life. *Gerontologist, 15,* 176–178.

Athens, L. H. (1980). *Violent criminal acts and actors: A symbolic interactionist study.* Boston: Routledge.

Auerbach, J. D. (1990, December). Employer-supported child care as a women-responsive policy. *Journal of Family Issues, 11*(4), 384–400.

AVERT. (2008). *AIDS orphans.* Retrieved from http://www.avert.org/ aidsorphans.htm

Bagne, P. (1992). High-tech breeding. In J. M. Henslin (Ed.), *Marriage and family in a changing society,* (4th ed.; pp. 226–234). New York: Free Press.

Bai, M. (1999, May 3). Anatomy of a massacre. *Newsweek,* pp. 25–31.

Bailey, J. (1992, June 2). Economics of trash shift as cities learn dumps aren't so full. *Wall Street Journal,* pp. A1, A7.

Baldo, M. H. (2008). Caesarean section in countries of the Eastern Mediterranean region. *La Revue de Santé de la Méditerranée orientale, 14*(2).

Ball, D., & O'Connell, V. (2006, February 15). As young women drink more, alcohol sales, concerns rise. *New York Times.* Retrieved from http://www.nytimes.com

Ball, J. (2008, April 12). U.N. effort to curtail emissions in turmoil. *Wall Street Journal.* Retrieved from http://www.online.wsj.com

Bandura, A., & Walters, R. H. (1963). *Social learning and personality development.* New York: Holt.

Bansal, R., John, S. & Ling, P. M. (2005). Cigarette advertising in Mumbai, India: Targeting different socioeconomic groups, women, and youth. *Tobacco Control, 14,* 201–206.

Barber, J. A., Jr. (1972). The military-industrial complex. In S. E. Ambrose & J. A. Barber, Jr. (Eds.), *The military and American society: Essays and readings,* New York: Free Press.

Bardwick, J. M. (1971). *Psychology of women: A study of bio-cultural conflicts.* New York: Harper & Row.

Barkley, R. A. (2006). *Attention-deficit hyperactivity disorder: A handbook for diagnosis and treatment* (3rd ed.). New York: Guilford.

Barnes, E., & Shebar, W. (1987, December). Quitting the mafia. *Life,* 108–112.

Baron, L. (1987, July-August). Immoral, inviolate or inconclusive? *Society,* 6–12.

Barringer, F. (2005, August 12). Growth stirs a battle to draw more water from the Great Lakes. *New York Times.* Retrieved from http://www.nytimes.com

Barron, J. (2008, February 7). Medical examiner rules Ledger's death accidental. *New York Times.* Retrieved from http://www.nytimes.com

Bart, P. B., & O'Brien, P. H. (1984). How the women stopped their rapes. *Signs, 10.*

Bart, P. B., & O'Brien, P. H. (1985). *Stopping rape: Successful survival strategies.* New York: Pergamon.

Bartlett, D. L., & Steele, J. B. (1998, November 23). Paying a price for polluters. *Time,* pp. 72–80.

Bartoi, M. G., & Kinder, B. N. (1998). Effects of child and adult sexual abuse on adult sexuality. *Journal of Sex & Marital Therapy, 24,* 75–90.

Batalova, J. A., & Cohen, P. N. (2002, August). Premarital cohabitation and housework: Couples in cross-national perspective. *Journal of Marriage and Family, 64,* 743–755.

Baumann, M. (2006, September 14). U.S. Senate Historical Office. Personal communication.

Bayles, F. (2004, May 17). Mass. to allow gay marriage Monday. *USA Today.* Retrieved from http://www.usatoday.com

Beals, R. L., & Hoijer, H. (1965). *An introduction to anthropology* (3rd ed.) New York: Macmillan.

Beasley, B., & Standley, T. C. (2002). Shirts vs. skins: Clothing as an indicator of gender role stereotyping in video games. *Mass Communication and Society, 5*(3), 279–293.

Becker, H. S. (1966). Editor's introduction. In H. S. Becker (Ed.), *Social Problems: A Modern Approach* (pp. 1–31). New York: Wiley.

Becker, H. S. (1967, June). History, culture, and subjective experience: An exploration of the social bases of drug induced experiences. *Journal of Health and Social Behavior, 7,* 163–176.

Beckett, K. (2005). Choosing cesarean: Feminism and the politics of childbirth in the United States. *Feminist Theory, 6*(3), 251–275.

Beddoe, C., Hall, C. M., & Ryan, C. (2001). *The incidence of sexual exploitation of children in tourism.* Madrid: World Tourism Organization.

Beech, H. (2004, July 26-August 2). Unhappy returns. *Time.*

Beeghley, L. (2005). *The structure of social stratification in the United States* (4th ed.). Boston: Allyn & Bacon.

Bell, D. (1960). *The end of ideology.* New York: Free Press.

Bell, D. A. (1991). An American success story: The triumph of Asian-Americans. In L. Cargan & J. H. Ballantine (Eds.), *Sociological footprints: Introductory readings in sociology* (5th ed.; pp. 308–316). Belmont, CA: Wadsworth.

Bell, J. (2006, March 22). Aspirin may help women cut heart attack risk, study says. *Sun-Sentinel.*

Belluck, P. (1998, October 4). Forget prisons: Americans cry out for the pillory. *New York Times.* Retrieved from http://www.nytimes.com

Benenson, C., & Geib-Cole. (2008). *Aggressive Behavior.* Retrieved April 24, 2009, from Aggressive Behavior: http://faculty.mckendree.edu/scholars/winter2009/marin.htm

Bengtson, V. L., Rosenthal, C. & Burton, L. (1990). Families and aging: Diversity and heterogeneity. In R. H. Binstock & L. K. George (Eds.), *Handbook of aging and the social sciences* (3rd ed.; pp. 263–287). San Diego: Academic Press.

Bennice, J. A., & Resick, P. A. (2003, July). Marital rape: History, research, and practice. *Trauma, Violence, and Abuse, 4*(3), 228–246.

Benning, L. (2005). *Granny-nanny: A guide for grandparents who provide full, part-time, or temporary daycare for their grandchildren.* Cleveland: Cleveland Clinic Press.

Benson, M. L. (1985, November). Denying the guilty mind: Accounting for involvement in white-collar crime. *Criminology, 23,* 585–607.

Berger, P. L. (1963). *Invitation to sociology.* New York: Doubleday.

Bergström, H. (1992, July). Pressures behind the Swedish health reforms. *Viewpoint Sweden, 12,* 1–5.

Bernard, J. (1971). *Women and the public interest: An essay on policy and protest.* Chicago: Aldine-Atherton.

Bernard, V. W., Ottenberg, P., & Redl, F. (1971). Dehumanization: A composite psychological defense in relation to modern war. In R. Perucci & M. Pilisuk (Eds.), *The triple revolution emerging: Social problems in depth* (pp. 17–34). Boston: Little, Brown.

Bernhardt, E. M., & Goldscheider, F. K. (2001, August). Men, resources, and family living: The determination of union and parental status in the United States and Sweden. *Journal of Marriage and the Family, 63*(3), 793–803.

Bernstein, E. (2001). The meaning of the purchase: Desire, demand, and the commerce of sex. *Ethnography, 2*(3), 389–420.

Bhattacharya, S. (2005, February 14). Multi-drug-resistant HIV strain raises alarm. *New Scientist.* Retrieved from http://www.newscientist.com.

Bianchi, S. M., Milkie, M. A., Sayer, L. C., & Robinson, J. P. (2000, September). Is anyone doing the housework? Trends in the gender division of household labor. *Social Forces, 79*(1), 191–228.

Biddle, R. (2001, April 1). The ghost of energy crisis past. *Reason.*

Biederman, J. (2003). Pharmacotherapy for attention-deficit/hyperactivity disorder (ADHD) decreases the risk for substance abuse: Findings from a longitudinal follow-up of youths with and without ADHD. *Journal of Clinical Psychiatry, 64*(Suppl. 11), 3–8.

Biello, D. (2006, April 5). Vegetable compounds combat cancer. *Scientific American.* Retrieved from http://www.sciam.com

Bilmes, L., & Stiglitz, J. E. (2006, January). *The economic costs of the Iraq War: An appraisal three years after the beginning of the conflict.* Paper presented at the ASSA meetings.

Births, marriages, and divorce. (2004, February 13). National Center for Health Statistics. *National Vital Statistics, 52*(3), Table A.

Bishop, J. E., & Wells, K. (1989, March 24). Two scientists claim breakthrough in quest for fusion energy. *Wall Street Journal,* pp. A1, A5.

Blackstone, Sir W. (1899). *Commentaries on the Laws of England* (4th ed.) Thomas M. Cooley (Ed.). Chicago: Callaghan.

Blau, F. D. (1975). Women in the labor force: An overview. In Jo Freeman (Ed.), *Women: A Feminist Perspective* (pp. 211–226). Palo Alto, CA: Mayfield.

Block, R., & Skogan, W. G. (1982). Resistance and outcome in robbery and rape: Nonfatal, stranger to stranger violence. *Mimeo.*

Blok, A. (1974). *The Mafia of a Sicilian village: A study of violent peasant entrepreneurs.* New York: Harper Torchbooks.

Blum, R. H., Blum, Eva, & Garfield, E. (1976). *Drug education: Results and recommendations.* Lexington, MA: Heath.

Blum, R. H., et al. (1969). *Drugs I, Society and drugs: Social and cultural observations.* San Francisco: Jossey-Bass.

Blumberg, A. S. (1967). The practice of law as confidence game: Organizational cooptation of a profession. *Law and Social Review, 1,* 15–39.

Blumemthal, R. (1981, June 8). Polluted Midwest rain is killing New York lakes. *Alton Telegraph.*

Blumer, H. (1971). Social problems as collective behaviour. *Social Problems, 18*(3), 298.

Blumstein, A., et al. (1988). *Criminal careers and "career criminals.* Washington, DC: National Academy Press.

Bogo, J. (2001, March 1). Consider the source: How clean is your bottled water? *E/The Environmental Magazine.*

Bohn, K. (2008, August 8). Suspect took leave to mail anthrax letters. *CNN.* Retrieved from http://www.cnn.com

Boot, M. (1998, March 4). Your money or your life? That depends. *Wall Street Journal,* p. A18.

Booth, A, & Dabbs, J. M., Jr. (1993, December). Testosterone and men's marriages. *Social Forces, 72*(2), 463–477.

Boston, G. D., O'Brien, K., & Palumbo, J. (1977, March). *Terrorism: A selected bibliography* (2nd ed.) Washington, DC: National Institute of Law Enforcement and Criminal Justice.

Bottcher, J., & Ezell, M. E. (2005, August). Examining the effectiveness of boot camps: A randomized experiment with a long-term follow up. *Journal of Research in Crime and Delinquency, 42*(3), 309–332.

Bowen, C. (1972). Donora, Pennsylvania. In R. R. Campbell & J. L. Wade (Eds.), *Society and environment: The coming collision* (pp. 163–168). Boston: Allyn & Bacon.

Brace, C. L. (1880). *The dangerous classes of New York and twenty years' work among them* (3rd ed.). New York: Wynkoop & Hallenbeck.

Bramlett, M. D., & Mosher, W. D. (2002, July). Cohabitation, marriage, divorce, and remarriage in the United States. Hyattsville, Md.: National Center for Health Statistics, *Vital Health Statistics,* Series 23, Number 22.

Brannigan, A. (1987, July-August). Is obscenity criminogenic? *Society,* 12–19.

Brecher, E. M., & the Editors of Consumer Reports. (1972). *Licit and illicit drugs.* Boston: Little, Brown.

Bremer, L. P. III. (1988, May). Terrorism: Myths and reality. *Department of State Bulletin, 63.*

Brewer, D. D., Potterat, J. J., Garrett, S. B., Muth, S. Q., Roberts, J. M., Kasprzyk, D., Montano, D. E., & Darrow, W. W. (2000, October 24). Prostitution and the sex discrepancy in reported number of sex partners. *Proceedings of the National Academy of Sciences, 97,* 22, 12385–12388.

Bridges, G. S., & Stein, Sara. (1998, August). Racial disparities in official assessments of juvenile offenders: Attributional stereotypes as mediating mechanisms. *American Sociological Review, 63,* 554–570.

Broad, W. J. (2006a, November 7). In ancient fossils, seeds of a new debate on warming. *New York Times.* Retrieved from http://www.nytimes.com

Broad, W. J. (2006b, November 3). U.S. web site is said to reveal a nuclear primer. *New York Times.* Retrieved from http://www.nytimes.com

Broad, W. J., & Miller, J. (1998, August 7). Rocky start for U.S. plan to stockpile vaccines to fight germ warfare. *New York Times.* Retrieved from http://www.nytimes.com

Brockerhoff, M. P. (2000, September). An urbanizing world. *Population Bulletin, 55*(3), 1–44.

Brockman, J. (2006, April 5). Child sex as Internet fare, through eyes of a victim. *New York Times.* Retrieved from http://www.nytimes.com

Broder, M. S., Kanouse, D. E., Mittman, B. S., & Bernstein, S. J. (2000 February). The appropriateness of recommendations for hysterectomy. *Obstetrics and Gynecology, 95,* 199–205.

Brody, E. M. (1978, July). The aging of the family. *Annals of the American Academy of Political and Social Science, 438,* 13–27.

Brody, J. E. (1976, November 5). 1,100 tested in Michigan for effects of toxin that poisoned food in '73. *New York Times,* p. 65.

Broff, N. (1989, January). Statements supplied to the author from NARAL.

Brooke, J. (1999, March 26). Deep desert grave awaits first load of nuclear waste. *New York Times.* Retrieved from http://www.nytimes.com

Brooks, J. (1985). *HHS' failure to enforce the Food, Drug, and Cosmetic Act: The case of cancer-causing color additives.* Eleventh Report of the Committee on Government Operations. Washington, DC: U.S. Government Printing Office.

Brooks, J. (1987). *FDA continues to permit the illegal marketing of carcinogenic additives.* Twenty-fifth Report of the Committee on Government Operations. Washington, DC: U.S. Government Printing Office.

Brown, D. A. (2001, Fall). The ethical dimensions of global environmental issues. *Daedalus, 130*(4), 59–69.

Brown, J. W. (n.d.). *Environmental Defense Fund Letter.* New York.

Brown, L. R. (1985, February 25). "Human element," not drought, causes famine. *U.S. News & World Report,* 71–72.

Brown, L. R. (1987). Food growth slowdown: Danger signal for the future. In J. Price Gittinger, J. Leslie, & C. Hoisington (Eds.), *Food policy: Integrating supply, distribution, and consumption* (pp. 89–102). Baltimore: Johns Hopkins University Press.

Brown, M. H. (1979, December). Love Canal and the poisoning of America. *Atlantic Monthly, 235,* 33–47.

Brown, R. M. (1969). Historical patterns of violence in America. In H. D. Graham & T. R. Gurr (Eds.), *Violence in America: Historical and comparative perspectives.* New York: Bantam.

Brownfield, D., & Sorenson, A. M. (1993, July–September). Self-control and juvenile delinquency: Theoretical issues and an empirical assessment of selected elements of a general theory of crime. *Deviant Behavior, 14,* 243–264.

Brownmiller, S. (1975). *Against our will: Men, women, and rape.* New York: Simon & Schuster.

Buck, K. J. (1998, December 9). Recent progress toward the identification of genes related to risk for alcoholism. *Mammalian Genome, 12,* 927–928.

Budiansky, S. A. (1987, February 9). The trees fell—and so did the people. *U.S. News & World Report,* 75.

Buff, S. A. (1987, May). Lois Lee takes back children from the night. *ASA Footnotes, 15*(5), 1, 2.

Bulkeley, W. M. (1995, February 27). Untested treatments, cures find stronghold on on-line services. *Wall Street Journal,* p. A1, A7.

Bunn, M., & Weir, A. (2004, September 12). Preventing a nuclear 9/11. *Washington Post.* Retrieved from http://www.washingtonpost.com

Burgess, A. W., & Holmstrom, L. L. (1974). Rape trauma syndrome. *American Journal of Psychiatry, 131,* 981–986.

Burgess, E. W. (1925). The growth of the city: An introduction to a research project. In R. E. Park, E. W. Burgess, & R. D. McKenzie (Eds.), *The City* (pp. 47–62 in the 1967 edition). Chicago: University of Chicago Press.

Burgess, E., & Locke, H. (1945). *The Family.* New York: Appleton-Century-Crofts, Inc.

Burns, J. F. (1994). Bangladesh, still poor, cuts birth rate sharply. *New York Times,* p. A10.

Burros, M. (1999, March 14). Experts worry about the return of a deadly germ in cold cuts. *New York Times.* Retrieved from http://www.nytimes.com

Burroughs, W. (1975). Excerpts from "Deposition: Testimony concerning a sickness." In M. Wilson & S. Wilson (Eds.), *Drugs in American life* (pp. 133–158). New York: Wilson.

Butler, R. N., et al. (2006). *Ageism in America*. New York: Open Society Institute.

Butterfield, F. (1999, January 11). Prison population increases as release of inmates slows. *New York Times*. Retrieved from http://www.nytimes.com

Butterfield, F. (2005, April 8). Indians' wish list: Big-city sites for casinos. *New York Times*. Retrieved from http://www.nytimes.com

Cahoun, L., Cox, L., & Chitale, R. (2008, February 22). Celebrity addictions: Painkillers and Hollywood. *ABC News Medical Unit*. Retrieved from http://abcnews.go.com/

Calle, E. E., Rodriguez, C., Walker-Thurmond, K., & Thun, M. J. (2003, April 24). Overweight, obesity, and mortality from cancer in a prospectively studied cohort of U.S. adults. *New England Journal of Medicine, 348,* 17.

Callick, R. (2008, September 20). China's food chain now at risk. *The Australian*. Retrieved from http://www.theaustralian.news.com.au/

Cameron, P. (1999). *Violence and homosexuality*. Family Research Institute. Retrieved from http://www.familyresearchinst.org/FRI_EduPamphlet4.html

Campbell, D. (1995, August 12). Electronic tagging may be used for prisoners released on parole. *Guardian*.

Campbell, J. L. (1987, February). The state and the nuclear waste crisis: An institutional analysis of policy constraints. *Social Problems, 34*(1), 18–33.

Campo-Flores, A. (2002, September 2). A crackdown on call girls. *Newsweek*. Retrieved from http://www.newsweek.com

Canada tries to bar pro-Nazi view on the Internet. (1998, August 2). *New York Times*. Retrieved from http://www.nytimes.com

Caplan, B. (2006). The economics of Szasz: Preferences, constraints, and mental illness. *Rationality and Society, 18*(3), 333–366.

Caplow, T., et al. (1982). *Middletown families: Fifty years of change and continuity*. Minneapolis: University of Minnesota Press.

Carey, B. (2005, August 16). In the hospital, a degrading shift from person to patient. *New York Times*. Retrieved from http://www.nytimes.com

Carlson, K., & Chaiken, J. (1987, September). *White collar crime*. Special Report of the Bureau of Justice Statistics. Washington, DC: U.S. Department of Justice.

Carlson, L. H., & Colburn, G. A. (1972). *In their place: White America defines her minorities, 1850–1950*. New York: Wiley.

Carlson, R. J. (1975). *The end of medicine*. New York: Wiley.

Carnevale, A. P., & Rose, S. J. (2003, March). *Socioeconomic status, race/ethnicity, and selective college admissions*. New York: Century Foundation.

Carnevale, M. L. (1990, July 12). New jolt for Nynex: Bawdy "conventions" of buyers, suppliers. *Wall Street Journal*, pp. A1, A6.

Carroll, C. R. (2000). *Drugs in modern society* (5th ed.). New York: McGraw-Hill.

Carton, B. (1994, November 29). At Jenny Craig, men are ones who claim sex discrimination. *Wall Street Journal*, pp. A1, A7.

Castaneda, C. (1968). *The teachings of Don Juan: A Yaqui way of knowledge*. New York: Ballantine.

Castaneda, C. (1971). *A separate reality: Further conversations with Don Juan*. New York: Simon & Schuster.

Castaneda, C. (1974). *Tales of power*. New York: Simon & Schuster.

Castells, M. (1977). *The urban question: A Marxist approach* (Alan Sheridan, Trans.) Cambridge, MA: MIT Press.

Castells, M. (1983). *The city and the grass roots*. Berkeley: University of California Press.

Castells, M. (1989). *The informational city*. Oxford, England: Blackwell.

Catanzaro, R. (1992). *Men of respect: A social history of the mafia*. New York: Free Press.

Cates, J. A., & Markley, J. (1992, Fall). Demographic, clinical, and personality variables associated with male prostitution by choice. *Adolescence, 27*(107), 695–706.

Cendrowski, S. (2008, October 27). Being Buffetted. *Fortune, 158*(8), p. 13.

Centers for Disease Control and Prevention. (2005). *HIV/AIDS surveillance report, 2004,* 16.

Centers for Disease Control and Prevention. (2006a). Cigarette use among high school students, United States, 1991–2005. *Morbidity & Mortality Weekly Report, 55*(26), 724–726.

Centers for Disease Control and Prevention. (2006b). *Deaths, percent of total deaths, and death rates for the leading causes of death: United States and each state, 2003*.

Centers for Disease Control and Prevention. (2006c). *Leading causes of death, 1900–1998*.

Chafetz, J. S. (1990). *Gender equity: An integrated theory of stability and change*. Newbury Park, CA: Sage.

Chagnon, N. A. (1988, February 26). Life histories, blood revenge, and warfare in a tribal population. *Science*, 985–992.

Chalkey, K. (1997, October). Female genital mutilation: New laws, programs try to end practice. *Population Today, 25*(10), 4–5.

Chambliss, W. (2001). *Power, Politics, and Crime*. Boulder, CO: Westview Press.

Chambliss, W. J. (2007). The saints and the roughnecks. In J. M. Henslin (Ed.), *Down-to-Earth Sociology: Introductory Readings* (14th ed.). New York: Free Press. (Original work published 1973 in *Society 11*(1): 24–31)

Chang, I. (1997). *The rape of Nanking: The forgotten holocaust of World War II*. New York: Basic Books.

Chase, M. (2006, January 20). Defying treatment, a new, virulent bug sparks health fears. *Wall Street Journal*. Retrieved from http://www.online.wsj.com

Chen, M. (2006, April 4). Texas court overturns conviction under "Fetal Rights" law. *The New Standard*.

Chen, M. (2007). Ground Zero: The most dangerous workplace. *The New Standard*. Retrieved from http://newstandardnews.net/content/index.cfm/items/1402

Cheng, V. (1995, June 27). 328 Useful drugs are said to lie hidden in tropical forests. *New York Times*, p. C4.

Cherlin, A. J. (2002, Spring). A "quieting" of change. *Contexts, 1*(1), 67–68.

Chernoff, N. W., & Simon, R. J. (2000, Summer). Women and crime the world over. *Gender Issues, 18*(3), 5–20.

Chilman, C. S. (1988). Public policies and families. In E. W. Nunnally, C. S. Chilman, & F. M. Cox (Eds.), *Mental illness, delinquency, addictions, and neglect* (pp. 189–197). Newbury Park, CA: Sage.

Cho, E., et al. (2004, July 7). Dairy foods, calcium, and colorectal cancer: A pooled analysis of 10 cohort studies. *Journal of the National Cancer Institute, 96*(13), 1015–1022.

Choi, K. H., Catania, J. A., & Dolcini, M. M. (1994). Extramarital sex and HIV risk behavior among U.S. adults: Results from the national AIDS behavioral survey. *American Journal of Public Health, 84,* 2003–2007.

Choo, R. E., Huestis, M. A., Schroeder, J. R., Shin, A. S., & Jones, H. E. (2004). Neonatal abstinence syndrome in methadone-exposed infants is altered by level of prenatal tobacco exposure. *Drug and Alcohol Dependence, 75*(3), 253–260.

Churchill, W., & Vander Wall, J. (1990). *Agents of repression: The FBI's secret wars against the Black Panther Party and the American Indian Movement*. Boston: South End Press.

Clarke, S. (2001). Earnings of men and women in the EU: The gap narrowing but only slowly. *Eurostat: Statistics in Focus: Population and Social Conditions*.

Clausing, J. (1998, July 22). Senate adds Internet proposals to spending bill. *New York Times*.

Cleaver, E. (1968). *Soul on ice*. New York: McGraw-Hill.

Clinard, M. B. (1990). *Corporate corruption: The abuse of power.* New York: Praeger.

Clinard, M. B., Yeager, P. C., Brisette, J., Petrashek, D., & Harries, E. (1979). *Illegal corporate behavior.* Washington, DC: U.S. Department of Justice.

Clines, F. X. (1998, June 18). Soviets now admit '57 nuclear blast. *New York Times.* Retrieved from http://www.nytimes.com

Clinton, H. R. (1997). *It takes a village: And other lessons children teach us.* New York: Touchstone Books.

Cloward, R. A., & Ohlin, L. E. (1960). *Delinquency and opportunity: A theory of delinquent gangs.* New York: Free Press.

Cockerham, W. C. (1991). *This aging society.* Englewood Cliffs, NJ: Prentice Hall.

Cockerham, W. C. (1997, June). The social determinants of the decline of life expectancy in Russia and Eastern Europe: A lifestyle explanation. *Journal of Health and Social Behavior, 38,* 117–130.

Cohen, A. K. (1955). *Delinquent boys: The culture of the gang.* New York: Free Press.

Cohen, E. (1997, January 17). Shrinks aplenty online, but are they credible? *New York Times.*

Cohen, J. (1978). The incapacitative effect of imprisonment: A critical review of the literature. In A. Blumstein, J. Cohen, and D. Nagin (Eds.), *Deterrence and incapacitation: Estimating the effects of criminal sanctions on crime rates.* Washington, DC: National Academy of Sciences.

Cohen, M. R. (1940, April). Moral aspects of the criminal law. *Yale Law Journal, 49,* 1009–1026.

Cohen, M., Seghorn, T., & Calamas, W. (1969, April). Sociometric study of the sex offender. *Journal of Abnormal Psychology, 74,* 249–255.

Coleman, J. W. (1989). *The criminal elite: The sociology of white collar crime.* New York: St. Martin's.

Coleman, J. W. (1995). Politics and the abuse of power. In J. M. Henslin (Ed.), *Down-to-earth sociology: Introductory readings* (8th ed.; pp. 442–450). New York: Free Press.

Colombia. (2006, October). U.S. Department of State, Bureau of Western Hemisphere Affairs.

Coltrane, S., & Messineo, M. (2000). The perpetuation of subtle prejudice: Race and gender imagery in 1990s television advertising. *Sex Roles: A Journal of Research, 42*(5–6), 363–389.

Comer, J. P. (1986). Education for community. In A. L. Schorr (Ed.), *In common decency: Domestic policies after Reagan* (pp. 186–209). New Haven, CT: Yale University Press.

Conahan, F. C. (1991, May 15). Statement of Frank C. Conahan, Assistant Comptroller General, National Security and International Affairs Division, US General Accounting Office, before the Committee on the Budget: Cost of Operation Desert Shield and Desert Storm and Allied Contributions, GAO/T-NSIAD-91-34.

Confronting confinement. (2006). *A report of the commission on safety and abuse in America's prisons.* Retrieved from http://www.prisoncommission.org/pdfs/Confronting_Confinement.pdf

Congress looks to fund efforts to beat back Fetal Alcohol Syndrome. (1994, March). *The Nation's Health, 24,* 3, 5.

Conley, D. (2001, January). Capital for college: Parental assets and postsecondary schooling. *Sociology of Education, 74*(1), 59–68.

Conner, R. L. (1990, February). Demographic doomsayers: Five myths about population. *Current,* 21–25.

Conrad, P. (1995). Learning to doctor: Reflections on medical school. In J. M. Henslin (Ed.), *Down-to-earth sociology: Introductory readings* (8th ed., pp. 420–430). New York: Free Press.

Conti, M. (1980, January). The famine controversy. *World Press Review, 27,* 56.

Cookson, P. W., Jr., & Persell, C. H. (2005). Preparing for power: Cultural capital and elite boarding schools. In J. M. Henslin (Ed.), *Life in society: Readings to accompany "Sociology: A down-to-earth approach"* (7th ed., pp. 175–185). Boston: Allyn & Bacon. (Original work published 1985 in P. W. Cookson & C. H. Persell, *Preparing for power*)

Cooper, P. F. (2002). Historical aspects of wastewater treatment. In P. Lens, G. Zeeman, & G. Lettinga (Eds.), *Decentralized sanitation and reuse: Concepts, systems and implementation* (pp. 11–38). London: IWA.

Corcoran, M., Duncan, G. J., Gurin, G., & Gurin, P. (1985). Myth and reality: The causes and persistence of poverty. *Journal of Policy Analysis and Management, 4*(4), 516–536.

Cornell, G. W. (1981, April 13). Modern persecutions mirror those of Jesus. Associated Press.

Corzine, J., & Kirby, R. (1977, July). Cruising the truckers: Sexual encounters in a highway rest area. *Urban Life, 6,* 171–192.

Cose, E. (1999, June 7). The good news about black America. *Newsweek,* pp. 29–40.

Coser, L. A. (1956). *The functions of social conflict.* New York: Free Press.

Coser, L. A. (1977). *Masters of sociological thought: Ideas in historical and social context.* New York: Harcourt.

Couch, K. A., Daly, M. C., & Wolf, D. A. (1999). Time? Money? Both? The allocation of resources to older parents. *Demography, 36*(2), 219–232.

Cowley, G. (2006, May 15). The life of a virus hunter. *Newsweek.* Retrieved from http://www.newsweek.com

Cowley, J. (1969). *Pioneers of women's liberation.* New York: Merit.

Cressey, D. R. (1953). *Other people's money.* New York: Free Press.

Cressey, D. R. (1969). *Theft of the nation: The structure and operations of organized crime in America.* New York: Harper & Row.

Crider, R. (1986). Phencyclidine: Changing abuse patterns. In D. H. Clouet (Ed.), *Phencyclidine: An update,* Rockville, MD: National Institute on Drug Abuse, 163–173.

Crime in the United States. (Annual). Washington, D.C.: Department of Justice, Federal Bureau of Investigation. Available from http://www.fbi.gov

Critchfield, R. (1986, January 13). China's agricultural success story. *Wall Street Journal,* p. 25.

Cross national comparison of rape rates: Problems and issues. (2004, October 28). Working Paper #18. Statistical Commission and UN Economic Commission for Europe.

Cuffel, B., Goldman, W., and Schlesinger, H. (1999). Does managing behavioral health care services increase the cost of providing medical care? *Journal of Behavioral Health Services and Research 26*(4), 372–380.

Cumming, E., & Henry, W. E. (1961). *Growing old: The process of disengagement.* New York: Basic Books.

Currie, Elliott. *Confronting Crime: An American Challenge.* New York: Pantheon, 1985.

Curry, P., & Klumpp, T. (2007). *Statistical Discrimination in the Criminal Justice System: The case for Fines instead of Jail.* B.C., Canada: Department of Economics, Simon Fraser University.

Cushman, J. H. (1999, January 3). Industries press plan for credits in emissions control. *New York Times.* Retrieved from http://www.nytimes.com

Dabbs, J. M., Jr., & Morris, R. (1990, May), Testosterone, social class, and antisocial behavior in a sample of 4,462 men. *Psychological Science, 1*(3), 209–211.

Dahl, R. A. (1961). *Who governs?* New Haven, CT: Yale University Press.

Dahrendorf, R. (1959). *Class and class conflict in industrial society.* Stanford, CA: Stanford University Press.

Dahrendorf, R. (1973). Toward a theory of social conflict. In A. Etzioni & E. Etzioni (Eds.), *Social change: Sources, patterns, and consequences,* New York: Basic Books.

Daly, M., & Wilson, M. (1988). *Homicide.* New York: Aldine de Gruyter.

Daniels, R. (1975). *The decision to relocate the Japanese Americans.* Philadelphia: Lippincott.

Dao, J. (1999, January 13). U.S. government joins Oneida Indians' suit against New York State. *New York Times.* Retrieved from http://www.nytimes.com

Dash, L. (1990, July–August). When children want children. *Society, 27*(5), 17–19.

Davies, J. C. III, & Davies, B. S. (1975). *The politics of pollution* (2nd ed.). Indianapolis, Ind.: Bobbs-Merrill.

Davis, A. (1974). *Angela Davis: An autobiography.* New York: Random House.

Davis, K. (1937, October). The sociology of prostitution. *American Sociological Review, 2,* 744–755.

Davis, K. (1966). Sexual behavior. In R. Merton & R. Nisbet (Eds.), *Contemporary social problems* (2nd ed.). New York: Harcourt.

Davis, K., & Moore, W. E. (1945). Some principles of stratification. *American Sociological Review, 10,* 242–249.

Davis, N. J. (1978). Prostitution: Identity, career, and legal-economic enterprise. In J. M. Henslin & E. Sagarin (Eds.), *The sociology of sex: An introductory reader* (pp. 297–322). New York: Schocken.

Davis, N. J., & Robinson, R. V. (1988, February). Class identification of men and women in the 1970s and 1980s. *American Sociological Review, 53,* 103–112.

Daws, G. (1994). *Prisoners of the Japanese: POWs of World War II in the Pacific.* New York: Morrow.

Day, C. R., Jr. (1990, March 5). Tear up the tracks. *Industry Week, 239*(5), 5.

De Beauvoir, S. (1953). *The second sex.* New York: Knopf.

De Mott, B. (1980, March). The pro-incest lobby. *Psychology Today, 13*(11–12), 15–16.

de Silva, R. (1980). Developing the Third World. *World Press Review,* 48.

Death Penalty Information Center. (2008). *Facts about the death penalty.* Retrieved from http://www.deathpenaltyinfo.org/FactSheet.pdf

Denes, M. (1976). *In necessity and sorrow: Life and death in an abortion hospital.* New York: Basic Books.

Denzin, N. K. (1992, July–August). The suicide machine. *Society,* 7–10.

DeOilos, I. Y., & Kapinus, C. A. (2002, Winter). Aging childless individuals and couples: Suggestions for new directions in research. *Sociological Inquiry, 72*(1), 72–80.

DeRios, M. D., & Smith, D. E. (1977). Drug use and abuse in cross-cultural perspective. *Human Organization, 36,* 14–21.

Deschner, A., & Cohen, S. A. (2003, October). Contraceptive use is key to reducing abortion worldwide. *The Guttmacher Report on Public Policy 6,* 4.

DeSouza, E., & Fansler, A. G. (2003, June). Contrapower sexual harassment: A survey of students and faculty members. *Sex Roles, 48*(11/12), 529–542.

Devine, M. A. (2004, September). A fresh look at cogeneration. *Energy User News, 29*(1), 13–15.

Diamond, M., & Uchiyama, A. (1999). Pornography, rape, and sex crimes in Japan. *International Journal of Law and Psychiatry, 22*(1), 1–22.

DiChiara, A., & Chabot, R. (2003). Gangs and the contemporary urban struggle: An unappreciated aspect of change. In L. Kontos, D. Brotherton, & L. Barrios (Eds.), *Gangs and Society: Alternative Perspectives* (pp. 77–94). New York: Columbia University Press.

Dickey, C., & Rogers, A. (2002, February 25). Smoke and mirrors. *Newsweek.*

Dickman, A. B., & Murnen, S. K. (2004, March). Learning to be little women and little men: The inequitable gender equality of nonsexist children's literature. *Sex Roles, 50,* 5.

Dickson, D. T. (1968, Fall). Bureaucracy and morality: An organizational perspective on a moral crusade. *Social Problems, 16,* 143–156.

Digest of Education Statistics. (2005, November). Washington, DC: U.S. Department of Education.

Dingell, J. D. (1985, March 27). *Sulfites: Hearing before the subcommittee on oversight and investigations of the Committee on Energy and Commerce, House of Representatives.* Washington, DC: U.S. Government Printing Office.

Dispute between EU and U.S. over beef now before WTO. (2004, November). *The Food Institute Report.*

Dobyns, H. F. (1983). *Their numbers became thinned: Native American population dynamics in Eastern North America.* Knoxville: University of Tennessee Press.

Doerner, W. G. (1978, May). The index of southernness revisited: The influence of wherefrom upon whodunnit. *Criminology, 16,* 47–56.

Dollard, J., Miller, N. E., Doob, L. W., Mowrer, O. H., & Sears, R. R. (1961). *Frustration and aggression.* New Haven, CT: Yale University Press. (Original work published 1939)

Domhoff, G. W. (1974). *The Bohemian Grove and other retreats: A study in ruling-class cohesiveness.* New York: Harper & Row.

Domhoff, G. W. (1978a). *The powers that be.* New York: Random House.

Domhoff, G. W. (1978b). *Who really rules?* New Brunswick, NJ: Transaction.

Domhoff, G. W. (1990). *The power elite and the state: How policy is made in America.* New York: Aldine de Gruyter.

Domhoff, G. W. (1998). *Who rules America? Power and politics in the year 2000* (3rd ed.). Mountain View, CA: Mayfield.

Domhoff, G. W. (2001). *Who rules America? Power and politics* (4th ed.). Mountain View, CA: Mayfield.

Donaldson, S. (1992, May 25). *World News Tonight.* ABC News.

Doran, B. (2006, August 24). How green is my plastic? *North Coast Journal.*

Douglass, J. D. (1998, March 10). A biological weapons threat worse than Saddam. *Wall Street Journal,* p. A22.

Douvan, E. (1980). *Is the American family obsolete?* University of California, University Extension, Courses by Newspaper, San Diego.

Dove, A. (n.d.). Soul folk "chitling" test or the Dove counterbalance intelligence test. Mimeo.

Dowie, M. (1977, September–October). Pinto madness. *Mother Jones, 2,* 18–32.

Dowie, M. (1979, November). The corporate crime of the century. *Mother Jones, 4,* 23–25, 37.

Downing, B. (2006, September 23). Coalition sees damage to Great Lakes growing. *Akron Beacon Journal.*

Draper, R. (1986, June 26). The history of advertising in America. *New York Review of Books, 33,* 14–18.

Drug dependence in pregnancy: Clinical management of mother and child. (1979). Rockville, MD: U.S. Department of Health, Education, and Welfare.

Drug Enforcement Administration. (2001). *Opium poppy cultivation and heroin processing in Southeast Asia.* Washington, DC: U.S. Department of Justice.

Dubar, H. (1980). American discovers child pornography. In J. R. Barbour (Ed.), *Human sexuality, 80/81.* Guilford, CT: Dushkin.

Dufay, J. (n.d.). Ten years after Chernobyl: A witness to the devastation. Greenpeace. Retrieved from http://www.greenpeace.org

Durkheim, E. (1938). *The rules of sociological method* (G. E. G. Catlin, Ed.). New York: Macmillan. (Original work published 1904; 8th ed. 1950.)

Durkheim, E. (1951). *Suicide* (J. A. Spaulding & G. Simpson, Trans.). New York: Free Press. (Original work published 1897.)

Durkheim, E. (1964). *The division of labor in society* (G. Simpson, Trans.). New York: Free Press. (Original work published 1893.)

Durning, A. (1990). Cradles of life. In L. W. Barnes (Ed.), *Social problems 90/91* (pp. 231–241). Guilford, CT: Dushkin.

Duskin, E. W. (2003, August 7). Environment continues to get better. *Southwest Farm Press.*

Duster, T. (1970). *The legalization of morality: Law, drugs, and moral judgment.* New York: Free Press.

Duster, T. (1988, May). From structural analysis to public policy. *Contemporary Sociology, 17*(3), 287–290.

Eberstadt, N. (1988). *The poverty of communism.* New Brunswick, NJ: Transaction.

Ebomoyi, E. (1987). The prevalence of female circumcision in two Nigerian communities. *Sex Roles, 17*(3/4), 139–151.

Eder, D. (1995). *School talk: Gender and adolescent culture.* New Brunswick, NJ: Rutgers University Press.

Ehrenfeld, R. (1990). *Narcoterrorism.* New York: Basic Books.

Ehrenreich, B., & English, D. (1973). *Witches, midwives, and nurses: A history of women healers.* Old Westbury, NY: Feminist Press.

Ehrlich, P. R., & Ehrlich, A. H. (1972). *Population, resources, and environment: Issues in human ecology* (2nd ed.). San Francisco: Freeman.

Ehrlich, P. R., & Ehrlich, A. H. (1981). *Extinction: The causes and consequences of the disappearance of species.* New York: Random House.

Eichenwald, K. (2005, December 19). Through his webcam, a boy joins a sordid online world. *New York Times.* Retrieved from http://www.nytimes.com

Eisenhart, R. W. (1975, Fall). You can't hack it, little girl: A discussion of the covert psychological agenda of modern combat training. *Journal of Social Issues, 31,* 13–23.

Eisenhower, D. D. (1972). From "Farewell Address to the Nation," January 17, 1961. In S. E. Ambrose & J. A. Barber, Jr. (Eds.), *The military and American society: Essays and readings* (pp. 61–63). New York: Free Press.

Eisinger, P. K. (1980). *The politics of displacement: Racial and ethnic transition in three American cities.* Campbell CA: Academic Press.

Ellis, H. (1897). Mescal: A new artificial paradise. *Annual Report of the Smithsonian Institution, 52,* 547–548.

Ellis, H. (1902). Mescal: A study of a divine plant. *Popular Science Monthly, 61,* 52–71.

Engelmayer, P. A. (1983, November 21). Violence by students, from rape to racism, raises college worries. *Wall Street Journal,* pp. 1, 18.

Englund, W., & Cohn, G. (1997, December 9). A Third World dump for America's ships? *Baltimore Sun.*

Environmental Protection Agency. (1994, February). *The Great Lakes: Report to Congress on the Great Lakes ecosystem.*

Environmental Protection Agency. (1998, November). *Reduction of toxic loadings to the Niagara River from hazardous waste sites in the United States.*

Epstein, C. F. (1986, September–October). Inevitabilities of prejudice. *Society,* 7–13.

Epstein, C. F. (1988). *Deceptive distinctions: Sex, gender, and the social order.* New Haven, CT: Yale University Press.

Epstein, C. F. (1989). Letter to the author.

Equality Now. (2007). *Words and deeds: Holding governments accountable in the Beijing + 10 review process.* Retrieved from http://www.equalitynow.org/english/wan/beijing10/beijing10_en.pdf

Escalante, J., & Dirmann, J. (1990, Summer). The Jaime Escalante math program. *Journal of Negro Education, 59*(3), 407–423.

Espenshade, T. J. (1990, February). A short history of U.S. policy toward illegal immigration. *Population Today,* 6–9.

Etzioni, A. (1998, November 3). Letter to the editor: Porn filters are a net benefit. *Wall Street Journal,* p. A23.

Facts about sexual harassment. (2006). U.S. Equal Employment Opportunity Commission. Retrieved from http://www.eeoc.gov

Faison, S., Jr. (1991, September 22). Friend says girl killed on train resisted robbery of other girls. *New York Times,* p. 34.

Fall colors: 2003–04 prime time diversity report. (2004). Oakland, CA: Children Now.

Farah, J. (1995, March 15). Crime and creative punishment. *Wall Street Journal,* p. A15.

Faris, R. E. L., & Dunham, W. W. (1939). *Mental disorders in urban areas.* Chicago: University of Chicago Press.

Farney, D. (1989, August 16). On the Great Plains, life becomes a fight for water and survival. *Wall Street Journal,* pp. A1, A12.

Faunce, W. A. (1981). *Problems of an industrial society* (2nd ed.). New York: McGraw-Hill.

Faupel, C. E., & Klockars, C. B. (1987, February). Drugs-crime connections: Elaborations from the life histories of hard-core addicts. *Social Problems, 34*(1), 54–68.

FBI uniform crime reports. (Annual). Washington, DC: U.S. Government Printing Office.

Federal Bureau of Investigation. (1998). *Terrorism in the United States, 1997.* Washington, DC: U.S. Department of Justice.

Federal Reserve Board. (2004). Survey of consumer finances. Retrieved from http://www.federalreserve.gov/PUBS/oss/oss2/2004/scf2004home.html

Feinsilber, M. (1981, September 24). Agent Orange may have fallen near U.S. bases. Associated Press.

Felsenthal, E. (1998, March 5). Justices' ruling further defines sex harassment. *Wall Street Journal,* B1, B2.

Ferguson, R. E. (2001). Community revitalization, jobs, and the well-being of the inner-city poor. In S. H. Danziger & R. H. Haveman (Eds.), *Understanding poverty* (pp. 417–443). New York: Russell Sage.

Fergusson, D. M., Horwood, L. J., & Beutrais, A. L. (2003). Cannabis and educational attainment. *Addiction,* 1681–1692.

Fernandez, F. G., Johnson, K. D., Terry, R. E., Nelson, S., & Webster, D. (2005, October 27). Soil resources of the ancient Maya at Piedras Negras, Guatemala. *American Journal of the Soil Science Society, 696,* 2020–2032.

Feshbach, M. (1992, May 14). Russia's farms, too poisoned for the plow. *Wall Street Journal,* A14.

Fialka, J. J. (1988, February 23). Pentagon outlines plans to use troops to join border "war" against drugs. *Wall Street Journal,* A10.

Fialka, J. J. (2004, November 16). Position available: Indestructible bugs to eat nuclear waste. *Wall Street Journal,* A1.

Field, M. G. (1998). The health crisis in the former Soviet Union: A report from the "post-war" zone. In W. C. Cockerham, M. Glasser, & L. S. Heuser (Eds.), *Readings in medical sociology* (pp. 506–519). Upper Saddle River, NJ: Prentice Hall.

Fields, G. (1986, November 10). Racism is accepted practice in Japan. *Wall Street Journal,* 19.

Finckenauer, J. O. (1982). *Scared straight and the panacea phenomenon.* Englewood Cliffs, NJ: Prentice Hall.

Finegold, B. (2006). Data points: Pregnant with implications. *Scientific American, 295*(3).

Finkelhor, D., & Yllo, K. (1985). *License to rape: Sexual abuse of wives.* New York: Holt.

Finkelhor, D., & Yllo, K. (1989). Marital rape: The myth versus the reality. In J. M. Henslin (Ed.), *Marriage and family in a changing society* (pp. 382–391). New York: Free Press.

Finsterbusch, K., & Greisman, H. C. (1975, February). The unprofitability of warfare in the twentieth century. *Social Problems, 22,* 450–463.

Firestone, S. (1970). *The dialectic of sex: The case for feminist revolution.* New York: Morrow.

First death sentence under new drug law. (1991, May 15). *New York Times,* p. A24.

Fischer, C. S. (1976). *The urban experience.* New York: Harcourt.

Fish, J. M. (1995). Mixed blood. *Psychology Today, 28*(6), 55ff.

Fisher, G. M. (1988, Spring). Setting American standards of poverty: A look back. *Focus, 19*(2), 47–52.

Fisher, S. (1986). *In the patient's best interest: Women and the politics of medical decisions.* New Brunswick, NJ: Rutgers University Press.

Fisse, B., & Braithwaite, J. (1987). The impact of publicity on corporate offenders: Ford Motor Company and the Pinto papers. In M. D. Ermann & R. J. Lundman (Eds.), *Corporate and governmental deviance: Problems of organizational behavior in contemporary society* (3rd ed.; 244–262). New York: Oxford University Press.

Flavin, C. (1987). Reassessing nuclear power. In L. R. Brown (Ed.), *State of the world* (pp. 57–80). New York: Norton.

Foley, D. E. (2006). The great American football ritual. In J. M. Henslin (Ed.), *Society: Readings to accompany core concepts* (pp. 64–76). Boston: Allyn & Bacon. (Original work published 1990.)

Food and Drug Administration. (1994, May). Food allergies—rare but risky. *FDA Consumer.*

Ford, C. S., & Beach, F. A. (1972). *Patterns of sexual behavior.* New York: Harper Colophon.

Forero, J. (2006, February 12). Bolivia's knot: No to cocaine, but yes to coca. *New York Times.* Retrieved from http://www.nytimes.com

Forward, S., & Buck, C. (1978). *Betrayal of innocence: Incest and its devastation.* New York: Penguin.

Fouts, G., & Burggraf, K. (1999, March). Television situation comedies: Female body images and verbal reinforcements. *Sex Roles: A Journal of Research, 40*(5-6), 473–481.

Fowler, L. (2008). *Breast implants for graduation? Parent and adolescent narratives.* Dissertation, University of North Texas.

Fox, J. A., & Levin, J. (2005). *Extreme killing: Understanding serial and mass murder.* Thousand Oaks, CA: Sage.

Fox, J. W. (1990, December). Social class, mental illness, and social mobility: The social selection-drift hypothesis for serious mental illness. *Journal of Health and Social Behavior, 31*(4), 344–353.

Frankenberg, E., & Lee, C. (2002, August). *Rapidly resegregating school districts.* The Civil Rights Project. Cambridge, MA: Harvard University.

Frazier, S., & Schlender, B. R. (1980, August 6). Huge area in Midwest relying on irrigation is depleting its water. *Wall Street Journal,* p. 1.

Freed, A. O. (1994). How Japanese families cope with fragile elderly. In R. B. Enright, Jr. (Ed.), *Perspectives in social gerontology* (pp. 76–86). Boston: Allyn & Bacon.

Freedman, A. M. (1994, October 26). How a tobacco giant doctors snuff brands to boost their "kick." *Wall Street Journal,* pp. A1, A6.

Freidson, E. (1961). *Patients' views of medical practice.* New York: Russell Sage.

Frequent tobacco use among U.S. youth declines. (1992, February). *Smokers' Advocate.*

Freund, M., Lee, N., & Leonard, T. (1991, November). *Journal of Sex Research, 28*(4), 579–591.

Friedan, B. (1963). *The feminine mystique.* New York: Norton.

Friedl, E. (1990). Society and sex roles. In J. P. Spradley & D. W. McCurdy (Eds.), *Conformity and conflict: Readings in cultural anthropology* (pp. 229–238). Glenview IL.: Scott, Foresman.

Friends of the Earth. (2004). Press release, online.

Friess, S. (2005, December 12). Betting on the studs. *Newsweek.*

Froman, I. (1994, November). Sweden for women. *Current Sweden, 407,* 1–4.

Fromm, E. (1973). *The anatomy of human destructiveness.* New York: Holt.

Fuller, R., & Schoenberger, R. (1991, December). The gender salary gap: Do academic achievement, internship experience, and college major make a difference? *Social Science Quarterly, 72*(4), 715–726.

Furchtgott-Roth, D. (2008, March 13). Are we in (or headed for) a recession? *The American.* Retrieved from http://www.american.com/archive/2008/march-02-08/are-we-in-or-headed-for-a-recession

Galbraith, J. K. (1979). *The nature of mass poverty.* Cambridge, MA: Harvard University Press.

Gale, R. P. (1972). From sit-in to hike-in: A comparison of the civil rights and environmental movements. In W. R. Burch, Jr., N. H. Cheek, Jr., & L. Taylor (Eds.), *Social behavior, natural resources, and the environment* (pp. 280–305). New York: Harper & Row.

Gall, C. (2006, February 17). Despite Afghan strictures, the poppy flourishes. *New York Times.* Retrieved from http://www.nytimes.com

Galliher, J. R., & Walker, A. (1977, February). The puzzle of the social origins of the Marihuana Tax Act of 1937. *Social Problems, 24,* 367–376.

Ganahl, D. J., Prinsen, T. J., & Netzley, S. B. (2003, November). A content analysis of prime time commercials: A contextual framework of gender representation. *Sex Roles, 49*(9/10), 545–551.

Gannon, M. (2008, October 16) Casino slot profits plunge in September. *Norwich Bulletin.* Retrieved from http://www.norwichbulletin.com

Gans, H. J. (1962). *The urban villagers.* New York: Free Press.

Gans, H. J. (1968). *People and plans: Essays on urban problems and solutions.* New York: Basic Books.

Gans, H. J. (2007). The uses of poverty: The poor pay all. In J. M. Henslin (Ed.), *Down-to-earth sociology: Introductory readings* (14th ed.). New York: Free Press. (Originally work published in *Social Policy,* July/August 1971:20–24.)

GAO delineates state use of tobacco funds. (2003, March 10). *Alcoholism and Drug Abuse Weekly, 15*(10), 3.

Garbarino, M. S. (1976). *American Indian heritage.* Boston: Little, Brown.

Garelik, G. (1996, June–July). Russia's legacy of death. *National Wildlife.*

Garreau, J. (1991). *Edge city: Life on the new frontier.* New York: Doubleday.

Garrett, L. (1999, March 1). Global warning. *Los Angeles Times.*

Gartner, M. (1988, December 22). A dream of peace, the reality of never-ending wars. *Wall Street Journal,* p. A13.

Gattari, P., Spizzichino, L., C. Zaccarelli, V. M., & Rezza, G. (1992). Behavioural patterns and HIV infection among drug using transvestites practising prostitution in Rome. *AIDS Care, 4*(1), 83–87.

Gaufberg, S. V. (2004, March 11). Russia. *E-Medicine.*

Gay, J. (1985, February). The "patriotic" prostitute. *The Progressive,* 34–36.

Gaylin, W. (1974). *Partial justice: A study of bias in sentencing.* New York: Knopf.

Gelles, R. I. (1980). The myth of battered husbands and new facts about family violence. In R. L. David (Ed.), *Social Problems 80–81,* Guilford, CT: Dushkin.

Gellhorn, M. (1959). *The face of war.* New York: Simon & Schuster.

Gemme, R. (1993, Winter). Prostitution: A legal, criminological, and sexological perspective. *Canadian Journal of Human Sexuality, 2*(4), 227–237.

George, D. T., Phillips, M. J., Doty, L., Umhau, J. C., & Rawlings, R. R. (2006). A model linking biology, behavior, and psychiatric diagnoses in perpetrators of domestic violence. *Medical Hypotheses.*

Gerbner, G. (1998, December). The 1998 Screen Actors Guild report: Casting the American scene. Online.

Gerlin, A. (1994, August 4). Quirky sentences make bad guys squirm. *Wall Street Journal,* pp. B1–B2.

Gerstl-Pepin, C. I. (2006, March). The paradox of poverty narratives: Educators struggling with children left behind. *Educational Policy, 20*(1), 143–162.

Gessen, M. (2001, February 26). The nuclear wasteland. *U.S. News & World Report.*

Gest, T. (1987, May 18). Teaching convicts real street smarts. *U.S. News & World Report,* p. 72.

Getter, L. (1999, March 1). Cancer risk from air pollution still high, study says. *Los Angeles Times.*

Getting the message. (1997). Children now. Online.

Gibbs, N. (1999, May 3). In sorrow and disbelief. *Time,* pp. 25–36.

Gibbs, N., & Bower, A. (2006, May 1). Q: What scares doctors? A: Being the patient. *Time.* Retrieved from http://www.time.com

Giddens, A. (1969). Georg Simmel. In T. Raison (Ed.), *The founding fathers of social science* (pp. 165–173). Baltimore: Penguin.

Giddens, A. (1976). *New rules of sociological method.* London: Hutchinson.

Giddens, A. (1984). *The constitution of society: Outline of the theory of structuration.* Cambridge, UK: Polity Press.

Giele, J. Z. (1978). *Women and the future: Changing sex roles in modern America.* New York: Free Press.

Gilham, S. A. (1989). The Marines build men: Resocialization in recruit training. In R. Luhman (Ed.), *The sociological outlook: A text with readings* (2nd ed.; pp. 232–244). San Diego, CA: Collegiate Press.

Gilmore, D. G. (1990). *Manhood in the making: Cultural concepts of masculinity.* New Haven, CT: Yale University Press.

Glascock, J. (2001, Fall). Gender roles on prime-time network television: Demographics and behaviors. *Journal of Broadcasting and Electronics Media, 45,* 656–669.

Glaser, D. (1978). *Crime in our changing society.* New York: Holt.

Glasser, S. B. (2005, May 1). Global terrorism statistics debated. *Washington Post.* Retrieved from http://www.washingtonpost.com

Glaze, L. E., & Bonczar, T. P. *Probation and parole in the United States, 2006.* Bureau of Justice Statistics. Retrieved from http://www.ojp.usdoj.gov/bjs/pub/pdf/ppus06.pdf

Goering, L. (1998, August 28). Paranoia pervasive in Amazon. *Seattle Times.*

Goetting, A. (2001). *Getting out: Life stories of women who left abusive men.* New York: Columbia University Press.

Goldberg, C., & Kishkovsky, S. (2000, December 16). Russia's doctors are beggars at work, paupers at home. *New York Times.* Retrieved from http://www.nytimes.com

Goldberg, S. (1974). *The inevitability of patriarchy* (Rev. ed.). New York: Morrow.

Goldberg, S. (1986, September–October). Reaffirming the obvious. *Society,* 4–7.

Goldberg, S. (1989, January 18). Letter to the author.

Goldberg, S., & Lewis, Michael. (1969, March). Play behavior in the year-old infant: Early sex differences. *Child Development, 40,* 21–31.

Goleman, D. (1987, August 2). Girls and math: Is biology really destiny? *New York Times,* p. 42–46.

Goode, E. (1989). *Drugs in American society* (3rd ed.). New York: Knopf.

Gooden, A. M., & Gooden, M. A. (2001, July). Gender representation in notable children's picture books: 1995–1999. *Sex Roles, 45*(1/2), 89–101.

Goodyear, C. (2007, March 28). S.F. first city to ban plastic shopping bags. *San Francisco Chronicle.* Retrieved from http://www.sfgate.com

Gordon, M. (1964). *Assimilation in American life.* New York: Oxford University Press.

Gordon, M. R. (1996, April 20). Russia struggles in long race to prevent an atomic theft. *New York Times.* Retrieved from http://www.nytimes.com

Gorman, S. (2005, November 18). Hollywood madam to open Nevada "stud farm." *New York Times.*

Gottfredson, M., & Hirschi, T. (1990). *A general theory of crime.* Stanford, CA: Stanford University Press.

GPS creates global jail. (1998, April 8). *Space Daily.* Retrieved from http://www.spacedaily.com

Granddaddy of all ghettos faces wrecking ball. (2006, October 8). Associated Press.

Graven, K. (1990, March 21). Sex harassment at the office stirs up Japan. *Wall Street Journal,* pp. B1, B7.

Green, G. S. (1993, January). White-collar crime and the study of embezzlement. *Annals of the American Academy of Political and Social Sciences, 525,* 95–106.

Greenall, R. (2003, September 16). Russia turns spotlight on abortion. *BBC News.* Retrieved from http://news.bbc.co.uk/

Greenberg, D. F. (1975, Summer). The incapacitative effect of imprisonment: Some estimates. *Law and Society Review, 9,* 541–579.

Greenberger, R. S. (1992, February 19). U.S., Russia will explore joint system for early warning of missile attacks. *Wall Street Journal,* p. A7.

Greenberger, R. S. (1994, September 29). U.S., Russia agree to faster timetable for destruction of nuclear arsenals. *Wall Street Journal,* p. A22.

Greenberger, R. S., & Bishop, J. E. (1995, March 21). Suspected toxic agent in attack is made of chemicals easily available in U.S. *Wall Street Journal,* p. A12.

Greenfield, L. A. Capital punishment 1990. *Bureau of Justice Statistics Bulletin,* September 1991.

Greenhouse, S. (1999, February 4). Doctors, under pressure from H.M.O.'s, are ready union recruits. *New York Times.*

Greer, G. (1972). *The female eunuch.* New York: Bantam.

Grimmett, R. F. (2006, October 23). *Conventional arms transfers to developing nations, 1998–2005.* Washington, DC: CRS Report for Congress.

Guardian of Brazil Indians faces many foes. (1997, June 10). Retrieved from http://forests.org/archive/brazil/guarind.htm

Gudkov, Y. (1980, January). The "respectable" mafia. *World Press Review, 27,* 51.

Gurvich, T., & Cunningham, J. A. (2000). Appropriate use of psychotropic drugs in nursing homes. *American Family Physician, 6,* 1437–1446.

Gusfield, J. R. (1963). *Symbolic crusade: Status politics and the American temperance movement.* Urbana: University of Illinois Press.

Guttmacher Institute. (2008). *Facts on American teens' sexual and reproductive health.* Retrieved from http://www.guttmacher.org/sections/abortion.php

Haas, J., & Shaffir, W. (1993). The cloak of competence. In J. M. Henslin (Ed.), *Down-to-earth sociology: Introductory readings* (7th ed.). New York: Free Press.

Haber, J. (2003). *ADHD: The great misdiagnosis.* Dallas: Taylor.

Hacker, H. M. (1951 October). Women as a minority group. *Social Forces, 30,* 60–69.

Hackett, G. (1988, January 11). Kids: Deadly force. *Newsweek,* pp. 18–19.

Hadden, J. K., & Barton, J. J. (1973). An image that will not die: Thoughts on the history of anti-urban ideology. In L. H. Masoti & J. K. Hadden (Eds.), *The urbanization of the suburbs* (pp. 79–116). Beverly Hills, CA: Sage.

Hagan, F. E. (1997). *Political crime: Ideology and criminality.* Boston: Allyn & Bacon.

Hage, D. (2004). *Reforming welfare by rewarding work.* Minneapolis: University of Minnesota Press.

Hagedorn, J. M. (2005, May). The global impact of gangs. *Journal of Contemporary Criminal Justice, 21*(2), 153–169.

Hagerty, J. R., Langley, M., & Pulliam, S. (2008, July 21). *Mortgage giant Freddie Mac considers major stock sale.* Retrieved from http://www.online.wsj.com

Hale, M. (1980, October 3). In courts, defendant's color counts. *Fort Lauderdale News.*

Hall, S. (1972). *Gentleman of leisure: A year in the life of a pimp.* New York: New American Library.

Hampson, R. (2005, April 19). Studies: Gentrification a boost for everyone. *USA Today.* Retrieved from http://www.usatoday.com

Hanson, D. J. (1995). *Preventing alcohol abuse: Alcohol, culture, and control.* Westport, CT: Praeger.

Hanssen, M. (1997). *The new additive code breaker.* Port Melbourne, Australia: Lothian Books.

Hardin, G. (1968, December). The tragedy of the commons. *Science, 162,* 1243–1248.

Harlan, C. (1988, November 4). Come out with your hands up and no funny stuff with the peas. *Wall Street Journal*, p. B1.

Harrington, M. (1962). *The other America*. New York: Macmillan.

Harrington, M. (1977). *The vast majority: A journey to the world's poor*. New York: Simon & Schuster.

Harris, C., & Ullman, E. (1945, November). The nature of cities. *Annals of the American Academy of Political and Social Science, 242*, 7–17.

Harris, D. K., & Benson, M. L. (2006). *Maltreatment of patients in nursing homes: There is no safe place*. New York: Haworth Pastoral Press.

Harris, G. (2006, March 23). Panel advises disclosure of drugs' psychotic effects. *New York Times*. Retrieved from http://www.nytimes.com

Harris, M. (1977, November 13). Why men dominate women. *New York Times Magazine*, 46ff.

Harris, S. H. (1994). *Factories of death*. New York: Routledge.

Harrison, P. M., & Beck, A. J. (2005, May). Prison and jail inmates at midyear 2005. *Bureau of Justice Statistics Bulletin*.

Hart, C. W. M., & Pilling, A. R. (1979). *The Tiwi of North Australia* (Fieldwork Edition). New York: Holt, Rinehart and Winston.

Hart, H. (1957). Acceleration in social change. In F. R. Allen, H. Hart, D. C. Miller, W. F. Ogburn, & M. F. Nimkoff (Eds.), *Technology and Social Change*. New York: Appleton.

Haskins, R. (2006, July 30). The welfare check. *Wall Street Journal*. Retrieved from http://www.online.wsj.com

Haub, C. (2005). *2005 World population data sheet*. Washington, DC: Population Reference Bureau.

Haub, C., & Cornelius, D. (1999). *1999 World population data sheet*. Washington, DC: Population Reference Bureau.

Hauser, P., & Schnore, L. (Eds.). (1965). *The study of urbanization*. New York: Wiley.

Haveman, R. H., & Scholz, J. K. (1994–1995, Winter). The Clinton welfare reform plan: Will it end poverty as we know it? *Focus, 16*(2), 1–11.

Hawkins, D. N., Amato, P. R., King, V. (2007). Nonresident father involvement and adolescent well-being: Father effects or child effects? *American Sociological Review, 72*(6), 990–1010.

Hayden, F. G., Wood, K. R., & Kaya, A. (2002, September). The use of power blocs of integrated corporate directorships to articulate a power structure: Case study and research recommendations. *Journal of Economic Issues, 36*(3), 671–706.

Hayes, A. S. (1991, October 11). How the courts define harassment. *Wall Street Journal*, p. B1, B3.

HealthGrades. (2005, October 17). The eighth annual HealthGrades hospital quality in America study.

Heins, M. (1991, November). The war on nudity, continued. *Playboy*, 53.

Hello Kitty robot receptionist debuts in Japan. (2006, January 26). *ABC News Online*. Retrieved from http://www.abc.net.au

Helmer, J. (1975). *Drugs and minority oppression*. New York: Seabury.

Hench, D. (2006, September 28). Jail sends TB patient to hospital in Boston. *Portland Press Herald*.

Hendin, H. (1997, May 8). Euthanasia and physician-assisted suicide in the Netherlands. *New England Journal of Medicine, 336*(19), 1385–1387.

Hendin, H. (2000, January). Suicide, assisted suicide, and mental illness. *Harvard Mental Health Letter, 16*(7), 4–7.

Henriques, F. (1966). *Prostitution and society*. New York: Grove.

Henslin, J. M. (1970). Guilt and guilt neutralization: Response and adjustment to suicide. In J. D. Douglas (Ed.), *Deviance and respectability: The social construction of moral meanings*. New York: Basic Books.

Henslin, J. M. (2007a). On becoming male: Reflections of a sociologist on childhood and early socialization. In J. M. Henslin (Ed.), *Down-to-earth sociology: Introductory readings* (14th ed.). New York: Free Press.

Henslin, J. M. (2007b). *Sociology: A down-to-earth approach* (8th ed.). Boston: Allyn & Bacon.

Henslin, J. M., & Biggs, M. A. (2007). Behavior in pubic places: The sociology of the vaginal examination. In J. M. Henslin (Ed.), *Down-to-earth sociology: Introductory readings* (14th ed.). New York: Free Press.

Herbert, B. (1988, August 10). In America: The hate virus. *New York Times*. Retrieved from http://www.nytimes.com

Herbert, B. (1998, August 13). In America: Don't flunk the future. *New York Times*. Retrieved from http://www.nytimes.com

Herper, M. (2006, February 27). The best-selling drugs in America. *Forbes*. Retrieved from http://www.forbes.com

Hersh, S. (2002, December 23). Manhunt. *New Yorker*. Retrieved from http://www.newyorker.com

Hertsgaard, M. (2004, May 24). Bhopal's legacy. *The Nation*. Retrieved from www.thenation.com

Heyl, B. S. (1979). *The madam as entrepreneur: Career management in house prostitution*. New Brunswick, NJ: Transaction.

Hibbert, C. (1963). *The roots of evil: A social history of crime and punishment*. New York: Minerva.

Hill, C., & Silva, E. (2005). *Drawing the line. Sexual harassment on campus*. Washington, DC: American Association of University Women Educational Foundation.

Hilliard, A., III. (1991, September). Do we have the will to educate all children? *Educational Leadership, 49*, 31–36.

Hills, S. L. (1980). *Demystifying social deviance*. New York: McGraw-Hill.

Hills, S. L. (Ed.). (1987). *Corporate violence: Injury and death for profit*. Totowa, NJ: Rowman & Littlefield.

Hiltz, S. R. (1989). Widowhood. In J. M. Henslin (Ed.), *Marriage and family in a changing society* (pp. 521–531). New York: Free Press.

Himmelhoch, J., & Fava, S. F. (Eds.). (1955). *Sexual behavior in American society: An appraisal of the first two Kinsey reports*. New York: Norton.

Hindelang, M. J. (1978, February). Race and involvement in common personal crimes. *American Sociological Review, 43*, 93–109.

Hirschi, T. (1969). *Causes of delinquency*. Berkeley: University of California Press.

Historical statistics of the United States: From colonial times to the present. (1976). New York: Basic Books.

Hochschild, A., & Machung, A. (2001). Men who share the "second shift." In J. M. Henslin (Ed.), *Down-to-earth sociology: Introductory readings* (11th ed., pp. 395–409). New York: Free Press.

Hodgson, J. F. (1997). *Games pimps play: Pimps, players and wives-in-law*. Toronto: Canadian Scholars' Press.

Hoffman, A. (1968). Psychotomimetic agents. In *Drugs affecting the central nervous system* (vol. 2). New York: Marcel Dekker.

Hoffman, S. (2006, August 10). The foreign policy the U.S. needs. *New York Review of Books, 53*, 13.

Hogan, B. (2001, September 1). The wages of synfuels. *Mother Jones*. Retrieved from http://www.motherjones.com

Holdren, J. P., & Ehrlich, P. R. (1974, May–June). Human population and the global environment. *American Scientist, 62*, 282–292.

Holman, R. L. (1994, July 28). World wire. *Wall Street Journal*, p. A10.

Holtzman, A. (1963). *The Townsend movement: A political study*. New York: Bookman.

Homblin, D. J. (1973). *The first cities*. Boston: Little, Brown.

Hooton, E. A. (1939). *Crime and the man*. Cambridge, MA.: Harvard University Press.

Hope, C. A., & Stover, R. G. (1987). Gender status, monotheism, and social complexity. *Social Forces, 65*, 1132–1138.

Hornblower, M. (1993, June 21). The skin trade. *Time*, pp. 45–51.

Horowitz, R. (1983). *Honor and the American dream: Culture and identity in a Chicano community*. New Brunswick, NJ: Rutgers University Press.

Hosenball, M. (1999, May 3). A plutonium mystery. *Newsweek*, pp. 62–64.

Hotchkiss, S. (1978, December). The realities of rape. *Human Behavior, 12,* 18–23.

Hotz, R. L. (1999, January 8). Early humans' fire use linked to extinctions. *Los Angeles Times.*

Howard, J., & Strauss, A. (Eds.). (1975). *Humanizing health care.* New York: Wiley.

Howell, K. K., Lynch, M. E., Platzman, K. A., Smith, G. H., & Coles, C. D. (2006). Prenatal alcohol exposure and ability, academic achievement, and school functioning in adolescence: A longitudinal follow-up. *Journal of Pediatric Psychology, 31*(1), 116–126.

Hsu, F. L. K. (1971). *The challenge of the American dream: The Chinese in the United States.* Belmont, CA: Wadsworth.

Huber, J. (1990, February). Micro-macro links in gender stratification. *American Sociological Review, 55,* 1–10.

Huddle, D. (1993). The net national cost of immigration. Washington, DC: Carrying Capacity Network.

Hudson, R. B. (1978, October). The "graying" of the federal budget and its consequences for old-age policy. *The Gerontologist, 18,* 428–440.

Huff-Corzine, L., Corzine, J., & Moore, D. C. (1986). Southern exposure: Deciphering the South's influence on homicide rates. *Social Forces, 64,* 906–924.

Huff-Corzine, L., Corzine, J., & Moore, D. C. (1991, March). Deadly connections: Culture, poverty, and the direction of lethal violence. *Social Forces, 69*(3), 715–732.

Huggins, M. K. (1993). *Lost childhood: Assassinations of youth in democratizing Brazil.* Paper presented at the annual meetings of the American Sociological Association.

Huhtala, M. T. (2004). *Measures to combat trafficking in persons.* Unpublished speech given April 13, 2004, Kuala Lumpur, Malaysia. http://www.usembassymalaysia.org.my/amsp041304 .html

Hull, J. D. (1987, August 24). Life and death with the gangs. *Time,* pp. 21–22.

Human Rights Watch (1996). *No escape: Male rape in U.S. prisons.* http://www.hrw.org/reports/2001/prison/report.html

Humphreys, L. (1970). *Tearoom trade.* Chicago: Aldine. (Expanded version, Chicago: Aldine-Atherton, 1975.).

Humphries, D., Dawson, J., Cronin, V., Keating, P., Wisniewski, C., & Eichfeld, J. (1992). Mothers and children, drugs and crack: Reactions to maternal drug dependency. *Women and Criminal Justice, 3*(2), 81–99.

Huxley, A. (1954). *The doors of perception.* New York: Harper & Row.

Hybrid car market revs up. (2004, May 3). *USA Today.* Retrieved from http://www.usatoday.com

Iannelli, V. (2008, April 30). *ADHD Symptoms.* (M. R. Board, Editor, & Health's Disease and Condition) Retrieved April 30, 2009, from About.com: http://pediatrics.about.com/od/adhd/a/ adhd_symptoms.htm

Ilminen, G. R. (2006, April). New strategies ramping up quality in Wisconsin Medicaid managed care. *Home Health Care Management & Practice, 18*(3), 235–238.

Implementation of measures to prevent sexual harassment of national civil servants. (2000). *Woman in Japan Today.*

Inciardi, J. A. (1986). *The war on drugs: Heroin, cocaine, crime, and public policy.* Mountain View, CA: Mayfield.

Inciardi, J. A., & Pottieger, A. E. (1994, Winter). Crack-cocaine use and street crime. *Journal of Drug Issues, 24*(2), 273–292.

Ingersoll, B. (1988, December 20). FDA is proposing limits on sulfites in range of foods. *Wall Street Journal,* p. C21.

Ingersoll, B. (1990, November 16). Faster slaughter lines are contaminating much U.S. poultry. *Wall Street Journal,* pp. A1, A6.

Iovine, N. M., & Blaser, M. J. (2004, June). Antibiotics in animal feed and spread of resistant campylobacter from poultry to humans. *Emerging Infectious Diseases* [serial on the Internet]. Retrieved from http://www.cdc.gov/ncidod/EID/vol10no6/04-0403 .htm

Iran test fires longer range missile as part of new maneuvers. (2006, November 9). *International Herald Tribune.* Retrieved from http://www.iht.com

Isbell, H. (1969). Historical development of attitudes toward opiate addiction in the United States. In S. M. Farber & R. H. L. Wilson (Eds.), *Man and Civilization: Conflict, and Creativity* (pp. 154–170). New York: McGraw-Hill.

Izaak Walton League of America. (2000). *Conservation policies.* http://www.iwla.org

Izumi, L. (n.d.). *Cutting Through the Smoke: Facts on the Cigarette Tax.* Retrieved April 24, 2009, from Mensch Magazine: http://www .forces.org/articles/files/tobacco1.htm

Jacobs, J. (2004). *Dark age ahead.* New York: Random House.

Jaffe, J. H. (1965). Drug addiction and drug abuse. In L. S. Goodman & A. Gilmann (Eds.), *The pharmacological basis of therapeutics* (pp. 285–311). New York: Macmillan.

Jain, A. (2005, March 28). Is arranged marriage really any worse than Craigslist? *New York.* Retrieved from http://nymag.com

Jain, S. (2006, September 6). It's official: Asbestos is crippling Alang workers. *Indian Express.* Retrieved from http://www .indianexpress.com

James, J., & Davis, N. J. (1982, Winter). Contingencies in female sexual role deviance: The case of prostitution. *Human Organization, 41*(4), 345–350.

James, J., & Meyerding, J. (1977). Early sexual experiences in prostitution. *Archives of Sexual Behavior, 7,* 31–42.

Janowitz, M. (1970a). The twentieth-century race riot, commodity type: The summer of 1967. In R. Maxwell (Ed.), *American violence* (pp. 147–155). Englewood Cliffs, NJ: Prentice Hall.

Janowitz, M. (1970b). The twentieth-century race riot, communal type: Chicago, 1919. In R. Maxwell (Ed.), *American violence,* (pp. 126–136). Englewood Cliffs, NJ: Prentice Hall.

Jefferson, T. (1977). *Notes on the state of Virginia* (B. Wishy & W. C. Leuchtenburg, Eds.). New York: Harper & Row. (Original work published 1784.).

Jekielek, S. M. (1998, March). Parental conflict, marital disruption and children's emotional well-being. *Social Forces, 76*(3), 905–935.

Jenkins, B. M. (1987, July–August). The future course of terrorism. *The Futurist, 8.*

Joffe, C. (1978, May–June). What haven? For whom? *Social Policy, 9,* 58–60.

Johnson, B. D., Anderson, K., & Wish, E. D. (1988, April). A day in the life of 105 drug addicts and abusers: Crimes committed and how the money was spent. *Sociology and Social Research, 72*(3), 185–191.

Johnson, B. D., Goldstein, P. J., Preble, E., Schmeidler, J., Lipton, D. S., Spunt, B., and Miller, T. (1985). *Taking care of business: The economics of crime by heroin abusers.* Lexington, MA: Lexington Books.

Johnson, D. (1988, August 8). Murder charges are met by cries of compassion. *New York Times,* p. A14.

Johnson, D. R. (1992, December). Tobacco stains: Cigarette firms buy into African-American groups. *The Progressive, 56*(12), 26–28.

Johnson, T. R., Pozdena, R. J., & Steiger, G. (1979, October). *The impact of alternative negative income tax programs on non-durable consumption.* Menlo Park, CA: SRI International.

Johnston, L. (2006, December 21). *The University of Michigan News.* Retrieved April 30, 2009, from The University of Michigan News Service: http://www.ns.umich.edu/htdocs/releases/story .php?id=3066

Johnston, L. D., O'Malley, P. M., Bachman, J. G., & Schulenberg, J. E. (2003). *Monitoring the future: National results on adolescent drug use.* Washington, DC: U.S. Department of Health and Human Services.

Johnston, L. D., O'Malley, P. M., Bachman, J. G., & Schulenberg, J. E. (2007). *Monitoring the future: National results on adolescent*

drug use. Washington, DC: U.S. Department of Health and Human Services.

Johnston, L. D., O'Malley, P. M., & Terry-McElrath, Y. M. (2004) Methods, locations, and ease of cigarette access for American youth, 1997–2002. *American Journal of Preventative Medicine, 27,* 267–276

Johnston, L. D., Schulenberg, J. E., & Bachman, J. G. (2005). *Monitoring the future: National survey results on drug use, 1975–2004, Vol. 1: Secondary Students.* Washington, DC: U.S. Department of Health and Human Services.

Jones, R. G. (2008, January 13). Heroin's hold on the young. *New York Times.* Retrieved from http://www.nytimes.com

Jordan, J. (2001). Worlds apart? Women, rape and the police reporting process. *British Journal of Criminology, 41,* 679–706.

Josephy, A. M., Jr. (1970, June). Indians in history. *Atlantic Monthly,* 67–72.

Julien, R. M. (2001). *A primer of drug action.* New York: Worth Publishers.

Kahn, J. (2006, March 17). Sane Chinese put in asylum, doctors find. *New York Times.* Retrieved from http://www.nytimes.com

Kalb, C. (2000, March 6). Drugged-out toddlers. *Newsweek.* Retrieved from http://www.newsweek.com

Kane, E. (2006, April). "No way my boys are going to be like that!" Parents' responses to children's gender nonconformity. *Gender and Society, 20*(2), 149–176.

Kanin, E. J. (2003). Date rapists: Differential sexual socialization and relative deprivation. In M. Silberman (Ed.), *Violence and society: A reader* (pp. 207–225). Upper Saddle River, NJ: Prentice Hall.

Kantor, G. K., & Straus, M. A. (1987, June). The "drunken bum" theory of wife beating. *Social Problems, 34*(3), 213–230.

Kaplan, C. S. (1998, November 20). Anti-porn law enters court; Delay soon follows. *New York Times.* Retrieved from http://www.nytimes.com

Kaplan, S. (1990, Summer). Historical efforts to encourage White-Indian intermarriage in the United States and Canada. *International Social Science Review, 65*(3), 126–132.

Karlen, N., & Burgower, B. (1985, January 7). Dumping the mentally ill. *Newsweek,* p. 17.

Karmen, A. (1980). The narcotics problem: Views from the left. In H. Etzkowitz (Ed.), *Is America possible? Social problems from conservative, liberal, and socialist perspectives* (2nd ed.; pp. 171–180). St. Paul, MN: West.

Karp, D. A., Stone, G. P., & Yoels, W. C. (1991). *Being urban: A sociology of city life* (2nd ed.). New York: Praeger.

Katz, M. B. (1989). *The undeserving poor: From the war on poverty to the war on welfare.* New York: Pantheon.

Kelly, E., & Hillard, P. J. A. (2005). Female genital mutilation: Adolescent and pediatric gynecology. *Current Opinion in Obstetrics & Gynecology, 17*(5), 490–494.

Kemp, J. (1990, Winter). Tackling poverty: Market-based policies to empower the poor. *Policy Review, 51,* 2–5.

Kemper, P., Komisar, H. L., & Alexcih, L. (2006). Long-term care over an uncertain future: What can current retirees expect? *Inquiry, 42*(4), 335–350.

Kettl, D. F. (1991, September). The savings-and-loan bailout: The mismatch between the headlines and the issues. *PS, 24*(3), 441–447.

Keyes, K, Jr. (n.d.). *The hundredth monkey.* St. Mary, KY: Vision Books.

Kids count data sheet. (2004). Baltimore, MD: Annie E. Casey Foundation.

Kilborn, P. T. (1998, October 5). Reality of H.M.O. system does not live up to hopes for health care. *New York Times.* Retrieved from http://www.nytimes.com

Kilman, S. (2006, October 31). Seed firms bolster crops using traits of distant relatives. *Wall Street Journal.* Retrieved from http://www.online.wsj.com

King, M. L., Jr. (1958). *Stride toward freedom: The Montgomery story.* New York: Harper.

King, S. A., & Poulos, S. T. (1999). Ethical guidelines for on-line therapy. In J. Fink (Ed.), *How to use computers and cyberspace in the clinical practice of psychotherapy* (pp. 121–132). Lanham, MD: Jason Aronson.

King, V. (1994). Nonresident father involvement and child well-being: Can dads make a difference? *Journal of Family Issues, 15*(1), 78–96.

King, W. (1979. March 15). Violent Klan group gaining members. *New York Times,* p. A18.

Kinsey, A. C., Pomeroy, W. B., & Martin, C. E. (1948). *Sexual behavior in the human male.* Philadelphia: Saunders.

Kinsey, A. C., Pomeroy, W. B., Martin, C. E., & Gebhard, P. H. (1953). *Sexual behavior in the human female.* New York: Saunders.

Kirkham, G. L. (1971). Homosexuality in prison. In J. M. Henslin (Ed.), *Studies in the sociology of sex* (pp. 325–349). New York: Appleton.

Kirkpatrick, M. (1992, April 23). On the abortion barricades. *Wall Street Journal,* p. A14.

Kirkpatrick, T. (1981, June 26). A new breed of pioneers are homesteading America's cities. *Alton Telegraph.*

Kitano, H. H. L. (1974). *Race relations.* Englewood Cliffs NJ: Prentice Hall.

Kitty Genovese. (2005, April 15). *A picture history of Kew Gardens, NY.* Retrieved from http://kewgardenshistory.com/kitty_genovese.html

Kleck, G., & Sayles, S. (1990, May). Rape and resistance. *Social Problems, 37*(2), 149–162.

Klein, S., Petersilia, J., & Turner, S. (1990, February 16). Race and imprisonment decisions in California. *Science, 247*(4944), 812–816.

Kleinman, P. H., Wish, E. D., Deren, S., Rainone, G., & Morehouse, E. (1987). Daily marijuana use and problem behaviors among adolescents. *International Journal of the Addictions, 22,* 12.

Kluger, J. (2006, April 3). Global warming heats up. *Time.* Retrieved from http://www.time.com

Knights, R. (1999, January 22). Electronic tagging in practice. *Teleconnect.*

Koball, H., & Douglas-Hall, A. (2006). *The new poor: Regional trends in child poverty since 2000.* National Center for Children in Poverty. Available at http://nccp.org/publications/pub_672.html

Kocieniewski, D., & Sullivan, J. (2006, January 16). In Newark, a ward boss with influence to spare. *New York Times.* Retrieved from http://www.nytimes.com

Kohn, A. (1988, June). Make love, not war. *Psychology Today,* 35–38.

Komisar, L. (1971). The image of woman in advertising. In V. Gornick & B. K. Moran (Eds.), *Woman in sexist society: Studies in power and powerlessness* (pp. 207–217). New York: Basic Books.

Konrad, K., Gunther, T., Hanisch, C., & Herpertz-Dahlmann, B. (2004). Differential effects of methylphenidate on attentional functions in children with attention-deficit/hyperactivity disorder. *Journal of the American Academy of Child and Adolescent Psychiatry, 43,* 191–198.

Korda, M. (1973). *Male chauvinism: How it works.* New York: Random House.

Kornhauser, W. (1961). "Power elite" or "veto groups"? In S. M. Lipset & L. Lowenthal (Eds.), *Culture and social character* (pp. 252–267). Glencoe, IL: Free Press.

Kozel, N. J. (1996, June). *Epidemiologic trends in drug abuse.* Community Epidemiology Work Group. Bethesda, Maryland: National Institutes of Health.

Kozol, J. (1999). Savage inequalities. In J. M. Henslin (Ed.), *Down-to-earth sociology: Introductory readings* (10th ed., pp. 343–351). New York: Free Press.

Krieger, L. (1985, June 7). Abortion foes, proponents intensify battle. *American Medical News, 28,* 2–3.

Kristoff, N. D. (2002, July 23). Interview with a humanoid. *New York Times.* Retrieved from http://www.nytimes.com

Kruk, J., & Aboul-Enein, H. Y. (2006, February). Environmental exposure, and other risk factors in breast cancer. *Current Cancer Therapy Reviews, 2,* 1, 3–21.

Kumanyika, S. (2005, October). Obesity, health disparities, and prevention paradigms: Hard questions and hard choices. *Preventing Chronic Disease, 2,* 4.

Kurella, H. (1911). *Cesare Lombroso: a Modern Man of Science.* London: Rebman, Ltd.

Kurth, J. R. (1974). American military policy and advanced weapons. In L. Rainwater (Ed.), *Social problems and public policy: Inequality and Justice* (pp. 336–352). Chicago: Aldine.

Kurtz, S., Inciardi, J., Surratt, H., & Cottler, L. (2005). Prescription drug abuse among Ecstasy users in Miami. *Journal of Addictive Diseases, 24*(4), 1–16).

Kusum. (1993, April). The use of pre-natal diagnostic techniques for sex selection: The Indian scene. *Bioethics, 7*(2–3), 149–165.

Kutchinsky, B. (1973). The effects of easy availability of pornography on the incidence of sex crimes in Copenhagen: The Danish experience. *Journal of Social Issues, 29,* 163–181.

La Barre, W. (1954). *The human animal.* Chicago: University of Chicago Press.

La Gory, M., Ward, R., & Juravich, T. (1980). The age segregation process. *Urban Affairs Quarterly, 16,* 59–80.

LaBastille, A. (1979, October). The deadly toll of acid rain: All of nature is suffering. *Science Digest, 86,* 61–66.

Labaton, S., & Andrews, E. L. (2008, September 7). In rescue to stabilize lending, U.S. takes over mortgage finance titans. *New York Times.* Retrieved from http://www.nytimes.com

Lacayo, R. (1991, October 21). Crusading against the pro-choice movement. *Time.* Retrieved from http://www.time.com

Lacey, M. (2003, February 7). African activists urge end to female mutilation. *International Herald Tribune,* 10.

LaFree, G. D. (1980, October). The effect of sexual stratification by race on official reactions to rape. *American Sociological Review, 45,* 842–854.

Lalumiere, M. L., Harris, G. T., Quinsey, V. L., & Rice, M. E. (2005). *The causes of rape: Understanding individual differences in male propensity for sexual aggression.* Washington, DC: American Psychological Association.

Lamar, J. V., Jr. (1986, August 11). An inmate and a gentleman. *Time,* pp. 17.

Lamptey, P. R., Johnson, J. L., & Khan, M. (2006, March). The global challenge of HIV and AIDS. *Population Bulletin, 61,* 1.

Landes, D. S. (1998). *The wealth and poverty of nations: Why some are rich and some so poor.* New York: W.W. Norton.

Lang, K., & Lang, G. (1968). Racial disturbances as collective protest. In L. H. Masotti & D. R. Bowen (Eds.), *Riots and rebellion: Civil violence in the urban community* (pp. 121–130). Beverly Hills, CA: Sage.

Lang, R. E. (2003). *Edgeless cities: Exploring the elusive metropolis.* Washington, DC: Brookings Institution Press.

Langan, P. A., & Levin, D. J. (2002, June). *Recidivism of prisoners released in 1994.* Bureau of Justice, Special Report.

Laqueur, W. (1977). *Terrorism.* Boston: Little, Brown.

Larned, D. (1977). The epidemic in unnecessary hysterectomies. In C. Dreyfus (Ed.), *Seizing our bodies: The politics of women's health.* New York: Random House.

Larson, M. S. (2001, Winter). Interactions, activities and gender in children's television commercials: A content analysis. *Journal of Broadcasting and Electronic Media, 45,* 41–51.

Larsson, S. C., Bergkvist, Leif, & Wolk, Alicja. (2004, November). Milk and lactose intakes and ovarian cancer risk in the Swedish mammography cohort. *American Journal of Clinical Nutrition, 80* (5), 1353–1357.

Lasch, C. (1977). *Haven in a heartless world: The family besieged.* New York: Basic Books.

Laslett, B. (1980). *Family, social change can often spell trouble.* University of California, University Extension, Course by Newspaper, San Diego.

Laumann, E. O., Gagnon, J. H., Michael, R. T., & Michaels, Stuart. (1994). *The social organization of sexuality: Sexual practices in the United States.* Chicago: University of Chicago Press.

Law enacted to protect Ainu culture, tradition. (1997, June 19). Foreign Press Center of Japan.

Leaf, C. (2004). Enough is enough. In K. Finsterbusch (Ed.), *Sociology* (33rd ed., pp. 52–59). New York: McGraw-Hill/Dushkin.

LeBlanc, S. (2007, January 2). Mass. lawmakers advance proposed gay marriage ban. Associated Press/*Boston Globe.* Retrieved from http://www.boston.com

Lee, D. (1959). *Freedom and culture.* Englewood Cliffs, NJ: Prentice Hall.

Lee, S. M. (1998, June). Asian Americans: Diverse and growing. *Population Bulletin, 53*(2), 1–39.

Lehrer, J. (2005). Corporate crime. *Online NewsHour Special Report: Corporate Ethics.* Retrieved from http://www.pbs.org/newshour/bb/business/july-dec05/crime_7-14.html

Leigh, B. C., Temple, M. T., & Trocki, K. F. (1993). The sexual behavior of US adults: Results from a national survey. *American Journal of Public Health, 83,* 1400–1408.

Leighty, K. E. (1981, October 31). Germ testing by Japanese killed POWs. Associated Press.

Leinwand, D. (2004, February 24). Judges write creative sentences. *USA Today.* Retrieved from http://www.usatoday.com

Leland, J. (2003, August 7). A new Harlem gentry in search of its latte. *New York Times.* Retrieved from http://www.nytimes.com

Lender, M. E., & Martin, J. K. (1982). *Drinking in America: A history.* New York: Free Press.

Leonard, R., & Locke, D. C. (1993, March). Communication stereotypes: Is interracial communication possible? *Journal of Black Studies, 23*(3), 332–343.

Lerner, G. (1986). *The creation of patriarchy.* New York: Oxford University Press.

Lerner, R., Nagai, A. K., & Rothman, S. (1990, January–February). Abortion and social change in America. *Society, 2*(27), 8–15.

Lesser, A. (1968). War and the state. In M. Fried, M. Harris, & R. Murphy (Eds.), *War: The anthropology of armed conflict and aggression.* Garden City, NY: Natural History.

Lester, D. (1972, November). Incest. *Journal of Sex Research, 8,* 268–285.

Leuchtag, A. (2004). Human rights, sex trafficking, & prostitution. In K. Pinsterbusch (Ed.), *Social Problems* (32nd ed.; pp. 88–93). New York: McGraw-Hill/Dushkin.

LeVay, S. (1993). *The sexual brain.* Cambridge, MA.: MIT Press.

Levine, A. (1986, October 13). Drug education gets an F. *U.S. News & World Report,* 63–64.

Levine, J. W. (2004, December 16). National educators meet to discuss success of small public school in New York's *El Barrio. Siempre.*

Levine, S. (2004, April 5). Who'll stop the mercury rain? *U.S. News & World Report.* Retrieved from http://www.usnews.com

Lewin, T. (1998, June 26). 1 in 8 boys of high-school age has been abused, survey says. *New York Times.* Retrieved from http://www.nytimes.com

Lewis, D. L. (1996, February 5). Bias in drug sentences. *National Law Journal.*

Lewis, J. (1990, November). The Ogallala Aquifer: An underground sea. *EPA Journal, 16*(6), 42–44.

Lewis, K. J. (1988, September 13). *Abortion: Judicial control.* Washington, DC: Congressional Research Service, American Law Division. Mimeo.

Lewis, O. (1959). *Five families.* New York: Basic Books.

Lewis, O. (1966, October). The culture of poverty. *Scientific American, 115,* 19–25.

Lewis, P. W., & Peoples, K. D. (1978). *The Supreme Court and the criminal process: Cases and comments.* Philadelphia: Saunders.

Lewnes, A. (2005). *Changing a harmful social convention: Female genital mutilation/cutting.* Paris: UNESCO.

Lewontin, R. C. (2006). *Confusions about human races.* Retrieved from http://raceandgenomics.ssrc.org/Lewontin/

Liazos, A. (1981). Corporate crime and capitalism. Paper presented at the annual meeting of the Society for the Study of Social Problems.

Light, D. W., Jr. (1973). Treating suicide: The illusions of a professional movement. *International Social Science Journal, 25,* 473–488.

Light, D. W., Jr. (1992, March). Perestroika for Russian health care. *Footnotes, 20*(3), 7, 9.

Lightfoot-Klein, H. (1989). Rites of purification and their effects: Some psychological aspects of female genital circumcision and infibulation (pharaonic circumcision) in an Afro-Arab society (Sudan). *Journal of Psychological Human Sexuality, 2,* 61–78.

Linden, E. (1991, September 23). Lost tribes, lost knowledge. *Time,* pp. 46–56.

Lindner, K. (2004, October). Images of women in general interest and fashion magazine advertisements from 1955 to 2002. *Sex Roles, 51*(7/8), 409–421.

Linton, R. (1936). *The study of man.* New York: Appleton.

Linz, D., Donnerstein, E., & Penrod, S. (1987, October). The findings and recommendations of the Attorney General's Commission on pornography: Do the psychological "facts" fit the political fury? *American Psychologist,* 946–953.

Liptak, A. (2004, October 16). Ex-inmate's suit offers view into sexual slavery in prisons. *New York Times.* Retrieved from http://www.nytimes.com

Liptak, A. (2005, October 22). Kansas law on gay sex by teenagers overturned. *New York Times.* Retrieved from http://www.nytimes.com

Little, P. D., & Horowitz, M. M. (Eds.). (1987). *Lands at risk in the Third World: Local-level perspectives.* Boulder, CO: Westview.

Littleton, H., & Breitkopf, C. R. (2006). Coping with the experience of rape. *Psychology of Women Quarterly, 30,* 106–116.

Liu, Y. (2004, July). China's public health-care system: Facing the challenges. *Bulletin of the World Health Organization, 82*(7), 532–538.

Livernash, R., & Rodenburg, E. (1998, March). Population change, resources, and the environment. *Population Bulletin, 53*(1), 1–40.

Livingston, K. (1997, April, 15). Ritalin: miracle drug or cop-out? *The Public Interest.* Retrieved from http://donpugh.dyndns.org/Psych%20Interests/ADD/Ritalin.htm

Lloyd, J. (2006). The link between environment and disease. *UN Chronicle,* 1.

Locy, T., & Biskupic, J. (2003, June 23). Anti-porn filters in libraries upheld. *USA Today.* Retrieved from http://www.usatoday.com

Lohn, M. (2005, February 17). Minnesota may expand meth boot camp program. Associated Press.

Lombroso, C. (1911). *Crime: Its causes and remedies* (H. P. Horton, Trans.). Boston: Little, Brown.

Lopez, A. (Ed.). (1980). *The Puerto Ricans: Their history, culture, and society.* Cambridge, MA: Schenkman.

Lopman, B. A., et al. (2006). Assessing adult mortality in HIV-1-afflicted Zimbabwe (1998–2003). *Bulletin of the World Health Organization, 84*(3).

Lorber, J. (1980). Beyond equality of the sexes: The question of children. In J. M. Henslin (Ed.), *Marriage and family in a changing society* (pp. 522–533). New York: Free Press.

Lorenz, K. (1966). *On aggression.* New York: Harcourt.

Loven, J. (2006, March 9). Religious charities get more money. Associated Press.

Low, S. (2008, September 6) Hydrogen is driving change. [Letter to the editor]. *The Globe and Mail* [Toronto], p. A24.

Lowi, T. J. (1977). Machine politics—Old and new. In J. J. Palen (Ed.), *City scenes: Problems and prospects.* Boston: Little, Brown.

Lucas, A. M. (2005). The work of sex work: Elite prostitutes' vocational orientations and experiences. *Deviant Behavior, 26,* 513–546.

Luckenbill, D. F. (1986, April). Deviant career mobility: The case of male prostitutes. *Social Problems 33*(4), 283–296.

Luker, K. (1975). *Taking chances: Abortion and the decision not to contracept.* Berkeley: University of California Press.

Lundberg, O. (1991). Causal explanations for class inequality in health: An empirical analysis. *Social Science and Medicine, 32*(4), 385–393.

Lutz, H. J. (1959). *Aboriginal man and white man as historical causes of fires in the Boreal Forest, with particular reference to Alaska.* New Haven, CT: Yale University School of Forestry. No. 65.

Luy, M. L. M. (1977, February 15). Rape: Not a sex act—A violent crime, an interview with Dr. Dorothy J. Hicks. *Modern Medicine,* 36–41.

Lynch, M. C. (1980, September 18). Old ice indicates acid was present in rain long ago. *Wall Street Journal,* pp. 13.

Lynd, R. S., & Lynd, H. M. (1929). *Middletown.* New York: Harcourt.

Lynd, R. S., & Lynd, H. M. (1937). *Middletown in transition.* New York: Harcourt.

Mackellar, L., & Horlacher, D. (2000, December). Population ageing in Japan: A brief survey. *The European Journal of Social Sciences, 13,* 4.

MacKenzie, D. L., & Souryal, C. (1995). Inmate attitude change during incarceration: A comparison of boot camp with traditional prison. *Justice Quarterly, 12,* 2.

MacKinnon, C. A. (1979). *Sexual harassment of working women: A case of sex discrimination.* New Haven, CT: Yale University Press.

MacNamara, D. E. J., & Sagarin, E. (1977). *Sex, crime, and the law.* New York: Free Press.

Madigan, L., & Gamble, N. (1991). *The second rape: Society's continued betrayal of the victim.* New York: Free Press.

Magee, E. A., Edmond, L. M., Tasker, S. M., Kong, S. C., Curno, R., & Cummings, J. H. Associations between diet and disease activity in ulcerative colitis. *Nutrition Journal, 4,* 7.

Mahran, M. (1978). Proceedings of the Third International Congress of Medical Sexology. Littleton, MA: PSG.

Mahran, M. (1981). Medical dangers of female circumcision. *International Planned Parenthood Federation Medical Bulletin, 2,* 1–2.

Malamuth, N. M., Addison, T., & Koss, M. (2000). Pornography and sexual aggression: Are there reliable effects and can we understand them? *Annual Review of Sex Research, 11,* 26–91.

Malthus, T. R. (1926). *First essay on population.* London: Macmillan. (Original work published 1798).

Mamdani, M. (1973). *The myth of population control: Family, caste, and class in an Indian village.* New York: Monthly Review. (As contained in Simon 1981).

Mandel-Campbell, A. (2001, June 25). A breath of fresh(er) air. *U.S. News & World Report.*

Manpower Report to the President. Washington, D.C.: U.S. Department of Labor, Manpower Administration, April 1971.

Manski, C. F. (1992–1993, Winter). Income and higher education. *Focus, 14*(3), 14–19.

Marger, M. N. (1987). *Elites and masses: An introduction to political sociology* (2nd ed.). Belmont, CA: Wadsworth.

Martin, P. S. (1967). Prehistoric overkill. In P. S. Martin & H. E. Wright, Jr. (Eds.), *Pleistocene extinctions: The search for a cause.* New Haven, CT: Yale University Press.

Martin, P., & Midgley, E. (1999, June). Immigration to the United States. *Population Bulletin, 54*(2), 1–43.

Martinez, J. F. E. (2003). Urban street activists: Gang and community efforts to bring peace and justice to Los Angeles neighborhoods. In L. Kontos, D. Brotherton, & L. Barrios (Eds.), *Gangs and society: Alternative perspectives* (pp. 95–115). New York: Columbia University Press.

Marx, K. (1967). *Das kapital.* New York: International. (Originally work published 1867–1895).

Marx, K., & Engels, F. (1906). *Capital: A critique of political economy* (E. Aveling, Trans.). Chicago: Charles Kerr.

Marx, K., & Engels, F. (1964). *The Communist manifesto* (S. Moore, Trans.). New York: Washington Square. (Originally published in 1848).

Mascio, B. (2007). *The daughters and sons of elder care.* Retrieved from http://www.seniorsapprove.com/daughter.html

Massey, D. S. (2001, September–October). As quoted in *Footnotes,* (29)6.

Mauer, M. (2004). Race, class, and the development of criminal justice policy. *Review of Policy Research, 21*(1), 79–92.

Maynard, D. W. (1984). *Inside plea bargaining: The language of negotiation.* New York: Plenum.

Mayne, S. T., Janerich, D. T., Greenwald, P., Chorost, S., Tucci, C., Zaman, M. B., et al. (1995, January 5). Dietary beta carotene and lung cancer risk in U.S. nonsmokers. *Journal of the National Cancer Institute, 86*(1), 33–38.

McCain, C. (2004, June 25). The pros of preventing cons. *Business First of Columbus.*

McCool, C. (2006, April 29). More contamination found at Bay Harbor. *Traverse City Record Eagle.*

McCormick, J. (1999, June 7). Change has taken place. *Newsweek,* p. 34.

McDonald, P. (2001, August–September). Low fertility not politically sustainable. *Population Today, 3,* 8.

McDowell, B. (1984). Mexico City: An alarming giant. *National Geographic, 166,* 139–174.

McGarigle, B. (1997, May). Satellite tracking for house arrest. *Geo Info.*

McGinley, L. (1999, February 18). Health-care debate heats up over control of medical decisions. *Wall Street Journal.*

McGinty, J. C. (2006, April 28). New York killers, and those killed, by numbers. *New York Times.* Retrieved from http://www.nytimes.com

McIntyre, J., Myint, T., & Curtis, L. (1979). *Sexual assault outcomes: Completed and attempted rapes.* Paper presented at the annual meeting of the American Sociological Association. Boston.

McKeown, T. (1977). *The modern rise of population.* New York: Academic Press.

McKeown, T. (1980). *The role of medicine: Dream, mirage, or nemesis?* Princeton, NJ: Princeton University Press.

McKinley, J. C., Jr. (2006a, October 30). Mexico: Grisly message from drug gang. *New York Times.* Retrieved from http://www.nytimes.com

McKinley, J. C., Jr. (2006b, October 26). With beheadings and attacks, drug gangs terrorize Mexico. *New York Times.* Retrieved from http://www.nytimes.com

McKinley, J. C., Jr., & Lacey, M. (2006, October 25). Mexico's drug war brings new brutality. *New York Times.*

McLanahan, S. (1996). Child support enforcement and child well-being: Greater security or greater conflict? *Child Support and Child Well-Being.* Washington: Urban Institute Press, pp. 239–56.

McManus, M. J. (1986). Introduction. In *Final Report of the Attorney General's Commission on Pornography* (pp. ix–1). Nashville, Tenn.: Rutledge Hill.

McNeely, R. L., & Pope, C. E. (1981). Socioeconomic and racial issues in the measurement of criminal involvement. In R. L. McNeely & C. E. Pope (Eds.), *Race, crime, and criminal justice* (pp. 31–41). Beverly Hills, CA: Sage.

Meadows, M. (2001). Prescription drug use and abuse. *FDA Consumer Magazine.* Washington DC: U.S. Food and Drug Administration.

Meese Commission. (1986). *Final report of the Attorney General's Commission on Pornography.* Washington, DC: U.S. Department of Justice.

Meier, B. (1987, March 26). As food imports rise, consumers face peril from use of pesticides, *Wall Street Journal.*

Melloan, G. (1994, December 12). Europe struggles with the burdens of old age. *Wall Street Journal,* p. A15.

Melman, S. (1970). *Pentagon capitalism.* New York: McGraw-Hill.

Melody, G. F. (1969, November). Chronic pelvic congestion in prostitutes. *Medical Aspects of Human Sexuality, 3,* 103–104.

Mendels, P. (1998, November 23). Judge rules against filters at library. *New York Times.*

Merton, R. K. (1957). *Social theory and social structure* (Rev. ed.). Glencoe, IL: Free Press.

Merton, R. K. (1968). *Social theory and social structure* (enlarged ed.). New York: Free Press.

Merton, R. K., & Nisbet, R. (Eds.). (1976). *Contemporary social problems* (4th ed.). New York: Harcourt.

Merwine, M. H. (1993, November 24). How Africa understands female circumcision. *New York Times.*

Messner, M. A., Duncan, M. C., & Cooky, C. (2003, February). Silence, sports bras, and wrestling porn. *Journal of Sport and Social Issues, 27*(1), 38–51.

Meyer, H. (1954). *Old English coffee houses.* Emmaus, PA: Rodale.

Michelman, K. (1988). As quoted in NARAL, pamphlet published by the National Abortion Rights Action League, 1.

Milbank, D. (1994, May 20). In his solitude, a Finnish thinker posits cataclysms. *Wall Street Journal,* pp. A1, A8.

Miles, S. (1980, April 8). Intellectualism meant death in Cambodia. *St. Louis Post-Dispatch,* D3.

Miller, J. (1999, May 25). U.S. and Uzbeks agree on chemical arms plant cleanup. *New York Times.* Retrieved from http://www.nytimes.com

Miller, J., & Broad, W. J. (1999, January 22). Clinton describes terrorism threat for 21st century. *New York Times.* Retrieved from http://www.nytimes.com

Miller, L. L. (2007). Women in the military. In J. M. Henslin (Ed.), *Down-to-earth sociology: Introductory readings* (14th ed.). New York: Free Press.

Miller, M. W. (1994, October 27). Quality stuff: Firm is peddling cocaine, and deals are legit. *Wall Street Journal,* pp. A1, A8.

Miller, W. B. (1958). Lower-class culture as a generating milieu of gang delinquency. *Journal of Social Issues, 14,* 5–19.

Millett, K. (1970). *Sexual politics.* Garden City, NY: Doubleday.

Millett, K. (1973). *The prostitution papers: A candid dialogue.* New York: Avon.

Mills, C. W. (1958). *The causes of World War Three.* New York: Simon & Schuster.

Mills, C. W. (1959a). *The power elite.* New York: Oxford University Press.

Mills, C. W. (1959b). *The sociological imagination.* New York: Oxford University Press.

Mills, K. M., & Palumbo, T. J. (1980). *A statistical portrait of women in the United States: 1978.* Washington, DC: U.S. Government Printing Office.

Milner, C., & Milner, R. (1972). *Black players*. Boston: Little, Brown.

Milvy, P. (1979, April 12). Cancer from the radiation. *New York Times*, p. 19.

Mintz, M. (1979, May 18). Error placed H-Bomb secrets on library shelf. *St. Louis Globe-Democrat*, 5A.

Moffitt, R. A. (2004, Summer). The idea of a negative income tax: Past, present, and future. *Focus, 23*, 2.

Mokdad A. H., Marks, J. S., Stroup, D. F., & Gerberding, J. L. (2004). Actual causes of death in the United States. *Journal of the American Medical Association, 291*, 1238–1245.

Mokhiber, R., & Shen, L. (1981). Love canal. In R. Nader, R. Brownstein, & J. Richard (Eds.), *Who's Poisoning America: Corporate Polluters and Their Victims in the Chemical Age* (pp. 268–310). San Francisco: Sierra Club Books.

Montagu, M. F. A. (1964). *The concept of race*. New York: Free Press.

Monto, M. A. (2004, February). Female prostitution, customers, and violence. *Violence Against Women, 10*(2), 160–188.

Moore, B. A., Augustson, E. M., Moser, R. P., & Budney, A. J. (2004). Respiratory effects of marijuana and tobacco use in a U.S. sample. *Journal of General Internal Medicine, 20*, 33–37.

Moore, G. (1979, October). The structure of a national elite network. *American Sociological Review, 44*, 673–691.

Morash, M. A., & Anderson, E. A. (1978, June). Liberal thinking on rehabilitation: A work-able solution to crime. *Social Problems, 25*, 556–563.

Morash, M., & Rucker, L. (1990, April). A critical look at the idea of boot camp as a correctional reform. *Crime and Delinquency, 36*(2), 204–222.

Morgan, P. A. (1978, Winter). The legislation of drug law: Economic crisis and social control. *Journal of Drug Issues, 8*, 54–62.

Morgenson, G. (2008, July 13). Silence of the lenders: Is anyone listening? *New York Times*. Retrieved from http://www.nytimes.com

Morrison, D. E., Hornback, K. E., & Warner, W. K. (1972). The environmental movement: Some preliminary observations and predictions. In W. R. Burch, Jr., N. H. Cheek, Jr., & L. Taylor (Eds.). (1972). *Social behavior, natural resources, and the environment* (pp. 259–279). New York: Harper & Row.

Morrison, D., & Cherlin, A. J. (1995). The divorce process and young children's well-being: A prospective analysis. *Journal of Marriage and the Family, 57*, 800–812.

Mukamal, K. J., Chung, H., Jenny, N. S., Kuller, L. H., Longstreth, W. T., Jr., Mittleman, M. A., et al. (2006). Alcohol consumption and risk of coronary heart disease in older adults: The cardiovascular health study. *Journal of the American Geriatrics Society, 54*, 30–37.

Mulvihill, D. J., Tumin, M. M., & Curtis, L. A. (1969). *Crimes of violence: A staff report to the National Commission on the Causes and Prevention of Violence*. Washington, DC: U.S. Government Printing Office.

Murphy, K. (1999, January 10). Last stand of an aging Aryan. *Los Angeles Times*, p. A-1.

Murphy, T. (2003, December 1). Hybrids, FCVs, oddities abound. *Ward's Auto World*. Retrieved from http://wardsautoworld.com

Murray, C. (1993, October 29). The coming white underclass. *Wall Street Journal*, p. A-14.

Murray, C. (2006, Spring–Summer). A plan to replace the welfare state. *Focus, 24*(2), 1–4.

Murray, C. J. L., Kulkarni, S. C., & Ezzati, M. (2006, September). Eight Americas: Investigating mortality disparities across races and counties in the United States. *PloS Medicine*.

Murray-West, R. (2004, January 23). *First Death, then Shag*. (Telegraph Media Group) Retrieved April 30, 2009, from Telegraph.co.uk: http://www.telegraph.co.uk/finance/2872930/First-Death-then-Shag—welcome-to-the-world-of-cult-student-cigarettes.html

Mydans, S. (1991, June 16). Bullets and crayons: Children learn lessons of the 90s. *New York Times*, p. 14.

Myers, M. A., & Talarico, S. M. (1986, February). The social contexts of racial discrimination in sentencing. *Social Problems, 33*(3), 236–251.

Myrdal, G. (1944). *An American dilemma*. New York: Harper.

1969 Handbook on women workers. (1969). Washington, DC: U.S. Department of Labor, Woman's Bureau.

Naj, A. K. (1992, May 15). Kuwait oil-well fires did little damage to the global environment, study says. *Wall Street Journal*, p. B5.

Nash, G. B. (1979). *The urban crucible*. Cambridge, MA: Harvard University Press.

National Conference of State Legislatures. *Women's Legislative Network of NCSL*. Retrieved from www.ncsl.org.

National Resources Defense Council. (2002, February 13). *Diesel exhaust may cause asthma, not just aggravate it*. Retrieved from http://www.nrdc.org/media/pressreleases/020213b.asp

National strategy for combatting terrorism. (2006, September). Washington, DC: The White House.

National Women's Political Caucus. (1998, November 5). *News & opinions: 1998 election results*.

Neergaard, L. (1998, December 31). Strong tainted food warnings urged. Associated Press. Retrieved from http://archives.foodsafety.ksu.edu/fsnet/1998/12-1998/fs-12-31-98-01.txt

Nelan, B. W. (1998, July 27). Sudan: Why is this happening again? *Time*, pp. 29–32.

Nelson, T.F., Naimi, T.S., & Brewer, R.D. (2005). *The state sets the rate: The relationship of college binge drinking to state binge drinking rates and selected state alcohol control policies*. Harvard School of Public Health College Alcohol Study. *American Journal of Public Health, 95*(3), 441–446.

Nettler, G. (1974, January). Embezzlement without problems. *British Journal of Criminology, 14*, 70–77.

Nettler, G. (1976). *Social concerns*. New York: McGraw-Hill.

Newdorf, D. (1991, May). Bailout agencies like to do it in secret. *Washington Journalism Review, 13*(4), 15–16.

Newman, D. J. (1966). *Conviction: The determination of guilt or innocence without trial*. Boston: Little, Brown.

Newman, D. K., Amidei, N. J., Cater, B. L., Day, D., Kruvant, W. J., & Russell, J. S. (1978). *Protest, politics, and prosperity: Black Americans and White institutions, 1940–1975*. New York: Pantheon.

Newsday. (1974). *The heroin trail*. New York. Holt, Rinehart, & Winston.

Nishio, H. K. (1994). Japan's welfare vision: Dealing with a rapidly increasing elderly population. In Laura Katz Olson (Ed.), *The graying of the world: Who will care for the frail elderly?* (pp. 233–260). New York: Haworth.

NOAA. (2006, October). Has Prince William Sound recovered from the spill? National Ocean Service, Office of Response and Restoration. Retrieved from http://response.restoration.noaa.gov

Norris, R. S., & Kristensen, H. M. (2005, September–October). India's nuclear forces, 2005. *Bulletin of the Atomic Scientists, 61*(5), 73–75.

North, A. (2004, November 18). Following the Afghan drugs trail. BBC News. Retrieved from http://news.bbc.co.uk

NPR. (2007, June 21). *Blacks and bypass surgery*. Transcript from broadcast aired June 21, 2007.

Nucleus: A report to union of concerned scientists sponsors, 3. (Spring–Summer 1981). Union of Concerned Scientists.

Nuland, S. (1995, February 3–5). The debate over dying. *USA Weekend*, pp. 4–6.

Nurge, D. (2003). Liberating yet limiting: The paradox of female gang membership. In L. Kontos, D. Brotherton, & L. Barrios (Eds.), *Gangs and society: Alternative perspectives* (pp. 161–182). New York: Columbia University Press.

O'Connell, P. L. (1998, August 13). Web erotica aims for new female customers. *New York Times*. Retrieved from http://www.nytimes.com

O'Hare, W. P. (1992, December). America's minorities: The demographics of diversity. *Population Bulletin, 47*(4), 1–47.

O'Keefe, B. (2008, November 10). Is buy-and-hold dead? *Fortune, 158*(9), p. 94.

Oakley, R. B. (1985, June). Combating international terrorism. *Department of State Bulletin,* 73–78.

Of birds and bacteria. (2003, January). *Consumer Reports.*

Oilism: Crude oil resources, prices, history, and analysis. (2008, April 4). Retrieved from www.oilism.com

Oliver, M. L., & Shapiro, T. M. (1995). *Black wealth/White wealth: A new perspective on racial inequality.* New York: Routledge.

Olivo, A. (1999, April 19). Doctor shortage severe in poor areas. *Los Angeles Times,* p. A1.

Olshansky, S. J., Passar, D. J., Hershow, R. C., et al. (2005, March 17). A potential decline in life expectancy in the United States in the 21st century. *New England Journal of Medicine, 352*(11), 1138–1145.

Olson, J. S., Baxter, M., Tetzloff, J. M., & Pierson, D. (1997). *Encyclopedia of American Indian civil rights.* Westport, CT: Greenwood Press.

Olson, W. K. (2002, Autumn). Give it back to the Indians? *City Journal.* Retrieved from http://www.city-journal.org

Onion, A. (2004, July 7). Getting better . . . virtually. ABC News online.

Organized crime: Report of the Task Force on Organized Crime. (1976). Washington, DC: National Advisory Committee on Criminal Justice Standards and Goals.

Osborne, L. (2002, June 15). Got silk. *New York Times Magazine.* Retrieved from http://www.nytimes.com

Oster, S., & Spencer, J. (2006, September 30). A poison spreads amid China's boom. *Wall Street Journal.* Retrieved from http://www.online.wsj.com

Otten, A. L. (1995, January 27). People patterns. *Wall Street Journal,* p. B1.

Ozturk, M., Ozcelik, H., Sakcali, S., & Guvensen, A. (2004, July). Land degradation problems in the Euphrates Basin, Turkey. *International Society of Environmental Botanists, 10,* 1–5.

Paddock, R. C. (1999, March 13). Patient deaths point to depth of Russian crisis. *Los Angeles Times,* p. A1.

Page, J. (2007, February 19). Hospital mass grave found as India cracks down on female infanticide. *The Times* (London). Retrieved from http://www.timesonline.co.uk/

Pagelow, M. D. (1992). *Protecting the fetus from its mom: A new form of social control.* Paper presented at the annual meeting of the Society for the Study of Social Problems.

Palen, J. J. (2005). *The urban world* (7th ed.). New York: McGraw-Hill.

Pamuck, E. (1998, July 30). A study for the National Center for Health Statistics, as reported in America Online, Rich get richer, poor get sicker in U.S.

Park, R. E. (1941, January). The social function of war. *American Journal of Sociology, 46,* 551–570.

Parmesan, C., & Yohe, G. (2003, January). A globally coherent fingerprint of climate change impacts across natural systems. *Nature,* 37–42.

Partington, D. H. (1965). The incidence of the death penalty for rape in Virginia. *Washington and Lee Law Review, 22,* 43–75.

Passel, J. S. (2005, June 14). *Unauthorized migrants: Numbers and characteristics.* Washington, DC: Pew Hispanic Center.

Passell, P. (1996, May 10). Race, mortgages and statistics. *New York Times,* pp. D1, D4.

Pattis, N. (2005, October 17). A plea on plea bargains: Don't tie hands of justice. *Connecticut Law Tribune.* Retrieved from http://www.law.com/jsp/PubArticle.jsp?id=900005439177

Paul, B. (1987, March 2). Cogeneration is rapidly coming of age. *Wall Street Journal,* p. 6.

Paul, P. (2005). *Pornified: How pornography is transforming our lives, our relationships, and our families.* New York: Henry Holt.

Peele, S. (1987). The addiction experience. In P. J. Baker & L. E. Anderson (Eds.), *Social Problems: A Critical Thinking Approach* (pp. 210–218). Belmont, CA: Wadsworth.

Penn, S. (1982, October 5). Organized crime finds rich pickings in rise of union health plans. *Wall Street Journal,* pp. 1, 26.

Penn, S. (1985, July 5). How public defenders deal with the pressure of the crowded courts. *Wall Street Journal,* pp. 1, 22.

Pereira, J. (1993, December 17). Toys "R" Us decides to pull night trap from store shelves. *Wall Street Journal,* p. A9A.

Pereira, L. A. A., de Sousa, C., Gleice, M., & Braga, A. L. F. (2004, July). Cardiovascular effects of air pollution in adults in Cubatao, Sao Paulo, Brazil. *Epidemiology, 15*(4), S21.

Persell, C. H., Catsambis, S., & Cookson, P. W., Jr. (1992). Family background, school type, and college attendance: A conjoint system of cultural capital transmission. *Journal of Research on Adolescence, 2*(1), 1–23.

Persell, C. H., & Cookson, P. W., Jr. (1985, August). Where the power starts. *Signature,* 51–57.

Pestka, E. L. (2006). Genetic counseling for mental health disorders. *Journal of the American Psychiatric Nurses Association, 11*(6), 338–343.

Petersilia, J. (1983, June). *Racial disparities in the criminal justice system.* Santa Monica, CA: Rand.

Peterson, I. (2003, July 30). Neighbors see lesson in Oneida casino deal: What not to do. *New York Times.* Retrieved from http://www.nytimes.com

Pettigrew, T. (1976, January–February). How the people really feel. *The Center Magazine, 9,* 35.

Physicians and surgeons. (2006). *Occupational outlook handbook.* U.S. Department of Labor, Bureau of Labor Statistics.

Piliavin, I., & Briar, S. (1964, September). Police encounters with juveniles. *American Journal of Sociology, 70,* 206–214.

Pillemer, K., & Moore, D. W. (1989). Abuse of patients in nursing homes: Findings from a survey of staff. *The Gerontologist, 29* (3), 314–320.

Piot, P. (2008). *Independent Commission on AIDS in Asia calls for countries to craft new responses.* Retrieved from http://www.unaids.org/en/KnowledgeCentre/Resources/FeatureStories/archive/2008/20080326_asia_commission.asp

Piotrow, P. T. (1973). *World population crisis: The United States' response.* New York: Praeger.

Pittman, D. J. (1971, March–April). The male house of prostitution. *Transaction, 8,* 21–27.

Piven, F. F., & Cloward, R. A. (1971). *Regulating the poor.* New York: Vintage.

Piven, F. F., & Cloward, R. A. (1982). *The new class war: Reagan's attack on the welfare state and its consequences.* New York: Pantheon.

Piven, F. F., & Cloward, R. A. (1989). *Why Americans don't vote.* New York: Random House.

Piven, F. F., & Cloward, R. A. (1997). *The breaking of the American social compact.* New York: New Press.

Platt, A. M. (1979). *The child savers.* Chicago: University of Chicago Press.

Polgreen, L., & Simons, M. (2006, October 2). Global sludge ends in tragedy for Ivory Coast. *New York Times.* Retrieved from http://www.nytimes.com

Pollack, A. (2004, May 18). U.N. unit sees great promise in biotech research on crops. *New York Times.* Retrieved from http://www.nytimes.com

Pollay, R. W. (1997). Hacks, flacks, and counter-attacks: Cigarette advertising, sponsored research, and controversy. *Journal of Social Issues, 53*(1), 43–74.

Pope, C. E. (1988). The family, delinquency, and crime. In E. W. Nunnally, C. S. Chilman, & F. M. Cox (Eds.), *Mental illness, delinquency, addictions, and neglect* (pp. 108–127). Newbury Park, CA: Sage.

Popenoe, D. (1998). An American dilemma. *Testimony before the House of Representatives, Committee on Small Business, Subcommittee on Empowerment, Washington, DC, July 16, 1998.* Retrieved from http://marriage.rutgers.edu/Publications/pubteenp.htm

Potterat, J. J., Woodhouse, D. E., Muth, J. B., & Muth, S. Q. (1990, May). Estimating the prevalence and career longevity of prostitute women. *Journal of Sex Research, 27*(2), 233–243.

Pozdena, R. J., & Johnson, T. R. (1979, March). *Income maintenance and asset demand.* Menlo Park, CA: SRI International.

Preidt, R. (2003, August 7). Tobacco companies target women in developing countries. *HealthDay.*

Prescott, C. A., Cross, R. J., Kuhn, J. W., Horn, J. L., Kendler, K. S. (2004). Risk for alcoholism mediated by individual differences in drinking motivations? *Neurobiological, behavioral, and environmental relations to drinking. Alcoholism: Clinical & Experimental Research, 28*(1), 29–39.

Price, D. O. (Ed.). (1967). *The 99th hour.* Chapel Hill: University of North Carolina Press. (As contained in Simon 1981.)

Pridemore, W. A., & Freilich, J. D. (2006). A test of recent subcultural explanations of White violence in the United States. *Journal of Criminal Justice, 34,* 1–16.

Pruitt, D. G., & Snyder, R. C. (1969). Motives and perceptions underlying entry into war. In D. G. Pruitt & R. C. Synder (Eds.), *Theory and research on the causes of sar.* Englewood Cliffs, NJ: Prentice Hall.

Prus, R., & Irini, Styllianoss. (1988). *Hookers, rounders, and desk clerks: The social organization of the hotel community.* Salem, WI: Sheffield.

Ra'anan, U., Pfaltzgraff, R. L., Jr., Shultz, R. H., Halperin, E., & Lukes, I. (Eds.). (1986). *Hydra of carnage: The international linkages of terrorism and other low-intensity operations, the witnesses speak.* Lexington, KY: Lexington Books.

Rabinovitz, J. (1998, July 7). Three Mile Island: Cleaned up, and for sale. *New York Times.* Retrieved from http://www.nytimes.com

Rabinowitz, D. (2004). *No crueler tyrannies: Accusation, false witness, and other terrors of our times.* New York: Simon & Schuster.

Raghunathan, V. K. (2003, February 8). Millions of baby girls killed in India. *The Straits Times.*

Rakow, L. F. (1992, Winter). "Don't hate me because I'm beautiful": Feminist resistance to advertising's irresistible meanings. *Southern Communication Journal, 57*(2), 132–142.

Raloff, J. (1990, March 17). The colloid threat. *Science News, 137*(11), 169–170.

Ramaekers, J. G., Berghaus, G., van Laar, M., & Drummer, O. H. (2004). Dose related risk of motor vehicle crashes after cannabis use. *Drug and Alcohol Dependence, 73,* 109–119.

Ramo, A. (2003, Fall). The environmental justice clinic at the Golden Gate University School of Law. *Human Rights, 30*(4), 6.

Rates of cesarean delivery among Puerto Rican women—Puerto Rico and the U.S. Mainland, 1992–2002. (2006). *Journal of the American Medical Association, 295,* 1369–1371.

Ray, O. S. (1998). *Drugs, society, and human behavior* (8th ed.). New York: McGraw-Hill.

Ray, O., & Ksir, C. J. (2004). *Drugs, society, and human behavior* (10th ed.). New York: McGraw-Hill.

Reasons, C. E. (Ed.). (1974). *The criminologist: Crime and the criminal.* Pacific Palisades, CA: Goodyear.

Reay, D., Davies, J., David, M., & Ball, S. J. (2001, November). Choice of degrees or degrees of choice? Class, "race," and the higher education choice process. *Sociology, 35*(4), 855–876.

Reckless, W. C. (1973). *The crime problem* (5th ed.). New York: Appleton.

Redlich, F., & Kellert, S. R. (1978, January). Trends in American mental health. *American Journal of Psychiatry, 135,* 22–28.

Reed, T., & Cummings, J. (1994). *Compromised: Clinton, Bush, and the CIA.* Kew Gardens, NY: Clandestine Publishing.

Reeves, T., & Bennett, C. (2003). The Asian and Pacific Islander population in the United States: March 2002. *Current Population Reports.*

Regaldo, A. (2004, October 22). When a plant emerges from melting glacier, is it global warming? *Wall Street Journal,* p. B1.

Rehm, J., Gmel, G., Sempos, C. T., & Trevisan, M. (2003). Alcohol-related morbidity and mortality. *Alcohol Research and Health, 27*(1), 39–51.

Reich, M. (1972). The economics of racism. In R. C. Edwards, M. Reich, & T. E. Weiskopf (Eds.), *The capitalist system* (pp. 313–326). Englewood Cliffs, NJ: Prentice Hall.

Reich, M. (1981). The economic impact in the postwar period. In B. P. Bowser & R. G. Hunt (Eds.), *Impacts of racism on White Americans* (pp. 165–176). Beverly Hills, CA: Sage.

Reichert, L. D., & Frey, J. H. (1985, July). The organization of bell desk prostitution. *Sociology and Social Research, 69*(4), 516–526.

Reiss, A. J. (1961, Fall). The sociological integration of queers and peers. *Social Problems, 9,* 102–120.

Revzin, P. (1989, January 9). U.S. claims progress at global meeting discussing ban on chemical weapons. *Wall Street Journal,* p. A3.

Reynolds, J. (1973). The medical institution: The death and disease-producing appendage. In L. T. Reynolds & J. M. Henslin (Eds.), *American society: A critical analysis* (pp. 198–224). New York: McKay.

Reynolds, J. (1976). Rape as social control. In J. M. Henslin & L. T. Reynolds (Eds.), *Social Problems in American Society* (2nd ed., pp. 79–86). Boston: Holbrook.

Richardson, L. F. (1960). *Statistics of deadly quarrels.* Chicago: Quadrangle.

Riesel, V. (1982a, January 16). Crackdown on mobsters. Syndicated column.

Riesel, V. (1982b, January 25). Racketeers infest New Jersey construction trade. Syndicated column.

Riesman, D., Glazer, N., & Denney, R. (1951). *The lonely crowd: A study of the changing American character.* New Haven, CT: Yale University Press.

Riley, K. J. (1998, December 12). Crack, powder cocaine, and heroin. Drug purchase and use patterns in six U.S. cities. National Institute of Justice. Available at http://www.ncjrs.gov/pdffiles/167265.pdf

Risen, J., & Johnston, D. (2002, December 15). Threats and responses: Hunt for al Qaeda; Bush has widened authority of C.I.A. to kill terrorists. *New York Times.* Retrieved from http://www.nytimes.com

Ritzer, G. (2002). *Contemporary sociological theory and its classical roots: The basics.* New York: McGraw-Hill.

Roach, J. (2003, October 7). Rain forest plan blends drug research, conservation. *National Geographic News.* Retrieved from http://news.nationalgeographic.com

Roberts, S. (2006, October 15). It's official: To be married means to be outnumbered. *New York Times.* Retrieved from http://www.nytimes.com

Rockwell, D. (1972, Fall). Social problems: Alcohol and marijuana. *Journal of Psychedelic Drugs, 5,* 49–55.

Roe, K. M. (1989). Private troubles and public issues: Providing abortion amid competing definitions. *Social Science and Medicine, 29*(10), 1191–1198.

Roffman, R., & Stephens, R. S. (Eds.). (2006). *Cannabis dependence: Its nature, consequences, and treatment.* Cambridge: Cambridge University Press.

Rolo, M. A. (n.d.). Marked media. *The Circle.* Online.

Rosaldo, M. Z. (1974). Women, culture, and society: A theoretical overview. In M. Z. Rosaldo & L. Lamphere (Eds.), *Women, culture, and society.* Stanford, CA: Stanford University Press.

Rosen, L. Savitz, L., Lalli, M., & Turner, S. (1991, Fall). Early delinquency, high school graduation, and adult criminality. *Sociological Viewpoints, 7,* 37–60.

Rosen, M. (1996). *On voluntary servitude: False consciousness and the theory of ideology.* Retrieved from www.equalitynow.org

Rosen, Y. (1999, March 14). Exxon Valdez oil spill of 1989 crippled Sound, Alaskans say. Reuters.

Rosenberg, C. E. (1987). *The care of strangers: The rise of America's hospital system.* New York: Basic Books.

Rosenberg, M. (2006). *Population growth rates and doubling time.* Retrieved from www.about.com/od/populationgeography/a/populationgrow.htm

Rosenfeld, R. A., & Kalleberg, A. L. (1990, July). A cross-national comparison of the gender gap in income. *American Journal of Sociology, 96*(1), 69–106.

Rosenthal, E. (2006, September 6). "Virtually untreatable" TB raises fears. *International Herald Tribune.* Retrieved from http://www.iht.com

Rosett, C. (1994, October 27). Big oil-pipeline spill in Russia may be a sign of things to come. *Wall Street Journal,* p. A14.

Ross, J. I. (2003). *The dynamics of political crime.* Thousand Oaks, CA: Sage.

Rothman, D. J. (1971). *The discovery of the asylum.* Boston: Little, Brown.

Rothman, D. J., & Rothman, S. M. (1972). *On their own.* Reading, MA: Addison-Wesley.

Rowland, H. (2006). *Two Feminist Classics: Bachelor Girls.* Addison Oaks Books.

Rubenstein, R. E. (1987). *Alchemists of revolution: Terrorism in the modern world.* London: I. B. Tauris.

Rubin, T. (2004, February 8). Nuclear "supermarket" another concern for U.S. *Philadelphia Inquirer.*

Ruethling, G. (2006, March 16). 27 charged in international online pornography ring. *New York Times.* Retrieved from http://www.nytimes.com

Ruggles, P. (1989, June). *Short and long term poverty in the United States: Measuring the American underclass.* Washington, DC: Urban Institute.

Ruggles, P. (1990). *Drawing the line: Alternative poverty measures and their implication for public policy.* Washington, DC: Urban Institute.

Ruggles, P. (1992, Spring). Measuring poverty. *Focus, 14*(1), 1–5.

Rumbaut, R. G., & Weeks, J. R. (1994). *Unraveling a public health enigma: Why do immigrants experience superior perinatal health outcomes?* Paper presented at the annual meeting of the American Public Health Association.

Rumney, P. N. (2008). Policing male rape and sexual assault. *Journal of Criminal Law, 72,* 67–86.

Russell, D. E. H. (1980). *Rape in marriage: A case against legalized crime.* Paper presented at the annual meeting of the American Society of Criminology.

Russell, D. E. H. (1986). *The secret trauma: Incest in the lives of girls and women.* New York: Basic Books.

Sagan, S. D. (1994, Spring). The perils of proliferation: Organization theory, deterrence theory, and the spread of nuclear weapons. *International Security, 18*(4), 66–107.

Sager, I., Elgin, B., Elstrom, P., Keenan, F., & Gogoi, P. (2002, September 2). The underground web. *Business Week.* Retrieved from http://www.businessweek.com

Saguy, A. (2006, Spring). Are we eating ourselves to death? *Contexts,* 11–13.

Sakharov, A. (1977, January 29). Text of Sakharov letter to Carter on human rights. *New York Times,* p. 2.

Sanchez-Jankowski, M. (1991). *Islands in the street: Gangs and American urban society.* Berkeley: University of California Press.

Sanchez Taylor, J. (2001). Dollars are a girl's best friend: Female tourists' sexual behavior in the Caribbean. *Sociology, 35,* 749–764.

Satcher, D. et al. (1999). *Mental Health: A Report of the Surgeon General.* National Institutes of Health.

Satyananda, G. J. (2006). *Chinese capitalism and the modernist vision.* New York: Taylor & Francis.

Saunders, K., & Kashubeck-West, S. (2006). The relations among feminist identity development, gender-role orientation, and psychological well-being in women. *Psychology of Women Quarterly, 30*(2), 199–211.

Savitch, H. V., & Vogel, R. K. (2004, July). Suburbs without a city: Power and city-county consolidation. *Urban Affairs Review, 39*(6), 758–790.

Sawhill, I. V. (1988, September). Poverty in the U.S.: Why is it so persistent? *Journal of Economic Literature, 26*(3), 1073–1119.

Schaefer, R. T. (2004). *Racial and ethnic groups* (9th ed.). Upper Saddle River, NJ: Prentice Hall.

Scherer, M. (2003, May 19). The return of the poppy fields. *Mother Jones.*

Schlafly, P. (1979, November). *The Phyllis Schlafly report, 13.*

Schmidt, G., & Sigusch, V. (1970, November). Sex differences in response to psychosexual stimulation by films and slides. *Journal of Sex Research, 6,* 268–283.

Schmitt, R. B. (1982, February 2). Some towns jail indigents illegally and get free labor. *Wall Street Journal,* pp. 1, 16.

Schneider, K. (1992, February 26). Nuclear disarmament raises fear on storage of "triggers." *New York Times,* p. A1.

Schneider, K. (1994, October 11). Burning trash for energy: Is it an endangered industry? *New York Times,* p. A18.

Schoenfeld, A. C., Meier, R. F., & Griffin, R. J. (1979, October). Constructing a social problem: The press and the environment. *Social Problems, 27,* 38–61.

Schoepfer, A., & Piquero, A. R. (2006). Self-control, moral beliefs, and criminal activity. *Deviant Behavior, 27,* 51–71.

Schottland, C. I. (1963). *The social security plan in the U.S.* New York: Appleton.

Schreiber, J. (1978). *The ultimate weapon: Terrorists and the world order.* New York: Morrow.

Schrieke, B. J. (1936). *Alien Americans.* New York: Viking.

Schumpeter, J. A. (1955). *The sociology of imperialism.* New York: Meridian. (Original work published 1919)

Schuster, L. (1985, April 15). Industrialization of Brazilian village brings jobs at cost of heavy pollution and even death. *Wall Street Journal,* p. 28.

Schwidrowski, K. (1980, March). Italy's mafia blight. *World Press Review, 17,* 56.

Schwyzer, H. (2007).Why divorced men remarry more often than divorced women: A preliminary reflection. *Feminism, Marriage and Men and Masculinity.* [blog post] Retrieved from http://hugoschwyzer.net

Scott, G. (2004). "It's a sucker's outfit:" How urban gangs enable and impede the reintegration of ex-convicts. *Ethnography, 51*(1), 107–140.

Scott, J. (2001, February 25). White flight: This time toward Harlem. *New York Times.* Retrieved from http://www.nytimes.com

Scott, M. K. (1994). *Monster: The autobiography of an L.A. gang member.* New York: Penguin Books.

Scully, D. (1990). *Understanding sexual violence: A study of convicted rapists*. Boston: Unwin Hyman.

Scully, D. (1994). Negotiating to do surgery. In H. D. Schwartz (Ed.), *Dominant issues in medical sociology* (3rd ed.; pp. 146–152). New York: McGraw-Hill.

Scully, D., & Marolla, J. (2007). "Riding the bull at Gilley's": Convicted rapists describe the rewards of rape. In J. M. Henslin (Ed.), *Down-to-earth sociology: Introductory readings* (13th ed.; pp. 48–62). New York: Free Press. (Original work published 1985 in *Social Problems, 32*(3), 251–263.)

Seib, G. F. (1981, September 15). U.S. aides say toxins on a Cambodian leaf hint at chemical war. *Wall Street Journal*, p. 22.

Seligman, L. (2008) Anti-rape group reaches out to fraternities. *The Daily Pennsylvanian*. Retrieved from http://media.www.dailypennsylvanian.com

Seligmann, J. (1984, April 9). The date who rapes. *Newsweek*, pp. 91–92.

Sellin, T. (1928, November). The Negro criminal: A statistical note. *Annals of the American Academy of Political and Social Sciences, 140* (Part II), 52–64.

Serum results study update. (2006, Spring). *Love Canal Health News*. Troy, NY: Center for Environmental Health.

Seto, T. P. (2002). The morality of terrorism. *Loyola of Los Angeles Law Review, 35*, 1227. DOI: 10.2139/ssrn.341600

Seventh special report to the U.S. Congress on alcohol and health. (1990). Rockville, MD: U.S. Department of Health and Human Services.

Sewall, S. B., & Kaysen, C. (Eds.). (2000). *The United States and the international criminal court: National security and international law*. Lanham, MD: Rowman & Littlefield.

Shaffer, H. G. (1986, May). $1,000,000,000,000. *Republic*, 24.

Shafir, G., & Peled, Y. (1998, May). Citizenship and stratification in an ethnic democracy. *Ethnic and Racial Studies, 21*(3), 408–427.

Shapiro, J. P. (1997, January 17). Euthanasia's home: What the Dutch experience can teach Americans about assisted suicide. Retrieved from http://www.usnews.com

Shaw, S. (1987, March). Wretched of the Earth. *New Statesman, 20*, 19–20.

Shellenbarger, S. (1994, July 22). Companies help solve day-care problems. *Wall Street Journal*, p. B1.

Shellenbarger, S. (1995, January 24). Sales offers women fairer pay, but bias lingers. *Wall Street Journal*, pp. B1, B14.

Sheppard, N., Jr. (1980, August 6). Chicago project dwellers live under siege. *New York Times*, p. A14.

Shibutani, T. (1970). On the personification of adversaries. In T. Shibutani (Ed.), *Human nature and collective behavior* (pp. 223–233). Englewood Cliffs, NJ: Prentice Hall.

Shim, K. H., & DeBerry, M. (1988, August). *Criminal victimization in the United States, 1986*. Washington, DC: U.S. Department of Justice, Bureau of Justice Statistics.

Shinnar, R., & Shinnar, S. (1975, Summer). The effects of the criminal justice system on the control of crime: A quantitative approach. *Law and Society Review, 9*, 581–611.

Shishkin, P., & Crawford, D. (2006, January 18). In Afghanistan, heroin trade soars despite U.S. aid. *Wall Street Journal*. Retrieved from http://www.aegis.com/news/wsj/2006/WJ060103.html

Shively, J. (1999). Cowboys and Indians. In J. M. Henslin (Ed.), *Down-to-earth sociology: Introductory readings* (10th ed.; pp. 104–116). New York: Free Press.

Shribman, D. (1989, March 9). Even after 10 years, victims of Love Canal can't quite escape it. *Wall Street Journal*, pp. A1, A8.

Silverman, D. (1981). Sexual harassment: The working women's dilemma. *Building Feminist Theory: Essays from Quest* (pp. 84–93). New York: Longman.

Simmel, G. (1904, January, March, May). The sociology of conflict. *American Journal of Sociology, 9*, 490–525; 672–689; and 798–811.

Simon, D. R. (1981). The political economy of crime. In S. G. McNall (Ed.), *Political economy: A critique of American society* (pp. 347–366). Glenview, IL: Scott Foresman.

Simon, J. L. (1977). *The economics of population growth*. Princeton, NJ: Princeton University Press.

Simon, J. L. (1980, Winter). Global confusion, 1980: A hard look at the Global 2000 Report. *Public Interest, 62*, 3–20.

Simon, J. L. (1981). *The ultimate resource*. Princeton, NJ: Princeton University Press.

Simon, J. L. (1982, March 23). Conversation with the author.

Simon, J. L. (1986). *Theory of population and economic growth*. New York: Blackwell.

Simon, J. L. (1991, Winter). The case for greatly increased immigration. *The Public Interest, 102*, 89–103.

Simon, J., Patel, A., & Sleed, M. (2005, August). The costs of alcoholism. *Journal of Mental Health, 14*(4), 321–330.

Simon, S. (2004). The new terrorism: Securing the nation against a messianic foe. In K. Finsterbusch (Ed.), *Sociology* (33rd ed.; pp. 215–220). New York: McGraw-Hill/Dushkin.

Simons, M. (2005). Social change and Amazon Indians. In J. M. Henslin (Ed.), *Life in society: Readings to accompany sociology: A down-to-earth approach* (7th ed., pp. 158–165). Boston: Allyn & Bacon.

Simons, R. (1996). *Understanding differences between divorced and intact families*. Thousand Oaks, CA: Sage.

Simpson, G. E., & Yinger, J. M. (1972). *Racial and cultural minorities: An analysis of prejudice and discrimination* (4th ed.). New York: Harper & Row.

Sindler, A. P. (1978). *Bakke, De Funis, and minority admissions: The quest for equal opportunity*. New York: Longman.

Sitomer, C. J. (1986, March 13). Fencing out pornography without fencing in free speech. *Christian Science Monitor*, p. 23.

Skinner, B. F. (1948). *Walden two*. New York: Macmillan.

Skinner, B. F. (1953). *Science and human behavior*. New York: Macmillan.

Skinner, B. F. (1971). *Beyond freedom and dignity*. New York: Knopf.

Skinner, J., Weinstein, J. N., Sporer, S. M., & Wennberg, J. E. (2003, October 2). Racial, ethnic, and geographic disparities in rates of knee arthroplasty among Medicare patients. *New England Journal of Medicine, 349*(14), 1350–1359.

Slikker, W., Jr. (1992). Behavioral, neurochemical, and neurohistological effects of chronic marijuana smoke exposure in the nonhuman primate. In L. Murphy & A. Bartke (Eds.), *Marijuana cannabinoids neurobiology and neurophysiology*, Boca Raton, FL: CRC Press.

Smedley, B. D., Stith, A. Y., & Nelson, A. R. (Eds.). (2003). *Unequal treatment: Confronting racial and ethnic disparities in health care*. Washington, DC: The National Academies Press.

Smith, B. E. (1987). *Digging our own graves: Coal miners and the struggle over black lung disease*. Philadelphia: Temple University Press.

Smith, C. (1980). Oral history as "therapy": Combatants' accounts of Vietnam War. In C. R. Figley & S. Leventman (Eds.), *Strangers at home: Vietnam veterans since the war* (pp. 9–34). New York: Praeger.

Smith, D. A., & Visher, C. A. (1981, December). Street-level justice: Situational determinants of police arrest decisions. *Social Problems, 29*, 167–177.

Smith, H. (1986, December). A colossal cover-up. *Christianity Today*, 16–17.

Smith, H. (2001). Gender and sexuality. Review of *The power of feelings: Personal meaning in psychoanalysis, gender, and culture, by*

N. J. Chodorow. [book review]. *Journal of the American Psychoanalytic Association, 49,* 1427–1431.

Smith, J. P., & Edmonston, B. (Eds.). (1997). *The new American: Economic, demographic, and fiscal effects of immigration.* Washington, DC: National Academy Press.

Smith, K. F., & Bengtson, V. L. (1979, October). Positive consequences of institutionalization: Solidarity between elderly parents and their middle-aged children. *Gerontologist, 19,* 438–447.

Smith, W. J. (1999, February 25). Dependence or death? Oregonians make a chilling choice. *Wall Street Journal.*

Snipp, C. M., & Sorkin, A. L. (1986). American Indian housing: An overview of conditions and public policy. In J. A. Momeni (Ed.), *Race, ethnicity, and Minority housing in the United States* (pp. 147–175). New York: Greenwood.

Snow, R. W., & Cunningham, O. R. (1985). Age, machismo, and the drinking locations of drunken drivers: A research note. *Deviant Behavior, 6,* 57–66.

Snyder, H. (1988). *Court careers of juvenile offenders.* Washington, DC: Office of Juvenile Justice and Delinquency Prevention.

Social Darwinism in Sweden. (2001, July 9). *Report* (Alberta Edition), *28*(14), 4.

Solomon, D. (2006, March 9). Shift in federal bench spurs governors, legislators to battle Roe. *Wall Street Journal.* Retrieved from http://www.wsj.com

Solomon, J. (1988, December 29). Companies try measuring cost savings from new types of corporate benefits. *Wall Street Journal,* p. B1.

Solomon, J. (Producer), & Rather, D. (Interviewer). (1980, November 9). The Kyshtym disaster [Television series episode]. *60 Minutes.* New York: CBS Broadcasting.

Some facts about members of new Congress. (2007, January 3). Associated Press.

Sorensen, J. B. (1990, September). Perceptions of women's opportunity in five industrialized nations. *European Sociological Review, 6*(2), 151–164.

Sorokin, P. A. (1941). *Social and cultural dynamics* (4 vols.). New York: American Book.

Sourcebook of criminal justice statistics. (Annual). Washington, DC: U.S. Government Printing Office.

Spaeth, A. (1989, February 22). Court settlement stuns Bhopal survivors. *Wall Street Journal,* p. A10.

Specter, M. (1992, October 14). TB carriers see clash of liberty and health. *New York Times,* pp. A1, A20.

Specter, M. (1995, August 1). Plunging life expectancy puzzles Russians. *New York Times,* pp. A1, A6.

Specter, M. (1998, July 10). Population implosion worries a graying Europe. *New York Times.* Retrieved from http://www.nytimes.com

Speer, A. (1970). *Inside the Third Reich* (R. & C. Winston, Trans.). New York: Avon.

Spivak, J. (1980, December 3). Israel's discrimination problem. *Wall Street Journal,* p. 28.

Spunt, B. (2003). The current New York City heroin scene. *Substance Use and Misuse, 38*(10), 1539–1549.

Squires, G. D. (2003). Racial profiling, insurance style: Insurance redlining and the uneven development of metropolitan areas. *Journal of Urban Affairs, 25*(4), 391–410.

Srole, L, et al. (1978). *Mental health in the metropolis: The midtown Manhattan study.* New York: New York University Press.

Stafford, L., Kennedy, S. R., Lehman, J. E., & Arnold, G. (1986–1987, Winter). Wealth in America. *ISR Newsletter.*

Stakeholders and radiological protection: Lessons from Chernobyl 20 years after. (2006). Committee on Radiation Protection and Public Health. Nuclear Energy Agency.

Stalenheim, P., Fruchart, D., Omitoogun, W., & Perdomo, C. (2006). Military expenditures. *Stockholm International Peace Research Institute Yearbook,* 15–16.

Stanford, S. (1968). Madamhood as a vocation. In C. H. McCaghy, J. K. Skipper, Jr., & M. Lefton (Eds.), *In their own behalf: Voices from the margin* (pp. 204–207). New York: Appleton.

Stanley, S. (2007). *What really is the divorce rate?* Retrieved from http://www.prepinc.com/main/Docs/what_really_div_rate.html

Starfield, B., Robertson, J., & Riley, A. W. (2002, July–August). Social class gradients and health in childhood. *Ambulatory Pediatrics, 2*(4), 238–246.

Starr, M. (1985, March 4). Violence on the right. *Newsweek,* pp. 23–26.

State of food insecurity in the world 2005. (2005). Food and Agriculture Organization of the United Nations.

Statistical abstract of the United States. (Annual). Washington, DC: U.S. Bureau of the Census.

Stein, P. J. (1992). The diverse world of single adults. In J. M. Henslin (Ed.), *Marriage and family in a changing society* (4th ed.; pp. 93–103). New York: Free Press.

Steinhauer, J. (1999a, January 10). Angry at managed care, doctors start fighting back. *New York Times News Service.*

Steinhauer, J. (1999b, March 1). For women in medicine, a road to compromise, not perks. *New York Times.* Retrieved from http://www.nytimes.com

Steinhauer, J. (2001, April 1). So, the tumor is on the left, right? *New York Times.*

Steinhauer, J., & Fessenden, F. (2001, March 27). Medical retreads: Doctors punished by state but prized at the hospitals. *New York Times.* Retrieved from http://www.nytimes.com

Steinhoff, P. G., & Diamond, M. (1977). *Abortion politics: The Hawaii experience.* Honolulu: University Press of Hawaii.

Steinmetz, S. K. (1988). *Duty bound: Elder abuse and family care.* Newbury Park, CA: Sage.

Steinmetz, S. K., & Straus, M. A. (Eds.). (1992). *Violence in the family.* New York: Dodd Mead. Original publication 1974.

Stevens, A. (1992, April 8). Sensible victims will be hoping their burglar drives up in a Rolls. *Wall Street Journal,* p. B1.

Stevens, C. W. (1980, September 29). Integration is elusive despite recent gains; social barriers remain. *Wall Street Journal,* p. 1.

Stevens, C. W. (1989, March 8). Advance in hydrogen storage may make use of abundant element more practical. *Wall Street Journal,* p. B4.

Stevens, W. K. (1996, May 28). Great Plains or great desert? *New York Times.* Retrieved from http://www.nytimes.com

Stevens, W. K. (1998, April 22). Science academy disputes attack on global warming. *New York Times.* Retrieved from http://www.nytimes.com

Stockard, J., & Johnson, M. M. (1980). *Sex roles: Sex inequality and sex role development.* Englewood Cliffs, NJ: Prentice Hall.

Stokes, M., & Zeman, D. (1995, September 4). Detroit: Is apathy to blame for a brutal death? *Newsweek.* Retrieved from http://www.newsweek.com

Stolberg, S. G. (1998, June 29). Epidemic of silence: A special report.; Eyes shut, black america is being ravaged by AIDS. *New York Times.* Retrieved from http://www.nytimes.com

Stolberg, S. G. (2001, May 10). Blacks found on short end of heart attack procedure. *New York Times.*

Stolz, M., & Wald, M. L. (2006, September 9). Interior department rejects interim plan for nuclear waste. *New York Times.* Retrieved from http://www.nytimes.com

Stouffer, S. A., Lumsdaine, A. A., Harper Lumsdaine, M., Williams, R. M., Jr., Smith, M. B., Janis, I. L., et al. (1949). *The American soldier: Combat and its aftermath* (vol. 2.). New York: Wiley.

Strand, S. D., & Smith, I. J. (2006). Sex differences in cognitive abilities test scores: A UK national picture. *British Journal of Educational Psychology, 76*(3), 463–480.

Straus, M. A. (1980, May-June). Victims and aggressors in marital violence. *American Behavioral Scientist, 23,* 681–704.

Straus, M. A. (1992). Explaining family violence. In J. M. Henslin (Ed.), *Marriage and family in a changing society* (4th ed.; pp. 344–356). New York: Free Press.

Straus, M. A., & Gelles, R. J. (1988). Violence in American families: How much is there and why does it occur? In E. W. Nunnally, C. S. Chilman, & F. M. Cox (Eds.), *Troubled Relationships* (pp. 141–162). Newbury Park, CA: Sage.

Straus, M. A., Gelles, R. J., & Steinmetz, S. K. (1980). *Behind closed doors: Violence in the American family.* New York: Anchor/Doubleday.

Strobel, L. (1980). *Reckless homicide: Ford's Pinto trial.* South Bend, IN: And Books.

Strohschein, L. A. (2005). Parental divorce and child mental health trajectories. *Journal of Marriage and Family, 67,* 1286–1300.

Strom, S. (2006, August 13). A charity's enviable problem: Race to spend Buffett billions. *New York Times.* Retrieved from http://www.nytimes.com

Stroud, J. S. (2006, August 16). Ogallala Aquifer starting to run on empty. *Express-News.*

Struck, D. (2006, October 5). Canada in quandary over gas emissions. *Washington Post.*

Struckman-Johnson, C. & Struckman-Johnson, D. (1992). Acceptance of male rape myths among college men and women. *Sex Roles, 27*(3–4), 85–98.

Stutchbury, M. (2008, September 16). Too green is no good. *The Australian.* Retrieved from http://www.theaustralian.news.com.au/

Suicide rates. (2004). United Nations: World Health Organization.

Suit settled by Neil Bush. (1992, March 29). *New York Times,* p. A43.

Surgeon General of the United States. (2007). *Surgeon General's report.* Washington, DC: Centers for Disease Control and Prevention.

Sutherland, E. H. (1937). *The professional thief.* Chicago: University of Chicago Press.

Sutherland, E. H. (1947). *Principles of criminology* (4th ed.). Philadelphia: Lippincott.

Sutherland, E. H. (1949). *White collar crime.* New York: Dryden.

Suttles, G. D. (1968). *The social order of the slum: Ethnicity and territory in the inner city.* Chicago: University of Chicago Press.

Suzuki, B. H. (1985). Asian-American families. In J. M. Henslin (Ed.), *Marriage and family in a changing society* (2nd ed.; pp. 104–119). New York: Free Press.

Swedish health care in the 1990s. (2002, July). Stockholm: Federation of Swedish County Councils.

Swedish Institute. (1992, February). Fact sheets on Sweden.

Sykes, G. M., & Matza, D. (1957, December). Techniques of neutralization: A theory of delinquency. *American Sociological Review, 22,* 664–670.

Szasz, T. (1961). *The myth of mental illness.* Harper & Row.

Szasz, T. (1975). *Ceremonial chemistry: The ritual persecution of drugs, addicts, and pushers.* Garden City, NY: Anchor.

Tabuchi, H. (2008, July 2). Japan tobacco tax could triple prices. *Wall Street Journal,* p. A6.

Taslitz, A. E. (2005). Willfully blinded: On date rape and self-deception. *Harvard Journal of Law & Gender,* 381–446.

Tavernise, S., & McNeil, D. G., Jr. (2006, October 10). Iraqi dead may total 600,000, study says. *New York Times.* Retrieved from http://www.nytimes.com

Tax Foundation. (2006, April). America celebrates tax freedom day. Available at http://www.taxfoundation.org/files/sr140.pdf.

Taylor, M. M. (2002). *Harlem: Between heaven and hell.* Minneapolis: University of Minnesota Press.

Taylor, P., Funk, C., & Clark, A. (2007, March 14). Generation gap in values, behaviors: As marriage and parenthood drift apart, public is concerned about social impact. *A Social and Demographic Trends Report.* Washington, D.C.: Pew Research Centers.

Teaford, J. (1986). *The twentieth century American city.* Baltimore: Johns Hopkins University Press.

Teller, E. (1980). *The energy crisis: No contingency plan.* San Diego, CA: World Research.

Templeton, S-K., & St. Quinton, L. (2006, January 29). NHS patients pay cash for superior care. *The Times* (London). Retrieved from http://www.timesonline.co.uk

Teresa, V., with Renner T. C. (1973). *My life in the Mafia.* Greenwich, CT: Fawcett.

Tetreault, S. (2006, September 28). Judge dismisses suit, But state is happy. *Las Vegas Review-Journal.*

Thayer, F. C. (1997, Fall). The holy war on surplus Americans: Soviet dogma, old-time religion and classical economics. *Social Policy, 28*(1), 8–18.

The price of success. (2004, April 17). *Economist, 371,* 8371.

The wild wild East. (1995, March 12). CNN.

The world of the child 6 billion. (2000). Population Reference Bureau.

Thio, A. (1978). *Deviant behavior.* Boston: Houghton Mifflin.

Thomas, P. (1992, October 9). Boston fed finds racial discrimination in mortgage lending is still widespread. *Wall Street Journal,* p. A3.

Thomasson, M. (2003).Health insurance in the United States. *EH.Net Encyclopedia.* Retrieved from http://eh.net/encyclopedia/article/thomasson.insurance.health.us

Thornburgh, N. (2006, February 6). Inside the life of the migrants next door. *Time,* pp. 35–42.

Thorsheim, P. (2004). Interpreting the London fog disaster of 1952. In E. M. DuPuis (Ed.), *Smoke and mirrors: The politics and culture of air pollution* (pp. 154–169). New York: New York University Press.

Thrasher, F. M. (1927). *The gang.* Chicago: University of Chicago Press.

Tierney, J. (1986, January 20). The population crisis revisited. *Wall Street Journal,* p. 16.

Tierney, J. (1990, December 2). Betting on the planet. *New York Times.* Retrieved from http://www.nytimes.com

Tiger, L., & Fox, R. (1971). *The imperial animal.* New York: Holt.

Tilove, J. (2006, November 9). Election finds secure place in annals of Black politics. Newhouse News Service Online.

Timasheff, N. S. (1965). *War and revolution* (J. F. Scheuer, Ed.). New York: Sheed & Ward.

Timmons, H., & Romero, S. (2005, December 13). Energy, the hot deal field, is likely to get still hotter. *New York Times.* Retrieved from http://www.nytimes.com

Tinker, J. N. (1981). *Ethnic bias in California courts: A case study of Chicano and Anglo felony defendants.* Paper presented at the annual meeting of the Society for the Study of Social Problems.

To restore and protect the Great Lakes. (2005, December). Great Lakes Regional Collaboration Survey.

Toffler, A. (1971). *Future shock.* New York: Bantam.

Tolchin, M. (1991a, April 19). Mildest possible penalty is imposed on Neil Bush. *New York Times,* p. D2.

Tolchin, M. (1991b, June 9). Fund established to help pay legal fees for president's son. *New York Times,* pp. 1–31.

Tönnies, F. (1957). *Community and society.* East Lansing: Michigan State University. (Original work published 1887).

Toth, M. (1998, March 10). According to Professor Ehrlich, shouldn't the world be over by now? *Stanford Review.*

Treas, Judith. (2000). Sexual infidelity among married and cohabiting Americans. *Journal of Marriage and the Family, 62,* 48–60.

Trebach, A. S. (1987). *The great drug war: And radical proposals that could make America safe again.* New York: Macmillan.

Trust, C. (1986, January 15). Presidential panel says 4 major unions have connections to organized crime. *Wall Street Journal,* p. 48.

Tsuda, S., Murakami, M., Matsusaka, N., Kano, K., Taniguchi, K., & Sasaki, Y. F. (2001, May). DNA damage induced by red food

dyes orally administered to pregnant and male mice. *Toxicological Sciences, 61*(1), 92–99.

Turner, J. H. (1978). *The structure of sociological theory.* Homewood, IL: Dorsey.

U.S. Census Bureau. (2006a). *Current Populations Survey.*

U.S. Census Bureau. (2006b). Estimates of metro and non-metro populations by state, 2005. FSCPE Population Estimates Program.

U.S. Census Bureau. (2006c). International Data Base.

U.S. Department of Justice. (2001). *Terrorism 2000–2001.* Retrieved from http://www.fbi.gov/publications/terror/terror2000_2001.htm

U.S. Department of State. (1997, April 22). *Environmental diplomacy: The environment and U.S. foreign policy.*

U.S. Environmental Protection Agency. (2008). *Protecting the stratospheric ozone layer.* Retrieved from http://www.epa.gov/air/caa/peg/stratozone.html

U.S. greenhouse gas inventory. (2006, October). Washington: Environmental Protection Agency.

U.S. pesticide exports and the circle of poison. (1994, January 26). Committee on Foreign Affairs, Subcommittee on Economic Policy, Trade and Environment, House of Representatives.

Uchitelle, L. (2001, May 28). How to define poverty? Let us count the ways. *New York Times.* Retrieved from http://www.nytimes.com

Ullman, S. E. (1998, April). Does offender violence escalate when rape victims fight back? *Journal of Interpersonal Violence, 13*(2), 179–192.

Umberger, A. (2005, Spring). The transatlantic dispute over genetically modified organisms. Culture, politics and economics. *International Affairs Review, 14*(1).

UNICEF. (2005, November). *Female genital mutilation/cutting: A statistical exploration.* New York: United Nations.

United Nations Office on Drugs and Crime. (2002). *The Eighth United Nations Survey on Crime Trends and the Operations of Criminal Justice Systems.* Information retrieved via NationMaster: http://www.nationmaster.com/graph/cri_tot_cri-crime-total-crimes

United Nations Schoolbus. (2006, October). *Habitat at Unit 1.* Online data.

United Nations surveys of crime trends and operations of criminal justice systems. (2004). New York: United Nations Office of Drugs and Crime.

United Nations. (2002). *Fact sheet: Sub-Saharan Africa.*

Useem, M. (1979, August). The social organization of the American business elite. *American Sociological Review, 44,* 553–572.

Useem, M. (1984). *The inner circle: Large corporations and the rise of business political activity in the U.S. and U.K.* New York: Oxford University Press.

Valocchi, S. (1994, August). The racial basis of capitalism and the state, and the impact of the New Deal on African Americans. *Social Problems, 41*(3), 347–362.

van den Haag, E. (1975). *Punishing criminals: Concerning a very old and painful question.* New York: Basic Books.

van den Haag, E., & Conrad, J. P. (1983). *The death penalty: A debate.* New York: Plenum.

Veevers, J. E. (1973, April). Voluntarily childless wives. *Sociology and Social Research, 57,* 356–366.

Veevers, J. E. (1980). *Childless by choice.* Toronto: Butterworths.

Vidal, D. (1977, January 30). Bilingual education is thriving but criticized. *New York Times.*

Vigil, J. D. (2002). *A rainbow of gangs: Street cultures in the mega-city.* Austin: University of Texas Press.

Waddington, C. H. (1978). *The man-made future.* New York: St. Martin's.

Wagley, C., & Harris, M. (1958). *Minorities in the new world.* New York: Columbia University Press.

Wagman, R. (1981, November 27). Is Japanese mafia threat to U.S.? Syndicated column.

Wain, B. (1981, January 29). Cambodia: What remains of the killing ground. *Wall Street Journal,* p. 24.

Waitzkin, H., & Waterman, B. (1974). *The exploitation of illness in capitalist society.* New York: Bobbs-Merrill.

Wald, P. M. (1974, Fall). Making sense out of 12 rights of youth. *Human Rights, 4,* 13–29.

Walker, A., & Parmar, P. (1993). *Warrior marks: Female genital mutilation and the sexual binding of women.* New York: Harcourt Brace.

Wallace, J. N. (1980, July 28). Green revolution hits double trouble. *U.S. News & World Report,* 37, 40.

Wallace, L. J. D., Calhoun, A. D., Powell, K. E., O'Neil, J., & James, S. P. (1996). *Homicide and suicide among Native Americans, 1979–1992.* Atlanta, GA: National Center for Injury Prevention and Control.

Walsh, E., & Goldstein, A. (2000, June 29). Supreme Court upholds two key abortion rights. *Washington Post.*

Walsh, M. (1996, July 1). Supreme Court refuses to weigh race-based college admissions. Education Week online.

Walsh, M. (2004, September 27). Supreme Court endorses race-conscious admissions, with limits. *Education Week.* Retrieved from http://www.edweek.org

Walters, D. (2008, September 2). *U.S. Census Bureau Reports Drop in Number, Percentage of Uninsured.* Retrieved April 30, 2009, from CaliforniaHealthline.org: http://www.californiahealthline.org/articles/2008/9/2/US-Census-Bureau-Reports-Drop-in-Number-Percentage-of-Uninsured.aspx?topicID=39

Ward, L. M., Hansbrough, E., & Walker, E. (2005, March). Contributions of music video exposure to Black adolescents' gender and sexual schemas. *Journal of Adolescent Research, 20*(2), 143–166.

Ward, R. A. (1991). Patient-provider ties and satisfaction with health care. *Research in the Sociology of Health Care, 9,* 169–190.

Watanabe, T. (1998, December 25). The green movement is getting religion. *Los Angeles Times.*

Wax, M. L. (1971). *Indian Americans: Unity and diversity.* Englewood Cliffs, NJ: Prentice Hall.

Wax, M. L., & Wax, R. H. (1964, January 15–18). Cultural deprivation as an educational ideology. *Journal of American Indian Education, 3,* 1964.

Wax, M. L., & Wax, R. H. (1965, Fall). Indian education for what? *Midcontinent American Studies Journal, 6,* 164–170.

Wax, R. H. (1967, May). The warrior dropouts. *Trans-Action, 4,* 40–46.

Webber, M. M. (1973). Urbanization and communications. In G. Gerbner, L. P. Gross, & W. H. Melody (Eds.), *Communications technology and social policy; Understanding the new cultural revolution.* New York: John Wiley.

Weber, D. L., & Wade, T. J. (1995). Individual differences in overt and covert measures of sexism. *Social Behavior & Personality, 23*(3), 303.

Weber, M. (1921). Collected Political Miscellanies. *Gesammelte Politische Schriften.* Germany.

Weber, M. (1964) *Theory of social and economic organization.* London: Free Press. (Original work published 1921)

Weitzman, L. J., Eifler, D., Hokada, E., & Ross, C. (1972, May). Sex role socialization in picture books for pre-school children. *American Journal of Sociology, 77,* 1125–1150.

Wells, J. W. (1970). *Tricks of the trade.* New York: New American Library.

Wells, K. (1990, March 23). Hazelwood is acquitted of most charges. *Wall Street Journal,* pp. A3, A4.

Wells, K., & McCoy, C. (1989, April 5). Exxon says fast containment of oil spill in Alaska could have caused explosion. *Wall Street Journal,* p. A3.

Wertheimer, R. & Papillo, A. R. (2008). An update on state policy. Initiatives to reduce teen and adult nonmarital childbearing. *Child Trends 2008*. Retrieved from www.urban.org

West, R. W., & Steiger, G. (1980, May). *The effects of the Seattle and Denver income management experiments on alternative measures of labor supply*. Menlo Park, CA: SRI International Research Memorandum, 72.

Whitaker, M. (1984, December 17). "It was like breathing fire" *Newsweek*, pp. 26–32.

White, H. R. (1991, Spring). Marijuana use and delinquency: A test of the "independent cause" hypothesis. *Journal of Drug Issues, 21*(2), 231–256.

Whitehurst, C. A. (1977). *Women in America: The oppressed majority*. Santa Monica, CA: Goodyear.

WHO/Europe. (2006, October 9). *Highlights on health, Russian Federation 2005*. World Health Organization.

Whyte, W. F. (1943). *Street corner society*. Chicago: University of Chicago Press.

Whyte, W. F. (1995). Street corner society. In J. M. Henslin (Ed.), *Down-to-earth sociology: Introductory readings* (8th ed.; pp. 59–67). New York: Free Press.

Widdowson, M., Sulk, A., Bulens, S. N., Beard, R. S., et al. (2005, January). Norovirus and foodborne disease, United States, 1991–2000. *Emerging Infectious Diseases, 11*(1).

Wilcox, A., II. (1957, November 21). Letter from Hooker Electro-chemical Company to the President of the Niagara Falls Board of Education.

Willhelm, S. M. (1980, December). Can Marxism explain America's racism? *Social Problems, 28*, 98–112.

Williams, R. C. (1980, October). Three Mile Island as history. *Washington University Magazine, 50*, pp. 56ff.

Williams, T. M., & Kornblum, W. (1985). *Growing up poor*. Lexington, MA: Lexington Books.

Williamson, C., & Cluse-Tolar, T. (2002, September). Pimp-controlled prostitution. *Violence Against Women, 8*(9), 1074–1092.

Willing, R. (2005, February 4). U.S. prisons to end boot camp program. *USA Today*. Retrieved from http://www.usatoday.com

Wilson, J. Q. (1975, March 9). Lock 'em up and other thoughts on crime. *New York Times Magazine*, pp. 11, 44–48.

Wilson, W. J. (1978). *The declining significance of race: Blacks and changing American institutions*. Chicago: University of Chicago Press.

Wilson, W. J. (1987). *The truly disadvantaged: The inner city, the underclass, and public policy*. Chicago: University of Chicago Press.

Wilson, W. J. (1992, June 14). Scholar in Residence lecture at Southern Illinois University, Edwardsville.

Winick, C. (1961, Fall). Physician narcotic addicts. *Social Problems, 9*, 174–186.

Wirth, L. (1938, July). Urbanism as a way of life. *American Journal of Sociology, 44*, 1–24.

Wirth, L. (1945). The problem of minority groups. In R. Linton (Ed.), *The science of man in the world crisis*, New York: Columbia University Press.

Wirtz, J. J. (2006, March). Do U.S. nuclear weapons have a future? *Strategic Insights, 5*(3).

Wolfensohn, J. D., & Fuller, K. S. (1998, May 7). Making common cause: Seeing the forest for the trees. *International Herald Tribune*, p. 11.

Wolfgang, M. E. (1958). *Patterns in criminal homicide*. Philadelphia: University of Pennsylvania Press.

Wolfgang, M., E., & Reidel, M. (1975, July). Rape, race, and the death penalty. *American Journal of Orthopsychiatry, 45*, 658–668.

Women in the Riksdag. (2006, November). Swedish Parliament Factsheet. Online.

World population profile. (Various). Washington, DC: Bureau of the Census, U.S. Department of Commerce.

Worm, B., et al. (2006, November 3). Impacts of biodiversity loss on ocean ecosystem services. *Science, 314*(5800), 787–790.

Wren, C. S. (1998, October 3). Holding an uneasy line in the long war on heroin; Methadone emerged in city now debating its use. *New York Times*. Retrieved from http://www.nytimes.com

Wright, E. O. (1979). *Class structure and income determination*. New York: Academic Press.

Wright, E. O. (1985). *Classes*. London: Verso.

Wright, L. (2007). *The looming tower: Al Queda and the road to 9/11*. New York: Vintage.

Wright, Q. (1942). *A study of war* (2 vols.). Chicago: University of Chicago Press.

Wu, Q. (2006, October 4). China cools down coal liquefication. *China Business*. Retrieved from http://www.atimes.com

Wurmbrand, R. (1970). *Torturado por cristo: La iglesia martir de hoy*. Cuernavaca, Mexico.

Wyatt-Brown, B. (2003). Anatomy of a wife-killing. In M. Silberman (Ed.), *Violence and society: A reader* (pp. 182–189). Upper Saddle River, NJ: Prentice Hall.

Yablonsky, J. (1981, May 20). Survey finds world trend toward more liberal abortion laws. Associated Press.

Yonas, M. A., O'Campo, P., Burke, J. G., & Gielen, A. C. (2006, July 21). Neighborhood-level factors and youth violence: Giving voice to the perception of prominent neighborhood individuals. *Health, Education, and Behavior OnlineFirst*.

Yuan, D. Y. (1963, Fall). Voluntary segregation: A study of New York Chinatown. *Phylon, 24*, 255–265.

Zaitseva, L., & Hand, K. (2003, February). Nuclear smuggling chains: Suppliers, intermediaries, and end-users. *American Behavioral Scientist, 46*(6), 822–844.

Zawitz, M. W. (Ed.). (1988, July). *Report to the nation on crime and justice* (2nd ed.). Washington, DC: U.S. Department of Justice, Bureau of Justice Statistics.

Zernike, K. (2006, January 18). Hospitals say meth cases are rising, and hurt care. *New York Times*. Retrieved from http://www.nytimes.com

Zhou, M., & Xiong, Y. S. (2005, November). The multifaceted American experiences of the children of Asian immigrants: Lessons for segmented assimilation. *Ethnic and Racial Studies, 26*(6), 119–1152.

Zibechi, R. (2005, July 22). Brazilian military getting ready for Vietnam-style US invasion. *Brazzil Magazine*.

Zielbauer, P. (2000, November 29). Study finds Pequot businesses lift economy. *New York Times*. Retrieved from http://www.nytimes.com

Zimbardo, P. G. (2007). The pathology of imprisonment. In J. M. Henslin (Ed.), *Down-to-Earth Sociology: Introductory Readings* (14th ed.). New York: Free Press. (Original work published 1972: The pathology of imprisonment. *Society, 9* (6), 4–8)

Zimmerman, A. (2006, October 25). As shoplifters use high-tech scams, retail losses rise. *Wall Street Journal*.

Zinn, M. B., & Eitzen, D. S. (1990). *Diversity in families* (2nd ed.). New York: HarperCollins.

Zoucha-Jensen, J. M., & Coyne, A. (1993, November). The effects of resistance strategies on rape. *American Journal of Public Health, 83*(11), 1633–1634.

Zundel, Ernst. (2004). *Setting the record straight: Letters from Cell #7*. New York: Soaring Eagles Gallery.

NAME INDEX

Names spelled out in full indicate people who are discussed in the text, while names using first initials only indicate authors cited.

Child labor, 362, 373, 435
Childrearing, 137, 370
Children
    Brazilian death squads and, 229
    changing ideas about, 167–168, 373
    day care, 361, 363–364, 395
    divorce and, 366, 367
    economics of having, 362, 431, 434–436
    hunger, global, 430–431, 432
    hyperactivity and, 94
    infant mortality rate, 248, 326–328, 355
    juvenile delinquency in history, 167–168
    in pornography, 67–68, 69, 72, 73–74, 75
    in poverty, 43, 49, 221, 233–234, 239,
        430–431, 432
    prostitution and, 55, 60, 62, 64,
        73–74, 75
    rights of, 393
    runaways and "pushouts," 371
    of single parents, 367, 368–371
    socialization of, 282–283, 288–292,
        296–297, 314–315, 375
    as soldiers, 527
    violence towards siblings, 381
Children of the Night, 73
Children's literature, sex discrimination in,
    295
Child support, 222, 234
China
    capitalism in, 160, 204
    earthquake in, 443
    food pollution in, 481
    food production in, 451
    health care in, 355
    nuclear weapons in, 522
Chinatowns, 270
Chinese Exclusion Act (1882), 269
Chinese immigrants, 87, 88, 90, 269–270
Cholera, 322
Cholesterol, alcohol and, 98
Chop shops, 177
CIA (Central Intelligence Agency), 534–535
Circumcision, female, 285, 286
Cities. *See also* Urbanization; Urban
    problems
    concentric zones in, 406, 407
    definition of, 400
    edge cities, 420–421
    evolution of, 399–400, 401
    fastest growing and shrinking, 403,
        406–407, 421
    government of, 417–420
    growth of, 403, 406–407
    in-migration, 401, 402, 403, 425–426
    mobility in, 406–408
    murder rates in, 150
    U. S. population, 401–402
    world's largest, 400, 401, 402
City of Richmond decision, 272
Civil disobedience, 265–266
Civil Rights Act (1964), 272, 315
Civil Rights Act (1968), 266

Civil unions, 310
Class. *See* Social class
Class consciousness, false, 216, 217, 258
Closed-ended questions, 20
Club drugs, 93
Coal, 473, 495
Coca-Cola, 107
Cocaine, 79, 82, 93, 106–109, 119
Coca plant, 107
Code of the street, 406
Coffee, 80
Cohabitation, 378, 388, 390, 397
Cold turkey, 113
Cold War, 204, 503, 507–508, 519–520
Collateral damage, 518
Collective violence, 128, 275
Colombia, drug dealers in, 119, 532
Colonialism, economic, 228–229
Colonialism, internal, 243, 244
Columbine High School shootings, 127
Combat stress reaction, 519
Commodity riots, 416
Common sense
    drugs and, 89, 115
    legal system and, 172
    pornography and, 69
    social policy and, 193
    sociology and, 15, 17
Communal riots, 416
Communication styles, inner-city, 405
Community
    city life and, 407, 408, 409–413
    definition of, 400
    in education, 426
    environmentalism, 499
    establishing, 422
    Harlem, reclaiming, 419
    urban policies and, 427
Community Right to Know Act of 1986,
    492
Community spaces, 499
Compartmentalization, 254
Computer-enhanced therapy, 346
Concentration camps, 268–269, 517
Concentric zone theory, 406, 407
Condominium in-filling, 422
Conflict theory, 32–36
    on aging, 32–36, 47
    applying, 34–35
    on crime, 152, 166–167, 173
    definition of, 32–33
    development of, 32–34
    on drug abuse, 87, 89–90, 118
    on employment, 33, 216–217, 218,
        257–258
    on the environment, 467–470
    on families, 376–377
    on health care, 336–337
    on homosexuality, 309–310
    on murder, 150, 152
    on organized crime, 177
    on population, 440–441

    on pornography, 67
    on poverty, 150, 216–217, 234
    on power, 33, 35
    on power elites, 226
    on prostitution, 57, 62–63
    on race and ethnic relations, 257–258
    on rape, 141
    on sex discrimination, 284–288, 302
    social problems and, 26, 32–36
    on urban problems, 408
    on violence, 137–138, 155
    on violence against women, 314
    on war, 510–511
    on workforce segregation, 302
Conformists, 164
Conservation, 495, 497
Conservation movement, 466
Conservative extremists, 315
Conspiracy theories, 179
Constitutional amendments
    Hyde Amendment, 11
    race and citizenship, 270
    race–ethnicity and gender, 272
Containment theory, 137
Continued subjugation, 243
Control groups, 18
Controlled style, 143
Control theory, 137, 150, 165
Convention prostitutes, 57
Conversion therapy, 331
Corporate crime, 166, 167, 171, 172–173
Corporate culture, 172
Corporate executive officers (CEOs), 166
Corporate prostitution, 54, 58–59
Corporate welfare, 469
Corporations. *See also* Advertising; Industry
    crime against, 173–174
    crime on behalf of, 166, 167, 172–173
    day care and, 395
    farming, 442
    pornography industry, 65–66, 71
    power and, 173, 225–228
Correlation, 69
Cosa Nostra, 177
Covert observation, 19
Crack, 107, 108–109
Cravings, 84
Crime, 158–201. *See also* Criminal justice
    system; Murder; Rape
    arrests, 18, 146, 168–171, 180, 184, 201
    as business/work, 175, 176–177
    conflict theory on, 152, 166–167, 173
    corporate, 166, 167, 171, 172–173
    costs of, 174, 178
    cultural relativity of, 160
    definition of, 159
    deterrence of, 192–193, 196
    drug sales/dealers, 116, 118–119
    drug use and, 82, 86, 89, 115–116
    drug use as, 80, 87, 89–90
    embezzlement, 174–175, 201
    functionalism on, 164–166

PHOTO CREDITS

Chapter 1: p. 1: Mark Peterson/Redux; p. 7: Amit Bhargava/Corbis; p. 9: John Watney/Photo Researchers, Inc.; p. 13: David Kadlubowski/Corbis; p. 18, L: A. Ramey/PhotoEdit, Inc.; p. 18, R: Kurt Rogers/San Francisco Chronicle/Corbis

Chapter 2: p. 24: David Young-Wolff/PhotoEdit, Inc.; p. 28: The London Art Archive/Alamy; p. 29, L: Gary Saltzer/zefa/Corbis; p. 29, R: Blend Images/Alamy Royalty Free; p. 31: Kimimasa Mayama/Bloomberg News/Landov; p. 33: The Print Collector/Alamy; p. 34: Brown Brothers; p. 35, Pauline Lubens/Detroit Free Press Inc.; p. 39: Courtesy of Phyllis Moen; p. 40: David Young-Wolff/PhotoEdit, Inc.; p. 41: Boston Globe/Bill Greene/Landov; p. 45, L: Josef Polleross/The Image Works; p. 45, R: Corbis Super RF/Alamy Royalty Free; p. 46: Michelle D. Bridwell/PhotoEdit, Inc.

Chapter 3: p. 50: Pictures Colour Library/Newscom; p. 53: Courtesy of Edward O. Laumann; p. 54: The London Art Archive/Alamy; p. 56: Paul Simcock/The Image Bank/Getty Images; p. 58: Courtesy of Lori Fowler; p. 60: Chung Subg-Jun/Getty Images; p. 61: ND/Roger-Violett/The Image Works; p. 62: AP Images; p. 64: Frederic Neema/Gamma Presse/Newscom; p. 65: Steve Marcus/Reuters/Corbis; p. 71: Mark Mellett/Stock, Boston; p. 73: REUTERS/Adam Tanner/Landov; p. 74: Kayte M. Deioma/PhotoEdit, Inc.; p. 75: ThinkStock/SuperStock Royalty Free

Chapter 4: p. 78: AP Images/Israel Leal; p. 81, T: AP Images/Karl DeBlaker; p. 81, BL: Getty Images Royalty Free; p. 81, BR: Tony Freeman/PhotoEdit, Inc.; p. 88: George A. Hiriliman Productions, Inc./20th Century Fox/Photofest; p. 89: UPI Photo/Terry Schmitt/Landov; p. 91, L: Noel Hines/Landov; p. 91, R: AP Images/Michael Caulfield; p. 92: SW Productions/Getty Images Royalty Free; p. 93: Courtesy of James A. Inciardi; p. 99: Margaret Bourke-White/Time Life Pictures/Getty Images; p. 101: SSPL/The Image Works; p. 104: Richard Levine/Alamy; p. 106: Jeffrey L. Rotman/Corbis; p. 108: Alpha/Landov; p. 109: AP Images/Chuck Robinson; p. 111: Reuters/Corbis; p. 112: Faces of Meth/Multnomah County Sheriff's Office; p. 114: Heidi Levine/Sipa; p. 117: ©The Courier-Journal; p. 121: Michael Reynolds/epa/Corbis

Chapter 5: p. 126: Maxppp/Philippe De Poulpiquet/Landov; p. 130: Alain Daussin/Photographer's Choice/Getty Images; p. 136: Courtesy of Ruth Horowitz; p. 138: Rebecca Cook/Reuters/Corbis; p. 144: Deborah Davis/PhotoEdit, Inc.; p. 149: Reuters/Corbis; p. 152: James M. Henslin; p. 154: ©Houston Chronicle

Chapter 6: p. 158: Reuters/Corbis; p. 165: Todd Plitt/Getty Images; p. 167: Andrew Hetherington/Redux; p. 168: Courtesy of William Chambliss; p. 171: AP Images/Ann Johansson; p. 172: Bettmann/Corbis; p. 176: AP Images; p. 177: Interfoto USA/Sipa; p. 178: D. Hurst/Alamy; p. 180: AP Images/Bedford, N.H. Police Department; p. 187: STR/AFP/Getty Images; p. 189: Mike Simons/AFP/Getty Images; p. 191: Boston Globe/Stan Grossfeld/Landov; p. 192: REUTERS/Shannon Stapleton/Landov; p. 193: AP Images/John Russell; p. 194: John Eastcott and Yva Momatiuk/Photo Researchers, Inc.; p. 196: Bob Daemmrich/The Image Works

Chapter 7: p. 202: Newscom; p. 205, L: Brunei Department of Information via Getty Images; p. 205, R: Reuters/Rupak De Chowdhuri; p. 211: Alison Wright/Corbis; p. 217: Michael Newman/PhotoEdit, Inc.; p. 218: Courtesy of Warna Oosterbaan/Photo provided by Herbert Gans; p. 219: Michael Newman/PhotoEdit, Inc.; p. 222: Ebby May/Taxi/Getty Images; p. 224: Peter Turnley/Corbis; p. 225: Margot Granitsas/The Image Works; p. 232: AP Images/Works Progress Administration; p. 235: Dan Lamont/Corbis

Chapter 8: p. 240: Najlah Feanny/Corbis Sygma p. 245: AP Images/Frank Polich; p. 246: Digital Vision Ltd./SuperStock Royalty Free; p. 247: Robin Nelson/PhotoEdit, Inc.; p. 249: Boston University ©2007, Photo Provided by Nazli Kibria; p. 251: William Thomas Cain/Getty Images; p. 254: REUTERS/Fred Prouser/Landov; p. 255: Courtesy of Rafael Ezekiel; p. 261: B.S.P.I./Corbis; p. 263: Kayte M. Deioma/PhotoEdit, Inc.; p. 264: Andrew Holbrooke/Corbis; p. 265: AP Images/Gene Herrick; p. 266, 269: Bettmann/Corbis; p. 267: Kyodo/Landov; p. 275: Najlah Feanny/Corbis Saba

Chapter 9: p. 278: Thinkstock/Corbis Royalty Free; p. 281: Juice Images/Corbis Royalty Free; p. 282: UPN/Landov; p. 287: Bob Thomas/Popperfoto/Getty Images; p. 290: Courtesy of Steven Goldberg; p. 291: Courtesy of Cynthia Fuchs Epstein; p. 292: Stockbyte/Getty Images Royalty Free; p. 296: ©Disney Channel/Courtesy Everett Collection; p. 297, T: Bill Aron/PhotoEdit, Inc.; p. 297, B: AP Images/Ed Betz; p. 303: Ezra Shaw/Getty Images; p. 304: Tibor Bognar/Corbis; p. 306: Courtesy of Kirsten Dellinger; p. 309: TIMOTHY A. CLARY/AFP/Getty Images/Newscom; p. 310: CBS/Cliff Lipson/Landov; p. 312: Shepard Sherbell/Corbis Saba

Chapter 10: p. 318: Paul Burns/Photodisc/Getty Images Royalty Free; p. 321: Reuters/Anthony P. Bolante/Landov; p. 324: Thomas Photography LLC/Alamy; p. 326, L: Mark Richards/PhotoEdit, Inc.; p. 326, R: Tom Stewart/Corbis; p. 331: Darren McCollester/Newsmakers/Getty Images; p. 332: Spencer Grant/PhotoEdit, Inc.; p. 334: Bill Aron/PhotoEdit, Inc.; p. 338: Sean Sprague/The Image Works; p. 340: Les Gibbon/Alamy; p. 341: REUTERS/Mario Anzuoni/Landov; p. 345, L: CBS/Tony Esparza/Landov; p. 345, R: Robin Nelson/PhotoEdit, Inc.; p. 348: Peter Widmann/Alamy; p. 350: Ace Stock Limited/Alamy; p. 351: Bubbles Photolibrary/Alamy; p. 352: Courtesy of Dr. Cockerham; p. 354: REUTERS/STR/Landov; p. 357: AP Images/Richard Sheinwald

Chapter 11: p. 360: John Birdsall/The Image Works; p. 362: ClassicStock/Alamy; p. 364: Bob Daemmrich/PhotoEdit, Inc.; p. 369: JUPITERIMAGES/Thinkstock/Alamy Royalty Free; p. 370: Richard B. Levine/Frances M. Roberts; p. 372: JupiterIMAGES/Brand X/Alamy Royalty Free; p. 373: AP Images/Truman Family; p. 376: Siri Stafford/Taxi/Getty Images; p. 377: SSPL/The Image Works; p. 380: Courtesy of Lori Fowler; p. 382: Courtesy of Kathleen Ferraro p. 384: Jeff Greenberg/PhotoEdit, Inc.; p. 385: Courtesy of Lori Fowler; p. 387: PNC/Brand X/Corbis Royalty Free; p. 389: Adam Smith/Taxi/Getty Images; p. 395: AP Images/Jacquelyn Martin

Chapter 12: p. 398: John Birdsall/The Image Works; p. 403: Sean Sprague/The Image Works; p. 405: Courtesy of Professor Elijah

Anderson; p. 410: Angel Franco/The New York Times/Redux; p. 412: Tim Boyle/Getty Images; p. 413: Journal-Courier/Steve Warmowski/ The Image Works; p. 415: Jerome Sessini/In Visu/Corbis; p. 417, L: Bettmann/Corbis; p. 417, R: R. Duyos/Sun Sentinel/Corbis Sygma; p. 419: Lee Snider/The Image Works; p. 426: Chris Hondros/ Newsmakers/Getty Images; p. 430: Karin Retief/Trace Images/The Image Works; p. 432: Courtesy of Carl Haub; p. 435: Paula Bronsteain/Getty Images; p. 438, T: Gabriel Jecan/Bettmann/Corbis; p. 440: AP Images/Wong Maye-E; p. 441: AP Images/Eau Claire; p. 443: AP Images/David Guttenfelder; p. 445: Clay Caviness; p. 447: David Barber/PhotoEdit, Inc.; p. 456: Johner Images/Getty Images Royalty Free

Chapter 13: p. 460: WorldFoto/Alamy; p. 462: Warren Morgan/ Bettmann/Corbis; p. 464: China Photos/Getty Images; p. 465, L: Phil Gilham/Getty Images; p. 465, R: AP Images/Denis Farrell; p. 466: Corbis; p. 469: Sam Kittner/National Geographic/Getty Images; p. 474: Zoriah/The Image Works; p. 475: ©David Fisher Architect.

ALL RIGHTS RESERVED ©2008. International Pantent Pending; p. 480: Rachel Epstein/The Image Works; p. 481: James M. Henslin; p. 484: AP Images/Walter Astrada; p. 486: James Marshall/The Image Works; p. 490, L: Photo provided courtesy of Anne Ehrlich; p. 490, R: Copyright ©2006 by Transaction Publishers. Reprinted by permission of the publisher; p. 491: Oxford Picture Library/Alamy; p. 493: Tony Savino/The Image Works; p. 496: Norman Rowan/The Image Works; p. 498: David Cooper/Toronto Star/ZUMA/Corbis; p. 499: Courtesy of Robert Gottlieb

Chapter 14: p. 502: REUTERS/Mike Segar/Landov; p. 505: Topham/The Image Works; p. 510: Bettmann/Corbis; p. 513: Courtesy of Morten Ender; p. 517, T: Kathy Ferguson-Johnson/ PhotoEdit Inc.; p. 517, B: Bettmann/Corbis; p. 521: Fred Ramage/ Keystone/Getty Images; p. 525: Thomas White/Reuters/Corbis; p. 527: David Turnley/Corbis; p. 531: Rob Elliott/AFP/Getty Images; p. 533: James M. Henslin; p. 534: Monika Graf/The Image Works; p. 538: Chris Fitzgerald/The Image Works.